ROUTLEDGE ENCYCLOPEDIA OF TRANSLATION STUDIES

ROUTLEDGE ENCYCLOPEDIA OF TRANSLATION STUDIES

Second edition

Edited by
MONA BAKER
and
GABRIELA SALDANHA

Routledge
Taylor & Francis Group

LONDON AND NEW YORK

First published in 1998 by Routledge

Second edition published in 2009 by Routledge
Published in paperback in 2011 by Routledge
2 Park Square, Milton Park, Abingdon, OX14 4RN

Simultaneously published in the USA and Canada by Routledge
711 Third Ave, New York, NY 10017

Routledge is an imprint of the Taylor & Francis Group, an informa business
© 1998, 2009, 2011 Mona Baker and Gabriela Saldanha

Typeset in Minion Pro 9.5pt by Fakenham Photosetting Ltd, Fakenham, Norfolk
Printed and bound in Great Britain by CPI Antony Rowe, Chippenham, Wiltshire

British Library Cataloguing in Publication Data
A catalogue record for this book is available from the British Library

Library of Congress Cataloging in Publication Data
Routledge encyclopedia of translation studies / edited by Mona Baker and Gabriela Saldanha. -- 2nd ed.
p. cm.
1. Translating and interpreting--Encyclopedias. I. Baker, Mona. II. Saldanha, Gabriela.
P306.E57 2008
418'.0203--dc22
2008007761

ISBN13: 978-0-415-36930-5 (hbk)
ISBN13: 978-0-203-02911-4 (ebk)
ISBN13: 978-0-415-60984-5 (pbk)

Contents

Part I: General

Part II: History and Traditions

Contents

List of figures and tables

Figures

Tables

Consultant editors

Contributors

Note: * indicates deceased

Gunilla Anderman *
University of Surrey, UK

Dimitris Asimakoulas
University of Surrey, UK

Harry Aveling
La Trobe University, Australia

Aliki Bacopoulou-Halls
University of Athens, Greece

Mona Baker
University of Manchester, UK

Matthijas Bakker
Universiteit Utrecht, The Netherlands

Paul Bandia
Concordia University, Canada

Heloisa Gonçalves Barbosa
Universidade Federal do Rio de Janeiro, Brazil

Georges L. Bastin
Université de Montréal, Canada

Francesca Billiani
University of Manchester, UK

Jean Boase-Beier
University of East Anglia, UK

Lynne Bowker
University of Ottawa, Canada

Gordon Brotherston
University of Manchester, UK

Siobhan Brownlie
University of Manchester, UK

Andrew Chesterman
University of Helsinki, Finland

David Connolly
University of Athens, Greece

Guy Cook
The Open University, UK

Michael Cronin
Dublin City University, Ireland

Kathleen Davis
Princeton University, USA

Dirk Delabastita
Facultés Universitaires Notre-Dame de la Paix, Belgium

Jean Delisle
University of Ottawa, Canada

Ebru Diriker
AIIC Training Committee and Boğaziçi University, Turkey

Riccardo Duranti
Università di Roma 'La Sapienza', Italy

Roger Ellis
University of Wales, Cardiff

Peter Fawcett
UK

Muhammad Y. Gamal
University of New South Wales, Australia

Daniel Gile
Université Paris 3 Sorbonne Nouvelle, France

Rainier Grutman
University of Ottawa, Canada

Terry Hale
University of Hull, UK

Sandra Halverson
University of Bergen, Norway

Sameh Fekry Hanna
University of Salford, UK

Lorna Hardwick
The Open University, UK

Basil Hatim
The American University of Sharjah, UAE

Theo Hermans
University College London, UK

Juliane House
University of Hamburg, Germany

Eva Hung
The Chinese University of Hong Kong, Hong Kong

Moira Inghilleri
University College London, UK

Riitta Jääskeläinen
University of Joensuu, Finland

Francis R. Jones
University of Newcastle, UK

Ji-Hae Kang
Ajou University, Suwon, Republic of Korea

Ahmad Karimi-Hakkak
University of Maryland, USA

David Katan
University of Trieste, Italy

Ke Ping
Nanjing University, People's Republic of China

John Kearns
Kazimierz Wielki University, Bydgoszcz, Poland

Dorothy Kelly
Universidade de Granada, Spain

Louis G. Kelly
Darwin College, Cambridge, UK

Dorothy Kenny
Dublin City University, Ireland

Harald Kittel
Georg-August-Universität Göttingen, Germany

Kinga Klaudy
University of Budapest, Hungary

János Kohn *
Hungary

Vilen N. Komissarov
Moscow State Linguistic University, Russia

Masaomo Kondo
Daito Bunka University, Japan

Cees Koster
Utrecht University, The Netherlands

Ramesh Krishnamurthy
Aston University, UK

Zlata Kufnerová
Literary translator, Prague, Czech Republic

Keneva Kunz
University of Iceland, Reykjavik, Iceland

Gillian Lathey
Roehampton Univeristy, UK

Sara Laviosa
Università di Bari, Italy

Lorraine Leeson
Trinity College Dublin, Ireland

Kitty van Leuven-Zwart
The Netherlands

Anna Lilova
Literary translator, Bulgaria

Allison Beeby Lonsdale
Universitat Autònòma de Barcelona, Spain

Carol Maier
Kent State University, USA

Anne Martin
Universidade de Granada, Spain

Ian Mason
Heriot-Watt University, Scotland

Jeremy Munday
University of Leeds, UK

Hassan Mustapha
Alhosn University, United Arab Emirates

Liz Oakley-Brown
Lancaster University, UK

Minako O'Hagan
Dublin City University, Dublin

Maeve Olohan
University of Manchester, UK

Ewald Osers
Literary translator, Reading, UK

Saliha Paker
Boğaziçi University, Turkey

Jerry Palmer
London Metropolitan University

Viggo Hjørnager Pedersen
University of Copenhagen, Denmark

Luis Pérez González
University of Manchester, UK

Loredana Polezzi
University of Warwick, UK

David Pollard
The Chinese University of Hong Kong, Hong
Kong

Andreas Poltermann
Georg-August-Universität Göttingen, Germany

Anthony Pym
Universitat Rovira i Virgili, Tarragona, Spain

Per Qvale
Literary translator, Norway

György Radó *
Hungary

Paolo Rambelli
University College London, UK

Myriam Salama-Carr
University of Salford, UK

Gabriela Saldanha
University of Birmingham, UK

Christina Schäffner
Aston University, UK

Reinhard Schäler
University of Limerick, Ireland

Mark Shuttleworth
Imperial College London, UK

James St André
University of Manchester, UK

Ubaldo Stecconi
The European Commission, Belgium

Kate Sturge
Aston University, UK

Elżbieta Tabakowska
Jagiellonian University, Poland

Şehnaz Tahir Gürçağlar
Boğaziçi University, Turkey

Ira Torresi
Università di Bologna, Italy

Gideon Toury
Tel Aviv University, Israel

Lawrence Venuti
Temple University, USA

Luise von Flotow
University of Ottawa, Canada

Cecilia Wadensjö
University of Linköping, Sweden

Judy Wakabayashi
Kent State University, USA

Wang Hui
Hong Kong Baptist University

Lars Wollin
Institutionen för nordiska språk, Uppsala,
Sweden

Lia Wyler
Pontificia Universidade Católica do Rio de
Janeiro, Brazil

Teri Shaffer Yamada
California State University, USA

Federico Zanettin
Università di Perugia, Italy

Lynell Zogbo
United Bible Societies

Introduction to the first edition

In May 1991, I received a phone call from Simon Bell, former Language Reference Editor at Routledge, who wanted to know if I had any suggestions for a reference work on translation studies, possibly a dictionary. Simon, among many others, had begun to see translation studies as an exciting new discipline, perhaps *the* discipline of the 1990s. And indeed translation studies has not only fulfilled our expectations but greatly exceeded them. We need only think of one area in which translation studies has flourished beyond anyone's expectations, namely the academicization of translator and interpreter training, to appreciate the phenomenal speed with which the discipline as a whole has established itself in the 1990s. The entry on Translator-training institutions by Caminade and Pym (this volume) documents the dramatic rise in the number of university-level institutions which offer degrees in translation and/or interpreting: 'From 49 in 1960 then 108 in 1980, the global number had risen to at least 250 in 1994'.

New disciplines, disciplines 'in the making' as it were, are particularly exciting for the rich research potential they hold and the sheer intellectual energy they are capable of generating. This intellectual energy can attract – as it has done in the case of translation studies – the interest of scholars working within more traditional disciplines, because it can revitalize a staid framework with new challenges, new avenues of enquiry, and new perspectives on pursuing such enquiry. Hence the current interest in translation across a variety of disciplines, from linguistics to ethnography and from cultural studies to psychology, to name only a few.

The vivacity and diversity that we find so attractive in new disciplines are a consequence of the fact that their potential is as yet unrealized, or is in the process of being realized. And this is precisely why the 'state of the art' of an emerging discipline such as translation studies is notoriously difficult to capture in a work of reference. All encyclopedias, this one included, are inevitably out of date before they hit the press – such is the nature and speed of intellectual progress in any field of study. A pioneering work of reference which sets out to chart a territory that has hitherto not been charted, to capture the core concerns of a discipline in a state of flux, cannot hope to be totally comprehensive. But it can and should aim to offer a balanced, non-partisan view of the discipline.

Translation studies is at a stage of its development when the plurality of approaches that inform it or are capable of informing it can be overwhelming, and the temptation for many has been to promote one approach with which they feel particularly comfortable and dismiss the rest. Throughout the editing of this *Encyclopedia*, I have tried to keep an open mind on what constitutes a viable perspective on the study of translation and what might legitimately be seen as a relevant area of concern or method of research in translation studies. An encyclopedia of a scholarly subject has a duty to open up rather than unduly restrict the scope of the discipline it sets out to describe. Thus, in addition to traditional issues such as EQUIVALENCE, SHIFTS OF TRANSLATION and TRANSLATABILITY, the reader will also find substantial entries which discuss less traditional but increasingly popular issues, including translation as a metaphor for relations which exist between objects outside language (METAPHOR OF TRANSLATION), the metaphorics of gender and sexuality in discussions of translation (GENDER METAPHORICS IN TRANSLATION), the application of model theory to the study of translation (MODELS OF TRANSLATION), the process by which books are chosen to be translated and published in other languages (PUBLISHING STRATEGIES), and the use of computerized corpora in studying universals of translation (CORPORA IN TRANSLATION STUDIES).

So much for Part I. Part II of this *Encyclopedia* offers a very brief overview of national histories of translation and interpreting in some thirty linguistic and cultural communities. These entries are inevitably restricted in terms of space and can only offer a glimpse of what a full-scale history of each tradition might have to offer. When the plan for the *Encyclopedia* was first drawn in 1991, no significant initiatives had been announced in terms of a general history of translation; nothing had then appeared on the FIT History of Translation (Delisle and Woodsworth 1995) nor on the forthcoming de Gruyter Encyclopedia, and I was not aware at that stage that these projects were being planned. The rationale for including a historical section and for covering as many traditions as possible, albeit very briefly, was to stimulate interest in what I then felt was a seriously neglected area of translation studies. Inevitably for a relatively short section of this type, not all traditions could be represented, and the divisions in terms of linguistic and/or geographical communities are inherently arbitrary to a large extent. Irrespective of possible methodological weaknesses and unavoidable brevity of treatment, a reading of these histories can lead to interesting insights on such issues as the overall profile of translators and interpreters during different historical periods, the role of the translator and/or interpreter as it has been conceived by different communities, the range of incentives that have led to periods of intensive translation activity across the ages, the amazing variety of activities that have been subsumed at different times under the general heading of 'translation', and the kinds of contexts in which translators and interpreters have sometimes had to operate. These 'global' insights would be difficult if not impossible to draw from a small number of more detailed histories. A brief outline of a number of these global patterns may be useful at this point.

Profile of translators and interpreters

One of the most interesting and potentially productive areas of research to emerge from the historical section of this encyclopedia concerns the kind of social or ethnic groups that translators and interpreters have typically belonged to during various periods.

Translators and interpreters, on the whole, seem to have historically belonged to minority groups of one type or another. For example, many interpreters in the New World, during the early expeditions, were native Indians, often servants and the like: a minority group not in terms of numbers at this stage, but in terms of political and economic power. In fact, the first generation of interpreters in the New World were largely natives who were captured and trained as interpreters by explorers such as Jacques Cartier in Canada and Christopher Columbus in Latin America. In the United States, Squanto – a prominent Indian interpreter – was initially captured by an English captain and taken to England. A similar pattern exists outside the New World, in both European and non-European countries. In Turkey during the fifteenth and sixteenth centuries, translators and interpreters were chosen from Greek, Italian, German, Hungarian and Polish converts to Islam. In Egypt in the early nineteenth century, the best-known literary translators were Christians, of one denomination or another (Protestant, Orthodox, Maronite), and often of Lebanese or Syrian origin. In the 1940s and 1950s in Czechoslovakia, simultaneous interpreting was provided by wartime émigrés (in the case of English), by Jewish survivors of concentration camps (in the case of German), and by second-generation Russian émigrés (in the case of Russian). These are all minority groups and migrants. It is quite possible that a similar profile exists for community and court interpreters today in countries such as Britain, Sweden, the US and Australia: the majority may well prove to be second-generation immigrants belonging to ethnic minority groups.

The pattern is not totally consistent of course, but then patterns never are. In Africa, for instance, in very early times, interpreting was a hereditary and highly revered profession, performed by 'wise men' born to other 'wise men'. In China, the most active and prominent translators in early times were mainly Buddhist monks. These groups cannot be thought of as minorities in the political or economic sense, nor in terms of power. And of course being members of minority groups does not necessarily mean that translators and interpreters did not achieve a high status. In Turkey, for instance, 'dragomans' were held in high esteem and earned very high incomes between the fifteenth and nineteenth centuries; there was even a Translators' Mosque built in Istanbul in the sixteenth century, which is surely a sign of respect for the profession. Also, translators and interpreters who belonged to religious minorities enjoyed great privileges: they were exempt from the capitation tax levied on non-Muslims in the Islamic world in general and were allowed a wide range of privileges that could normally only be enjoyed by Muslims; for example a non-Muslim translator was allowed to grow a beard and ride a horse.

There are also patterns within patterns. As far as interpreters in the colonial context are concerned for instance, the profile is mixed: there are essentially two groups. One group consists of native interpreters and another consists of members of the colonial culture – in Latin America, Canada and the United States, both are prominent. The role of native interpreters is of course socially and psychologically more complex and many were often branded as traitors by their people. *Malinchista* is a term of abuse in Mexico and among the Chicano community in America: it is used to refer to someone who sells out or betrays a cause, because Malinche (Doña Marina), who interpreted for Hernán Cortés in the early sixteenth century, was heavily implicated in his colonial schemes, acting as his informant and warning him of ambushes by her people. The status of native interpreters in these contexts was not particularly high, unlike their colonial counterparts, and we see in Africa for instance a distinct deterioration in status with the arrival of colonialism.

Women, an important minority group, were often not allowed to work as translators; for example, the profession of sworn translator in Brazil was regulated by Royal Decree in 1851, and women were explicitly barred from the profession.

Role and status of translators and interpreters

In the colonial context, we find translators and interpreters, but particularly interpreters, taking on an amazing range of responsibilities which go far beyond linguistic mediation. Interpreters in the colonial context acted as guides, explorers, brokers, diplomats, ambassadors and advisers on Indian or local affairs; that is why they were sometimes branded as traitors, because they were indispensable to the colonial authorities. In other contexts, too, translators and interpreters were expected to perform a wide variety of tasks. Translators, or more specifically interpreters, in oral traditions such as the African tradition were expected to act as spokesmen for their communities, not just as linguistic mediators. In the eighteenth century in Turkey, the duty of the Naval Dragoman included the supervision of the collection of taxes from non-Muslim subjects, though later on the 1839 Tanzimat limited his responsibility to interpreting again, i.e. strictly linguistic mediation.

In terms of status, the highest status attained by translators and interpreters seems to have been linked to the profession being hereditary, as in the case of the 'wise men' in the oral tradition of Africa, who passed on their skills to their sons. Other examples include the *tsujiis* in Japan, who exercised family monopolies on interpreting in this area from the seventeenth century until the end of Japan's isolation in the second half of the nineteenth century. There are also the Greek Phanariots in Turkey in the seventeenth and eighteenth centuries, who similarly had sole control of the profession. All these groups were highly regarded by their communities and earned a very respectable living.

Working contexts

Another interesting area worth investigating concerns the use of interpreters in contexts where we very rarely see them used today. The role of interpreters in educational contexts is of particular interest here. This seems to have been fairly common at various periods, though it is hardly ever discussed in the literature, except perhaps with reference to sign language interpreting for deaf children.

In the early Byzantine period the Greek *antikinsores* (professors of law) used to make Latin texts accessible to their students in class by first providing a detailed introduction in Greek to the particular Latin section of a given law. This was not a word-for-word translation but a general explanation of the law. Then the students would be asked to attempt a translation of the Latin text, and if they ran into difficulty the *antikinsores* would provide them with the translations of particular terms. This was known as interpreting *kata poda* (lit. 'on foot').

In China in the early centuries AD, interpreters played an important role in Buddhist translation forums, which were both intensive seminars on Buddhist sutras and also meant to produce Buddhist texts in Chinese translation. Interpreters acted as intermediaries between a 'Chief Translator', who often knew no Chinese but who was a Buddhist monk and provided explanations of the Buddhist texts, and a Chinese 'Recorder', who was the person responsible for producing a translation on the basis of the monk's explanation.

In Turkey, dragomans were used in institutions such as the School of Military Engineering in the eighteenth century to interpret for foreign instructors who did not speak Turkish. And the same happened in Egypt around the mid-nineteenth century, when the various schools set up by Muhammed Ali relied on foreign instructors who had to have interpreters in the classroom to communicate with their students.

Incentives for translation activity

The incentives which gave rise to periods of intensive translation activity in different parts of the world have varied a great deal over the centuries. One such incentive was the spread of Buddhism in China; the need to translate Buddhist sutras into Chinese, starting around the mid-second century, supported a massive translation movement, often sponsored by the government, lasting for some nine centuries.

Other incentives include the massive campaigns to translate the Bible in most of Europe, as well as Greek classics and learning in general in the Islamic World and later in Europe. The Qur'ān, unlike the Bible, has never supported a serious translation movement anywhere in the world, because of the belief in its untranslatability (see QUR'ĀN (KORAN) TRANSLATION), but it has supported a tradition of commentary, which very often included long stretches of word-for-word translation.

Most of us tend to take such incentives for granted, because they are often too close to home for us to realize that they are culture- and period-specific. So we might not think that there is anything special about saying that the Bible has provided the main impetus for translation activity in much of Europe since the birth of Christianity. It is only by comparison with what was happening in other parts of the world, and at different periods of time, that we can see what is specific about this pattern. For instance, when we come to look at the history of translation in Greece, we find that there is an almost total lack of interest in translation from the early days until fairly recent times, and this is precisely because the two main incentives to early thinking about translation in other countries – namely, the translation of ancient Greek texts and of the New Testament – were not present in Greece, since the original texts remained relatively accessible to Greek readers for a long time.

Another major incentive for massive translation activity, more typical of the nineteenth and twentieth centuries, is the establishment of official bilingualism in countries such as Canada, Finland and Belgium, which tends to support large-scale programmes of administrative and legal translation (rather than translation of religious or academic texts), and of course simultaneous interpreting in such contexts as parliamentary sessions. And linked to this type of incentive is the official recognition of the rights of linguistic and ethnic minorities to be provided with interpreters in courts and similar situations, as well as official documents in their own languages. Today, it would seem, the main impetus for translation is no longer specific religious movements or interest in the classics but rather official policies which recognize and support linguistic heterogeneity, including official bilingualism, recognition of minority rights, the establishment of political and economic unions (such as the EU), and so on. Again, this kind of statement seems rather banal until one places it against the backdrop of other incentives during different historical periods.

Types of translation/interpreting

One of the most fascinating things about exploring the history of translation is that it reveals how narrow and restrictive we have been in defining our object of study, even with the most flexible of definitions. When we read about how African interpreters regularly translated African drum language into actual words, for instance, we begin to realize that the current literature on translation has hardly started to scratch the surface of this multifaceted and all-pervasive phenomenon. Similarly, intralingual translation is not such a minor issue as the existing liter-ature on translation might suggest. Intralingual translation figures far more prominently in the Greek tradition than interlingual translation: the major preoccupation in Greece has been with translating ancient Greek texts into the modern idiom. I know of no research that looks specifically at the phenomena of intralingual or intersemiotic translation. We do have classifica-tions such as Jakobson's, which alert us to the possibility of such things as intersemiotic and intralingual translation, but we do not make any genuine use of such classifications in our research.

An ingenious annotation system was used in Japan around the ninth century; this was known as *kambun kundoku*, or interpretive reading of Chinese. The system was used to enable the Japanese to read Chinese texts without 'trans-lation'. Special marks were placed alongside the characters of Chinese texts to indicate how they can be read in accordance with Japanese word order, and a system of grammatical indicators was used to show inflections. This directly converted the Chinese texts into understandable, if unnatural, Japanese. But was it translation? It seems to be something in between intralingual and interlingual translation, and I do not believe we have any theories that can account for this type of practice either.

What the historical research done for the *Encyclopedia* seems to suggest is that we still know very little about the history of our own profession, that what we know of it indicates that its profile has varied tremendously from one era to another, and – equally important – that the activities of translation and interpreting have taken such a wide variety of forms and have occurred in such a multitude of contexts over the years that we are obliged to look at the historical facts before we can even begin to develop theoretical accounts for this complex phenomenon.

Acknowledgements

This *Encyclopedia* has been six years in the making, during which time a great many people have worked hard to ensure that the end result is as representative of the discipline and as error-free as is humanly possible. In addition to the ninety-four contributors who made it possible to put this substantial volume together in the first place and the seven consultant editors who patiently checked every entry after I edited it to weed out some of the remaining errors and infelicities, I must thank the staff at Routledge for their support over an extended period of time. Simon Bell and Louisa Semlyen in particular have been exceptionally patient and supportive. Helen Coward, Alison Foyle, Helen McCurdy, Claire Trocmé, Sarah Foulkes and Sarah Hall all helped at various stages of the project and have been a pleasure to work with.

I am grateful to a number of colleagues for valuable advice on some of the less 'traditional' topics that were eventually included in Part I and for putting me in touch with suitable contributors for entries in both Part I and Part II; in particular, I wish to acknowledge my debt to Lawrence Venuti, Douglas Robinson, Anthony Pym, Dirk Delabastita, Theo Hermans, Marilyn Gaddis Rose and Susan Bassnett. Dirk Delabastita kindly spent many hours checking the bibliography for missing accents and other errors. Theo Hermans, Clive Holes, Myriam Salama-Carr, Maeve Olohan, Peter Fawcett and Paul Bennett took on the difficult task of 'editing the editor', providing detailed comments on my own contributions to this volume and saving me some potential embarrassment in the process.

Kinga Klaudy revised the final section of the

entry on the Hungarian tradition to bring it up to date, following the unfortunate death of Dr György Radó in 1994. Sara Laviosa-Braithwaite provided invaluable support as my Research Assistant for practically the whole of 1995. Juan Sager helped me edit a number of entries when I started to run out of energy in the summer of 1996, and Kirsten Malmkjær stepped in later that summer to give the editing a final push.

Even with so much good will and generous assistance from a large number of people, there are bound to be some errors and infelicities left in this volume, given the scope of the enterprise. For these I have to take full responsibility.

MONA BAKER
APRIL 1997

Introduction to the second edition

The *Routledge Encyclopedia of Translation Studies* has been the standard and most authoritative reference in the field since it first appeared in 1998. Much has changed since then, however, and the first edition was certainly beginning to 'show its age'. By 2005 it was necessary to begin planning for a new, extensively revised and extended edition to reflect the concerns and priorities of a much enlarged and better established community of scholars.

The growth of translation studies as a discipline is well charted in many recent publications (Kuhiwczak and Littau 2007, Trivedi 2007, Tymoczko 2007, among others), all of which have commented extensively on such developments as the increase in the number of journals dedicated to translation and/or interpreting, the increase in the number of institutions offering degree courses in translation and interpreting, the number of publishers now launching series dedicated to the subject, the availability of dedicated abstracting services (from St Jerome and John Benjamins), and the stream of encyclopedias (beginning with the first edition of this volume), dictionaries, readers and other anthologies of primary material which have steadily appeared since 1997, with various large projects still under preparation. Trivedi refers to these developments as 'the new embarrassment of riches available in the field' (2007: 279), no doubt to stress the meteoric speed with which the discipline has taken off in recent years, moving from a position of extreme obscurity and poverty of resources to one in which it is at least as visible and as well endowed with resources as any of the newly established disciplines in the humanities.

Translation studies has traditionally been strongly Eurocentric in orientation, and in some parts of the world continues to be dominated by theoretical paradigms that originated in the West and that are oblivious to the rich and substantially different experiences of translation outside Europe and North America. However, as translation studies continues to gain a strong foothold in the academy and establish itself as a fully-fledged discipline, one important and welcome trend at the turn of the century has been a sustained growth of interest in non-western perspectives. Titles which focus heavily on non-western experiences and theorizing of translation include Fenton (2003), Kothari (2003), Chan (2004), Hung and Wakabayashi (2005b), Cockerill (2006), Hermans (2006), Lindsay (2006), Kenny and Ryou (2007), Bandia (2008), Gentzler (2008) and Tahir Gürçağlar (2008), among others. These and similar titles invite us to reconsider the scope and central preoccupations of the discipline. Cheung's (2006) *Anthology of Chinese Discourse on Translation*, for instance, introduces us to the monumental project of Buddhist sutra translation which lasted for nearly ten centuries, drawing our attention to the work of central figures such as Kumarajiva and Xuan Zang (as important in the Chinese tradition as St Jerome and Luther in the West, but hitherto largely ignored in our theorizing on translation), and to very different ways of thinking about familiar topics such as translatability and translation criticism.

Engagement with non-western perspectives at the turn of the century did not simply emerge accidentally or spontaneously. It is a deliberate act of intervention undertaken by a number of leading scholars in the field in order to effect a radical and long overdue repositioning of translation studies internationally. Cheung, for example, declares in her introduction to the *Anthology* that she set out 'to make available for study a major non-western perspective from which to look at general, technical or theoretical issues relating to translation, and thereby to promote an international translation studies, one that is less limited by the Eurocentric mode that dominates the present scene' (2006: 2). Hung and Wakabayashi deplore 'the bias in the contemporary field of Translation Studies, which remains highly Eurocentric both in its theoretical explorations and its historical grounding' and declare their aim as 'demonstrating that Asian voices on translation are not merely an echo of the Western voice' (2005b: 1). Hermans's two-volume collection of studies focusing on Asia, Africa and the Middle East explicitly sets out to 'put translation studies on a global map' and to bring to the fore those 'countless others who translate, in their own way, for their own reasons, in their own world', others that 'the traditional discipline of translation studies never even saw' (2006: 9). This commitment to opening up translation studies to the world outside the West is also evident in the establishment of the International Association for Translation and Intercultural Studies in 2004.

Another interesting phenomenon to emerge at the turn of the century has been a sustained growth of interest in translation and interpreting *outside* translation studies, a remarkable development given the traditional marginalization of translation studies in the academy. One facet of this interest has involved 'appropriating' the concept of translation itself as a trope through which the local concerns of the appropriating discipline may be addressed. Examples include the now popular concept of cultural translation as elaborated in the work of Homi Bhabha. Trivedi (2007: 285) sees this particular development as somewhat threatening to translation studies, arguing that 'given the usurpation that has taken place, it may be time for all good men and true, and of course women, who have ever practised literary translation, or even read a translation with any awareness of it being translation, to unite and take out a patent on the word "translation", if it is not already too late to do so'. But much of the more recent engagement with translation and interpreting outside the discipline proper has been more focused on these activities as understood in mainstream translation studies. The prevalence and pervasiveness of translation, in all its guises, together with the increased blurring of boundaries between translation and other types of linguistic mediation, have both enticed a variety of disciplines to engage with these phenomena directly. For one

thing, leading scholars in other disciplines have increasingly been writing on translation on an individual basis; examples include historians (Dodson 2005), critical discourse analysts (van Leeuwen 2006), philosophers (Sampson 2006), literary theorists (Bal 2007) and scholars of journalism (Palmer and Fontan 2007), among others. Some are actively introducing translation studies to their colleagues and encouraging them to engage with it (Miguélez-Carballeira 2007). But even more interestingly, a wide range of international scholarly journals have started to publish entire special issues dedicated to translation and/or interpreting in recent years. These include the following, by no means exhaustive list:

- *The International Journal of Speech, Language and the Law: Forensic Linguistics*, Volume 6, Number 1 (1999). Special issue on 'Legal Interpreting', guest-edited by Diana Eades, Sandra Hale and Michael Cooke.
- *Public Culture*, Volume 13, Number 1 (2001). Special issue on 'Translation in a Global Market', guest-edited by Emily Apter.
- *The Yale Journal of Criticism*, Volume 16, Number 2 (2003). Special issue 'On Translation', guest-edited by Jessica Brantley and Joseph Luzzi.
- *Wasafiri*, Number 40 (2003). Special issue on 'Translation', guest-edited by Theo Hermans and Harish Trivedi.
- *Language and Literature*, Volume 13, Number 1 (2004). Special issue on 'Translation and Style', guest-edited by Jean Boase-Beier.
- *Journal of Pragmatics*, Volume 38, Number 3 (2006). Special issue on 'Translation and Context', guest-edited by Mona Baker.
- *TRANSIT* (published by the Department of German at the University of California Berkeley, and dedicated to the critical inquiry of travel, migration, and multiculturalism in the German-speaking world). Special Topic (2006): Translation and Mobility.
- *Journal of Visual Culture*, Volume 6, Number 1 (2007). Special issue on 'Acts of Translation', guest-edited by Mieke Bal and Joanne Morra.
- *Social Semiotics*, Volume 17, Number 2 (2007). Special issue on 'Translation and Conflict', guest-edited by Myriam Salama-Carr.
- *Theatre Journal*, Volume 59, Number 3 (2007).

Special issue on 'Theatre and Translation', guest-edited by Jean Graham-Jones.

The second edition of the *Encyclopedia*

Against this rich and stimulating backdrop, the second edition of the *Encyclopedia* set out to reflect new concerns in the discipline, its growing multidisciplinarity, and its commitment to break away from its exclusively Eurocentric origins, while holding on to the achievements of the past decades. This has not always proved doable. Thus, for example, in trying to expand the historical part to include more non-western traditions (within the restrictions on space imposed by the publisher), we have either been unable to identify suitable contributors with the relevant expertise, or were promised entries that never materialized. We ended up with only one new entry, on Southeast Asian Traditions, and a revised and slightly expanded entry on the Arabic Tradition. Our only consolation here is that the first edition had already incorporated many non-western traditions: indeed, commitment to challenging the Eurocentric focus in the discipline was one of the main motivations for undertaking that project in the early 1990s. At the same time, more entries in Part I now actively incorporate non-western perspectives than in the first edition; see, for example, the entries on Classical texts, History of translation, Institutional translation, Machine Translation, Postcolonial approaches, Relay, and Retranslation, all of which are written from and devote considerable space to non-western perspectives.

New and developing themes in the discipline are also reflected in a wide range of new entries; these include Censorship, Cultural translation, Deconstruction, Ethics, Fictional representations, Gender and sexuality, Globalization, Hermeneutics, Minority, Mobility (which covers travel and diasporic contexts), Postcolonial approaches, Rewriting, and Sociological approaches. The range of genres and contexts

of translation has also been expanded considerably. In addition to various entries on literary and religious translation, as in the first edition, this edition also includes entries on Advertising, Children's literature, Classical texts, Comics, Commercial translation, Institutional translation, Localization, News gathering and dissemination, and Scientific and technical translation. The growth of interest in interpreting is similarly reflected in additional entries: Asylum, Dialogue Interpreting, and Conference interpreting (sociocultural perspectives). Several entries that appeared in the first edition have been amalgamated to avoid fragmentation, and some have been recommissioned (for example, Audiovisual translation, Machine Translation, Strategies, Terminology). The remaining entries in Part I have all been revised and updated. The bibliographical references at the end of each entry are now ordered chronologically rather than alphabetically, to give a sense of the evolution of concepts and perspectives.

It remains for us to thank the contributors to this second edition for their professionalism and the quality of their contributions, and to acknowledge our gratitude to numerous colleagues who gave us advice and contributed to this volume in various capacities. In particular, we thank Theo Hermans, Moira Inghilleri, Francis Jones, Dorothy Kenny and Carol Maier for stepping in to write excellent entries at rather short notice when initially commissioned contributions failed to materialize. Martha Mutesayire provided valuable administrative support. Our consultant editors – Annie Brisset, Martha Cheung, Hoda Elsadda, Theo Hermans, Jeremy Munday, Mahasweta Sengupta, Elżbieta Tabakowska and Kumiko Torikai – offered sound advice throughout. We are also grateful to the staff at Routledge, in particular Andrea Hartill, Ursula Mallows, Andrew Watts and Samantha Vale Noya, who helped at various stages and whose support has been invaluable, and to Mariam Alfarra for preparing the index.

MONA BAKER AND GABRIELA
SALDANHA

PART I
GENERAL

Adaptation

Adaptation may be understood as a set of translative interventions which result in a text that is not generally accepted as a translation but is nevertheless recognized as representing a source text. As such, the term may embrace numerous vague notions such as appropriation, domestication, imitation, REWRITING, and so on. Strictly speaking, the concept of adaptation requires recognition of translation as non-adaptation, a somehow more constrained mode of transfer. For this reason, the history of adaptation is parasitic on historical concepts of translation.

The initial divide between adaptation and translation might be dated from Cicero and Horace (see LATIN TRADITION), both of whom referred to the *interpres* (translator) as working word-for-word and distinguished this method from what they saw as freer but entirely legitimate results of transfer operations. The different interpretations given to the Horatian verse *Nec verbum verbo curabis reddere fidus interpres* ('and you will not render word-for-word [like a] faithful translator') – irrespective of whether they were for or against the word-for-word precept – effectively reproduced the logic by which adaptations could be recognized.

Adaptation has always existed, since it is a 'normal' part of any intellectual operation; but the golden age of adaptation was in the seventeenth and eighteenth centuries, the epoch of the *belles infidèles*, which started in France and then spread to the rest of the world (see FRENCH TRADITION). The very free translations carried out during this period were justified in terms of the need for foreign texts to be adapted to the tastes and habits of the target culture. The nineteenth century witnessed a reaction to this 'infidelity' (see GERMAN TRADITION), but adaptation continued to predominate in the theatre. In the twentieth century, the proliferation of technical, scientific and commercial documents has given rise to a preference for transparency in translation, with an emphasis on efficient communication; this could be seen as licensing a form of adaptation which involves REWRITING a text for a new readership while maintaining some form of EQUIVALENCE between source and target texts.

Generally speaking, many historians and scholars of translation continue to take a negative view of adaptation, dismissing the phenomenon as a distortion, falsification or CENSORSHIP, but it is rare to find clear definitions of the terminology used in discussing this and other related controversial concepts.

Main definitions

Since Bastin (1998), there has been no comprehensive definition of adaptation. The concept continues to be part of a fuzzy metalanguage used by translation studies scholars. Today, adaptation is considered only one type of 'intervention' on the part of translators, among which a distinction must be made between 'deliberate interventions' (Bastin 2005) and deviations from literality.

It is possible to classify definitions of adaptation under specific topics (translation strategy, genre, metalanguage, faithfulness), though inevitably these definitions tend to overlap.

As one of a number of translation STRATEGIES, adaptation can be defined in a technical and objective way. The best-known definition is that of Vinay and Darbelnet (1958), who list adaptation as their seventh translation procedure: adaptation is a procedure which can be used whenever the context referred to in the original text does not exist in the culture of the target text, thereby necessitating some form of re-creation. This widely accepted definition views adaptation as a local rather than global strategy, employed to achieve an equivalence of situations wherever cultural mismatches are encountered.

Adaptation is sometimes regarded as a form of translation which is characteristic of particular genres, most notably DRAMA. Indeed, it is in relation to drama translation that adaptation has been most frequently studied. Brisset (1986: 10) views adaptation as a 'reterritorialization' of the original work and an 'annexation' in the name of the audience of the new version. Santoyo (1989: 104) similarly defines adaptation as a form of 'naturalizing' the play for a new milieu, the aim being to achieve the same effect that the work originally had, but with an audience from a different cultural background (see also Merino Àlvarez 1992, 1994).

Adaptation is also associated with ADVERTISING and AUDIOVISUAL TRANSLATION. The emphasis here is on preserving the character and function of the original text, in preference to preserving the form or even the semantic meaning, especially where acoustic and/or visual factors have to be taken into account. Other genres, such as CHILDREN'S LITERATURE, also require the re-creation of the message according to the sociolinguistic needs of a different readership (Puurtinen 1995). The main features of this type of adaptation are the use of summarizing techniques, paraphrase and omission.

Adaptation is, perhaps, most easily justified when the original text is of a metalinguistic nature, that is, when the subject matter of the text is language itself. This is especially so with didactic works on language generally, or on specific languages. Newmark (1981) points out that in these cases the adaptation has to be based on the translator's judgement about his or her readers' knowledge. Coseriu (1977) argues that this kind of adaptation gives precedence to the function over the form, with a view to producing the same effect as the original text. However, while such writers start from the principle that nothing is untranslatable, others like Berman (1985) claim that the adaptation of metalanguage is an unnecessary form of exoticism.

Definitions of adaptation reflect widely varying views *vis-à-vis* the issue of remaining 'faithful' to the original text. Some argue that adaptation is necessary precisely in order to keep the message intact (at least on the global level), while others see it as a betrayal of the original author's expression. For the former, the refusal to adapt confines the reader to an artificial world of 'foreignness'; for the latter, adaptation is tantamount to the destruction and violation of the original text. Even those who recognize the need for adaptation in certain circumstances are obliged to admit that, if remaining 'faithful' to the text is a *sine qua non* of translation, then there is a point at which adaptation ceases to be translation at all.

Modes, conditions and restrictions

By comparing adaptations with the texts on which they are based, it is possible to elaborate a selective list of the ways (or modes) in which adaptations are carried out, the motivations (or conditions) for the decision to adapt, and the limitations (or restrictions) on the work of the adapter.

In terms of **mode** of adaptation, the procedures used by the adapter can be classified as follows:

- *transcription of the original*: word-for-word reproduction of part of the text in the original language, usually accompanied by a literal translation
- *omission*: the elimination or implicitation of part of the text
- *expansion*: the addition or EXPLICITATION of source information, either in the main body or in a foreword, footnotes or a glossary
- *exoticism*: the substitution of stretches of slang, dialect, nonsense words, etc. in the original text by rough equivalents in the target language (sometimes marked by italics or underlining)
- *updating*: the replacement of outdated or obscure information by modern equivalents
- *situational or cultural adequacy*: the recreation of a context that is more familiar or culturally appropriate from the target reader's perspective than the one used in the original

- *creation*: a more global replacement of the original text with a text that preserves only the essential message/ideas/functions of the original.

The most common factors (i.e. **conditions**) which cause translators to resort to adaptation are:

- *cross-code breakdown*: where there are simply no lexical equivalents in the target language (especially common in the case of translating metalanguage)
- *situational or cultural inadequacy*: where the context or views referred to in the original text do not exist or do not apply in the target culture
- *genre switching*: a change from one discourse type to another (e.g. from adult to children's literature) often entails a global re-creation of the original text
- *disruption of the communication process*: the emergence of a new epoch or approach or the need to address a different type of readership often requires modifications in style, content and/or presentation.

These conditions (which in practice may exist simultaneously) can lead to two major types of adaptation: **local adaptation**, caused by problems arising from the original text itself and limited to certain parts of it (as in the first two conditions), and **global adaptation**, which is determined by factors outside the original text and which involves a more wide-ranging revision.

As a local procedure, adaptation may be applied to isolated parts of the text in order to deal with specific differences between the language or culture of the source text and that of the target text. In this case, the use of adaptation as a technique will have a limited effect on the text as a whole, provided the overall coherence of the source text is preserved. This type of adaptation is temporary and localized; it does not represent an all-embracing approach to the translation task. Local, or as Farghal (1993: 257) calls it, 'intrinsic' adaptation is essentially a translation procedure which is guided by principles of effectiveness and efficiency and seeks to achieve a balance between what is to be transformed and highlighted and what is to

be left unchanged. Except in the case of local replacement of metalanguage, local adaptation does not need to be mentioned in the target text in a foreword or translator's note.

As a global procedure, adaptation may be applied to the text as a whole. The decision to carry out a global adaptation may be taken by the translator him- or herself (deliberate intervention) or by external forces (for example, a publisher's editorial policy). In either case, global adaptation constitutes a general strategy which aims to reconstruct the purpose, function or impact of the source text. The intervention of the translator is systematic and he or she may sacrifice formal elements and even semantic meaning in order to reproduce the function of the original.

As in the case of translation, adaptation is carried out under certain restrictions, the most obvious of which are:

- *the knowledge and expectations of the target reader*: the adapter has to evaluate the extent to which the content of the source text constitutes new or shared information for the potential audience
- *the target language*: the adapter must find an appropriate match in the target language for the discourse type of the source text and look for coherence of adapting modes
- *the meaning and purpose(s)* of the source and target texts.

Theoretical boundaries between adaptation and translation

Some scholars prefer not to use the term 'adaptation' at all, believing that the concept of translation as such can be stretched to cover all types of transformation or intervention, as long as 'the target text effect corresponds to the intended target text functions' (Nord 1997: 93), be the latter those of the source text or different. Others view the two concepts as representing essentially different practices. Michel Garneau, Quebec poet and translator, coined the term **tradaptation** to express the close relationship between the two activities (Delisle 1986). The very few scholars who have attempted a serious analysis of the phenomenon of adaptation and its relation to translation insist on the tenuous nature of the borderline which separates the two concepts.

The controversy surrounding the supposed opposition between adaptation and translation is often fuelled by ideological issues. This becomes evident when one considers the heated debates that have raged over the translation of the BIBLE ever since the first versions began to appear. It is this apparent lack of objectivity about the adaptation process that has prompted Gambier (1992: 424) to warn against what he calls the 'fetishization' of the original text. After all, it is often argued that a successful translation is one that looks or sounds like an original piece of work, which would seem to imply that the translator is expected to intervene actively (i.e. adapt) to ensure that this ideal is achieved.

The study of adaptation encourages the theorist to look beyond purely linguistic issues and helps shed light on the role of the translator as mediator, as a creative participant in a process of verbal communication. Relevance, rather than accuracy, becomes the key word, and this entails a careful analysis of three major concepts in translation theory: meaning, purpose (or function, or *skopos*: see FUNCTIONALIST APPROACHS) and intention. We could say that translation – or what is traditionally understood by the term translation – stays basically at the level of meaning: adaptation seeks to transmit the purpose of the source text, and exegesis attempts to spell out the intentions of the author. Adaptation may constitute deliberate intervention on the part of the translator, but for functional purposes. Most deliberate interventions such as appropriation, imitation and manipulation imply a shift in authorship (Bastin 2005). This kind of analysis will inevitably lead translation studies to consider the inferential communication pattern (Sperber and Wilson 1986/1995), rather than the traditional code model, as the most appropriate frame of reference for the discipline (see PSYCHOLINGUISTIC AND COGNITIVE APPROACHES).

Adaptation has always been defined in relation to something else – a specific style, linguistic conventions or a communication model. Translation studies as an independent discipline now enables us to study adaptation on its own terms, as both a local and a global procedure. It is imperative to acknowledge adaptation as a type of creative process which seeks to restore the balance of communication that is often disrupted by traditional forms of translation. Only by treating it as a legitimate strategy can we begin to understand the motivation for using it and to appreciate the relationship between it and other forms of conventional translation.

See also:
CHILDREN'S LITERATURE; DRAMA TRANSLATION; IDEOLOGY; LATIN TRADITION; REWRITING; STRATEGIES.

Further reading
Delisle 1986; Foz 1988; Gailliard 1988; Santoyo 1989; Brisset 1990; Nord 1991a/2006; Donaire and LaForge. 1991; Gambier 1992; Merino Álvarez 1992; Farghal 1993; Merino Álvarez 1994; Nord 1997; Bastin 1998, 2005; Ámorim 2005.

GEORGES L. BASTIN

Translated from Spanish by Mark Gregson

Advertising

Advertising texts have been widely studied from the linguistic and sociological points of view, and have also been one of the favoured objects of semiotic analysis (from Barthes and Eco to the recent developments of visual and social semiotics). They have not, however, received the same treatment in translation studies. Especially before 2000, promotional materials (including sub-genres such as advertising, publicity and tourist brochures) were mainly used in general translation handbooks or textbooks as examples, or 'special cases' of translation (see COMMERCIAL TRANSLATION). Although several specialized articles had already been published, systematic research into advertising translation *per se* started only very recently, with monographs (Guidère 2000a; Bueno García 2000) and edited volumes (Adab and Valdés 2004) beginning to appear from 2000 onwards. Recent research also marked a shift away from purely linguistic or verbal-only approaches, opening up new insights into the intersemiotic and multimodal nature of advertising texts, while also highlighting the need to take the cultural dimension of advertising translation into account.

A possible reason for the reticence of early translation scholars to address the question of translating advertising material may lie in the verbal connotation traditionally attached to the term 'translation', which may explain why the crosslinguistic and cross-cultural transfer of multimodal promotional texts is often termed LOCALIZATION, ADAPTATION or (less frequently) transcreation or REWRITING. The latter set of terms suggests a kind of transfer which is less concerned with issues of 'faithfulness' and more, perhaps, with functional EQUIVALENCE and adequacy. These terms, rather than 'translation', may therefore appear more appropriate for use in connection with advertising, where the QUALITY of the 'translated' text is usually assessed according to functionalist criteria.

Another factor which makes it conceptually difficult for translation scholars to engage in a systematic analysis of advertising material is the current practice, adopted by several multinational companies, of developing local campaigns simultaneously from a brief that avoids culture-specificity as much as possible. In this process – which Adab (2000: 224) calls **glocalization** – there is no single advertisement or campaign that can be easily recognized as a 'source' text. Thus, the very TRANSLATABILITY of advertising and promotional texts can only be accepted on the condition that the term 'translation' is taken in its etymological meaning of 'transfer' (across languages and cultures), irrespective of the extent of 'departure' from some 'source text' (which might not be retrievable). It is in this broad sense, then, that the term 'translation' is used in this entry.

Verbal-only approaches to advertising translation

Early research into advertising translation, carried out during a period when multimodality had not yet gained prominence in translation studies, tended to focus on the linguistic analysis of the verbal copy. While these studies did invoke a functional perspective, their scope was limited to identifying the function of single pay-offs or sentences in the copy, not the function of the advertisement as a whole. For instance, Tatilon, who advocates 'traduire non la lettre *mais l'esprit, non les mots mais les fonctions*' (1990: 245, emphasis in the original – 'translate not the letter but the spirit, not the words but the functions'), offers as good examples of what he advocates a few English and French slogans where assonance and puns are recreated in the target language. Similarly, when Quillard (1998) focuses on the rendering of humour in French translations of English ads, she mentions the role of pictures in activating puns but does not include them in her paper; in other words, she isolates the humorous sentences from the rest of the verbal text, which does not appear in the discussion. In this type of research, 'function' is taken to be the ability of a pun to amuse the reader, or attract his or her attention. And the assumption is that for the target text to constitute a good translation, this ability or potential must be recreated. This justifies the extraction of selected fragments of the copy from the rest of the advertisement.

A different type of linguistic analysis restricted to the verbal level attempts a broader understanding of advertising translation by providing verbal-based evidence for the study of cultural adaptation. For example, Quillard (1999) investigates differences between the Canadian English, Canadian French and French versions of the same advertisements to demonstrate the importance of the localization of cultural values across two communities that share (almost) the same language but not the same geographical and cultural space (French and French Canadians), as well as across two communities that share (almost) the same geographical space but not the same language (English- and French-speaking Canadians). Similarly, in her analysis of a small corpus of Spanish and German advertisements for cosmetic products, Montes Fernández (2003) explores the way in which different conventions in advertising language may reflect different cultural conventions.

As these examples suggest, studying the verbal aspects of texts is fully compatible with studying cultural aspects of advertising in translation (see below); it also does not necessarily exclude the analysis of other semiotic dimensions in the translation of promotional material.

Multimodality and intersemiotic translation

Referring to the translation of advertising and promotional websites, Calzada Pérez (2005) argues that 'images need translating as much as words and cyberspace is nothing if not a huge meeting point which provides information that is constantly translated back and forth'. This statement summarizes a new trend in the study of advertising translation, one that attempts to take into account the range of constraints imposed upon and opportunities offered to the translator of advertising material by virtue of the modes of expression involved in each advertising text.

It has been argued that no text is strictly monomodal (Baldry 2000). For instance, a novel or textbook without illustrations may appear to have only a verbal dimension, but typographical choices (Schopp 2002, 2005) and the physical qualities of the paper it is printed on give the words a particular rendering or **inscription** (Kress and Van Leeuwen 1996: 230–32) that contributes to the construction of textual meaning. At the same time, advertising texts on the whole display a high level of multimodality with respect to other genres, because of their simultaneous reliance on different kinds of stimuli. For instance, print advertisements usually have verbal and visual components, radio commercials rely on verbal and aural (sound/music) effects, and street advertising makes use of verbal and/or visual signs combined with geosemiotic cues such as position relative to the viewer, proximity with other texts, and spatial context (see Scollon and Scollon 2003 on geosemiotics). Thus, the multimodality of advertising texts does not depend only on the fact that campaigns for the same products may span various media – in other words, that the same campaign may be run in identical or slightly different forms on television, street posters, radio, etc. Rather, multimodality is achieved within each advertising text, even in the case of texts that are traditionally excluded from the definition of 'multimedia', such as print advertisements.

A multimodal approach to the translation of advertisements and promotional material tends to prioritize three areas. First, it advocates training translators of advertising material and translation students to analyse relationships among the different semiotic (rather than merely linguistic) elements of the text (see, for example, Laviosa 2007; Torresi 2007a). Second, intersemiotic translation is advocated as a means of effectively localizing the advertising message by working on the text *as a whole* – for instance replacing a visual element in the source text with a new one which can compensate for an unavoidable loss of meaning in the verbal component of the text, or building an entirely new verbal text *around* the visual one to accommodate market differences (Torresi 2007b). Third, on a more theoretical level, scholars of translation are encouraged to 'move beyond the written word' to incorporate 'the visual, and multimodal in general' in their research (Munday 2004: 216).

Examples of multimodal, intersemiotic approaches to the study of advertising in translation include Chiaro's (2004) contrastive analysis of intrasemiotic and intersemiotic strategies in international websites and print advertisements for Italian food products, and Simões Lucas Freitas's (2004) study of the way in which meaning is conveyed across different modes of expression in multimedia campaigns. While other scholars who have studied the translation of advertising do not explicitly use the term 'intersemiotic translation', they implicitly draw on the same concept. For instance, Millán-Varela (2004) contrasts a corpus of European, Asian and South American TV commercials of Cornetto ice cream within the framework of Kress and Van Leeuwen's (1996) visual grammar. Bueno García (2000) highlights the importance of elements such as sound and image in the translation of advertising, while Guidère (2000b: 28) states that 'les signes linguistiques du texte publicitaire sont en relation d'étroite dépendance avec les signes iconiques de l'image' (the linguistic signs of advertising texts are directly dependent on the iconic signs of the image). Nomura (2000) similarly emphasizes the importance of the visual in constructing the advertising message, and discusses the implications for translators. A more subtle analysis is provided by Valdés (2000), who reveals the importance of what might appear as slight changes in terms of typography and adjustment of visuals to accommodate national stereotypes.

And as early as 1996, de Pedro proposed a scale for describing the transnational adaptation of TV advertisements based on the degree to which both the verbal and the visual are changed, including those cases where an entirely new campaign is created.

Finally, many of these studies also engage with cultural issues, often identifying such issues as the very motivation for intersemiotic translation.

Cultural transfer

There are several ways of making an advertising text as persuasive as possible. Each, however, is largely culture-specific and has to be examined carefully when an advertising or publicity text is transferred across different languages and/or social groups.

In their study on multinational organizations, Hofstede (1980/2001, 1991) and Hofstede and Hofstede (2005) found that different national populations show different orientations towards what the authors call **dimensions of culture** (see also CULTURE). De Mooij (1998/2005, 2003, 2004) applies Hofstede's model to advertising, mapping these dimensions onto different consumer behaviours and advertising styles. For instance, Italians appear to score high on the 'uncertainty avoidance' dimension, meaning that they value being reassured by what they already know more than being surprised by something new. This may explain why advertising campaigns in Italy tend to adopt a style that complies with the target group's expectations (Brancati 2002: 76–7), rather than resorting to humour, puns and other creative resources which are popular in Great Britain, for instance (Pennarola 2003).

But it is not only the form, or style, of advertising campaigns that change across cultures and languages. In order to fulfil their persuasive purpose, publicity material and advertisements have to *motivate* the target group to change their consumer or public behaviour by appealing either to their aspirations or fears. Such aspiration or fears, however, are often culture-specific and should be carefully handled in the translation of advertising material, even in the case of values, such as cleanliness, which may be assumed to be universal (Torresi 2004).

Cultural values and stereotypes have important implications for professional practice and training: Fuentes Luque and Kelly (2000: 241) point out that 'the role of the translator in international advertising ... can in no way be limited to "purely linguistic" issues', and suggest that training courses should help would-be translators of advertising material to become 'intercultural experts'. Guidère (2001) agrees that 'to accomplish his mission successfully, the translator is required to think and to integrate a certain amount of data, not only about marketing and basic communication, but also about geopolitics and ethnology'. Adab (2000, 2001) similarly stresses the importance of cultural values, placing them in a broader functionalist view that takes into account situational factors as well as linguistic ones in the context of advertising.

The discussion of cultural issues in the translation of advertising material would particularly benefit from insights on the cultural adaptation of European or American advertising campaigns and messages for non-Western audiences. Important research has been carried out in this area by scholars such as Guidère (2000a), who highlights the difficulties of translating advertisements into Arabic, Zequan (2003), who traces some of the terminological choices made in the translation of a beauty spa advertisement from English into Chinese to differences in religious traditions, and Chuansheng and Yunnan (2003), who provide an extensive overview of brand name translation strategies in China. Ho (2004) analyses the cultural adjustments he introduced in his own translation of commercial advertising for Singapore as a tourist destination, again from English into Chinese.

As far as promotional genres are concerned, an obvious example of the importance of cultural adaptation (and appropriation) to ensure customer motivation can be found in the translation of tourist brochures. If, as Sumberg (2004) points out, the profile of the advertised destination is poorly adjusted to the target readership's tourist expectations, the brochure will fail to *sell* the destination – even though that brochure might very well reflect the actual profile and reality of the place better than a heavily adapted translation. This highlights a certain tension between the translation of promotional material, which tends to domesticate Otherness in order to comply with its ultimate persuasive function, and the general preference for foreignizing STRATEGIES in other genres, in particular LITERARY TRANSLATION. In the real-life practice of promotional translation, foreignization does not appear to be a viable choice, inasmuch as strategies of advertising (and of translating advertising material) that do not take into account local cultural orientations and preferences are simply likely to fail (De Mooij 2004: 181). At the same time, in educational contexts, as Calzada Pérez (2007a) has argued, domestication in advertising translation can be exposed and used as a tool to encourage consumers to develop a critical gaze on consumerist values.

See also:

ADAPTATION; AUDIOVISUAL TRANSLATION; COMICS; COMMERCIAL TRANSLATION; CULTURE; GLOBALIZATION.

Further reading

De Mooij 1998/2005; Bueno García 2000; Guidère 2000a; Schopp 2002; De Mooij 2003; Adab and Valdés 2004; Calzada Pérez 2007a; Laviosa 2007; Torresi 2007b.

IRA TORRESI

Asylum

Translators and interpreters play a pivotal role in global processes of communication. Some of the key issues surrounding GLOBALIZATION are enacted in the political asylum context; these include national sovereignty, the construction of individual/collective identities and rights, and the question of territorial borders. The right to asylum is simultaneously a national and an international issue. The granting of political asylum, which guarantees the applicant temporary or permanent residence in the country of application, involves an array of contexts in which interpreters and translators are involved. Although the contexts and accompanying bureaucratic procedures will vary from one country to another, all countries are obliged to follow certain basic procedures as signatories to the 1951 United Nations Geneva Convention and 1967 Protocol.

Instances of interpreted oral communication exchanges take place at the initial port of entry interview, through the development of narratives that are elaborated within solicitors' offices or, more spontaneously and often without the benefits of any professional legal advice, in the substantive interview with immigration officials; interpreting ultimately also takes place in yet another context, namely in the appeals courts. Written documents in the form of identity cards or certificates, newspaper clippings, affidavits of support, etc. (where available) must also be translated in order to be included as verification evidence of an individual claim. The purpose of both oral and written forms of communication is to determine the credibility of an asylum applicant's claim of a 'well-founded fear of persecution' for reasons of race, religion, nationality, membership of a particular social group or political opinion.

Research in this field has encompassed four overlapping areas of practical and theoretical concern: the analysis of micro-interactional exchanges; theorizations of the status and construction of narratives in the interviewing process; the macro-social position and positioning of interpreters in the asylum system; and the role of interpreters in psychotherapeutic sessions with trauma and torture victims.

Analysis of micro-interactional exchanges, either exclusively with regard to asylum interviews (Pöllabauer 2004, 2006, 2007) or including asylum interview excerpts in a broader corpus (Mason 2006a), details misunderstandings and mistranslations in actual asylum interviews, audio-taped and transcribed for close textual analysis. The research draws on a range of methodological and theoretical approaches, including interactional sociolinguistics, conversational analysis and critical discourse theory and considers such factors as the interactionally-derived coordination and control of utterances, participant alignment, face-saving strategies and identity. Work in this area focuses on the role of discourse and power in constructing and communicating identities across languages and cultures. In particular, it has demonstrated the visibility of interpreters' participation in substantive asylum interviews, the contingency of the interpreter's role in relation to the needs and expectations of the other participants, and the problematic relationship between interpreter practices and existing codes of ETHICS that purport to define this practice.

The focus on the role of narratives in establishing applicants' credibility has contributed significantly to research in this area (Barsky 1996, 2001; Blommaert 2001; Jacquemet 2005; Maryns 2006). In the asylum process, applicants' explanations and defence of their asylum case are presented in an interview or series of interviews involving the construction of a narrative account of their individual case of persecution. Barsky's pioneering work in this area examined the ways in which both INSTITUTIONAL and discursive constraints impacted on applicants' and immigration officials' ability to reach more culturally-nuanced understandings through a survey of written records of Canadian Convention Refugee hearings. He suggested that asylum claimants were overburdened with the task of projecting a self through their narrative accounts that coincided with the expectations of the interviewing officers. He further suggested that interpreters be encouraged to act as intercultural agents and active intermediaries between applicants and the immigration service in order to compensate for both cultural and linguistic gaps in understanding.

In related work, Blommaert's (2001) and Maryns's (2006) studies of asylum seekers' narratives in the Belgian asylum system explore in detail what happens when sociolinguistic repertoires and resources are transferred, forcibly or otherwise, across cultural and linguistic boundaries. They explore the impact of applicants' cultural and physical dislocation from their countries and communities of origin on narrative production and interpretation in eligibility determination interviews. Their work highlights the bureaucratic processing of individual narratives which collapses the idiosyncratic and culturally-bound experiences of an applicant into a generalizable institutional frame and interactively denies applicants their right to locally-derived, experiential, personalized accounts. The transfer of spoken to written accounts in interpreted interviews is also explored. In certain cases, for example, interpreters will create a written translation for the interviewing officers from an initial oral exchange. This form of entextualization of the applicant's narrative is a further instantiation of the institutional framing of discourse; as a record of the encounter, it represents yet another move away from the original account, contributing to the process of localization, delocalization and relocalization of the applicant's original text. In this research, interpreters are seen to play a role in the institutionalization of culturally specific, locally derived narratives in so far as they contribute to the construction of versions of applicants' narratives that correspond to the needs and expectations of the bureaucracies in which they are situated and evaluated.

In other cases, as seen in Jacquemet's (2005) account of the United Nations High Commission for Refugees' (UNHCR) registration interviews of Kosovars and Albanians during the Balkan conflict, Kosovar interpreters functioned to curtail applicants' attempts at providing narrative evidence in order to demonstrate their Kosovar origins, which was a crucial factor in earning them refugee status. As Kosovar refugees themselves, interpreters were given the task of assessing the credibility of an applicant's claim by distinguishing speakers of the Gheg variety of Albanian spoken in Kosovo from that spoken in Northern Albania. With this as a priority, experiential narratives of place and time were deemed irrelevant to the purpose of the interview, in which the interpreters' role was transformed to that of communicative detective. Jacquemet's research highlighted the perceived importance of the narrative format for applicants themselves in order to adequately represent their experiences and the frustrations and uncertainties that arose when this opportunity was inexplicably denied to them. In addition, the research provides evidence for what in a number of countries has emerged as an officially sanctioned – though highly unethical and unreliable – practice of using interpreters to conduct linguistic identification in order to determine the nationality of asylum applicants (Eades *et al.* 2003).

Overlapping in its concerns to theorize the role of interpreters in the asylum system is research which takes as its starting point the nature and impact of the macro-social and ideological spaces in which the micro-settings identified above are situated (Inghilleri 2003, 2005a, 2007a, 2007b). This research theorizes the social position and positioning of interpreters in the asylum system using Toury's concept of NORMS and Bourdieu's concepts of *habitus*, field, capital and *illusio* as a starting point (see SOCIOLOGICAL APPROACHES). It examines these in relation to the principal legal and political institutions involved in the political asylum process as well as interpreter TRAINING programmes to determine the extent to which observable socially and institutionally derived interpreting norms and expectations influence the professional practice of interpreters. It also considers the social and biological trajectories of interpreters and asylum applicants themselves and the relationship between these and any expectations or constraints on discursive practices. This research is concerned with configurations and reconfigurations of the social in local, interactional contexts of interpreting where interpreters may challenge the normative practices specific to their own or others' professions, and where linguistic and cultural understandings are constituted and reconstituted, including others' perceptions of interpreters themselves. It suggests that while at the local level interpreters do frequently participate in the reproduction of the existing social order, they also contribute to the production of interactively reconfigured social relations of power. The overwhelming conclusion of this research – which considers the asylum systems of Europe, North America and Australia – is that interpreted asylum interviews occur within a climate of national and international policies of exclusion that significantly restrict the right of refugees and asylum seekers to be adequately heard. At the same time, however, it suggests that translation and interpreting play a central role in the development of expansive conceptions of human rights and transnational norms which have the potential to expand applicants' rights to participate in a constructive inclusive dialogue within the global politics of asylum.

Another important area of research on interpreting for refugees and asylum seekers that is also concerned with the generation of a constructive inclusive dialogue focuses on the issue of mental health. A majority of those seeking refuge through the asylum system suffer from the effects of physical and mental torture, the loss of family members through separation or war, and the difficulties of adjusting to major disruptions and distortions of their life prior to displacement. Many of those who seek or find help through some form of counselling rely on interpreters to communicate in the psychotherapeutic sessions. The quality and choice of interpreter will influence the adequate reporting of symptoms, psychological assessment and diagnosis and the overall progress of treatment. An interpreter's presence can be a positive force, serving to reassure clients and providing an invaluable source of information about a client's culture and language to the therapist. Alternatively, the interpreter can become a source of additional fear if perceived or known by the client to be on an opposing side of the political conflict which is the very source of his or her trauma (Nicholson 1994; Tribe 1999; Tribe and Raval 2003).

A major piece of research by Bot (2005) draws on a range of methodological and theoretical approaches which relate to the interactional nature of the therapeutic encounter and also those derived from psychotherapeutic research traditions, including concept mapping, psychotherapeutic categorization systems, and intercultural mediation. This research explores the question of how the therapist–patient relationship is affected by the set of potential roles adopted by the interpreter and which of the different communicative models available in interpreter training and research may be most effective in psychotherapeutic treatment of refugees and asylum seekers. It examines the interplay between communicative practices and psychotherapeutic ones, revealing the presence of a multitude of factors that challenge and constrain the communicative behaviour of therapist, interpreter and client alike. Drawing on conversational analysis, it focuses on the assignment of turns as indicators of negotiation over control, conversational alignments and interactional status amongst the participants. It also examines models of cooperation operating in the therapeutic encounter which generate distinctive moves regarding, for example, information chunking, overlap and pause, gaze and gesture.

Research in the area of political asylum makes clear that interpreters and translators operate as pivotal players within the asylum system. They enable the system to function by ensuring both the flow of communication and of applicants. Interpreters and translators serve as active social agents in the global political space of the asylum system. They contribute consciously and unconsciously to both inclusionary and exclusionary practices as they negotiate linguistic and cultural meanings in the context of institutional and political agendas and national and international relations of power.

See also:
COMMUNITY INTERPRETING; GLOBALIZATION; INSTITUTIONAL TRANSLATION; MINORITY; MOBILITY.

Further reading
Barsky 1996, 2001; Blommaert 2001; Inghilleri 2003; Pöllabauer 2004; Bot 2005; Inghilleri 2005a; Jacquemet 2005; Maryns 2006; Pöllabauer 2006; Inghilleri 2007a, 2007b.

MOIRA INGHILLERI

Audiovisual translation

Audiovisual translation is a branch of translation studies concerned with the transfer of multimodal and multimedial texts into another language and/or culture. Audiovisual texts are **multimodal** inasmuch as their production and interpretation relies on the combined deployment of a wide range of semiotic resources or 'modes' (Baldry and Thibault 2006). Major meaning-making modes in audiovisual texts include language, image, music, colour and perspective. Audiovisual texts are **multimedial** in so far as this panoply of semiotic modes is delivered to the viewer through various media in a synchronized manner, with the screen playing a coordinating role in the presentation process (Negroponte 1991).

Since the 1970s, screen-based texts have become increasingly ubiquitous. Scholars have been quick to bring the investigation of new textual manifestations – ranging from software to videogames – into the remit of audiovisual translation research, thus extending the boundaries of this area of study (see also LOCALIZATION). Chaume (2004) has documented the successive stages of this expansion by looking at the terms used to designate this field of enquiry during the period in question. Considering that the mainstream forms of audiovisual translation – i.e. subtitling and dubbing – were born on the back of sound motion pictures, it is only natural that the terms 'film dubbing' and 'film translation' came to feature prominently in early scholarly work (Fodor 1976; Snell-Hornby 1988). The subsequent emergence of television as a mass medium of communication and entertainment provided new avenues for the dissemination of translated audiovisual texts, with labels such as 'film and TV translation' (Delabastita 1989) and 'media translation' (Eguíluz *et al.* 1994) gaining visibility in the literature. The most recent developments relate to the exponential growth in the volume of audiovisual texts produced by and for electronic and digital media. Terms like 'screen translation' (Mason 1989; O'Connell 2007) and 'multimedia translation' (Gambier and Gottlieb 2001) illustrate the extent to which audiovisual translation has outgrown its core domain of enquiry and annexed neighbouring fields under an all-inclusive research agenda.

The genealogy of audiovisual translation

Even during the silent film era, exporting films to foreign markets involved some form of interlingual mediation. The turn of the twentieth century witnessed the incorporation of written language into the conglomerate of film semiotics in the form of intertitles (Ivarsson 2002). The use of these texts placed between film frames grew in parallel with the emergence of increasingly complex filmic narratives. Intertitles situated the action in a specific temporal and spatial setting, provided viewers with insights into the characters' inner thoughts and helped them negotiate the discrepancies between screen time and real time, during a period when filmic techniques were rudimentary (Dick 1990). Removing the original intertitles and inserting a new set of target language texts back into the film was all that was required to exploit it commercially in a foreign market. But intertitles also served as the springboard for the development of new forms of audiovisual translation. In-house commentators were employed to fill the same gaps as the intertitles (Dreyer-Sfard

1965; Díaz Cintas 2003), although these enter-tainers often sought to enhance the viewer's experience by spreading gossip about the film stars or even explaining how the projector worked (Cazdyn 2004). The national industries of the USA and a number of European countries thrived on this absence of linguistic barriers to film exports until the aftermath of World War I took its toll on the financial capability of European industry to fund new projects. By the early 1920s, American films had come to secure a dominant market share throughout Europe, pushing some national film industries (e.g. British and Italian) close to the brink of collapse (Nowell-Smith and Ricci 1998).

According to Forbes and Street (2000), the advent of sound in the late 1920s put a temporary end to the American domination of European film industries, as the big studios became suddenly unable to satisfy the demand of European audiences for films spoken in their native languages. Experimental attempts to appeal to local European sensibilities – e.g. the 'multilingual filming method' and the 'dunning process' (Ballester 1995) – failed to earn the American industry its lost market share back, and it soon became obvious that new forms of audiovisual translation were required to reassert its former dominance. During the second half of the 1920s, technological developments made it possible to 'revoice' certain fragments of dialogue or edit the sound of scenes that had been shot in noisy environments through a process known as 'post-synchronization' (Whitman-Linsen 1992; Chaves 2000). Despite being conceived as a means of improving the quality of an original recording, post-synchro-nized revoicing was soon used to replace the source dialogue with a translated version, and is therefore acknowledged as the immediate forerunner of dubbing as we know it today. Concurrent advances in the manipulation of celluloid films during the 1920s allowed distrib-utors to superimpose titles straight onto the film strip images through optical and mechanical means (Ivarsson 2002). By the late 1920s it had become customary to use this evolved version of the primitive intertitles to provide a translation of the source dialogue in synchrony with the relevant fragment of speech, thus paving the way for the development of modern subtitling.

The perfection of these new techniques

and their acceptance by European audiences ended the moratorium on American control of European markets (Forbes and Street 2000), with American films regaining a market share of 70 per cent in Europe and Latin America by 1937 (Chaves 2000). This second wave of domination was regarded as a threat not only to the sustain-ability of Europe's national film industries, but also to their respective languages, cultures and political regimes – in the mid-1930s, the latter ranged from democratic systems to fascist dicta-torships. The multiplicity of European interests and ideologies would soon lead each country to adopt its own protectionist measures and/or CENSORSHIP mechanisms (Nowell-Smith and Ricci 1998), which were, in many cases, enforced through the choice of specific policies and forms of audiovisual translation. Despite these efforts, and except for brief exceptional periods like World War II, these dynamics of domination were to remain unchanged.

Subtitling

A typology of subtitling procedures

Subtitling consists of the production of snippets of written text (**subtitles**, or **captions** in American English) to be superimposed on visual footage – normally near the bottom of the frame – while an audiovisual text is projected, played or broadcast. In so far as it involves a shift from a spoken to a written medium, subtitling has been defined as a 'diasemiotic' or 'intermodal' form of audiovisual translation (Gottlieb 1997). **Interlingual subtitles** provide viewers with a written rendition of the source text speech, whether dialogue or narration, in their own language. In communities where at least two languages co-exist, **bilingual subtitles** deliver two language versions of the same source fragment, one in each of the two constitutive lines of the subtitle (Gambier 2003a).

Each of the fragments into which subtitlers divide the speech for the purposes of trans-lation must be delivered concurrently with its written rendition in the target language via the subtitle. And given that 'people generally speak much faster than they read, subtitling inevitably involves ... technical constraints of shortage of screen space and lack of time' (O'Connell

1998:67). Subtitles composed according to widely accepted spatial parameters contain a maximum of two lines of text, each accommodating up to 35 characters (Karamitrouglou 1998). The actual number of characters that can be used in each subtitle then depends on the duration of the corresponding speech unit (Titford 1982).

Since the 1970s, we have witnessed the proliferation of **intralingual subtitles**, which are composed in the same language as the source text speech. Intralingual subtitles were traditionally addressed at MINORITY audiences, such as immigrants wishing to develop their proficiency in the language of the host community or viewers requiring written support to fully understand certain audiovisual texts shot in non-standard dialects of their native language (Díaz Cintas 2003). However, intralingual subtitling has now become almost synonymous with **subtitling for the deaf and hard of hearing** in the audiovisual marketplace, where accessibility-friendly initiatives are receiving increasing attention. Subtitles for the hard of hearing provide a text display of the speech but also incorporate descriptions of sound features which are not accessible to this audience. To compensate for their higher density (Wurm 2007), this type of subtitle complies with specific conventions in terms of timing, text positioning and use of colours (Neves 2005). Although subtitles for the deaf were for a long time restricted to films and programmes recorded in advance, the development of **real time** or **live subtitling technologies**, ranging from the stenograph and stenotyping methods to speech recognition systems (Lambourne 2006), has increased the accessibility of live news, live chat shows and reality TV to the deaf community (see also SIGNED LANGUAGE INTERPRETING).

Historically, the terms 'interlingual' and 'intralingual subtitles' correlated with **open** and **closed subtitles**, respectively. Interlingual subtitles have tended to be printed on the actual film, thus becoming part of the audiovisual text itself. Given that they are visually present throughout the screening and universally accessible to all viewers (except for the visually impaired), interlingual subtitles are said to be open. Intralingual subtitles, however, have tended to be encoded in the broadcast signal using a number of technologies, mainly teletext (Neves 2007). They are known as 'closed subtitles' because they are accessible only to viewers whose television sets are equipped with the relevant decoder and who choose to display them on the screen while watching the programme. The advent of DVD and digital television represents a departure from this tradition as both media provide viewers with closed intralingual and interlingual subtitles, normally in more than one language.

The subtitling process

The subtitler's basic working materials have traditionally included a time-coded VHS copy of the source film or programme and a 'dialogue list'; i.e. an enhanced post-production script containing a transcription of the dialogue, a description of relevant visual information and sometimes notes for the translator (Díaz Cintas 2001). The text is typically subjected to a 'spotting' process, during which the dialogue is divided into segments that are time-cued individually. Each dialogue segment is then translated or transcribed in compliance with certain segmentation and editing conventions (Karamitrouglou 1998), including time–space correlation standards. The output of this process, normally an electronic list of spotted subtitles, is then returned to the commissioner of the translation. In recent years, increased circulation of audiovisual texts in digital format and the development of dedicated software applications have brought about important changes in the subtitling process. Although these new technologies are not necessarily available to all freelance professionals, they now allow subtitlers to complete a project – including the actual transference of subtitles onto the text – using a standard computer.

Advantages and limitations of subtitling

Empirical evidence suggests that subtitles can deliver 43 per cent less text than the spoken dialogue they derive from (de Linde and Kay 1999). Given the constraints arising from the synchronous alignment between spoken sound and written subtitles that the industry requires (Naficy 2001), subtitlers are expected to prioritize the overall communicative intention of an utterance over the semantics of its individual lexical constituents (Gottlieb 1998). Deleting, condensing and adapting the source speech are thus some of the most common subtitling STRAT-EGIES deployed by professionals. Under such tight medium-related constraints, subtitling is claimed to foster cultural and linguistic stand-ardization (Fawcett 2003; Díaz Cintas 2005) by ironing non-mainstream identities – and their individual speech styles – out of the trans-lated narrative. Pragmatically, this streamlining process can affect, for instance, the impression that viewers form of characters in terms of friendliness (Remael 2003). In terms of Venuti's 'domestication/foreignization' dichotomy, the subtitling process typically leads to the domesti-cation of the source dialogue and the effacement of the translator (Ulrych 2000).

Subtitling can be viewed as a form of 'overt translation' (Battarbee 1986) since it allows viewers to access the original speech (see QUALITY). Effectively, this empowers viewers who have some knowledge of the source language but are unaware of how the subti-tler's work is conditioned by media-related constraints to monitor and criticize the trans-lation. Criticisms are often levelled at subtitling because it represents an intrusion on the image and its processing requires a relatively intensive cognitive effort on the part of the viewer, thus detracting from the overall viewing experience. On the positive side, advocates of subtitling highlight the fact that it respects the aesthetic and artistic integrity of the original text. The viewer's exposure to a foreign language has also been found to promote the target audience's interest in other cultures (Danan 1991). And finally, subtitling is a comparatively cheap and fast form of audiovisual translation (Dries 1995).

Revoicing

Although there is a lack of consensus on the scope of the term 'revoicing' (Luyken *et al.* 1991; Baker and Hochel 1998), it technically designates a range of oral language transfer procedures: voice-over, narration, audio description, free commentary, simultaneous interpreting and lip-synchronized dubbing. In practice, 'revoicing' tends to encompass all

these procedures, except for lip-synchronized dubbing, which is commonly referred to as 'dubbing'. Although all these methods involve a greater or lesser degree of synchronization between soundtrack and on-screen images, the need for synchronization is particularly important in the case of dubbing.

Voice-over or **'half-dubbing'** (Gambier 2003a) is a method that involves pre-recorded revoicing: after a few seconds in which the original sound is fully audible, the volume is lowered and the voice reading the translation becomes prominent. This combination of realism (the original sound remains available in the acoustic background throughout) and almost full translation of the original text (Luyken *et al.* 1991) makes voice-over particu-larly suitable for interviews, documentaries and other programmes which do not require lip synchronization. Voice-over is also used today to translate feature films for some small markets in Europe and Asia because it is substantially cheaper than dubbing (O'Connell 2007).

Although it is not always pre-recorded, **narration** has been defined as 'an extended voice-over' (Luyken *et al.* 1991: 80). This form of oral transfer aims to provide a summarized but faithful and carefully scripted rendition of the original speech, and its delivery is carefully timed to avoid any clash with the visual syntax of the programme. In recent years, a very specific form of pre-recorded, mostly intralingual narration has become increasingly important to ensure the accessibility of audio-visual products to the visually impaired: this is known as **audio description**. An audio description is a spoken account of those visual aspects of a film which play a role in conveying its plot, rather than a translation of linguistic content. The voice of an audio describer delivers this additional narrative between stretches of dialogue, hence the importance of engaging in a delicate balancing exercise to establish what the needs of the spectator may be, and to ensure the audience is not overburdened with excessive information.

As opposed to these pre-recorded transfer methods, other forms of revoicing are performed on the spot by interpreters, presenters or commentators by superimposing their voices over the original sound. **Free commentary**, for example, involves adapting the source speech to meet the needs of the target audience, rather than attempting to convey its content faithfully (Gambier 2003a). Commentaries are commonly used to broadcast high-profile events with a spontaneous tone. **Simultaneous interpreting** is typically carried out in the context of film festivals when time and budget constraints do not allow for a more elaborate form of oral or written language transfer (see CONFERENCE INTERPRETING). Interpreters may translate with or without scripts and dub the voices of the whole cast of characters featuring in the film (Lecuona 1994).

Lip-synchronized dubbing

Lip-synchronized (or **lip-sync**) **dubbing** is one of the two dominant forms of film translation, the other being interlingual subtitling. In the field of audiovisual translation, dubbing denotes the re-recording of the original voice track in the target language using dubbing actors' voices; the dubbed dialogue aims to recreate the dynamics of the original, particularly in terms of delivery pace and lip movements (Luyken *et al.* 1991). Regarded by some as the supreme and most comprehensive form of translation (Cary 1969), dubbing 'requires a complex juggling of semantic content, cadence of language and technical prosody ... while bowing to the prosaic constraints of the medium itself' (Whitman-Linsen 1992: 103–4). In the last three decades, there have been several attempts to map out the set of variables moulding this transfer method, mainly by diluting the importance of lip synchrony proper within a wider range of synchrony requirements. These new and more elaborate models of dubbing synchrony advocate the need to match other features of the original film which contribute to characterization or artistic idiosyncrasy (Fodor 1976; Whitman-Linsen 1992; Herbst 1994; Chaume 2004). At any rate, the relative weighting of lip matching *vis-à-vis* other types of synchrony depends on the target market, with American audiences, for example, being more demanding than Italians in this respect (Gambier 2003a).

The lip-sync dubbing process

The translation of a source language dialogue list is one of the earliest stages in the dubbing process. Although access to a working copy of the film is crucial for translators to verify non-visual information and make appropriate decisions on aspects such as register or pragmatic intention, this is not always made available to them (Hensel 1987). The translators' participation in the dubbing process often ends with the production of a dialogue list in the target language; in practice, translators do not concern themselves with lip movements as they usually lack experience in dialogue adaptation and adjustment techniques (Luyken *et al.* 1991). A 'dubbing writer' who is adept at lip reading (Myers 1973) but not always familiar with the source language takes over at this point to 'detect' the text. This involves identifying those sounds delivered by screen actors in close-up shots that will require maximum synchrony on the part of dubbing actors and marking their presence on the relevant frames of the film strip (Paquin 2001). Once the adaptation is ready, the film dialogue is divided into passages of dialogue, called 'loops' (Myers 1973) or 'takes' (Whitman-Linsen 1992), whose length depends on the country where the dubbed version is produced. These takes become the working units during the revoicing of the dialogue track, which is carried out under the supervision of a dubbing director and a sound engineer. The involvement of so many professionals in the dubbing process explains why this form of audiovisual translation is up to fifteen times more expensive than subtitling (Luyken *et al.* 1991). The actual translation and adaptation of the dialogue amounts to only 10 per cent of the overall cost (Dries 1995), although this depends on the genre – with action and humour films being the cheapest and most expensive, respectively (Muntefering 2002).

Advantages and limitations of lip-sync dubbing

Dubbing allows viewers to watch a film or programme without dividing their attention between the images and the written translation (Goris 1993). This reduces the amount of processing effort required on the part of the audience and makes dubbing the most effective method to translate programmes addressed at children or viewers with a restricted degree of literacy. In so far as dubbing is a spoken translation of an oral source text, it is possible for the target text to convey more of the information contained in its source counterpart. Also, dubbing allows for the reproduction of the original dialogue's interactional dynamics, including stretches of overlapping speech and most other prosodic features. On the negative side, dubbing is expensive and time-consuming. Furthermore, it tends to draw on a restricted range of voices to which viewers may become over-exposed over a number of years, which detracts from the authenticity of the dubbed film. In relation to the translation process itself, the concern of dubbing practitioners with synchronization and the take-based approach to the revoicing process has often resulted in a 'compartmentalization' of the source text. This adherence to the constraints of micro-equivalence often proves detrimental to the 'naturalness' and 'contextual appropriateness' of the translated dialogue (Herbst 1997; Pérez González 2007). It is also held accountable for most of the so-called 'universals' of dubbed language, including its failure to portray sociolinguistic variation and its overall tendency towards cultural neutralization (Pavesi 2005). The transmission of culture-specific terms and values in dubbed audiovisual texts remains a highly problematic issue. In principle, the revoicing of the dialogue allows for an easy domestication of the original text, including the replacement of source cultural references by their naturalizing counterparts, i.e. their functional equivalents in the target viewer's cognitive environment (Chiaro 1992). However, these attempts to maintain the illusion of authenticity may backfire and damage the commercial success of the dubbed product when the foreign language and culture draw attention to themselves, e.g. through poor synchronization of mouth movements or the reliance on culturally idiosyncratic visuals (Fawcett 1996).

Translation in the audiovisual marketplace

Lip-synchronized dubbing, the most expensive method of audiovisual translation, has traditionally been the preferred option in countries with a single linguistic community – and hence a large potential market to secure a sizeable return on the investment. In some cases (e.g. France), the dissemination of a single dubbed version across the length and breadth of the national territory has been instrumental in achieving linguistic uniformity, to the detriment of regional dialects or minority languages (Ballester 1995). On the other hand, the predominance of dubbing in Germany, Italy and Spain in the 1930s and 1940s was fostered by fascist regimes. Revoicing a whole film became an effective instrument of CENSORSHIP, enabling the removal of inconvenient references to facts and values that clashed with the official doctrine (Agost 1999). Voice-over, on the other hand, became the transfer method of choice in most Soviet bloc countries and other Asian markets (e.g. Thailand), either because the national language was unchallenged (Danan 1991) or because budget constraints made the cost of lip-sync dubbing simply prohibitive (Gottlieb 1998). Subtitling, on the other hand, thrived in a group of rich and highly literate countries with small audiovisual markets (Scandinavian countries) and bilingual communities (the Netherlands and Belgium), as well as in other states with lower literacy rates but much poorer economies (Portugal, Greece, Iran and most Arab countries), for whom other forms of audiovisual translation were unaffordable.

Until the mid-1990s, the audiovisual marketplace remained divided into two major clusters: subtitling versus dubbing countries (Luyken et al. 1991). Since then, however, we have witnessed a series of changes in the audiovisual landscape, including the ever growing volume of programmes and broadcast outlets, the development of digitization techniques and the emergence of new patterns in the distribution and consumption of audiovisual products (Pérez González 2006b). This has contributed to blurring the lines between the formerly opposing camps: in any given market, 'dominant' or traditional forms of audiovisual transfer now co-exist with other 'challenging' or less widespread types (Gambier 2003a). The combined use of several established methods within a single programme constitutes developments that continue to contribute to the hybridization of the media industry worldwide (ibid.).

Research in the field of audiovisual translation

Although the available body of research on audiovisual translation has grown exponentially in the last two decades, scholars have tended to gravitate to a small range of issues, including the effects of medium-related constraints on the translator's discretion, transfer errors arising from the search for synchronization and the failure of translated dialogue to recreate social and geographic variation. Luyken *et al.*'s concerns over the lack of systematic theorization (1991: 165) and Fawcett's warnings against the excessive degree of anecdotalism and prescriptivism in audiovisual translation scholarship (1996: 65–9) continued to resonate in subsequent work (e.g. Chaume 2002).

On the basis of a relatively small number of experimental studies on viewers' processing habits, reading strategies or reception patterns (e.g. d'Ydewalle *et al.* 1987; Gottlieb 1995; de Linde and Kay 1999; Fuentes 2001), some researchers have sought to articulate frameworks of rules, time-space correlations and mediation priorities for subtitling and dubbing practitioners. Such frameworks of seemingly undisputed assumptions on viewers' needs require systematic validation and updating, particularly in view of the increasing ubiquity of screen-based texts in everyday life and the ongoing fragmentation of audiences into specialized niches (Pérez González 2008). The need for robust insights into the perceptual and cognitive dimension of audiovisual translation, however, has been overshadowed in the early part of the twenty-first century by technological developments in the field, including speech-recognition techniques (Eugeni 2007) as well as the use of CORPORA and translation memory tools (Armstrong *et al.* 2006; see COMPUTER-AIDED TRANSLATION); these developments seek to respond to the industry's demand for fast delivery of automated output.

Audiovisual translation scholars have relied heavily on descriptive translation studies, both under the umbrella of POLYSYSTEM and NORM theories. In their attempt to understand what guides the choice of translation STRATEGIES, specialists have examined the status of the source and target cultures *vis-à-vis* one another within the global audiovisual arena (Delabastita 1990); explored how the interaction of power, prestige and other market factors within a given country has led to the dominance of a specific form of audiovisual transfer (Lambert and Delabastita 1996; Karamitrouglou 2000); and looked into the universality of certain filmic rhetorical devices (Cattrysse 2004). A plethora of studies has drawn on these same theories to identify the operational norms that guide the actual transfer of textual material in the main forms of audiovisual transfer. Some of these studies have resulted in descriptions of widely accepted translation standards (Karamitrouglou 1998), techniques and strategies (Díaz Cintas and Remael 2007). A descriptive agenda also informs a series of new corpus-based studies of dubbed language, which seek to demonstrate the limited influence of the source text on the configuration of emerging target text norms (Pavesi 2005).

Against the backdrop of increased attention to processes of contextualization, recent publications on audiovisual translation have drawn on theories from neighbouring disciplines, including pragmatics (Hatim and Mason 1997; Kovačič 1994) and GENDER studies (Baumgarten 2005). As in other fields of translation studies, researchers have also investigated the impact of clashes of IDEOLOGY and power differentials on dubbed or subtitled dialogue (Ballester 1995, 2001; Remael 2003) and looked at the translator's mediation in terms of domesticating and foreignizing strategies (Ulrych 2000; Fawcett 2003). Amateur subtitling cultures such as fansubbing (Pérez González 2006b) – which emerged as a result of the increasing compartmentalization of subtitling audiences – represent an extreme example of foreignization, known as 'abusive subtitling' (Nornes 1999). Amateur translators exploit traditional meaning-making codes in a creative manner and criss-cross the traditional boundaries between linguistic and visual semiotics in innovative ways, thus paving the way for new research informed by multimedia theory (Pérez González 2008).

See also:
ADAPTATION; ADVERTISING; COMICS; GLOBALIZATION; LOCALIZATION; NEWS GATHERING AND DISSEMINATION; RELAY.

Further reading
Delabastita 1989; Luyken *et al.* 1991; Whitman-Linsen 1992; Dries 1995; Herbst 1997; Agost 1999; de Linde and Kay 1999; Chaves 2000; Karamitrouglou 2000; Díaz Cintas 2003; Fawcett 2003; Gambier 2003b; Remael 2003; Chaume 2004; Neves 2005; Pavesi 2005; Pérez González 2007, 2008.

LUIS PÉREZ GONZÁLEZ

B

Bible, Jewish and Christian

The Bible, from the Greek *biblia*, meaning 'books', is the sacred text of both Jews and Christians. The Jewish Scriptures are composed of the Old Testament (OT), a collection of 39 books written for the most part in Hebrew, with a few passages in Aramaic. The Christian Bible contains these Scriptures plus the New Testament (NT), and in some traditions, the Deuterocanon. The New Testament comprises 27 books, written in *koiné* Greek between 50 and 100 CE. The Deuterocanon or Apocrypha, also written in Greek, is recognized as 'canonical', i.e. authoritative in matters of religious doctrine, by the Roman Catholic and Orthodox traditions, but not by the Anglican or any other Protestant denominations.

Bible translation (meaning the translation of both Old and New Testaments) has been a major preoccupation of the Christian church for the past two millennia. As of 2006 (UBS World Report), the whole Bible (OT and NT) has been translated into 426 languages, the New Testament into 1100, with parts of the Bible now available in 2,403 languages.

History of Bible translation

The beginnings of Bible translation can be traced back to an incident recounted in the book of Nehemiah (8: 5–8) many centuries before the birth of Christ. After living for several decades in exile in Babylon, many Jews no longer spoke or even understood Hebrew. Thus, when the exiles returned to Jerusalem, and Ezra called the people together to listen to the reading of the Law of Moses, the Levite priests had to translate the meaning of the sacred texts into Aramaic so that people could understand. Since that time, Jews and Christians have continued to emphasize the importance of the Scriptures being understood by all believers.

The earliest known written translation of the Bible is the Septuagint, a translation from Hebrew into Greek of the Old Testament texts, carried out primarily for Greek-speaking Jews living in the Graeco-Roman diaspora. According to tradition, this version, which includes the Deuterocanonical books, was the joint work of 72 Jewish scholars who completed the task in 72 days, leading to its name and abbreviation (Latin *septuaginta* = 70, LXX). The translation was started under Ptolemy II of Egypt and carried out in or around Alexandria during the third and second centuries BCE. Although this translation and its interpretations of the Hebrew text have been criticized since its inception, the Septuagint has nevertheless served as a standard reference since that time. It is the source of most of the OT quotes in the NT. To this day, the Septuagint retains considerable influence on questions of interpretation and textual matters, and its study continues to shed light on the principles of translation used in the ancient world. However, in the second century CE, Jewish scholars – Aquila, Theodotion, and Symmachus – produced new translations and/ or revised versions of the Septuagint, which were preserved by Origen (*c.*185 – *c.*245 CE). The Targum, literally 'translation', is a kind of running paraphrase of and commentary on the Hebrew text in Aramaic, originating from before the time of Christ but still read publicly in synagogues around the world today.

As the New Testament was compiled and its content fixed by 367 CE under Athanasius, the bishop of Alexandria, translations were undertaken in various European and Middle Eastern languages. The NT was translated into Latin, the language of the former Roman

Empire (including Northern Africa), as well as into Coptic, spoken by Egyptian Christians, and into Syriac. This latter translation served newly converted Jews and/or new Christians in the Mesopotamian region (Syria). The revised Syriac Bible, known as the Peshitta, the 'simple' version, is widely referred to in discussions of the biblical text.

In 383 CE, Pope Damasus I commissioned Jerome to produce the whole Bible in Latin, a task completed in 406. This version, known as the Vulgate, served for centuries as a reference for translations into numerous languages, including Armenian, Georgian, Ethiopic, Arabic, Persian and Gothic.

In the meantime, scholarly work continued on the OT Hebrew texts, whose original writing system included only consonants. Though tentative systems to mark vowels and accents ('masorah') were devised in Babylonia and Palestine, basic standardization only came about in the ninth century, through the work of Moshe ben Asher and the scholars at Tiberius. This Masoretic text (MT) has served as the source text for major Jewish and Christian translations since that time. Its latest complete edition, the *Biblia Hebraica Stuttgartensia*, is used throughout the world as the primary source text of the Old Testament.

The invention of the printing press around the time of the Reformation and the growing interest in national languages such as German, English, French and Spanish led to the publication of Bible translations in various European vernaculars. Martin Luther, John Wycliffe and William Tyndale were among the pioneers who translated the Bible in a language accessible to all, often at great personal sacrifice. Many considered the translation of sacred texts from 'sacred languages' (Hebrew, Greek and Latin) into vernaculars to be heretical. However, despite serious opposition, this period saw the birth of many versions of the Bible, which still serve as references today: the King James or 'authorized version' (AV) in English (1611), Olivétan's French translation (1535) and the Luther version, among others.

Progress in the translation of Scriptures on the European continent steadily continued for the centuries that followed, with a sharp increase in Bible translation activity in the early nineteenth century. This major thrust has continued, almost unhindered, into the twenty-first century. The 1800s began what might be called the missionary era of Bible translation. Rising interest in taking the Gospel to the remotest parts of the world was accompanied by all-out efforts to translate the Bible into 'unknown tongues'. In the first wave were the 'missionary greats', whose life work included learning, and reducing to writing, major languages around the globe: Adoniram Judson (Burmese), Robert Morrison (Chinese), William Carey (Bengali, Sanskrit, Marathi, Hindi), Henry Martyn (Urdu, Persian and Arabic). During this period, portions of Scripture were published in literally hundreds of languages worldwide: Thai or Siamese in the east, Maya and Quechua in the Americas, Swahili in Africa. Though at times unmentioned, mother tongue translators were major contributors to Bible translation during this period. For example, in 1843, Bishop Samuel Ajayi Crowther, a Yoruba speaker, began work on the Yoruba Bible in Nigeria, which was finally completed in 1884. This period of missionary activity coincided with the birth of the influential British and Foreign Bible Society (1804), as well as many other Bible societies throughout the world: Dublin (1804), East Pakistan (1811), Ceylon (1812), Ethiopia (1812), Mauritius (1812), the US (the American Bible Society, 1816) and South Africa (1820).

Alongside the many translations carried out in languages never before written, the late nineteenth century and the twentieth century witnessed an increase in the number of Bible translations done in major European languages. Taking English as an example, following the publication of the English Revised Bible in 1885, there has been a steady stream of new translations: the *American Standard Version* (1901), the *Revised Standard Version* (1952), the *Jerusalem Bible* (1966), the *Revised English Bible* (1970), the *New American Bible* (1970), the *New Living Bible* (1971, 1989, 1996), the *New Jerusalem Bible* (1985), the translation of the OT by the Jewish Publication Society (TANAKH, 1985), as well as Bible translations done by individual scholars, including Edgar J. Goodspeed, James Moffatt, Eugene Peterson, J. B. Phillips and Ken Taylor, among others.

A kind of turning point occurred in the 1950s and 1960s, as a number of factors led to a new focus on Bible translation theory and procedures. In 1947, significant archaeological discoveries were made at Qumran, with the Dead Sea Scrolls providing new texts and giving more information on the cultural and historical context of Scripture formation. At around the same time, new developments in linguistic and anthropological studies contributed to reflection on the theory and practice of Bible translation. In response to the growing desire for Scriptures in non-European languages, emphasis was put on readers being able to read and understand the Bible. Guidelines were proposed to ensure natural, comprehensible renderings that would remain faithful to the source texts (Nida 1964; Nida and Taber 1969; Beekman and Callow 1974; Callow 1974; Barnwell 1975/1986). Decisions taken at Vatican II (1965) promoted the use of vernacular translations, alongside Latin, in liturgical settings. All these factors combined to raise interest in and support for what is known today as 'common language versions', translations meant to communicate to the 'common man'. These translations, many of which were inter-confessional, first met with resistance but eventually became best-sellers; they include in English: *Today's English Version*, also known as the *Good News Bible* (TEV 1966, 1976, 1994; GNB, 1976), and the *Contemporary English Version* (CEV 1995); in French, *Français Courant* (1982, 1997) and *Parole de Vie* (2000); in Spanish, *Dios Habla Hoy* (1966, 1979); and in German, *Die Gute Nachricht* (1982, 1997). Today some translations are being produced in simplified language, for example the Spanish *Versión en Lenguaje Sencillo* (2003), which can be used by children as well as second-language users.

Through time, the Bible translation cause, once championed mainly by missions, churches and individuals, has become the work of worldwide organizations focused on this one particular task. The United Bible Societies (UBS), with its translation efforts spearheaded by Eugene A. Nida, was founded in 1946 and currently groups together over 200 national Bible societies, whose primary task is the translation and distribution of Scriptures worldwide. The Summer Institute of Linguistics (SIL, also known as Wycliffe Bible Translators), founded in 1942 by Cameron Townsend and until recently led by the missionary-linguist Kenneth

L. Pike, continues to support the work of Bible translation teams around the world. Made up of expatriates and mother-tongue speakers, the work of these teams often involves language learning and analysis, in order to establish a suitable alphabet, written grammar and dictionary, all of which are useful in pursuing the translation task. While SIL teams initially concentrated on the translation of the NT, perceived to be more pertinent to evangelistic needs, interest is now extending to the whole Bible. Both SIL and UBS have a system of quality control, carried out by PhD-level translation consultants. These two worldwide organizations are joined in their efforts by many other agencies, including Pioneer Bible Translators, Lutheran Bible Translators and International Bible Translators.

At the beginning of the twenty-first century, Bible translation activity has in no way waned, as more and more Bible translation projects are being put in place and revisions undertaken. Scripture use has generated new interest in providing Scriptures in varying formats: study Bibles, comics, Scripture 'storying', as well as non-print media renderings, including music cassettes, videos, radio, TV, on-line Bibles, etc. Bibles in Braille as well as signed Scriptures are also becoming available in different sign languages around the world (see SIGNED LANGUAGE INTERPRETING).

As interest in Bible translation remains at an all-time high, the procedures and profile of personnel involved in Bible translation continue to evolve. During the missionary era, the role of mother-tongue speakers was ill defined, and 'native assistants' often remained unnamed. However, today, with colonialism arguably relegated to history and the role of expatriate missionaries diminishing, a new era in Bible translation has begun (Bessong and Kenmogne 2007; Sánchez-Cetina 2007). While in the 1970s translator training was being discussed and encouraged, today, mother-tongue exegetes and translators are being trained at a very high level around the world. Undergraduate and graduate training programmes, including studies in linguistics, communication theory, biblical exegesis, Hebrew and Greek, along with translation theory and practice, are producing highly qualified mother-tongue personnel. Whereas in the past most Bible translation consultants were

Western expatriates, today's Bible translation consultants come from every continent on the globe.

Bible translation teams are also now equipped with new technology. Computers enable translators to bypass the numerous hand-written drafts of the past. Through innovative programs such as Paratext (a program designed by UBS and supported by SIL), translators can have instant access on their screens to dozens of Bible versions, including the source texts, as well as to dictionary definitions and parsing of Hebrew and Greek forms. Manuscript spelling and punctuation checks, which in the past took months of tedious work, are today carried out in far less time, with the assistance of computer programs. Though attempts at MACHINE TRANSLATION and ADAPTATION have produced uneven results in the first instance, or controversial versions in the second, new technology has given Bible translation teams around the world a new sense of autonomy.

In some ways, twenty-first-century Bible translators can be compared to the earliest pioneers – Jerome, Luther and Tyndale – since today, once again, the major goal is to have qualified mother-tongue translators using biblical languages to consult the source text, in order to produce understandable and faithful renderings in their own languages. The difference is that today's Bible translators have the advantage of 2,000 years of scholarship, interpretation and translation models, as well as access to powerful technical tools.

Translation theory and approaches

It is difficult to speak of translation theory during the earliest years of Bible translation. Examination of the first known translations reveals that different translators have always used different approaches and conventions. However, despite centuries and even millennia of reflection and discussion, the basic issues in Bible translation remain surprisingly the same. These include whether a translation tends to be more or less literal, that is, how closely the forms and structures of the source language are reflected in the translation, how consistently words are rendered (especially 'key' terms of special theological importance), how much the translation adapts the source text to allow for natural modes of expression in the target language, and how much 'foreignization' is accepted, allowing readers to experience the 'otherness' of a foreign text. A brief overview of the developments in the last decades of theory and practice in Bible translation provides some insights into these issues.

In the early part of the twentieth century, the more accepted translations were those which stayed close to Hebrew and Greek grammatical structures. In the Anglophone world, for example, the Authorized or King James Version remained a standard reference, despite its difficult and increasingly archaic language. Some versions had a goal of verbal consistency, whereby a word in the source text would be consistently rendered by a single word in the target language. Such literal translations gave high priority to the form of the source text and tried to stay close to its word order, sentence structure, etc. But such translation approaches often resulted in unnatural, and sometimes incomprehensible, renderings. For example, the RSV's literal rendering of St. Paul's expression 'having girded their loins with truth' (Ephesians 6: 14) is not immediately understood by the majority of English speakers.

In their *Theory and Practice of Translation* (1969), Nida and Taber put forth proposals (referred to as the TAPOT approach) for producing a more comprehensible rendering of such expressions: translators examine and analyse the source text, extract its meaning (by identifying the content of the 'kernels' of each sentence as well as semantic components of each lexical item) and transfer that meaning into the target language. This process leads to a *dynamic equivalence* translation. Though this approach was modified to emphasize the communicative functions of language and renamed *functional equivalence* translation (de Waard and Nida 1986), in both equivalence models meaning has priority over form (see EQUIVALENCE). Thus, faced with a phrase such as 'girding the loins with truth', translators would 'unpack' the phrase to determine what Paul meant, and then look for the closest natural equivalent expression in their own language. In the search for a meaning-based translation, many translators would reject RSV's rendering as too literal. They would drop the archaic verb *gird*, as well as the confusing Old English *loins*, and attempt to substitute them with modern equivalents. Some common language versions in English have tried to retain the original image by rendering the passage as 'stand ready, with truth as a belt tight around your waist' (TEV). However, according to the principles of dynamic/functional equivalence, if the relevance of *belt* as part of this defensive military attire is not understood in the target culture, it is possible to drop the image and express the meaning directly, as in 'Always be ready to defend yourself with the truth'.

Another of the basic tenets of dynamic equivalence translation is that what is implicit in the text can be made explicit, if this is necessary for the reader or hearer to correctly understand the message of the source text. In the case of Ephesians 6: 14, a Bible translator might be justified in making explicit 'the truth *of (the word of) God*', an acceptable exegetical interpretation in this context. Using the dynamic or functional equivalence approach, it might also be noted that certain languages need to make explicit where this 'truth' is kept, which might lead to an even wider rendering, as in 'Always keep the truth of God in your heart/mind/liver, being ready to defend yourself' (see EXPLICITATION).

The dynamic equivalence approach thus adapts the translation to the realities of the target language and culture, so that the meaning or message of the source text can be clearly understood. Translators are free to use different terms, different grammatical constructions, and even different word and sentence orders, in order to express the meaning of the source text. In translation parlance, this approach 'domesticates' the text, by removing difficult expressions and images which would be incomprehensible or poorly understood if rendered literally.

An advantage of this approach is that it gives translators the freedom to make difficult theological concepts clear. For example, comparing RSV's rendering of Romans 3: 28 to common language versions (TEV and CEV), the latter convey the message more clearly to today's speakers of English than the earlier version does:

RSV   For we hold that a man is justified by faith apart from works of law.

TEV   For we conclude that a person is put right with God only through faith, and not by doing what the Law commands.

CEV   We see that people are acceptable to God because they have faith, and not because they obey the Law.

However, this approach can easily be misapplied. Over-eager or patronizing translators may end up paraphrasing the text. Some translations of this type have thus been widely criticized for being too explicit, i.e. adding or even changing ideas of the source text. This is one of the reasons many of these versions are undergoing revision today. Indeed, translators can inadvertently (or advertently!) introduce theological and other ideological biases into their translations (see IDEOLOGY), a practice deemed unacceptable by most Bible translation agencies today (Ogden 1997; Zogbo 2002).

Another criticism of this approach is that translators using this model may take too much liberty, thereby violating historicity. For example, is it permissible for translators to substitute an animal such as a seal in the key phrase 'the lamb of God', in Arctic cultures where sheep are not well known? Does the use of a local fruit juice or distilled liquor to refer to wine made from grapes violate the historical accuracy of the translation and/or rob the text of an important leitmotiv? Along the same lines, by trying to make everything in the biblical text 'clear and natural', translators may flatten out poetic lines and images, or 'over-translate' literary forms, whose beauty is reflected precisely through brevity and possible multiple readings. This domestication of both the form and content of the text pulls the translation away from the historical and literary bearings of the source text. For a detailed assessment of Nida and Taber's TAPOT approach, see Wilt (2003a) and Stine (2004).

In the past, where expatriate and/or indigenous translators have had little or no access to the source texts in the biblical languages, a method known as the *base-models* approach has often been used alongside the dynamic/functional equivalence framework. Thus, if a translation team does not have a member qualified in Hebrew or Greek, translators are encouraged to use a more literal version in a language they know, such as RSV in English, as the *base* text, with more dynamic versions (TEV, CEV) serving as *models* of what a good translation might be. Though many New Testaments and some Bibles produced using this approach have yielded highly readable and popular texts, in some cases this method has produced translations quite far from the form and meaning of the source text. Some teams end up translating a model text literally, often overlooking an excellent solution available in their own language. For example, translators may look for an equivalent of the dynamic 'God has given you victory over the Midianites' (Judges 7.16, TEV) when the target language might already have a structure identical to the one in Hebrew: 'God has given the Midianites into your hands'.

However, despite the shortcomings and possible misapplications of this approach, the principles of dynamic/functional equivalence have liberated translators from a rigid system whereby word-by-word consistency, especially in relation to key terms, was considered the ideal. Thus, a word like *grace* (*charis* in Greek), which is used in many different ways in many different contexts in the NT, can be rendered contextually. For example, in standard greetings ('Grace to you and peace...'), a natural equivalent in the language may be used, while another term may be used to translate the theologically crucial concept of grace in contexts where this is necessary (e.g. 'by grace you are saved'). By giving priority to meaning over form and translating contextually, translators may better render the message of the source text, providing a more faithful rendering, as established by the norms of this translation theory.

Common language translations have also popularized supplementary materials and Bible helps. In the past, the text was considered so sacred that certain versions put in parentheses or italics any word that was not actually present in the Hebrew or Greek text. Nowadays, almost all Bibles published by UBS have explanatory prefaces, introductions to each book of the Bible, footnotes explaining textual variants and word plays, and are equipped with helpful glossaries, maps, charts, illustrations, etc.

Since the introduction of the dynamic/functional equivalent approach, reflection on Bible translation theory and practice continues to evolve. Much thought is now given to the role of the audience in determining which type of translation needs to be produced. Scholars speak less of a strict dichotomy between literal and dynamic translations, tending rather to acknowledge a continuum. For example, a community may request a translation to be used in worship services, leading to the production of a liturgical version which preserves the literary beauty and poetic nature of the Hebrew source text (Zogbo and Wendland 2000). Another community may need a common language version due to their unfamiliarity with the Scriptures, while other special audiences, e.g. youth, may well appreciate a translation which exploits the stylistic features of oral genres of the target language.

Today, before a Bible translation project is begun, great care is taken to define the context and influences related to a given translation. In *Bible Translation, Frames of Reference* (Wilt 2003a), the sociocultural, organizational, textual and cognitive 'frames' involved in shaping and interpreting texts are explored. Questions of who is requesting, sponsoring and managing the translation (see Lai 2007), who will be using it and for what purposes, and who is actually doing the translation, have become fundamental. Audience considerations have also led to the publication of Bibles with clear ideological and theological slants, for example, Bibles with feminist, liberation theology, Africanist, or Afro-American agendas (Yorke 2000). The close interaction between IDEOLOGY, theology, ETHICS and translation is today the subject of much debate, raising important theoretical issues (such as inclusive-exclusive language and GENDER sensitivity; see Bratcher 1995; Simon 1996; von Flotow 1997), as well as very practical ones (copyright, marketing strategies, low vs. high cost editions, etc.).

Today the field of translation is alive with discussion and debate, and there is more communication between theoreticians of Bible translation and those dealing with translation theory in general. Theorists and Bible translation practitioners are giving more thought to literary theory (Wendland 2006), discourse ('top-down') analysis of both source and target languages (Longacre 1989; Grimes, 1972; Bergman 1994; Levinsohn 1987, 2000; Wendland 2002), pragmatics and communication theory, in particular relevance theory (Gutt 1990,

1991/2000, 2005; Hill 2006). Theorists writing from a non-Western perspective have further enriched our understanding of the impact of biblical translation on a wide range of societies (Wickeri 1995; Rafael 1998; Naudé and van der Merwe 2002; Lai 2007, among others). Consideration of the SKOPOS or function/goal of a text within its community has become a main focus of discussion. The question of whether it is possible, necessary or desirable to reconstruct the source author's intent, in order to reflect this in translation, remains a much debated issue to this day.

Despite these new avenues for reflection and research, the basic parameters for discussing Bible translation remain much the same, as translations continue to be described as more or less literal, more or less foreign, more or less natural. Some questions of faithfulness have been resolved or simplified as text sources for the Old and New Testament, to which translators adhere, are becoming more universally accepted. On the other hand, faithfulness remains a complex and intriguing issue in relation to new forms of Bible translation in non-print media, such as video, song, theatre and other forms of art (Soukoup and Hodgson 1999).

See also:
BRITISH TRADITION; GENDER AND SEXUALITY; GREEK TRADITION; HEBREW TRADITION; INSTITUTIONAL TRANSLATION; LATIN TRADITION; QUR'ĀN; RETRANSLATION; STRATEGIES.

Further reading
Nida 1964; Nida and Taber 1969; de Waard and Nida 1986; Gutt 1991/2000; Wickeri 1995; Soukoup and Hodgson 1999; Zogbo and Wendland 2000; Naudé and van der Merwe 2002; Wilt 2003a; Stine 2004; Wendland 2004, 2006; Noss 2007.

LYNELL ZOGBO

C

Censorship

Censorship is a coercive and forceful act that blocks, manipulates and controls cross-cultural interaction in various ways. It must be understood as one of the discourses, and often the dominant one, articulated by a given society at a given time and expressed through repressive cultural, aesthetic, linguistic and economic practices. Censorship operates largely according to a set of specific values and criteria established by a dominant body and exercised over a dominated one; the former can often be identified with either the state or the Church, or with those social conventions which regulate one's freedom of choice at both public and personal levels. In contrasting fashions, both censorship and translation influence the visibility and invisibility, as well as the accessibility and inaccessibility, of the cultural capital enjoyed or produced by a given text or body of texts.

In his seminal work on knowledge, power and repression, Foucault (1975) argues that the production and representation of knowledge depend on the ways in which any social system articulates a set of rules. These visible and invisible rules, however, are not only to be read as repressive instances, but also as a means of generating further knowledge and power (ibid.: 177, 187, 201–2). The censorship of translations does not act simply according to the logic of punishment, but also according to the principle of correction, or in some cases of self-correction. Thus, when censors punish and regulate the circulation of the cultural capital of translations, they can also foster further knowledge (Foucault 1975: 170–94; Sammells 1992: 5–6). For instance, in his work on sexuality, Foucault argues that in the Victorian era the ban on evocation of sexuality did not obstruct the production of more discourses on the issue;

instead, it encouraged their regulated and diverse proliferations (Foucault 1981: 6–9; Saunders 1992; Brownlie 2007b; see also GENDER AND SEXUALITY).

Similarly to Foucault, Pierre Bourdieu's sociological theory emphasizes the relationship between the agent and the structure (Inghilleri 2005c) and analyses their implications for shaping the cultural habitus and field (Bourdieu 1984: 170, 63–95, 232; see SOCIOLOGICAL APPROACHES). In *Distinction* (1979), Bourdieu defines the *habitus* as 'both the generative principle of objectively classifiable judgements and the system of classification (*principium divisionis*) of these practices'; in other words, as 'a creative and organising principle' (Bourdieu 1984: 170). Specifically, Bourdieu argues that to understand fully how censorship operates, one needs to take into consideration its relationship with the *habitus* (dynamics of tastes) of the field in which it circulates. Bourdieu names this censorial condition 'structural censorship', and argues that it is determined by the *habitus* of the agents belonging to the field within which a text circulates (Bourdieu 1982: 168; Bourdieu 1984: 170; Krebs 2007a; Thomson-Wohlgemuth 2007). Furthermore, in its consideration of transnational dynamics of taste, Bourdieu's definition of structural censorship allows us to view the phenomenology of translation and censorship in terms of both its national specificity and a repertoire of universal themes (for instance sexuality, religion and IDEOLOGY) shared by different communities at different times of their history (Bourdieu 1982: 168–73). In this respect, censorship has to be seen not as an institutional set of rules, or even as an overtly repressive means of controlling public opinion and discourses, but rather as a set of unwritten rules, shaped both by current *habitus* and by the symbolic capital a text enjoys in a certain field (ibid.: 172–3). Translators thus act as agents who, in a visible or invisible guise, can emphasize the text's otherness or familiarity from a target culture point of view (Venuti 1995a, 1998b). As a result, depending on the degree of visibility and acceptability with which translators wish to endow a text, they will employ different STRAT-EGIES of foreignization and domestication. Hence, the relationship between censorship and translation can challenge current assumptions on the notion of accessibility of CULTURE, both in overtly repressive contexts and in seemingly neutral cultural scenarios (Billiani 2007a; see also the General Censorship Resources website for a wide range of examples of censorial operations).

Censorship in practice

Censorship may be divided into two main categories: INSTITUTIONAL and individual. As an institutional phenomenon, censorship has existed since at least 399 BC, when Socrates was accused of introducing new divinities and corrupting the young and thus exposed to the punishment of the State. The history of the application of censorship measures to translation, however, remains difficult to trace (Jones 2001: xi; Haight 1970). In particular, the relationship between censorship and translated texts has always been questioned in terms of the extent to which translations themselves allow the circulation of ideas beyond the boundaries imposed by a certain authority; in other words, in terms of the extent to which translation is a means of evading censorship (Billiani 2007b). Religious texts, including the BIBLE and QUR'ĀN, are a case in point. In 553, for example, Emperor Justinian issued a decree commanding exclusive use of the Greek and Latin versions of the Bible and forbidding the use of the Midrash, the Jewish stories that explain or elaborate on the Bible (Jones 2001: 229–32). In this case, the original Midrash texts in Hebrew were subjected to censorship but translations were deemed unthreatening.

Examples of translations that have been subjected to censorship abound, however. Famous instances of banned individual trans-lations belonging to diverse literary domains (canonical texts, high and lowbrow culture, CHILDREN'S LITERATURE) and demonstrating

the range and practices of censorship include the following: Macchiavelli's *The Prince* (banned in France in 1576); *The Thousand and One Nights* (banned in the USA in 1927); H. B. Stowe's *Uncle Tom's Cabin* (banned in Russia in 1852); and Lewis Carroll's *Alice's Adventures in Wonderland* (banned in China in 1931), among many others. Similarly, the translations of entire oeuvres have been banned at different times; for example, André Gide's works were banned in 1938 in the Soviet Union and in 1954 in East Berlin, and Upton Sinclair's were banned in 1929 in Yugoslavia, in 1933 in Germany and in 1956 in East Germany. The official reasons for these bans on well-known transla-tions, which cover a broad chronological and geographic spectrum, are diverse and largely dependent on the cultural and political specifi-cities of the relevant national context. On the whole, although many of these bans affected the political and ideological spheres, they seem to have been mostly concerned with the moral acceptability of a text. Victorian England is a key example of the complex relationship between the social and moral sphere in the context of direct or indirect censorship. Examples of censorship of English texts and translations alike abound in the Victorian era. The most famous case of censorship, which gave rise to the term 'bowdlerization', is that of Dr Bowdler's (1724–1825) expurgated texts: bowdlerization in this case resulted in the simultaneous circulation of expurgated and full editions which differed in price and thus addressed diverse audiences (Perrin 1969, 1992; Ó Cuilleanáin 1999: 37–9). It was however the Obscene Publications Act (1857) that marked the beginning of official censorship of texts which were deemed offensive to readers in Britain. Henry Vizetelly (1820–1894) was the first publisher to be tried for circulating obscene translations of literary books by the French writer Émile Zola: *Nana* (1880/1884), *Pot-bouille* (1882) and *Piping Hot!* (1886), but especially *La Terre* (1887) and *The Soil* (1888) (Jones 2001: 2584–5; King 1978). Vizetelly pleaded guilty in his first trial in 1888, but he persisted in publishing five more translations of Zola. In 1889, by then totally impoverished, he was tried again and imprisoned for three months. Nonetheless, expurgated translations, not only of Zola but also of Maupassant and Bourget, continued to be available. In order to avoid prosecution, various strategies of translation could be, and were, employed. One such strategy involved leaving the 'offensive' word in the original language (i.e. opting for non-translation); another consisted of using paraphrase or innuendo to communicate the message indirectly (Brownlie 2007b). At times, CLASSICAL TEXTS which had gained aesthetic respectability had to be censored, often by the translator him- or herself, in order to be made available to a wider audience (Jones 2001: 164–6).

Censorship does not necessarily always apply to individual texts. In the context of censorship, the name of the author and that of the translator can gain considerable importance: in other words, institutional censorship can officially reject a text not only because of its content but also because of the author's profile or indeed the translator's identity. In Fascist Italy, translations by authors such as Thomas Mann and André Gide were banned because they were believed to be Jewish (Fabre 1998). Similarly, entire genres may be subjected to censorship. Both in Fascist Italy and in Nazi Germany, translations of detective stories, for example, were banned as a genre a priori during the last years of the dictatorship because of the popularity they had gained among readers. These stories were thought to constitute a vehicle for importing perilous and immoral examples of antisocial behaviour.

Imported cinema has often been subjected to various forms of censorship through dubbing and subtitling (Rabadán 2000; Ballester 2001; Vandaele 2002; Gutiérrez Lanza 2002; see AUDIOVISUAL TRANSLATION). While reading might be seen as a private act, screening occurs in front of a purportedly vulnerable and visible audience (Jones 2001: 164–7). Creative censorship, or at times the translator's own self-censorship, has been applied to subtitled films, two well known examples being the *Last Tango in Paris* (1972; Jones and Platt 1991) and the renowned Japanese film *Ai No Corrida* by Ōshima Nagisa (*In the Realm of Senses*, 1976). Although once censored (in the original as well as in the subtitled versions), both films are now regarded as masterpieces. The Japanese film was censored for obscene content, but its main purpose was to address the repressive politics of 1930s Japan (Jones 2001: 797–812, 817–20).

By targeting only the erotic content of the film, the institutional censorial power was able to set, albeit in a contradictory fashion, the boundaries of the circulation of the film as well as its modes of reception. Similarly, and in relation to another genre, until 1968 dramatic productions in the UK were subject to approval by the Lord Chamberlain's office, which determined what plays could or could not be performed (Krebs 2007a, 2007b; Walton 2006, 2007; see DRAMA).

Institutional censorship often operates more overtly in contexts in which political freedom is severely constrained. Fascist Italy, Nazi Germany and Franco's Spain put into practice a censorial preventive apparatus which specifically and selectively targeted those translations which were ideologically destabilizing. In these contexts, censorship functioned as a preventive measure which worked effectively because of the relevant regimes' ability to recruit the publishing industry and bring it in line with the political order. Translations were rarely sequestrated, because the publishers themselves pre-empted censorship by guaranteeing their acceptability (Rundle 2000; Van Steen 2007). Here, as elsewhere when censorship does not involve a complete ban, translations are identified with a 'stranger' who needs to be presented in a particular fashion in order to become part of the discourse of dominant institutions and political leaders. One area of translation which generally seems to attract the censor's attention under dictatorships is that of CHILDREN'S LITERATURE, due to the alleged vulnerability of its readers (Craig 2001; Thomson-Wohlgemuth 2007). On the whole, however, recent studies have demonstrated that preventive censorship allowed agents (publishers, translators, authors) a certain freedom of manoeuvre, so that they could occasionally succeed in having some potentially subversive texts published (Fabre 1998; Sturge 2004).

In addition to institutional censorship, translators can also function as self censors; in other words, they can apply a form of *individual* censorship. Self censorship can assume either a private or public significance, depending on the circulation of the translation in the target culture. Since translating can easily become a political act of resistance or of acquiescence, the main question to address is whether this censorial act is conscious or unconscious, visible or invisible. Philpotts (2007) discusses the translations and adaptations of radio plays selected by the celebrated post-war German writer Günter Eich to broadcast on National Socialist radio in 1930; these often consisted of the REWRITING of popular historical and literary material to serve as lightweight entertainment. Philpotts demonstrates how in anticipating the censorial response the author-translator denied himself his function as author and engaged in self censorship in order to conform to the regime's restrictions (see also for theatre, Krebs 2007a).

The relationship between translation and (all forms of) censorship has often been surprisingly productive (Boase-Beier and Holmann 1998: 1–17). The constraints imposed by censorship on individual creativity can paradoxically result in further production of knowledge, provided there is a degree of shared mutual understanding among communities (Ó Cuilleanáin 1999: 31–44; Tourniaire 1999: 71–80). Ultimately, censorship acts against what lies in that space between acceptance and refusal: the ambiguous, the composite and, more importantly, what disturbs identity, system and order. This means that translation has been and will continue to be a frequent target of censorship in its various forms, but that it also continues to function as a space for negotiating, and at times evading, these forms of censorship. It also explains the growing interest in studying the relationship between censorship and translation, as evidenced in the range of volumes dedicated to the theme since the beginning of the 21st century (Rabadán 2000; Ballester 2001; Craig 2001; Merkle 2002; Sturge 2004; Billiani 2007a).

See also:

ADAPTATION; AUDIOVISUAL TRANSLATION; CHILDREN'S LITERATURE; COMICS; ETHICS; GENDER AND SEXUALITY; IDEOLOGY; PSEUDOTRANSLATION; REWRITING.

Further reading
Perrin 1969; Bourdieu 1982; Jones and Platt 1991; Fabre 1998; Ó Cuilleanáin 1999; Tourniaire 1999; Jongh 2000; Rabadán 2000; Rundle 2000; Ballester 2001; Craig 2001; Jones 2001; Merkle 2002; Vandaele 2002; Sturge 2004; Billiani 2007a, 2007b.

FRANCESCA BILLIANI

Children's literature

Translation for children encompasses such diverse forms as the toddler's board book, the young adult novel or the illustrated information text, and requires an understanding of both developmental factors and the world of childhood. Hollindale's definition of 'childness' as 'the quality of being a child – dynamic, imaginative, experimental, interactive and unstable' (1997: 46) underpins the fine balance of affective content, creativity, simplicity of expression and linguistic playfulness that characterize successful writing, and therefore successful translation, for the youngest readers. At the other end of the age-range, novels addressing the fragility of the adolescent's self-image demand up-to-date information on rapidly changing youth cultures.

Central to a discussion of translation for children is the adult–child duality that raises the question of exactly what counts as children's literature: texts intentionally written for children by adults, texts addressed to adults but read by children, texts read by both children and adults? Definitions of children's literature may include any of these interactions, with the adult presence taking on many guises in children's books, from the spectre of the didactic narrator of the eighteenth-century moral tale to the playful ironic asides intended for the adult reading aloud to a child in *Winnie-the-Pooh*. Translation may, however, alter the nature of the adult–child relationship implicit in the source text. Shavit's (1986) analysis of the transfer of both *Robinson Crusoe* and *Gulliver's Travels* from the adult to the children's literary canon via translation points to antecedents of the modern phenomenon of 'crossover' fiction, i.e. fiction that is read by or addresses readers of all ages (Beckett 1999). Another example is provided in O'Sullivan's (2000) account of the removal of the layer of irony in the first German translation of A. A. Milne's classic stories, resulting in a loss of dual address.

Translating image and sound

A further and fundamental difference between texts for adults and children is the history of children's literature as a visual medium. Whether they are used to create visual narratives in COMICS or in picture books, or to punctuate a prose text, images add a new dimension to the dynamics between source and target languages. Oittinen (2000) argues that translating illustrated texts requires specialized training, combining translation studies with classes in art appreciation. A similar integration of image and language is essential in the rapidly expanding fields of AUDIOVISUAL TRANSLATION (O'Connell 2003) and video-game LOCALIZATION.

Sound, too, is a vital element in translating for the young, since children have stories read to them and translating for reading aloud demands considerable competence from the translators (Dollerup 2003). Whether read aloud or silently, children's stories require a clear narrative line and close attention to rhythm. Puurtinen (1995) is one of the few scholars to have examined the effect of syntactic alterations on readability in children's literature in her study of two different Finnish translations of Frank. L. Baum's *The Wizard of Oz*. She found that one of the two versions has a more fluent and dynamic style and is easier to read aloud. The aural texture of a story, or indeed of lullabies, nursery rhymes and jingles, is of paramount importance to a child still engaged in discovering the power and delights of the phonology of her or his native language. Repetition, rhyme, onomatopoeia, word-play, nonsense, neologisms and the representation of animal noises are therefore all common features of children's texts and require a considerable degree of linguistic creativity on the part of the translator.

Theoretical and critical developments

Critical interest in the translation of children's literature has developed at an accelerating pace over the last thirty years, as Tabbert's (2002) comprehensive international review of publications and Lathey's (2006) collection of English-language articles on the subject indicate. Klingberg, Swedish co-founder of the International Research Society for Children's Literature (IRSCL), was one of the first scholars to pay serious academic attention to translations for children. In *Children's Fiction in the Hands of the Translators*, Klingberg adopted a prescriptive approach to the practice of 'cultural context adaptation' – the domestication of foreign names, coinage and foodstuffs – for a child audience, arguing that the literary integrity of the source text should be respected as much as possible (1986: 17). Yet translators and editors are not always prepared to trust the child's ability to delight in and assimilate the unfamiliar, often citing a lack of life experience as grounds for domestication. Award-winning English translator Anthea Bell has advocated flexibility and autonomy for the translator who has to 'gauge the precise degree of foreignness, and how far it is acceptable and can be preserved' (1985: 7).

Since the 1970s the general trend in the study of translation has moved away from an emphasis on EQUIVALENCE and faithfulness, towards descriptive approaches focusing on the purpose, function and status of the translation in the target culture (see DESCRIPTIVE VERSUS COMMITTED APPROACHES). Shavit's (1986) application of Even-Zohar's POLYSYSTEM to children's texts locates translations for a child audience within a model of literary hierarchies. Shavit argues that the low status of children's literature, different cultural constructs of childhood and different notions of what is 'good for the child' have led to radical CENSORSHIP and abridgement, particularly of classic texts such as *Gulliver's Travels*. Sutton (1996) offers further evidence of ADAPTATION to the NORMS of the target culture in nineteenth-century translations of Grimms' Tales where violent and scatological passages were removed. Didactic interventions in the process of translation, too, are plentiful, with the toning down of Pippi Longstocking's wayward and anarchic behaviour in the first translation into French of Astrid Lindgren's modern Swedish classic as a telling example (Heldner 1992). Similarly, the dialect or slang of a source text may be transposed into standard language in the process of translation because of pedagogical concerns, a practice that is particularly significant in children's fiction with its high proportion of dialogue. Although there are indications of a greater concern to find an equivalent register in the target language in recent translations, Hagrid's non-standard English is changed to standard French and German in translations of J. K. Rowling's *Harry Potter and the Philosopher's Stone* (Jentsch 2002).

Issues of IDEOLOGY in the adoption of different translation STRATEGIES for a young audience have attracted the attention of a number of scholars. Fernández López (2000) discusses intercultural ideological factors in the translation into Spanish of the work of Roald Dahl and Enid Blyton. The eradication of racist and sexist language from the work of these authors during the 1970s and 1980s was ignored in Spanish translations that returned to earlier, 'unpurified' versions of source texts, thereby creating a mismatch between English and Spanish versions published in the same period. Fernández López regards this practice as indicative of political and social factors in the Franco and post-Franco eras in Spain. An extreme example of translation under political control is provided by Thomson-Wohlgemuth (2003), whose investigation into the selection of children's texts for translation in the German Democratic Republic reflects the primacy of ideological content in a period when the child was central to the socialist enterprise.

Narrative communication and the child reader

Two major studies published at the turn of the millennium (O'Sullivan 2000 and Oittinen 2000) take a different direction by addressing the complexities of narrative communication with the child reader. In *Kinderliterarische Komparatistik* (2000), of which a shortened English version was published in 2005, O'Sullivan applies the insights of a comparatist to books written for the young, offering a number of case histories that inspire a fresh look at the international history of children's literature. Adapting existing theories of narrative communication by Schiavi and Chatman, O'Sullivan also proposes a model that distinguishes between the implied child readers inscribed in source and target texts. She cites instances where translators have inserted additional material or explanations for the attention of the child reader in the target culture, thereby creating an implied reader who needs information that the author of the source text could take for granted. Such additions also demonstrate a further aspect of O'Sullivan's model: the presence of the implied translator whose voice can be detected within the translated text.

Drawing on Bakhtin's theories of dialogism, Oittinen (2000) argues that translation for children constitutes a series of playful and subversive social interactions that take place between the translator and the source text, between the translator and the potential child reader, and between the child reader and the translated text. She encourages freedom and creativity in the translator whose goal should be child-friendly translation that constitutes a 'positive' manipulation of the source text. Other professional translators besides Oittinen have made thought-provoking contributions to debates on translating for children, notably Anthea Bell's witty 'notebooks' (1985 and 1986) on the translation of names, tense, gendered nouns and other 'delicate matters', and Cathy Hirano's (1999) depiction of the challenges presented by subtle degrees of politeness inherent in personal pronouns in Japanese young adult fiction.

Current developments

The GLOBALIZATION of the children's book market and of children's culture generally has had a marked effect on translation, as the international marketing strategies of recent volumes of the Harry Potter series and the rapidly decreasing interval between the publication of the original and worldwide translations demonstrate. Translation into the English language continues to lag behind translation from English into other languages; nonetheless, prizes for the translation of children's literature into English such as the Marsh Award in the UK and the Mildred L. Batchelder Award in the USA testify to the range and quality of translation for children and young people within a limited market. The international exchange of children's books has always been uneven, partly because stories enjoyed by children do not constitute a separate 'children's literature' in all cultures and languages. At the same time, interest in the field continues to grow as children's literature and translation scholars work towards a more complete picture of the role of translation in the dissemination of children's literatures across the world. In addition to the publication of a dedicated reader on translation for children (Lathey 2006), recent edited volumes (Van Coillie and Verschueren 2006) and monographs (Frank 2007) demonstrate a diversity of approaches and theoretical perspectives. Desmet's (2007) investigation of the translation into Dutch of narrative fiction for girls reaffirms Shavit's emphasis on literary status as a determining factor in the degree of ADAPTATION and abridgement in translations for children, while historical research has uncovered evidence not only of changes in translation practices according to contemporary constructions of childhood, but also of the impact of translations on the target culture (Lathey 2006, in press). Seifert (2005) and Frank (2007) draw on developments in image studies for their case studies on the translation of Canadian fiction into German and Australian children's fiction into French respectively, demonstrating ways in which images of a nation and locale are constructed as children's texts move from one language and culture to another.

Looking to the future, children's responses to translations are still a matter of speculation and a greater emphasis on empirical research is required to discover just how much 'foreignness' young readers are able to tolerate, especially in view of research on the degree of sophistication with which young readers respond to texts (Fry 1985; Appleyard 1990). Research into reader response to translations may lead to a review of the widespread practice of contextual adaptation for children at a time when the practice in general is regarded as exploitative in its appropriation of the source culture (Venuti 2000b: 341). Moreover, the development of new research methods in translation studies has the potential to offer new insights into the translation of children's literature. In particular, advances in process-oriented studies (see PSYCHOLINGUISTIC AND COGNITIVE APPROACHES and THINK-ALOUD PROTOCOLS) may shed light on how translating for children differs from translating for adult audiences, and large-scale computer analysis of CORPORA may pinpoint cultural trends and linguistic patterns in translations for the young.

See also:
ADAPTATION; AUDIOVISUAL TRANSLATION; CENSORSHIP; COMICS; LITERARY TRANSLATION; LOCALIZATION.

Further reading
O'Sullivan 2000; Oittinen 2000, 2003; Tabbert 2002; Lathey 2006; Van Coillie and Verschueren 2006.

GILLIAN LATHEY

Classical texts

Translations from ancient Greek and Latin contribute perspectives on most of the key issues in translation studies as well as offering insights into related areas such as reception studies and the history of the book. Types of translation STRATEGIES applied to classical texts range from the most literal ('cribs'), through close translation to creative literary and theatrical ADAPTATION of classical material across forms and genres. Translation from classical languages has some distinctive features: the languages are no longer spoken; the corpus of extant texts is (apart from some fragmentary additions) finite; manuscript traditions are sometimes disputed and some foundational texts, such as Homer's epics, present problems because of their oral composition. Classicists sometimes display ambivalent attitudes towards translations, since they represent both a lifeline for the texts and their influence and a threat to the continuing study of the languages. Access to and appropriation of the texts has been ideologically loaded (in terms of power relations, class, GENDER and ethnicity) and their translations have been used to entrench ideas as well as to extend and liberate them (see IDEOLOGY). Translations have had a continuing impact on how Greek and Roman culture is perceived and valued and on how concepts of 'the classical' have developed and changed. In this respect, they provide an important index to critical thought (Armstrong 2005; Leezenberg 2004). The major threads in the translation history of Greek and Latin texts also overlap with those relating to classical texts in other languages and are part of wider debates about CULTURAL TRANSLATION.

Cross-cultural migrations of classical texts

The conceptualization and practices of translation in antiquity laid the basis for modern theories. Translation and linguistic exchange were part of everyday public and commercial life in the context of the ancient Mediterranean, Near East and North Africa. The Greek language, in particular, was crucial to the expansion of Roman power and cultural development (see LATIN TRADITION). Translation from Greek into Latin led to debates about 'word-for-word' versus 'sense for sense' approaches and about the pragmatics of domestication, strategies for interpretation and the impact of performance requirements (in politics as well as theatre). 'Sense for sense' translation was central to the approach developed by Cicero (first century BCE) and refined for sacred texts by St. Jerome (fourth century CE). The Roman poet Horace turned the focus to the creative impact in the target language (*Ars Poetica* 133–34, first century BCE). Even Schleiermacher's model of preserving the alterity of the source for the target audience was to some extent anticipated in the development of a Roman critical vocabulary for describing different kinds of relationship between Greek texts and their Latin analogues. This recognized different translation practices involved in transmission and REWRITING, including variation, exchange, transfer and transformation. There was a sometimes uneasy relationship between recognition of the authority of the source text and the more culturally confident desire for the target text to acquire a status of its own. Latin translation of Greek texts included early versions of Greek plays and of Homer that led to an autonomous Latin literature in which intertextuality supplemented translation as the main aesthetic driver.

In late antiquity and the medieval period (when Latin remained the official language of the Christian church in the West), Christian attitudes to the religious and moral values of the texts reshaped transmission patterns. Translation of material collected in Alexandria and other libraries proved vital in preserving Greek medical, mathematical and philosophical texts. In the Abbasid period (second and third centuries H., equivalent to the eighth and ninth centuries CE), these were translated into Arabic, sometimes with Syriac as an intermediary language (see ARABIC TRADITION). This activity was epitomized in the work of *Dar El Hikmah* (Wisdom House) in Baghdad (Etman 2008). Together with the work of the twelfth-century Cordovan physician and philosopher Ibn Rushd (Averroës), which was often mediated through Hebrew and Latin translations, these translations led to the recuperation of Greek science and philosophy and their incorporation into the Western intellectual tradition during the Renaissance (Etman 2004; Haddour 2008).

The work of the translators into Arabic was essentially scholarly. However, other strands of migratory translation developed through creative work, such as the rewriting of Greek and Roman texts by neo-classical dramatists in France and the creative translation of epics within the BRITISH TRADITION. In the late seventeenth and eighteenth centuries, the responses to Virgil by John Dryden (1631–1700) and to Homer by Alexander Pope (1688–1744) not only contributed to debates about the relationship between the source text and the target language but also became canonical literary works in their own right. Dryden's interest in satire led him to translate from Latin (Persius and Juvenal) and demonstrate once more the capacity of classical texts to be used as a vehicle for contemporary political critique, already pioneered by Denham (Poole and Maule 1995: xxxvi). Denham saw translation as involving a process similar to alchemy ('transfusion'), while Dryden's preferred approach was 'paraphrasing', i.e. keeping the author 'in view' but following the words less strictly than the sense. This approach was less free than 'imitation' but more creative than 'metaphrase' (Hopkins 2008). Dryden's translation of Virgil's *Aeneid* (1697) was extensively excerpted in the commonplace books of poetry that shaped eighteenth-century tastes. His LITERARY translations directly influenced later poets such as Pope, Gray, Byron, Burns, Coleridge, Hopkins, Tennyson and Browning. Dryden's work shows how a web of translation practices combines both 'domesticating' and 'foreignizing' elements and how categorizations of these can shift. He used previous translations; absorbed the language of his predecessors Spenser, Shakespeare and Milton, itself already classicized (Haynes 2003), and in turn influenced practice and aesthetics in both translation and literature, making the boundaries between the two more porous.

The classical translation/transmission symbiosis also activates the crossing of boundaries of culture and class. For example, Arab translators influenced the Renaissance in Europe; European tradition reciprocated at the time of the Arab *Nahda* (Awakening, c. 1870–1950), when the impact of classical texts was partly shaped by the links with French culture. Following Napoleon's influence, students and scholars from Egypt had been able to work in Paris, and this enabled Rifa'a Rafi' El Tahtawi (1801–72) to translate Fénelon's *Les Aventures de Télémaque* (1699) into Arabic (see ARABIC TRADITION). Fénelon's work had been inspired by Homer's *Odyssey*. Subsequently, interest in Greek texts that had not previously been translated into Arabic profited from the availability of French translations. These stimulated the pan-Mediterranean cultural work of Taha Hussein, who, in 1925, founded the Classics department at Cairo University (Pormann 2006) and led to the translation of the plays of Sophocles into Arabic (1939), which in turn influenced Arab theatre. Since then, four Arabic versions of Sophocles' *Oedipus Tyrannos* have been translated into English (Carlson 2005) and have encouraged the re-engagement between Arabic and Anglophone classical scholarship and theatre criticism.

The history of translation into English also maps the history of education, historiography and popular culture and is sometimes distinctive for its use of less well-known texts (Hall 2008). In the nineteenth and twentieth centuries, social, gender and educational barriers were increasingly breached and redefined by the availability of inexpensive popular translations (for example those published by Bohn, Everyman, Penguin and the bilingual Loeb series) and the more prominent role taken by female translators (Hardwick 2000). In the early twentieth century, the best-selling translations of Greek plays by the Oxford Regius Professor Gilbert Murray also led to commercially successful London theatre productions and to the development of a strong BBC radio broadcast tradition (Wrigley 2005). In the USA, the demands made by undergraduate humanities and 'great books' courses from the 1920s and 1930s onwards created a

huge market for translations of classical texts, especially epic, DRAMA and historiography (Schein 2007). Translations by scholars such as Richmond Lattimore (1951, 1965) and Robert Fitzgerald (1961, 1974), and by Robert Fagles (1984, 1990, 1996) who collaborated with the classicist Bernard Knox, influenced both literary criticism and popular conceptions of the ancient world. E. V. Rieu's prose translations of Homer (1946, 1950) sold millions of copies and were publicized as eroding differences between ancient and modern idiom. Rieu's work made direct speech colloquial (with the unintended result of dating it) and was criticized for losing the 'nobility' that had been attributed to Homer by Matthew Arnold (Hardwick 2000). One of Rieu's readers was Patrick Kavanagh, whose poem 'On Looking into EV Rieu's Homer' (1951) alluded to the influence of translations on poets who did not know Greek (cf. John Keats's 'On Looking into Chapman's Homer', 1817) and, by using images from Homer to link parochial squabbles in rural Ireland with global conflict, also braided into the Irish poetic tradition a sense of the alignment of ancient and modern experience that contributed to the use of close translations of classical texts by Michael Longley and Seamus Heaney (Harrison 2008; Hardwick 2007a).

Relationships of power between source, mediating and target languages and cultures

Because of the historical and cultural status of the classical languages there is a sense in which even the most powerful target language can be perceived as subaltern in relation to them. Paradoxically, in imperial and POSTCOLONIAL contexts the appropriation of classical literature and ideas in education systems has provided counter-texts that both challenged imperial domination and provided themes and forms for the development of postcolonial debates and of new senses of identity (Budelmann 2005). Examples of the exchange between west African and Greek mythology and theatrical practices include Soyinka's *The Bacchae of Euripides: A Communion Rite* (1973), Femi Osofisan's *Tegonni: An African Antigone* (1999) and Ola Rotimi's *The Gods Are Not To Blame* (1971), each of which employs close translation alongside linguistic and formal variations from the Greek (Goff 2007; Simpson 2007). South African workshop theatre, in which both actors and spectators take part in a transformative experience of resistance and reconstruction, has drawn extensively on Greek plays as a source of raw material (Hardwick 2007b). A feature of this development has been multilingual translations and performances that combine the languages normally spoken by the actors and/or those prominent among the audience.

In theatrical contexts, the term 'translation' also covers the semiotics of performing the play-text – costume, acting style, gesture, movement, masks and make-up, music, sound and lighting (see DRAMA). The conventional but problematic criteria of 'performability' add a practical dimension to the aesthetics and philology brought to bear on the rewriting of the source text (Bassnett 2000; Walton 2006). An initial close translation may be followed by the preparation of the play-text by a dramatist who may not be familiar with the source text and language. The preparation of the play-text may be interwoven with the rehearsal process and the design and direction by theatre practitioners whose knowledge of the source play and its context of production has been mediated via the theatrical traditions to which they belong. Interestingly, this process gives an extended influence to scholarly translations which are used to mediate the source text. Examples include Heaney's use of Jebb's late-nineteenth-century translations for *The Cure at Troy: after Sophocles' Philoctetes* (1990) and for *The Burial at Thebes* (2004).

New translations also involve overt or covert statements about the capabilities and aspirations of the target language. One example is the blending of literary Scots (pioneered by Gavin Douglas in his sixteenth-century translation of Virgil's *Aeneid*) with demotic idiom to create a 'theatrical' Scots that aimed to by-pass the English language and to link Scottish theatre with the European tradition. The Scottish poet laureate Edwin Morgan's *Phaedra* (2000), which was based on Racine's *Phèdre* and thus drew on Seneca's *Phaedra* and Euripides' *Hippolytus*, was written in Glaswegian Scots. In South Africa, different languages have come

together in a new translation of Homer's *Iliad* into Southern African English (SAE) by the classicist Richard Whitaker, who judged that the hybrid SAE would convey the resonances of the source text better than a translation in standard English, which tends to inflate Homeric institutions and titles. For example, in SAE the Homeric term *basileus* is translated as 'chief' rather than 'king', and this is both more historically accurate and more attuned to the cultural horizons of readers in South Africa (Whitaker 2003).

Thus the translation of classical texts continues to be a means of negotiating intellectual, aesthetic and cultural status and of practising realignments (Johnston 2007). It provides a prime example of how rigidly polarized models of alterity and domestication need to be refined in order to take into account the fluidity and contingency of the interaction between translation and cultural practices. Furthermore, because of the richness of its comparative material it not only provides an index of scholarly trends but also maps symbiotic relationships with literary and theatrical creativity. The global role of classical translations provides cultural geographies as well as temporal genealogies.

See also:
ADAPTATION; ARABIC TRADITION; DRAMA; GREEK TRADITION; LATIN TRADITION; RETRANSLATION; REWRITING; STRATEGIES.

Further reading
Poole and Maule 1995; Bassnett, 2000; France 2000; Hardwick 2000; Armstrong 2005; Walton 2006; Schein 2007; Hall, 2008.

LORNA HARDWICK

Comics

Comics may be seen as a continuation of other forms of visual sequential art, from prehistoric graffiti to medieval tapestries to eighteenth- and nineteenth-century prints and 'protocomics' (McCloud 1993; Groensteen 1999). However, the emergence of comics in their present form 'is closely related to the emergence of mass media, due to new means of mass reproduction and an increasing readership of the printed media' (Mey 1998).

Comics developed into a text type of their own thanks to their growing commercial value in the journalistic field (Kaindl 1999). They first appeared in colour in the Sunday pages of American newspapers at the end of the nineteenth century, and were accompanied by daily strips in black and white (B&W) over the course of the following years. Collections of comics began to be published in book form shortly afterwards (Carlin 2005; Restaino 2004; Horn 1976/1999). From the 1920s onwards, comics began to be published and to gain popularity in other areas of the world, at first in Europe (most notably in France, Belgium and Italy) and South America (most notably in Argentina), then in the rest of the world (most notably in Japan). Today, almost every nation in the world has its own comics industry. The Japanese comics industry, the largest in the world, has grown steadily and exponentially since World War II. It is now fifty times as large as the US comics industry – the second largest – and accounts for some 40 per cent of all printed material published in the country, compared to approximately 3 per cent in the US (Pilcher and Brooks 2005: 90). Japanese comics, or manga, have developed their own style and conventions and comprise a vast range of genres targeted at specialized readerships. They currently fall into five main categories: *shonen* ('boys'), *shojo* ('girls'), *redisu* or *redikomi* ('ladies'), *seijin* ('adult erotica') and *seinen* ('young men'). Each category is further subdivided into a myriad of genres which often overlap and cut across categories.

A large number of all comics published in the world have traditionally been translated American comics, a situation which led to American comics conventions merging with and shaping local traditions of 'visual storytelling' (Eisner 1985) as they brought with them a set of genres (funny animals, familiar comedy, adventure, detective story, etc.), themes and narrative devices, as well as a repertoire of signs. Conventions which came to be recognized as characteristic of the art form – even though some of them in fact pre-date American comics – include the use of balloons for dialogues and thoughts, the use of speed lines to represent movement, onomatopoeias to represent feelings and sounds, and pictograms to represent concepts or emotions (Gasca and Gubern 1988). Japanese comics have been translated in other Asian countries since the 1960s, but remained practically unknown in Western countries until the 1980s. From the 1990s onwards translated manga began to circulate widely also in the USA and in Europe, where they currently represent a considerable share of the comics market. Japanese comics are now increasingly replacing American comics as a source of inspiration for Western authors, who tend to adopt Japanese reading pace, page layout, type of transition between panels, pictograms and ways to represent the human body and facial expressions, among other conventions.

Comics come in a number of formats (paper size, number of pages, colour vs. B&W, periodicity, etc.), each usually originating in a specific country or region. Anglophone and North-European countries are especially familiar with the comic strip format of daily newspapers, in colour (on Sunday) and B&W (on weekdays), with the comic book format (typically of the superhero genre, based on serialization and distributed as cheap four-colour booklets), and with the more recent 'graphic novel' format (a one-off rather than periodical publication addressed to an adult or 'high-brow' readership). More typical European formats include the up-market large size, full-colour French album, and the smaller B&W popular, periodical Italian notebook format. Japanese Manga (and Taiwanese and Chinese Manhua) are B&W, rather lengthy volumes with stories which run into hundreds of pages. European and Japanese readers are perhaps more familiar with anthological magazines than American readers. A change in the publication and distribution format of comics in translation may affect the visual reading experience as well as orient translation strategies (see Rota, 2008; Scatasta 2002).

The publication of a comic in translation typically involves securing reproduction rights from a foreign publisher, acquiring the films or files from the original publisher, and 'adapting' the product for the local readership. This 'adaptation' can be done in-house or commissioned to an external agency, or may involve a mix of the two. The translator receives a copy of the comic and produces a text which is usually subdivided into pages and numbered paragraphs, each corresponding to a balloon or caption in the source text. In some cases English may function as a vehicular or transitional language (see RELAY). For example, Japanese comics are sometimes translated into other languages based on an American translation (Jüngst 2004), while Disney comics, which are mostly produced and published in European countries and are often written in languages such as Italian or Danish, are often translated on the basis of a working English version (Zanettin, 2008a). The translation is then delivered to the publisher, where it is often subjected to further revision before a letterer erases the source text from balloons and captions and replaces it with the translation. The art director and graphic editors are then responsible for effecting any changes deemed necessary or appropriate to the visual text (editing or removing pictures, adding/removing/altering colours, changing layout and pagination); they are also responsible for 'packaging' the product with appropriate paratext (covers, titles, flyleaves, advertisements, etc.).

Before the advent of computers, the whole process was manual, and letterers used to erase the source text with a shaving blade and write the target text by hand. Graphics represented an additional cost for publishers which was often perceived as unnecessary, unless dictated by institutional or self-censorship. Words used as pictures (i.e. onomatopoeias, graffiti) and pictures used as words (i.e. calligrams, ideograms) were often left unaltered in translated American comics, thus becoming part of the comics conventions of importing countries. In recent years, however, digital technologies brought about many changes in the comics industry. Computers and the Internet have not only changed the way many comics are now produced and distributed (see McCloud 2000 and 2006 on Webcomics and processes of comics production), but have also changed translation practices. Introducing changes to a computer file rather than film has made both lettering and retouching easier and less expensive.

Comics have mostly been relegated to a marginal position in translation studies. They are hardly mentioned in general works on translation. Even studies which adopt a semiotic approach to translation, either in general terms (e.g. Jakobson 1960: 350; Eco and Nergaard 1998) or in discussions of a specific subfield of translation studies such as film dubbing (e.g.

Gottlieb 1998), usually mention comics only in passing. The majority of individual articles dealing with comics in translation have been written in languages other than English, often on topics such as the translation of proper names, puns and onomatopoeia (notably in the foreign translations of *Astérix*), while volumes entirely or mainly devoted to the translation of comics are extremely rare, a notable exception being Kaindl (2004); see also Zanettin (2008b). The number of research articles on the translation of comics has been growing since the mid-1990s, but it remains relatively limited.

The translation of comics has often been regarded as a type of 'constrained translation' (Mayoral *et al.* 1988; Rabadán 1991; Zanettin 1998; Valero Garcés 2000). This term, initially applied by Titford (1982) to subtitling, is now usually understood to include the translation of comics, songs, ADVERTISING, and any type of AUDIOVISUAL or multimedia translation, from film subtitling and dubbing to software and website localization (Hernández-Bartolomé and Mendiluce-Cabrera 2004). Although 'constrained translation' approaches stress the semiotic dimension and the interdependence of words and images in comics, they remain primarily concerned with the translation of verbal material. Words are seen as subordinated to the images, and the non-verbal components of comics are discussed only in so far as they represent visual constraints for the translator of the verbal components.

This approach assumes that pictures in translated comics are not modified, and thus often restricts the scope of investigation to linguistic analysis. However, comics are primarily visual texts, and meaning derives from the interaction between images and written language, both within and across panels and pages. When comics are published in translation they are often manipulated at both textual and pictorial level. Such modifications may range from the omission of panels, or even pages, to the retouching or redrawing of (part of) the layout and content. Furthermore, images are not universally perceived to have the same meaning, since non-verbal signs are as culture-bound as verbal signs. The same graphic convention may have different meanings in comics and in manga; for example, cloud-like bubbles with a tail of increasingly smaller circular bubbles are used to represent thought (in comics) or whispered dialogue (in manga). Even when images are apparently not manipulated, they are 'translated' by readers according to culture-specific visual conventions. The prevailing norm for Japanese comics published in translation now seems to be to retain the original right to left reading direction, a strategy favoured by fans of Japanese pop ACG (anime-comics-games) subculture. Not only does the reading of words conflict with the reading of images in this case, but their interpretation is also filtered through culture-specific ways of reading visual signs such as the direction of movement and the disposition of bodily masses in a panel (Barbieri 2004). When translated manga are instead published as mirror images to conform to Western reading habits, they entail changes in asymmetry (e.g. left rather than right handedness). The role played by the manga fan subculture in orienting translation practices is also evident in scanlation, which consists in the scanning, translating and distributing through the Internet, by and for communities of fans, of foreign comics that have not yet been officially published (Ferrer Simó 2005).

While constrained translation approaches are often prescriptive, either explicitly or implicitly, other approaches adopt a more descriptive stance, complementing linguistic with cultural and semiotic analysis. Kaindl (1999) proposes a taxonomy of elements which may be usefully adopted in the analysis of comics in translation: typographical signs (font type and size, layout, format), pictorial signs (colours, action lines, vignettes, perspective), and linguistic signs (titles, inscriptions, dialogues, onomatopoeias, narration). All of these may be subjected to different STRATEGIES of 'translation', such as replacement, subtraction, addition, retention, etc. In a similar vein, Celotti (2000, 2008) discusses a number of strategies (translation, non-translation, footnotes, cultural adaptation, etc.) which are used in relation to the trans-lation loci of comics, these being the four areas containing verbal messages: balloons, captions, titles and paratext. Celotti also describes the interplay between visual and verbal messages in translated comics. Zanettin (2008a) suggests that the translation of comics may be usefully investigated within a localization framework,

understood in its broadest sense as the ADAPTATION and updating of visual and verbal signs for a target locale (see LOCALIZATION). In addition to the translator 'proper', different actors are involved in the process, and the work of the 'translator' is considered in relation to the general context and workflow. If translated comics are understood as commercial products and textual artefacts in which 'translation' in the sense of 'replacement of strings of natural language' is only one component of the process, the publication of a comic in translation may be regarded as a form of LOCALIZATION.

See also:
ADVERTISING; AUDIOVISUAL TRANSLATION; CHILDREN'S LITERATURE; GLOBALIZATION; LOCALIZATION.

Further reading
Zanettin 1998; Kaindl 1999; Celotti 2000; Scatasta 2002; Jüngst 2004; Ferrer Simó 2005; Zanettin 2008b.

FEDERICO ZANETTIN

Commercial translation

The question of classifying translation activity by subject domains, topics, genres, text types, text functions or other criteria is not unprob-lematic. Some theorists (e.g. Sager 1994, 1998) attempt to group all translation activity which is not of literary or religious texts into a category called 'industrial' or 'non-literary' translation. The term 'pragmatic translation' was introduced by Casagrande (1954: 335) to refer to translation where 'the emphasis is on the content of the message' as opposed to the literary or aesthetic form, and this term now appears to be used frequently to refer to non-literary translation, particularly in the commercial sphere.

SCIENTIFIC AND TECHNICAL TRANSLATION may be defined in relation to subject domains (science and technology) which are recognized by classification systems such as the Dewey Decimal Classification or the Universal Decimal Classification. However, commercial translation, financial translation, economic translation, business translation and other, similar terms do not correspond so readily to existing classifications of knowledge. There is thus no consensus on how to label or define this translation activity. The term used here is one of convenience, intended to cover the translation of all texts used in business contexts, excluding technical and legal texts. It should be noted, in addition, that 'commercial translation' is sometimes used to designate translation services rendered for payment, as opposed to 'voluntary translation'; this distinction is not pursued here.

Studies of commercial translation

Given the difficulty of classifying this translation activity and the wide range of text types it encompasses, it is hardly surprising that translation studies as an academic discipline has paid commercial translation relatively little attention. However, it can also be argued that it is neglected due to the high esteem in which LITERARY texts are held, compared with genres considered culturally less prestigious and therefore perceived as less worthy of study (see also Aixelá 2004: 33).

Within studies of commercial translation, the main focus in recent years has been on activities related to the GLOBALIZATION of trade in goods and services. The stimulation of demand for products across borders through ADVERTISING and the translation of advertising campaigns has provided a rich source of material for translation scholars. Most studies (e.g. Jettmarová 1997, 1998; Chiaro 2004; Smith 2006) have focused on the STRATEGIES used in translating advertising material in particular linguistic and cultural contexts. Some researchers (e.g. Séguinot 1995) have also examined the range of competencies or knowledge (business and marketing, legal frameworks, cultural conventions, etc.) required by translators working on commercial texts.

Closely connected to the translation of advertising material is the phenomenon of language contact and code switching in commercial texts (see also MULTILINGUALISM). Recent work on multilingual discourse focuses on the use of English in non-Anglophone advertising. For example, Piller (2001, 2003) reports a shift towards multilingual advertising in a corpus of German advertisements, which is attributed to the perceived status of English as the language of progress. Similarly, English is used to signal prestige and quality in the Russian market (Ustinova 2006) and in the Mexican context (Baumgardner 2006). In Martin's (2006) study of French advertising, the tendency to use English and global imagery is correlated with social trends, consumer attitudes and legislative frameworks. Hornikx (2007) provides an example of an investigation to gauge reception of multilinguality in advertising material by testing the associations evoked by the foreign language and examining the ways in which those associations are transferred to the product being advertised.

A number of scholars (e.g. Snell-Hornby 1999) have focused on the translation of commercial documents from the tourism sector. Sumberg (2004), for example, analyses how different strategies to attract British tourists to Spain and France are reflected in the respective tourist brochures and in target text production strategies. Navarro Errasti et al. (2004) bring together a collection of papers which present pragmatic analyses of diverse aspects of tourist literature and its translation.

Other commercial texts with a persuasive function which have been researched by translation scholars include company financial reporting documents (see, for example, Böttger and Bührig 2003; Böttger 2004). Introductory sections of annual reports (e.g. the letter to the shareholders) are often the focus of attention due to the way in which they reflect corporate cultures and the possibility for variation in how corporate philosophies are expressed in different cultures. Baumgarten et al. (2004), for example, find that German translations of letters to shareholders are typically more distant, more neutral, more formal and more factual than their English source texts.

Theoretical and methodological frameworks

Much of the research on the translation of marketing material is informed by theories from neighbouring disciplines of cross-cultural communication (e.g. Katan 1999/2004), semiotics (e.g. Freitas 2004), interpersonal communication (e.g. de Mooij 2004), pragmatics (e.g. Navarro Errasti *et al.* 2004) and models of multimodal communication and visual design (e.g. Millán-Varela 2004). In addition, studies of commercial documents have often drawn on a range of linguistic frameworks, in particular Hallidayan linguistics (e.g. Baumgarten *et al.* 2004) and cognitive linguistics (e.g. Charteris-Black and Ennis 2001).

One of the few attempts to develop a theory of translation applicable specifically to commercial translation is offered by Sager's work (1994). He views the translation process as an industrial one and identifies the various components of this process: the input material (documents); operations performed on the material (human translation, MACHINE TRANSLATION, COMPUTER-AIDED TRANSLATION); the scope and capabilities of the operator (skills, experience, expertise); and possible end-products (range of documents produced) (Sager 1994: 151). The translation process may be instigated in various ways: by the writer of a source text; by a prospective reader of a translation, or by agents acting for writer and/or reader (ibid.: 140). The type of end-product produced may be determined by the end-user requirements, by a particular relationship between the source and target documents or by the operation that is performed on the source document. Sager (ibid.: 140–2) also outlines the pre-conditions of translation. They include, for example, the existence of a set of instructions for the translator and the presence of a client who is the recipient of the translation. Conditions such as these exclude translation performed in training settings, translating for pleasure, or translations done by readers for their own benefit, thus defining more clearly the scope of professional translation activity.

While Sager's (ibid.: 116–17) approach requires the translation to bear some similarity to the source document, it also accommodates the production of substantially different document types. Based on the status of the source text and the relationship between the source and target documents, he puts forward a functional typology of translation which recognizes three types of translated texts: autonomous, interdependent or derived (ibid.: 179–84). The autonomous document is a translation arising from a draft or provisional source text which has no status once the translation is available.

Interdependent texts may co-exist in parallel in bilingual or multilingual versions and the source text is no longer recognizable; in some cases, e.g. European legislation, the parallel documents are also functionally equal. The category of derived documents represents the prototypical translation. Sager further classifies derived documents depending on whether the translation serves the same or a different function to that of the source text, and whether it is a full, selective or reduced translation. He presents a model of the translation process based on these principles, which he later uses to identify specific characteristics of BIBLE translation, LITERARY TRANSLATION and technical translation (Sager 1998).

Sager's approach is useful because it accommodates a range of activities which occur in professional contexts sometimes overlooked in translation research or training (see TRAINING AND EDUCATION). In addition, it acknowledges the role played by situational factors (e.g. time and cost) and personal factors (e.g. the translator's ability to tackle the job, the writer's and reader's awareness of translation in the process of disseminating information, the end-user's expectations) in the specification and performance of the translation task. Pym's (1995b, 2001c) discussion of transaction costs, cooperation, mutual benefits and translatorial ETHICS provides an alternative framework within which to approach the notions of social effort and to examine the impact and relevance of different forms of translation activity. Finally, some translator training manuals (e.g. Gouadec 2007) also offer practical guidance on various types of commercial translation activity and the translation process.

It has been argued that the wider cultural and social significance of commercial translation activity has been underestimated. Cronin (2003: 2), for example, asserts that 'the cultural and intellectual stakes of non-literary translation are rarely spelled out in any great detail and are generally referred to in only the vaguest possible terms ("promoting understanding", "encouraging trade")'. This viewpoint provides the motivation for his study of non-literary translation in its cultural, economic and societal context. In line with current developments within the humanities more generally, translation studies is now giving greater prominence to social and SOCIOLOGICAL APPROACHES to translating, and agency and resistance are key themes in this discussion (see DESCRIPTIVE VERSUS COMMITTED APPROACHES). There is considerable scope for future research on commercial translation to consider critically, not just what this activity entails and how students might be trained to undertake it, but also how and why it is done, its impact on society, and what roles the translator and his or her translations play in shaping economic, cultural, societal and political developments.

See also:
ADVERTISING; FUNCTIONALIST APPROACHES; GLOBALIZATION; LOCALIZATION; SCIENTIFIC AND TECHNICAL TRANSLATION.

Further reading
Sager 1994; Séguinot 1995; Sager 1998; Katan 1999/2004; Snell-Hornby 1999; Charteris-Black and Ennis 2001; Böttger and Bührig 2003; Cronin 2003; Navarro Errasti *et al.* 2004.

MAEVE OLOHAN

Community interpreting

The term 'community interpreting' refers to interpreting which takes place in the public service sphere to facilitate communication between officials and lay people: at police departments, immigration departments, social welfare centres, medical and mental health offices, schools and other institutions. Community interpreting is typically carried out consecutively, but can also involve instances of interpreting performed simultaneously (in the form of whispering). The term covers both interpreting in face-to-face situations and interpreting provided over the telephone (see DIALOGUE INTERPRETING).

Growth of interest in interpreting from the 1990s onwards, including interpreting performed in community settings, has led to a proliferation of terms referring to this type of activity. The variety of terms can be explained by the diversity of conceptualizations of the activities and actors involved. For instance, in most countries interpreting between spoken and signed languages in the same settings detailed above is traditionally termed SIGNED LANGUAGE INTERPRETING rather than community interpreting. This area has its own established organizations and journals but is increasingly included in collected volumes on community interpreting (e.g. Hertog and van der Ver 2006; Hale 2007). Dialogue interpreting (Wadensjö 1992; Mason 1999), liaison interpreting (Gentile *et al.* 1996; Erasmus *et al.* 2003) and public service interpreting (Corsellis *et al.* 2000) are other terms used more or less synonymously with community interpreting, though each term tends to emphasize a specific characteristic of the same activity – the communicative format (involving face-to-face, bi-directional interpreting) in the first two cases, and the social setting in the third. Some authors tend to avoid the term 'community interpreting' since it has been associated in some contexts with amateurism and ad hoc solutions, and with interpreting performed by people with little or no professional training.

At one time performed only by volunteers, untrained bilinguals, friends and relatives, sometimes including children – what Hall (2004) refers to as 'language brokering' – interpreting in community settings has developed into a profession over the past decades, in response to international migration and the consequent linguistic heterogeneity of most nations (see MOBILITY). Increasingly, community interpreting seems to be further developing into a number of distinct areas of professional expertise, such as 'healthcare interpreting', 'mental health interpreting', 'educational interpreting' and 'legal interpreting' (the latter including COURT INTERPRETING, interpreting at police stations and in immigration and ASYLUM hearings). Nevertheless, community interpreting continues to be performed by untrained individuals, what Harris (1990) calls 'natural translators'. This partly has to do with the fact that the need for community interpreting fluctuates, sometimes very quickly, with global streams of migration. National and international organizations regularly attempt to set standards and promote a professional attitude to community interpreting among those who undertake it as well as their clients. However, the wide variety of languages involved and the fluctuating demand for interpreter services for each language tend constantly to frustrate these efforts. Community interpreters who can only secure few assignments are also likely to enjoy limited opportunities for developing their professional skills. Generally speaking, the level of funding available for appointing professionals and for professional training programmes tends to fluctuate in response to the current political climate.

Community interpreting vs. other types of interpreting

The role of the community interpreter is as vital to successful communication as that of any other type of interpreter. In addition, involvement in face-to-face interaction emphasizes the community interpreter's role as both a language and social mediator. While the textual material for conference interpreting largely consists of prepared (often written) monologues in the source language, community interpreters have to handle real-time dialogue – more or less spontaneous and unpredictable exchanges of talk between individuals speaking different languages – and they also have to interpret in both directions. This is often the case also in face-to-face interpreting undertaken in business, media and diplomatic settings. However, professional community interpreting differs from most other types of DIALOGUE INTERPRETING in that it is often understood and/or required to involve a high level of neutrality and detachment; the community interpreter is generally expected not to side with either party. The principle of neutrality and detachment, which is taken for granted in COURT INTERPRETING, has been a major issue of debate among professional community interpreters and those who train them. Attempts to define the appropriate level of involvement vs. detachment on the part of the community interpreter are fraught with difficulties. In practice, a community interpreter often has to suffer the dilemma of being simultaneously seen as the immigrants' advocate and the official's 'tool' and helping hand. This also means that community interpreters can be regarded, from two opposing points of view, as potential renegades. Their dilemma as mediators is further exacerbated by the prevalence of social antagonism, ethnic tensions and racial prejudice in most countries.

Many community interpreters are themselves members of minority groups in the host country, but compared to other members of these groups they are relatively assimilated into the host society and familiar with its institutions. Compared to conference, business and diplomatic interpreting, community interpreting remains a low-status profession which does not attract high levels of remuneration. This is indirectly reflected in the level of training made available: where courses are specifically designed for community interpreters, they tend to be run by colleges rather than universities. However, since the 1990s courses in community interpreting (especially legal interpreting) have increasingly been taught as part of undergraduate and master's programmes in interpreting at university level. For a discussion of the role of the interpreter in various settings, see Angelelli (2004).

Content and aims of training programmes

Training programmes for community interpreters vary in both scope and aims. A general goal is to achieve a high level of accuracy by improving students' command of their working languages. In addition to knowledge of linguistic structures, this covers training in the use of specialized terminology and familiarizing students with the subject areas and administrative procedures of the particular domains in which they wish to specialize, for example health services, local government, social services and legal services. Most programmes are also designed to develop awareness of potential cultural differences between participants involved in the interpreting event. It is not uncommon for community interpreters to feel the urge to intervene to smooth cultural differences by, for instance, explaining or adjusting conventions concerning the degree of formality in addressing the other party. Differences in conventions concerning when and where it is appropriate to bring up what to one or both parties might be taboo topics – such as money, sex and religion – may also require deliberate interventions on the part of the interpreter to avoid communicative breakdown. Such intervention by the community interpreter could mean preventing the parties concerned from acquiring familiarity with each other's conventions of politeness and correctness. Opinions therefore vary among trainers concerning the role of the community interpreter and the notion of efficiency in the interpreting context. Ultimately, efficiency can only be measured against a particular goal, and goals of course differ, coincide and are generally negotiated in face-to-face interaction.

Some scholars consider it the community interpreter's professional duty to inform each (or one) of the parties about what is considered appropriate, normal, rational and acceptable by another party. Shackman says of the (UK) community interpreter that 'she is responsible for enabling the professional and client, with very different backgrounds and perceptions and in an unequal relationship of power and knowledge, to communicate to their mutual satisfaction' (1984: 18). Empirical research has also shown that in practice interpreters are inclined to prevent possible threats to a smooth exchange from surfacing in interaction (Jansen 1995; Wadensjö 1998; Davidson 2002). As a result, the interacting parties may experience 'mutual satisfaction' at one level, but at the cost of an illusory mutual understanding. Research has also demonstrated that interpreters tend to give higher priority to their role as co-ordinators, rather than translators (of spoken discourse), in the sense that they devote much effort to sustaining interaction, sometimes at the cost of accuracy in rendering interlocutors' utterances (Wadensjö 1992, 1998, 2004). This situation does have its dangers: in assuming the position of the 'expert' on language and culture, and hence taking control of the inter-action, the community interpreter runs the risk of depriving the monolingual parties of power (and responsibility), following a patron-izing model, more or less deciding for them what they optimally want to achieve in and by their encounter. This becomes evident when we consider that the monolingual parties in institutional settings may occasionally lack the interest and motivation to actually talk to one another. For instance, a suspect meeting a police officer or a child meeting a doctor may prefer to remain silent. Professional training can be designed to raise awareness of these and other issues specific to the community interpreter's

work. As a rule, most training aims to ensure the interpreter's commitment to a professional code of ethics and guide to good practice that involves supporting existing standards on how the monolingual parties' needs and expectations should be met.

Most programmes provide training in consecutive and simultaneous interpreting. They pay varying degrees of attention to note-taking techniques and to developing relevant skills for sight translation, as well as for written translation. They generally also include a component on interpreting theory, in addition to practical exercises and linguistic and termi-nology training in the languages in question. Practical exercises involve role-play, language laboratory work and analysis of audio and video recordings of interpreting practices.

Guidelines instructing public service officials and others on how to communicate through community interpreters are provided by various institutions, such as NAATI (the National Accreditation Authority for Translators and Interpreters) in Australia and the Institute of Linguists in the UK. These guidelines include, for instance, advising officials to speak directly to the other party rather than saying to the community interpreter 'tell him to …', etc. Such guidelines are both influenced by and reflected in existing training programmes, where community interpreters are instructed to speak in the first person. Users of community interpreting services are also advised to pause frequently so as not to tax the interpreter's memory, to plan ahead for interviews in which the assistance of an interpreter is required, to avoid discussing issues directly with the inter-preter in order not to exclude the other party, and to hire accredited community interpreters wherever possible.

Accreditation of community interpreters

In many countries, a number of university programmes that specialize in interpreter training offer a degree or a certificate upon completion of a given course. These degrees are seldom designed specifically for community interpreting. Some types of community inter-preting, such as legal interpreting, are relatively more likely to be included in a degree programme than others, such as social service, health and mental health interpreting.

In some countries, accreditation is available through professional organizations; in others it is available through state-controlled institutions. In the USA, a Registry of Interpreters for the Deaf (RID) was established in 1964. RID offers two certifications for Deaf interpreters, the Certified Deaf Interpreter (CDI) and the Conditional Legal Interpreting Permit-Relay (CLIP-R) (see SIGNED LANGUAGE INTER-PRETING). The CDI is a generalist exam and the CLIP-R is a legal specialist exam. There is no corresponding registry or testing for spoken language interpreters in the USA, but the American Translators Association (ATA) has an Interpreters Division that constitutes a network of professionals in the field. Sweden was among the first to organize national accreditation for community interpreters, which has been available since 1976 and is awarded by a state institution, the Swedish Legal, Financial and Administrative Services Agency. Once authorized, interpreters may take additional tests for specialist qualifications as 'court interpreter' and 'health services interpreter', respectively (Idh 2007). Accreditation in Norway and Denmark is also undertaken by a governmental body. In Australia, accreditation of community interpreters has existed since 1977. It is provided by the National Accreditation Authority for Translators and Interpreters (NAATI). NAATI accredited interpreters can become members of the Australian Institute of Interpreters and Translators (AUSIT). In New Zealand, accreditation has been available since 1987 for community interpreters in English–Maori. These interpreters are certified by the Maori Language Commission after passing language exams only. For other languages, interpreters can receive accreditation through the Australian NAATI, generally accepted as providing a *de facto* standard.

In South Africa, the South African Translators Institute (SATI) conducts accreditation exams for conference interpreters as well as for sign language interpreters and, starting mainly with the work of the Truth and Reconciliation Commission, also for 'liaison interpreters' (in the Commission's terminology). In the United Kingdom, the Institute of Linguists Educational Trust is the main awarding body; it offers vocationally related qualifications in a wide variety of languages. These include the Interpreting Diploma in Public Service Interpreting (accredited for England, Wales and Northern Ireland). A National Register of Public Service Interpreters, NRPSI LTD, has existed since 1994 (Corsellis *et al.* 2007).

Community interpreters in society

The professionalization of community interpreting (including setting up training programmes, systems of certification and professional associations) reflects an official concern for the legal and social welfare of MINORITY, immigrant and refugee populations. Community interpreting enables those who lack fluency in and knowledge of the majority language(s) and culture(s) to receive full and equal access to public service facilities. Support for the professionalization of community interpreting can also be seen as reflecting the authorities' concern for ensuring their own ability to carry out their duties when dealing with people who are unable or unwilling to communicate in the official language(s). For instance, a doctor can only provide adequate health care if the patients are able to discuss their problems clearly and frankly; confidentiality must therefore be guaranteed. Professional community interpreters are obliged to ensure that the confidentiality of any interaction in which they are involved is always maintained. In this sense, community interpreters form an integral part of the social service system of a modern society and are instrumental in ensuring that all parties have equal access to and control over those systems. Civil rights and civil responsibilities are two sides of the same coin. Professional training may focus on avoiding errors and omissions that might be costly to the public purse, but seen from a wider perspective, community interpreting is not just about enabling efficient communication to take place: it is also bound to play a crucial role in social processes of segregation and integration.

Research on community interpreting

Community interpreting has attracted the interest of researchers from a diverse range of academic disciplines. Starting in the 1990s, community interpreting also began to emerge as a field of study in its own right, which meant that research on community interpreting has contributed to the interdisciplinary character of translation studies. Pöchhacker (2004) offers an overview of studies on interpreting and a detailed discussion of developmental trends within this empirical field. He describes how research initiatives designed to explore and explain community-based interpreting led to the broadening of an area which used to be dominated by investigations of simultaneous interpreting performed at international conferences. Such studies of simultaneous interpreting were for the most part quantitative and informed by cognitive psychology (see CONFERENCE INTERPRETING, HISTORICAL AND COGNITIVE PERSPECTIVES). Research interest in community interpreting, by contrast, brought in a variety of new theoretical approaches and methodologies. Pöchhacker attributes much of the growth and diversification of interpreting studies generally to the emergence of research which focuses on interpreting as social interaction, and which applies detailed discourse analyses as a method of inquiry, following Wadensjö (1998) and others. Wadensjö's *Interpreting as Interaction* (1992, 1998) features analyses of naturally occurring, Russian–Swedish interpreter-mediated discourse data, drawn from medical and immigration interviews. Interpreting is examined in this context as a set of linguistic and social practices that are embedded in layers of contexts and that involve various constellations of people. As in many other studies of interpreter-mediated face-to-face interaction, Toury's (1995) descriptivist theory of translation is adopted as a basic point of departure (see NORMS).

Investigations of the dynamics of community interpreting in terms of turn-taking procedures, face-work and other theoretical frameworks from pragmatics and conversational analysis have been undertaken by Apfelbaum (1995) and Roy (2000), who looked specifically at educational settings; by Bolden (2000), Davidson (2000, 2002) and Valero Garcés (2002), who

explored medical encounters, and by Pöllabauer (2004, 2005), who examined ASYLUM hearings. Pöchhacker and Kadric (1999) and Meyer (2004) explored doctor–patient interaction mediated by relatives acting as interpreters, in Austrian and German health care, respectively. A thematic issue of the journal *Interpreting* features five studies of healthcare interpreting based on recorded and transcribed naturally occurring, spoken interaction (Shlesinger and Pöchhacker 2005). Some authors have relied – partly or exclusively – on recorded and transcribed interpreter-mediated role play (e.g. Cambridge 1999; Metzger 1999), on questionnaire-based surveys, on interviews, ethnographic fieldwork and/or written discourse data. For instance, Kaufert and Koolage (1984) adopt an anthropological approach in investigating the social role of medical interpreters in the Canadian Arctic. Barsky (1996) interviews asylum applicants to investigate the institutional processes involved in securing refugee status in Canada. Inghilleri (2003, 2005a, 2005c) and Maryns (2006) explore the impact of macro-social features on the interpreting activity, applying Bourdieu's macro-social theory and discourse analysis. Bischoff and Loutan (1998) bring in additional theoretical concepts from the field of nursing. Bot's (2005) study of interpreter-mediated, therapeutic encounters is informed by sociological and psychotherapeutic theories and methods. Community interpreting naturally also interfaces with the study of law, not least in the context of COURT INTERPRETING, as in Berk-Seligson's *The Bilingual Courtroom* (1990) and Hale's *The Discourse of Court Interpreting* (2004). The wide range of theoretical and methodological approaches to community interpreting reflects the fact that this practice forms part of a variety of social situations that are more extensively explored in the social sciences, medicine and law than in the language sciences.

Since 1995, a series of international conferences devoted entirely to issues of community interpreting have taken place every three years. The first 'Critical Link' conference took place in Toronto, Canada. Like the rest of this conference series, it brought together practising interpreters, agencies, policy makers, teachers of interpreting and interpreting researchers. The publications that came out of these conferences

(Carr *et al.* 1997; Roberts *et al.* 2000; Brunette *et al.* 2003; Wadensjö *et al.* 2007) demonstrate a growing ambition to link research, training and practical concerns, an ambition also evident in other publications on community interpreting (e.g. Hertog and van der Ver 2006; Hale 2007).

See also:
ASYLUM; CONFERENCE INTERPRETING, HISTORICAL AND COGNITIVE PERSPECTIVES; CONFERENCE INTERPRETING, SOCIOCULTURAL PERSPECTIVES; COURT INTERPRETING; DIALOGUE INTERPRETING; SIGNED LANGUAGE INTERPRETING.

Further reading
Gentile *et al.* 1996; Carr *et al.* 1997; Bischoff and Loutan 1998; Wadensjö 1998; Roberts *et al.* 2000; Brunette *et al.* 2003; Erasmus *et al.* 2003; Hertog and van der Ver 2006; Hale 2007; Wadensjö *et al.* 2007.

CECILIA WADENSJÖ

Computer-aided translation (CAT)

The term Computer-aided Translation (CAT) refers to a translation *modus operandi* in which human translation (HT) is aided by computer applications. A competing term, Machine-aided Translation (MAT), is also in use, particularly within the software community involved in developing CAT applications (Quah 2006: 6). A key characteristic of CAT is that a human translator takes control of the translation process and technology is used to facilitate, rather than replace, HT.

Technology-based solutions to translation needs are a natural consequence of the shortened timeframe available for translation and increasing budgetary constraints resulting from GLOBALIZATION, as well as the progressive digitization of source content. CAT has become the predominant mode of translation in SCIENTIFIC AND TECHNICAL TRANSLATION and LOCALIZATION, where technology is employed to increase productivity and cost-effectiveness as well as to improve quality. The technology applications in CAT – commonly referred to as CAT tools – include 'any type of computerized tool that translators use to help them do their job' (Bowker 2002a: 6). Thus, CAT tools range from general-purpose applications such as word-processors, optical character recognition (OCR) software, Internet search engines, etc., to more translation-oriented tools such as multilingual electronic dictionaries, corpus analysis tools, terminology extraction and terminology management systems (see CORPORA; TERMINOLOGY). Having emerged as one of the earliest translation technologies in the 1970s, translation memory (TM) was commercialized in the mid-1990s (Somers 2003a: 31), becoming the main CAT tool since the late 1990s.

Translation Memory technology

TM allows the translator to store translations in a database and 'recycle' them in a new translation by automatically retrieving matched segments (usually sentences) for re-use. The TM database consists of source text and target text segment pairs which form so-called translation units (TUs). After dividing a new ST into segments, the system compares each successive ST segment against the ST segments stored in the translation database. When a new ST segment matches an ST segment in the database, the relevant TU is retrieved. These matches are classified as 'exact matches', 'full matches' and 'fuzzy matches' (Bowker 2002a). An exact match means that the ST segment currently being translated is identical, including formatting style, to a segment stored in the memory. A full match means that the ST segment matches one stored in the memory with differences only in 'variable' elements such as numbers, dates, time, etc. A fuzzy match is one where the ST segment is similar to a segment in the memory, which can be re-used with some editing. The fuzzy matching mechanism uses character-based similarity metrics where resemblance of all characters in a segment, including punctuation, is checked (Bowker 2002a: 200).

TM technology relies on text **segmentation** and alignment. Segmentation is the process of splitting a text into smaller units, such as words or sentences. Most TM systems use the sentence as the main unit, but also recognize as segments other common stand-alone units such as headings, lists, table cells or bullet points. The user is normally able to override the default segmentation rules by setting user-specific rules and also by shrinking or extending the proposed segmentation in interactive mode. In Latin-based scripts, where white space or a punctuation mark generally indicate a word boundary, segmentation is relatively straight-forward. This is not the case in non-segmented languages such as Chinese, Japanese and Thai, which do not use any delimiters between words. A non-segmented source language can therefore affect TM performance, even though TM systems are designed to be largely language independent. On the basis of segmentation, the process of **alignment** explicitly links corre-sponding segments in the source and target texts to make up TUs. Alignment algorithms are usually based on 'anchor points' such as punctu-ation, numbers, formatting, names and dates, in addition to the length of a segment as a measure for correspondence. When a memory is created in interactive mode, alignment is verified by the translator. However, when automatic alignment is used to create memories retrospectively from past translations, known as 'legacy data', misalignments may occur. Misalignments may be caused by instances of asymmetry between the source and target texts, for example when one ST segment is not translated into one TT segment, or when the order of sentences is changed in the TT. These problems may be exacerbated in translations between less closely-related language pairs.

In a relatively short time-span, TM technology has evolved from a first-generation 'sentence-based memory', only able to search exact matches on the level of the full sentence, to a second generation where fuzzy matches can also be retrieved. A third generation of TM technology is now emerging where repetitions below sentence level – sub-sentential matches – are exploited (Gotti *et al.* 2005). Translation researchers have discussed the disadvantages of using the sentence as the key processing unit from the viewpoint of translator produc-tivity (e.g. Schäler 2001) as well as from the perspective of the translator's cognitive process (e.g. Dragsted 2004). More efficient approaches to identifying useful matches for the translator

have been explored (Bowker 2002b; Macklovitch and Russell 2000), but an ideal translation UNIT which optimizes precision and recall of matches, while facilitating but not interfering with the human translator's cognitive process, is still to be identified.

Translation workflow in CAT

TM systems are usually provided in the form of a translator's 'workbench', where different tools such as terminology management systems and concordancers are integrated into the translation environment to facilitate a streamlined workflow. A distributed translation mode is supported in most TM products to allow a translation job to be divided and allocated to a number of trans-lators in separate physical locations connected via an electronic network (O'Hagan 2005). This client–server architecture enables a team of translators to share simultaneously the same TM and a termbase on a network, irrespective of their physical locations. Such a distributed workflow is usually further supported by trans-lation management tools to monitor and keep track of the progress of several concurrent trans-lation projects. The need to be able to exchange linguistic data between different proprietary TM systems has led to the development of standards such as translation memory exchange (TMX), termbase exchange (TBX) and, more recently, segmentation rules exchange (SRX) formats. The localization industry has led this initiative through the OSCAR (Open Standards for Container/Content Allowing Re-use) group, part of the Localization Industry Standards Association (LISA). The main advantage of these standards is the freedom of using different CAT tools for different projects, as required by each client or agency, while still being able to exploit the previously accumulated data in any other system.

CAT tools such as TM have introduced new processes in the translation workflow. For example, a text destined to be translated with TM is likely to undergo a pre-analysis process. The use of the analysis tool, which is usually a component of the TM system, provides information on repetitions within a new ST and matches against an existing TM database. The statistics gained from these processes have various implications, including deductions on translation fees for the segments with existing matches. TM has also introduced a 'pre-translation' process where TM is used in a non-interactive context prior to beginning the actual translation process. The pre-translation function compares the new ST against the contents of the TM database and automatically replaces any ST matches with the corresponding target-language segments, thus producing a hybrid text, partly in the source language and partly in the target language. This function enables clients to avoid giving the translator direct access to their TM database as well as overcoming the issue of data format incompatibility between different TM products. However, the resulting text poses a new challenge to the translator, who not only has to translate the source language fragments but also to verify and transform into an acceptable translation the target language fragments which may only partially correspond to given ST segments. Wallis (2006) suggests that the use of the TM pre-translation function could have a negative impact in terms of translators' job satisfaction as well as translation QUALITY.

Widespread impact of TM

The benefit of re-using previous human translations for the same or similar segments has been largely accepted in the commercial translation world. Accordingly, it has become common practice to obtain discounts in translation fees if there are pre-existing TM matches (Austermühl 2001: 141; Heyn 1998: 136). As a result, TM has occasionally created unrealistic expectations that it instantly provides substantial cost savings without any negative consequences for the quality of the translation. Even when there are exact matches, the translator still needs to consider the text as a whole, and in the light of the new context in which the matched segments are to be inserted. It is possible for TM to create a 'sentence salad' effect (Bédard 2000) when sentences are drawn (without adequate contextual information) from various translation memories created by different translators with different styles. A related problem, described as 'peep-hole translations' (Heyn 1998: 135), concerns the cohesion and readability of the

translation, which can be compromised for the sake of facilitating TM – for example, when translators avoid the use of anaphoric and cataphoric references, opting instead for lexical repetitions that can yield more exact or full matches. A study on consistency and variation in technical translation (Merkel 1998) suggests that while the consistency facilitated by TM is in keeping with the general aim of technical translation, it is not always welcomed by some translators when the same segment appears in different functional contexts. Industry sources have also reported anecdotal evidence of TM's negative impact on the development of translation competence, although this needs to be substantiated by in-depth empirical studies (Kenny 2007). The cost of the software and the steep learning curve are also seen as negative aspects of TM.

Another controversial issue concerns the ownership of the content of a translation memory, which can be a commercially valuable asset. The ethical question of whether or not the particular memory data belong to the commissioner of the job or to the translator escapes the parameters of conventional copyright agreements (Biau Gil and Pym 2006: 10; Topping 2000: 59). The use of the pre-translation function mentioned above is generally motivated by the client's desire to maintain exclusive access to their TM content. At the same time, various initiatives are now emerging to share TM data on a cooperative basis, as proposed by the Translation Automation User Society (TAUS), or a commercial basis, such as TM Marketplace licences (Zetzsche 2007: 38), with far reaching implications for the scope of translation recycling.

Future of CAT

CAT is likely to be enhanced by the use of a wide range of technology components which have not been developed specifically with translation tasks in mind. For example, speech recognition systems are becoming a popular CAT tool among translators, including their integration into TM systems (Benis 1999). In the area of AUDIOVISUAL TRANSLATION, speech recognition technology is being applied to the production of intralingual subtitles for live TV programmes in a mode called 're-speaking', where subtitles are generated in real time by the subtitler dictating, instead of typing, subtitles to the computer (see Eugeni and Mack 2006). In terms of the use of Internet-related technology, Bey *et al.* (2006) have proposed to design and develop an online CAT environment by exploiting Web-based collaborative authoring platforms such as *Wiki* with a view to facilitating translation work by volunteer translators who collaborate online.

The increasing availability of CORPORA is also likely to impact the future of CAT. A feasibility study on the application of Example-based Machine Translation (EBMT) to AUDIOVISUAL TRANSLATION (Armstrong *et al.* 2006), for example, was inspired by the potential re-usability of prior translations of subtitles which are becoming increasingly available in electronic form. In parallel with further automation involving the integration of TM and MACHINE TRANSLATION into the translation workflow (Zetzsche 2007), fine-tuning of TM technology continues to focus on how to assist the human translator. The enhancement of CAT applications is likely to benefit from translator-focused investigations, such as empirical process-oriented translation research (see PSYCHOLINGUISTIC/ COGNITIVE APPROACHES). Dragsted (2004, 2006), for example, has highlighted a discrepancy between technology-imposed segmentation of TM and the cognitive segmentation inherent to the human translation process, and O'Brien (2006) has looked at differences in translators' cognitive loads when dealing with different types of TM matches. Market demands will continue to drive applied research on CAT but, as highlighted in recent studies eliciting users' views on TM systems (García 2006; Lagoudaki 2006), involvement of the professional community of translators in the research and development of CAT tools is crucial in shedding light on the practical implications of the use of technology in this field.

See also:
CORPORA; LOCALIZATION; MACHINE TRANSLATION; TERMINOLOGY.

Further reading
Austermühl 2001; Bowker 2002a; O'Hagan and Ashworth 2002; Somers 2003b; Quah 2006.

MINAKO O'HAGAN

Conference interpreting, historical and cognitive perspectives

Interpreting is the oral or signed translation of oral or signed discourse, as opposed to the oral translation of written texts. The latter is known as **sight translation**.

Interpreting as an official or professional activity seems to have been in existence since very early times, at least as far back as Ancient Egypt (Hermann 1956/2002). Interpreters have played an important role in history, especially during campaigns such as the Spanish incursions into Central and South America (Kurz 1991). Conference interpreters became most visible in the public eye between the two World Wars and during the Nuremberg trials after World War II (Baigorri Jalón 2000, 2004). Other forms of interpreting include business interpreting, COURT INTERPRETING, COMMUNITY INTERPRETING and SIGNED LANGUAGE INTERPRETING. This entry makes particular reference to conference interpreting.

Types and modes of interpreting

According to Herbert (1978), conference interpreting (CI) was born during World War I. Until then, important international meetings were held in French, the international language at the time. During the war, some high-ranking American and British negotiators did not speak French, which made it necessary to resort to interpreters. With the advent of simultaneous interpreting, and especially after the Nuremberg trials (1945–6), conference interpreting became more widespread. It is now used widely, not only at international conferences but also for radio and TV (in Japan, 'Broadcast Interpreting' is a recognized branch of interpreting provided by conference interpreters and interpreters with CI training), various courses and lectures, high-level meetings in multinational corporations, important political and business visits and negotiations, and even in high-level court proceedings. What distinguishes conference interpreting from other forms of interpreting today are its modes (cf. DIALOGUE INTER-PRETING) and its (ideally) high performance level, the latter as described in particular by AIIC, the International Association of Conference Interpreters created in 1953 (see TRAINING AND EDUCATION).

Most conference interpreters have two or three working languages, classified as A languages (native or native-like), B languages (non-native but mastered to a sufficient extent for the interpreter to work into them) and C languages (from which interpreters work into their active languages).

In **consecutive interpreting**, the interpreter listens to a speech segment of a few minutes or so, takes notes, and then delivers the whole segment in the target language; then the speaker resumes for a few minutes, the interpreter delivers the next segment, and the process continues until the end of the speech. Sentence-by-sentence interpreting often found in liaison and community interpreting is not regarded by conference interpreters as 'true consecutive', possibly because it does not involve note-taking and the cognitive pressure associated with it.

In **simultaneous interpreting**, the interpreter sits in an interpreting booth, listens to the speaker through a headset and interprets into a microphone at the same time. Delegates in the conference room listen to the target-language version through a headset. Simultaneous interpreting is also done by signed language interpreters (or interpreters for the deaf), generally from a spoken into a signed language and vice versa (see SIGNED LANGUAGE INTER-PRETING). Signed language interpreters do not sit in a booth; they stand in the conference room where they can see the speaker and be seen.

Whispered interpreting (or **chuchotage**) is a form of simultaneous interpreting in which the interpreter sits not in a booth but in the conference room, next to the delegate who needs the interpreting service, and whispers the target-language version of the speech in the delegate's ear.

Differences between translation and interpreting

While most scholars stress that translation and interpreting essentially fulfil the same function, many – especially interpreters – consider that the two are very different, even incompatible professions. This assertion, as well as alleged personality differences between translators and interpreters, have not been substantiated by research. However, as regards actual translation and interpreting practice, some differences are not controversial. The most obvious of these arise from the fact that translators deal with written language and have time to polish their work (at least minutes, but generally hours and often days), while interpreters deal with oral language, work online with a lag of a few seconds at most in the simultaneous mode and a few minutes at most in the consecutive mode, and have no opportunity to refine their output. These differences have a number of implications:

◆ Translators need to be competent writers while interpreters need to be good speakers, which includes using their voice effectively. Unlike translators, interpreters also need to achieve immediate understanding of the oral form of their passive language(s) for immediate processing of acoustic signals with a wide variety of voices, accents and prosodic features.
◆ Additional knowledge required for a specific translation task, be it linguistic or extra-linguistic, can be acquired *during* the written translation task but has to be acquired *prior* to interpreting to a large extent.
◆ Interpreters have to make decisions instantly, with strategies aimed at doing the best they can with what they have understood on the spot and under cognitive pressure, while translators' STRATEGIES are generally more ambitious because of the possibility of acquiring additional information and the availability of extra time for decision making.
◆ Interpreters' discourse needs to be adequate in both form and content for on-the-spot processing by their listeners; it does not aspire to the same stylistic standards as written translation, given that translators' target texts

need to meet QUALITY requirements that involve repeated scrutiny by readers.

These differences may explain why the central concerns of practitioners, thinkers and researchers in translation and interpreting have largely evolved in different directions. In translation, the concern has largely been to establish the best principles and strategies to overcome dissimilarities between the source language and culture and the target language and culture and produce target texts that are faithful to the original and its intentions at the same time and acceptable and effective in the target setting. Such preoccupations have led to far-reaching analyses and discussions of cultural, literary, philosophical and sociological issues. In conference interpreting, the main challenge has revolved around the more technical question of how to cope with the cognitive pressure involved in having to produce a target speech immediately after listening to the source speech once (in the consecutive mode) or while listening to the source speech (in simultaneous mode).

The Effort Models developed in the early 1980s (Gile 1995a) illustrate the main concerns of conference interpreters. They model simultaneous interpreting as the parallel unfolding of three 'Efforts' (each of which encompasses multiple cognitive operations): listening and analysing the source speech; producing the target speech and monitoring it; performing various short-term memory operations that involve the storage and retrieval of source-speech information over a period of up to several seconds. The Models assume that each of these Efforts requires attentional resources and that these requirements add up to a level close to saturation of the interpreters' total available resources (the 'Tightrope hypothesis' – Gile 1999). The Effort Model for consecutive interpreting defines a 'comprehension phase', during which the interpreter listens to the source speech and takes notes, and a 'reformulation phase', during which the target speech is reconstructed from the notes and from long-term memory. In Gile's model of translation (Gile 1995a), there is also a comprehension phase followed by a reformulation phase, but no short-term memory component is highlighted as playing an important role, and the time scale for problem solving is larger by

several orders of magnitude. This model also includes an important external information-acquisition component which is not found in the interpreting models.

Unlike translation errors, many recurrent interpreting errors are likely to result from cognitive saturation or improper management of the interpreter's processing capacity. Features of simultaneously interpreted speeches such as non-natural prosodic patterns (Shlesinger 1994; Williams 1995; Ahrens 2005) or certain syntactic patterns which result in a large amount of information being stored in working memory increase the risk of saturation.

History of research on conference interpreting

The history of research into conference interpreting may be conveniently divided into four periods: early writings, the experimental period, the practitioners' period and the renewal period (Gile 1994).

The early writings period covers the 1950s and early 1960s. During this period, some interpreters and interpreting teachers in Geneva (see in particular Herbert 1952; Rozan 1956; Ilg 1959) and Brussels (Van Hoof 1962) started thinking and writing about their profession in a didactic and professional mindset rather than an academic mindset. They identified intuitively many of the fundamental issues that are still debated today.

During the experimental period (the 1960s and early 1970s), a few psychologists and psycholinguists such as Treisman, Oléron and Nanpon, Goldman-Eisler, Gerver, and Barik (see Gerver 1976) became interested in interpreting. They conducted a few experimental studies on psychological and psycholinguistic aspects of simultaneous interpreting and examined the effect of variables such as source language, speed of delivery, ear–voice span (i.e. the interval between the moment a piece of information is perceived in the source speech and the moment it is reformulated in the target speech), noise, pauses in speech delivery, etc. on performance. Practitioners rejected both the methods and the results of such studies which, they argued, were not valid because subjects, tasks and the experimental environment had little to do with conference interpreting as it is practised.

During the practitioners' period, which started in the late 1960s and continued into the 1970s and early 1980s, interpreting teachers began to develop an interest in research. The first doctoral dissertation on interpreting by an interpreter (Ingrid Pinter, now Ingrid Kurz) was defended in Vienna in 1969. Numerous papers, as well as more than twenty MA theses and dissertations, were subsequently written by practising interpreters. The main thrust of this research came from ESIT (Ecole Supérieure d'Interprètes et de Traducteurs) in Paris under the charismatic leadership of Danica Seleskovitch, but there was also much activity in West Germany, East Germany, Czechoslovakia, Switzerland and other European countries, as well as in the USSR and in Japan. Most of the research was introspective and prescriptive, and most authors worked as individuals (as opposed to research teams). Relations with the scientific community of linguists, psycholinguists and cognitive psychologists were virtually non-existent except in the USSR, possibly because of the interpreters' defensive attitude rather than due to a lack of interest from non-interpreters (see Gerver and Sinaiko 1978). The prevailing paradigm was ESIT's INTERPRETIVE APPROACH, also known as *Théorie du sens*.

Towards the mid-1980s, a new generation of practitioners began to question the idealized view of interpreting modelled by the *Théorie du sens* and to call for a more 'scientific' study of interpreting and for an interdisciplinary approach to the subject. A conference on the teaching of translation and interpreting held at the University of Trieste (Italy) in November 1986 (Gran and Dodds 1989), which was followed by further initiatives from the same university, including the launching of the journal *The Interpreters' Newsletter* and a series of interdisciplinary studies with neurophysiologist Franco Fabbro, can be seen as a milestone marking a paradigm shift. Research on conference interpreting continues to be undertaken largely by teachers of interpreting, but they increasingly draw on ideas (and sometimes on findings) from other disciplines, in particular cognitive psychology and linguistics. There are more empirical studies (35 per cent of the studies listed in the bibliography of CIRIN – The

Conference Interpreting Research Information Network – for 2000–2006, as opposed to 10 to 20 per cent before 2000). This is however still very low by the standards of established empirical disciplines.

Theoretical and research issues

Reflection and research on conference interpreting have developed in three clusters: around the cognitive dimension of interpreting, around training, and around professional topics.

A large number of studies continue to focus on the central processes of simultaneous interpreting (cf. CONFERENCE INTERPRETING, SOCIO-CULTURAL PERSPECTIVES). The initial studies by psychologists in the 1960s were exploratory. The interpretive theory did not look at specific linguistic or cognitive mechanisms. Starting in the 1990s, these became central. In the Effort Models, linguistic issues are viewed as determining cognitive load to a significant extent. Setton (1999) developed a sophisticated model combining cognitive and pragmatic factors and claims that linguistic/syntactic differences are offset by pragmatic markers which facilitate anticipation and reduce the amount of information that must be kept in short-term memory.

The idea that limitations in attentional resources play an important role in interpreting is not new. It had already been formulated by Kirchhoff in the 1970s (Kirchhoff 1976c/2002) and developed into a probabilistic anticipation model by Chernov (1979/2002, 2004). However, since the 1990s this type of research has led to a growing interest in the interpreters' working memory (see in particular Padilla Benítez 1995; Liu 2001).

In the cognitive research cluster, interdisciplinarity has been a one-way flow, with conference interpreting researchers importing concepts and theories from cognitive psychologists, but very little integration of concepts from CI research taking place in cognitive science. While the work of psychologists on interpreting in the 1960s and 1970s was holistic, psychologists who have shown interest in conference interpreting from the 1990s onwards have focused on the interpreter's working memory. Findings in the beginning of the new century (Liu 2001; Köpke and Nespoulos 2006) seem to indicate that contrary to what was thought initially, interpreters do not develop a larger working memory space with experience, but rather acquire cognitive skills which make them less dependent on such space.

Some work on neurophysiological aspects of interpreting was also initiated in Trieste in the late 1980s (e.g. Gran and Taylor 1990); follow-up studies focused to a large extent on lateralization of brain functions associated with interpreting. Other neurophysiological studies looked at activation patterns in the brain during interpreting and other activities, using various indicators (e.g. Kurz 1996).

In the cluster of research on professional aspects of interpreting (e.g. Miram 2000; Huittinen 2001; Choi 2002; Kurz 2004; Noraini Ibrahim 2005), one important aspect of conference interpreting which has received considerable attention is QUALITY measurement. This is perhaps the area where the largest number of empirical studies have been conducted, focusing mostly on the relative importance of quality components in the context of user expectations and evaluations. Studies of user expectations initiated this type of research, one important pioneer in the field being Ingrid Kurz (e.g. Kurz 1996). These studies are problematic in so far as the users' discourse about quality components may overstate the importance of content and underrate the importance of form. Later studies have extended to user reactions (see for instance Collados Aís et al. 2003, 2007). Findings of these studies suggest that features of single quality components, and in particular form-related components (terminology, intonation, etc.), may strongly influence the users' perception of other quality components.

In the same cluster, some research has been conducted since the late 1990s on TV interpreting (BS Broadcast Interpreters Group 1998; Lee 2000; Kurz 2002a; Mack 2002), stress (Kurz 2002a) and remote interpreting (Braun 2004; Moser-Mercer et al. 2005; Mouzourakis 2005). Some of this research is done with a view to justifying demands relating to working conditions. The findings confirm that conference interpreting involves stress, but how interpreters cope with it in the short and longer term and how and to what extent it is affected by working conditions, including remote interpreting, remains unclear.

In the cluster on interpreter training (see TRAINING AND EDUCATION), there is an abundance of prescriptive literature (e.g. Seleskovitch and Lederer 1989) and of descriptions of courses and methods (Moser-Mercer and Setton 2005) and some discussion of the use of new technology in training (de Manuel Jerez 2003; Sandrelli and de Manuel Jerez 2007). With a few exceptions such as Sawyer (2004) and Soler Caamaño (2006), however, there is little empirical research in the field, in particular on the actual efficiency of the proposed methods of training.

Developments since the late 1990s

Since the late 1990s, there has been a dramatic increase in the number of publications arising from colloquia and other meetings around conference interpreting (Gambier et al. 1997; Englund Dimitrova and Hyltenstam 2000; Garzone and Viezzi 2002; Collados Aís et al. 2003; Chai and Zhang 2006). There is also more global interaction, with increasingly active Asian countries, in particular Japan, Korea and China. In Japan, general interest in conference interpreting is as old as in the West (see Meta 33: 1); what is new is Japanese scholars' growing engagement in academic research. This has led to the setting up of JAIS, the Japanese Association for Interpretation Studies, which publishes the journal Tsuuyaku Kenkyuu/Interpretation Studies, and to the publication of more than 100 texts on conference interpreting between 1990 and 1999. In Korea, CI research is more recent. Only a handful of publications are found in the CIRIN bibliography for 1990 to 1999, but there are more than 60 from 2000 to 2006. The development of CI research in China has been most spectacular, from less than 10 publications between 1990 and 1999 to several hundred items since 2000.

A further development concerns the increasing integration of the emerging discipline of interpreting studies into the larger discipline of translation studies, as shown by the active participation of scholars specializing in interpreting in all events and bodies involved in translation studies, be they conferences, journals, editorial and advisory boards, learned societies where CI scholars often hold offices, or doctoral programmes of translation. This has perhaps been supported by another trend, namely CI authors' growing interest in other types of interpreting, in particular COMMUNITY INTERPRETING, where the central issues are not necessarily cognitive, but rather sociological and ethical; on the coming together of translation studies and interpreting studies, see Schäffner (2004).

One important topic where the interests of researchers into interpreting and translation converge is DIRECTIONALITY: whereas a rather strong Western tradition prescribed interpreting into one's A language and an equally strong Soviet and East-European tradition prescribed interpreting into one's B language, this is being reconsidered, just as the principle of work into one's A language only is being reconsidered in research into translation (Kelly *et al.* 2003; Godijns and Hinderdael 2005). However, the jury is still out on the relative merits of the two options, because they have not been investigated empirically to a sufficient extent to allow any clear conclusions to be drawn.

Finally, it is worth noting that some sectors of conference interpreting may be losing ground as an increasing number of politicians, international and national civil servants, medical and other scientists now use English in international encounters, while other forms of interpreting, which have wider social significance, are constantly developing.

See also:
ASYLUM; COMMUNITY INTERPRETING; CONFERENCE INTERPRETING, SOCIOCULTURAL PERSPECTIVES; COURT INTERPRETING; DIALOGUE INTERPRETING; PSYCHOLINGUISTIC/COGNITIVE APPROACHES; SIGNED LANGUAGE INTERPRETING; TRAINING AND EDUCATION.

Further reading
Herbert 1952; Gerver 1976; Gile 1995a; Pöchhacker and Shlesinger 2002; Baigorri-Jalón 2004; Pöchhacker 2004; Schäffner 2004; Chai and Zhang 2006.

DANIEL GILE

Conference interpreting, sociocultural perspectives

As a result of the boom in international meetings after World War II, and with the impact of GLOBALIZATION, simultaneous conference interpreting (SCI) flourished as a technology-assisted solution to the growing demand for efficient cross-cultural contact. From the 1950s until around the 1990s, SCI remained the most visible type of interpreting and the main focus of attention in interpreting research, with a considerable share of the scholarly attention being devoted to the cognitive processes of the task. While research in the neighbouring field of COMMUNITY INTERPRETING placed significant emphasis on the interpreter as an active agent of communication in a variety of settings, ranging from healthcare settings to ASYLUM hearings (see also DIALOGUE INTERPRETING), research into conference interpreting largely remained focused on describing cognitive processes, using psycholinguistic methods to explore issues such as attention, working memory and multiple-tasking (see CONFERENCE INTERPRETING, HISTORICAL AND COGNITIVE PERSPECTIVES). Within a field dominated by cognitive and psycholinguistic paradigms, markedly less attention came to be devoted to the position of conference interpreters as professionals working and surviving in sociocultural contexts, and to the interdependence between the presence and performance of conference interpreters and the social contexts in which they operated.

This, however, is not to say that the importance of viewing simultaneous conference interpreting as a form of situated action was never acknowledged by scholars in the field. As early as 1976, Anderson argued that interpreting took place 'in social situations – situations amenable to sociological analysis', contending that 'in any such setting the role played by the interpreter is likely to exert considerable influence on the evolution of the group structure and on the outcome of the interaction' (1976: 209). In a paper exploring 'interpreter roles' published two years later, Anderson went on to highlight discrepancies between what interpreters claimed interpreting entailed and what they did in actual situations (Anderson 1978). At about the same time, Kirchhoff (1976a, 1976b) also stressed the importance of considering interpreting as a communicative system that is influenced by a number of linguistic and extra-linguistic variables, drawing attention to the role of context in shaping the meaning of utterances. By the early 1980s, scholars such as Stenzl were beginning to call for more observational and descriptive research in simultaneous conference interpreting, stressing the importance of SCI as an interlingual communicative task that involves the speaker, the interpreter and the target-culture receiver in a specific context of situation (1983: 48).

Calls to adapt and apply theories and concepts developed mainly in translation studies marked a turning point in SCI research by introducing new notions such as 'NORMS' and by highlighting the significance of product-oriented investigations. Shlesinger's (1989b) pioneering call to extend the notion of norms to interpreting in general was followed by a number of pleas for adopting a more sociologically-oriented approach in interpreting studies, one that involved close examination of actual behaviour during interpreting so as to gain a better understanding of the norms that govern it (Schjoldager 1995a, 1995b; Gile 1998; Diriker 1999; Garzone 2002; Inghilleri 2003, 2005b; Marzocchi 2005; Duflou, in progress).

In a similar vein, aiming to test the viability of applying the FUNCTIONALIST theory developed by Vermeer (1983b, 1989a) and Holz-Mänttäri (1984) to conference interpreting, Pöchhacker (1994) investigated a 'real-life' SCI event, evaluating the interpreters' output as 'text-in-situation-and-culture'. This was the first study in which simultaneous conference interpreting was approached as complex situated action. Pöchhacker investigated various aspects of SCI at a three-day conference of the International Council for Small Business, transcribing the recordings of original speeches and their interpretations to explore – among other aspects – how interpreters dealt with forms of address and humour (see also Pöchhacker 1995).

Pöchhacker's pioneering study on real-life interpreting behaviour was followed by several

studies conducted by various researchers such as Kalina and Setton, who worked on authentic instances of interpreting and acknowledged the importance of social contexts, though with different aims and from different theoretical perspectives. Kalina (Kohn and Kalina 1996; Kalina 1998), for instance, adopted a discourse-based mental modelling approach and worked on the recordings of a conference on fraud to explore interpreting strategies. She complemented her analysis of simultaneous conference interpreting STRATEGIES with interpreters' introspective comments on their own behaviour, thus complementing studies of listeners' views with those of interpreters in a conference situation. Monacelli (2000, 2005) and Kent (2007) similarly examined the views of interpreters; Pöchhacker (2005) offers a review of user surveys in general. Setton (1999), on the other hand, has drawn mainly on Relevance Theory and used both authentic and simulated data to develop a cognitive-pragmatic approach to exploring the way in which meaning is cognitively processed in conference interpreting contexts.

The strongest call for approaching SCI from a sociocultural perspective came with Michael Cronin's (2002) appeal for a 'cultural turn' in interpreting studies. Pointing out that the field had remained largely unaffected by theoretical developments elsewhere in translation studies, Cronin forcefully underlined the need for fresh perspectives to examine all forms of interpreting 'as they are grounded in the economic, cultural and political aspects of people's lives' (ibid.: 391).

Perhaps a preliminary sign of such a 'cultural turn' is the emergence in the first decade of the twenty-first century of a strand of sociologically-oriented research on conference interpreting that involves investigating the interdependence between the presence and performance of conference interpreters and the larger and more immediate social contexts in which they operate (see also SOCIOLOGICAL APPROACHES). Diriker (2004), Vuorikoski (2004), Monacelli (2005) and Beaton (2007a, 2007b) all explore various aspects of this interdependence, thus addressing one of the most persistent lacunae in SCI research, namely the lack of holistic conceptions of text, situation, CULTURE and the entire course of action in interpreting settings (Pöchhacker 1995: 33). Diriker (2004), for instance, combines participant observation, interviews with conference participants and analysis of recordings at a two-day conference on politics and metaphysics to demonstrate that the behaviour of simultaneous interpreters in actual conference settings is more complex than is generally assumed. She argues that this complexity is most palpable in the relationship between the speaker and the interpreter who share the same 'subject position' (i.e. the first person singular *I*) in the interpreter's delivery. Vuorikoski (2004) analyses a corpus of speeches recorded in the plenary sessions of the European Parliament, looking at how rhetorical devices in original speeches are rendered in interpretation. In addition to source speech-related factors such as speech density and rate of presentation, Vuorikoski stresses the importance of affinity with the sociocultural context of the European Union, highlighting 'exposure to the EU genre' as a determining factor in shaping the outcome of the delivery (ibid.: 183). Monacelli (2005), on the other hand, combines analysis of interpreting data gathered at the Italian Parliament with introspective comments by interpreters to explore self-regulatory (survival) moves of interpreters. Viewing simultaneous conference interpreting as inherently constraining and face-threatening for interpreters, she cites distancing, de-personalization and mitigation of illocutionary force as some of the strategies widely used by interpreters in her corpus to ensure professional survival. Beaton (2007a, 2007b) looks at simultaneously interpreted political debates during the plenary sessions of the European Parliament to investigate how certain ideologies are interpreted and whether interpreter-mediated communication in this context is influenced by the interpreter's agency and subjectivity. Based on the analysis of three cohesive devices (metaphor strings, lexical repetition and intertextuality), she suggests that simultaneous interpretation in the European Parliament tends to strengthen EU institutional ideology, and that 'the very fact that institutional communication is interpreted is, in itself, ideologically significant' (2007b: 293); see also IDEOLOGY.

Growing interest in exploring authentic performances of simultaneous conference interpreting from a sociocultural perspective is also evident in other publications which appeared during the same period, including Garzone and Viezzi (2002), where a number of papers review theoretical and methodological aspects of approaching SCI as situated action. Two further volumes edited by Schäffner (2004) and Pym *et al.* (2006), as well as a special issue of *The Translator* edited by Inghilleri (2004), all devote considerable attention to the social dimension of interpreting research.

Despite growing attention to sociocultural aspects of simultaneous conference interpreting since the early- to mid-1990s, several relevant areas remain largely unexplored. The most pressing of these include the impact of gender, agency, IDEOLOGY and power on the behaviour of simultaneous interpreters and the dynamics of interpreter-mediated interaction in the conference setting. At the same time, the political and social effects of GLOBALIZATION are beginning to be felt in the discipline and among practitioners, leading to the emergence of new avenues of research that were not foreseen by scholars writing in the 1990s. Relevant, often overlapping areas of research that have begun to attract attention include the positionings available to and taken up by members of the conference interpreting community in relation to a number of controversial issues, in particular neutrality, activism, political engagement, and volunteering for civil society. Babels, the international network of volunteer conference interpreters which aligns itself with the Social Forum, has received particular attention, from both practitioners and researchers (see Boéri and Hodkinson 2004; de Manuel Jeréz *et al.* 2004; Hodkinson and Boéri 2005; Naumann 2005; Baker 2006a, 2006b; Pöchhacker 2006; Boéri 2008). Growing interest in exploring the ETHICS of conference interpreting marks a new point of departure in the discipline, and a willingness to discuss the interdependence between conference interpreting, ideology and social contexts.

See also:
ASYLUM; COMMUNITY INTERPRETING; CONFERENCE INTERPRETING, HISTORICAL AND COGNITIVE PERSPECTIVES; COURT INTERPRETING; DIALOGUE INTERPRETING; IDEOLOGY; SOCIOLOGICAL APPROACHES.

Further reading
Anderson 1976, 1978; Shlesinger 1989b; Pöchhaker 1994, 1995; Cronin 2002; Diriker 2004; Monacelli 2005; Beaton 2007a; Boéri 2008.

EBRU DIRIKER

Corpora

A **corpus** (plural: corpora) is a collection of texts that are the object of literary or linguistic study. In contemporary corpus linguistics, such collections are held in electronic form, allowing the inclusion of vast quantities of texts (commonly hundreds of millions of words), and fast and flexible access to them using corpus-processing software. While most definitions stress the need for corpora to be assembled according to explicit design criteria and for specific purposes (Atkins *et al.* 1992), Kilgarriff and Grefenstette (2003) allow for more serendipitous collections of texts, even the entire World Wide web, to be considered as corpora, as long as their contents are the focus of linguistic (or related) study. No matter how the corpora they work with come into being, however, all corpus linguists insist on the primacy of authentic data, as attested in texts, that is, instances of spoken, written or signed behaviour that have occurred 'naturally, without the intervention of the linguist' (Stubbs 1996: 4). Corpus linguists thus take an approach to the study of language that is consistent with the empiricism advocated in descriptive translation studies since the 1970s. At that time, scholars became particularly critical of the use of introspection in translation theory (Holmes 1988: 101) and of approaches that viewed translations as idealized, speculative entities, rather than observable facts (Toury 1980a: 79–81). While Toury conceded that isolated attempts had been made to describe and explain actual translations, he called for a whole new methodological apparatus that would make individual studies transparent and repeatable. It was Baker (1993) who saw the potential for corpus linguistics to provide such an apparatus, and her early work in the area (Baker 1993, 1995, 1996a) launched what became known as 'corpus-based translation studies', or CTS. Researchers in CTS now

pursue a range of agendas, drawing on a variety of corpus types and processing techniques, and these are addressed below, following some more general remarks on corpus design and processing.

Corpus creation and basic processing

Best practice in corpus creation requires designers to make informed decisions on the types of language they wish to include in their corpora, and in which proportions. Design criteria crucially depend on the envisaged use of the corpus but have, in the past, centred on the idea that corpora should somehow be 'representative' of a particular type of language production and/or reception. The statistical notion of representativeness is, however, extremely difficult to apply to textual data, and many commentators now prefer to aim for a 'balanced' sample of the language in which they are interested (Kenny 2001: 106–7; Kilgarriff and Grefenstette 2003). A general-purpose monolingual corpus might thus have to include both (transcribed) spoken and written language, and, within each, samples of a variety of text types, dating from specific time periods. There may also be a trade-off between including fewer but more useful, full-length texts on the one hand, and more, but textually 'compromised' partial texts on the other (Atkins *et al.* 1992; Baker 1995: 229–30; Sinclair 1991). Once a suitable breakdown of text types, author profiles, etc. has been decided upon, the actual texts chosen for inclusion in a corpus can be selected randomly, or through more deliberate 'handpicking'. The texts thus selected may then have to be converted to electronic form (through key-boarding or scanning), if they are not already available in this form, and permission to include them in the corpus may have to be sought from copyright holders. Depending on the intended use of the corpus, various levels of structural or linguistic annotation are desirable. Basic mark-up may involve indicating (using a standard mark-up language like XML) the main divisions in a text (headings, paragraphs, sentences, etc.) or the addition of 'headers' that describe the content of texts, name their authors, and so on. More linguistically oriented annotation includes part-of-speech tagging, where each word in a running text is assigned to a word category (e.g. 'noun' or 'verb'), as well as syntactic parsing and semantic annotation. A number of sources (Kenny 2001; Meyer 2002; Olohan 2004) provide guidance on the creation and annotation of corpora. Kilgarriff *et al.* (2006) is particularly useful for those interested in including web data in their corpora.

The level of mark-up that a corpus is subjected to will have implications for the kind of electronic processing the corpus can undergo. Raw corpora – that is, untagged, unparsed corpora – can be treated as sequences of characters delimited by spaces (in languages like English); in other words, as sequences of running or orthographic words. The number of different orthographic words (types) in a corpus can be easily computed and compared with the total number of running words (tokens), to yield the type–token ratio, a primitive measure of the lexical variety in a text (see Kenny 2001 and Daller *et al.* 2003 on the limitations of type–token ratios). Values for average sentence and paragraph lengths can also be fairly easily computed in a raw corpus (using sentence-ending punctuation marks and paragraph symbols). Another measure, lexical density, gives the percentage of running words in a corpus made up by lexical (vocabulary), as opposed to grammatical words. Put simply, a low lexical density indicates high levels of redundancy and thus predictability in a text (Stubbs 1996: 73), perhaps making it easier to process than a lexically more dense text. As long as the analyst can supply a finite list of grammatical words to be excluded in this calculation, lexical densities are also fairly easily computed. All these measures have the signal merit of being applicable to every verbal text, but their interpretation is not straightforward, and they should be used with care. Other types of processing allow more qualitative analysis of corpus data. The generation of word lists and clusters, for example, allows the analyst to focus on particular words or recurring groups of words. A further type of processing outputs a KWIC (keyword in context) concordance for an input word, revealing the contexts in which it occurs. Recurring patterns may be discerned across contexts, pointing to the existence of statistically significant collocates of the input word. In order to discover regularities in the behaviour of a word form occurring in a certain

part of speech (see Olohan 2004: 70–71), however, a tagged corpus is usually required. Concordancing and basic statistical processing of raw corpora are discussed in Sinclair (1991). More translation-oriented discussions are available in Kenny (2001) and Olohan (2004).

Translation-oriented corpus typology

Several scholars have proposed corpus typologies that are of particular relevance to translation studies (see, especially, Laviosa 1997, 2002). At a high level of abstraction, corpora can be divided into those that contain texts in a single language – **monolingual corpora** – and those that contain texts in two or more languages – **bilingual** or **multilingual corpora**, although, for the sake of economy, bilingual corpora are sometimes subsumed under 'multilingual' corpora (Altenberg and Granger 2002: 7). Another broad characterization depends on whether the texts were originally written in the language in question, or whether they were translated into that language. By far the best-known corpora outside of translation studies are large monolingual reference corpora like the British National Corpus (Burnard 2007), which contains 100 million words originally uttered or written in British English. Laviosa (2002: 37) calls such corpora **non-translational**. The Translational English Corpus (Olohan 2004: 59–60), on the other hand, is perhaps the best-known monolingual **translational corpus**. It continues to be developed under the stewardship of Mona Baker at the University of Manchester, and currently contains roughly ten million words of text translated into English from a variety of source languages.

Corpora may also be characterized by the relationship that holds between their subcorpora, where these exist. Thus, a monolingual corpus may consist of two subcorpora; one translational, the other non-translational. If the two sets of texts cover the same genre(s) in roughly the same proportions, were published in the same time period, cover the same domains, etc., then we can speak of a **monolingual comparable corpus**. Monolingual comparable corpora allow systematic investigations of how translated text differs from non-translated text in the same language, and thus are a vital resource in research that seeks to isolate characteristic features of translation (see below). Well-known monolingual comparable corpora include Laviosa's English Comparable Corpus (1998a, 1998b) and the Corpus of Translated Finnish (Mauranen 2004). Likewise, the subcorpora in a bilingual corpus may be related through shared values for attributes such as genre, date and place of publication, domain, etc., and thus combine to form a **bilingual comparable corpus**. The New Corpus for Ireland (Kilgarriff *et al.* 2006), designed in the first instance as a resource for English–Irish (Gaelic) lexicography, is one such corpus. Bilingual (or multilingual) comparable corpora are sometimes used as a data source in contrastive linguistics, and are valued precisely because they are free from 'various translation effects' (Altenberg and Granger 2002: 8). They are not without problems, however: as with monolingual comparable corpora, it can be difficult to ensure comparability between the subcorpora (see Bernardini and Zanettin 2004), and searching for 'cross-linguistic equivalents' (Altenberg and Granger 2002: 9) is not straightforward. Baker (1995: 233) has also expressed reservations about their usefulness in theoretical translation studies, claiming that their use is based upon the erroneous assumption that 'there is a natural way of saying anything in any language, and that all we need to do is to find out how to say something naturally in language A and language B'.

The subcorpora in a bilingual (or multilingual) corpus may, on the other hand, be related through *translation*, that is, the corpus may contain texts in one language, alongside their translations into another language (or other languages). Such corpora are commonly known as **parallel** corpora, although the term **translation corpus** is also used (Altenberg and Granger 2002). Parallel corpora are usually **aligned** (Véronis 2000). That is, explicit links are provided between units of the source and target texts, usually at the sentence level. This enables bilingual concordancing, where a search for a word in one language returns all sentences containing that word, along with their aligned equivalent sentences in the other language. Parallel corpora exist for several language pairs/ groups of languages. Some are a by-product of bilingual or multilingual parliaments: the

English–French Hansards in Canada (Church and Gale 1991) and the multilingual Europarl corpus (Koehn 2005), which contains the proceedings of the European Parliament, are two well-known examples. Other, more handcrafted, parallel corpora are created specifically for use in translation studies and contrastive linguistics, and a number of variations on the basic design are possible: a bilingual parallel corpus can be uni-directional or bi-directional, for instance. Given that bi-directional corpora such as the English–Norwegian Parallel Corpus (Johansson 1998) contain source texts (or 'originals') in both languages, they can also be used as bilingual comparable corpora, provided, of course, that conditions of comparability obtain. Other parallel corpora may contain, on their target sides, two or more translations into the same language of the same source text (Winters 2005), or progressive drafts of the emerging target text (Utka 2004). Parallel corpora have been used in translation TRAINING AND EDUCATION to support students in finding solutions to problems that characteristically arise in translation but not other sorts of writing (Pearson 2003), and in research into translation SHIFTS (Munday 1998a, 2002). They have also been used for the extraction of de facto translation equivalents in bilingual terminography and lexicography (Bowker and Pearson 2002: 171–2; Teubert 2002, 2004), and to provide empirical data for corpus-based MACHINE TRANSLATION systems (Hutchins 2005a).

Corpus-based translation studies

Much early work in CTS set out to pursue the research agenda put forward in Baker's seminal 1993 article and investigated, on a scale that had not been possible before, those recurrent features that were thought to make translation different from other types of language production. These features, also called UNIVERSALS of translation, included the reported tendency of translated texts to be more explicit, use more conventional grammar and lexis, and be somehow simpler than either their source texts or other texts in the target language. Much of this work was concerned with operationalizing abstract notions like simplification and EXPLICITATION (see, especially, Baker 1996a), and with investigating the potential of the quantitative techniques that corpus linguistics offered. The shift in focus from global statistics (lexical densities, sentence lengths, etc.) to the distributions of particular words and phrases marks a transition to more qualitative research. As CTS developed, researchers also began to integrate insights from related fields to enrich their analyses. Thus Olohan and Baker (2000), for example, draw on cognitive linguistics in their investigation of explicitation in original and translated English. Laviosa (2002) and Olohan (2004) sum up much of the corpus-based research into features of translation conducted to date, and Olohan's own case studies (ibid.) are a particularly rich source of quantitative and qualitative analysis.

The search for generalizations that characterized this early research inevitably led to the recognition of particularities, and before long researchers in CTS began focusing on the distinctive behaviour of individual translators. Particular translators' styles are addressed in a variety of studies, including Baker (2000), Bosseaux (2007), Kenny (2001), Saldanha (2004, 2005) and Winters (2005). All but the first of these are conducted using parallel corpora, and these sources again draw increasingly on areas such as narratology, semantics, pragmatics, and even typography, to enable theory and data-rich studies of the translator's otherwise elusive presence in translation. Like the studies into general features of translation mentioned above, these studies are made possible by the computer's ability to retrieve and display in useful ways sometimes many thousands of examples of textual features (from personal pronouns to modal particles, instances of italics, and hapax legomena) that would otherwise be difficult to study. Corpus-processing software cannot do the analysis, however, and researchers in CTS are often faced with the particularly onerous task of accounting, as exhaustively as possible, for vast numbers of instances of selected phenomena, including those instances that buck the general trend. Most of these studies are predominantly descriptive, but efforts are made to establish connections between translators' agendas, or the conditions under which they work, and the translation product. Citing Munday (2002) as a promising model, Olohan (2004: 192) argues for increased contextualization of corpus-based studies, more integration of analytical tools from other areas, and a greater focus on trans-

lators, in a bid to strengthen CTS's ability to feed into research that can better account for causes and effects in translation (Chesterman 2000).

Not all CTS is, strictly speaking, descriptive however: Kenny (2006) is concerned with the contribution, if any, that CTS can make to translation theory; and corpora have become indispensable in applied studies. The use of corpora in translation pedagogy is a particularly dynamic area of research (Zanettin *et al.* 2003), and scholars such as Bowker and Pearson (2002: 193–210) and Sánchez-Gijón (2004) have shown how corpora can be of particular value as an aid in specialized translation.

As the variety of corpora continues to grow – we now have substantial SIGN LANGUAGE corpora (Leeson *et al.* 2006), subtitle corpora (Armstrong *et al.* 2006), multimedia corpora of original and dubbed films (Valentini 2006), and dialect and other 'unconventional' corpora (Beal *et al.* 2007a, 2007b) – as do the number of languages and language pairs covered, and given increased ease of access to corpora, in particular as derived from the world wide web (Kilgarriff and Grefenstette 2003), we can expect CTS to develop in as yet unpredictable ways. The current trajectory, however, suggests that the area will remain a dynamic force in translation studies, and that initial fears that the area would become bogged down in unnecessary quantification (Tymoczko 1998: 652) have proved unfounded. Rather we are seeing the emergence of the multi-vocal, decentred, inclusive paradigm that Tymoczko (ibid.) predicted CTS could become.

See also:

EXPLICITATION; LINGUISTIC APPROACHES; NORMS; TERMINOLOGY; UNIVERSALS.

Further reading

Sinclair 1991; Baker 1993, 1996a; Stubbs 1996; Laviosa 1998c; Kenny 2001; Bowker and Pearson 2002; Laviosa 2002; Zanettin *et al.* 2003; Kruger 2004; Olohan 2004.

DOROTHY KENNY

Court interpreting

The term 'court interpreting' is widely used to refer to any kind of legal interpreting, but the courtroom is in fact only one of several contexts in which legal interpreting may take place. Non-courtroom contexts include interpreting in police departments (Krouglov 1999), customs offices, immigration authorities (Barsky 1996; Inghilleri 2003, 2005a; see also ASYLUM); and barristers' chambers. Courtroom interpreting, however, has come to occupy a more prominent position and has received more scholarly attention than other types of legal interpreting.

The history of official court interpreting, as we know it today, is fairly short. Although it started with the famous war trials which took place in Nuremberg between November 1945 and October 1946 and in Tokyo between June 1946 and November 1948, the experience of these trials gave rise not to court interpreting as such but to simultaneous interpreting (de Jongh 1992), which is only one of the techniques that may be used in court under certain circumstances. Irrespective of the range of techniques it uses, what most distinguishes court interpreting from other types of interpreting is its close attention to ethical issues which arise from the function of the courtroom. In terms of interpreting strategies, this tends to be reflected in an insistence on fidelity, impartiality and confidentiality. In theory, the evidence given by a witness has to be preserved in its entirety, not only through a close rendering of the sentences and words but also the 'ers' and 'ums' uttered by the speaker. The argument here is that what is at issue is a human being's life and liberty, and that the court judges the credibility and veracity of an individual by his or her demeanour to a large extent. Nevertheless, Gonzalez *et al.* (1991) and O'Tool (1994a) have observed that prosodic elements and paralinguistic features are frequently left uninterpreted, and that a witness's testimony suffers accordingly. Shlesinger (1991) similarly reports a general tendency on the part of court interpreters to 'grammticize' ungrammatical utterances and observes that 'the overriding tendency of the interpreter to delete a false start may in fact lead to the omission of a self-correction which,

it would seem, was expressly intentional' (ibid.: 150). Hale (1997) documents consistent patterns of register variation in the courtroom, with interpreters between Spanish and English in Australian courts raising the level of formality when interpreting into English and lowering it when interpreting it into Spanish.

Modern court interpreting has made limited progress in its brief history. This is primarily due to the complex nature of legal interpreting and the judiciary's ambivalent attitude to interpreters in the courtroom. On the one hand, the law is reluctant to accept interpreters as professionals who are capable of rendering linguistic messages efficiently (O'Tool 1994b), and therefore as officers of the law (Morris 1995; Colin and Morris 1996). On the other hand, it insists on treating the product of interpreting as a legally valid equivalent of the original utterance. Morris (ibid.: 29) reports that in the English-speaking world, '[t]ape recordings of non-English utterances produced in the courtroom hardly ever exist; written transcripts are almost never provided'. Challenges to the interpreter's performance and credentials, including challenges by defence lawyers, are not uncommon. For example, in *Holliday v. State* in Fulton County, Georgia (reported in Eustis 2003), lawyers for Holliday argued that the interpreter left utterances uninterpreted which could have led to a different result. The court hearing the appeal conceded that errors in translation are inevitable but rejected the appeal on the basis of available evidence. The lawyers commented that they might consider hiring independent interpreters to monitor the performance of court-appointed interpreters. The basis of the argument was that if lawyers wish to object to errors in interpretation, they have to do it when the errors are made rather than after the event.

The provision of court interpreting as a legal right

For justice to be done, the legal system administering it has to be seen to be fair. One of the essential tenets of a fair trial is the legal presence of the accused during the trial. The concept of 'legal presence' includes 'linguistic presence' (Gonzalez 1994; Colin and Morris

1996). This means that the accused must be able to hear and understand what other witnesses are saying and has to be able to follow the legal proceedings. Consequently, a person in a foreign country (be it a tourist or a worker), an immigrant who does not have adequate command of the official language of the court, the aboriginal populations in countries such as Australia and the United States, members of MINORITY groups in multi-racial societies such as Malaysia and Singapore, not to mention the speech or hearing-impaired population (see SIGNED LANGUAGE INTERPRETING), should all be legally entitled to an interpreter.

The right to an interpreter in a court setting is a legal issue which has received much attention but remains supported by little legislation in most countries (Hertog 2002; Tsuda 2002). At an international level, the right to an interpreter is provided for in the International Covenant on Civil and Political Rights, in the European Convention on Human Rights, and in the American Convention on Human Rights; it was also expressed in procedure at the Nuremberg and Tokyo Trials. At the national level, very few legal systems have formalized this right. In Australia, for instance, only the state of South Australia has protected it by a statute. In other states with a large population of immigrants, for example Victoria and New South Wales, the provision of an interpreter is made or withheld at the discretion of the trial judge. Common practice in both states indicates that interpreters are provided as a matter of course, but this does remain a question of common practice rather than legal right (*Access to Interpreters* 1991).

A witness who is only partly fluent in the language of the trial may be denied an interpreter on the premise that limited knowledge should not be the passport to an unfair advantage before the court. However, a witness might sound fluent in a language and be disastrously ignorant of the linguistic subtleties and cultural traits of that language. A report by the New South Wales Commission in Australia thus acknowledges that '[t]he notion of advantage deriving from the use of an interpreter arises out of a fundamental misunderstanding of the nature of interpreting', and that 'there is no evidence that ... any advantage is actually secured' (*Multiculturalism and the Law* 1991).

The judiciary has long failed to recognize the complexity of legal interpreting and has consequently expected the court interpreter to act as a conduit, transmitting messages between the accused, witnesses and members of the court without any intervention, and irrespective of linguistic and cultural differences among participants (Softic 1993; Tsuda 2002). This situation has been further exacerbated by a lack of adequate training in the techniques of court interpreting (see TRAINING AND EDUCATION) and a general lack of definition of the court interpreter's role, leading to deficient interpreting in many cases (Edwards 1995; Hale 2004). As Roberts-Smith (1989: 71) has observed,

> Untrained interpreters, far from facilitating communication, can cause many problems. Their language skills may be deficient, they may not have the necessary appreciation of relevant cross-cultural differences, they may not have interpreting skills (as opposed to conversational abilities); their choice of words may be imprecise and consequently misleading and they may have a tendency to flavour the interpretation with their own views and perception of the facts.

Incompetent interpreting has therefore contributed to the fact that interpreted evidence is rarely perceived as truthful or reliable (Carroll 1994). Consequently, rather than benefiting from the availability of an interpreter, and in addition to the difficulty of understanding the procedures of the court, a linguistically-handicapped individual may be faced with the added dilemma of whether to use an interpreter and risk being labelled as evasive, unresponsive and untrustworthy.

The mechanics and logistics of court interpreting

Broadly speaking, court interpreting is concerned with enabling the client (whether the accused, witness, or other participant) to understand what is going on in the courtroom. Different forms of interpreting, and translation, may be used to achieve this end. An interpreter might be asked to carry out consecutive interpreting when a witness is in the dock, simultaneous interpreting when the witness or accused is listening to another testimony or following other events in the courtroom (from depositions to sentencing), liaison interpreting outside the courtroom with council, and even chuchotage (i.e. whispered interpreting) in some cases (see CONFERENCE INTERPRETING, HISTORICAL AND COGNITIVE PERSPECTIVES for an explanation of various modes of interpreting). For instance, Shlesinger (1989b) reports that chuchotage was used in *The State of Israel* v. *Ivan John Demjanjuk* (1987–8) to render the entire proceedings into Ukrainian for the defendant.

Court work also includes sight translation of documents produced in court. Moreover, it is not uncommon for the bench to ask the interpreter, over a short recess, to produce a written translation of an exhibit, a transcript of a telephone conversation or subtitles for a video recording. The various methods of interpreting used in the courtroom all have their shortcomings. For instance, O'Tool (1994b) observes that consecutive interpreting leads to lack of spontaneity and naturalness of communication, and Morris (1995) reports the unease created in the courtroom by acoustic interference from whispered interpreting. In the UK Lockerbie trial (2000–2001), the two Libyan defendants complained to the bench that they were unable to follow the four simultaneous interpreters appointed by the United Nations. The simultaneous mode inevitably means that the interpreter has to anticipate information and deliver the interpreted utterances at a fast pace. The interpreters were equipped with a 'slow-down' button in this case, but the bench was concerned about and drew the prosecutor's attention to the fact that the interpreters were lagging behind. One strategy used by simultaneous interpreters to avoid lagging behind is anticipation, but this is problematic in the context of the court: unlike conference interpreting, courtroom interpreting requires attention to detail, chronology and facts that may seem redundant to the interpreter. The shortcomings associated with different modes of interpreting suggest that while allowing communication to take place in the courtroom, interpreting often slows down the court procedures, especially in cases where inexperienced interpreters are used (Roberts-Smith 1989).

To enable communication to proceed smoothly in the courtroom, all interlocutors are generally instructed to speak in the first person, which entails ignoring the physical presence of the interpreter. The place where the interpreter is seated therefore plays a significant role in aiding or hindering the communication process. Seating the interpreter too far away creates acoustic difficulties for the court and the interpreter alike. Conversely, seating him or her too close to one party can give the impression that the interpreter is not impartial.

Impartiality, which is the *raison d'être* of court interpreting, places a special constraint on the court interpreter, who has to distance him- or herself from witnesses and their immediate families, even when they themselves are in need of the interpreter's services. The task is made more difficult by the fact that judicial concern for guaranteeing the impartiality of the interpreter has given rise to the principle of excluding the interpreter from pre-trial conferences and the viewing of relevant documents prior to the commencement of a trial (Gonzalez *et al.* 1991: 177, 291). The judicial view that prior knowledge of the case could affect the interpreter's impartiality is, to some extent, understandable. However, it seems unrealistic to expect an interpreter to walk into a courtroom without any knowledge of the topic, terminology or chronology of the case and still be able to perform efficiently, especially given the fact that backtracking and requests for clarification on the part of the interpreter are generally discouraged and seen as interrupting court procedures. It is also unrealistic to expect an interpreter to remain totally unaffected by the narratives recounted in court. The Acholi interpreter Julian Ocitti reportedly broke down during the trial of Ugandan opposition leader Dr Kizza Besigye in April 2006 as one state witness narrated how he killed ten people. WBS Television reported that '[c]ourt was then adjourned for a ten minute break to allow her [the interpreter] to compose herself, before another interpreter was brought in' (Ntimbal 2006). Similar traumatic experiences of court interpreting have been reported in connection with the Truth and Reconciliation trials held after the fall of apartheid in South Africa (Baker 2006a: 32) and cases of child abuse (Brennan and Brown 1997: 62).

Like other professionals such as lawyers, court interpreters are bound by professional ETHICS, and there should arguably therefore be no need to exclude them from certain procedures in order to ensure their impartiality. Like conference interpreters, they too need to be briefed about the material they have to deal with, the topics likely to be raised and the documents to be sight-translated. Prior access to information in court interpreting is among the most hotly debated issues between the court interpreting profession and the judiciary.

In addition to these difficulties, court interpreters also have to contend with extra-linguistic pressures such as speed, interrupted delivery, stress and mental fatigue, and the extreme variety of topics raised and issues discussed. These, and the wide range of interpreting modes that have to be mastered and used skilfully (consecutive, simultaneous, chuchotage and sight translation), all contribute to the complexity of court interpreting and highlight the importance of specialized and regular training for court interpreters.

The training of court interpreters

A number of countries such as the United States and Australia have made some effort to ensure the availability of formal training, examinations, and certification systems for court interpreters. In the United States, the Court Interpreter Act of 1978 and its amendment in 1988 sought to regulate the profession (Angelelli 2004). COMMUNITY INTERPRETING in Australia tends to involve a great deal of legal interpreting, and this has led to professional ethics becoming an integral part of the induction process for newly accredited interpreters. Australia has also pioneered the provision of leaflets on 'How to Work with Interpreters'; these aim to educate the public to make the best use of interpreters.

There are virtually no academic institutions that provide training in court interpreting specifically. However, some colleges, particularly in the United States and Canada, offer short courses specifically designed for court interpreters. With the emergence of translation studies as a fully-fledged academic discipline, more attention is now being paid to the need to provide full academic training in court interpreting (Laster

and Taylor 1994). In an attempt to bridge the gap between 'generalist' academic training in interpreting and the specific standards and skills required in the professional world, serious steps have also been taken in Australia, the United States and elsewhere to provide certification of court interpreters. Berk-Seligson (1990/2002) points out that no matter how ethically aware court interpreters might be, quality interpreting can only be guaranteed through formal training. In Australia, the Community Relations Commission in the state of New South Wales, the largest provider of translating and interpreting services in the country, introduced a mandatory one-week induction programme for practising court interpreters in 2000, in a bid to ensure better quality.

The situation is also changing in South Africa where a Diploma in Legal Translation and Interpreting was introduced at UNISA (University of South Africa) in 1998 (Moeketsi and Wallmach 2005). In Japan, the eight High Courts which maintain a list of more than 3000 'qualified' interpreters have been offering a general two-day induction course since 1997 (Arai 1997). Tsuda (2002) describes a Master's programme in Translation at the Osaka University of Foreign Studies which has a strong component of court interpreting.

Finally, it is worth noting that AIIC (the International Association of Conference Interpreters) does not recognize even regular court interpreting experience as equivalent to its '200 conference days' mandatory requirement for membership. There is no international association that represents court interpreters, but the United States does have an online network of judicial interpreters (NAJIT). The International Association of Forensic Linguists (IAFL) dedicates a great deal of its work to courtroom discourse and the practice of court interpreting.

See also:
ASYLUM; COMMUNITY INTERPRETING, CONFERENCE INTERPRETING, HISTORICAL AND COGNITIVE PERSPECTIVES; CONFERENCE INTERPRETING, SOCIOCULTURAL PERSPECTIVES; DIALOGUE INTERPRETING; SIGNED LANGUAGE INTERPRETING; TRAINING AND EDUCATION.

Further reading

Altano 1990; Berk-Seligson 1990/2002; Gonzalez

et al. 1991; Shlesinger 1991; de Jongh 1992; Brown 1993; Laster and Taylor 1994; Robinson 1994; Edwards 1995; Morris 1995; Colin and Morris 1996; Brennan and Brown 1997; Hale 1997; Hertog 2002; Hale 2004.

MUHAMMAD Y. GAMAL

Cultural translation

The term 'cultural translation' is used in many different contexts and senses. In some of these it is a metaphor that radically questions translation's traditional parameters, but a somewhat narrower use of the term refers to those practices of LITERARY TRANSLATION that mediate cultural difference, or try to convey extensive cultural background, or set out to represent another culture via translation. In this sense, 'cultural translation' is counterposed to a 'linguistic' or 'grammatical' translation that is limited in scope to the sentences on the page. It raises complex technical issues: how to deal with features like dialect and heteroglossia, literary allusions, culturally specific items such as food or architecture, or further-reaching differences in the assumed contextual knowledge that surrounds the text and gives it meaning (see STRATEGIES). Questions like these feed long-standing disputes on the most effective – and most ethical – ways to render the cultural difference of the text (see ETHICS), leaning more towards naturalization or more towards exoticization, with the attendant dangers of ideologically appropriating the source culture or creating a spurious sense of absolute distance from it (Carbonell 1996). In this context, 'cultural translation' does not usually denote a particular kind of translation strategy, but rather a *perspective* on translations that focuses on their emergence and impact as components in the ideological traffic between language groups (see IDEOLOGY).

Anthropological 'translation of cultures'

More elaborated uses of the term 'cultural translation' have been developed in the discipline of cultural anthropology, which is faced with questions of translation on a variety of levels. In the most practical sense, anthropological fieldwork usually involves extensive interlingual translation, whether by anthropologists themselves or by their interpreters (Rubel and Rosman 2003: 4). As linguistically challenged outsiders trying to understand what is going on, fieldworkers may encounter cultural difference in a very immediate and even painful way: 'participant observation obliges its practitioners to experience, at a bodily as well as intellectual level, the vicissitudes of translation' (Clifford 1983: 119). Secondly, when the fieldworker's multidimensional, orally mediated experiences are reworked into linear written text, this is not simply a matter of interlingual, or even intersemiotic, translation, but also a translation between cultural contexts. Since anthropologists assume that language and culture filter our experiences of the world to a very great extent, evidently it will be difficult to grasp and convey experiences that take place within a different system of filters, outside our own frames of reference. The degree to which speakers of different languages can share a common ground of understanding, and communication can proceed in the face of potential incommensurability or untranslatability between viewpoints, has been explored by Feleppa (1988), Needham (1972) and Tambiah (1990); see TRANSLATABILITY.

Alongside these epistemological worries, ethnography involves writing down the complex worlds of other people's meaning in a way that is intelligible in the receiving language. How much use of transferred source-language terms is required in that process, how much contextualization, how much approximation to target-culture genres and narrative forms are questions that are hotly debated in the literature. Like the literary 'cultural translator', the ethnographer has to reconcile respect for the specificity of the 'native point of view' with the desire to create a text comprehensible to the target readership. As Crapanzano puts it, the ethnographer like the translator 'must render the foreign familiar and preserve its very foreignness at one and the same time' (1986: 52). In ethnographic practice the balance between these goals varies. Much debate has focused on the twin dangers of, on the one hand, an 'orientalizing' translation style associated with hierarchical representations of other cultures as primitive and inferior to a normative 'western' civilization, and, on the other, an 'appropriative' style that downplays the distinctiveness of other world views and claims universal validity for what may in fact be domestic categories of thought (see Pálsson 1993 for an interesting discussion of these points).

Some objections to 'translation of cultures'

These debates are not always formulated explicitly in terms of translation, but as Asad explains in an influential 1986 essay, the phrase 'translation of cultures' is a conventional metaphor in anthropological theory. Gaining ground from the 1950s, especially in British functionalist anthropology, the 'translation of cultures' approach saw its task as searching for the internal coherence that other people's thinking and practices have in their own context, then re-creating that coherence in the terms of Western academia. Asad's critical discussion of the metaphor shows that in the 'translation of cultures' perspective, the ethnographer-translator assumes authority to extract the underlying meanings of what the 'natives' say and do, as opposed to the sayers and doers themselves determining what they mean. As a result, the 'cultural translator' takes on authorship and the position of knowing better than the 'cultural text' itself, which is relegated to the status of an unknowing provider of source material for interpretation. This imbalance of power arises from political inequality between source and target languages, and itself feeds into dominant 'knowledge' about colonized societies. Thus 'the process of "cultural translation" is inevitably enmeshed in conditions of power – professional, national, international' (1986: 162). Although Asad does not reject the viability of cultural translation as a whole, he insists that it must always be approached through awareness of the 'asymmetrical tendencies and pressures in the languages of dominated and dominant societies' (ibid.: 164).

Asad thus challenges the model of cultural translation which assigns to a dominating target language the authority to survey the source culture and detect intentions hidden to its members. But the idea of cultures as being text-like, and thus susceptible to 'translation' in the first place, has also been questioned. The textualizing approach of interpretive anthropology was set out by Clifford Geertz in *The Interpretation of Cultures* (1973), which takes a hermeneutic view of cultures as complex webs of meaning capable of being 'read'. Much influenced by Geertz, the critics often labelled as 'Writing Culture' (after the title of Clifford and Marcus's ground-breaking 1986 collection) focus on ethnographic descriptions themselves as texts – 'fictions' that conventionally make use of particular tropes and genres and that have served to reinforce hegemonic relationships between anthropologizers and anthropologized. The concept of translation is frequently employed by these critics, who are interested in the power of texts to form and re-form dominant knowledge (see also Clifford 1997). However, their detractors argue that culture should not necessarily be viewed as system or language, let alone as text, but perhaps rather as historically contingent conversation and interaction (Pálsson 1993). Additionally, *Writing Culture*'s focus on textuality has been accused of sidestepping the concrete political practices which far more powerfully determine the relationships between cultures (Abu-Lughod 1991).

A more fundamental criticism of the concept of 'cultural translation' questions the very existence of 'cultures'. The many anthropological critiques of the notion of cultures, usefully presented by Brightman (1995), show how it can falsely construct human communities as being homogeneous, monolithic, essentially unchanging, and clearly bounded by national or other borders. As the *Writing Culture* critics pointed out, cultural descriptions based on this conception participated in constructing the alleged 'primitivism' of non-western peoples by representing them as radically separate and sealed off from the describing western societies. For example, the history of contact, especially the violent contact of colonialism, was repressed in classic ethnographies so as to present the quintessential ethnographic 'culture' as pure, primordial and untouched by outside influences. The notion of discrete cultures, then, provided the dubious framework for the ethnographic description and guided what could be seen and said about the people being 'translated'.

Intersections, internal conflict, mixing and historical change had no place in such a model of the ideal 'cultural unit'; these features were attributed to target-language societies alone. A similar argument is made by Niranjana (1992) for the case of India: translation in both the textual and the more metaphorical senses helped to construct an essentialized and ahistorical 'Indian culture' that could be conveniently inserted into a position of inferiority *vis-à-vis* the British colonial power.

Cultural translation as processes of hybrid identification

In view of these thorough-going attacks on the model of cultures as distinct languages that can be translated into other languages, 'cultural translation' too is undermined, at least as a model of *inter-*'cultural' translation between boundaried, quasi-national entities. Here a related but more figurative and far-reaching use of the term 'cultural translation' comes to the fore: the notion, common in POSTCOLONIAL studies, that translation is less a procedure to which cultures can be subjected than itself the very fabric of culture. In this case, 'translation' is not meant as interlingual transfer but metaphorically, as the alteration of colonizing discourses by the discourses of the colonized and vice versa. For Bhabha, the resulting 'hybridity' in language and cultural identity means culture is both 'transnational and translational' (1994a: 5) – constituted via 'translation' as exchange and ADAPTATION, especially through the phenomenon of migration (see MOBILITY; GLOBALIZATION). In this view, translation is not an interchange between discrete wholes but a process of mixing and mutual contamination, and not a movement from 'source' to 'target' but located in a 'third space' beyond both, where 'conflicts arising from cultural difference and the different social discourses involved in those conflicts are negotiated' (Wolf 2002: 190).

Cultural translation in this sense offers a dissolution of some key categories of translation studies: the notion of separate 'source' and 'target' language-cultures and indeed binary or dualistic models in general. Rather than being clear-cut *locations* of coherent identity,

argues Doris Bachmann-Medick, cultures are *processes* of translation, constantly shifting, multiplying and diversifying; the idea of cultural translation can 'act as an anti-essentialist and anti-holistic metaphor that aims to uncover counter-discourses, discursive forms and resistant actions within a culture, heterogeneous discursive spaces within a society' and enable 'a dynamic concept of culture as a practice of negotiating cultural differences, and of cultural overlap, syncretism and creolization' (2006: 37).

Although this kind of approach does not specifically rule out the meaning of 'translation' as an interlingual practice, clearly it is interested in much wider senses of translation than the movement from language one to language two. The danger here, in Trivedi's view (2005), is that the notion of 'cultural translation' might drastically undervalue the linguistic difference and co-existence upon which translation in the more traditional sense relies. Trivedi accuses Bhabha of marginalizing bilingualism and translation as specifically interlingual practices, the precondition for polylingual cultural diversity. He calls for translation studies to insist on the centrality of translation's polylingual aspect and to refute the generalization of 'cultural translation' into an umbrella term for all aspects of MOBILITY and diasporic life.

Trivedi's criticism might be extended to uses of the translation metaphor in anthropological and cultural studies which exclude or do not address language difference, thus potentially presenting a false sense of monolingualism to western audiences. Metaphorical usage could at worst hollow out the word 'translation', not just into something that need not necessarily include more than one language but into something that primarily *does not* include more than one language – a factor, instead, of shifts and layering within globally dominant English without the need for bilingual translation to take place. As Bachmann-Medick (2006) hints, in a nightmare scenario 'cultural translation' could mean the adaptation of everything to the dominant idiom of western capitalism, thus destroying difference or relegating it to unheard margins of global society. For critics such as Trivedi, the challenge to translation studies is thus to reassert the crucial role of translation in all its senses within interdisciplinary debates on cultural difference and GLOBALIZATION.

See also:
CULTURE; ETHICS; GLOBALIZATION; IDEOLOGY; LITERARY TRANSLATION; MOBILITY; POSTCOLONIAL APPROACHES; STRATEGIES; TRANSLATABILITY.

Further reading
Geertz 1973; Asad 1986; Clifford and Marcus 1986; Feleppa 1988; Niranjana 1992; Pálsson 1993; Bhabha 1994b; Brightman 1995; Sturge 1997; Wolf 2002; Rubel and Rosman 2003; Trivedi 2005; Bachmann-Medick 2006; Sturge 2007.

KATE STURGE

Culture

Until the birth of anthropology, culture referred exclusively to the humanist ideal of what was considered 'civilized' in a developed society. Since then, a second meaning of culture as the way of life of a people has become influential. With the development of disciplines such as cultural studies, a third meaning has emerged which attempts to identify political or ideological reasons for specific cultural behaviour (see Katan 1999/2004: 29). Hence, depending on the definition adopted, culture may be formally learnt, unconsciously shared, or be a site of conflict. To complicate matters further, anthropologists themselves now seriously question 'the old idea of "a people" possessing "a shared culture"' (Erikson and Nielson 2001: 162).

In translation studies, theorists and practitioners are equally divided over the meaning and importance of culture, though most would tacitly accept that there is some form of 'cultural filter' (House 2002: 100) involved in the translation process

Culture as a system of frames

We can clarify the apparently contradictory definitions of culture by presenting them as hierarchical frames or levels, each one (to some extent) embedded within larger frames. This hierarchy is based on the Theory of Types (Bateson 1972), which allows for each of the

competing types of culture (i.e. definitions) to be valid for translation, albeit within their own level. In an extensive treatment of culture in the context of translation and interpreting, Katan (1999/2004: 26) proposes a definition of culture as a shared 'model of the world', a hierarchical system of congruent and interrelated beliefs, values and strategies which can guide action and interaction, depending on cognitive context; '[e]ach aspect of culture is linked in a [fluid] system to form a unifying context of culture'. The levels themselves are based on Edward T. Hall's popular anthropological *iceberg model*, the 'Triad of Culture' (1959/1990), which serves to introduce one dimension of the system, dividing aspects of culture into what is visible (above the waterline), semi-visible and invisible (Figure 1). The frames below the water line are progressively more hidden but also progressively closer to our unquestioned assumptions about the world and our own (cultural) identities. A further, sociological, dimension may be described as operating on the iceberg itself. The levels also reflect the various ways in which we learn culture: technically, through explicit instruction; formally, through trial-and-error modelling; and informally, through the unconscious inculcation of principles and world views.

The extent to which a translator should intervene (i.e. interpret and manipulate rather than operate a purely linguistic transfer) will be in accordance with our beliefs about which frame(s) most influence translation. Translation scholars tend to focus on the more hidden levels, while practitioners are more concerned with what is visible on the surface.

Technical culture: civilization

The first cultural frame is at the tip of the iceberg and coincides with the humanist concept of culture. The focus is on the text, dressed (adapting Newmark 1995: 80) in its best civilized clothes of a particular culture. At this 'Technical' level, language signs have a clear WYSIWYG (What-You-See-Is-What-You-Get) referential function, and any associated hidden values are 'universal'. The task of the translator at this level is to transfer the terms and concepts in the source text abroad with minimum loss (from literature and philosophical ideas to software

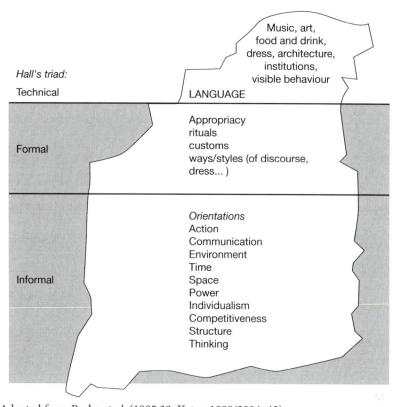

Figure 1: Adapted from Brake *et al.* (1995:39; Katan 1999/2004: 43)

manuals), so that 'what you see' in the source text is equivalent to 'what you see' in the target text. As long as the two cultures 'have reached a comparable degree of development', some have argued, there is no reason why meaning, reader response and uptake should not be 'universal' (see, for example, Seleskovitch, in Newmark 1988: 6, and Wilss 1982: 48). This is what Newmark (1981: 184–5) calls 'the cultural value' of translation, and indeed the bylaws of the International Federation of Translators (n.d.) similarly assume that the value of translation is that it 'assists in the spreading of culture throughout the world'. The chapter headings in *Translators through History* (Delisle and Woodsworth 1995) give us an idea of what is involved at this level: the invention of alphabets and the writing of dictionaries; the development of national languages and literatures, and the spread of religions and cultural values. Depending on the asymmetries of power, spreading the new terms and concepts might

be perceived as enlightenment, 'the white man's burden', an affront, the wielding of hegemony or a much-valued addition to intellectual debate. However, the main concern of translators intervening at this level is the text itself and the translation of 'culture-bound' terms, or 'culturemes' – defined as formalized, socially and juridically embedded phenomena that exist in a particular form or function in only one of the two cultures being compared (Vermeer 1983a: 8; Nord 1997: 34). These culturemes, or 'cultural categories' in Newmark's terms (1988: 9 5), cover a wide array of semantic fields: from geography and traditions to institutions and technologies. Since Vinay and Darbelnet (1958), various scholars have offered a plethora of STRATEGIES to compensate for lack of EQUIVALENCE at this level (see Kwieciński 2001 for a useful summary).

Formal culture: functionalist, appropriate practices

Hall's second, 'Formal', level of culture derives from the anthropological definition, focusing on what is normal or appropriate (rather than what is civilized). Hans Vermeer's definition of culture, accepted by many translators as 'the standard', belongs to this level: 'Culture consists of everything one needs to know, master and feel, in order to assess where members of a society are behaving acceptably or deviantly in their various roles' (translated in Snell-Hornby 2006: 55).

Culture here is a predictable pattern of shared practices which guide actual (technical level) language use, for example culture-specific genre preferences, protopypes and schemata, or even simply 'good style'; see, for example, Clyne (1991), Ventola (2000) and Candlin and Gotti (2004). What is judged as good translation practice is also guided by culturally-specific translation NORMS, rules and conventions, including, among other things: which texts are accepted for translation; the type of translation and compensation strategies to employ; and the criteria by which a translation is judged (Chesterman 1993; Toury 1995). Intervention at this level focuses on the SKOPOS of the translation and on tailoring the translation to the expectations of receivers in the target culture. In practice, however, it is often project managers and 'cultural interpreters' within the language industry who ultimately mediate Formal culture, leaving 'the translator' with the Technical, 'lingua' part of 'linguaculture' (Agar 1994).

Informal culture: cognitive systems

Hall calls his third level of culture 'Informal' or 'Out-of-awareness', because it is not normally accessible to the conscious brain for meta-cognitive comment. At this level, there are no formal guides to practice but instead unquestioned core values and beliefs, or stories about self and the world. As such, one's culture, inculcated for example though family, school and the media, becomes a relatively fixed internal representation of reality, Bourdieu's *habitus* (see SOCIOLOGICAL APPROACHES), which then both guides and constrains one's orientation in the

real world. Psychological anthropology defines culture in terms of a *Weltanschauung*, a shared model, map or view of the perceivable world (Korzybski 1933/1958); 'mental programming' (Hofstede 1980/2001); 'the form of things that people have in their mind' (Goodenough 1957/1964: 36) and which orients individual and community ways of doing things. These are 'core, primary ethical values' (Chesterman 1997: 149) or 'transcendental values' (Walter Fisher, in Baker 2006a) that guide Formal culture choices. The hierarchy of preferred value orientations is seen as the result of a community response to universal human needs or problems (Kluckhohn and Strodtbeck 1961), such as relations to time, and between the individual and the group. With their coining of the term 'cultural turn', Lefevere and Bassnett (1990: 1; see also Bassnett 1980/2002) were among the first to popularize the view that translation is a bicultural practice requiring 'mindshifting' (Taft 1981: 53) from one linguacultural model of the world to another, and mediating (or compensating) skills to deal with the inevitable refraction between one reality and another. Linguacultures have been studied through, for example, the description of their 'cultural grammar' (Duranti 1997: 27; Goodenough 2003: 5), defined by Wierzbicka (1996: 527) as 'a set of subconscious rules that shape a people's ways of thinking, feeling, speaking, and interacting'. Her emic 'cultural scripts' (e.g. Wierzbicka 2003, 2006) provide strong linguistic evidence for the need to translate at the informal level. For a more etic approach based on orientations, see, for example, de Mooij (2004) and Katan (2006); see also Manca (2008) for a corpus-driven perspective.

Outside the iceberg: power relations

Sociologists and scholars of cultural studies tend to focus on the influence that culture exercises on society and institutions in terms of prevailing ideologies. Culture here is seen as the result of the 'pressures that social structures apply to social action' (Jenks 1993: 25). These pressures mould, manipulate or conflict with the individual but shared models of the world discussed above.

Two other fundamental differences distinguish this approach from the traditional anthropological model. First, individuals (and texts) cannot be assigned to 'a culture' in this view. Instead they have many cultural provenances, are variously privileged or suppressed from different perspectives, and will negotiate a position within a set of complex cultural systems that are constantly jockeying for power. Within translation studies, scholars drawing on POLYSYSTEM theory (Even-Zohar 1990), POSTCOLONIAL theory (Bassnett and Trivedi 1999) and narrative theory (Baker 2006a) all share this assumption. Secondly, the system of culture itself is constantly subject to questioning (as is the idea of cultural relativity). At this level, translators intervene between competing (and unequal) systems of power, no longer to facilitate but to participate in constructing the world, acknowledging that texts (and they themselves) are carriers of ideologies (Hatim and Mason 1997: 147). The decision to translate Salman Rushdie's *The Satanic Verses* (1988) or *Did Six Million Really Die?* (Harwood 1977) are clear cases in point. The translator at this level is no longer a detached mediator but is conscious of being 'an ethical agent of social change' (Tymoczko 2003: 181), or 'an activist' involved in renarrating the world (Baker 2006b). In a similar vein, Venuti's preference for foreignizing strategies 'stems partly from a political agenda ... an opposition to the global hegemony of English' (Venuti 1998b: 10), a hegemony that communicates and normalizes specific (e.g. capitalist, colonial) cultural values. Intervention at this level clearly raises many ethical questions (see ETHICS); on a practical level the difficulty of unsettling the third level of culture (Informal or Out-of-awareness) means that only a fine line separates a successful translation which resists generic conventions to introduce a new way of writing or way of thinking and an unread translation; as Baker (2006a: 98) puts it, 'even breaches of canonical storylines have to be effected within circumscribed, normative plots [i.e. Formal culture] if they are to be intelligible at all'.

Ultimately, culture has to be understood not only as a set of levels or frames but as an integrated system, in a constant state of flux, through which textual signals are negotiated and reinterpreted according to context and individual stance.

See also:
CULTURAL TRANSLATION; ETHICS; GLOBALIZATION; IDEOLOGY; NORMS; SEMIOTICS; TRANSLATABILITY.

Further reading
Hall 1959/1990; Bassnett 1980/2002; Jenks 1993; Duranti 1997; Katan 1999/2004; House 2002; Snell-Hornby 2006.

DAVID KATAN

Deconstruction

The issues considered most basic to translation theory, such as those of signification, meaning, interpretation and intention, also form the core of the Western philosophical tradition. Deconstruction puts this philosophical, or 'metaphysical', tradition into question, particularly its method of conceptualizing meaning as a presence that can exist outside or before language, and that can be transferred unchanged between languages. At every point, therefore, deconstruction is involved with the concerns and the processes of translation.

The term 'deconstruction' was coined by Jacques Derrida in the late 1960s as part of his larger engagement with and critique of the Western metaphysical tradition, and throughout the 1960s and 1970s this critique focused strongly on issues of language and translation. Deconstruction does not offer a theory or a strategy of translation; rather, it thoroughly rethinks the linguistic, semantic and political operations involved in translation. In so doing, it repositions translation with respect to the 'original' and to language more generally. Directly and indirectly, deconstruction has altered understandings of the cultural, institutional and political conditions in which translation occurs.

The works of Jacques Derrida, the most influential figure associated with deconstruction, consistently discuss the problem of philosophy as one of translation:

> What does philosophy say? … What does the philosopher say when he is being a philosopher? He says: What matters is truth or meaning, and since meaning is before or beyond language, it follows that it is translatable. Meaning has the commanding role, and consequently one must be able to fix its univocality or, in any case, to master its plurivocality. If this plurivocality can be mastered, then translation, understood as the transport of a semantic content into another signifying form, is possible. There is no philosophy unless translation in this latter sense is possible.
> (Derrida 1982/1985: 120)

Deconstruction shows that philosophy in this sense is not possible, that it necessarily must fail. Meaning is an *effect* of language, not a prior presence merely expressed in language. But it does not follow that neither philosophy nor translation are possible at all. On the contrary, the work of deconstruction shows that the *limit* of language, which prevents pure meaning and total translation, is also precisely what makes translation possible in the first place, since this limit ensures that meaning can never be absolute, closed off, or shut down. Deconstruction rethinks many issues crucial to translation, some of which will be discussed here under two topics: *différance* and *iterability*.

Différance

Pursuing the implications of Ferdinand de Sausssure's observation that 'in language there are only differences *without positive terms*' (Saussure 1959: 120; emphasis in original), Derrida notes that a signified concept is never present, or a presence, in and of itself; rather, 'every concept is inscribed in a chain or in a system within which it refers to the other, to other concepts, by means of the systematic play of differences' (Derrida 1972b/1982: 11). This play of differences is both spatial and temporal. It is spatial because the sign does not mark the place of some positive presence; rather, it marks differential relations to other signifiers. It is temporal because signification cannot refer directly to the present: it can only make meaning with respect to *already* constituted relations among signifiers, and in its very constitution it is necessarily open to future relations. Pursuing meaning is therefore not a matter of revealing a content that is already 'there'; on the contrary, it is a relentless tracking through an always moving play of differences. For this reason, deconstruction often speaks not of the signifier, but of the *trace*. Each element of discourse is 'constituted on the basis of the trace within it of the other elements of the chain or system' (Derrida 1972a/1981: 26).

In order to express the differential movement of language succinctly, Derrida coined the neologism (or, more precisely, the neographism) ***différance***. The French verb *différer* has two meanings, roughly corresponding to the English 'to defer' and 'to differ'. The common French noun *différence*, however, retains the sense of 'difference' but lacks a temporal aspect. Spelling *différence* with an *a* evokes the formation in French of a gerund from the present participle of the verb (*différent*), so that it recalls the temporal and active kernel of *différer* (see Derrida 1972b/1982: 6–7). *Différance* is not a concept and cannot be assigned a meaning, since it is the condition of possibility for meanings, which are effects of this systemic movement, or play of differences. The implications for translation are important: since meaning cannot precede *différance*, there can be no pure, unified, static 'original' and no absolute division, let alone a hierarchy, of original and translation. Indeed, the 'original' relies upon translation for survival. This is not an argument for an 'anything goes' approach. On the contrary, it demonstrates the importance of scrupulous attention both to the *singularity* of a text's particular historical and rhetorical conjunctions, and to a text's *generality*, its openness and its participation in the mobile weave of differences.

Following through on this thinking about *différance*, deconstruction uses some terms, such as *text* and *writing*, in a revised sense. Language performs as part of an open weave with the social, cultural, political, sexual, familial, economic, etc., so that everything meaningful to us participates in the play of differences, or 'general text' (see Derrida 1988). No sign – whether a body part that indicates gender, a skin colour that indicates ethnicity, or a title that indicates institutional status – gives access to a 'real' presence that can be experienced outside an instituted system of differences. Likewise, the boundaries between categories, whether between 'natural' languages such as English and French, between races or genders, or even between the linguistic and non-linguistic, do not precede but emerge with such an instituted system.

Every 'identity' is therefore both *singular* and *general*. On the one hand, each language or culture has a *singular* way of meaning due to its particular set of differential relations, and this singularity precludes perfect translatability (Derrida 1988, 1979; de Man 1986: 73–93). On the other hand, the boundaries of any given language or culture are in the first place constituted as relations to other languages and cultures, and therefore participate in a *general* code, or 'text'. This generality precludes the possibility of absolute singularity and total untranslatability. The important point here for translation is that translatability and untranslatability are not mutually exclusive, nor are they poles on a scale of relativity. Singularity and generality are mutually constitutive, and their structural interdependence allows for meaning and *at the same time* prevents both total translatability and total untranslatability. The *limit* of any language is both a boundary and a structural opening to its outside. Just as this structure makes translation between languages possible, it also makes possible new 'translations' of identities such as race, gender, culture or ethnicity. 'Translation' in this more general sense has therefore become important in fields such as POSTCOLONIAL and feminist theory (see GENDER AND SEXUALITY) (Arrojo 1994; Bhabha 1994a; Godard 1990; Spivak 1992b, 1994, 1999).

Deconstruction also stresses that there is no clear-cut boundary between speech and writing as it is conventionally understood. Contravening a long tradition that posits speech as 'natural' and writing as a derived system that simply represents speech, Derrida points out that the structure of signification in general depends upon characteristics typically associated with writing: 'If "writing" signifies inscription and especially the durable institution of a sign (and that is the only irreducible kernel of the concept of writing), writing in general covers the entire field of linguistic signs' (Derrida 1967a/1974: 44). This 'writing in general' (*écriture*) thus corresponds to the revised sense of textuality, or the 'general text', discussed above. Signifiers (as Saussure had shown) are not 'natural' but arbitrary and conventional: they are always and can only be instituted, and thus the phonic signifier, like the graphic, relies upon the durable institution of a sign and its *iterability*, which guarantees translatability.

Iterability

The verb *iterate* is defined as 'to say or perform again; repeat' (*American Heritage Dictionary*). It derives from the Latin *iterum*, 'again', and is also related to *iter*, 'journey' or 'route'. This conjunction is useful for thinking about the implications for translation of deconstruction's work on the structural interrelation of the *singularity* and the *generality* of every text. If, as discussed above, each element of discourse is 'constituted on the basis of the trace within it of the other elements of the chain or system', then these elements rely for their meaning upon their own repetition of past usages, which accrue a fairly stable history. Without this stability, interpretation and translation would not be possible at all. Nonetheless, each repetition must also be different from all the others, since each occurs in a new context and therefore produces its effect within a different set of systemic relations. The same repetition that builds stability, then, also builds up a history of differences, so that this stability always offers multiple routes for meaning, and is thus always capable of being destabilized. Every meaning effect is *disseminated* throughout the entire system, which we can think of as innumerable routes, or pathways of differential meanings.

This dissemination guarantees that every sign and every text is *iterable*, or repeatable, differently. As Derrida puts it, 'This has to do with the structure of a text, with what I will call, to cut corners, its iterability, which both puts down roots in a unity of a context and immediately opens this non-saturable context onto a recontextualization' (1992: 63). It may seem a statement of the obvious to say that signifiers or texts can always be repeated: *of course* words, phrases and actions can be repeated or cited,

plays can be restaged in new circumstances, etc. The structure of *iterability*, however, shows that ideas about 'correct' and 'incorrect' translation, like translatability and untranslatability, are structurally interdependent. Deconstruction does not suggest that 'anything goes', but it does point out that the conditions that make 'mistakes' possible are the *same* conditions that make meaning possible in the first place.

It may help to return to the connections of *iter* to both repetition and travel, and to think about the dissemination of meaning as similar to a postal system. The conditions that make it possible to address and to deliver a letter – for example, numbers and letters of the alphabet can be rearranged and transposed; streets intersect; multiple routes and detours facilitate travel – are the same conditions that make 'mistakes' possible. In order for a letter to be written and addressed, it must *already* be implicated in a differential system full of detours, so that it always may not arrive. Again, this may seem obvious: we all know that our letters may not arrive, just as our 'intended meanings' may be misunderstood. Conventional wisdom labels such events as errors or exceptions that somehow escape or break the rules of the system. Deconstruction reverses this assumption, positing that detours and multiple pathways *constitute* any system that enables meaning; they are not 'accidents' belonging to its outside, but are the conditions of possibility for signification, and for translation.

Deconstruction therefore points out that the decisions involved in translation are not mere choices between predetermined options, in which case they would not really be decisions at all. They are decisions in the 'strong' sense: that is, they are made in the face of undecidability. Decision-making 'positively *depends upon* undecidability, which gives us something to decide' (Caputo 1997: 137). Because meaning cannot be *pre*-determined, translation must 'respond' to its source by deciding in this strong sense, and thus entails responsibility and ETHICS. The translator's decisions are not dissociable from other kinds of political and ethical delimitations about what is possible or permissible in a language or culture. Indeed, in responding to a text *as* foreign, translation simultaneously defines the 'same' and the 'other', and puts itself in an ethical relation with this 'other'.

Translation, then, enacts the problem not only of philosophy, but of ethics. This is why deconstruction is at every point fully involved with the concerns and the processes of translation.

See also:
EQUIVALENCE; ETHICS; HERMENEUTICS; SEMIOTICS; TRANSLATABILITY.

Further reading
Derrida 1967a/1974, 1972a/1981, 1979; Culler 1982; Arac *et al* 1983; Derrida 1985; de Man 1986; Derrida 1987/1988, 1988; A. Benjamin 1989; Derrida 1992; Niranjana 1992; Pasanen 1992; Spivak 1992b; Venuti 1992; Bhabha 1994a; Derrida 1996/1998, 1999/2001; Spivak 1999; Chesterman and Arrojo 2000; Davis 2001.

KATHLEEN DAVIS

Descriptive vs. committed approaches

Historically, much of the discourse about translation has revolved around prescribing certain modes of translation, right from the earliest statements of the famed Cicero and St Jerome, and has centred on the perennial debate over literal versus free translation. Reflections on translation have been made mainly by translators who were also scholars or poets themselves, and who defended their chosen mode of translation in prefaces or other writings (see STRATEGIES). For example, in his preface to the translation of Ovid's *Epistles* (1680/1992), Dryden, the famous poet and dramatist who also translated various Greek and Latin poets into English, made a three-way distinction between metaphrase (word-by-word translation), paraphrase (sense-for-sense translation), and imitation (very free translation), and expounded his preference for paraphrase. Prescriptive approaches remained influential throughout the twentieth century and continue to be so today because of the importance of translator training (see TRAINING AND EDUCATION). Within this context, the study of translation has been seen as an ancillary

discipline, a part of linguistics, which serves the practical purpose of producing better translations and better translators. Newmark, for example, argues that 'translation theory's main concern is to determine appropriate translation methods for the widest possible range of texts or text-categories' (1981: 19).

Descriptive Translation Studies

The emergence of Descriptive Translation Studies (DTS) in the 1970s, embodying the aim of establishing translation research as an empirical and historically oriented scholarly discipline, can be considered a reaction to centuries-long speculative and prescriptive writing on translation. Holmes (1972) conceived of translation studies as a discipline which espouses the structure, goals and methods of the natural sciences. There were to be pure and applied branches, with the pure branch further subdivided into theoretical and descriptive branches. The core activity of the discipline was to be theoretical and descriptive, with any prescriptive orientation relegated strictly to the applied branch. The main objectives were to describe, explain and predict translational phenomena.

Toury (1980, 1995), who developed Holmes's vision and made important theoretical and methodological additions to Holmes's model, was heavily influenced by Even-Zohar's (1979) POLYSYSTEM theory. He argued that translational phenomena could ultimately be explained by their systemic position and role in the target culture. Another source of explanation proposed by Toury is the concept of NORMS: translators are influenced by the norms that govern translation practice in the target culture at a certain place and time. Norms are arguably Toury's lasting conceptual contribution to the field.

Toury's approach is firmly target-oriented, since he considers that translations are facts of the target culture, their characteristics being conditioned by target culture forces. Another specificity of Toury's approach is that he chooses not to offer an abstract definition of translation (since what translation is will be revealed by the studies undertaken), and he takes as objects of study 'assumed translations', texts that are considered to be translations in the society concerned. There are different types of descriptive study that can be undertaken. The most common perhaps is the study of a corpus of translations and their source texts. The relationship between source texts and translations is described, and explanations for the findings are proposed. Apart from systemic position and norms, a third potential source of explanation is 'laws of translation' (the use of 'laws' is in line with the scientific paradigm to which Toury subscribes). For Toury, the goal of the discipline is to amass a large number of studies of different genres of translation in different eras and cultures; based on the findings of such studies, it should then be possible to propose a series of laws of translational behaviour. Laws express the likelihood that given types of behaviour will occur under given sets of specifiable conditions. An example of a law proposed by Toury is that 'the more peripheral the status of translation in a community, the more translation will accommodate itself to established models and repertoires' (1995: 271).

Toury and other pioneers of the descriptive approach, such as Hermans (1985a) and Lambert (1988), were tremendously important in putting translation studies on a firm footing as an academic discipline. The descriptivist approach also laid the foundations for further developments, notably approaches using CORPORA and tools from corpus linguistics, as well as approaches that are sometimes referred to as the 'cultural turn' in translation studies and which foreground the role of translation as a cultural vector.

Critiquing descriptivism

DTS has been criticized for its scientificity and rigidity. While supporting many of the accomplishments of DTS, Hermans (1999) points out such problematic features as the goal of establishing laws of translation – a 'positivist chimera' according to Tymoczko (1998) – and the concomitant neglect of individual agency and individual translating situations. Particular contexts of production of a translation can act as a source of explanation for translational phenomena. Rather than there being only a few sources of explanation, or even one final source (the systemic position) as in the case of Toury's theory, the complex phenomenon of translation

calls for multiple sources of explanation (Pym 1998). Toury's uncompromising target orientation is also seen as an oversimplification which overlooks various types of complex translational setting.

Other areas of neglect in early descriptivism include the role of values and the political and ideological effects of translation. Lefevere (1992a) demonstrates strikingly, for example, how translations normally reflect target culture ideologies and mores of particular eras (see REWRITING; IDEOLOGY). Translations may thus support reigning ideologies and poetics in some cases and promote non-conformative ideologies in others. Effects also encompass the readership's reaction to a translation. Chesterman (1999) argues that the study of both causes and effects of translations should be given equal importance in research.

The strict division made in early DTS between descriptive and prescriptive approaches has also been questioned. Concepts which describe practices have ethical implications: for example, to say 'X is a translator' implies 'X ought to do what a translator ought to do'. Furthermore, the study of effects can involve the testing of prescriptive statements about translation (Chesterman 1999).

Another important criticism of DTS is that it adopts a positivistic stance which assumes that the researcher is able to take an objective position with regard to the object of study, whereas it is clear that interpretation and perspectival judgements inevitably enter into descriptions. Arrojo points out that statements about norms are not in themselves prescriptive, but they are not merely descriptive either, since they reflect the viewpoint, interests and perspective of those who elaborate them (Chesterman and Arrojo 2000). Hermans (1999), too, calls for a more self-critical stance on the part of translation researchers, and for researchers to fully recognize that they filter translational data through their individual conceptions and those of the societies in which they are immersed. For Hermans, the task of the discipline is to theorize the historical contingency of different modes and uses of translation and of discourses on translation, including discourses elaborated within translation studies. In spite of its questioning of the objectivity of descriptivism, the approach outlined by Hermans still distinguishes itself from prescriptivism in that it does not seek to interfere in the practice of translation; it seeks rather to account for what happens in translation practice and in the discourse on translation. Like DTS, it is descriptive, but unlike DTS it is self-reflexive and self-critical. We might thus call this development 'Critical Descriptive Translation Studies'.

Committed approaches

The cultural turn which began in the 1990s heralded a range of approaches which viewed translation from a cultural perspective. Translation was studied in terms of cultural systems, including ideological influences emanating from those systems. Influenced by literary and cultural studies, translation has also come under the purview of special interest groupings, such as women's studies, queer studies and postcolonial studies. Studies of translation undertaken within these frameworks may remain descriptive. One example is Harvey (2000), who adopts a descriptive-explanatory approach in his case studies of the translation of American gay literature into French and vice versa. On the other hand, research undertaken from the perspective of GENDER and POSTCOLONIAL APPROACHES may make judgements on existing translations and advocate particular modes of translation in line with specific ideologies (see below). There has thus been a politically motivated revival of prescriptive approaches towards translation, based on the recognition of unfair power differentials in and between cultures and languages. More broadly, we might call these 'committed approaches', because they stem from a concern with the importance of political commitment. Committed approaches can be divided into approaches which espouse a particular political commitment and approaches which are based on a more general recognition of the importance and even inevitability of political engagement.

A researcher who is directly motivated by a particular political engagement in undertaking his or her research may prescribe a certain way of translating which entails an activist and interventionist role on the part of the translator. With specific reference to the Indian context, Niranjana (1992) argues convincingly that translation has been an instrument of colonial domination, producing hegemonic representations of the colonized. However, Niranjana considers that translation is not doomed to play such a role. The issue here is not one of presenting a more 'accurate' version of the colonized nor of glorifying some pre-colonial utopia, because that would be buying into the notions of truth, fixed reality and univocality that Niranjana has already rejected. Rather, Niranjana advocates modes of translation that reveal the diversity of the indigenous population. An example might be literalness which foregrounds heterogeneity in the translation through a mixture of natural and non-natural target language expressions and both familiar and foreign elements. French-speaking Canada is another part of the world which has given rise to developments in translation studies that are driven by political commitment. The aims in this case have been the valorization of a region and its language, and the promotion of women's writing and feminist translation. De Lotbinière-Harwood (1991) is one of a number of vocal feminist translators who argue that only feminist-friendly texts should be translated in the first place, and that they should be rendered using creative feminist translation strategies. De Lotbinière-Harwood terms this 'rewriting in the feminine'. In order to convey the highly playful language used in the source text to highlight a feminist stance, de Lotbinière-Harwood resorts to creative linguistic and typographical inventions and to paratexts such as notes and prefaces, thus making her presence highly visible in the translation.

Venuti (1995a) is another politically committed theorist who has been concerned with the (in)visibility of translators, and with the ethical implications of translation (see ETHICS). He critiques the current predominance of neo-capitalist values in the English-speaking world and argues that fluent, 'invisible' translation into English insidiously inscribes those values in translated texts, suppressing the foreignness of the source text and resulting in ethnocentric violence. Venuti thus promotes foreignizing translation STRATEGIES. Foreignizing translation can take the form of choosing to translate a foreign text excluded by target culture literary canons, maintaining source text features in the translation, or using a marginal target-language discourse or a heterogeneous mix of discourses.

By signalling the foreignness of the translated text and/or disrupting dominant target discourses, these strategies challenge the status quo in the target culture.

The second group of committed approaches is in a sense more subtle than the first, since a particular political commitment is not promoted in this case. Rather, translation is studied as an activist and interventionist cultural activity *per se*. This approach is represented by Baker (2005a, 2006a) and Tymoczko (1999a, 2000a, 2003), both of whom share a strong personal belief in the importance of political engagement, which they have put into practice in their lives outside academia. As far as their research in translation studies is concerned, Baker and Tymoczko do not overtly promote a particular political agenda but emphasize the importance of political engagement more generally. Arguing against the notion of translators as neutral go-betweens, and of translation as an activity which takes place in a third space beyond or between specific cultural settings, Baker and Tymoczko stress the culturally and politically embedded nature of translators and translation. Tymoczko (2000a) offers a telling example of the active role played by translation in Irish history. Late nineteenth- and early twentieth-century English translations of early Irish literature produced a hero figure, Cú Chulainn, who became the emblem for militant Irish nationalists participating in the struggle for Irish independence. Years later, the same hero figure was used by both sides during 'the troubles' in Northern Ireland. However, a 1969 RETRANSLATION of the tale *Táin Bó Cúailnge* revealed that this hero was a highly romanticized version of a rather comic and earthy source text character. The aim of the retranslation was in part to contest the repressive and regressive movement that Irish nationalism had become.

Descriptive versus committed approaches

Hermans (1999) considers the relative virtues of descriptive approaches and those committed approaches where the researcher's political views lead him or her to advocate a particular mode of translation. He suggests that the direct link to practice (prescribing what translators should do) in committed approaches is detrimental to a critical stance. As mentioned above, for Hermans, the task of translation theory is to account for the practice and conceptualization of translation in different time periods. Hermans argues that committed approaches are not the best equipped to accomplish this task because their engagement limits their ability to adopt a critical perspective, and their blind spots may constrain their interpretations. It could be said that all studies, both descriptive and committed, are constrained by interpretative conceptions. However, Hermans argues that the difference between critical descriptivism and committed approaches is situated at a deeper level than that of interpretative constraints, namely the level of presuppositions. Committed approaches do not question their presuppositions; the particular political stance of each approach is a given. A critical descriptive approach, on the other hand, could provide space for self-reflection, for questioning presuppositions, for eclecticism, and for openness to various viewpoints which may be adopted in undertaking a given study (Brownlie 2003). Although researchers in the second group of committed approaches described above do not overtly promote particular political stances in translation practice, one may assume that these researchers necessarily hold strong political opinions which may inform their research and remain unquestioned. They may thus also be liable to the type of criticism outlined by Hermans (1999).

The strengths of committed and critical descriptive approaches in translation research could perhaps be combined by adopting Derrida's (1990) notion of a 'just decision', which involves both engagement in the sense of making firm and justified decisions and the necessity of putting into question one's existing conceptions in light of the singularity of particular contexts in which decisions are undertaken (Brownlie 2007).

See also:
CORPORA; ETHICS; GENDER AND SEXUALITY; IDEOLOGY; NORMS; POLYSYSTEM; POSTCOLONIAL APPROACHES.

Further reading
Lefevere 1992a; Niranjana 1992; Toury 1995;

Hermans 1999; Tymoczko 2000a, 2003; Baker 2006a; Brownlie 2007.

SIOBHAN BROWNLIE

Dialogue Interpreting

Among the many designations of various kinds of interpreting, dialogue interpreting (DI) is a term that seeks to encompass a group of activities seen as sharing an overall mode of interaction rather than a particular setting. Thus, whereas professionally recognized terms such as CONFERENCE INTERPRETING, COMMUNITY INTERPRETING, 'public service interpreting' and COURT INTERPRETING reflect defined areas of social activity as well as actual professional categories, DI transcends these boundaries by focusing on the characteristics of a particular mode of interaction, shared in many, quite diverse socio-professional contexts.

Four essential characteristics may be identified in defining dialogue interpreting and are reviewed in greater detail below. First, DI involves **dialogue**, the two- or three-way exchange of utterances and meanings that are the basis of conversation, rather than monologue, the most frequent mode of conference interpreting and of some sign-language interpreting. This fact in turn involves the interpreter in bi-directional translation, requiring active communicative skills in both languages and a facility for constant code switching. Second, what is translated is, in nearly all cases, **spontaneous speech** and only occasionally the speaking of what has been written. Typically too, DI is conducted **face-to-face**, requiring of interpreters that they manage the exchange and 'co-ordinate' (Wadensjö 1998) interaction between participants. Lastly, the mode of interpreting is mostly **consecutive**, exposing the interpreter to greater prominence and scrutiny than is the case for simultaneous interpreting.

It follows from this perspective, then, that a wide range of institutionally diverse interpreting events qualifies as instances of dialogue interpreting. For example, interpreter-mediated business encounters, although not institu-

tionally within the domain of COMMUNITY INTERPRETING, belong to a similar interactional framework and are amenable to the same methods and techniques of investigation. Indeed, conference interpreters, when they leave the booth to facilitate face-to-face ad hoc meetings, find themselves facing many of the interactional issues that are familiar within DI: they temporarily become dialogue interpreters.

Because DI is a denomination that seeks out interactional similarities between different fields of interpreting, what follows is not divided into the well-recognized domains of healthcare interpreting, ASYLUM interpreting, COURT INTERPRETING, media interpreting and so on. Rather, this entry describes the factors that characterize DI as a whole and presents aspects of DI behaviour as well as avenues of investigation within this field.

Dialogue and participation

In the simplest configuration – assumed by most outsiders and some users of interpreting services to apply to interpreting in general – the interpreter acts as a neutral intermediary between two interlocutors of equal status. He or she co-ordinates a turn-taking routine (Participant 1 – Interpreter – Participant 2 – Interpreter – Participant 1 – Interpreter – Participant 2, etc.), that may be only temporarily interrupted for purposes of clarification, repetition and so on. It is assumed that all of – and only – what is said is interpreted. Such a situation is, however, rare. Participants may provide their own interpreters, opening up perceptions of in-group allegiance. Even where interpreters are provided by third parties, in-group/out-group distinctions may be maintained on account of ethnic identities or simply because the interpreter is perceived as working for – and therefore acting in the interests of – a service provider. Usually, participants do not enjoy equal status in the exchange, as a result of disparities of power (e.g. police interviews) and/or knowledge and expertise (e.g. doctor/patient consultations).

Frequently, the event involves more than the three participants of the idealized situation described above, and a variety of configurations among them. For example, in a courtroom cross-examination, an attorney (addresser) may be putting questions to a witness (addressee) in order to convince a judge and jury (who are 'auditors', that is, ratified participants in the event but not at this time being directly addressed; see Goffman 1981). In the public gallery are 'overhearers', that is, people who are not ratified participants in the exchange but who witness it and who, by their behaviour (e.g. laughter), may exert influence on the unfolding of the event. All these categories of participant are relevant to – indeed, exert pressure in one way or another on – the interpreter's behaviour. A wholly different participation framework is apparent in the TV chat show (Straniero Sergio 1999; Katan and Straniero Sergio 2001; Seferlis 2006). In this configuration, a host may address questions, via an interpreter, to a guest (addressee) but may equally turn to camera and address comments to the television audience who, in this instance, shift from the category of overhearers to that of addressees. The interpreter will then either relay these comments for the benefit of the guest or simply omit them, thus relegating the guest to excluded status. Moreover, the host frequently addresses remarks directly to the interpreter (compliments, admonitions, etc.) that are not intended to be translated at all.

Now, whereas in this latter setting, the interpreter's opportunities for gate keeping and turn management may be circumscribed – these being partly ceded to the chat-show host – in other situations the interpreter adopts the pivotal role of co-ordinator of others' talk (Wadensjö 1998). An important aspect of this scenario is the changes of 'footing' (Goffman 1981) or alignment that each participant adopts towards the others. There is first the interpreter's choice to represent another's speech in the first person (e.g. 'I want you to tell me …') or the third person ('he wants you to tell him …'). The choice however may be influenced by the questioner, who often prefers to address the interpreter directly and refer to the intended recipient of the question in the third person: 'Tell her to … Ask her whether …'. This direct communication between, say, a doctor and an interpreter often leads to an extended dyadic exchange between these two participants in which the interpreter is positioned as a medical expert discussing a patient's symptoms but, for a while, excluding the patient from the exchange (see Bolden 2000). Alternatively, the interpreter may strive

to sustain a genuinely triadic exchange in which each participant is fully recognized and everything said is made available to every participant. Even here, though, the co-ordinating role comes to the fore when interpreters feel the need to explain their moves to other participants (e.g. 'I'm just asking her what she means by …').

Spontaneous speech

Another distinctive feature of dialogue interpreting is that it invariably involves spontaneous speech (and only occasionally the translation of prepared statements). The representation in another language of spontaneous speech requires the interpreter to make a range of judgements and decisions. There is, for example, the question of how to treat utterances that are, to varying degrees, incoherent. Barsky (1996: 53) provides a telling example of an inarticulate utterance in French, spoken by a Pakistani asylum seeker, but represented in coherent standard English by his Pakistani interpreter, clearly acting in what he saw as the best interests of his client. Hale (1997) provides evidence of interpreters' accommodation to the speech style of their addressees, raising the level of formality in interpreting for the court but lowering it when interpreting for Spanish-speaking witnesses. The handling of interruptions, interjections, back-channelling and other features of spontaneous speech also involves the interpreter in immediate decision making that can determine the direction an exchange will follow. Frequently, back-channelling markers and utterance-initial items such as 'okay', 'alright' and 'yeah' function as signals of uptake of what has been said and thus constitute a form of feedback. They may also however simply serve as an indication that a speaker is taking (or wishes to take) the floor. A decision to translate them may have the consequence of making them more prominent in the exchange than they were intended to be; conversely, ignoring an interjection that was intended as a turn at talk may close down lines of communication between the participants (other than the interpreter). In ways such as these, the gatekeeping role of the interpreter is crucial to the establishment of common ground (Davidson 2002) in three-way communication or in separate dyadic exchanges (e.g. interpreter + patient in language A; interpreter + doctor in language B) that tend to exclude participants from full awareness of what has been or is being said (or transacted or decided).

Face-to-face interaction

The face-to-face situation of DI entails a whole dimension of non-verbal communication that does not feature (or at least is much less prominent) in simultaneous CONFERENCE INTERPRETING. Normally, each participant can establish eye contact with each other participant. In such circumstances, avoidance or withdrawal of eye contact will in itself communicate meaning. Since the pioneering work of Lang (1976, 1978), who showed the importance of gaze for signalling involvement or exclusion, little attention has been paid to this paralinguistic feature of DI encounters – perhaps on account of the difficulty of making video-recordings of such material. The direction of gaze, in addition to its structural role (in attributing or declining turns at talk), is yet another instrument of power and control, especially where it is non-reciprocal. The immigration officer, for example, may seek to look her interviewee in the eye while the latter may (unwittingly) signal powerlessness by directing gaze only towards the interpreter. The doctor may engage the patient with reciprocal eye contact but then redirect gaze towards the interpreter when he or she has something negative to report (the results of tests or a diagnosis, for instance; see Tebble 1999). Other paralinguistic features such as gesture, posture and facial expression are equally important, constituting forms of feedback on interlocutors' responses to each other's talk. Given these multiple – and interacting – features of DI encounters, it follows that such physical details as the arrangement of chairs may also be more important than is sometimes assumed by users of interpreting services. Wadensjö (2001), for example, provides some evidence that the physical positioning of the interpreter in a therapeutic encounter, either within or outside the sight-lines (or 'communicative radius') of the other participants, affects the degree of affinity or involvement – and hence willingness to recall and narrate painful events – experienced by the patient.

The consecutive mode, power and control

One of the consequences of the consecutive mode employed in most instances of dialogue interpreting is that the interpreter's output becomes available for immediate scrutiny by other participants (including overhearers) and comparison with the other-language utterances it is intended to represent. It is, of course, frequently the case that participants know at least a little of each other's languages, allowing them to monitor the interpreter's moves, to interrupt or even to override them. This factor constitutes an inhibiting constraint on the power of the interpreter as the sole bilingual within the exchange. Generally, though, the interpreter does enjoy power within the exchange. Gatekeeping, turn-management and general co-ordination of others' talk are all mechanisms of power and control invested in the interpreter by dint of the consecutive mode of interpreting. But this form of power is to be distinguished from the institutional power invested in the doctor, immigration officer, business executive, chat-show host, etc., through their social/institutional position. They are, in effect, the decision makers, initiating the exchange, steering it, closing it down and, often, deciding outcomes. They may temporarily share this power by treating the interpreter as an institutional insider; on the other hand, their power may come into conflict with the power of the interpreter, on whom they are dependent for effective communication – as in utterances such as 'Try to translate as faithfully as possible' (Baraldi 2006: 238) or 'Would you break off now and just say what he has said?' (Wadensjö 1998: 173). Finally, the distribution of power is affected by who has access to the discourses that are required within particular institutional frameworks and genres. By controlling these, the interpreter can position her- or himself as an authoritative institutional voice and/or can reposition the client who does not have access to the required discourse into a convincing interlocutor for the agent of the institution.

In all of the above, it will be apparent that the dialogue interpreter is likely to experience multiple problems of role conflict and identity (Hale 2005; see also COMMUNITY INTERPRETING). The growing body of research in DI adopts a variety of methodological approaches in order to describe and analyse these and other features of participant behaviour in DI encounters: conversation analysis (e.g. Bolden 2000); pragmatics (e.g. Pérez González 2006a); critical discourse analysis (e.g. Pöllabauer 2004). Increasingly, historical and ethnographic approaches (e.g. Fenton 2001; Cronin 2002; Inghilleri 2003, 2005a) are seeking to make good a long-standing deficit in interpreting research by examining the interpreter's social and cultural role, their agency at the interface between the colonizer and the colonized (see POSTCOLONIAL APPROACHES; MINORITY) or between local, interactional practices (of the kind reviewed here) and socially constituted norms that serve to govern and control behaviour (Inghilleri 2003).

See also:

ASYLUM; COMMUNITY INTERPRETING; CONFERENCE INTERPRETING, HISTORICAL AND COGNITIVE PERSPECTIVES, CONFERENCE INTERPRETING, SOCIOCULTURAL PERSPECTIVES; COURT INTERPRETING; SIGNED LANGUAGE INTERPRETING.

Further reading
Wadensjö 1998; Mason 1999; Straniero Sergio 1999; Davidson 2000, 2002 ; Roy 2000; Inghilleri 2003; Pöllabauer 2004; Inghilleri 2005a.

IAN MASON

Directionality

Directionality in contemporary Western translation studies usually refers to whether translators are working from a foreign language into their mother tongue or vice versa. The practice of different directions in translation/interpreting depends on the context in which the activity is carried out. Attitudes towards directionality also vary in relation to contextual factors, such as market and political conditions.

There is no consensus about the terminology used to refer to directions in translation. In English the unmarked direction of translation is **into the mother tongue** or **language of habitual use**. Traditionally, the 'other' direction was

prose translation (in French ***thème*** as opposed to *version*), but this was associated with the academic exercise of making school children translate into Greek or Latin. Newmark's **service** translation (1988: 52) is not often used. Russian, German and Japanese have no specific terminology for directionality, whereas in Spanish, Italian, Portuguese, Arabic and Chinese translations are **direct** (into the mother tongue) or **inverse** (into the foreign language). This terminology has also been used in English, but the AVANTI research group at Granada University (Kelly *et al.* 2003: 37–40) reject the term 'inverse' translation for its negative connotations and suggest using combinations of A, B and C languages, as defined by AIIC (Professional Conference Interpreters Worldwide) and used in interpreting. The advantage of this proposal is that it can account for a variety of directions and variations in a translator's linguistic competence over the years. For example, in Catalonia, translators work from one language of habitual use into another (Catalan to Spanish/Spanish to Catalan/A→A). Some translators also work from one foreign language into another (C→B/ B→B).

Directionality only began to be studied at the end of the twentieth century when some scholars in countries where A→B translation is common practice questioned the assumption (particularly widespread in English-speaking countries) that B→A translation was the only viable professional option (Kelly 1997; Snell and Crampton 1989; McAlister 1992; Beeby 1996; Campbell 1998; Lorenzo 1999). At first, the debate centred on B→A versus A→B translation, but more recently it has widened to include: the difficulties involved in defining a mother tongue; ethno-linguistic democracy; new models of translation competence; the role of the Internet and technology; the existence of other common directions of translation in an increasingly multilingual, multicultural world with a dominant global language (Grosman *et al.* 2000; Kelly *et al.* 2003; Pokorn 2005; Godijns and Hinderdael 2005; Neunzig and Tanqueiro 2007).

In popular belief, linguistic competence is symmetrical: the general public makes no distinction between B→A and A→B and assumes that a translator will have no difficulty translating in both directions. This belief often extends to employers. On the other hand, translators, interpreters, translation companies, linguists and translation scholars know that translation competence is rarely symmetrical. Today, the most common reaction to this complex issue is to equate quality with native speaker translation. This tendency has its roots in Romanticism, and after Herder (1767) the assumption was that translation away from one's own language was not worth mentioning except to stress the difficulties involved (Kelly 1979: 111). Ladmiral's position is typical: he recognized A→B translation only as a pedagogical exercise to test the B language; from a professional point of view, he considered it an absurd requirement and a hopeless task (1979: 40–50). Most international organizations expect translators to work in the direction B→A. UNESCO's *Recommendations on the legal protection of translators and translations and the practical means to improve the status of translators* (1976) state: 'A translator should, as far as possible, translate into his, or her, mother tongue or into a language of which he or she has a mastery equal to that of his or her mother tongue' (Picken 1989: 245).

This prescriptive position has been reinforced by English-speaking scholars and practitioners enjoying a privileged position with English as the global *lingua franca*, despite the fact that A→B translation is common practice in most countries: 'The convention in the UK is that translation is undertaken into the language of habitual use' (Keith 1989: 164). The Institute of Linguists Diploma in Translation in Britain only tests translation into the language of habitual use. Translation companies advertise native-speaker translators as a proof of quality, even though individual translators are often listed as bilinguals who can translate in both directions. *Language Monthly*'s pioneer survey of European translation agencies (Grindrod 1986) showed that it was usual for translators to translate into one or two languages other than the mother tongue; in fact, some translated into five or six other languages. Britain was an exception to the other European countries covered by the survey, with only 16 per cent of translators offering A→B (65 per cent in Germany). The case of Finland is typical of many countries with lesser-used languages: Betcke's 1987 survey of A→B translation in Finland (McAlister

1992) showed that between 69.7 per cent and 91.7 per cent of the 18 text types translated by agencies were from Finnish and yet 94 per cent of the members of the Finnish Translators and Interpreters Association claimed to be Finnish native speakers.

Historical background

At the beginning of the Christian era, directionality was not an issue in Europe since most translations were into Latin, the language of officialdom, religion and learning. The first Christian translators into Latin were probably Greek, and even for Latin speakers like St Hilary or St Jerome (see LATIN TRADITION), Latin was not their mother tongue (Kelly 1979: 109). It was only with the rise of the nation states, the Reformation and the development of the vernaculars that the idea of the superiority of direct translation appeared in Europe.

In China, in the second century AD, the first translations of the Buddhist sacred texts from Sanskrit to Chinese were by foreign missionaries, of whom An Shih-kao, a Parthian, and Chih-lou chia-ch'an, a Scythian, were the most important (Nienhauser 1986).

In the twelfth and thirteenth centuries, translators of the Toledo School made the learning of the East available to the West by A→B translations of Arabic and Hebrew texts, influenced by Greek, Syriac, Persian and Indian scholars. Most of these translations were done by pairs or teams of translators, which included Muslim or Jewish converts, and the texts were translated first into one of the vernacular languages and then into Latin (Vernet 1978) (see RELAY).

The earliest Humanists translated from the mother tongue as a matter of course. In his criticism of the medieval translations of Aristotle in *De interpretatione recta* (1420), Bruno Aretino insisted that a translator should have mastery of both source and target languages, in this case Greek and Latin, neither of which were the translator's mother tongue (Kelly 1979: 110).

Martin Luther (1483–1546) (see GERMAN TRADITION) was perhaps the first to assume that the best translations were always into the mother tongue (Schwarz 1963: 18), and translation out of the mother tongue began to be regarded only as a pedagogical exercise. However, there were important exceptions in science, religion and literature. Scientific treatises continued to be translated into Latin until the end of the eighteenth century.

In literature, the idea persisted in some quarters that writing in the vernaculars was like writing in sand, whereas writing in Latin or Greek was like working in marble. Because vernacular languages such as English were constantly changing and had a limited number of readers, some works were translated into Latin to reach a wider audience. For example, Milton's *Paradise Lost* was translated into Latin by Thomas Power (1691) in order to reveal Milton to the world as a great poet.

Context and directionality practice

Directionality is influenced by the context in which translation takes place: language combinations, the availability of translators with those language combinations and of subject specialists, genres, deadlines, different kinds of institutional controls and individual translators' expert competence. If the source language and the target language are in close contact (geographical, commercial and cultural proximity) there will be more B→A translators available. This is the case with French and English. French is taught in English schools as English is in French schools, and there are French native speaker translators in the United Kingdom and vice versa. When such proximity between source and target languages does not exist or only exists in one direction (English is taught in Finnish schools but Finnish is not taught in England), it will be harder to find B→A translators. However, the importance of geographical distance has been minimized by the Internet.

Among the most important factors that seem to have affected directionality practices in the twentieth and twenty-first centuries are: globalization and the increasing volume of translations; the Internet; the use of English as an international language and as a language of administration within certain multilingual countries (such as India or South Africa), higher education and business; the struggle for survival of lesser-used and lesser-translated languages;

immigration and the growth of community translation and interpreting (the 2006 American Translation and Interpreting Studies Association conference focused on how Spanish heritage students in the South West posed a threat to the classical definition of directionality).

Market conditions influence directionality. John Wheen (2006: 4), the Chairman of the ATC (Association of Translation Companies), reported among the SWOTs (Strengths, Weaknesses, Opportunities and Threats) identified in their 2005 general conference certain market conditions closely related to directionality: 'Weaknesses: Few British nationals with Far/ Middle East Languages; Internet marketing versus cheap global TSPs [Translation Services Providers]. Opportunities: Universal English; Web trade; Emerging countries import/export. Threats: Low cost overseas TSPs improving quality; Indian and Eastern European cheap English.'

Political conditions also influence directionality. In some countries directionality is determined by norms designed to assure the political allegiance of the translator. In Syria and North Korea, the official translators for Spanish language broadcasts have to be civil servants and, therefore, A→B translators. The broadcasters are Latin American, but they are not allowed to revise the scripts before going on the air. Martin (2003: 428) suggests that attitudes to directionality in interpreting (the Western European B→A model versus the Eastern European A→B model) also have an ideological basis.

Current approaches to understanding directionality

Despite the complexity of translation competence and directionality practices in different countries, the assumption that native speaker equals quality still prevails and a recent guide for clients, *Translations – Getting it Right* (Durban 2003), written for the ITI (Institute of Translation and Interpreting, UK) and endorsed by ATA (American Translators Association, USA) and FIT (International Federation of Translators) advises clients that 'professional translators work into their native language. As a translation buyer you may not be aware of this but a translator who flouts this basic rule is likely to be ignorant of other important quality issues as well.' This issue has been the topic of several heated Internet debates among translators. Those supporting direct translation tended to be English native speakers. In one debate, Chris Durban (2004), the author of the original guide, admitted that:

> There is hardly a single statement about translation or the industry that applies in all situations (e.g. dearth of Japanese to English translators reported here; same seems to apply for Finnish to English …). This problem is compounded by translators making categorically opposing statements/claims (each one usually being valid or partially so … if only they'd tell us precisely which section of the market and which market conditions they are referring to …).

Whereas attitudes amongst translation associations and companies still seem to be mainly prescriptive, there is increasing recognition of the complexity of the issue amongst translation scholars. The different approaches reflect the working contexts of the authors, many of whom are translator trainers. In the 1990s, some of the studies on directionality stressed the 'service' side of A→B translations. In Finland, McAlister (1992: 297) argued that the majority of A→B translations from Finnish to English were texts for international consumption, where the argument that the translator has to have native speaker competence in the target language and culture loses significance. Finnish tourist brochures in English are intended not only for English native speakers but also for Italian, Dutch and Japanese visitors. Translators working out of their native language can translate this kind of text competently, i.e. 'transmit the intended message in a language which is clear and sufficiently correct not to strain the reader's patience unduly' (ibid.). In Spain, Beeby (1996) was concerned with training translators to be aware of their limitations and strengths in A→B translation and to recognize which genres they can translate competently and how to go about preparing themselves for the task. The assumption was that A→B translation should be restricted to standardized, informative genres and interpreting in situations where less than

perfect pronunciation and syntax are acceptable if they do not interfere with the communicative situation. In Australia, Campbell (1998) evaluated the competencies of immigrants translating from their mother tongues into English as a second language. The study, which focused on the development of different aspects of translation competence amongst L2 translators, rather than the translation product as an inferior version of translation into the mother tongue, showed that those competencies were not merely linguistic.

Snell and Crampton (1989: 85) stressed the importance of understanding the source text: 'In specialized fields it might also be found that it was more suitable to use a subject specialist with knowledge of the source language than a mother tongue translator, especially if the text is subsequently to be edited.'

In the first decade of the twenty-first century, scholars are less apologetic about describing other forms of directionality and two international conferences have contributed to this more confident approach (Ljubliana 1997 and Granada 2002). Empirical studies have supplied more information about the relationship between context and directionality and the inadequacy of the terms 'mother tongue' or 'bilingual' to define the linguistic and cultural elements of translation competence. Pokorn's work (2003, 2005) on the reception of Slovene literature translated into English challenges the traditional axioms of the superiority of direct translation. Prunč (2003) provides a theoretical framework based on ethno-linguistic democracy for righting the ideological asymmetries of directionality and argues that there is no such thing as an *a priori* optimal translation because quality criteria vary in different contexts. According to Lorenzo (2003), dogmatic approaches to directionality derive from linguistic concepts of translation competence. Her studies of Danish (A)→Spanish (B) translations suggest that directionality is just one more factor that obliges translators to activate their strategic competence in order to minimize the risks involved in decision making. Expert B→A translators are competent A→B translators, regardless of the genre. She claims that theoretical frameworks are being left behind by the technology that has revolutionized documentation strategies for translators. The sections on teaching A→B translation and interpreting in Kelly *et al.* (2003) provide an introduction to some of the new teaching methods being used to develop strategic and documentation competencies – for example the use of contrastive rhetoric to develop genre literacy (Beeby 2003), information technology and specialized translation (Neunzig 2003) – as well as making the most of multilingual, multicultural and multidirectional teaching situations that are the result of immigration and exchanges within the European Union.

See also:
FOREIGN LANGUAGE TEACHING; RELAY; SELF-TRANSLATION; TRAINING AND EDUCATION.

Further reading
Kelly 1979; Grindrod 1986; Grosman *et al.* 1987; Newmark 1988; McAlister 1992; Beeby 1996; Campbell 1998; Grosman *et al.* 2000; McAlister 2000; Kelly *et al.* 2003; Lorenzo 2003; Martin 2003; Pokorn 2003; Prunč 2003; Godijns and Hinderdael 2005; Pokorn 2005.

ALLISON BEEBY LONSDALE

Discourse analysis

Since it was first used by Zellig Harris in 1952 to refer to the manifestation of formal regularities across sentences in combination, the term 'discourse analysis' has come to mean different things to different people. That what is involved is the study of language beyond the level of the sentence may in fact be the only thing that unites a broad array of otherwise disparate approaches. For example, for some researchers, the term 'discourse' includes all forms of writing and speaking (Gilbert and Mulkay 1984), while for others, it covers only the way talk is 'put together' (Sinclair and Coulthard 1975). Another influential notion of discourse is that proposed by Foucault (1972), who conceives discourse as social structure and discursive practice as social practice. Translation studies has not been less indeterminate in this respect, and translation-oriented models of discourse have been taking shape along varied and diverse lines since the early 1980s.

From an applied linguistics perspective, it has been found useful to distinguish two basic kinds of discourse analysis deriving from two different senses of the term 'discourse' itself (Candlin 1985). The first kind, a text-analytic approach to discourse analysis, covers the way texts are 'put together' in terms of product and form, sequential relationships, intersentential structure and organization and mapping. Subsumed under this purely text-linguistic trend of analysing discourse would be conversational analysis and work done within corpus linguistics. The second basic sense of discourse is that which concerns the way texts 'hang together' in terms of negotiative procedures, interpretation of sequence and structure and the social relationships emanating from interaction. Included within this more pragmatics-oriented trend would be Critical Discourse Analysis (CDA; see LINGUISTIC APPROACHES) and various branches of the study of language in social life, including 'Foucauldian' discourse analysis (see Holstein and Gubrium 2005; Scheurich and McKenzie 2005). In actual practice, however, the two approaches inevitably complement each other, and translational models of discourse have thus been necessarily eclectic. Yet, within this eclecticism, one can still detect a certain tendency to focus on the former, more procedural sense of discourse (see, for example, House and Blum-Kulka 1986; Gambier and Tommola 1993; Snell-Hornby *et al.* 1994; Dollerup and Lindegaard 1994).

Text-analytic approaches to discourse analysis

The more formal kind of discourse analysis has aimed to portray the structure of suprasentential entities or social transactions. This is an explicit or implicit framework-imposition which plays a structure-portraying role. The object is the determination of interactive acts, and the primary concern on the part of the researcher is with sequential relationships, working towards the identification of 'rules' which will capture certain useful generalizations to account for relationships between product and form, emphasizing organization and mapping (Candlin 1985).

This kind of predominantly quantitative discourse analysis has flourished in applied linguistics and is in evidence in such areas of research as conversational analysis and corpus linguistics (see CORPORA). Translation research, particularly into text types and literary genres (Hatim 1997), and interpreting research, particularly into such modes as liaison/community interpreting (Parnell and Villa 1986), have stood to benefit from insights yielded by this textual approach to discourse.

Conversational analysis concerns the study of talk and other forms of conduct (such as posture or facial expression) and ongoing activities in the conversational setting, including turn taking and organization, action formation and sequence organization. Of particular importance to the analysis of COMMUNITY and COURT INTERPRETING, as well as interpreting within the ASYLUM seeking process, has been conversational analytic research into the practices of 'repair'. Repair involves stopping the ongoing course of action to address a trouble/problem (Barsky 2005). Attention has also been paid to word/usage selection, recipient design and the overall structural organization of the occasion of interaction (Wadensjö 1998).

Pragmatics-oriented discourse analysis

In certain quarters of Applied Linguistics, the textual product that is subjected to quantitative analysis has been found lacking as conclusive evidence of discourse practice, a mere static abstraction. According to Widdowson (2000: 7), 'the texts which are collected in a corpus have a reflected reality: they are only real because of the presupposed reality of the discourse of which they are a trace'. Widdowson goes on to argue that studies of CORPORA provide us with the description of text, not discourse: 'Although textual findings may well alert us to possible discourse significance and send us back to their contextual source, such significance cannot be read off from the data' (ibid.: 9). Such misgivings have paved the way for more critical, PRAGMATICS-oriented, approaches to the analysis of discourse.

Discourse, genre, text

Alongside the duality of 'form' and 'procedure' in the various competing definitions of discourse, another useful distinction has been established in translation studies between 'discourse', on the one hand, and 'genre' and 'text', on the other (Hatim and Mason 1990a). At a general level, *text* refers to a sequence of sentences serving an overall rhetorical purpose (e.g. counter-arguing), *genre* refers to the conventional linguistic expression associated with speech and writing in certain contexts of situation (e.g. the letter to the editor), and *discourse* refers to the material out of which interaction is negotiated and themes addressed.

Within this three-way distinction, discourse has been accorded supremacy and is seen as the institutional–attitudinal framework within which both genre and text cease to be mere vehicles of communication and become fully operational carriers of ideological meaning (Hatim and Mason 1997). For example, by employing the rebuttal as a counter-argumentative text strategy, and the 'letter to the editor' as a genre, one could conceivably engage in any of a number of discursive practices, such as expressing racism or camouflaging real intentions. The general argument underlying this understanding of language use has been that, while awareness of the conventions governing the appropriate use of a particular genre or textual practice is essential in translation, it is awareness of what discourse implies that ultimately facilitates optimal transfer and renders the much sought-after translation EQUIVALENCE an attainable objective.

Cross-cultural communication: worldview and perspective

Within and across cultural and linguistic boundaries, different cultural assumptions and different ways of linguistically acting on these assumptions underlie people's capacity to communicate with each other in order to achieve both personal and global objectives (Tannen 1984). Translation and interpreting studies have benefited considerably from the application of discourse analysis to the study of cross-cultural communication beyond traditional translation/interpreting settings (Barsky 1993; Shakir and Farghal 1997). For example, in one particular study of the kind of discourse in which two parties converse with one another via a non-professional interpreter/ mediator, it has been found that different types of mediating roles emerge in the process and that the mediator's perception of his or her role determines the criteria for what constitutes an adequate interpretation (Knapp-Potthoff and Knapp 1987). As Knapp-Potthoff and Knapp point out, in situations like these, the interaction tends to drift into two parallel discourses, and the major difficulty of the mediator's task consists in managing both while trying to relate them to one another.

Within cross-cultural communication studies, 'discourses' are sometimes understood as 'the many different ways of speaking that are associated with different social contexts' (Lee 1992: 51). Adopting such a view, a number of translation scholars have attempted to tackle the issue of sociocultural practices, their role in discourse production and the wider implications they have for the work of the translator and interpreter (see, for example, Baker 2006a).

One of the more interesting hypotheses underlying work in this area has been that, while all literate language communities possess a number of modes of text development (e.g. an aural or a visual mode), a particular preference for some of these and not for others is usually observed. Such preferences reflect different world views and are motivated by a variety of sociolinguistic factors, including shared experience, receiver expectations and feedback, power, solidarity, politeness and so on. For example, the aural mode, which is drawn upon heavily in a language such as Arabic, is normally not acceptable for written prose in English. In translation, the failure to switch modes results in negative transfer and breakdown of interaction (Sa'adeddin 1989).

Extending the scope of cross-cultural studies to include what may be termed ideological perspectives (Fowler 1991; Kress 1985), discourse analysis has in recent years been particularly active in tackling not only political discourse (Fairclough 1989) but also other modes of communication, including academic and industrial encounters (Kress and Fowler

1979). The general thrust of the argument in this kind of perspective-analysis relates to the tendency in given discourses to suppress unpalatable semantic features and give more prominence to other, more favourable shades of meaning.

An example of this kind of discourse analysis in translation is provided by Crick (2002) in her assessment of the translation of Freud into English, which exhibits a number of distinctive features. First, there is a tendency to replace a humanistic perspective (i.e. way of thinking and writing) by a clinical, quasi-medical, Greco-Latin terminology (for example, *Ich* becomes *Ego,* and so on). Second, there is a tendency towards de-personalization, by changing actives into passives, for instance. Finally, the variety of registers and mobility of tones apparent in the source text are consistently replaced by a uniform medical/scientific style. It may be instructive here to recall the words of A. Strachey, one of the translators of Freud (and one of the culprits, according to Crick): 'The imaginary model I have kept before me is of the writings of some Englishman of science of wide education born in the middle of the nineteenth century' (Strachey, in Crick 2002:1057).

In this domain of discourse, translation scholars have thus focused on the constraints placed on the translation process by the sociocultural content of communication. The ideological and cultural background initiated in the text by the author and read off by both reader and translator governs the way in which the overall meaning potential is realized at both ends of the communicative channel. Furthermore, the way in which a reader constructs a representation of the text and relates this to the real world seems to be of crucial importance in dealing with discoursal meanings (Campbell 1993).

The metaphorical process exploited

The metaphorical process has perhaps been one of the more significant markers of worldview and ideological perspective in the kind of discourse analysis under discussion. This may be illustrated from areas of language use as varied as ADVERTISING and persuasion, on the one hand, and POETRY, on the other. One basic fact about figurative expression may be underlined as being particularly relevant to the task of translating; this relates to what in discourse circles has recently become known as the **intimacy theory**: metaphors do not operate singly, they form a 'network', as it were. Thematic/poetic links are established not only within the same stretch of language (say, a paragraph or a single oral encounter) but also within much wider spans, as in the case of a short story or novel (Abu Libdeh 1991). This has not only enabled translators to see metaphoric expression in a new light, but it has also encouraged translation theory to support a 'beyond-mere-embellishment' view of figurative expressions. In poetry, for example, aspects of the message such as sound symbolism, rhyme, metre, alliteration and so forth are no longer seen as divorced from semantic content, but as part and parcel of the text's overall import and effect (Campbell 1993).

The utilization of metaphor in relaying point of view, expressing perspective and generally propounding a particular brand of IDEOLOGY may be illustrated from an interesting domain of discourse at work, namely Nuclear Discourse. The nuclear industry has always been concerned with people's negative reaction, and to counter this, what came to be known as nukespeak developed (Chilton 1985). Nukespeak is the language used to refer to nuclear weapons in a rather deceptive way, with the intention to mask what such weapons really are. Examples include *Vanguard*, *Polaris*, *cruise*, and even *Strike*: the latter may simply suggest a slap with the hand rather than incinerating thousands of people. Translators and interpreters are constantly called upon to deal with the kind of material that primarily serves opaque discoursal purposes such as nukespeak.

Another domain that has attracted the attention of both discourse analysts and translation theorists is sexist discourse. A number of principles underpinning sexist expression of attitude have been identified, and awareness of these rules, which regulate the PRAGMATICS of communication, have been seen as indispensable tools for the translator (see GENDER AND SEXUALITY).

Courtroom interaction

Courtroom interaction has been another fertile area for discourse analysis that has yielded more immediately accessible insights in translation studies, particularly into the process of interpreting. The central hypothesis entertained by this kind of research claims that, due to different modes of class- and sex-socialization, some defendants will be more able to cope with the power differentials at court than others; for example, middle-class defendants are likely to know the role expectations better than working-class defendants. The questions addressed by studies within this brand of discourse analysis thus include the following: Are those who are unfamiliar with the system discriminated against? Does the defendants' linguistic behaviour contribute to the outcome of the hearing? Would the interpreter make it a priority on his or her list to preserve the overall coherence of an incoherent defence? Perhaps more to the point, would the interpreter train him/herself to resist the temptation of stepping in to help an incoherent defendant? These are some of the problems with which practitioners are concerned and which have attracted the attention of the translation theorist (Berk-Seligson 1988, 1990; Morris 1995; Barsky 1996; Hale 1997; see also: ASYLUM; COURT INTERPRETING; ETHICS).

Competing discourses

A particularly interesting phenomenon, and one with which translators often have to wrestle, is that of discourse within discourse, or the notion of competing discourses. This is when a given discourse borrows from or effectively 'hijacks' another discourse (Bakhtin 1981), relaying in the process all kinds of marked meanings that the translator has to preserve by mastering: (a) the pre-discourse norms of linguistic usage; (b) the unmarked discourse to be departed from; and (c) the discourse being borrowed for a rhetorical purpose.

An example can be seen in Sykes (1985), who focuses on the expression 'immigrants and their offspring', which Enoch Powell, a British politician known at the time the speech was given for his contentious views on race relations, was fond of using in preference to, say, 'immigrants and their children'. Within the analytic trend covering this type of discourse, elements such as 'offspring' are analysed both textually and intertextually. The textual analysis would involve assessing the choice of given linguistic elements in both syntagmatic and paradigmatic terms, that is in terms of what is included, and how, and what is excluded and why. As Sykes (ibid.) points out, Powell's lexicon for family relationships is a limited one. These are the terms relevant to immigrants and their children, together with their frequency of use in the speech analysed: immigrants and their offspring (2); the offspring of immigrants (1); immigrant offspring (1); immigrant and immigrant descended population (2). In this particular domain of family relationships, terms which could have been used but were excluded are, among others: 'husbands', 'wives', 'mothers', 'fathers', 'parents', 'sons', 'daughters', 'families'. The rule governing inclusion and exclusion of terms is most relevant to the translator who has to operate within similar constraints and pay special attention to the overall effect of this kind of restricted texture.

Linguistic forms such as those from Powell's speech are intertextually seen by translators in terms of (a) a pre-discoursal linguistic norm in which synonymy could be said to exist (e.g. offspring = children); (b) an unmarked, register-based discourse (offspring = +legal); and (c) a marked, imported discourse which involves the hijacking of the normal discourse of (b), because Powell is not a lawyer but a politician. The competition of the various discourses can ultimately be reconciled by arriving at a reading which, while institutionally sound (the text producer could not be taken to court for libel), is intertextually pernicious: in the particular context under study, Powell's remarks are dehumanizing and reminiscent of statements often heard within racist discourse such as 'they breed like rabbits'. Translators work with this intricate network of relationships, each of which would constitute the limits of discoursal expression which has to be reached before real intentions are properly relayed.

Further reading

Chilton 1985; Sa'adeddin 1989; Hatim and Mason 1990; Barsky 1993; Campbell 1993;

Hatim and Mason 1997; Wadensjö 1998; Barsky 2005.

BASIL HATIM

Drama translation

Unlike the translation of a novel, or a poem, the duality inherent in the art of the theatre requires language to combine with spectacle, manifested through visual as well as acoustic images. The translator is therefore faced with the choice of either viewing drama as literature or as an integral part of a theatrical production (van den Broeck 1988: 55–6). Translators may approach the play as a literary work when, for instance, the translation of the complete works of a particular playwright is undertaken, as in the case of James McFarlane's translation of Ibsen's collected works. When performed on stage, however, the words spoken constitute only one element of a theatrical production, along with lighting, sets, costumes and music. Here, because it forms part of an integrated whole, greater demands are also placed on the translation with respect to its 'performability', thus increasing the tension between the need to relate the target text to its source (the adequacy factor), and the need to formulate a text in the target language (the acceptability factor) (Toury 1980a: 29; see NORMS).

Dialect, style and register

Satisfying the linguistic requirements of performability may entail adjustments at a number of different levels. If, for instance, a play was originally written in dialect, the translator will have to make a decision as to whether there is a suitable dialect in the TL into which it may be translated. Successful attempts to overcome this problem include Bill Findlay's translation of *The Weavers* by Gerhart Hauptmann, the 1912 recipient of the Nobel Prize for Literature. Findlay skilfully replaces the Silesian dialect of the striking loom workers by Scots and allows the numerous linguistic options made use of by Hauptmann in German to find their match in urban versus rural, regional versus standard, historic versus contemporary linguistic varieties. The availability of a particular dialect in the TL may also provide a welcome opportunity for successful transfer of sociolects in the SL text, which are normally difficult to capture in translation. This appears to be the case in Quebec, where québécois, marked by a proletarization of language, has made it possible to find natural equivalents for some Anglo-American sociolects of writers such as Tennessee Williams, Edward Albee and Eugene O'Neill (Brisset 1989).

Other adjustments which may need to be undertaken concern slang and terms of endearment or of abuse, which may provide an inappropriate audience response when rendered too literally in another language. Although taboo words are likely to be universal, the time and place of their use may vary from language to language. Topical allusions also require careful treatment. While replacements may be found in the TL, they may be out of character for the whole work itself, its setting, period or tone. Further difficulties arise if the play is in verse or, as in the case of a play like T. S. Eliot's *Murder in the Cathedral*, in a variety of verse and prose forms.

Socio-cultural differences

Customs and attitudes also differ markedly from one culture to another. Hamlet's dilemma, for instance, would obviously be incomprehensible to an island race whose culture makes it obligatory for a widow to marry her dead husband's brother (Gostand 1980: 3). The use of irony, to take another example, although commonly found in parts of the English-speaking world, is nevertheless not a universal phenomenon. In Eugene O'Neill's *Long Day's Journey into Night*, the colloquy between Edmund and his father, with its thrust and parry, is merely a game to hide the real emotional feelings between father and son; but this might mistakenly cause consternation in a culture where any ambiguity of familial relationships is foreign to an audience accustomed to clear and well defined roles in the family, as in the case of China (Ooi 1980).

Even in the case of more closely related European cultures, there is still the risk of concepts being either misinterpreted or not fully comprehended. A production of O'Casey's *Juno and the Paycock* in Germany grappled for a long time with the problem of conveying the idea of tenement houses: these belong to the slum district of Dublin and stand as a symbol of social degradation. Although an audience may be provided with an explanation in the programme note, the specific environment which constitutes the background of the message and which, as a microcosm, represents the macrocosm of Ireland, or even the world, cannot be maintained (Venneberg 1980: 127). In other cases, cultural norms or habits may be known but felt to be conjuring up the wrong associations. When Pinter's *The Caretaker* was staged in translation in France, a French critic reacted negatively to Davies, the tramp, drinking tea. He would have preferred him to be drinking wine since in France 'tea is a drink taken mainly by genteel old ladies' (Kershaw 1966: 61).

Problems such as these show the need for adjustments to be made before a play can be successfully performed in translation. Being present at the scene of the action, as immediate witness, is part of the experience of the audience in a performance situation and creates the impression of participation in the same system of communication. The audience thus occupies a different position from the reader of a book who can decide where to stop and reflect, and even consult relevant works of reference if further clarification is required. The extent to which adjustments need to be made in order to enhance rapid understanding, however, tends to depend on the literary norms prevailing in a given language community at a particular time.

Adaptations and versions

Translation is not a phenomenon whose parameters are fixed once and for all, as is shown by Heylen's (1993) discussion of different translations of *Hamlet* into French through the ages. The acceptability constraints to which translations of SHAKESPEARE have been subjected are also illustrated by Voltaire's French version of *Julius Caesar* (cf. Lefevere 1983a: 20–21; van den Broeck 1988: 61). Under the influence of neoclassical rules with respect to the unities of action, time, and place, Voltaire chose to omit two and a half acts: the rules dictated that the events related to Brutus and the remaining conspirators could not be included, and the play had to end with Caesar's death.

Because of the position of English as a global language, literature in translation inevitably takes up a less central position in the English-speaking world than it does in the literature of nations where less frequently used languages are spoken. Translation from English into such languages is likely to be closer to the original, as familiarity with English social and cultural customs can often be assumed on the part of such theatre audiences. Hence, a play such as *Educating Rita* by the British playwright Willy Russell, which tells the story of a Liverpool hairdresser who enrols at the Open University to study English literature, may at first seem riddled with problems for the translator, as books are discussed throughout the play which may not even be available in other languages. The play was, however, successfully translated into a large number of different languages, with titles of books, in some cases, simply retained in English.

Plays originating in less frequently used languages and performed in translation in English-speaking countries, on the other hand, often require a greater degree of adjustment because of English audiences' lack of familiarity with SL cultures and societies. Not infrequently, leading British playwrights are commissioned to perform this task, producing what is known as a new **version**. Recent examples of this type of ADAPTATION include *Pillars of the Community*, Sam Adamson's version of Ibsen's play, better known as *Pillars of Society,* for the National Theatre in the autumn of 2005 and Christopher Hampton's dramatization of Sándor Márai's Hungarian novel staged in London in the spring of 2006, titled *Embers*.

Another successful ADAPTATION for the National Theatre was Tom Stoppard's reworking of Johann Nestroy's nineteenth-century Viennese comedy *Einen Jux will er sich machen*. Crucial to Nestroy in the original is the language, in particular the remarkable games he plays with the Viennese dialect. *On the Razzle*, Stoppard's rewrite version (1982), makes no use of dialect, nor does it incorporate comic songs of the type Nestroy liked to interpose between scene changes. For comic effect, it relies solely on

Stoppard's own wit, on newly coined puns and other inventive word games.

In the translation of humour, a particularly difficult problem is presented by malapropisms, so called after Sheridan's Mrs Malaprop, inclined to making fatal mistakes in the form of 'unedu-cated blends' such as referring to 'epitaphs' instead of 'epithets'. Here the challenge to the translator is formidable. There appear for example to be few if any successful renderings of the malapropisms used by Gina in *The Wild Duck,* with the concomitant loss of the comic effect created in Norwegian. As a result, while Ibsen described his play as a tragi-comedy, in English translation it emerges as little more than a tragedy.

Adaptations which take the form of 'creative rewrites' (Billington 1984) are most likely to be successful in the case of more robust comedies, less so with plays concerned with social criticism, and least of all with psychological drama. This is acknowledged by Stoppard who, prior to his Nestroy adaptation, turned Arthur Schnitzler's *Das Weite Land* into *Undiscovered Country*, also for the National Theatre.

> In the case of *Undiscovered Country*, the Ibsenesque undercurrents of the play made it important to establish as precisely as possible what every phrase meant, root out the allusions, find the niceties of etiquette, and so on, and generally to aim for equivalence.
>
> (Stoppard 1981: 8)

The fate of other, less successful productions of plays adapted in translation confirms the need for attention to detail and faithfulness to the original in the case of psychological drama. Reid (1980) reports on a less than successful production of Anouilh's *Antigone* as the result of some minor, well-intentioned alterations undertaken by the translator. Feeling that this translation needed elaboration, the translator added a couple of glosses and deleted a few lines. In a second translation of the play, however, no such alterations were made. The dramatic effect of the unadapted translation turned out to be markedly different. Whereas reviewers of the London production based faithfully on the source text were in no doubt as to Anouilh's central themes, American and New Zealand reviewers expressed serious misconceptions about the true nature of the tragedy which the adapted text engendered (Reid 1980).

The inherent danger in an approach to translation that favours a great degree of adaptation is that it may shift the focus away from the source-language-bound aspects of a playwright's work. In the case of Chekhov, Anglicization has, according to Bassnett (1998: 94), reached the point where English translations have established a traditional way of reading his works that has resulted in a major shift of meaning and an alteration of the ideological basis of Chekhov's thinking: 'What we have, therefore, is not a Russian but an English Chekhov, and it is this playwright, invented through the translation process, whose work has entered the English literary system.'

Being true to the original playwright while at the same time allowing the target audience full enjoyment of a dramatic work may in fact be the most difficult problem facing the translator of drama for the stage (Zatlin 2005). Although not always easy, in the case of living authors the ideal situation often entails collaboration between writer, translator and director.

The observation that translators from different cultures and different time periods will render a play differently in translation (Heylen 1993) also shows that a framework is beginning to emerge for historical-relative and socio-cultural models of translation. The links between stage translation and cultural context have been the subject of attention in Aaltonen's (2000) *Time-Sharing on Stage: Drama Translation in Theatre and Society*. More recently, Anderman (2005) in *Europe on Stage: Translation and Theatre* dealt with the subject of the reception in English translation of the major modern playwrights. Cross-cultural reception has also been a major theme in Taviano's discussion in *Staging Dario Fo and Franca Rame* (2006).

See also:
ADAPTATION; CENSORSHIP; CLASSICAL TEXTS; LITERARY TRANSLATION; REWRITING; SHAKE-SPEARE.

Further reading
Bassnett 1980; Zuber 1980; Bolt *et al.* 1989; Scolnicov and Holland 1989; Bassnett 1991; Heylen 1993; Brisset 1996; Johnston 1996; Bassnett 1998; Findlay 1998; Aaltonen 2000; Upton 2000; Findlay 2004; Anderman 2005; Zatlin 2005; Taviano 2006.

GUNILLA ANDERMAN

E

Equivalence

Equivalence is a central concept in translation theory, but it is also a controversial one. Approaches to the question of equivalence can differ radically: some theorists define translation in terms of equivalence relations (Catford 1965; Nida and Taber 1969; Toury 1980a; Pym 1992a, 1995a, 2004; Koller 1995) while others reject the theoretical notion of equivalence, claiming it is either irrelevant (Snell-Hornby 1988) or damaging (Gentzler 1993/2001) to translation studies. Yet other theorists steer a middle course: Baker uses the notion of equivalence 'for the sake of convenience – because most translators are used to it rather than because it has any theoretical status' (1992: 5–6). Thus equivalence is variously regarded as a necessary condition for translation, an obstacle to progress in translation studies, or a useful category for describing translations. Given that the concept has been particularly associated with linguistic theories of translation – which were heavily critiqued in the 1980s and 1990s (see Pym 1995a; Kenny 2001) – and, sometimes unfairly, with the idea that translations could somehow convey the 'same', necessarily stable and language-independent meaning as their source texts (as argued, for example, by Rabin 1958), it is not surprising that equivalence has been in and out of fashion in translation studies (Pym 1992a). Yet LINGUISTIC APPROACHES to translation have proved tenacious (Malmkjær 2005), and it is difficult to find any contemporary theorists who subscribe to the 'same meaning' approach to translation (Baker 2004). Under the influence of post-structuralism and the analytical philosophy of Quine (1960) and Davidson (1973/1984) in particular, meaning is now more likely to be construed as fleeting and inherently unstable, highly subjective and context-bound, and thus not amenable to replication, whether in the same or another language (Malmkjær 2005:15). Thus, when contemporary theorists posit relationships of equivalence between texts, they do so without appeal to language-neutral, objective meanings, and they acknowledge the role of translating subjects, translators, in creating and maintaining these relationships (Pym 1992a, 2004; Teubert 2002; Eco 2003).

As already indicated, proponents of equivalence-based theories of translation now define equivalence as a relationship between two texts: a source text (ST) and a target text (TT). Equivalence relationships are also said to hold between parts of STs and TTs. In many cases, it is this relationship that allows the TT to be considered a translation of the ST in the first place. This definition of equivalence is not unproblematic, however. Pym (1992a: 37), for one, has pointed to its circularity: equivalence is supposed to define translation, and translation, in turn, defines equivalence. Unfortunately, few attempts have been made to define equivalence in translation in a way that avoids this circularity. Earlier theorists interested in equivalence concentrated, for the most part, on developing typologies of equivalence, focusing on the rank (word, sentence or text level) at which equivalence is said to obtain (see, for example, Baker 1992) or on the type of meaning (denotative, connotative, pragmatic, etc.) that is prioritized in particular instances of translation. Investigations of the essential nature of equivalence remain the exception.

Typologies of equivalence

At various levels, and loosely following Koller (1979: 187–91, 1989: 100–4), equivalence is commonly established on the basis that the

ST and TT words supposedly refer to the same thing in the real world, i.e. on the basis of their *referential* or *denotative equivalence*; the ST and TT words triggering the same or similar associations in the minds of native speakers of the two languages, i.e. their *connotative equivalence*; the ST and TT words being used in the same or similar contexts in their respective languages, i.e. what Koller (1989: 102) calls *text-normative equivalence*; the ST and TT words having the same effect on their respective readers, i.e. *pragmatic* (Koller 1989: 102) or *dynamic equivalence* (Nida 1964); the ST and TT words having similar orthographic or phonological features, or *formal equivalence*. Baker (1992) extends the concept of equivalence to cover similarity in ST and TT information flow and in the cohesive roles ST and TT devices play in their respective texts. She calls these two factors combined *textual equivalence*. Newman (1994: 4695) stresses that not all the variables in translation are relevant in every situation, and that translators must decide which considerations should be given priority at any one time, thus establishing a kind of *functional equivalence* (see also Neubert 1994).

Kade (1968) and other writers on lexical equivalence, in particular in the area of terminology (see, for example, Arntz 1993; Hann 1992a and b), combine the above qualitative distinctions with a quantitative scheme that categorizes equivalence relationships according to whether there is: a single expression in the TL for a single SL expression, i.e. *one-to-one equivalence*; more than one TL expression for a single SL expression, i.e. *one-to-many equivalence*; a TL expression that covers part of a concept designated by a single SL expression, i.e. *one-to-part-of-one equivalence*; or no TL expression for an SL expression, i.e. *nil equivalence*. This quantitative, lexical approach reflects an earlier concern with language systems (see below) and has been criticized precisely because it is restricted to the word level and also because it assumes that the language system can be equated with concrete realization in text (Snell-Hornby 1988: 20).

The nature of equivalence

Writers who have addressed the problem of the nature of equivalence include Catford (1965, 1994) and Pym (1992a). Catford posits an extra-linguistic domain of objects, persons, emotions, memories, history, etc. (**situation** in Firthian/Hallidayan terms), features of which may or must achieve expression in a given language. Translational equivalence occurs, he suggests, when STs and TTs are relatable to at least some of the same features of this extra-linguistic reality, that is when STs and TTs have approximately the same referents (1965: 50, 1994: 4739). Catford thus prioritizes referential meaning here, although his holistic view of situation in theory allows for other priorities to be established. Bassnett (1980/1991: 6), amongst others, has found this focus too narrow, and Frawley (1984) is sceptical of any approach to translation that appeals to identity of extra-linguistic referents: 'The worlds and possible worlds differ, and the question of referent is not even the question to pose' (ibid.: 164). Catford also comes under criticism (see Snell-Hornby 1988: 20) for using simplistic, invented sentences to exemplify his categories of translational equivalence, and for limiting his analysis to the level of the sentence. Catford's approach may have been criticized, but few alternatives have been put forward. The problem of pinning down the essential nature of equivalence seems to be related to the problem of pinning down the nature of linguistic meaning itself. Pym (1992a) avoids this difficulty by moving away from the strictly linguistic to viewing translation as a transaction, and equivalence as equality of exchange value. Equivalence becomes a negotiable entity, with translators doing the negotiation. The idea of translation as negotiation is developed by Eco (2003). Even in cases where a translation priority has already been established – for example, a translator may have decided to attempt to recreate in the translation the same effect as was intended in the original (dynamic equivalence) – many outcomes are possible; in this case there are many possible hypotheses as to the intention of the original text/author, and it is the translator who ultimately negotiates a solution (ibid.: 56).

Interlingual and intertextual equivalence

In earlier work on equivalence, theorists made a distinction between hypothetical mappings between elements of abstract language systems (at the level of *langue*) on the one hand, and actual observable mappings between elements of real STs and TTs (at the level of *parole*) on the other. Catford used the terms *formal correspondence* and *textual equivalence* respectively to refer to the two categories. Koller (1979: 183–4) made a similar distinction when he differentiated between *Korrespondenz*, formal similarity between language systems, and *Äquivalenz*, equivalence relations between real texts and utterances. Koller then went on to present *Äquivalenz* as the real object of enquiry in translation studies. Similarly, Toury (1980a: 24–6) charts the evolution of the notion of TRANSLATABILITY from an interlingual phenomenon to an intertextual one. Thus the general view in translation studies soon came to be that equivalence was a relationship between texts in two different languages, rather than between the languages themselves. This step liberated translation studies from debates on interlingual TRANSLATABILITY based on entire language systems with all their unactualized meaning potential (see Koller 1979; Pym 1995a: 157–8). Such debates had centred on incompatibilities between the worlds inhabited by speakers of different languages and on the structural dissimilarities between languages. Once attention was focused on texts and utterances, many of the potential multiple meanings and functions of words and structures in a language system could be eliminated by reference to their co-text and context, making translation not only more tractable, but also more realistic.

It is worth noting that the shift of focus from language system to text is one that has also occurred in related disciplines, for example, contrastive linguistics (see Altenberg and Granger 2002) and MACHINE TRANSLATION (Hutchins 2005a), and that has been facilitated in these disciplines by the availability of large parallel CORPORA.

Equivalence as an empirical and a theoretical concept

The narrowing down of the scope of the term equivalence to an intertextual relation still left plenty of room for competing notions of the concept. Toury (1980a: 39) identified two main uses of the term: first, equivalence could be 'a *descriptive* term, denoting concrete objects – actual relationships between actual utterances in two languages (and literatures), recognized as TTs and STs – which are subject to direct observation'. This definition regarded equivalence as an empirical category which could be established only after the event of translation. Toury contrasted this approach with equivalence as 'a *theoretical* term, denoting an abstract, ideal relationship, or category of relationships between TTs and STs, translations and their sources' (ibid.).

This dichotomy can be problematic, however: equivalence as a theoretical term, a prospective and often prescriptive notion, is responsible for acquiring a bad name for equivalence in some quarters in translation studies. Gentzler (1993: 4), for example, contends that standards of translation analysis that rely on equivalence or non-equivalence and other associated judgemental criteria 'imply notions of substantialism that limit other possibilities of translation practice, marginalize unorthodox translation, and impinge upon real intercultural exchange'. Newman (1994: 4694), on the other hand, describes translation equivalence as 'a commonsense term for describing the ideal relationship that a reader would expect to exist between an original and its translation'. Newman's equivalence is clearly prospective and ideal, although empirical approaches also feature in the analysis. Pym also speaks about equivalence as a 'fact of reception' (1992a: 64) and about the socially determined 'expectation' that TTs should stand in some kind of equivalence relation to their STs (1995a: 166).

Toury's empirical category of equivalence has much in common with Catford's textual equivalence. A textual equivalent is defined as 'any TL form which is observed to be the equivalent of a given SL form (text or portion of text)' (Catford 1965: 27). Equivalent forms can be matched by appealing to the intuition of bilingual informants or by applying more formal procedures such as commutation (ibid.: 27–8), a method of discovering textual equivalents which consists of asking a competent bilingual informant to translate stretches of text and then systematically introducing changes into the SL text to establish how each change is reflected in the translation. Textual equivalence, according to Catford, is an empirical, probabilistic phenomenon. The probability that a given ST form will be translated as a given TT form can be calculated on the basis of previous experience and recast as a probabilistic translation rule (ibid.: 31). Snell-Hornby (1988: 20) finds the same weakness with this view of equivalence as does Pym (1992a: 37): it is circular; translation equivalence is what is observed to be equivalent; but Catford's general approach has found application in areas such as example and statistics-based machine translation (see Hutchins 2005) and bilingual TERMINOLOGY extraction (Kraif 2003), and textual equivalence is the basis of much contemporary work in contrastive linguistics and natural language processing, where further distinctions are often made between commonly observed mappings between parts of STs and TTs, and less common, more idiosyncratic or unpredictable mappings (see, for example, Kraif 2003; Salkie 2002).

Toury's equivalence postulate

Equivalence as an empirical phenomenon in translation studies has seen perhaps its most powerful manifestation to date in Toury's (1980a, 1995) work. Whereas other theorists might ask whether two texts are equivalent according to some pre-defined, prescriptive criterion of equivalence, Toury treats the existence of equivalence between TTs and STs as a given. This equivalence postulate (1980a: 113) then allows him to state that 'the question to be asked in the actual study of translations (especially in the comparative analysis of ST and TT) is not *whether* the two texts are equivalent (from a certain aspect), but *what type* and *degree* of translation equivalence they reveal' (1980: 47). Toury's approach, and subsequently Koller's (1995: 196), makes appeal to a historical, relative notion of equivalence: 'Rather than being a single relationship, denoting a recurring type of invariant, it comes to refer to any relation which is found to have characterized translation under a specified set of circumstances' (Toury 1995: 61). The NORMS that determine the particular concept of equivalence prevalent at different stages in history, or amongst different schools of translators, or even within the work of a single translator, then constitute a valid object of enquiry for DESCRIPTIVE translation studies.

Toury's equivalence postulate, as well as his broad definition of a translation as whatever is regarded as a translation in the target culture (1980, 1995), allow him to broaden the scope of translation studies to investigate previously marginalized phenomena. Thus equivalence-based translation theories can escape the censure of other schools of thought, where it is widely held that equivalence implies a prescriptive, non-inclusive approach to translation. There are, however, objections to what is viewed as too wide a notion of equivalence: Snell-Hornby (1988: 21) suggests that the notion of equivalence in the English-speaking world has become so vague as to be useless, while Pym (1992a, 1995a), Neubert (1994) and Koller (1995) would like to see a more restrictive view of equivalence reinstated, not least because a more constrained view of equivalence allows translation to be distinguished from non-translation. Pym (2004: 56) quotes Stecconi (1994/1999: 171) to support this point: 'in most western cultures today, equivalence is that unique intertextual relation that only translations, among all conceivable text types, are expected to show'.

See also:
DECONSTRUCTION; FUNCTIONALIST APPROACHES; LINGUISTIC APPROACHES; QUALITY; SEMIOTICS; SHIFTS; STRATEGIES; TRANSLATABILITY; UNIT OF TRANSLATION.

Further reading
Catford 1965; Toury 1980a; Snell-Hornby 1988; Koller 1989, 1995; Pym 1995a; Toury 1995; Baker 2004; Pym 2004.

DOROTHY KENNY

Ethics

Ethical practice has always been an important issue for translators and interpreters, though historically the focus of concern has been the question of fidelity to the spoken or written text. In a special issue of *The Translator* published in 2001, Pym declared that translation studies had 'returned to questions of ethics' (Pym 2001a: 129). He linked this resurgent interest to a widening of the parameters of translation to include the translator's agency and to a move within the discipline away from the dominance of the descriptivist paradigm towards globalizing trends that demand increased attention to processes of cross-cultural communication (see GLOBALIZATION; DESCRIPTIVE VS. COMMITTED APPROACHES). In the same volume, Chesterman identified four overlapping theoretical models of, or orientations to, ethical practice: representation, service, communication and NORMS. He also highlighted the importance of such models to professional codes of ethics which guided best practice across a range of contexts (Chesterman 2001). In 2004, a volume dedicated to the theme of translation and ethics appeared as a special issue of *Traduction, Terminologie, Rédaction* (Fiola 2004), in which many of the discussions initiated in Pym's volume were developed further. And 2005 saw the publication of *Nation, Language and the Ethics of Translation* (Bermann and Wood 2005), a collection of essays, several of which had translation ethics as their primary theoretical focus.

Pym's declaration in 2001 coincided with the beginning of a post-9/11 era of global politics, thus sparking an even greater awareness amongst translators, interpreters and translation scholars of the significance of ethics. The new era threw the issue of conflicting beliefs and values amongst the producers and receivers of spoken and written texts, and their relationship to social, economic and political power, into sharp relief. Drawing on insights from a range of disciplinary bases, including philosophy, sociology, anthropology, literary theory, narratology and legal studies, scholars of translation have increasingly identified questions of ethical responsibility, social activism and personal integrity as urgent issues that must be considered central to academic and non-academic pursuits within the field. Despite a growing commitment amongst groups of translation scholars and practitioners to address such questions, however, we have not by any means reached a clear understanding of or agreement about what an 'ethical' approach actually means in the context of translation theory or practice, or the construction of the field itself.

One of the earliest attempts to elaborate an ethics of translation was Antoine Berman's *L'épreuve de l'étranger: Culture et traduction dans l'Allemagne romantique* (1984), which appeared in English translation in 1992. Berman developed a critique of the kind of literary translations that operated on the source text through ethnocentric, annexationist or hypertextual methods, deforming the text and sacrificing its poetics. He viewed such acts as inevitable submissions on the part of the translator to unconscious forces that caused translation to deviate from its essential aim – that of allowing readers to receive the translated source text as foreign, the Other as Other. Berman offered a psychoanalytic/textual method through which translators and translations could be freed from the deforming tendencies that worked against a more open confrontation between source and target language, a method that both embraced the notion of an 'original' meaning and sought to restore the original meaning of the source text to its translation (cf. DECONSTRUCTION).

Venuti has worked with these ideas too, for example, in his distinction between domesticating and foreignizing (later minoritizing) translations (see STRATEGIES) and in his focus on the translator's invisibility (Venuti 1986, 1995a, 1998b). Like Berman, and Schleiermacher before him, Venuti advocates translation techniques which challenge strategies of fluency and fidelity, arguing for approaches to translation that highlight the differences between source and target language and culture. Unlike Berman, however, and drawing on DECONSTRUCTION, Venuti supports an approach to translation which allows the translator greater freedom to play with meanings in the original, in the process challenging the very notion of an original text. His ethical approach calls for specific political and stylistic practices in translation. In this sense, he challenges the descriptivist tendency to refrain from an evaluation of translations as good or bad, correct or incorrect (see QUALITY). Venuti has been careful, however, to underscore the contingent nature of his approach to an ethics of translation, describing it as an 'ideal' grounded in specific cultural, historical and intellectual environments (Venuti 1998b: 6). Venuti's passage from ethics to politics has not been without its critics (cf. Pym 1996a; Tymoczko 2000a; Koskinen 2000a). Problems have been identified with Venuti's concepts *qua* concepts, with the elitist strand in his thinking, and its exclusively literary and overly prescriptivist orientation. Later work on ethics has sidestepped such criticisms in favour of engaging more fully with the philosophical traditions underlying Berman's and Venuti's interests in exploring how the Other can retain its otherness while caught up in the gaze of a (more powerful) observing subject.

For several decades, postmodernism, the intellectual tradition most associated with questions of alterity – and deconstruction, in particular – has been influential in the development of POSTCOLONIAL APPROACHES to translation, with Spivak's influential work on the politics of translation (1992b) being one of the earliest attempts to combine a deconstructionist ethics with a socially activist political agenda (Staten 2005; see also Arrojo 1998). Scholars working on feminist translations of literary texts have also attempted to combine post-structuralist theories of discourse with feminist politics (von Flotow 1991, 1997; Simon 1996; see GENDER AND SEXUALITY). More recent work in the field has explored one of the sources of the deconstructionist ideas that have informed translation studies, namely the philosophical work of Emmanuel Levinas. Interest in Levinas's writings on ethics and subjectivity (cf. Levinas 1989) has coincided with a heightened awareness within translation studies of the responsibility of the translator as an active agent in geopolitical conflicts and the ensuing uncertainties over how to act ethically or politically in encounters with a text, an individual or a community, without relying on the traditional foundations of identity, IDEOLOGY or rationalist/univeralist moral judgement. Interpretations and applications of Levinas in the field, though varied (see Staten 2005; Eagleston 2005; Larkosh 2004; Laygues 2004; Basalamah 2005; Inghilleri, 2008), share a common interest in understanding what occurs

at the moment of encounter with the Other, whether in the form of a literary text, its author, a refugee, a fellow citizen or a declared enemy.

For Levinas, the question of how 'I' as subject respond to 'You' as other/Other – an other I cannot fully comprehend and who calls my very being into question – is central to any attempt to conceptualize ethical subjectivity (see CULTURAL TRANSLATION). For Levinas, the origin of subjectivity is founded on subjection to rather than reciprocity with the other/Other, a subjection that precedes consciousness, identity and freedom. Our very existence, our 'right to be' is called into question by the prior existence of the other/Other, whose presence unremittingly reminds us of our ethical responsibility. The other speaks to us, makes an ethical claim on us, interrupts and disrupts our speaking for ourselves; the presence of the other's 'face' before me inspires a wish to destroy it, to do violence to it in order to preserve my own; at the same time it makes an ethical demand on me that I am not free to refuse.

Levinas's conceptualization of ethical responsibility has been interpreted in different ways within the field. For some, it carries an implication that there are ethical grounds to be suspicious of the idea of translation, given Levinas's identification of our inherent tendency to wish to take power over and reduce the other to sameness, to comprehension on our own terms (Eagleston 2005). Others have read in Levinas an ethical-political imperative for the field to accept and direct its ethical responsibility through the development of a complex transcultural consciousness and greater reflection on the cultural preconceptions about translation found both in fictionalized accounts of translators and interpreters and within the discipline itself (Larkosh 2004; Basalamah 2005; FICTIONAL REPRESENTATIONS). Levinas has also been read as pointing the way towards foregrounding the ethical relationship between translator and author/text at a more interpersonal level, creating a space where reciprocity, equality and, ultimately, humanity become possible (Laguyes 2004).

Importantly for Levinas, the ethical imperative cannot be accounted for by social or historical forces, although it can lead to social or political action. Levinas thus insists on the primacy of ethics over politics. The passage from ethics to politics in the ethical encounter is identified by Levinas through the presence of the 'third' party (*le tiers*), that is, a political context within which ethical obligations open onto wider questions of justice. A certain contradiction, however, can be said to emerge from Levinas's wish to situate the ethical encounter as primary, based in the belief that such an encounter depends for its immediacy on its detachment from social or historical forces. For Levinas, such a detachment is crucial in eliminating the risk that the Other will be identified as other than primordially Good. But once the Other is remembered as of the world, one of many others, questions that are implicated in every relationship, to do with identity, loyalty, power, difference and indifference, inevitably emerge (Inghilleri, 2008; and see Gouanvic 2001).

However differently interpreted in the field, the idea of the ethical in Levinas's writings corresponds to views concerning the ethical and political responsibility of the translator represented in a number of recent publications (Simon 2005; Salama-Carr 2006; Baker 2006a; Sturge 2007; Timoczko 2007). These individual and edited works share the insight that translators and interpreters are unavoidably and actively involved and implicated in questions of responsibility to others, whether in actual situations of judicial, political, military or ideological conflict or in the representation of such situations in fictionalized accounts that they undertake to translate. From this position, they experience firsthand the tension between self-preservation and real or symbolic violence towards others of the kind indicated in Levinas. Once the space between translator and text or interpreter and another speaking subject is acknowledged as irrefutably ethical, the task of the translator cannot be viewed as simply one of linguistic transfer, where this is understood as segregated from an ethical injunction.

This creates a further set of questions, particularly with regard to codes of ethics and codes of practice to which translators and interpreters are professionally and institutionally tied. The relationship between ethics and professional services or societies, what is sometimes referred to as the 'deontology of ethics' – i.e. ethics perceived as a set of objective rules or duties that decide ethical behaviour irrespective of their

consequences – has been explored only to a limited degree. It poses a major challenge for the field of translation when it suggests the possibility of establishing a set of codes that could distinguish an ethically 'correct' course of action in a given situation from an ethically 'good' or 'bad' one. A call has been made for a movement back to the deontological, to the establishment of actual guidelines or codes from professional associations that would support 'altruistic alterity' in the face of social, cultural and institutional demands and constraints (Pym 2001a: 134). Timoczko, however, has stressed the need to situate any codified translation ethics within a context of self-reflexivity and a recognition of the circles of affiliation and responsibility to which translators and interpreters are linked, as well as contemporary views of ethical action (2007: 316–17).

There is little evidence, however, that these ideas have been taken up in any comprehensive and sustained way, and there is no current consensus on the nature and status of professional codes of ethics. The view that codes of ethics are needed in order to establish guidelines and enhance professionalism continues to be widely adopted, with or without the additional caveat that they must not and cannot always be adhered to. Generally speaking, codes of ethics within the profession reveal a continued strong emphasis on notions of impartiality, neutrality, accuracy and fidelity across a range of professional contexts, including medical, judicial and literary translator and sign language and conference interpreting associations. There is, however, a growing awareness amongst some translation scholars and practitioners, including internationally-based, socially-activist organizations such as ECOS and Babels, that translation and interpreting are socially- and politically-directed professions, not simply specialized, language-related activities (Baker 2006a, 2006b; Simon 2005).

The question of whether developments towards an ethical imperative indicate a turn away from descriptivism towards a new approach to prescriptivism and deontology remains unclear. It is perhaps more accurate to suggest that approaches to ethics can be either, or both, depending on how one views the very question of what an 'ethics' of translation entails, and one's theoretical/disciplinary location. Philosophical or sociological insights tend to do more to reveal the (pre)ontological or epistemological bases of ethical subjectivity and political judgement than suggest how subjects *ought* to act ethically or politically, though such insights do not preclude a more socially activist stance. Likewise, although the growing interest in ethics within the field may be motivated by an increasing acknowledgement of the social and political role of translators and interpreters, whether working in public contexts such as hospitals, courts, detention centres and war zones, in technologically-based or corporate contexts, or translating literary texts, views about what counts as ethical practice and social responsibility still vary considerably.

Situated somewhere between descriptivism and prescriptivism is the recent application of a narratological approach in translation studies by Baker (2006a), which draws on the work of communication studies' theorist Walter Fisher (1987). Fisher argues that human beings decide whether something counts as an ethical practice – that is, whether something has been done for a 'good reason' – based on the narratives they have come to embrace about the world(s) in which they live, not on an abstracted rationality rooted in transcendent ideals. Thus, ethical choices are grounded in forms of rationality that are inherently subjective. Applying Fisher's model, which provides a framework for both analysing and assessing the underlying values expressed in all narratives, to a close reading of the narrative of a group of volunteer translators operating as an offshoot of a commercial translation agency, Baker illustrates how the relationship between the agency's humanitarian agenda and its acknowledged commercial interests can be read alternatively as coherent *or* incoherent, based on sound *or* contradictory values, depending on different assessments of the rational basis of the agency's presentation of itself.

A narratological approach can provide the means for a closer reading of the narratives of professional translation and interpreting associations in order to assist translators and interpreters to make better informed decisions about their own reasons for and the possible social or political consequences of adhering to or challenging these values. Baker also suggests that a critical understanding of how narratives function can lead to greater resistance to the normalizing effects of all narratives, not just those pertaining to professional codes of practice. This is important given that the interpretation of and commentary on oral and written narratives – including how they function and are assessed in particular contexts as legitimate stories – is a vital task that is undertaken by translators and interpreters in a variety of contexts, particularly in situations where asymmetries of power exist between storyteller and recipient (see Baynham and De Fina 2005).

A commitment to ethical translational practices is likely to engender both descriptive and prescriptive research, training and practice. It does seem important, however, that a renewed focus on ethics is not seen as a panacea for the inevitable and unresolvable tensions and dilemmas that arise in translation and interpreting encounters, nor as a quest for the holy grail of universal cultural or linguistic meanings and values. Directed and collective engagement with an ethics of translation can, on the other hand, serve as a means of strengthening the possibility of elaborating a role for translation as a positive force for social and political change. It can also help to create more effective pedagogical tools for training translators and interpreters to reflect upon their personal and/or social commitments and challenge existing norms established in codes of ethics that are untenable in actual contexts of practice (Arrojo 2005; Timoczko 2007: 318–22; see also TRAINING AND EDUCATION). Perhaps most importantly, increased focus on translation ethics within the field can help to guide translators, interpreters and translation scholars towards their 'right' to act responsibly, and to take their visibility and accountability seriously (Maier 2007). This does not mean that there is likely to be a consensus on what responsible action entails. A shared aim, however, could be to shift the debate from questions of impartiality and loyalty to questions of justice and the 'need to decide', and to remain as fixed as possible on the instrumental and utopian social and political goals that translation and interpreting can help to adjudicate.

See also:
ASYLUM; CULTURAL TRANSLATION; DESCRIPTIVE VS. COMMITTED APPROACHES; GENDER AND SEXUALITY; GLOBALIZATION; HERME-

NEUTICS; IDEOLOGY; MINORITY; POSTCOLONIAL APPROACHES.

Further reading
Berman 1984/1992; Levinas 1989; Venuti 1998b; Koskinen 2000a; Pym 2001a; Fiola 2004; Arrojo 2005; Bermann and Wood 2005; Baker 2006a; Maier 2007; Tymoczko 2007; Inghilleri, 2008.

MOIRA INGHILLERI (AND CAROL MAIER)

Explicitation

Explicitation is the technique of making explicit in the target text information that is implicit in the source text. Explicitation (and implicitation) STRATEGIES are generally discussed together with addition (and omission) strategies (Vinay and Darbelnet 1958/1965). Some scholars regard addition as the more generic and explicitation as the more specific concept (Nida 1964), while others interpret explicitation as the broader concept which incorporates the more specific notion of addition (Séguinot 1988; Schjoldager 1995a). The two are handled as synonyms by Englund Dimitrova (1993), who uses the terms 'addition-explicitation' and 'omission-implicitation'. Explicitation has now developed into a cover term which includes a number of obligatory and optional translational operations (Klaudy 2001, 2003). Pápai (2004) distinguishes between explicitation as a strategy used in the *process* of translation and explicitation as a feature of the *product* of translation, the latter being manifested in a higher degree of explicitness in translated than in non-translated texts in the same language.

Defining explicitation

The concept of explicitation was first introduced by Vinay and Darbelnet, who defined it as 'a stylistic translation technique which consists of making explicit in the target language what remains implicit in the source language because it is apparent from either the context or the situation' (1958/1995: 342). Implicitation, on the other hand, is defined as 'a stylistic trans-

lation technique which consists of making what is explicit in the source language implicit in the target language, relying on the context or the situation for conveying the meaning' (ibid.: 344). The results of explicitation and implicitation are often discussed in terms of gains and losses: for example, because the Hungarian pronoun system is not marked for gender, part of the meaning of the English personal pronoun *she* is lost in translations into Hungarian.

The concepts of explicitation and implicitation were further elaborated by Nida (1964), though he does not actually use the terms 'explicitation' and 'implicitation'. Nida deals with the main techniques of adjustment used in the process of translating, namely additions, subtractions and alterations. Additions are divided into the following types (1964: 227):

(a) filling out elliptical expressions
(b) obligatory specification
(c) additions required because of grammatical restructuring
(d) amplification from implicit to explicit status
(e) answers to rhetorical questions
(f) classifiers
(g) connectives
(h) categories of the receptor language which do not exist in the source language
(i) doublets

Amplification from implicit to explicit status (category (d) above) takes place when 'important semantic elements carried implicitly in the source language may require explicit identification in the receptor language' (ibid.: 228). Nida lists several examples from the BIBLE to illustrate the range and variety of this type of addition. For example, ' "queen of the South" (Luke 11: 31) can be very misleading when neither "queen" nor "South" is familiar in the receptor language... Accordingly in Tarascan one must say "woman who was ruling in the south country" ' (ibid.: 229).

Throughout the 1970s and the 1980s most publications on the subject of partial translation theories, especially in the field of language-restricted, area-restricted and culture-restricted theories (Holmes 1972), followed Nida's example: explicitation and implicitation were seen as only two among a variety of methods for addition and omission in translation. For example, Barkhudarov (1975: 223) identifies four types of transformations in translation: *perestanovka* ('transposition'), *zamena* ('substitution'), *dobavleniye* ('addition') and *opushcheniye* ('omission'). He argues that the most important reason for additions in translation from English into Russian is ellipsis in nominal structures in English, that is, the omission of certain semantic components in English surface structure which were present in the deep structure. Since ellipsis is not characteristic of Russian, the omitted semantic components are reconstructed in the Russian surface structure: *pay claim* thus becomes *trebovaniye povisit zarplatu* (demand to raise the pay) and *gun licence* becomes *udostovereniye na pravo nosheniya oruzhiya* (licence for right to carry weapon).

A very detailed typology of lexical and grammatical transformations, including grammatical additions in Bulgarian–Russian and Russian–Bulgarian translation, can be found in the work of the Bulgarian scholar Vaseva (1980). In Vaseva's view, additions are generated when 'linguistic asymmetry' necessitates explicit expressions in the target language to encode meaning components that are contained implicitly in the source language. She explains grammatical additions with reference to so-called 'missing categories' and categories with different functions: Bulgarian has articles, while Russian has none; the possessive pronoun and the copula can be omitted in Russian, but not in Bulgarian; the direct object can in certain rare cases be omitted in Russian, but never in Bulgarian. Besides grammatical additions, Vaseva refers briefly to so-called pragmatic additions, which are introduced when concepts generally known by the source language audience may be unfamiliar to the target language audience and therefore require explanation in the translation.

The explicitation hypothesis

The so-called **explicitation hypothesis** was formulated by Blum-Kulka (1986) in what is considered by many to be the first systematic study of explicitation. Drawing on concepts and descriptive terms developed within discourse analysis, she explores discourse-level explicitation, that is, explicitation connected with SHIFTS of cohesion and coherence (overt and covert textual markers) in translation. Shifts of cohesive markers can be attributed partly to the different grammatical systems of languages. For instance, in English–French translation gender specification may make the French text more explicit than the English. Other shifts in the use of cohesive markers are attributable to different stylistic preferences for certain types of cohesive markers in different languages. For example, in English–Hebrew translation preference for lexical repetition rather than pronominalization may make the Hebrew text more explicit (1986: 19). However, according to the explicitation hypothesis, it is the translation process itself, rather than any specific differences between particular languages, which bears the major part of the responsibility for explicitation (ibid.):

> The process of interpretation performed by the translator on the source text might lead to a TL text, which is more redundant than SL text. This redundancy can be expressed by a rise in the level of cohesive explicitness in the TL text. This argument may be stated as 'the explicitation hypothesis', which postulates an observed cohesive explicitness from SL to TL texts regardless of the increase traceable to differences between the two linguistic and textual systems involved. It follows that explicitation is viewed here as inherent in the process of translation.

According to Séguinot (1988: 108), however, the definition is too narrow: 'explicitness does not necessarily mean redundancy'. Séguinot also points out that 'the greater number of words in French translation, for example, can be explained by well-documented differences in the stylistics of English and French' (ibid.). In her view, the term 'explicitation' should be reserved for additions which cannot be explained by structural, stylistic or rhetorical differences between the two languages, and addition is not the only device of explicitation. Explicitation takes place not only when 'something is expressed in the translation, which was not in the original' (ibid.), but also in cases where 'something which was implied or understood through presupposition in the source text is overtly expressed in the translation, or an element in the source text is given a greater importance in the translation through focus, emphasis, or lexical choice' (ibid.).

Séguinot examines translations from English into French and from French into English, and in both cases she finds greater explicitness in translation, resulting from improved topic-comment links, the addition of linking words and the raising of subordinate information into coordinate or principal structures (ibid.: 109). Her study suggests that the increase in explicitness in both cases can be explained not by structural or stylistic differences between the two languages but by the editing strategies of the revisers.

However, support for a version of the explicitation hypothesis may be found in Vehmas-Lehto's study (1989), which compares the frequency of connective elements in Finnish journalistic texts translated from Russian with their frequency in texts of the same genre, originally written in Finnish. She finds that the Finnish translations are more explicit than the texts originally written in Finnish. It is possible, therefore, that explicitation strategies inherent in the translation process lead to translated texts in a given genre being more explicit than texts of that genre originally composed in the same language.

Another application of the concept is to be found in Hewson and Martin's study of DRAMA translation, which suggests that implicitating/explicitating techniques shift 'certain elements from the linguistic to the situational level and vice versa' (1991: 104). In drama translation, in other words, 'meaningful elements are transferred from situation into the staging text (stage directions) or integrated into character's words' (ibid.).

Types of explicitation

Obligatory explicitation

Obligatory explicitation is dictated by differences in the syntactic and semantic structure of languages (Barkhudarov 1975; Vaseva 1980; Klaudy 1993, 2003; Englund Dimitrova 1993). Syntactic and semantic explicitation is obligatory because without it target-language sentences would be ungrammatical.

The most obvious cases of obligatory explicitation are triggered by the so-called 'missing categories'. For example, there is no definite article in Russian. Translation from Russian into English, which uses the definite article prolifically, will thus involve numerous additions, as will translation from the preposition-free Hungarian into languages such as Russian and English, which use prepositions.

While syntactic explicitation generally entails an increase in the number of words (tokens) in the target text, semantic explicitation consists of choosing more specific words in the target text. Because of the different linguistic structuring of reality in different languages, certain concepts such as body parts, colours and kinship terms may have more detailed vocabularies in some languages than in others. For example, the English terms 'brother' and 'sister' cannot be translated into Hungarian without explicitation, because Hungarian has different terms for 'younger brother' (*öcs*) and 'younger sister' (*hug*), and for 'older brother' (*báty*) and 'older sister' (*nővér*).

Optional explicitation

Optional explicitation is dictated by differences in text-building strategies (cf. Blum-Kulka's cohesive patterns) and stylistic preferences between languages. Such explicitations are optional in the sense that grammatically correct sentences can be constructed without their application in the target language, although the text as a whole will be clumsy and unnatural. Examples of optional explicitation include sentence or clause initial addition of connective elements to strengthen cohesive links, the use of relative clauses instead of long, left branching nominal constructions, and the addition of emphasizers to clarify sentence-perspective, among others (Doherty 1987; Vehmas-Lehto 1989).

Pragmatic explicitation

Pragmatic explicitation of implicit cultural information is dictated by differences between cultures: members of the target-language cultural community may not share aspects of what is considered general knowledge within the source language culture and, in such cases, translators often need to include explanations in translations. For example, names of villages and rivers, or of items of food and drink, which are well known to the source language community may mean nothing to the target-language audience. In such cases, a translator might, for instance, write 'the river Maros' for *Maros*, or 'Lake Fertő' for *Fertő*.

Translation-inherent explicitation

Translation-inherent explicitation can be attributed to the nature of the translation process itself. Séguinot draws a distinction between 'choices that can be accounted for in the language system, and choices that come about because of the nature of the translation process' (1988: 18). The latter type of explicitation is explained by one of the most pervasive, language-independent features of all translational activity, namely the necessity to formulate ideas in the target language that were originally conceived in the source language (Klaudy 1993).

Corpora in explicitation research

As one of the potential UNIVERSALS of translation, research on explicitation gained a new impetus in the 1990s, thanks to the introduction of electronic CORPORA as research tools in translation studies. Corpus-based studies revealed new evidence of explicitation as a strategy of translation and of explicitness as a characteristic feature of translated texts. Olohan and Baker (2000), for instance, found that the optional connective was more common in a corpus of translated English texts (the Translational English Corpus) than in a corpus of non-translated texts in the same language (a subset of the British National Corpus). Pápai (2004), using the ARRABONA corpus which consists of English and Hungarian parallel texts and Hungarian–Hungarian comparable texts, identified sixteen types of explicitation strategies (frequent use of punctuation marks, filling in of elliptical structures, addition of conjunctions, lexical explanation and addition of discourse-organizing items, among others) in English–Hungarian translation. The study also revealed a higher level of explicitness in translated Hungarian texts than in non-translated Hungarian texts.

Explicitation vs. implicitation: the asymmetry hypothesis

Klaudy (2001) examined the relationship between explicitation and implicitation in operations carried out by translators translating literary works from Hungarian into English, German, French and Russian and vice versa. Obligatory explicitation shifts are generally symmetrical, that is, explicitation in one direction is matched by implicitation in the other. Optional explicitation in one direction may also be in a symmetrical relationship with implicitation in the opposite direction; however, due to its optional nature, this type of explicitation is not always counterbalanced by optional implicitation in the opposite direction. Klaudy (1996a) demonstrated that translators carrying out English–Hungarian back translation do not omit elements added in Hungarian–English translation. Quantitative analysis of semantic variability of reporting verbs in English–Hungarian and Hungarian–English translations indicated that, while translators tend to choose more specific reporting verbs in translation from English into Hungarian (for example, 'say' would be replaced by the equivalent of 'mutter', 'burst on', 'accuse', etc.), they do not choose more general verbs in the Hungarian into English direction (Klaudy and Károly 2005). These findings seem to verify the *asymmetry hypothesis* postulated by Klaudy (2001), according to which explicitation in the L1→L2 direction is not always counterbalanced by implicitation in the L2→L1 direction because translators – where they have a choice – prefer to use operations involving explicitation, and often refrain from introducing optional implicitation. Should this hypothesis be verified, it would underpin the assumption that explicitation is a universal strategy of translation, independent of language-pair and direction of translation.

New developments in explicitation research

Research on explicitation as a strategy and explicitness as a supposed universal of translated texts has become a testing ground for new experimental methods in translation studies, such as

THINK-ALOUD PROTOCOLS and keystroke logging (Englund Dimitrova 2005), and has benefited from new theoretical approaches (House 2004a; Pym 2005a; Heltai 2005). Englund Dimitrova (2005) investigated the translation process using the language pair Russian–Swedish, focusing on the explicitation of implicit logical links. The data analysed show that certain types of explicitation appear to function as translation NORMS and are adopted by professional translators as part of a highly automatized decision-making process, while others occur as the result of intralingual paraphrasing in the target language, as part of the translator's revision of the target text.

Pym (2005a) attempts to model explicitation within a risk management framework, arguing that 'since translation involves communication into a context with a fewer shared references, it involves greater risks than non-translation, which does not consistently have this feature. And where there are greater risks, there are greater opportunities for risk minimization' (ibid.: 41). Heltai (2005) raises the question of the relationship between explicitness and processability: if translations are more explicit than non-translations why is it often more difficult to read translations? Explicitation may increase redundancy, but increased redundancy does not always help processing. Heltai offers a detailed description of the effect of redundancy and ellipsis on the readability of translated texts.

It is especially revealing to investigate the occurrence of explicitation in modes of language mediation where time and space constraints might preclude it. In this respect, studies conducted so far suggest that explicitation is indeed a feature of interpreting (Shlesinger 1995; Ishikawa 1999; Gumul 2006) and subtitling (Perego 2003).

See also:

CORPORA;   EQUIVALENCE;   LINGUISTIC
APPROACHES;   NORMS;   SHIFTS;   UNIVERSALS.

Further reading
Vinay and Darbelnet 1958/1995; Séguinot 1985; Blum-Kulka 1986; Doherty 1987; Séguinot 1988; Vehmas-Lehto 1989; Baker 1993; Englund Dimitrova 1993; Baker 1996a; Puurtinen 2001; Klaudy 2003; House 2004a; Pápai 2004; Englund Dimitrova 2005; Heltai 2005; Klaudy and Károly 2005; Pym 2005a.

KINGA KLAUDY

Fictional representations

With translation (including interpreting) being ubiquitous in the real world, it is not surprising that it has emerged as a theme or plot device in fiction. Even in its most imaginative and fantastic shapes, fiction always has a mimetic dimension in the broad sense of referring back somehow to our understanding of reality and commenting on it.

There are several other basic conventions of the narrative genre that would seem to invite the 'emplotment' of MULTILINGUALISM and translation. Most narratological models recognize the importance of conflict as the driving force of plots. Conflicting wants and needs may develop within the same linguistic community, but in stories describing cosmopolitan fictional realities (e.g. borderlands, modern cities, international diplomacy, espionage) or stories involving shifts along the spatial axis (e.g. travel, exploration, conquest, migration) they may well find expression on the linguistic plane. In that case, translation may play a part in the conflict's resolution, or the absence or mismanagement of interlinguistic mediation may become an obstacle to its solution. Independently of all the symbolic and sociocultural values that translation may acquire, the figure of the translator can in this way be central to the 'mechanics' of the plot as protagonist, antagonist or helper, possibly in various roles (the translator-as-helper may become the protagonist, or turn enemy, etc.).

Since, in a more rhetorical perspective, the art of narrative largely depends on the manipulation of the reader's knowledge and curiosity, translation can be employed for the sake of mystery and suspense-management too. From Sherlock Holmes's adventure with 'The Greek Interpreter' (1893) to Dan Brown's *The Da Vinci Code* (2003), one finds countless examples of fiction where translation serves to encode and then, at the appropriate moment, to unlock a crucial piece of information, such as a prophecy or a secret message. Rhetorical effects of a very different nature may be found in COMIC texts where interlingual misunderstandings and mistranslations are mobilized for humorous purposes.

Despite all these and other possibilities, in many cases fictional texts will fail to reflect the multilingualism which is known or can be assumed to exist in the fictional world. The possibilities that exist in this respect have been summarized by Sternberg (1981) as follows:

- **vehicular matching** means the allotment of different languages or language varieties to characters and groups of characters in accordance with our knowledge of the historical reality represented;
- the **homogenizing convention** is operative when a monolingual text describes what we know or believe to be a multilingual reality; the credibility gap that such a non-mimetic policy may entail is mostly taken care of by the viewer's or reader's 'willing suspension of disbelief';
- **referential restriction** applies to texts which are monolingual because the social milieu of the fictional world is monolingual;
- in the much rarer case of **vehicular promiscuity**, multilingual textual means are used to express monolingual realities, as in Joyce's *Finnegans Wake* (1939).

It is mainly in fictional texts that show vehicular matching where one expects translation to become an issue.

A more fine-grained analysis could describe the exact degrees and types of code-mixing and code-switching as well as the quotation techniques that may be employed in textual representations of MULTILINGUALISM and translation. Moreover, the data always need to be interpreted in terms of *why* the fictional text renders (or significantly fails to render) assumed multilingualism or translation in a certain way. The linguistic skills of authors and of their entourage and intended audience are to be regarded as enabling conditions rather than as ultimate explanations. In many cases, the orchestration of different languages and language varieties in a text implies some kind of comment on linguistic hierarchies in the real world (see MINORITY). Thus, the way in which Shakespeare in a play such as *Henry V* exploits the differences and stages problematic passages between English, French, broken English, broken French, English spoken with Irish, Scottish and Welsh accents, with a sprinkling of other languages added for good measure, is partly a mimetic reflection of historical realities but partly also an ideological projection which reconfigures these realities to show a confident Britain on the way to unity under firm English guidance and with superiority over its overseas rivals.

In discussing matters of translation and fictional representations alike, we are well advised to use an open and flexible concept of 'language' which accommodates not only the 'official' taxonomy of languages but also the whole range of subtypes and varieties existing within the various officially recognized languages (e.g. dialect, sociolect, slang) and indeed sometimes challenging our neat linguistic typologies (e.g. Spanglish, artificial languages). Institutionalized power relationships which have taken the form of habit and convenience continue to prop up the conventional distinction between 'languages' and 'language varieties' or 'dialects', but the dividing line is historical and problematic. What matters in each instance is the hierarchical patterns according to which the textual space is divided between the different idioms (e.g. narrative vs. character voices, main text vs. paratexts, translation or not) and the question of their function and effect.

Gods, aliens, colonizers, subjects

In fiction as in real life, the translator's power can be assessed in terms of two variables: the intrinsic importance of the message, and the distance between the two cultures which enter into communication via the translator.

Divine messages (e.g. sacred books) provide an extreme example of the translator's power. What messages could have a more profound significance than those coming from an omnipotent God, and what could be more radically different than the spheres of divine perfection and those of human error? Different religions and faiths seem to have incorporated an awareness of this into their belief systems by developing mythical accounts of how God's divine message was translated and/or multiplied in languages that humans can understand, with divine inspiration guiding the human and thus fallible translators so as to guarantee the EQUIVALENCE, sacrality and orthodoxy of their work (see BIBLE, JEWISH AND CHRISTIAN). Such accounts of the origin of sacred texts and their translations constitute a fascinating body of myths involving translation, but not without reminding us of the blurred line between 'fact' and 'fiction'. Whereas sceptics and agnostics will see stories about divinely inspired translation as fictional projections, more orthodox believers will believe them to be literally true. Such issues of fictionality and truth also arise, albeit with a totally different range of implications, in stories in which the account of translation has an (auto) biographical or historical dimension (e.g. Antjie Krog's *Country of My Skull*, 1998).

One level below the sacred/human interface we find another body of narratives in which translators may have crucial responsibilities, namely in the realm of science fiction, where storylines often include communicative problems on an interplanetary or even intergalactic scale. Here too, the intrinsic importance of the messages is huge inasmuch as the very survival of a race, planet or galaxy may be at stake, with mind-boggling linguistic and cultural distances to be bridged by the translator. But translation appears to be less of a central theme in science fiction than one would perhaps have expected; the translation problem is usually 'either passed over in silence or dispensed with in one of three ways that reflect received ideas: telepathy, lingua franca and machine translation' (Mossop 1996:2). Technology or pseudoscience can thereby take the place of divine inspiration as the fictional sleight of hand helping translators to bridge the unbridgeable. The so-called Babelfish in Douglas Adams's *The Hitchhiker's Guide to the Galaxy* from 1979 (an earplug with inbuilt translation facility that renders any message heard into the hearer's language) is essentially the acoustic equivalent of the transparent stones through which Joseph Smith, founder of the Mormon Church in 1830, had to read the *Book of Mormon* in order to have the divine message visually revealed to him in his native English.

Coming down one more step to reach a level where stories about translation start referring to chronicled human history in a more tangible manner, we find ourselves dealing with stories which describe – and fictionalize – the encounters and struggles between continents and peoples. Many of these writings can be subsumed under the labels of colonial and postcolonial writing (see POSTCOLONIAL APPROACHES). They are typically stories in which explorers and settlers in the crucial first stages of the colonization process, or administrators in the later stages of imperial government, depend on the services of local translators. In these stories translators may have crucial control over flows of information which determine the fate of entire communities, possibly continents, and they have to negotiate ocean-wide linguistic and cultural gaps, aggravated by the opposed interests of indigenous populations and colonizers. Not surprisingly, the problems of interlinguistic and intercultural mediation in colonial settings have given rise to a large number of narratives, some of which have gone on to lead a life of their own as powerful myths in the grey zone between fact and fiction. Examples include La Malinche and other interpreters of the *conquistadores* (see LATIN AMERICAN TRADITION) and the local interpreters in Africa's French-speaking colonies (e.g. Ahmadou Kourouma's *Monnè, outrages et défis*, 1990 and Amadou Hampâté Bâ's *L'étrange destin de Wangrin*, 1973; see also AFRICAN TRADITION).

The translator's ability to 'make a difference' can have potentially heroic or tragic dimensions, as in the three kinds of stories just surveyed. But in many narratives, the translator's agency and impact on history will have more modest dimensions that might correspond to the endeavours of 'ordinary' people simply going about their everyday business, trying to preserve their moral integrity as well as character and circumstances permit. This fourth category typically includes stories involving the multilingual encounters and experiences of individual travellers, immigrants, nomads, expatriates, refugees and the like (involving changes of geographical space) and stories set in multicultural cosmopolitan settings (where interlingual and intercultural contacts occur regardless of changes of place). Their success and topicality today follow from the processes of internationalization in our recent history and from the resistance and anxieties these seem to be engendering. Like 'travel', 'translation' has become a kind of master metaphor epitomizing our present *condition humaine* in a globalized and centreless context, evoking the human search for a sense of self and belonging in a puzzling world full of change and difference.

These stories are likely to describe multilingualism and translation in terms of subjective experience and personal identity rather than in the larger perspective of human history. History is of course present in them, conditioning experience and agency, but the translator is not necessarily portrayed as being in a position to substantially change the course of events. The translator's experience often shows the following affective components: **trust** (the interlocutors who do not know the 'other' language lay their fate in the hands of the translator) and **loyalty** (how to balance the conflicting loyalties that the translator may have or develop towards the sender of the original and/or the ultimate receivers?); **invisibility** and **personal ambition** (given the frequent lack of social recognition of the translator's work, how to resist frustration and the temptation to 'usurp' the original author's role?); **untranslatability** (given all these pressures, how can translation ever be unproblematic or straightforward?); **trauma** (how to live with the weight of terrible experiences that the translator may have to absorb and express in his or her own words?); and last but not least, **identity** (how can translators prevent the permanent oscillations of empathy and sympathy, the never-ending switching and adjusting to other parties, from fragmenting, eroding or dislocating their sense of self, leaving them in a space 'in-between'?).

The more such issues are brought into play, the more the focus shifts from the 'objective' reality of the translator's impact to the subjective, emotional and experiential dimension of how the process affects individuals and communities. Something along these lines happens in a wide range of plays (e.g. Brian Friel's *Translations*, 1981), aphoristic notes (Carlos Batista's *Bréviaire d'un traducteur*, 2003), diaries (Michel Orcel's *Les larmes du traducteur*, 2001), films (*Lost in Translation*, dir. Sofia Coppola, 2003), and especially short stories and novels: Isaac Babel's 'Guy de Maupassant' (1932), Deszö Kosztolanyi's 'Le traducteur cleptomane' (1933/1985), Ingeborg Bachmann's *Simultan* (1972), Francesca Duranti's *La casa sul lago della luna* (1984), Ólafur Jóhann Ólafsson's *Absolution* (1991), Just Ward's *The Translator* (1991), Javier Mar'as's *Corazón tan blanco* (1992), Michael Ondaatje's *The English Patient* (1992), David Malouf's *Remembering Babylon* (1993), Barbara Wilson's *Trouble in Transylvania* (1993), Suzanne Glass's *The Interpreter* (1999), Mikael Niemi's *Populärmusik från Vittula* (2000), José Carlos Somoza's *La caverna de las ideas* (2000; translated by Sonia Soto as *The Athenian Murders*, 2001), John Crowley's *The Translator* (2002), Jonathan Safran Foer's *Everything is Illuminated* (2002), and Claude Bleton's *Les nègres du traducteur* (2004), among others. Some of these narratives reflect the growing fascination of novelists with the very process of textual representation which has produced the highly self-referential works known as metafiction. Not surprisingly, in metafictional writing by the likes of Borges, Cortázar, Garc'a Márquez, Vargas Llosa, Nabokov and Calvino, translation is the object of much speculation. In a number of cases, the recourse to PSEUDOTRANSLATION is part of a wider metafictional strategy.

One is struck by the growing number of fictional texts that stage polyglot characters and translation scenes. Moreover, at the meta-level of translation criticism and translation studies, these fictional representations are attracting increasing levels of attention, indeed to the point that 'the fictional turn' in translation studies has recently begun to serve as a catchphrase. In several cases, this trend signals a postmodern and counter-cultural critique of

rational science: narrated singular experience is trusted more than the lifeless generalities of empirical research.

See also:
MOBILITY; MULTILINGUALISM.

Further reading
Sternberg 1981; Thieme 1995; Mossop 1996; Hoenselaars and Buning 1999; Cronin 2000; Pagano 2000; Delabastita 2002; Gentzler 2002b; Pagano 2002; Cronin 2003; Strümper-Krobb 2003; Barnett 2004; Delabastita 2004, 2005; Delabastita and Grutman 2005a; Maier 2006.

DIRK DELABASTITA

Foreign language teaching

Despite the widespread popular assumption that translation should play a major and necessary part in the study of a foreign language, recent theories of language teaching and learning have at best ignored the role of translation and at worst vilified it. From the end of the nineteenth century onwards almost all influential theoretical works on language teaching have assumed without argument that a new language (L2) should be taught without reference to the student's first language (L1).

The grammar-translation method

The reasons for the rejection of translation are complex; but both the popular perception and the academic reaction against it derive from the widespread influence of the **grammar-translation method**, which has become the stereotype of the use of translation in language teaching.

In a grammar-translation syllabus, the structures of the L2 are graded and presented in units (often equivalent to a lesson or the chapter of a textbook). In each unit a list of new vocabulary items is presented together with translation equivalents, grammar rules are explained in the L1 and there are sentences for translation, both into and out of the L2, employing only the vocabulary and grammar encountered in the current and earlier units.

Introduced in the Gymnasia of Prussia in the mid-nineteenth century, the grammar-translation method spread rapidly and it is still used widely today (Howatt and Widdowson 2004: 151–8). Under its influence written translation exercises became the central feature of language teaching syllabuses in textbooks for self-study, in schools and in universities. These exercises are regarded as a means of instruction, practice and assessment; L2 competence is measured by the accuracy of the lexical and grammatical equivalence attained in translation.

Direct method and the rejection of translation

Grammar-translation soon came under attack. At the turn of the twentieth century, the self-styled 'Reform Movement' criticized it for ignoring the spoken language, for encouraging false notions of EQUIVALENCE and for presenting isolated sentences rather than connected texts (Howatt 2004: 187–98). The influential phonetician and language-teaching theorist Henry Sweet ([1899] 1964: 101) ridiculed the kind of sentence found in a typical translation exercise as 'a bag into which is crammed as much grammatical and lexical information as possible' and produced parodies in illustration such as 'The merchant is swimming with the gardener's son, but the Dutchman has the fine gun' (Sweet [1899] 1964: 74). Such sentences, as many have observed, are highly artificial, divorced from purpose, context and actual use (Firth 1957: 24) although these factors do not in themselves invalidate such sentences as a pedagogic device (Cook 2001). Other attacks on grammar-translation have cited the demotivating difficulty of translating from L1 to L2, the reinforcement of reliance on processing via the L1, strengthening of L1 interference and a detrimental effect on the acquisition of native-like processing skill and speed (for a summary of such arguments see Stern 1992: 282–7)

Such criticisms have been devastatingly effective in influencing academic opinion against the use of translation in language teaching. Opposition to the use of translation has led to its replacement by the **direct method**: the teaching of an L2 using that language (and only that language) as a means of instruction. Attitudes to translation have varied from a total ban (as in the Berlitz schools), to an indulgent if reluctant admission of it as a necessary last resort, 'a refuge for the incompetent' (see Koch 1947). Almost all twentieth-century methodologies are species of the direct method (for descriptions and discussion see, *inter alia*, Johnson 2001: chapter 10; Richards and Rodgers 2001; Stern 1992).

Meanwhile, grammar-translation has continued to be used, especially in secondary schools in many parts of the world. It is one of the few methods which can be adopted in very large classes and, being structured and predictable, can give students a sense of confidence and attainment. It is also suited to teachers whose own command of the L2 may be limited. The typical teacher of grammar-translation is one whose L1 is the same as his or her students, and who has learned the L2 as a foreign language; such teachers have the advantages of understanding the language-specific problems of their students.

Political and demographic influences

In any discussion of language teaching theory and practice, it is important to remember the consequences of the position of English as the world's most widely learned foreign language (Crystal 1997a: 360–61). In recent years, the most influential ideas about language teaching have often been developed with explicit reference to English Language Teaching (ELT), accompanied by an implicit assumption that they apply to foreign language teaching in general. This view is strengthened by the focus of attention, deriving from Chomskyan linguistics, on universal rather than language-specific aspects of language and language acquisition. Arguments concerning the pedagogic use of translation are no exception to the influence of these general trends. The relevance of ideas from ELT to the teaching of other languages, however, should not be taken for granted. The case for and against translation may vary with the social and linguistic relationship between a student's L1 and L2. The growing ascendancy of English as the world's main international language (Crystal 1997b; Coulmas 1992: 187–9; Phillipson 1992: 17–37) makes the issues surrounding its teaching in many ways atypical.

In the twentieth century, the theoretical rejection of translation fitted well with demographic and economic changes which created new motivations for learning English, and with changes in the composition of student groups. From the nineteenth century onwards, immigration into the USA led to a demand for utilitarian courses focusing upon the rapid development of a functional command of the language. Increased world trade and tourism, and the growing dominance of English as a world language, have perpetuated this pedagogic situation. Language schools in English-speaking countries cater for classes of visitors and immigrants from mixed linguistic background, making translation impossible. The typical teacher in such schools is a native English speaker whose expertise is in direct-method teaching skills and rarely includes command of the students' L1. English-speaking countries, moreover, especially Great Britain, have promoted the employment of such teachers abroad, even in situations where students share an L1 and translation can consequently be used. A highly questionable assumption has developed that the native-speaker teacher is necessarily the best (Phillipson 1992: 193–9; Seidlhofer 1999). International publishers have had an interest in the demise of translation too, as monoglot materials can be distributed without regard to the students' first language.

Influence of second language acquisition theory (SLA)

Further opposition to translation in language teaching has been fuelled by successive theories of second language acquisition (SLA), which in turn derive from theories of children's first language acquisition (FLA), where, by definition, translation has no role to play. Among major theories of FLA have been: behaviourism, which sees language acquisition as a process of habit formation; Chomskyan nativism, which views a disposition to acquire language as a genetic endowment; and functionalism, which sees

language acquisition as the result of a need to convey social meaning. All have in turn had a vicarious influence on teaching practices, almost none making use of translation. A widespread belief in the 1970s and 1980s, deriving from a combination of nativism and functionalism, was that student attention should be exclusively focused on meaning and communication rather than on form, as this would stimulate the subconscious acquisition of the language system (Krashen 1982; Prabhu 1987). Translation, which implies a conscious knowledge of two language systems, and the deliberate deployment of both, is not among the activities compatible with this belief. A later return to some limited direction of student attention to linguistic form in language teaching in the 1990s (Doughty and Williams 1998) still did not reinstate translation as a means of achieving this end.

The assumptions underlying current SLA theory and attempts to apply them to language teaching are all highly questionable, especially in their denial of the inevitable wish of teachers and learners to attempt a conscious and systematic relation of L1 to L2 via translation. It is clear that, before translation can be reinstated as an aid to language acquisition, there needs to be explicit recognition that adult SLA need not necessarily attempt to repeat the stages of a child FLA, but can be essentially different in kind.

The revival of translation

Most criticisms of translation apply only to the limited and idiosyncratic uses of translation in the grammar-translation method and overlook the fact that translation can be used in many other ways (Duff 1989: 5–18; Deller and Rinvolucri 2002). Grammar-translation holds no monopoly, and translation may be used both more imaginatively and as a complement to the direct method of teaching rather than an exclusive alternative to it. Activities may involve oral as well as written practice and focus on connected text rather than isolated sentences. Successful translation, moreover, may be judged by other criteria than formal lexical and grammatical equivalence. Students may be assessed for speed as well as accuracy. They may be encouraged to translate for gist, to seek pragmatic or stylistic equivalence, to consider the features of genre (Swales 1990), or to produce different translations according to the needs of the audience. Yet, so strong has been the influence of the grammar-translation method that many critics have been unable to envisage any other approach to translation in language learning and believe that, in criticizing this one methodology, they are dealing with the use of pedagogic translation in general.

Recent years have seen the beginnings of a reappraisal of the role of translation in language learning and a number of writers have expressed doubts about its banishment from the classroom (Howatt and Widdowson 2004; Duff 1989; Stern 1992; Cook 2000: 187–8; Butzkamm 2001; Cook 2001, 2007, forthcoming). The extremism of its earlier rejection is being recognized and the use of translation is being readmitted, not only as a matter of expediency (translation is often the quickest and most efficient way to explain the meaning of a new word), but also as a theoretically justified activity aiding acquisition. A number of factors have contributed to this reappraisal. It is acknowledged that the good practice of translation is an end in itself for many students rather than simply a means to greater proficiency in the target language. There is a strong movement in favour of promoting bi- and multilingual practice in schools for political reasons (Skutnabb-Kangas 2000). It is no longer assumed, as it was in direct method teaching, that the use of English will take place in an exclusively monolingual setting. There has been criticism of the chauvinism and illogicality of the view that native speaker teachers are always the best (Medgyes 1994; Braine 1999). It is recognized that translation involves far more than formal EQUIVALENCE.

There is a growing awareness of the formal inaccuracy which can result from an exclusive focus on communication and a realization that translation can, as it was traditionally believed to do, develop accuracy. One of the virtues of translation as an exercise is that the learner, being constrained by the original text, is denied resort to avoidance strategies and obliged to confront areas of the L2 system which he or she may find difficult. Another virtue is that translation can focus attention upon subtle differences between L1 and L2 and discourage the naive view that every expression has an exact equivalent.

There are thus signs that the outlawing of translation may be coming to an end. As Kelly (1969: 217) observes, the twentieth century was unique in its vilification of the use of translation in language teaching. Howatt and Widdowson (2004: 312) comment that '[t]here has long been a strong case for reviewing the role of translation in language teaching and particularly its educational value for advanced students in schools and universities. Properly handled, it provides a useful antidote to the modern obsession with utilitarian performance objectives, but the pitfalls that were identified by the nineteenth-century reformers have not gone away, and the activity remains a demanding one.'

See also:
DIRECTIONALITY; TRAINING AND EDUCATION; MINORITY.

Further reading
Duff 1989; Widdowson 2003; Howatt and Widdowson 2004; Cook 2007.

GUY COOK

Functionalist approaches

In broad terms, functionalist approaches look at translation as an act of communication and understand meaning in terms of function in context. In a more specific sense, functionalist approaches define translation as a purposeful transcultural activity and argue that the linguistic form of the target text is determined by the purpose it is meant to fulfil. These approaches draw on action theory, communication theory and cultural theory, and include: Vermeer's (1978, 1996) Skopos theory, Reiß and Vermeer's (1984, 1991) general theory of translation, and Holz-Mänttäri's (1984) theory of translatorial action. In addition to Vermeer and Holz-Mänttäri, other scholars who have made significant contributions to the development of functionalist theories include Hönig and Kußmaul (1982/1991) (see also their individual contributions, e.g. Hönig (1995; Kußmaul 1995,

2000b); Nord (1988, 1997), Kupsch-Losereit (1986); Witte (2000), Risku (1998); Kiraly (2000) and Ammann (1990).

Language function, text function, communicative function

There have been many attempts to classify the functions of language. Among the most influential are those of Bühler (1934), Jakobson (1960) and Halliday (1973). Bühler's *Darstellungsfunktion, Ausdruckfunktion* and *Appelfunktion* refer, respectively, to the representation of objects and phenomena, the attitude of the text producer towards such phenomena and the appeal to the text receiver. These three functions correspond broadly to Jakobson's referential, expressive and conative functions, although the latter additionally distinguishes phatic (the use of language to create and maintain social contact), metalingual and poetic functions. Halliday distinguishes three macrofunctions: the ideational (representation of experience), the interpersonal (the speaker's expression of attitude) and the textual (the internal organization of language, or the way links are established within the text and between the text and its context of situation). There is, then, a degree of consensus among these alternative formulations.

Reiß (1971, 1976, 2000) developed a translation-oriented text typology with the aim of deriving strictly objective criteria for assessing the QUALITY of translations. Based on Bühler's three functions of language, Reiß identified three corresponding text types (informative, expressive, appellative) which she linked to translation methods. In the translation of informative texts (examples of which would be reports and textbooks), the aim is invariance of content and the translation is deemed successful if the information has been transmitted in full. In the case of expressive texts (e.g. literary texts), the aim is the communication of artistically organized content and the translation method involves identifying the artistic and creative intention of the ST author and conveying it in an analogously artistic organization. The translation of appellative or operative text types (e.g. ADVERTISING) aims to provoke in the target readers identical behavioural reactions to those of the reader

of the source text, and the translation method called for is ADAPTATION. Reiß's approach is source-text based, i.e. she judges translation quality with reference to the source text (type). Her translation-oriented text typology is thus, strictly speaking, not a functionalist theory of translation in the more specific sense in which this label is now used in translation studies.

There can be no doubt that language functions and communicative functions impinge significantly on the translator's task. However, no actual text will exhibit only one language function, and many texts cannot be assigned to one specific text type only. Hatim and Mason (1990a), who add pragmatic and semiotic dimensions to their characterization of the communicative domain of context, argue that all texts are multifunctional, even if one overall rhetorical purpose will generally tend to predominate and function as the ultimate determinant of text structure.

Functionalist theories of translation

The theories developed by Hans J. Vermeer (1978) and Justa Holz-Mänttäri (1984) reflect a paradigm shift from predominantly LINGUISTIC APPROACHES and rather formal translation theories, firmly situated within the framework of applied and comparative linguistics, to a more functionally and socioculturally oriented concept of translation.

The main point of functionalist approaches is the following: it is not the source text as such, or its effects on the source text recipient, or the function assigned to it by the author, that determines the translation process and the linguistic make-up of the target text, as is postulated by EQUIVALENCE-based translation theories, but the prospective function or purpose of the target text as determined by the initiator's (i.e. client's or commissioner's) needs. Consequently, the purpose (skopos) is largely constrained by the target text user (whether reader or listener) and his or her situation and cultural background. A theoretically sound definition of translatorial action must therefore take account of all the elements involved in human communicative action across cultures; in particular, it must take into consideration the client's culture, the process of text production in its widest sense, and the concept of expert action. Thus, in addition to linguistic theory, functionalist approaches draw inspiration from (intercultural) communication theory, action theory (e.g. von Wright 1971, see also Allwood 1995) and text theory, as well as from theories of literary reception (e.g. Iser 1978).

Vermeer's *skopos* theory

Skopos theory takes seriously factors which have always been stressed in action theory, and which were brought into sharp relief with the growing need in the latter half of the twentieth century for the translation of non-literary text types (see COMMERCIAL TRANSLATION; SCIENTIFIC AND TECHNICAL TRANSLATION). Translation is viewed not as a process of transcoding, but as a specific form of human action which is determined by its purpose. The word *skopós*, derived from Greek, is used as a technical term for the purpose, aim, goal or objective of a translation. *Skopos* must be defined before translation can begin; in highlighting skopos, the theory adopts a prospective attitude to translation, as opposed to the retrospective attitude adopted in theories which focus on prescriptions derived from the source text. This prospective view is reflected in the following definition: 'To translate means to produce a text in a target setting for a target purpose and target addressees in target circumstances' (Vermeer 1987: 29).

Vermeer (1978: 100) postulates that, as a general rule, it must be the intended purpose of the target text that determines translation methods and strategies. From this postulate, he derives the *skopos* rule: Human action (and its subcategory: translation) is determined by its purpose (skopos), and is therefore a function of its purpose. Two further general rules are postulated: the **coherence rule** and the fidelity rule. The coherence rule stipulates that the target text must be sufficiently coherent to allow the intended users to comprehend it, given their assumed background knowledge and situational circumstances. The starting point for a translation is a text, written in the source language, which is part of a world continuum. This text has to be translated into a target language in such a way that it becomes part of a world continuum that can be interpreted by the recip-

ients as coherent with their situation (Vermeer 1978: 100). The **fidelity rule** concerns intertextual coherence between the text that is the outcome of the **translational** action (the translatum in Vermeer 1989b: 174; the **translat** in Reiß and Vermeer 1991: 2) and the source text, and stipulates that some relationship must remain between the two once the overriding principle of skopos and the rule of (intratextual) coherence have been satisfied.

One practical consequence of this theory is a reconceptualization of the status of the source text. It is up to the translator as the expert to decide what role a source text is to play in the translation action. The decisive factor is the precisely specified skopos, and the source text is just one constituent of the commission given to the translator. The skopos must be decided separately in each specific case. It may be ADAPTATION to the target culture, but it may also be to acquaint the reader with the source culture. Fidelity to the source text is thus one possible or legitimate skopos. Skopos theory should not, therefore, be understood as promoting (extremely) free translation in all, or even a majority of cases. The important point is that no source text has only one correct or preferred translation (Vermeer 1989b: 182) and, consequently, every translation commission should explicitly or implicitly contain a statement of skopos. The skopos for the target text need not be identical with that attributed to the source text; but unless the skopos for the target text is specified, translation cannot, properly speaking, be carried out at all.

The general translation theory of Reiß and Vermeer

Vermeer's general skopos theory was further developed and combined with Reiß's specific translation theory to arrive at a general translation theory (Reiß and Vermeer 1984, 1991). This theory is presented as sufficiently general (*allgemeine Translationstheorie*) and sufficiently complex to cover a multitude of individual cases. A text is viewed as an **offer of information** (*Informationsangebot*) made by a producer to a recipient. Translation is then characterized as offering information to members of one culture in their language (the target language and culture) about information originally offered in another language within another culture (the source language and culture). A translation is thus a secondary offer of information, with the translator offering information about certain aspects of the source text-in-situation, according to the target text skopos specified by the initiator and considering the needs, expectations, etc., of the target text receivers (Reiß and Vermeer 1984/1991). Translation, by definition, involves both linguistic and cultural transfer; in other words, it is a culture transcending process (Vermeer 1992: 40, 1986).

Whether the skopos of the target text and of the source text is different or the same for the two texts (that is, whether we have *Funktionskonstanz* or *Funktionsänderung* in Reiß and Vermeer's terminology), the standard for the translation will be **adequacy** or appropriateness to the skopos, which also determines the selection and arrangement of content. Although Reiß and Vermeer depart from traditional approaches that see EQUIVALENCE as a constitutive feature of (any) translation, they do use the label 'equivalence' in the sense of adequacy to a skopos that requires functional constancy: for example, if the translation brief requires a faithful reproduction of the words and structures of the target text, as happens frequently in pedagogical situations (1991: 140). For functionalists, then, the long-standing debate about literal versus free translation becomes superfluous, since all forms, whether literal translation, communicative translation, or adaptation, whether documentary or instrumental translation (Nord 1997: 138), are equally valid translational procedures, depending on the skopos.

Although the terms 'skopos', 'purpose' and 'function' are often used interchangeably by Reiß and Vermeer (1984/1991), **function** is also used in a more specific sense which derives mainly from Reiß's text typology. In this sense, it is linked to aspects of genre (*Textsorte*) and text type (*Texttyp*). That is, Reiß's original idea of correlating text type and translation method was presented as a specific theory to fit into a general translation theory; it has repeatedly been argued that the two parts of the book 'do not really form a homogenous whole' (Nord 1997: 12). In assigning the source text to a text type and to a genre, the translator can decide on the hierarchy of postulates which has to be

observed during target text production (Reiß and Vermeer 1984/1991: 196). Such a classification of the source text is relevant only in cases where functional constancy is required between source and target texts.

However, both Vermeer (1989b) and Reiß (1988) have expressed reservations about the role of genre: the source text does not determine the genre of the target text, nor does the genre determine *ipso facto* the form of the target text, or, indeed, the skopos; rather, it is the skopos of the translation that determines the appropriate genre for the translatum, and the genre, being a consequence of the skopos, is secondary to it (Vermeer 1989b: 187).

Theory of translatorial action

The theory of 'translatorial action' (*translatorisches Handeln*, also translational action) was developed by Justa Holz-Mänttäri (1984). Translation is here conceived primarily as professional acting, as a process of intercultural communication whose end product is a text which is capable of functioning appropriately in specific situations and contexts of use. In this conception, neither source and target text comparison, nor linguistics, has any significant role to play, and translation is situated within the wider context of cooperative interaction between professionals (experts) and clients. In developing her approach, Holz-Mänttäri draws on communication theory and on action theory. Communication theory enables her to highlight the components involved in a process of communication across cultural barriers, while action theory provides the basis for a delineation of the specific characteristics of translatorial action. In order to set her theory apart from more traditional approaches, Holz-Mänttäri develops, in German, a distinctive and highly abstract terminology, at times eschewing even the term 'translation' (*Übersetzung*) in order to avoid the connotations and expectations traditionally attached to that term (Holz-Mänttäri 1986: 355).

Holz-Mänttäri's aim is to provide a theoretical basis and conceptual framework from which guidelines for professional translators may be drawn. The primary purpose of translatorial action is to enable cooperative, functionally adequate communication to take place across cultural barriers. In Holz-Mänttäri's terms, the purpose of the translatorial action process is to produce a **message transmitter** (*Botschaftsträger*; literally: 'message conveyor') that can be utilized in superordinate **configurations of actions** (*Handlungsgefüge*) whose function is to guide and co-ordinate communicative, cooperative action (Holz-Mänttäri 1984: 17). Translation and other forms of (foreign language) text production are conceived as part of, rather than constitutive of, translatorial action. Texts act as **message-conveyor compounds** (*Botschaftsträger im Verbund*) of content (*Tektonik*), structured according to function and represented by formal elements (*Textur*). One purpose of the translatorial text operations is to establish whether the content and form components of the source text are functionally suitable for the target text. In making this decision, the translator cannot be guided by the source text alone, but must research, in addition, the target culture's conception of the subject matter, of text classes and of genres.

Because an action is determined by its function and purpose, its outcome, too, must be judged by these criteria. The textual profile of the target text is determined by its function, and whether this is or is not similar to the textual profile of the source text can only be established through systematic translatorial analysis (Holz-Mänttäri 1984, 1993). The notion of function is central in two respects. On the one hand, it forces the translator to embed the product of translatorial action in a complex situation of human needs. On the other hand, it forces the translator to embed translatorial action in the social order, i.e. in a society organized by a division of labour. The main roles in a translation process are played by one or more persons or institutions. The roles include the initiator, the commissioner, the text producer, the translator, the target text 'applicator' and the receptor, and each role is highly complex.

In establishing a **product specification** (*Produktspezifikation*), that is, a description of the required properties and features of the target text, text-external factors pertaining to the commissioning of the target text influence to a great extent the framework within which all the textual operations involved in translatorial action are to take place. These factors include the aim of the action, the mode in which it is to be realized, the fee to be paid and the deadline for delivery, all of which are negotiated with the client who has commissioned the action. The roles of all actors involved, the overall aim of the action, the purposes of individual actions within the configuration of actions in which the text to be produced will be used, the circumstances in which these actions will take place, and the functions of message transmitters are all subjected to careful analysis and evaluation.

As experts in translational action, translators are responsible for carrying out a **commission** in such a way that a functionally appropriate text is produced. They are responsible for deciding whether, when and how a translation can be realized. Whether a commission can be realized depends on the circumstances of the target culture, and the translator must negotiate with the client in order to establish what kind of optimal translation can be guaranteed, given a specific set of circumstances. The translatorial text operations are based on analytical, synthetic, evaluative and creative actions that take account of the ultimate purpose of the text to be produced and of aspects of different cultures for the distances between them to be narrowed (see also Risku 1998).

The translator is the expert whose task it is to produce message conveyors for use in transcultural message transfer. Translators produce texts to enable others to cooperate (*professionelles fremdbedarfsorientiertes Handeln* – Witte 2000: 168). Holz-Mänttäri's theory adopts a much wider conception of the translator's task, thus creating new professional perspectives (professional profiles are discussed in Holz-Mänttäri 1986: 363ff.). For example, the ethical responsibility of the translator is seen to derive from his or her status as an expert in the field of transcultural message transfer, because only translators with the requisite expertise can succeed in producing a functionally adequate text (cf. ETHICS). This has clear consequences for the training of translators (as illustrated, for example, by Vienne 2000; Mackenzie 2004; see TRAINING AND EDUCATION).

Although Holz-Mänttäri's theory has much in common with Vermeer's skopos theory, her approach is even more radical than Vermeer's in rejecting the paradigm of linguistics that was still dominant in the early 1980s. Vermeer himself comments that her model suggests 'a wider possibility of approaching and describing translational acting from a general theory's point of view' (1996: 26).

Criticism of functionalist theories

The main objections to both skopos theory and the theory of translational action concern the theoretical foundations, the concepts used, and the applicability of the approach (for a more in-depth engagement with a range of criticisms, see Vermeer 1996; Nord 1997: 109–22). It has been argued that Reiß and Vermeer's use of the labels 'skopos', 'purpose', 'function' and 'aim' interchangeably has created terminological confusion. The very term skopos is criticized as being too broad since it may refer to the translation process (the goal of this process), or to the translation result (function of the *translatum*), or to the translation mode (the intention of this mode). For Vermeer, 'intention, skopos and function are individually ascribed concepts (by the producer, sender, commissioner, translator and recipient)', and if they coincide, they mean 'the same seen from different points of view' (Vermeer 1996: 8; see also Nord 1997: 27ff. for a discussion and distinctive definitions). With respect to Holz-Mänttäri's theory, Newmark finds fault with the 'modernistic abstract jargon of contemporary Public Relations' and the 'businesslike manner of writing' which, he believes, obscure 'the real issues in translation' (1991: 106).

Criticism of functionalist approaches on the basis that they transgress the limits of translation proper and that they do not respect the original (Nord 1997) rests on the definition of translation and the resulting need to reconceptualize the status of the source text. In Holz-Mänttäri's model, the source text is viewed as a mere tool for realizing communicative functions; it is totally subordinate to its purpose, is afforded no intrinsic value and may undergo radical modification in the interest of the target reader. The translator is unilaterally committed to the target situation because it is primarily the message and the commission, rather than the text itself, that have to be rendered for the client. Newmark (1991: 106) criticizes the emphasis on the message at the expense of

richness of meaning and to the detriment of the authority of the source text. It is mainly because the source text may be thus 'dethroned' (ibid.) that Holz-Mänttäri's theory in particular has met with objections or reservations, even from theorists who themselves apply a functionalist approach to translation (e.g. Nord 1991a: 28). The concept of 'dethronement' of the source text had been used by Vermeer himself, but in the context of stressing that in a target-oriented theory of translation the source text is no longer the exclusive factor determining the structure of the target text.

It has also been argued that in their attempt to establish a truly general and comprehensive translation theory, Reiß and Vermeer force totally disparate cases of text relations into a frame which they attempt to hold together by means of the notion of information offer (Schreitmüller 1994: 105), and that there should be a limit to what may legitimately be called translation as opposed to, for example, ADAPTATION (Koller 1993). Koller points out that if translation theory does not 'strive to differentiate between (original) text production and translatory text *re*production' (1995: 194; emphasis in original), it will face a fundamental dilemma since it will not have delimited its object of research.

However, proponents of skopos theory argue for a wide definition of translation (e.g. Reiß 1990), which in Snell-Hornby's words (2006: 53) is 'indeed closer to the realities of translation practice'. Any attempt to accommodate the purpose of a translation will involve using STRATEGIES that are often listed under adaptation, for example reformulation, paraphrase and textual explication. Moreover, a narrow definition of translation would seriously constrain the scope of research, discouraging scholars from examining various forms of translational activity that do occur in professional practice and should therefore be addressed by translation studies (a view shared by Toury 1995).

Reiß and Vermeer's approach has also been judged less applicable to LITERARY TRANSLATION than to other text types because of the special status and 'apurposive' nature of literary texts (Kohlmayer 1988; Zhu 2004). Snell-Hornby (1990: 84) argues that the situation and function of literary texts, where style is a highly important factor, are more complex than those of non-literary texts. Thus, although skopos theory is by no means irrelevant to literary translation, a number of points need rethinking before the theory can be made fully applicable to this genre. It has been argued, for example, that to assign a skopos to a literary text is to restrict its possibilities of interpretation. In literary theory, a distinction is often made between text as potential and text as realization, and skopos theory appears to see the text only as realization, and not as a potential which can be used in different situations with different addressees and different functions. However, Vermeer (1989b: 181) argues that a text is composed with an assumed function, or a restricted set of functions, in mind. The suitability of skopos theory for literary texts, and for practically all kinds of text (including interpreting), has been supported by numerous case studies (e.g. Ammann's 1990 model of translation critique; see also Snell-Hornby 2006: 64).

A further point raised by Chesterman (1994: 153), who otherwise acknowledges the important contributions of skopos theory, is that even though a translation may indeed fulfil its intended skopos, it may be assessed as inadequate on other counts, particularly as far as lexical, syntactic, or stylistic decisions on the micro level are concerned. Moreover, the focus on translations being 'commissioned' by clients has led some scholars to argue that functionalism turns translators into mercenaries (Pym 1996b) who simply do what their clients want them to do. Vermeer's skopos rule allows for the interpretation that any end (the purpose as specified by clients) justifies the means (the choice of linguistic structures). Kadric and Kaindl (1997) therefore argue for the inclusion of ethical aspects into skopos theory in order to avoid a misinterpretation of the skopos rule for unethical purposes and to ensure that translators base their decisions on intersubjectively valid criteria. Nord introduced the concept of **loyalty** to highlight the 'responsibility translators have toward their partners in translational interaction' (Nord 1997: 125). Function plus loyalty is thus Nord's specific variety of functionalist approaches. Whereas concepts such as faithfulness or fidelity usually refer to relationships between the texts themselves, loyalty stresses the translator's responsibilities towards people,

i.e. not only with regard to clients and users of their translations, but also with regard to the author(s) of the source text. For Nord, the skopos of the target text must be compatible with the intentions of the source text author(s). The concept of loyalty thus means a limited range of justifiable target text functions. This view is supported by Hönig (1997: 12), whereas for Witte (2000: 43) 'loyalty' to the intention of the source text author constitutes a sub-skopos of the overall skopos and is therefore redundant as a separate concept.

In sum, the shift of focus away from source text reproduction to the more independent challenges of target text production for transcultural interaction has brought an important element of innovation to translation theory. As attention has turned towards the functional aspects of translation and the explanation of translation decisions, the expertise and ethical responsibility of the translator have come to the fore. Translators have come to be viewed as target text authors and as competent experts in translational action, a development which releases them from the limitations and restrictions imposed by a narrowly defined concept of fidelity to the source text alone.

See also:
ADAPTATION; COMMERCIAL TRANSLATION; EQUIVALENCE; LINGUISTIC APPROACHES; QUALITY; REWRITING; SCIENTIFIC AND TECHNICAL TRANSLATION; UNIT OF TRANSLATION.

Further reading
Reiß 1971, 1976; Vermeer 1978; Hönig and Kußmaul 1982/1991; Holz-Mänttäri 1984, 1986; Reiß and Vermeer 1984/1991; Vermeer 1986, 1987; Nord 1988; Vermeer 1989b; Ammann 1990; Hatim and Mason 1990a; Newmark 1991; Nord 1991a/2006; Holz-Mänttäri 1993; Koller 1993; Hönig 1995; Kußmaul 1995; Vermeer 1996; Hönig 1997; Nord 1997; Kußmaul 2000b; Reiß 2000; Witte 2000.

CHRISTINA SCHÄFFNER

G

Gender and sexuality

The two concepts – sexuality and gender – are closely related, but tend to be considered separately in translation studies. Generally speaking, 'sexuality' refers to the linguistic representations of sexual practices, while 'gender' designates the cultural trappings that accompany biological sexual difference: the behaviours, dress codes, views, belief systems and treatments that are part of being male or female in any particular place, time, and group – and the linguistic representations of these trappings. 'Gender' as a concept and an analytical category entered the field of translation studies in the late 1980s, and since then a substantial number of books (Simon 1996; von Flotow 1997; Messner and Wolf 2001; Santaemilia 2005) and articles have been written on the topic. 'Sexuality' is a currently developing analytical category in translation studies (Larkosh 1996), addressing issues such as forms of CENSORSHIP imposed on representations of sexuality in translation.

Gender and language: Does the term man include woman?

In the 1970s and 1980s, the connections between gender and language were examined in numerous studies throughout the West that applied feminist ideas and considered the significance of 'gender' in relation to linguistics, literary studies, anthropology, historiography, philosophy, psychology, politics and, finally, translation. Virtually every academic discipline in the humanities and social sciences engaged with this issue, and the general public also took considerable interest in it. While no consensus on the extent and exact type of relationship between gender and language use may have been reached as a result, the fact that such a relationship exists has been established (Cameron 1985; Sunderland 2006). The same goes for the relationship between gender and literary or historical fame, and the gendered content and meaningfulness of philosophical, sociological and political texts (where, for example, the term *man* has traditionally been assumed to include *woman*).

The general aim of gender-focused work has been to explore the importance of 'gender' as an analytical category where social phenomena are concerned, demonstrating that the term *man* cannot, and does not, in fact, include *woman*, confirming the inherently sociopolitical connections between gender and language, and revealing how language reflects power relations between the sexes.

In the late 1980s and the 1990s, when the focus on female and male as the major gender categories broadened with the arrival in the academy of gay activism and queer theory, the neat binary opposition between 'men' and 'women' that had been so useful to feminisms was challenged. Queer theory brought with it ideas of contingent, performative gender with similarly contingent meaning and language use; flexibility and individual choice in regard to gender came to imply similarly contingent approaches to language use, where the social and subjective contexts can arguably be as powerful as any learned or acquired behaviours or belief systems. An approach developed that recognizes gender as a continuum, and the linguistic identity politics that followed have accordingly had an important impact on translation studies.

Research integrating the category of gender into translation studies does so on a number of different levels:

- by focusing on gender as a sociopolitical category in macro-analyses of translation phenomena, such as the production, criticism, exchange, and success of works, authors and translators;
- by examining gender issues as the site of political or literary/aesthetic engagement through micro-analyses of translated texts; and
- by shaping the theories applied to or derived from translation praxis.

Gender and sexuality as sociopolitical issues in macro-analyses of translation

Gender as a category informing macro-analyses of translated texts is largely revisionist, exposing the fact that women and other gender minorities have essentially been excluded from or presented negatively in the linguistic and literary histories of the world's cultures. Researchers have re-evaluated historical texts, their translations, authors, translators and sociopolitical contexts from the perspective of gender. Often large areas of writing and translating such as women writers and translators in Renaissance England (Hannay 1985; Krontiris 1992), the translation of sexuality in eighteenth-century Russia (Tyulenev 2008), or English women translators of science texts in the 1700s (Healy 2002) are explored in order to examine the effects of gender politics across a wide swath of society. Such research has raised many further questions, and not all studies have focused only on the female gender.

One very important area of research has been the revision of translations of key cultural texts such as the BIBLE or the QUR'ĀN from a gender-aware perspective, revealing new readings, and REWRITING them for a contemporary audience. Feminist critiques and RETRANSLATIONS of parts of the Bible have appeared in several European languages from the late 1970s (Haugerud 1977; *Inclusive Language Lectionary* 1983; Korsak 1992), focusing on the need for inclusive language that directly addresses women in the congregation and recognizes them in the texts themselves. The Qur'ān has attracted somewhat less attention, but a few studies are beginning to appear (see *The Feminist Sexual Ethics Project*

and Edip Yuksel's collection of 'Unorthodox Articles', n.d.). Revisionist studies of the Bible have shown that translations have traditionally hardened Christian attitudes against women, interpreting these ancient texts 'creatively' in order to define women as the root of evil (Korsak 1994/1995, 2005) or as untrustworthy and incapable (Stanton 1898/1985), and casting the human male in the image of a male God. Centuries of interpretation and translation have fostered the cultural and political denigration of women in Christian countries and cultures. While gender-conscious retranslations of the Bible in the late twentieth century initiated some turbulent discussions and changes in certain churches and congregations, they also caused a backlash from the Vatican in the 2001 document entitled *Liturgiam Authenticam* (Vatican 2001). This document asserts Vatican control of Bible translations and insists that a generic male term does refer to all humans (e.g. *man/homme/ Mann* includes *woman/femme/Frau*). Further, it re-instates the traditional masculine vocabulary for God, Jesus Christ, and the Holy Spirit, re-aligning these figures once more with the human male.

Historical revision from a gender-conscious perspective has also been undertaken in relation to other textual, largely LITERARY, phenomena. Previously undocumented work of women translators in colonial and modern-day Korea (Hyun 2003), eighteenth- and nineteenth-century Germany (Messner and Wolf 2001) and eighteenth- and nineteenth-century France (Sirois 1997) has been unearthed and discussed. The output of numerous neglected or forgotten women writers from the past or from many other cultures has also been identified, and their works collected, translated or retranslated. Examples include women writers in India (Tharu and Lalita 1991/1993), abolitionist women writers in eighteenth- and nineteenth-century France (Kadish and Massardier-Kenney 1994), women translators (Delisle 2002) and women writers of post-Cold War East Central Europe (von Flotow and Schwartz 2006). The impetus for such research derives from feminist literary historiography, which has sought to counter the effects of the literary canon that has promoted and recognized male writers and translators at the expense of female writers and translators, thus depriving cultures and societies of the work and ideas of an important and different sector of the population. Work on the translations of women writers has focused on the roles that translators play in furthering knowledge and transporting texts across cultures, as well as on their subjective involvement and intervention in such texts. Thus, the story of Julia Evelina Smith, the mid-nineteenth-century American Bible translator, shows not only the interventionist power of the individual woman translator working against the grain of her cultural context, but also the political impact of this work on others around her (von Flotow 2002). Similarly, the French translations of Charles Darwin by Clémence Royer have been shown to be strongly influenced by her personal views on his research and contemporary ideas about eugenics (Brisset 2002).

Similar work is currently underway with regard to homosexual and gay authors and references to gay sexuality in translation. Recent research on the role played by LITERARY TRANSLATION in the westernization of Russia (Tyulenev 2008) shows to what extent sexuality was a more sensitive issue in translation than in the local literature. A fascinating piece of work on the English translations of German nineteenth-century sexologists Ulrichs, Krafft-Ebing and Hirschfeld demonstrates the power of translation to both respond to and reflect target culture mores, in this case adapting source texts that study and describe phenomena of human sexuality in such a way as to criminalize and condemn the phenomena (Bauer 2003).

Gender and sexuality as categories in micro-analyses of translation

When gender serves as a lens for the micro-analysis of individual translations, the focus is on the minute details of language that (may) reflect the gendered aspects of a text, or seek to conceal them (often in the case of homosexual writings). Translations can be shown to be sensitive to such manifestations of gender, exaggerate them or ignore and obscure them. Often, the translation effects discerned through such analyses provide clues about the cultural and political literary climate of the translating culture, or can be understood as a facet of this climate. Such work also offers valuable re-readings of key

writers, exploring the synchronic or diachronic connections between a writer and his or her translators, revealing the positioning of writers, translators and researchers engaged in a triangular struggle for the power to interpret and assign meaning.

Critical translation analyses, or re-readings, of key writers include work on a number of women writers viewed as important for the feminist movement, such as Sappho, Mary Wollstonecraft and Simone de Beauvoir. The poetic fragments that survive from the work of the Greek poet Sappho, one of the few women known to have been a public literary figure in ancient Greece, have been translated in many different ways, with translators often filling in the gaps from their own imagination. Prins (1999), Rayor (1991) and DeJean (1989) study the way in which English translations of Sappho have historically adapted her work to the surrounding literary environment and its gender interests, serving, for example, to support lesbian literary movements in nineteenth-century England or trite lyricism in 1950s compendia of ancient poets. Similarly, a study of three different twentieth-century German translations of Mary Wollstonecraft, one of the first women to publish on the rights of women in eighteenth-century England, shows that the translating cultures (both pre- and post-1989 East and West Germany) adapt the text for their own purposes – to support women's bourgeois education – and thus obscure much of the political intent, intelligence and difficulty of the work (Gibbels 2004). Finally, the case of Simone de Beauvoir in English translation provides many examples of intellectual and literary CENSORSHIP (Simons 1983; von Flotow 2000a) that has truncated and misrepresented her thought, making her work appear confused, conventionally patriarchal, unpalatable, and hardly relevant to late twentieth-century readers. English translations of Beauvoir also provide excellent examples of censored sexuality in translation: 1950s male translators working in the US simply excised her daunting descriptions of awkward contraceptive contraptions and erotic love scenes.

Studies of the connections between one specific writer and (her) translators have had a noteworthy impact on the theorization of gender and translation: Nicole Brossard, a Quebec writer of experimental avant-garde poetry and prose whose work has foregrounded gender in language since the late 1970s, has triggered a series of translations as well as theorizations that set off work on feminist translation in the 1980s and 1990s (see CANADIAN TRADITION). Written in French, her work has been translated into dozens of languages, thus posing and re-posing the problem that every woman writer must face: the nefarious aspects of gender in the language she has at her disposal and which work against her as a *woman writer*. Brossard's work – like that of Monique Wittig, Mary Daly, Hélène Cixous, Clarice Lispector and other experimental twentieth-century women writers – seeks to undermine this conventional language and develop experimental forms for preferred use in women's writing. Since she writes in French, where nouns, adjectives and participles need to be gender-identified (as in any Romance language, and many others), Brossard deliberately overuses this capacity to feminize language by coining words such as *maternell, homoindividuell, essentielle* and *ma continent* to write 'the feminine' back into French. The translations of these new forms as well as the commentaries and theoretical approaches developed by translators on the topic of rendering feminist neologisms now make up a large corpus on feminist experimental translation (Godard 1984; Wildeman 1989; de Lotbinière-Harwood 1991; von Flotow 2004; Wheeler 2003), also furthering reflection on the act of 'woman-handling' texts (Godard 1990), or intentionally intervening in translation to express political and personal identity (see DESCRIPTIVE VS. COMMITTED APPROACHES).

Ideas derived from these struggles around gender identities in experimental language and translation are also present in work on gay writing and translating. For example, a certain type of language use identified as 'camp' in English writing and described as 'language features [that] have come to stand for certain gendered and subcultural differences' (Harvey 2000: 298) and that are often 'extrasexual performative gestures' (Harvey 1998: 305) denotes and generates gay self-identificatory activity. Studies of the translation of this coded neologistic language into another sociocultural and political context and time have shown how contingent (gay) identity in language is and to what extent it is negotiated and devised within a certain source community and, later, within the translating culture, where such identity issues are often differently expressed, viewed and handled. Keenaghan's article (1998) on the 'gayed' American rewriting of Federico Garcia Lorca's encrypted homosexual images traces some of the issues around identity-reinforcing or celebratory translation of quietly homosexual writing, while a detailed study of Plautus translations into German (Limbeck 1999) traces the power of centuries of CENSORSHIP of homosexual references in the target culture.

Research questions and agendas

The relationship between gender affiliations of the writer and those of the translator has led to theorization about whether biological sex or gender identification play a role in translation, and if so, under what circumstances. Questions posed include whether men can translate women's texts and vice versa; whether gender identification plays a role in this process; whether a translator needs to be gay in order to successfully translate a gay writer's work (Kinloch 2007); and how women translators have fared in the past with the male authors they translated (Simon 1996; Delisle 2002).

The practice of feminist translation, as a particular approach to rendering a text in translation (Godard 1990; von Flotow 1991; de Lotbinière-Harwood 1992; Massardier-Kenney 1997), has raised overarching theoretical and ethical questions; these include the extent to which the literary and cultural politics of the moment do or should offer translators the freedom and the political justification to view and present themselves as creative and deliberately interventionist, and what constitutes an ETHICS of interventionist translation in the name of gender politics.

Studies of the gendered metaphors of translation (Chamberlain 1988/2004, 1998/2001) have raised questions about how perceptions of translation both reflect and structure a society's conception of gender relations, tie it in with its understanding of translation, and reveal the power plays involved in both the operations of text transfer and male/female relations. In this respect, it is worth examining how these metaphors mould translators', writers', publishers' and readers' experiences and uses of translation. Moreover, given the strong link such metaphors establish between the reproduction of texts and the reproduction of humans, it is interesting to speculate whether the development of 'new reproductive technologies' will affect this thinking and the treatment of texts (Orloff 2005).

Littau (2000) raises the question of the extent to which psychoanalytic approaches to gender can help explain and formulate translation theories; more specifically, she explores how Freudian/Lacanian theories that posit male heterosexuality as the norm have affected text production and the conceptualization of translation, and how feminist revision of these theories – by Irigaray, for example – also revise our understanding of translation.

Differences within so-called 'gendered minorities' (see MINORITY) – such as women, or GBLT (gay, bi-sexual, lesbian, transsexual) – raise theoretical questions about the conceptual and actual limits of considering such groups as homogeneous entities which can be represented or misrepresented by a certain discourse, or by certain texts in translation (von Flotow 1998; Spivak 1992b). How much difference within such groups – due to class, race, ethnicity, IDEOLOGY and other factors – is allowed/accounted for in the identity-forming discourses around gender, sexuality and translation (Arrojo 1995; Harvey 2000)?

An as yet undeveloped area of gender-focused research concerns AUDIOVISUAL TRANSLATION, where the role played by the sound effect of gendered voices raises interesting questions, such as how sound carries gender authority and affects meaning, what connotations and associations it triggers, and how it plays out in translations of media and audiovisual work.

See also:
CENSORSHIP; DESCRIPTIVE VS. COMMITTED APPROACHES; ETHICS; IDEOLOGY; LITERARY TRANSLATION; MINORITY.

Further reading
Chamberlain 1988/2004; Godard 1990; von Flotow 1991; de Lotbinière-Harwood 1992; Arrojo 1995; Simon 1996; Massardier-Kenney 1997; von Flotow 1997, 1998; Harvey 1998,

2000; Keenaghan 1998; Maier 1998; Bauer 2003; Santaemilia 2005.

LUISE VON FLOTOW

Globalization

The term 'globalization' has been used to broadly describe the profound nature of changes affecting economies, cultures and societies worldwide from the late twentieth century onwards. Anthony Giddens has defined globalization as 'the intensification of worldwide social relations which link distant localities in such a way that local happenings are shaped by events occurring many miles away and vice versa' (1990: 64).

A central feature of the new, global economy which has emerged in the context of intensified relations is that it is informational. That is to say, the productivity and competitiveness of firms in the new economic order depend on their ability to create, process and apply knowledge-based information efficiently. Alongside the centrality of information and knowledge, a further distinct feature is the nature of economic organization which has emerged in late modernity. The central activities of production, consumption and circulation, as well as their components (capital, raw materials, management, information, technology, markets), are organized on a global scale, either directly or through a network of connections between different economic agents. The importance of the information technology revolution from the 1970s onwards was that it provided the tools or the material basis for this new economy. Although the history of empires shows that economic activity on a supra-national scale is by no means a novelty in human history, the crucial difference with a global economy is that it is able to work as a unit in real time on a planetary scale. For the economy to work as a unit in a multilingual world, however, the mediation of translation is necessary.

The emergence and exponential growth of the LOCALIZATION industry in the late twentieth century was the most obvious consequence of the need to satisfy the translation needs generated by the informational economy in the era of global markets. Evidence of the scale of the translation challenge was provided by the second version of Microsoft *Encarta*, which involved the translation into a variety of languages of approximately 33,000 articles, 10 million words, 11,000 media elements, 7,600 photos and illustrations, 2,000 audio elements, 1,250 maps and charts, 1,500 web links and 3,500 bibliographical entries. The rise of the World Wide Web has meant a shift to web localization, with a shift from project-based to program-based localization. In other words, rather than simply taking a web site at a point in time and putting it into another language a provision must now be made to translate continuously updated and revised content. An important impetus for the growth in web localization is the increasing numbers of web users who are non-English speaking and who prefer web content in their own language. Indeed, much of the commentary on translation studies to date, in this context, has focused on issues raised by localization practice (Sprung 2000b; Pym 2004). What this development points to is the fundamental ambiguity of the role played by translation in the context of globalization. If information is acknowledged to be the basic raw material of the new global economy and significant economic gains are to be made from the production of goods with a high cognitive content, then not only is language a key factor in the expression of that information but language also represents a crucial means of accessing the information. One translation consequence is that speakers of different languages seek to translate themselves into the language perceived to have the greatest information-density. This is the translation movement that results in a language perceived as information-poor gradually being abandoned for a language deemed to be information-rich. Another consequence is the increase of pressure on translators and the translation industry to translate ever-increasing volumes of material more and more quickly, precisely because access to information is so important and because the availability of such access is an evidence of a language's ability to function in the modern world and thus remain an important source of symbolic identification.

A readily available example of the spread of global relations is the exponential growth in supra-national institutions in the latter half of the twentieth century. In 1909, for example,

there were 37 inter-governmental and 176 international non-governmental organizations; by the end of century, this number had grown to 300 inter-governmental and 4,200 international non-governmental organizations (Goldblatt 1995: 28). The growth in these institutions is seen both as a shift from an exclusive focus on the sovereign nation state as the locus of governance and as evidence of an increasing awareness of the need to tackle political, military, cultural and ecological issues at a global level. Given that these organizations operate in a multilingual world and have in certain instances (European Union, Amnesty International) a foundational multilingualism as a feature of their internal organization, translation is a key element of their ability to function effectively. Indeed, one of the striking features of the impact of globalization is the manner in which organizations such as Babels have emerged. Babels is an international network of volunteer interpreters and translators whose main objective is to cover the interpreting and translation needs of the Social Forum (Boéri and Hodkinson 2005; Hodkinson and Boéri 2005; Baker 2006b). The Social Forum brings together groups critical of the political, economic and cultural impacts of globalization. The existence of such a network and other similar groupings guarantees that linguistic and cultural diversity is maintained as a core value in movements contesting the assimilationist tendencies of hegemonic languages sustained by economic and military might. A further dimension to the issue of translation and resistance in the contemporary age is the implication of translators and interpreters in military conflicts. Baker (2006a), for example, uses theories of narrative to explore the implications for translation and translators of their involvement in situations that produce real and often deadly tensions between global ambitions and local realities.

In a fundamental sense, what is repeatedly at stake in the relation between the phenomenon of globalization and translation practices is a tension between what might be loosely labelled centrifugal and centripetal forms of globalization (Pieterse 1995: 45–67). On the one hand, there is the centripetal form, the notion of globalization as homogenization – implying imperialism, subjection, hegemony, Westernization or Americanization. On the other hand, there is the centrifugal form, suggesting globalization as resulting in interdependence, interpenetration, hybridity, syncretism, creolization and crossover. Thus, we can see translation as the *sine qua non* of the cultural dominance and an agent of centripetal globalization if we consider that without the services of dubbers and subtitlers Hollywood dominance of global cinema markets would be inconceivable (see AUDIO-VISUAL TRANSLATION). Conversely, translation can be seen as the quintessential expression of centrifugal globalization if we reflect that it is translation which alone allows speakers of a language under threat to retain full autonomy, whether this means using software in their own language on the computer or taking an active part in public life in a language of their own choosing.

One of the most obvious consequences of globalization for many societies has been the phenomenon of inward and outward migration (see MOBILITY). In 2002, the United Nations Population Division reported that over 175 million people were residing in a country other than the one in which they had been born, and in the period between 1975 and 2002 the total number of migrants in the world had more than doubled. An ageing population in the developed world, the insatiable labour needs of the tertiary sector and the continued presence of warfare and persecution provide a powerful impetus for migratory movements. Migrants can be those who travel elsewhere to find opportunities equal to their skills and qualifications or they can be post-industrial migrants who are available to work anywhere at low rates of pay. The presence of and increasing awareness of migration results in, among other things, a perceived need to deal with language issues. Migrants not only translate themselves in the literal, physical sense of uprooting themselves from one place and moving to another but they also find themselves having to translate themselves into another language and culture. It is no surprise, therefore, that the most visible outcome of the impact of migration on translation studies has been the burgeoning of interest in COMMUNITY INTERPRETING (Brunette *et al.* 2003).

The very global nature of migration, with peoples travelling great distances to find work, means that alongside proximate we have extended migration. That is to say, the languages spoken by migrants will no longer generally be the language of a neighbouring nation state or of an economically disadvantaged region within the nation state, but will often be from very distant and distinct language groups. Thus, translation as an issue is especially visible in a world of increasingly extended migratory networks, where the operations of a global economy in real time bring citizens in a variety of countries into immediate and daily juxtaposition with language and cultural difference. Questions of power and identity are very much to the fore in the realm of migration and translation. Gaining access to interpreting services is at one level an acknowledgement that a language community must enjoy the same rights as other citizens in terms of their dealings with various public bodies; at the same time, access to interpreting also implies the right to a language identity, to retain and foster one's own language and culture. Indeed, a notable feature of the response of nation states such as the United States, Britain, Denmark and the Netherlands in the era of globalization has been to focus on language and translation questions in debates around citizenship and entitlement.

Fundamentally, migration policies divide into policies of translational assimilation and translational accommodation (Cronin 2006). Under a regime of translational assimilation, the stated objective of the state is that migrants will only qualify for citizenship if they can demonstrate satisfactory proficiency in the language of the state, and policies will be generally aimed at encouraging migrants to assimilate as rapidly as possible to the dominant or official language of the country, to translate themselves in other words into the language of their hosts. On the other hand, a regime of translational accommodation is one which acknowledges the importance of linguistic and cultural diversity in a society and the contribution of language and culture to the psychological and social well-being of migrants and therefore supports translation practices as a way of protecting diversity while ensuring communication. Needless to say, neither regime tends to exist in isolation, though depending on the vagaries of domestic politics, one model will come into the ascendant.

Underlying the opposition between the two regimes of translation is another issue which is very much to the fore in debates around globalization, namely the relation between translation and multiculturalism. If, as Marion Young argues, 'groups cannot be socially equal unless their specific experience, cultural and social contributions are publicly affirmed and recognised' (1990: 37), it follows that equality involves the policy of active support of linguistic and cultural difference, a policy generally referred to as one of multiculturalism. It is the rights discourse of multiculturalism which often serves to legitimize or justify, for example, the provision of community interpreting services to a particular group. The difficulty is that a multiculturalism signalled exclusively through difference can end up defining ethnic groups as unchanging cultural communities, predicated on a static notion of CULTURE which ignores the constant flux and changing nature of human, social groups. Interculturalism as distinct from multiculturalism is more concerned with the dynamics of interaction and developing reciprocal relations of understanding. Given that translation, by definition, is engaged with the business of communication and understanding, albeit sharply circumscribed by the power relationships present in any situation, it inevitably finds itself in greater dialogue with the emerging interdisciplines of intercultural communication and intercultural studies in the human and social sciences. Thus, if the 1960s and 1970s have been loosely periodized as the time of the 'linguistic turn' in translation studies and the 1980s and 1990s as the period of the 'cultural turn', it is apparent that translation studies in the context of accelerated globalization has shown evidence of an 'intercultural turn'.

When discussing the nature of globalization, it is commonplace to argue that one of the most important features of the phenomenon is space-time compression. It takes less and less time to cross greater and greater distances. A letter can take days or weeks to arrive, an e-mail message arrives in seconds. The compression is of course partly a question of circumstance. Those who are not connected to global networks as a result of economic or social disadvantage can find themselves even more isolated or marginal than they were previously. It is nonetheless striking in translation studies itself that one of the consequences of globalization has been a greater geographical and institutional dissemination of centres of translation study and research, so that scholars from, for example, Brazil, South Africa, Australia, China and the Arab world are challenging the dominance of translation studies research by writers and thinkers from Europe and North America (Wakabayashi 2005; Hermans 2006). It is without doubt the increased interaction between scholars from non-traditional centres of translation research which will be globalization's most enduring legacy to the discipline.

See also:

ASYLUM; COMMUNITY INTERPERTING; ETHICS; INSTITUTIONAL TRANSLATION; LOCALIZATION; MOBILITY; NEWS GATHERING AND DISSEMINATION.

Further reading
Giddens 1990; Young 1990; Goldblatt 1995; Pieterse 1995; Cronin 2003, 2006.

MICHAEL CRONIN

Hermeneutics

Hermeneutics is the discipline concerned with understanding and explicating what is not immediately intelligible. It operates in the first instance within a given tradition, when the accidents of time and change have rendered access to the meaning of texts problematic and in need of explication. It can also be applied across languages and cultures. Viewing translation in relation to hermeneutics highlights the contiguity of intra- and interlingual translating as the negotiation of difference and otherness. As an INTERPRETIVE practice translation is framed by hermeneutic concerns.

Hermeneutics takes its name from the ancient Greek god Hermes, who ran messages between the gods and between gods and mortals. To carry out his task Hermes needed to be able to translate between the divine and the human orders.

The ancient Greek verb *hermeneuein*, from which the term 'hermeneutics' derives, means to interpret, explain, narrate, clarify, translate. Its Latin counterpart *interpretari* means likewise to interpret and elucidate.

The development of modern hermeneutics is rooted in the separate disciplines of exegesis and philology. Exegesis dealt primarily with canonical and sacred texts, especially the BIBLE. There is a long and rich Jewish tradition of kabbalistic readings of the Bible. They tease out meanings from a text regarded in principle as inexhaustible. Christianity too developed sophisticated ways of interpreting the Bible. The early Church discerned four levels of meaning in the Christian Bible (literal, figural, anagogical and eschatological). Philology, a secular discipline, came into its own in Early Modern Europe as part of the Humanist engagement with Ancient texts. These texts, transmitted in often corrupt manuscripts, were collated, compared and studied for both authenticity and meaning. Their interpretation called for detailed knowledge of the relevant language and historical context.

Modern hermeneutics proper is usually said to begin in the Romantic period with Friedrich Schleiermacher. Among the major names since then are Wilhelm Dilthey, Martin Heidegger, Hans-Georg Gadamer, Paul Ricoeur and Jacques Derrida. All have dealt with questions of translation in their work, sometimes in considerable and illuminating detail.

Before Schleiermacher, several thinkers in different disciplines had reflected on the general principles of interpretation. In the Early Modern period, the theory of translation tended to be subsumed under this heading. This was the case, for instance, with Lawrence Humphrey's *Interpretatio linguarum* (1559) and Pierre Daniel Huet's *De optimo genere interpretandi* (1661, 1683; DeLater 2002). In the eighteenth century, Johann Martin Chladenius presented perhaps the most thorough account of hermeneutics until then. His *Introduction to the Correct Interpretation of Reasonable Discourses and Writings* (1742) held, in line with Enlightenment ideas, that while understanding required knowledge and practical skill, for example in comparing different viewpoints, it was not fundamentally problematic, provided both speaker and interpreter were led by common sense or 'reason'. The hermeneutic task consisted in removing obstacles of language, genre, perspective or historical distance so as to allow a full and clear view of the meaning of a text. That such a view could be achieved was not in doubt.

The Romantic conception of language was destined to change all that. For the Romantics, language was constitutive of thought. Different languages embodied different ways of conceptualizing the world. As a result, understanding and translating others became fundamentally problematic. For Friedrich **Schleiermacher** (1768–1834), who worked on his hermeneutics for decades without gathering his notes into a book, 'understanding is an unending task' because 'the talent for misunderstanding is infinite' (1977a: 41; Ellison 1990: 78).

In Schleiermacher's view understanding is especially problematic because linguistic usage and thought are not only interdependent but also highly individual. Works of art in particular are expressions of creative selfhood which shape language as much as they are shaped by it. To grasp this individuality, one must put oneself 'inside' an author and even awaken meanings the author may have remained unaware of. Historical and cultural distance and differences between languages only compound the problem. In his *Dialectic* of 1814–15 Schleiermacher put it starkly: 'No knowledge in two languages can be regarded as completely the same; not even … A = A' (1998: xxi).

On a practical level Schleiermacher divides hermeneutics into 'grammatical' and 'technical' (subsequently called 'psychological') interpretation. The former is concerned with pre-given linguistic structures, the latter with the sovereign transformative power of individual thought. The two forms of interpretation operate together and are supplemented by comparison and divination, the former an exercise in criticism, the latter an imaginative leap into the author's subjectivity. By thus attempting a holistic reading and by contextualizing the utterance as a moment in a life, the interpreter can strive to 'understand the utterance at first as well as and then even better than its author' (1977a: 112). The continual movement back and forth between the parts and the whole and between textual detail and context which this type of analysis requires, is known as the hermeneutic circle.

Schleiermacher's 1813 lecture 'On the Different Methods of Translating' is an offshoot of his hermeneutic concerns. It is informed by the two kinds of interpretation mentioned above and locates the difficulty of translation in insuperable difference. The translator must seek to articulate by means of his own language, and in mimetic form, the specific understanding that he, as an outsider, has reached in engaging with an author writing in a different tongue that

exhibits a different lifeworld and is being handled in a uniquely individual manner. The preferred modality of this articulation, the often-quoted 'bringing the reader to the foreign author', is altogether secondary compared with the formidable nature of the hermeneutic challenge.

If Schleiermacher marks the Romantic break with the Enlightenment, Wilhelm **Dilthey** (1833–1911) wrote at a time when positivism provided the model of the sciences. He is best known today for the distinction he made between the aims of the natural and the human sciences. Whereas the former seek explanation, the latter pursue understanding. This understanding is concerned with history, which does not repeat itself, and with unique creations, which are expressions of lived experience. Indeed for Dilthey the act of understanding itself is lived experience in an historical context. In this way hermeneutics begins to shift from a theory of knowledge, an epistemology, to a theory of being, an ontology (Ricoeur 1981: 53–4).

'Tell me what you think of translation and I will tell you who you are', Martin **Heidegger** (1889–1976) observed in an essay on the poet Hölderlin in 1942 (1996: 63), confirming the ontological dimension of the new philosophical hermeneutics. Heidegger's attempt to rethink Western metaphysics led him to question the imposition, ever since Greek philosophy, of overarching schemes on pre-reflexive thought and language. Language for Heidegger is even more fundamental than for his predecessors. It has the power to open up the world and point to the totality of existence or 'Being'. The meaning of a text consequently exceeds any authorial intention.

Much of Heidegger's own work, like Jacques Derrida's later practice, is grafted on existing texts and seeks to uncover what remains unsaid and unthought in them. It does this by patiently and sometimes idiosyncratically tracing their presuppositions and limits, their incompleteness, the ground that underpins but is not part of the logic they display. When this listening to the speaking of the language itself is verbalized in critique or translation, it requires the reporting language to be stretched as well and may even provide access to its own unthought. Heidegger's translations of pre-Socratic fragments by Anaximander,

Heraclitus and others (Heidegger 1975) are extraordinary exercises, extensive meditations that incorporate repeated and increasingly radical attempts at translation, going beyond dictionaries and philology and pushing his own German to the limits of intelligibility.

Hans-Georg **Gadamer** (1900–2002) also regards language as man's distinctive characteristic, but he is concerned less with metaphysics than with methodology. Gadamer highlights the dialectic of participation and distancing that marks the effort to understand, and stresses the historicity of the interpreter who is confronted with the 'otherness' of the data to be interpreted, even though the latter are part of a historical continuum that comprises the interpreter as well. Being exposed to history is the precondition for understanding but makes self-understanding problematic. While it prevents a globalizing view from above, it permits a 'fusion of horizons', the always provisional and hard-won meeting at the intersection between the familiar and the alien. This explains Gadamer's invocation of translation as illuminating the hermeneutic endeavour, since 'from the structure of translation [is] indicated the general problem of making what is alien our own' (Gadamer 1977: 19). In the pages devoted to translation in *Truth and Method* (1960) Gadamer stresses that translation cannot be a reproduction of an original, it can only be an interpretation reflecting both empathy and distance (1989: 385–90).

More than any other writer on hermeneutics Gadamer has influenced theorists and critics of translation, notably George **Steiner**. Steiner too asserts 'the primacy of the matter of translation' in all cross-cultural comparative work (1995: 11) and thinks of translation as operating both intralingually and interlingually. He has recast the idea of fidelity in translation in terms of a 'hermeneutic motion' in four steps (1975: 296–303): initial confidence that the foreign text has something valuable to communicate, then an aggressive move of incursion into the alien territory and extraction of meaning from it, followed by incorporation of new material into the receiving language, and finally the satisfaction that the original too has been enhanced by being translated. In Germany Fritz **Paepcke** (1986) also took his cue from Gadamer. His analyses favoured a holistic rather than a linguistic or analytical approach.

If for Gadamer conversation was the archetypal hermeneutic model, Paepcke stressed translation as a personal encounter which called for the translator's emotional and physical as well as intellectual investment, an idea that would be reprised in Douglas Robinson's *The Translator's Turn* (1991).

The dialogic principle informing Gadamer's hermeneutics has led Paul **Ricoeur** (1913–2005) to posit that the self only knows itself through the Other. But whereas spoken conversation may provide a model for direct understanding as grasping an interlocutor's intended meaning, written texts are typically divorced from such originary intentions and contexts. This is what makes translation as well as interpretation difficult. Ricoeur (2006) stresses that translation has to labour to overcome resistance: that of the original which cannot be grasped in its entirety and thus defies translation, and that of the receiving language, which cannot hope for a perfect translation. Yet he also dismisses the twin utopias that would overcome translation: that of an original language which can never be recovered and that of a universal language which remains forever to be devised. Instead, Ricoeur celebrates the Babel myth as symbolizing diversity. It allows him to make translation the paradigm of what he calls 'linguistic hospitality', the site where similarity across languages and cultures is constructed rather than found and where the host language opens itself up to accommodate the foreign.

The deconstructive practice of Jacques **Derrida** (1930–2004) is perhaps best described as a hermeneutics of suspicion (see DECONSTRUCTION). Derrida shares Heidegger's scepticism regarding the Western metaphysical tradition and its vocabulary, including its two vital translation moments (the creation of a philosophical terminology in Greek, then the transition to Latin). Like Heidegger, Derrida explores translation not by trying to dominate it through theorizing from above but by close engagement with it. His most incisive essay on translation (Derrida 1985) starts by demonstrating the aporia of translation conceived as transfer of meaning and continues by translating, in highly ironic vein, an essay on translation (Walter Benjamin's 'The Task of the Translator') which rejects the idea of language as a vehicle for meaning. Elsewhere Derrida has explored, in patient detail, the 'double bind' of translation as both impossible and necessary. Perhaps no other contemporary thinker has lavished such attention on the eminently hermeneutical problems and paradoxes of language, meaning and translation.

See also:
BIBLE, JEWISH AND CHRISTIAN; CULTURAL TRANSLATION; CULTURE; DECONSTRUCTION; ETHICS; INTERPRETIVE APPROACH; TRANSLATABILITY

Further reading
Heidegger 1942/1996; Gadamer 1960/1989; Heidegger 1975; Steiner 1975/1992; Schleiermacher 1977a; Derrida 1985; Ricoeur 2004/2006.

THEO HERMANS

History

Interest in the history of translation has been growing steadily since the early 1990s. Woodsworth (1998) provides a comprehensive overview of developments up until 1995; this entry focuses on developments from 1995 onwards.

Like most fields within the humanities and social sciences, history has taken a 'cultural turn' under the influence of postmodernism. There has been a shift from a (presumably) factual and objective, Eurocentric, top-down history, concerned with great men, great ideas and discrete political events and nations, to a history that is seen as narrative in nature, subjective, bottom-up, concerned with either local or worldwide systems, with ordinary people, popular culture, and the development of social institutions across political borders and over longer periods of time. As a result, the 'great men of history' approach (Cary 1963) has given way to studies of individual translators considered in their larger social, political or cultural context (Wilhelm 2004b). The individual translator is now seen as representative of a larger social group, for example middle-class Spanish participants in the conquest and governance of South America (Fossa 2005).

There has been a concomitant tendency to take into account issues such as GENDER AND SEXUALITY (Krontiris 1992), POSTCOLONIAL contexts (Tymoczko 1999a) and the interplay between history and CULTURE (Frank 1992). Two related recent developments include examining paratexts (prologue, epilogue, notes, etc.) as data for historical research (Lavigne 2004; St André 2004) and looking at the role of translation in the writing and shaping of history (Payàs 2004; Bastin and Echeverri 2004).

Aims and methods

Despite the growing volume of literature on translation history since the early 1990s, there have been few attempts at reflecting on how and why the history of translation should be researched and documented. Scattered individual articles have appeared, more often asking questions such as 'what is the history of translation?' than answering them, or simply calling for more studies (Berman 1984; D'hulst 1991; Lambert 1993; Pym 1992b; Bastin 2004). The one salient exception is Pym's *Method in Translation History* (1998). Pym argues that a history of translation should focus on translators rather than texts, address the social context and be relevant to the present. He gives concrete and detailed advice on how to locate, compile and interpret the material necessary to achieve those aims. For example, Pym suggests the use of CORPORA as a methodological tool to systematize data for historical analysis, although this suggestion pulls him away from the translator and towards bibliographic research of translations. His discussion of the need for reliable data harks back to Bragt's (1989) call for such work and puts the spotlight on resources such as UNESCO's *Index translationum*, a database of titles in translation which was begun in the 1930s. Originally covering just five languages in six countries, and with a hiatus in publication due to World War II, the *Index translationum* expanded rapidly in the 1950s and an online version has been available since 2000. There are, however, some inaccuracies in the information provided, and the almost total lack of records dealing with translations into certain languages (most notably Chinese) means that such resources must be used with caution, bearing in mind potential inbuilt biases and cross-checking with other sources whenever possible (see Foz and Serrano 2005 for insights into the problems and pitfalls of compiling bibliographies of translations from databases).

Scope

The scope of a history of translation concerns questions relating to the boundaries of legitimate inquiry: What counts as a translation? Who counts as a translator? What other types of activities, either associated with translation (such as editing, printing, publishing) or with translators (their background, finances, other professional activities, etc.), can or should be discussed when writing a history of translation? Historically, translation has not been pursued as a career (Pym 1998), and many works that were considered translations at the time they were produced would not be considered so by current professional standards. To what extent do we wish to use modern criteria to evaluate the past? If we choose to be more inclusive, what are the implications for the contemporary relevance of a history of translation? Finally, the role of PSEUDOTRANSLATION; ADAPTATION, summary and other grey areas needs to be tackled.

Due to the lack of consensus around these issues, and to practical concerns regarding delimitation and focus (a comprehensive history of translation would involve countless languages, be unmanageably long and probably unreadable), in practice each historian draws their own boundaries.

History of translation theory and criticism

Many historians of translation are attracted to writing the history of translation CRITICISM and theory rather than of translation proper, perhaps because such works form a relatively restricted set. Some have dealt with the development of ideas in one geographical region over a limited period of time. D'hulst (1990), for example, focuses on the history of translation in France, and Balliu (2005a) on Russia. A pan-European approach, generally from Greco-Roman times

until the early twentieth century, has also been popular (Ballard 1992; Robinson 1997c).

Steiner (1975/1992) combines a history of European translation theory along with his own theoretical model of translation. Steiner is not alone in combining historical research and theoretical arguments of his own; indeed, the potential for a history of translation theory to offer useful insights or correctives to the development of contemporary or future theoretical models is one of its strengths. Such a use of history can be traced as far back at least as Johnson's use of translation history to advocate and justify free translation (Johnson 1759/1963: 211–17). Venuti (1995a), too, uses historical material to advance a theoretical argument, and critics of that work have also used historical data to challenge his theory (Pym 1996a). Gile (2001) is unique in tracing the history of research into conference interpreting.

History of translation practice

Although some fairly ambitious works covering a wide geographic and temporal area have been attempted (Kelly 1979), historians working individually commonly use delimiters from political history, such as the nation (Delisle 2005). An example can be seen in Wyler (2005), who focuses on the Brazilian tradition. Such studies may be further restricted in terms of time period, as is the case in Milton and Euzebio (2004), who focus on the 1930s–1950s, also within the Brazilian context. The medieval and early Renaissance period in Europe seem to have attracted a great deal of attention, although this was perhaps more true in the late 1980s and 1990s (see Woodsworth 1998).

Other studies tend to be even more sharply focused, often on the works of a particular writer or one particular text (Foz and Serrano 2005; Léger 2004). Such studies frequently touch on the issues of RETRANSLATION and RELAY (St André 2003a). Moving the spotlight from the author to the translator, Moyal (2005) discusses how Guizot, a French Restoration translator, used his translations of SHAKESPEARE and Gibbon to advance his ideological agenda in France; Wilhelm (2004b) looks at Mme de Staël and the emergence of liberalism, while St André (2004) situates the translator George Staunton within British debates on the nature of law and Chinese society.

Greek and Roman classics, despite having been translated several times through European history, have attracted surprisingly little attention to date in translation studies, although endless debates over the 'best' or 'proper' way to translate Homer echo down the ages (see, for example, Arnold and Newman 1914; see CLASSICAL TEXTS). By contrast, translation of the BIBLE was one of the first areas to attract the attention of twentieth-century historians (Norlie 1934) and remains popular today (Sneddon 2002; Delisle 2005). Translation of the Bible often merges into other areas of historical inquiry, such as LITERARY TRANSLATION (Barnstone 1993), print culture (Van Kempen 1997) and TERMINOLOGY (Prickett 1993). The translation activities of missionaries have also begun to receive attention (Rafael 1993; Demers 2004; Lai 2007). Perhaps because both the Jewish and Islamic traditions insist that believers recite holy texts in the original language, there has been less written on the history of translation in these religions, although there have been some studies of the translation of the QUR'ĀN (Bobzin 1993; Versteegh 1991). The translation of Buddhist scriptures has attracted more attention (Zacchetti 1996; Cheng 2003; Tajadod 2002; see CHINESE TRADITION).

In general, the history of translation has focused on literary (Corbett 1999; Thomson-Wohlgemuth 2004) and religious texts. However, a few other areas have received coverage, most notably science (Montgomery 2000; see SCIENTIFIC AND TECHNICAL TRANLATION).

Due to its ephemeral nature, the history of interpreting has received relatively little attention, although there have been a few articles on the history of CONFERENCE INTERPRETING (Keiser 2004; Baigorri-Jalón 2005), at least one book (Roland 1999), and some interesting uses of indirect documentation to study the role of interpreters in pre-modern society (Demers 2003; Karttunen 1994; Kaufmann 2005; Lung and Li 2005).

Moving outside Europe

Sánchez and Pinilla (2004) note that certain traditions in Europe, such as the Portuguese tradition, are relatively neglected. Scattered articles indicate that various other cultures have rich and varied historiographical traditions in translation (Baccouche 2000), but because of the lack of translation of scholarly articles into European languages, they remain little known to the Western reader. A notable exception is Bandia (2005) on Africa. Articles concerning the history of translation criticism in China and Asia have also begun to appear in English (Yu 2000; Cheung 2006; Hung and Wakabayashi 2005b; see also SOUTHEAST ASIAN TRADITION). The Chinese have a highly developed historiographical tradition which has long featured the history of translation to and from Chinese as a significant area of research. Chen (1975) collects together many significant essays from 1895 to 1965, including works on the history of the translation of Buddhist texts and the translation of Western scientific works into Chinese. An entire book is dedicated to the history of translation in Central Asia from the remote past down to the thirteenth century (Maitiniyazi 1994), and many articles have been published on the translations by the Jesuits in the Ming and the Qing dynasties (Li 2000, 2001).

A 'Canadian School'?

Credit for fostering some of the most recent developments in translation history must be given to several members of the Canadian Association for Translation Studies, including Jean Delisle, Judith Woodsworth, Georges Bastin and Paul Bandia. In 2004 and 2005 they produced two special issues of META devoted to the history of translation, plus an edited volume based on the special theme for their 2004 annual meeting 'Translation and History' (Bastin and Bandia 2006). They have also been responsible for pioneering work on the history of translation in Central and South America (Milton and Euzebio 2004; Payàs 2004; Bastin and Echeverri 2004; Fossa 2005).

The Canadian School has also led the way in collective approaches, but with mixed results. A FIT project launched in the 1960s languished for some years before eventually coming to partial fruition as Delisle and Woodsworth (1995), which opted for a selective and representative approach rather than the grand narrative of world history that was originally envisaged. Baker (1998) and the present volume collect essays on various regions, but no attempt is made to connect them together.

Reflections on the practice of translation history

There has been a concerted effort to argue for the increased visibility and recognition of translators through the examination of their influence in one culture or in a wide variety of cultures over one millennium (Delisle and Woodsworth 1995). This type of history may be perceived as a sort of 'lobbying' by a professional organization to show the world that translation matters and that translators should therefore be treated better. However, this desire to celebrate the role of the translator threatens to turn all history of translation into hagiography. In a curious way, the history of translation today resembles early twentieth-century American history, which uncritically celebrated the founding fathers. To date, few historians of translation have followed in the footsteps of revisionist American histo-

rians such as Beard (1925). There is a need for critical reflection on what uses translation has and may be put to, either by the translator, the client, or the reader. The history of translation is inevitably bound up with ethical considerations (see ETHICS) and must ultimately address questions such as why we are writing the history of translation, who the intended audience of this history is, and what possible impact our research might have, both on our evaluation of the past actions of other people and on our future plans.

See also:
BIBLE, JEWISH AND CHRISTIAN; CENSORSHIP; CLASSICAL TEXTS; PSEUDOTRANSLATION; QUR'ĀN; RELAY; RETRANSLATION; REWRITING.

Further reading
D'hulst 1991; Ballard 1992; Frank 1992; Lambert 1993; Delisle and Woodsworth 1995; Robinson 1997c; Pym 1998; Woodsworth 1998; Liu 1999; Tymoczko 1999a; Fossa 2005; Kaufmann 2005; Bastin and Bandia 2006; Cheung 2006.

JAMES ST ANDRÉ

Ideology

A significant problem with the study of 'ideology' in any discipline is its definition and scope. First used in 1796 by Count Destutt de Tracy to refer to a new rationalist 'science of ideas', from the nineteenth century onwards 'ideology', from the French *idéologie*, came to acquire a negative Marxian sense of illusion or false consciousness (the misguided way of thinking that characterizes others, such as the ruling classes, for example), and this negative sense has had a significant impact on the way it was studied (Williams 1983: 153–4). Although more contemporary uses of the term in the humanities cover neutral phenomenological as well as negative senses, the word 'ideology' remains problematic, as emphasized by Woolard (1998: 8), who states that 'arguably, even the most doggedly neutral social-scientific uses are tinged with disapprobation, the truly neutral stance more often encoded by the choice of other labels such as culture, worldview, belief, *mentalité*, and so on'.

The terminological confusion associated with 'ideology' is exemplified by the various theoretical frameworks from other disciplines that have informed translation studies. Thus, for example, the term 'worldview' is used by Simpson (1993: 5) to frame his definition of an ideology as 'deriv[ing] from the taken-for-granted assumptions, beliefs and value-systems which are shared collectively by social groups ... [and] mediated [through] powerful political and social institutions like the government, the law and the medical profession'. This definition is taken up by Hatim and Mason (1997) in their discussion of ideological mediation in translation and, using almost the same phrasing, by Faiq (2004), but in his case to refer to 'CULTURE'. Other important models used for uncovering implicit ideology in translation are drawn from critical discourse analysis (Fairclough 1989/2001; see DISCOURSE ANALYSIS), sociology (Bourdieu 1991) or the multidisciplinarity of van Dijk (1998), which brings together aspects of cognition, discourse and society. Some translation theorists have posited their own terminology and models: Lefevere (1998b: 48), for instance, describes ideology as 'the conceptual grid that consists of opinions and attitudes deemed acceptable in a certain society at a certain time and through which readers and translators approach texts' and argues that translation is governed above all by patronage, which consists of ideological, economic and status components (Lefevere 1992a: 16; see REWRITING).

In part, then, the problem of discussing translation and ideology is one of definition and category, giving rise to a range of challenging questions. Is all human activity ideologically motivated? When is something 'ideology' rather than just 'culture', and what is the difference between the two? Can we invoke the notion of ideology to explain what is only our 'life-world', our concrete human situation (Gadamer, quoted in Bandia 1993: 62)? When the publishers of Anne Frank's diary remove allusions to her sexuality, is that, as Lefevere suggests, because there is an 'ideologically sanctioned image of what a fourteen-year-old should be' (1992a: 62–4), or is it simply a matter of modesty? When Gutzkow, in preparing Büchner's *Dantons Tod* for the stage, 'deletes what may be taken to be offensive to the taste of the middle- and upper-class readers' (ibid.: 153), is that an ideological move or a matter of taste? And what can we say about Lefevere's own hidden ideology which decrees that the middle and upper classes are a monolith about whose taste sweeping judgements may be made?

The essence of ideological intervention in the case of translation is that the selections made during the translation process (not only by the translator but by all those involved, including those who decide the choice of texts to translate) are potentially determined by ideologically based STRATEGIES governed by those who wield power. These can be uncovered by analysing the various target text selections that impact on the target reader who, nevertheless, generally and crucially reads the text as though it were a transparent, unmediated rendering of the original, more or less unaware (or at least willingly suspending the knowledge) that it is a translated text. The perceived truth status of the words of the target text can only be uncovered if the source and target texts and their paratextual framings are compared side by side, even though the motivation for any SHIFTS may remain open to conjecture.

Translation studies' interest in ideology is thus firmly linked to the concept of language and power relations and the distortion, manipulation (Hermans 1985a) or 'REWRITING' (Lefevere 1992a) of the source text and culture in the process of translation. This interest is explained by what Gentzler and Tymoczko (2002: xviii) call the inherent 'partiality' of translation, its status as an inevitably partial representation of the source text. The textual and other choices made by the translator(s), editor(s), commissioners and other actors must be selective and therefore also 'partisan', since they condition the image, function and impact of the text in the target culture and may be repressive or subversive (ibid.).

The ideology of translation strategy

The 'partisan' role of translation is highlighted in the assertion by Penrod (1993: 39) that 'since we are always required when translating to "take a position" relative to other cultures and languages, we must as well remain ever vigilant as to the nature of the position assumed' (see ETHICS). Penrod interprets in terms of power relations Schleiermacher's (1813/1963) philosophical distinction between what are now known as domesticating and foreignizing strategies of translation (see GERMAN TRADITION; STRATEGIES). However, the distinction has been redefined many times by many people, among

them Berman (1984) who, writing explicitly about translation and ideology, talks of ethnocentric and hypertextual translation, and Venuti (1995a, 1998b), who critiques the dominant, transparent translation strategies of the Anglo-American tradition. This demonstrates the extent to which the debate about translation strategies (essentially literal versus free) has tended to be ideologically motivated, even in its more modern manifestations.

The practice of translation was for a long time, and in some cases remains, deeply implicated in religious ideology, as can be seen in the grim fate of translators such as Tyndale in Britain (see BRITISH TRADITION) and Dolet in France (see FRENCH TRADITION), both burnt at the stake, a fate mirrored in the twentieth century by the assassination of the Japanese translator of Salman Rushdie's *Satanic Verses* and the subsequent refusal by other publishers to produce a translation. In many instances, literal translation, or non-translation (see QUR'ĀN), of religious and other sensitive texts in traditions such as the Arabic or medieval European was an attempt to prevent what was seen as a potential sacrilegious distortion of the sacred word of God.

While the extremes of literal translation attempt to fix and control meaning, the deconstructionists would claim that all deviations are permissible, needing only the motivation of an ideology to justify them, because there is no original to be copied and because the 'violent hierarchy' which gives primacy to the source text can be overturned in favour of the target scheme (see DECONSTRUCTION). If original meaning does not exist and if the work lives on in the endlessly deferred meaning of the play of the signifier, then various forms of ADAPTATION become justified as the main translation techniques (see below).

As well as (and perhaps even more so than) the textual practices of translation, ideology reveals itself in recontextualization, the use of paratextual devices such as prefaces and other material which frame the text (Baker 2006a, 2007), and in the policy choices of those who control the publication process. The latter include the decision of whether to commission and publish a translation or not. In the most obvious cases of ideological manipulation, there is a concerted policy: thus, in Germany from 1933 to 1945 there was a clear ideology behind the selection of texts, with a high number of Scandinavian and Flemish/Dutch texts translated because of the feeling of kinship the Nazis considered they shared with the German *Volk* (see CENSORSHIP). Ideological orientation can also be gleaned from bibliographical data of books the Nazis published every year, and by examining reviews in the Party and book-trade press that supported the racist official policy of eliminating 'all elements alien to the German character' and those felt to be characteristic of foreign literature (Sturge 2004).

The ideological struggle within translation studies

As well as examining the expression of ideology in translation, it is interesting to consider the ideological struggle that has been taking place to make translation studies accepted within the academy in many countries. This struggle is motivated in part by the lower status that has long been accorded to translation compared to 'original' writing, and in part by the strength and interests of more established disciplines: first the Classics, Latin and Greek, which were prestigious and dominant in many Western education systems until the second half of the twentieth century, and then Modern Languages. As translation studies has established itself over a number of decades (from the 1970s onwards), so research foci have shifted from a 'scientific' linguistic categorization of translation phenomena to studies that centre principally on the macro-sociocultural context in which the translation act is performed (see LINGUISTIC APPROACHES). Both types of study are underpinned by an ideological agenda. While the scientific study of EQUIVALENCE drew strength from the absolutist, logocentric philosophy of Plato that was central to Western rationality, and in which the referential function of language predominated, so the more 'cultural' approaches to translation are also founded on an underlying and partial ideological base.

In the scientific and technological atmosphere of the early and mid-twentieth century, there was for a time a feeling that linguistic theory had provided a 'scientific' basis for grounding translation in a way that should eliminate subjective evaluations of 'accuracy' and transfer of meaning. One of the main proponents of this trend was Eugene Nida, who believed that he had found a neutral point of observation on which to base his concept of dynamic equivalence. Nida is therefore understandably the prime target of deconstructionist critiques of 'closure', which aim to lay bare the ideological bases not only of individual acts of translation but also of translation theories in general. Meschonnic (1986: 77), for example, accuses Nida of 'pseudo-pragmatism' and manipulative behaviourism, and Gentzler points to the 'non-dit' of 'the Protestant sub-text' in Nida's linguistic approach (1993/2001: 59).

To some extent, criticisms of Nida are themselves ideologically motivated. One of the most frequent criticisms of Nida's methodology is that its justification for translating the biblical phrase 'to greet with a holy kiss' by 'to give a hearty handshake all round' amounts to complicity on the theory's part with the dominant white, heterosexual, male, Western Anglo-American understanding of what is an acceptable mode of greeting between men. Yet Gentzler, a severe critic of Nida, has no comparable denunciation to offer of Barbara Godard's declaration that the feminist translator 'flaunts the signs of her manipulation of the text' (Godard 1990: 94; see GENDER AND SEXUALITY).

The ideological perspective of the analyst thus always plays a role in shaping the course of his or her argument; this inherent subjectivity and bias of the viewer and commentator, along with the concomitant relativism of truth, can be traced back to the Greek Sophists (Hawkes 2003: 22–3) and finds its most outspoken voice in Nietzsche. Even those working firmly within the branch of descriptive translation studies (Toury 1980a, 1995) which has placed descriptivism at the heart of inquiry into translation and has proposed a solid basis for the study of translation as an empirical science (see DESCRIPTIVE VS. COMMITTED APPROACHES), must respond to the criticism that such observation can never be totally dispassionate and value-free (Hermans 1999: 36). Other translators and translation studies theorists have an openly ideological and political agenda, and espouse what Brownlie (2007a: 136) calls 'committed approaches'. For instance, Canadian feminist translators such as Godard and de Lotbinière-Harwood deliberately distort the norms of language to highlight the female experience, while the US translator-academic Suzanne Jill Levine has chosen to work on the apparently most unpromising ideological texts, in Levine's case the machista *Three Trapped Tigers* by the Cuban Guillermo Cabrera Infante (Levine 1991). Elsewhere, Cheyfitz (1991) and Niranjana (1992), among many others, have focused on the unequal power relations between colonizer and colonized, and between colonial language–native languages, in a concerted effort to deconstruct these relations and to counter the relevant imbalance (see POSTCOLONIAL APPROACHES). Similarly, as a translator Venuti (1998: 10) sets out 'an opposition to the global hegemony of English' and the erasure of the foreign by choosing to translate 'minority' texts and to translate in a non-fluent style. This 'positionality' of the translator and translation theorist (von Flotow 2000b: 18), from a postcolonial, post-structuralist or gender perspective, has its counterpart in the committed work of critical linguists who seek to uncover the 'insidious discursive practices in language' and thereby to 'challenge' the ideological practices they enact (Simpson 1993: 6). Tymockzo (2003), too, asserts that the translator is necessarily located in an ideological position in the target culture, a claim which runs counter to those translation theorists who depict the translator as a 'mediator' or 'communicator' (Hatim and Mason 1997) or in an 'in-between' or hybrid 'third space' (Wolf 2000).

Much of the work in translation studies has been centred on major world, especially major European, languages and ideologies, and this has created its own imbalance to the detriment of lesser-used languages (Cronin 2003: 140; see MINORITY). But the ideological focus on concepts that are rooted in Western models of translation is increasingly being challenged. Tymoczko (2006: 22) discusses some of the alternative perspectives on translation in non-Western cultures: the very words and metaphors for 'translation' used in India (*rupantar* = change of form; *anuvad* = 'speaking after', 'following'), in the Arab world (*tarjama* = 'biography') and China (*fan yi* = 'turning over'), for example, indicate a radically different focus, one where the goal of close lexical fidelity to an original is not a given. Furthermore, there are contexts and forms of translation which challenge traditional

thinking in Western translation studies: thus, Bandia (1993: 56–7, 2008) discusses African authors writing in European languages and argues that translation of their works requires a source culture-oriented approach which takes particular care to avoid 'negative stereotyping' in the transfer into the colonizer's language; Japan developed the practice of 'kambunkundoku', where Chinese texts were read in Japanese but where no written target text was produced (Wakabayashi 2005: 59); the greater bilingualism and lower literacy rates in India, as in some other countries, to some extent obviate the need for formal written or spoken translation (Trivedi 2006), though such diglossia contains its own hierarchy.

From a historical perspective, then, general questions of power and ideology are constantly tied up with the relative power of different languages, which has an important effect on what is translated and how translation takes place. This is particularly noticeable in the history of Bible translation in a Christian context, where desire for dissemination of the texts led to translation first into the international languages of Greek and later Latin, and then in the Reformation into the new vernacular European languages, all the while against a tense backdrop of a Church that sought to control that translation and dissemination. In current times, it is English that occupies a hegemonic position as the overriding international language, increasingly influencing and even undermining the viability of scientific and technological genres in other languages (see Anderman and Rogers 2005). The consequences of such imbalances of power and the way they convey and frame ideology have attracted growing interest within translation studies in the first decade of the twenty-first century. This is illustrated by the publication of a range of volumes on the issue of ideology in translation, including von Flotow (2000c), which contains mainly historical case studies; Gentzler and Tymoczko (2002) and Calzada Pérez (2003), which embrace more interdisciplinary approaches and cover a variety of forms of translation and interpreting; Cunico and Munday (2007), which examines ideology in the translation of scientific, political and other non-literary texts; and Munday (2007), which explores how the translator's ideology, sometimes expressed subconsciously, may be detected through an examination of specific textual and stylistic choices.

See also:

ADAPTATION; CENSORSHIP; CHILDREN'S LITERATURE; CULTURAL TRANSLATION; DECONSTRUCTION; DESCRIPTIVE VS. COMMITTED APPROACHES; ETHICS; GENDER AND SEXUALITY; HERMENUETICS; POSTCOLONIAL APPROACHES; REWRITING; SOCIOLOGICAL APPROACHES; STRATEGIES.

Further reading
Hermans 1985a; Lefevere 1992a; von Flotow 2000c; Gentzler and Tymoczko 2002; Calzada Pérez 2003; Cunico and Munday 2007.

PETER FAWCETT AND JEREMY MUNDAY

Institutional translation

'Institutional translation' broadly refers to a type of translation that occurs in institutional settings. The term is problematic, in part due to the categorical ambiguity of the concept of *institution* – indeed, translation itself is arguably an institution in its own right – but also because, somewhere between the commissioning of a translation project and the publishing of a translation, translators and translations inevitably become associated with an institution, such as a multinational manufacturer that commissions a translation or a publishing house that puts it into print. Nevertheless, 'institutional translation' is generally used by translation scholars to refer either to translating *in* or *for* specific organizations such as the Translation Bureau of the federal government of Canada (Mossop 1988, 2006), or to institutionalized social systems such as the legal system (Colin and Morris 1996) or the health care system (Davidson 2000). Based on this definition, the study of institutional translation is concerned with organizational, structural, relational, ideological or historical aspects of a translating institution and their impact on translators and the process and product of translation.

The importance of institutions to the study of translation was first underlined by Mossop, who pointed out that translating institutions are a 'missing factor in translation theory' (1988: 65). While approaches to the study of institutional translation are heterogeneous, they all share the assumption that translation is a socially situated practice (see SOCIOLOGICAL APPROACHES). This assumption is evident in the theoretical frameworks employed as well as the topics of research. Discourse Analysis, Bourdieu's concepts of *habitus*, field and capital, and Latour's Network Theory are among a wide range of theoretical tools and methods that are borrowed from other disciplines and increasingly being used to describe and explain translation in an institutional setting. Research topics range from a critical investigation of the texts selected for translation (Tahir-Gürçağlar 2003) to an analysis of textual features of institutionally produced translations (Kang 2007); from a scrutiny of the role of the institutional translator as a social and cultural agent (Rudvin 2006) to the problematization of the production and reproduction of discursive practices via translation (Blommaert 2005); from an examination of the translator's work routines, status and issues of power and control (Berk-Seligson 1990/2002) to an investigation of institutional NORMS and culture (Inghilleri 2003); and from the analysis of institutional goals and IDEOLOGY (Koskinen 2000b) to a historical description of practices of institutional translation (Hung 2005). Increased attention to institutional translation is indicative of a shift in the discipline towards more contextualized explanations of translational practices and more socially informed approaches to the study of translation.

The history of institutional translation

Although scholarly interest in institutional translation is a relatively recent phenomenon, the practice of institutional translation has a long history. One of the earliest and best known examples is the translation of the Pentateuch of the Old Testament into Greek, commonly known as the Septuagint. According to the *Letter of Aristeas*, this translation enterprise began with Demetrius of Phaleron, Director of the Royal Library of Alexandria, persuading Ptolemy II

Philadelphus, ruler of Egypt in the third century BCE, to arrange for the Pentateuch to be translated for the library. After much negotiation between the relevant parties, seventy-two elders, all knowledgeable in Hebrew and Greek, were brought to the island of Pharos from Jerusalem to carry out the translation under the direction of Demetrius, with 'all their requirements being lavishly supplied' by Ptolemy II (Hadas 1973: 119).

Many such instances of institutional translation activities are documented by historians of translation. BIBLE translation in particular has a long history of institutional translation practice, although examples of Bible translation as a private endeavour are also numerous. Some generalizations may be adduced from such historical accounts: institutional translation is carried out by teams of individuals with complementary knowledge and skills, working under established procedures and translating on the basis of explicit principles and language guidelines. These features can be identified in another well-known seventeenth-century Bible translation project commissioned by King James I of England. Non-theological discussion of this project has tended to focus more on its literary influence and the political agenda behind the King's commissioning of the translation. However, the systematic character of the work format and translation procedures adopted in this project, which involved forty-seven scholars divided into six committees entrusted with revising each other's work in addition to translating their own part of the text – all working with specific guidelines provided by King James I – have since been replicated in many institutional projects of Bible translation. For example, Wilt (2003b), a translation consultant working for the United Bible Societies, describes contemporary translation projects at this institution as involving the following roles and processes: translators reviewing the work of others; the team's exegete(s) checking translations for faithfulness; reviewers checking dialect use, style and translation approach; a translation consultant examining the exegesis, translation approach, content and presentation of supplements; a manuscript examiner checking the quality of manuscript presentation; and translators reviewing a camera-ready copy before it is sent to the printer. In addition, translation work is hierarchically coordinated to 'assure satisfactory content and quality of products developed in view of organizational goals' (ibid.: 51).

This continuity in work format and participation structure is evident throughout the history of institutional translation, despite the great diversity of this practice. In China, institutional translation played a critical role in the transmission of Buddhism, the implementation of trade and diplomatic policies, and the introduction of Western learning (see CHINESE TRADITION). Translation of sutras from Central Asian languages and Sanskrit into Chinese was instrumental in ensuring the spread of Buddhism in China and other parts of East Asia, such as Korea and Japan. Isolated attempts to translate Buddhist scriptures, which began around the second century CE, evolved into large-scale, and often government sponsored projects that were carried out in teams. The process became more organized and systematic in the third and fourth centuries CE, with explicit procedures being adopted and various team members collaborating in distinct roles: *yizhu* (Chief Translator), a highly revered master, presided over the translation by orally explicating the Buddhist concepts; *chuanyu* (Interpreter) interpreted the Chief Translator's explication into Chinese; and *bishou* (Recorder) compiled the text in Chinese. The final stage of translation involved checking the Recorder's notes and cross-checking them against those taken by the monks and scholars in the audience for verification. During the earlier period of sutra translation, the Chief Translator was often a foreign monk who could not speak Chinese. However, even after the linguistic need for adopting this format disappeared with the emergence of Chinese monk-translators, teamwork in sutra translation continued. Teamwork has thus come to be viewed as an important practice that sets the Chinese translation tradition apart from other traditions, as evident in Lefevere's comment that 'the Chinese tradition emphasizes what we would now call teamwork, while the Western tradition has often frowned upon that very concept' (1998a: 22). However, the history of translation in Europe and other parts of the world features comparable translation practice in terms of adopting organized procedures, distinct roles and collective translation. In the European context, the practice of collective Bible translation mentioned above is one example. In thirteenth-century Spain, translations were undertaken by collective teamwork under the direction of King Alfonso the Learned. Members of translation teams assumed such roles as *enmendador* (Reviser), *glosador* (Writer of Glossess) and *capitulador* (Organizer into Chapters), in addition to the usual translator role (Pym 2000a). Other instances of teamwork in institutional translation are documented in the history of translation into Arabic: in the seventh and eighth centuries, large-scale government translation projects were carried out in Baghdad (see ARABIC TRADITION).

According to Hung and Wakabayashi (2005a: 6), government translation in the Chinese context constitutes the 'only continuous translation tradition in history'. The most prevalent mode of government translation in China was indirect translation or *chongyi* (RELAY translation), a practice which reflects the strong sense of superiority that prevailed among the Chinese in general and the educated elite in particular. The Chinese belief in the existence of acute cultural differences between 'alien' people and themselves and the resulting Chinese disapproval of direct communicative interaction with foreigners such as tribute-bearers may partly explain the prevalence of this mode of translation, which sometimes involved as many as eight or nine translators in the communication process. Relay translation continued from the tenth century BCE until the end of the Ching Dynasty in the early twentieth century. The pervasiveness of the relay mode of government translation in Chinese translation history is indicative of the way an institution's prestige and ideology can often outweigh concerns for efficiency and effectiveness in interlingual communication. This is also evident in the case of European Union translation, considered in more detail below.

Work modes and the translating agent

Contemporary modes of institutional translation vary considerably across institutional and cultural boundaries. While working in in-house translation departments was the general mode of employment for institutional translators in the past, perhaps due to the centralized organization of cultures in which many translators traditionally worked, increased attention to issues of cost and flexibility mean that partial or complete outsourcing structures now complement or entirely replace in-house translation (see Pym 2001b and Dollerup 2000a for discussions of translation in the EU and the UN, respectively). Many institutions continue to draw on internal resources to meet their translation demands: Lee *et al.* (2001), for example, found that translation in 72.6 per cent of the 223 South Korean public institutions surveyed (including central and local government, governmental agencies, public corporations and associations) is undertaken by in-house personnel, mostly working in teams. Nevertheless, institutions are increasingly making use of freelance translators and sub-contracting structures, and exerting different degrees of control over the recruitment of translators, the quality of translations and text production procedures. This shift towards outsourcing was made possible by the World Wide Web and the resulting 'de-materialization of space' (Cronin 2003: 43; see GLOBALIZATION). The spatial decentring of translators has also been supported by increased reliance on COMPUTER-AIDED TRANSLATION, including various electronic resources, translation memories, terminology-management systems, LOCALIZATION, web-page translation tools, and MACHINE TRANSLATION, all of which have significantly shortened the time spent on translation and streamlined work procedures. Although the dependence on technological tools at present may be more prominent in certain parts of the world, such as Europe, or industries (e.g. the localization industry), this trend is likely to expand globally in the future.

Translation in an institutional setting is thus developing into an intricate process that involves multiple mediators, or more specifically a network of humans and technological tools. The institutional production of translation often involves complex, collaborative work among translators, revisers, editors, experts and sometimes even source text drafters, as well as a range of electronic resources. Although collectively produced translations tend to be associated with issues of speed and quality control in an institutional context, there are other factors which motivate this practice, most

notably the fact that the distribution of responsibility for producing a translated text among
several layers means that the text selected for
translation is taken through a series of processes
designed to ensure that the translated output
functions seamlessly as part of the discourse of
a given institution. As such, the notion of *the
translator* in our common conceptualization of
translation may no longer be serviceable in an
institutional context: 'the translator' is no longer
an individual who translates a text solely on
the basis of personal training and experience,
but also a participant in a situated institutional
practice that has become routinized and habit-
uated over time. The distinction between 'the
translator' and 'the translating agent' in an institutional context and the reconfiguration of the
way in which the role of 'translator' is understood in a translating institution are both issues
that require further investigation.

Research on institutional translation

One institution that has been the focus of
sustained scrutiny in translation studies since
the 1990s is the Translation Service of the
Commission of the European Union, the largest
translating institution in the world. Interest in
this particular institution may be motivated by
its sheer size and complexity, and the consequent light that its description can thus shed on
many theoretical and practical issues of language
policy, IDEOLOGY, economics, GLOBALIZATION
and intercultural communication. It may also
originate, in part, from a long-standing bias in
translation studies, which remains Eurocentric
in orientation. That said, the perspectives and
topics taken up in the discussions are diverse and
have enriched our understanding of translation.

One topic that has been addressed by several
researchers is the way in which textual features
of EU translations (e.g. vocabulary, syntax,
style) clash with target language conventions. These features have been discussed in
terms of the EU policy of MULTILINGUALISM,
collective and complex translation processes
and procedures, and the concept of 'hybridity';
the latter, according to Trosborg, refers to
features of translated text that are ' "out of
place"/"strange"/"unusual" for the receiving

culture' (1997: 146). Hybridity in EU translations, in particular, has been associated less with
'translationese', or lack of translational competence, and more with a convergence between
cultures or institutional patterns of behaviour.
Another area that has received some attention
in the literature is the institutional culture of the
EU. For example, Koskinen (2000b: 49) suggests
that EQUIVALENCE is an 'a priori characteristic
of all translations' within the EU since the EU
policy of linguistic equality presupposes equal
value for all language versions. As an inherent
and automatic quality of all translations, the
equivalence relationship holds not only between
the source and the target text but among various
translations of the same source text. Koskinen
thus argues that EU translations are 'intracul-
tural' in that they are reflective of a distinct
EU culture that cannot be accounted for by the
dichotomous conceptions of source and target
cultures or by the concept of 'interculture' as
theorized by Pym (2000a). Other scholars have
since attempted to describe this 'distinct' institutional culture of the EU (e.g. Wagner *et al.*
2002; Hermans and Stecconi 2002; Pym 2000b),
but Mason rightly argues that 'the whole issue of
institutional cultures of translating … is worthy
of a more systematic exploration, across a range
of institutions and language pairs' (2004: 481).

Like many other terms in the discipline,
'institutional translation' continues to evolve
and encompass new meanings. While it has
so far mostly centred on translation practice at
large and important institutions, the concept
is slowly but clearly being used as a means of
understanding and studying translation practice
in general: in other words, there is a growing
trend to view and analyse all forms of translation
in institutional terms. This is not surprising
given that translation itself is arguably an institution. It might thus be more productive to
adopt an institutional perspective on all forms
of translation. The diachronic, synchronic and
panchronic study of translation practice in institutional terms might then render new insights
about different forms of translation practice
and provide more systematic explanations,
alternative explanations and specific empirical
detail that have so far been largely lacking in the
discipline.

Further reading
Mossop 1988; Trosborg 1997; Koskinen 2000b;
Pym 2000b, 2001b; Calzada-Pérez 2001;
Wagner *et al.* 2002; Koskinen 2004; Hung and
Wakabayashi 2005b; Inghilleri 2005b; Mossop
2006; Pym *et al.* 2006.

JI-HAE KANG

Interpretive approach

The interpret(at)ive approach or 'the interpretive
theory of translation' (*la théorie interprétative de
la traduction*) has also been known as the 'theory
of sense' (*la théorie du sens*). It is an approach to
interpreting and translation adopted by members
of the ESIT group (*École Supérieure d'Interprètes
et de Traducteurs,* of the University of Paris III/
Sorbonne Nouvelle), sometimes referred to as
'the Paris School'. Developed in the 1960s on
the basis of research on CONFERENCE INTER-
PRETING, the interpretive theory of translation
remains one of the main paradigms in interpreting studies research. It was initially applied
to TRAINING AND EDUCATION in interpreting,
where it has been very influential (for example,
it informs the practice of simultaneous interpreting at the European Union Institutions),
and was subsequently extended to the written
translation of non-literary or 'pragmatic' texts
(Delisle 1980/1988; see COMMERCIAL TRANS-
LATION) and to the teaching of translation.

The Paris School was founded by Danica
Seleskovitch. Drawing on her extensive
experience of professional conference interpreting, Seleskovitch (1975, 1977) developed
a theory based on the distinction between
linguistic meaning and non-verbal sense,
where **non-verbal sense** is defined in relation
to a translating process which consists of three
stages: interpretation (as understanding) of
discourse, deverbalization and reformulation.

A detailed model of simultaneous interpreting
that draws on this distinction is elaborated in
Lederer (1981).

The theoretical background

Drawing on experimental psychology, neu-
ropsychology, linguistics and Jean Piaget's work
on developmental psychology, researchers of
the Paris School study interpreting and translation in real situations, with particular emphasis
on the mental and cognitive processes involved
(see PSYCHOLINGUISTIC AND COGNITIVE AP-
PROACHES). Their research focuses on the translating process, particularly on the nature of
meaning as *sense* – as opposed to linguistic
or verbal meaning. Sense is composed of an
explicit part (what is actually written or spoken)
and an implicit part (what is unsaid but nevertheless meant by the author and understood by
the reader/listener), the latter not to be confused
with the author's intention. Full comprehension
of sense depends on the existence of a sufficient
level of shared knowledge between interlocutors, without which the confrontation between
text and cognitive structures does not lead to
the emergence of sense. Cognitive structures
include both the **encyclopaedic** or real-world
knowledge (*bagage cognitif*), and the **contextual** knowledge (*contexte cognitif*), which is the
knowledge acquired through the specific and
immediate listening to the speech to be interpreted, or reading of the text to be translated.

According to the interpretive theory of
translation, ambiguity, an issue which has long
preoccupied translation theorists and linguists
(see MACHINE TRANSLATION), is in most cases
a direct result of a lack of relevant cognitive
'inputs' to verbal meaning. The possibility of
multiple interpretation arises in situations in
which only the surface or verbal meaning of the
text/speech is available and the translator or the
interpreter do not have at their disposal all the
cognitive elements and complementary information needed to extract sense.

Proponents of this approach see all translation as interpretation and acknowledge the
contribution made by Cary (1956), a practising
interpreter and translator who based his
description and explanation of written translation on 'oral' translation or interpreting.

Although different in their modalities, the translation of a written text and that of oral discourse are both seen as communicative acts. The link between discourse and the real world becomes increasingly tenuous as written texts age or when one crucial factor, the '*vouloir dire*' or intended meaning of the author as expressed in the specific contextual sense, is lost. Interpreting is considered the ideal communicative situation: all interlocutors are present, sharing the same spatial and temporal situation, circumstances and (normally) knowledge relevant to the topic of discourse.

Interpreting is not based on verbal memory but on the appropriation of meaning, followed by reformulation in the target language. Translators, too, reconstruct the meaning of the source language text and convey it to the readers of the translation. But they normally go one step further than interpreters, by attempting to 'equate the expression of sense, to a certain extent, with the linguistic meanings of the source language' (Seleskovitch 1977: 32).

Seleskovitch distinguishes between two levels of perception, that of the linguistic tool (rather transient) and that of sense as awareness: 'Sense [in the listener's awareness] results from the merging of pre-established linguistic meaning with a concomitant perception of reality' (ibid.: 31). The translation process is seen not as a 'direct conversion' of the linguistic meaning of the source language but as a 'conversion from the source language to sense and then an expression of sense in the target language' (ibid.: 28). Translation is thus not seen as a linear transcoding operation, but rather as a dynamic process of comprehension and re-expression of ideas.

Delisle developed a more detailed version of the interpretive approach applied to translation, with particular reference to the methodological aspects of the teaching of translation. In Delisle's view, which is based on text analysis, the interpretation of the text is defined with regard to specific criteria such as contextual analysis and the preservation of textual organicity (Delisle 1980/1988, 1993/2003). Delisle focuses on the intellectual process involved in translation, the cognitive process of interlingual transfer, and stresses the non-verbal stage of conceptualization. He views translation as a heuristic process of intelligent DISCOURSE ANALYSIS involving three stages. The first stage is that of **comprehension**: this requires decoding the linguistic signs of the source text with reference to the language system (i.e. determining the semantic relationships between the words and utterances of the text) and defining the conceptual content of an utterance by drawing on the referential context in which it is embedded (Delisle 1988: 53–6). The two operations are performed simultaneously. The second stage, namely **reformulation**, involves reverbalizing the concepts of the source utterance by means of the signifiers of another language; this is realized through reasoning, successive associations of thoughts and logical assumptions. Finally, the third stage is termed **verification** and can be described as a process of comparison of the original and its translation, which allows the translator to apply a qualitative analysis of selected solutions and EQUIVALENCE. Its purpose is to confirm the accuracy of the final translation, in terms of both content and form (see QUALITY).

Relationship to other approaches

By distancing itself from LINGUISTIC APPROACHES in order to explain the translation and interpreting processes, the interpretive theory of translation played a pioneering role in the 1960s and 1970s. Although linguistics and applied linguistics are not seen as constituting adequate frameworks for the description of the translating process, the interpretive approach is nevertheless indebted to developments in the fields of PRAGMATICS, text-linguistics and DISCOURSE ANALYSIS, particularly when applied to written translation.

The 'theory of sense' is not to be confused with Newmark's notion of **interpretative translation** which 'requires a semantic method of translation combined with a high explanatory power, mainly in terms of the SL culture, with only a side glance at the TL reader' (Newmark 1981: 35). The interpretive approach advocated by members of the Paris School in fact argues the opposite of this position and places much emphasis on the target reader, on the clarity and intelligibility of the translation and its acceptability in the target culture in terms of writing conventions, use of idioms, etc., as well as the communicative function of oral or written discourse. Nor should this approach be confused with the ontological approach to translation which emphasizes the subjective conditions of the interpreter and the role played by intuition in text interpretation and exegesis (Steiner 1975/1992).

The Paris School initially doubted the applicability of the interpretive approach to LITERARY TRANSLATION. Attention was focused on the kind of discourse that is aimed at informing, explaining and convincing, and literary translation was therefore excluded from its field of study. In recent years, however, the fact that form is seen as a means rather than an end in the interpretive approach has been evoked to reject the notion of the untranslatability of literature (Seleskovitch 1988; Lederer and Israël 1991; Lederer 1994/2003; see TRANSLATABILITY).

The languages used for exemplification in the publications of the Paris School are mostly English, French and German, and the examples provided are normally drawn from authentic interpreting and translating situations. Yet, although the main publications have been translated into several languages, including English, the interpretive approach as expounded by Seleskovitch, her colleagues and students has not been widely acknowledged in the English language literature on translation studies. With the development of interpreting studies as an independent area of research, however, the approach has acquired renewed visibility (see, for instance, Setton 1999; Pöchhaker 2004; Pöchhacker and Shlesinger 2002).

An overall account of the interpretive theory can be found in Seleskovitch and Lederer (1984), a collection of articles which also includes some earlier work. Lederer (1994/2003) offers a clear presentation of the approach and addresses a number of the criticisms that have been levelled against the theory. Some of these criticisms include a lack of statistical and quantitative studies (Gile 1995b) and the unproblematized use of key concepts such as 'context' (Setton 1999). To its credit, however, the interpretive approach has strived to define a clear terminology to refer to aspects of sense and meaning, which contrasts with the terminological fuzziness in a number of writings in translation studies. A three-volume collection of essays (Israël and Lederer 2005) provides a comprehensive and useful retrospective of the genesis and development of the interpretive theory of translation, and of its engagement and encounters with alternative and complementary paradigms as translation and interpreting studies have grown into fully-fledged disciplines.

See also:
CONFERENCE INTERPRETING, HISTORICAL AND COGNITIVE PERSPECTIVES; CONFERENCE INTERPRETING, SOCIOCULTURAL PERSPECTIVES; DISCOURSE ANALYSIS; LINGUISTIC APPROACHES; PSYCHOLINGUISTIC AND COGNITIVE TRAINING AND EDUCATION.

Further reading
Lederer 1981; Seleskovitch and Lederer 1984; Cormier 1985; Seleskovitch 1987, 1988; Delisle 1988; Larose 1989; Seleskovitch 1989; Lederer 1990, 1993/2003; Delisle 1993; Lederer 1994; Israël 2002; Israël and Lederer 2005; Widlund-Fantini 2007.

MYRIAM SALAMA-CARR

L

Linguistic approaches

The term 'linguistic approaches' has been used to refer to (a) theoretical MODELS that represent translation and/or interpreting as a (primarily) linguistic process and are therefore informed mainly by linguistic theory (for example, Catford 1965; Nida 1964; House 1977/1981; Hatim and Mason 1990a, 1997; Davidson 2002), and (b) a diverse range of studies that apply findings, concepts and methods from linguistics on an ad hoc basis to explain specific aspects of the phenomenon of translation and/or interpreting. The meaning of any term, however, is not only a function of what it *includes* but also of what it *excludes*, and in the past linguistic approaches have come to be perceived as distinct, in particular, from so-called 'cultural approaches'.

Cultural, or cultural studies approaches, are largely based on a mixture of cultural studies and literary theory (Baker 1996b). If linguistic and cultural approaches to translation were to be understood as differentiated purely on the basis of the disciplines that inform them, they should logically be seen as complementary rather than opposing paradigms. Arguments in favour of cross-fertilization have been put forward by Baker (1996b), Tymoczko (2002b), Crisafulli (2002) and Chesterman (2002b, 2004b), among others. However, the cultural-studies paradigm emerged later than the linguistic one and built much of its reputation around the inadequacy of previous linguistically oriented theories, thus setting itself in opposition to rather than in a complementary relation with linguistic approaches.

Notwithstanding the truth in some of the criticisms levelled against linguistic approaches by proponents of the 'cultural turn' in trans-

lation (Bassnett and Lefevere 1990), much of that criticism assumes a view of linguistics that has long ceased to be representative of current trends in the field and, in particular, of the linguistic theories that have informed the great majority of the discussions of translation at least since the late 1980s and 1990s (see below). The opposition between cultural and linguistic approaches is therefore arguably artificial. Another reason why the linguistic/cultural dichotomy has become obsolete is that recent developments in translation studies have benefited from input from a wider range of fields of study, such as sociology (see SOCIOLOGICAL APPROACHES), narrative theory (Baker 2006a) and anthropology (Blommaert 2005; Sturge 2007), making the study of translation and interpreting a truly interdisciplinary field.

Along with models and concepts imported from other fields, linguistics has consistently continued to inform studies of translation along the years. Course material in translator training has always tended to rely on linguistic theory, in particular text-linguistics (e.g. Nord 1988/1991a) and systemic functional linguistics (e.g. Baker 1992; see TRAINING AND EDUCATION). The *Thinking Translation* series published by Routledge since 1992 provides a good example of the enduring relevance of linguistic theory. More recent publications, such as Malmkjær (2005), provide further evidence of the continued appeal that linguistic knowledge holds for translators and translation scholars. Apart from discussing a range of linguistic issues – from rhyme and collocation to implicatures – that are particularly relevant to practical translation, Malmkjær explores the implications for translation of different theories derived from the philosophy of language, in particular universalism and relativism. Vandeweghe *et al.* (2007) go as far as claiming that the increasing number of conferences and publications focusing on linguistic aspects of translation might be taken as an indication that translation studies is experiencing a 'linguistic re-turn'.

Early linguistic approaches

Fawcett (1997) offers a comprehensive overview of linguistic theories of translation and how they developed, as well as a balanced assessment of their strengths and weaknesses. The taxonomies of translation STRATEGIES developed by Vinay and Darbelnet (1958), for example, represent the first attempts at systematically classifying some of the linguistic procedures that are used when attempting to map lexis and syntactic structures across languages. Despite their lasting influence, such taxonomies were based on knowledge of contrastive linguistics rather than on how translators work in practice and therefore failed to describe the operational strategies that guide the actual translation process (Fawcett 1997: 50).

Other linguistically-oriented theorists have attempted to explain translation in terms of EQUIVALENCE, the most influential being Catford (1965) and Nida (Nida 1964; Nida and Taber 1969). Both Catford and Nida stress that translation is not about achieving equivalence of meaning; Catford argues that it is about finding target text meanings that are interchangeable with source text meanings in a given situation, that is, when the two relate to some of the same features of extra-linguistic reality. Catford's model never goes beyond the level of the sentence and is out of touch with what translators actually do (Fawcett 1997: 56). However, as Kenny (this volume) points out, there have been few attempts to produce a similarly complete theoretical model, and Catford's notion of SHIFTS is still widely discussed.

Nida attempts to formalize general, non-language-specific strategies of translation, based on transformational grammar and the concept of deep structure. However, his attempts at moving towards a 'science' of translation are undermined by a prescriptive attitude that sometimes borders on the patronizing, frequent references to – and lack of definitions for – notions such as the 'genius' of language and 'natural' translation, and his insistence on the use of reader response as a measure of equivalence, particularly in the context of Bible translation, which seems to serve evangelical purposes rather than scientific interests (see Fawcett 1997: 57–8; Gentzler 1993).

The prescriptive orientation of early linguistic approaches to translation (see also Newmark 1988) has been challenged by scholars who have argued that it does not serve the interest of translation studies as an empirical discipline, whose aim ought to be to explain what translation *is* rather than what it *should be* (Toury 1980a, 1995). The descriptive focus on translations as facts of the target culture also stressed that ideals of QUALITY are inevitably historical and contextually-bound. This latter argument relates to another criticism of linguistic approaches to translation, namely that they are 'essentialist', that is, they assume that translation is a question of successfully transferring stable, language- and culture-independent meanings between source and target texts (see, for example, Arrojo 1998). These arguments stress that meanings are dynamic, subjective and therefore not amenable to being 'reproduced' (even when they are *iterable*, see DECONSTRUCTION).

Incorporating pragmatics and semiotics

Without going to the same lengths as deconstruction and postmodernism in terms of denying the possibility of stable meanings, attempts at theorizing language as an instrument of communication begin by acknowledging that language cannot be divorced from the context of situation and culture where it is produced. The work of Firth (1956a, 1956b) is frequently cited in this context. The assumption that cross-linguistic equivalence cannot be posited at the level of linguistic structures and semantics but must be established instead at the level of real-world events that involve human verbal and non-verbal actions is also evident in the work of Catford and Nida.

However, mainstream traditional linguistics has its limitations when it comes to dealing with the notion of context (Fawcett 1997: 72–3), and various scholars have therefore resorted to neighbouring disciplines such as PRAGMATICS and SEMIOTICS to account for the phenomenon of translation as performed by real-life translators/interpreters and experienced by readers/

listeners. Typical examples include Baker (1992), House (1997), Hatim and Mason (1990a, 1997), Hickey (1998), and Carbonell i Cortés (2003). Interpreting studies in particular have drawn heavily on pragmatics to demonstrate how interpreters reconstruct contextually relevant meanings (Davidson 2002; Perez González 2006a; Setton 1999; Wadensjö 2000, 2004).

House, whose concern is with translation assessment, insists that translation is a 'linguistic-textual phenomenon and can be legitimately described, analysed and assessed as such' (1997: 118–19), but clearly distinguishes her model of quality assessment from purely text-based approaches such as Reiß's (1971) and Koller's (1979/2004), where pairs of source and target texts are compared with a view to discovering syntactic, semantic, stylistic and pragmatic regularities of transfer. The model proposed by House (1977/1981, 1997), based on pragmatic theories of language use, claims that QUALITY in translation is achieved when the translation has a function which is equivalent to that of the original, and employs equivalent pragmatic means for achieving that function.

Hatim and Mason (1990a) look at communicative, pragmatic and semiotic dimensions of context, focusing on translation as a form of inter-semiotic transfer that involves constraints at the level of genre, discourse and text (see DISCOURSE ANALYSIS). *Genre*, the conventionalized forms of texts employed by members of a linguistic community in certain social situations, and *discourse*, understood, following Foucault, as ritualized modes of expression that reflect ideological positioning, present problems that are resolved in *texts*, where different discourses and genres need to be articulated in a coherent manner (i.e. within textual constraints). Hatim and Mason (ibid.) argue that the semiotic system formed by genre, discourse and text provides a suitable framework for analysing the way IDEOLOGY is mediated through translation. Their work represents one of the clearest attempts at introducing insights from more critical linguistic approaches to the study of translation. Hatim and Mason (1997) bring further issues of ideology, politics and market forces to bear more explicitly upon their theory.

Critical linguistics

Linguistics has gradually moved from using words and clauses as the unit of analysis to considering texts as a whole and finally to seeing texts as instances of discourses that are constantly engaged in the dynamic representation and construction of knowledge and IDEOLOGY.

Two fields of inquiry that have proved particularly influential in translation studies are **critical linguistics** (CL) and **critical discourse analysis** (CDA). The former is a critical approach to DISCOURSE ANALYSIS that uses Halliday's systemic functional grammar as an analytic methodology. CDA is not a single theory or methodology, but rather an umbrella term used to refer to a series of theories and practices that share certain principles in terms of their approach to language study. Although heavily influenced by linguistic theory, CDA also draws from other sources, in particular the work of Foucault and Bourdieu. Crucial to both critical linguistics and CDA is the view that discourse is both socially conditioned *and* shapes social relationships, and that it is necessary to adopt a critical stance towards the relationship between analysis and the practices analysed. Both approaches also agree on the need to analyse authentic instances of verbal interaction in context. Critical linguistics was pioneered by Roger Fowler and other socially concerned linguists at the University of East Anglia in the late 1970s, while CDA is associated with the names of Norman Fairclough, Teun Van Dijk and Ruth Wodak, among others. Despite the fact that they initially followed slightly different paths (see Fowler 1996), the terms 'critical linguistics' and 'critical discourse analysis' are now used interchangeably.

From the point of view of CDA, translation is seen as a process of mediation between source and target world views, a process that is inevitably influenced by the power differentials among participants. Mason (1994) offers a particularly good example of how detailed linguistic analysis can provide fascinating insights into the motivations behind translators' choices. He examines the translation of a text on social history and shows how ideologically loaded textual patterns (for instance, the recurrence of words such as *memory* (which evokes and links together the past and the present) are downplayed in the target text through (subconscious) manipulation of theme-rheme structure and breaking up patterns of lexical cohesion, in such a way that source and target texts end up relaying different world views.

CDA scholars have tended to focus on certain genres and types of discourses, and these preferences are also reflected in CDA-informed work in translation studies. In particular, the discourses of the media (e.g. ADVERTISING and NEWS GATHERING AND DISSEMINATION), politics and institutions have attracted considerable attention. Calzada Pérez (2007b), for instance, presents a thorough analysis of transitivity patterns in the translation of EU parliamentary speeches, revealing the complex implications of individual translation choices within an INSTITUTIONAL setting. Schäffner (2003) describes how the portrayal of a political party's identity is influenced by decisions taken at the micro-linguistic level in the production of a bilingual document. Baumgarten (2007) carries out a meticulous textual analysis of eleven English translations of Hitler's *Mein Kampf* in order to demonstrate how decision makers in translation position the source text author in relation to resistant or compliant discourses within the target culture.

Valdeón (2007) examines the ideological implications of the terms *separatist/separatista* and *terrorist/terrorista* in a corpus of media texts from the BBC and CNN and their Spanish services. Drawing on the notion of 'audience design' as well as the conceptual apparatus of CDA, Kuo and Nakamura (2005) look at patterns of omission/inclusion and stylistic patterns in the Chinese translations of a news story which first appeared in an English newspaper, as well as the use of headlines and quotations in other reports of the same event in two Chinese newspapers, revealing how such choices reflect the newspapers' different stances and conceptualization of their own audiences. Kang (2007) offers a similar analysis of the recontextualization of news on North Korea published in *Newsweek* and its South Korean edition, *Newsweek Hankuk Pan*.

There is, however, no reason why the insights provided by CDA should be limited to those areas where ideology tends to be more obviously reflected in discourse. Olk (2002) demonstrates that mediation during the actual process of translation can be observed by applying CDA to THINK-ALOUD PROTOCOLS. The results of Olk's small-scale study point to a rather low level of critical discourse awareness among students of translation, which suggests that critical linguistic approaches may well have applications in applied translation studies (see also Alves a Magalhães 2006; TRAINING AND EDUCATION).

Taking stock and moving on

Some of the criticisms levelled against CDA are reminiscent of the criticisms that have been levelled – explicitly or implicitly – against cultural-studies approaches to translation. They have both been criticized for ignoring or misinterpreting the existence of work in linguistics that, without calling itself 'critical', does question the connection between discourse and social structures by drawing on a wide range of fields of theoretical inquiry, such as anthropology and sociology (Baker 1996b, 2005b; Blomaert and Bulcaen 2000; Toolan 1997). Although cultural-studies approaches have not been explicitly challenged in terms of methodology by more linguistically oriented scholars, repeated calls for empiricism and systematic linguistic analysis (House 1997; Malmkjær 2005; Chesterman 1998) can be seen as implicit criticism of what are perceived as unfalsifiable and impressionistic claims (Toolan 1997: 88), and as analyses based on 'sketchy' patterns of power relations that are projected onto the data in CDA (Blomaert and Bulcaen 2000: 455–6).

Stubbs (1997: 107) points out that few CDA studies compare the features they find in texts with typical norms in a given language, which is essential if reliable generalizations are to be made concerning the effects of different linguistic choices in society at large. This concern with the relation between micro-linguistic events and macro-social structures (see also Halliday 1992) is not exclusive to linguistics but also crucial to the social sciences (Giddens 1979), and the fact that translation studies has started to look towards the social sciences in order to reconcile the tension between linguistic research and social structures (see, for example Inghilleri 2005b; Wolf and Fukari 2007) might be seen as a move in the right direction.

The concerns expressed by Stubbs (1997) and Toolan (1997) in relation to methodological weaknesses do not hold true in much of the recent work in translation studies that is informed by CDA, where a critical stance has been fruitfully combined with methods derived from empirical linguistics and insights from other social disciplines. It now seems to be generally accepted that acknowledgement of the analyst's subjectivity does not necessarily lead to the projection of bias on to the data, nor does striving for rigour in analysis mean ignoring the fact that language is a socially-conditioned instrument that can be and is manipulated (consciously or subconsciously) to serve diverse ends. The debate is now moving on to another question raised by Toolan (1997), namely, whether CDA should be politically committed (prescriptive) rather than simply politically aware (see DESCRIPTIVE VS. COMMITTED APPROACHES).

In any case, the language/culture tension does not need to be seen as a problem to 'solve'. According to Blommaert (2007), debates on whether to separate language, culture and society in linguistic anthropology have had positive outcomes, such as the emphasis on *function* as a bridge between language structure and sociocultural patterns. The same could be said about translation studies (see FUNCTIONALIST APPROACHES). Blommaert also points out that the quest for functions of language-in-use encouraged linguistic ethnography to engage with the notion of 'context', and praises work in this area for revealing the ethnographic object as 'always a composite, complex and layered one' (ibid.: 687). In translation studies, the concept of 'context' has been frequently invoked but rarely treated in any depth (Baker 2006c). This may be the next challenge to address in the attempt to map the interaction between language and culture as expressed in translation.

See also:
CORPORA; CULTURE; DESCRIPTIVE VS. COMMITTED APPROACHES; DISCOURSE ANALYSIS; EQUIVALENCE; FUNCTIONALIST APPROACHES; IDEOLOGY; MODELS; PRAGMATICS; SEMIOTICS; SHIFTS.

Further reading
Hatim and Mason 1990a; Baker 1996b; Fawcett 1997; Hatim and Mason 1997; Blommaert and Bulcaen 2000; Baker 2005b; Malmkjær 2005; Calzada Pérez 2007b; Vandeweghe *et al.* 2007.

GABRIELA SALDANHA

Literary translation

Texts are often popularly viewed as either literary or non-literary, implying that literature should be seen as a large 'super-genre' – with 'genre' being regarded as a category of communication act whose rules are roughly pre-agreed within a 'discourse community' of users, but which the producers and audience of an actual text may also negotiate on the spot (Andrews 1991: 18; Stockwell 2002a: 33–4). (Super-)genre rules may be seen in terms of typical features. Typical features attributed to literary texts include the following (Stockwell 2002a; Venuti 1996; Pilkington 2000; Berman 1985/2000: 296): they have a written base-form, though they may also be spoken; they enjoy canonicity (high social prestige); they fulfil an affective/aesthetic rather than transactional or informational function, aiming to provoke emotions and/or entertain rather than influence or inform; they have no real-world truth-value – i.e. they are judged as fictional, whether fact-based or not; they feature words, images, etc., with ambiguous and/or indeterminable meanings; they are characterized by 'poetic' language use (where language form is important in its own right, as with word-play or rhyme) and heteroglossia (i.e. they contain more than one 'voice' – as with, say, the many characters in the Chinese classic *Shui Hu Zhuan / Water Margins Epic*); and they may draw on minoritized styles – styles outside the dominant standard, for example slang or archaism.

Alternatively, literature may be seen as a cluster of conventionally-agreed component genres. Conventional 'core literary' genres are DRAMA, POETRY and fictional prose; even here, however, a text may only display some of the features listed above. There also appear to be 'peripherally literary' genres, where criteria such as written base-form, canonicity or fictionality are relaxed, as in the case of dubbed films (see AUDIOVISUAL TRANSLATION), CHILDREN'S LITERATURE and sacred texts (see BIBLE, JEWISH AND CHRISTIAN, QUR'ĀN). Conversely, genres conventionally seen as non-literary may have literary features: ADVERTISING copy, for example. Thus, while understanding and (re)writing literary texts forms part of the literary translator's expertise, literary translators' real-time working STRATEGIES and text transformation techniques may vary between literary text and genre but overlap with those used in other genres.

Traditionally, translation theories derived largely from literary and sacred-text translation. Thus the interminable debates over EQUIVA-LENCE, whether framed as a word-for-word vs. sense-for-sense opposition or as a literal-communicative-elegant triangle (Yan Fu, in Sinn 1995), are relevant to literary translation but much less so to SCIENTIFIC AND TECHNICAL TRANSLATION, say. Tymoczko (1999a: 30) argues that the focus on literary translation provides the discipline with high-quality evidence about 'interfaces' between cultures and about the linguistic challenges of translating. Hence it can inform theories, models of practice and research methodologies relevant to other genres, and vice versa.

The discipline's engagement with literary translation may be summarized from three viewpoints: translation as text, translating processes, and links with social context.

Translation as text

Literary translation studies have traditionally concentrated on source–target text relations. Theoretical discussions focus on two closely-related issues: equivalence and communicative purpose. In terms of **equivalence**, the question is whether translators can ever replicate the complex web of stylistic features found in many literary texts. If not, what should translators prioritize? Or should they see the quest for equivalence as senseless and focus instead on communicative effectiveness (Holmes 1988: 53–4; Jones 1989)? In terms of **communicative purpose**, the question is how far translators should prioritize loyalty to the source writer versus producing a text that works in receptor-genre terms. How far, for example, should they adapt or update?

Another concern is the translation of **style** (Parks 1998/2007; Boase-Beier 2006a). Style

is important in the context of literature for two reasons. First, it inadvertently defines the writer's 'cultural space-time'. To a modern Italian reader, for example, the style of Dante's *Divina commedia* signals that it was written by a medieval Tuscan. Secondly, writers may deliberately use non-standard styles – archaism, dialect, or a style idiosyncratic to the writer, for example – to encode their attitude towards the text's content, to mark out different voices, and/or to structure the text (Boase-Beier 2004: 28; Jones and Turner 2004; Armstrong and Federici 2006). Thus, in *Kameni spavač* (*Stone Sleeper*, 1973), Bosnian poet Mak Dizdar alternates between modern standard Serbo-Croat and medieval/religious diction. This marks a dialogue between a modern narrator-figure and a medieval heretic, respectively – a dialogue that presents today's Bosnians as the heretic's descendants.

Translators mediate both aspects of style via their own inadvertently signalled stylistic space-time, via deliberate stylistic choices, or both. Markedly non-standard and/or non-modern source text style confronts translators with various choices. These may include: (a) replicating the (modern) source reader's experience by calquing – for example translating Dante's *Divina commedia* into medieval English with a Northern tinge; (b) using different stylistic means to indicate this experience – for example translating Dante's *Divina commedia* into formal literary Japanese (Venuti 1996); and (c) prioritizing semantic content by normalizing the style: translating Dante's *Divina commedia* into modern standard Polish, say (Allén 1999). In order to use calquing and other stylistic devices, translators need expertise in writing multiple styles. Normalizing arguably risks losing the style's textual function.

Literary text may also refer intertextually to other texts. Thus, in Joseph Heller's *Catch 22* (1961), when Yossarian asks 'Where are the Snowdens of yesteryear?' he refers not only to his dead comrade Snowden, but also to French poet François Villon's lament at life's transience (in English, 'where are the snows of yesteryear?'). This sets Heller's translators a considerable challenge.

Part of the literary translator's 'habitus' (see SOCIOLOGICAL APPROACHES; Inghilleri 2005c: 134–5) appears to be the convention that the translator 'speaks for' the source writer, and hence has no independent stylistic voice. Some scholars, however, advocate that the translator's voice should be made distinctly present in the translated text, while others have argued that individual translators inevitably leave their own stylistic imprint on the texts they produce (Baker 2000).

Literary translators may express a separate voice in paratexts – the texts that accompany a core text, such as introduction, translator's notes, etc. Paratexts and metatexts (texts about the translated work, such as reviews, publishers' promotional web-pages, etc.) can provide data about a translation 'project' (Berman 1995) and its context. As they may be written by various 'actors' (translators, editors, critics, etc.), they can also provide evidence on attitudes towards translation within wider communities of literary translation and production (Fawcett 2000; Jones and Turner 2004; see REVIEWING AND CRITICISM).

Translation as process

Literary translating may also be seen as a communication process. Two broad translation-studies approaches address this aspect: one largely data-driven, and one largely theory-driven.

The first, data-driven, approach treats translation as **behaviour**. Data here derives mainly from translators' written reports about their own practice, plus some interview and THINK-ALOUD studies (e.g. Honig 1985; Flynn 2004; Jones 2006). Written reports tend to be text- or source writer-specific, often focus on special problems rather than routine practices, and can lack awareness of recent translation theory. Nevertheless, written reports and interview studies can provide data on literary translators' techniques (i.e. how source text structures are modified in the target text, and why), and on working relationships with informants or source writers. The relative lack of literary-translation THINK-ALOUD studies, however, means that less is known about the process of arriving at such decisions – though it appears, for example, that poetry translators can spend considerable time brainstorming ways of reproducing a source text item's multi-valency (e.g. its style-marking, associative meaning, etc.; see Jones 1989, 2006).

The complexity of many literary messages means that literary translators are conventionally allowed a wide range of text-transformation options. Research based on creativity as problem solving explores what this might mean in process and product terms. Here, creativity means generating target text solutions that are both novel and appropriate (Beylard-Ozeroff et al. 1998: xi; Sternberg and Lubart 1999: 3) – that is, not directly predictable by source text features, but constrained by factors such as the translator's preferred balance between source text loyalty and target text effectiveness, *habitus* (seeing oneself as a 'translator' or as a 'poet', say), etc.

The second approach to literary translation as a process is more theory-driven and may be termed **cognitive-pragmatic**. The analysis of literary translation processes here may be informed by literary cognitive stylistics and the pragmatics of translation (e.g. Kwan-Terry 1992; Hickey 1998; Gutt 1991/2000; Pilkington 2000; Stockwell 2002a). These studies attempt to model communication between source writer, translator-as-reader, translator-as-rewriter and target reader. Source writers are seen as providing 'interpretive potentials' in their text. Readers, including translators-as-readers, infer a most likely communicative intent from these potentials on the basis of pre-existing linguistic knowledge, genre knowledge (e.g. how novels conventionally develop), world knowledge, author knowledge, their developing knowledge of the 'text world' (events, characters, etc., in the text), their own personal background, and so on. There is also a cost–benefit aspect, which raises questions such as whether the added value for the reader of a complex word-play, for example, is worth the added effort exerted in understanding it.

Literary translators-as-rewriters communicate with target readers in a similar way, though interactants usually also know that the translator is reporting on an earlier writer-to-reader communication (Holmes 1988: 10). Thus, when a modern translator translates Dante's early-fourteenth-century *Divina commedia* into Chinese verse modelled on seventh-century Tang-dynasty poetry, he or she assumes that Chinese readers know that the source work is a medieval classic, that they realize the target style is meant to signal the work's medieval-classic status, and that this enhanced stylistic experience justifies the extra writing and reading effort involved.

Links with social context

Literary translation is also a form of action in a real-world context. This context may be examined in terms of gradually-widening networks: translation 'production teams'; the 'communities of interest', 'fields' and 'systems' with which teams interact; and the 'imagined communities' in which they operate. Other issues which are central to the real-world context of literary translation are connected with the subject-setting relationship: IDEOLOGY, identity and ETHICS.

A **production team** is an example of what Milroy calls a 'first-order network': a relatively small group of people interacting tightly together for a certain purpose (Milroy 1987: 46–7). Production-team research assumes that literary translation involves not only translating, but also source-text selection, source- and target-text editing, publishing and marketing. Teams involve various actors and roles: source writer, translator, editor and publisher, among others. This implies that the whole team, not just the translator, is responsible for a translation's form, sociopolitical effects, and other aspects of its functioning.

Key analytic frameworks used in researching literary translation production teams include the following: (a) *Actor Network Theory*, which sees actors as negotiating, collaborating and/or opposing each other to form a working network, formulate its goals and achieve them (Buzelin 2004, 2005, 2006). Actors may be human (e.g. translators, editors), but also non-human (e.g. source texts, computers); (b) *Activity Theory*, which examines the way goals are structured and pursued within the individual, within the team, and between teams (Axel 1997; Engeström and Miettinen 1999); and (c) Goffman's *Social-Game Theory* (Goffman 1970, 1959/1971; Jones and Arsenijević 2005), which focuses on how actors play socially-defined roles – a translation production team acting as an 'embassy' empowered to communicate with one group on behalf of another, for example. Alongside these theoretically-grounded studies, reports provide information about practices at production-team level, such as copyright, contracts, pay and conditions, working procedures, etc. (Hamburger 2004; Bush 1998/2001).

In terms of **communities, fields and systems**, various groupings proposed by literary translation researchers resemble what Milroy calls 'second-order' networks: larger networks than first-order teams, where goals are vaguer or absent, and not all members need to interact directly with each other (1987: 46–7). Venuti's 'community of interest' (2000a: 477) comprises those affected by a published literary translation: target-language readers and target-language writers, among others. Other communities of interest are possible to envisage, however: the source-language enthusiasts, commissioners and supporters who, along with the production team, wish to see a translation published, for example. Communities may also be 'transnational', encompassing both source- and target-language users. They typically interact with other communities in the same social space. Poetry translations from Bosnia during the 1992–5 war, for instance, were supported by transnational communities involving both Bosnian and non-Bosnian players, which aimed to portray Bosnia as a unitary society in the European cultural mainstream; these communities opposed other communities which presented Bosnia as barbaric mayhem (Jones and Arsenijević 2005).

Bourdieu's concept of 'field' (Inghilleri 2005c: 135; see SOCIOLOGICAL APPROACHES) focuses on how second-order networks generate and are shaped by discourse and action. For a translator of novels, say, a relevant field would be the network of fiction translators to which he or she feels allegiance, including institutions such as national, regional or international associations of literary translators. Other relevant fields may be those governing the production of novels in the target country, or the broad field of professional translation. The rules or NORMS that condition literary translators' *habitus*, in Bourdieu's terms, are negotiated and communicated within such fields; they include genre and style conventions, norms of professionalism, and accepted attitudes to EQUIVALENCE and creativity. The mid-twentieth-century shift from widespread approval to widespread disapproval of archaizing style in English literary translation, for example, shows how conventions evolve through discourse within literary and literary-translation fields (Jones and Turner 2004).

POLYSYSTEM theory sees literary works as forming networks ('systems') in their own right: one example might be translated poetry in Korean. These determine the canon of high-prestige works and interact with other literary systems, such as non-translated Korean poetry (Hermans 1999; Even-Zohar 2000). Arguably, however, textual systems cannot be viewed separately from their social and interpersonal contexts (Hermans 1999: 118).

The above models enable translation production to be viewed in a wider context of processes such as (a) *gatekeeping*: selecting or failing to select an author for translation; (b) *commissioning*: editors seeking translators, or translators seeking publishers; and (c) *extra-translation events*: for example, the release of Spielberg's film *The Color Purple* inspiring Chinese translations of the Alice Walker novel on which it was based (Lee, in progress). They also provide a framework for analysing the way literary translation networks operate in a number of respects. These include the following:

* The way literary translation networks engage with other literary networks. During the Cold War, for example, UK readers expected Eastern European literature to convey raw experience in powerful metaphors, and this filtered the type of poetry that was translated at the time; this translated poetry, in turn, influenced the work of British poets such as Ted Hughes (Doce 1997: 48; Jarniewicz 2002).
* The way they interact with non-literary networks: those concerned with the economics of publishing, for example, or politics (Chang 2000); and the way they interact with networks of subvention, support and patronage, such as organizations that finance literary translation from a certain language (e.g. the Dutch NLPVF or the Cervantes Institute).
* The way they differ in terms of Bourdieu's 'capital', i.e. power, resources and prestige. Those supporting the import of a translated Brazilian novel into the USA, say, may have less capital than those supporting the import

of a translated US novel into Brazil, which results in different sales figures.
* The way they use and generate capital internally. Thus literary translation might be inspired by a source writer's existing symbolic capital, but – especially with translation into a globalized language – may also consecrate a writer as a figure of international worth (Casanova 1999/2005, 2002/in press).
* The way they enjoy more or less capital relative to non-translation literary networks, as shown by the relative sales and prestige of translated and non-translated literature (ibid.).
* The way they may increase the capital of a marginalized source or target language – as in the case of literary translation into Scots (Barnaby 2002; Findlay 2004).
* The way they may encourage RETRANSLATION of canonical works as norms change.

In terms of **imagined communities**, members of first- and second-order networks also participate in 'third-order networks' – communities so heterogeneous that their grounds for membership and boundaries are best seen as 'imagined', i.e. determined largely by a subject's belief and self-image (Anderson 1991/2004). Two imagined communities often seen as relevant to literary translation are those of CULTURE and nation.

Culture can refer not only to the behaviours, products and ideas seen as typifying a community, but also to the community itself. Culture's imagined status reminds us that the term 'Hungarian culture', for instance, may have powerful metaphoric value for teams and communities involved with translations of Hungarian literature, but also that it is more a discourse of identity than a coherent set of real-world properties or people.

Literary translators are often seen as 'communicators between cultures'. This trope embraces several different sub-metaphors, including cultural partisanship, intercultural embassy and globalized hybridity. *Cultural partisanship* (Álvarez and Vidal 1996; cf. Tymoczko 2000a) conceptualizes the source and receptor cultures as separate and holding potentially different amounts of symbolic and economic capital. Literary translation inevitably 'manipulates': because there are few compulsory solutions, translators make choices, and these choices may reveal a sociopolitical stance. Manipulation may be either hegemonic or emancipatory, depending on whether it favours the more or the less powerful culture. Venuti links source- vs. receptor-culture partisanship not only to text selection, but also to the choice between source- and receptor-oriented style (1995). Arguably, however, a source-oriented style may stereotype source-culture identity in some contexts (Shamma 2005) and validate it in others. Similarly, seeing a canonical text from a hegemonic source culture – for example a SHAKESPEARE play in South America (Modenessi 2004) – as material for creative 'cannibalization' may challenge the hegemonic relationship. *Intercultural embassy* metaphorizes literary translation as bridging intercultural divides by representing the best interests of the source writer and culture to the receptor culture. *Glocalized hybridity* (Hermans 2002; Gentzler 2002a: 217; Pym 2003) metaphorizes literary translators as operating in and owing allegiance to a transcultural space. They 'glocalize' by adapting local and/or global concerns in the source text for an international and/or other local audience. They also 'hybridize', merging or juxtaposing source and receptor ideas and forms, each of which may derive from discourses, tensions and collaborations between various intertexts and interest groups.

Literary translation also engages with discourses of nation: nineteenth-century translations of Irish literature, for example, helped build a sense of Irish nationhood in resistance to British colonial domination (Tymoczko 1999a).

Finally, in terms of the relationship between **subject** and **setting**, selection decisions and manipulation of source and target text may reveal literary-translation actors' IDEOLOGY and identity: what they believe in, or who they feel they are (in terms of GENDER or sexuality, for instance). Or they may deliberately debate or contest issues of ideology and identity.

Ideology is linked to ETHICS. Here, for example, a translator-*habitus*-based ethic of loyalty to source text features may conflict with an ethic of social justice which might demand deviation from the original text. Ideological decisions by translators or other actors may also result in CENSORSHIP or resistance to censorship. Thus, in late nineteenth-century

English translations of Irish literature, heroes were made cleaner and more noble in order to support the nationalist cause; after Irish independence, however, unexpurgated retranslations of these texts aimed to subvert such 'pieties of Irish nationalism' (Tymoczko 2000: 29–30).

See also:
CHILDREN'S LITERATURE; CLASSICAL TEXTS; DRAMA; FICTIONAL REPRESENTATIONS; POETRY; POLYSYSTEM; PUBLISHING STRATEGIES; RETRANSLATION; REVIEWING AND CRITICISM; REWRITING; SHAKESPEARE; SOCIOLOGICAL APPROACHES.

Further reading
Holmes 1988; Venuti 1995a; Álvarez and Vidal 1996; Bush 1998/2001; Hickey 1998; Parks 1998/2007; Venuti 1998b; Allén 1999; Casanova 1999/2005; Hermans 1999; Even-Zohar 2000; Bassnett 2000a; Casanova 2002/in press; Stockwell 2002a; Tymoczko and Gentzler 2002; Jones and Turner 2004; Buzelin 2005; Armstrong and Federici 2006; Boase-Beier 2006a.

FRANCIS R. JONES

Localization

Localization can be defined as the linguistic and cultural adaptation of digital content to the requirements and locale of a foreign market, and the provision of services and technologies for the management of multilingualism across the digital global information flow. By including related services and technologies, this definition goes beyond that generally provided in the literature, for example by Dunne (2006b: 115), who defines it as the 'process by which digital content and products developed in one locale (defined in terms of geographical area, language and culture) are adapted for sale and use in another locale'.

Parrish (2003) points out that the general idea behind localization is not, of course, new: artists, traders, marketers and missionaries realized hundreds of years ago that their products and ideas sold better if they were adapted to the expectations, culture, language and needs of their potential customers. It is therefore important to highlight what makes localization, as we refer to it today, different from previous, similar activities, namely that it deals with *digital* material. To be adapted or localized, digital material requires tools and technologies, skills, processes and standards that are different from those required for the adaptation of traditional material such as paper-based print or celluloid, as Shadbolt (2003) and Scattergood (2003) point out.

In 2007, the localization industry was estimated to be worth in excess of US$10 billion per annum (Benninato and DePalma 2006) and to generate around 60 per cent of the overall income of many large multinational digital publishers such as Microsoft, Oracle and SAP (Sprung 2000a: ix). For these companies and their service providers, localization is predominantly 'big business'. Although Fry (2003: 10) sees localization as a means to 'level the playing field and redress economic inequalities, helping to create a better world in which no one is left out' by allowing 'speakers of less common languages [to] enjoy access to the same products that those in major markets use', other observers, such as Kenniston (2005), believe that localization in its current form is actively contributing to widening what has become known as the 'digital divide' (see also MINORITY).

Origins

In the mid-1980s, large software publishers were looking for new markets for their products, mainly word processors and spreadsheet applications. They quickly realized that there was a demand for those products in countries such as France, Italy, Germany and Spain, where potential customers had the financial means to pay for them, but would only do so if they were translated into their respective languages. The multinationals learned their lesson quickly, a lesson neatly encapsulated in the former German Chancellor Willy Brandt's famous quote: 'If I'm selling to you, I speak your language. If I'm buying, *dann müssen Sie Deutsch sprechen!*' (then you must speak German). As a consequence, 'localization has become the showcase market strategy of international capitalism' (Pym 2004: 47).

Many early localization projects turned out to be extremely difficult, and some ended in financial disaster for the companies involved. They underestimated the technical difficulties involved in translating text ('strings') buried in thousands of lines of code. Some translators simply deleted the code surrounding the strings they were asked to translate (and in the process rendered the now translated digital content unusable), while computer programmers did not see the point of, and in effect deleted, those 'funny characters', such as accents or *umlauts*, on top of what they considered to be perfectly well-formed words (and in the process rendered the content displayed to users meaningless). Educating the translators, as well as the designers and developers of digital content, quickly became (and still is) one of the most important tasks of localizers.

As the digital content to be localized became more sophisticated, so did the localization process. The focus on short-term return on investment drove the large multinational digital publishers to concentrate on two areas to reduce the cost of the localization effort: recycling translations and internationalization. The ability to *recycle* or leverage previous translations using Translation Memory Systems has been a milestone in the history of localization (see COMPUTER-AIDED TRANSLATION). Internationalization is the process of designing (or modifying) software so as to enable users to work in the language of their choice (even if the software is not localized) and to isolate the linguistically and culturally dependent parts of an application in preparation for localization. The better digital content is internationalized, the lower the cost of localization. The return on investment in internationalization obviously grows significantly as the number of target languages increases. The ultimate, ideal aim of this effort is that a product works out-of-the-box in any language; that is to say, users can input and generate output in their own language and writing system, even though the user interface might still be in the original language (in most cases English). If the objective of the internationalization effort was ever to be achieved, localization could be reduced to *just* translation (Schmitt 2000), with no engineering and testing effort required.

Process

Localization teams handle projects in different ways, depending on, for example, whether they work for a publisher (the client) or for a localization service provider (the vendor). While localizers rightly claim that each project is different and that the way projects are tackled depends on a large number of variables – such as the type of content, its release cycle, size, accessibility and target audience – most projects have a number of standard tasks and stages in common, as described by Esselink (2000) and Schäler (2003):

- **Analysis**. Before any work on a localization project can start, the original content needs to be analysed and a number of important questions answered, among them: Can this product be localized for the target market? Some material is not suitable for certain markets or is so specific that localization would come close to redevelopment of the original product. Does the original product support the specific features of the target language (characters, script)? Are all strings to be translated and is all material to be localized (images, symbols, etc.) available to the localizers? What tools and technologies are necessary and suitable to support translators, engineers and testers? What is the estimated effort necessary to localize the product (word count, number of pictures, dialog boxes, etc.)? One of the strategies used during the analysis stage is the so-called *pseudo-translation*, where original strings are automatically replaced with strings expanded by a certain percentage and containing characters from the target language according to pre-defined algorithms in order to mimic a translation and to determine the effect this translation would have on a particular product. Pseudo-translation is a quick and inexpensive way to show, for example, whether a product supports the characters of the target language, what effect string expansion will have on the layout of the user interface and to what extent concatenation was used by developers to create messages. The outcome of this stage is a report.
- **Preparation**. Based on the outcome of the project analysis and once a project has

been given the go-ahead, project managers, engineers and 'language leads' (linguistic coordinators) put together a project plan and a localization kit. The project plan outlines the tasks, milestones and financial details of the project and is under constant review throughout the project's lifecycle. The localization kit contains all the material needed to localize a product successfully, from source material to tools, localization and translation guidelines, test scripts, problem-reporting mechanisms, delivery instructions and contact details for all individuals involved in a project. This localization kit is made available to translators, engineers and managers.
- **Translation**. As a consequence of dealing with digital material, translators working in localization will be required to perform extremely technical and demanding administrative tasks in addition to translating, such as preparing TERMINOLOGY databases; maintaining translation memories; analysing and pre-translating text using automated translation systems; using and maintaining MACHINE TRANSLATION applications and resources; managing thousands of source and target files; updating previous translations and checking the consistency of translations, across product lines, versions and computing platforms. The pressure to produce high-quality translations within short time frames and at low cost is extremely high, and although this is seldom officially stated, time and financial constraints are often more important than the QUALITY of the translation. While visual localization environments – which allow the translators to translate strings in context and to see the positioning of these translated strings in relation to other strings, controls and dialog boxes on the screen – are available for some computing environments and platforms (such as Microsoft Windows), it is in the nature of translating digital material that translators often have to translate (sub-) strings out of context. These strings are later assembled, at runtime, to become the messages presented to the user on the screen. Concatenation at runtime can cause significant problems in the localized digital content and requires careful checking and linguistic quality assurance.
- **Engineering/Testing**. Properly executed

internationalization of a product and the availability of visual localization platforms can dramatically reduce the number of problems introduced during translation. In particular, problems impacting on the core functionality of digital products are minimized. However, layout and linguistic problems will always be quite common and must be identified and fixed before a product can be released. Testers and Quality Assurance (QA) personnel use test plans, test scripts and sophisticated error reporting and tracking procedures to ensure the quality of the localized products. Once the localization engineers have removed all significant problems, the localized product is signed off by the QA team and passed on to the release lab, from where it is released to the customers.

+ **Project Review**. Every localization project undergoes a thorough review by the project team and managers from both the client and vendor site. The quality of the service provided by the vendor is assessed and strategies to address problems that were identified during the project are discussed and, where possible, agreed on, so as to prevent their recurrence in future projects.

Localization projects can differ significantly in their size and the number of languages addressed. Some are relatively small and confined, but large localization projects can involve millions of words and dozens of languages, thus requiring a translation and localization operation that is active around the clock, across the globe, every day of the week. They involve thousands of people working for different operations or product groups of the same digital publisher as well as people working for service providers to which distinct localization tasks were outsourced.

Future directions

Changes in the economic, technical and socio-political arenas are reflected in the localization industry. At a time when the academic world is finally beginning to conduct research into localization and to include localization modules on their degree programmes (see TRAINING AND EDUCATION), teaching desktop-based localization tools, technologies and processes, the

localization processes are evolving into huge, complicated, standardized, automated and web-based activities where the tasks performed by localizers of the early days, i.e. translating strings and performing manual testing, are becoming less and less important. Automated **localization factories** are currently being developed to cope with the increasing demand for localized material; these are automated localization environments capable of managing localization processes and automating many of its tasks, and indeed require a much reduced level of human intervention.

A product such as Microsoft *Vista* was already being localized into ninety-nine languages in 2007 (Microsoft 2007), a number that is set to increase in the future. More localized versions of digital products are now simultaneously shipped with the original version (simship). Instead of well-defined release cycles, many publishers are switching over to a continuous stream of small releases delivered to their customers over the Internet. Large-scale **enterprise localization** projects are complemented by smaller-scale, on-demand **consumer localization** projects, providing users with ad hoc localized versions of, for example, websites or customer service information.

Developments are also taking place – for example in the context of the European Union funded IGNITE (2007) project and the newly established Irish-based research centre funded by the Science Foundation Ireland – that will eventually transcend many of the by now well-established concepts in localization: translation memories (storing and managing previous translations) will become localization memories (storing and managing process, technical and linguistic information on previous projects); the idea of different *locales* (country and language settings) will be replaced by personal preferences, allowing individuals to *personalize* their production and consumption of digital material.

Another dramatic change in localization will most likely be the growing presence of developing regions in the digital world, which should firmly establish **development localization** in addition to current mainstream short-term localization efforts driven by return on investment. This may lead to a shift in focus from the exclusively commercial to the wider political, social and cultural dimensions of localization (Schäler and Hall 2005). So far, localization has predominantly serviced rich countries. Decisions by large multinational digital content developers on whether a product should be localized into a particular language and locale continue to be made based on the purchasing power of the target market, i.e. on the gross domestic product (GDP) in a particular country, rather than on the number of speakers of a language. Most large mainstream localization projects will thus include Danish (spoken by approximately 5 million people) or Swedish (spoken by approximately 9 million people), but very few, if any, will include Amharic (spoken by approximately 17 million people) or Bengali (spoken by approximately 100 million people). By contrast, development localization works on the basis that access to and a presence in the digital world is a right for speakers of any language and should not be dependent on their income. Promoters of development localization believe that access barriers to the digital world, causing what has been described as the 'digital divide', can be lowered or even removed, rather than raised, through localization. Examples of development localization include initiatives funded by the Canadian government's International Development Research Centre (2007) in Asia, the Global Initiative for Local Computing (2007) and moves by some of the world's largest digital publishers like Microsoft (Cronin 2005) to develop alternative localization models that allow localization projects for markets previously considered not economically viable.

'**Crowdsourcing**' as proposed by *Wired* magazine author Jeff Howe (2006) and the '**wikifization**' of translation raised by Alain Désilets (2007) of the National Research Council of Canada are two examples of emerging localization frameworks that are no longer focused on predominantly commercial concerns. Crowdsourcing involves the *outsourcing* of localization tasks to a large group of people in an open call; wikifization is the impact of massive online collaboration on the world of localization and translation. Ultimately, localization may be seen as an instrument of GLOBALIZATION: it facilitates the movement towards greater interdependence and integration of countries, societies and economies. The different constituents of the localization community have just begun to put their interests on the map, to take ownership and to chart the future course of localization as is demonstrated by the recent establishment of new, targeted educational programmes (such as the Certified Localisation Professional Programme, or *CLP*, by the Institute of Localisation Professionals), professional associations, trade events and research activities (Locke 2003; Folaron 2006; Schäler 2007).

See also:
ADAPTATION; COMMERCIAL TRANSLATION; COMPUTER-AIDED TRANSLATION; GLOBALIZATION; MINORITY.

Further reading
Esselink 2000; Sprung 2000; Localisation Research Centre 2003–6; Schäler and Hall 2005; Dunne 2006a; Schäler 2007.

REINHARD SCHÄLER

Machine Translation

Machine Translation (MT) involves the use of computer programs to translate texts from one natural language into another automatically. It is usually subsumed under the category of computer(-based) translation, together with COMPUTER-AIDED TRANSLATION.

MT has been the subject of research for more than half a century, ever since the invention of the electronic computer in the 1940s (see Hutchins 2006 for an overview of the history of MT). Although high-quality, general-purpose MT is still a somewhat elusive goal, a number of systems have been in use in specific areas of human activity for some time, and new approaches are being explored which hold the promise of enhancing the output quality of MT systems substantially .

Types of MT systems

Computer(-based) translation can be classified according to a number of criteria, such as: (i) degree of intervention by human translator, (ii) whether the system provides generic or customized translation, and (iii) what system architecture or approach is employed.

In **unassisted** or **fully automatic MT**, the translation engine translates whole texts without the intervention of human operators. These systems are sometimes referred to as 'batch' systems since the whole text is processed as one task. The raw output is known as 'informative translation' or 'translation for assimilation' (Hutchins 2001a) and is generally a 'quick and dirty' draft rendition of the original. Assisted MT is generally classified into **human-assisted MT** (HAMT) and machine-assisted human translation (MAHT). In human-assisted MT (HAMT), also known as interactive MT, human translators intervene to resolve problems of ambiguity in the source text or to select the most appropriate target language word or phrase for output. In **machine-assisted human translation** (MAHT), computer programs are used to help human translators carry out the translation. An increasingly popular form of MAHT is COMPUTER-AIDED TRANSLATION (CAT).

Generic MT systems are general-purpose systems that translate texts in any subject area or domain. They can be used, for example, to get the gist of the information contained on a web page in a foreign language. **Customized** or special-purpose systems are targeted at groups of users who work in specific areas or fields (domains). Customized MT is much more effective than generic MT.

In terms of the system's architecture, MT can be broadly categorized as **rule-based** or **corpus-based**. Rule-based MT (RBMT) is essentially based on various kinds of linguistic rules. Two major paths are taken in the development of such systems: the direct approach and the indirect approach. Systems developed before the 1980s largely adopted the **direct approach**. These systems work between pairs of languages on the basis of bilingual dictionary entries and morphological analysis. They translate the source text word by word, without much detailed analysis of the syntactic structures of the input text or of the correlation of meaning between words, and then make some rudimentary adjustments to the target text in accordance with the morphological and syntactic rules of the target language. This is the most primitive kind of approach to MT, but some commercial systems still use it.

During the 1980s, the **indirect approach**, which is more sophisticated in architecture, became the dominant framework in MT design. Translation engines using this approach analyse the syntactic structure of a text, usually creating an intermediary, abstract representation of the meaning of the original, and generating from it the target language text. The parsing process involves successive programs for identifying word structure (morphology) and sentence structure (syntax) and for resolving problems of ambiguity (semantics). According to the nature of the intermediary representation, two specific indirect approaches can be distinguished: the transfer-based approach and the interlingua approach.

Transfer-based MT consists of three basic stages: (i) parsing an input sentence into a formal meaning representation which still retains the deep-structure characteristics of the source text; (ii) 'transferring', i.e. converting, the ST formal representation into one which carries the deep-structure characteristics of the target language, and (iii) generating a target sentence from the transferred meaning representation. Most of today's major commercial mainframe systems, including METAL, SYSTRAN, and Logos, adopt this approach. Two widely known research projects, Eurotra (funded by the Commission of the European Communities) and Ariane (at GETA in Grenoble), also used this approach (Hutchins 1999).

In **interlingua** MT, the abstract representation of the meaning of the original is created using an 'interlingua' or pivot language, i.e. an (ideally) source/target language-independent representation, from which target texts in several different languages can potentially be produced. Translation thus consists of two basic stages: an analyser 'transforms' the source text into the interlingua and a generator 'transforms' the interlingua representation into the target language. The most obvious advantage of this approach is that, for translations involving more than one language pair, no transfer component has to be created for each language pair. The interlingua is used to provide a semantic representation for the source language which has been abstracted from the syntax of the language. However, finding language-independent ways of representing semantic meaning is an extremely difficult task which generally involves either making arbitrary decisions as to what specific language (natural, artificial, or logical) conceptualizations should be taken as the basis, or multiplying the distinctions found in any of the languages concerned, with the result that a

vast amount of information is required. In the latter case, one will obtain, for example, several primitive interlingual items representing 'wear' as a concept because the Japanese translation of this verb depends on where the object is worn, so that a different verb will be required depending on whether the object worn is a hat or gloves, for example (Dorr *et al.* 2006). The tremendous difficulties involved in finding language-neutral ways of representing semantic meaning led some researchers to argue that interlingua MT may not be a viable option within the rule-based MT paradigm; but successful interlingual systems do exist, the best known being the Fujitsu system in Japan.

A variant of interlingual MT is **knowledge-based MT** (KBMT), which produces semantically accurate translations but typically needs, for the purpose of disambiguation, massive acquisition of various kinds of knowledge, especially non-linguistic information related to the domains of the texts to be translated and general knowledge about the real world. This knowledge is usually encoded using painstaking manual methods. Examples of KBMT systems include Caterpillar (Carnegie Mellon University) and ULTRA (New Mexico State University).

In the 1990s, researchers began to explore the possibility of exploiting CORPORA of already translated texts for automatic translation. Corpus-based MT can be classified into two categories: statistical MT and example-based MT. In **statistical machine translation** (SMT), words and phrases (word sequences) in a bilingual parallel corpus are aligned as the basis for a 'translation model' of word–word and phrase–phrase frequencies. Translation involves the selection, for each input word, of the most probable words in the target language, and the determination of the most probable sequence of the selected words on the basis of a monolingual 'language model' (Hutchins 2006). Since the translation engine works on the basis of corpora, building quality bilingual text corpora is essential to the success of SMT. Where such corpora are available, impressive results can be achieved when translating texts of a similar kind to those in the training corpus.

Example-based MT (EBMT) systems also use bilingual parallel corpora as their main knowledge base, at runtime. In this case, translation is produced by comparing the input with a corpus of typical translated examples, extracting the closest matches and using them as a model for the target text. Translation is thus completed in three stages: matching, which involves finding matches for the input in the parallel corpus; alignment, which involves identifying which parts of the corresponding translation are to be re-used, and recombination, which involves putting together those parts of the examples to be used in a legitimate (or grammatical) way. The process is similar to that used in translation memory (TM) (see COMPUTER-AIDED TRANSLATION). Both EBMT and TM involve matching the input against a database of real examples and identifying the closest matches. The main difference between the two is that the TM system identifies the corresponding translation fragments but it is up to the human translator to recombine them to generate the target text, while in EBMT the entire process of identifying corresponding translation fragments and recombining them to generate the target text is carried out automatically by the MT engine. This approach is said to be more like the way humans go about translating since the target text is produced basically by analogy, and the process can be viewed as an instance of case-based reasoning (the process of solving new problems based on the solutions of similar past problems). EBMT is also claimed to result in more stylish, less literal translations, since fundamentally it is not based on structural analysis of the input by computer programs (Somers 1999).

Rule-based MT and corpus-based MT represent the two major avenues of research into MT. The most obvious distinction between the two is that RBMT is characterized by an effort to interpret – on various linguistic levels – the meaning of the original, while CBMT is concerned essentially not with interpreting the original but with finding out the best matching patterns for source text and target text segments on the basis of an aligned corpus of translation examples. Within the RBMT paradigm, direct, transfer and interlingual methodologies differ in the depth of their analysis of the source language and the extent to which they attempt to reach a language-independent representation of meaning or communicative intent in the source and target languages. The Vauquois triangle (Vauquois

1968; cited in Dorr *et al.* 2006) illustrates these levels of analysis.

Starting with the shallowest level at the bottom, direct transfer is achieved at word level. In syntactic and semantic transfer approaches, the translation is based on representations of the source sentence structure and meaning, respectively. Finally, at the interlingual level, the notion of transfer is replaced with a single underlying representation – the interlingua – that represents both the source and target texts simultaneously. The interlingual method typically involves the deepest analysis of the source language. Moving up the triangle reduces the amount of work required to traverse the gap between languages, at the cost of increasing the required amount of analysis (to convert the source input into a suitable pre-transfer representation) and synthesis (to convert the post-transfer representation into the final target surface form) (Dorr *et al.* 2006).

MT from the user's point of view

As far as users are concerned, the most popular MT systems of today are special-purpose systems, speech translation systems, and online translation systems.

Special-purpose systems

Current general-purpose MT systems cannot translate all texts reliably. **Post-editing** is indispensable if the MT output is intended for dissemination (see Hutchins 1999 for a description of the four major uses of MT). Post-editing involves human translators consulting the source texts and hence can be time-consuming and expensive (Allen 2003). Another way of improving a system's output quality is to design the system to deal with only one particular domain (sub-domain) and/or to **pre-edit** the source material (input text) using 'regularized', controlled vocabulary and syntax to make it compatible with the expectations of the MT system. MT systems working with such sub-languages or domain-specific languages (specialized languages of sub-domains) and/or controlled or restricted languages (specially simplified versions of a natural language) to minimize incorrect machine output and reduce editing hours are known as '**special-purpose systems**' or '**customer-specific systems**' (see Kittredge 2003 and Nyberg *et al.* 2003 for a discussion of sub-languages and controlled languages in MT).

Special-purpose systems are particularly effective in domains where formulaic or technical language is typically used, e.g. product specifications, maintenance manuals, government bulletins, legal documents, etc. In some cases such systems can produce output that can be used without post-editing. For example, METEO, which was designed for translating Canadian meteorological bulletins between English and French, has been in use at the Canadian Meteorological Center in Dorval, Montreal since 1977 without any significant human intervention whatsoever (Arnold *et al.* 1995).

Speech translation systems

Made feasible by speech technology in the 1980s, speech translation synthesizes speech recognition, speech generation and MT technologies. It has probably been the most innovative area of computer-based translation research and experienced rapid development since the 1990s. JANUS, a system under development by Carnegie Mellon University's Language Technologies Institute (LTI) in collaboration with other research partners of the C-STAR consortium, addresses speech translation of spontaneous conversational dialogs in multiple languages using primarily an interlingua-based approach. The current focus of the project is on the travel domain (Language Technologies Institute at Carnegie Mellon University 2004).

Online translation systems

With the fast growth of the Internet, more and more MT vendors are collaborating with Internet service/content providers to offer on-demand online translation services, with human post-editing as optional extras. In the mid-1990s, CompuServe began to offer on-line translation of emails and SYSTRAN made its systems available online for text and webpage translation in AltaVista's Babel Fish service. Today, most Internet portals, including Google and Yahoo, offer free online MT services.

The demand for online translation has given a huge impetus to the development of MT systems. For example, the need for the translation of Internet content has prompted most stand-alone PC-based MT software developers to incorporate in their products the function of translating webpages and email messages. Moreover, by providing a vast number of customers and potential customers with easy access to multiple translation engines on a free or trial-use basis, MT developers are able to engage an unprecedented number of people in the testing and evaluation of MT systems, which will certainly help improve the systems' quality over time and promote the need for research and development in the field.

Challenges in MT

The slow improvement of the output quality of MT is rooted in problems inherent to language as a form of human communication. Some of these are problems also faced by human translators, while others are specific to MT. Broadly speaking, translation requires at least two categories of knowledge: (i) linguistic, i.e. grammatical, semantic and pragmatic knowledge; and (ii) extra-linguistic, including knowledge of the subject matter and knowledge about the real world, or common-sense knowledge. For instance, when asked whether $35,000 \times 58,000$ is greater or smaller than 1, human beings will readily give the answer 'greater' without actually performing the calculation: they resolve the question by using their real-world knowledge – in this case, basic arithmetic knowledge about what an operation of multiplying positive integers will yield; a computer, however, needs to perform the calculation before giving an answer. Depending on whether primarily linguistic or primarily non-linguistic knowledge is required for their resolution, problems in MT can be categorized into linguistic and extra-linguistic ones. The treatment of extra-linguistic problems is more difficult than that of linguistic problems because extra-linguistic knowledge is much harder to codify.

Linguistic problems encountered in MT are primarily caused by the inherent ambiguities of natural languages and by the lexical and structural mismatches between different languages.

Ambiguity

Disambiguation, the resolution of ambiguities, has always been one of the greatest challenges for MT researchers and developers. There are two kinds of ambiguity: lexical and structural. **Lexical ambiguity** is typically caused by polysemy and homonymy. **Structural** or **grammatical ambiguity** arises where different constituent structures (underlying structures) may be assigned to one construction (surface structure). Typical cases include alternative structures and uncertain anaphoric reference. **Alternative structures** are constructions which present two or more possible interpretations but presuppose that only one is true. For example, from a purely grammatical point of view, 'pregnant women and babies' can be interpreted as '(pregnant women) and babies' or 'pregnant (women and babies)', although only the former is semantically accurate.

Uncertain anaphoric reference occurs when an expression can refer back to more than one antecedent, as in the following example: 'There's a pile of inflammable trash next to your car. You are going to have to get rid of it.' Here, it is not possible to determine, without reference to the context, whether 'it' refers anaphorically to 'trash' or 'car'. To disambiguate the second sentence, MT system developers must encode a great deal of real-world knowledge and develop procedures to use such knowledge. Specifically, they would have to encode facts about the relative value of trash and cars, about the close connection between the concepts of 'trash' and 'getting rid of', about the concern of fire inspectors for things that are inflammable, and so forth.

A special type of alternative structure exists in non-segmented languages such as Chinese, where characters and words are not typographically set off from each other by an orthographic space (see also COMPUTER-AIDED TRANSLATION for a discussion of segmentation problems in natural language processing). For example, the Chinese sentence 'Bai tian ee zai hu li you yong. [白天湖在湖里游泳。]', meaning, literally, 'white sky/day goose in lake swim' may be segmented in two different ways, resulting in two totally different interpretations of the sentence:

Baitian ee zai huli youyong. [白天|湖|在|湖里|游泳。] 'By day geese swim in the lake'.

Bai tianee zai huli youyong. [白|天湖|在|湖里|游泳。] 'White swans are swimming in the lake'.

To translate such potentially ambiguous sentences from Chinese into other languages, the MT system must be programmed first to segment words and phrases in a context-sensitive way. In this process, ambiguous lexical chunks and sentence constructions must be disambiguated, with unacceptable and unsuitable word combinations excluded from processing in the next step of analysis.

Problems can also be caused by word groupings as idioms/metaphors or ordinary phrases. Since idioms and metaphorical expressions are not to be interpreted literally, sophisticated syntactic and semantic analysis is necessary for the translation engine to determine whether a phrase is an idiom/metaphor or not. One way of disambiguating word senses is to incorporate compounds in the MT system's dictionaries and to have the translation engine consult dictionaries of compounds first for the meaning of a lexical unit before looking it up in dictionaries of individual words. For example, incorporating the French 'pomme de terre' ('potato') into the machine dictionary of compounds and giving it priority in the translation engine's dictionary lookup procedure should prevent the mistranslation of the phrase into English as 'apple of earth'.

Source and target language mismatches

Source and target language mismatches (also known as cases of non-correspondence or transfer problems) arise from lexical and structural differences between languages. **Lexical mismatches** are due to differences in the ways in which languages classify the world. For example, Chinese consanguineous kinship terminology is classified on the basis of five parameters: generation from ego, lineality vs. collaterality, male vs. female, seniority vs. juniority, and paternal vs. maternal; its English counterpart involves only three parameters: generation from ego, male vs. female, and lineality vs. collaterality. In translating from English into Chinese, a term denoting a kinship relationship requires specification of the relationship with regard to all the above-mentioned five parameters. For example, in order to render *cousin* into Chinese, the translator needs to determine if it is a *tangxiong*, *tangdi*, *tangjie*, *tangmei*, *biaoxiong*, *biaodi*, *biaojie*, or *biaomei*. A correct translation of the term requires knowledge beyond what is there in the text, and will even be impossible if sufficient contextual clues are not available.

Structural mismatches occur when different languages use different structures for the same purpose, and the same structure for different purposes. The relative clause construction in English, for example, generally consists of a head noun, a relative pronoun and a sentence with a 'gap' in it. The relative pronoun (and hence the head noun) is understood as filling the gap in that sentence. In English, there are restrictions on where the 'gap' can occur, e.g. it cannot occur within an indirect question. In Italian, however, such a restriction does not obtain. So, while the following Italian original is perfectly well-formed, its literal English translation is ungrammatical: 'L'uomo che mi domando chi abbia visto fu arrestato' (*The man that I wonder who (he) has seen was arrested). Problems of this kind are beyond the scope of current rule-based MT systems.

Cases where the same structure is used for different purposes include the use of passive constructions in English and Japanese. In the following example, the Japanese particle *wa* (glossed as TOPIC) marks the 'topic' of the sentence, i.e. what the sentence is about:

Satoo-san wa shyushoo ni
erabaremashita.
Satoo-HONORIFIC   TOPIC   Prime
Minister in was-elected.
Mr. Satoh was elected Prime Minister.

This example indicates that Japanese, like English, has a passive-like construction, but the Japanese passive differs from its English counterpart in that it tends to have an extra layer of adverse implication, suggesting in this case that either Mr Satoh did not want to be elected, or that the election is somehow bad for him (Arnold *et al.* 1995).

The convergence of different approaches and technologies

The success of rule-based MT ultimately rests on the successful computer modelling of the structure of human language and the codification of subject-matter knowledge and real-world knowledge for computer manipulation. Rapid breakthroughs in this respect, however, do not seem very likely in the near future. This is because, on the one hand, computer modelling of the structure of human language and the codification of relevant knowledge places enormous engineering demands on the IT industry, giving a rather low return on investment. Human crafted rules for creating an MT system capable of translating any kind of text, for example, are considered to require an effort in the order of 500 to 1,000 person years, and building a specialized bilingual system (in the order of 10,000 concepts) would require approximately 100 person years (Murzaku 2007). On the other hand, progress on investigating the formal structure of human language has been slower than that of computer technology (Liu 2002:1). Thus, while the dominant approach to MT research today is largely rule-based, there has been an increasing interest in the integrated use of both rule-based and corpus-based technologies in the so-called 'hybrid systems', which are expected to yield output of higher quality than purely rule-based systems. Hutchins (1995) notes that linguistic rules in a hybrid system can be somewhat less complex than in a purely rule-based system. For example, syntactic analysis may be limited to the recognition of surface phrase structures and dependencies, lexical information extracted mainly from standard sources such as general-purpose dictionaries, and corpus-based methods would then be used to refine the rule-based analyses, to improve lexical selection and to generate more idiomatic target language texts. An example of a hybrid system is CATALYST, a large-scale knowledge-based and controlled-language system for multilingual translation of technical manuals developed jointly by Carnegie Mellon University (CMU) and Caterpillar. The knowledge-based approach at CMU was combined with developments in statistical analysis of text corpora for the rapid prototyping and implementation of special-purpose systems (DIPLOMAT), e.g. for translation of Serbo-Croatian in military operations (Hutchins 2001b).

A number of systems that integrate CAT technologies into MT were developed in the past two decades. The Institute of Computational Linguistics (ICL) of Peking University (PKU/ICL), the Institute of Computing Technology of the Chinese Academy of Sciences, and the State Key Laboratory of Intelligent Technology and System of Tsinghua University at Beijing jointly developed a Chinese–English MT system, primarily oriented towards journalistic translation, which incorporates corpus-based translation memory (TM) technologies in a multiple-engine architecture (Bai *et al.* 2002: 124). Fujitsu's software package ATLAS, which translates from Japanese to English and English to Japanese, also uses both MT and TM technologies (ATLAS V13).

Since Eurotra, a research project funded by the Commission of the European Communities, failed to produce the working system that the Commission hoped would replace the commercially-developed SYSTRAN systems it had been using, research funded by the European Union has focused more generally on projects within the broad field of language engineering. Many of these multilingual projects involve translation of some kind, usually within a restricted subject field and often in controlled conditions (Hutchins 2005b). However, MT is usually not used alone but along with computer-aided translation and other (multilingual) information processing technologies, such as concordancers and terminology management tools, which are usually compatible with the word processing systems professional translators customarily use, and are integrated in 'translator workstations'.

Promising research directions

Among the many research directions explored in MT in the past decade or so, two stand out as particularly promising: knowledge-based machine translation (KBMT) and statistical machine translation (SMT).

Knowledge-based machine translation (KBMT)

Artificial intelligence research discovered that adding heuristics (rules of thumb) enabled computer programs to tackle problems that were otherwise difficult to solve. The discovery inspired efforts to build knowledge-based systems to help solve traditional problems in MT. A knowledge-based system is based on the methods and techniques of AI and is programmed to imitate human problem solving by means of artificial intelligence and reference to a knowledge base (KB), i.e. a database of knowledge providing the means for the computerized collection, organization and retrieval of knowledge on a particular subject. The core components of a KBMT are the KB and the inference mechanisms. Developing relevant knowledge bases or resources (including dictionaries of grammatical and semantic rules, specialized dictionaries or glossaries, term banks, translation memories, aligned parallel corpora, world models, etc.) is expected to improve the accuracy of MT output. A dictionary that contains useful information on word segmentation, for example, can dramatically reduce the complexity usually associated with the use of a parser in segmentation (Wu and Jiang 1998: 1). Characterized by a tight integration of automatic translation technologies with the expertise and experience of highly skilled linguists/translators, KBMT is viewed as a bridge between the two extremes of human-only high-quality translation and machine-only low-quality translation, and generally yields higher-quality output.

The best known KBMT project is KANT, founded in 1989 at the Center for Machine Translation at Carnegie Mellon University. One example of a re-designed, object-oriented C++ implementation of KANT technology for MT is KANTOO, which features a tool ('the Knowledge Maintenance Tool') for knowledge source development. Intended primarily for the developer and end-user maintainer, the tool provides an interface for structured editing of grammar rules and domain knowledge and can be used by customers who wish to continue customizing the grammar and domain knowledge after the delivery of a finished system.

The Institute of Computational Linguistics at Peking University (PKU/ICL) has plans to build an integrated, comprehensive Language Knowledge Base to support Chinese information processing tasks (including Chinese–English translation). The Knowledge Base will consolidate a number of important language-data resources the Institute has developed in the past two decades, which include, among other things, the Grammatical Knowledge-base of Contemporary Chinese (GKB), the POS-Tagged Corpus of Contemporary Chinese, the Semantic Knowledge-base of Contemporary Chinese (SKCC), the Chinese Concept Dictionary (CCD), a bilingual parallel corpus, and a multi-disciplinary term bank (Yu *et al.* 2004). KBMT technologies have also been applied in commercial systems such as SDL International's SDL Kb T System and Caterpillar Inc.'s Caterpillar Corporate Translations.

Statistical machine translation (SMT)

Statistical analysis of huge, aligned bilingual corpora allows for the automatic construction of MT systems by extracting lexical and syntactic translation equivalents from such corpora on a statistical probability basis. For language pairs such as Chinese–English or Arabic–English, statistical systems are already the best MT systems currently available (SMT Group at the University of Edinburgh 2006).

The statistical approach to MT has been developed by teams at IBM, Johns Hopkins University, University of Pennsylvania, and the Information Sciences Institute of the University of Southern California (USC/ISI), among other partners. Knight and Marcu at USC/ISI, for example, devoted twenty person-years to the development of SMT systems. The key to their SMT software is the translation dictionaries, patterns and rules (known as 'translation parameters') that the program develops and ranks probabilistically on the basis of previously translated documents. Knight and Marcu founded a company called Language Weaver which sells systems for Arabic, Chinese, French, German, Persian, Romanian and Spanish translation to and from English (Knight 2005; Hutchins 2006).

Google too has reported promising results obtained using its proprietary SMT engine and its massive text databases. It currently uses SYSTRAN for most of the language pairs it

handles, but is working on a statistical translation method to implement in most of its online 'Google Translate' services in the future. Although the statistical translation method is now used only in Arabic–English, Chinese–English, Japanese–English and Korean–English translation, more language pairs will soon be migrated from the SYSTRAN engine to the statistics-based Google engine. In 2007, Google improved this engine's translation capabilities by inputting approximately 200 billion words from United Nations materials to train their system. The accuracy of translations provided by Google has since improved dramatically (Hutchins 2006).

See also:
COMPUTER-AIDED TRANSLATION; CORPORA; LOCALIZATION.

Further reading
Hutchins and Somers 1992; Arnold *et al.* 1995; Trujillo 1999; Hutchins 2001b; Liu 2002; Quah 2006.

KE PING

Minority

The relationship between translation and minority languages has been a relatively neglected topic for much of the existence of translation studies. Translation theory anthologies rarely included contributions from minority language perspectives, and little or no allowance was made for the fact that attitudes towards translation might significantly alter depending on whether the source or target language was in a majority or minority position. Although a number of the significant theorists in translation studies in the 1970s and 1980s, for example, came from smaller countries such as Belgium, Israel and the Netherlands, this did not translate into a specific concern with the position of minority languages. It was in the areas of anthropology, area studies, literary and cultural studies – rather than in translation studies *per se* – that questions began to be asked about the relationship between the role of translation for communities in a subordinate position. Yet, in cultural studies the problem was further compounded by the tendency of POSTCOLONIAL theorists to treat the 'West' or 'Europe' as a homogeneous bloc and to overlook the significant asymmetry in power relationships between the different languages of European nation states and within these nation states (Niranjana 1992). A signal irony of the neglect or oversight is that minority-language cultures are of course translation cultures *par excellence* as they are heavily dependent on translation to supply informational needs in the language. Translation is a central and inescapable fact of the economic, scientific and cultural life of a minority language.

It is important to note that for translation studies the concept of minority is always dynamic and never static. The concept of minority is the expression of a *relation* not of an *essence*. A language may be displaced from the public sphere and thus increasingly marginalized from use in various areas of life because of invasion, conquest or subjection by a more powerful group. The speakers of the minority language thus occupy the same territory as before, but their language is no longer in a dominant position. A historical example would be the situation of Irish Gaelic in Ireland. In other instances, it might be the redrawing of national boundaries after the collapse of empire which results in a once dominant language now finding itself in a minority position. This was the case with Russian in the Baltic Republics after the break-up of the Soviet Union. A crucial distinction between the former and latter situation is that in the latter, there is a larger linguistic hinterland that translators can draw on for reference tools, publishers, educational institutions, infrastructural support – all of which are largely absent in the case of the former.

The relational and dynamic nature of minority status is of fundamental importance for translation studies as it points to the fact that all languages are potentially minority languages. Thus, in certain areas such as science and technology (see SCIENTIFIC AND TECHNICAL TRANSLATION), or in certain circumstances such as any number of international conferences, the speakers of major world languages such as Chinese, Arabic, Russian, Hindi and Portuguese can find that their language has a peripheral or marginalized status. The relentless expansion of English and the increased incidence of language death in the late modern period mean that many languages, even those used by millions of speakers, can find themselves in a minoritized position. This is why Albert Branchadell uses the term 'less translated-language', which 'applies to all those languages that are less often the source of translation in the international exchange of linguistic goods, regardless of the number of people using these languages' (Branchadell and West 2005: 1). A consequence of this observation is that the translation experiences of minority languages become relevant to a much wider community of scholars as the questions of where, what, when and how to translate become issues for many different languages and language communities across the globe.

Drawing on the work of Gilles Deleuze and Félix Guattari, Lawrence Venuti pointed out that a 'minor language is that of a politically dominated group, but also language use that is heterogenous, that deviates from the standards, varies the constants' (1998a: 136). The German of Franz Kafka, the English of James Joyce, the French of Michèle Lalonde thus demonstrate the creative tension of a movement between 'major' and 'minor' varieties of a language as its location shifts from a point of geographical or historical origin. The increasing prominence of sociolinguistics in translation studies and the interaction with DISCOURSE ANALYSIS allowed for greater cognizance to be taken of language varieties and of the social and political situatedness of utterances in translation (Hatim and Mason 1997). Conceiving of minority as a function of political or cultural subjection also meant that in translation studies issues of GENDER or sexual orientation could be seen from a minoritarian perspective (Simon 1996; Harvey 2003).

One important reason for factoring in minority status to any consideration of translation is that theoretical claims are challenged by the specific circumstances of translation practice in a minority culture. In the context of powerful, hegemonic cultures to advocate a foreignizing, refractory or abusive approach to translation could be seen as a subversive, progressive practice which undermines the homogenizing pretensions of the dominant languages and cultures. Seen from the point of view of a minority language, however, subject to constant pressures to engage in substantial translation from the major language, an unthinking foreignizing strategy is the default value which could ultimately lead to the disappearance of the language. There would no longer be any distinct language into which translation might be done as the language would in a sense have been translated out of existence. In this context, a domesticating strategy attentive to the distinctive features of the minority language and culture could indeed provide a more vivid example of subversion or resistance than a foreignizing approach (Tymoczko 1999a); see STRATEGIES. This position would have to be qualified, however, by the observation that translation does contribute to heterogeneity in minority cultures and cannot simply be annexed to essentialist forms of identity politics. The development of the novel form in Catalan, for example, was greatly facilitated by the translation of British English novels into the language in the pre-World War II period. In a sense, the problematic for minority languages bears similarities to a more general question with regard to the role of translation in cultures, whether translation functions to assimilate or to diversify. That is to say, the question is whether speakers and writers of minority languages allow themselves to engage in collective SELF-TRANSLATION, in wholesale assimilation into the major language, or whether they look to translation as a guarantor of diversification, as a way of maintaining identity through difference.

An important dimension to translation-as-diversification is the contention that a basic right of a language community is to be able to live a full life in the minority language. One consequence has been to challenge the tendency in translation studies to consider languages and cultures in a minoritized position principally in the context of LITERARY TRANSLATION. As language groups based their arguments for sovereignty and self-determination on the cultural legitimacy of a distinctive past as illustrated by the evidence of written or oral literature, the focus of translation theory and history was inevitably on the translation record of literary exchanges between groups and languages. Such a focus brought with it the inevitable risk of an antiquarian perspective on minority languages and cultures. While idealized for a glorious

aesthetic past, the languages and cultures in question were deemed wholly unsuitable to a commercial present or a scientific future. As a result, Maria Tymoczko has argued, 'to a very high degree philological approaches have remained the norm for translating the native texts of minority and non-Western cultures' (1999a: 269). However, the recognition that communities also function linguistically in the areas of science, technology, business and administration has led to the extension of minority language issues in translation studies to the fields of SCIENTIFIC, TECHNICAL and COMMERCIAL translation (Cronin 2003). The relationship between minority languages and science and technology, for example, does not simply relate to what does or does not get translated into the minority language. There is the issue of the availability of machine-readable forms of the language for translation research. A further topic is the cultural minoritization of major languages in translation through the existence of extensive intertextual resources on electronic media sourced predominantly in one major language such as English. For this reason, there is an obvious convergence of interest between research on language planning and investigation of minority-language translation. The issue of linguistic normalization, involving the standardization and spread of a language, has been the focus of work by a number of Catalan translation scholars, and the contribution of translation to normalization is a constant feature of nation-building projects, whether these are to be found in the Western or non-Western world (Branchadell and West 2005). A dimension which is often specific to minority languages in translation is the importance of the symbolic as opposed to the informational function of language. That is to say, for political or other reasons speakers of minority languages may have a perfectly good knowledge of a dominant language (Catalans knowing Spanish) but still insist on translation from and into that language. Translation in this instance is not about making communication possible but about establishing identity or enacting a form of resistance to the claims of the hegemonic language.

Whether the object of inquiry is pragmatic or aesthetic translation, a basic problem confronting translation scholars working with minority languages is the INSTITUTIIONAL TRANSLATION of their work in the field of translation studies. The difficulties here emerge at two levels. First, there is the existence of translation research published in languages other than major languages and which is not read and therefore not cited in international translation studies research. Indeed, a notable trend in translation studies research in recent decades has been the further narrowing of the language range of the citational base so that at present any work not published in English has a diminishing chance of featuring in translation studies debate or research. Almost all languages other than English have now become minor languages in the translation research community. Second, the presentation of material in languages that are not widely known leads to difficulties of exemplification, as examples must be continually translated into a vehicular language or a form of periphrasis must be used. The complexities of articulation and presentation involved can therefore lead to a greater reluctance to engage in minority-language translation research. It is not altogether surprising therefore that much of the translation studies research in the area of minority languages has tended to be on languages in contact with English, such as Scots, Irish Gaelic and (Quebec) French (Corbett 1998; Cronin 1996; Brisset 1996), though in addition to work on Catalan mentioned earlier, other scholars have discussed the situation with respect to languages such as Hebrew, Orissa and Indonesian Malay (Shavit 1997; Pattanaik 2000; Fitzpatrick 2000; St-Pierre and Kar 2007). The research has frequently been of a historical nature as translation scholars working with minority languages either engage in a process of retrieval, unearthing an ignored or undervalued translation past, or consider the consequences of earlier translation policies for the development of the language or the evolution of the culture.

More broadly, the notion of the minoritization of major languages through heteroglossia has proved to be an important source of inspiration for scholars looking at the impact of translation from native languages on the body of POSTCOLONIAL writing in languages such as English, French and Portuguese (Bandia, 2008). If postcolonial writers have often found themselves living and writing in the former imperial centres, it is also true that migration from former colonies has been a continuous feature of population shift in the developed world (see MOBILITY). The impact of economic GLOBALIZATION has further contributed to accelerated migration so that migrant languages are increasingly becoming a notable feature of the societies of migrant host countries. Thus, another context emerges in which translation studies has to engage with the notion of a minority language and indeed, in translation terms, languages which previously enjoyed rights as minority languages must renegotiate their terms of co-existence with the new migrant languages as well as the host language.

Minority languages were a much neglected topic in translation studies for a relatively long period but the recent resurgence of interest promises to be sustained by the global importance of ostensibly local concerns.

See also:
ASYLUM; COMMUNITY INTEPRETING; ETHICS; GLOBALIZATION; LOCALIZATION; MOBILITY; MULTILINGUALISM; POSTCOLONIAL APPROACHES; SIGNED LANGUAGE INTERPRETING.

Further reading
Venuti 1998a; Tymoczko 1999a; Cronin 2003; O'Connell 2003; Branchadell and West 2005.

MICHAEL CRONIN

Mobility

The connection between translation and mobility is often traced back to etymological roots, the Latin word *translatio* indicating the movement or transfer of objects and people across space (Campbell 1988: 1–2). Travel and its textual accounts are associated with a form of translation of the Other and the new in terms familiar to a home audience. Translation, in turn, is configured as a form of transportation or appropriation of the foreign within the language and culture of the nation. The coupling between the figures of the traveller and the translator (or interpreter) is also well established and encompasses historical as well as phenomenological parallels, starting from the way in which travellers have to either rely on language mediators or take up that role for themselves. Specialists of subjects ranging from ethnography to postcolonial theory have approached these concepts and widened their scope in order to underline the increasingly pervasive role played by various forms of travel, including the movement across languages and cultures, within contemporary societies. The links drawn between spatial and linguistic mobility are both of a theoretical nature – drawing metaphorical connections between two sets of concepts – and an applied one – relating to the historically determined realities of two sets of practices and to the way in which they have been connected over the centuries (Bassnett 1993; Bauman 1987; Forsdick 2005: 158; Hulme and Youngs 2002: 9).

A substantial impulse to the adoption of translation as a wide-ranging theoretical model and to its frequent conjunction with notions of mobility has come, in particular, from the shift towards a cultural, rather than strictly linguistic, understanding of translation processes, which in turn produced what Bassnett called the 'translation turn' in cultural studies (Bassnett 1998b). Treating translation as a broadly intercultural phenomenon invited the reading of intercultural communication as a translation process. This trend has made 'translation' an increasingly popular term in a number of theoretical fields. During the same period, notions of place and mobility were also becoming more popular within literary theory and historical criticism, the latter being increasingly sensitive to the question of narrativity. Michel de Certeau's often quoted statement that 'every story is a travel story, a spatial practice' (1984: 115) is indicative of this tendency, inviting attention to the textual dimension of mobility as well as to the spatial qualities of text.

At the same time, the connection between geographic and cultural movement was also being brought to the fore by a number of historical phenomena which have come to be seen as characteristic of the late twentieth century. These include postcoloniality and attendant forms of neo-colonialism; GLOBALIZATION, accompanied by renewed localism; and the impulse given by these trends to both physical mobility and the creation of wider and faster communication networks. Such phenomena

have instigated a radical rethinking of notions of identity and belonging, stressing the role played by asymmetrical relationships of power with respect to individual choices as well as group affiliations (Papastergiadis 2000). Increasing attention has been devoted to a variety of forms of mobility, inflecting the notion of 'travel' to include gendered and class-related perspectives as well as notions of economic migration, exile, diaspora or mass tourism (see GENDER AND SEXUALITY; ASYLUM), and taking into account transnational forms of identification such as nomadism and cosmopolitanism. Many of these perspectives, in turn, are connected to questions of language, translation and TRANSLATABILITY.

Textual and historical studies

A growing number of studies linking travel and translation are concerned with the way in which both practices have been used in order to construct images of the foreign, especially, though not exclusively, within Western cultures. Here, the two terms, 'translation' and 'travel', are usually understood in a restrictive rather than open-ended sense, and they are taken as indicative of well-established practices characterized by fixed points of departure and clearly defined destinations, by specific source and target texts as well as cultures, and by neatly (if at times hastily) defined boundaries between these and other, related polarities. Within these rather narrowly defined confines, travellers and translators have, for a long time, played the role of intermediaries between cultures. They have also shared an ambiguous status as, at one and the same time, privileged witnesses of diversity and potential liars, or even double agents intent on infiltrating the home community. As a result, questions of faithfulness and objectivity, transparency and visibility have been common to the debates which have characterized the fields of translation and travel writing for centuries (Bassnett 1993, 2002b; Fabbri 2000).

The acknowledgement of these historical similarities has opened up a rich field of research concerned with establishing the relative prestige, superimposition or contraposition of translations and travel accounts as parallel yet not fully interchangeable genres relating to the ferrying and elaboration of cultural difference (St André

2006). A related and equally promising area of study concerns the way in which translation and travel (as well as the written and figurative accounts they produce) contribute to the establishment of national or regional stereotypes, to their endurance over long periods of time, and – at least in cases where the cultures being represented and appropriated are less prestigious than those actively doing the translating – to the eventual re-absorption of dominant, fixed images within the source culture itself; this latter phenomenon can take the form of auto-stereotypes, images which are given widespread credibility in popular as well as official self-representations of a group, for instance as part of the discourse produced by the heritage industry in order to support modern forms of mass tourism (Cronin 1995; Pfister 1996; Polezzi 2000). Such studies in the parallel history of translation and travel writing can highlight mechanisms through which translators and travellers play a crucial role in constructing images of foreign cultures under the sign of difference, at times relegating those cultures into the realm of the exotic, or even representing them as devoid of 'civilization' and therefore pushing them outside the boundaries of the human (Cheyfitz 1991). Alternatively, however, the focus of both travel writing and translation can be on the positive aspects of a foreign culture, and both travellers and translators can use their experience of the foreign in order to introduce and support innovative practices, or to establish an ongoing dialogue between two cultural poles. An illustration of this trend and, specifically, of the role played by translation and travel in mediating and highlighting issues of gender across European cultures, can be found in Agorni (2002), a study which examines the way in which eighteenth-century British women writers used translations and travelogues (as well as fictional genres such as the gothic novel) in order to produce images of Italy which could sustain their own 'proto-feminist' attitudes and agenda. On the gendering of travel and translation, see also Bassnett (1993, 2002b) and Monticelli (2005).

This type of work is also typical of a tendency for studies in the interconnected history of travel, travel writing and translation to combine, at a methodological level, the analysis of micro- and macro-textual features. Attention to both kinds of phenomena is evident, for instance, in

the essays collected in Di Biase (2006), a volume which traces detailed portraits of translators/travellers who moved across Europe (and, in some cases, beyond its boundaries) during the early modern period. These travelling translators – ranging from Martin Luther to John Milton, from Erasmus to Leo Africanus and Garcilaso el Inca – had an undeniable impact on the development of translation theory and practice, and on the evolution of Western culture as a whole. Their itineraries are both textual and geographical (and inextricably so), while their work traces a web of interconnections which is fundamental for understanding not just literary but also political and religious history. Combined attention to macro- and micro-textual phenomena is also central to research which traces the migrations not of travellers but rather of travel books across languages (Polezzi 2001; Smecca 2003). Given the role played by travellers' tales in the creation of images of self and Other, an examination of the foreign travel accounts translated by a culture at any particular point in time, of the STRATEGIES adopted by the translators, and of the marketing choices selected by publishers to promote these texts is potentially revealing of wider cultural trends. Research of this kind also shows how representational phenomena do not simply work according to a binary system of oppositions (self/Other; observer/observed; subject/object; source/target), but rather form part of a complex web of travelling images and multiple refractions which often involve several layers of writing, REWRITING and translation. Ultimately, such readings of translation call into question established views of national cultures as self-contained systems, stressing, instead, the constant mutability and dynamic interpenetration of cultural phenomena.

Migrant writing, postcolonial theory and the question of world literature

The practices and notions of travel and translation, together with their multiple superimpositions, are also a constitutive element of a growing range of contemporary creative literature. In spite of the fact that travel writers have often tended to overlook or gloss over the role played by translation as a communicative strategy and by translators as active participants in their journeys (Cronin 2000), the beginning of the twenty-first century saw the publication of a number of travelogues which centre on issues of language and translation (e.g. Abley 2003; Drysdale 2001). Additionally, the growth in global mobility experienced in the second half of the twentieth century has produced a marked increase in the range of works which can be classed as 'migrant literature' (King *et al.* 1995). A number of authors have produced autobiographical or semi-autobiographical works which centre on the experience of travel, in the form of forced exile, economic migration, or even privileged cosmopolitanism. Significantly, language and translation are crucial aspects of many such works (see also FICTIONAL REPRESENTATIONS), whether in the form of a prolonged examination of the relationship between linguistic and personal identity (Aboulela 1999; Hoffman 1989) or of the dramatization of the complex mechanisms of allegiance and belonging which affect dislocated subjects (Gurnah 1996, 2001; Iyer 2000; Kubati 2000).

This is an area which is attracting increasing critical attention, especially from specialists in LITERARY TRANSLATION (Malena 2003; Polezzi 2006). One point of particular interest concerns the intricate relationship between translation and SELF-TRANSLATION, as well as between explicit and implicit uses of translation, activated within this kind of writing. A further, related issue raised by such works concerns the way in which linguistic choices characterize the relationship between migrant writing and its multiple readerships. Adopting a host language and being adopted by a host public can constitute a double gesture of hospitality. That same strategy, however, can also sustain an effective erasure of difference (rooted in far less welcoming and more discriminatory motives) and ultimately entrap migrant writing within a condition of invisibility and marginalization (see MINORITY). Employing a number of languages within the same text (see MULTILINGUALISM) – sometimes in ways which make the presence of each idiom immediately evident, or, in other cases, hiding the presence of such polylingualism underneath an apparently homogeneous surface – also plays games of inclusion and exclusion which are

characteristic of GLOBALIZATION, its ambiguities and its unevenness at more than one level (Gentzler 2006). In an early article devoted to the complexities of Francophone North-African texts, for instance, Mehrez stressed how the works of 'Third World postcolonial plurilingual writers' have managed to forge 'a new language that defies the very notion of a "foreign" text that can be readily translatable into another language' (1992: 121). Tymoczko (1999a, 1999b, 2002a) has also underlined the subversive potential of translation processes in colonial and postcolonial contexts, analysing in detail the connections between translations and texts produced by multilingual authors, whose linguistic and cultural allegiances defy the traditional association between language and nation. Such texts are doubly connected to issues of mobility, through the identity of their authors on the one hand and, on the other, by virtue of their interpellation of multiple and often dislocated audiences. The writers are marked, both biographically and intellectually, by processes of displacement as well as translation: they are the product of historical phenomena which involve linguistic and cultural hybridization, resulting in what Salman Rushdie has described as 'translated men' (1992: 17). Most of them also produce works which address (often provocatively) readerships that are equally complex, mobile and hybrid. A number of postcolonial intellectuals – such as Ngũgĩ wa Thiong'o (1986), Gayatri Spivak (1993) and Sujit Mukherjee (1981/1994), all of whom are also significantly involved in translation or self-translation – have posed crucial questions about who is writing in what language as well as who is translating and for whom. The mobility of the postcolonial writer is thus compounded by the mobility of his or her public and the ensuing mutability of reading. Migrant writers, in particular, are often compelled to take up the role of group representatives while also striving to assert an individual identity, so that their work takes on the quality of personal as well as collective testimony (Parati 2005). That voice, with its strong connotations of foreignness and alterity, finds a way of 'talking back' to its multiple audiences, its multiple homes, through translation – whether this is already implicitly inscribed within a text marked by MULTILINGUALISM and heterogeneity, or whether it is an explicit process of transformation aimed at gaining further visibility and audibility.

Acknowledging the connection between postcolonial reality and enforced forms of mobility – including diaspora, exile or economic migration – is also a constitutive element of the recent tendency to extol the value of dislocation and of the subsequent 'translated' condition understood as an intellectual stance. In proposing the notion of 'translated men', Rushdie, for instance, remarked: 'it is normally supposed that something always gets lost in translation; I cling, obstinately, to the notion that something can also be gained' (1992: 17). Edward Said, on the other hand, offered as an *exemplum* of both personal ETHICS and scholarly practice the figure of the exiled Erich Auerbach writing his seminal texts on comparative literature in Istanbul in the 1930s and 1940s, stressing that it is not in nation, but rather 'in culture that we can seek out the range of meanings and ideas conveyed by the phrases *belonging to* or *in* a place, being *at home in a place*' (1983: 8; emphasis in original). While both Said's humanism and Auerbach's Eurocentric vision of literary history have been subject to criticism, later re-readings of notions of world literature and cosmopolitanism have underlined the connection between displacement, multilingualism and possible transnational models of cultural production.

Focusing on another European expatriate living in Istanbul, Leo Spitzer, Apter has proposed a notion of 'global *translatio*' which is based on the recognition of 'a worldly paradigm of *translatio studii* with strong links to the history, both past and present, of *translatio imperii*', but which also 'emphasizes the critical role of multilingualism within transnational humanism' (2004: 108, 104). Apter's positive reading of practices aimed at disturbing complacent monolingualism has found favour with a number of translation scholars. Cronin, in particular, has argued that 'the strategy of partial or non-translation is signalling not so much the failure of translation … as the necessary complexity of language and culture without which translation would not exist and which justifies its existence in the first place' (2006: 130). Cronin's positive reading of language (and cultural) difference in a world increasingly characterized by mobility and hybridization embraces not just global perspectives, but also local ones, managing to offer a viable critique of recent notions of world literature based on macro-analysis and systemic models, such as those offered by Moretti (1998, 2004) and Casanova (2004). While both these authors assign an important role to translation processes and multilingualism – embodied, in Casanova's study, by polyglot cosmopolitan writers travelling from the margins to the centre of the literary world (see LITERARY TRANSLATION) – Cronin points out that the vision they propose tends to overlook the importance of local and vernacular dimensions of literary circulation, as well as the inevitable interconnections between local and global communication systems. Ultimately, for Cronin, 'there is no "world literature" without translation' (2006: 132). Cronin's reading of contemporary literary as well as sociological theory is thus linked to his call for a micro-cosmopolitanism which would allow a new perspective on such oppositions as centre–periphery, urban–rural, modernity–tradition, and could sustain solidarities, as well as language and translation practices, which are 'both *local* and *global*' (ibid.: 19). Cronin's notion of 'a micro-cosmopolitan transnationalism' (ibid.: 24) draws on his own work on translation and globalization (2003) and on the relationship between translation and travel (2000) to stress the role of individual agency and its links with notions of citizenship and participatory action. This vision is meant to complement theorizations of a globalized world, such as Appadurai's portrait of a social reality in which 'moving images meet deterritorialized viewers' to create 'diasporic public spheres' (1996: 4).

Postcolonial writers and scholars have also underlined the importance of language policies and politics within the colonial context, as well as the impact of those strategies for postcolonial subjects and communities. In the early 1990s, the work of scholars such as Rafael (1988), Cheyfitz (1991) and Niranjana (1992), while grounded in specific historical contexts, opened up the field to historical reflection on the role played by translation and by what Niranjana calls its 'strategies of containment' (ibid.: 21) in processes of colonial domination. At the same time, within the field of travel writing, Mary Louise Pratt introduced the notion of 'contact zones' (a phrase she modelled, significantly, on the linguistic term 'contact languages'), in order to describe the cultural productivity of colonial encounters and their spatial as well as temporal dimensions (Pratt 1992: 6–7). Her work stresses the role played, within the contact zone, by transculturation phenomena set within the context of asymmetrical power relationships, thus providing a viable model for the analysis of specific colonial and postcolonial scenarios in which language and cultural politics are inextricably linked. Pratt has not fully developed the implications of such encounters in terms of language dynamics and translation practices and, in subsequent work, she has explicitly queried the usefulness of the notion of translation as an all-encompassing metaphor for the 'traffic in meaning', stressing that a translation-based model of cultural transactions runs the risk of underlining difference rather than 'entanglements' and proposing alternative ideas on which to construct models for the movement of cultural forms, such as 'resonance', 'intersection', and 'doubling' (2002: 32–4). At a more abstract theoretical level, Bhabha's notion of translation as 'the performative nature of cultural communication' (1994b: 228) has also proven extremely influential for conceptualizations of translation in postcolonial contexts marked by high levels of ethnic and cultural hybridity, as well as by pervasive mobility. Starting from the Benjaminian notion of the foreignness of languages, which he interprets as an apt description of 'the performativity of translation as the staging of cultural difference', Bhabha relates translation to the notions of newness, hybridity and liminality – elements which, in turn, he sees as constitutive, irresolvable and potentially disruptive components of migrant discourse, thus reinforcing the inherent link between spatial and linguistic mobility (ibid.: 224, 227). Scholars of migration have begun to use these notions in order to stress the transformative, dynamic nature of all journeys, as well as the role played by translation in the construction and negotiation of cultural difference (Papastergiadis 2000).

Mobility and translation practices

What is common to studies of colonial/postcolonial cultural exchange, world literature models, and the emerging field of migrant writing is the stress on the way in which (cultural) translation processes are neither innocent nor transparent, but are rather enmeshed within uneven relationships of power and (at least potential) exploitation. These fields also share, however, a certain ambiguity in their use of the notion of translation, which becomes a wide-ranging metaphor for almost all kinds of negotiation and transformative influence between cultures (see POSTCOLONIAL APPROACHES). This broadening of the idea of translation often results in the total or partial erasure of actual processes of linguistic mediation. Criticisms of this apparent blind spot have come mostly from within the field of translation studies and have stressed the need to underline the continuing centrality of language exchange, even within an increasingly 'global' perspective on intercultural communication (Cronin 2000; Sturge 2007). A relevant example of this type of influential yet ambiguous theorization can be found in the work of the cultural ethnographer James Clifford. His assertion that 'travel' is to be considered 'a translation term' which, like all such terms, 'used in global comparisons … get[s] us some distance *and* fall[s] apart' (1997: 39; emphasis in original) has been seminal for a number of works examining the social as well as textual implications of the overlap between geographical movement and linguistic displacement, yet it has also invited an extremely wide and at times rather diluted understanding of the notions of 'translation' and 'travel'.

A more prolonged and critical engagement with the notion of CULTURAL TRANSLATION and its connection to travel (both as a material and textual set of practices) is to be found in the work of Talal Asad (1986, 1995) and in his analysis of the way in which anthropology traditionally misused translation due to the flawed assumption of an equivalence between 'culture' and 'text'. For Asad, it is only through a profound misunderstanding of the notion of translation as a literal activity based on 'matching written sentences in two languages, such that the second set of sentences become the "real meaning" of the first', that Western anthropologists have been able to maintain a position of superiority with respect to the objects of their observations (1986: 155). According to Asad, on the other hand, 'translation is … at once a sequence of human acts and a narrative recounting it, both being and representation' (1995: 325). Asad's critique of the notion and practice of cultural translation underlines both the pervasive role of language phenomena in the negotiation of cultural difference and the relation between such processes and the relative positions of power occupied by those involved in them. As a result, 'cultural translation' emerges as a set of practices in which 'translation' in its narrower linguistic sense plays a crucial and pervasive role, ultimately stressing the need for the explicit acknowledgement of the role played by language difference in encounters between cultures (first and foremost those fostered by all forms of mobility), while also denouncing the fallacy implicit in any vision of individual cultures as self-contained, monolingual and coherent systems (Papastergiadis 2000; Sturge 2007).

These observations remind us of the need to focus on translation and travel as sets of located practices, rather than (or at least as well as) on their theoretical interpretations and interpellations. If the textual products of mobility and translation are constituted by forms of representation, it is also the case that they have substantial material consequences and ask us to adopt consciously ethical positions (see ETHICS). Asad's admonitions on the limits of cultural translation, like Pratt's caveats concerning the limits of translation as a metaphor for intercultural negotiations, are well placed: there may indeed be a risk of dilution in recent wide-ranging theorizations of the nexus between translation and mobility; yet such risks can be countered by the antidote of ethically grounded translation as well as travel practices. The increased role of mobility in contemporary society raises a number of queries relating to established associations between national, linguistic and ethnic identities (Cohen 1997; Simon 2002). While the enhanced presence of multilingual realities within and across communities does not solve inequalities and asymmetries of power, it does foster new or renewed forms of multi- and interlingual communication and solidarity, as attested by recent attempts to ground contemporary models of cosmopolitan identity – seen as an alternative to the fragmented nature of intercultural society – on notions of multiple linguistic and cultural affiliation (Mudimbe 1997; Breckenridge et al. 2002; Vertovec and

Cohen 2002). Such phenomena are accompanied by a growing pervasiveness of translation practices. These can take explicit forms, such as the increased role of COMMUNITY INTERPRETING in attempting to ensure access on the part of refugees, economic migrants and other minority groups to human rights, citizenship and, more specifically, freedom of movement and expression (Baker 2006a; Cronin 2006). They can also, however, take the form of a textual (and especially but not exclusively literary) production which is constructed on multilingual and intercultural experience, relies on multiple layers of individual and collective memory, and addresses a range of constituencies and readerships. The results of such practices have the additional effect of querying the binary model on which translation studies has traditionally been based, exploding the linear oppositions between source and target text (culture, language) and calling for a theorization of translation practices which is in itself more sensitive to the complexity of geographic as well as cultural mobility.

See also:
ASYLUM; CULTURAL TRANSLATION; ETHICS; GLOBALIZATION; IDEOLOGY; MULTILINGUALISM; POSTCOLONIAL APPROACHES; SELF-TRANSLATION.

Further reading
Asad 1986; Mehrez 1992; Bassnett 1993 (pp. 92–114); Asad 1995; Clifford 1997 (pp. 17–46); Tymoczko 1999a, 2000; Cronin 2000; Papastergiadis 2000; Polezzi 2001; Agorni 2002; Apter 2004; Cronin 2006; Di Biase 2006; Gentzler 2006; Polezzi 2006.

LOREDANA POLEZZI

Models

Although model theory is a field of study in itself, a comprehensive definition of the concept of 'model' remains problematical. This is partly because models can be of very different kinds, ranging from iconic or diagrammatic representations (known as 'analogue models') to conceptual and theoretical models, and partly because there is little agreement among theorists about the classification of models into types. Nevertheless, some common properties of models can be distinguished.

First, a model is always a model of something, called the object, or the original, or the **prototype**. In this sense a model, when perceived in terms of its modelling function, is a vicarious object, i.e. a substitute. It represents, reproduces, refers to something else, which is necessarily anterior to it. Model and prototype therefore have a different ontological status which arises from the fact that one represents while the other is represented. Neither model nor prototype need to be physical realities: they can be abstract, mental or hypothetical entities.

Secondly, a modelling relation is not an objectively given fact or a state of affairs existing naturally between two entities. A model requires a human subject to recognize it as a model of something. That is, a model can only be a model of something if there is someone who perceives it as such and who apprehends an appropriate relation between model and prototype. The modelling operation therefore involves three components: a prototype, a model and a human subject.

Thirdly, the model represents its prototype through approximation. It is not a reproduction of the prototype in its entirety and in all its aspects. The model reduces the complexity of the prototype by retaining only certain features of it, and in so doing establishes a certain similarity or correspondence, between itself and the object to which it refers. The similarity or correspondence established on this basis is of a certain kind (it may, for example, be isomorphic), deemed by the human subject to be functionally relevant. The model exhibits the relevant similarity or correspondence in a certain manner and to a certain degree.

Finally, while from the point of view of the modelling relation only the representational aspects of a model are normally regarded as pertinent, every model of necessity also contains other, non-functional or 'contingent' features.

It is possible to consider the relevance of models in the context of translation from four different angles: (i) the use of theoretical models as heuristic tools in translation studies; (ii) the use of diagrammatic or analogue models to represent certain aspects of translation; (iii) the view of translating as a modelling activity; and (iv) the relation between models and NORMS.

Theoretical models

Theoretical, or conceptual, models are hypothetical constructs which operate at a higher level of abstraction than the concrete detail of individual phenomena and may be used as an explanatory framework to account for the world of phenomena. One can also tentatively project a theoretical model derived from an established field of knowledge onto a new, wholly or partly unknown domain. Because the model is first mapped on one field and then applied to another, it employs language appropriate to the first field to speak about the second. This enables a conceptual model to function heuristically: the researcher may derive cognitive gain from deploying the model as a probing instrument, a prism or searchlight which allows new things to come into view or to perceive familiar things in a new light. At the same time, theoretical models inevitably construct the object in their own image: they apply their own terms, categories and distinctions to the new domain, illuminating certain aspects while obscuring others.

In translation studies, various theoretical models derived from other domains and disciplines have been applied. They range from linguistic and semiotic to literary and sociocultural models. Several of these in turn make use of terms and concepts imported from other disciplines such as philosophy, history or sociology. In each case, particular currents of thought within the fields concerned have served as more refined research tools. For example, the linguistic model has tended to see translation primarily as a linguistic operation (see LINGUISTIC APPROACHES). Within this conceptual frame, structuralist models of translation have focused on relations between linguistic systems, pragmatic models concentrate on the human interaction in given communicative situations, psycholinguistic models look at linguistic aspects of the mental operations involved in the translation process, and cognitive models are interested in how the mind maps and processes information (see PRAGMATICS; PSYCHOLINGUISTIC AND COGNITIVE APPROACHES).

Relevance theory, for instance, combines pragmatics with cognitive science and views translation in this light (Sperber and Wilson 1986/1995; Gutt 1991/2000). Semiotic models see the field of enquiry as extending to forms of transfer between signifying systems other than natural languages (see SEMIOTICS). Sociocultural models and social action theories emphasize contextual features of translation and the interactive social web tying the various participants in translation-driven communication together (see FUNCTIONALIST APPROACHES). Literary models have approached translation in terms of the categories of literary criticism, literary history and literary theory (see LITERARY TRANSLATION; POETRY). In recent years gender studies, postcolonial studies, the theory of social narratives and the sociology of Pierre Bourdieu have served as new conceptual models (see GENDER AND SEXUALITY; POSTCOLONIAL APPROACHES; SOCIOLOGICAL APPROACHES). All have led to redescriptions of the phenomenon of translation.

The models are complementary and they often overlap and conflict. In mapping the domain of translation in their own terms they also delimit it in different ways, or highlight precisely the problematical nature of such delimitation. Each model will prioritize certain kinds or aspects or areas of translation; put differently: each model constructs translation in its own terms.

Analogue models

Analogue models are used to represent those characteristics of a prototype considered to be relevant in a given context. They serve an intellectual and pedagogic purpose in visually foregrounding pertinent features while ignoring others. In the study of translation, flow charts and other diagrammatic representations are commonly used to represent certain processes and relations.

As a rule, communication that involves translation is represented as an extension of the by now traditional scheme 'sender→message →receiver'. The extension features a translator who first acts as a receiver of a message in one language and then as the sender of a new (translated) message, in another language, to a new receiver; hence: 'sender1→message1→receiver1

= translator = sender2→message2→receiver2'. The model and its symbolic representation derive from the information theory of Claude Shannon and Warren Weaver (1949), and in turn gave rise to the so-called conduit metaphor which casts language as the vehicle of thought and of translation as a process of decoding and recoding messages. The model separates the signifier from the signified and envisages translation as keeping the signified intact while exchanging one signifier for another across languages. The conduit metaphor has been challenged by Michael Reddy (1979), among others. Relevance theory also abandoned it and replaced it with a stimulus and inference model. In translation studies, skopos theory also adopted this latter model (see FUNCTIONALIST APPROACHES).

The translation process itself is a mental operation that remains inaccessible to direct observation. It has nevertheless been hypothetically reconstructed, especially by psycholinguists and by researchers operating with THINK-ALOUD PROTOCOLS. In these studies, too, the process of translation is represented diagrammatically. While the input (the source utterance and its reception) and the output (the generation of the target utterance) tend to remain stable in these representations, the considerable differences between the diagrams reflect different assumptions about the way in which the human mind processes the incoming information, brings about a conversion of one kind or another and constructs a new utterance in another language or medium.

Diagrams are also frequently used by philologists to map a variety of textual filiations, textual and contextual relations between source and target utterances and the communicative relations within and between the two systems involved. While flow charts purporting to represent the translation process serve a cognitive purpose, diagrams of textual, contextual and communicative relations are mostly pedagogical in nature.

Translating as modelling

Translating can be seen as a modelling activity in that the result of the operation, the translated text, commonly claims, explicitly or implicitly, to represent an anterior discourse in a way comparable to the representational function of models. This makes a translation into a vicarious object, a substitute or a metatext. Also, like a model, a translation is a derived, second-order product, which means that the relation between a translation and its prototype is neither symmetrical nor reversible. Moreover, a translation can stand as a representative or substitute of a source text only if a (collective) subject will recognize it as such. A translation that goes unrecognized as a translation is, functionally speaking, not a translation at all, because its modelling aspect remains ineffective. Conversely, a translation which purports to represent an original and is accepted as such is, functionally speaking, a translation, even if no prototype can be identified; this is the case with so-called PSEUDOTRANSLATIONS.

In contrast to models, translations may replace and even displace their prototypes. They can do so mainly because translation typically involves one or more semiotic transformations, as a result of which the original is left at the other side of at least one of these semiotic barriers (such as a natural language) and may thus become inaccessible to those on this side of the barrier. The modelling relation itself, however, is not affected by this. Another objection might be that translations, as opposed to models, constitute objects of the same order as their prototypes. However, many cultures maintain the ontological distinction by assigning different places in value and classification systems to translated as opposed to non-translated texts (see POLYSYSTEM). The two kinds of text are likely to be ranged in the same class only in cultural situations where all texts are perceived essentially as transformations of other texts. In those cases, the notions of translation and of related forms of textual processing and modelling tend to encompass virtually all text production.

While under their representational and representative aspects translations can be seen as approximations of their prototypes, all translations also exhibit contingent features, a material surplus not reducible to the modelling function.

Models and norm theory

Translating involves a process of continuous decision-making which takes place in a communicative context. Descriptive translation studies in particular have invoked norm theory in an effort to explain why translators make certain decisions in preference to other equally available options (see DESCRIPTIVE VS. COMMITTED APPROACHES). NORMS may be regarded as social regulation mechanisms which make certain choices and decisions by the translator more likely than others. They can be understood as particular kinds of expectations which are shared among most members of a community and tell them how to behave in certain situations. Whereas conventions are expectations about how individuals will probably behave, norms are expectations about how people *should* behave.

Norms consist of a directive aspect which urges members of a community – here, translators – to operate in certain ways, and a 'content' comprising an intersubjective 'notion of correctness'. The latter is a notion of what is proper or correct in particular situations. Because correctness notions are abstract values, more concrete models of correct behaviour are derived either directly from the values and attitudes which make up the correctness notions or from concrete instances and occurrences which have come to be regarded as exemplifying such notions. These models can, in turn, serve as prototypes to be imitated, as examples of good practice.

Compliance with a set of translation norms regarded as pertinent in a given context means that the product, the translation, is likely to exhibit the requisite relation with the original and conform to the relevant textual or discursive model or models (see QUALITY). In other words, establishing conformity with relevant models occurs both at the level of the translation as representation and at the level of its contingent features. The former concerns the translation as a model of its original, the latter bears on those textual elements which are not directly relevant to the translation's modelling function but affect its quality as a text in relation to other texts of the same genre.

Cultures and their subdivisions are complex

entities containing a diversity of competing, conflicting and overlapping norms, conventions and models embedded in different spheres of activity, which themselves form part of changing historical configurations (see HISTORY). It is one of the tasks of the historical study of translation to identify translation norms and models and explain their nature and functioning.

See also:
PSYCHOLINGUISTIC AND COGNITIVE AP-PROACHES; DESCRIPTIVE VS. COMMITTED APPROACHES; FUNCTIONALIST APPROACHES; LINGUISTIC APPROACHES; NORMS; POSTCOLO-NIAL APPROACHES; SEMIOTICS; SOCIOLOGICAL APPROACHES.

Further reading
Shannon and Weaver 1949; Stachowiak 1965; Reddy 1979; Sperber and Wilson 1986/1995; Bartsch 1987; Pazukhin 1987; Hermans 1991; D'Andrade and Strauss 1992; Hermans 1993.

THEO HERMANS

Multilingualism

Though both are widespread intercultural phenomena, multilingualism and translation are rarely considered in connection with each other. Whereas multilingualism evokes the co-presence of two or more languages (in a society, text or individual), translation involves a substitution of one language for another. The translating code does not so much supplement as replace the translated code: except in a classroom setting perhaps, translations are not meant to be read side by side with originals. Schleiermacher's ideal reader, 'who is familiar with the foreign language' yet to whom 'that language always remains foreign' (quoted in Lefevere 1992b: 152), remains the exception, not the rule. Far from having its origin in 'a certain ability for intercourse with foreign languages … among the educated part of the population' (ibid.), translation is today more commonly assumed to cater for monolingual readers by disclosing unknown literatures to them, thus effectively restricting bilingual competence to the translators themselves.

Denison (1976) framed the relationship between translation and multilingualism in an unusual yet stimulating fashion. Whilst popular belief considers translation 'a more natural and necessary human undertaking than the active, functional plurilingualism of whole communities in daily life', he argues, 'it turns out that where groups of people find themselves obliged to participate in heterolinguistic communication networks, functional plurilingualism is the solution [most] often adopted' (1978: 313). Translation tends to occur in two types of cases, the first of which being those instances 'where individuals and groups from mutually remote parts of a continuum lacking a *lingua franca* need to interact' (ibid.). The fact that those living in the Western world, where communication typically needs to bridge long distances, consider this to be the default situation does not imply that it actually is: Denison gives many examples (from the Amazon area, as well as from Africa and New Guinea) where adult multilingual competence is the rule, not the exception. Likewise, he goes on to say, 'translation is seldom necessary for purely informative needs' but tends to be employed for 'considerations other than the straightforward communication of information' (ibid.). Many of those considerations could be called tactical, in that translation is often invoked 'for reasons of ritual, dignity, civil rights or [even] time-gaining' (ibid.: 314) by participants who *do* have a passive understanding of what was said in the other language but prefer to have it repeated in their own. Communication of information alone, then, cannot account for the use of Gaelic place names in Wales or for the presence of English road signs (including important ones like *slow* and *danger*) in Pakistan (ibid.: 314–15). In those and many more instances, translation is not carried out in order to 're-encode basic semantic information for the benefit of a monolingual' but rather 'to convey a different set of social presuppositions' (ibid.: 316).

The poetics and politics of multilingual writing

This might be all the more true in literature, where conveying semantic information can hardly be said to be the main issue. More often than not, something else is at stake when the decision is made to (re)translate a text of literary and cultural significance. Thus, when Mexican-American Ilan Stavans (2003: 253–8) was provoked into producing a 'Spanglish' version of the opening lines of Cervantes' *Quixote*, this gesture caused quite a stir, not least in America's Latino communities. Whereas some language purists simply did not think the mixed speech of illiterate immigrants was 'worthy' of such an endeavour, other critics pointed out that those educated enough to be able to write in Spanglish should just stick with the original Castilian text (Kunz 2005). But these reactions miss the point Stavans was trying to make. He did not intend his translation to act as a replacement for the original, but rather as proof of the stylistic and indeed literary possibilities Spanglish could offer to whoever is willing to explore them (on bilingualism in Chicano literature in general, see Keller 1984; Bassnett 1985; Flores 1987; Reyes 1991; Arteaga 1994; Rudin 1996).

In literary poetics, 'multilingualism' stands for the use of two or more languages within the same text (Bem and Hudlett 2001; Canonica and Rudin 1993; Sarkonak and Hodgson 1993; Grutman 1997). In principle, texts can either give equal prominence to those languages or merely add a liberal sprinkling of foreign tongues to a dominant language clearly identified as their central axis. The latter solution is much more commonly encountered, with the actual quantity of foregrounded linguistic material varying widely. For a Romantic poet like Gérard de Nerval, a short Spanish title (*El desdichado*) was enough to conjure up exotic landscapes and valiant knights. The writer of fiction, on the other hand, may want to either incorporate larger foreign language samples – taking up entire paragraphs or even pages, as in Tolstoy's *War and Peace* and Sterne's *Tristram Shandy* – or make repeated use of them in order to obtain the desired effect.

The study of textual multilingualism does not always involve a close examination of a writer's actual language skills, since writers have been known to consult either their entourage or a nearby library (or both). Philologists like J. R. R. Tolkien, who devised an ingenious linguistic system for *The Lord of the Rings*, tend to be rare. Even if a biographical link can be shown to exist, it is questionable whether it enhances our understanding of this writing practice.

Does Charlotte Brontë's stay in Brussels, for instance, explain the role of Adèle's French in *Jane Eyre*? Secondly, polyglot writing does not always require a polyglot public, though its deciphering more often than not requires some imagination (compare Forster 1970: 12–13 to Baetens Beardsmore 1978: 93 and Sternberg 1981: 226). While such knowledge no doubt adds to our reading pleasure, we need not master Russian to enjoy Anthony Burgess's *Clockwork Orange* or Latin for Umberto Eco's *Name of the Rose*. Thirdly, from the vantage point of textual analysis, it matters relatively little whether dialects, slang, classical, national or indeed artificial languages make up the multilingual sequences. The impact of these varieties will depend as much on the ways in which they are textually embedded as on the values attached to them in society (Grutman 1993, 2002).

Multilingualism translated

The romantic discovery and subsequent fetishizing of 'national mother tongues' has undoubtedly affected the ways in which 'foreign' languages are viewed, learned, and hence used in literature (Forster 1970). The degree of multilingualism in a text might even be said to be commensurate with the status of the corresponding literary system: literatures that are either young, postcolonial (Ashcroft *et al.* 1989) or belong to linguistic minorities (Lagarde 2001) tend to show more openness to linguistic diversity than the firmly established canons of the former imperial powers (see POSTCOLONIAL APPROACHES; MINORITY). In literatures belonging to the latter category, such as England's or France's, exotic languages presumably spoken by foreign characters are either sampled to provide comic relief or, worse, dismissed 'as an irrelevant, if not distracting, representational factor' (Sternberg 1981: 224). It is not by chance that Shakespeare's Caliban, Crusoe's Friday, and Voltaire's Ingénu all speak their master's language.

Writers can of course also decide to incorporate translations into their text, thereby creating a buffer for those unable (or unwilling) to read foreign languages. In Walter Scott's day, for instance, Latin was still a must for the educated classes. He therefore could let one of his characters, when requested to give his opinion on the outcome of the Jacobite uprising, quote a Roman historian in Latin: 'Why, you know, Tacitus saith *"In rebus bellicis maxime dominatur Fortuna"*, which is equiponderate with our own vernacular adage, "Luck can maist in the mellee"' (Scott 1985:335). Scott's decision to append an approximate version as an intratextual gloss (a more literal translation would be: 'In matters of war Fortune mostly rules') shows he did not want to alienate his less-educated readers – he was, after all, one of the first to write what we now call best-sellers. At the same time, he established a particular rapport with those 'happy few' who actually did share his knowledge and love of the Classics.

It has been argued that such 'cushioning' of foreign words and expressions reduces them to mere exotic signs without questioning the power relations between representing and represented codes: 'the forceful proximity of both items represents the failure to achieve cultural symbiosis' (Zabus 1990: 354). For bilingual readers, such tagged-on translations might indeed seem unnecessary. Yet for monolingual readers they create a suspense by only progressively revealing the secret of the foreign language. Instead of excluding monolingual readers from a bilingual text, they guide them 'through it with utter carefulness' (Rudin 1996: 225–7, in response to Dasenbrock 1987: 16).

When language is itself a topic, translations accompanying heterolinguistic utterances may focus less on referential meaning and highlight more subdued cultural connotations. In Lawrence's *Women in Love*, for example, Ursula Brangwen calls the dominant behaviour of a tomcat 'a lust for bullying – a real *Wille zur Macht* – so base, so petty', to which Rupert Birkin replies:

> I agree that the *Wille zur Macht* is a base and petty thing. But with the Mino, it is the desire to bring this female cat into a pure stable equilibrium, a transcendent and abiding *rapport* with the single male. Whereas without him, as you see, she is a mere stray, a fluffy sporadic bit of chaos. It is a *volonté de pouvoir*, if you like, a will to ability, taking *pouvoir* as a verb.
>
> (Lawrence 1960:167)

By joining translations that have such a different ring in English ('a lust for bullying' and 'a will to ability'), yet are supposed to mean the same in German and in French (*la volonté de pouvoir* is the common French translation of Nietzsche's *Wille zur Macht*), Birkin's comments become metalinguistic in nature, albeit in a stereotypical way. The harsh German sounds suggest violence, while French confirms its penchant for rhetorical niceties, as Ursula stresses in her answer: 'Sophistries!'.

What happens to multilingualism in translation (Delabastita 2002; Delabastita and Grutman 2005b; Frank and Bödeker 1991; Kunz 1998; Lefevere 1995; Meylaerts 2006; Mezei 1988, 1998)? According to Henry Schogt, who compared Western translations of the Russian classics, 'as a rule only the main language of the text is replaced, the foreign elements remaining unchanged' (1988: 114). Antoine Berman (1985: 79–80; 2004: 284–5), on the other hand, believes most translators will rather reduce the interlingual tension found in the original. Additional complications arise when the target language happens to be the embedded foreign language of the source text. In his version of Thomas Mann's *The Magic Mountain*, French translator Maurice Betz successfully maintained the distinction between the narrator's voice and those of Hans Castorp and Madame Chauchat, in spite of the fact that the latter two already spoke French in the original German text. Such feats are rare. Usually, multilingual texts undergo the fate of Lawrence's novel, as becomes clear from a cursory look at the French rendering of the passage quoted above:

> Je suis d'accord que la volonté de puissance est quelque chose de vil et de mesquin. Mais avec Minou, c'est le désir d'amener cette femelle à un équilibre stable et parfait, à un rapport transcendant et durable avec le mâle célibataire. Tandis que sans lui, comme vous voyez, elle est un simple fragment égaré, une parcelle ébouriffée et sporadique du chaos. C'est une volonté de pouvoir, si vous voulez, en prenant «*pouvoir*» pour un verbe.
>
> (Lawrence 1974: 210)

All traces of foreignness have been conveniently erased. Gone is Nietzsche's German, and with it, the pseudo-philosophical gist of the conversation. Gone, as well, is the stylistic contrast between English and French as the preferred idiom for making love. This is almost completely neutralized, except for a footnote mentioning that the second *'pouvoir'* (set apart in the text by quotation marks and italics) already figured in French in the original. But so did *rapport* and the earlier *volonté de pouvoir*, which go undocumented. Because of such 'technical' problems – but also because linguistic diversity flies in the face of many perceived notions of language, culture and identity – foreign languages are usually at considerable risk of disappearing or having their subversive potential downplayed in translation (Grutman 2006: 20–24).

See also:
GLOBALIZATION; MINORITY; MOBILITY; POSTCO-LONIAL APPROACHES.

Further reading
Traugott 1981; Vidal 1991; Canonica and Rudin 1993; Sarkonak and Hodgson 1993; Grutman 1997; Hoenselaars and Buning 1999; Serrano 2000; Bem and Hudlett 2001; Levy 2003; Marín Ruano 2003; Delabastita and Grutman 2005a; Meylaerts 2006.

RAINIER GRUTMAN

News gathering and dissemination

Translation in news gathering and dissemination (or 'news translation' for short) can be considered with respect to two different sets of concerns. The first of these is the question of the relationship between two texts; the second is the nature of the process within which the translation is undertaken. The first is not – if taken in isolation from the second – very different from translation considered in other contexts: the relationship is influenced by a range of factors, which include the translator's understanding of the context and purpose of the original. The second takes as its focus the nature of organizations involved in news gathering and dissemination and is concerned primarily with who undertakes translation, in what context, for what purposes. The first is concerned primarily with news output, or news considered as a series of statements about the world; the second is concerned with the process within which that output is produced. The two may also be considered in combination, typically in order to investigate the extent to which the process has an impact upon the relationship between the two (or more) texts.

News translation occurs primarily (but not exclusively) at the point where news crosses national boundaries; this is because of the traditional association linking news media with the nation state and national language (Anderson 1982) and has implications for the nature of news translation, as discussed later in this entry. However, this traditional association is no longer universal because of the rise of MINORITY (or lesser-known) language media in previously monoglot states, and transnational media operating in widely used transnational languages. Moreover, many nation states are inhabited by linguistically diverse populations, with associated media, and indeed may not have a single national language (for example, India, Switzerland and many African nations).

While there are many studies of the language of news (for example, van Dijk 1991; Bell 1991; Fowler 1991; Fairclough 1995), such studies largely ignore the role of translation; their predominant focus is the discursive structure of news and a frequent concern is the extent to which particular articulations of words and expressions – especially recurrent ones – may impact upon public opinion (see Ackerman 2006 for a particularly detailed example). This focus is also to be found in some studies of news translation (see various examples in Baker 2006a). Other recent studies in translation focus on the information needs of a global economy, which include information transfers in the form of news (Bielsa 2005; Cronin 2005). Central to such concerns is a debate about the relationship between 'globalization' and 'localization' (see GLOBALIZATION), in which the functional needs of transnational linguistic transfer are poised in an unstable equilibrium between the demands of transfer (for example, speed and comprehensibility across cultural boundaries) and the demands of local reception, where comprehensibility may be subject to the dynamics of spatially limited cultural forces. Here, the relationship between source and target texts is understood as a product of the process in which the linguistic transfer is undertaken.

If news translation is studied as a phenomenon in its own right, it is because it can be considered an articulation of discourse which produces its own range of effects: here, the act of translation is assumed to potentially produce transfers of meaning independently of other activities which produce such transfers. Thus, such analyses commonly take as their primary evidence divergences in meaning between original texts and derived texts in the target language and treat them as clear evidence of transfers of meaning that have occurred exclusively in the act of translation (Schäffner 2005; Baker 2006a: 137–79; Valdeón 2005; Kang 2007).

News translation occurs at various points in the overall process of news gathering and dissemination. Any given item of reported information may be translated at any of these points, or indeed more than one of them, which may lead to divergent translations of the same original text circulating simultaneously (see Steele 2006 and Norouzi 2007 for discussions of a problematic example). Additionally, the overall process of news gathering and dissemination is divided between organizations with different roles in the process. These fall into three main categories: (a) media accessed directly by the public, such as broadcast channels, newspapers and magazines; (b) news agencies, which are typically not accessed directly by the public but only by client organizations such as publicly accessible news media; and (c) monitoring organizations, such as government departments, NGOs and activist/advocacy groups, which circulate reports to clients, colleagues or supporters and potential supporters. Public access media and news agencies are sometimes distinguished as 'retail' and 'wholesale' news (Boyd-Barrett 1980). Some broadcasting organizations act as both, for example the BBC, CNN and Al Jazeera. News agencies, especially outside the Western parliamentary democracies, are frequently owned or controlled directly by government (Boyd-Barrett and Rantanen 1998).

The location and nature of translation in the news process depend on two factors: the internal structure of the news organization and its clientele. The three categories of news organizations have different editorial practices, which lead to different translation strategies (see below). The points at which translation may occur are as follows: during the reporting (initial news gathering) stage; during the editing stage, where reports are transformed into output text – which may derive from more than one original report; and during the dissemination process, where reports are transferred between different news organizations.

At the reporting stage, translation commonly occurs where a reporter is unable to communicate directly with relevant sources of information; this is frequent in international reporting, where journalists employed by media from one nation work temporarily in another nation. It is increasingly the case that international correspondents spend only short periods of time in particular posts abroad (Kalb 1990: xiv), and foreign reporting is increasingly done from transnational 'hubs', where a team of reporters covers the affairs of a group of nations (Hess 1996: 99–100). There has been vigorous recent debate, especially in the USA, over the extent to which these arrangements may have negative effects upon such reporting (Hamilton and Jenner 2004; Arnett 1998). The debate focuses primarily on the role of reporters employed by 'retail' media rather than news agencies, whose reporters are commonly nationals of the host nation. Translation 'in the field' is usually done by personnel who are not specialized in translation and interpretation (usually called 'fixers'), for whom translation is only part of the job description, and may not even be its most important part (Palmer and Fontan 2007; Tumber and Webster 2006: 106–15). Translation here consists of advising journalists about the content of local media and interpreting interviews with relevant sources of information; such translation commonly consists of summary rather than *in extenso* translation (Palmer and Fontan 2007). Translation in this context may consist of multiple stages, for example from a local language into a more commonly spoken national language and on into the target language or a transnational language. Thus, a journalist who has worked in Darfur (Ostian 2004) explains that a local language is typically translated into Arabic by a local translator, and the Arabic is then translated into the ultimate target language by a second interpreter. No survey currently exists of the extent to which such multi-stage or RELAY translations are practised in news gathering. The use of a vehicular transnational language such as English by all participants is of course also common.

Where reporting is done directly by a journalist working for 'retail' media, it is common for contextualizing material to be incorporated at the moment of original composition. Agency reports, however, are usually restricted to the event being reported, intended as they are for incorporation into the reports put out by a wide variety of client organizations. Reports produced by commercial, transnational agencies carefully use terminology which is as 'neutral' as possible, as client organizations may have very different cultural or political affiliations. The editorial policies of government-owned agencies, or activist organizations, as well as the language used in their reports, commonly reflect the policy of the controlling organization. These factors impact upon translation strategies; they also influence textual choices in material accompanying video footage put out by agencies (usually called 'dope sheets'), which is commonly provided in a vehicular transnational language.

At the editing stage, journalists commonly assemble documents from disparate sources – typically, agency reports and reports from one or more of their own reporters. Where such amalgamation also involves translation – for example, from a foreign national agency or media – it is normal for this to be undertaken by a journalist working on the story who has relevant bilingual competence, since translation is viewed as only one component of the process of transfer from one news organization to another (Orengo 2005: 169–70; Schäffner 2005: 158; Tsai 2005). Among other implications, this means that an act of news translation undertaken at the editing stage is frequently – if not usually – based upon more than one 'original' text, with these texts commonly summarized and amalgamated in the same process as translation.

At the dissemination end, translation may be undertaken either at the output or reception stages. Many news agencies produce output material both in the national language of the nation to which the agency belongs and also in a transnational language, most commonly English. Middle Eastern news agencies benefit from the fact that the commonest national regional language, Arabic, is also a transnational language – as, of course, do English language agencies, and to a more limited extent Spanish news agencies. Major agencies which translate their own material (or some selection of it) include the European Broadcasting Union (which circulates in English and French), Xinhua (China) and Agence France Presse, both of which circulate material in English as well as the original agency language. There are also agencies which specialize in bringing news from particular areas of the world and making it available in a target language; Outherenews, for example, specializes in making news from the Arabic-speaking world available in English (Outherenews 2006). Alternatively, bilingual journalists in 'retail media' may take incoming texts and adapt them, by both editing and translation, for the audience in question.

Translation may also be undertaken by media monitoring organizations, which access a wide range of media in a variety of languages and disseminate versions of the reports they retrieve to clients and other interested parties. Probably the largest of these are the two main English language media monitoring organizations: the BBC and the American Open Source Center (OSC). The BBC maintains a monitoring section which monitors media from outside the UK and is administratively and financially separate from the rest of the organization; it serves a wide variety of clients, including UK government departments. The OSC similarly monitors media external to the USA. Many organizations undertake translinguistic media monitoring, the results of which are circulated as a working tool: for example the US military in Iraq has a monitoring service for Arabic language media (and rumours) called the 'Baghdad Mosquito' (Shanker 2004).

Because of the association between news translation and national boundaries, translation tends to occur in the category of foreign news, which is commonly subject to editorial processes different to those of domestic news. It has often been pointed out that large sections of the planet are condemned to silence in the media of the industrial West, a situation that is exacerbated by the fact that the media of 'Third World' nations depend upon the big Western-owned transnational news agencies for news about these nations' own neighbours. In addition, foreign news is widely regarded in the USA as uninteresting to most of the media audience (Arnett 1998). In general, news from abroad is more frequently subject to summary, abbreviation and editorial selection than domestic news, a process sometimes brutally summarized as 'McLurg's Law', according to which publication of news depends upon this equation: the scope, importance or drama of events must increase in proportion to the distance separating the event from the reporting medium (Palmer 2000: 28; Schlesinger 1987: 117). This has a particular impact upon news translation: it means that translation in this context primarily takes the form of summary rather than *in extenso* translation. Indeed, translation strategies in news gathering and dissemination must generally be acknowledged as a mixture of selection, summary, contextualizing commentary and *in extenso* translation (see STRATEGIES).

As a result of the processes described above, translated material may exist in several, sometimes divergent, versions. For example, when President Ahmedinejad of Iran was quoted in English language media as saying that 'Israel should be wiped off the map', this quotation was taken from versions of a speech published in Farsi by the official Iranian Government news agency on 26 October 2005. During the following hours, three translations of this speech were widely circulated among international and transnational media; one was done by the Farsi section of the BBC Monitoring department, one by correspondents of the *New York Times* working in Teheran, and one by the pro-Israeli, US-based monitoring organization MEMRI (Middle East Media Research Institute). The translations differed in significant ways (Steele 2006) and have since been heavily contested (Norouzi 2007). There was also an English language translation put out by the Iranian news agency itself, in two divergent versions (IRNA 2005a, 2005b), and subsequent summaries and partial translations appeared in reports by other English language news agencies.

Although this last example is only a single case, it illustrates the principles outlined here. First, it indicates the centrality of the institutionally embedded process involved, where translation is undertaken by both journalists and employees of media monitoring organizations. Secondly, as a result of the insertion of translation into other editorial processes, particular translations become accepted as the equivalent of the original text as they move along the chain of information transfer. Thirdly, it illustrates the relationship between *in extenso* translation and summary, since the phrase in question was only a small part of an extensive text which was already summarized in the trans-

lations referred to here. Fourthly, it indicates the multifarious nature of the transfer process, where a small number of original translations give rise to a large number of quoted reports, due to the insertion of translation into other editorial processes. And finally, it shows – by being the exception that tests the rule – how rarely translation in news is questioned. This translation was questioned, and as a result it was seen to be problematic. It is impossible to know to what extent news translation is the source of problematic language transfers, as such questioning is rare – but see Radin (2004) for another problematic example.

See also:
GLOBALIZATION; INSTITUTIONAL TRANSLATION; STRATEGIES.

Further reading
Hess 1996; Boyd-Barrett and Rantanen 1998; Hamilton and Jenner 2004; Bielsa 2005; Orengo 2005; Schäffner 2005; Tsai 2005; Valdeón 2005; Ackerman 2006; Kang 2007; Palmer and Fontan 2007.

JERRY PALMER

Norms

The notion of 'norms' was first introduced by the Israeli scholar Gideon Toury in the late 1970s to refer to regularities of translation behaviour within a specific sociocultural situation (Toury 1978, reprinted in Toury 1980a). The concept proved influential during the 1980s and 1990s and has supported an extensive programme of research in translation studies, though mainly in the domain of written translation (see CONFERENCE INTERPRETING, SOCIOCULTURAL APPROACHES).

Historical and theoretical background

The impetus for Toury's work, including his notion of norms, came from the POLYSYSTEM approach developed in the early 1970s by his colleague Itamar Even-Zohar. Prior to the development of the polysystem approach, studying translation often consisted of an evaluative comparison of source and target texts, in isolation from both the source and target contexts of literary production. Even-Zohar's work effected a shift away from this treatment of translated texts as isolated elements and towards a historical and social understanding of the way they function collectively, as a sub-system within the target literary system. One of the main achievements of polysystem theory then has been to shift attention away from the relationship between individual source and target texts and towards the relationships which exist among the target texts themselves (Baker 1993).

Apart from directing attention towards translated texts as a body of literature worth investigating in its own right, there are other aspects of the polysystem approach and of Even-Zohar's work in general which prepared the ground for Toury's concept of norms and the research methodology which he went on to elaborate under the umbrella of 'Descriptive Translation Studies', or DTS for short (see DESCRIPTIVE VS. COMMITTED APPROACHES). These include: an explicit refusal to make a priori statements about what translation is, what it should be, or what kinds of relationship a translated text should have with its original; an insistence on examining all translation-related issues historically, in terms of the conditions which operate in the receiving culture at any point in time; and an interest in extending the context of research beyond the examination of translated texts, in particular to include examining the paratextual and evaluative writing on translation, for example prefaces, reviews, reflective essays, and so on (see REVIEWING AND CRITICISM).

Toury is primarily interested in making statements about what translation behaviour consists of (rather than what it should consist of). Moreover, given the systemic framework which provides the theoretical basis of his work, these statements cannot consist of a random selection of observations. They have to take the form of generalizations that are applicable to a particular class or subclass of phenomena and to be 'intersubjectively testable' (Toury 1995: 3). The notion of norms provides a descriptive category which makes it possible to elaborate precisely such non-random, verifiable state-

ments about types of translation behaviour. Rather than attempting to evaluate translations, the focus here is on investigating the evaluative yardstick that is used in making statements about translation in a given sociocultural context.

Investigating norms

Toury (1978, 1980a) proposed a tripartite model in which 'norms' represent an intermediate level between 'competence' and 'performance'. **Competence** is the level of description which allows the theorist to list the inventory of options that are available to translators in a given context. **Performance** concerns the subset of options that translators actually select in real life. And norms is a further subset of such options: they are the options that translators in a given sociohistorical context select on a regular basis. What Toury has done, then, is to take the dualism common in mainstream linguistics at the time (competence and performance in Noam Chomsky's terms, or *langue* and *parole* in Ferdinand de Saussure's terms) and introduce an interlevel which allows him to investigate what is *typical* rather than simply what *is* or what *can be*. This interlevel of norms enables the analyst to make sense of both the raw data of performance and the idealized potential of competence.

The notion of norms assumes that the translator is essentially engaged in a decision-making process. Toury (1995) further suggests that being a translator involves playing a social role, rather than simply transferring phrases and sentences across a linguistic boundary. The translator fulfils a function specified by the community and has to do so in a way that is considered appropriate in that community. Acquiring a set of norms for determining what is appropriate translational behaviour in a given community is a prerequisite for becoming a translator within that community. However, Toury has always stressed that norms are a category of descriptive analysis and not, as the term might imply, a prescriptive set of options which are thought by the analyst or scholar to be desirable. One identifies norms of translational behaviour by studying a corpus of authentic translations and identifying regular patterns of translation, including types of strategies that are typically opted for by the translators represented in that corpus. Thus, as Hermans puts it (1995: 215–16), this approach 'liberated the study of translation by urging researchers to look at translations as they had turned out in reality and in history, not as some armchair critic thought they should have turned out'.

Toury (1978/1980a: 53–7, 1995: 56–61) discusses three types of translational norms: initial norms, preliminary norms and operational norms. The **initial norm** involves a basic choice between adhering to the norms realized in the source text (which, it is assumed, reflect the norms of the source language and culture) and adhering to the norms prevalent in the target culture and language. Adherence to source norms determines a translation's *adequacy* with respect to the source text; adherence to norms originating in the target culture determines its *acceptability* within that culture (cf. the more politicized notions of foreignizing and domesticating STRATEGIES). **Preliminary norms** concern the existence and nature of a translation policy (in terms of the choice of source text types, individual source texts, authors, source languages, etc.) and the directness of translation, i.e. a particular society's tolerance or intolerance towards a translation based on a text in an intermediate language rather than on the source language text (see RELAY). And finally, **operational norms** concern decisions made during, rather than prior to, the actual act of translation. Toury discusses two types of operational norms: (a) *matricial* norms, which have to do with the way textual material is distributed, how much of the text is translated, and any changes in segmentation, for example as a result of large-scale omissions, and (b) *textual-linguistic* norms, which concern the selection of specific textual material to formulate the target text or replace particular segments of the source text.

Translational norms can be investigated using two main sources: textual sources, namely the translated texts themselves, and extratextual sources, i.e. the theoretical and critical statements made about translation in general or about specific translations.

Toury (1995) offers another perspective on the notion of norms. Instead of the competence/performance framework, it is possible to view norms from a social angle in terms of their *potency*: sociocultural constraints in general can be seen as lying along a continuum, with **absolute rules** at one end and **pure idiosyncrasies** at the other. Norms occupy the middle ground between these two extremes; seen from this angle, norms 'always imply *sanctions* – actual or potential, negative as well as positive' (ibid.: 55). Norms themselves in turn form a graded continuum , with some being stronger/more rule-like and others being weaker, tending towards idiosyncrasy. This gradation will vary within a given socio-culture, so that an overall weak translational norm may be almost rule-like in certain types of translation. For example, avoiding cultural substitution as a translation strategy may be a relatively weak norm today in dealing with canonized authors and texts; but in COURT INTERPRETING, the norm is much stronger: cultural substitution is simply not allowed. The interpreter typically has no latitude to replace an element which he or she thinks might be opaque for the audience with one that has a broadly similar function in the target culture. This injunction is likely to render the occurrence of cultural substitution highly atypical in a corpus of interpreted utterances in court.

Other scholars have discussed norms in terms of their potency, making a distinction between norms and conventions and/or between constitutive and regulatory norms (Chesterman 1993; Hermans 1991, 1993, 1996; Nord 1991b, 1997). The difference between norms and conventions is that the latter are not binding and only express preferences. In terms of the distinction between **constitutive** and **regulatory norms**, the former concern what is or is not accepted as translation (as opposed to ADAPTATION, for instance), and the latter concern translation choices at the lower levels, i.e. the kind of EQUIVALENCE a translator opts for or achieves.

Chesterman (1993) attempts to refine the notion of norms further by distinguishing between professional norms and expectancy norms. **Professional norms** emerge from competent professional behaviour and govern the accepted methods and strategies of the translation process. They can be subdivided into three major types: *accountability norms* are ethical and call for professional standards of integrity and thoroughness (see ETHICS); *communication norms* are social and emphasize the role of the translator as a communication expert; *relation norms* are linguistic and require the translator to establish and maintain an appropriate relation between source and target texts on the basis of his or her understanding of the intentions of the original writer/commissioner, the projected readership and the purpose of the translation (ibid.: 8–9; see FUNCTIONALIST APPROACHES). **Expectancy norms** 'are established by the receivers of the translation, by their expectations of what a translation (of a given type) should be like, and what a native text (of a given type) in the target language should be like' (ibid.: 9). In attempting to conform to the expectancy norms operating in a given community, a translator will simultaneously be conforming to the professional norms of that community (ibid.: 10).

From norms to laws

Consistent with his and Toury's overall empirical approach that seeks to emulate scientific modes of enquiry, Even-Zohar had suggested as early as 1986 that no scientific activity and no theory is conceivable without the formulation of laws of behaviour (1986: 75). Such laws have to describe the relations between variables or constraints which apply in a particular domain. Toury incorporated the notion of laws into his research programme from the beginning, as outlined in the maiden issue of *Target* (Toury and Lambert 1989; see also Hermans 1999: 91), and went on to elaborate it in some detail from there on (Toury 1991, 1993), eventually devoting an entire chapter to it in his 1995 book.

Toury begins by specifying two types of statement that do not and cannot constitute theoretical laws, namely, lists of possibilities that are not connected with specific constraints operating in a given domain, and directives, or lists of prescriptions, since there is no guarantee that these reflect actual behaviour. Laws have to be derived from actual behaviour and have to be expressed in a conditional form that signals the relationship between behaviour and constraint: *if X, then the greater/the lesser the likelihood that Y*, where *Y* stands for observed behaviour and *X* for the constraint or conditioning factor that influences that behaviour. The idea, clearly, is to endow theorizing about translation with a predictive and explanatory power similar to that attained in the sciences.

An example of a translation law is the 'law of interference', where the 'observed behaviour' is interference and the conditioning factor is the relative dominance of the languages/cultures involved: 'tolerance of interference – and hence the endurance of its manifestations – tend to increase when translation is carried out from a "major" or highly prestigious language/culture, especially if the target language/culture is "minor", or "weak" in any other sense' (1995: 278). Problems with terms such as 'minor' and 'weak' aside, what this 'law' predicts is greater levels of interference (syntactic, lexical, stylistic, etc.) in translations from, say, English into Arabic or French into Swahili than from Arabic into English or Swahili into French. The law may be further refined by introducing additional conditioning factors, relating to genre or time span, for example.

Assessment

The concept of norms ultimately gives priority to the target text, rather than the source text, and has therefore effectively replaced EQUIVALENCE as the operative term in translation studies (Hermans 1995: 217). More importantly, the concept of norms 'assumes that the primary object of analysis in translation studies is not an individual translation but a coherent corpus of translated texts' (Baker 1993: 240). This position has had far-reaching consequences in terms of elaborating an explicit definition of the object of study in the discipline and providing the basis for a relevant research programme that has informed numerous studies to date (see, for example, Hyun 1992; Du-Nour 1995; Øverås 1998; Karamitroglou 2000, among many others). It has also been instrumental in preparing the ground for corpus-based studies of translation, a development which has proved highly influential (see CORPORA). Nevertheless, the concept of norms, and particularly that of 'laws', have not been without their critics.

Hermans (1999) offers the most extended and critical assessment of Toury's work to date. Hermans (1995, 1999) points out that the choice of 'adequacy' and 'acceptability' as the polar alternatives for Toury's initial norms is unfortunate (because confusing) and conceptually suspect. On the one hand, the idea of reconstructing *the* 'adequate' translation with which a given choice in the target text could be compared is utopian and unworkable. On the other hand, what is 'adequate' is ultimately a matter of individual judgement on the part of readers, who invest the text with meaning. A better alternative, Hermans argues, is to replace these terms with 'source-oriented' and 'target-oriented' (1999: 77). Hermans further argues that it is unproductive to think of norms as involving choices between two alternatives (adequacy/acceptability): 'If translation is a sociocultural activity, as the norms concept suggests, there seems little point in trying to conceptualize it in terms of a choice along a single axis' (ibid.).

Baker (2007, in press) criticizes norm theory more broadly for focusing on repeated, abstract behaviour rather than the intricacy of concrete, everyday choices. By focusing our attention on repeated behaviour, she argues, norm theory 'privileges strong patterns of socialization into that behaviour and tends to gloss over the numerous individual and group attempts at undermining dominant patterns and prevailing political and social dogma' (ibid.: 152). Crisafulli (2002: 35) similarly suggests that the abstractions of norm theory downplay the importance of 'human translators living in historically determined circumstances', and Pym (1998: 111) argues that 'theorists and describers of translational norms spectacularly sideline questions concerning power relationships or conflictual groups'.

The notion of 'laws' has been met with limited enthusiasm on the whole. One objection is that it assumes a clearly bounded, discrete category ('translation') whose various manifestations across time and space can be reduced to a common denominator (Hermans 1999: 92; Tymoczko 2007: 155). As with norms, the search for laws, argues Crisafulli, 'also isolates certain features in an abstract realm where historical problems have no or very little bearing' (2002: 34).

Nevertheless, although translation studies has generated a highly diverse range of theoretical and methodological agendas and approaches since the mid-1990s, some of which have restricted the influence of what was once *the* major paradigm of research in the discipline, the concept of norms, and DTS more broadly, continues to inform a considerable volume of the research conducted in the field, even as scholars persist in questioning some of its basic premises.

See also:

CONFERENCE INTERPRETING, SOCIOCULTURAL PERSPECTIVES; CORPORA; DESCRIPTIVE VS. COMMITTED APPROACHES; EQUIVALENCE; EXPLICITATION; MODELS; POLYSYSTEM; SHIFTS; STRATEGIES; UNIVERSALS.

Further reading

Toury 1978, 1980a; Lambert and van Gorp 1985; Toury and Lambert 1989; Hermans 1991; Toury 1991; Baker 1993; Chesterman 1993; Hermans 1993, 1995; Toury 1995; Hermans 1999; Schäffner 1999; Crisafulli 2002.

MONA BAKER

Poetry

The central question that all studies of the translation of poetry have asked, implicitly or explicitly, is whether poetry can be translated (see TRANSLATABILITY). It may seem obvious that it can, for poetry has always been widely translated, and some poets, such as Catullus or Rilke, have been translated many times. In fact, translated poetry plays such a large part in the literature of most cultures that it is taken very much for granted (Honig 1985: 1). English readers of Virgil or Omar Khayyám or Alvarez's (1992) anthology *Modern European Poetry*, for example, might see the poems as foreign without necessarily reading them as translations. This could be taken as evidence that they have been successfully translated, if translation is viewed as a type of writing which avoids drawing attention to itself.

The opposite view – that poetry translation is difficult or even impossible – arises from the coincidence of two assumptions: (i) translated poetry should be poetry in its own right (see, for example, Coleridge 1990: 200); (ii) poetry is difficult, cryptic, ambiguous and exhibits a special relationship between form and meaning (Furniss and Bath 1996: 13). These two assumptions together have led many writers – such as Weissbort (1989: x) and Raffel (1988: vii) – to suggest that the translation of poetry, more than that of any other genre, demands both special critical abilities and special writing abilities. One way of negotiating this difficulty is to translate poetry into prose, an approach sometimes favoured (see, for example, Arnold 1954: 316; Selver 1966: 13ff.; Weissbort 1989: xii) for writers such as SHAKESPEARE. This might be because prose is seen as easier to write, although Scott (2000: 163) argues that prose translations of poetry have their own 'resourcefulness' and

their own freedoms. Prose translations are, however, the exception.

Another way of dealing with the supposed difficulty of poetic translation is to move away from the original, producing what Lowell called *Imitations* (1958) or what Paterson calls versions (2006: 73ff.). Hamburger (1989: 51) sees such deviation from the original as 'an admission of defeat'; yet many translators of poetry feel it is the only way to produce translated texts which aim 'to be poems in their own right' (Paterson 2006: 73).

The *skopos* of poetic translation

One way of expressing the fact that translated poetry aims, in general, to be itself poetry, is to say that the aim or skopos (Nord 1997: 27) of its translation is to carry over the source text function into the target text; it is thus an instrumental translation (see FUNCTIONALIST APPROACHES). However, if it is to avoid being what Hamburger saw as merely a 'springboard' for one's own work, then it must aspire also to be documentary, to give 'some idea of what the original is actually like' (Honig 1985: 177, 179), and especially to allow its readers to see those very difficulties which make it poetic. The common tendency to publish translated poetry bilingually, especially in recent years, points to this documentary aspect. Especially for the bilingual reader, the relationship of the translated poems with the source text is highlighted by a similar layout in both languages. Thus recent books such as the Welsh anthology by Minhinnick (2003), Crucefix's version of Rilke's *Duino Elegies* (2006) or Gardner's translations of Dutch poet Remco Campert (2007) suggest that successful translation of poetry does not depend upon the reader's belief that the translated poem is an original. Yet translators like Minhinnick point out that they attempt to 'restyle' (2003: x) the poems where necessary. The notion that translation means in essence documentary writing, and therefore we need a new term ('version' or 'imitation') to describe translation of poetry which is also instrumental, was behind Jakobson's suggestion that what poetry required was not translation but 'creative transposition' (1959/2000: 118).

Other writers do not see the need for instrumentality in translated poetry as running counter to the idea of translation. Gutt, for example, argues that poetic texts demand 'direct translation' (1991/2000: 167): they must preserve the stylistic qualities of the original. The focus on poetic style as a way of combining documentation of the poetics of the source text with the necessary instrumentality of the target text (even if not put in the same terms) is shared by a number of theorists of poetic translation (e.g. Tabakowska 1993; de Beaugrande 1978; Boase-Beier 2006a) who argue that the translation of poetry must take into account the special nature and language of poetry and the type of reading it demands.

Translation and the nature of poetry

The idea that there is something peculiar to poetry which, if captured in translation, will allow the poetic effects (Gutt 1991/2000: 164) of the original to be recreated is implicit in descriptions of poetic translation as writing which captures what Pope called the 'spirit' (Lefevere 1992b: 64f.) or Rowan Williams the 'energy' (2002: 8) of the original poem. One way of making this abstract notion more concrete is to equate it with style, because style can be seen as the result of the poet's choices (Verdonk 2002: 9), and therefore the embodiment of poetic voice (Stockwell 2002b: 78) or mind (Boase-Beier 2003a), as well as that which engages the reader (Boase-Beier 2006a: 31ff.). This focus on style as central to poetic translation is found especially in the writings of: (i) translators who are themselves poets and can be assumed to have an inherent (perhaps unconscious) knowledge of how poetry works (e.g. Pope, Paterson or Williams), and (ii) critics who take the view that a theoretical understanding of poetry is essential not only to the reading of translated

poetry but also to the act of translation (e.g. Tabakowska 1993; Boase-Beier 2006a).

There have been many debates about the characteristics of poetic style and whether they distinguish poetry from prose or indeed literary from non-literary texts (e.g. Fowler 1981: 162ff.; see LITERARY TRANSLATION). Some of the elements that have been put forward as distinctive of poetic style are:

- its physical shape (Furniss and Bath 1996: 13), including use of lines and spaces on a page
- its use of inventive language (Eagleton 2007: 46) and, in particular, patterns of sound and structure (Jakobson 1960: 358)
- its openness to different interpretations (Furniss and Bath 1996: 225)
- its demand to be read non-pragmatically (Eagleton 2007: 38)

The layout in lines can be seen as a signal to read the text in a particular way: as a text in which style is the main repository of meaning (Boase-Beier 2006a: 112). Typically, writers will speak of recreating particular aspects of style such as metaphors (Newmark 1988/1995: 104–13), repetition (Boase-Beier 2003b) and ambiguity (Boase-Beier 2004); all these are stylistic resources which, though present in non-poetic language, are used in greater concentration in poems and add up to Eagleton's sense of 'inventiveness'. Ambiguity, in particular, is a stylistic device which allows for different interpretations and thus its preservation in translation enables the poem to retain its ability to fit different contexts (Verdonk 2002: 6f.). Discussions on the nature of poetry suggest that there might be poetic characteristics that are universal; yet poetic traditions vary from one culture to another and, as Connolly (1998: 174) points out, this is also an important consideration in translating poetry.

How to translate poetry: theory and process

Concerning the processes involved in poetry translation, a common question asked is whether the process of interpretation and creation are separate or not. Some writers appear to suggest that they are: Sayers Peden (1989) speaks of 'dismantling' the original poem and 'building' the translation, Bly speaks of the eight 'stages' of translation (1984), Barnstone of two (1993: 49) and Diaz-Diocaretz (1985) explicitly distinguishes the process of reading from the production of the new poem. Others differ: Jones (1989: 188) says that such stages are 'helical rather than unilinear'; Scott (2000) goes further, maintaining that reading and translation are inextricably linked. In this latter view, creativity is an element in reading as much as in writing. This seems also to be what Felstiner (1989: 36) implies in calling his translation of Celan 'the closest act of reading and of writing'. Yet Hamburger (interviewed in Honig 1985) maintains that translation is, for him, a less creative act than writing his own poetry.

A further question that translation (or any activity which has been theorized) faces is that of the relationship between theory and practice. It is generally held to be the case (see Chesterman and Wagner 2002) that theory describes practice in a way which offers a (partial) explanation for observed phenomena. Others, especially practising translators who are not themselves theorists (ibid.), tend to see theory as dictating practice. Though this view is often frowned on as being prescriptive rather than descriptive, and therefore denying theory its true character as MODEL, the distinction is not, in fact, so clear-cut. Toury, for example, says that descriptive theory can help make predictions about practice (1985: 34–5). Moreover, it is reasonable to assume that theory can enhance the translator's knowledge of what is possible (Boase-Beier 2006a: 111).

For the translation of poetry, two main types of theory are of relevance: theory of the literary text and theories of translation. That theory which explains how poetry works will help the translator of poetry is the view expressed by Tabakowska (1993: 1) and Boase-Beier (2006a: 111), as mentioned above. Other literary and linguistic theories may lead us to question the authority of the author (Lecercle 1990: 127), of the source text (Montgomery *et al.* 2000: 279) or the notion that there is one correct interpretation (Scott 2000); see DECONSTRUCTION; HERMENUETICS. Theory may thus help free the translator from the constraints of the source

text, and could therefore be seen as a source of creativity for the translator (Boase-Beier 2006b).

Theories of translation can be important in increasing awareness of particular issues, such as translation politics (see GENDER AND SEXUALITY; DESCRIPTIVE VERSUS COMMITTED APPROACHES) and ETHICS. Venuti's concern with foreignization (1995a: 20), for example, might lead the translator to consider to what extent poetic language is itself foreignized language. Theories that specifically aim to describe the translation of poetry include the 'seven strategies' described by Lefevere (1975).

Theories of poetics, stylistics and translation are also of value in the TRAINING AND EDUCATION of translators, and in reading translated poetry. Just as students can be taught to read poetry critically, and to acknowledge the need for multiple interpretations, so they can be made aware of the consequences of such stylistically aware reading for translation.

There are, then, several different ways of translating poetry, but it would be fair to say that most poetry translators aim to create translations that work as poetry in the target language. In fact, it could be argued that if poetry, by nature, uses language which is strange and devices which both draw the reader's attention and allow freedom of interpretation, then translated poetry is in the best possible position to embody what it means to be poetic.

See also:
ADAPTATION; CLASSICAL TEXTS; DECONSTRUCTION; DRAMA TRANSLATION; HERMENEUTICS; LITERARY TRANSLATION; REWRITING; TRANSLATABILITY.

Further reading
Lefevere 1975; Bly 1984; Diaz-Diocaretz 1985; Honig 1985; Raffel 1988; Biguenet and Schulte 1989; Jones 1989; Weissbort 1989; Boase-Beier 2004, 2006a.

JEAN BOASE-BEIER

Polysystem

Originally arising from the work of a group of Russian literary theorists, the concept of the **polysystem** has received considerable attention in the work of certain groups of translation scholars since the mid-1970s. While offering a general model for understanding, analysing and describing the functioning and evolution of literary systems, its specific application to the study of translated literature – an area frequently marginalized by literary theory – has given rise to much useful discussion and research.

The origins of the polysystem model and the work of Itamar Even-Zohar

In the early 1970s, Itamar Even-Zohar, a scholar from Tel Aviv, developed the polysystem model on the basis of his work on Hebrew literature. Its roots, however, lie in the writings of the late Russian Formalists Yury Tynyanov, Roman Jakobson and Boris Eikhenbaum. Matejka and Pomorska (1971) provide a good English-language introduction to the ideas of Russian Formalism.

Although many aspects of their thinking are taken up by Even-Zohar, probably the most significant contribution of the Formalists is the notion of system. This term, which was originally defined by Tynyanov (1929), was used to denote a multi-layered structure of elements which relate to and interact with each other. As a concept, this was flexible enough to be applicable to phenomena on various levels, thus enabling Tynyanov to view not only individual works, but also whole literary genres and traditions – and ultimately even the entire social order – as systems (or even 'systems of systems') in their own right. Furthermore, within the wider framework of his work on the process of literary evolution (Tynyanov 1971), the use of the systemic concept led to this process being viewed as a 'mutation of systems' (ibid.: 67).

Using the work of Tynyanov and other Formalists as his starting point, Even-Zohar took up the systemic approach in the early 1970s more or less from the point where they had left off. His immediate aim at the time was to resolve certain problems connected with translation theory and the historical structure of Hebrew literature, and his application of the Formalists' ideas in these areas resulted in the formulation of what he termed polysystem theory.

In Even-Zohar's writings, the terms 'system' and 'polysystem' are to a large extent synonymous. However, the latter term was proposed in order to stress the dynamic nature of his conception of the 'system' and to distance it from the more static connotations which the term had acquired in the Saussurean tradition; an account of the provenance and rationale of the term polysystem can be found in Even-Zohar (1990: 9–13). It should also be pointed out that Even-Zohar's use of the terms 'system' and 'systemic' is quite distinct from that associated with Michael Halliday's systemic functional grammar, which forms the theoretical basis of Catford's (1965) model of translation (see LINGUISTIC APPROACHES).

According to Even-Zohar's model, the polysystem is conceived as a heterogeneous, hierarchized conglomerate (or system) of systems which interact to bring about an ongoing, dynamic process of evolution within the polysystem as a whole. From the first part of this definition, it follows that polysystems can be postulated to account for phenomena existing on various levels, so that the polysystem of a given national literature is viewed as one element making up the larger sociocultural polysystem, which itself comprises other polysystems besides the literary, such as the artistic, the religious or the political. Furthermore, being placed in this way in a larger sociocultural context, 'literature' comes to be viewed not just as a collection of texts, but more broadly as a set of factors governing the production, promotion and reception of these texts.

Essential to the concept of the polysystem is the notion that the various strata and subdivisions which make up a given polysystem are constantly competing with each other for the dominant position. Thus, in the case of the literary polysystem there is a continuous state of tension between the centre and the periphery, in which different literary genres all vie for domination of the centre. The term 'genre' is understood in its widest sense, and is not restricted to 'high' or 'canonized' forms, i.e. 'those literary norms and works ... which are accepted as legitimate by the dominant circles within a culture and whose conspicuous products are preserved by the community to become part of its historical heritage' (Even-Zohar 1990: 15). It also includes 'low' or 'non-canonized' genres, 'those norms and texts which are rejected by these circles as illegitimate' (ibid.). Thus the literary polysystem is made up not only of 'masterpieces' and revered literary forms (such as the established verse forms), but also of such genres as CHILDREN'S LITERATURE, popular fiction and translated works, none of which have traditionally fallen within the domain of literary studies. The new, non-elitist, non-prescriptive approach which this rejection of value judgements has made possible has had far-reaching consequences for the field of translation studies.

Although so-called low forms tend to remain on the periphery, the stimulus which they give to the canonized forms occupying the centre is one of the main factors which determines the way in which the polysystem evolves. Thus, for Even-Zohar literary evolution is not driven by a specific goal but is rather brought about as a consequence of 'the unavoidable competition generated by the state of heterogeneity' (1990: 91). Another facet of this competition can be seen in the further tension which exists between primary (innovative) and secondary (conservative) literary principles: once a primary form has been accepted into the centre and has managed to achieve canonized status by maintaining its position there for some time, it will tend to become increasingly conservative and inflexible as it attempts to fight off challenges from newer, emerging literary ideas. However, it will eventually – and inevitably – succumb to a newer model which will ultimately evict it from its privileged position at the centre of the polysystem.

Polysystem theory and translation

While the polysystem concept was designed specifically in order to solve certain problems connected with the study of translation, it is clear from the above that as a theory it accounts for systemic phenomena of a considerably more general nature. However, much of Even-Zohar's writing is devoted to a discussion both of the role which translated literature plays in a

particular literary polysystem, and also of the wider theoretical implications which polysystem theory has for translation studies in general.

Regarding the first of these questions, Even-Zohar argues for the recognition of limited systemic relationships between the seemingly isolated translated texts which exist in a given literary polysystem (1990: 45–6). These relationships concern the principles of selection imposed on prospective translations by the dominant poetics, and also the tendency for translated texts to conform to the literary NORMS of the target system. Having established the systemic status of translated literature, Even-Zohar then proceeds to discuss its role and significance within the literary polysystem.

Although it might be tempting, on the basis of the scant attention traditionally accorded to translated literature by most branches of literary studies, to conclude that it will invariably occupy a peripheral position in the polysystem, it would in fact be a mistake to do so. While a peripheral situation is of course normal, Even-Zohar identifies three sets of circumstances in which translated literature can occupy a more central position (ibid.: 46–8). The first of these involves the situation in which a 'young' literature in the process of being established has not yet been crystallized into a polysystem. In this case, translated literature becomes one of its most important systems as the emerging literature looks to other, older literatures for initial, ready-made models for a wide variety of text types. The second instance in which translated literature may occupy a central position in a given literary system is when the original literature of that system is 'peripheral' or 'weak', as for example occurs when the literature of a small nation is overshadowed by that of a larger one. The third set of circumstances occurs at moments of crisis; at such turning points in the evolution of a polysystem, the vacuum left when older, established models cease to be tenable can frequently only be filled by an influx of new ideas via translation. At times other than these, however, translated works tend to be representative of more conservative, secondary NORMS, and consequently come to act as a means of maintaining traditional, even outdated models. However, it should be pointed out that regardless of the overall state of the literary polysystem, the translated literature within it will not necessarily all behave in the same way; like any other literary form, it comprises its own stratified polysystem.

Given the fact that translated literature can take on a variety of roles in the target polysystem – either by conforming to already existing models or by introducing original elements into the system – it inevitably follows that the ways in which translation is practised in a given culture are themselves dictated by the position which translated literature occupies within the polysystem. To use Even-Zohar's words, 'translation is no longer a phenomenon whose nature and borders are given once and for all, but an activity dependent on the relations within a certain cultural system' (1990: 51). This new insight inevitably leads to a widening of the definition of translation itself. Past definitions have frequently been formulated in highly prescriptive terms, and texts not conforming to accepted theoretical preconceptions have frequently been denied the full status of 'translations', instead being dubbed 'imitations', 'adaptations' or 'versions' (see ADAPTATION). The work of Even-Zohar, on the other hand, suggests that translation scholars have been asking the wrong questions, and aims at a new definition of the discipline itself by acknowledging the fact that the parameters within which the translation process is carried out in a given culture are themselves dictated by the models which are currently operative within the target literary polysystem. This fundamentally non-prescriptive approach has led to three extremely important insights (see DESCRIPTIVE VS. COMMITTED APPROACHES).

The first of these is the suggestion that it is more profitable to view translation as one specific instance of the more general phenomenon of inter-systemic transfer. This has the advantage not only of enabling us to examine translation within a wider context, but also of allowing those features which are genuinely peculiar to translation to stand out against the backdrop of this wider context (see Even-Zohar 1990: 73–4). The other two insights follow on from this first one. The second concerns our conception of the translated text. Instead of limiting the discussion to the nature of the EQUIVALENCE which exists between source and target text, the translation scholar is now free to focus on the translated text as an entity existing in the target polysystem in its own right. This new target-oriented approach, now chiefly associated with the name of Gideon Toury, has led to a large volume of descriptive work investigating the nature of the target text, for example in terms of the features which distinguish it from other texts originating within a particular polysystem (see UNIVERSALS). Furthermore, translated texts cease to be viewed as isolated phenomena, but are rather thought of as manifestations of general translation 'procedures' which are determined by the conditions currently prevalent in the target polysystem (Even-Zohar 1990: 74–5). The third insight concerns these translation procedures themselves. Once it has been recognized that the target text is not simply the product of selections from sets of ready-made linguistic options but is rather shaped by systemic constraints of a variety of types (concerned not only with language structure but also, for example, with questions of genre and literary taste), it becomes possible to suggest explanations for translation phenomena (such as the appearance in a translated text of functions native only to the source system) within the more general context of inter-systemic transfer (ibid. 75–7).

Further developments

Three substantial early case studies that use polysystem theory are Yahalom (1980, 1981) and D'hulst (1987). Further systemic concepts have been proposed to supplement the model: Lefevere (1983b: 194), for example, suggests the addition of notions of polarity, periodicity and patronage (see REWRITING). A number of scholars have questioned the necessity of the primary/secondary distinction (Lefevere 1983b:194; Gentzler 1993: 122). Gentzler further suggests that the influence of Russian Formalism is too strong, and that polysystem theory needs to break free from some of its more restrictive concepts (1993: 122–3). However, the influence of Even-Zohar's thinking has been considerable, the new approach which it has engendered being particularly associated with groups of scholars in Israel, Belgium and the Netherlands. Probably the most significant extension of the model is found in Toury (1980a), where Even-Zohar's target-oriented approach is consolidated and the notion of translation NORMS – the factors and constraints which shape standard translation practices in a given culture – is introduced and developed (Toury 1995 is a continuation of this work). Hermans's (1985a) collection of largely descriptive essays by a variety of scholars is another important expression of this approach, contributing in particular the notion of translation as the manipulation of literature. In a later work (1999), Hermans observes that the polysystem approach is able to accommodate a 'range of traditionally neglected texts' that permit translation to be located within the broader context of cultural history (1999: 118). However, in the same work, he discusses a number of limitations to polysystem theory (ibid.: 118–19). First, he highlights the danger of depersonalization. Ultimately text-based, the approach does not concern itself with individuals, groups or institutions, revealing an unwillingness to engage with the underlying causes of the phenomena that are of interest to it. Hermans also characterizes the 'primary versus secondary' opposition as a 'self-fulfilling prophecy' because, unlike the other oppositions, it may not be deduced from statements deriving from within the system that forms the object of study but is imposed retrospectively by the researcher. Finally, he points out that real-life case studies reveal phenomena that are too 'ambivalent, hybrid, unstable, mobile, overlapping and collapsed' for polysystem's binary logic.

Polysystem theory has provided the theoretical framework for numerous case studies focusing on different kinds of translation activity within a wide range of linguistic, cultural and historical contexts. These include the representation of Ireland in Finnish realist drama (Aaltonen 1996); British New Wave film adaptation, screenwriting and dialogue (Remael 2000); Malraux in English translation (Fawcett 2001); French Existentialism in post-World War II Jewish-American literature (Codde 2003); the translation of Shakespeare's *The Tempest* into German and Japanese (von Schwerin-High 2004); and translated children's books (Thomson 2005).

Polysystem theory as articulated by Even-Zohar and other scholars is not a complete, watertight package but rather a point of departure for further work. As long as it is viewed as such, it is likely to continue to give rise to fruitful investigation, of both a theoretical

and a descriptive nature. Although it remains very much 'work in progress', open to further modification and refinement, the contribution of polysystem theory to our understanding of the nature and role of translation has been significant and highly influential.

See also:
DESCRIPTIVE VS. COMMITTED APPROACHES; LITERARY TRANSLATION; MODELS; NORMS; PSEU-DOTRANSLATION; REWRITING.

Further reading
Even-Zohar 1978a, 1978b; Holmes *et al.* 1978; Toury 1980a; Lefevere 1983b; Hermans 1985a; Even-Zohar 1990; Gentzler 1993; Hermans 1995, 1999; Toury 1995.

MARK SHUTTLEWORTH

Postcolonial approaches

Translation is increasingly being investigated as a cultural artefact that is deeply entrenched in the historical reality of its production. POLYSYSTEM theory and Descriptive Translation Studies (see DESCRIPTIVE VS. COMMITTED APPROACHES) have directed scholarly attention to studying translation within the target culture, but as a product of intercultural transfer, translation also signals the relationship between the cultures it traverses. Since cultures rarely, if ever, meet on equal terms, a postcolonial approach to translation inevitably poses the crucial but long-neglected question of how blatant power differentials, particularly in the age of European colonialism, have influenced the practice of translation. A second, crucial question of interest to postcolonial theorists concerns how translation might contribute to exposing, challenging and decolonizing the legacy of colonialism and various forms of neo-colonialism in a postcolonial era.

Translation served colonial powers in many ways. To start with, translation is a form of intelligence gathering. The natives can be conquered with brutal military force and coercion, but colonial rule must be sustained through persuasion and knowledge of the other. The fact that the East/Rest was turned into a formidable province of European learning during the period of European colonialism clearly attests to the complicity between power and knowledge (Said 1978). As a primary means of making sense of Europe's Other, translation took pride of place in nineteenth-century Orientalism, with translated knowledge informing the colonial project of ruling and transforming the colonized in the interests of the colonizers.

Translation from and into dominated/dominating cultures

Translation **from dominated cultures** not only informs and empowers the colonizers but also serves to interpellate the colonized into colonial subjects (Niranjana 1992). As a form of representation, translation constructs a whole set of orientalist images of dominated cultures, images which come to function as 'realities' for both dominant and dominated peoples. This is accomplished through various means:

(a) *The choice of translation materials.* Texts which help create a desired image of the colonized or confirm prevalent orientalist images are more readily translated and circulated. Sengupta (1995: 162) notes that Indian texts translated by English orientalists, most notably William Jones, 'were either religious or spiritual, saturated with mysticism, or portrayed a simple and natural state of existence that was radically different from the metropolitan self of the target culture'. Jacquemond (1992: 150–51) similarly points out that *The Arabian Nights*, which has been translated numerous times into French throughout the last two decades, 'has undoubtedly been the main literary source of French representations of the Arab world, in both their negative (the "barbarian" Orient) and positive (the "magical" Orient) dimensions'.

(b) *The orientalist paradigm of translation.* Canonical texts from dominated cultures often appear in imposing scholarly translations, which are painfully and pedantically literal and loaded with an awesome exegetical and critical apparatuses. Such scholarly translations reinforce the image of the 'orient' as stagnant, mysterious, strange, and esoteric, of interest to and penetrable only with the help of a handful of orientalist 'experts' (Jacquemond 1992: 149). Indeed, in spite of their meticulous care and apparent servitude to the words of dominated-language texts, orientalist translators often pose as authoritative interpreters and judges of things oriental. Science, rationality and Christian 'truths' could all be rallied to deconstruct, denigrate, or desacralize the canons of other cultures. The refusal to see non-Western cultures on their own terms is manifested either in the translation proper or in the critical apparatus: orientalist translators may feel constrained to represent native views in the main body of the translation, but they are seldom shy of turning the paratextual space – prefaces, introductions, notes, appendixes, and so forth – into a colonizing space where cultural differences are interpreted as signs of the inferiority of non-Western cultures (Wang Hui 2007).

Translations produced in this orientalist or philological tradition, identified by Tymoczko as 'the norm for translating the native texts of minority and non-Western cultures' (1999a: 269), have the potential of 'constructing a posture of esthetic … and … cultural imperialism' because through them 'the literature of other cultures is reduced to non-literature and segments of world literature come to be represented by non-literature', leading to 'the sort of judgment about non-Western literatures epitomized in Macaulay's infamous remarks that he had not found an Orientalist "who could deny that a single shelf of a good European library was worth the whole native culture of India and Arabia".' (ibid.).

(c) *Fluent, domesticating translations.* In the popular tradition of translating non-Western cultures, translators often domesticate foreign texts to suit Western values, paradigms and poetics. According to Venuti (1995a), fluent, domesticating translations create the illusion of invisible translators and transparent representations, which helps to conceal their imperialistic, ethnocentric reduction of cultural difference.

If translations from dominated cultures construct an image of non-Western cultures as inferior, creating a need and justification for Western civilizing missions, translations **from dominant cultures**, much larger in quantity than those from dominated cultures, serve the very purpose of intellectual colonization. The gross trade imbalance in translation between dominant and dominated cultures, as documented by Jacquemond (1992: 139) and Venuti (1992: 5–6, 1995a: 12–17), clearly reflects the dynamics of cultural hegemony and dependency.

In contrast with the orientalist representation of dominated-language texts as esoteric and strange, texts from dominant cultures often appear in readable versions as embodying universal truths and values. In the initial contact with dominant cultures, dominated societies tend to naturalize foreign literary production, a tendency interpreted by Jacquemond (1992: 142) as a sign of cultural independence. As political and economic domination deepens, however, the cultural confidence of dominated societies wanes, and translation becomes a primary tool of modernization, or rather Westernization, viewed as a means of strengthening the domestic culture. During this period of intense cultural and linguistic colonization, Western texts tend to be translated more accurately, with their cultural and linguistic specificities foregrounded to serve as a powerful model and stimulation for 'stagnant' native languages and cultures.

Strategies of resistance and decolonization

Translation is not solely a channel of colonization; it can also be a site of active resistance to colonial and neocolonial powers. A number of studies that approached translation from a postcolonial perspective have revealed traces of resistance inscribed in translations undertaken in colonial contexts and proposed ways of putting translation at the service of decolonization.

Rafael (1988) argues that a series of playful mistranslations of the Spanish Christian missionaries' more 'prestigious' languages helped the Tagalogs in the Philippines to negotiate the terms of their conversion under Spanish rule. The examples he provides demonstrate that translation is never a site where one language-culture can claim complete victory over the other. Rather, it is a 'space of hybridity' where 'newness enters the world', 'newness' which undermines the 'purity' of the dominant language-culture (Bhabha 1994b).

Tymoczko's (1999a) sympathetic and nuanced analysis of early Irish literature in English translation reveals how different metonymic aspects of Irish hero tales have been suppressed, foregrounded or transformed by Irish translators at different historical moments to advance anti-colonial, nationalist agendas. Her analysis suggests that resistant translations can employ a wide range of STRATEGIES to undermine the colonizer and empower the colonized, and that sweeping dismissal of domesticating or assimilationist strategies is therefore historically naive.

Perhaps more fundamental than the choice of translation strategy in a specific text is the ethical issue of helping translators adopt an anti-colonial stance in their interaction with other cultures (see ETHICS). Postcolonial approaches recognize that translation is never neutral, that it is a site of intense ideological and discursive negotiation (see IDEOLOGY). For translators to promote a genuine respect for alterity, they need first of all to decolonize their own minds, to dislodge traces of colonialist ideologies, and to recognize the basic right to equality of all languages and cultures (see MINORITY).

Scholars who adopt a post-structuralist stance tend to valorize foreignizing translation strategies. As a leading discourse which has informed a significant number of postcolonial studies of translation, post-structuralism (including DECONSTRUCTION) has initiated a radical reconsideration of many concepts which underwrite traditional theorization of translation, concepts such as the originality of the source text (which relegates translation to servitude); the idea of a stable meaning waiting to be decoded from one language and encoded into another, and the image of a transcendental translator unconstrained by the sociocultural conditions of his or her time. A keen awareness of the power of language in constructing, rather than reflecting, meaning and reality has led to a shift in attention, from the transcendental signified to 'the chain of signifiers, to syntactic processes, to discursive structures, to the incidence of language mechanisms on thought and reality formation' (Lewis 1985: 42). Venuti advocates foreignizing translation as a means of resisting 'ethnocentrism and racism, cultural narcissism and imperialism' and promoting 'democratic geopolitical relations' (1995a: 20). Niranjana follows Walter Benjamin in advancing extreme literalism as the preferred mode of translation, opting for a type of interlinear, word-for-word translation which 'provides a literal rendering of the syntax', 'lovingly and in detail incorporates the original's mode of signification', and 'holds back from communicating' (1992: 155). Spivak similarly argues that the task of the translator is 'to surrender herself to the linguistic rhetoricity of the original text' (1992b: 189), a task that 'holds the agency of the translator and the demands of her imagined or actual audience at bay' (ibid.: 181) and confines the translator, most of the time, to the position of 'literalist surrender' (ibid.: 190). Over the years, the call for adopting foreignizing translations has thus become closely associated with postcolonial translation discourse, but its effectiveness and theoretical underpinnings remain open to question for many scholars (Robinson 1997a: 107–13; Dharwadker 1999; Tymoczko 2000a, among others).

Because the ultimate goal of 'decolonized' and 'decolonizing' translation is to understand other cultures on their own terms, the concept of 'thick translation', developed by Appiah (1993) and applied by a number of scholars (Wolf 2003; Hermans 2003; Cheung 2004/2007; Sturge 2006), has naturally proved appealing. Thick translation 'seeks to locate a text (i.e. the translation) in a rich cultural and linguistic context in order to promote, in the target language culture, a fuller understanding and a deeper respect of the culture of the Other' (Cheung 2004/2007: 3). In thick translation, an attempt is made to go beyond translating an individual text; the aim is to activate much of the tradition behind the text through a process of layered contextualization.

Postcolonial translation is mainly concerned with preserving the alterity of dominated languages and cultures. When it comes to the translation of dominant-language texts, the task of the postcolonial translator is often reformulated as one of resisting neocolonial linguistic and cultural hegemony. Jacquemond

(1992: 156) maintains that in the postcolonial moment translation should be situated within the framework of an 'Occidentalism', that is, western intellectual production should be sifted, appropriated and naturalized in the service of dominated languages/cultures. In Brazil, a similar postcolonial poetics of translation has become known metaphorically as 'cannibalism': cannibalistic practices value creative translation of foreign texts on local terms, so that foreign nourishment can be absorbed and combined with one's own for greater vitality (Vieira 1999).

Strengths and limitations

During the past two decades, postcolonial studies of translation have redefined our understanding of translation, particularly its relation to power, ideology and empire building. In addition to exposing the shameful history of exploiting translation to justify and maintain colonial dominance, postcolonial studies of translation have also been instrumental in exploring various ways of putting translation at the service of anti-colonial and decolonizing agendas. Nevertheless, postcolonial studies of translation are not without their limitations.

If postcolonial approaches to translation were born out of 'anthropology, ethnography and colonial history' (Robinson 1997a: 1), they have been slow and reluctant to cut their umbilical cord. The four major theorists discussed in Robinson's (1997a) survey of the field are postcolonial scholars who 'find little in the field (of translation studies) to hold their interest' (ibid.: 2). What allows Robinson to bring them together and present them as part of the translation studies landscape is a common interest they share in using the term 'translation' metaphorically for a variety of colonial transactions: for Asad (1986), anthropological representation of cultures is a form of 'translation'; for Rafael (1988), Christian conversion is an act of 'translation'; Cheyfitz (1991) applies the term 'translation' to the introduction of the European concept of property right in order to lawfully dispossess American Indians; and Niranjana (1992) similarly treats the Orientalist interpellation of the Indians into colonial subjects as an act of 'translation'. When colonialism itself is seen as a huge 'translation' project, as an attempt to 'translate' other cultures into Europe's servile copies, research that has no more than a tangential relation to interlingual translation can easily be incorporated into the field. This is why many essays which might more properly belong to 'postcolonial studies' have found their way into volumes of collected essays on 'postcolonial translation studies'.

In line with this all-embracing, metaphorical use of 'translation', the concept of CULTURAL TRANSLATION has also become popular; Robinson (1997a: 43) defines 'cultural translation' as the process 'not of translating specific cultural texts but of consolidating a wide variety of cultural discourses into a target text that in some sense has no "original", no source text'. This development threatens to undermine the specificity of translation studies by expanding it to include practically all forms of representation and discourses. In addition, it introduces a certain level of confusion and overgeneralization into some discussions of translation. For example, in critiquing William Jones's deployment of translation in constructing the 'Hindu' subjects of the empire, Niranjana deems it unnecessary to interrogate his actual translations against 'the so-called originals' (1992: 13). Instead, she proposes 'to examine the "outwork" of Jones's translations – the prefaces, the annual discourses to the Asiatic society, his charges to the Grand Jury at Calcutta, his letters, and his "Oriental" poems' (ibid.). Niranjana's dismissal of 'the so-called original' is informed by a post-structuralist concept of textuality. But translation *per se* – not 'cultural translation' in its broad, metaphorical sense – presupposes the existence of a source text. To reveal the instability of the source text is one thing (here one needs to be mindful of the cultural imperialism potent within a radically deconstructive stance towards third world texts, particularly their sacred canons); to dismiss the relevance of comparative textual study is quite another. Without in-depth textual case studies to reveal the manifold ways in which colonialist ideologies have shaped, and taken shape in, actual translations, postcolonial studies of translation cannot address the core questions posed from within the discipline. Failure to address these questions adequately cast doubt on the legitimacy of postcolonial approaches' claim to a central position in translation studies

See also:
CULTURAL TRANSLATION; DECONSTRUCTION; ETHICS; GLOBALIZATION; IDEOLOGY; MINORITY; STRATEGIES .

Further reading:
Rafael 1988; Niranjana 1992; Spivak 1992b; Venuti 1992; Sengupta 1995; Venuti 1995a; Robinson 1997a; Bassnett and Trivedi 1999; Tymoczko 1999a; Simon and St-Pierre 2000; Tymoczko and Gentzler 2002; Cheung 2004/2007; Branchadell and West 2005.

WANG HUI

Pragmatics

In 1955 at Harvard, psychologists were buzzing with excitement about the lectures being given by Noam Chomsky on his theory of Transformational Generative Grammar. In the same year, also at Harvard, the British philosopher John Austin was to deliver the prestigious William James lectures and present what was to have an equally strong impact on a wide range of disciplines. This was a new perspective which was to radically reshape our view of language and the way it operates. Since then, the domain of pragmatic inquiry has emerged as a discipline in its own right, attending to such matters as 'the study of the purposes for which sentences are used, of the real world conditions under which a sentence may be appropriately used as an utterance' (Stalnaker 1972: 380).

Speech acts

Speech acts are those we perform when, for example, we make a complaint or a request, apologize or pay someone a compliment. The pragmatic analysis of speech acts sees all utterances in terms of the dual function of 'stating' and 'doing things', of having a 'sense' and a 'force'. An utterance, in this view, has:

(a) a **sense** or reference to specific events, persons or objects;
(b) a **force** which may override literal sense and thus relay added effects such as

those associated with, say, a request or an admonition;

(c) an **effect** or consequence which may or may not be of the kind conventionally associated with the linguistic expression or the functional force involved.

For example, 'Shut the door' is in a sense an imperative that could conceivably carry the force of a request, which in turn could be used simply to annoy the hearer. To these three aspects of message construction Austin (1962) assigned the labels: **locution**, **illocution** and **perlocution**, respectively. These distinctions have proven to be extremely important in translation and interpreting studies, particularly when force departs from conventional sense, or when the ultimate effect defies the expectations based on either sense or force.

In pragmatics-oriented models of the translation process, the assumption generally entertained has been that striving to achieve 'equivalence' in the act of translation is an attempt at the successful (re)performance of speech acts. That is, in the quest to approximate to the ideal of 'sameness' of meaning, translators constantly attempt to (re-)perform locutionary and illocutionary acts in the hope that the end product will have the same perlocutionary force in the target language (Blum-Kulka 1981). Actual examples of pragmatics at work in the general domain of translation can be found in Baker (1992), Hervey (1998), and in the collection of papers on the pragmatics of translation edited by Hickey (1998). Within the general field of translation quality assessment, insights yielded by pragmatic theories of language use have been put to optimal use in building up textual profiles for both source and target texts (House 1977, 1997).

Within interpreting, it has been argued that the Paris School theory of 'sense' (Seleskovitch 1991; see INTERPRETIVE APPROACH), which has practically revolutionized interpreting pedagogy, could have had a more lasting impact on interpreting research had it invoked pragmatics more explicitly (Gile 1995a). Serious cases of communication breakdown tend to be caused more often by speech act misperception than by mere miscomprehension of linguistic expression. To take one practical example, in response to the question 'what were the contents of the letter you handed to King Fahad?', a Tunisian minister is reported to have replied rather curtly what should have been interpreted as 'this is a matter solely for the Saudis to consider'. Not aware of the pragmatic meaning involved, the interpreter rendered the Arabic literally as: 'This matter concerns the Saudis'. The statement was obviously intended to carry the pragmatic force 'do not pursue this line of questioning any further', a 'rebuke' which would have been appreciated by the English journalist had it been rendered properly. However, lured by the kind of inviting answer he received through the interpreter, the journalist did pursue the initial line of questioning, only to be more explicitly rebuked the second time round (Hatim 1986; Hatim and Mason 1997).

Speech acts are certainly rule-governed, but, as various studies on the use of speech act theory in a variety of domains have shown, the problem with such rules is not only that they are more procedure-like but also that they are not necessarily followed through in the same way in all languages and cultures. This gives rise to a number of difficulties which, to overcome, translators and interpreters are urged to opt for a systematic observation of the speech acts being performed, and a careful monitoring of the output to ensure that the response evoked in the hearer of the source text remains intact in the translation (see Anderman 1993 on DRAMA TRANSLATION).

In assessing the potential of speech act analysis, translation and interpreting theorists have shared some of the misgivings expressed by critics of speech act theory. The theory, at least in the initial period of its development, was primarily concerned with combating alternative philosophical views rather than attending to the practical aspects of language use in natural situations. Naturalness is a key term for the practising translator or interpreter, and actual use of language can and does throw up different kinds of problems from those that mainstream speech act theory would wish us to focus on. For instance, there is a huge difference between acts such as 'promising' or 'threatening', on the one hand, and more diffuse acts such as 'stating' or 'describing', on the other. Yet, both types of act tend to be merged under the single heading of 'illocutionary force' (cf. Searle 1969; see critique in de Beaugrande's 1978 study of poetic translating).

Appropriateness conditions beyond the single speech act

In attempting to apply speech act theory to translation and interpreting, translation theorists soon become aware of the fact that a text is not a one-dimensional, linear succession of elements glued one onto the other evenly; rather it is a complex, constructed edifice with some elements enjoying a higher communicative status, some a less prominent one, within an emerging, evolving hierarchic organization (de Beaugrande 1978). It is this insight into the way texts are perceived which underpins an influential body of work on the extension of speech act analysis. Both theoretically and in various domains of applied pragmatics, it has been demonstrated that the interpretation of speech acts depends crucially on their position and status within sequences. The variation in status which underlies the interrelationship of speech acts within sequences leads to the notion of the 'illocutionary structure' of a text, determining its progression and defining its coherence (Ferrara 1980).

In translation studies, it is now accepted that it is this overall effect which has to be relayed and not a series of unstructured sequences whose EQUIVALENCE in the target language is determined piecemeal (i.e. speech act by speech act). A global, more comprehensive view of the force of action has been made possible by the emergence in pragmatics of the notion of the **text act**. Here, the force of a given speech act is assessed not only in terms of its contribution to the cohesion of the 'local' sequence in which it is embedded, but also in terms of the contribution it makes to the 'global' coherence of the entire text (Horner 1975).

In an attempt to extend the analysis beyond the individual speech act, there has been a considerable shift of focus in the analysis of the translation process, and entire text formats began to be considered from the viewpoint of pragmatics. For example, argumentative texts have been found to display a global problem-solving structure, with the 'problem' section being typically 'assertive' in its illocutionary value, and the 'solution' section typically 'directive'. Such global characterizations are informed by both functional and hierarchical criteria governing the various speech acts involved, and ought to

be heeded in their globality by the translator (Tirkkonnen-Condit 1986).

In text type-oriented translation studies, a major issue addressed has been that of the indeterminacy which a particular speech act can exhibit and which can only be resolved by reference to the global organization of the text (Hatim and Mason 1990a). For example, describing a given peace plan as *slightly better* than the previous ones could pragmatically mean 'only slightly and therefore negligibly better' or 'appreciably better', depending on whether the overall stance is pro- or anti-plan. The initial sequence is indeterminate and is settled only when we subsequently read *but there are reasons for hope*. There are languages (e.g. Arabic) which have to mark such distinct meanings and where a number of alternative lexico-grammatical structures are available to cater for the alternative readings intended.

Implied meaning

The study of implied meaning has marked another influential development in the discipline of pragmatics, and one that has had a considerable impact on the theory and practice of translation and interpreting (Malmkjær 1998b; Thomson 1982). Implication may best be understood with reference to the basic assumption of pragmatic analysis that, in communication, being sincere is a social obligation (Austin 1962; Searle 1969, among others). Though not exclusively, implied meanings can be located in the paradigmatic axis of the communicative act, or the level of interaction best captured by the familiar stylistic principle of dealing with 'what is said' against a backdrop of 'what could have been said but wasn't' (Enkvist 1973).

The trend of assessing various degrees of opacity in linguistic expression was led by Grice who, rather than elaborating rules for successful communication, preferred to concentrate on where, how and why the smooth ongoingness of interaction may be intentionally thwarted, leading to various kinds of implicature (Grice 1975). Within what he calls 'the Cooperative Principle', Grice has identified a number of Maxims to which language users conventionally adhere, unless there is a 'good reason' for them not to do so. These Maxims are:

1. Quantity: Make your contribution as informative as is required;
2. Quality: Do not say that for which you lack adequate evidence;
3. Relevance: Be relevant
4. Manner: Be communicatively orderly.

The Maxims may be obeyed or disturbed. Disturbance can take the form of blatant 'breaking' of a Maxim (e.g. due to lack of knowledge), 'violation' (i.e. failure on the part of the speaker to secure the hearer's uptake or acceptability), or 'flouting' (non-compliance with the rules in a motivated, deliberate manner).

The notion of 'implicature' emanating from flouting any of the cooperative Maxims has been shown to be particularly helpful to practising translators and interpreters. In purely receptive terms, appreciation of implied meaning facilitates comprehension, which would otherwise be partial and blurred. In terms of reproducing the message in the target language, on the other hand, the meanings which are implied and not stated could be an important yardstick in assessing the adequacy of a translation, that is, in estimating whether and to what extent intervention on the part of the translator is necessary to secure a reasonable degree of equivalence. This last point is particularly relevant in working with languages which are both culturally and linguistically remote from one another, and where different pragmatic means may have to be chosen to achieve a given ultimate effect.

Within this cross-cultural domain of pragmatic analysis as applied to translation, an interesting assumption has been that, by examining the various rules that govern textual competence in using any language, it might be possible to make predictions regarding the plausibility or otherwise of reconstructing the same degree of 'indirectness' in another language (Blum-Kulka 1981; Thomson 1982). Thus, for example, through failure on the part of the translator to assess the effectiveness of target renderings in preserving implied meanings in the source text, it has been argued, Edward Said's *Orientalism* has lost quite a large chunk of its irony in the published translation into Arabic (Hatim 1997).

Politeness and implicature

Motivated disobedience of any Maxim within the Cooperative Principle, then, gives rise to implicatures. But compliance with these maxims does not fully guarantee total avoidance of producing implied meanings. 'Implying' as opposed to 'explicitly stating' is possible even when a given maxim is adhered to, provided such adherence is opted for in contexts where non-adherence would be the expected norm. One such context may be illustrated by the following example:

Dentist: ...	Why didn't you let me give you gas?
Young Lady:	Because you said it would be five shillings extra.
Dentist:	[shocked] Oh, don't say that. It makes me feel as if I had hurt you for the sake of five shillings.
Young Lady.	[with cool insolence] Well, so you have.

This example is from Shaw's *You Never Can Tell*, analysed in Leech (1993). Typical of Dolly's bluntness of character, the Maxim of Quality is meticulously adhered to and truth is valued no matter what. It is speaking the truth when a white lie would do, however, that in its own way constitutes a flouting of some principle or other, giving rise to an implicature all the same. What is being flouted here is politeness, which sanctions flouting Quality as a norm and deems not doing so a deviation (Leech 1983). This and similar examples have raised important questions for a translation theory that intends to confront cross-cultural pragmatic failures and accounts for the problems thrown up by this particular area of language use. In translating a play like Shaw's into Arabic or Japanese, for example, the hypothesis widely accepted in pragmatically oriented theories of translation is that the more language-bound the rules governing the performance of any indirect speech act, the lower the degree of TRANSLATABILITY (Blum-Kulka 1981). Studies of politeness in translation include Hatim and Mason (1997, chapter 5), Hatim (1998), House (1998), Cambridge (1999), Krouglov (1999), Hickey (2001), Mason and Stewart (2001), and Zitawi (2008), among others.

Relevance in translation

Drawing on Sperber and Wilson (1986/1995), Gutt (1991/2000) describes translation in terms of a general theory of human cognition. This builds on the basic premise that the ability of human beings to 'infer' what is meant may be accounted for in terms of observing the principle of **relevance** (i.e. the tendency to achieve maximum benefit at minimum processing cost). In dealing with what are essentially 'form vs. content' problems, the relevance model of translation invokes a range of communicative criteria, including the issue of 'ordinary' vs. 'non-ordinary' text-based information (de Beaugrande 1978).

According to the theory of relevance, two ways of using language are distinguished: 'descriptive' and 'interpretive'. These reflect two ways through which the mind entertains thoughts. An utterance is said to be 'descriptive' if it is intended to be true of a state of affairs in some possible world. Conversely, an utterance is said to be 'interpretive' if it is intended to represent someone else's thought or utterance. Translation is said to be an instance of 'inter-lingual interpretive use' (Gutt 1991/2000: 136).

The relevance theory of translation deals with situations in which the translator needs to provide not only the same information content as the original, but also the same form in which this information is presented: to reproduce exactly not only what is said, but also how it is said, not only the content but also the style. In relevance theory, the notion of 'communicative clues' is proposed as a possible solution to the problem of inter-linguistic disparity. Communicative clues may be found in any domain and at any level of linguistic analysis. For example, focal effects (such as emphasis) may be achieved by such formal means as prosodic stress in some languages, but not in others. Stress would be a communicative clue which, if unavailable in the target language, can be replaced by syntactic means (e.g. clefting as in 'it is X which ...' or the use of illocutionary particles). In these target languages, **clefting** (like stress) would be a crucial communicative clue.

Based on the distinction between descriptive and interpretive use, Gutt further distinguishes between direct and indirect translation. **Indirect translation** is a case of interpretive use, but so too, ultimately, is **direct translation**. Because languages differ in their structural and lexical make-up, direct translation 'cannot be understood in terms of resemblance in actual linguistic properties' but only in terms of an intention to reproduce the ST's communicative clues (ibid.: 170). Direct translation is therefore a special case of interpretive use (ibid.: 169). Gutt (1991/2000: 210) further argues that 'the distinction between translation and non-translation hinges first and foremost on *the way the target text is intended to achieve relevance*' (emphasis in original), and that therefore 'attempts of looking for a definition of translation in terms of intrinsic structural properties of the text ... must be of questionable validity' (ibid.: 211).

Serious reservations about the value of relevance theory in translation have been expressed by a number of translation theorists (e.g. Tirkkonnen-Condit 1993; Malmkjær 1992; Thomas 1994) on a number of grounds, including the vexed question of how and by whom the various 'rankings of relevance' are to be determined in particular contexts of translation. Gutt attempts to respond to these criticisms systematically in a lengthy Postscript he attaches to the 2000 edition of his 1991 book (Gutt 1991/2000: 202–38). Extended applications of relevance theory to translation include Setton (1999) and Hill (2006).

See also:
CULTURE; DISCOURSE ANALYSIS; FUNCTIONALIST APPROACHES; LINGUISTIC APPROACHES.

Further reading
Blum-Kulka 1981; Gutt 1991/2000; Andermann 1993; Hickey 1998; Mart'nez 1998; Setton 1998, 1999; Hickey 2001; Mason and Stewart 2001; Hill 2006; Mason 2006b.

BASIL HATIM

Pseudotranslation

The compound noun *pseudo-translation*, as the Greek etymon *pseudés* (= false) suggests, refers to a target-oriented practice of imitative composition which results in texts that are perceived as translations but which are not, as they usually lack an actual source text. In other words, it refers to a relationship of imitation which does not link a target text to a specific source text but rather to an ideal one, possibly abstracted from a group of texts identifying a particular genre. In the latter case, pseudotranslators often draw on a class of texts (which might constitute a specific literary genre or an entire literary system), selecting and condensing certain features that they aim to introduce into their own literary system. See LOCALIZATION for a different use of the term 'pseudotranslation' in the computing industry.

The first use of the term 'pseudotranslation' dates back to 1823, in a review of Alexis's *Walladmor* for *The Literary Gazette and Journal of the Belle-Lettres, Arts, Sciences*, as a synonym of 'free translation'. Since then, the term has been applied to a wide range of literary products (see, for example, Radó 1979; Genette 1982; Torrens 1994; O'Sullivan 2004–2005). However, it is the character of pseudotranslation as a reciprocal relationship between a present text and its sources, in spite of the apparent absence of the latter, that has gained ground in translation studies, in particular in Descriptive Translation Studies (see DESCRIPTIVE VERSUS COMMITTED APPROACHES).

Establishing a tradition a posteriori

The starting point for the dissemination of the concept of pseudotranslation was Popovič's definition of it as an 'original work' published by its author 'as a fictitious translation' with the explicit aim 'to win a wide public, thus making use of the reader's expectation' (1976: 20). This definition, which already proposed a possible reason for authors to hide their identities, was immediately appropriated and integrated into studies by scholars working within the framework of POLYSYSTEM theory. In 1980, for example, Toury redefined pseudotranslations as 'TL texts which are regarded in the target culture as translations though no genuine STs exist for them' (1980a: 31). The following year, Yahalom underlined their use as a literary strategy, putting them on the same level as other literary 'forgeries' that do not necessarily involve movement across linguistic systems, such as pseudo-letters and pseudo-memoirs

(1981: 153). In 1984, Lefevere, in turn, spoke of pseudotranslations as 'refractions of texts' even if those texts 'on closer scrutiny, turn out not to exist at all' (1984: 233).

What characterizes pseudotranslations is therefore the reference to a source or proto-text, or rather, to a group of texts to which the alleged source text belongs. To effect this reference, authors have several tools at their disposal: they can explicitly present a text as a translation, or they can 'creolize' it, by scattering across its pages signals of 'translationese', such as lexical items and syntactic constructs peculiar to the source language and culture. By privileging pseudotranslation over translation, the target culture author signals an interest in certain aspects of the source culture in their entirety, rather than in one single literary expression of it. We could therefore say that at the very moment in which a pseudotranslator writes a text, he or she also shapes its source text by gathering together all the elements of the source culture they aim to transfer into their own culture.

Motivations

Underlying Popovič's (1976) claim that pseudotranslations exploit the reader's expectations in order to win a wider public is the assumption that cultures are inclined to accept innovations more easily from outside, in the belief that they can confine such changes within the boundaries of the exotic. From this standpoint, Lefevere sees the strategy of pseudotranslating as a sort of 'strong patronage', under which innovative – and possibly subversive – material can gain 'the necessary manoeuvring space' for itself (1984: 233; see also REWRITING). Likewise, Toury, from the perspective of literary evolution, describes it as an effective way – 'sometimes the only way' (1984: 83) – at a writer's disposal to renovate their literary system. Contemporary examples of pseudotranslations that fulfil this function are particularly common in the field of science fiction (Sohár 1998). Santoyo (1984) further points out that pseudotranslations result in a shift in the author's narrative standpoint which enables them to bring to the fore their role as readers without completely denying their status as authors.

A pseudotranslation becomes recognized

as such only when the overlapping identity of its author and translator is brought to light: until then, the text is simply a translation. Pseudotranslators can therefore substantially preserve the authoritativeness associated with original authors without being subject to the same restrictions. This allows them, as Santoyo (1984: 46–8) observes, to exploit the prestige of supposed originals in order to overcome readers' reservations (as in the case of *El caballero Cifar*, pseudotranslated in the fourteenth century from Chaldean into Latin: that is, from an extremely ancient work – authoritative in itself – through the mediation of an equally authoritative language). It also allows them to keep their names secret for social reasons – as in the case of Horace Walpole, son of a former Prime Minister, who ascribed his *The Castle of Otranto* to Onuphrio Muralto (in 1764) – or for humorous purposes, as Nathaniel Hawthorne did by ascribing *Rappacini's Daughter* in 1844 to 'Monsieur de l'Aubepine', a translation of his surname into French. Pseudotranslations also allow their writers to criticize the norms and traditions of their own countries by adopting the persona of the 'ingenuous traveller' (cf. the 1684 novel *L'esploratore turco* by Giovanni Paolo Marana, ascribed to the Arab spy Mahmut).

Toury (1995) identifies other reasons for authors resorting to this device. One such reason is the intention to try their hand at new genres without compromising their previous reputation: a good example is *Gengaeldsens veje* by Karen Blixen, who ascribed her 1944 novel to Pierre Andrézel and its translation into Danish to her secretary Clara Svendsen. Another reason is an author's 'fear of censorial measures', as in the case of the satirical *Lettres Persanes* (1721) by Montesquieu, who did not hesitate to pillory both political and religious aspects of contemporary French society, including the monarchical system itself (see CENSORSHIP). Toury also notes that the prestige of the alleged source text (or genre) can be partly transferred to its pseudotranslation, so that the latter can establish itself as a model of the same literary genre in the target culture, turning from metatext into prototext.

Pseudotranslations have often served as prototypes for new literary genres. This was the case in Italy, where Boiardo's *Orlando Innamorato* (1483, a pseudotranslation from French) provided a model for chivalrous poetry; in Spain, with Cervantes' *Don Quijote* (1605, ascribed to the Arab historian Cide Hamete Benengeli), often referred to as the 'first modern novel'; and in Germany, where Holz und Schlaf's *Papa Hamlet* (1889, a pseudotranslation from Norwegian) was one of the most important forerunners of the so-called 'konsequenter Naturalismus'.

Venuti (1998b) includes new conceptions of authorship among the innovations that pseudotranslations can introduce into the target culture, thus going beyond the formal and content aspects of the texts and highlighting the social role and position of their authors, as well as issues of patronage, readership and book market. This function of pseudotranslations is illustrated by the numerous eighteenth-century novels dedicated to the figure of the *philosophe*, usually ascribed to French or English authors. One of the most eloquent examples, the novel *Le Lord Impromptu* (1767) by Cazotte, is particularly interesting because of the way paratexts are used to frame not only the fictitious source text but also its fictitious author (Rambelli 2004). Cazotte states in his preface that he translated the work from the English novel *The White Witcherast*, by an anonymous writer. In 1805, *Le Lord Impromptu* was translated into Italian by an anonymous writer who decided to go back to the alleged original title (translated as *La magia bianca*) and to further elaborate the figure of its alleged author, whom he called Fassdown. The Italian translator added to the novel a dedicatory letter by the fictitious Fassdown to an Italian friend, and a second letter by a French acquaintance of Fassdown, the abbot Parruque-Blonde, to the anonymous translator. All these 'disguises' allow the Italian writer to describe and compare the difficulties experienced by intellectuals in finding a new social position after the disappearance of the courtier system in three different cultural polysystems (Italian, French and British). Du Pont (2005) offers a detailed discussion of similar attempts to frame a non-fictitious writer, Robert Graves, as the author of a pseudotranslation, using various strategies to explain stylistic differences between existing writings by Graves and the pseudotranslation attributed to him.

A device for cultural transitions

As previous examples demonstrate, it is possible to find pseudotranslations in any epoch, but this practice tends to intensify in periods of profound political and social transformation, since it enables intellectuals to introduce innovations into their own cultural polysystems more easily, while at the same time drawing readers' attention to the role of these intellectuals as cultural mediators. Pseudotranslations have thus often played a prominent part in the establishment of national identities and consciousness, endowing texts such as the *Historia Regum Britanniae* (1136–48), the *Parzival* (1200–16, linked to French and Arab originals), Boiardo's *Orlando Innamorato* (1483, ascribed to the French bishop Turpin) and the Ossianic poems (1760–63) with prestige by virtue of the antiquity and intrinsic authoritativeness of the language of the alleged source text. Wolfram von Eschenbach, for example, pretended to refer to a non-existent Provençal poem in order to reinvigorate the subject of *Perceval*, while Geoffrey of Monmouth claimed that he translated his *Historia Regum Britanniae* from 'a certain very ancient book written in the British language' (Geoffrey of Monmouth 1966: 51).

Moving from the Middle Ages to the eighteenth century, the best-known case is James Macpherson's pivotal pseudotranslation of the Ossianic poems (*Fragments of Ancient Poetry, Fingal* and *Temora*), allegedly from Gaelic, which supported the romantic hypothesis that poetry was not a matter of rhetorical devices but a natural and primitive form of expression. The poems consequently not only constituted a major point of reference for Scottish national pride but also served as a model for other cultures which sought epic cycles of foundation, such as Finland, where Elias Lönnrot's *Kalevala* (1835–44) drew on genuine folk poetry.

Further developments

As a relatively recent discipline, translation studies has often adopted terms and concepts developed in other fields. The concept of pseudotranslation, however, seems to have travelled in the opposite direction, proving extremely productive in cultural studies, particularly in the study of phenomena such as transnationalism and postcolonialism. Pseudotranslations highlight both the role of writers as cultural mediators and the strategies, methods and reasons of cultural transfer and innovations, even in the borderline case in which they do not involve any textual transformation (see, for example, Borges's apologue on Pierre Menard who, by rewriting the *Quixote* word-for-word, ends up composing a novel perfectly identical to the original but, at the same time, totally new, because the same words take on a completely different meaning when they are written by a Spaniard in the eighteenth century or by a Frenchman in the nineteenth century).

See also:
ADAPTATION; CENSORSHIP; DECONSTRUCTION; FICTIONAL REPRESENTATIONS; LITERARY TRANSLATION; POLYSYSTEM.

Further reading
Thomas 1951; Popovič 1975, 1976; Radó 1979; Toury 1980a; Even-Zohar 1981; Yahalom 1981; Lefevere 1984; Santoyo 1984; Toury 1984; Torrens 1994; Toury 1995; Venuti 1998b; O'Sullivan 2004–5; Rambelli 2004; Du Pont 2005; Rambelli 2006.

PAOLO RAMBELLI

Psycholinguistic and cognitive approaches

The loose grouping of psycholinguistic and cognitive approaches to the study of translation and interpreting subsumes a number of quite disparate theoretical views and empirical/ methodological practices. Developments in this area of translation studies have been and still are driven by developments in cognitive psychology, (cognitive) linguistics, psycholinguistics and computational linguistics, these being the main sources of theoretical and methodological insight. The influence of these 'feeder' disciplines (Malmkjær 2000: 165) is found in issues related to theory, data and method. Importantly, however, this area of translation research has reached a stage in its evolution where developments are also internally generated: theory and method, in particular, are developing along paths that are motivated by translational questions, in addition to more general linguistic or cognitive ones.

The diversity of approaches encompassed by the label 'psycholinguistic/cognitive' share a basic foundation: a concern with the role of knowledge, linguistic and otherwise, and cognitive processes in translation and/or interpreting. This basic concern is manifested in a number of ways, primarily in the focus on investigating processing phenomena through a set of shared methods. Despite this broad common interest there are also important differences between the practitioners of different research programmes. Even key assumptions such as those relating to the relationship between general cognitive processes and linguistic ones vary within theories of cognition and language. This is indeed a heterogeneous area.

It is difficult to maintain a strict division between the study of translation and the study of interpreting in this field. The boundaries of these two categories do not correspond consistently to relevant distinctions of any kind – theoretical, empirical or methodological. For that reason, a distinction between translation and interpreting will be pointed out in this entry only where necessary or particularly relevant.

Research that is identified as being inspired by the disciplines of cognitive psychology or psycholinguistics is also often identified as 'process-oriented'. This term is often used in contrast to 'product-oriented' research, which is then assumed to represent a concern with translations as linguistic artifacts. This distinction, though perhaps expedient for some purposes, is becoming increasingly difficult to uphold, thanks to new sets of theoretical assumptions and methodological developments (see Toury 1995:11ff.). The term will be used where relevant in discussing the work of scholars who opt to use it.

Key issues

In the preface to one of the few volumes specifically dedicated to cognitive processes in translation and interpreting, Shreve and Danks suggest a number of initial questions that the work presented in that volume seeks to address:

♦ What are the unique characteristics of translation and interpreting relative to monolingual languaging processes?
♦ How are the cognitive processes of translation and interpreting the same as, and different than, monolingual reading, writing, speaking, and listening?
♦ What is the relationship between bilingual language processing and translation/interpreting skill?
♦ What cognitive learning mechanisms can account for the development of translation and interpreting abilities?
♦ What are the important cognitive parameters of the translation and interpreting tasks?
♦ What methods and models can be used to investigate the cognitive processes of translation and interpreting?
                    (Shreve and Danks 1977: viii)

Although this list is now several years old, it continues to present a relevant set of issues for this particular area of translation and interpreting research. Recent and ongoing research presents further refinement or more specific perspectives on these basic concerns. For instance, ongoing research in bilingualism is contributing to knowledge that is pertinent to the first, second and third questions on the list, while recent developments in cognitive linguistics allow for further elaboration of the penultimate question concerning cognitive parameters that pertain to linguistic tasks and the final question on research models and methods. Research within translation and interpreting studies itself addresses all of these questions, though some are more central than others.

In sum, researchers within this area of translation and interpreting research are interested in general characteristics of bilingual language processing, specific characteristics of translation/interpreting and the cognitive constraints on such processing, the relationships between the overall skill and the various subskills that comprise these complex activities, the development of translation/interpreting abilities in bilinguals and the effects of particular developmental pathways on specific performance variables.

Data and methods

Researchers interested in translation and interpreting processes have incorporated models and methodologies from cognitive psychology and psycholinguistics for several decades, with an early bulk of work dating from the 1970s (for a review of relevant interpreting studies, see Moser-Mercer 1997). This entry focuses on work done primarily from the 1990s up to the present, as this is work that still enjoys some currency in the field.

Traditional experimental methods that have been applied to or borrowed for translation and interpreting research include psycholinguistic experiments used in bilingualism research and THINK-ALOUD PROTOCOLS of various types, borrowed from cognitive psychology. A third type, keystroke logging, is a method that has emerged more recently within translation studies research. This is an adaptation of a methodology used in cognitive studies of text production (see Jakobsen 2006, and other papers in the same volume). These three basic types of experimental methods will be discussed in turn.

Studies in the psycholinguistic area of bilingualism research have a long tradition of incorporating translation-related tasks. Importantly, such studies are not designed for the purposes of researching translation as such. Translation/interpreting tasks are seen as a means to an end, and that end is the elaboration or testing of theories of bilingual semantic representation or bilingual language processing. The methods involved here include variations on word-translation tasks: normal word translation, cued word translation (in which the first letter of the target word is given) and 'translation recognition', with the dependent variables usually being response time, percentage errors and percentage omissions (in production tasks) (de Groot 1997: 33–4). Studies within this research paradigm involve laboratory experi-

ments and primarily quantitative analyses of the data. There are variations on the type of task, and later studies also incorporate context into word- and sentence-translation tasks. De Groot summarizes her review of this work as follows:

> the scattered studies have already revealed many of the relevant variables: the signal-to-noise ratio and input rate in simultaneous interpretation as well as structuredness, syntactic ambiguity, and word characteristics of the input. They have also suggested that the language switch and the conversion (rephrasing) process that are both required in translation contribute separately to the complexity of the full task. Finally they have pointed at a number of the sources of the effects of the variables that have been identified.
>
> (1997: 56)

Thus in de Groot's view, these findings from psycholinguistic bilingualism research clearly indicate avenues for further work on translation and interpreting.

The main criticism levelled by translation and interpreting scholars at experimental psycholinguistic methods has been what is claimed to be a lack of 'ecological validity' (Tirkkonen-Condit 2000: vii). The argument here has been that the isolation of sub-skills and the use of translation involving linguistic units in isolation make the results invalid for theorizing translation and interpreting. This criticism is not trivial. On the other hand, as de Groot points out,

> disclosing many of the determinants of the translation of isolated words has been worthwhile, if only because during the translation of text, all bilinguals, also those with a high level of proficiency in both SL and TL, as well as experts in translation occasionally seem to relapse into word-to-word translation.
>
> (1997: 43)

In addition to the point raised by de Groot, one might also suggest that while the results of these tests may not be *directly* applicable to translation and interpreting issues, the models of bilingual processing and semantic representation that they address and support are (see Christoffels and de Groot 2005 for a good example). In other words, translation and interpreting studies may not always be able to make direct use of the results, but the discipline can ill afford to disregard theoretical accounts of bilingual language processing and semantic representation.

The second experimental method to be dealt with here, unlike the first one, has been widely used within the translation and interpreting studies community itself: THINK-ALOUD PROTOCOLS (TAPs). Originally borrowed from cognitive psychology, this method has evolved into several varieties, all of which involve verbalization of thought processes during a translation or interpreting exercise. The objective is to gain insight into the translation/interpreting process through introspection. Indeed, the use of TAP methodology has been nearly synonymous with 'process-oriented' research.

TAPs research has produced book-length investigations (e.g. Krings 1986; Lörscher 1991; Jääskeläinen 1999) as well as collections of articles (e.g. Tirkkonen-Condit and Jääskeläinen 2000) and numerous journal articles. The method has developed over time, and there are now several versions of it, including real-time verbalization, retrospective verbalization and joint verbalization/dialogue, though some authors (cf. THINK-ALOUD PROTOCOLS) restrict their use of 'TAPs' to methods that involve *concurrent* verbalization. Criticism aimed at the method has raised questions regarding the accessibility of automated knowledge (which represents a sizable portion of translational/interpreting activity) and the danger that verbalization might disturb or distort the translation/interpreting process, thus yielding unreliable data.

The third method used in investigating cognitive aspects of the translation process is of more recent origin, and goes under the generic label of keystroke logging. Developed by Arnt Lykke Jakobsen in Denmark specifically to support research into translation, keystroke logging is a means of acquiring information about a translator's real-time decision-making processes. The software logs all keystrokes, including backspacing and deletions, and also records the time the strokes were made and the intervals between them. Jakobsen describes

the log data as a source of information on the various stages of creating a translation and the timing of the various actions taken along the way. Jakobsen argues that '[t]he rhythm and speed with which a target text was produced could then be studied as a kind of prosody of writing reflecting the cognitive rhythm of meaning construction' (2006: 96). Various process-related phenomena are amenable to keystroke logging investigation: text revision, text segmentation (see Dragsted 2004 for a full-length study), links between pauses and various adjacent text actions, the distribution of sub-tasks, and the 'pulse' as Jakobsen calls it, i.e. the 'rhythm arising from the alternation of key tapping and pausing, which is a reflection of "cognitive rhythm"' (2006: 104).

A number of scholars are implementing studies in which keystroke log data is supplemented by other types of data, as Jakobsen points out (2006: 103–4). Jakobsen himself has used log data in combination with TAPs (2003); Hansen (2005) has combined log data with retrospection data; Ida Rambek of the University of Oslo is currently combining log data with screen logging. The most commonly used logging program, TRANSLOG, may now be used in conjunction with multiple data collection modes, including audio recording and eye-tracking. Halverson (2006) has argued for a combination of corpus, log data and eye-tracking data: in other words, a combination of linguistic (textual) and processing data.

These new empirical approaches, often working towards triangulation of methods to test their hypotheses, represent real advances in the study of the cognitive processes involved in translation and interpreting.

Theoretical developments

Translation and interpreting scholars who adopt psycholinguistic or cognitive approaches in their work draw on theoretical developments within their respective feeder disciplines while framing their work to ensure relevance for theory development in their own field. As far as psycholinguistic theories of bilingualism are concerned, there are numerous developments that are relevant to the study of translation and interpreting. In a recent review of this area of bilingualism research, Kroll and Tokowicz (2005: 531–2) point out the key areas in which our understanding of bilingual language processing and the bilingual lexicon are currently changing. These include discrimination between different levels of representation (e.g. representation of orthography, phonology, semantics and syntax), discrimination between what is processed and how it is represented, the separation of the various sub-skills which comprise the whole (comprehension, production, memory), and finally taking into account the consequences of differences in bilingual acquisition histories. The immediate relevance for translation and interpreting research lies in the more highly refined process models being elaborated, the new models of bilingual representation, and the recognition of the effect of varying bilingual histories on language performance (for a state-of-the art review, see Kroll and de Groot's *Handbook of Bilingualism* 2005).

Cognitive perspectives on translation and interpreting follow the generational developments of cognitive science at large. What have sometimes been referred to as first-generation models conceptualize cognition as an information processing activity, and the models devised resemble broader information processing models. One comprehensive (and representative) translational model of this type is Bell (1991); early interpreting models developed along similar lines include Gerver (1976) and Moser (1976, 1978). These are gradually being replaced by so-called second-generation models in which distributed processing, spreading activation and network models of knowledge representation, are favoured. Certain aspects of this type of work, or work related to it, have been or are being adapted from cognitive linguistics for the purposes of translation research by Snell-Hornby (1988, 2005), Tabakowska (1993, 2000), Kussmaul (1994, 2000a), Halverson (1998, 1999, 2003, 2006), Risku (2002), Jansen (2004) and Sergo and Thome (2005), among others. An intermediate position is represented by relevance-theoretic views of cognitive processes. From this perspective, a modular theory of mind and a theory of cognition are linked to a theory of communication. This approach has been applied to translation by Gutt (1991/2000) and to interpreting by Setton (1999). The latter also incorporates other cognitive theoretical approaches.

Findings and areas of future research

Psycholinguistic and cognitive approaches to the study of translation represent a continuation of the discipline's long tradition of interdisciplinary dialogue. In this area, the dialogue has revolved primarily around issues of theory, data and method in the investigation of the translation process. The work undertaken so far has contributed to issues addressed in the final two questions outlined in the introduction to this entry: the cognitive parameters of translation and interpreting tasks and the methods and models that can be used in their investigation. Three main issues that demonstrate aspects of both theoretical and methodological development are discussed below: translational expertise, directionality, and semantic representation and processing.

Translational expertise has been investigated in several TAP and TRANSLOG studies. Differences between novices and experts have been found along such dimensions as problem identification and resolution (Krings 1986; Lörscher 1991; Jääskeläinen 1999) and automization. For instance, experts are found to identify more problems, and problems at a more global level, than novices; experts have been found to switch between more automatic and more deliberate modes (see THINK-ALOUD PROTOCOLS). In addition, experts have been found to process larger segments than novices; in one study the difference was identified as clause versus phrase segments for experts and novices, respectively (see Dragsted 2004: 354–5). The clause is also identified by Christoffels and de Groot as the unit of processing in interpreting (2005: 457).

Directionality is attracting increasing interest in the discipline today (see DIRECTIONALITY, this volume). The direction of translation is also a highly relevant topic in the bilingualism community, as it touches on issues such as language dominance, bilingual acquisition history and language atrophy. In one key model, the acquisition pathway followed by each bilingual is assumed to affect the pattern of linkages within his or her bilingual lexicon (Kroll and Stewart 1994; Kroll and Tokowicz 2005). The strength and type of these connections then affect translation performance in a bilingual's two directions; the effects will also change over the course of bilingual development. In their review of interpreting studies, Christoffels and de Groot state that 'there is little experimental evidence in support of any directional effect' (2005: 464) and argue that the actual language combination might be more significant for the interpreting process than the translation direction (ibid.: 465). If this proves to hold also for translation, it will indeed be an important finding. Translation and interpreting scholars must therefore make a concerted effort to test for direction effects and for evidence of changes in any pattern of effects that might be found over the course of bilingual development and translator/interpreter training.

Both of these issues, expertise and directionality, are inherently linked to models of bilingual semantic representation and processing. The issues at stake here are many; for the purposes of translation and interpreting studies, the most relevant one is arguably the extent of conceptual versus lexical processing, or what Christoffels and de Groot describe as 'meaning-based' and 'transcoding' (2005: 459). These two modes of processing imply different roles for the linguistic form itself. In an extreme 'meaning-based' translation process, the linguistic form would serve only as a means of accessing the conceptual level, and selection of a target structure would take place on the basis of meaning comprehension. In 'transcoding', on the other hand, links between linguistic forms in a bilingual's two languages may allow a short cut from one language to another. In other words, less meaning is activated, and the forms do more of the work in moving from one language to another. According to Christoffels and de Groot (2005: 471), both forms of processing are likely to occur in translation. This was also the conclusion reached in a study of lexical similarity vs. dissimilarity in which the author suggests that the degree of form-based processing in interpreting might be greater than previously assumed (Dam 1998). Pressing research questions thus include the extent of both kinds of processing, the variation between the two modes in different types of bilinguals and/or translators, and variation in modes as related to translation direction.

As outlined here, the findings in this area seem disparate and fragmented. This is, perhaps, a natural result of the fact that the feeder disciplines are evolving rapidly. Our knowledge of cognition, including language representation and processing, is expanding and developing at an extraordinary pace. As regards translation and interpreting studies, the most productive research in this area has been the process-oriented research based on TAPs and keystroke logging methods. However, it is imperative that the findings of these investigations be linked, or at least made interpretable, within broader frameworks of language representation and processing in bilingual or multilingual individuals.

On a related note, the findings mentioned here make it imperative that the links between the translation process and its tangible products be dealt with in a more critical fashion. Theoretical models that incorporate features of semantic representation and of processing, and methodological approaches that combine, for instance, corpus data, keystroke logging and eye-tracking, or keystroke logging and retrospective introspection, and even keystroke logging on its own (which provides both a translation and a record of its creation in real time), all indicate that a clear distinction between process and product is becoming increasingly problematic. Clearly, it is a relevant distinction to uphold in some cases. But developments in this area have demonstrated the promise of considering product and process in a more holistic way, and we may therefore expect psycholinguistic and cognitive approaches to translation and interpreting to yield more significant findings in the decades to come.

See also:
CONFERENCE INTERPRETING, HISTORICAL AND COGNITIVE PERSPECTIVES; DIRECTIONALITY; THINK-ALOUD PROTOCOLS.

Further reading
Gerver 1976; Danks *et al.* 1997; Dam 1998; Halverson 1999; Tirkkonen-Condit and Jääs-keläinen 2000; Halverson 2003; Dragsted 2004; Christoffels and de Groot 2005; Kroll and de Groot 2005; Jakobsen 2006.

SANDRA HALVERSON

Publishing strategies

The term 'publishing strategies' refers to the speculative process by which books are chosen to be translated and published in other languages: despite their cultural significance, the production of books is generally regulated by entirely commercial forces. Although the results of this speculative process are uneven both in historical terms and across cultural boundaries, the process itself is neither random nor unmotivated. Indeed, according to Venuti (1995a), the very choice of a foreign text to translate is dependent on domestic cultural values. Although this entry largely addresses the issue within a European and North American context, similar underlying principles may be seen in operation elsewhere.

Translation rate, category and flow

The number of books published every year in translation varies significantly from country to country. In 1991, for example, although some 67,628 books were published in the UK, only 3 per cent of these (1,689 titles) were translations. In Germany, a country with a comparable output, some 67,890 books were published of which 14 per cent (9,557 titles) were translations. Meanwhile, in Portugal, although only 6,430 books were published, 44 per cent of these (2,809 titles) were in translation. Though the number of new titles published each year in all three countries has risen dramatically in the course of the last fifteen years, there is little evidence to suggest any significant changes in the underlying rate of translation. In 2005, though Britain produced some 206,000 new titles, the translation rate remained static at around 3 per cent (or even dipped slightly to nearer 2 per cent). In Germany and Portugal, on the other hand, the rate of translation has remained robust despite significant expansion in the publishing industry.

Falling between these extremes of high output/low translation rate as represented by the UK and the USA, and low output/high translation rate as represented by Portugal, we find countries such as Italy (40,487 books published in 1991 of which 26 per cent were translations),

Spain (43,896 books of which 24 per cent were translations), and France (39,525 books, 18 per cent of which were translations). (These statistics are drawn from a report prepared for the Council of Europe by BIPE Conseil in 1993; more recent statistics with regard to the UK are taken from the UK Book Publishing Statistics Yearbook 2007 produced by the Publishers Association.)

Although the translation rate may be broadly indicative of the cultural acceptance of translation in a particular country, from the point of view of publishing strategies two further sets of statistics are required before it is possible to draw any general conclusions: the category of works published (i.e. Academic/Professional; School/ELT; Children's; Non-Fiction/Reference; and Fiction) and translation flow (i.e. the language of origin of translations). With respect to category, for example, of the total number of books published in the UK in 2006, Academic and Professional (which includes the highly lucrative STM, or SCIENTIFIC, TECHNICAL and Medical field) accounted for 8 per cent of market share; School/ELT for 21 per cent; Children's books for 24 per cent; Non-Fiction/Reference (including biographies, for example) for 20 per cent; and Fiction for 27 per cent. One reason why it is difficult to compare statistics across cultures, however, is the fact that other language areas present different profiles with regard to publishing category. The situation in Belgium, for example, is complicated by the country's linguistic diversity and the problems encountered by a publishing industry which is competing, with regard to French-language publishing, with powerful and well-organized Parisian publishing houses and, with regard to Flemish-language publishing, with Dutch publishing houses with well-defined expertise in areas such as the social sciences. One consequence of this is that, historically, Belgium has not sought to compete in the area of science and technology but has developed a niche in the market for CHILDREN'S LITERATURE and COMIC strips (which in the early 1990s accounted for more than 40 per cent of new titles). More generally, the Belgian situation is typical of small countries situated in larger language areas where the domination of foreign publishing houses tends to force local firms into specialization. In China, on the other hand, the world's fastest growing market (with 190,000 books published in 2003), almost 50 per cent of purchases relate to text books.

In terms of translation flow, 60 per cent of translations published in Europe are of works originally written in British or American English; a further 14 per cent are originally written in French and another 10 per cent in German. Nonetheless, it is possible to distinguish 'zones of influence' specific to particular language areas. In the LITERARY field, for example, the cultural cohesion of northern European countries (Belgium, Denmark and the Netherlands) is demonstrated by the fact that German is the second most translated language after English, while in southern Europe French is everywhere the second most translated language. Obviously, it is not possible here to present a picture of the global publishing industry, but it is likely that an analysis of publishing practices in other regions according to translation rate, category and flow would reveal similar patterns.

General trade publishers

Given the extent of Anglo-American hegemony (not only in Europe but also in Africa, Asia and South America), it is useful to discuss the organization of the publishing industry in Britain and the USA. As Feather (1993: 171) has noted, the 1970s and 1980s were characterized in both countries by a pattern of conglomeration. By 2007, this has resulted in a situation whereby the publishing industry in Britain, North America, and increasingly in much of Europe, is dominated by a small number of international groups. The largest players are Reed Elsevier (an Anglo-Dutch media company); Pearson (a UK media company); Rupert Murdoch's News International (which owns HarperCollins, the latter created by the takeover of Collins in the UK and Harper and Row in the USA in the early 1980s); the German media group Bertelsmann (which owns Random House); and Hachette Filipacchi (which is in turn part of a much larger French conglomerate and which owns a tranche of well-known UK publishing imprints). The Random House 'family', for example, now includes Knopf (acquired in 1960), Doubleday, Bantam, Dell, Ballantine, Dial Press, Clarkson Potter, Three Rivers and Delacorte (amongst

others) in the US; and the Bodley Head, Chatto & Windus (acquired in 1987), Jonathan Cape and Virago (amongst others) in the UK. As will be seen from the example of Random House, the process of conglomeration has resulted in the *de facto* disappearance of a large number of independent publishers, some with histories dating back a hundred years or more.

Chatto & Windus, for example, emerged in 1873 when Andrew Chatto, a junior partner of the disreputable John Camden Hotten, entered into business with a minor poet named W. E. Windus. Unlike other emergent Victorian publishers, such as Vizetelly (who clearly saw translation from French as the primary strategy on which to create a successful business), Hotten's strategy involved producing pirate editions of North American writers, particularly Mark Twain. Though Chatto & Windus developed into a highly reputable publishing house in the twentieth century, the initial problem for any publisher, but especially those specializing in fiction, concerns the recruitment of a suitable stable of authors. In the 1920s, the American publisher Alfred A. Knopf regularly travelled as far afield as Sweden, Norway, Denmark, Germany and South America in search of authors: his firm's 1925 list, for example, included Knut Hamsum, André Gide and Thomas Mann (Tebbel 1987: 229–31).

Even after the Second World War, American publishers still continued to issue a 'large but select body of translations mostly from European languages' (Venuti 1992: 5). Since then, however, there has been a steady decline in the publishing of translations – a decline which has coincided with the conglomeration of the American publishing industry. The pursuit of profit or, more precisely, the redirection of investment towards more potentially profitable areas of a conglomerate's activities, can lead to the eclipse of culturally significant imprints, including those specializing in translations. In terms of English-language publishing, recent years have also been marked by a decline in the phenomenon of the occasional translation which becomes a best-seller, such as Umberto Eco's *The Name of the Rose* (1983) or Peter Høeg's *Smilla's Sense of Snow* (1993; UK title: *Miss Smilla's Feeling for Snow*).

One particularly important issue is the changing role of the editor. In larger firms, specialist editors are responsible for different parts of the list. With respect to the social sciences, for example, they frequently visit academic institutions in order to seek out potential authors. Editors, who are often only salaried employees of the company, are subject to financial pressures to discover titles which will not only bring prestige to the firm but also prove to be profitable. Consequently, they will only take on authors who have already established considerable reputations in their own country and, preferably, already been translated into English. Schulte (1990: 2), amongst others, has further suggested that 'the presentation of new writers is further complicated by the fact that most editors at [English-speaking] publishing houses are unable to read works in their original language in contrast to editors at European publishing houses who are in general quite familiar with English – and must therefore rely on the advice and taste of others'. Schulte also argues that since translators are 'in a position to initiate the flow of works from other countries into English', they should become 'the key figure in the establishment of cross-cultural communication' (ibid.: 1). With respect to literature, however, there is an increasing tendency for English and American editors to rely, at least in the first instance, on agents and events such as the annual Frankfurt Book Fair rather than on the advice of translators.

In countries where family publishers are still the norm, editors build up formal or informal networks of informants (including translators) whose role it is to write reports on manuscripts which have been offered to the firm or even to propose titles of their own accord. In the latter case, they may be paid a small royalty on sales (such as 1 per cent), even if they take no further part in preparing the manuscript for press. The extent of these networks and the informal rules regulating their behaviour varies from publishing house to publishing house and from country to country.

Cultural and academic presses

Venuti (1992: 5) has suggested that the small rise in the number of English-language translations being brought out by Anglo-American publishers towards the end of the 1980s was a consequence of general trade publishers being forced 'to compete against new translation initiatives at university and small presses'. Although the total number of titles issued each year by academic and what might better be termed 'cultural' presses is small in comparison to that achieved by general trade publishers, they are worth discussing here since collectively and even, in some cases, individually they are capable of exerting a not inconsiderable cultural influence.

From a purely economic point of view, publishing offers a number of advantages. Publishing is not capital-intensive; the entrepreneur can concentrate on developing a specialist or niche market; alternative marketing strategies, especially involving the Internet, may help maximize profits; and overheads may be minimized, especially if the publisher operates from his or her own premises. More generally, the economies of large-scale ventures are not so great as to preclude small-scale operations: a general trade publisher might consider a print run of three thousand as financially unjustifiable; a cultural press might judge a similar print run a great success. And finally, there are no impediments to entering the market. Nonetheless, the financial existence of such presses not only in the USA and western Europe but elsewhere is often precarious, and those involved (whether as publishers, translators or authors) frequently depend on salaries earned from activities such as teaching. More worrying is the belief held by many commentators that print media is experiencing a slow but steady worldwide decline. Indeed, British and North American fiction publishing, which is increasingly dependent on heavy discounting (especially to supermarkets), is also showing signs of an accelerated polarization. In 2006, the fifty best-selling titles accounted for a quarter of all fiction sales in the UK.

It is encouraging, therefore, that of the two thousand publishers in existence in the UK, the majority might be described as cultural presses. Immune from the exigencies of corporate finance, many take a long-term view of their own success and not a few are motivated primarily by a quest for prestige, whether on behalf of their founders, their authors or, more generally, the literary or political tendency which they advance. Cultural presses, however, are capable of producing works of a highly innovative nature, particularly in the fields of contemporary literature (including translation and poetry), special/regional interests, and social/political commentary. Indeed, as Schulte (1990: 2) has remarked, '[t]he burden of bringing new international writers onto the American [and, one should also add, British] market falls upon the small presses'. For cultural publishers of this kind, the selection of material and the identification of new authors provides the focus for their activities. Having their own specific cultural agenda, they do not necessarily rely on soliciting new manuscripts from the general public. Instead, as they grow, they develop an informal (though often extensive) network of like-minded informants to complement the editorial acumen of their founders.

Although cultural publishers are responsible for only a fraction of the number of titles produced each year, they may be looked towards by certain groups for a specific kind of title not available elsewhere. This, too, is highly important since the formation of nationalistic literary canons tends to discriminate against translation. In Britain, for example, F. R. Leavis advanced for many years a highly persuasive (though now largely discredited) notion of an English 'tradition'. Schulte argues that teachers and university lecturers, frequently perceived as a likely market for new literary works in translation, tend to be unadventurous in their reading habits and unlikely to include a particular writer on a curriculum until he or she has already received widespread academic approval.

Academic presses are likewise relatively immune to commercial pressures, though some generate considerable revenues (Oxford University Press has an estimated turnover of £425 million per annum). The existence of such a press brings prestige and credibility to the host institution and the means of participating in academic debate. Although the publishing of translations, whether of a literary or scholarly nature, is not their main activity, academic presses do nonetheless issue a number of important texts in translation every year. Equally significantly, the kudos of a university imprint can help raise the profile of a particular writer or school of thought and so play a major part in the reformulation of canons.

Subsidies and state intervention

Democracies tend to view state intervention in publishing with some mistrust as characteristic of totalitarian regimes (Feather 1993: 167–8). The political and social changes which swept through Central Europe in the 1980s led to the disintegration of much of the state and parastatal publishing apparatus which, for more than half a century, had held a near monopoly on book production in those countries. Besides seeking to promote its own political ideology in other countries by means of translation, that state apparatus also supported the translation of serious literary work, for example of novels by authors such as Graham Greene or William Faulkner into minority languages such as Estonian. Many translators working in those countries developed good relationships with their respective state publishing houses, such that they were in a position to recommend titles which appealed to them. With the decline of that parastatal apparatus (though some publishing companies have remodelled themselves as commercial publishing houses along Western lines), those translators have generally had to turn their attention to more popular titles. In Poland, for example, the 1990s witnessed one of the fastest-growing markets for translations not only of thrillers and 'best sellers' but also of women's light romantic fiction, along the lines of that published by Harlequin (US) or Mills & Boon (UK).

Matters are even more complicated in China where an estimated 30,000 private publishing companies are tolerated by the political system without actually benefiting from an official legal status. Since the state controls the issuing of ISBNs, these private publishing houses are forced to act as 'packagers': their role is to find suitable titles, purchase the rights, and enter into some form of agreement with one of the state-owned publishers, who can then publish them under the state imprimatur. Apparently, about 6 per cent of titles are translations, though the predominant trend is for works which may be broadly labelled as 'self-help' manuals (Meyer 2005).

Though European and North American publishers may benefit from a defined legal status, there is little funding available for the support of LITERARY TRANSLATION or other publishing ventures. The European Commission provided limited funds to promote the translation of contemporary works (including DRAMA) from and into MINORITY languages in the 1980s and 1990s, but most of these programmes have now been abandoned. Similarly, funding which was formerly available to support a European network of translation centres has also largely dried up. Though national cultural agencies (such as the National Endowment for the Arts in the United States, the Canadian Arts Council, and the Arts Council of England in the UK) have shown willingness to support specific translation projects, the funding available has never been sufficiently large to sustain any viable large-scale project.

In part, the disengagement of the state from the field of cultural intervention is fuelled by the erosion of the distinction between 'literary' and 'popular' fiction. Some distinctly 'literary' authors, such as Marguerite Duras, command large markets, while some so-called 'popular' writers are not without literary merit, for example Ruth Rendell. However, while the translation market may remain buoyant in many parts of the world, there can be little doubt that publishing in Britain and North America is more introspective and inward-looking than it was even ten years ago. In the nineteenth century, the low translation rate in Britain and North America could be ascribed to the influence of a linguistically sophisticated elite which had little need for translation with regard to standard languages such as French (Hale 2006); whether the present-day ambivalence to literary translation is due to the self-sufficiency of the English-speaking world, or to changes in publishing practice, or is simply an aristocratic residue is more difficult to determine.

See also:
LITERARY TRANSLATION; POLYSYSTEM; RE-WRITING.

Further reading
Tebbel 1987; Schulte 1990; Venuti 1992; BIPE Conseil 1993; Feather 1993; Venuti 1995a, 1995b; Hale 2006; *UK Book Publishing Industry Statistics Yearbook* 2007.

TERRY HALE

Quality

Translation quality assessment presupposes a theory of translation. Different views of translation itself lead to different concepts of translation quality, and different ways of assessing it. The following discussion of various approaches to translation will focus on two issues: the relationship between source and target text, and the relationship between features in the text itself and how they are perceived by human agents.

Approaches to translation quality assessment

Approaches to translation quality assessment fall into a number of distinct categories: anecdotal and subjective, including neo-hermeneutic approaches; response-oriented approaches; text-based approaches.

Anecdotal and subjective approaches

Anecdotal and subjective views on translation quality have long been offered by practising translators, philosophers, philologists, writers and many others. A central problem in such treatments is the operationalization of concepts such as 'faithfulness to the original', or 'the natural flow of the translated text'. Such intuitive treatments of translation quality are atheoretical in nature, and the possibility of establishing general principles for translation quality is generally rejected (see for example Cary and Jumpelt 1963; Savory 1957). Proponents of this approach tend to see the quality of a translation as solely dependent on the translator and his or her personal knowledge, intuitions and artistic competence.

An equally subjective and intuitive treatment of translation quality has more recently been proposed within the 'neo-hermeneutic' approach (e.g. Stolze 1992), where the hermeneutic interpretation of the original and the production of a translation are individual, creative acts that defy systematization, generalization and the development of rules (see HERMENEUTICS). In Stolze's view, a 'good' translation can only come about when the translator identifies him- or herself fully with the text to be translated. Whether such identification enables or in fact guarantees a translation of quality, and how this quality might be assessed, remains unclear.

Response-oriented, psycholinguistic approaches

Response-oriented approaches to evaluating translations are communicatively oriented and focus on determining the **dynamic equivalence** (Nida 1964) between source and translation, i.e. the manner in which receptors of the translated text respond to it must be equivalent to the manner in which the receptors of the source text respond to the source text. Nida postulated three criteria for an optimal translation: general efficiency of the communicative process, comprehension of intent and equivalence of response. Upon closer scrutiny, these criteria prove to be as vague and non-verifiable as those used by proponents of the intuitive-anecdotal approach. Nida and Taber (1969: 173) propose another set of criteria: the correctness with which the message of the original is understood through the translation, the ease of comprehension and the involvement a person experiences as a result of the adequacy of the form of the translation. But the tests suggested for implementing such criteria, such as **cloze tests** or elicitation of a receptor's reactions to different translations, are not rigorous enough to be considered theoretically valid or reliable.

In the 1960s, and predominantly in connection with experiments with machine translation, psycholinguists such as Carroll (1966) suggested the use of broad criteria such as 'intelligibility' and 'informativeness' for assessing translation quality, together with a number of testing methods such as asking the opinion of competent readers, etc. The major weakness of all such response-based suggestions for evaluating translation quality is the same as that which characterizes all behaviouristic approaches: the 'black box', the human mind, is not taken into account, so that tests involving expert judges, for example, simply take for granted certain criteria that are not developed or made explicit in the first place. This approach is also reductionist in that the overall quality of a translation is made dependent on measures of, for example, intelligibility and informativeness. What we have here is a norm against which the results of any behavioural test are to be judged.

One view of translation evaluation that is both contextually and cognitively motivated is Gutt's (1991/2000) 'relevance-theoretic approach'. Gutt stresses the point that meaning in a translation depends on the addressees' ability to make inferences on the basis of their interaction with various contextual factors. These factors are bound to the addressees' assumptions about the world, which they use to interpret a translated text. Translation is here seen as an instance of 'interlingual interpretive use', with the principles of translation being applications of the principle of relevance. Reducing the complex, multidimensional phenomenon of translation to the cognitive-communicative dimension is however arguably as one-sided as previous behaviourist attempts to take performance as the one and only yardstick of translation quality.

Text-based approaches

Text-based approaches may be informed by linguistics, comparative literature or functional models.

In linguistically-based approaches, pairs of source and target texts are compared with a view to discovering syntactic, semantic, stylistic and pragmatic regularities of transfer (see LINGUISTIC APPROACHES). An early and influ-

ential text-based approach to translation quality assessment is Reiß (1971). Reiß suggested that the most important invariant in translation is the text type to which the source text belongs, as it determines all other choices a translator has to make. She proposed three basic text types on the basis of Bühler's (1934) three language functions: content-oriented, form-oriented and conative. However, exactly how language functions and source text types can be determined, and at what level of delicacy, is left unexplained. Nor is the exact procedure for source text analysis given in another influential publication, namely Koller (1979/2004). Koller suggests that the evaluation of a translation should proceed in three stages: (a) source text criticism, with a view to assessing transferability into the target language, (b) translation comparison, taking account of the methods used in the production of a given translation, and (c) translation evaluation on the basis of native speaker metalinguistic judgements, based on the text-specific features established in stage (a). However insightful, this proposal remains programmatic in nature.

A combined micro- and macro-textual approach to translation quality assessment, which also tries to unite quantitative and qualitative dimensions, is suggested by Williams (2004). Similar to Tirkkonen-Condit (1986), Williams applies argumentation theory to translation evaluation. The drawback of the standardized, norm-based procedure which he suggests is that, in assuming the universality of argumentative structure, he totally disregards the context- and culture-boundness of texts. Even if such universality did exist, there might still be culture-conditioned differences in the degree of explicitness of argumentative structures in texts. Further, argumentative structure may only be relevant for specific types of texts.

In approaches which draw on comparative literature, the quality of a translation is assessed according to the function of the translation in the system of the target language literature (see POLYSYSTEM). The source text is thus of little importance in this approach, and the hypothesis that translations belong to one system only (Toury 1995), namely the literary system of the target culture, determines how the issue of translation quality assessment is to be tackled: first the translated text is criticized without reference to the source text, then specific solutions to translation problems are analysed by means of the mediating functional-relational notion of translation equivalence. Such solutions, however, presuppose linguistically defined source and target units that can be related to one another. Further, it is not clear how one is to determine when a text is a translation and what criteria one is to use for evaluating a translation.

In their functional theory of translation, Reiß and Vermeer (1984) claim that it is the **skopos**, i.e. the purpose of a translation, which is all important (see FUNCTIONALIST APPROACHES). The way the translated text is adapted to target language and culture NORMS is then taken as the yardstick for evaluating a translation. The authors distinguish between EQUIVALENCE and **adequacy**. Equivalence refers to the relationship between an original and its translation, where both fulfil the same communicative function; adequacy is the relationship between source and translation where no functional match obtains and the 'skopos' of the translation has been consistently attended to. Whether such a terminological distinction is necessary and sound is open to debate. Of more relevance here is the failure of the authors to spell out exactly how one is to determine whether a translation is either adequate or equivalent, let alone how to assess its skopos. Also, given the crucial role assumed by the purpose or skopos of a translation in this model, it follows that the source text is of secondary importance; in fact, the source text is degraded to a mere 'source of information' that the translator may change as he or she sees fit.

By its very nature, translation is simultaneously bound to the source text and to the presuppositions and conditions governing its reception in the target linguistic and cultural system. Any attempt at evaluating translations must take this basic fact as a starting point. What is needed then is a model which attempts to transcend anecdotalism, reductionism, programmatic statements and intuitively implausible one-sided considerations of the source or target text alone. Such a model would provide a linguistic description and explanation of whether and how a translation is equivalent to its source.

A functional-pragmatic model for translation quality assessment

House (1977, 1997, 2004b, 2007) proposes a model based on pragmatic theories of language use; this model provides for the analysis of the linguistic-situational particularities of source and target texts, a comparison of the two texts and the resultant assessment of their relative match. The basic requirement for equivalence of original and translation in this model is that the translation should have a function (consisting of an ideational and an interpersonal functional component, in the Hallidayan sense) which is equivalent to that of the original. The translation should also employ equivalent pragmatic means for achieving that function.

The operation of the model involves initially an analysis of the original according to a set of situational dimensions, for which linguistic correlates are established. The resulting textual profile of the original characterizes its function, which is then taken as the norm against which the translation is measured; the degree to which the textual profile and function of the translation (as derived from an analogous analysis) match the profile and function of the original is the degree to which the translation is adequate in quality.

In evaluating the relative match between original and translation, a distinction is made between dimensional mismatches and non-dimensional mismatches. Dimensional mismatches are pragmatic errors that have to do with language users and language use; **non-dimensional mismatches** are mismatches in the denotative meanings of original and translation elements and breaches of the target language system at various levels. The final qualitative judgement of the translation then consists of a listing of both types of errors and of a statement of the relative match of the two functional components.

The model has been developed on the basis of contrastive German–English discourse analyses (House 1996). Empirical work with the model has resulted in a distinction between two basic types of translation, **overt translation** and **covert translation**. An overt translation is required whenever the source text is heavily dependent on the source culture and has independent status within it; a covert translation is required when neither condition holds, i.e. when the source text is not source-culture specific. Functional equivalence is only possible in covert translation, which is more difficult than overt translation because differences in the cultural presuppositions of the source and target language communities may require the translator to apply a **cultural filter**, i.e. a set of cross-cultural dimensions along which members of the two cultures differ in socio-cultural predispositions and communicative preferences. This also makes evaluation difficult because it involves assessing the quality of the cultural filters introduced in translation, as well as operationalizing the concept of 'context' (House 2006).

Recent and potential developments

Insights into what goes on in the translator's mind can be used both to supplement translation evaluation and to validate hypotheses about the cross-cultural dimensions that characterize cultural filters. Such introspective studies of the translational process (for example Tirkkonen-Condit and Jääskeläinen 2000) are potentially useful in that translators indicate how and why they choose certain options or translational strategies, thus making the decision path in the process of translation more transparent (see PSYCHOLINGUISTIC/COGNITIVE APPROACHES; THINK-ALOUD PROTOCOLS). While translation quality assessment is obviously and necessarily product-based, such process-oriented work is important because it can shed light on to the mysterious cause-and-effect chain in translational behaviour.

Future approaches to translation quality assessment need to be more transdisciplinary in nature (cf. Lee-Jahnke 2001; House and Baumgarten 2007). An interesting suggestion in this direction has also recently been made by Bolanos Cuellar (2007). He integrates both product- and process-oriented perspectives on translation as well as linguistic, literary and culturally oriented views in his dynamic translation model, combining textual-contextual aspects with considerations of the communicative nature of translation.

Future work on translation quality assessment needs to develop beyond subjective, one-sided or dogmatic judgements by positing intersubjectively verifiable evaluative criteria on the basis of large-scale empirical studies. Large CORPORA of translations from and into many different languages (cf. Bowker 2001; Olohan 2004; Kenny 2006) must be analysed in order to formulate hypotheses about why, how, and to what degree one translation may be deemed better than another.

See also:
EQUIVALENCE; FUNCTIONALIST APPROACHES; LINGUISTIC APPROACHES; REVIEWING AND CRITICISM.

Further reading
Koller 1979/2004; House 1997; Williams 2004; House 2006a, 2006b; House and Baumgarten 2007; Colina 2008.

JULIANE HOUSE

Qur'ān (Koran)

The Qur'ān is the holy book of Islam and the most important of the sources of authority which underpin Muslim religious life, others being accounts 'relating to the deeds and utterances' of the Prophet Muhammad during his life (*The Concise Encyclopedia of Islam* 1989: 141): the *hadith* ('sayings') and the Prophet's own practice (*sunna*, 'tradition'). The singular importance attached to the Qur'ān stems from the belief that it contains, verbatim, the Word of God, as revealed gradually to Muhammad by the Angel Gabriel between 610 and 632 AD. It is therefore considered inimitable, and this has important implications for both the possibility, legitimacy and (authorized) methods of translating it.

The Qur'ān consists of 114 *sura*(s), i.e. chapters, each divided into *aya*(s), i.e. verses. Each *sura* has a name (for example *al-fatiha*, 'the Opening', *al-baqara*, 'the Cow'). With the exception of *al-fatiha*, a short *sura* that always appears first in printed editions, the rest of the *sura*(s) are mostly ordered by length rather than chronologically, with the longest appearing at the beginning and the shortest at the end. The word *Qur'ān* itself also means 'recitation', and the *sura*(s) in the book are in fact meant for oral recitation, with some being written in rhyming prose.

Uthman ibn Affan (d. 656), the third Guided Caliph, was responsible for ordering a group of scholars to produce a canonical written text of the Qur'ān, which he then sent to all major Islamic cities, ordering them to burn any unauthorized versions they might have possessed. Nevertheless, there are still seven legitimate readings (*ahruf*) in circulation, which differ mainly in the manner in which the verses are recited orally and the interplay between the recited and written forms. Abul Aswad al-Du'aly (*c*.605–88) and al-Khalil ibn Ahmad (*c*.718–86) were responsible for determining the more exact and now widely accepted spelling of the Qur'ān. Directly or indirectly, they also had a significant impact on determining the pronunciation of the words in isolation and in context. While there are still some residual differences between the readings in circulation, mostly at word level, these are minor and there are therefore no 'versions' of the Qur'ān in the strict sense of the word, as used in the context of the New Testament (Zidan and Zidan 1991: 5); see BIBLE, JEWISH AND CHRISTIAN.

Linguistically and stylistically, the Qur'ān is viewed by followers of the faith and erudite speakers of the language as the unparalleled masterpiece of Arabic. Its grammatical structure, for instance, is specific to it and in many cases different from the grammatical structure of non-Qur'ānic Arabic. So much so that there is a field of linguistic study dedicated to Qur'ānic grammar and syntax (al-Ansari 1405H). In other words, there is Arabic and there is Qur'ānic Arabic. It is this distinct character of the linguistic composition of the Qur'ān which Muslims cite as 'the strongest argument in favour of the genuineness of their faith' (Hitti 1937/1970: 91) as well as the miraculous nature of the text. Some scholars therefore suggest that 'the triumph of Islam was to a certain extent the triumph of a language, more particularly of a book' (ibid.).

The translatability and legitimacy of translating the Qur'ān

It is interesting to note that whereas *hadith* (the sayings of the Prophet) may be legitimately translated and quoted in translation, it has traditionally been considered illegitimate to translate the Qur'ān. The quintessentially divine nature of the Qur'ān and the clearly human character of the *hadith* are basically the reasons for these two diametrically opposed views towards translating them. The issue of legitimacy is difficult to separate from the more general question of TRANSLATABILITY in discussions of the Qur'ān. Proponents of the absolute untranslatability of the Qur'ān find explicit support for their view in *aya* number 2 of the *sura* of *Yusuf*: 'We have sent it down / as an *Arabic* Qur'ān' (*The Holy Qur'ān*: version of the Presidency of Islamic Researches, p. 623; emphasis added).

Even today, there is still a strong and influential school of thought that subscribes to the view that the Qur'ān cannot be translated and that any existing 'translations' of it are illegitimate. Many believe that if it is to be translated at all, the Qur'ān can only be translated by a Muslim. Even then, in the context of the Qur'ān the term 'translation' and all its derivatives must always be placed between quotation marks or some such graphic marker to point out that the term is used in a uniquely context-sensitive sense. If and when used, translation would function merely as a commentary, explaining or paraphrasing the source text but not replacing it. Translations of the Qur'ān may thus help the reader, for example non-Arab Muslims who have to learn to read and recite the Qur'ān in Arabic, understand its meanings, especially if more than one translation is read in conjunction with the original in Arabic. The Qur'ān in translation is thus considered an aid to understanding, but is not in itself 'holy'.

The belief in the illegitimacy of translating the Qur'ān has always had its opponents, however, even in the early decades of Islam. Abu Hanifa, the Iraqi scholar and theologian (*c*.700–67), believed it was legitimate to translate all the verses of the Qur'ān into a foreign tongue but 'it was not lawful to put the whole together in one volume unless the Arabic text was placed opposite the translation throughout'

(Pickthall 1931: 442). Moreover, Abu Hanifa declared that it is 'permissible for one who could not speak Arabic to express the meaning of the Arabic words in his own language when reciting the prescribed prayers' (ibid.). However, he reportedly retracted this radical view at a later stage and followed the more orthodox line (Mousa and Dahroug 1992: 126ff.), according to which a Muslim who cannot read the Qur'ān in Arabic is deemed virtually illiterate.

Any attempt at translating the Qur'ān is essentially a form of exegesis, or at least is based on *an* understanding of the text and consequently projects a certain point of view; hence the preference given to Muslim as opposed to non-Muslim translators. Terms such as 'explanation', 'interpretation' and 'paraphrase' take on exegetic hues in the context of translating the Qur'ān, and this has implications for legitimizing any such attempt. Andalus-born Imam Shatby (c.1133–93), for example, based his view that the Qur'ān is untranslatable on the premise that the book has 'senses' that are exclusive to Qur'ānic Arabic, so that attempting to render such senses even in non-Qur'ānic Arabic is doomed to failure (Mehanna 1978). He did not, however, object in principle to translating the Qur'ān provided such translation as may be produced is seen as a translation of the 'meanings' of the book, i.e. a paraphrase or basic interpretation. This wording continues to function as a 'condition', attached to 'approved' translations; Pickthall (1931: 432) relates how the Rector of al-Azhar (the authoritative, traditional centre of Islamic studies in Cairo) gave his consent only when he was told that Pickthall would not call his 1930 translation '*Al-Qur'ān*' but would call it '*ma'aniu'l-Qur'āni' l-majid*' (The meanings of the Glorious Qur'ān), to which he added 'if he does that … then there can be no objection'.

The decade or so beginning in 1925 and ending in 1936 in Egypt witnessed some particularly vigorous polemics concerning the translation of the Qur'ān. Senior Azhar personalities expressed strong views, arguing for or against the legitimacy of such an enterprise. Most were initially opposed to the very idea of translating the Qur'ān, and many actually supported the banning and burning of an English translation by a Muslim, Muhammad Ali, which had arrived in Egypt

at the time; the translation is cited variously as being published in 1917 or 1918 (Mehanna 1978). The decision by the Turkish statesman Kemal Ataturk (1881–1938) to commission a translation of the Qur'ān into Turkish brought matters to a head: one view held at the time was that the translation was designed to distance Muslim Turks from their holy book in its original language (Mehanna 1978: 27). In the general context of Ataturk's policies, it was also perceived as an attempt to sever a significant link between Turkey and the Arabic-speaking Muslim world in order to move the former closer to Europe.

In 1936, Sheikh Mustafa al-Maraghi, Rector of al-Azhar, formally announced in a letter to the prime minister of the time that rendering the meanings of the Qur'ān into any language could not be termed 'Qur'ān' (Mehanna 1978; al-Zafzaf 1984). Sheikh Maraghi's views eventually resulted in a *fatwa* (formal legal opinion) to the effect that translating the Qur'ān was allowed from a *Shari'a* (religious jurisdiction) point of view (*Shorter Encyclopaedia of Islam* 1974). On 16 April of the same year, the *fatwa* was approved by the Council of Ministers. One of the stipulations attached to this approval was that any such translation must be called 'a translation of an interpretation of the Qur'ān' or 'an interpretation of the Qur'ān in language X', and not 'a translation of the Qur'ān' (Mehanna 1978; al-Zafzaf 1948). To this day, when al-Azhar and similar bodies in the Islamic world grant permission for a translation of the Qur'ān to be published it is explicitly stated that the work concerned is a translation of the 'meanings' of the Qur'ān.

Pronouncements by religious leaders aside, the strong link between the Qur'ān and the type of Arabic in which it was revealed means that the difference between *the* revealed book and one of its translations (whether approved or not) has never gone unnoticed. Thus, readers of the Gospels in a language such as English may have some awareness that the verses being read are a translation of some original text, but this awareness would not particularly mar the text concerned or detract from its authority or holiness (see BIBLE, JEWISH AND CHRISTIAN). In the eyes of a Muslim, by contrast, the difference between the Qur'ān and any of its translations is ultimately the difference between God as the

Author, Authority and Source on the one hand, and man as a mere translator/interpreter on the other. Pickthall (1931: 423) asserts that 'No non-Arab Muslims ... ever had the least idea of elevating a translation of the Scripture [i.e. the Qur'ān] in their language to the position of the English translation of the Bible among English-speaking Protestant Christians – that is to say, of substituting it for the original.' At a more practical level, there is, by implication, no universally recognized or authorized single translation, or edition in translation, of the Qur'ān.

Translations of the Qur'ān: a historical overview

Early messages from the Prophet Muhammad to political rulers of the time, such as Emperor Heraclius (c.610–41) of the Eastern Roman Empire and al Muqawqis, his viceroy in Coptic Egypt, included an *aya* from the Qur'ān. It can only be assumed that translations of these messages were undertaken by translators employed by the receivers, or at least by persons familiar with Arabic in their particular country. The first *aya* which may have been translated in this fashion is likely to be number 64 in the *sura* of *al Imran* (al-Zafzaf 1984). Pickthall (1930/1992) translates it as follows:

> Say: O People of the Scripture! Come to an agreement between us and you: that we shall worship none but Allah, and that we ascribe no Partner unto Him, and that none of us shall take others for lords beside Allah and if they turn away, then say: Bear witness that we are they who have surrendered (Unto him).

The other candidate is *aya* number 29 in the *sura* of *al Tawba*, translated by Zidan and Zidan (1991) as:

> Fight those who do not believe in GOD and the Last Day, who do not forbid what GOD and His Messenger have forbidden, and do not adopt the True Religion (Islam), from among the people of earlier Scripture, until they pay the Jizyah (tax) with willing submission and feel themselves subdued.

The first 'translations' of the Qur'ān appeared in Persian during the reign of the Abbasids (c.750–1258). Undertaken by Persian converts to Islam, these were primarily commentaries, but they nonetheless contained much word-for-word translation (see PERSIAN TRADITION). The first 'proper' translation of the full text, by Robert of Chester, was into Latin; it was sponsored in 1143 by Peter the Venerable, Abbot of Cluny, with the explicit aim of refuting the beliefs of Islam (Hitti 1937/1990: 126). Since then, the book has been translated into almost all languages of the world, and more than once into many of them. In Europe, the Arabic text of the Qur'ān was first printed in Venice in 1530, followed shortly by the Latin translation of Robert of Ketton in Basle in 1543 (Watt and Bell 1970).

The first translation into English was made by the Scotsman Alexander Ross in 1649. This was an indirect translation (see RELAY), based on a French version by the Sieur du Ryer (Watt and Bell 1970: 201; Hitti 1937/1990: 126) and, like the Latin translation sponsored by the Abbot of Cluny, had dubious aims, as can be seen from its title '... And newly Englished, for the satisfaction of all that desire to look into the Turkish vanities'. More careful and scholarly translations followed. Notable among these were the translations into Latin by Ludovici Marracci in 1698, into English by George Sale in 1734 and Bell in 1937/1939 (Watt and Bell 1970, chapter 11 and pp. 200–1).

Bell's translation is of particular interest since it was not just a translation but also a 'critical re-arrangement of the Surahs' (ibid.: 177). By and large, there is consensus among most Qur'ānic translators to use as source text the 'Uthmanic Recension', i.e. the canonical version sanctioned by Uthman ibn Affan in the seventh century, referred to earlier, which has a set order based mainly on the length of each *sura*. Bell was one of a small number of translators, including Rodwell (1861), who saw fit to rearrange the *sura*(s) of the Qur'ān on chronological grounds. Most translations in print do not just follow the order of the Uthmanic Recension but also ensure that the individual *aya*(s) in each *sura* are given numbers in the same fashion as the Arabic texts, which makes for ease of cross-referencing, comprehension, accuracy and interpretation of both source and target texts. Rodwell (1909) and Arberry (1955) are among those who do not follow this practice.

Style and strategies of Qur'ānic translation

Qur'ānic translations adopt a variety of styles and strategies in terms of both format and content. As far as format is concerned, many translations are printed in the form of parallel texts, with the Arabic text facing the translation. Some are printed on the same page while other editions print the parallel text on opposite pages. Pages of some parallel translations are sequenced to be read from left to right, others from right to left (the latter in recognition of the fact that Arabic is written from right to left) (see SCRIPT). Parallel texts of this type serve various purposes, such as confirming the secondary role of the translation while ensuring the presence of immediate and direct means of cross-referencing and verification. But perhaps the most important motivation for this format (of parallel texts) is the 1936 *fatwa* referred to earlier, which stipulated that 'translations of the meanings … should be printed next to the text concerned' (Mehanna 1978: 22).

In terms of style, Arberry's (1955) translation tries to emulate the quality of the original. It does so with some success and seems, at least partially, to have influenced other translations that aimed at the same effect, such as the translation by Zidan and Zidan (1991). Rodwell's (1909) quasi-versified translation tries to balance accuracy with the need to reproduce a similar effect on the target reader. Pickthall (1930/1992) is considered particularly successful (see, for example, Hitti 1937/1970: 127), showing erudition and sensitivity. Yusuf Ali's (1934) edition is an example of an approach that attempts to be literal at times while tending to over-translate at others (Irving 1992: xviiff.).

Most translations of the Qur'ān are source-oriented (see STRATEGIES); accommodating the target audience is not generally favoured given that the Qur'ān is the Word of God, revealed in Arabic to the Prophet Muhammad. This may explain the extensive use of notes in many translations, and the lengthy introductions that tend to precede them. It is also interesting to note that Arabic-speaking preachers who normally use formal Arabic in general, and especially in Friday's congregational prayers, may interpret or reword a *sura* or *aya* in colloquial or simplified Arabic. This type of simplification is not a feature of written 'translations' into other languages. Nevertheless, a translation in simple English 'to suit the reading and comprehension of 6–16 year old individuals' (Ahamed 2003) has been approved by Al Azhar and other religious bodies in the Arab and Muslim world.

Every translation of the Qur'ān has had to confront the issue of its own legitimacy at some point, in addition to the usual questions of accuracy, relevance and stylistic impact. However, throughout its long history, it has been the question of the very TRANSLATABILITY of the Qur'ān that has mostly dominated debates over this unique text and particular translation context.

See also:

ARABIC TRADITION; BIBLE, JEWISH AND CHRISTIAN; LATIN TRADITION; PERSIAN TRADITION; TRANSLATABILITY; TURKISH TRADITION.

Further reading

Pickthall 1931; Watt and Bell 1970; Mehanna 1978; al-Bundaq 1983; al-Zafzaf 1984; Kidwai 1987; Fischer and Abedi 1990; Ali 1992; Watt 1994; Holes 1999; Cook 2000, Abdul-Raof 2001.

HASSAN MUSTAPHA

Relay

Relay translation is the translation of a translated text (either spoken or written) into a third language (for example, from Chinese to English, then from English to French). It is sometimes considered a subset of RETRANSLATION (see, for example, Idema 2003), although Gambier (1994) more usefully distinguishes the two by defining retranslation as a translation of an already translated message into the same language (e.g. Chinese to English and then again into English). Dollerup (2000b) proposes to further differentiate relay translation from **indirect translation** (where the intermediary translation is not intended for publication, but only as a stepping stone to the second translation), and **support translation** (where translators consult earlier translations while preparing their own new one); the latter would seem to be at the limit of retranslation.

Relay translation has received very little attention by either critics, theoreticians or historians of translation. This should come as no surprise, given the privileging of original texts over translation in most times and places. If translation is a poor copy, then why discuss poor copies of poor copies? Informal discussions (for example, among practitioners and trainers) tend to stress that mistakes made in the original translation are passed on to the relay translation, and more mistakes and distortions are added as one moves further away from the original. A posting on the Chartered Institute of Linguists discussion forum, under the topic 'European standard in translation', is typical in this respect: 'I find the concept of "relay" translation appalling. I wonder sometimes when I translate a document into English and discover that the client is a Japanese company just how the "Chinese whisper" phenomenon will affect

the understanding of the final result' (Dina 2006). Relay translation is thus seen, at best, as a necessary evil, and the assumption is that it is always preferable to translate from the original, just as it is always preferable to read the original rather than a translation. The perception is that studying it will add nothing to the total sum of human knowledge.

Interestingly, Benjamin (1968/1996) believed that there was something different involved in the two processes – direct and relay translation. He argued that the difference arises from the changes that occur between an original text and its translation: the translation's relation to the work of art is like a rich robe draped around a kernel; whereas the original language fits the work of art like the skin of a fruit. Since the fit between the language and the work of art is different in the translation, no translation can be used to create a further translation of the work of art; the translator must always work from the original. The difference between the original and the translation, then, precludes relay translation – although it does not preclude retranslation, which in fact Benjamin encouraged. No one seems to have followed up on this discussion by Benjamin of relay translation and its possible implications.

However, just as translation has always been an important human activity despite the fact that it is seen as derivative, relay has also been a widely used strategy in both oral and written translation. The first insight that relay translation affords us, then, is the extent to which the devaluation of translation has been internalized within the translation community itself, where the disdain and mistrust of translation has been replicated in a disdain and mistrust of relay translation.

Relay translation is one of the few areas of translation studies in which interpreting has probably enjoyed more visibility than translation. Due to economic and technical constraints, it is often not possible to provide 'direct' simultaneous interpreting feeds for every language combination at meetings where several languages are in use. For a meeting using six languages (say, for a meeting in Southeast Asia involving Chinese, French, English, Bahasa Indonesia, Thai and Burmese), even if we assume that for every language combination the same interpreters could work in both directions, 15 booths and 15 audio channels would be needed, and delegates would have to be constantly switching channels. If, however, one language (say French) is used as a 'clearing house', then only 5 booths are needed (French–Chinese, French–English, French–Bahasa, French–Thai, French–Burmese), with a total of 6 channels and no need for delegates to ever switch between them. Given the difficulty of finding good interpreters in all language combinations, the relevant costs and the problems involved in having enough booths and channels, it is no wonder that relay interpreting is common in CONFERENCE INTERPRETING where more than three or four languages are used. A BBC online article in 2004 noted that the recent expansion of the EU meant 20 languages and almost 200 possible combinations; faced with this plethora of unusual combinations, the EU has no choice but to increasingly use relay (Roxburgh 2004).

Training programmes in simultaneous interpreting often make students aware of the fact that relay interpreting poses special problems, and special programmes have been set up to train relay interpreters of languages of limited diffusion (Mikkelson 1999; see TRAINING AND EDUCATION). Students are taught that in a relay situation certain points must be observed by both the first booth and the relay booths. Interestingly, it is the interpreters providing the feed (i.e. those translating into the pivot – or mediating – language as opposed to those translating out of it) who are subject to most pressure, since they are held or hold themselves responsible not only for the translation into their target language but also for all relay translations out of that language. In particular, they are enjoined to avoid long silences. Thus, relay interpretation may directly affect the 'original interpretation'; in other words, interpreters may produce a different sort of interpretation when they know that it will be relayed into

other languages. Unfortunately, to date there are no studies in this area, although there are intriguing possible links to postmodern models of translation (see DECONSTRUCTION).

Another interesting area of research where insights into relay interpretation might be useful concerns the impact of economic and technical limitations on the act of interpreting. There is much anecdotal material shared amongst interpreters and trainers of interpreters in this area, but to date the only study which deals with these issues in relation to relay is Pihkala (1998).

Studies of relay in written translation have also been scarce. Two have appeared since the beginning of the twenty-first century: one discussing the relay translation of Ibsen into Chinese through English (He 2001), the other dealing with subtitling of films from Danish to Hebrew, again through English (Zilberdik 2004); see AUDIOVISUAL TRANSLATION. In line with the established idea that relay translation is at best a necessary evil, both articles focus on problems involved with relay translation and ways to reduce error. The fact that English is the mediating language in both cases is no accident (see MINORITY). English's increasing dominance in the world of international exchange, be it economic, political or cultural, has meant that 'International English' is fast becoming the clearing house language for most relay translation. Japanese manufacturers of electronic goods often have their manuals translated into English, and then from English into other European languages (Álvarez 2005). Here we see relay being used, not because of a lack of translators trained in other languages, but for economic reasons: translations to and from Japanese tend to be more expensive than between English and other European languages.

We find frequent instances of relay translation in the HISTORY of translation. For example, an article tracing the translation and influence of one or more works of literature (or science) might list or even discuss relay translations to indicate the extent of the work's influence (Pym 1998). Relay translation is also discussed in relation to the diffusion of CULTURE and knowledge. The role of Arabic as a mediating language of Greek works (which were then translated into Latin and other European languages) in instigating the European Renaissance, for instance, is often mentioned (see CLASSICAL

TEXTS; ARABIC TRADITION; LATIN TRADITION). Relay translations can also be discussed as an instance of cultural mediation; see, for example, Pajares (2001) and Toledano Buend'a (2001) for discussions of translations of literary works from English into Spanish via French.

A closer look at the history of translation reveals that relay plays an important role in many different times and places. In general, it can be said that it occurs mainly when there is a lack of competent trained translators in various language combinations. Besides the few examples listed above, one of the largest areas that merits more research is the role that relay translation has played in developing contacts between European and non-European cultures from the sixteenth to the twentieth century. St André (2006) notes the importance of relay translation in shaping British knowledge of East and Southeast Asia, and the fact that, at a time when translations from Chinese were few and far between, any translation into a European language was likely to be quickly relayed into other European languages (see also Idema 2003 on relay translations from Chinese into Dutch through Latin, English, French and German). During this period, there was often considerable anxiety about the accuracy of translations from non-European into European languages, and the frequent phenomenon of PSEUDOTRANSLATION raised doubts as to the status of genuine translations (St André 2003b). However, there was no such anxiety concerning relay translations of Chinese texts into other European languages. This phenomenon indicates a 'closing of ranks', or sense of community, among European languages. The difficulty of translating from more distant languages, such as Chinese, Arabic or Sanskrit, makes the problems involved in translating from French or German appear trivial. This then allows a 'we Europeans' versus 'you Others' dichotomy, with Europeans sharing information about non-European peoples through relay translation (St André 2003a).

In the other direction, it was often common in colonized territories for all knowledge of Europe to be mediated by one language, that of whichever European country happened to have control of the area. Translation into Tagalog, for example, during the eighteenth and nineteenth centuries, was almost exclusively from Spanish, including relay translations of works from other European languages (Batnag 2002). The colonizing language (Spanish, Dutch, Portuguese, English, German) thus became the 'portal' or 'mediating' language between the colonized country and Europe.

Liu (1995) examines the role of relay translation from European languages through Japanese in the early twentieth century as a mediator for Chinese modernity. Unlike some of the other studies mentioned here, Liu is not interested in deploring the fact that relay translations are full of mistakes, but focuses rather on how the Japanese understanding of European modernity played an important role in influencing the development of modern China.

Finally, relay translation tends to surface in discussions where historians wish to emphasize the 'messy' nature of the translation process and the blurring of lines between original, translation, ADAPTATION and PSEUDOTRANSLATION. What, for example, is the status of 'the wondrous tale of Han' in Marryat's nineteenth-century novel *The Pacha of Many Tales*? Based upon an 1829 translation of a Chinese tale, the tale of Han has been significantly altered to fit Marryat's needs, but this new 'version' is neither a 'retranslation', since Marryat did not know Chinese, nor a 'relay', since the 1829 version and Marryat's version are in the same language. 'Adaptation of a translation' is perhaps the closest (but still rather messy) name for this phenomenon – which, like relay translation, is much more common than one would suppose from looking at the secondary literature. In sum, relay translation remains one of the most understudied phenomena in translation studies today, and one that could and should receive more attention from theoreticians and historians alike.

See also:
HISTORY; PSEUDOTRANSLATION; RETRANSLATION; SHAKESPEARE.

Further reading
Gambier 1994; Liu 1995; He 2001; St André 2003a, 2003b; Zilberdik 2004.

JAMES ST ANDRÉ

Retranslation

The term 'retranslation' most commonly denotes either the act of translating a work that has previously been translated into the same language, or the result of such an act, i.e. the retranslated text itself. 'Retranslation' is sometimes also used to refer to an 'indirect', 'intermediate' or RELAY translation, i.e. a text that is translated through a mediating source language (Shuttleworth and Cowie 1997: 76; Gambier 1994: 413). This entry focuses on the former meaning of the term.

Research on retranslation traditionally focused on literary material, and indeed the most frequently retranslated works continue to be sacred texts, canonical literary works and dramatic texts (Brownlie 2006: 146; Aaltonen 2003). On the other hand, non-literary retranslations in fields such as literary theory (Susam-Sarajeva 2003, 2006), retranslations of various types of text produced in the European Union institutions (Paloposki and Koskinen 2003) and of scientific texts (Jianzhong 2003; Brisset 2004) are also undertaken and have received some attention. Retranslation in the field of literature is usually regarded as a positive phenomenon, leading to diversity and a broadening of the available interpretations of the source text (see HERMENEUTICS). In some fields such as DRAMA, retranslation is not only desirable but also often inevitable: with each staging of a foreign play a new retranslation is normally required (Aaltonen 2003). Non-literary retranslation of SCIENTIFIC AND TECHNICAL texts, on the other hand, is generally viewed as redundant repetition, a practice that is best avoided (Koskinen and Paloposki 2003: 24) and, with few exceptions, should even be 'banned' (Jianzhong 2003: 195).

Traditional views of retranslation that were common in the 1990s have been challenged in a number of case studies published during the first decade of the twenty-first century (Koskinen and Paloposki 2003, 2004; Susam-Sarajeva 2003, 2006; Hanna 2006). These studies have revealed the complexity of the phenomenon and the need to embed it within a broader discussion of historical context, NORMS, IDEOLOGY, the translator's agency and intertextuality.

Retranslation hypothesis

Theoretical assumptions on retranslation formulated in the 1990s are often referred to as the 'retranslation hypothesis' (Koskinen and Paloposki 2003; Brownlie 2006). The 'retranslation hypothesis' originated in an article written by the French translation scholar Antoine Berman in a special issue of the journal *Palimpsestes*. Speaking strictly of literary retranslations, Berman argued that translation is an 'incomplete' act and that it can only strive for completion through retranslations (1990: 1). The kind of completion Berman had in mind concerned the success of a translation in getting closer to the source text and in representing the encounter between the translator and the language of the original (ibid.: 3). Berman talks of an inherent 'failure' marking all translations, a failure that makes itself felt both as an 'incapacity' and a 'resistance' to translate. According to Berman, this 'failure' is at its peak in the first translations (ibid.: 5). Driven by cultural and editorial considerations, first translations are assumed to suppress the alterity of the translated text and to feature cuts and changes that are motivated by a concern for higher levels of readability (Gambier 1994: 414). They naturalize foreign works and serve to introduce them into a given target culture (Bensimon 1990: ix). Subsequent translations, by contrast, pay more attention to the letter and style of the source text and maintain a cultural distance between the translation and its source, reflecting the singularity of the latter (ibid.: ix–x). Gambier (1994: 414) suggests that this 'logocentric' view offers a model of retranslation as a process of improvement over time and is based on the illusion of an 'immanent meaning' contained in the source text. This teleological view of retranslation as a unidirectional move towards 'better' target texts has been critiqued as adopting a 'history-as-progress model' (Susam-Sarajeva 2003: 2) and oversimplifying a complex phenomenon (Milton and Torres 2003: 2). Brisset (2004) argues that an approach which foregrounds 'novelty' as opposed to linear progress can better explain the phenomenon of retranslation, and a number of case studies have challenged the earlier hypothesis by demonstrating that first translations are not always domesticating, and neither are all subsequent ones progressively more foreignizing (Koskinen and Paloposki 2003: 22).

A second aspect of the retranslation hypothesis pertains to the issue of ageing. Berman suggests that while originals remain forever 'young', translations will age with the passage of time, thus giving rise to a need for new translations (1990: 1–2). However, not all translations are equally affected by the passage of time, and not all translations will necessarily 'age'. Those that stand the test of time and match the endurance of the original may be thought of as 'great translations' (ibid.: 2), a view that is extensively problematized by Brisset, who invites a critical discussion of 'greatness' which, she suggests, will inevitably involve the difficult question of literary value (2004: 52–7). The ageing of translations and the ensuing need for retranslation have also traditionally been associated with language change and the need to update the wording and terminology used in earlier translations (Hanna 2006: 194). However, no straightforward link can be assumed to exist between the passage of time and the need for retranslation since there are many cases of retranslations of the same source texts undertaken within a short span of time (Susam-Sarajeva 2003; Pym 1998, 2005b; Hanna 2006; Jenn 2006). The decision to retranslate or to publish a retranslation, then, cannot be reduced to a single factor such as the ageing of the initial translation.

The question of why certain texts are repeatedly translated while others are translated only once has been posed by various scholars (Rodriguez 1990: 64; Gambier 1994: 414; Susam-Sarajeva 2003: 5; Paloposki and Koskinen 2004: 29). The answer probably has more to do with the context of the retranslations than any inherent characteristic of the source text that makes it 'either worthy or in need of retranslation' (Paloposki and Koskinen 2004: 29).

Motives for retranslation

Changing social contexts and the evolution of translation NORMS are often cited as major factors influencing the choice to retranslate specific texts (Brownlie 2006: 150). In a study of retranslations of CHILDREN'S LITERATURE into Hebrew, Du-Nour examined retranslations in order to trace the 'linguistic and translational norms' prevailing at different periods (1995: 327). Her study demonstrates close correspondence between the evolution of linguistic and stylistic norms and the publication of new retranslations: 'readability' is shown to be a major concern in later retranslations, while earlier translations were marked by a less readable, bible-like style which reflected the prevailing norm for translation in the 1920s (ibid.: 331). Kujamäki's study of German translations of the Finnish novel *Seitsemän veljestä* by Aleksis Kivi similarly uses retranslation as data to examine the historical dynamics of literary translation, and concludes that retranslations are largely governed by 'the context of time-bound normative conditions' (2001: 65), in particular by shifts in the ideological context of reception and Finland's changing image in Germany. Such ideological and political factors have often motivated new retranslations of canonical literary texts in particular. Examples include competing retranslations of *Tom Sawyer* and *Huckleberry Finn* by Communist and pro-American publishers in postwar France (Jenn 2006: 247–52); retranslations by the Brazilian author, translator and publisher Monteiro Lobato, who inserted his own political views in his retranslations of children's classics (Milton 2003); and retranslations and re-editions of many adult and children's classics during the first decade of the twenty-first century by Islamist publishers in Turkey (Aktaş Salman 2006; Boztepe 2006). Apart from retranslations of literary classics, less canonical texts are sometimes retranslated within a new ideological context and are thus re-positioned in the target culture. Venuti (2003: 27) mentions the case of some feminist retranslations (see GENDER AND SEXUALITY) and argues that retranslations may also be published in order to reaffirm the authority of certain social institutions, including academic or religious establishments (ibid.:26).

There are other, sometimes simpler explanations for retranslation. For example, some retranslators may not be aware of the presence of an earlier translation (Venuti 2003: 25); similarly, lack of coordination and communication among publishers may result in the simultaneous publication of two different translations, in which case each translation can be considered 'initial' and 'retranslation' at the same time. The need to update or modernize the language of a translation, the publication of a revised or expanded source text, and the discovery of mistakes or misinterpretations in the first translation all serve as legitimate justifications for retranslation. A retranslation may also be carried out with the aim of introducing a new interpretation of the source text, sometimes addressing a different readership or creating a new readership altogether. Typical examples of such attempts at reinterpretation/reorientation of previously translated works include issuing children's versions of adult classics and vice versa (Gambier 1994; Jenn 2006). In such cases, retranslations stand in a special intertextual relationship with each other, as well as with their source texts (Brownlie 2006: 153), and are characterized by mutability and border-crossing (Jenn 2006: 236). Koskinen and Paloposki refer to the 'supplementary' nature of retranslation, which enables translators to target different audiences or re-categorize source texts (2003: 22). The notion of supplementarity suggests that 'texts and their interpretations function simultaneously on several layers, denying easy classification into assimilative first and source text oriented new translations' (ibid.: 23). Retranslations may be supplementary not only in terms of complementing or reorienting their source texts, but also in terms of introducing novel material and ideas to the target culture. Toury (1999) suggests that retranslations set out to overcome a deficiency or fill a gap in the target system and to bring in something that was not there before. He argues that retranslation, like translation, should be considered an act of planning because it always involves an element of change, however slight, on behalf of the receiving culture.

Retranslating canonical literature and/or 'recycling' existing translations by reprinting them in a new format continues to be familiar practice for publishing houses attracted by the prestige, cost-effectiveness and guaranteed sales associated with the publication of literary classics (Milton 2001: 62; Koskinen and Paloposki 2003: 26; Venuti 2003: 30). These and other motivations provide the broader background against which retranslations are carried out and published, often with a certain degree of tension and competition with each other.

Tension and competition

By contrast with the linear progression model that informs the retranslation hypothesis put forward by Berman and others, later research on retranslation portrays it as a field marked by a constant struggle between individuals and institutions for the control and production of new interpretations. Venuti maintains that retranslations undertaken with the awareness of a pre-existing translation 'justify themselves by establishing their difference from one or more previous versions' (2003: 25). This difference can be traced in the retranslation STRATEGIES that inscribe competing interpretations formed on the assumption that previous versions are no longer acceptable (ibid.: 26). This assumption is usually based on social or ideological premises, rather than an evident linguistic or literary lack in the previous translations. Venuti offers the example of English translations of Thomas Mann's works, which became a site of open rivalry between academia and commercial publishers in 1995, with each party defending a competing interpretation of Mann's source texts (2003: 27).

Pym draws a distinction between two types of retranslations. 'Passive retranslations' are separated by geographical distance or time and do not have a bearing on one another (1998: 82), whereas 'active retranslations' share the same cultural and temporal location and are indicative of 'disagreements over translation strategies', challenging the validity of previous translations (ibid.: 82–3). A number of case studies have revealed the resistance and tension that mark active retranslations. In her study of the Turkish translations of works by Roland Barthes, Susam-Sarajeva (2003) argues that retranslations carried out during the fifteen years between 1975 and 1990 were not prompted by linguistic change or the ageing of previous translations; rather, they were initiated by translators who were trying to create an indigenous Turkish discourse on literary criticism. She maintains that 'retranslations may also emerge as a result of a synchronous struggle in the receiving system to create the target discourse into which these translations will be incorporated' (ibid.: 5). In the same study, Susam-Sarajeva draws attention to an area of retranslation that has been largely ignored, namely the 'non-existence' of retranslations (ibid.). Like non-translations, works that are only translated once can reveal the mechanisms and conditions of inclusion and exclusion of foreign works in a given culture.

In his study of translations of SHAKESPEARE's plays in Egypt, Hanna (2006) introduces an alternative perspective on retranslation that is also characterized by active competition. Drawing on Bourdieu's sociology (see SOCIOLOGICAL APPROACHES), Hanna argues that retranslators of Shakespeare's tragedies into Arabic in the late nineteenth and early twentieth century made use of various forms of 'distinction' to set their translations apart from earlier ones, claiming, for example, that they had better access to the source text, the source culture or the author (ibid.: 208). As another form of distinction (in the Bourdieusean sense), some retranslators tried to discredit previous translations by pointing out various deficiencies in them (ibid.: 223). Others sought distinction by claiming that their translations served a function in the target culture that had not been served by earlier translations (ibid.: 227). In drawing attention to the active struggle in which retranslators often engage as they attempt to legitimize and distinguish their translations from earlier ones, both Hanna's and Susam-Sarajeva's studies foreground the retranslator's agency, an element that is not given much attention in studies informed by norm theory.

Although retranslations, like first translations, cannot be studied outside their historical context, relying on a strictly social-causational model to explain them runs the risk of overlooking the human element involved in the process. Brisset thus draws attention to the importance of studying retranslations not only from a diachronic but also a synchronic perspective, suggesting that this would reveal those factors that distinguish the work of different 'translating subjects' and highlight the cognitive and creative aspects of translation (2004: 64). Venuti similarly foregrounds the role of the individual retranslator and argues that 'retranslations typically highlight the translator's intentionality because they are designed to make an appreciable difference' (2003: 29). He draws attention to the fact that some retranslations may originate purely from a translator's personal appreciation of a text (ibid.: 30). Retranslators may also set out to displace the prevailing translation NORMS in a given culture (ibid.: 29).

In the nineteenth century, some sinologists tried to define the norms of translation from Chinese by openly criticizing earlier translations (St André 2003a: 68); St André offers the example of Sir John Francis Davis, whose desire to establish himself as an authority on Chinese culture motivated his retranslation of *Hao qiu zhuan* in 1829 (ibid.: 64). Nevertheless, individual choices are naturally embedded in a larger social context, and as Venuti notes, 'transindividual factors inevitably enter into translation projects' (2003: 30). The interaction between the individual translator and the larger context in which retranslations are produced reminds us that retranslation is a function of the dynamics of the target context, rather than a response to any inherent properties of the source text.

See also:
BIBLE, JEWISH AND CHRISTIAN; CLASSICAL TEXTS; GENDER AND SEXUALITY; LITERARY TRANSLATION; NORMS; RELAY.

Further reading
Berman 1990; Gambier 1994; Milton and Torres 2003; Susam-Sarajeva 2003; Venuti 2003; Brisset 2004; Brownlie 2006.

ŞEHNAZ TAHIR GÜRÇAĞLAR

Reviewing and criticism

Reviewing and criticism are distinct but related evaluative practices concerned with literature in the broadest sense, of not only imaginative writing but also non-fiction. The differences cited conventionally between them also hold true for literature in translation: the reviewer alerts a reader to new books, describing them and passing judgement as to whether they are worth reading and buying; the critic addresses books that may or may not be new, considering them in detail and usually assuming a reader's familiarity with them (Berman 1986, 1995; Oates 1990; Ozick 2007; Leonard Woolf 1939: 29; Virginia Woolf 1939: 7). Neither the reviewing nor the criticism of literary translations has developed fully as a tradition, however – unlike the reviewing and criticism of literature. This can be explained only in part by the multiple difficulties inherent in establishing appropriate criteria for analysing and passing judgement on creative activity. The general lack of value – or 'literary capital' (Casanova 1999/2004: 16) – associated with translation in the West has been an additional factor, possibly an equally determinant one (Bassnett 1980: 10; Santoyo 1985: 28–36; Holmes 1988: 78; Vilikovský 1988: 72). As Leighton (1991: xi–xix and ff.) has indicated, translation criticism flourishes in a national-cultural condition where translation is highly esteemed.

Despite the challenges that evaluation presents, translators and translation scholars alike increasingly recognize its importance. As a 'special kind of critical activity' (Vilikovský 1988:74), it must be distinguished from the forms of criticism implicit in the activity of translation itself (van den Broeck 1985: 61; Lefevere 1987; di Stefano 1982; Berman 1986, 1984/1992: 7, 41). At least one scholar has suggested that translation criticism be considered a separate area of applied translation studies (Holmes 1988: 78). Others have stressed its importance as a 'link' between translation theory and practice (Newmark 1988:184) and a 'weapon in defence of the profession' (Dodds 1992: 4). For Berman, criticism, when performed as rigorous analysis or critique, offers the possibility of releasing a translation's 'truth' (1995: 13–14). Translators and reviewers of literary translation have also indicated a need for evaluations that discuss a translation with more than a single adjective and refrain from trashing a translator's work on the basis of isolated errors (Douma 1972; Christ 1982; Maier 1990–91; Hearne 1991; PEN American Center 2004). In the case of both reviewing and criticism, an interest in and concern for evaluation is leading to the study of past evaluative practices, discussions about the criteria appropriate for the evaluation of translations, and the scrutiny of current trends in reviewing and criticism.

The study of past evaluative practices presents a particular set of challenges. The absence of a 'universal canon according to which texts may be assessed' (Bassnett 1980: 9) and the changes that occur continually in the criteria used to measure the success or value of translations make it difficult to identify fixed patterns and trends. John Dryden may have spoken confidently about 'good' and 'bad' likenesses (1680), but the distinction between them has always depended on 'ethnocentric approaches to the task of criticism' (Kelly 1979: 47). Perhaps even more importantly, many of the evaluations that have proved most influential are, like translation itself, not immediately visible. For the unwritten history of translation reviewing and criticism is not only characterized by the unacknowledged, covert, implicit and verbal acts of evaluation that occur in all evaluative practices (Smith 1987/1990: 18–82), but even the 'highly specialized *institutionalized forms of evaluation*' (ibid.: 182) frequently contain value judgements made without reference to explicit criteria. In addition, such judgements have often appeared, and continue to appear, in forms not specifically identified as evaluative, such as translators' prefaces and annotations, complimentary poems and essays about the work of other translators, scholarly writing about translation theory and practice, and appraisals embedded in fictional commentary.

Translators' prefaces and annotations often provide insightful observations about translation practice. RETRANSLATIONS, however, are frequently undertaken with the intent of improving or even rectifying existing versions, and the evaluative comments they contain must themselves be evaluated in the light of their possible role in a translator's own project (Vanderschelden 2000b). The same is true of writing by translators about the work of other translators. Such commentary is often both highly metaphorical and highly motivated with respect to a translator's effort or to the profession of translation itself. This means that commentary must be read in the context of prevailing rhetorical conventions, and this makes the task of extracting general principles of evaluation treacherous if not impossible. The compliments found in such Renaissance poems as Constantijn Huygens's verses on translations by Jacob Westerbaen or those by James Wright on Dryden's translations were in fact a deliberate strategy to improve the subordinate position of translations (Hermans 1985b: 117). Commentary also provides translators with a vehicle for enhancing the status of their work by emphasizing the challenges it presents or by asserting the superiority of their own versions (Raffel 1992). Evaluations that prove influential are even found in works of fiction, for example, the comments about translation and translators that Cervantes included in *Don Quijote* (Moner 1990: 519–22).

By examining the judgements of critics and reviewers from the past, current translation scholars have begun to document the often complex contexts in which evaluation occurs. This work brings to light both the motivation of individual critics and the fact that their assessments were often based on information apparently unrelated to the activity of translation. Williams (1993: 187, 75) has argued that Alexander Pope's critics judged him as a translator of Homer in terms of his 'poetic virility', using evidence 'only tangentially relevant to their observations'. In his study of Matthew Arnold's 'On Translating Homer', Venuti (1995: 118–45) has shown not only that Arnold's attack on Francis Newman's translation of the *Iliad* (see BRITISH TRADITION) served to marginalize Newman's work, but also the extent to which a polemics about acceptable translation STRATEGIES can be simultaneously about cultural politics. May's discussion about Constance Garnett reveals that the long-lived popularity of Garnett's many translations from the Russian did not result from critical acclaim of her work. Rather, it was due to Garnett's ability to make Russian works readable to the English-language public and to the unquestioning acceptance on the part of critics and readers alike once her reputation was established (May 1994: 30–42).

From Alexander Tytler (see BRITISH TRADITION) to George Steiner and others writing more recently, critics have described translations as 'good' or 'bad' without seriously questioning or qualifying those adjectives (Tytler 1813: 13–14; Steiner 1975: 396). At the same time, however, thoughtful efforts to bring increased attention to bear on evaluation and establish systematic evaluative criteria do exist. The error identification and highly subjective appraisals that characterize much translation criticism have no doubt been largely responsible for both critics who argue exclusively for linguistics-based evaluations and those who adopt more eclectic approaches for evaluations grounded on thorough analysis and description (see QUALITY). Some critics uphold the desirability of value judgements and question the possibility of 'pure description' (Dodds 1992: 3), but those who tend to eschew value judgements, preferring not to proclaim one translation better than another, are more numerous (Hatim and Mason 1990b: 1). Concerned less with traditional concepts of quality than with understanding the way translated texts work (van den Broeck 1985: 58–60), they speak instead of defining a translator's methods (Vilikovský 1988: 75) and purpose (Newmark 1988: 186); these are to be discussed with respect to a given translation and, in some instances, also to a critic's own, individual purpose (Newmark 1988: 186–9).

The majority of critics expect that both description and criticism will involve originals as well as translated texts, even when they advocate varying degrees of comparison, seek to answer different questions, or document the possibility of more than one competent translation (Nida 1982). Vilikovský's model, for example, is based on an understanding of translation criticism as 'an instrument for describing the observational facts of interliterary contact' (1988: 74). This model consists of three principal relationships; one is limited to the 'literary context' of the translation, but the other two relationships – between the 'original and the metatext' and between 'the two literary contexts' – involve both the original and the translation. A description of the translator's methods and a discussion of the translation's 'degree of adequacy' and 'level of equivalence' pertain to the first relationship (ibid.: 74, 77, 75). Newmark's five-part model also includes the analysis of the source language text, a comparison of it and the translation, and comments about the translation's potential role as a translation; the comparative study is the 'heart' of this model (1988: 188). Dodds (1985: 191) describes the translation critic as a 'text analyst' whose threefold analysis must encompass the language of the source text, that of the target text and a comparison between the two. Hatim and Mason (1990b: 10) outline a set of comparative parameters that can be used to analyse and compare translations. Their principal interest lies in the 'cultural semiotics of language'; they focus not on individual words but on a 'thread of discourse which is sustained through a communicative transaction'.

Other comparative models include de Beaugrande's discussion of translating POETRY, in which the critic is urged to establish criteria for evaluation that address the 'presuppositions and expectations about texts' shared by readers and writers in each language (1978: 122). Van den Broeck (1985: 56) posits as the starting point of his description 'a comparative analysis of the source and target texts' that includes both 'text structures' and 'systems of texts'. Wilss (1982: 220) argues for a principally empirical, linguistic approach that rests on a comparison of source and target language texts, and Simpson (1975: 255) similarly recommends a linguistic approach that is primarily comparative; Kirkov (1988: 231) suggests more comprehensive 'aesthetic-linguistic criteria' but still considers both translation and original. The seven features of textuality proposed by Neubert and Shreve (1992) also provide a framework that could be used for comparative analysis and evaluation, as do Snell-Hornby's analyses (1988).

Comparative models, however, do not represent the only approach to translation criticism, despite an insistence on the part of some scholars that translation criticism must not be performed without taking the original into account (Vilikovský 1988: 75; de Beaugrande 1978: 121). Nor are the critics who study only the translated text and its context necessarily the reviewers and editors who overlook the fact of translation entirely. On the contrary, Lefevere (1981: 55, 59) has explained the POLYSYSTEM hypothesis and its focus on the product of translation in the context of the target culture rather than on the translation process. Toury's work with translational NORMS also suggests evaluative criteria centred on the target system alone (1978, 1980b). Although Toury argues that comparative study might have some role in translation criticism, he notes that comparisons between translations and originals often lead to an enumeration of errors and a reverence for the original (1978: 26). His comments are echoed, albeit in different frameworks, by Jorge Luis Borges and Tom Conley. Borges points to the crippling effect that bilingual editions can have on a reader's ability to read, and implicitly, to evaluate a translation (Alifano 1984: 51), and Conley (1986: 48) states that 'critics fabricate "something [to be] lost in translation" at the very instant they place their eyes between two versions of a canonical text'. Berman elaborated and argued for a 'productive critique'

in which the 'confrontation' of a translation and the original is a decisive, but not the sole component of an ethical and aesthetic evaluation that considers a translation in relation to its own language and literary tradition (1995: 83–96) and to the experience of the foreign it makes possible in them (1999: 74–5).

Recent work in literary criticism and theory, linguistics, anthropology, philosophy and cultural studies has direct, albeit at times contradictory implications for the evaluation of literary translations. On the one hand, not only the 'deconstructionists' entire project' (Gentzler 1993/2001: 146; see DECONSTRUCTION) but also the entire range of challenges presented by post-structuralism to prevailing definitions of textual authority and integrity have rendered obsolete conventional evaluative terms, putting in question even the notion of 'between' in the context of translation (Tymoczko 2003). On the other hand, the work of postcolonial scholars has documented the extent to which translations can go 'wrong', even 'respectfully' (Spivak 1992b: 183) when inequalities and power relationships between cultures are not understood and acknowledged appropriately (see POSTCOLONIAL APPROACHES). In both instances the practice of translation becomes newly visible and the role of the translator is scrutinized; in both instances value judgements are made according to new and shifting criteria.

Despite the unquestionable freedom that the radical decentring associated with poststructuralism offers translators, the very requirement of decentring itself carries a set of expectations and implicit evaluative criteria. For if post-structuralism granted a new agency to translators (Venuti 1992: 11), it also imposed on them an increased burden of responsibility. In the absence of universal definitions, translators have been called on to make explicit the strategies and goals that govern their practice (see, for example, Arrojo 1998). They are also encouraged to write prefaces, afterwords, and other forms of commentary. Especially in the case of innovative, transgressive texts, they are expected to translate transgressively, and their work has been measured against criteria such as 'abusive' (Lewis 1985: 56) or 'destructive' (Conley 1986: 49) fidelity. In this measurement, words like *accurate* and *incorrect* are not relevant. Instead, failure is associated with an inability to continue the linguistic momentum of a text, with an 'excess of reverence' that can make it impossible for a translator to 'take the necessary distance from the original' – which must function not as an absolute but as a point of departure (Sartiliot 1988: 28). Consequently, translations are often measured as well in the light of the translators' own words about their work or in terms of the context in which the work appears. Such criticism, in addition to concerning itself with new translations, implies the re-evaluation of translations performed in the past (Conley 1986; Porter 1991). It also implies the acceptance of multiple versions and the evaluation of individual versions with respect to the purposes for which each version is intended – 'the different values behind what makes a "good" translation' (Cohen 1988: 111).

The simultaneous agency and responsibility accorded the translator by contemporary theories of literature and translation also characterize the translator's work as defined by translators and critics who position themselves with respect to a specific location or ideology. For when translation is defined in terms of a 'site for raising questions of representation, power, and historicity' (Niranjana 1992: 1), the expectation is that those questions will be raised. This is a definition that challenges translators to rethink the conventional use of *equivalence, difference* and *communication*. In the face of not merely difference but decided inequalities between languages and cultures, translators have been asked to construct a 'site' in which there is 'overlap without equivalence' (Bhabha 1994a: 186) and urged to make their work not fluent and readable but 'thick' (Appiah 1993) with the factors that can make smooth interaction an illusion on the part of the more powerful party. This can occur in texts themselves or in the various commentaries that accompany them as 'combat weapons' against time (Mukherjeee 1994: 73), but also against transparency on the part of the translation. Consequently, a translation may not be evaluated on the basis of its readability and the 'communication' it makes possible but in terms of a newly defined literalism (Robinson 1993: 124; Gaddis Rose 1995: 84), the extent to which it prompts a crisis in communication, or even the extent to which translation is withheld (Spivak 1992a: 192–5, 1992b: 792). Translators themselves may be evaluated in terms of their qualifications

to represent 'another' identity – nationality, race, religion, GENDER (Voldeng 1984; de Lotbinière-Harwood 1991: 139–91; Spivak 1992a: 178–92). In a similar way, translations can be judged in terms of the (mis)representations and the 'exotic and essentializing stereotypes' they perpetuate (Payne 1993: 3).

The co-existence of such numerous and diverse evaluative criteria and approaches offers a challenge to contemporary critics, readers and translators. Whether critics work to evaluate contemporary translations or those performed in the past, they find themselves obliged to inform themselves about the cultural context of a given translation and also to be cognizant of their own evaluative criteria and the context within which they apply them. Likewise, readers and translators must formulate evaluative criteria that will enable them to assess divergent, even contradictory critical evaluations. For example, Venuti has discussed the innovative, subtly 'foreignizing' STRATEGIES in the translations of the work by writers such as Argentine Julio Cortázar that during the 1960s altered both the 'canon of foreign fiction in Anglo-American culture' and 'British and American fiction' (Venuti 1995: 266). Payne, on the other hand, finds that translations of the '"big four" of the Latin American boom' have reinforced, rather than challenged, North American stereotypes about Latin America (1993: 30–31, 33).

An additional example is provided by recent evaluations of the work of Sir William Jones, whose translations into English of Indian literature were highly influential in the late eighteenth century (see INDIAN TRADITION). Cannon praises Jones's work without qualification, particularly his translation of Kalidasa's *Sakuntala* (1789), stating that his work prompted Europeans to have a new respect for Indian literature (1986: 181). Figueira, however, finds that Jones's translation, like those of other translators of the *Sakuntala*, was often 'erroneous', generating misrepresentations of the Indian work (1991: 198–9). Niranjana (1992) and Sengupta (1995) offer still harsher evaluations. Sengupta emphasizes the oversimplification of Kalidasa's work that occurred as Jones shaped an 'image' for it that Europeans would find acceptable (1995: 161–2); Niranjana details his participation, through his translation, in the construction of the English-language Hindu character, psyche and way of life (1992: 13–14, 60).

Looking towards the future, it is possible to note two trends in evaluative practices. Translators and translation scholars are devoting increased attention to reviewing, criticism, the study of reception (see, for example, Bush 2004/2005; Cohn 2006; Fawcett 2000; Munday 1998b, 2007; Vanderschelden 2000a) and the effectiveness of the alienating strategies advanced by Venuti and others (see, for example, Abel 2005; Leppihalme 2000); the proposal of more comprehensive approaches to reviewing (Tymoczko 2000b); and the advocacy for reviews of translations that address the translator's work (PEN). In addition, the rise is well underway of an interactive, international discussion on the Internet that includes general readers and bloggers as well as critics, scholars and professional reviewers. One hopes that these exchanges will raise the level of commentary about the evaluation of literature in translation and counter, at least to an extent, the cursory, and in some places significantly decreased coverage of literature in translation found in the print media.

See also:
LITERARY TRANSLATION; POETRY; QUALITY.

Further reading
Woolf 1939; Douma 1972; de Beaugrande 1978; van den Broeck 1985; Newmark 1988; Smith 1987/1990; Vilikovský 1988; Hatim and Mason 1990b; Maier 1990–91; Hearne 1991; Munday 1998b; PEN American Center 2004; Bush 2004/2005.

CAROL MAIER

Rewriting

The theory of rewriting proposed by André Lefevere (1945–96) draws on systemic/descriptive approaches and treats translation as a discursive activity embedded within a system of literary conventions and a network of institutions and social agents that condition textual production (see POLYSYSTEM; DESCRIPTIVE VS. COMMITTED APPROACHES). Translating, according to Lefevere, is one of several types of

practice that result in partial representations of reality. These forms of **rewriting** include editing, reviewing and anthologizing – with translation being a particularly effective form of rewriting that has been instrumental throughout the ages in the circulation of novel ideas and new literary trends. Rewriting and **refraction** (the latter a term used in Lefevere's earlier work) refer to the projection of a perspectival image of a literary work (novel, play, poem) (Lefevere 1982/2000: 234–5, 1992a: 10). Lefevere nevertheless questions the concept of originality (see DECONSTRUCTION), arguing that the notion of authorial genius and the idea that there can be access to an author's intention stem from the poetics of Romanticism and are untenable given that no 'original' is sacred and that all 'originals' draw on prior sources (1982/2000: 234). As Hermans (1999: 124) puts it, the picture Lefevere draws 'does not quite amount to a postmodern hall of mirrors and simulacra without a trace of any "originals", but it certainly highlights both the quantitative and the qualitative significance of these "refractions" for the perception and transmission of cultural goods'.

Rewriting is subject to certain 'intra-systemic' constraints: *language, the universe of discourse* and *poetics*; it is also subject to the influence of regulatory forces, namely, *the professionals* within the literary system, and *patronage* operating from outside the system. Both types of constraint operate as 'control factors' in Lefevere's model. Under **language**, Lefevere discusses differences between the source and target language and linguistic SHIFTS of various kinds that are dictated, for example, by the dominant aesthetic criteria and IDEOLOGY of the time (Lefevere 1992a: 103–9). **Universe of discourse** refers to 'the knowledge, the learning, but also the objects and the customs of a certain time, to which writers are free to allude in their work' (Lefevere 1985: 233), in other words, to 'cultural scripts' (1992a: 87; see CULTURE). **Poetics** refers to aesthetic precepts that dominate the literary system at a certain point in time. Poetics consists of two components, an *inventory* component (a repertoire of genres, literary devices, motifs, certain symbols, prototypical characters or situations) and a *functional* component, which concerns the issue of how literature has to or can function within society (Lefevere 1982/2000: 236, 1992a:

26). Both components of poetics are subject to processes of deferred fossilization; in other words, there is an ongoing process of literary trends coming into and going out of fashion, with certain genres and authors dominating certain stages in the evolution of a literary system (e.g. *tanka*, *renga*, and *haiku* in Japanese literature, in that order) (1992a: 35). **The professionals** are the individuals (critics, translators, and so on) who elaborate aesthetic criteria, control the literary system and filter material in or out of it. Strictly regulated literary systems even appoint individuals or create institutions with the express purpose of bringing about aesthetic stability in the system; the Académie Française and similar language institutions are good examples (Lefevere 1985: 232). **Patronage** can be understood as the powers, be they persons or institutions, which can further or hinder the reading, writing or rewriting of literature and is usually more concerned with the ideology of literature than its poetics (Lefevere 1992a: 15). Patronage can be exercised by individuals (Louis XIV, for instance), by groups of people, religious bodies (see Lai 2007), political parties, social classes, royal courts, publishers, and the media (printed or otherwise) (Lefevere 1992a: 15).

Patronage consists of three components, the ideological, economic and status components, with all three interacting in complex ways. IDEOLOGY, an inherently slippery term, is briefly defined by Lefevere as a general world view that guides people's actions, as well as a diffuse, taken-for-granted frame of mind. The influence of ideology on the translation process may be traced in omissions, shifts and additions of various kinds. The economic component of patronage concerns the translator's economic survival. The patron sees to it that writers and rewriters are able to make a living by giving them a pension, appointing them to some office, paying royalties on the sales of books or employing (re)writers as teachers and reviewers (1985: 227). The economic component also acts as a control factor on a more global level, for example by regulating royalties and production costs nationally and internationally (1982/2000: 245–6). Acceptance of patronage signals integration into and acceptance of the style of life of a group or subculture of some kind, or an elite in the sense of the most talented and powerful group of individuals (1985: 228). This is precisely what the *status* component refers to. It is status conferred upon a writer in a given society that allows him or her to be integrated into a certain 'support group' or its lifestyle (Lefevere 1982/2000: 236, 1992a: 16).

Patronage can be undifferentiated or differentiated. In undifferentiated patronage, the three components (ideological, economic and status) are all dispensed by one source, i.e. one patron (Lefevere 1992a: 17). Totalitarian regimes and the monarchies of the past are good examples. Differentiated patronage is typical of (contemporary) democratic or liberal societies, where an array of different patrons are active at the same time and assume disparate ideological positions, and where, for instance, financial success does not necessarily confer status (Lefevere 1982/2000: 228, 236).

Limitations

Lefevere's theory of rewriting attempts to incorporate a wide range of complex factors in an essentially flat model; the strain is evident in the terminology employed as well as the structure of the model. Hermans (1999: 124) acknowledges the strength and appeal of Lefevere's work but stresses that it is 'also frequently superficial, inconsistent, and sloppy'.

As explained above, the theory posits that there are two factors that *control* the literary system, the group of professionals within and patronage outside the system (with apparently no overlap, or none discussed by Lefevere). Thus, individuals or institutions within and outside the system assume a gatekeeping role, serving as guardians of poetics and ideology and rewriting works accordingly. In addition, the theory builds in the dominant poetics, language and universe of discourse as control factors. But it is difficult to see how institutions and gatekeepers of any kind can function as constraints in the same way as language or universe of discourse might. The lack of a clear distinction between the mainly literary/systemic product of rewriting and gatekeepers with a potential influence on rewriting results in a certain level of vagueness. Lefevere seems to adopt a Foucaultian approach to patronage and translation as determining and determined, but fails to clarify this dynamic in his case studies. Patronage may mean exercising strategic behaviour in society and imposing constraints on others, but it may also be circumscribed by the patron's position in the sociopolitical environment. Similarly, translation is conditioned by constraints within or outside the system, but it is also a shaping force in the system. Moreover, Lefevere's list of constraints varies from one publication to another, and sometimes within the same publication: for example, in Lefevere (1992a), there is a simple scheme of two factors that 'determine the image of a work projected by a translation'; in order of importance, these two factors are the translator's ideology and poetics, which jointly determine solutions to problems posed by the universe of discourse and language (ibid.: 41). Although language is not presented as a constraint from the beginning of the book (or in any of his essays in general), Lefevere nonetheless goes on to present it as such in a dedicated chapter, where he compares translations of a poem by Catullus which were produced in the last 200 years, offering a list of what he calls 'illocutionary strategies': morphosyntactic patterns, lexical choice and connotation and metric patterning (ibid.: 101–10).

The fluidity of terminology allows for the free 're-writing' of the main concepts of Lefevere's model in secondary sources: Gentzler refers to two constraints, ideology and poetics (1993/2001: 136–8); Chesterman mentions five constraints: patronage, poetics, the universe of discourse, the source-target languages (treated as one category), and the translator's ideology (1997: 78); Hatim talks about a double control factor, poetics and ideology, and then lists eight different factors that influence translation (2001: 63, 64); Munday refers to three factors that control the literary system in which translation functions: professionals within the literary system, patronage outside the literary system, and the dominant poetics (2001: 128–9). This indicates that sociocultural, ideological and literary constraints are not sufficiently delineated in Lefevere's model. At any rate, and irrespective of issues of overlap and vagueness of terminology, it is perhaps unrealistic to assume that such dissimilar sets of constraints can be neatly grouped together in a flat model, or that a complete list can be identified for something

as complex as rewriting. More constraints, for instance, can easily be added to the model, the audience (potential reception and presupposed knowledge) being an obvious candidate.

The notion of patronage is unduly rigid in Lefevere's model. First, the tripartite internal structure of patronage is much more diffuse in real life. Lefevere argues that the three components of patronage (economic, status and ideological) can 'enter various combinations' (1992a: 16), but this does not explain how they can be distinguished from each other or from other types of constraints for the purposes of descriptive analysis, nor why this separation is deemed productive. The economic factor, which can determine whether or not a given work or works will be translated (in their entirety), is inextricably linked to the status of the text and the ideology of the patrons. Thus, the English translation of Henriette Walter's *Le Français dans tous les sens* (1985) could only be undertaken after the French government agreed to pay a subsidy to the UK publisher, in order to promote what they saw as a token of Frenchness in the English system (Fawcett 1995: 181). Even in cases where economic considerations mean little more than making profit, ideology does not simply become inoperative: some institutions of patronage subscribe to corporate values, competition and the achievement of a high turnover more than others. These values influence the selection of works that are deemed 'good' or worth translating. Nor can ideology, perhaps the least satisfactorily defined factor in Lefevere's model, be divorced from components outside the system of patronage. Language, which occasionally features as a separate constraint in Lefevere's model, is clearly not ideologically neutral (Fairclough 1989; Fowler *et al.* 1995; see DISCOURSE ANALYSIS; LINGUISTIC APPROACHES).

Another shortcoming of the model concerns the binary distinction between differentiated and undifferentiated patronage. Studies on totalitarian regimes have repeatedly demonstrated that power is exerted in a less monolithic way than Lefevere's model would seem to suggest. For instance, both in Italy under Mussolini and in Nazi Germany, the state (in the case of Germany it was the educational and library system collaborating with Party institutions) controlled cultural production and translation intermittently, at times allowing for loopholes and some margin for negotiation, especially during the first few years before the war (Rundle 2000; Kohlmayer 1992; Sturge 1999). As these countries edged closer towards war, they began to close such loopholes and regulate the functional and inventory components of poetics more strictly (see case studies in Billiani 2007a; CENSORSHIP).

Applications

Despite its limitations, Lefevere's model has been instrumental in situating translation within a broader set of activities to which it is inextricably linked, and in drawing researchers' attention to social and INSTITUTIONAL factors that influence all processes of rewriting. Lefevere reiterated the importance of the interdependence of poetics, social agency and ideology throughout his work and provided an impressive battery of examples from various traditions, from Europe to Africa and America. This has inspired a range of case studies that drew heavily on his model or some elements of it, especially patronage (Zhao 2005, 2006; Lai 2007, among others). Drawing on Lefevere's model, particularly the notions of patronage, poetics and ideology, Zhao (2006) demonstrates how Hu Shi, a prominent Chinese intellectual, became a major proponent of the New Culture Movement in China (1919–1923), a movement fuelled by a massive import of foreign ideologies and poetics. Hu Shi's complex treatment of Ibsen illustrates the full range of rewritings discussed by Lefevere and demonstrates the extent to which the conceptualization of the activities that constitute translation can be stretched. Hu Shi managed to introduce sinicized foreign ideas into China by means of subtle domesticating and contextualizing translation techniques in strategically selected plays by Ibsen (see STRATEGIES). His own 'original' play, *Life's Greatest Event*, was an imitation of Ibsen's *A Doll's House*; it promoted an ideology of individualism and focused on political issues rather than dramatic technique. Hu Shi's influential essay entitled *Ibsenism* ventriloquized and (re)interpreted Ibsen's views, projecting Hu Shi's own agenda of internationalism and social critique (Zhao 2005: 162, 168, 241).

In a similar study that draws on Lefevere's model of rewriting to explain a series of theatrical performances and demonstrate the influence of socio political conditions and personal agendas, McNeil (2005) examines the various rewritings of Brecht's *Leben des Galilei* in English. The 1947 premiere of *Galileo* in America was the fruit of a close and 'respectful' collaboration between Charles Laughton (who was working from literal translations into English) and Brecht (who was still revising his 'history play' version of 1938). The result was a play that was much sharper, faster, with fewer scenes, a play that brought out the contradiction between individual and social morality, between science's potential and its historical applications (McNeil 2005: 67). This was a play that engaged with immediate dilemmas in the aftermath of Hiroshima. The 1980 production for the National Theatre in the UK, on the other hand, was the result of a different division of labour and authority. The National Theatre commissioned Howard Brenton, who worked from literal as well as existing translations of the play and who sought to imitate, appropriate and (aggressively) supersede Brecht in order to produce a modernized version that can serve as a riposte to Thatcherism (ibid.: 74). The director, John Dexter, on the other hand, saw Brecht's *Life of Galileo* as a concealed autobiography of someone who 'sold out'; he sought to 'get rid of the Marxist rubbish' in order to portray Brecht as a survivor and modified the text accordingly to produce a faster piece that would be more appropriate as a National Theatre production (ibid.: 84, 89). The end-product was a barometer of the tensions pervading socialist theatre in England, given the limitations imposed by a conservative government on left theatre: this tension took the form of a dialectic relation between a rejection of the mainstream, bourgeois values and institutional outlets and a compromise that allowed Brenton and Dexter to send out a message even to a bourgeois audience that is not necessarily responsive (ibid.: 94) (see DRAMA).

The appeal of Lefevere's model lies in the fact that it identifies important contextual factors that impinge on translation, irrespective of how well it weaves these factors into a coherent model. The way in which these factors operate, and the promotion of political and other interests through translation, are not restricted to the area of literature (Lefevere's main preoccupation).

The same can be said to apply to other types of translation and to polymedial products such as ADVERTISING material, AUDIOVISUAL material, and COMICS. Examples include the rewriting of the Treaty of Waitangi into Maori, with political repercussions that continue to reverberate in contemporary New Zealand (Fenton and Moon 2003), and Croatian nationalistic 'rewritings' of the Asterix series after the dissolution of Yugoslavia (Kadric and Kaindl 1997). These and other non-literary instances of rewriting can be productively analysed using some version of Lefevere's model. In order to investigate cases such as these, it is necessary to take into account the interplay between textual variables and power/patronage in the broader socio political context in which translation takes place, and Lefevere's theory of rewriting provides at least a stimulating first step in this direction.

See also:

ADAPTATION; CENSORSHIP; CLASSICAL TEXTS; DESCRIPTIVE VS. COMMITTED APPROACHES; LITERARY TRANSLATION; POLYSYSTEM; PUBLISHING STRATEGIES; SHAKESPEARE; SOCIOLOGICAL APPROACHES.

Further reading
Lefevere 1982/2000, 1985, 1992a; Hermans 1999; Zhao 2006; Lai 2007.

DIMITRIS ASIMAKOULAS

S

Scientific and technical translation

The binominal phrase 'science and technology' occurs frequently in corpora of news and academic prose (Biber *et al.* 1999: 1033) and it is perhaps its familiar nature which leads us very readily to use the term 'scientific and technical translation'. This nomenclature appears to indicate that there is a useful distinction to be made between 'scientific and technical translation', COMMERCIAL TRANSLATION, 'legal translation', etc. At first glance, the topic-based distinction might be regarded as clear-cut. However, in practice, it is not unusual for the term 'technical translation' to be used to refer to the translation of texts from domains other than technology/applied science. For some scholars, 'technical translation' is synonymous with 'specialized translation' or the translation of language for special purposes (LSP), as exemplified by the definition of technical translation offered by Wright and Wright (1993: 1). There is also widespread use of the term 'pragmatic translation', introduced by Casagrande (1954: 335) to refer to translation where the purpose is 'to translate a message as efficiently and as accurately as possible' and where 'the emphasis is on the content of the message' as opposed to its aesthetic or literary form. This topic-independent label is frequently used in relation to translation of text types common in scientific, technical and commercial domains.

Proceeding from an understanding of scientific and technical translation as the translation of texts from the domains of science and technology, another point of contention arises: namely, the extent to which it is meaningful to group these two together. Byrne (2006: 8), for example, argues that it is not, because scientific and technical texts exhibit differences in 'subject matter, type of language [and] purpose'.

Notwithstanding the difficulties with classification, it is widely acknowledged that translation has played a major role in the dissemination of knowledge – often scientific or technical – throughout the ages. Though under-represented in translation studies, there has been some historical research which takes scientific and technical texts as a basis for in-depth theoretical reflection on the role of translation; for example, Pym's (2000a) case study of translation of medicine, mathematics and astronomy from Arabic into Latin in twelfth-century Toledo, and Delisle and Woodsworth's (1995) discussion of the translation of science in the Chinese and Indian historical contexts. From a history of science perspective, Montgomery, who argues that 'translation is involved at every level of knowledge production and distribution in the sciences' (2000: ix), has carried out studies of scientific translation activity in several historical periods. Likewise, Burnett (e.g. 2005) has conducted extensive research on the transfer of mathematics and science from the Arab world to Europe through translation.

Scientific texts are now increasingly written with international consumption in mind and in the lingua franca of English. However, technical translation activity is flourishing in today's global economy and information society, in which there is strong demand for product specifications, instruction leaflets, user guides, etc., in many languages, as well as for the LOCALIZATION of software applications.

Guides to scientific and technical translation

The majority of publications which focus on scientific and technical translation have aimed to serve as guides to those performing translation in these fields. Paradigmatic shifts in translation studies are mirrored, with word-based or sentence-based approaches gradually ceding to more FUNCTIONAL and user-based approaches.

One of the first publications in Europe was Jumpelt's (1961) *Die Übersetzung naturwissenschaftlicher und technischer Literatur*, a guide to the translation of scientific and technical texts, with examples from German and English. His approach is based on the assumption that while there are some translation choices which are 'subjective', i.e. which an individual translator is free to make, there are other choices which are 'objective', i.e. determined by other factors which make certain constructions, formulations or shifts 'compulsory' or 'likely' (ibid.: 175, my translation). Jumpelt focuses on the 'objective' choices, seeking to uncover regularities which are recognized by the discourse community and can therefore be analysed and compared across languages to aid translators in their task. His analysis first focuses on obligatory translation SHIFTS and transpositions at the levels of the word and the grammatical structure; these are necessitated by features of the target language system. Jumpelt then discusses 'complex units of meaning' (e.g. compounds and complex noun phrases) where the context and conventions of use play an important role in determining translation options. While Jumpelt regards most translation decisions as linguistic, he sees genre conventions and the need for accuracy as important constraints on scientific and technical translation; it is these constraints which render scientific and technical translation at least as difficult as other kinds of translation and which also make this translation activity a valid object of study (Jumpelt 1961: 186). Here, he departs from the views of theorists before him (e.g. Ortega y Gassett 1937/2000: 50) who argue that scientific translation is easier than translation of LITERARY texts, due to a perceived universality of the language of science and/or of scientific thought.

In relation to stylistic considerations – which, Jumpelt argues, are just as relevant for scientific and technical translation as for any other kind of translation – he stresses that the basic requirements are simplicity, clarity and precision. He asserts that a translation should read like a text on the same subject written originally in the target language; stylistic choices are determined by the target language and purpose of the translation and they are independent of the source text (Jumpelt 1961: 171). EQUIVALENCE is used as a criterion for establishing correspondence between source text and target text, but is seen as dependent on context and situation, i.e. taking usage, institutional and genre conventions into account (ibid.: 51).

Jumpelt's work was perceived as filling an important gap (Oettinger 1963: 350), and it raised issues which continue to be pertinent; these include the question of style in scientific and technical writing; the prioritization of the target text, target readers and target text purpose; the notions of equivalence, adequacy and accuracy as parameters of QUALITY; the processes of simplification and EXPLICITATION in translation; the role of text-type or genre conventions and, finally, the imbalance between the extent of scientific and technical translation activity in the professional world and the lack of attention it receives in the academic discipline.

By way of contrast, one of the first books in English on the subject was Finch's (1969) *An Approach to Technical Translation*, aimed primarily at scientists with some foreign language ability. Finch, who believes that technical translation is less difficult than translation of literary works, outlines as specific, unique features of scientific text and scientific translations the fact that they are intended to be read by scientists and that therefore 'obtrusive "style" should be notable by its absence', that they are usually of recent scientific work and are intended to be read immediately, and that usually there will be only one translation produced (ibid.: 4–5). It is possible, Finch asserts, to produce a 'perfect' translation, 'one which fulfils the same purpose in the new language as the original did in the language in which it was written' (ibid.: 3–4). The ideal situation is when the translation is not recognized as a translation. It is also possible to produce a translation which is 'better' than the original, 'by clarification and avoidance of clumsy phrases' (ibid.: 5). Problems arise when new ideas are being discussed and new TERMINOLOGY may be required. Looking beyond the preponderance of prescriptive statements about translation into 'literate English' and the stereotypical discussion of false friends in the Romance languages, word order in German texts, etc., there is some evidence of a FUNCTIONALIST APPROACH in Finch's anecdotal work. He insists, for example, on the importance of knowing for what purpose the information is required, asserting that 'a statement of the user's requirements can be a valuable help to the translator', and acknowledges that a full, unabridged translation (as opposed to summary or translation of only parts of the text) may not always be required (ibid.: 8). One of the main questions arising from Finch's work continues to be discussed today in relation to the competencies of the technical translator; those who seek to identify an 'ideal' translator's profile tend to compare the relative merits of a linguist who has specialist domain knowledge with those of a domain specialist who has linguistic competence.

Most of the works which followed those of Finch and Jumpelt were written by professional scientific or technical translators. They were aimed at translators or trainees, and therefore had a strong didactic and normative function. They focused their predominantly terminological analysis on specific language combinations. Maillot, for example, published *La traduction scientifique et technique* in 1969, with an extended second edition in 1981. His stated aim is to move away from studies which focus entirely on vocabulary, and to prioritize instead the precision and rigour required in the translation of scientific and technical texts, seeking to establish laws or rules which are valid for scientific and technical translation and which could perhaps be extended to other forms of translation (Maillot 1981: 3). In spite of this, Maillot's discussion is firmly focused on terminological and lexical matters, with chapters on equivalence of terms and concepts, synonymy and other semantic relations, faux amis, word formation, complex terms, proper nouns, bilingual and multilingual dictionaries, nomenclature and terminology, terminology standardization, transcription and translit-

eration, symbols and units of measurement, abbreviations, punctuation and typography. He illustrates his discussion with examples from French, English, German and Russian. This book was translated into Spanish in the late 1990s, which would indicate that its content continues to be considered useful in translator TRAINING. Similarly, Pinchuck, in *Scientific and Technical Translation* (1977), develops principles for solving technical translation problems, using translation from German into English as exemplification, and this book, together with Bédard's (1986) *La traduction technique: principes et pratique*, still figures on reading lists and in bibliographies.

The approach changed somewhat with Hann's (1992a, 1992b) contribution, *The Key to Technical Translation*. Volume 1 is concerned with concept specification, while Volume 2 deals with terminology and lexicography. Hann's approach is first to provide translators with an understanding of key concepts which may be used in technical texts, i.e. to impart a basic subject knowledge, and then to familiarize them with the German and English terminology related to these key concepts. The subjects covered range from material science to electronic engineering, from automotive engineering to computing, and a range of terminological resources are offered to aid the novice technical translator. This is an approach which is continued and extended in Hann's (2004) *A Basis for Scientific and Engineering Translation*. Underlying this work is the view that, first, translators require a conceptual understanding of science or technology and, second, they can benefit from a translation-oriented organization and presentation of this summarized knowledge.

Byrne (2006) may be indicative of a new perspective on technical translation which is much less focused on terminology-oriented analysis of LSP texts and more interested in the function and reception of those texts. He concentrates on the issue of usability of technical documentation and draws on technical writing and cognitive engineering to do so. Finally, in keeping with a growing interest in issues of TRAINING AND EDUCATION, Montalt and Gonzalez Davis (2007) offer a reflective approach to the teaching and learning of medical translation.

Theories applicable to scientific and technical translation

In his seminal paper of 1972, Holmes wrote about 'text-type restricted' theories of translation, i.e. theories which would 'deal with the problem of translating specific types or genres of lingual message' (Holmes 1972/2000: 180). He argued that there had been long-standing efforts to produce theories for the translation of literary or sacred texts, but that attempts to develop theories for the translation of scientific texts were relatively new. However, Holmes also believed that such theories would not succeed because the discipline lacked 'anything like a formal theory of message, text or discourse types' (1972/2000: 180). In his view, writing on scientific and technical translation was overly focused on the word and word-group level, but he saw potential for new approaches based on the then emerging work in linguistics on defining text types, communication types and language varieties (ibid.: 179).

Such an approach is offered by Sager (1994), who, in aiming to provide 'an industrially oriented analysis of translation' (ibid.: xix), brings together insights from LSP, communication theory and theories of text type and messages to produce a model of the translation process and a discussion of translation technology (principally MACHINE TRANSLATION). On the basis of translation practice, he develops classifications of text types, types of translation activities and functional types of translation (including selective translation), and describes the translation process step by step (see COMMERCIAL TRANSLATION for a more detailed discussion of Sager's model).

Other theoretical approaches to translation studies which were to follow Holmes's paper and which were to prove particularly applicable to technical and scientific translation include those of the functionalist school. Most strongly associated with scientific and technical translation are Vermeer's (e.g. 1989b) 'skopos theory' (see FUNCTIONALIST APPROACHES) and subsequent refinements (e.g. Nord's 1997 addition of the notion of loyalty).

In research terms, there is a dearth of studies on this 'ugly duckling of translation' (Byrne 2006: 1), as demonstrated by Aixela's (2004) bibliographic survey. Diverse contributions on scientific and technical translation may be found in some journals (especially *Meta* and *JoSTrans*) and in collected volumes, e.g. Wright and Wright (1993), Fischbach (1998), Gotti and Sarcevic (2006). The study of terminology continues to be seen as relevant (e.g. Bowker and Pearson 2002), while CORPORA have also been used to analyse other features of scientific and technical translations, such as ADAPTATION to target language NORMS (e.g. Baumgarten *et al.* 2004). As noted above, user-based perspectives have gained in prominence, and it is possible that future theoretical developments in scientific and technical translation may draw increasingly on COGNITIVE and SOCIOLOGICAL models of knowledge construction and communication (see, for example, Bennett 2007).

See also:
COMMERCIAL TRANSLATION; INSTITUTIONAL TRANSLATION; LOCALIZATION, TERMINOLOGY.

Further reading
Wright and Wright 1993; Delisle and Woodsworth 1995; Montgomery 2000; Pym 2000a; Aixelá 2004; Baumgarten *et al.* 2004; Hann 2004; Byrne 2006; Bennett 2007.

MAEVE OLOHAN

Script

The topic of script in the context of translation keenly raises the question of how to define the notion of script itself, of what may properly constitute writing. Exploring the concept of grammatology, Derrida exposes a strong Western prejudice against scripts that are not phonetic or – worse – not alphabetic, these often being denied the status of writing proper (see DECONSTRUCTION). He detects what he calls a 'phonologism' that persistently underrates the formal resources of visible language (Derrida 1976: 102; cf. Davies 1987: 35). And yet, since his concerns are mainly philosophical he proposes no workable scheme in its stead. From a point of view that is both literary and practical, one thing is certain: however reified and subservient to speech a script-type may be (Herrick 1975), it may nonetheless always function in its own right as a significant factor in a given text, and hence in the translation of it. Technically, script establishes, if nothing else, a reading order and direction which, as in the different cases of Chinese (downwards), early Greek (alternately left to right and right to left, or **boustrophedon**), Arabic (right to left), and English (left to right), may much complicate the task of interlinear or parallel translation. In ideological terms, it may be actively set against any form of transcription or translation, as in the case of the divinely arranged characters of the QUR'ĀN.

The use of visible language merely to convey speech, in what Jakobson (1959) has termed a cognitive fashion, is of course most pronounced in alphabetic systems; yet it is present wherever there is phoneticism. Hence, faced with ancient hieroglyphic scripts like those of the Egyptians and of the Maya, which make an undeniable visual statement in their own right, decipherers have aimed primarily at their phonetic elements, seeking to crack their linguistic code (Coe 1992) as if it were a case of artificial language used for military intelligence. At the same time, the characters of any script may have or be accorded a non-phonetic value of their own, a fact which demands a different order of deciphering or translation. Such is the case with the brush-stroked ideogram of a type of Japanese poem known as *haiku*, or the alphabetic letter integrated into a concrete poem by Ian Hamilton Finlay (Henderson 1958; Bann 1977).

The clearest and commonest type of value that may inhere in a written character, regardless of any phonetic message, is visual or pictorial **image**, the proper reading of which has provoked intense debate among translators of Chinese ideograms. Besides being image, a character may also be a **cipher** and have numerical value, like the syllables of Hebrew or the alphabetic letters of Greek. And finally, a character may conventionally convey a concept through an attributed **name**, like those of the Germanic runes. In order to explore what is at stake here for the translator, we may in the first instance best refer to scripts from the Old World, since to date these have been far more thoroughly analysed and interrelated than have those of the New (Diringer 1968; Gelb 1974; Harris 2001).

Old World scripts: image, cipher and name

Character as image: the pictorial element. As Gardiner's *Grammar* confirms, Egyptian hieroglyphs, being phonetic, can generally be transcribed into the alphabet and translated without particular loss. However, early hieratic texts used by priests in ancient Egypt, for example the murals in the Theban tombs, deliberately bring out their pictorial origin and quality as water, bird, human face or fish, to the degree of setting up an alternative visual reading (Gardiner 1973). Further, certain of the hieroglyphs in any case primarily serve as pictures since, though formally indistinguishable from the rest, they are not phonetic at all. These are the **generic determinatives** that indicate an area of meaning, for example, canals of irrigated land, mountains of foreign country, sun, the sailing boat of the gods and kings, a cup, the raised arms of height, the gnawing of a tooth, or the age of an old man leaning on his stick. In the Book of the Dead, the pictorial message is strongly reinforced through the visual echoing of these determinatives in figures and other elements featured in the vignettes or scenes that introduce chapters. Overall, these images vividly convey the logic and beliefs assumed in an otherwise (for us) remote dialogue with the world of the dead. In his edition of this work from the Papyrus of Ani, Wallis Budge (1967) offers both 'an interlinear transliteration and translation', which includes the hieroglyphic original complete with non-phonetic images, and 'a running translation', which does not include the hieroglyphic original and attends only to phonetic meaning. Comparing them even for a moment makes clear the huge loss sustained in the second version.

Authorities on Chinese script inform us that when its characters are read rapidly they function as logographs, mere signs for words and no more (Needham 1958; Cooper 1978). However, with the pondered reading required by poetry in any language, the make-up of characters may assume some importance, so that in a stanza about mountains a whole series of characters may occur in which the mountain element is present (Teele 1949). The distinction, in other words, again does not have to do with the putative nature of the characters but with their actual functions in different kinds of texts and readings, though professional Sinologists continue to insist that the characters are essentially non-poetic in the visual sense. With astounding insight, Ezra Pound drew on the visual and paratactic functions of Chinese script in his edition of Fenellosa's essay 'The Chinese written character as a medium for poetry' (1936) and in his translations of poetry (*Cathay* 1915) and of writings by Confucius. At all events, the effect of the Chinese example on Pound's own poetry is indisputable: indeed, his imagist techniques radically transformed poetry in English and several other Western languages (Yip 1969; Kenner 1970; Steiner 1975; 358; Po-Fei Huang 1989). Chinese script likewise prompted the visual brilliance of *Calligrammes*, the work of Pound's French contemporary Guillaume Apollinaire. As adapted to the *tanka* and other highly structured verse forms in Japanese, the sheer layout of these characters and the links between them further lay behind the experiment *Renga: a Chain of Poems* (1969) that coordinated, in vertical and horizontal readings, sonnets and stanzas of sonnets composed by the four poet-translators Octavio Paz, Jacques Roubaud, Edoardo Sanguinetti and Charles Tomlinson (Tomlinson 1979). Reciprocally, translations of Western verse into Japanese script have put particular emphasis on set structures of syllabic characters (Naito 1993).

Character as cipher: hidden meanings. A visual element also inheres in the early stages of the Semitic script tradition which eventually issued into the alphabets of Europe: witness the Greek *alpha* and *beta* which, turned through ninety degrees, are still legible as the ox head *aleph* and the town *beth*. Yet, with the fixing of a finite and small number of syllabic signs (contrast the 214 radicals of the Chinese dictionary *Tz'u Hai*) numeracy has had greater importance, to the extent that Hebrew and Greek letters automatically denote the cardinal number of their position in the overall series. In Hebrew, the physical alignment of the twenty-two characters on the page in rows and squares, and their equation with numbers through the *Albam* and *Atbash* formulae, were taken to great lengths in the literature of the Kabbala, as part of a philosophy that sought to contain the universe in a text. Kabbalistic messages can be deciphered in the Old Testament and even in the New, for example in verses in the Book of Jeremiah (25: 26; 51: 1) and Revelation (13: 18); the first of these specifically invokes Babel or Babylon, that source of script and mathematics alike (Cook and Ginsburg 1911). Although Bible translations into European languages that use the Latin alphabet of western Christendom typically fail to make explicit this ciphered value of the Hebrew text, it has found literary echoes. Consider, for instance, the concept of the *Tetragrammaton*, which literally means 'four letters' and refers to the Hebrew name of God, a name consisting of the four consonants Y, H, V and H and considered too sacred to be pronounced. The Tetragrammaton and other key Kabbalistic concepts are for example translated into modern plots in the *Ficciones* of the Latin American writer Jorge Luis Borges (1944/1999).

Character as name: the self-referential element. Beyond conveying an image or a cipher, the characters of a script may signify through the name by which they are known and recognized. A classic case here are the runes of northern Europe whose origin remains in dispute but which, in Anglo-Saxon and other Germanic literatures, are perceived to represent an ancient pagan force. Known as the *Futhorc* in Anglo-Saxon, after its first six letters, the set itself is the subject of a major text in that language ('The Runic Poem'); this draws on the meaning of each letter's name, obliging the translator both to retain the original name and to supply a translation: *Feoh* ('wealth') is a comfort to every man, and so on (Anderson 1949: 180–2; Shippey 1972: 156).

Runes also play an intricate role in the Anglo-Saxon riddles in the Exeter Book. One (no. 19) inserts four noun clues written backwards in runes (horse, man, warrior, hawk); another (no. 42) integrates seamlessly the names of runes into the text so that deciphering it involves identifying and transcribing the runes in question and arranging them so that they spell out the answer to the riddle (Rodrigues 1989). A fine piece of poetry in its own right, this latter piece reflexively draws attention to the upright form and poetic power of the rune staves, or characters, which resist easy decipherment. Among translators of texts in this tradition, Michael Alexander

(1966), an admirer of Pound, is one of the few to strive to convey their literary ingenuity.

New World scripts

In discussing translation with regard to New rather than Old World scripts, the prime difficulty is that so few of these scripts have been adequately identified or described (Brotherston 1992; Boone and Mignolo 1994; Gelb 1974: 57–8 typifies a demeaning view held by many scholars). A convenient starting point is provided by the hieroglyphic script of the lowland Maya, now much better understood as a phonetic system than it was two or three decades ago (Coe 1992; Martin and Grube 2000). For this very reason it has become susceptible to the sort of observation made above about Egyptian and Chinese script. In other words, although most of these glyphs undoubtedly register the sounds of Maya speech, in the sequence consonant–vowel plus consonant (-vowel), others do not. The latter notably include calendrical signs and the 'emblem' glyphs appended to the proper names of people and places, which may sooner be read as images. Moreover, the visual potential of these non-phonetic elements is often reinforced by the regular grid pattern typical of the hiero-glyphic text as a whole, and by accompanying illustrations like those in the trilogy of panels inscribed in the late seventh century AD in honour of Pacal, ruler of the city of Palenque, near Mexico's border with Guatemala. Visual potential is also brought out by variant hiero-glyphic forms which portray human and animal figures. The major example of this last convention, the text inscribed on Stela D at Copan in Honduras, shows the time periods of the calendar as living creatures literally borne or carried by other creatures who function as their numerical co-efficients: for example '3 years' expressed as '3' carries the period year. When, after the European invasion, the hieroglyphic texts began to be transcribed into alphabetic Maya, in the Chilam Balam books of Yucatan and other texts, such features of Maya philosophy were often highlighted by the retention of certain calendar glyphs. The glyphic statement of time as a load has in turn informed American works as diverse as *Los pasos perdidos* by the Cuban novelist Alejo Carpentier and

Charles Olson's *Mayan Letters* (both of 1953). Of the major versions of the Chilam Balam books, Mediz Bolio's Yucatec version (1930) is palpably more sensitive to the glyphic palimpsest and to the idea of Maya literary tradition than is that of Ralph Roys (1933). A good test of the difference between them is to compare their respective approaches to the constant puns and riddles found in the Chilam Balam text, which in the case of the Zuyua Than chapter are explicitly related back to the Maya intellect that fostered the hieroglyphic tradition (Mediz Bolio 1973: 37–60; Roys 1967: 88–97).

Historically, the Maya hieroglyphic system emerged from the broader Mesoamerican base that is shared by the 'Mixtec-Aztec' or iconic system of highland Mexico to the west (Benson 1973; Bricker 1988). This script is known as *tlacuilolli* in the Aztec or Nahuatl language (Nowotny 1961) and is likewise recorded in inscriptions and in screenfold books of skin and native paper. Used by speakers of various languages and tied phonetically to none, a fact which greatly extends its conceptual as opposed to verbal range (Tedlock 1989), *tlacuilolli* script defies Western definitions of writing in the ingenuity with which it fuses image, number and name into one holistic statement (Figure 2; Brotherston 1992: 50–9; León-Portilla 2003). This script served historically as a palimpsest or prior formulation for many texts written subse-quently in the alphabet by Nahuatl authors, notably in the genres of the annals and of the ritual books. In the annals, the script confirms time depth through embedded numeracy (for example, a knot for the 'tying' of the 52-year cycle). In ritual books, dazzling images of 'flower-song' underlie the Twenty Sacred Hymns and the poems collected in the *Cantares mexicanos* manuscript, a major source in turn for modern Mexican and Central American writers. In presenting the Rain god *Tlaloc* as the 'Jaguar-Snake' (*ocelo-coatl* in Nahuatl), one of the Sacred Hymns gives the key to the ingenious construction of his persona in *tlacuilolli*, that is the rain that results from the jaguar's thunder-roar and snake-like lightning: the construction is also arithmetical since, in the set of Twenty Signs fundamental to Mesoamerican ritual and calendrics, *Tlaloc's* mask of rain is Sign 19, the sum of Jaguar and Snake, Signs 14 and 5 respectively.

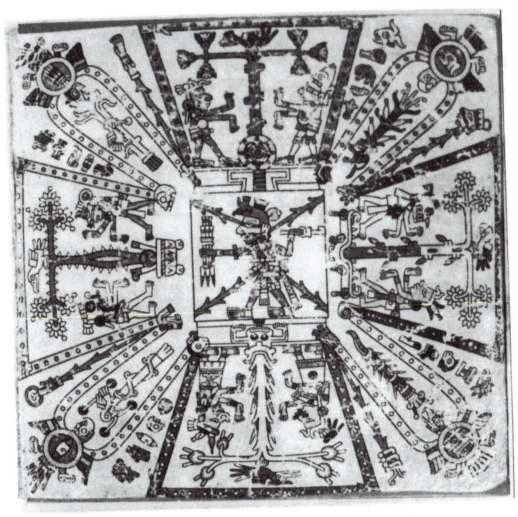

Figure 2: Hieroglyphic forms of humans and animals on Stela D at Copan, Honduras

Beyond Mesoamerica, the New World nurtured other examples of writing, for the most part quite undertheorized in Western scholarship. These include the pictographs found on Algonkin birchbark scrolls from the Great Lakes region (Dewdney 1975; Rothenberg 1986: 270–5) amongst a range of texts that includes treaty signatures that are animal *totems* (an Algonkin word). A sample is transcribed in one of the finer passages of *Hiawatha* (1855; Canto 14): H. W. Longfellow's tetrameters succeed in making poetry out of these Algonkin characters by recording the detail of their outline, as agents of genesis ('as an egg, with points projecting/ To the four winds of the heavens') or as ancestral totems ('Figures of the Bear and Reindeer,/ Of the Turtle, Crane, and Beaver'. See also Townsend 2004). Finally, to the south there is the highly sophisticated knotted string script of the Andes known as the *quipu*, of which a scholar has said: 'With pieces of string, the Inca developed a form of recording that forces a reconsideration of writing as we generally understand that term' (Ascher and Ascher 1981: 158. See also Salomon 2004). Alphabetic transcriptions into Quechua and Spanish are now being mapped (Julien 2000), the quipu being explicitly named as the source of several texts in the Inca language Quechua, among them a hymn to Viracocha and passages of an elaborate chronicle composed by Guaman Poma (1613). In the Quechua play *Apu Ollantay*, this particular form of literacy is reflexively commented upon at two moments when quipus are introduced into the action by bearers of messages: in the second the knots are unravelled in a literal denouement (Brotherston 1992: 208–9; see also Arnold and de Dios Yapita 2006). Overall, these American scripts make a strong collective impact in *Homenaje a los indios americanos* (1969) by Ernesto Cardenal (a Nicaraguan who also learned much from Pound), the homage being a set of poems which respond in detail to, and even transcribe, the particular forms and qualities of these scripts (Cardenal 1992).

Concrete poetry and its antecedents

In the Western tradition, Guillaume Apollinaire's *Calligrammes* (1918) and the Mexican José Juan Tablada's *Li-Po* (1920, Paz 1966: 444, 449–54) mark a turning point in so far as they strive to recover in alphabetic script itself an image-value more readily available in non-alphabetic systems. Through sheer layout and deployment of letters these poems translate the effect of the painted characters of Chinese and Japanese poetry. In Apollinaire's 'La Colombe poignardée et le jet d'eau' (Figure 3), the *C* of *Chères* forms the throat of the bird seen in right-facing profile: in this context to render *Chères* as *Dear*, as one published English translation does, swells the throat into a goitre and hence defeats the prime visual message of the text (Apollinaire 1970, trans. Anne Hyde Greet). For their part, the five lines of the poem 'Il pleut' (Figure 4) read downwards, like oriental characters, as threads of falling rain. In this case the English translation must struggle with a greater problem, of how to convey the fluid fall of the French, here emphasized through the vertical alignment ('il pleut des voix de femmes …'), in syllables that accumulate unvoiced consonants and glottal stops ('It's raining women's voices …'). Translating this same poem into a language that uses the Cyrillic alphabet would physically distort the even fall of the rain threads,

given that Cyrillic characters are less constant in breadth.

From *Calligrammes* and the intervening experimental placards of the Soviet poet Vladimir Mayakovsky, it is but a step to the type of concrete poetry theorized and practised in the 1950s by Eugen Gomringer (a Swiss-Peruvian) in German and Augusto de Campos and other members of the Brazilian *Noigandres* group in Portuguese, and later by Edwin Morgan and Ian Hamilton Finlay in English (Campos 1975; Bann 1977). In Finlay's river poem in *Telegrams from my window* (1965), rows of unspaced words – *redboat-bedboat* – form solid banks between which other words free-float as if in a stream of consciousness – *dream touch catch sleep fish* (twice) *say* (twice) *do* (thrice). That is, by the sheer arrangement of script on the page, this piece transcends the rigid demands of normal syntax, taking advantage of English words that are identical as nouns and verbs (*dream touch*, etc.). For that reason, the poem defies translation into a Romance language like Spanish or French, where nouns and verbs are formally not identical.

The visual effects on the page created by Apollinaire and the Concrete poets appear to be reflected in the work of an important US school of anthropologist translators identified with Dell Hymes and those who set up the review *Alcheringa* in 1970, namely, Jerome Rothenberg, Dennis Tedlock, Nathaniel Tarn and others (Rothenberg 1985, 1986; Tedlock 1989). Concentrating on native American sources, these translators first of all have excelled at rescuing verse from the amorphous prose of existing transcriptions by the simple but decisive use of line (Swann 1992). Then they have gone on to make ingenious use of typography and layout on the page, appealing to Gestalt and visually patterned text. Nonetheless, their prime loyalty has always been to the medium of speech rather than script, and as translators they have been concerned to convey as much as possible of originals that are spoken and sung in performance, their pace, pitch and volume. So that, rather than explore the potential of visible language in its own right, in this ethnopoetic vein they merely continue the age-old story of its subjection to the features and needs of speech.

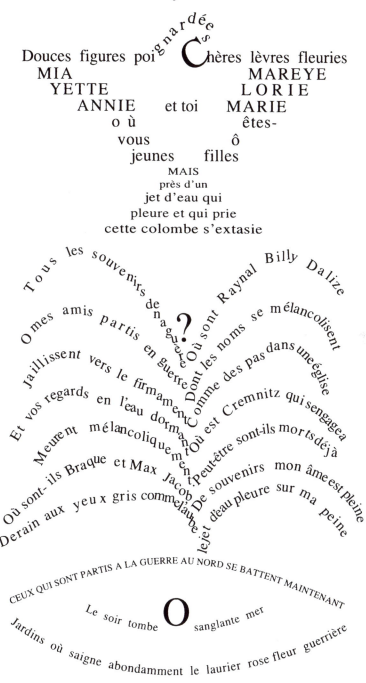

Figure 3: 'La Colombe poignardée et le jet d'eau' by Guillaume Apollinaire

Il pleut

Figure 4: 'Il pleut' by Guillaume Apollinaire

See also:
DECONSTRUCTION; POETRY.

Further reading
Cook and Ginsburg 1911; Teele 1949; Henderson 1958; Alexander 1966; Budge 1967; Pound 1969; Bann 1977; Warren 1989; Brotherston 1992; Coe 1992; Harris 2001; Arnold and de Dios Yapita 2006.

GORDON BROTHERSTON

Self-translation

The term 'self-translation' can refer both to the act of translating one's own writings into another language and the result of such an undertaking. Once thought to be a marginal phenomenon (as documented in Santoyo 2005), it has of late received considerable attention in the more culturally inclined provinces of translation studies. Several special issues have been devoted to the topic by journals in Spain (*Quimera*, Vol. 210, 2002), the UK (*In Other Words*, Vol. 25, 2005) and Romania (*Atelier de traduction*, Vol. 7, 2007). Hokenson and Munson's *The Bilingual Text*, the most ambitious attempt thus far to chart the *terra incognita* of self-translation, also appeared in 2007.

Self-translators do not just master, but choose to create in more than one language. Their conscious awareness of this option cannot be overstated: while 'bilinguals frequently shift languages without making a conscious decision to do so, polyglot and bilingual *writers* must deliberately decide which language to use in a given instance' (Beaujour 1989: 38; emphasis in original). Since self-translation involves an equally important decision, it may prove useful to consider, in addition to the actual use authors make of their languages, the attitudes and feelings they develop towards them.

Language use and attitude

A few questions may help to flesh out the portrait of a particular (group of) self-translator(s). At which point in their careers do they decide to translate their own writings? Does this practice become systematic or does it remain a single experience? Are writers constant in their choice of source and target languages or do they switch directions? Is their mother tongue reserved for original texts only, or is it used for translations (see DIRECTIONALITY)? Does there appear to be a 'division of labour' between the languages involved, one being predominantly used for 'high literature', the other for more popular genres? And last but not least: are second versions produced some time after the first versions have been published or do they evolve more or less simultaneously, cross-fertilizing each other as it were?

Having thus determined *how* self-translators' languages relate to each other, one has to ask a far trickier question: *why* do some writers choose to repeat what they have already written in another language? Dissatisfaction with existing translations alone hardly explains a choice that, to some at least, seems as absurd as 'redoing a painting in a different shade' (Devarrieux 1993: 15). Apart from material conditions (exile, marriage, financial gain), there must be some ulterior motive that helps them overcome their initial reluctance. For neither Vladimir Nabokov nor Samuel Beckett, arguably the two most famous examples of sustained self-translation, looked forward to what the former described as 'sorting through one's own innards, and then trying them on for size like a pair of gloves' (Beaujour 1989: 90), the latter as the 'wastes and wilds of self-translation' (Cohn 1961: 617).

While it is hard to pinpoint a single factor, some pattern usually emerges from the consideration of a group of writers whose bilingualism can be related to sociocultural circumstances. In Renaissance Europe, for instance, it was not uncommon for poets to translate their own Latin musings, as finger exercises. Trained in Latin, they had reached a level of competence unequalled even in their native language, and needed 'to form their poetic diction in the vernacular' (Forster 1970: 30). A well-known example was Joachim du Bellay, a founding member of the French Pléiade school (Demerson 1984). Leonard Forster (1970: 30–35) mentions the case of Antwerp-born Jan van der Noot, whose *Olympia* (1579) appeared in a bilingual edition, with French and Dutch texts side by side, the latter a free rendering of what was already an 'imitation' of Pierre de Ronsard. The fact that these poems were invariably translated into the mother tongue from models directly composed in an acquired language shows how much language attitudes have changed over the centuries.

In more recent times, despite the paradigm shift caused by romanticism (which favoured self-expression along linguistic and national lines), Eileen Chang (Li 2006), Isak Dinesen (Kure-Jensen 1993), Julian Green (1987), Nancy Huston (Danby 2004; Klein-Lataud 1996), Manuel Puig (Larkosh 2006), Jorge Semprun (Tanzmeister 1996) and many other bilingual writers have continued to belie widely held assumptions about the impossibility of creating in a so-called 'foreign' language (Grutman 2007). Of particular relevance are instances of asymmetrical language contact, where for a variety of political or market-related reasons, speakers of MINORITY languages might feel compelled to translate their work into the dominant language. This practice was not uncommon among writers from the more outlying republics of the former Soviet Union (Dadazhanova 1984). It has its supporters as well as opponents in present-day Ireland and Scotland (Brown 1992; Whyte 2002). In most bilingual Gaelic/English poetry publications, the English version is the work of a Gaelic self-translator. However, the unintended effect of this way of promoting minority literatures is that it tends to confirm the dominant status of the majority language. Because of their very nature, bilingual editions allow the anglophone reader to do little more than glance at the text in the 'other', less widespread language (Krause 2005).

Self-translation is also prevalent in language minorities that are in a much less precarious situation. Post-Franco Spain has seen a resurgence of self-translational activity as writers from Catalonia, Galicia and the Basque country are increasingly educated in their native languages and no longer solely rely on (Castilian) Spanish. The Catalan-speaking regions in particular spearheaded the reaction against centralization. They have produced a wide array of writers who switch between languages and translate their own work, be it only on occasion (Terenci Moix, Carme Riera, Eduardo Mendoza) or on a more regular basis (Baltasar Porcel, Andreu Mart'n). For the newer generations, better equipped to write in Catalan than their parents, Spanish is not (yet) a foreign language, which makes them ideal linguistic and cultural mediators (Arnau i Segarra et al. 2002; Lagarde 2004; Azevedo 1996; Heinemann 1998: 211–29). One could apply to them Beaujour's view of self-translation as 'a rite of passage' or even 'the pivotal point in a trajectory shared by most bilingual writers' (1989: 51).

Catalonia's self-translators seem to be in a position similar to that of Belgium's bilingual writers between and shortly after the World Wars (Grutman 1991, 2003). In this particular case, the 'vogue' of self-translation, spanning two generations and involving only Flemish writers, can roughly be dated between 1920 and 1970. Whereas members of the older group (Jean Ray/John Flanders, Roger Avermaete, Camille Melloy) tended to publish a local Flemish text shortly after writing the original in the acquired yet fully mastered French language, younger self-translators such as Marnix Gijsen and Johan Daisne wrote novels and plays in a much more standardized version of Dutch and subsequently marketed their own French translation, sometimes years later. This switch in direction between source and target languages can be linked to major social and political changes in the 1930s, when linguistic rights were enshrined in a new federal constitution recognizing territorial unilingualism. Today, bilingual writing is very much a thing of the past in Belgium: while all Walloons and most Brusselers continue to write in French, Flemings have massively opted for the Dutch language. Only in Brussels (where the language laws mentioned above do not apply) does one encounter the occasional self-translator (Gunneson 2005).

Textual relations

One question worth posing concerns the way in which self-translations relate as *texts* to 'normal' translations. Can they be said to possess distinct characteristics? In an essay on James Joyce's own Italianizing of two passages from his *Work in Progress* (the future *Finnegans Wake*), Jacqueline Risset answers in the affirmative. Unlike translations 'in the usual sense of the word' (1984: 3), that attempt to be 'hypothetical equivalents of the original text', Joyce's versions, she argues, represent 'a kind of extension, a new stage, a more daring variation on the text in process' (1984: 6; see Lamping 1992 for similar conclusions on Stefan George and Rainer Maria Rilke). This allows Risset to set off Joyce's self-translation against the 'fidelity and uninventiveness' (1984: 8) of the French translation, prepared by a team that included no less than Philippe Soupault, Yvan Goll, Adrienne Monnier and Samuel Beckett. What is ultimately at stake here is the old notion of authority, of which original authors traditionally have lots and translators none (Filippakopoulou 2005). Since Joyce himself wrote these second versions in idiomatic and creative Italian, they seem to be invested with an authority that not even an 'approved' translation by diverse hands could match.

The public's reception of an author's own translation is often based not so much on an extensive study of the textual product's intrinsic qualities – though Risset does conduct such an examination – as on an appreciation of the process that gave birth to it. In Menakhem Perry's words, 'Since the writer himself is the translator, he can allow himself bold shifts from the source text which, had it been done by another translator, probably would not have passed as an adequate translation' (1981:181). The reason for this unusual degree of acceptance is explained by Brian Fitch, who suggests that 'the writer-translator is no doubt felt to have been in a better position to recapture the intentions of the author of the original than any ordinary translator' (1988: 125; see also Tanqueiro 1999, 2000; Bueno García 2003: 268). It is indeed in terms of their production that self-translations strike us most as being different. A double writing process more than a two-stage reading–writing activity, they seem to give less precedence to the original, whose authority is no longer a matter of 'status and standing' but becomes 'temporal in character' (Fitch 1988: 131). The distinction between original and (self) translation therefore collapses, giving way to a more flexible terminology in which both texts can be referred to as 'variants' or 'versions' of comparable status (Fitch 1988: 132–3; see also Fitch 1983, 1985).

This is especially the case in 'simultaneous self-translations' (which are produced even while the first version is still in progress), as opposed to what might be called 'consecutive self-translations' (which are prepared only after completion or even publication of the original). Samuel Beckett, arguably the self-translator who has received most critical attention (Cohn 1961; Hanna 1972; Simpson 1978; Federman 1987; McGuire 1990; Clément 1994; Arndorfer 1997; Scheiner 1999; Collinge 2000; Oustinoff 2001; Sardin-Damestoy 2002; Montini 2007), resorted to both modes at different stages in his career. With the help of Alfred Péron, he started out by translating *Murphy*, a novel published in English before World War II, but whose French equivalent was to come out only a decade later. In this case, the English text had already led an autonomous existence, thereby limiting the possibilities of innovation: Cohn (1961: 616) explains that '[b]y and large, the translation follows the original, of which, obviously, no one could have more intimate knowledge than its author-translator'. Soon after, Beckett would initiate his (often English) rewritings while still working on the (mostly French) versions: in the process of completing *Ping*, for instance, he does not 'work simply from the final version of [*Bing*], but on occasion takes as his source the earlier drafts of the original manuscript' (Fitch 1988:70). The latter practice can be most aptly described as a type of cross-linguistic creation, where the act of translation allows the bilingual writer to revisit and improve on earlier drafts in the other language, thereby creating a dynamic link between both versions that effectively bridges the linguistic divide. Thus, even though Beckett's individual texts might not be bilingual (see MULTILINGUALISM), his work taken as a whole clearly is, with each monolingual part calling for its counterpart in the other language. As Fitch (1988: 157) puts it, 'one might say that while the first version is no more than a *rehearsal* for what is yet to come, the second is but a *repetition* of what has gone before, the two concepts coming together in the one French word *répétition*'.

See also:
LITERARY TRANSLATION; MINORITY; MULTI-LINGUALISM.

Further reading
Palacio 1975; Grutman 1994; Jung 2002,

2004; Grutman 2007; Hokenson and Munson 2007.

RAINIER GRUTMAN

Semiotics

Semiotics studies how people make sense of their experience of the world and how cultures share and give currency to this understanding. The core assumption is that these abilities entail the use of signs. In this broad description, a sign is anything that stands for something else and gives meaning to it. Thus, semiotics is a theory of how we produce, interpret and negotiate meaning through signs. No comprehensive theory of semiotics exists at present. However, there are several approaches which ultimately derive from different and sometimes conflicting accounts of meaning-making. This varied landscape can be divided for convenience into two broad regions, each referring to semiotic models which originated at the turn of the nineteenth century. One is the tradition initiated by Ferdinand de Saussure (1857–1913), often referred to as *sémiologie* or 'structural semiotics'; the other is the theory elaborated by C. S . Peirce (1839–1914), known as 'interpretive semiotics'.

Structural and interpretive semiotics

According to Saussure's structural view of language, subsequently extended to other sign systems (Lévi-Strauss 1949; Barthes 1964; Greimas 1966), 'each language is regarded as a *system of relations* (more precisely, a set of interrelated systems) the elements of which – sounds, words, etc. – have no validity independently of the relations of equivalence and contrast which hold between them' (Lyons 1968: 50; emphasis in original). This view implies that, in principle, distinct semiotic systems are incommensurable and therefore difficult to compare. In practice, however, translators routinely compare semiotic structures. Two texts – one the translation of the other – can be compared on various grounds, including lexical items, isotopies or sense levels,

narrative structures, and other narratological features such as narrators, characters, implied authors and readers. Thus, although structural semiotics can provide useful heuristic and analytical tools, it is unsuitable for other tasks, such as distinguishing translations from nontranslations and addressing the question of TRANSLATABILITY.

Whereas the system of relations is the overriding principle in structural semiotics, interpretive semiotics is centred on the notion of sign-action, or semiosis. Semiosis is 'an action, an influence, which is, or involves, a cooperation of *three* subjects, such as a sign, its object and its interpretant, this three-relative influence not being in any way resolvable into actions between pairs' (Peirce 1931–58 5: 484; also in Peirce 1992–8: II, 411; emphasis in original). This quotation offers a general account of how semiosis works. It outlines a model in which the sign stands for another entity called object. The representative function of the sign is directed towards a third entity, called interpretant. The interpretant is an effect of the sign, and often itself a sign, which says something more about the object.

Interpretants may belong to different semiotic systems. Indeed, when Peirce coined the term he had oral translation in mind: 'Such a mediating representation may be termed an interpretant, because it fulfils the office of an interpreter, who says that a foreigner says the same thing which he himself says' (Peirce 1931–58 1: 553). This suggests that Peirce's theory of signs is intimately linked to the discursive logic of translation. The fact that what Peirce refers to as 'genuine semiosis' involves three entities at all times – i.e. that sign relations are triadic – marks the main difference with structural models, which are based on binary relations. Another important difference concerns the conception of ground and the goal-directedness of representation, which always tends towards an interpretant. Signs represent their objects from a given point of view – or ground – selected within a range of possible ones. As to the interpretant, the variety that is most relevant to our argument can be described as an idea that signs give rise to in the mind of a person (cf. Peirce 1931–58 1: 339). Thus the model provides for two degrees of freedom for semiosis: one along the sign-object relation and the other along the sign-interpretant relation. This corresponds to the familiar feeling that meaning-making – including translation – always involves probabilistic inferences that are based on 'interpretive bets' (Eco *et al.* 1992: 63).

Semiotics and translation

Several authors have called for drawing on semiotics to enrich translation theory. Major contributions in the structuralist tradition include Toury (1986), who made a compelling case for the semiotic nature of translating and attempted a definition of it as 'an act (or a process) which is performed (or occurs) over and across systemic borders' (ibid.: 1112). The issue of the boundaries between semiotic systems is also taken up in the work of Torop (e.g. 2000). With reference to Lotman's concept of the **semiosphere** (2005), Torop described the boundary not as a limiting factor but as a mechanism that 'translates external messages into the internal language of the semiosphere, discriminates one's own from the alien, [and] turns external non-messages into messages' (ibid.: 605). Chesterman (2002a), in contrast, used insights from another semiotic tradition – Greimas's generative semiotics – to investigate translation causality.

In the interpretive semiotics camp, a notable early voice was Roman Jakobson, who identified the nexus between Peirce's theory of signs and the theory of translation in what is probably the single most quoted essay in the field (Jakobson 1959). Jakobson, who regarded Peirce as 'the deepest inquirer into the essence of signs' (ibid.: 233), based his call for a semiotic understanding of translation on Peirce's insight that 'the meaning of any linguistic sign is its translation into some further, alternative sign' (ibid.: 232). In other words, translation was identified as a crucial element of all meaning-making and of ordinary language use. This allowed Jakobson to extend the scope of translation beyond interlinguistic translation or 'translation proper' ('cheese' → Russian *syr/tvorog*), to include intralinguistic translation ('bachelor' → 'unmarried man') and intersemiotic translation ('sunrise' → the picture of a rotating planet).

Two authors began to engage more extensively with interpretive semiotics towards the end of the 1980s: Deledalle-Rhodes (1988–9, 1996) and Gorlée (1989, 1994). More recent contributions include Nergaard and Franci (1999), Eco (2001), Cosculluela (2003), Petrilli (2003) and Stecconi (2004a). These authors have taken on the task of redefining the traditional categories of translation studies in the belief that interpretive semiotics represents the future of translation theory. For instance, Gorlée proposed to change the core image of translation in the West from transfer to growth: 'Indeed, the image of translation that emerges from a Peircean semiotics is one of change and growth, of expansion through transformation' (Gorlée 1994: 231).

Finally, the term 'semiotics' is also used as shorthand for research that goes beyond verbal language (Poyatos 1997), for instance, in studies that explore the translation of advertising (Adab and Valdés 2004) and multimedia/multimodal material (Gottlieb 2005), without necessarily engaging with either structural or interpretive semiotics as described above.

Applications

Apart from strengthening the theoretical underpinnings of translation, sustained engagement with semiotics may open new paths to applied research. One application could involve revisiting the long-standing debate over EQUIVALENCE. Peirce showed that all interpretation is inferential, and the kind of interpretation involved in translating is no exception. Code-based theories imply that translators search the target environment for forms which are supposedly already equivalent to certain elements in the source environment – whatever is meant by 'equivalence'. Their task in this perspective is merely to note the equivalence and match source and target forms. By contrast, interpretive-semiotic accounts would recognize the inferential and creative work carried out by translators. The task of translators would then evolve accordingly: they would use signs from both source and target environments to *constitute* equivalence relations (cf. Stecconi 1994/1999). Drawing on semiotics to make a case for the inferential nature of translation can also provide sound arguments to support other theories of translation which either implicitly presuppose or explicitly discuss inferential processes, for example FUNCTIONALIST APPROACHES (e.g. Reiss and Vermeer 1984), the model of translatorial action (Holz-Mänttäri 1984), and the research strand based on Relevance Theory (e.g. Setton 1999; Gutt 2000), in which the inferential character of human interpretation is made explicit.

Semiotic explanations can also help clarify two commonly observed phenomena: the **non-reversibility** of translation and **interference**. Toury stated that 'translating has to be conceived as an *irreversible* process, and the equivalence relationships – as *unidirectional*' (Toury 1986: 1116; emphasis in original). In semiotic terms, these claims can be explained as follows. When a translator starts processing a source sign, he or she spends semiotic energy to power the series of transformations that ends when other signs are released in the target environment. A good image for the process is that of a wave that originates in the source environment and propagates all the way to the target environment. When a certain strand of translation semiosis comes to an end, the energy carried by the wave is spent and the process cannot be reversed. At most, additional energy would have to be invested to translate the new signs back into the source environment; but that would be a distinct strand of translation semiosis altogether.

Interference, on its part, is an effect produced by **iconicity**. Icons are part of Peirce's most famous classification of signs, together with indexes and symbols. This classification focuses on the relation of signs to their objects. Symbols represent their objects thanks to an agreed-upon rule and are constituted by interpretation. Ordinary words and sentences in a natural language are examples of symbols. In contrast, indexes have a real and factual connection to their objects. Peirce's own example is a weathervane, which is an index of the direction of the wind. An index would not exist without its object. Finally, icons represent their objects merely by virtue of likeness and their existence does not depend on anything else. Diagrams are examples of strongly iconic signs. The three classes are like Russian dolls: symbols include indexes and icons, and indexes include icons. For example, 'The Balcony' is a symbol of *Le Balcon* because it is a natural language

expression; it is an index because it is linked by a cause–effect relation to the title of Baudelaire's poem; and it is an icon because it resembles *Le Balcon* in many respects.

These classes can help us analyse interference; a common feature which Toury identified as a law of translation (Toury 1995: 275ff.; see NORMS). From a semiotic perspective, interference may be seen as a phenomenon that reinforces the image of translation as a continuous, wave-like process. If translation semiosis were like a wave, then interference would be one of its natural (if often undesirable) properties. In this hypothetical reasoning, interference would occur when a strand of semiosis proceeding from a source sign like *libreria* in Italian meets and amplifies another wave that originated from a target sign like 'library'. Drawing on the icon–index–symbol classification, interference occurs when translators are misled into believing that because the two forms iconically resemble one another, 'library' would be like *libreria* under indexical and symbolic respects as well, including meaning.

Semiotics and translation theory

Perhaps the most innovative contribution of interpretive semiotics is the possibility it provides of distinguishing translation from other kinds of sign-action. The scope of the term 'translation' has arguably become too wide in the past few years, with 'translation' being used as a synecdoche for most types of ordinary communication, such as writing, reading and conversing. Because of its power of abstraction, the theory of signs can treat translation as a special case of semiosis and help delimit it as an independent and consistent field of research (cf. Stecconi 2004b, 2007 for a fuller treatment of this issue). Given the variability of the concept of translation in space and time, it is futile to attempt substantive or essentialist descriptions of the form of semiosis that is specific to translation (translation semiosis or *T-semiosis* for short). However, it is possible to state the logico-semiotic conditions of translation – the conditions that set it apart from non-translation. These are *similarity*, *difference* and *mediation*. The argument can be briefly illustrated as follows. T-semiosis presupposes

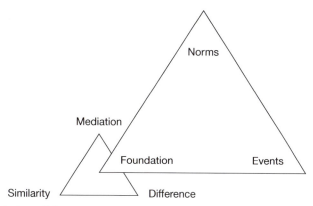

Figure 5: The foundation of T-semiosis

the effort to make a new text similar to existing semiotic material in the source environment. This is a metaphysical goal – so to speak – because the kind of similarity which, at any given time, is regarded as relevant and proper for translation is specified by historical agents and communities. It is equally impossible to conceive of T-semiosis without reference to a gap or difference which justifies it and which normally obtains between source and target environments. Finally, it is logically impossible to label as translation a text that is not perceived as speaking on behalf of another – i.e. that does not mediate between source and target environments. Together, these existential conditions constitute the *foundation* of T-semiosis. The foundation describes T-semiosis only in general and potential terms. In practice two additional and familiar conceptions are required if one is to develop a complete and workable model: **events** and **norms**.

Examples of translation events include individual translation projects and translated texts circulating in the target environment. In turn, these events are regulated by translation NORMS, as they are understood in the literature at least since Toury (1980a). To be more precise, norms are Peircean habits. As such, translation norms are rules for action (Peirce 1931–58 5: 397) that social groups establish and expect at given times. In so far as these norms are interiorized by translators, they represent tendencies to act in a certain way when certain conditions hold (Peirce 1931–58 5: 12 n.1). The three conditions included in the foundation and the two additional categories

come together in a two-layered model, as shown in Figure 5.

The six concepts featured in Figure 5 can be used to trace an edge around T–semiosis, distinguishing it from other types of semiosis. For any form of sign-action to be *potentially* regarded as T-semiosis, the three conditions included in the foundation must be jointly met. However, if one stopped there, one could only say what translation is not, rather than what it is. For a complete answer, one has to examine the category of events and the norms that prevail at the relevant point in the space-time continuum.

See also:
NORMS; TRANSLATABILITY.

Further reading
Peirce 1992–8; Gorlée 1994; Torop 2000; Eco 2003; Petrilli 2003; Misak 2004; Stecconi 2007.

UBALDO STECCONI

Shakespeare

The fact that the present volume has entries on the translation of the BIBLE and of Shakespeare but not of, say, Homer, Cervantes, Racine, or Joyce probably has more to do with the unique cultural functions Shakespeare and the Scriptures have fulfilled, each in their own way, than with any concern for the intrinsic difficulties involved in translating them. Like the Bible, Shakespearean texts and references are ubiquitous, and in either case there has been a great deal of doctrinal discord on the adjacent textual battlefields of translation and commentary (exegesis, interpretation, critisism). If from the Reformation onwards the issues of the true ownership and orthodox reading of the Scriptures have created deep divisions along religious as well as political lines, the post-Renaissance period has seen how the ownership and orthodox reading of Shakespeare have divided Europe and the wider world along aesthetic and political lines.

The cultural importance of Shakespearean translation could be measured in quantitative terms (Shakespeare is among the most widely translated writers and the most frequently performed playwrights in world literature) as well as in qualitative terms (Shakespeare has helped shape cultural identities, ideologies, and linguistic and literary repertoires across the world, and the challenge of translating him has attracted leading writers, politicians and many other captains of culture). Its cultural importance is reflected in the plethora of publications devoted to the subject and further attested by the fact that many translation scholars have elected to test their views against the case of Shakespeare in translation, using it as a touchstone for the relevance and validity of their theoretical constructions (e.g. the influence of Descriptive Translation Studies on Heylen 1993 and Delabastita 1993). It is however useful to be aware of the intrinsic differences among all these critical writings, each having been produced with a certain public and purpose in mind and, consciously or unconsciously, incorporating certain theoretical presuppositions or even value judgements.

Normative and descriptive attitudes to the translation of Shakespeare

Many discussions of Shakespeare in translation are normative, in that their perception of existing translations is determined by a pre-defined concept of what translation is or should be. This normative stance may take the form of explicitly prescriptive statements of the kind 'This is how to translate Shakespeare for the stage'. It may also manifest itself more subtly, for instance in the various attempts to draw the borderline between ADAPTATION and translation, or in the many historical accounts describing the development of Shakespeare in translation in terms of a progress or growth from the crudely disrespectful first attempts to the scholarly accuracy or artistic excellence of contemporary translations. Such teleological accounts of translation history tend to frown upon, or even pass over, those versions which supposedly caused stagnation or a relapse in the process. In this way many scholars have felt called upon to come to the Bard's rescue and have shown a dismissive attitude towards translations of Shakespeare which attempt to achieve acceptability (in the sense of adhering to the norms of the target language and culture) at the expense of the revered original author. Such source-oriented views on translation have typically caused the neoclassical tradition in Shakespearean translation to be ignored or treated with disdain.

A very different kind of norm-based engagement with Shakespeare translation is found in those cases where appreciation is expressed for more creative, interventionist and overt forms of translation (or adaptation). Such a defence of translational freedom may come from critics with a background in the theatre whose commitment to revitalizing Shakespeare for the modern stage implies a rejection of the kind of museum theatre which they feel is the outcome of philological orthodoxy in translation; it will typically be heard when the translators in question hold a canonized position in the receiving literature or theatre, which is taken to entitle them to the privilege of a more personal artistic response to Shakespeare. In the context of postmodern culture and cultural studies, translation norms are often inspired by political motives, whereby translators/adapters who show what is regarded as healthy disrespect for Shakespeare's canonized status and rewrite him freely to serve a worthwhile political agenda – for example, in relation to GENDER or MINORITIY groups – can count on understanding and approval.

Trying to situate themselves beyond these positions, and indeed playing them off against each other, descriptively oriented scholars will attempt to look at Shakespearean translation with a more relativistic perspective, posing questions such as: what kinds of translations were made, by whom, for whom, why, and with what effect?

Translating Shakespeare: the technicalities and beyond

The range of technical problems that the translator of Shakespeare may be faced with is quite formidable, including as they do the many textual cruxes, Shakespeare's obscure cultural and intertextual allusions, his archaisms and daring neologisms, his contrastive use of words of Anglo-Saxon and Romance origin, his use of homely images, of mixed metaphors and of iterative imagery, the repetitions of thematic key words, the personifications (which in some languages may lead to contradictions between natural sex and grammatical gender), Shakespeare's puns, ambiguities and malapropisms, his play with *y-* and *th-* forms of address, his elliptical grammar and general compactness of expression, his flexible iambic patterns (not easily reproducible in certain other prosodic systems) and the musicality of his verse, the presence of performance-oriented theatrical signs inscribed in the text, the embedding of dialects and foreign languages, and so on.

Real enough though these technical problems may be in many cases, they are not the be-all and end-all of the question of translating Shakespeare. First, several of them are specific to particular language-pairs. Second, as translators of Ovid, Rabelais or Joyce will readily confirm, none of the potential problems listed above is limited to the case of Shakespeare. Last but not least, the problems experienced by translators in practice have a relative status in so far as they are always subject to certain prior decisions. For example, the difficulty of finding an optimal prosodic equivalent for Shakespeare's iambic verse obviously depends on the preliminary choice of verse over prose, and history teaches us that especially philologically oriented Shakespeare translators have often preferred prose as the most suitable textual format throughout. As opposed to these all-prose versions, verse of some kind has often been used for renderings intended for the 'stage' rather than the 'page', including the passages where Shakespeare actually had his characters

speak in prose. Of course, all-prose and all-verse renderings equally override Shakespeare's deliberate combination of both forms. The notion that this very combination had to be reproduced in translation was applied methodically for the first time in the German Schlegel–Tieck project (1797–1833) (see GERMAN TRADITION), which drew on the Romantic view of the work of art being an indivisible structure in which form and content have fully fused into a strictly unique organism, springing from the creative powers of the author and therefore being beyond and above any external system of rules (such as that of neoclassicism, for instance). The true translator therefore has to aim for an integral rendering that re-creates this organism in the receiving language, and this requires relentless attention to form (including Shakespeare's prosodic modulations) as well as to content. It is noteworthy that the systematic observation of Shakespeare's prose/verse distinctions is a fairly recent phenomenon in several of the major Shakespeare cultures, such as the French (e.g. Jean-Michel Déprats) and the Spanish (e.g. Angel Luis Pujante).

It is also useful to bear in mind that many of the problematic features in question have at times disturbed Shakespeare's English-speaking readers and rewriters as well, appearing no less perplexing, alienating or unacceptable to them than to his overseas readers and translators. Indeed, modern-language versions in English of the *Shakespeare Made Easy* kind (which in Jakobson's famous typology may count as a form of intralingual translation) seem to fulfil an increasingly real function. In other words, the understanding and evaluation of Shakespeare rests on textual, cultural and ideological codes and on semiotic mechanisms which are to some extent independent of the linguistic barrier (unless one wishes to call Early Modern English a different language from contemporary English) and which therefore tend to confront editors, critics, directors, adapters and other English-speaking rewriters of Shakespeare with much the same dilemmas as the translators abroad. Not surprisingly, a certain rapprochement seems to be taking place between the study of the critical and theatrical afterlives of Shakespeare in English and the study of his translations (Hoenselaars 2006), even though a large part of the anglophone critical establishment in Shakespeare Studies still finds it difficult to put down the anglophone blinkers and regard any translation as one of the 'alternative Shakespeares' (Delabastita 2003).

Texts, mediation and languages

Translators usually prefer to start from the current critical editions of Shakespeare's texts rather than from the original quartos and folios. This means that many translations somewhat belatedly reflect trends in English text editing. For example, editions prepared under the influence of the New Criticism have been instrumental in making translators more aware of certain subtleties of Shakespeare's verbal textures, including word-play, ambiguity, imagery and the like. The Internet now brings a wealth of different editions, versions and hyperlinked commentaries to the translator's computer screen, expanding even further the massive Bibliotheca Shakespeareanea. On further reflection, this situation prompts certain fundamental questions about the identity and stability of the source texts in so far as the ever-growing body of editorial and critical traditions interposes itself willy-nilly between the elusive Elizabethan Shakespeare and his translator.

Very often, it turns out that translators have not only used English editions of the original, but also intermediate translations in their own or even another language. Several translators of Shakespeare have actually been known to possess little or no English. Far from being a rare curiosity, in certain situations, including eighteenth- and nineteenth-century Europe, indirect translation (see RELAY) of Shakespeare was the rule rather than the exception. In the days of the neoclassical hegemony, Shakespeare was imported into Europe largely via France. For example, the late eighteenth-century neoclassical versions by Jean-François Ducis (see Golder 1992) were further translated into Dutch, Italian, Polish, Portuguese, Russian, Spanish and Turkish, and eventually reached several colonial territories. France however gradually lost its grip on the reception of Shakespeare in Europe, as opposition to the neoclassical domination became stronger. With Germany having emerged as the champion of anti-classicism, translators increasingly turned

to German intermediate translations of a more 'faithful' kind. The translations by Christoph M. Wieland (1762–6), Johann Joachim Eschenburg (1775–82), and August Wilhelm Schlegel (1767–1845) and Ludwig Tieck (1797–1833) began to influence translators elsewhere in Europe either directly, in terms of serving as a basis for further translations, or indirectly as a general blueprint for a viable approach to the task of translating Shakespeare. In this way, international networks of relations connecting the various so-called national Shakespearean traditions in Europe (and beyond) clearly reflect the shifting power relations among its cultural communities. The binary model positing a direct spiritual link between source text and target text is a particularly unhelpful abstraction with a writer like Shakespeare.

The ties between cultural or political entities and the dominant national language spoken within them are too easily taken for granted: French is not the only language spoken in France for instance, nor has its use been restricted to that area. This insight points to yet another aspect of Shakespeare's cosmopolitanism by drawing attention to the cultural reality of MULTILINGUALISM as well as to 'non-translation' as a means of dealing with the language barrier. The status of English, French and German as a lingua franca in certain areas and at certain times has indeed strongly determined the international spread of Shakespeare's works, leading to bilingualism and biculturalism in theatrical or literary life and so bringing about a complex interplay between different translation traditions. In the nineteenth century, the same audiences may well have been able to variously enjoy Shakespeare in English (visiting troupes), in French (e.g. Ducis, Berlioz), in Italian (operas including but not restricted to Verdi) and/or in the local language.

The use of a foreign lingua franca alongside, or as a substitute for, the local vernacular is very often enforced by a politically stronger and/or culturally more prestigious group rather than being the outcome of a free choice. This colonial pattern largely accounts for the immense worldwide success of untranslated Shakespeare, a major export product especially in Britain's (former) colonies and dependencies, where the seeming stability of the sacrosanct originals could be used to serve Western ideology and avert the danger of Shakespeare 'going native' (see POSTCOLONIAL APPROACHES). However, as the British Empire fell apart and gave way to the pressures of postcolonial nationalisms arising worldwide, the 'authentic' British Shakespeare formerly taught under the imperial flag was increasingly rejected and the local cultures began to appropriate and recycle him for their own purposes. This happened either in the local vernacular or in a hybridized English, in what some critics have termed a cannibalizing form of translation (e.g. Welcome Msomi with his Zulu *Macbeth*). Comparable processes of decentralization have occurred in the Western sphere too, with translators strategically promoting suppressed languages or language varieties as a new Shakespearean idiom (e.g. Catalan, Basque, and *joual* in Quebec) in a bid to claim greater cultural legitimacy for them. Thus, two *Macbeths* came out in Scots in 1992.

From Globe to globe

It is a commonplace of dramatic history that Shakespeare's work presents a blend of Greco-Roman and popular-vernacular elements. This underlies Shakespeare's ambivalent relationship to later neoclassical poetics, many of whose principles he flouted to the point of exasperating its supporters: witness his juxtaposition of high tragedy with broad farce and of prose with verse, his ignorance of social decorum, his disrespect for the unities of place, time and action, the bloodshed, ghosts and spectacular effects on stage, the indecencies, word-play, undisciplined imagery and verbal obscurity, and so on. This incompatibility with neoclassical poetics hardly mattered in the first stage of Shakespeare's reception in Europe. During Shakespeare's lifetime and the next few decades, the English strolling players brought simplified stage versions of Shakespeare to the Continent, first in English with strong dependence on body language and spectacular stage action and later followed by translations.

Shakespeare's name gradually began to emerge in canonized European culture, not least via mentions in translated English magazines and novels and through Voltaire's widely influential criticism (for instance in his *Lettres philosophiques*, 1734). This incipient interest in

Shakespeare's work led to the earliest published translations, including those by Pierre-Antoine de La Place in France and C. W. von Borck's German version of *Julius Caesar* in 1741, and was further encouraged by them. However, growing familiarity with Shakespeare's work – for instance via the more source-oriented prose versions of all the plays by Pierre Le Tourneur (1776–83) – also brought home the extent of its unacceptability by neoclassical standards, barring the way to the prestigious theatres, except in strongly adapted versions, and leading to fierce controversy between detractors and defenders of Shakespeare, who posthumously became the standard-bearer of the anti-classical campaign. Many eighteenth- and nineteenth-century critics and translators used his works as a testing ground for literary and theatrical experimentation, often aligning Shakespeare with other innovatory trends or genres of English provenance, including non-dramatic ones such as the Gothic novel, Ossianic poetry or the historical novel. Similarly, many European artists in non-dramatic and even non-literary genres appealed to the authority of the Shakespearean model and adapted it for their own purposes. Clearly, what was being challenged in Shakespeare's name was not just a particular concept of the tragedy, but the entire genre-system, indeed the whole cultural and political paradigm of neoclassicism which the tragedy epitomized as its most respectable genre. But the so-called real Shakespeare that the (pre-)romantics tried or pretended to resurrect remained above all a writer of anthology pieces and closet dramas: the free neoclassically inspired rewritings of the eighteenth century continued to dominate the stage until well into the nineteenth century.

The opposition between Shakespearean and French neoclassical poetics was clearly a very effective force. Among other things, it helps us understand why the reception of Shakespeare remained largely restricted to some of his tragedies for a long time, entailing the partial exclusion of the comedies, the histories and even more the non-dramatic works. Translations of the *Sonnets*, for instance, systematically appeared much later and often have to be ascribed to an interest in their presumed autobiographical content. Even so, one should resist the temptation to reduce the opposition between Shakespeare and neoclassicism to a radical or static polarity and so overlook the particulars of each concrete situation. First, those who used Shakespeare to liberate their culture from French rule by trying to create a truly national theatre, literature or even language were acting in their own interest and not in Shakespeare's. The critics' and translators' versions of Shakespeare were thus biased in accordance with prevailing personal or more collective convictions. For example, in the German context Shakespeare really became a pawn in the strategies of the promoters of the domestic tragedy, the *Sturm und Drang* movement, the closet drama, the notion of popular poetry, the Weimar production style, and so forth. Even the celebrated Schlegel–Tieck translations are no exception to this in so far as they prove strongly tributary to the ruling stylistic conventions of the Goethe era. Second, neoclassically oriented rewriters such as Voltaire or Ducis were not the arch-conservatives they are usually made out to be: they were using Shakespeare to renew the classical tragedy from within by borrowing Shakespearean elements such as movement and spectacle and adding elements of the bourgeois drama. Third, in many nations Shakespeare also catered for expanding middle-class audiences in popular theatres which could more safely ignore the conventions of high neoclassical tragedy and welcome a variety of Shakespearean adaptations (such as comedies, prose versions, operatic versions, parodies, melodrama and vaudeville).

After the Romantic debates merged into new aesthetic developments in the nineteenth and early twentieth centuries, the now secure standing of Shakespeare as a genius has boosted even further the production of new translations and adaptations in a wide range of regional, national and international contexts. In cultures where they did not exist yet, the complete works were made available in translation.

As a broad generalization, the following can be said to be important aspects of Shakespearean translation in the twentieth and twenty-first centuries:

(a) the continued political uses and implications of Shakespearean translation – in contexts as diverse as postcolonialism, nation-building projects, the Cold War, the Middle East, etc. (see Abend-David 2003);

(b) the spread of English as the vehicle and symbol of a globalized economy and culture involving enhanced MOBILITY and the diminishing importance of territorially based cultural identities, creating a paradoxical situation in which Shakespeare simultaneously requires *less* and *more* translation;

(c) the spread and professionalization of English Studies in non-anglophone countries (in various cases speeded up after the collapse of totalitarian regimes), leading to greater philological expertise and dispensing with the pragmatic need to rely on second-hand translation;

(d) the spread of translation studies, furnishing translators with conceptual tools and a greater sense of historical perspective, and thereby enabling them to define more lucidly their positions, methods and objectives;

(e) the mediatization of Shakespeare, not only giving his international afterlife a very powerful further boost (via Hollywood, among other outlets) but also giving rise to an exciting range of new applications for Shakespearean translation (film, television, digital media, surtitles in theatres, etc.);

(f) society's greater permissiveness in the areas of sexuality and violence, which has given translators as well as film and theatre directors from the 1960s onwards a higher degree of expressive freedom.

The postwar years have witnessed the progressive establishment of a postmodern cultural climate which promotes notions like playfulness, experiment, overt textual intervention and hybridity at the expense of the axioms and values which inspire the more traditional ethics of equivalent translation, such as fidelity, submissiveness, invisibility, and a general belief in textual cohesion and the controllability and reproducibility of meanings. This has tended to result in translations (adaptations, tradaptations) which highlight their own textuality and manipulative nature by the use of techniques such as: archaism/neologism; anachronism; eclecticism (language, style/register, genre, media); juxtaposition of different translation techniques, ranging from hyperliteralism (or even non-translation) to free adaptation (even original composition); free verbal association and punning; and citation, among others.

Meanwhile the ideal of equivalent translation for the page and/or the stage is still around, of course, and many older Shakespeare versions have continued to be present in the theatre repertoires, in reprints and on library shelves, often proving more resilient than the newcomers that may have wanted to supersede them. The resulting range of Shakespeares on offer today or at any point in the past is extraordinary, but then, it is hardly surprising that the endless complexity of culture should be mirrored by the heterogeneity of interpretive and translational responses to Shakespeare.

See also:
ADAPTATION; DRAMA; IDEOLOGY; REWRITING.

Further reading
Monaco 1974; Golder 1992; Delabastita 1993; Delabastita and D'hulst 1993; Heylen 1993; Brisset 1996; Kocourek *et al.* 1997/1998; O'Shea 1999; Abend-David 2003; Delabastita 2003; Hoenselaars 2004; Homem and Hoenselaars 2004; Hoenselaars 2006.

DIRK DELABASTITA

Shifts

The term **shifts** commonly refers to changes which occur or may occur in the process of translating. Since translating is a type of language use, the notion of shift belongs to the domain of linguistic performance, as opposed to that of theories of competence. Hence, shifts of translation can be distinguished from the systemic differences which exist between source and target languages and cultures. Systemic differences, which pertain to the level of competence, are part of the opening conditions for translation. Shifts, on the other hand, result from attempts to deal with systemic differences. Translation involves the transfer of certain values of expression or content across a semiotic border; shifts are concomitant with this transfer. The relation between any two systems confronted in the process of translation is asymmetric, and the way the transfer is carried out is not determined a priori. It is because the translation operation performed on

an initial semiotic entity can lead to different resultant entities that 'shift' is not a category of competence (see also SEMIOTICS). The description and explanation of shifts in translation as performance therefore ought to be concerned with the dynamics of CULTURE rather than the static contrastive description of languages and cultures which takes place within the framework of various comparative disciplines (Toury 1980a: 11–18).

Shifts and invariance

Translation, like every transfer operation, involves an 'invariant under transformation' (cf. Toury 1980a: 12). The transformation which is occasioned by the translation process can be specified in terms of changes with respect to the source texts, changes which are termed 'shifts'. The two concepts of **invariant** and shift are therefore interdependent, such that any classification or definition of shifts entails a definition of the invariant (Bakker and Naaijkens 1991: 204–5). Definitions of the concept of invariant (i.e. those elements which remain unchanged in the process of translation) necessarily serve a certain theoretical purpose, while presupposing a certain point of view. A very rough and schematic division can be made between those conceptions of invariance in which the point of view lies 'before' translation (be it actual or ideal), and those in which it lies 'after' the fact. In accordance with this division, two classes of definitions of the invariant can be distinguished. The first consists of those definitions in which the invariant is postulated as a necessary condition to be met before the transfer operation can qualify as translation; here, the invariant coincides with the *tertium comparationis* of translation (cf. Steiner 1975: 319; Lefevere and Bassnett 1990: 3). In definitions of the second type, the invariant is meant for use as a descriptive, purely heuristic construct; here, the *tertium comparationis* is a device in the methodology of the description.

Invariance defined 'prior' to translation

When a certain type of invariance is considered a requirement for appropriate translation behaviour, the corresponding notion of shift is likely to be a normative or prescriptive one. The directive statements in which this notion is found can be cast either in an affirmative form as *do*, or in a negative form as *don't* (van Leuven-Zwart 1990b). The choice of either the positive or the negative formulation depends on the way the initial differences between source and target codes or systems are taken into account. In both types of statement the concept of shift is especially relevant to the applied branches of translation studies: TRAINING AND EDUCATION and criticism (see REVIEWING AND CRITICISM).

In negative formulations, shifts are looked upon as unwelcome results of the translation act, as something to be avoided: the implied performance instruction is *don't*. The term, then, refers to transformations of certain source text values or properties which ought to remain, or have remained, unaltered; the result is described as an error or mistranslation. Since shifts are thus seen as unnecessary deviations from the due course of the translation process, the concept could be said to operate within a restricted theory of TRANSLATABILITY (cf. Toury 1980a: 26–8). While being derived from the source text, this theory already allows for systemic differences between the source and target languages to a certain, variable extent: the source text-based theory is modified to accommodate target language possibilities and impossibilities, whether only linguistic, or textual and cultural as well. Consequently, shifts are shifts with respect to a specific translation ideal and some postulated concept of EQUIVALENCE. If, for instance, it is stipulated as an invariance condition that the translation be (at least) the maximal reconstruction of the conceptual semantic meaning of the source text, any deviation from this potential reconstruction will be marked as a shift.

In positive formulations, on the other hand, shifts are seen as required, indispensable changes at specific semiotic levels, with regard to specific aspects of the source text. Their supposedly necessary, or desirable, occurrence is a consequence of systemic differences. Shifts are the means which allow the translator to overcome such differences. In other words, changes at a certain semiotic level with respect to a certain aspect of the source text benefit the invariance at other levels and with respect to other aspects. With this notion of

shift, the focus is not on departures from a given normative concept of translatability but on the systemic differences which, in the projected translatability model, remain to be provided for. It is these systemic differences which are rewritten in terms of performance instructions (*do*). The concept of shift, then, is instrumental within a set of translation procedures. Examples of shifts postulated as *do's* include changes at the level of formal linguistic means which are brought about in favour of functional or text-pragmatic equivalence (see FUNCTIONALIST APPROACHES; PRAGMATICS). For instance, Nida's notion of **dynamic equivalence**, where 'the focus of attention is directed, not so much toward the source message, as toward the receptor response' (Nida 1964: 166), adopts a functional-pragmatic concept of invariance and presupposes shifts away from static, or formal hierarchies of source text properties. Two of the translation procedures discussed in Vinay and Darbelnet (1958) provide further examples of positive performance instructions: **transposition**, where an SL word is rendered by a TL word of a different word class, and **modulation**, '[a] translation method consisting of changing a point of view, an evocation, and often a category of thought' (Vinay and Darbelnet 1995: 346). Chesterman (1997: 87–116) elaborates on the categories of Vinay and Darbelnet in his classification of translation STRATEGIES (which conceptually can be viewed as the methodological mirror image of shifts) on syntactic, semantic and pragmatic levels.

Invariance defined 'after' translation

As a descriptive category, shifts are defined and identified retrospectively. They are reconstructed or established during the description of actual, existing translations. The descriptive focus may be on the reconstruction of the translation process or on the product, particularly with respect to its relation to the source. However, the distinction between process-oriented and product-oriented description is not clear cut. Process-related elements may play a role within the description of translation as a product, and the study of the product is the principal means for describing translation as a process.

When the focus is on the process, typologies of shifts generally attempt to account for the nature of translation operations and the considerations underlying certain decisions taken during the course of translation. Because the translation process is essentially a 'black box' (Holmes 1972: 72), any classification of shifts at this level has to be based on translation competence, that is, on the possible relationships and differences between systems or codes. But, since the empirical testing of cognitive processes involved in translation is problematical (see THINK-ALOUD PROTOCOLS; PSYCHOLINGUISTIC AND COGNITIVE APPROACHES), process-oriented typologies tend to reduce theoretical, general translation competence to a specific translation ideal. A distinction is often made between obligatory and optional shifts (van den Broeck and Lefevere 1979; Toury 1980a; van Leuven-Zwart 1989). **Obligatory shifts** are dictated by differences between linguistic systems, for example a lack of correspondence between related lexical items in the source and target languages (Kade 1968: 79 ff.). **Optional shifts** are those opted for by the translator for stylistic, ideological or cultural reasons. This distinction is similar to one made by Popovič between constitutive and individual shifts (see below), but according to Popovič constitutive shifts are not exclusively linguistic.

As far as the product-oriented view of shifts is concerned, the following definition by Popovič (1970: 79) may serve as a starting point: 'All that appears as new with respect to the original, or fails to appear where it might have been expected, may be interpreted as a shift'. In this definition, three elements can be discerned: (a) a relationship between the source and target texts ('new with respect to the original'); (b) a relationship between the target text and its reception in the target system ('where it might have been expected'); and (c) a descriptive point of view ('may be interpreted'). The descriptive focus can be either on (a) or on (b). For example, a zero-shift established at specific textual or linguistic levels in the source/target text relationship (i.e. an instance of invariance, where nothing new appears) may still be interpreted as a shift in terms of (b): by violating the expectations of the target system, a target text may acquire a function other than that fulfilled by the source text in the source system. This double point of view implies that there is always the possibility of a description in which shifts are shown to occur in translation. For this

reason, shifts are sometimes called a **categorial quality** (van den Broeck 1984–5: 117) of the class of translation. This quality can be causally linked to the double status of the translation as a reconstruction of another text and a text functioning in its own right in the target culture (see, for instance, Levý 1969: 72).

Definition and classification of shifts in product-oriented descriptions

Any typology of shifts presupposes a descriptive point of view (see DESCRIPTIVE VS. COMMITTED APPROACHES). This point of view can be made explicit in terms of criteria or parameters for comparative analysis. One might suggest that the relationship between a translation and its original may be defined as a 'network of correspondences and shifts' (Koster 2002: 34). For any given parameter, the degree of correspondence that will be taken as invariance has to be established.

Catford (1965) discusses shifts within the framework of a linguistic theory of translation (see LINGUISTIC APPROACHES). Within this framework, shifts occur on the grammatical and lexical levels, and their investigation is therefore pursued within the boundaries of the sentence as an upper rank. Catford distinguishes between a **textual equivalent**, 'any TL text or portion of text which is observed on a particular occasion ... to be the equivalent of a given SL text or portion of text', and a **formal correspondent**, 'any TL category (unit, class, structure, element of structure, etc.) which can be said to occupy, as nearly as possible, the "same" place in the "economy" of the TL as the given SL category occupies in the SL' (Catford 1965: 27). He limits his theory of shifts to instances of translation which satisfy the condition that the relationship between source and target utterances can be identified by a competent bilingual as textual EQUIVALENCE. The invariant of comparison Catford employs is formal correspondence. Shifts, in his definition, are 'departures from formal correspondence in the process of going from the SL to the TL' (ibid.: 73). If, from a descriptive point of view, a given TL instance is observed to be a textual equivalent of a given SL form, this does not entail that formal correspondence exists between the units under comparison, since the TL categories cannot necessarily 'be said to occupy, as nearly as possible the "same" place in the economy of the TL as the given SL category occupies in the SL' (ibid.: 32). The type and degree of divergence between formal correspondence and translation equivalence can be detailed in terms of shifts. Catford distinguishes two major types, **level shifts** (where an SL item at one linguistic level, for example grammar, has a TL equivalent at a different level, for instance lexis) and **category shifts**, which involve (a) changes of structure (**structure shifts**, for example a subject–predicate–object structure may be translated as a predicate–subject–object structure), (b) changes of rank (**unit shifts**, for example a word may be translated by a morpheme or a group by a clause), (c) changes of class (class shifts, for example an adjective may be translated by a noun or a verb), or (d) changes of term (**intra-system shifts**, shifts which occur internally, within a system, when source and target language systems have the same formal constitution but translation involves the selection of a non-corresponding term in the TL system) (Catford 1965: 73 ff.).

In Popovič (1970), the main concern is with LITERARY TRANSLATION, and shifts are therefore defined as a stylistic category and termed 'shifts of expression'. For Popovič, 'a systematic evaluation of the shifts of expression that occur in a translation', and hence 'the objective classification of differences between the translation and its original' (ibid.: 84), should be based on a theory of expression, such as can be found in Miko (1970). The linguistic means employed in the source and target texts cannot be compared in isolation, but only 'in relation to the entire system of expression' (Popovič 1970: 84). It is this system of expression which allows us to determine the expressive values of the respective linguistic devices, a necessary precondition for the establishment of shifts 'in the sphere of style' (ibid.: 83). Style, for Popovič, is a multi-layered and hierarchically organized concept. It is because it covers abstract and general categories and qualities, as well as more specific stylistic means, that it can be used as an invariant for the comparison of source and target texts. For the evaluation of shifts, it is necessary to examine the respective differentiation of stylistic quali-

ties in the source and target languages and texts. Popovič distinguishes between **constitutive shifts** and **individual shifts**. Constitutive shifts are system-bound, but the concept is wider than that of obligatory shifts. Popovič defines a constitutive shift as '[a]n inevitable shift that takes place in the translation as a consequence of differences between the two languages, the two poetics and the two styles of original and translation' (1976: 16). One might also conceive of these shifts as constitutive in the sense that they are constitutive for the style of the translation (cf. the notion of shifts as a categorial quality of translation above). According to Popovič, the style of the translation, conceived of as the 'integrative principle' in the development of its structure (1970: 79), is necessarily determined by shifts because of its 'dual character' (ibid.: 82): it has to comply both with the norms of the original and with a given target 'translation ideal'. Individual shifts differ from constitutive shifts in that they are prompted by the stylistic propensities and the subjective idiolect of the individual translator. When changes at the level of macro-stylistics cause the translation to fit a literary genre different from that of the original (see ADAPTATION), Popovič speaks of a generic shift (see also van den Broeck 1986).

Within the methodology of Toury (1980a: 89–121, 1985: 32), the invariant of the comparison is the adequate translation (AT) and the unit of comparison is the texteme. An **adequate translation** is a reconstruction of source text textemes and consists of an EXPLICITATION of the textual relations and functions of the source text. As such, it is not an actual text but a hypothetical construct, serving only methodological purposes (see Hermans 1995: 218–20 for a critical assessment of this concept). The degree of correspondence taken as invariance within this method is adequacy at the textemic level, and shifts are defined as deviations from adequacy. The purpose of comparison is to determine the distance between the 'actual equivalence' found between source and target texts and the maximal norm of adequate translation, inasmuch as this distance can be attributed to norm-governed translational behaviour. Since obligatory shifts are rule-governed, they cannot be taken to reflect translational NORMS and are therefore not taken into consideration; methodologically, they are accounted for in the invariant itself (the weak version of adequacy, see Toury 1980a: 69). The comparative procedure starts by assuming equivalence at the textual-functional level, hence the parameter of comparison is textual-functional. When the dominant relationship between target text texteme and source text unit is found at that level, the translational relationship is one of adequacy. When there is no textual-functional correspondence, the procedure is to look for correspondence at lower textual and linguistic levels. Norms determine the position of the actual translation equivalence between adequacy and acceptability, and the establishment of individual shifts ultimately leads to the establishment of the translational norms governing the text in question. When, after further generalization and expansion of the investigated corpus, shifts show a certain pattern or statistical regularities, they can be explained by the existence of a historically and culturally determined poetics of translation or translation ideal.

In later stages of Toury's thinking (1985, 1990), the above procedure became part of a larger one in which an additional unit of comparison was introduced: the 'coupled pair of "problem + solution"' (see UNIT OF TRANS-LATION). The notion of shift gradually became less central in his method of description (see, especially, Toury 1995).

Within the methodology of van Leuven-Zwart (1984, 1989, 1990a), a distinction is made between shifts at the level of a text's microstructure (comparative model) and the effects of these shifts at the macrostructural level (descriptive model). At the microstructural level, the invariant of the comparison is the **archi-transeme** (ATR), which expresses the common denominator(s) in the relation between specific textual units of the source and target texts; these textual units are called **transemes**. Inasmuch as the descriptive model is comparative, it works with an invariant at the macrostructural level as well. The invariant in this case is based on a theory of the genre to which the texts under comparison belong. Van Leuven-Zwart limits her methodology to the domain of narrative texts, and the invariant is therefore derived from specific narratological concepts such as 'story level' and 'focalization'. The ATR has to be established separately for each pair of transemes, the invariant at the macrostructural level will be established a priori.

Esssential to the method of van Leuven-Zwart is the priority given to the concept of relation. Any comparative description involves establishing the relation between elements as well as attributing certain features to those elements. According to Van Leuven-Zwart, a comparison based on the prior attribution of features is only a 'second degree comparison', since it departs from a descriptive operation, and the relationship between the elements is established afterwards. In a direct comparison, the order is reversed. According to this scheme, a **texteme**, for instance, would be a unit of description rather than a unit of comparison. At the microstructural level, a relation of complete conjunction between the transemes and archi-transemes (in which case there is a relation of synonymy between transemes) is assumed as a starting point, and shifts occur when there are aspects of disjunction between transemes and the ATR. Van Leuven-Zwart distinguishes three main categories: **modulation** (where a source *or* target transeme shows one or more aspects of disjunction with the ATR; a relation of hyponymy between transemes), **modification** (where a source *and* target transeme show one or more aspects of disjunction with the ATR; a relation of contrast between transemes), and **mutation** (where there are no aspects of conjunction, and therefore no ATR can be established; no relation between transemes). The purpose of this method is to arrive at hypotheses about the interpretation and the strategy underlying the translation involved in the comparison. As a consequence, shifts that do not reflect a translator's interpretation or strategy are not taken into account: only optional shifts and substantial shifts are considered. As far as the distinction between obligatory and optional shifts is concerned, van Leuven-Zwart expresses a reservation as to its applicability. In the first instance, the decision whether shifts are to be considered optional or obligatory is suspended. Not until the effects of the microstructural shifts on the macrostructural level have been established will it be possible to determine to what extent the shifts are due to other than purely linguistic factors. Initially, all substantial shifts are noted; that is, all the shifts that have some bearing on one of the substantial levels, namely the semantic, stylistic or pragmatic level. As to syntactic shifts, only those that affect these substantial levels are taken into account. Purely formal shifts are disregarded. On the distinction between formal and substantial shifts, see also van den Broeck and Lefevere (1979). In more relativistic terms, Koster (2000: 131–2, 153) relates substantiality to the purpose of a descriptive procedure. Substantial shifts, from that perspective, are those shifts which are relevant to what the procedure sets out to describe (NORMS, STRATEGIES or the translational interpretation).

See also:

EQUIVALENCE; EXPLICITATION; LINGUISTIC APPROACHES; NORMS; TRANSLATABILITY; UNIT OF TRANSLATION.

Further reading
Catford 1965; Popovič 1970, 1976; Holmes 1972, 1978; Toury 1980a; van den Broeck 1986; Van Leuven-Zwart 1989, 1990a; Koster 2000.

MATTHIJS BAKKER, CEES KOSTER AND KITTY VAN LEUVEN-ZWART

Signed language interpreting

The term 'signed language interpreting' (or 'sign language interpreting') refers most typically to interpreting between a signed and a spoken language, though it may also involve interpreting between a spoken language and a signed form of that language, a practice known as 'transliteration' (or 'fingerspelling'). Transliteration, as opposed to interpreting (in the context of signed languages), involves the transfer of information from a spoken language to an artificially created signing system that follows the syntax and morphology of a spoken language. For example, signed English marks morphological alterations like –ED to indicate past tense (WALK+ED) and – S to mark plural (GIRL+S). This differs significantly from the way time and plurality are expressed in signed languages (Cokely 2005; McDonnell 1997; Isham 1998). The distinction between 'interpreting' and 'transliteration' largely reflects the distinction between those who were born deaf and regard themselves as members

of a MINORITY group (typically referring to themselves as Deaf, with a capital D) and those who suffered some form of hearing loss later in life, after acquiring a spoken language (Ladd 2003; Lane *et al.* 1996).

Signed language interpreting (including transliteration) occurs in a range of domains, including CONFERENCE and COMMUNITY INTERPRETING, and diverse contexts, such as medical, mental health, legal and educational settings. Signed language interpreting thus takes place and is required in any situation where a d/Deaf and a hearing person do not share a common language for the purpose of direct interaction, bearing in mind that a d/Deaf person may be fluent in the written form of the spoken language of his or her country but may not be able to or wish to use spoken language in interactive settings. This can include face-to-face interaction (meetings, police interviews, university lectures, etc.) and, more recently, remote interpreting via telephone, Internet or video phone links (Frishberg 1990; Napier *et al.* 2006).

Signed language interpreting may also involve interpretation between signed languages. Today, this is more frequently carried out by Deaf interpreters (Boudreault 2005; Collins and Walker 2006). Deaf interpreters also increasingly work in TV interpreting, often from written scripts or autocue, thus introducing an element of translation to their task (Stone 2007). In many countries, Deaf interpreters translate information relating to state services into their national signed language in order to ensure that public service information is accessible to Deaf communities: working from text-based information (e.g. autocue), signed language versions are prepared for broadcast on TV, via the Internet, or for distribution on DVD. Some broadcasts (e.g. news) are interpreted live, but there is still a translation element involved since the Deaf interpreters work from a text-based source.

It has been suggested that Deaf people prefer to have information presented on TV (and, by inference, in other visually recorded and disseminated media) by Deaf rather than hearing interpreters, because Deaf interpreters typically bring first language competence to the task, as well as a heightened awareness of Deaf cultural norms (Kyle 2007). But despite the increasing public profile of Deaf interpreters, they have not developed a clearly defined role so far (Boudreault 2005; Collins and Walker 2006). In addition to the kinds of interpreting/translating work described above, Boudreault (2005: 329) notes that Deaf interpreters also interpret for Deaf-blind people, working from a signed language to a tactile mode of communication, and that they carry out a range of tasks that do not necessarily involve working into another language:

> For the DI, the work does not necessarily always involve two languages, but instead can mean working from one language to some other form of communication, such as gesturing, drawing, using props, idiosyncratic signs, International Sign, etc., which are not considered as actual language systems.

Deaf interpreters thus function as interpreters, translators and facilitators for Deaf clients whose knowledge and/or use of the dominant signed language in a specific region may deviate from what is considered normative for that signed language community due to a variety of educational, language and cultural factors – for example because they acquired the relevant signed language late in life, are recent immigrants to a country, or suffer from some form of mental illness (Boudreault 2005; Collins and Walker 2006). In such settings, Deaf interpreters facilitate communication between the Deaf client and the hearing client, typically via RELAY to a hearing signed language interpreter. In the past, Deaf interpreters were therefore typically referred to as 'Relay Interpreters'. However, it is important to distinguish between the method of interpreting and the interpreters who implement it. Relay interpreting between signed and spoken languages (e.g. French Sign Language to French, and then to English), or between signed languages (e.g. from English to American Sign Language to Langue des Signes Québécoise) occurs in similar ways to those of relays in spoken language interpreting. Thus, Deaf interpreters functioning as facilitators clearly operate using relay methods, but in terms of their work between signed languages, the interpreting is often direct, from one language to another. The difference here is one of modality rather than method.

Modality issues: spoken versus signed languages

While spoken languages are received and expressed via the auditory-vocal channels, signed languages are visual-spatial in nature: they are expressed in space. Signers make use of their head, face, torso, arms and hands in order to express themselves in three-dimensional space. Space is used to represent space; for example the relative location of entities in the real world can be re-established in signing space (Sutton-Spence and Woll 1999; Liddell 2003). Motion is used to express motion; for instance, the path of movement and manner of movement are encoded in some verbs that are expressed in signing space, giving very accurate information regarding the relative location of entities in an environment. Such information is not usually encoded with the same level of specificity in spoken languages, and as such, one of the main challenges facing signed language interpreters working from spoken languages is accuracy regarding the relative location of entities and the path and manner of interaction: exactly where on the road was the car when it hit the man, and where exactly was the man when he was hit? Did the man slap, hit or punch the woman? And where on her body was she hit? Was it one punch or many? In the same place or in many places? The modality effect is particularly crucial in legal contexts, as the accuracy of information relating to location, interaction and manner of interaction is perhaps even more important than in any other context (Brennan and Brown 1997; Brennan 1999).

The visual aspect of signed language interpreting differentiates it from some types of spoken language interpreting in other respects. Signed language interpreters are physically visible. They are required to be seen in order to be 'heard' by signers and, additionally, when working from a signed language to a spoken language, the interpreter must be audible to ensure that their non-Deaf audience can hear the interpretation of what the Deaf person is signing. In other words, signed language interpreters work bilingually and bi-modally. This has technical implications for their work into a signed language: lighting in a venue must be appropriately bright to allow the interpreter to be seen, but not so glaring as to cast shadows on the interpreter's face or body since this would impede 'reading' the interpretation. For example, a spotlight must be placed on an interpreter in a theatre interpretation, or in contexts where the lights will be lowered in an auditorium, which means that the interpreter stands on stage, beside the speaker or adjacent to the actors as they work for the duration of the performance (Turner and Pollitt 2002). In community settings, seating arrangements must be conducive to interaction: the Deaf person must be able to have easy eye contact with the interpreter and the hearing person must be able to see the Deaf person (the interpreter's primary goal is to facilitate interaction between the Deaf and hearing parties). Thus, seating arrangements in triadic exchanges are typically triangular, so that all parties can see each other, while in group discussions or small-group facilitated sessions, U-shaped seating arrangements, with the interpreter standing/seated close to the facilitator, are common (Frishberg 1990; Napier *et al.* 2006; Humphrey and Alcorn 1996; Stewart *et al.* 1998).

The interpreters

Leeson (2001) notes that in Europe, the signed language interpreter is typically female and learns the signed language of her region or country as a second language. Despite the tradition of people who have Deaf parents (CODAs – Children of Deaf Adults) acting as interpreters, in recent times it has been noted that a relatively small percentage of CODAs seem to consider interpreting as a profession. The average signed language interpreter does not have a third working signed language or spoken language, though in order to work at European level (e.g. in international conferences, working with European institutions, etc.) knowledge of English is necessary. Although there has been an increase in the number of interpreters who do work with more than one spoken and one signed language, this is not yet the norm. With the exception of Tècnic superior en interpretació del llenguatge de signes in Catalonia, which offers spoken Catalan and Spanish, Catalan Sign Language and Spanish Sign Language, training programmes do not typically offer more than one spoken and one

signed language to students. Primary focus is typically placed on skill development in the one signed language being taught. As the European Deaf community becomes more multilingual in its signed language use, this situation will probably need to change. Increased MOBILITY due to GLOBALIZATION may also increase the demand on signed language interpreters to be multilingual at a global level.

Signed language interpreting is usually bi-directional. That is, interpreters must be able to work between both of their primary working languages: for example, Irish Sign Language and English (or Irish), Polish Sign Language and Polish, Palestinian Sign Language and Arabic, etc. In some regions, the linguistic situation is more complex, and interpreters potentially have to work across several language boundaries, as is the case in South Africa (Akach 2006).

The profession

Signed language interpreters work to a Code of Ethics that makes reference to confidentiality and impartiality (amongst other things). Codes of ethics are normally specified by national associations of signed language interpreters. While many signed language interpreters are professionally trained, and there are protocols in place in many countries for their professional certification, they do not form a licensed profession.

The profession of signed language interpreter is relatively new. The first interpreters were professionally trained in the USA from 1964 onwards, and the Registry of Interpreters of the Deaf (RID) began assessing interpreting and transliterating skills in 1972 (Cokely 2005). TRAINING varies across the US, with some programmes offered at community college level and some to associate degree, bachelor's postgraduate degree level. Cokely (2005) and Moody (2007) offer excellent overviews of the evolution of interpreting in the USA.

In Europe, training has been in place in some countries at least since the early 1970s. However, the duration of training varies significantly from country to country (Leeson 2001, 2005b). Sweden was the first European country to initiate training in the late 1960s. Initial training consisted of a two-week programme, but today the majority of full-time interpreter training programmes in the European Union are between two and four years in length. As in the USA, some are undergraduate programmes leading to qualifications such as Bachelors degrees or Diplomas. Other courses lead to a Masters degree. Some are offered at university level, others at vocational training institutes, and others are run through Deaf organizations, with many programmes (often part-time or evening courses) having no state accreditation. This variability demonstrates that there is still no standardization regarding how signed language interpreters should be trained or agreement regarding the minimum standard for performance required on completion of training, despite the fact that core competencies have been identified by the Conference of Interpreter Trainers (CIT) in the USA.

In many EU countries, such as Belgium, only part-time training options exist. In some, such as Luxembourg, no ongoing programme exists. This contrasts with training in Denmark, for example, where a national three-and-a-half-year programme for signed language interpreters is in place. This degree of variation seems to hold across the globe, with the worst (in terms of provision of training) being countries in war zones or those emerging from colonialism or situations of conflict (Mweri 2006; Alawni 2006; Akach 2006; Aquiline 2006).

Against this background, there is inevitably significant variation in terms of assessment and accreditation of signed language interpreters worldwide. The most developed systems operate in the USA (Registry of Interpreters for the Deaf, RID), Canada (The Association of Visual Language Interpreters of Canada, AVLIC), Australia (The National Accreditation Authority for Translators and Interpreters Ltd, NAATI), the UK (The Council for the Advancement of Communication with Deaf People, CACDP) and Sweden (Kammarkollegiet, 'The Legal, Financial and Administrative Services Agency'). Some of these bodies assess both spoken language interpreters in the public service arena and signed language interpreters (Australia, Sweden) while others only assess signed language interpreters (Canada, USA, UK).

Despite the lack of training standards, there is an increased sense of cohesion and professionalism among signed language interpreters. For example, in the European Union, almost every country has a national association of signed language interpreters; together these form the European Forum of Sign Language Interpreters, which was established in 1993. EFSLIT (the European Forum of Sign Language Interpreter Trainers) facilitates interaction between institutions delivering interpreter education and creates a forum for them to discuss matters of interest to the profession and the development of standards and best practices in interpreting. The World Association of Sign Language Interpreters (WASLI) was established in 2003 with the aim of supporting further collaboration with respect to best practices in interpreter education and assessment, among others (Hema 2007; see also Ojala-Signell and Komarova 2006).

With the evolution of an interpreting profession, the relationship between Deaf people and interpreters has shifted in many countries. Cokely (2005) presents a comprehensive overview of the way signed language interpreting evolved as a profession in the USA: initially interpreters were helpers, volunteers, closely aligned to the Deaf communities they served, and came from or were chosen by the Deaf community (i.e. they were people with Deaf parents or siblings, teachers of the Deaf, chaplains, etc.). Over time, interpreters came to see themselves as 'professionals', and with this shift came a disassociation from the Deaf Community. Whereas the idea of establishing training for signed language interpreters came originally from Deaf communities, the direct input of Deaf communities in (a) influencing who gains access to interpreter training, and (b) what (from a Deaf community perspective) constitutes quality interpreting, has reduced over time while, critically, the demand for more highly skilled interpreters has increased. As Cokely (2005: 24) notes,

What began as a relationship largely evolved from personal connections with members of the Community became a relationship based on commerce and often rooted in detachment. The shifted positionality was heightened by the exponential growth of employment opportunities brought about by federal legislation. The most significant consequence of this shift was a loss of Community control over who would be viewed as interpreters/transliterators.

Research on signed language interpreting

Several disciplines have been influential in shaping the course of research on signed language interpreting, most significant amongst these being the field of sign linguistics. The very first linguistic analysis of a signed language was undertaken by Tervoort in 1953, for Sign Language of the Netherlands, followed by Stokoe (1960) for American Sign Language, both focusing on the analysis of the sign. These groundbreaking studies led to work on the morpho-syntax, semantics and sociolinguistics of signed languages worldwide. Research on interpreting emerging from this strand includes work that looks at the relationship between the content of the source and target languages, identifying 'miscues' that occur during interpretation. These include additions, omissions, substitutions, intrusions and anomalies (Cokely 1992). Other work looks at the impact of modality difference on target language completeness (e.g. Brennan and Brown 1997; Johnston 1992) and discourse-level analysis of data, for example the way in which the signed language interpreter manages turn-taking (Roy 2000).

A second key influence comes from the field of psychology (see PSYCHOLINGUISTIC AND COGNITIVE APPROACHES). The focus on cognition has resulted in studies that examine issues relating to language processing, including aspects of attention, and visual memory, including working memory for signed languages (Kyle 1986; Isham 1994; Ingram 1992, among others). Other studies have examined how d/Deaf people experience signed language interpreting (e.g. Marschark *et al.* 2004, 2005a).

A third strand of influence comes from translation and interpreting studies. For example, the work of scholars like Wadensjö (1998) has prompted much discussion and further research regarding how signed language interpreters manage triadic encounters (Metzger 1999). The methodology of THINK-ALOUD PROTOCOLS has been imported from translation studies to signed language interpreting studies with some success (Stone 2006, 2007).

The volume of research on signed language interpreting has grown with the evolution of university-based training programmes, and this has increased the potential for closer collaboration with colleagues who focus on spoken language interpreting. Networks of researchers have formed, for example via the establishment of The Critical Link conferences in 1992, which have offered researchers working in the broad field of COMMUNITY INTERPRETING the opportunity to engage in dialogue. Major publications on interpreting (e.g. Pöchhacker and Shlesinger 2002) have thus come to include reference to signed language interpreting. At least two major European projects have included both signed and spoken language interpreting within the remit of a major review of access to justice across languages and cultures in the EU (Hertog 2001, 2003b). The multidisciplinarity of interpreting studies has been critical in promoting comparative analyses of interpreting service provision and practice (e.g. Hertog 2001, 2003b; Colin and Morris 1996). This has implications not only for improving our understanding of various aspects of the interpreting task, but also for policy development and service provision.

Other major fields which have also had a growing impact on research in signed language interpreting since the late 1990s are sociology, philosophy, gender studies, equality studies and anthropology. For example, empirical analyses have been undertaken of the performance of signed language interpreters in a range of settings, including legal contexts (Brennan and Brown 1997; Russell 2003a, 2003b), educational contexts (Marschark *et al.* 2005a; Russell 2007; Leeson and Foley-Cave, 2007) and medical contexts (Metzger 1999). These studies draw on the full spectrum of research from the three key domains and beyond, leading to the elaboration of a shared perspective on what interpreters do, irrespective of the specific issue of modality. This in turn has led to growing interest in conducting contrastive analyses of what Deaf and non-deaf interpreters/translators do in terms of preparing their output (Stone 2007), what Deaf clients think interpreters should do versus what interpreters report doing (Leeson 2005b), and how interpreting strategies are affected by the modality of the languages involved (Leeson 2005a) or the method used (e.g. consecutive versus simultaneous) (Russell 2003a, 2003b).

The challenges that face researchers seeking to analyse authentic data are multiplied for those looking at signed language interpreting, where video recording is necessary and raises additional issues, including the requirement of informed consent from participants, the privacy of participants, and data protection concerns. Nevertheless, several key themes have been identified as priorities for empirical research. These include re-examining the way interpreter training meshes with Deaf community demands and requirements; ways of developing research-driven TRAINING; and elaborating appropriate assessment protocols. Pöchhacker (2004) also identifies GLOBALIZATION and technical enhancement as key themes for future research. The establishment of the Conference of Interpreter Trainers (CIT) in the USA and the European Forum of Sign Language Interpreter Trainers (EFSLIT) allows for the exchange of research knowledge and the opportunity to consider how research can impact on practice. The launch in 2007 of a journal dedicated to the dissemination of research about signed language interpreting and translation, *The Sign Language Translator and Interpreter*, constitutes an important landmark for promoting scholarship in the field and creates further opportunities for collaboration at an international level.

See also:

ASYLUM; COMMUNITY INTERPRETING; CONFERENCE INTERPRETING, HISTORICAL AND COGNITIVE PERSPECTIVES; CONFERENCE INTERPRETING, SOCIOCULTURAL PERSPECTIVES; COURT INTERPRETING; DIALOGUE INTERPRETING; MINORITY; RELAY; TRAINING AND EDUCATION.

Further reading

Humphrey and Alcorn 1996; Brennan and Brown 1997; Stewart *et al.* 1998; Brennan 1999; Metzger 1999; Mindess 1999; Harrington and Turner 2001; Cokely 2005; Janzen 2005; Marschark *et al.* 2005b; Locker McKee 2006; Napier *et al.* 2006.

LORRAINE LEESON

Sociological approaches

In the past decade, a range of sociological perspectives on research in translation studies has emerged which provide new sets of analytical concepts and explanatory procedures to theorize the social nature of translation practices. Research in this area has focused on a diverse array of actual and potential sites and activities. These include: the educational institutions where TRAINING is provided; training pedagogies; the relationship between training and professional work conditions; the relationship between research and training; the social constitution of professional organizations; and the social and biological trajectories of translators and interpreters. In addition, the sociology of translation takes as its object of investigation questions concerning: the function of translation in the global distribution and reception of cultural goods; the influence of market forces on translation practices; the role of translation and interpreting in articulating socio political and symbolic claims of the nation state; translation and globalization; translation and activism; and translators' agency.

As well as stimulating research across a diverse range of contexts, the different sociological perspectives emerging within the field have introduced a number of methodological approaches for investigating translation and interpreting activity as a social phenomenon. In relation to both theory and methods, there is a distinction to be made between research which identifies itself as sociocultural and applies a more eclectic set of observational and explanatory frameworks to specific translation activity taken, for example, from cultural studies, DISCOURSE ANALYSIS or sociology (see Pym *et al.* 2006) and research which relies on theoretical and methodological frameworks that originate in the social sciences. Within the field of translation, while each approach to research may be considered, broadly speaking, to constitute a 'social-theoretical' perspective, there are clear and significant differences that should not be overlooked.

The French social theorists Pierre Bourdieu and Bruno Latour, along with Niklas Luhmann from Germany, have so far been the most influential in approaches that originate in the social sciences. Although their respective understandings of what constitutes the social are varied, within the field of translation their work has been used, separately or in combination, to explore fundamental questions shared by translation scholars interested in the social nature of acts of translation. A brief summary of their respective work and its application to translation studies is provided below in order to illustrate the actual and potential influence of their work thus far.

Bourdieu's sociology involves a critique of structuralist attempts to develop conceptual schema abstracted from concrete analytical objects or projects and a rejection of a philosophy of the subject that concentrates exclusively on individuals as calculating, rational actors. His view of the social foregrounds social practices, not individual actions. For Bourdieu, individuals act in habitual, conventionalized ways that are to a large extent the product of the incorporation of social structures, structures that are themselves the product of historical struggles and which are therefore subject to change.

Taken together, Bourdieu's central concepts of *habitus*, field, capital and *illusio* formulate his theoretical approach to the relationship between agency and structure (Bourdieu 1977, 1990, 1991). **Fields** are sites for the confrontation of various forces, individual and institutional, and for the production, dissemination and authorization of different forms of symbolic/material **capital**. Fields are viewed as the relatively autonomous social microcosms that constitute a network of objective relations between objectively defined positions of force within social space. Each field is defined by specific stakes and interests which operate both in relation to other fields and within the same field. It is within the context of particular fields and through the **habitus** – embodied dispositions acquired through individuals' social and biological trajectories and continually shaped and negotiated *vis-à-vis* fields – that social agents establish and consolidate their positions in social space. Bourdieu's concept of **illusio** refers to the feel for and belief in the game, i.e. the tacit knowledge that allows social agents, relatively unquestioningly, to make sense of what is happening around them and to make

decisions as to how to act appropriately in the moment. Crucially, for Bourdieu, these concepts, as applied to the examination of concrete practices, serve as a means both to describe, explain and potentially transform the social world, while at the same time revealing the limits of social scientific knowledge itself.

Latour, in contrast to Bourdieu, would argue that attention to social 'forces' neglects or masks the elements, associations and contradictory voices that do not already form part of the familiar social repertoire, but which are indicative of the social being performed and created anew in increasingly complex and constantly evolving contemporary societies. Drawing significantly on ethnomethodology, Latour (1979/86, 1987, 2005) argues that the observation and description of these heterogeneous elements – both human and non-human – and the tracing of their associations for individuals themselves should be the primary work of social theorists. Social theory needs to be able to recognize the **actor-networks** and examine the **associations** being made or extended by actors themselves. Actors must be granted their own theories of what makes up the social. The task of describing a social group, for example, cannot be solely the responsibility of the social scientist, for group formation is also a constant task of social actors themselves. The task of the social scientist should be to document innovations with regard to the (social) collectives that individuals have taken up or transformed; describe the strategies they have undertaken to make certain heterogeneous elements fit together; and reproduce actors' own definitions and understandings of the new associations they have established.

Latour and Bourdieu share a commitment to ethnographic methods and to social practices as the starting point in sociological inquiry. They share a belief in the importance of examining the existence and relevance of objects, strategies and networks. Where Bourdieu and Latour differ fundamentally, however, is in the explanatory weight given to their ethnographic data. Bourdieu would argue that the descriptions given by Latour's social actors are themselves dependent upon the actors' location in the world. Latour takes these descriptions to be sufficient accounts of social reality as constituted in actors' experiences of everyday practices. He is content to leave unanswered (and unanswerable) the question of who or what is influencing their actions. For Bourdieu, to limit social scientific observation to the point of view of agents is to treat agents as instruments of knowledge, leaving unexamined the objective structures that have produced this knowledge. His ultimate aim is not to give priority to the explanation of the social scientist or the social actor, but to apprehend the limits imposed on scientific knowledge itself. In Bourdieu's view, these limits do not originate in socially-determined subjects, whether informants or social analysts, but in the social determinants of different forms of social practice, including sociology itself.

Niklas Luhmann offers a radically different view of society, although like Latour he conceives of contemporary society in terms of complexities and contingencies rather than as the social totality (albeit based in struggle) implied in Bourdieu's work. For both Latour and Luhmann, there is no overarching, integrating space from where the development of society can be measured or co-ordinated. Luhmann elaborates a view of society that is structured according to a principle of functional differentiation (Luhmann 1985, 1995, 2006). The world is constituted by a multiplicity of **functional systems** (e.g. law, fine arts, science, education, media) and what he refers to as the **environments**, inhabited by humans and non-humans alike, that surround them. In contrast to Latour, however, Luhmann's theory reduces human individuals to mere observers. Although social systems interact with environments, they remain essentially free from the influence of human actors. Functional systems are operationally closed and incommensurable; they establish and reproduce themselves *autopoietically* – i.e. they are self-referential and self-organized – drawing on past and present resources for their continued existence. Interactions between system and environment, whilst leaving the system's operational closure intact, can, however, set off perturbations or *irritations*, which may precipitate changes in the system's behaviour.

Central to Luhmann's theorization of the social are his views on meaning and what he refers to as **communications**. Drawing on phenomenology, Luhmann suggests that social systems operate in a similar way as human minds or intentional subjects; they process informational input from the world in the form of utterances and then select what is meaningful. For Luhmann, social systems also process meanings selectively, effectively producing themselves in and through communications just as minds produce themselves through thoughts. Importantly, however, minds and systems are kept apart in Luhmann's world; communications produce only communications. Communications produce themselves by encoding in binary terms other communications perceived as relevant to the system – for example, in translation, the historical source/target, literal/free dichotomies – and discarding others as mere irritations, unless these are important enough to force the system to adjust its coding orientations. Social systems develop rules and regularities such that, in time, they become structured in predictable ways. Patterns of expectations become established which, together with high levels of efficiency and specialization, allow that system to further distinguish itself from another – thus contributing to and maintaining both their functional differentiation and the complex character of modern society.

Translation scholars have explored the relevance of these theories to the field of translation and interpreting in a number of ways. These include the relationship between, for example, translator agency and social structure, historical, social and cognitive processes, human and non-human actors, and translation products, processes and relations of power. The work of these theorists has contributed to the endeavour to make translators and interpreters more visible, or in the case of Luhmann, invisible as social actors. It has also informed the conceptualization, at both the theoretical and methodological level, of empirical research designed to examine translation activity, including training, in the contexts of its occurrence. Bourdieu's work, the most widely discussed within the field, has been applied to a range of empirical and theoretical issues from literary and non-literary translation to sign language and public service interpreting (Simeoni 1998; Gouanvic 1997, 1999, 2001; Inghilleri 2003, 2005a; Wolf 2006; see also the collection of articles in Heilbron and Sapiro 2002; Inghilleri 2005b). Latour's Actor-Network-Theory has been taken up particularly, though not exclusively, to theorize the translation process from the perspectives of the actors involved, including the pivotal role of translators themselves (Buzelin 2005). Luhmann's theory has been used to conceptualize translation itself as a functionally differentiated system, to explore the self-referential nature of translation communications as metacommunications and to examine the autonomous relationship between translator training and professional practice (Hermans 2007).

These emergent sociological perspectives constitute both a new direction for work in the field of translation and a potential shift in the relationship between this field and the social sciences. Sociological perspectives have expanded the focus of analysis beyond literary texts to include non-literary and spoken and signed texts. They have highlighted the central position of translators and interpreters themselves in the translation process. And unlike FUNCTIONALIST APPROACHES, where the analysis of the translator's role is concerned to describe this position in largely neutral terms within a wider functional network, sociological approaches have identified translators' professional trajectories and social positionings as crucial to both the process and products of translation activity.

The developing interest in sociological perspectives within translation studies research may also impact on discussions taking place within the social sciences more broadly. The role of social theory in the analysis of contemporary society has come under increasing scrutiny as the visible and invisible factors that shape individual and collective lives appear to some to defy traditional sociological or philosophical attempts to categorize, stabilize or transform social phenomena. The emergent sociological perspectives in translation and interpreting research are reflective of significantly distinctive epistemological and ontological positions with regard to what constitutes knowledge and understanding of the world and how social theorists can best intervene in or comment on it. Latour and Luhmann argue for better observation and description of multiple, autonomous social realities while Bourdieu would support the possibility and validity of a transformative agenda for sociology through description and scientific explanation. These differences have implications for what form of intervention each believes social theory can or should make in complex contemporary societies. Translation scholars undertaking work in sociocultural or sociological research paradigms deal directly with these issues in their focus on the role of translation and multiple meanings in the multicultural and multilingual settings that comprise modern social systems. Translation research in this area, therefore, has the potential to play a critical role in current debates in the social sciences about modernity and the inevitability of differentiation, contingency and incommensurability in contemporary social life.

See also:
ASYLUM; ETHICS; GLOBALIZATION; IDEOLOGY; REWRITING.

Further reading
Gouanvic 1997; Simeoni 1998; Casanova 1999/2005; Heilbron 1999; Heilbron and Sapiro 1999; Gouanvic 2002; Inghilleri 2003, 2005a, 2005b; Buzelin 2005; Wolf 2006.

MOIRA INGHILLERI

Strategies

The term 'strategy' connotes a teleological course of action undertaken to achieve a particular goal in an optimal way. Problems arise, however, in defining the concept more precisely. As Chesterman (2005) has noted, not only is the term 'strategy' itself often used in different ways in translation studies, but a variety of other terms can be used to mean the same thing: 'procedures', 'techniques of adjustment', 'transformations', 'transfer operations' etc. Molina and Hurtado Albir (2002: 507) observe two different strands in definitions of 'translation strategy': (a) the procedural sense (often used by those investigating PSYCHOLINGUISTIC AND COGNITIVE APPROACHES to translating), and (b) the textual sense. The distinction here is metonymic of the greater distinction which some have proposed between prospective and retrospective translation studies (Koster 2002: 27; Wilss 1977: 67).

Procedural and textual strategies

A good example of the use of 'strategy' in the 'procedural' sense may be found in Lörscher (1991: 68–81), who distinguishes strategies from 'methods' (which are less subject to individual circumstances), 'rules' (which are more socially prescriptive), 'tactics' (which are less sequential) and 'plans' (which are more concerned with mental representation than with procedural knowledge). With regard to these last two distinctions, it should be noted that some commentators differ from Lörscher, for example in seeing strategies as a subcategory of tactics (van Dijk and Kintsch 1983: 66) or of plans (Færch and Kasper 1980: 60).

Lörscher is keen to break with earlier prescriptivist accounts (e.g. Hönig and Kußmaul 1982) by developing a descriptive definition of a translation strategy as 'a potentially conscious procedure for the solution of a problem which an individual is faced with when translating a text segment from one language into another' (1991: 76). As mental phenomena, strategies in this sense are themselves unobservable, although they may be reconstructed by researchers through analysis of strategy indicators. Since Lörscher's study, the notion of 'strategy' has gained greater currency in translation studies parlance, particularly given the rise in interest in empirical research into translation procedures in the 1990s. Much of the work on translation strategies has since focused specifically on their role in solving translation 'problems', though this in itself begs the question of what constitutes such a problem in the first place. As Chesterman notes, 'A problem for translator X may not be a problem for translator Y; but both translators may arrive at the same solution' (2005: 21). Would we then say that translator X had used a strategy but Y had not? Lörscher concedes that researchers analysing empirical data of strategy indicators (e.g. THINK-ALOUD PROTOCOLS) must proceed speculatively and hypothetically: 'They often do not interpret signs to be indicators because they know the respective entity, i.e. the strategy, but rather on the basis of considerations of probability' (Lörscher 2005: 599).

A second use of the term strategy, referred to here as 'textual', applies to descriptions of the results of procedures rather than the procedures themselves. The choice of 'strategy' to refer to this phenomenon again appears to be fairly recent, with earlier studies speaking of 'procedures' (Vinay and Darbelnet 1995/1958) and 'SHIFTS' (Catford 1965; Popovič 1970) between source and target texts. Chesterman (2005: 20) suggests that, in English, confusion in the use of 'strategy' to refer to both procedures and their results may be a consequence of the fact that many words used to describe textual translation procedures are nominalizations of verbs: 'compensation', 'omission', etc. Yet the discussion of strategies along these lines (as evidenced in texts such as Hatim 2001: 87–96; Munday 2001: 121–3; and Hatim and Munday 2004) generally follows very different lines of enquiry to procedural discussions of strategies, and tends to focus on the free/literal translation dichotomy or on issues of TRANSLATABILITY.

Local and global strategies

Another pervasive division is that between 'local' and 'global' strategies (Jääskeläinen 1993: 115–16; Séguinot 1989; Lörscher 1991: 71). 'Local strategies' relate specifically to the translation of particular language structures and lexical items, while 'global strategies' operate at a more general level and pertain to broad questions of textual style and the choice between suppressing or emphasizing specific aspects of the source text. This division is not uncontroversial, with Chesterman in particular recanting on his earlier use of it because it gives rise to (or perhaps fails to resolve) the ambiguity between procedural and textual senses (2005: 22, with reference to his earlier discussion 1997: 90).

In his classification of (mainly local) translation strategies, Chesterman (1997), drawing on Gile (1992, 1995a), distinguishes between 'comprehension strategies' (relating to the cognitive analysis of the source text) and 'production strategies' (relating to the production of the target text). While some research exists on translation comprehension strategies (e.g. Kupsch-Losereit 2000), scholars have devoted far greater attention to production strategies, with detailed classifications being proposed by, among others, Vinay and Darbelnet (1958/1995), Nida (1964), Catford (1965), Malone (1988), van Leuven-Zwart (1989/1990a), and Chesterman (1997). Often the development of production strategies at this level is explicitly didactic (e.g. Kiraly 1995; Kußmaul 1995; Piotrowska 2002). Chesterman (1997: 92–112) proposes that such strategies can largely be divided into three (somewhat overlapping) categories of syntactic/grammatical strategies (involving purely syntactic changes of one kind or another, e.g. literal translation, loans/calques, phrase and sentence structure changes, etc.), semantic strategies (changes mainly relating to lexical semantics and clause meaning, e.g. synonymy, antonymy, paraphrase and trope changes) and pragmatic strategies (involving selection of information in the TT governed by the translator's knowledge of the prospective readership of the translation, e.g. cultural filtering, information changes, illocutionary changes, partial translation, transediting, etc.). The often radical reorganizations of textual arrangement resulting from pragmatic strategies might lead one to consider them to be more akin to global strategies.

Writers like Lörscher (1991, 2005) and Muñoz Martin (2000: 130) contend that translation strategies refer to specific instances in the translation of text segments; this would initially appear to preclude discussion of more global strategies of the kind which have concerned writers like Venuti (1995a, 1998b). Nevertheless, consideration of such issues in strategic terms has exerted a major influence in translation studies in recent years.

While it might seem unusual to consider in strategic terms the decision of whether to translate or not to translate a text, the practices of certain translators demonstrate how such an issue may serve to further inform the translator's activity. Susanne de Lotbinière-Harwood's decision, based on broadly feminist grounds, not to translate any more male poets following her translation of Lucien Francoeur appears more strategic when it is seen as acknowledging a different relationship between women and language, a relationship which itself goes on to influence her further translations (de Lotbinière-Harwood 1995: 64; Simon 1996: 31–2) (see GENDER AND SEXUALITY). Similarly, recent years have seen the rise of groups of translators such as Babels, Translators for Peace, and the Translators' and Interpreters' Peace Network which engage in translation with explicitly humanitarian and political agendas

at the outset, agendas which exert a major influence on their translation practice (Baker 2006b). Again, since these agendas impinge on far more than just the translation of 'text segments', discussion of these groups' work in terms of global strategies may be largely without precedent. Nevertheless, the ensuing praxis produces target texts which are shaped by conscious and coherent series of language-mediation tactics that are consonant with most scholars' understanding of strategies.

Arguably, the key historical dichotomy which has dominated thinking about global translation strategies – and indeed much of the general discourse on translation theory up to the late twentieth century – has been that of 'literal' vs. 'free' translation. This division has been expressed in many different ways down through history, from St Jerome's espousal of the 'sense-for-sense' approach to more recent distinctions between 'formal' and 'dynamic' equivalence (Nida 1964: 159–77), 'semantic' and 'communicative' translation (Newmark 1981: 38–56), 'documentary' and 'instrumental' translation (Nord 1991a: 72–3), 'overt' and 'covert' translation (House 1981, 1997; see also QUALITY), and others (for a fuller list and more detailed discussion, see Kwieciński 2001). All of these oppositions relate to the degree to which strategies may involve manipulating a source text in its transition to a target text, with the extent of this manipulation often being determined by the relationship of target text receivers to the source culture. Perhaps as a result of its dominance over such a long period in the history of translation theory and criticism, the 'literal vs. free' debate has been criticized for being relatively unfruitful in the consideration of translation strategies and for oversimplifying a complex issue with blunt dichotomous analysis (Steiner 1975/1992).

In recent years, the work of Lawrence Venuti has been influential in the area of global translation strategies, particularly in his consideration of 'foreignizing' and 'domesticating' translation strategies (Venuti 1995a). Venuti derives these terms from his reading of Schleiermacher's famous discussion of the translator's choice between moving the reader towards the author or the author towards the reader (Schleiermacher 1977b: 74, quoted in Venuti 1991: 129). Schleiermacher's espousal of the former is supported also by Venuti, who praises this 'foreignizing' strategy for its contemporary potential to 'restrain the ethnocentric violence of translation … [as] a strategic cultural intervention in the current state of world affairs, pitched against the hegemonic English language nations and the unequal cultural exchanges in which they engage their global others' (Venuti 1995a: 20). For Venuti, this foreignization transcends mere literalism to become a more general strategy of intervention, impinging even on the choice of text to translate. He gives the example of how foreign texts which are marginal in the target culture may be translated with a canonical discourse (e.g. transparency) while other source-language texts which are part of the target-culture canon may be translated with a marginal discourse (e.g. archaism): 'In this foreignizing practice of translation, the value of a foreign text or a discursive strategy is contingent on the cultural situation in which the translation is made' (1995a: 310).

The manner in which Venuti harnesses the opposition to strategic ends has given rise to considerable discussion. Some have criticized his laxness in defining terms and developing his arguments to their conclusions (cf. Pym 1996a; Tymoczko 2000a). Tymoczko further criticizes his assumptions of a universality resulting from the fluency afforded by domestication – she notes that the prioritizing of domestication is highly culture specific, with more philological (non-domesticating) translation practices being valorized in various non-globalized language cultures at different stages in history. The textual and cultural deformation of translated texts is not, Tymoczko asserts, the result of particular translation strategies, but rather of cultural dominance itself (ibid.: 35). In subsequent work, Venuti has stressed (after Berman 1984/1992, 1995) that translation involves an 'inevitable domestication' (Venuti 1998b: 11) and has focused on the notion of a 'minoritizing' translation meta-strategy which generally aims to defamiliarize the target majority language by opting for non-standard discourse solutions, compensations and innovations (Venuti 1998b; for critical reaction see Tymoczko 2000a; Pym 1999).

In keeping with the general move from EQUIVALENCE-based to NORM-based theoretical models augured by the rise of Descriptive Translation Studies, particularly from the 1990s onwards, thought on both local and global translation strategies has aimed to take stock of such developments, most explicitly perhaps in the proposal by Chesterman that strategies are 'ways in which translators seek to conform to norms … not to achieve equivalence, but simply to arrive at the best version they can think of' (1997: 88). This may well point to new research trajectories in strategy studies in the future, trajectories which may well demand new categories and classifications for critical reflection on translation strategies.

See also:
ADAPTATION; BIBLE, JEWISH AND CHRISTIAN; CULTURAL TRANSLATION; EQUIVALENCE; EXPLICITATION; IDEOLOGY; NORMS; REWRITING; SHIFTS; UNIT OF TRANSLATION.

Further reading
Lörscher 1991; Jääskeläinen 1993; Venuti 1995a; Chesterman 1997; Muñoz Martin 2000; Kwieciński 2001 (pp. 115–65); Chesterman 2005.

JOHN KEARNS

T

Terminology

Terminology is concerned with the naming of concepts in specialized domains of knowledge. This field has developed rapidly since the middle of the twentieth century, but there has been an ongoing debate as to whether terminology can truly be considered a discipline. While some commentators (e.g. Jaekel 2000; Sprung 2000a) consider terminology to be a discipline in its own right, others, such as Sager (1990), argue that it still has some way to go in order to achieve this status. Although Sager affirms the value of terminology as a subject worthy of study, he rejects the claim that it is an independent discipline, viewing it instead as a number of practices, based on methodologies, that deal with the creation, collection, explication and presentation of terms. According to Sager, disciplines establish knowledge *about* things, whereas methodologies, which focus on *how to do* things, are only a means to an end. Scholars such as Sager argue that everything of importance that can be said about terminology is more appropriately said in the context of other disciplines, such as linguistics, information science or computational linguistics. Whether or not it is considered an independent discipline, terminology clearly has very close ties to other areas of applied linguistics, including specialized translation, and while terminological investigations can certainly be carried out in a monolingual setting, one of its most widely practised applications is in the domain of translation.

Fundamental notions

There are three key notions associated with terminology, namely **concept**, **definition** and **term**. Essentially, concepts are units of thought that are used to organize our knowledge and perceptions of the world around us. Moreover, we tend to understand concepts not in isolation but rather in relation to other concepts, in a structured system (Wright 1997).

Once it has been identified, it is necessary to define a concept. This definition is what provides a bridge between the concept and the term that is used to designate it (de Bessé 1997). A terminological definition must be as detailed as is necessary to differentiate a concept and its associated term from other concept-term units.

Terms are the linguistic designations assigned to concepts. Because terminology deals with specialized domains of knowledge, terms refer to the discrete conceptual entities, properties, activities or relations that constitute knowledge in a particular domain. Ideally, then, behind each term there should be a clearly defined concept which is systematically related to the other concepts that make up the knowledge structure of the domain. Moreover, the choice of the term should reflect this concept effectively and the form of the term should be generally acceptable within the language in question (Sager 1997).

Theories of terminology

Concepts, definitions and terms provide the foundation for a theory of terminology. Knowledge of theories of terminology is important for translators because they will need to apply it in order to carry out tasks such as determining relationships between concepts, dealing with instances where concepts are similar rather than identical, creating target language terms for new concepts and finding terms that correspond to the same concept in two languages, which sometimes involves selecting one term from among a number of possible alternative expressions.

There are various different theoretical approaches to terminology. The classical approach, known as the General Theory of Terminology (GTT), grew out of the work of Eugen Wüster (1968, 1976), an Austrian engineer. Wüster was particularly concerned with facilitating communication in specialized fields and sought to eliminate ambiguity from scientific and technical communication by using precisely defined concept-term units. The main principles embodied in this theory include those of onomasiology (i.e. beginning with the concept and working towards the term), the clear-cut nature of concepts (i.e. concepts have precise limits and a fixed place within a system of concepts), univocity (i.e. a one-to-one relationship between concept and term), and synchrony (i.e. focusing on current use of concepts and terms rather than on their evolution).

Each of these principles helps to achieve the primary objective of the GTT, which is standardization. This is normally a two-step process: first, the concept is fixed; then its designation is standardized. This process is analogous to that used in industry to standardize manufactured goods and processes; once the goods and processes have been standardized, they are labelled with appropriately standardized terms, and these terms are then firmly associated with the clearly defined properties of the entities they label. Standardization often involves selecting one term from among a range of competing terms. Pragmatic criteria for selecting one term rather than another are generally based on considerations such as economy (one term may be shorter and easier to write or remember correctly than another), transparency (one term may be more precise and less ambiguous than another), and appropriateness (one term may be more widely used than another) (ISO 704 2000). The task of standardizing terms is usually carried out by national and international standards institutes, such as the International Organization for Standardization (ISO) and its member bodies.

The process of standardization has also been applied to the language used in electronic information collections (e.g. databases and ontologies) to increase the effectiveness of information retrieval. This work has both a mono- and multilingual dimension and may use thesaurus-like devices to create links between the natural language of the searcher and the artificial language of the query system. Regular users of such systems readily adopt standardized expressions to maximize success when consulting the collection.

While the GTT has been successfully applied in contexts such as terminological standardization and ontology-based information retrieval, it has been criticized for its inability to function as an all-embracing theory of terminology. This has, in turn, spurred the development of a number of new theories, such as socioterminology, sociocognitive terminology and the Communicative Theory of Terminology (CTT).

Socioterminology adopts a more descriptive approach to terminology (see, for example, Gambier 1991; Gaudin 1993; Boulanger 1995), focusing on performance or real language use rather than on prescriptive standardization. It incorporates the study of synonymy and polysemy and calls into question the existence of clearly delineated concepts and domains. It also encourages the diachronic study of the processes of conceptualization and naming.

While the GTT is an objectivist theory, sociocognitive terminology is an experientialist theory. The basic premise of experientialism is that reality does not exist independently of the subject perceiving it; rather, all knowledge comes from experience and is perceived and expressed through an inescapable filter (i.e. language). Therefore, the sociocognitive theory of terminology (see, for example, Temmerman 2000) argues that terms are more likely to represent fuzzy and dynamic categories, whose members may exhibit differing degrees of prototypicality, rather than clear-cut concepts.

Sager (1990) was perhaps the first scholar to actively call for the addition of a communicative dimension to terminology, with the consequence that terms are now studied in texts rather than being considered as context-independent labels. Researchers such as Cabré Castellv' (2003) have taken up this call and argue for the development of a Communicative Theory of Terminology (CTT) in which the linguistic, cognitive and communicative dimensions are taken into account.

Applications

In terminology, theory and application are even more closely linked than in other fields. Indeed, terminology exists mainly because of its applications, and it is probably the applied work that is most familiar to translators. **Terminography**, sometimes known as **applied terminology** or **terminology work**, refers to the group of practices concerned with the collection, description, processing and presentation of concepts and terms in a specialized field. In most cases, it is terminologists who engage in the systematic research of one or more domains in order to compile bi- or multi-lingual resources, such as glossaries or term banks, for use by translators. However, as noted above, translators themselves may engage in a kind of ad hoc terminographic activity when they endeavour to establish a terminological equivalent or find a translation solution to a particular terminological problem encountered in a text. Translators may even need to create a new term in the target language if one does not already exist to describe the concept in question. Several methods of term formation exist, including borrowing, loan translation, explanatory paraphrase, adaptation and complete new creation. Whatever method is chosen, it is likely that the new term will be influenced by existing patterns of term formation in the domain in question, and terminologists, translators, technical writers and subject specialists can refer to a number of different guidelines for assistance (e.g. ISO 704 2000; Sager 1997).

The modern-day practice of terminography is highly reliant on technology, and researchers now use the term **terminotics** to refer to terminographic operations carried out with the help of computer tools. As documents become increasingly available in electronic form (e.g. via the Internet or full-text databases), a wide array of tools is being developed to help process them for terminological purposes. For instance, because terminologists and translators are faced with an overwhelming amount of electronic material to process – not all of which is necessarily relevant – tools have been designed to help with the construction of specialized high-quality CORPORA (i.e. collections of texts that meet certain criteria, such as topic, language, period, etc.). This type of (semi-) automatic corpus

construction tool allows a user to enter keyword information and then, using a combination of statistical and pattern-matching techniques, the tool attempts to retrieve documents available online that contain knowledge-rich contexts pertaining to those key search terms (Barrière 2006).

Once a corpus has been constructed, other tools, such as term extraction systems, can be used to identify automatically and extract a list of candidate terms contained in the corpus (Cabré Castellv' et al. 2001). Some term extraction tools work on monolingual corpora, but others can process bilingual parallel corpora, retrieving both candidate terms and their potential equivalents (Gaussier 2001). Once again, term extraction systems combine techniques such as pattern-matching and statistical processing to come up with the list of possible term candidates. Still other tools, such as concordancers, are available to allow terminologists or translators to conduct a more in-depth investigation of a given term or candidate by examining it in the range of contexts in which it appears within the corpus (Bowker and Pearson 2002).

Once the terminological research is complete, the next step is to present the information in a form in which it can be stored and disseminated to users. It is still possible to prepare printed glossaries or lexicons; however, such information is increasingly being provided in electronic form, in term banks or termbases. Term banks are large-scale collections of electronic term records, which are entries that contain information about terms and the concepts they represent (e.g. definitions, contexts, foreign language equivalents, grammatical and usage information, conceptual relations). Term banks date back to the 1960s, when they were among the first linguistic applications of computers. Early term banks were originally developed by large corporations or institutions to serve as resources for in-house translators. Translators continue to be primary users of such resources, though the contents of many term banks are now made available to a wider audience, including technical writers and subject specialists. Some term banks can be accessed freely on the World Wide Web, while others are available via subscription and may be distributed on CD-ROM or through a password-protected Web interface. Some long-established term banks include *Eurodicautom*, *Termium*, *Lexis*, *Normaterm*, and the *Grand dictionnaire terminologique* (formerly the *Banque de terminologie du Québec*).

Term banks are almost always multilingual and typically cover a broad array of specialized subject fields. While the aim is generally to produce a detailed record for each concept (i.e. containing both linguistic and extra-linguistic information), some records are more detailed than others. Term banks are a very dynamic resource and are updated frequently. Most institutions that maintain term banks also have a team of terminologists who conduct terminological research and compile the term records. Users may be invited to submit data for possible inclusion in the term bank, but this data is always vetted by the term bank's quality control officers.

There is no doubt that term banks constitute valuable and frequently used translation resources; however, since specialized subject fields and the language used to describe these fields are constantly expanding and evolving, it is not possible for any term bank to provide exhaustive up-to-date coverage. Moreover, clients may have terminological preferences that are not reflected in the term banks maintained by other institutions. Therefore, most translators find that it is also necessary to compile their own collection of term records in order to ensure that the appropriate subject fields and client preferences are adequately represented. There are a number of different options for managing personal terminology collections (e.g. using word processors or spreadsheets), but it is becoming increasingly common for translators to use purpose-built terminology management systems (TMSs), particularly when these are integrated with other COMPUTER-AIDED TRANSLATION tools, such as translation memory systems. These more personalized electronic collections of term records are generally referred to as termbases.

Early TMSs had a number of limitations, such as fixed templates or limits on the number of characters that could be entered in a given field; however, the more modern systems are highly flexible in terms of both record creation and search and retrieval features. Users can design their own templates and define their own fields, and they can create and maintain different termbases for different subject fields or clients. Moreover, if desired, these termbases can be exchanged or shared with other translators. With regard to retrieval, users cannot only search using the precise term in question; they can also use techniques such as fuzzy searching or wildcard searching to expand the range of the search.

When TMSs are combined with other tools, such as translation memories, the contents of the termbase can be searched automatically. So, for example, any time there is a termbase entry that corresponds to a term in the translator's source text, the translator will be notified and can consult the relevant term record or opt to have the translation equivalent retrieved from the term record pasted directly into the target text. Increased consistency and productivity are the oft-cited benefits of working with terminological resources such as term banks and termbases.

The increased application of technology to terminographic work has brought about other changes too. For instance, while traditional terminology textbooks recommend that term records should be strictly concept-based and that only the canonical form of a term should be recorded on a term record, translators who work with TMSs that are integrated with translation memories have found that it can be beneficial to create records for multiple forms of a term (e.g. in an inflected or conjugated form) in order to facilitate the copying and pasting of the term into the running text of the target document. Moreover, the tools used today, which often take a pattern-matching approach, may identify lexical items that do not strictly qualify as terms, but which could nonetheless be useful to translators (e.g. a frequently used phrase or other fixed or semi-fixed expression). From the point of view of a translator whose goal is to produce an acceptable translation on a short deadline, any type of information that may be recyclable – term or otherwise – could potentially be useful. Therefore, translators are beginning to fill their termbases with records containing a mixture of terms and non-terms, which goes against the principles put forth in the traditional terminology literature. Moreover, the popularity of translation memories means that translators are increasingly turning to translated material as a resource for conducting terminological research – a practice that was discouraged in the past. Resources such as corpus analysis tools and term extraction systems are encouraging terminologists and translators to adopt a somewhat more semasiological approach to the work (i.e. beginning with the term and working towards the concept) rather than the strictly onomasiological approach advocated in earlier times. For instance, because the only means for a tool to access a corpus is through a character string, rather than through a concept, the former may sometimes represent the starting point for terminographic research.

Finally, it is worth mentioning that other types of tools are being developed to assist with other aspects of terminological research, such as terminometric tools, which can help to measure the degree to which a term has been successfully implanted into a given language (Quirion 2005). Such tools could be of great use to the standardizing bodies mentioned above.

See also:
COMPUTER-AIDED TRANSLATION; CORPORA; EQUIVALENCE; SCIENTIFIC AND TECHNICAL TRANSLATION.

Further reading
Sager 1990; Cabré 1999; ISO 704 2000; Bourigault *et al.* 2001; Dubuc 2002; Bowker 2003; L'Homme 2004; Picht 2006.

LYNNE BOWKER

Think-aloud protocols

Translators and translation scholars have always been interested in the translation process. Translators have also analysed their own translation methods and solutions to translation problems (e.g. Bly 1984; Lefevere 1992a). In the 1980s, experimental methods were borrowed from psychology to gain access to what goes on in the translator's mind. To begin with, the most popular means of collecting data on translation processes involved 'thinking aloud', which means that a subject is asked to translate a text and, simultaneously, to verbalize as much of his or her thoughts as possible. Subjects' task performances are recorded on audio-

or videotape. The written transcripts of the recordings are called **think-aloud protocols** (**TAPs**).

At the most general level, the purpose of TAP studies is to gain a better understanding of the psychological and linguistic mechanisms involved in the activity of translation. More specific topics include problem-solving strategies (Krings 1986; Lörscher 1991), criteria for decision making (Tirkkonen-Condit 1990), and creativity in translation (Kußmaul 1991), among others. At the early stages of process-oriented empirical research, the emphasis was on formulating, testing and refining hypotheses about what translators do when they translate (Jääskeläinen 1999). Later research has focused on specific features of translation, such as EXPLICITATION (Englund Dimitrova 2005), or on a specific part of the process, for example revision (Shih 2006).

Thinking aloud as a method of data collection

The fact that the contents of human minds are inaccessible to direct observation poses a challenge to research. In psychological research, various methods have been developed to acquire access, albeit indirect, to mental processes. Thinking aloud is one of the methods of data collection known as 'verbal report procedures' or 'introspective methods'. These also include (traditional) **introspection**, which means that a subject carries out a self-analysis of his or her thought processes, and **retrospection**, which takes place after the task is completed. By contrast, thinking aloud is concurrent (simultaneous with the task performance) and undirected (subjects are not asked to verbalize specific information; it is the researcher who analyses the data). As a result, TAP data are considered to be more complete (because less is forgotten) and more reliable (because there is less distortion) than introspective or retrospective reports (Ericsson and Simon 1984). To facilitate verbalizing and to prevent subjects from analysing their own thoughts (i.e. introspecting), it is recommended that subjects be trained by having them perform warm-up tasks before the experiment proper (Ericsson and Simon 1984, 1987).

Verbal reports have a controversial history in psychology, spanning the whole range from unconditional acceptance by structuralists to total rejection by behaviourists. Contemporary assessments tend to be less extreme, maintaining that when elicited with care and analysed with an awareness of their limitations, verbal reports provide rich and useful data (Ericsson and Simon 1984/1993), and thinking aloud is thus routinely used to study writing (Hayes and Flower 1980; Bereiter and Scardamalia 1987) and expertise (Chi *et al.* 1988).

In psychology, the most controversial question is whether verbal report data provide access to mental processes or to the (intermediate) products of these processes (also known as 'mental content'; Nisbett and Wilson 1977). The answer depends largely on the definition of 'process': if mental processes are defined as neural activities, they are obviously inaccessible via any method of verbal reporting. By contrast, Ericsson and Simon (1984) view human thought processes as information processing. According to their theory of verbalization, the part of information processing which takes place in working memory, i.e. which is at the focus of conscious attention, is accessible to verbalization. However, making a distinction between mental processes and mental content – the latter including, for example, prior experiences, focus of attention at any given moment, attitudes, emotions and plans (Nisbett and Wilson 1977) – may be less relevant to translation research. Verbalizations produced in the course of a translation process provide additional information about the otherwise hidden stage between the source text and the target text. Whether these data reflect mental processes or mental content may be of marginal importance at this stage for translation research.

Nevertheless, TAPs have their limitations. One such limitation is the inevitable incompleteness of the data. Because only that which is consciously attended to can be verbalized, TAPs can provide no more than an incomplete account of the processing involved in any cognitive task. This rules out, for example, processes which have become automatized due to extensive practice with a task. On the other hand, some mental processes which take place at the unconscious level may not be of direct interest to translation researchers (for example, basic perceptual

processes). Translating also tends to raise into the level of awareness certain phenomena, such as nuances of meaning, which require little or no conscious attention in everyday language use. Audio- or videotapes which record the event provide supplementary observational data, such as intonation patterns, pauses and, in the case of videotapes, eye movements, gestures and facial expressions. Observational data can also provide clues about what might be going on at the unconscious level. In the case of translation, the written end product is an additional source of information. In addition, research software such as *Translog* has been designed to log the translator's keyboard activities during the translation process.

Thinking aloud may also interfere with the process under investigation. On the basis of an extensive survey of research evidence, Ericsson and Simon (1984: 78–107) argue that verbal reporting does not change the course or the structure of thought processes. However, in the absence of a thorough methodological survey of the effects of verbalization on translation processes, it is difficult to determine whether a similar degree of optimism can be justified within translation studies. Indeed, Jakobsen's (2003) findings indicate that in addition to slowing down the process, thinking aloud may affect segmentation and force professional translators to work with smaller chunks of text, which can result in less coherent target texts (see also UNIT OF TRANSLATION).

In sum, although think-aloud protocols cannot unravel all the mysteries of translation, they do provide access to valuable information about the nature of translating. Other methods of acquiring similar information include interviews, questionnaires and joint translating or dialogue protocols (translators working in pairs or small groups); see, for example, House (1988) and Matrat (1995). Collecting converging evidence from different sources, also known as 'triangulation' (see below), is likely to yield the most complete and reliable picture of the contents of the translator's mind.

Overview of TAP studies

TAP studies of translation offer a prime example of the interdisciplinary nature of translation research. Data collection methods originate from psychology, while the methods used to describe and analyse TAP data come from psycholinguistics, translation studies and cognitive and social psychology, among other disciplines. Because methods of analysis are usually modified, even tailor-made, to describe a particular body of data, TAP studies represent such a wide spectrum of research traditions that instead of forming a clearly uniform approach within translation studies, many of them seem to share no more than the basic methodology of eliciting data.

Thus, for instance, the source and target languages have varied, as has the DIRECTIONALITY. Usually subjects have produced a written translation of a written source text, except in Lörscher's study (1991) in which foreign language students produced an oral translation of a written text. The source texts have represented different text types, ranging from travel brochures to political satire and from popularized science to government documents. POETRY translation (Jones 2006) and BIBLE translation have also been studied with TAPs. Access to reference material has sometimes been allowed, sometimes denied with the purpose of eliciting richer inferencing strategies. Subjects, in turn, have represented various levels of linguistic and translational competence and have included, for example, foreign language learners, translation students, competent bilinguals and professional translators. The translation processes of language learners can be dismissed as not being representative of professional translation; on the other hand, it is necessary to have control groups for comparison, otherwise it would be impossible to determine what constitutes professional behaviour in translation.

Not surprisingly, such a multiplicity of approaches creates problems. Comparing the results and using the comparisons as a basis for generalizations becomes highly complicated. Yet combining evidence from several studies is extremely important, because subject populations have in general been rather small (ranging from one to twelve in most cases). On the other hand, the variation within TAP studies has certain advantages; different studies shed light on different aspects of different kinds of translation processes, thus illustrating the complexity of translational phenomena and the

need for further research. Indeed, the findings of TAP studies clearly demonstrate that there is no single monolithic translation process. The nature of the process varies considerably depending on several factors, including type of text, type of task and type of translator.

Limitations of research methodology aside, the evidence which has gradually become available from TAP studies has given rise to some intriguing hypotheses for further research. In addition to some predictable results, for instance that language learners focus on lexical transfer (Krings 1986; Lörscher 1993) whereas professional translators focus on style and the needs of the target audience (Jääskeläinen 1999; Tirkkonen-Condit 1990), TAP studies have offered a few surprises. For example, it was assumed initially that professional translators' processing would be highly automatized and would contain few problems and little conscious decision making (Börsch 1986; Krings 1986). Séguinot's case study (1989) of a Canadian government translator supported this hypothesis. However, further research has demonstrated that professional translators often identify more problems and spend more time and resources on solving them than language learners (Jääskeläinen 1999; Krings 1988; Rothe-Neves 2003). On the basis of these findings, the automaticity hypothesis can be refined: language learners are unaware of potential problems in translation, while increasing competence leads to a heightened awareness of problems in the case of professional translators (Jääskeläinen and Tirkkonen-Condit 1991). Furthermore, professional translators are able to shift between automatized processing in routine tasks (as in Séguinot 1989) and conscious processing in novel situations (Jääskeläinen 1999; Krings 1988; Laukkanen 1993).

Since the 1990s, increasing attention has been paid to the role of affective factors such as attitude and motivation in translation processes (Fraser 1993; Kußmaul 1991; Laukkanen 1997). Preliminary results suggest that a positive attitude and high level of motivation form part of professional competence and may even contribute to enhancing the QUALITY of translation. These findings are supported by psychological research on expertise, where it is hypothesized that the decisive factor in the development of expertise may not be giftedness (nature) or extensive practice (nurture) alone: in order to sustain the long period of training required to gain the relevant expertise, a high level of motivation needs to be created and maintained (Posner 1988).

Research on translation expertise has attracted growing attention since the late 1980s. Translation expertise shares features with expertise in other fields (Chi *et al.* 1988). These include allocation of time (experts spend more time on planning and revision), domain-specificity (experts excel in their specialized domains), and segmentation (experts work with larger chunks); see Englund Dimitrova (2005), Jakobsen (2005), and Sirén and Hakkarainen (2002).

TAP studies have progressed in terms of research design and have expanded to new areas. Among other things, one of the former short-comings of process research has been addressed: longitudinal studies which focus on the development of translation competence in the same individuals over a longer period of time are being undertaken (see below). Nevertheless, much ground remains to be covered. More research is required to test the results and refine the hypotheses documented so far. No large-scale, systematic study of the use of TAPs as a methodology to study the process of translating has yet been attempted. Such a study could have something to offer to other disciplines, such as psychology, where the focus has always been on monolingual and monocultural settings, and where the multilingual and multicultural settings typical of TAP studies conducted with translators could yield interesting results. Indeed, language-typological and cultural differences may be one source of contradictory findings in relation to the subjects' ability to verbalize fluently, an issue that does not arise in monolingual and monocultural settings.

Research software

To provide a source of 'hard' quantitative data on the translation process, research software has been developed to record the translator's keyboard activities during the translation process (deletions, back and forward movements, pausing, etc.). The most widely used software is *Translog*, developed by Jakobsen (1999) and

Schou at the Copenhagen Business School. Often the log-files created by the software are complemented with 'soft' qualitative data, TAPs, dialogue protocols or retrospective reports.

The availability of research software has facilitated the creation of large-scale projects to study translation processes. Among the first to be initiated was the Translation Process (TRAP) project at the Copenhagen Business School (Hansen 1999, 2002). The TRAP project also introduced the notion of triangulation in process-oriented research. Triangulation means that the object of study, the translation process, is approached from different angles, using a variety of sources to obtain a more complete and reliable account of the phenomenon under investigation. The second stage of Hansen's (2005) extensive longitudinal study of forty-seven students of translation investigates the translation processes of graduates in their work places.

Other projects include PACTE (Process in the Acquisition of Translation Competence and Evaluation) at the Universitat Autónoma de Barcelona, which focuses on the development of translation competence (PACTE 2003). The PRONIT project at the Universidade Federal de Rio de Janeiro investigates the translation processes of language students and experienced professional translators in order to design a framework for a translator training programme (Barbosa and Neiva 2003). These large-scale projects, with more rigorous and uniform research designs, are better placed to overcome the problems of limited generalizability and fragmentation of earlier process studies.

See also:
PSYCHOLINGUISTIC   AND   COGNITIVE
APPROACHES; UNIT OF TRANSLATION.

Further reading
Ericsson and Simon 1984; Krings 1986; Tirkkonen-Condit 1990; Lörscher 1991; Hansen 1999; Jääskeläinen 1999; Hansen 2002; Alves 2003; Englund Dimitrova 2005.

RIITTA JÄÄSKELÄINEN

Training and education

There has been a boom in institutional training of translators and interpreters since the mid-twentieth century, and in particular since the 1980s. The terms 'training' and 'education' are both used in the literature and reflect some of the diversity of approaches to the subject. In very general terms, 'training' tends to be preferred by those who adopt a more vocational or market-driven approach to developing translator and interpreter skills, while 'education' is favoured by those who situate the acquisition of these skills in the broader social context of higher or tertiary education, although this split is not entirely clear-cut (see Bernardini 2005). The term 'pedagogy' is sometimes used to encompass both approaches.

A brief history

Unlike the training of other professionals, there is no long-standing tradition of institutional interpreter and translator education until the mid-twentieth century. Historical antecedents tend to point to specific responses to concrete social or political needs at particular points in time: for example, the 1669 Colbert decree in France set up formal training for interpreters between French and Turkish and Arabic and Persian (Caminade and Pym 1998). Translators and interpreters tended to be language specialists or bilinguals who were either self-taught or had some form of apprenticeship or mentoring alongside more experienced colleagues. The well-known Toledo School in mediaeval Spain, for example, took on the form of a loose grouping of experienced and less-experienced scholars who learned together from collaborative work over time, but without setting up formal training as has often been assumed (Pym 2000a; see also SPANISH TRADITION; ARABIC TRADITION; CLASSICAL TEXTS). Self-teaching and apprentice approaches still survive today, both in contexts with institutional programmes and in contexts where these do not (yet) exist, and it may well

be that self-taught and informally trained interpreters and translators will continue to join the ranks of the professions, given the nature of the activities and the sectors in which they are carried out. However, they now account for a much smaller proportion of those employed or self-employed as professional interpreters and translators as the institutionalization of training has proved to be a powerful and irreversible movement.

The oldest institutions devoted to generalist translator and/or interpreter training are the Moscow Linguistic University (ex-Maurice Thorez Institute, founded in 1930), the Ruprecht-Karls-Universität Heidelberg (1933), the Université de Genéve (1941) and the Universität Wien (1943). A second group appeared after World War II, including the Universität Innsbrück (1945), the Karl-Franzens-Universität Graz (1946), the Universität Johannes Gutenberg Mainz (at Germersheim, 1947), and the Universität des Saarlandes (at Saarbrücken, 1948). Two French institutions, the École Supérieure d'Interprètes et de Traducteurs (ESIT) and the Institut Supérieur d'Interprètes et de Traducteurs (ISIT), followed in the 1950s. During this decade, the prestigious CIUTI (Conférence Internationale Permanente d'Instituts Universitaires de Traducteurs et d'Interprètes) was formed in order to 'ensure the quality of professional translation and interpretation and … contribute to the development of research in translation and interpretation and to the continued development of the training of professional translators and interpreters across the world' (CIUTI website).

The growing need for professional translators and interpreters has now led to the founding and expansion of programmes in an increasing number of countries around the world. Under the auspices of the Training and Qualification Committee of the Fédération Internationale des Traducteurs (FIT), the Intercultural Studies Group (ISG) maintains a list of existing translator training institutions. In 1998, the list contained some 250 references (Caminade and Pym 1998); by April 2006 it featured 380 programmes in 63 countries (Intercultural Studies Group website).

A curricular perspective

Institutional training

The ISG database reveals the wide variety of forms that programmes can take: from full undergraduate courses lasting three, four or even five years (for example, in Germany, Belgium, Spain, Canada) to postgraduate degrees lasting one or two years (in France, the USA, and the UK). Some are fully integrated into the university system and linked to academic departments which also conduct research; these tend to include a higher proportion of theoretical elements. Others are offered by institutions which do not belong entirely to the university system and grant vocational diplomas which tend to include only a minimum of theoretical content, or none at all.

Programme content depends heavily on the aims of individual programmes. In the case of translation, taking generalist undergraduate education as the paradigmatic form of institutional teaching and learning, several trends can be identified. The first is related to language combinations, where there is a strong tendency for students to be required to work with two foreign or acquired languages, reflecting the influence of early programmes designed to feed the translation services of international organizations. The vast majority of institutions work with only one mother tongue or A language, the exception being institutions in diglossic and international communities. Curricula are thus organized around students' language combinations, despite the fact that increased student mobility and the internationalization of higher education mean that many students find themselves learning in artificial language combinations.

The second major trend is that of organizing translation programmes into modules or courses in the following areas: language skills, culture or civilization, translating, interpreting, instrumental skills such as COMPUTER-ASSISTED TRANSLATION, documentary research or TERMINOLOGY management, and subject area options. These correspond roughly to the major areas of competence required by professional translators. This kind of organization, however, involves a clear risk of compartmentalization of learning. No institutions seem to have attempted cross-curricular learning for whole undergraduate programmes based on alternative organizational concepts such as the translation problem, although several authors have made the case for innovation of this kind (e.g. Mayoral Asensio 2001) and there are interesting experiences at postgraduate and/or course unit level (Kiraly 2000; Gouadec 2002).

A third major trend is that of placing specialized translation at the end of programme structures, thus implying stating that it is more complex than what is understood to be non-specialized translation. This tends to go hand in hand with classifications of specialized translation corresponding roughly to the major subject areas where translation work is carried out: SCIENTIFIC AND TECHNICAL, COMMERCIAL, legal and, less frequently, LITERARY. New areas of specialization have also been introduced, including LOCALIZATION, multimedia translation and AUDIOVISUAL TRANSLATION, where the basis of the classification is not the subject area but the medium through which texts are made public. Particularly germane here is the issue of the relationship between translator and interpreter education. Some traditions have linked the two and offer full-length programmes covering both areas of competence; others offer a joint foundation of anything from one to four years and then fork into two distinct specializations; others offer entirely separate training from the outset, particularly at postgraduate level. It is perhaps true to say, at the risk of overgeneralization, that the most common model situates the training of conference interpreters at postgraduate level, whereas translator training is strongly represented at undergraduate level. This may well be a result of the powerful influence exercised from the 1950s and 1960s by AIIC, the Association Internationale d'Interprètes de Conférence, on curricular and syllabus design for the training of conference interpreters.

In sharp contrast with translation, specialization in interpreting tends to be categorized by technique rather than subject area and on what is generally assumed to be a scale of increasing difficulty, from liaison interpreting through to consecutive and progressing to simultaneous. The prevailing trend is to focus all instruction on interpreting exercises or exercises directly related to interpreting technique (note taking, public speaking, attention-sharing skills)

(Gile 2005: 131). Occasionally, aspects such as documentation, conference preparation, terminology and professional ETHICS are covered, but rarely as separate units: they are clearly intended to complement interpreting techniques.

The introduction of consecutive before simultaneous interpreting is informed by the model pioneered by Seleskovitch and Lederer (1989/2002) at ESIT, Paris, and has been largely accepted by the vast majority of interpreter training institutions. It is based on the premise that consecutive obliges trainees to analyse content and dissociate words from meaning, rather than lapsing into word-for-word transcoding, and thus constitutes an appropriate grounding for the more cognitively exacting technique of simultaneous (Gile 2005).

For many years the term 'interpreting' was understood by many to mean CONFERENCE INTERPRETING. However, the end of the twentieth century saw the rise of COMMUNITY INTERPRETING (also known as 'public service interpreting', and understood here to include COURT INTERPRETING for the sake of brevity) as a separate discipline for research and training (see also DIALOGUE INTERPRETING). Although the basic skills involved are the same, the way in which the profession has developed and is still developing, the contexts in which community interpreters work, the different situational and communicative factors which come into play, the language combinations and many other aspects combine to make specific training desirable (Adams *et al.* 1995). In many countries this type of interpreting is done by family members and volunteers, and professionalization is urgently required for a number of reasons, including the need to guarantee the rights of migrants in the host societies (see ASYLUM; MINORITY). Few countries in the world have developed comprehensive training systems for their community interpreters, Australia and Sweden being the most notable cases, followed by Canada, the UK and the USA in the case of court and, more recently, medical interpreters. But even in these countries, training approaches are quite diverse and are conditioned by historical and cultural factors, such as immigration and language policy, amongst others. A recent survey of community interpreter training around the world (Abril Marti 2006) indicates that training initiatives come from a wide variety of sources, including

universities, public services, local authorities and NGOs. Only in countries with highly developed structures for the provision and accreditation of community interpreters is training primarily, although not exclusively, provided at university level (Australia) or under the auspices of a university level institution (Sweden). Given the urgency with which courses are set up to respond to pressing needs, traditional trends in translator/interpreter education are now challenged and novel formulas adopted: courses given in one common language, distance learning, adult education, part-time courses, itinerant courses offered on contract, creation of networks that share resources and programmes. Unlike conference interpreting programmes, courses on community interpreting do not generally focus on interpreting techniques but rather on factual information about the functioning of the public service concerned and/or intercultural mediation techniques.

Non-institutional training

Non-institutional training is offered by two major stakeholders in translation: professional bodies and major employers. Most countries have at least one association which brings together professional translators and/or interpreters with the aim of jointly defending their interests, promoting the profession and protecting standards. The vast majority of these organize professional development programmes for members, normally in the form of short courses designed to deal with very specific aspects of translators' and/or interpreters' work: new technologies, marketing, tax, copyright, terminology management, revision, and so on. Some organize longer-term programmes, such as the American Translators' Association (ATA) mentoring scheme, whereby senior experienced professionals offer guidance to novices over a period of time, thus facilitating their entry into the profession. ATA also has a Continuing Education programme that requires members to earn a minimum of 20 points every three years in order to maintain their accreditation.

Academic associations and societies in the field of Translation and Interpreting Studies, such as EST (European Society of Translation Studies) and IATIS (International Association for Translation and Intercultural Studies), tend to have training committees which organize seminars, compile bibliographical data (see for example the unique *Bibliography of Publications on Translator and Interpreter Training* compiled by Kearns (2006a) for the IATIS training committee) and promote research into the training of translators in general.

Conference interpreter training in the Western world is strongly influenced by AIIC training recommendations, which were developed at successive conferences held under the auspices of AIIC from 1969 onwards (AIIC 1979). This has given conference interpreting in Europe much cohesion with regard to training methods. The work of the Association's Training Committee includes organizing training workshops (for interpreters and interpreter trainers) as well as publishing guidelines for best practice for interpreter training and a guide to interpreter training institutions graded according to compliance with the association's criteria. Although AIIC is nominally an international organization, 70 per cent of its members are domiciled in Europe. Practices in non-Western contexts are often little known outside the countries where they are implemented, the prime example being the Soviet Union before 1989, whose high-quality interpreting research and training activity did not filter through to the West at the time (Denissenko 1989; Chernov 1992).

As for major employers in the private sector, larger translation companies run short staff induction and development courses. Many of these essentially cover technological aspects of professional translation and LOCALIZATION. It is also common for such companies to have agreements with universities whereby they offer work placements to advanced level students and thus complement more academic training. In the public sector, international organizations such as the European Union have a particularly strong interest in promoting training in specific areas. The European Commission's interpreter training programme began in 1964 (Van-Hoof Hafercamp 1989) and ran until 1997. Although the training programme has now been discontinued, the Directorate General for Interpretation (formerly Joint Interpreting and Conference Service (SCIC)) is still active in interpreter training through a number of mechanisms: the temporary secondment of DGI interpreters as trainers to those training institutions which request them, granting of subsidies to universities so that information concerning interpreting for EU institutions can be added to their course programme, and the promotion of the European Masters' Programme in Conference interpreting, which began in 1997 in an attempt to cover the demand for language combinations necessary for enlargement to include the countries of Eastern Europe. A similar initiative focusing on translation, the European Masters in Translation (EMT), is being mooted. Interestingly, there are also European Union recommendations regarding the level, length and content of court interpreter training courses, with the aim of harmonizing practices in different member states and guaranteeing access to justice for members of language minorities in the EU (Hertog 2003a). Such harmonization would bring the European model closer to the US system, where training of court interpreters has been organized from the outset by the University of Arizona.

As for public service interpreting, the main initiators of training in many countries are the public institutions themselves, in an attempt to solve their own urgent communication problems, in collaboration with NGOs and interpreter recruitment agencies (Abril Marti 2006). Community interpreting has thus been described as an institution-driven profession (Ozolins 2000).

Theoretical approaches to teaching and learning

Early training approaches reflect both the incipient state of the discipline and the teaching trends of the 1950s and 1960s. Trainers, a mixture of professionals co-opted on part-time contracts and linguists with no professional experience of translation or interpreting, worked on the often unspoken premise that the only way to learn was simply to translate or interpret, and then to compare the frequently unsatisfactory result of students' efforts with the trainer's own superior version. A combination of the development of the discipline and of teaching and learning theories at tertiary level has gradually led to new approaches being introduced. Skopos theory (see FUNCTIONALIST APPROACHES), descriptive translation studies (see DESCRIPTIVE

VS. COMMITTED APPROACHES) and PSYCHOLIN-GUISTIC AND COGNITIVE APPROACHES to the translation and interpreting process have all had a clear impact on training, encouraging more informed and reflective practice in the classroom. Higher education has witnessed a move from teacher-centred transmissionist approaches to more student-centred, and often outcomes-based approaches.

One of the first authors to propose the application of modern pedagogical principles to translator training was Delisle (1980, 1993/2003, 1998). His work, based on the *théorie du sens*, centres on the concept of teaching objectives, a forerunner, after a fashion, of the outcomes-based approach adopted by many university systems worldwide and by the European Bologna Process. The *théorie du sens*, with its triangular model of interpreting centred on the concept of deverbalization, or dissociation between words and meaning (see INTERPRETIVE APPROACH), was the first model to explain the process of interpreting from the standpoint of the practitioners. It clearly marked the difference between interpreter training and language teaching, and between interpreting and translation. It also rejected the restrictive linguistic theories of the time and their narrow concepts of EQUIVALENCE (see Lederer 2007). The main contribution of the *théorie du sens* was a practical pedagogical model presented in numerous publications, the most representative being *Pédagogie Raisonnée de l'Interprétation* (Seleskovitch and Lederer 1989/2002). No doubt the practical, prescriptive and simple nature of this model accounts for its considerable impact, even though it is aimed at training interpreters for one particular market. It continues to form the basis of the AIIC Training Committee's criteria, as reflected in its list of best practices.

Functionalist authors, in particular Nord (1991a/2006), have also contributed greatly to the modernization of training, encouraging professional realism and the gradual acquisition of skills. The influence of *skopos* theory can also be seen in training proposals put forward by Kußmaul (1995) and Kiraly (1995), who incorporate findings based on cognitive research. Kiraly (2000) has subsequently distanced himself from his previous work and gone on to adopt a social constructivist approach to training, based on real (or highly realistic) collaborative translation experience. A similar development took place in interpreter training, for example in the work of Pöchhacker (1995), whose functionalist perspective has shifted from a previously overriding concern with cognitive, process-based aspects to a communicative, situated approach, taking in external aspects and product-based considerations.

Vienne (1994) and Gouadec (2002) also adopt a project-based perspective, although these authors approach the issue from a more professional and less openly pedagogical point of view. The task-based approach developed by Hurtado (1999) and González Davies (2004), by contrast, is based on very carefully planned classroom activity around highly detailed tasks leading to a very specific outcome. Authors such as Marco (2004) and Kelly (2005), however, argue that the project-based and task-based approaches are compatible within the same training programme, the task-based activity being more appropriate for early stages and projects for later stages. Both approaches tend to incorporate much collaborative (group) work.

The move away from prescriptivism in interpreter training has led to the inclusion of activities such as the use of shadowing in training for simultaneous, simultaneous into B languages, the interpretation of non-spontaneous speech, the use in class of recorded source speeches and recognition of the link between translation and interpreting, all previously rejected or restricted by the ESIT model. This development in interpreter training methods is reflected in much of Gile's work, particularly *Basic Concepts and Models for Interpreter and Translator Training* (1995a), based on theories of human information processing (specifically the efforts model; see CONFERENCE INTERPRETING, HISTORICAL AND COGNITIVE PERSPECTIVES). Other authors whose research has influenced interpreting pedagogy include Moser-Mercer (Lambert and Moser-Mercer 1994; Moser-Mercer 2000, 2008), Kurz (1989, 1992, 2002b) and Setton (1999). Sawyer (2001, 2004) has applied principles used in education theory to interpreter education, in particular curriculum design and assessment.

Two major elements which have somewhat lagged behind in the development of new approaches to translator and interpreter training are assessment and trainer training.

Much as translation QUALITY assessment in general continues to be a complex and controversial area of the discipline (House 1977, 1997; Waddington 1999; Maier 2000), and the assessment of student learning is thus underdeveloped in relation to other aspects of teaching and learning design, with few exceptions (e.g. Colina 2008). The training of trainers began to attract more interest in the early part of the twenty-first century (see Englund Dimitrova 2002). The Consortium for Training Translation Teachers has run seminars and a certificate programme since 2000 at various European universities, and the ETI in Geneva has been running a comprehensive series of initiatives, including a postgraduate certificate and a Virtual Learning Environment for trainers under the direction of Barbara Moser-Mercer. Nevertheless, there is still much to be done in this area.

Interesting research is being carried out into the innovative application of new technologies to teaching and learning, rather than to translation practice (e.g. Bolaños 2002). The possibilities offered by virtual learning environments (VLEs) are of particular interest, and some programmes (such as Tradutech) have also been implemented using multilingual virtual collaborative professional simulation. The incorporation of new IT technology is also reflected in the development of interpreter training software and class material, for example the *Marius* database and training DVDs produced by De Manuel Jerez (2003, 2006), Interpretations/The Black Box (Sandrelli 2003), and the IRIS database (Carabelli 2003). Sandrelli and De Manuel Jerez (2007) offer an overview of developments in IT technology in the field of interpreter training.

Research

Although much has been written on translator and interpreter training, empirical research into training is arguably still in its infancy. Much early writing is anecdotal in nature (Kearns 2006a) and recounts individual, institutional or national experiences. Much of it was also published as conference proceedings, in particular the Elsinore conferences held in the 1990s (Dollerup and Loddegaard 1992;

Dollerup and Lindegaard 1994; Dollerup and Appel 1996; Hung 2002).

As far as research on translator training is concerned, there is considerable diversity of approaches and subjects. These include longitudinal studies of the acquisition of translator competence in general (PACTE 2003, 2005) and of more specific skills such as documentary research (Pinto and Sales 2008) or cultural and intercultural competence in particular (Lee-Jahnke 2006); aptitude profiles and admission testing (Timarová and Ungoed-Thomas 2008); the impact of collaborative activity (Kiraly 2005); the impact of international mobility (Soriano 2007); student expectations and motivations (Morón and Calvo 2006); learning assessment (Way, 2008); DIRECTIONALITY in training (Kelly *et al.* 2006; Pavlović 2007); the application of VLEs (Kenny 2007); interdisciplinary cooperation (Way 2004); graduate employability (Fraser 2007); curricular design (Kearns 2006b); and the development of computer tools for teaching and learning (Vandaele 2003; Boudreau and Vandaele, forthcoming).

At a round table on the interaction between interpreter training and research held at a conference in Turku, Finland in 1994, Dodds (Dodds and Katan 1997) reached the conclusion that the participants were not very interested in the application of research to training. According to Pöchhacker (2003: 106), the absence of research on interpreter training is due to the fact that interpreting research has focused too intently on the cognitive mechanics of the process, especially in simultaneous interpreting, with no great breakthroughs being made. As for COMMUNITY INTERPRETING, although there is a surprising level of quality research centring on interactive processes in DIALOGUE INTERPRETING from a sociolinguistic and discourse analysis standpoint (Berk-Seligson 1990/2002; Wadensjö 1998; Mason 1999, 2001; Hale 2004), little of that research is concerned with teaching and learning – and that which is has not, as yet, had a widespread direct impact on classroom practices, probably due to the great variety of forms taken by training in this field, together with the incipient nature of the profession in most countries. Nevertheless, an interesting and positive move has been the publication since 2007 of *The Interpreter and Translator Trainer*, an international refereed journal dedicated to research on the training of translators and interpreters.

See also:
COURT INTERPRETING; DIRECTIONALITY; FOREIGN LANGUAGE TEACHING; FUNCTIONALIST APPROACHES; INTERPRETIVE APPROACH; SIGNED LANGUAGE INTERPRETING.

Further reading
AIIC 1979; Delisle 1980; Gran and Dodds 1989; Seleskovitch and Lederer 1989/2002; Nord 1991a/2006; Delisle 1993/2003; Adams *et al.* 1995; Gile 1995a; Kiraly 1995; Robinson 1997b; Hurtado Albir 1999; Kiraly 2000; Schäffner and Adab 2000; Baer and Koby 2003; Colina 2003; De Manuel Jerez 2003; González Davies 2004; Malmkjær 2004; Sawyer 2004; Balliu 2005b; Kelly 2005; Tennent 2005; Moser-Mercer 2008.

DOROTHY KELLY AND ANNE MARTIN

Translatability

Can anything be translated? The question itself is likely to be untranslatable in some languages, up to a point and depending on context. This is because it can be read as meaning either 'is it possible to translate anything at all?' or 'is it permissible to translate just anything?', or both. When both meanings are to be kept in play at the same time, it is a matter of luck whether the translating language possesses a grammatical structure that allows the ambiguity to be reproduced with the same economy.

Debates about translatability concern primarily the question whether translation from one language into another is possible at all, or in what sense or to what degree it is possible. They extend to more social and ideological issues concerning what should or should not be translated. Historically, the social issues may well pre-date the linguistic ones, and be rooted in the belief that sacred texts containing arcane truths must not be profaned by explicating, disseminating or translating them (see BIBLE, JEWISH AND CHRISTIAN; QUR'ĀN). The debates, moreover, invariably turn on what one understands by the term 'translation'. Most Western

discussions of translatability and untranslatability project a conception of translation as integral interlingual representation involving not only notions of EQUIVALENCE but also, as hinted above ('with the same economy'), texts of comparable length (Pym 1992a: 67ff.); Derrida (1999/2001) speaks of the 'quantitative measure' of translation. When translation is taken in the broadest sense as the condition that enables communication in the first place, translatability tends to be accepted more readily. HERMENEUTICS, for example, sees in translation the model of all understanding (Gadamer 1960/1989).

Total translatability and total untranslatability are best regarded as limiting concepts. Full translatability, in the sense of an integral reproduction of a text's full signification, may be possible only in the case of artificial formal languages. Complete untranslatability would be beyond words, as it would imply the impossibility of communication or even semiosis. Linguistically speaking, the different approaches to the question of translatability derive from fundamentally opposing views of the nature of language and meaning. Steiner (1975: 73ff.) has characterized them as universalist versus monadist views. The former affirm the possibility of translation, the latter either deny it or regard translation as highly problematical.

Translatability

The universalist view considers the differences between languages to be surface phenomena only. They can cause practical problems for translation, but in principle translatability is guaranteed by biological factors and cultural considerations. All human brains are wired in the same way, hence there is a common human rationality. Moreover, we all inhabit the same physical world, hence there is a common core of human experience. Different languages may package meaning differently, but ultimately all languages are able to convey all possible meanings. In Roman Jakobson's words, 'All cognitive experience and its classification is conveyable in any existing language' and '[l]anguages differ essentially in what they *must* convey and not in what they *may* convey' (1959: 234, 236; emphasis in original). In the universalist perspective, language is typically seen as comprising two layers, a surface and a deep structure. Ideas and meaning are generated at the deeper layer and can be represented by a variety of surface linguistic structures. This view was held in the medieval period by Roger Bacon and dominated Early Modern and Enlightenment thinking; it is echoed in Noam Chomsky's transformational grammar of the 1960s.

The idea of language as two-layered promotes a dissociation between form and meaning, or, in Saussurean terms, signifier and signified (see SEMIOTICS). Form is material and perceptible, and varies from language to language, while meaning is invisible and can be extrapolated from the form that carries it. This is what Reddy (1979/1993) described as the conduit metaphor of language. It holds that meaning is transmitted, and can be preserved intact, as it travels along its conduit. The conduit metaphor also guarantees translatability, as translation transfers meanings by substituting one carrier for another. Translation thus constantly practises the separation of signifier and signified, as Derrida has pointed out (see DECONSTRUCTION). It makes us assume that different signifiers somehow convey a signified that remains identical to itself. This points up an aporia in Saussure's concept of language, in which signifier and signified are like two sides of a piece of paper and hence inseparable. Translation, however, is predicated on the separability of signifier and signified (Derrida 1972a/1981).

In the West, translatability was taken for granted from Roman antiquity onwards, the West's first copying culture, as Kelly (1979) called it. After the Roman empire, *translatio studii* accompanied the westward *translatio imperii*, again providing little ground to doubt translatability, whether linguistic or more broadly intellectual (Stahuljak 2004). The Christian Bible was overwhelmingly read and subsequently exported in translation, giving rise to the idea that its 'truth' could be expressed in any language and therefore existed independently of language.

Untranslatability

The day-to-day practice of translators appears to show overwhelmingly that translation is possible. If it happens all the time, surely it can be done? The argument against translatability does not usually posit absolute untranslatability but rather questions whether fully adequate translation can be achieved. The monadist case may be summed up as follows. In their different grammatical and lexical structures, individual languages embody and therefore impose different conceptualizations of the world. The structural asymmetries between languages prevent conceptual mapping from one language to another due to the lack of analogues and the absence of a language-independent mapping tool. The way different languages divide up the colour spectrum or organize kinship terms are among the classic examples of such asymmetries, but they affect all aspects of language. The French linguist Emile Benveniste (1958) even argued that the supposedly universal logical categories of the ancient Greeks were based on features of their language. The consequence, subsequently explored by ethnographers and philosophers, is that different languages may give rise to incommensurable logics (Winch 1964). Languages, that is, are embedded in the cultural environment of which they are a constitutive part. This reciprocity between language and CULTURE and the asymmetries between different lifeworlds, which are also language-worlds, make translation impossible (see also CULTURAL TRANSLATION).

The monadist view was articulated by the German Romantics, notably Johann Gottfried Herder, Wilhelm von Humboldt and Friedrich Schleiermacher, and taken up in the twentieth century by Edward Sapir and Benjamin Lee Whorf (hence the 'Sapir–Whorf hypothesis'). For Herder, all cross-cultural comparison was deeply problematic because each culture, and its language, had to be assessed on its own terms. Von Humboldt paradoxically asserted the impossibility of translation in the preface to a translation (the *Agamemnon* of Aeschylus, 1816) and presented untranslatability as a challenge to be taken up. In his famous 1813 lecture, Schleiermacher too asked whether translation was not a foolish undertaking, and went on to outline it as a task as unending as that of hermeneutic understanding (Lefevere 1977).

In doubting the possibility of translation, the monadist view clearly invokes the 'quantitative measure' mentioned above. It does not hold that we cannot learn another language or explicate in one language concepts proper to another. It claims that, due to the asymmetries between languages and cultures and the organic link between language and culture, translation understood as a linear discourse replicating another discourse with regard to both length and meaning is not possible. Approximate renditions can be achieved, or explanatory paraphrase; texts may also be translatable up to a point or in certain limited respects.

Untranslatability, then, mostly appears in relative form, as a matter of aspect, kind or degree. There always remains an untranslatable rest, for instance in the shape of connotation, nuance or poetic quality. Among the least translatable texts would be those that consciously exploit the idiomatic resources of a given tongue, or those that are encoded in multiple ways. In POETRY, for example, words may be woven into semantic, metrical, rhyming, intertextual and other patterns. This led Jakobson (1959) to claim that poetry is untranslatable and only 'creative transposition' is possible – leaving wide open the question of exactly how creative transposition differs from translation.

Since the case for untranslatability bears both on linguistic structure and on the relation between language and culture, it is often subdivided into two kinds, linguistic and cultural. For J. C. Catford (1965), linguistic untranslatability occurs in cases where ambiguity or polysemy is functionally relevant in a text, cultural untranslatability when situational features that are referred to in an original (for example, sauna, igloo) are absent in the culture of the translating language. Catford wondered whether cultural untranslatability should not be treated as simply a type of linguistic untranslatability: for any item unknown in the receptor language a loanword could be imported or an explanatory phrase devised, even if that would result in an unusual, linguistically marked collocation.

If a prohibition against translating certain texts or kinds of text is regarded as instancing untranslatability, then perhaps institutional untranslatability is a species of cultural untranslatability that is not reducible to linguistics. In this sense, the QUR'ĀN is institutionally untranslatable to the extent that the Islamic world will not recognize a version in another language as having religious authority. Adolf Hitler's *Mein Kampf* has become untranslatable because the current copyright holder, the German State of Bavaria, routinely refuses permission (Hermans 2007). In this case, the prohibition can only affect publication under the terms of international copyright law. Conversely, a language may be deemed incapable of accommodating certain concepts or be regarded as an inappropriate host for them due to its ties with an alien culture. Christian missionaries in the colonial Philippines or Spanish America reckoned some of their key doctrinal terms could or should not be rendered into native languages but were to be used by the natives in Latin or Spanish to avoid contamination by pagan beliefs (Rafael 1993).

The colonial context also provides examples of how cultural incommensurability, however radical in theory, may be overridden in practice to enable translation nonetheless. Colonial settlement meant that European ideas of property were imposed on native populations so as to allow the colonizers to claim territorial sovereignty and transfer ownership on their terms, regardless of the way the natives related to the land on which they lived (Cheyfitz 1991; Patton 2000). Using the somewhat unfortunate example of an anglophone linguist encountering a native speaking a 'jungle language', Quine (1959) explored the possibility of translation in situations of radical linguistic and cultural difference from a philosophical angle, suggesting that the construction of meaning across such divides remained hostage to an ineradicable indeterminacy.

Another key

In the twentieth century, both translatability and untranslatability were taken up in unexpected ways by influential thinkers. Walter Benjamin's 1923 essay 'The Task of the Translator' posits translatability as that which resides in the original as mere potential and which translation will adumbrate more fully. Just as the German Romantics held that a literary work is 'criticizable' in that criticism can point up the direction in which the work's latent striving towards pure art might be developed, a text is translatable if that translation can show a glimmer of the 'pure language' lying dormant in it. In developing this potential, translation adds to and liberates something in the original. In this sense the original invites translation.

Jacques Derrida, who more than any other modern philosopher lavished attention on issues of translation, cast untranslatability as both a critical asset and a positive challenge. Making his own writing virtually untranslatable through the insistent use of puns and polysemy, he focused on the 'double bind' of the simultaneous necessity and impossibility of translation. He highlighted instances of untranslatability in texts that draw on more than one language at the same time (as in James Joyce's phrase 'and he war', which plays on both English and German; see MULTILINGUALISM), use proper names that double up as common nouns (like the word 'Babel', which, confusingly, also means 'confusion'), make self-referential statements which re-mark the language in which they are written (René Descartes stresses, in French, that he has written his *Discours de la méthode* in French), or contain words of foreign origin not yet fully integrated into the language in which the text is written (like the word 'relevant', still in the process of migrating from English into French). Since translation theory, like philosophy, has no choice but to translate, the demonstration of untranslatability leaves the discipline in a quandary. However, like Von Humboldt, Derrida reads the untranslatable as holding out an invigorating challenge, inviting and daring the translator to tackle the impossible. The more untranslatable a text, the more insistently it begs and demands to be translated. Conversely, a wholly translatable text would not be worth translating.

See also:
BIBLE, JEWISH AND CHRISTIAN; CULTURAL TRANSLATION; CULTURE; DECONSTRUCTION; EQUIVALENCE; HERMENEUTICS; POETRY; QUR'ĀN; SEMIOTICS.

Further reading
Jakobson 1959; Quine 1959; Winch 1964; Catford 1965; Steiner 1975; Derrida 1985.

THEO HERMANS

U

Unit of translation

The unit of translation has been considered from a variety of perspectives. One early treatment comes from the comparative stylistics of Vinay and Darbelnet (1958/1995), who define the translation unit as 'the smallest segment of the utterance whose signs are linked in such a way that they should not be translated individually' (1995: 352). Vinay and Darbelnet's approach has been criticized for being overly prescriptive, too focused on the source language and based on idealized translations, factors which limit its ability to account for much real-world translation (see, for example, Ballard 1997). Their approach has been largely superseded by more recent, empirical research in translation, although it remains influential in translation pedagogy (e.g. Jones 1997) and the issues that arise from their discussion of translation units remain current. These include: whether or not such units are units of the source language/text, whether they are semantic or syntactic, at what linguistic rank they are realized, whether they have any cognitive basis, and whether they are conventionalized to any significant extent.

The growing diversity in research related to translation units has been accompanied to a modest extent by terminological differentiation, with Bennett (1994) proposing the term **translation atom** to label the smallest segments that must be translated as a whole. Bennett acknowledges that such atoms may themselves form part of larger units that are operational in translation. Bennett also proposes the term **translation focus** for the segment of a source text on which a translator focuses his or her attention at any one time (a concern in process-oriented translation studies), and interprets Bell's (1991: 29) claim that translators generally process clauses (as opposed to structures of other rank) as

a statement about the commonest translation focus. Similarly, Malmkjær (1998a: 286) argues on theoretical grounds that the clause 'seems a sensible structure to aim for as translation unit', amongst other things, because 'the clause is a manageable unit of attentional focus'. Finally, Bennett (1994: 13) reserves the term **translation macro-unit** for 'the largest linguistic unit which the translator needs to consider' (ibid.) in making local translation decisions. The full text is often the macro-unit, but given the limitations of working memory, it will rarely constitute the translation focus.

The unit of translation in process-oriented translation studies

In process-oriented translation studies, which is concerned principally with investigating translators' cognitive activity while they are translating (see PSYCHOLINGUISTIC AND COGNITIVE APPROACHES), scholars have considered the translation unit to refer to 'the stretch of source text on which the translator focuses attention in order to represent it as a whole in the target language' (Malmkjær 1998a: 286). That is to say, they have been concerned with Bennett's translation focus. Notwithstanding Malmkjær's comments on the clause as a sensible translation focus, scholars working in this paradigm generally stress the dynamic nature of translation units. Alves and Gonçalves (2003: 10–11) maintain that the translation unit 'is a segment in constant transformation that changes according to the translator's cognitive and processing needs'. According to this view, it is not possible to identify translation units a priori on the basis of source language structures or stretches of source text of a specified length. Rather, their identification can happen only in real time, as translators translate. In order to isolate such units, researchers have traditionally relied on concurrent THINK-ALOUD PROTOCOLS (TAPs), that is, translators' own attempts to verbalize their thought processes as they translate. One difficulty with this method, however, is that only a small proportion of any particular TAP is likely to give information about attentional focus on the source text (Krings 2001: 314). Moreover, because verbalizations related to the source text tend to occur only when subjects are experiencing particular problems with that text, some researchers come to equate 'translation unit' with 'translation problem'. Livbjerg and Mees (2003: 129), for example, define 'translation units' as 'Any word or phrase in the [source] text, or any aspect of such a word or phrase, which is verbalised by any single participant and for which he or she expresses any degree of doubt about its proper translation'. Barbosa and Neiva (2003: 138–9), on the other hand, suggest that translation units are not so much defined by problems as demarcated by problems which cause breaks in the translation 'flow'.

More recently, pause data obtained by means of keystroke logging has been used to explore the way translators segment or chunk their processing (see, for example, Alves 2005; Jakobsen 2002, 2005), the assumption being that distributions of pauses in the translation processing stream would give an indication of 'how much is being processed at any one time' (Jakobsen 2005: 173).

Even though process-oriented translation scholars stress that translation units are dynamic and cannot be equated with structural units of any particular rank, some studies have come to conclusions about the ranks at which translators with different levels of expertise tend to operate. Thus, Gerloff (1988) and Kiraly (1990) – both cited in Krings (2001) – and Lörscher (1991, 1993) conclude that professional translators tend to focus on source text units of higher rank than do semi-professionals or non-professionals, and Barbosa and Neiva (2003: 139) found that more advanced foreign language learners translating into L1 process longer translation units, at higher linguistic levels, than do less advanced students. Jakobsen (2005: 183) also found that expert translators work with longer segments

than translation students and when translating in the L2 to L1 direction than when translating into their second language.

The unit of translation in product-oriented translation studies

While process-oriented approaches to translation units give priority to source text segments, product-oriented approaches start with target texts and view the unit of translation as 'the target text unit that can be mapped onto a source-text unit' (Malmkjær 1998a: 286). There are few detailed descriptions of how such mappings can be carried out, but Toury (1980a, 1995) gives some relevant guidance. Toury is interested in identifying coupled pairs of target solutions ('replacing' segments) to source problems ('replaced' segments), but concedes that the boundaries of such **coupled pairs** are difficult to determine, given their dynamic nature and high context dependency. He thus advocates the application of a 'no leftovers' principle whereby the analyst goes about establishing 'a segment of the target text, for which it would be possible to claim that – beyond its boundaries – there are no leftovers of the solution to a translation problem which is represented by one of the source text's segments, whether similar or different in rank and scope' (1995: 78–9). For Toury, and Zabalbeascoa (2000), who offers a similar treatment, 'problems' and 'solutions' – combined by Zabalbeascoa (ibid.) into a single 'translation unit' – are mutually defining, dynamic, and specific to individual pairs of texts. They are also arrived at subjectively, and are, to a certain extent, an artefact of the analysis, as implied by Toury when he advises that 'whatever units one chooses to work with should be *relevant to the operation which would then be performed on them*' (1995: 88; emphasis in original). Although Toury's coupled pairs serve primarily to assist translation analysts in reconstructing translation decisions, he does suggest (ibid.: 99) that they may also have a function in the implementation of translation decisions, with translators potentially storing coupled pairs in long-term memory, and retrieving them in subsequent translation tasks.

The unit of translation in computer-aided translation and corpus linguistics

In COMPUTER-AIDED TRANSLATION, 'translation unit' tends to be used in a way that gives equal emphasis to source and target text. In translation memory (TM) systems, for example, a translation unit is a source text segment stored in memory along with its corresponding translation (Bowker 2002a: 155). Such segments tend to be stored at the sentence level, reflecting the relative ease with which the boundaries of sentences can be identified automatically and also the editing environments in which translators using these tools work. While attempts are made to automatically extract subsentential translation units from parallel CORPORA, for example, in bilingual TERMINOLOGY extraction, computational linguists concede that even if the translation *process* can somehow be seen as compositional – that is, the translation of a text is seen as a function of the translation of its parts – this compositionality remains a relative notion as far as translation *products* are concerned (Kraif 2002: 274), and it is not obvious after the event – to humans or machines – where the boundaries of individual translation units are to be drawn (Kay 2000; Kraif 2002, 2003). Having said that, if repeated stretches of source text consistently receive the same translation in a target language, then this can be taken as quantitative evidence that there are units of source and target texts between which a relatively stable translation relationship exists.

Recurrence in a parallel corpus is also used as a criterion for spotting translation units in the lexically-oriented corpus linguistics of Teubert (2002, 2004) and Kondo (2007). For Teubert, translation units are source text segments, usually compounds, multi-word units, collocations or set phrases (2002: 193) 'that are large enough to be monosemous' so that for each translation unit 'there is only one equivalent in the target language, or, if there are more, then these equivalents will be synonymous' (2004: 184–5). Translation units, although segments of source texts, are seen here through the prism of the target language, in a move that has much in common with Vinay and Darbelnet's (1958) original formulation of the concept, except, of

course, that Teubert's treatment has an explicit empirical base. Kenny (forthcoming) has also sought to develop a specifically corpus-based approach to the study of translation units, drawing on Toury's 'coupled pair' approach, and providing evidence to suggest that Bennett's (1994) terminological distinction between translation atom, translation focus and translation macro-unit is indeed well motivated.

See also:
EQUIVALENCE; PSYCHOLINGUISTIC AND COG-NITIVE APPROACHES; SHIFTS.

Further reading
Lörscher 1991; Bennett 1994; Kraif 2002, 2003; Kondo 2007; Kenny forthcoming.

DOROTHY KENNY

Universals

Universals of translation are linguistic features which typically occur in translated rather than original texts and are thought to be independent of the influence of the specific language pairs involved in the process of translation (Baker 1993: 243).

Toury conceives translation universals to be conditioned and probabilistic regularities in translation, and prefers the term 'laws' mainly because 'it should always be possible to explain away [seeming] exceptions to a law with the help of *another* law, operating on *another* level' (Toury 2004: 29; see NORMS). The value of probabilistic laws of translational behaviour, he argues, lies in their '*explanatory power*' rather than their '*existence*' (ibid.). Toury puts forward two laws of translational behaviour by way of illustration: the **law of growing standardization** and **the law of interference**. According to the former, source text **textemes** (signs which assume specific functions deriving from the special relationships they create within the text) tend to be converted into target-language **repertoremes** (signs which belong to an institutionalized repertoire, that is, a group of items which are codifications of phenomena that have semiotic value for a given community) (Toury 1995: 267–8). Age, extent of bilingualism, the knowledge and experience of the translator, cognitive factors and the status of translation within the target culture may influence the operation of the law (ibid.: 270–2). According to the law of interference, phenomena pertaining to the make-up of the source text tend to be transferred to the target text. The extent to which interference is realized depends on the professional experience of the translator and the sociocultural conditions in which a translation is produced and consumed, so that experienced translators tend to be less affected by the make-up of the source text, and tolerance towards interference tends to increase when translation is carried out from a highly prestigious culture. The prestige value assigned to different text types in the target language also has an impact on the operation of the law. Technical translation, for example, may display a lower degree of interference compared with literary translation (ibid.: 275–9).

In line with Toury, Chesterman (2000, 2004a) views the quest for universals as one way in which descriptive scholars propose and look for generalizations about translation. These general regularities or laws, he explains, are explored by putting forward, operationalizing and testing general descriptive hypotheses about the existence of similarities between different types of translation, without disregarding either the differences between them or the uniqueness of each particular case. Chesterman makes a useful distinction between **S-universals**, 'universal differences between translations and their source texts', and **T-universals**, 'universal differences between translations and comparable non-translated texts' (Chesterman 2004a: 39). If universals are supported by extensive empirical evidence, they can have explanatory force as regards the occurrence of a given feature in a particular translation (Chesterman 2000: 26). The reasons for the existence of universals, on the other hand, are to be found in the nature of translation as a communicative act, the translator's awareness of his or her sociocultural role, and in neighbouring fields of scientific enquiry, such as human cognition.

Drawing on Croft's (1990: 246) 'scalar concept of generalization', Halverson posits that universals are second-level (or internal) generalizations made on the basis of numerous empirical studies, and as such they are *'explanatory* with respect to individual studies of

particular linguistic realizations and/or language pairs' (2003: 232). By contrast, third-level (or external) generalizations are made on the basis of cognitive factors. Halverson further argues that various universal lexical/semantic patterns observed in ST–TT pairs, parallel corpora and monolingual comparable corpora can be explained by the existence of asymmetries in the cognitive organization of semantic information, whereby the nodes which function as category prototype and highest-level schema are more prominent and important than others, mostly as a result of their high frequency of use (Langacker 1987). Conversely, the absence of these asymmetries is assumed to produce the opposite effect in translated text.

The notion of universals has also been the subject of some criticism. Tymoczko (1998: 653) maintains that the search for universal laws of translation follows the tradition of empirical research, whose claims about scientific objectivity have been seriously challenged by twentieth-century explorations of subjectivity in the social sciences. Similarly, Arrojo argues that any regularities identified in translation 'will reflect the interests of a certain translation specialist, or a research group, at a certain time, in a certain context' (Chesterman and Arrojo 2000: 159).

The introduction of electronic corpus analysis as a research methodology in translation studies in the mid-1990s has acted as a stimulus to empirical research into universals (see CORPORA). Thanks to the increasing availability of parallel and comparable corpora in a growing number of languages, corpus-based studies have refined, extended and diversified previous descriptive research into linguistic translation universals, most notably simplification (Blum-Kulka and Levenston 1983; Toury 1995; Vanderauwera 1985), EXPLICITATION (Blum-Kulka 1986; Klaudy 1996b; Shlesinger 1989a, 1995; Toury 1995; Vanderauwera 1985) and normalization (Vanderauwera 1985; Shlesinger 1991; Toury 1995).

In terms of *simplification*, four 'core patterns of lexical use' were identified by Laviosa in the English Comparable Corpus (ECC), a multi-source-language monolingual comparable corpus made up of translational and non-translational narrative and newspaper texts (Laviosa 1998b: 565):

(a) translated texts have a relatively lower percentage of content words versus grammatical words (i.e. their lexical density is lower);

(b) the proportion of high frequency words versus lower frequency words is relatively higher in translated texts;

(c) the list head of a corpus of translated text accounts for a larger area of the corpus (i.e. the most frequent words are repeated more often);

(d) the list head of translated texts contains fewer lemmas.

The findings confirm the general hypothesis of lexical simplification in translation, defined by Blum-Kulka and Levenston (1983:119) as 'the process and/or result of making do with *less* words'. The above patterns of lexical use, argues Halverson (2003: 218–19), support and can be accounted for by the idea of a gravitational pull from category prototypes in semantic networks, since prototypes are selected more frequently than more peripheral structures or items.

Explicitation has been explored by Øverås (1998), who tested Blum-Kulka's 'explici-tation hypothesis' (1986: 19) in a corpus of literary translations drawn from a bidirectional English–Norwegian Parallel Corpus (ENPC). The explicitation hypothesis 'postulates an observed cohesive explicitness from SL to TL texts regardless of the increase traceable to differ-ences between the linguistic and textual systems involved' (ibid.). Based on the assumption that a rise in the level of cohesion in the target text is an aspect of explicitation, Øverås hypothesized that English and Norwegian target texts would be more cohesive than their source texts. The results confirmed this prediction: **expliciting shifts**, involving the addition and specification of lexical and grammatical items, were found to outnumber **implicitating shifts** in both direc-tions of translation. In addition to the process of interpretation inherent in translation, Øverås considers various factors that may explain the phenomenon of explicitation, such as stylistic preferences of source and target languages, their systemic differences, and culture-bound trans-lation norms.

Baker's notion of explicitation, which refers to 'an overall tendency to spell things out rather than leave them implicit in translation' (Baker 1996a: 180), was investigated by Olohan and Baker (2000) at the level of syntax. Their analysis of the use of the optional *that* in reporting struc-tures in translated narrative texts drawn from the Translational English Corpus (TEC), *vis-à-vis* comparable non-translated texts drawn from the British National Corpus (BNC), revealed a higher number of occurrences of *that* after the verbs SAY and TELL in translated texts compared to non-translated texts, thus suggesting a higher level of grammatical explicitness in translational English. Drawing on Günter Rohdenburg (1996), Olohan and Baker suggest that the cognitive complexity involved in translation could explain the over-representation of the optional *that* in translated texts.

Normalization, defined by Baker (1996a: 176–7) as 'the tendency to conform to patterns and practices which are typical of the target language, even to the point of exaggerating them', is the starting point of Kenny's (2001) study of lexical creativity and lexical normali-zation in a parallel corpus of contemporary German literary texts and their English transla-tions (GEPCOLT). Kenny identified three sets of creative lexis in the German subcorpus: creative hapax legomena, writer-specific forms, and creative collocations. Although overall findings pointed to lexical normalization being a feature of translation, the study also revealed evidence of lexical creativity. Closer examination of the corpus revealed that the extent to which creative lexis is normalized is influenced by how translators see their brief and by the systemic resources of the source language. For example, creative lexis linked to the derivational possi-bilities offered by German or involving puns might be particularly difficult to render in the target language.

Some evidence of normalization is also provided by Øverås's (1998) study of explici-tation discussed earlier, which shows a tendency in translation to prefer typical rather than unusual collocations and neutralize metaphorical expressions. The findings of these studies lend some support to Toury's law of growing standardization.

Finally, Toury's law of interference has also been investigated in a number of studies. Using the Corpus of Translated Finnish (CTF), Mauranen (2000) showed that Finnish academic texts translated from English use more multi-word strings with the functions of organizing the text, providing comments and guiding the reader's interpretation, *vis-à-vis* comparable original Finnish texts. Moreover, translations of popular non-fiction were found to depart more frequently from target language norms than translations of academic prose. Possible reasons for this difference may be related to the professional status of the translator of academic texts, who may devote more time to the translation task, and the more prestigious status of translated academic writing, whose linguistic qualities may be more closely scrutinized (Mauranen 2000: 137).

Tirkkonen-Condit's proposed *Unique Items Hypothesis* (UIH) states that target-language-specific elements, which do not have equivalents in the source language, tend to be under-represented in translated texts, since 'they do not readily suggest themselves as translation equivalents' (Tirkkonen-Condit 2004: 177–8). This hypothesis was tested on academic and fictional texts from the Corpus of Translated Finnish. Two sets of elements specific to Finnish were investigated: verbs of sufficiency and the clitic particles *–kin* and *–hAn*. The findings strongly support the hypothesis, notwithstanding some differences between the two genres. The Unique Items Hypothesis is further supported by Eskola (2004), whose study of translated narrative prose in English, Russian and comparable original Finnish texts found substantial evidence of under-representation of referative non-finite structures, which are used in Finnish to shorten an affirmative *that*-clause and have no straightforward equivalents in either English or Russian. Conversely, temporal and final non-finite constructions, which have straightforward equivalents in both source languages, were over-represented in translation.

Pedagogical applications

Stewart's (2000) research into the use of the British National Corpus (BNC) for translating Italian tourist texts into English as L2 shows that translator trainees can produce naturally sounding collocations by examining the frequency of occurrence and concordance lines of assumed target language equivalents of source language noun phrases. A large corpus

such as the BNC can therefore be a very useful resource for students translating into English as a foreign language. However, the use of CORPORA in the translation classroom, argues Stewart, may contribute to reinforcing the normalizing tendency evident in translated texts and thus inhibit creativity.

In the first phase of an experiment carried out by Kujamäki (2004) to test the Unique Item Hypothesis, thirty-six students were asked to back-translate into Finnish the German and English translations of a Finnish original text created ad hoc on the topic of driving in Finland. The text included several language-specific items with no straightforward equivalents in either German or English. These translations were then compared with the students' use of original Finnish as revealed by a cloze test designed to elicit 'unique items'. Even where TL-specific items were part of their lexical repertoire, students tended to overlook unique items and opt for straightforward lexical or dictionary equivalents.

Finally, Scarpa (2006) has investigated simplification and explicitation as possible indicators of translation quality. Specialized English–Italian translations carried out by advanced translator trainees were compared with the English source texts for overall length, number of sentences, average sentence length, standardized type/token ratio, and lexical density. A correlation was found between higher translation quality assessment grades and translations with a higher level of explicitness and a lower level of simplification.

Research into universals is now supported by a substantial volume of observational and experimental data. However, some studies have also provided counter evidence to these assumed universals (e.g. Puurtinen 1997; Saldanha 2004), and various scholars continue to debate the plausibility, types and sociocultural determinants of universals. What can be envisioned for the future is an improved methodology that combines comparable and parallel corpora in a wider range of languages and integrates textual and contextual data. Greater emphasis on exploring the cognitive factors that might account for regularities of translational behaviour, and more sustained attention to the specific sociocultural conditions that shape or constrain this behaviour, should further consolidate and refine findings in this field of study.

See also:
CORPORA; EXPLICITATION; NORMS.

Further reading
Baker 1993; Toury 1995; Baker 1996a; Laviosa
1998c; Kenny 2001; Laviosa 2002; Mauranen
and Kujamäki (eds) 2004; Olohan 2004.

SARA LAVIOSA

PART II
HISTORY AND TRADITIONS

African tradition

The practice of translation in Sub-Saharan Africa is virtually as old as communication through the spoken word. Numerous studies have shown that multilingualism is part and parcel of the very make-up of Sub-Saharan Africa (Greenberg 1955). Given the multiplicity of ethnic communities in this region (there are over 100 in Cameroon alone), translation has always been, and still is, the order of the day. The history of translation in Sub-Saharan Africa can be subdivided into three major eras: pre-colonial, colonial and postcolonial. In all three eras, translation played a crucial role in the political, economic and cultural survival of the African people.

The pre-colonial era

Research in oral history, particularly the works of oral tradition historians such as Vansina, Bascom, Finnegan and Okpewho, has been instrumental in uncovering information concerning the history of translation in pre-colonial Africa. Also of great help has been the work of some European missionaries and explorers who managed to record aspects of African oral tradition in writing during the period following the initial contacts between Europe and Africa.

The ancient history of Africa was mainly recorded in oral literature and handed down by word of mouth, from generation to generation. In this oral tradition, the closest thing to today's translator/interpreter is what some scholars have referred to as the 'professional linguist': something like an official spokesperson for a village or an ethnic group, who was believed to be endowed with special talents to record and narrate the history and culture of his people. In most African societies, the 'professional linguist' belonged to a long line of such gifted linguists of the same family. Many worked in the courts of great kings of ancient African kingdoms, such as the Mali, Zimbabwean and Ghanaian kingdoms. These linguists were often great orators and spokesmen for kings and chiefs, and consequently had a privileged position in society and wielded considerable political power. Referring to the Ashanti 'linguists', Danquah (1928: 42) points out that 'not only were they charged with repeating the words of their patron after him, acting as herald to make it clear to all his audience and to add to his utterances the extra authority of remoteness, but they were also expected to "perfect" the speech of a chief who was not sufficiently eloquent, and to elaborate his theme for him'. However the 'linguist' was not expected to 'add any new subject-matter, but … he may extend the phrases and reconstruct the sentences and intersperse the speech with some of the celebrated witty and philosophical reflections for which they are justly celebrated to the credit of both himself and his chief' (ibid.). In French-speaking Africa, linguists were known as 'griots'. Unfortunately, hardly any griot was identified by name by those who benefited from their knowledge.

The highly esoteric language used by rulers and elders in traditional Africa often required the mediation of an 'interpreter' to facilitate communication with the common people. Sometimes, interpreters would be needed to simplify the language used by members of a secret society, or to gloss speeches made during public occasions such as religious injunctions, sermons or solemn marriage transactions. The language used on such occasions often followed strict conventions of style and set phraseology, and was frequently replete with proverbs and wise sayings not known to the non-initiate.

The role of traditional interpreters as mediators between the ruling classes and the common people, in what were often highly organized nations marked by an extreme degree of hierarchy, earned them a great deal of respect. However, since they were a class set apart from those who needed their services, they were also feared, mistrusted and disliked by other members of society.

Another form of 'translation' prevalent in many pre-colonial African societies is that associated with 'drum language'. African drum literature is a form of communication which involves using instruments to communicate through direct representations of the spoken word. The instruments simulate the tone and rhythm of actual speech. This type of communication is linguistic since the message can be 'translated' into words, and it is only then, in fact, that it can be fully appreciated. African drum language can express words through instruments because the African languages involved are highly tonal. The drum language is built on the tonal patterns of the words which are being directly transmitted.

Pre-colonial Africa is also thought to have had a flourishing writing tradition. Scholars of African history are quite divided on this issue, for many believe that writing, or the recording of African oral narrative in writing, only began with the arrival of Arabs around A.D. 800 and Europeans in the fifteenth century. Opponents of this theory point to a plethora of writing conventions employed by Africans before any significant foreign incursions. They point to the advanced literate cultures that thrived in the Nile Valley established by the Nubian, Pharaonic Egyptian, Meroe, Ethiopian and Kush civilizations. This discussion is important because it has been suggested that translated literary and scientific documents had been available in Africa for centuries before the arrival of foreigners. A system of writing based on picture signs was widely used in pre-colonial Africa, and scholars of ancient African history have often relied on the expertise of specialists who can decipher the meaning of this pictorial writing. Much of ancient African history has been constructed through a systematic translation of such pictograms into modern Arabic or Roman script. This kind of translation is highly scholarly and is still practised in certain parts of Africa, where

pictorial languages are still used in spite of the presence of Arabic and Roman scripts. Mveng (1980: 90) refers to traces of pictorial writing in Ghana among the Akan, Ashanti, Adinkra and Baoulé, in Cameroon among the Bamileke and the Bamoun, and in Zaire among the Baluba and the Bakuba. The Amharic languages in Ethiopia and the hieroglyphics in Egypt are believed to have existed in written form long before the arrival of foreigners.

The colonial era (fifteenth century – mid-twentieth centuries)

The colonial era begins with the first encounter between Africans and Europeans in the fifteenth century and ends with the period immediately preceding the independence of African nations around the 1950s. The history of translation in this era can be divided into two main periods: (a) the early arrival of Europeans in Africa in the fifteenth century, a period marked by flourishing of the slave trade, and (b) the period from the nineteenth century onwards, referred to as the pre-independence era, marked by the partitioning of Africa.

The arrival of Europeans

The Portuguese are generally credited with establishing the earliest contacts between Europe and Black Africa. Portuguese sailors reached the Senegal River in 1445 in their search for a sea route to India. The Arabs had already been on the continent for some time, and the arrival of the Europeans now gave an impetus to the trading activities that already existed among Africans and between Africans and Arabs. The need for communication among the Africans, Arabs and Europeans led to an unprecedented need for translation/interpreting (African into African; African into Arabic; African into European).

Once the Portuguese established themselves securely on the continent, they proceeded to teach some Africans how to write (in Roman script). Some of the earliest translations of African literature into European languages are in Portuguese, and there is historical evidence that African literature in Portuguese translation flourished in the nineteenth century.

Early Portuguese missionaries were determined to provide Africans with some elementary education. Some schools were established by Jesuits, who taught Portuguese as well as Latin and showed some interest in studying local African languages. The missionaries soon realized that they could spread the Gospel among Africans more effectively in the local languages and thus proceeded to develop written forms of these mainly oral languages, which made it possible to produce catechisms, grammars and dictionaries in two, three and even four languages. It was these early efforts by the Portuguese, and the educational institutions they set up, which later inspired the literary movement known as the 1880 Group (Hamilton 1975). The 1880 movement launched a bilingual Portuguese/Kimbundu journal, *O Echo de Angola* (The Echo of Angola), which published some of the earliest translation works from European into African languages. The 1880 Group produced one of Africa's first translator-terminologists, Joaquim Dias Cordeiro Da Matta (1857–94), who wrote *Philosophia popular em proverbios angolanos* (Popular Philosophy in Angolan Proverbs), a collection of Kimbundu proverbs and riddles in Portuguese. Da Matta also published a Kimbundu–Portuguese dictionary which is considered a 'monument of scholarship' (Hamilton 1975: 15). These linguistic endeavours of the early Catholic missionaries, which could have laid the groundwork for thriving African literatures, were thwarted by the Portuguese authorities' ethnocentric quest to assimilate the natives.

A few Africans who were enslaved and then educated produced works in Latin that were generally thought to be translations from their respective oral traditions. One such case was that of Juan Latino (1516–94), a Negro slave who entered the service of a Spanish general in 1530 and went on to become a professor of Latin at the University of Granada. The panegyric poetry that Latino produced is thought to have been based on merely 'transposing' the model of the African praise poem and adapting it to a European setting. He wrote mainly in Latin as was required by the scholarly customs of the time. Although a slave, Juan Latino, like a few other Latinists, contributed a great deal to the literature and thought of the Classic tradition; this historical fact was only documented in the middle of the twentieth century by the African scholar and historian Cheikh Anta Diop (1923–86) (see Diop 1974).

The tradition of African writing in Latin began to die out towards the end of the sixteenth century, as slavery had become even more ruthless and Negroes were increasingly being deprived of education. Some of the Nordic nations had now entered the slave trade, which had become immensely profitable. Dutch merchants were particularly active during this period, and the few scholars of African descent whose works can throw some light on the history of translation at that time were educated mainly in Dutch and German. One such scholar is a Ghanaian by the name of Amo; he was born around 1703 and sent to Holland by a local minister of the Dutch Reformed Church. Amo became the protégé of a German nobleman and was sent to university to study under Christian Wolff, a well-known disciple of Leibniz. This African slave thus became a highly erudite scholar and philosopher and is said to have been familiar with Dutch, German, French, Latin, Greek and Hebrew. After teaching at the universities of Wittenberg and Jena, and serving as a court councillor for Frederick II of Prussia, he returned to his native Africa.

Apart from works produced by Africans in non-African languages, Gérard (1986) also mentions an African alphabet and a secret language invented by Sultan Njoya (1865–1933) of the Bamun people of Cameroon. The Sultan had found out about Arabic script through Hausa traders and Fulani emirates of a neighbouring territory. When the Germans arrived in 1899, Njoya noticed that the Europeans used a different kind of writing. Full of admiration for this mode of communication, he instructed some of his councillors to create an iconographic script. By 1918, hundreds of original signs had been successfully trimmed and given phonetic significance. Under Njoya's supervision, a 548-page manuscript on the history and customs of the Bamun was written using this system. However, Sultan Njoya, like most rulers in traditional Africa, craved for a secret language that would be completely esoteric to the people. Having learnt a few German, French and English words from German missionaries of the Basel mission, he created a new language by ascribing entirely arbitrary meanings to the words, mixing them with local Bamun words whose meanings had also been distorted. The manuscript on the history and customs of the Bamun was then translated into this 'private' language.

Translation of the Bible into African languages began around the seventeenth century. Nama (1993: 420) mentions that by 1658, Ge, an African language spoken by the Ewes (Republic of Benin), was included in a major document, *Doctriana Christiana*, a handbook for missionary purposes. However, it was not until the nineteenth century that large-scale translation of the Bible into African languages began in earnest.

It was in the area of religious translation that Christian, Islamic and traditional Africa vied for predominance. Although Islam had existed in Sub-Saharan Africa since around A.D. 800, it had been spread exclusively in Arabic. In order to win the hearts and minds of local African populations, it became necessary, much later on, to translate Islamic works, particularly the Qur'an, into some African languages. For instance, the Qur'an and other religious texts have been translated into Hausa and Yoruba. It is also thought that some Islamic texts were translated into Ajani (Yoruba written in Arabic script) by Yoruba 'malams' (teachers/learned men) and that some of the translations were done long before the adoption of the Roman script. A class of Africans fluent in Arabic and one or several African languages had now emerged, and there was a great deal of translation activity in this area.

The partitioning of Africa

The Berlin Conference on Africa (1884–5) triggered the full-scale colonization of the continent. In the 1890s, Africa was carved up into European spheres of influence, without any regard for natural or ethnic boundaries. The development of African literatures in Portuguese, English and French is a by-product of colonial domination by European nations which ensued after this 'scramble for Africa'.

The history of translation in Africa during this period is closely linked to the policies adopted by the European colonial administrations. While the French and the Portuguese pursued an aggressive policy of assimilation of the natives, the British implemented a policy of indirect rule. These policies determined the ensuing linguistic make-up of the colonies. In the French and Portuguese colonies, vernacular education was virtually non-existent; in the English colonies it was greatly encouraged, albeit for reasons of expedience.

Vernacular literature was mainly encouraged by Protestant missionaries whose main aim was to convert Africans to Christianity. An impressive volume of writing was produced in African languages with the sole aim of spreading the Gospel. Nonetheless, areas that were under British rule developed a bilingual literary tradition at an early stage, creating literature in the vernacular languages and then producing works in English at a later stage.

The French were mainly concerned with creating a sort of 'France outre-mer', which meant that the colonial subjects had to be converted into 'proper' French citizens by mastering the French language and culture. Attempts made by some Africans to produce creative works in French were unsuccessful; these works were not taken seriously because they were written in imperfect French. This attitude, canonized by the Académie Française, made matters worse for people in French Africa who could not 'translate' their oral narratives into French with the same flexibility and ingenuity enjoyed by their Anglophone counterparts. As a result, there were many more creative works in English than in French during this period.

The colonial era also saw a marked decline in the importance of the professional 'linguist' (or griot). Once revered and feared for his political clout in the royal courts, the pioneer of African translators and interpreters was reduced to a mere guide to his colonial masters. He was occasionally called upon to join a colonial expedition to 'translate', mediate and advise the colonialists. He was expected to have a thorough knowledge of the territory and to have the physical endurance to sustain long, tedious and often dangerous journeys. Though he still enjoyed some respect because of his association with the European colonialists and his (rudimentary) knowledge of a European language, the professional linguist was often despised by the local population and considered a 'traitor' for showing colonialists around and helping them gain access to the tribal lore and secrets of the people. Indeed, the professional linguist had become nothing more than the servant of the European colonialist, and he was generally disposed of as soon as his task was completed, to be called back only if and when he was needed.

During the late nineteenth and early twentieth centuries, a wave of 'liberal Romanticism' and a fascination with all forms of symbolism swept across Europe, resulting in increased interest in the oral traditions of non-Western cultures (Horton and Finnegan 1973). Africa, like most pre-industrialized societies, received wave after wave of Western scholars interested in studying its folklore. However, these scholars often relied on inadequate second-hand sources as they collected pieces of African oral tradition. With no access to today's recording technology, they had to rely on written records of the oral literature they needed to collect. These records were less than adequate as they were unreliable translations carried out by school children and other Africans working for Europeans, with hardly any skill in the artistry of the oral narrative. Quite often, the translations and transcriptions were subjected to a great deal of adaptation to suit the exotic tastes of Western audiences. It was not until the latter years of the colonial era that African oral narrative was made available to the public by a group of African writers who had the advantage of being bilingual and bicultural.

The postcolonial era

The period just before and after independence (the 1950s and 60s) witnessed the emergence of a new stage in the history of translation in Africa. Translation activity during this period can be subdivided into three main categories: religious translation, literary translation and public service translation.

Religious translation, which began in the colonial era, continued well into the postcolonial period. European missionaries continued to learn local languages for purposes of evangelization, and especially for the translation of the Bible and other religious texts. Some of the pioneers of Bible translation in Africa include the Nigerian Bishop Samuel Ajanji Crowther who is highly reputed for translating the Bible into Igbo and Yoruba – S. W. Koealle and J. F.

Schon. Today, the Bible has been translated into about 100 African languages. Eugene Nida has personally been involved with Bible translation projects in Africa, working with the American Bible Society, in Edea, Cameroon (Nama 1993: 420) among other areas. Although the majority of Bible translations produced in Africa are into vernacular languages, it is also worth noting that in many parts of West Africa the Gospel has been translated into pidgin English, a hybrid lingua franca resulting from contact between African languages and English.

Literary translation is not a lucrative business in Africa. Occasionally, some publishing houses which specialize in African literature written in European languages may need the services of a translator, but this happens rather infrequently and, when it does, the jobs often go to European rather than African translators. However, there is another type of literary translation between African and European languages which has flourished in Africa.

The late 1950s and early 1960s saw the emergence of a new class of African writers with a good command of both the European language of writing and the language of African oral narrative. African oral texts collected during the colonial era often posed a major paradox for translation, as they were produced via the mediation of colonial scribes in the language of European domination. The efforts of the colonialists to transcribe and translate African oral literature at best produced 'colonized' versions of that literature. Anxious to right the wrongs of the past and set the records straight, a new generation of African writers set out to 'translate' pieces of African oral literature into European languages. Such writers from Francophone Africa include Birago Diop, the Senegalese poet famous for his collection of short stories entitled *Nouveaux Contes d'Amadou Koumba* (The New Tales of Amadou Koumba, 1961), and Bernard Dadié, the Ivoirian known for his *Légendes Africaines* (African Legends, 1973). A similar phenomenon took place in Anglophone Africa. In West Africa, Amos Tutuola's *The Palm-Wine Drinkard and his Dead Palm-Wine Tapster in the Dead's Town* (1952) was among the first such African works of fiction to appear; *drinkard* is a modified form of *drunkard*, meant to mimic the language of a semi-literate drunkard. All these works by Francophone and Anglophone writers are essentially liberal translations of African oral texts. Tutuola, for example, literally translated some Yoruba mythology into English. In an attempt to capture Yoruba syntax in English (and given that he was a public service clerk with just an elementary school education), he produced curious syntactic patterns that endeared him to European readers. Apart from such 'translations' of African oral literature, the works of well-known African writers such as Achebe, Soyinka, Okara and Senghor have also been translated into several European languages.

The situation in East Africa is highly influenced by what has been described as East Africa's triple heritage – African, Islamic and European. While there have been many translations from the ethno-African heritage into European languages, there has been relatively less European language literature translated into African languages, and hardly any translation between African languages. Ethno-African literature reflects the ethnic divisions in East Africa, where the literatures of ethnic groups such as the Kikuyu, Baganda, Chagga, Acholi and Luo have remained separate. The Ugandan Okot p'Bitek is well known for his translation of the poem 'Song of Lawino' into English, which he had originally written in his native Acholi. The poem was subsequently translated into French, Spanish and Portuguese; p'Bitek's work had much more impact through the translation than through the original version in Acholi. P'Bitek is also a very knowledgeable linguist-terminologist. He makes his translations accessible to non-Acholi readers by including an analytical glossary of Acholi words and expressions that do not have English equivalents.

The famous Kenyan author Ngugi Wa Thiong'o, who wrote in English for several years, became frustrated with the inability of the English language to express the essence of his native culture and switched to writing in his native Kikuyu and then translating some of his works, such as his novel *Devil on the Cross*, into English.

There has also been some translation activity on the Afro-Islamic front. Swahili is essentially the product of contact between Islam and the Bantu civilization. A large volume of ethno-African literature has been translated into Swahili. The Afro-Islamic heritage in Swahili has been made available in English by scholars such as Lyndon Harries, James de Vere Allen, Ibrahim Shariff, Jan Knappert and others (Gérard 1986: 1049). There have also been translations from English into Swahili. Famous among these are the translations by Julius Nyerere (the founder-president of Tanzania) of Shakespeare's *Julius Caesar* and *The Merchant of Venice*. These translations won critical acclaim since Swahili has become a home-bred lingua franca of East Africa, spoken by over 100 million people.

The significance of Swahili as a lingua franca of such a vast region of Africa has led Mhina (1970) to argue in favour of producing works in Swahili and translating internationally recognized works into Swahili. Unlike the rest of Africa south of the Sahara, where there is no widely used home-grown international language, East Africa has the unique advantage of having Swahili as a viable international language outclassing many foreign languages.

Since independence, public service translation has continued to flourish as the governments of various African states attempt to cope with Western-style bureaucracies left behind as a colonial legacy. When most African countries became independent in the 1960s, they were left with a linguistic situation that was bound to enhance the role of translators and interpreters. Several of these newly-independent African countries already had many indigenous African languages spoken within their borders, to which was added the colonial language(s) which, though foreign, had become the official language(s) of these countries. Ironically, instead of a flourishing translation activity between African languages, as one might have expected in a postcolonial situation, translation evolved mainly in two directions: African into European languages and vice versa, and European to European languages. Faced with the need to cope with world affairs and the international economic market, it became increasingly necessary for African countries to communicate not only with other African nations, but also with other countries of the world, particularly their former colonial masters. In this context, European-to-European language translation thrived in Africa in the field of foreign affairs, as well as in administrative, economic and cultural areas.

The present day

Since independence, many economic and international organizations have been formed to enhance cooperation among African states, thus strengthening the need for European language translators. When the Organization of African Unity (OAU) was founded in 1962, English, French, Portuguese, Spanish and – on a smaller scale – Arabic were declared the official working languages. The decision to use European rather than African languages as a medium of communication among member states has been strongly criticized by many scholars and is said to have been indicative of the fate that awaited Africa.

During the early years of independence, the Western-style governments in various African countries were left with the legacy of colonial languages but without any personnel or infrastructure to carry out the immense translation work that the new linguistic situation entailed. In many instances, government civil servants with barely an elementary education and a smattering of knowledge in two European languages were called upon to provide translations. But as time went by, it became increasingly obvious that, given the amount of work to be done and the need for quality translations, governments had to take an interest in the training of professional translators. For almost two decades after independence many African governments sponsored some of their brightest graduates to study in translation schools in Europe and North America.

Cameroon provides a good example of how translator training has evolved since independence. Having adopted English and French as official languages, Cameroon is the only African country with official bilingualism in European languages. Hence, it is often cited as the centre for European-to-European language translation in Africa; it is also often compared to Canada, where English and French are similarly official languages. Yet, for a very long time, Cameroon's translators were trained in Europe or North America. It was not until the 1980s, that the Advanced School of Translators and Interpreters was established in Buea, Cameroon.

Translator training is therefore a relatively recent phenomenon in most African countries, and for this reason, trained and competent translators are in short supply. Simpson (1985: 107) mentions a study commissioned by UNCTAD 'on the need for a sub-regional translation, interpretation and staff language-training support service and to assess the feasibility of setting up such a service if it turned out to be needed'. Among the recommendations made is the creation of a sub-regional Translation and Interpretation School.

Political changes in South Africa since the 1990s brought about the need for a massive overhaul of translation training programmes. The ANC's Constitution for a post-apartheid South Africa recognizes eleven official languages, most of which are African languages. Unlike past translation programmes which dealt mainly in English and Afrikaans, current translation programmes must include African languages. It has been recommended that translation training programmes should aim at promoting multilingualism and eliminating the kind of linguistic prejudices and social inequality that have existed in South Africa for so long. In order to achieve this, translators should be trained not only at the postgraduate level, but also at the undergraduate and pre-tertiary levels. Adding a critical language awareness component to the training programme, it is thought, might help fight linguistic prejudice and instil respect for the language rights of all citizens in a post-apartheid democratic society. It is also believed that the enshrining of language rights in the new Constitution will lead to a major expansion and professionalization of language services. Community interpreting and translation are also being actively supported, especially at the level of health care and social services provision, so as to avoid alienating non-English and non-Afrikaans speakers. Terminology research plays an important role, particularly in programmes designed to meet the needs of African language translators (Kruger 1994).

The status of the translator/interpreter has undergone a considerable transformation since the time of the griot. Unlike the griot who was revered and even feared in pre-colonial Africa, today's translator is often perceived as a disenchanted civil servant who toils away without receiving any recognition in his or her country's public service. The only language specialists who seem satisfied with their lot are conference interpreters, who enjoy the glamour of criss-crossing the continent to attend international conferences. Translators, irrespective of country, complain about the low status attributed to their profession.

Not surprisingly, many African translators would prefer to work for international organizations, where they are often better paid and sometimes rise to important administrative functions. There are many African translators working in the linguistic services of various agencies of international organizations such as WHO, UNICEF, UNESCO and IMF. Some leave their countries because they are not needed. In Senegal, for instance, there are more professionally trained translators and interpreters than the needs of the country would justify. As a consequence, Senegalese translators often seek work in neighbouring West African countries and in international organizations in Africa and elsewhere.

A certain amount of freelance translation is undertaken in some African countries. Freelance translators often serve the needs of the African branches of multinational companies and of local businesses in the private sector. The governments rarely use freelance agencies as they rely heavily on civil servants as translators. Freelance translation can be quite lucrative, but it is still largely unregulated, and it tends to be a free-for-all type of venture which attracts a great number of unemployed university graduates from fields completely unrelated to translation.

In Sub-Saharan Africa, we are thus faced with a situation where there is a relatively high calibre of translation practice, where some countries have more translators than they need, and where, with a few exceptions, most countries still train their translators abroad.

In October 1982, FIT, in collaboration with UNESCO, organized a consultative meeting of African specialists in Lomé, Togo, with the aim of exploring professional problems in Africa. This meeting took place six years after that of the African Ministers of Education held in Nairobi in 1976, where some recommendations were made regarding the organization of the translation profession, translator training and questions of terminology in Africa (a full list of the recommendations can be found in Simpson 1985: 109–10). These meetings had the positive effect of catapulting the translation profession to a higher sphere by getting various African governments and professional translators involved in establishing a genuine professional status for translation. It was recommended, among other things, 'that encouragement should be given to the creation of associations of translators which should combine to form regional structures so as to intensify their action' and that 'governments grant translators the legal status and protection provided for in the … Nairobi recommendation'.

Further reading
Finnegan 1970; Mhina 1970; Diop 1974; Hamilton 1975; Mveng 1980; Ihenacho 1985; Simpson 1985; Gérard 1986; Bgoya 1987; Ihenacho 1988; Okpewho 1992; Nama 1993.

PAUL BANDIA

American tradition

Translation played an essential role in the origins and development of the United States, and it continues to do so, given the linguistic and cultural diversity of the country's more than 255 million inhabitants. English is the dominant language, but it is only one of the many languages that have been spoken in North America. The speech of the native Indian tribes was first encountered during the sixteenth century by Spanish and French explorers in present-day Florida and Louisiana. English expeditions to Virginia and Massachusetts began in earnest during the early seventeenth century, requiring a familiarity with Indian languages that helped to increase the colonists' cultural and economic autonomy from England. The nationalist fervour released by the Revolution brought a new self-awareness that fostered the translation of foreign-language literatures to develop American culture. A distinctly American version of English was recognizable by the 1850s, although characterized by various regional modulations as the country expanded its southern and western borders (Simpson 1983: 3). The great waves of European immigration that started in the mid-nineteenth century created an urgent need for English-language translating and interpreting which has remained constant ever since, with the immigrant pool widening to include numerous ethnic groups and nationalities from Latin America, Asia, the Middle East and the Caribbean. Today, more than 31 million inhabitants speak a language other than English at home, ensuring that translation is a fact of daily life for many Americans.

Throughout American history translation has been double-edged in its social functions and effects, serving English-language interests and agendas through exploitative encounters with foreign languages and cultures. On the one hand, translation enabled the United States to grow in size and power: it made possible the colonization, dispossession, and assimilation of peoples whose native language was not English, and it continues to support the political and economic hegemony that the country has enjoyed since World War II. On the other hand, translation contributed to the formation of a definably American identity: it was instrumental in constructing a national literary and political tradition, while simultaneously working to diversify American culture and to precipitate cultural innovation and social change.

Colonization, expansion, immigration (1607–1920)

Among the first American translators were Indians who acted as interpreters and assistants to the English colonists struggling to establish a viable existence in the North American wilderness. William Bradford, one of the first governors of the Massachusetts Bay Colony, described the Puritan settlers' meeting with Samoset, an Algonquian from Maine 'where some English ships came to fish … amongst whom he had got his language' (Bradford 1952: 79). Although Samoset spoke 'broken English', Bradford observed that 'he became profitable to them in acquainting them with many things concerning the state of the country' (ibid.). Bradford felt that Squanto, another Indian interpreter, 'could speak better English than himself' because he had been kidnapped by an English captain and 'entertained by a merchant in London' (ibid.: 80–81). To the pilgrims who landed at Plymouth in 1620, Squanto was essential for survival: he taught them how to grow corn and where to fish, and he negotiated a peace treaty between the colonists and the

Wampanoag Indians whereby they agreed to defend each other from warring tribes.

Although these relations benefited both colonists and Indians, they were hardly symmetrical, and translation quickly became a practice by which the English sought to alter an Indian culture they judged to be inferior because it was pagan. The royal charter issued to the Massachusetts Bay Company in 1629 asserted that 'the principall ende of this plantation [was] to wynn and incite the natives of [the] country to the knowledg and obedience of the onlie true God and Savoir of mankinde, and the Christian fayth' (Morgan 1964: 320). As a result, the first American translators included Puritan ministers who learned Indian languages to convert the natives. With the help of an Indian informant, 'a pregnant witted young man, who had been a Servant in an English house', the minister John Eliot (1604–90) wrote *A Catechism in the Indian Language* (1653) and then translated the Bible and several homiletic tracts into Algonquian (Eliot 1666: 66).

Conversion went hand in hand with conquest, so that translation also facilitated the expropriation of Indian lands. Here translators and interpreters mediated between significant cultural differences that were inscribed in the translating languages. Most of the Algonquian place names, for instance, 'related not to possession but to use', while the English colonists 'most frequently created arbitrary place names which either recalled localities in their homeland or gave a place the name of its owner' (Cronon 1983: 65, 66). In the translating that enabled colonists to purchase land from the Indians, the English concept of private property displaced the Indian understanding of communal ownership (Cheyfitz 1991). The colonists recognized such differences from the start. Yet driven by an imperialist impulse, they rendered Indian language and culture into characteristically English terms – legal, commercial, political. This is even apparent in *A Key to the Language of America* (1643), a dictionary in the Narragansett language written by the dissident Puritan Roger Williams (1603–83). Williams questioned the property rights granted by the royal charter of the Massachusetts Bay Colony and criticized the 'sinfull opinion amongst many that Christians have right to *Heathens* Lands' (Williams 1973: 167). Nonetheless, his book aimed to translate

Narragansett words and phrases into English equivalents so as to assist the colonist 'whatever [the] occasion bee either of Travell, Discourse, Trading &c.' (ibid.: 90).

During the eighteenth century, translation continued to be a crucial cultural practice in submitting the Indians to the colonists' interests. Conrad Weiser (1696–1760), a German immigrant's son who lived with the Mohawks for fifteen years, served as the official interpreter of Pennsylvania, arranging conferences in which Indian lands were deeded to the provincial government and Indian trade was extended to the Mississippi River. Simon Girty (1741–1818), an Irish immigrant's son who was kidnapped as a boy and adopted by the Senecas, learned a variety of Indian languages which he used in the service of the British during the Revolutionary War period. For over forty years, Girty interpreted for British military commanders and enlisted Indian tribes in raids on settlements in Pennsylvania, Ohio, Kentucky and Detroit, gaining a reputation as a 'renegade' and a 'white savage' (Thrapp 1988: II, 560–1). Girty was paid handsomely for his interpreting services, undoubtedly because they performed a military function: in 1778 he was hired at $2 (16 shillings) per day.

By the beginning of the nineteenth century, many Indians on the eastern coast of North America had been taught English and converted to Christianity. The newly instituted American republic, however, was pursuing a policy of expansion. The increasing profitability of the Indian trade, combined with the political goal of preventing further French and Spanish colonialism on the continent, motivated a redrawing of the western frontier, and this created a demand for interpreters to deal with unfamiliar Indian languages. In 1803, Thomas Jefferson, second president of the United States, commissioned Meriwether Lewis and William Clark to explore the Missouri River as far as the Pacific Ocean in an effort to locate 'the most direct and practicable water communication … for the purposes of commerce' (Bergon 1989: xxiv). Lewis and Clark relied heavily on interpreters both to navigate the wilderness and to deliver speeches that stressed American sovereignty, inter-tribal peace, and trade (Ronda 1984: 83). These interpreters included foreign traders and Indians who lived in the western territories. Lewis and

Clark's journals frequently mention Touissaint Charbonneau (c.1759–c.1843), a Canadian employed by the North West Company, and his wife Sacajawea (c.1780/1812–1884), a captured Shosone girl whom he had won through gambling. Charbonneau later became an interpreter for the American Bureau of Indian Affairs in the Upper Missouri area.

This government agency carried out American Indian policy, which assisted settlers and speculators seeking Indian lands by relocating eastern tribes on reservations west of the Mississippi. Agents were also interpreters who persuaded Indians, sometimes by fraud or coercion, to enter into treaties that ceded land to the United States (Satz 1974). By 1850, American Indian policy had achieved remarkable success partly because of the agents' linguistic proficiency. Lawrence Taliaferro (1794–1871), an agent at Saint Peter's in Minnesota, spoke over a dozen Indian languages (ibid.:188).

The displacement and dispossession of the Indians inevitably caused conflicts, both among the different tribes and with the United States. Yet the agents' interpreting skills enabled them to act as mediators and occasionally as advocates of the Indians. Taliaferro was called to intervene in a long-standing feud between the Sioux and the Chippewa, and his support of the Indians incurred the opposition of traders, particularly those associated with the American Fur Company, who tried to get him dismissed from the agency. Sarah Winnemucca (1844–91), a Paiute who learned English while living with an American military officer's family, aided in negotiations between hostile tribes and later became an interpreter at the Malheur reservation in Oregon, earning $40 per month plus lodging (Canfield 1983: 96). Her most significant interpreting, however, may have occurred in the lectures she delivered during the 1880s in eastern cities, where she reported the injustices that the government was inflicting on her people and raised funds to start an Indian school in Nevada.

While Indian tribes were gradually being acculturated and sequestered on reservations, increasingly large numbers of Europeans were entering the United States, making English-language translating and interpreting necessary for their assimilation into American society. Between 1851 and 1920, the peak period of immigration, the total was well over 31 million foreign nationals, mostly from Germany, Ireland, Italy, Poland, Russia, the Scandinavian countries and the United Kingdom. Approximately 5,000 immigrants per day passed through Ellis Island in New York harbour, where notices were printed in nine different languages. To process the masses of people, the American government employed a staff of interpreters who were certified by civil service examinations and commanded an average of six languages (Heaps 1967: 68). In 1907, when over 11,000 people were processed in one day, the interpreters included Fiorella La Guardia (1882–1947), an Italian immigrant's son who had worked in the consular service in Europe and was subsequently elected mayor of New York. For interpreting on Ellis Island, La Guardia was paid $1,200 per year. In so far as the immigrants were mainly agricultural and industrial workers, the diverse kinds of translation they required and performed contributed to the enormous economic growth that the United States witnessed during the twentieth century.

Building a national culture (1640–1954)

Translation has been indispensable to the development of a uniquely American culture, even if the linguistic and ethnic diversity of the country guaranteed that it would consist of various cultural constituencies, each with their own dialects and discourses, values and beliefs.

The first English-language book written and printed in North America was in fact a translation, *The Whole Booke of Psalmes Faithfully Translated into English Metre* (1640), commonly known as *The Bay Psalm Book*. A collaborative work produced by a group of Puritan ministers, this hymnal offered a very literal rendering of the Hebrew text, and since it was intended for singing, the translation was cast in ballad metre. In a preface, translator John Cotton (1584–1652) explained that the literal strategy conformed to a Puritan aesthetic: 'If therefore the verses are not always so smoothe and elegant as some may desire or expect, let them consider that God's Altar needs not our polishings' (Haraszti 1956: A4v). The religious values of the translation carried political implications. *The Bay Psalm Book* expressed the Puritans' dissent from the

liturgy of the Anglican Church and the literature of the royal court. The avowedly 'plain' language rejected the 'poetical license' that characterized Thomas Sternhold and John Hopkins's verse translation, which had been bound with the Book of Common Prayer since 1562 (ibid.). And the ballad meter linked the new versions to the popular song tradition in opposition to the metrical refinements of aristocratic poetry, including the translations of the Psalms made by such courtiers as Sir Philip Sidney and Thomas Carew.

As translation increased the cultural autonomy of the American colonies from England, it also contributed to the decisive political break by importing revolutionary political ideas from abroad. In this case, the translating took diverse forms. The works of French Enlightenment thinkers such as Voltaire and Rousseau were available in eighteenth-century America, although in French editions and in English-language versions first published in London and Edinburgh (May 1976: 41). Learned politicians such as Benjamin Franklin and Thomas Jefferson were able to read these works in French, incorporating the ideas they found there in documents like the *Declaration of Independence* (1775–6). And during the political crisis that precipitated the Revolutionary War, pamphleteers used their own and others' translations to disseminate Enlightenment thinking and to sway public sentiment against England. In *The Rights of the British Colonies Asserted and Proved* (1764), James Otis offered a democratic critique of the British monarchy that quoted his own renderings from Rousseau's *Social Contract* (Bailyn 1965: II, 436).

While the United States was emerging as an international political power, translation was enlisted in nationalist projects to develop an American culture that could vie with Europe. Perhaps the most ambitious of these projects was *Specimens of Foreign Standard Literature*, a 14-volume anthology of translations edited by George Ripley (1802–80). The first two volumes consisted of Ripley's own translations of several French philosophers, Benjamin Constant, Theodore Jouffroy, and Victor Cousin. In subsequent volumes, he relied on the translating skills of the New England Transcendentalists, intellectuals such as Margaret Fuller (1810–50) and John Sullivan Dwight (1813–93) who had been inspired by French and German literature and whose translations in turn inspired others, notably the quintessential American philosopher Ralph Waldo Emerson.

Ripley felt that translation could contribute to the creation of a national culture that respected democratic principles. 'The best productions of foreign genius and study', he argued, 'should not be confined to the few who have access to the original languages, but should be diffused among enlightened readers of every class and condition' (Ripley 1838: xi). Yet the 'standard' that guided his selection of foreign texts conformed to the cultural values of the elite intellectual minority who composed his primary readership as well as his stable of translators. There was indeed a mass audience for translations during the nineteenth century, but its tastes favoured melodrama and romance, not poetry and philosophy. William Dunlap (1766–1839), a New York playwright and theatre manager whose own works failed to draw at the box office, successfully staged numerous translations from the sentimental drama of the German August von Kotzebue. Henry William Herbert (1807–58), an English immigrant who published fiction, history and sports writing, reached many more readers by translating sensationalistic French novels, including six by Eugène Sue. During the 1840s Herbert was earning $3,000 per year.

Such translation patterns point not only to the heterogeneity that lay beneath any notions of a national American culture, but also to the dependence of American cultural developments on encounters with foreign literatures. Even when respected American poets translated the canonical works of Western literature, their strategies reflected translation theories that first emerged in foreign cultural traditions. William Cullen Bryant (1794–1878), whose early poetry gained him a national reputation, wrote a version of the *Iliad* (1876) that followed the prescriptions for translating Homer presented by the British critic Matthew Arnold some ten years earlier. Bryant wanted to render precisely those qualities of Homeric verse that Arnold defined as the prevailing scholarly reading of the Greek text: 'simplicity', 'fluent narrative', 'dignity' (Bryant 1876: iv–vi). The result was a strongly domesticating translation that adhered to current English usage, avoided archaic syntax and diction, and employed the Latin names

for the Greek gods because, Bryant observed, they 'have been naturalized in our language for centuries' (ibid.: vii). The foreign origins of Bryant's strategy can be detected even in his choice of meter: like the British poet William Cowper, he used blank verse, 'the vehicle of some of the noblest poetry in our language', although unlike Cowper he had in mind Shakespeare rather than Milton (ibid.: vii, v).

Bayard Taylor (1825–78), a journalist and travel writer whose poetry earned his contemporaries' praise but later fell into neglect, produced a version of Goethe's *Faust* (1871) influenced by the German translation tradition. Following Goethe's view that in the 'highest' translating 'the translator … attaches himself closely to his original' (Lefevere 1992b: 76), Taylor wrote 'a nearly literal version in the original metres' (Taylor 1871: xi). And just as Goethe felt that 'the taste of the multitude must first be shaped to accept' literal translations, Taylor saw himself issuing a challenge to American readers, whose 'intellectual tendencies', he argued, 'have always been somewhat conservative', making them 'suspicious of new metres and unaccustomed forms of expression' (Lefevere 1992b: 77; Taylor 1871: x). Taylor's German-inspired translation strategy undoubtedly worked to bring about a lasting change in American literary taste, at least as far as translations of Goethe were concerned: his version continued to be reprinted as late as 1950, when the commercial press Random House published it in the noted series of classic works called 'The Modern Library'.

With the advent of the modernist movement, the American translation tradition entered a period of striking innovation that centred on the translation of poetry. The most important figure in this development was Ezra Pound (1885–1972). Pound saw translation as a means of cultivating modernist poetic values, provided that the translator chose certain foreign poetries capable of supporting those values; his greatest successes occurred with the Anglo-Saxon lament *The Seafarer* (1912), the thirteenth-century Italian poet Guido Cavalcanti (1912, 1932), the Chinese poet Li Po (1915), and the Provençal troubadour Arnaut Daniel (1920). Pound experimented with a range of dialects and discourses, assimilating the foreign texts to pre-existing cultural forms: Anglo-Saxon patterns of accent and alliteration, pre-

Elizabethan English, Pre-Raphaelite medievalism, modernist precision, American colloquialism. This strategy clearly involved a process of domestication, but ultimately the effect was foreignizing: the resulting translation signified the cultural and historical difference of the foreign text because the English-language forms Pound used were so heterogeneous, culled from different moments in British and American culture.

After Pound, American translators began to regard their translations as autonomous literary works, although few were willing to take up his most daring experiments with translation strategies. By the middle of the twentieth century, American translation of both poetry and prose was for the most part modern, not Modernist. It eschewed Pound's experimentalism for a linguistic homogeneity that produced an illusory effect of transparency, whereby the translation seems to be not a translation, but the foreign original (Venuti 1995a). The transparency, however, actually conceals a thoroughgoing domestication, in which the foreign text is inscribed with cultural values that prevail in contemporary America. Thus Dudley Fitts (1903–68), who established a reputation as a leading translator of ancient Greek poetry and drama, admitted that his modern versions of Greek poems 'risked a spurious atmosphere of monotheism by writing "God" for "Zeus"' (Fitts 1956: xviii).

American global hegemony since World War II

Translating and interpreting have served American political and economic interests over the past several decades, enabling the United States to achieve and maintain its pre-eminence in world affairs. The Foreign Service in the State Department has long contained a language section to review translations of diplomatic documents and to provide for interpreting at international conferences. By the mid-1980s, this Language Services Division was providing an annual total of $8 million in translating and interpreting for various government agencies (Obst and Cline 1990: 12). In the State Department, translation has also performed explicitly ideological functions. Throughout the Cold War, the United States Information Agency operated the Voice of America radio broadcasts in thirty-five languages while issuing propagandistic materials in print and electronic media (Roland 1982: 130).

American businesses have increasingly turned to translation as a way of developing overseas markets, relying on firms that specialize in translating contracts, instruction manuals and technical information. These firms have in turn grown and multiplied, creating a translation industry that was valued at $10 billion in the early 1990s (Levy 1991: F5). For example, All-Language Services, a privately owned company founded in 1946 with five translators, employed ninety working in fifty-nine languages by the end of the 1990s. Since the 1980s, the translation division of Berlitz International, a subsidiary of the publisher Macmillan, has acquired six translation companies in the United States and Europe, yielding annual revenues of $30 million.

The American publishing industry has been relatively less interested in investing in translation. Although book production has increased fourfold since the 1940s, the proportion of translations has generally remained between 2 and 4 per cent of the annual total, in contrast to significantly higher percentages in other countries (see Venuti 1995a: 12–13). American publishers sell translation rights for more and more English-language books, including the global best-sellers, but spend disproportionately less on the rights to publish English-language translations of foreign books. As a result, the United States has exercised a hegemony over foreign countries that is not simply political and economic, as the particular case may be, but cultural as well. Publishers have profited from successfully imposing American cultural values on a vast foreign readership, while creating a domestic culture that is aggressively monolingual and receptive to the foreign only when it meets American expectations.

These expectations have decisively influenced the choice of foreign texts for translation. American publishers capitalized on reader curiosity about foreign nations that were allies or antagonists, as well as reader optimism that cultural exchange would facilitate better international understanding and more peaceful political relations. Since World War II, the languages most frequently translated into English have been French, German, Russian, Italian and Spanish. With Russian literature, publishers appealed to American anti-Communist sentiment by focusing on works that criticized Marxism or the Soviet government, novels like Boris Pasternak's *Doctor Zhivago* (1958) and Alexander Solzhenitsyn's *One Day in the Life of Ivan Denisovich* (1962), both of which became best-sellers in translation. In contrast, 'translations of Soviet (that is, nondissident) prose of the 1950s–1970s are relatively few and far between' (May 1994: 47).

Similar patterns of admission and exclusion have occurred with less frequently translated literatures. In the decades after World War II, American publishers emphasized a few modern Japanese novelists, mainly Junichiro Tanizaki, Yasunari Kawabata and Yukio Mishima. Consequently, they created a well-defined stereotype of Japanese culture (elusive, inconclusive, melancholic) which expressed a nostalgia for a less belligerent and more traditional Japan. The novels selected for translation 'provided exactly the right image of Japan at a time when that country was being transformed, almost overnight in historical terms, from a mortal enemy during the Pacific War to an indispensable ally during the Cold War era' (Fowler 1992: 6). A canon of Japanese fiction was established in English, one that was not simply unrepresentative, excluding comic and proletarian novels among other kinds of writing, but also enormously influential, determining readers' tastes for roughly forty years.

Apart from such political motivations, American publishers have generally issued translations for both literary and commercial reasons, and these books have had a diverse impact on American culture. Most of these books have had little or no impact on American culture, although in one instance the literary repercussions were significant. During the 1960s and 1970s, the so-called boom in Latin American literature was fostered by novelists and critics who valued its experimentalism over the realistic narratives that have always dominated American fiction (Payne 1993). Publishers brought out many translations from the work of such authors as the Argentine Julio Cortázar and the Columbian Gabriel García Márquez, forming a new canon of foreign literature in English as well as a more sophisticated American readership. This trend continued partly because the translations were profitable. García Márquez's novel *One Hundred Years of Solitude* was a notable success in Gregory Rabassa's eminently readable version: when the first paperback edition appeared in 1970, it stayed on *The New York Times* Bestseller List for several weeks (Castro-Klarén and Campos 1983: 326–7). At the same time, the influx of Latin American writing was altering the canon of contemporary American literature, encouraging writers like John Barth to develop various narrative experiments.

American publishers have tended to view translations as risky ventures, likely to sustain a loss. This situation has been most unfavourable to freelance translators. They have typically received work-for-hire contracts that require them to surrender any right in the translation for a flat fee with no royalty or share of the income from subsidiary rights sales (Keeley 1990). In 1965 a translator with a work-for-hire arrangement typically received $15 per thousand English words or roughly $1,200 for a 300-page book; in 1990, the rate varied between $40 and $90 or between $3,000 and $6,000 for a book-length project (Venuti 1995a: 10–11). Given the low volume of translations published in the United States, freelance translators have been forced to undertake several projects a year in order to earn their livelihood. Most supplement their translating with such other work as editing, writing and teaching.

Among the most notable translators of this period are Ralph Manheim (1907–92), whose translations from German and French included the writing of Freud, Brecht, Hitler, Céline, Grass and Handke; Helen R. Lane (1922–2004), whose translations from French, Spanish and Portuguese introduced American readers to a wide range of European and Latin American literature; and Richard Howard (1929–), who has translated many important French poets, novelists, philosophers, and literary critics, including Baudelaire, Proust, Barthes and Robbe-Grillet. These translators have not only been prolific, but accomplished and award-winning, so that their distinguished reputations have called attention to translation and helped to improve the conditions under which translators generally work.

Nonetheless, these conditions continue to be shaped most forcefully by economic developments. Since the 1980s, the American publishing industry has been transformed by the emergence of multinational conglomerates that pursue larger returns on investments, with the result that potential best-sellers have been favoured over difficult-to-market books such as translations (Whiteside 1981; Feldman 1986). Publishers are most attracted to foreign texts that were blockbusters abroad, hoping to repeat the same performance with American readers; or else they choose to invest in translations that are involved in 'tie-ins', film or theatre adaptations that ensure wider reader recognition and greater sales. This publishing strategy has worked quite well with classic foreign novels turned into Broadway musicals. After British composer Andrew Lloyd Webber successfully adapted *The Phantom of the Opera* to the musical theatre, American publishers scrambled to bring out translations of the Gaston Leroux novel. When the show opened in New York during the 1988 season, as many as four English versions were available in cheap paperback editions.

Economic considerations inevitably affect translation strategies, which have been dominated by fluent domestication since the 1940s. The dominance of fluent strategies and the transparency they make possible have undoubtedly limited the recognition of translation as a significant cultural practice. They have also led to the marginalization of experimental translations that seek to broaden the translator's discursive repertoire beyond the most familiar forms of English. The more radical the experiment, the greater the condemnation and neglect suffered by the translation (Venuti 1995a).

The 1990s brought signs that the dominance of fluency is weakening, at least in the case of certain languages and literatures whose peculiarities resist it. In their inventive translations of Dostoyevsky's novels, Richard Pevear and Larissa Volokhonsky have altered the general reader's conception of the Russian texts by refusing to assimilate them to the standard dialect of English or to English-language narrative styles. The new translations restore Dostoyevsky's 'oddities' and thereby evoke the polyphony of voices that characterize the Russian texts, as scholars have long recognized (Pevear and Volokhonsky 1990: xv; May 1994: 52–4).

The questioning of fluent translation may well betoken a greater respect for cultural difference, a new American openness towards foreign languages and literatures that will give translation more authority and improve the status of the translator. But American culture continues to exhibit a strong current of what can only be called xenophobia, a fear that multilingualism and the translating that a multilingual population must daily perform will undermine national unity. The 1980s saw the rise of movements that sought to repress translation by successfully making English the official language in states with substantial populations of recent immigrants: Arizona, California, Florida (Muller 1993: 235–7). All the same, translation remains a vital presence in contemporary America, even if it is underinvested, misunderstood and suspected. Perhaps the most visible reminder of its importance is the automated tellers at major banks in every metropolis. At Citibank in New York, the banking programmes render transactions in five languages: Spanish, Greek, Chinese, Korean, and English.

The marginality of translation in American culture is evident in the relative dearth of research, at least until the late 1990s. Commentary from the 1950s to the 1970s was generally belletristic, provocative reflections prompted by a translator's work with specific foreign texts and literatures. It was casual, occasional, likely to appear in a preface to a literary translation, in an interview, or in an essay for a poetry magazine. Despite this unsystematic presentation, the thinking about translation was often informed by theoretical assumptions that prevailed concurrently in academic literary scholarship and in translation workshops, particularly assumptions about literature that animated the New Criticism (Gentzler 1993). There were also emergent strands of other translation theories based in structural linguistics, cultural anthropology and analytic philosophy. Two pioneering anthologies that survey the range of translation commentary during this period are Brower (1959) and Arrowsmith and Shattuck (1961).

Much of this commentary shared the assumption that translation involves the communication of a fixed meaning located in the foreign-language text. As a result, notions of equivalence guided the research. Throughout the 1980s, this view was increasingly revised as American translation studies continued to draw on conceptual developments in several disciplines, including a variety of cultural and political discourses that are mostly European in origin: psychoanalysis, phenomenology, Frankfurt School Marxism, French feminism, post-structuralism. In these new lines of research, translation was considered less as communication between languages and cultures than as interpretation that provisionally fixes a meaning in the foreign-language text in accordance with an interpretive theory, cultural agenda and political standpoint in the domestic situation. Less attention was given to notions of equivalence than to the inevitable linguistic and cultural differences negotiated by the translator. The change in the direction of research can be glimpsed in *Translation Perspectives*, a series of occasional papers published since 1982 by the Translation Research and Instruction Program at SUNY (Binghamton) and edited by Marilyn Gaddis Rose. A watershed volume, which also originated in a conference at Binghamton, is Graham (1985), which represents post-structuralist styles of thinking.

Since the 1990s, as translation began to emerge as a scholarly discipline in its own right, two rather different paradigms appear to be driving research. On the one hand is an approach that can generally be called text linguistics, in which notions of equivalence are grounded in the classification of text types and functions. On the other hand is an approach that can generally be called cultural studies, which is concerned with how values, ideologies, and institutions shape practices differently in different historical periods. It is the latter approach that seems to be stimulating the most interest, attracting scholars from disciplines that have hitherto neglected translation – despite its importance in American cultural and political history.

Further reading
Pochmann 1957; De Sua 1964; Cunningham 1967; Apter 1987; Bowen 1990; Obst and Cline 1990; Cheyfitz 1991; Lecomte du Noüy 1991; Lefevere 1992a, 1992c, 1993; Barnstone 1993; Fowler 1993; Gentzler 1993; Payne 1993; May 1994; Neubert and Shreve 1994; Venuti 1995a; Baker 1996a.

LAWRENCE VENUTI

Arabic tradition

Arabic is a southern-central semitic language spoken by a large population in the Arab and Islamic worlds. It originated in the Arabian Peninsula but spread far beyond the confines of its birthplace with the rise of Islam in the seventh century.

Prior to the rise of Islam and the consolidation of the Arab nation, the various peoples who inhabited different parts of the territory now known as the Arab world were in many cases bilingual, speaking Arabic in everyday contexts and using a variety of languages such as Syriac and Aramaic for trade and learning (Hitti 1937: 70ff.), especially as Arabic did not develop a writing system until almost the time of the rise of Islam. They were of different ethnic backgrounds and followed very different ways of life, varying between a nomadic, tribal existence in the Peninsula (present-day Saudi Arabia, Yemen and the Gulf states) and a sedentary, merchant culture in the Fertile Crescent (Syria, Lebanon, Iraq and Palestine). The tribes in the Peninsula were not ruled by outside powers, whereas the inhabitants of other parts fell under the rule of either the Byzantine or Sassanian Empire.

The rise of Islam in the seventh century is the most important event in the history of the Arab peoples: it changed the political, cultural and linguistic map of the area forever. The spread of Islam began during the Prophet's lifetime and gathered phenomenal speed after his death in 632. By 698, Iraq, Syria, Egypt and North Africa had become part of the new political and religious order. At the height of its expansion, the Islamic Empire stretched from present-day Pakistan to Spain.

The political history of the Islamic world is rather complex, with the seat of empire moving from one capital to another as different dynasties rose to power, and with several caliphates at times existing in various parts of the world. The most important periods and caliphates are as follows:

- the orthodox period of the early caliphate, starting with the death of Muhammad in 632 and ending with the death of ʿAli, the fourth Guided Caliph, in 661. The seat of the caliphate during this period moved from Medina, in present-day Saudi Arabia, to al-Kufa and al-Basra in present-day Iraq;

- the Umayyad caliphate (661–750), with its seat in Damascus;
- the Abbasid caliphate (750–1258), with its capital in Baghdad;
- the Fatimid caliphate (909–1171), a Shi'ite offshoot of the main caliphate, with its capital in Cairo;
- an offshoot of the Umayyad caliphate which was established in Cordoba (929–1031);
- the Ottoman caliphate (c.1517–1924), with its seat in Constantinople. This last great caliphate of Islam was Turkish.

The office of caliph (i.e. leader of the Muslim community) was officially abolished in 1924.

From the point of view of the history of translation into Arabic, the orthodox period, the Fatimid caliphate and the offshoot of the Umayyad caliphate in Spain are of relatively little interest. Although the Arab conquest of Spain is associated with an important period of translation activity, much of this activity involved translation out of rather than into Arabic (see SPANISH TRADITION). The most important periods in the history of translation *into* Arabic are the Umayyad and Abbasid, which were followed by a long period of intellectual stagnation in the Islamic world from the twelfth to the eighteenth or early nineteenth centuries.

The widely celebrated flourishing of translation in the Islamic Empire is closely associated with and dependent on the growth of Arabic as a written literary language, which began with the need to standardize the text of the Qur'ān. The status of Arabic as lingua franca was established when the Umayyad Caliph ʿAbd al-Malik ibn Marawān (reigned 685–705) declared it the sole administrative language of the Empire. Since then it has been the official language of all Arab countries and continues to play a unifying role in the area, enabling the variety of religious and ethnic groups that make up the population of the Arab world to think of themselves as a 'nation'.

Translation in the Arab Islamic Empire (seventh to thirteenth century)

Some translation activity seems to have taken place on a small scale prior to the rise of Islam. A manuscript dating back to A.D. 513 and written in Greek, Syriac and Arabic was found near Aleppo. It lists, among other things, the names of men involved in building the church where the manuscript was found (ʿAli 1986: 51). Some translation and interpreting activities must also have existed in the very early days of Islam, though we have very few records of such activity. We do know, however, that the Prophet sent messages to various political rulers, such as the Viceroy of Egypt, urging them to adopt the new religion. This type of exchange between the Prophet and non-Arab rulers could not have taken place without some form of linguistic mediation. Moreover, the Qur'ān itself includes many words borrowed from Greek, Persian, Syriac and Hebrew.

The new cultural environment which developed following the rise of Islam and the expansion of the Islamic Empire was infinitely richer and more complex than anything previously experienced by the inhabitants of the Arabian Peninsula. The new empire lay at the intersection of eastern and western civilizations and brought together the most sophisticated cultural traditions of the period: Greek, Indian, Persian and Egyptian. One of the most important consequences of this development was the shift of Arabic from a mainly oral language, spoken by an ethnically homogeneous community of native speakers, to a written and spoken lingua franca of a vast civilization comprising many ethnic and linguistic groups.

The nomadic Arabs who came out of the desert had a great deal to learn from the nations they conquered; and they were eager learners. Inspired by the richness of the civilizations they were now encountering for the first time, and explicitly encouraged by the Qur'ān to seek knowledge wherever it could be found, they began a huge campaign to acquire the learning of the nations under their rule and naturally turned to translation as the means by which the new sources of knowledge could be accessed. The period from the eighth to the eleventh century in particular witnessed an unprecedented level of translation activity, greatly helped by the availability of paper, which was introduced to the Muslim world shortly after Samarqand was captured in 704 (Stock 1978: 13). With the introduction of paper, the process of transforming the oral Arabic culture into a literate one could proceed in earnest, with translation playing the main role in enabling this process to take shape.

The Arabs are credited with initiating the first organized, large-scale translation activity in history. This activity started during the reign of the Umayyads (661–750) and reached its zenith under the Abbasids (750–1258), particularly during the reign of Al-Ma'mūn (813–33), known as the Golden Era of translation. The centre of this activity was Baghdad, a fabulous city built by the Abbasid caliph al-Mansūr (reigned 754–75) and the scene of many episodes in the famous *Thousand and One Nights*.

This unprecedented commitment to translation can be distinguished from any translation activity the world had known before in terms of three factors (al-Khūry 1988: 24):

(a) Range of source languages: the Arabs translated voraciously from Sanskrit, Persian, Syriac, Greek, Aramaic and other languages.

(b) Range of topics and subjects: all aspects of knowledge interested the Arabs. They translated manuscripts on mathematics, astronomy, philosophy, logic, medicine, chemistry, politics, etc. Literature was of relatively less interest during this period, partly because it often included religious and mythical allusions which conflicted with Islamic teachings, and partly because the Arabs already had a strong literary tradition of their own.

(c) Most importantly, the translation movement which evolved under the Abbasid dynasty was organized and institutionalized. Translation was sponsored and supported by the government, and specific institutions, or translation chambers, were set up to initiate and regulate the flow of translations. The first such translation chamber was set up by al-Mansūr, the second Abbasid caliph (754–75), and expanded considerably by Al-Rashīd (786–809) and Al-Ma'mūn (813–33).

The Umayyad period

The first half of the eighth century witnessed a number of developments which laid the long-term foundations of the Empire: the development of a postal service, Arabic coinage and, most importantly, the establishment of Arabic as the official language of administration, replacing Greek in Damascus, Pahlavi in Iraq and the Eastern provinces and Coptic in Egypt.

Translation activity also started in earnest during this period. The most authoritative and comprehensive source for translation and writing activities in the Islamic Empire is *al-Fihrist* (lit. 'The Index'), compiled by Ibn al-Nadīm in 988. *Al-Fihrist* claims that it was Prince Khālid Ibn Yazīd, son of the second Umayyad caliph, who commissioned the first translations from Greek and Coptic (al-Nadīm, in al-Khūry 1988: 31), having turned to the pursuit of knowledge following his failure to acquire the position of caliph. Although the ascription of this activity to Khālid Ibn Yazīd is contested in the literature (Hitti 1937: 255), there is general agreement that the first translations were carried out during this period and were from Greek and Coptic. *Al-Fihrist* further suggests that the first treatises to be translated were on alchemy because Khalid ibn Yazīd believed it was possible to turn minerals into gold. At any rate, we do know that translations carried out during this period included treatises on medicine, astrology and alchemy. In addition, Arabizing the administration under Ibn Marawān naturally involved a certain amount of translation of official documents in the initial stages.

Byzantine and Persian songs also first began to appear in translation during this period. The translations were carried out by Saʿīd Ibn Misjāh, the first Meccan musician and one of the best known during the Umayyad period (Hitti 1937: 275).

A great deal of Greek gnomologia (wisdom literature) was translated into Arabic towards the end of the Umayyad period, including virtually all gnomologia connected with Aristotle and Alexander (Gutas 1975: 444). These translations were to have a strong influence on Arabic poetry in the ninth and tenth centuries. Two of the most celebrated Arab poets of the period, Abu al-ʿAtāhiya and al-Mutanabbi, used gnomic material in their poems.

The Abbasid period

Whereas the elite of the Umayyad Empire was largely Arab (ethnically speaking), the Abbasid Empire was overall more international in composition and character, with ethnic Arabs forming only one part of the nation and its elite. In due course, the word Arab came to refer to any Arabic-speaking Muslim, irrespective of racial background or affiliation. Thus it must be borne in mind that the many references to the large body of knowledge accumulated during this period as Arab (Arab medicine, Arab philosophy and so on) often apply to work which is not necessarily attributable to ethnic Arabs from the Peninsula. There were certain areas in which the ethnic Arabs excelled (in particular theology, jurisprudence and linguistics), but in almost all other areas it was the Persians, Syriacs and Jews who led the way, both in terms of translation and of original writing. The Persians in particular were instrumental in shaping the intellectual development of Muslim society. The fact that al-Mansūr was keen to maintain the loyalty of Persians to secure the stability of the then nascent Abbasid rule played a major role in the enrichment of Arabo-Islamic culture and the beginning of the translation movement, which lasted for more than two centuries. Many translations from Greek into Arabic were undertaken mainly through Pahlavi (Middle Persian of the Sassanians). By the tenth/eleventh centuries, Arabic had become more ornate under the influence of Persian. The Persian influence on translation activities is evident even in the first known translation institution in the Arabic tradition, Bayt al-Hikma (the House of Wisdom), which, as Gutas (1998: 54) suggests, was modelled on the Sassanian libraries. 'Bayt al-Hikma' itself is a translation of the Persian name of the Sassanian libraries.

Generally speaking, however, it is often very difficult to apportion credit for translation or original work to specific ethnic groups within this melting-pot of an empire. The earliest work of science to appear in Arabic (in 683), for example, was a translation by a Jewish physician of Persian origin (Masarjawayh of al-Basra) of a Syriac treatise on medicine, originally written in Greek by Ahrun, a Christian priest in Alexandria (Hitti 1937: 255). Similarly, it is often difficult to specify the boundaries between original and translated work, or for that matter, identify the exact source of a translation. The *Thousand and One Nights*, the best known work of Arabic literature in the West, is itself based on an old Persian work, *Hazar Afsani* (thousand tales; *Shehrazad* – the story-teller – is a Persian name); this in turn contained several stories of Indian origin. Some of the stories were also added much later and may have been inspired by the new context and written in Arabic.

Alexandria had been captured in 642 and the Arabs had begun to sample the riches of its great scholarly tradition. The first centres of education started to appear in the early eighth century in Egypt and Iraq, and early Abbasid caliphs subsequently began to take an active interest in translation. The second Abbasid caliph, al-Mansūr (reigned 754–75), commissioned a number of translations and set up a translation chamber. Al-Rashīd (reigned 786–809) similarly supported translation activity and enlarged the translation chamber set up by al-Mansūr. But it was al-Ma'mūn (reigned 813–33) who founded in 830 the most important institute of higher learning in Islam, which also became the most celebrated centre of translation in Arab history. Bayt al-Hikma (the House of Wisdom), in Baghdad, functioned as an academy, library and translation bureau, and produced translations from Greek, Syriac, Persian, Sanskrit and Nabatean.

A vast range of material was translated under the Abbasids. Ptolemy's *Geography* was translated into Arabic several times, most notably by Thabit Ibn Qurrah, either directly or through Syriac. Generally speaking, Greek material already available in Syriac was translated from Syriac, which still functioned as the liturgical language of the Nestorians who headed the translation chambers. Greek works which were not available in Syriac were either rendered directly into Arabic or first into Syriac and then into Arabic. Greek works on moral philosophy, starting with Aristotle's *Ethics*, were among the first to be translated and laid the foundation for the indigenous version of philosophy known as ʿilm al-Akhlāq (lit. science of manners/ behaviour). The scientific study of astronomy was inspired by the translation (c. 771) of an Indian treatise, *Sindhind*, by Muhammad Ibn Ibrāhīm al-Fazari, whose translations of this and other Hindu works also introduced into the Muslim world, and later Europe, the Hindu numeral system and the zero. The Old and New Testaments, or fragments of them, were translated several times. The most important, full translation of the Old Testament was done by Saʿīd al-Fayyūmī (882–942) in Egypt.

Overall, the Arabs translated essentially scientific and philosophical material from Greek and showed little or no interest in Greek drama and poetry. Even in translating such books as Aristotle's *Poetics* into Arabic they were not motivated by any perceived aesthetic or literary value, but rather by the need to learn Greek philosophical argumentation. Abū Bishr Matta ibn Yūnis (d. 940), probably the first to produce a full translation of Aristotle's *Poetics*, was not a man of letters, but a philosopher and logician ('Ayyād 1993: 177). The frequent religious debates between Muslims and non-Muslims and between the different sects of Islam during the reign of the Abbasid dynasty created a need for translating Greek works of philosophy and rhetoric. As far as literature was concerned, Persian – rather than Greek – provided most of the source texts during this period. India, on the other hand, was the chief source of wisdom literature and mathematics, though it must be borne in mind that much of Persian literature can be traced back to Indian sources. For example, as in the case of the *Thousand and One Nights*, *Kalilah wa Dimna* (another important work of literature in Arabic) is based on a translation from Pahlavi (Middle Persian), which in turn is based on Sanskrit sources. Sanskrit was also important as a source language for medical treatises, though the translations were often carried out via Persian, as in the case of the great Indian medical treatise *Charaka-Samhita* (Meyerhof 1937: 26).

In addition to Persian translators (for a full list, see al-Nadīm's *Fihrist*), a large number of the translators active during this period were Christian (Rosenthal 1975: 6), and many were scholars in their own right. The most notable was Yuhanna Ibn Māsāwayh (777–857), who headed Bayt al-Hikma and who wrote *Daghal al-ʿAyn* (Disorders of the Eye), the oldest systematic work on ophthalmology in Arabic. Other Christian translators included Yuhanna Ibn al-Bitrīq, 'Abd al-Masīh Ibn Na'īma al-Himsī, Qusta Ibn Lūqa and Yahya Ibn 'Adi.

One of the most outstanding translators

during this period is Hunayn Ibn Ishāq (809–73), known as Joannitius in the western tradition, who was paid by al-Ma'mūn in gold, matching the weight of the books he translated. Ibn Ishāq is credited with translating some 100 manuscripts into Syriac and 39 into Arabic, including the works of Aristotle, Plato and Ptolemy. A Nestorian Christian from al-Hīra (in modern Iraq), Ibn Ishāq was among the most gifted and productive translators during the Abbasid period. Bilingual in Arabic and Syriac, he studied medicine under the renowned physician and translator Yuhanna ibn Māsāwayh, went on to learn Greek and then began his career as physician and translator in Baghdad. He headed Bayt al-Hikma under the caliph al-Ma'mūn, where he took charge of all scientific translation work and, with his son, his nephew and other students and members of his school, translated into Syriac and Arabic the bulk of the Greek medical material known at the time, many of Aristotle's works (including *Categories*, *Physics* and *Magna Moralia*), Plato's *Republic*, works by Hippocrates, various treatises on mathematics and physics, as well as the Septuagint.

In the course of producing this enormous translation output, Ibn Ishāq enriched Arabic with a very large number of scientific terms. He was a conscientious and sophisticated translator who took great pains to verify the accuracy of a source text before proceeding with a translation. Ibn Ishāq adopted a sense-for-sense approach which distinguished his work from many crude, literal translations of the time. The most important document he left us is the treatise he wrote on the translations of Galen's work into Syriac and Arabic, including his own and his students' translations, known as *Risala*. Besides listing the translations of Galen's work, Ibn Ishāq comments on the translation practices of his time. This makes *Risala* the most important source for examining the discourse on translation during the Abbasid reign. Ibn Ishāq provides some detailed comments on the linguistic and stylistic qualities of Galen's translations and the proficiencies of the translators, their patrons and the impact of their work on medical education at the time (Meyerhof 1926).

Another prolific translator of the period was the Sabian Thābit Ibn Qurrah (c.836–901); the Sabians were a community of star worshippers who naturally had a long-standing interest in astronomy. Ibn Qurrah and his disciples were responsible for translating most of the Greek works on astronomy and mathematics, including the works of Archimedes and Apollonius of Perga (Hitti 1937: 314). As in the case of Ibn Ishāq, other members of Ibn Qurrah's immediate family followed in his footsteps and distinguished themselves as translators, including his son Sinān, his grandsons Thābit and Ibrāhīm, and his great-grandson Abu al-Faraj (ibid.).

Two methods of translation seem to have been adopted during this period (Rosenthal 1975: 17). The first, associated with Yuhanna Ibn al-Bitrīq and Ibn Nāʿima al-Himsi, was highly literal and consisted of translating each Greek word with an equivalent Arabic word and, where none existed, borrowing the Greek word into Arabic. This method was not successful overall and many of the translations carried out by al-Bitrīq were later revised under al-Maʾmūn, most notably by Hunayn Ibn Ishāq. The second method, associated with Ibn Ishāq and al-Jawhari, consisted of translating sense for sense, creating fluent target texts which conveyed the meaning of the original without distorting the target language. Ibn Ishāq and his followers thus gave priority to the requirements of the target language and the target reader from the outset, stressing readability and accessibility in a way which suggests that the translations were conceived as having a didactic function: Ibn Ishāq, for instance, explicitly praised his own translations for their 'pleasant and limpid style which can be understood by the non-expert in the field of medical science or by he who does not know anything of the ways of philosophy' (cited in Salama-Carr 1996).

In addition to comments concerning the most successful method of translation, there was also some reflection during this period on such issues as whether translation of certain text types was at all possible, whether translated texts in general offered a reliable source of information, and the effect of interference from Greek and Syriac on the structure of Arabic. Al-Jāhiz (d. 869), one of the best known writers of the period, was particularly caustic in his statements about translators and translation, insisting that 'the translator can never do [the philosopher] justice or express him with fidelity' (cited in Salama-Carr 1996). But apart from

such occasional criticism of their profession, translators generally enjoyed a most enviable position under the Abbasids. Their work was highly valued and they seem to have enjoyed a rather luxurious style of life, at least the more successful among them. Al-Nadīm (988, cited in Hitti 1937: 306) gives a lavish description of the daily routine of Hunayn Ibn Ishāq: he bathed, relaxed in a lounging robe, enjoyed a light drink and a biscuit, had his siesta, and on waking 'burned perfume to fumigate his person', had dinner, went back to sleep, woke up again and drank several rotls of wine 'to which he added quinces and Syrian apples if he felt the desire for fresh fruits'.

This Golden Era of translation under early Abbasid rule was followed by a rich period of original writing in many fields, including astronomy, alchemy, geography, linguistics, theology and philosophy. Here again, the most outstanding contributions came from Arabic-speaking subjects of the Empire (i.e. non-ethnic Arabs), especially Persians such as Ibn Sīna (Avicenna), al-Tabari and al-Rīzi (Rhazes). Much of this original writing included a substantial amount of commentary on Greek sources, such as Aristotle, by writers who often had no knowledge of Greek and who relied on existing Arabic translations in developing their own philosophical positions. This is true, for example, of the works of Ibn Rushd (Averroës) and the Jewish philosopher (as well as astronomer, theologian and physician) Mūsa Ibn Maymūn (Maimonides). Another interesting feature of the 'original writing' which followed the Golden Era of translation is that some of it, though written in Arabic, was either lost and later found only in Hebrew translations or Latin translations from the Hebrew (as in the case of Ibn Rushd's commentaries) or was written in Hebrew characters from the outset (as in the case of Ibn Maymūn's works (Hitti 1937/1970: 582ff.).

The flowering of knowledge that took place in the Islamic world during the tenth and eleventh centuries and that later provided the impetus for the development of all branches of knowledge in the West, including natural science and philosophy, could not have taken place had it not been for the intense programme of translation carried out under the Abbasids. Thus translation lay at the centre of *the* most important period of intellectual activity in the history of the Islamic World.

Translation under the Ottomans

Starting with the late tenth/early eleventh century, the Islamic Empire began to experience a long period of gradual disintegration, resulting in the establishment of rival caliphates in Egypt and Spain and endless petty dynasties in various parts of the Empire. A series of barbaric onslaughts by the Mongols eventually culminated in the destruction of Baghdad and the slaughter of the caliph and his officials by Hulagu in 1258. For a time, the Islamic world had no caliph to rule it. The Muslim Ottomans, a new power which was to endure well into the twentieth century, eventually took control of the region and claimed the title of caliph for their rulers in 1517.

Under this new political order, Arabic continued to be the language of learning and law, the latter because the Ottomans, being Muslim, had to rule the Empire according to Islamic jurisdiction. In other areas, Arabic began to lose ground to Turkish (now the language of government) and Persian (which became the language of polite letters). As the language of learning, Arabic continued to play a major role in the translation movement, though now it had to share this role with Turkish. As Muslims, the Turks were eager to access the resources of Islamic culture, and therefore more translation was done from Arabic into Turkish than vice versa (Oghli 2006). One of the most prominent translators into Turkish in the early nineteenth century was ʿUthmān Nūr al-Dī,n Pasha, who was the first to be sent by Muhammad Ali on an educational mission to Italy in 1809. On his return he embarked on translating books on military arts and industry into Turkish (for a full list of translators into Turkish under Muhammad Ali, see Oghli 2006: 183–5). In addition to books on Islamic religion and culture and military arts, the Turks were interested in history and politics.

The Arab world was largely isolated and deprived of cultural contact during the first few centuries of Ottoman rule. The first major contact with Europe came with the French invasion of Egypt in 1798, which lasted only

three years but had a considerable impact on the intellectual development of the area. Napoleon had brought with him a 'scientific expedition' which included a number of orientalists who set up the first Arabic press in the region. Initially, he brought his own translators and interpreters with him, including some Muslim sailors whom he had captured in Malta (al-Shayyāl 1950: 36). These 'foreign' translators prepared the Arabic circular that Napoleon distributed on landing in Alexandria, a circular designed to reassure the Egyptian populace and to incite them to rebel against their rulers. The circular, like much of what these foreign translators produced, was grammatically unsound and stylistically poor (al-Jabarti, cited in al-Shayyāl 1950: 36). The French also relied on foreign interpreters for reading out their decrees, and even for pacifying angry crowds. In addition, interpreters worked in the dīwān, where they interpreted lawsuits and read out letters and statements. Al-Jabarti tells us that these foreign interpreters often used French words while interpreting into Arabic.

Translators and interpreters during this period fell into three main groups: (a) Moroccan, Arab and Turkish sailors captured by the French in Malta and released to work as translators in Egypt; (b) French orientalists who accompanied the scientific expedition, the best known among them being Venture, Jauper and l'Homaca; (c) Christian Syrians who had a good knowledge of both French and Arabic, in addition to sharing the religion of the invaders. Some 500 of these Christian Syrians left with the French in 1801 and settled in Marseilles (al-Shayyāl 1950: 45ff.). Very few Egyptians were involved in the translation effort during this period. The best known was Père Antūn Raphaïl, a Christian priest of Syrian origin who became the only Arab member of Napoleon's Egyptian Academy of Science. Under French rule, Père Raphaïl became important enough to sign his name as Chief Translator on legal decrees and similar official documents. After the departure of the French he stayed in Egypt for two years, but then left for Paris where he was rewarded for his support of Napoleon in 1803 with an assistant professorship at the Oriental Institute in Paris (al-Shayyāl 1951/2000).

The greater part of translation activity under the French focused on official documents and legal decrees. However, a few interesting texts were also translated during this period, among them a grammar of spoken Arabic printed in a bilingual edition in 1801, and a treatise on smallpox translated by Père Antūn Raphaïl and printed in French and Arabic in 1800.

Translation under Muhammad Ali

In 1805, Muhammad Ali (reigned 1805–48), an Ottoman soldier who was originally sent to take control of Egypt on behalf of the caliph, managed to establish himself as the *de facto* governor of Egypt and later Syria and Sudan. Muhammad Ali had military ambitions, which he proceeded to support by initiating a substantial programme of foreign education and subsequently of translation, mainly of technical works. He set up professional schools, sponsored groups of students to study in Europe and, on their return, instructed them to translate the texts he required for modernizing his army and administration. Initially, most of the students sent to Europe were Turks or Christians from the Levant, but Egyptian students later began to join these educational missions.

Among the most active translators during this period and the decades that preceded it were the Maronite Christians of Lebanon and Syria, who translated or adapted various works of Catholic theology and who were used by political leaders such as Fakhr al-Dīn as interpreters in negotiations with the courts of Europe (Hourani 1962: 55–6). Under Muhammad Ali and his sons, this group enjoyed more freedom and were able to establish their own schools, where they also translated textbooks and printed them in their own presses. Students of these mission schools were later to act as interpreters for local government and foreign diplomats in the area and to form the first generation of journalists in the Arab World (ibid.: 67). Some of the translations which appeared during this period were done by Europeans, among them the French consul Basili Fakhr, who translated several French books on astronomy and natural science into Arabic.

French was the main source language during the eighteenth and early nineteenth centuries, and Muhammad Ali's sponsored student missions to Europe had France as their main destination. In 1826, one of Muhammad Ali's student missions to France was accompanied by a reli-

gious guide, a graduate of al-Azhar who was to become one of the most important figures in translation during this period and a leading educator of his time. Rifāʿa al-Tahtāwi (1801–73) spent five years in Paris, where he acquired an excellent command of French. On his return, he worked as a translator in one of Muhammad Ali's new specialist schools and later headed *al-Alsun* (lit. 'the tongues'), originally called *madrasat al-tarjama* (school of translation), which was set up by Muhammad Ali in 1835 on al-Tahtāwi's recommendation. Al-Alsun started out with eighty students, chosen by al-Tahtāwi himself from various regions. Within a few years, this number grew to some 150 students who studied Arabic, French and Turkish (and occasionally English) in addition to technical subjects such as geography and mathematics. Al-Tahtāwi would choose a number of books which he thought required translation and distribute them among the translation students. He would guide them through the translation and then revise each text himself before committing it to print. Al-Tahtāwi and his student translators were instrumental in making a vast range of European sources available in Arabic, covering numerous areas of knowledge. Among their most important translations were various histories of the ancient world and the Middle Ages, histories of various kings and emperors, Montesquieu's *Considérations sur les causes de la grandeur des Romains et de leur décadence*, as well as a large body of texts on medicine, geography, military science and other technical subjects.

Teaching in the various schools set up by Mohammed Ali was initially conducted by foreign instructors in French or Italian. These instructors relied on interpreters in the classroom to communicate with their students. Thus the use of interpreters in the educational context seems to have been fairly common practice at the time.

In 1841, a Translation Chamber was set up and attached to al-Alsun. This comprised four departments, three specializing in translating in a specific field of knowledge and the fourth focusing on Turkish translation. Each department was supervised by a high official, usually a graduate of al-Alsun, helped by a number of students. The translations were later sent to the Ministry of Education for final assessment. Al-Alsun continued to play a double role of teaching and producing translation until khedive Abbas I (reigned 1848–54) closed it down in 1849 and punished its director, al-Tahtāwi, by sending him to Sudan as headmaster of a primary school. During his years in Sudan al-Tahtāwi translated Fénelon's *Les aventures de Télémaque*, the first French novel to be translated into Arabic. Al-Tahtāwi's choice to 'domesticate' Fénelon's text, despite his claim to the opposite in the introduction, set an example that would later be followed by translators during what came to known by cultural historians as *nahda*, literally the revival or renaissance.

Muhammad Ali's translation programme lasted about twenty years. During this time the circulation of the translated books was restricted to a small group of academics, essentially the students and former students of al-Alsun, and government officials who needed access to specific information. However, the impact of the translation work done during this short period was quite considerable, for the new intellectual leadership in Egypt (which has since been the major cultural influence in the Arab world) came from the ranks of students who had access to translated books. Thanks to these students, Egypt, and with it the rest of the Arab world, started the twentieth century with a wealth of knowledge and an intellectual curiosity that have assured it a place in the modern world.

Translation and *nahda*

A period known as *nahda* (Arabic for renaissance or revival) followed from the activities initiated by Muhammad Ali and involved, in addition to Egyptians, Syro-Lebanese translators, theatre makers, journalists and writers who had been immigrating to Egypt since the eighteenth century for political and/or economic reasons. Translation was a key factor in initiating this cultural revival, so much so that Badawi refers to the Egyptian *nahda* as 'the age of translation and adaptation' (1993: 11).

Muhammad Ali believed that translation could only be a vehicle for the modernization of Egypt, helping to import the knowledge necessary for setting up the reliable infrastructure and societal institutions that would make Egypt a modern nation state. Hence his keen interest in translating books related to medicine, engineering, the structure and organization of the military and the structure and function of the legal system. Unlike Muhammad Ali, most Egyptian and Syro-Lebanese intellectuals associated with *nahda* believed translation could also be instrumental in achieving Arab modernity, in the sense of borrowing and introducing new modes of thinking as well as of literary and artistic expression.

Nahda translators focused on literary genres which were lacking in Arabic culture and which they felt were necessary to achieve modernity and cultural revival. Drama and fiction received most attention. Most, if not all, of the drama translations done during *nahda* were taken from French theatre. Even translations from English theatre were done through French. French was also the main language for translations of fiction. Among the few translators who worked direct from English were Ya'qūb Sarruf, Butrus al-Bustāni, translator of the first Arabic version of Defoe's *Robinson Crusoe*, Farīda 'Attiyya, Muhammad al-Sibā'i and others. It is worth noting that a small number of translators worked direct from Russian during *nahda*, most notably Khalil Baydas (1875–1949), a Palestinian who graduated from the Russian Teachers Higher College in Nazareth and who translated, among many other Russian works, Pushkin's *The Captain's Daughter* (Moosa 1983: 76). Other translators who worked directly from Russian included Rafa'īl Sa'd, Salīm Qub'ayn, Rashīd Haddād, Anton Ballān and Bebbāwi Ghāli al-Dwayri (ibid.: 77).

A number of significant non-literary translations were produced during *nahda*. The first complete modern translation of the Bible into Arabic was produced in the 1850s by missionaries in Cambridge, Britain. This was soon replaced by a version produced in 1865 by American missionaries in Beirut. The 1865 version was the first Arabic translation to be based on the original Greek, Hebrew and Aramaic (Somekh 1995). It took seventeen years to complete. The main translators, Eli Smith and Cornelius Van Dyck, employed three Arab translators to help them with the task. The Jesuit Arabic Bible, published in Beirut between 1876 and 1880, is very closely modelled on the Smith–Van Dyck version. This too was undertaken by a

Western scholar, Augustin Rodet, with the help of an Arab translator, Ibrāhīm al-Yāziji. Some of the most distinguished translators of the period, who were later to form the intellectual leadership of Egypt and Syria in particular, were involved in producing these new versions of the Bible. They included Fāris al-Shidyāq, Butrus al-Bustāni and Nasīf al-Yāziji.

Translation of material from the humanities, social and exact sciences remained marginal. Some scientific articles were translated in journals, especially Ya'qūb Sarrūf's *al-Muqtataf* and Shibli Shumayyil's medical journal *al-Shifā'*. Shibli Shumayyil translated Buchner's commentary on Charles Darwin's work in 1884, followed by a number of authored articles on the theory of evolution, and Ismā'īl Mazher translated Darwin's *The Origin of Species* in 1918. In philosophy, Ahmad Lutfi al-Sayyid translated a number of works by Aristotle from French, and Hanna Khabbāz translated Plato's *Republic* from English.

The present

The shortage of verifiable data about translation in the Arab world, especially during the second half of the twentieth century, makes it difficult to draw a clear picture of the realities of translation during this period. Statistics offered by the *Arab Human Development Report* (2003) about the translation output in the Arab world have been widely criticized as unreliable, incomplete, methodologically flawed and, at times, politically biased (Rogan 2004). A notable exception in terms of reliability of data is a report produced by the Next Page Foundation in 2004, entitled 'Lost or Found in Translation: Translations' Support Policies in the Arab World', which is based on field research, including questionnaires and interviews with publishers of translation and coordinators of translation projects in the Arab world.

According to the Next Page Foundation (2004), a total of twenty-two books were translated into Arabic between 1951 and 1998 as part of a UNESCO initiative which was discontinued as a result of the Lebanese civil war, during which the archives and documentation facilities of the project were destroyed. Western authors translated in this project included Aristotle,

Descartes, Leibniz, Durkheim, Montesquieu and Voltaire.

A number of translation projects sponsored by Arab governments were launched in the second half of the twentieth century. The One Thousand Book project, initiated by the Cultural Department of the Egyptian Ministry of Education in 1957, did not achieve its target, producing only 287 titles in five years (Klein 2003: 158); it ceased to exist in the early 1970s. A similar project called the Second Thousand Books was started by the General Egyptian Book Organization in 1986. By 2000, it had published a total of 361 books, 286 of which were translations (Next Page Foundation 2004: 18).

The National Translation Project, initiated by the Egyptian Higher Council for Culture in 1995, set out to widen the scope of translated languages. In addition to English, books were translated directly from French, Spanish, German, Russian, Urdu, Greek, Chinese, Hebrew, Polish, Syriac and Hieroglyphic. The translations covered various disciplines, including literature, linguistics, social sciences, history, geography, philosophy and psychology (Next Page Foundation 2004: 19).

The National Council for Culture, Arts and Literature (NCCAL) was established in Kuwait in 1973 with a similar remit of supporting translation work (Next Page Foundation 2004: 20). The most recent translation project to be launched in the Arab world is entitled *Kalima* (meaning 'word' in Arabic). Seeded by a grant from the Abu Dhabi Authority for Culture and Heritage and announced in 2007, *Kalima* aims to 'widen access to knowledge in the Arab world by funding the translation, publication, and distribution of high-quality works of classic and contemporary writing from other languages into Arabic' (*Al Bawaba* 2007).

Further reading
Hitti 1937/1970 (Chapter 24); Meyerhof 1937; al-Shayyal 1951/2000; Hourani 1962; Rosenthal 1975; Lindberg 1978; Stock 1978; Peled 1979; al-Khury 1988; Salama-Carr 1990; Sadgrove 1996; Gutas 1998; Next Page Foundation 2004; Rogan 2004.

MONA BAKER AND SAMEH FEKRY HANNA

B

Brazilian tradition

The 180 million inhabitants of Brazil, the largest country in Latin America, are of mixed descent: Brazilian Indian, African, Asian and European. But they share a common language, Portuguese, which is the official language of Brazil. Brazil is therefore part of the Lusophone, or Portuguese-speaking community, which includes Portugal and its former African colonies: Angola, Mozambique, Guinea-Bissau and the islands of São Tomé, Cape Verde and Príncipe.

Early history: sixteenth to eighteenth century

The history of Brazil is a history of translations and of linguistic change. Its documentation starts with the landing on Brazilian shores of the Portuguese fleet commanded by Admiral Pedro Álvares Cabral (1467–c.1520) on 21 April 1500, the first undisputed visit by Europeans to Brazil. Having claimed these western lands for the Portuguese Crown, Cabral, thinking that they were an island, initially called them *Ilha de Santa Cruz*, or the 'Island of the Holy Cross'. Within a few years, the land had come to be known as Brazil, because of the *pau-brasil*, or 'brazil-wood', that was found there in abundance. Since this wood produced a red dye that was difficult to obtain in Europe, the Portuguese soon started sending expeditions out to the new continent to find ways of exploiting it.

When the Portuguese arrived in Brazil, they found a population, according to various historians, of between one and five million natives, leading a neolithic, semi-nomadic life. Like the rest of the indigenous population of the New World, the natives of Brazil were called *índios* by Christopher Columbus, who applied this misnomer to them because he 'thought he had sailed so far west that he had reached India' (Partridge 1966: 308–9). The Brazilian Indians spoke thousands of different languages and dialects, which have now been classified by linguists and anthropologists into 102 language groups and three large linguistic families: Tupy, Macro-Ge and Arawak. This linguistic variety, which was accompanied by equally varied cultures, religions, cosmogonies and oral traditions, led to the development of at least two linguae francae: *Abanheenga*, spoken on the coast, and *Kariri*, spoken in the northeastern hinterland. Given that the languages in question lacked writing systems, any linguistic exchanges which took place between Indian tribes are likely to have included oral translation.

The first interpreters

The first recorded document about Brazil is a letter written by Pero Vaz de Caminha, the scribe in Cabral's fleet, to the Portuguese king, Manuel I (1475–1521), on 1 May 1500 to relate the finding of new lands (Caminha 1966; Cortesão 1967). The same document also records a translation act: it describes how the Portuguese and Indians attempted to communicate with each other by means of gestures, and how a deportee, Afonso Ribeiro, was left on shore with the Indians to learn their language. It also reports that another deportee and two sailors deserted the expedition in order to remain with the Indians. From then on, every expedition that went to Brazil left behind adventurers and deportees who learned the Indian languages and who then acted as interpreters between Indians and Europeans. These men were called *línguas*, or 'tongues', and their numbers continued to grow during early colonial times.

Foremost amongst these *línguas* were João Ramalho and Diogo Álvares. Ramalho (d. 1580) was a Portuguese lawyer who was shipwrecked off the coast of Brazil. He lived at Piratininga, in the highlands, near the modern day São Paulo, where he formed a half-Portuguese, half-Indian village. He then met Martim Afonso de Souza (*c*.1500–64), who had been sent to establish the first Portuguese settlement in Brazil, and the two men joined forces in founding São Vicente in 1532 on the coast of the São Paulo province. Diogo Álvares (1450–1557), another shipwrecked Portuguese, was nicknamed *Caramurú*, or 'firemaker', by the Indians after he supposedly saved his own life by an impressive display of musketry. He returned to Portugal briefly with his Indian wife but eventually settled in Brazil, where he helped Thomé de Souza (*c*.1515-73) establish the new city of Bahia in 1549. His exploits are commemorated in 'O Caramurú', an epic poem written by the Brazilian poet José de Santa Rita Durão (1721–84) in 1781.

The first translators

A new linguistic phase began in Brazil with the arrival of the Jesuit fathers in 1549. The Jesuits set out to convert the Indians to Christianity and turn them into obedient subjects of the Portuguese Crown. The Indians who inhabited the Brazilian coast between the present-day states of Amazonas in the north and Santa Catarina in the south spoke a variety of languages which belonged to the Tupy family and used a lingua franca, which they called *Abanheenga* or *Abanhéem*, for inter-tribal communication. The Jesuits saw the advantages to be gained from adopting this language in their missionary efforts and did everything in their power to learn it; they also wrote grammars for it, based on the Latin model. This simplified form of the language was named *Nheengatu*, or 'beautiful language', and was used for communication between Indians and Europeans, and, eventually, amongst Europeans in Brazil.

Translations of religious texts soon began to appear, with the Jesuits thus becoming Brazil's first translators. Father Azpicuelta Navarro (d. 1557) translated the *Summa da doutrina cristã*, 'Summary of Christian Doctrine', from Portuguese into *Nheengatu*. Upon Navarro's death, Father José de Anchieta (*c*.1533–97) took over as the expert in native tongues. He wrote the *Arte da gramática na língua mais usada na*

costa do Brasil ('Art of the grammar of the most used language on the coast of Brazil'), initially reproduced in manuscript form and later printed in Coimbra, Portugal, in 1595. In 1618, Father Antônio de Araújo (1566–1632) translated the catechism into *Nheengatu*; it was published in Lisbon as *Catecismo na língua brasílica*, or 'Catechism in the Brazilian language'.

Linguae francae

Indian languages were not used for religious purposes only; they were used to conquer and dominate the natives of Brazil. Starting in 1531, when the first forays into the interior of what was to become the Brazilian territory took place, interpreters who spoke *Nheengatu* and other Indian languages were sent along with the expeditions that set out to capture Indian slaves and find precious stones. Mém de Sá (*c*. 1500–72), General Governor of Brazil between 1557 and 1572, sent the Castilian interpreter Francisco Bruzo de Espiñoso with one such expedition in 1564. Diogo de Castro acted as interpreter for another such expedition in 1578.

Even as the Portuguese and Brazilian explorers tried to conquer the Brazilian interior, Brazil faced incursions and invasions by France, Holland and England from as early as 1503 and until 1887. Therefore French, Dutch, English and Spanish, which was widely used in Portugal by the educated classes for 300 years (Gonçalves Rodrigues 1992: 27), also helped to strengthen a tradition of multilingualism and translation throughout colonial times (Houaiss 1985: 94).

Education during that period, and until 1759, was bilingual. At the Jesuit colleges, children were taught Portuguese and *Nheengatu*, but the language of hearth and home was *Nheengatu*. Florence (1941: 174) notes that 'in 1780, the ladies from São Paulo talked naturally in the lingua franca of Brazil, which was the language of friendship and domestic life' (translated). Such was the widespread use of *Nheengatu* that interpreters between it and Portuguese were needed in courts of law. However, Sebastião José Carvalho e Melo Pombal, the Marquis of Pombal (1712–82), Portugal's War and Foreign Affairs Minister during the reign of José I and virtual dictator of Portugal and its colonies from 1750 to 1777, feared the growing power of the Jesuits. Their authority in the New World, where the Jesuits tended to protect the Indians against enslavement, seemed to be greater than that of the king. Pombal therefore expelled the Jesuits from Portugal and Brazil in 1759 and, at the same time, forbade the use of *Nheengatu* in Brazil and shut down all the Jesuit colleges.

By 1800, nearly two million of the total Brazilian population of three and a quarter million consisted of Negroes and mulattoes. Millions of Africans had been brought to Brazil as slaves since 1503; they spoke Yoruba, Kimbundu and other languages of the Bantu group. They also developed their own linguae francae: a form of Yoruba which prevailed in the north and northeast of Brazil, and Congoese in the south.

Recent history: eighteenth century to the present

The Indian population of Brazil had been decimated by that stage; they were killed by colonizers who wanted their lands, by the hardships of slave labour, by European diseases which ranged from the common cold to venereal diseases against which they had no immunity, or were eliminated by miscegenation. Deprived of Jesuit protection, they now scattered further inland into the marshes and jungles of west and northwest Brazil. Western-style progress continued to exacerbate the conditions of their demise, with the result that by the end of the twentieth century their number had been reduced to a mere 150,000, of whom 30 per cent spoke Portuguese as a first language.

Portuguese hegemony

These factors, combined with the arrival of the Portuguese royal family in Brazil in 1808 as they fled from Napoleon's troops, served to consolidate the position of Portuguese as the major language in the country. In 1815, the prince regent, Dom João (later Dom João VI; 1767–1826) elevated Brazil to the category of Kingdom, on an equal footing with Portugal. More importantly, he lifted the ban on printing which had been in force in the colony since 1500.

Although clandestine presses operated at different points and at different periods of time (printing leaflets and such like), the *Impressão Régia*, or 'Royal Printing Shop', established by Dom João in Rio de Janeiro in 1808, was the first legal establishment of its kind to be set up in Brazil. *Impressão Régia* was given the monopoly on printing in the country, a situation that prevailed until Brazilian independence in 1822. However, the stringent censorship exercised in Portugal was also imposed in Brazil, with the result that the importation of books into Brazil was severely restricted. Many books were nevertheless smuggled in, and it is said that various colonial officials made fortunes out of bribes received to turn a blind eye to this activity. Private libraries also thrived, particularly during the second half of the eighteenth century. The library of Canon Luís Vieira da Silva, one of the conspirators involved in an early attempt to obtain independence for Brazil in 1789, contained nearly 800 volumes (170 titles), representing most of Europe's leading thinkers, especially the French. All this points to the fact that educated Brazilians, like their counterparts in Portugal, did not really need literary translations, particularly not from French. By the late nineteenth century, the Portuguese gentry had taken to speaking French amongst themselves, using Portuguese only to address their servants. At any rate, both in Portugal and in Brazil, Portuguese was the language of administration and the language of print in general.

However, it was not until Brazil became independent, during the constitutional assembly of 1823 – when it was decided that Portuguese would continue to be the official language of the nation – that Brazilians from various parts of the country began to speak Portuguese to each other. And yet, *Nheengatu* and the other linguae francae have now been largely forgotten, and the average Brazilian usually has no idea that they ever existed. Most Brazilians are not aware that they continue to use many words of Indian origin on a day-to-day basis, a fact which makes the Portuguese currently spoken in Brazil very different from the Portuguese spoken in Europe. Indian and African languages have influenced it not only at the lexical, but also at the syntactic and morphological levels.

Successive waves of immigrants (German, Italian, Japanese, Lebanese, Polish, Portuguese,

Russian, Spanish, Swiss, Syrian and others) who arrived after independence have further contributed to developing a variety of Portuguese in Brazil which has become quite distinct from European Portuguese. For over a century, European immigrants tended to live in isolation, ignoring the customs and language of their new country. In 1938, President Getúlio Vargas (1883–1954) banned the exclusive use of foreign languages in instruction and imposed Portuguese as the medium of education (Dulles 1969: 41–2).

The history of written translation

The history of translation in Brazil is just beginning to be written. A pioneering contribution has been made by José Paulo Paes in his *Tradução, a ponte necessária*, or 'Translation, the Necessary Bridge' (Paes 1990), a reliable point of departure for further attempts at documenting the history of literary translation in Brazil. Paes (1990: 10) details the almost insurmountable difficulties encountered by researchers: the paucity of public libraries in Brazil, the restricted size of their collections, and deficient cataloguing. Two factors have contributed to this unfavourable state of affairs. One is that publishing houses were not allowed in Brazil until the early nineteenth century. The second is the late establishment of universities in Brazil. Law schools were established at Olinda and São Paulo in 1828, a military academy at Rio de Janeiro in 1810, and medical schools at Rio de Janeiro and Bahia in 1808, but the first university was not set up until 1920, in Rio de Janeiro.

It is possible to establish, however, that professional translators were first recognized officially in 1808 as staff members of Impressão Régia. Seventy-three years later, for reasons yet to be determined, their posts were eliminated and their work was taken over by multilingual copywriters. The first translation printed by Impressão Régia was Leonhard Euler's (1707–83) *Elementos de álgebra* ('elements of algebra'), translated by Manuel de Araújo Guimarães and published in 1809. This appears to have set the trend for this publishing house: most of the 1,100 works it published during the fourteen years in which it enjoyed a monopoly of the publishing trade were compendia and treatises on mathematics, engineering, economics, public health, geography and travel, astronomy and philosophy – an attempt, perhaps, to fulfil the country's technological needs at the time. The first literary translation to be published by the same publishing house was that of Alexander Pope's *Essay on Criticism*, translated and annotated in 1809 by Fernando José de Portugal, the Marquis of Aguiar (1752–1817).

After independence, Impressão Régia lost its monopoly over the printing industry, and it became possible to step up publishing activities. Many translations began to appear; these were chiefly of French authors, or of authors translated indirectly via French and, less often, via Spanish. Most of these, however, were reprints of translations published in Portugal. However, several factors hindered the production of books at a low cost in Brazil and, consequently, the publication of translations. The first was that all attempts at producing paper in the country prior to 1888 proved to be too costly, owing to a shortage of qualified workers and the high cost of importing equipment and raw materials. To circumvent these problems, books were usually printed at newspaper presses using imported paper and idle machinery time. Nevertheless, with the introduction of rotary presses for newspapers only in 1847, this practice had to be abandoned. Four years later, steamship lines were opened between Europe and Brazil, making it cheaper to import books than to produce them locally. During various periods in the nineteenth and twentieth centuries (1815–36; 1844–60; 1920–29; 1951–7), the taxes levied on imported paper and cellulose were 60 per cent higher than those levied on imported books. Until World War I, publishers therefore restricted their activities to printing textbooks and law books. Even major Brazilian authors such as José de Alencar (1829-77) and Joaquim Maria Machado de Assis (1839-1908) had their works published in Paris or London; publishing in Portuguese had become a flourishing business in Europe, with establishments such as the Livraria Garnier in Paris specializing in it. However, the seed sown in 1888 finally bore fruit. By 1920, the incipient Brazilian paper industry was boasting 120 paper mills and could supply local demand, but it depended heavily on imported cellulose.

The approach of World War II brought two major developments to the area. The first was that importing books became very difficult, and this favoured the growth of domestic publishing businesses. The second was the rise of the United States as a world power, with Brazil falling increasingly within its sphere of influence, which meant that English soon replaced French as the main source language in translation. Today, translation from lesser-known languages, such as Japanese or Czech, is also often done indirectly via English.

It was from the 1930s onwards, then, that the publishing business began to flourish in Brazil and, with it, translation activities. This flourishing business was aided by an increase in the reading public's income, literacy and leisure time. The growing gap between European and Brazilian Portuguese also encouraged publishers to commission new Brazilian translations, instead of reprinting European ones, as the reading public in Brazil was no longer so willing to accept European Portuguese as an alternative.

Two Brazilian writers are worth mentioning here for their activities as translators during this period. José Bento Monteiro Lobato (1882–1948), having had difficulty publishing his collection of short stories *Urupês* (1918), established his own publishing house and devoted his time to translating several major authors, including Rudyard Kipling, Jack London, Herman Melville, Antoine de Saint-Exupéry, Ernest Hemingway, Sholem Ash, and H. G. Wells. He also modernized and adapted a number of European Portuguese translations to Brazilian Portuguese. Monteiro Lobato's publishing house was later bought by Editora Nacional, also in São Paulo. Érico Veríssimo (1905–75), who started translating as a means of complementing his income from journalism, soon succeeded in persuading Editora Globo, a publishing house based in Porto Alegre in south Brazil, to bring out translations of a more literary character than the run-of-the-mill detective novels in which they specialized. His efforts were fruitful, and he was subsequently made a member of the editorial board of Editora Globo, where he coordinated the Nobel Collection, reputedly the best collection of foreign fiction ever published in Brazil. Editora Globo later brought out another collection of translations

of world classics called *Biblioteca dos Séculos*, or 'library across centuries'.

During the 1940s and 1950s, the main publisher of translations was Editora José Olympio of Rio de Janeiro. Not only did it publish the major Brazilian writers of the time, but it also commissioned them to translate foreign works. Among such translators were: Gastão Cruls, Manuel Bandeira, Raquel de Queirós, Carlos Drummond de Andrade, José Lins do Rego, Otávio de Faria, Lúcio Cardoso, Rubem Braga, Genolino Amado and many others. Other publishing houses in Rio de Janeiro and São Paulo have also published translations on a regular basis. They include Editora Civilização Brasileira, Pongetti, Martins, Diffel, Editora Nova Fronteira and others. Again, major writers have doubled as translators: Godofredo Rangel, Agripino Grieco, Sérgio Milliet, Jorge de Lima, Marcos Santarrita, Antônio Callado, Stela Leonardos and Paulo Leminski have translated fiction. Poets and writers such as Guilherme de Almeida, Manuel Bandeira, Cecília Meireles, Carlos Nejar, Ledo Ivo and Ivan Junqueira have translated poetry. Raimundo Magalhães Júnior, Guilherme Figueiredo and Millôr Fernandes, among others, have excelled in the translation of drama.

Today, Brazil has developed its own cellulose production industry to the extent that, since 1976, it has been an exporter rather than an importer of paper pulp; its printing industry has advanced significantly, thus giving translation a further boost. The number of published translations in Brazil increased to the extent that during the 1990s, although almost 400 new literary works written originally in Portuguese were being published every year (a number that practically equals the total for the rest of Latin America; Souza 1990), 80 per cent of all material published in Brazil was translated (Wyler 1993), a situation that applied to every genre. In the case of children's books, for example, 63 per cent of the works published between 1965 and 1974 were translations (though this total fell to 49.5 per cent in 1979).

These statistics apply to technical works as well, and it is in this area that foreign political interests play a particularly important role. In 1966, COLTED, the National Textbook Commission, was jointly financed by the Ministry of Education and USAID (United States Agency for International Development). The commission encouraged the publication of US technical works and textbooks where no Brazilian equivalent existed. The programme sponsored by USIS, the United States Information Service, represents another attempt to boost the number of translations of US material into Brazilian Portuguese. Published titles cover American history, economics, science, communism and literature, among other topics. Black (1977: 97) mentions that 'in the years 1965 through 1967, 442 books were published under this program'. France was quick to react and offered to subsidize the translation of French textbooks by paying authors' royalties.

Profession, training and research

The profession of sworn translators was regulated by a Royal Decree in 1851. Sworn translators had to prove their mastery of foreign languages, and to pay annual taxes. Women were barred from the profession at the time. A Business Code introduced in the late 1850s established that the translation of foreign language documents would only be accepted if the translation was done by a sworn translator. In the absence of one, a translator agreed upon by the parties concerned would be acceptable. Statements of accounts of foreign businessmen, on the other hand, would only be accepted if translated by a sworn translator. Translators were sworn in by the Trade Courts, which were eliminated in 1875 and replaced by Boards of Trade.

The Brazilian Civil Code of 1916 ensured the survival of the profession of sworn translator by maintaining the requirement that foreign language documents be translated into Portuguese. In 1943, a new decree allowed women to join the profession; today the majority of sworn translators are women. At present, admission into the profession of sworn translator is by competitive examination, coordinated independently by the Boards of Trade of the various Brazilian states. Associations of sworn translators were founded in and after 1959 to protect professional interests. The profession of translator in general, comprising literary, technical, drama, cinema and television translators, conference, consecutive and simultaneous interpreters as well as tape transcribers, was recognized by the Ministry of Labour in 1988.

Until the late 1960s, no specific training for translators was offered in Brazil. As a result, the translators of Brazil were mainly its renowned writers and those who had learned foreign languages at school or abroad, or those who had a university language degree. A decree passed by the Ministry of Education during the 1960s enabled Faculties of Arts to expand their language courses so as to provide training for translators at university level. The first such courses were offered at the Catholic University at Rio de Janeiro and Porto Alegre, and at the Federal University of Rio Grande do Sul.

It was the pioneer work of Paulo Rónai (1907–93) that had a major impact on the study of translation in Brazil. Rónai wrote several books on translation. *Escola de tradutores* ('School of Translators', 1952) was the first book on translation to be published in Brazil. It was followed by *Homens contra Babel* ('Men against Babel', 1964), *Guia prático da tradução francesa* ('A Practical Guide to French Translation', 1967) and *A tradução vivida* ('Translation Experienced', 1976). He also published numerous papers and lectured widely on the subject. Several of Rónai's books have been revised, enlarged and reprinted many times; they have also been translated abroad (in Germany and Japan, for example). At a time when translation studies was still trying to find its feet, Rónai adopted a practical outlook, derived from his experience as a translator, but never ceased considering translation as an art.

A large number of works on the theory, practice and teaching of translation have been published since then, as well as papers, essays and journals. The theoretical reflections of the brothers Augusto de Campos and Haroldo de Campos (1970, 1976a, 1976b, 1979, 1981, 1986; see Vieira 1999) on their translation practice are the closest thing to a theory of translation in Brazil. Being Concrete poets, the brothers devoted themselves to the translation of authors who they felt have radically transformed poetic styles, such as Pound, cummings, Joyce, Mallarmé, Maiakovsky, Valéry, Poe, Lewis Carroll and John Cage, among others. Their view of translation privileges form over content and favours the introduction of new forms into the target language. For these views, they draw on Walter Benjamin, Roman Jakobson and Ezra Pound. What has captured Western imagination is an element which they draw specifically from Brazilian culture. This is the idea of 'cannibalism', derived from the Modernist movement of 1922 and the writings of Oswald de Andrade, particularly his 'Cannibalist Manifesto' (Andrade 1970; Bary 1991). The cannibalist metaphor for the act of translation is one of the very few Brazilian contributions to be acknowledged outside Brazil (see Bassnett 1993). It expresses the experience of a colonized people who devour what is offered to them by their colonizers but do not swallow it whole: quite the opposite, they spit out what is noxious to them, but what they keep they make wholly theirs by altering and changing it to suit their nutritional needs.

Further reading
Putnam 1948; Calógeras 1963; Burns 1966; Dulles 1969; Black 1977; Burns 1980; Hallewell 1982; Bordenave 1990; Souza 1990; Bary 1991; Wyler 1993.

HELOISA GONÇALVES BARBOSA
AND LIA WYLER

British tradition

There are, of course, several British traditions, though this entry covers in detail only the tradition brought about by the arrival during the fifth century of invaders from what are now Holland, Denmark and Germany, who settled in the central parts of the island and drove the Celtic inhabitants to its western and northern fringes (and, later, colonized Ireland similarly). Invasion and colonization have characterized the linguistic and cultural situation of these islands almost from the beginning, and translation has played an active role throughout. Since their arrival, the English – as they became – have been more than once under threat of invasion, but their cultural and linguistic hegemony has been seriously challenged only twice: during the period of the Viking invasions (eighth–tenth centuries), where two languages were spoken in the region overrun by the Vikings, and for the three hundred years after the Norman Conquest, where Anglo-Norman was initially the language of the conquerors and English the language of the conquered. In both cases

we are struck by the power of the native traditions to absorb and finally take over from the traditions of the invaders. Other invasions were accomplished more peacefully – witness the regular accommodations of the native traditions to traditions of classical learning – but with an equally energetic and important part played by translators and their translations. Indeed, the cultural situation of these islands has been such that, though the Celtic traditions still survive in the fringes to which the invaders consigned them, their recessive position is, regrettably, a reflex of the dominance of English: which may explain, though not justify, their neglect in this entry.

Introduction

The tradition of translation in the British Isles is long and varied. Consequently, it is desirable to summarize a number of important features before proceeding to describe individual periods in more detail.

In the Middle Ages the Catholic Church played a central role in the generation and authorization of medieval translation, especially into and from Latin. But its attitude to translation into the vernacular was not as positive as that of the Orthodox church; the clergy often viewed Latin as the norm and the vernacular as corrupt and barbaric. Admittedly, vernacular and Latin were mutually supportive in the areas of scientific and medical writings (Voigts 1989). Likewise, translation into Latin was a necessary condition of a work's wider circulation and/ or the translator's claim to membership of the select club which Latin culture represented. But such translation generally represented a challenge, direct or indirect, to the learning from which it originated (Copeland 1991). In the Middle Ages, the Renaissance and the nineteenth century, translation into the vernacular helped to create and consolidate a national/literary consciousness; hence Bishop Bryan Walton's view, in 1659, that the 1611 Bible could stand comparison with any other European version (Norton 1993: I.219). In the Augustan period, translation helped underwrite national/literary self-confidence: for instance, in Alexander Pope's *Imitations of Horace* (1734–7), Latin original and English version, on facing pages, dramatize the latter's transformations of the former.

Translation from vernaculars into English never enjoyed the same authority as from Latin, but a hierarchy of sorts operated in favour of French in the later Middle Ages and again after the Restoration. Consequently, the English sometimes preferred to use French: hence, the *Mémoires … du Comte de Gramont* (1713) were written in French by the exiled Anthony Hamilton, and translated into English (1714) by the French émigré Abel Boyer (1667–1729). Nearer our own time, Oscar Wilde (*Salome*) and Samuel Beckett could be cited similarly. At other periods French dominance was challenged, by Italian in the sixteenth century, and by German in the nineteenth. Translations from the vernacular sometimes aimed to contribute to better relations between the two countries and/or advance the cause of reform at home: Francis Newman (1843) and Sir Frederick Lascelles Wraxall (1862) translated writings about England by Huber and the exiled Frenchman Esquiros to challenge English insularity, contrasting the objectivity of the foreigner with the prejudiced character of comparable work by English writers. By contrast, Charlotte Brontë used French in *Villette* (1853) to show her monolingual heroine's difficulties abroad among perfidious French-speaking Catholics. Exile, voluntary or involuntary, plays an ongoing part in this tradition.

Translators often translated by way of an intermediate version in another language, or used the intermediate version as a crib, especially when material was available only recently and/or in unfamiliar languages. The original text is then seen more as the first step in a process of textual transmission than as an absolute point of reference: hence John Stuart Mill viewed Goethe and his English followers/translators Samuel Taylor Coleridge and Thomas Carlyle as constituting 'a single cultural phenomenon' (Ashton 1980: 25). At the same time, a medieval writer's claim to be translating from non-existent texts (Geoffrey of Monmouth in his *Historia*), or following a source even as he departs from it (Sir Thomas Malory in his *Morte D'Arthur*), indicates the powerful force of the *idea* of an authoritative original. Then, too, the original text might reach the translator embedded with the accre-

tions of commentators, or in company with another translation: William Caxton's translation of the *Legenda Aurea* of James of Varaggio supplemented the Latin with French and English versions; A. D. Coleridge's 1868 version of Goethe's *Egmont* included piano transcriptions of Beethoven's incidental music.

Unsurprisingly, the line between original and translation proves difficult to draw. In the publisher's blurb for Morley's Universal Library (1883–8), some translated texts appear under author's, followed by translator's, name; some under author's name alone; one, *Six Dramas of Calderon*, under translator's name (Edward Fitzgerald). The Everyman Library Euripides (1906) uses translations by Percy Bysshe Shelley, Dean Milman, Michael Woodhull and Robert Potter, but identifies the contributions only of published *authors*, namely Shelley and Milman. Translations which continued in print for any length of time almost became original works: when the 1611 Bible was revised in the 1870s, the revisers introduced 'as few alterations as possible … consistent with faithfulness' (Norton 1993: II.219).

The ethics of a fully commercial production line are clearly in evidence towards the end of the nineteenth century, but can be traced much earlier, in the commissioning of works by, and dedication of works to, patrons. In the fifteenth century, noble households provided important centres of translation activity. Sir John Harington produced his translation of *Orlando Furioso* (1591) at the direction of Elizabeth I (1533–1603), Queen of England and Ireland (1558–1603). Jonathan Birch dedicated his two-volume *Faust* (1839–43) to the Crown Prince and King of Prussia. The patron could also turn translator: Earl Rivers and the Earl of Worcester produced translations printed by William Caxton; Elizabeth I, translations from Latin and Greek, including the *Consolatio Philosophiae* of Boethius in 1593, and works by Plutarch, Horace and Euripides.

Sometimes the translator worked alone; more often, collaboratively. Translations of major texts such as the Bible or Homer were often so undertaken. There is no firm evidence of schools of translation like those in second-century Alexandria, the French court of Charles V, or the 'factory of translations' (G. Steiner 1975: 246) at Rome during the papacy of Nicholas V. The institutionalization of translation as a profession had to wait till the twentieth century.

Occasionally bilingual authors translated themselves, as in the case of Charles Duke of Orleans in the fifteenth century. Otherwise, a living author might be consulted during the course of the translation, for example Goethe by Carlyle and Hugo by Wraxall; Abel Boyer supplemented his translation of the *Philological Essay* (1713) with new material provided by the author. Sometimes, the author approved the result (Venuti 1995a: 25–8), though not always: Huber criticized before its publication (1843) Newman's version of his *English Universities*, which Newman had based on an unpublished translation by J. Palgrave Simpson. From the eighteenth century on, authorization was increasingly dependent on copyright law (Venuti 1995b). Earlier, authorization was generally linked to considerations of commission and patronage: hence the different names under which the 1611 Bible was known, the 'King James Bible' or the 'Authorized' version.

Translators regularly authorize their work by referring to previous translations – of, for example, the Bible, in this way used in the Middle Ages to authorize translations by King Alfred, John of Trevisa and the Wycliffite Bible. A sense of evolving traditions of theory and practice is regularly evidenced: John Oldham's version of Horace's *Ars Poetica* (1681) acknowledges versions by Ben Jonson and the Earl of Roscommon; Ezra Pound's Cavalcanti acknowledges Dante Gabriel Rossetti.

Simultaneous translations of the same text occur quite frequently. In the Middle Ages difficulties of communication may account for this phenomenon (Pearsall 1989: 7). Other explanations also obtain: literary rivalry, or the desire to cash in on a work's popularity. A good instance of the former is the publication of Thomas Tickell's translation of the *Iliad* Book I on 8 June 1715, two days after Pope's of Books I–IV.

Generally, the choice of medium for a translation depended on the perceived hierarchy or uses of literary models in the target language rather than on any requirement of fidelity to the source text. Prose was probably favoured in the late Middle Ages, by contrast with the sixteenth century (Norton 1993: I.178), by analogy with the learned Latin prose of the schoolmen; used for verse originals in some twentieth-century

Loeb translations, it recalls the literary form most familiar to modern readers, the novel. In the same way, debate over the relative merits of the source and the readers was often resolved theoretically in favour of the source, but practically in favour of the projected or actual readers. Edward Fitzgerald was outspoken about the translator's right to omit, add or alter: his *Oedipus* was 'neither a translation, nor a paraphrase … but "chiefly taken"' from Sophocles, attending more to 'the English reader of today' than to 'an Athenian theatre … 2000 years ago' (Fitzgerald 1880); it also cannibalized the earlier popular translation (1788) of the Revd Robert Potter. Texts which challenged orthodox opinion were especially liable to modification: early translations of Goethe's *Faust* mostly omitted heterodox religious material; most translations of the *Decameron* before 1930 cut or replaced the bawdiest story (III.10) or reverted to the original Italian (McWilliam 1972: 25–43).

The Middle Ages

In the Old English period (*c*.600–1100), though translation occurs both before and after his time, the work of King Alfred is of the first importance. In reaction to a perceived decline in intellectual life in England, which had left few able to read English or translate Latin, Alfred produced and commissioned a number of translated works – including the *Pastoral Care* of Pope Gregory, the *Soliloquies* of St Augustine and the *Consolation of Philosophy* by Boethius, principally for the 'youth of free men … [able] to devote themselves to it' (Swanton 1993: 62). Mainland Europe provides later instances of monarchs who instituted comparable translation projects, for example Alfonso X in Spain and Charles V in France; England, if we except the commissioning of the 1611 Bible by James I, hardly any. Alfred's translation project was geared to leaders of Church and state, and happy to use English to express complex ideas. The other major Old English translation project was that of Ælfric (*c*.950–*c*.1010), Abbot of Eynsham, who produced numerous adaptations and translations of the Old Testament and other religious works and described his procedures in his *Tract on the Old and New Testament*. But Ælfric's project was orientated differently, towards the simple faithful, from whom the riches of Latin learning needed to be safeguarded.

Something of this division, between translation for an elite and for the masses, and between a writer's confidence in, and distrust of, the vernacular, resurfaces regularly throughout the Middle English period. Thus, immediately after the Norman Conquest, translators use Anglo-Norman, by contrast with English, confident of belonging to a social elite (Pearsall 1977: 90–91). Anglo-Norman translations are associated with court and monastic centres. Several were produced by women, including, in the twelfth century, nuns from Barking, where one Clemence produced a verse translation of the *Passio* of St Katherine of Alexandria, and an unnamed nun a *Life* of St Edward the Confessor (Legge 1963).

For much of the Middle English period (*c.*1100–1500), then, two vernaculars were available, Anglo-Norman and English, and translations could be undertaken into either, or from one to the other. Anglo-Norman was 'the prestige vernacular' during the thirteenth century (Pearsall 1977: 87); Robert Grosseteste (*c.*1175–1253), a native Englishman cited as an authority in the prologue to the Wycliffite Bible, legislated for the laity's religious instruction in English, but mainly used French. Widely in use early in the fourteenth century, Anglo-Norman was still being used at court in the fifteenth. In such a linguistic situation the choice of vernacular for a translation inevitably reflected complex social and political pressures.

Until the mid-fourteenth century most Middle English translations are anonymous, and, except for Richard Rolle (d. 1349), whose Psalter was still in use a hundred years and more later, few translators seem to have had much sense of contributing to an evolving tradition or to have reached a very wide readership. But one production, the Auchinleck MS, *c.* 1330, containing anonymous translations of Anglo-Norman romances, has been accorded greater importance and explained as the product of a commercial scriptorium where 'a general "editor" … supervised the work of his translators and scribes' (Pearsall 1977: 145–6). The existence of commercial scriptoria cannot be conclusively proven in England before the fifteenth century (Pearsall 1989: 4–6); never-

theless, translation, dramatically on the increase from the late fourteenth century on, is increasingly marked by the professionalism associated with the commercial scriptorium.

Two writers represent the new professionalism clearly. The first is Geoffrey Chaucer (*c.*1340–*c.*1400), the court poet and foremost English writer of his day. His close translations include part of the *Roman de la Rose* by de Lorris and de Meun, the *Consolatio Philosophiae* of Boethius, the *Liber Consolationis et Consilii* of Albertano of Brescia in the French version of Renaud de Louens, and a *Treatise on the Astrolabe* for his son (1391). *Troilus and Criseyde*, based on Boccaccio's *Il Filostrato*, alternates close translation with free invention and material from Boethius. Chaucer's importance was acknowledged by contemporaries at home and abroad – notably, by Eustache Deschamps, who called him a 'grant translateur' – and by followers at home (notable among the latter, Thomas Hoccleve and John Lydgate). The quantity and range of Chaucer's translated work are striking. Equally important is his decision to publish only in English, which contributed powerfully to the establishment of English thereafter as the principal literary language of England.

The principal translation of the second 'writer' (probably several, all anonymous) was equally important: the Wycliffite Bible. This was a collaborative venture, part of an ongoing debate about vernacular translation of the Bible. Names associated with its production have included John Wycliffe, John Purvey, Nicholas Hereford, and John of Trevisa. The work, possibly begun in the 1370s, survives in about 250 manuscripts.

The Wycliffite Bible survives in at least two major versions, the earlier more literal than the later: part of a collaborative project of book publication, distribution and ownership, well under way by 1388. The nature of the translation is revealed by the so-called General Prologue. Chapter 15 describes the practices of the translator(s), argues for a meaning at least 'as trewe and opin in English as … in Latyn', appeals to historical precedent, and describes the careful collaborative exercise that produced the translation (Hudson 1978: 67–72).

As important as the translators' concern for the truth and accuracy of their text is their developing understanding of the needs of their readers. Hence they replaced their literal translation, as less 'open' to understanding, by a later, slightly freer translation. There were few precedents in Bible translation in the Middle English period to suggest this approach. Most translations paraphrased the text and/or included secondary material; alternatively and exceptionally, the Rolle Psalter, though including an extensive commentary, translated the Bible verses very literally. Comparison with these other versions shows the considerable achievement of the Wycliffite translations.

Ecclesiastical reaction was swift and decisive. By 1409 the Archbishop of Canterbury had forbidden the making and use of all unlicensed Bible translations; thereafter the Wyclifffites mostly operated clandestinely. The prohibition ironically preceded a considerable increase in the range and variety of other translated texts in the fifteenth century, increasingly in prose, by named translators. Two names must suffice to suggest this range. In around 1440 Robert Parker produced a translation of Palladius which his patron, Humphrey Duke of Gloucester, corrected in draft, having commissioned it, with others, as part of a project to 'enrich English letters' (Pearsall 1977: 240); about 1470 Malory completed his *Morte D'Arthur*, a work partly from French, partly from an earlier English work, and partly original. The *Morte* was published in 1485 by William Caxton, with whose work we draw towards the Renaissance.

The sixteenth and early seventeenth centuries: Reformation and Renaissance

If Caxton's presses had immediate practical effects on the transmission of vernacular texts, the translations of the Wycliffite Bible and Chaucer indicate the two areas in which translation activity really took off in the sixteenth century – in particular, during the first ten years of Elizabeth I's reign (1558–68), when four times as many translations were produced as in the fifty previous years (Barnstone 1993: 203): the Bible and classical literature. Thanks to the erratic but powerful support of the monarchy, translation

helped forge a national identity both English and (religiously and intellectually) reformed. In this project, Bible translation, much of it published abroad, plays a crucial role.

Bible translations

In the run-up to and aftermath of Henry VIII's break with Rome, the pressure for religious reform, originating once more in clerical circles, led to an explosion of Bible translations. The first and most important was William Tyndale's translation of the New Testament (1525), based for the first time on the Greek edition of Desiderius Erasmus (1516; see DUTCH TRADITION). Faced with the ongoing ban on vernacular Bible translations, Tyndale travelled to the Continent to publish it. In 1526 it entered England illegally (Daniell 1994).

Within a decade relations had altered dramatically between Henry VIII and the papacy, and large numbers of vernacular Bibles were circulating in England. These included pirated editions of Tyndale's New Testament and his 1534 revision; Miles Coverdale's complete Bible, published in Zurich in 1535 and in England in 1537; and a Bible issued by John Rogers under the pseudonym of John Matthew (Antwerp, 1537), based on Tyndale and Coverdale. In 1539 a revision of the Rogers Bible appeared, by Richard Taverner, in the year that Thomas Cromwell, Henry VIII's Vicar-General, appointed Coverdale to oversee the printing of the Bible. The title-page of Coverdale's new edition, the Great (1539), showed Henry VIII handing Bibles to Cromwell and Archbishop Cranmer to distribute to a grateful crowd (Wilson 1976: 70; King 1982: 192): a clear representation of the involvement of the state in the publication of Bible translations.

From then until the 1611 version, a whole series of Bible translations was produced, the results of the 'wishes and counter wishes' (Kitagaki 1981: 45) of Henry's Protestant and Catholic successors. Amongst the Protestants who fled to the Continent after the accession of Queen Mary in 1553 were a team of translators who produced the Geneva Bible. This translation was the most widely read book in Elizabethan England (Jensen 1995: 31), reprinted as late as

1715 and used even by those who favoured the 1611 Bible (Norton 1993), although episcopal opposition prevented its printing in England until 1575: by then the Bishops had attempted unsuccessfully to replace it with an edition of their own, the Bishops' Bible (1568), a revision of the Great Bible (Norton 1993: I.116).

Lastly, King James I convened a conference at Hampton Court in 1604, at which agreement was given to a proposal for the creation of a new translation which would be, in the words of the proposer, John Reynolds, 'answerable to the truth of the Originall' (Kitagaki 1981: 48). Although, unlike the Great and Bishops' Bibles, this Bible was never officially authorized (Wilson 1976: 147), the King, with Bishop Bancroft, gave a set of rules for its making to six teams of translators. It was to be a revision, rather than a new translation; traditional readings (principally, those of the Bishops' Bible) should be preserved as far as possible; doctrinal tendentiousness was to be checked, and accuracy achieved, through a multiple checking system within and between committees. The mood was one of conciliation rather than, as before, of contestation, and the translators used the many translations from Tyndale onwards to create, in Reynolds's words, 'out of many good [Bibles] … one principall good one' (Kitagaki 1981: 63): the 1611 Bible. Of course, the huge success of this version owes as much to economic and political as to literary interests (Norton 1993: I.212ff.).

Meanwhile exiled Catholics had also produced a vernacular Bible, known as the Rheims–Douai version (1582–1610). The preface explains that this 'Catholic translation' precisely follows the 'old vulgar approved Latin' (Jones 1966: 111). Revised in the eighteenth century by Bishop Challoner, and again in the nineteenth, it remained the official translation for Roman Catholics until the twentieth century. Throughout that period the 'old vulgar approved Latin' was an integral part of Roman Catholic self-definition; if we except translations from the Greek in 1836 and from Greek and Hebrew in 1935–49, the Vulgate remained the base for Catholic translations until the appearance of the Jerusalem Bible in the 1960s: its last great monument is the translation of it (1945–49) by Ronald Knox (Dayras 1993: 44–59).

Classical and other secular literature

Although the translator's duties were less stringent in relation to secular than to sacred texts, the translation of secular material during the sixteenth and early seventeenth centuries runs broadly parallel to that of the Bible during this period. Latin was still the main language of scholarship, but one major difference between the sixteenth century and earlier periods is the direct influence of Greek literature. Translations of Demosthenes, Homer, Isocrates and Plutarch occur frequently, often by way of an intermediate source: thus Sir Thomas North's translation of Plutarch's *Lives* (1579) was based on Jacques Amyot's French translation.

As with the Bible translations, different translations of the same secular text were frequently in competition with each other, an economic rivalry associated with the increase in the publishing trade. Thus Thomas Peend complains, in the preface to his *Hermaphroditus and Salmacis* (1564), from Ovid's *Metamorphoses*, about Arthur Golding's having forestalled him with a translation of the complete text. Moreover, translators often discuss their work in terms of contestation: Philemon Holland, the 'translator general' of the age, described his enterprise as a conquest (Sampson 1941: 145). Secular translations were often the site of a debate both ongoing and ancient (and regularly focused by the question of Bible translation) about the adequacy of the vernacular to transmit the riches of classical learning, whether Greek, Latin, or even of the other European vernaculars.

Others saw the translative task, by contrast, as a patriotic act to improve the cultural position of the English nation. Nicholas Grimald, by translating Cicero's *Thre Bokes of Duties* (1556), wanted to 'do likewise for my countrimen: as Italians, Spaniardes, Dutchmen, and other foreins have liberally done for theyrs' (Jones 1966: 44). Not only Greek and Roman authors were translated. North translated the *Fables of Bidpai* (c.1589) from an intermediate Italian version of the Arabic. Other translators turned to European languages: Alexander Barclay's *Shyp of … Folys* (1509) was translated, by way of Locher's Latin version, from

Brandt's *Narrenschiff*; Thomas Hoby's *Book of the Courtier* (1561) came from Castiglione's Italian; a Spanish romance, by de Calahorra, was translated as *The Mirrour of Knighthood* (1580) by Margaret Tyler; Montaigne's French *Essays* were translated by John Florio (1603); Christine de Pisan's *Book of the City of Ladies*, in 1521, by Brian Anslay (the last English translation of any of her works until the late twentieth century).

There were opposing views, hindering access to certain texts. Some claimed that translating into the vernacular would hinder the study of Latin and Greek (Jones 1966: 19). Scholars continued to produce Latin texts, often later translated into English: for example, Sir Thomas More's *Utopia* (1516) and William Camden's *Britannia* (*c*.1586), translated by Ralph Robinson in 1551 and Holland in 1610 respectively. John Skelton, who produced a translation of Diodorus Siculus from the Latin version of Poggio, also wrote several works in Latin. Nor were all texts thought equally fit for translation. Christopher Marlowe's translations of Ovid, published clandestinely, were banned and burned as seditious in 1586 by order of the Archbishop of Canterbury. Until 1640 and Edward Dacre's translation of it, Machiavelli's *The Prince* was available only by way of a hostile French text, the *Contra-Machiavel* (1576) by Gentillet, translated by Simon Patericke in 1602. English readers had similarly to wait until 1620 for a complete text of Boccaccio's *Decameron*, and until 1694 for the whole of Rabelais' *Gargantua and Pantagruel* (begun before 1653 by Sir Thomas Urquhart; completed by Peter Motteux).

Though able to commission and read translations, women were largely restricted, as in the Middle Ages, to participating on the pious fringes of translation activity. In general, women translators (usually gently born, like Margaret More Roper and the Cooke sisters) produced literal religious translations (Lamb 1985: 124), though secular translations were produced by such as Elizabeth I, Margaret Tyler and Mary Sidney. Despite this marginality, the 'voices' of women translators, through their prefaces, construct other perspectives on the practice of translation, which briefly disrupt the dominant male traditions (Robinson 1995).

In this period translation aimed, generally, to advance eloquence and/or learning. On occasion, two audiences were addressed at once: the learned and the ignorant, the courtly and the

rude. Depending on the type of translation, the centres of translative activity were located now at the universities, now at the court. Original writing reflects the clear influence of newly-discovered or newly-valued forms. Thus the Italian sonnet is a vital element in the literary projects of the sixteenth century, translated and imitated by Thomas Wyatt and the Earl of Surrey, and 'naturalized' by Shakespeare; the pastoral, by way of Greek (Theocritus), Latin (Mantuan and Virgil) and Italian (Tasso and Guarini), takes root with Sir Philip Sidney and Edmund Spenser. Classical epics, especially those of Virgil and Homer – known to the Middle Ages but not translated in their own right until the sixteenth century: Virgil, by Gavin Douglas, Surrey, and Thomas Phaer; Homer, by George Chapman – gave rise to the epics of Spenser and John Milton; the epyllia of Ovid influenced Marlowe, Chapman and Shakespeare; translations from Greek and Roman drama contributed powerfully to the Elizabethan and Jacobean theatre.

The seventeenth and eighteenth centuries

This period of translation activity is dominated at the end of the seventeenth century by two figures, John Dryden and Alexander Pope, and, in the late eighteenth century, by the more complex figure of Alexander Tytler.

The distinctive emphases of Dryden and Pope, however, can be seen earlier, in embryo, in the prefaces to Chapman's *Iliad*, which had by stages attempted to negotiate and regularize a theoretical frame for the process of translation. At first, Chapman viewed translation as straightforward linguistic mimesis (preface to the *Seaven Bookes of the Iliad*, 1598). He then moved to more sophisticated discussions of a poetic art of translation (preface to the complete *Iliad*). He was not alone in so doing. Jonson's woodenly literal 1604 translation of Horace's *Ars Poetica* might have exemplified the first approach: the brilliant transformations of Roman satirists in his plays, the second.

Chapman's understandings anticipate developments during the next 200 years. First, during the exile of the court to France after the Civil War, court translators often practised a freer translation method for poetry, one evidenced in aristocratic circles since the 1620s (T. R. Steiner 1975: 64; Lefevere 1992a: 46). Notable exiles were John Denham, Abraham Cowley and Richard Fanshawe; both Denham and Cowley commented on their more liberal translative strategies, Denham in a poem on the translation by Fanshawe, of the *Pastor Fido* (1640) and in the preface to his own translation of *The Destruction of Troy* (1656), Cowley in the preface to his *Pindarique Odes* (1656).

The Restoration brought about major changes in literary attitudes, which owed much to the FRENCH TRADITION. Unsurprisingly, therefore, though Dryden praised Cowley and Denham, in his important preface to *Ovid's Epistles By Several Hands* (1680), 'for freeing translation from servility' (T. R. Steiner 1975: 63), he also distanced himself from what he saw as their excesses, and created a new model which would shape theory and practice for the following century, 'the earliest exhaustive division of translation' (ibid.: 28), under the three heads of metaphrase, paraphrase and imitation. He rejects both metaphrase (literalism in translation: the earlier of Chapman's positions) and imitation (abandonment of the source text: the 'excesses' of Cowley) in favour of the *via media* of paraphrase (translation with latitude). He modified this position in the *Dedication of the Aeneis* (1697), which talks of 'steer[ing] betwixt the two extreames of paraphrase and literal translation': understanding the spirit of the original author while adapting the translation to the aesthetic canons of the age. Dryden's *Aeneid* is widely regarded as a massive achievement. Pope's work clearly reflects Dryden's influence: the preface to his *Iliad* (1715–20) insists on moderation, and the need for an accuracy which avoids literalism or paraphrase.

Translations of Homer were, then as later – to put it mildly – a site of critical contention. Pope's translation situates itself adversarially in relation to earlier English versions by Chapman, Thomas Hobbes, John Ogilby and John Dryden, and was itself criticized by Thomas Bentley in 1735 on four counts: 'first [it is] in English, Secondly in Rhyme, thirdly not from the Original [Pope had used Latin, French and English sources], but fourthly from a French translation and that in Prose by a woman too [i.e. Mme Dacier]' (Levine 1991: 220). William Cowper also criti-

cized it when producing his own *Iliad* in 1791; so too, later, did Matthew Arnold.

The paradoxical obverse of this hostility is the fact that Pope's *Iliad* was to a degree, and his *Odyssey* (1725–6) still more, a collaborative venture; in the latter he was assisted by Elijah Fenton and William Brome, one of the translators of Mme Dacier's Homer. Another instance of collaboration occurred later in the century when Tobias Smollett gathered a group of translators together in his 'literary factory' (Sampson 1941: 423) in Chelsea and published a new translation of *Don Quixote* (1755), and a major translation of Voltaire's works (1761–74) in collaboration with Thomas Francklin.

The translation of Mme Dacier objected to by Bentley points to an important difference between women translators in this and the preceding periods. Though no English woman had yet ventured to translate Homer, women were translating a greater variety of texts than previously. At the start of the period Aphra Behn produced a version of De Brilhac's play *Agnes de Castro* (1688), contributed to Dryden's *Ovid's Epistles*, and in the preface to her translation of Fontanelle's *Discovery of New Worlds* (1688) 'sought to say something of [the] translation of prose', a subject which had previously received little comment (Kitagaki 1981: 282). In the eighteenth century Elizabeth Carter translated the complete works of Epictetus for the first time (1749–52), and Charlotte Brooke published the first anthology of translations of Gaelic poetry from Ireland in 1789.

The revival in Celtic literature, of which Brooke's work was part, had led during the century to translations from Welsh by Evan Evans (1764), and, by way of intermediate Latin versions, by Samuel Johnson and Thomas Gray; it had also resulted in the so-called translations, from the Gaelic of Ossian, of James Macpherson (c.1760). This revival accompanied a developing interest in the translation of oriental and Teutonic languages. George Sale translated the QUR'ĀN into English in 1734; Gray wrote texts in imitation of Old Norse in 1761; William Jones, the first English scholar to master Sanskrit, produced translations from Persian and other Asiatic texts. The nineteenth-century interest in medievalizing/orientalizing translations shown, for example, by Edward Fitzgerald and William Morris, is a natural development of this process.

The century ends, much as it had begun, with a major work of theory: Tytler's *Essay on the Principles of Translation* (1791). Tytler's theories resemble those of fellow Scot George Campbell, whose preface to his translation of the Gospels (1789) shares many of Tytler's conclusions about the translative process. Tytler's *Essay*, with a systematic approach typical of the period, reacts against Dryden's concept of paraphrase and the loose translations that resulted from it. According to Tytler, translation should give a complete transcript of the idea of the original work, the style and manner of writing should have the same character as in the original, and translation should have all the ease of the original. Granted, the *Essay* still uses eighteenth-century terminology ('genius', 'wit', 'taste'), and its standards for 'assessing success in composition are ... essentially aesthetic' (Huntsman 1978: xlii) or evaluative. Nevertheless, a sea change is observable in Tytler's claim that the original text provides the ultimate point of reference as well as in his published translations from Italian (Petrarch, 1784) and German (Schiller, 1792). Tytler is as prophetic as, in their different ways, the translations of Brooke and Gray had been.

The nineteenth century: Romanticism and the Victorian era

Romanticism distinguished itself sharply from the preceding age in several important ways.

After the Restoration, and for much of the eighteenth century, French had been the prestige vernacular. Late in the century there was a decisive shift from French towards German – in particular, the works of Goethe, Schiller and A.W. Schlegel (Bassnett 1991: 64–5) – often, initially, in intermediate French versions. Romantic writers cut their teeth on translations from the German: Sir Walter Scott on Goethe's *Goetz von Berlichingen* (1799), Samuel Taylor Coleridge on Schiller's *Wallenstein* (1800), Shelley on parts of Goethe's *Faust*. Within three years of Goethe's completed *Faust* (1832) there were five complete translations. Other German writers were made similarly accessible to Victorian readers by George Eliot, Sarah

Austin, J. C. Hare and Bishop Thirlwall, and William Wallace.

The ideas of the German Romantics were crucial in shaping a new self-understanding for the translator (George Steiner 1975; Robinson 1991). As previously noted, from the Renaissance to the eighteenth century translators had generally, if in different ways, 'domesticated' their work. Now, in Carlyle's words, 'the duty of a translator [was] ... to present the work exactly as ... in the [original]' (Ashton 1980: 84). Pope and Dryden both came in for criticism on this score. Admittedly, rejection of the earlier practices and/or theories was not total: Birch thought 'Pope-ish' practice inappropriate for his *Faust*, but was willing to invoke the Earl of Roscommon's authority.

At the same time, the Romantics were also rediscovering the literature of the Italian Renaissance, especially Dante, whose *Divina Commedia* was as important for nineteenth-century readers as *Faust*. Of first importance here is Henry Francis Cary's translation of 1814, one of the most successful translations of the century. Nor should we forget how artists like Gustave Doré and John Flaxman mediated the Dantes of Cary and Ichabod Wright to English readers, or how William Blake used Cary as a crib for his own 'translation', the *Illustrations to the Divine Comedy*.

The second half of the nineteenth century developed broadly along the same lines, though, arguably, its own 'translation' of Romantic theory and practice reveals a strongly 'domesticating' agenda in line with the overall imperial projects of the age. We can focus these generalizations by studying a few years, not entirely at random. Thus, in 1861–2, translations appeared of large parts of the *Iliad* and the *Odyssey* by Philip Worsley, Joseph Dart, James Landon and Dean Henry Alford; of Dante and his contemporaries by Dante Gabriel Rossetti; of the first two parts of the *Commedia* by Mrs C. H. Ramsay (1862); of Old Norse (*Burnt Njal*) by Sir George Dasent; of individual poems into and out of Greek and Latin, and out of Italian and German, with facing-page originals, by Lord Lyttelton and William Gladstone (1861); and an authorized translation of Hugo's *Les Misérables* by Wraxall, whose published translations in this two-year period include travel-cum-adventure stories, the autobiography of a French detective, and two works by Esquiros, who had helped with the Hugo. These productions are, admittedly, of varying significance. The Lyttelton–Gladstone venture – as Newman noted, amateur work, consisting of set-piece translations – was very different from Wraxall's adventure yarns. Alongside Rossetti's finely nuanced awareness that 'a translation … remains perhaps the most direct form of commentary' (Rossetti 1911), Wraxall was cutting an obscene expression 'which may be historical but is disgusting' (and, since the following chapter 'consist[ed] of a glorification of this abominable word', cutting that too) (Wraxall 1862). Moreover, the Homer translations were part of a booming industry: a reviewer of Morris's *Aeneid* (1875; Faulkner 1973: 216) noted the regularity of their publication.

Inevitably, the foregoing account omits important names and texts: the orientalizers Edward Fitzgerald, Robert Burton, James Legge (who translated from Chinese) and Max Müller (from Sanskrit); Lady Charlotte Guest (*Mabinogi*); revisions of the 1611 and Reims–Douai Bibles, the most important of the former (1881–95) known as the *Revised Version*; Eleanor Marx Aveling, and the Ibsen translators William Archer and Edmund Gosse.

It also omits Arnold's *On Translating Homer* (1861) which, like Pope and Cowper before him, criticized several translations of Homer, including those of Wright (1859–65) and Newman (1856), the latter already under attack for a translation of Horace (Venuti 1995a: 124–7). Both replied in kind; Arnold replied to the latter in *Last Words* (1862). For all their differences (ibid.:118–46), Arnold and Newman were both children of the Romantic revolution. Both shared with most of their contemporaries the Romantic view of the translator's 'duty … to be faithful' (Newman) to the original, as the translators of the 1611 Bible had been (Arnold), and of the necessary 'union of a translator with his original' in a good translation (Arnold). Their disagreement, then, was less about ends than about means. For Arnold, since Homer is a classic, the translation should adopt the language of that undoubted classic, the 1611 Bible. Its metre, however, should replicate the original's hexameters. Newman, who saw Homer as primitive and popular, used ballad metre and what he called a 'Saxo-Norman' language and a later writer 'Wardour Street

English' (Venuti 1995a: 141–2; Kelly 1979). Against Arnold's biblical model, Newman's was of the missionary whose translation for the 'Feejees' retained the phrase 'Lamb of God' and risked unintelligibility.

This protracted and largely pointless exercise in irony and acrimony cast long shadows. Arnold's authority was widely acknowledged in the nineteenth century (and well into the twentieth); his recommended 'King James English' was adopted by Benjamin Jowett and Andrew Lang. Newman's practice was largely ignored. But, as Venuti (1995a) notes, it represents an important tendency in nineteenth-century translation, one anticipated by the medievalizing translations of Robert Southey, and echoed in Robert Browning's *Agamemnon* (Robinson 1991: 245) and the very different work of Morris and Rossetti, to 'foreignize' the original (Venuti 1995a: 20) and make readers conscious of the gap between their own culture and the Other which the original embodies. This distinction between recessive 'foreignizing' and dominant 'domesticating' strains of translation resembles another made regularly in the nineteenth century – in the prefaces of Cary, Birch, Mrs Ramsay, Newman and Arnold – between what John Benson Rose called 'scholar's translations' (*Greek Dramas*, 1867–72) and those destined for the common reader, a distinction with clear echoes of the theorizings of German Romanticism.

The present

The twentieth century, and beyond, owes much of its agenda, in respect of translation, to the assumptions and practice of the nineteenth. Foreign classics have continued to be translated in popular imprints which appeal to an increasingly monolingual readership, such as World's Classics (1901), Everyman (1906–), Loeb (1912–), and Penguin Classics (1946–), the last-named distinguished by its decision to commission new translations of all published works. Important translations have been produced by Constance Garnett and Max Hayward (Russian classics), Arthur Waley (Chinese poetry), Helen Waddell (medieval Latin lyrics), W. Scott Moncrieff and E.V. Rieu (Greek classics). During the period 1948–86, according to the *Index Translationum*, literary translations of this sort accounted for 35 per cent of all translations published in Britain.

Similarly, the nineteenth-century 'foreignizing' translations by professional poets have their equivalents in the twentieth century, above all, in the translations of the American-born Ezra Pound. Foreignizing translations in Britain include the adaptations of Greek and Roman drama by Ted Hughes (Seneca's *Oedipus*, 1969) and Tony Harrison (Aeschylus's *Oresteia*, 1981).

Translation is now more professionally organized than ever before. Translation agencies have sprung up in large numbers; academic and professional courses and qualifications are becoming the order of the day in Britain, especially at postgraduate level. More importantly, a paradigm shift has taken place in the understanding of translation itself as a phenomenon since the 1970s. Terry Eagleton's review essay 'Translation and Transformation' (1977) illustrates this shift. The main thrust of Eagleton's account, in the light of 'recent semiotic enquiry', is to undermine the opposition of 'source' and 'target' text and the 'fetish of the primary text' (ibid.: 72) taken for granted in writing about translation, replacing it by 'the notion of *intertextuality*' (emphasis in original). Eagleton emphasizes the problematic hermeneutic issues of systems of signification of which translation is a paradigmatic case. At the centre of this new criticism is the attempted displacement of evaluative and purely formal criticism, and a recognition of the importance of new developments in cultural and critical theory.

In the light of these developments, the final decade of the twentieth century and the beginning of the twenty-first century witnessed an upsurge of interest in translation studies in Britain: new periodicals from very different perspectives (*Translation and Literature*, 1993–; *The Translator*, 1995–; *The Interpreter and Translator Trainer*, 2007–; *The Sign Language Translator and Interpreter*, 2007–; *Translation Studies*, 2008–); new series (such as *Topics in Translation*, *Translation Theories Explored*, *Translation Practices Explained*) and, as noted earlier, numerous courses on translation in all its aspects. The omens look good for developments in translation studies in Britain.

Further reading

Brand 1957; Cohen 1962; Legge 1963; Jones 1966; Hargreaves 1969; George Steiner 1975; T.R. Steiner 1975; Wilson 1976; Pearsall 1977; Kelly 1979; Ashton 1980; Bassnett 1980/1991; Kitagaki 1981; Hermans 1985b; Hudson 1985, 1988; McGerr 1988; Ellis *et al.* 1989; Copeland 1991; Godden and Lagidae. 1991; Levine 1991; Robinson 1991; Lefevere 1992a; Norton 1993; Robinson 1995; Venuti 1995a; Ellis *et al.* 1996.

ROGER ELLIS AND LIZ OAKLEY-BROWN

Bulgarian tradition

The earliest people known to have inhabited the Bulgarian lands in the Balkan Peninsula were the Thracians (an Indo-European tribe). They developed a rich culture and lived in close contact with Byzantium as well as the Persia of the Aechemenides and other Indo-European peoples in Asia Minor; in addition to Greek they understood the languages of the Huns, Sarmates and Avars. In the sixth century they gradually mixed with the tribes of the Eastern group of Southern Slavs, the Protobulgarians led by Khan Asparoukh (*c.*644–701), who came from the north and settled in present-day north-east Bulgaria at the end of the sixth century.

The year 681 saw the foundation of the first Slavonic Bulgarian state, established through the merger of Slavonic and Protobulgarian tribes which adopted the name 'Bulgarians'. The process of the formation and consolidation of the Bulgarian people and statehood continued from the seventh to the middle of the ninth century. In 865, Tsar Boris I (852–89) converted the country to Christianity; this helped overcome tribal differences, since there were many different pagan religions in the area at the time, and established a powerful medieval Slavonic state, emulating the cultural standards of neighbouring Byzantium.

Protobulgarian inscriptions preserved on stones, metal vessels and other surfaces reveal that both the Greek alphabet and Protobulgarian runes were used. The best known example is the Horseman of Madara: a stone relief depicting a ruler or deity from the eighth century, with

Protobulgarian inscriptions in the Greek language.

The medieval period: ninth to fourteenth centuries

Medieval Bulgarian literature started with the translations of Cyril (827–69) and Methodius (826–85) in the ninth century. Cyril and Methodius were brothers, natives of Thessaloniki; Slavonic enlighteners, inventors of the Slavonic/Cyrillic script, founders of Slavonic and Bulgarian literature and champions of an independent Slavonic church and culture. Cyril was educated in the Magnaur School in Constantinople and became a teacher of philosophy at the same school. He gave the first definition of philosophy in the Slavonic language and was an eloquent speaker and talented poet. Methodius served in the army and afterwards became the governor of a Slavonic principality. Both had excellent knowledge of the Byzantine culture and language as well as the ancient classics. They spoke Slavonic, Latin and Hebrew and were sent on diplomatic and preaching missions to the Saracens (Cyril, in 851), to Rome, where they defended the right of every people to be educated in their native language before the Pope, and to Moravia (862/3) to defend Christianity. Having created the Slavonic alphabet, Cyril and Methodius were the first in medieval Europe to try and assert the vernacular as the official Bulgarian language, replacing Latin as the language of the church.

The young Slavonic states in the area were gradually converted to Christianity as the rivalry between Rome and Constantinople grew. In the ninth century, the newly established Bulgarian state felt the spiritual need for enlightenment, a written culture and an alphabet; this was also true of other Slavonic peoples. The Slavonic/Cyrillic alphabet created by Cyril and Methodius played a major role in this process. The Old Bulgarian literary language was based on the vernacular of the Bulgarian Slavs. It performed the function of a common written language for all Slavonic peoples and served as a target language for translation, irrespective of whether the source text was in Greek (given that many adopted the Eastern Orthodox faith) or Latin (for those who joined the Catholic Church).

Cyril and Methodius used the new alphabet for the first translations from Greek of the New Testament, the Psalms, the Apostles, selected church masses, as well as books of various genres and styles, for example *Nomocanone* ('The Law on Judging People'; a legal treatise) and *Pateric*, a collection of essays on general topics. Their greatest feat, however, was the translation of the Bible; this translation played an important role in developing Slavonic culture.

The work of Cyril and Methodius constituted a cultural project of enormous dimensions. It proves that translation can instigate enduring changes in the cultural make-up of a nation. The creation of the Slavonic alphabet and the translation of the Christian Scriptures into Old Bulgarian had a number of important consequences. First, it broke the dogma of trilingual church service (Hebrew, Greek and Latin), thus leading to the recognition of the Slavonic language as an important element of European Christian culture. Second, it questioned the requirement for literal translation of the Bible and made possible a number of changes within Christian culture, thereby enabling the Slavonic culture to make the relevant connections with its own ancient traditions and specific world view. And finally, by translating the Bible and other religious works into Old Bulgarian Cyril and Methodius created a perfect cultural product in a language which had not previously had any written texts.

Cyril and Methodius developed a distinctive method of translation. They believed in word-for-word translation, based on a quantitative matching of key words in the original and the translated text. However, they also believed in the need for creative interpretation, so that the idea of word-for-word translation was not applied in its traditional form. Where the quantitative matching of words conflicted with what they perceived to be the meaning of the text or jeopardized the intelligibility of the translation, they gave priority to meaning as the invariant element and abandoned the principle of quantitative matching. In fact, their word-for-word translations were very close to what most people would see as free translation: they created neologisms, inserted additional words for clarification and elucidation of the broad context, and adjusted the translations to the linguistic and stylistic norms of Old Bulgarian.

Cyril and Methodius thus founded the first school of translation in Bulgaria, and their work provided a standard for other translators during that period. The influence of their great cultural project was, however, confined to Bulgaria; in the Slavonic regions under the Catholic Church, the idea of performing the liturgy in the Slavonic language remained unacceptable. Expelled from Moravia, Cyril and Methodius's disciples came to Bulgaria and continued their work with the support of the Bulgarian tsars.

We have no substantial evidence for the existence of interpreters in Bulgaria during the Middle Ages. However, we do know that Anastasius Librarian (800–80), a Roman clergyman and writer, acted as interpreter for the Pope when Rome attempted to convert the Bulgarians to Christianity and when Cyril and Methodius visited the Pope. Indirect evidence for the use of interpreters may also be drawn from the Latin clergy's stipulation that Cyril and Methodius, as well as their disciples, preach only in Latin, which implies that their sermons were interpreted into Bulgarian for the audience.

Schools of translation in medieval Bulgaria

From the ninth to the eleventh century the translation traditions established by Cyril and Methodius flourished in Ohrida and Preslav, the literary centres of feudal Bulgaria, where the disciples of the two brothers carried out intensive literary translation and educational work. Although operating with an identical language, the schools of translation which evolved in Ohrida and Preslav worked with different genres, employed different methods of translation and consequently developed different attitudes to the Greek source texts. The tension between the free approach of the Ohrida school and the formal approach of the Preslav school had a role to play in shaping the Old Bulgarian culture, which proves that attitudes to translation can generate different cultural and ideological paradigms that reflect the world view typical of a certain epoch.

In the Ohrida school (late 9th century), in the south-west of Bulgaria, church books were translated from Greek. The prevalent approach was one of free translation. While recognizing equivalence of meaning as the ultimate objective, preference was given to free translation in terms of syntax and word order, and the use of descriptive strategies was allowed. The work of Climent of Ohrida (c.840–916), founder of the Ohrida school, illustrates this approach. His translations of Byzantine writers such as John Chrysostom and John Damascene, as well as various religious texts and sermons, took the form of 're-tellings' of moral stories.

The Preslav school of translation was also established at the end of the ninth century, in the north-eastern parts of Bulgaria; Preslav was the capital city of the first Bulgarian kingdom. The Preslav translators tried to stay as close as possible to the Greek originals and to achieve equivalence of meaning by reproducing the morphological, syntactic and word-formation peculiarities of the original Greek syntax, even when this meant violating the norms of Old Bulgarian.

The principles of translation developed by the Preslav school were ideologically motivated. First, uncompromising faithfulness to the original meant that it was impossible for heretical ideas to find their way into the holy texts. Second, the preoccupation with accuracy with regard to classical texts reflected a concern on the part of Bulgarian culture to imitate the high models of Byzantine civilization. Even the selection of texts, with exclusively philosophical and polemic content, demonstrates the scope of the cultural and ideological project of the Preslav school of translation.

One of the best known translators during this period was John Exarch, who typically intermixed translations with his own creative work. His most important translations were *Six Days*, a compilation from several Byzantine authors which described the Christian cosmogony and the achievements of scientific thought, and the philosophical work *Source of Knowledge* by John Damascene, known in Old Bulgarian literature under the title 'Heaven' or 'Theology'. In the prefaces to these two translations, John Exarch expressed his theoretical views on the way in which Greek texts had to be translated into Bulgarian and on the practice of compilation, i.e. borrowing material from other authors. The idea that what matters is the translation of the meaning rather than mere sounds lay at the heart of the first Bulgarian and Slavonic theory of translation expounded by John Exarch. He rejected word-for-word translation and verbose explanations as deviations from the original and urged translators to aim for equivalence of meanings.

During the three centuries which followed the reign of Tsar Simeon (864–927), there was no specific school with uniform principles or conceptualized attitudes to translation. The overall tendency was to translate into an intelligible language, one that reflected the living speech of the people. This is clear, for instance, in the Apocrypha of the Bogomils; the Bogomils were Bulgarian heretics whose translations were intended to mediate between the high and low spheres of medieval Bulgarian culture. Their work was experimental and they sought to use translation as a means of transforming cultural and ideological paradigms.

The flourishing of literary and translation activity continued in the work of the Turnovo school in the fourteenth century. Its precursor was the Sveta Gora (Aton) school, which elaborated new principles of translation. Like Western humanists, the leader of the Turnovo school, Euthimius of Turnovo (c.1327–c.1401; Bulgarian patriarch, writer, philosopher and philologist), worked on 'the rectification of books' through new translations and editing of Greek originals. He initiated various linguistic, stylistic and spelling reforms which served the same purpose.

Attempts to purge the holy books of Christianity from heresies and distortions began in the thirteenth and continued in the fourteenth century, particularly in the Turnovo school. Translators were urged to review the existing translations of church books, but in order to do that they needed a 'pure' literary language. Emphasis on accuracy and the use of refined verbal forms meant that a versatile linguistic vehicle was needed to render such features of the original as prosodic effects and plays on words with the same root. The answer for the Turnovo school translators was to deliberately reproduce Greek word order as a way of approximating the norms of Greek as a high cultural model and of drawing on a pool of shared experience and aesthetic appreciation.

In the process of preparing the new translations of the Octoich, poetic and holy texts, hymns, panegyrics, sermons and speeches, the new theoretical principles of translation developed in accordance with the changing liturgical and aesthetic requirements of the fourteenth century, without abandoning Cyril and Methodius's tradition of faithfulness to meaning. The new attitude to meaning found its aesthetic realization in translations based on euphony and neologisms. As a result of this substantial cultural project, Bulgaria outstripped western Europe in its linguistic development during the thirteenth and fourteenth centuries. While the official European culture of the late Middle Ages still failed to recognize the vernacular languages, Bulgaria had developed a literary language of its own, established a system of classical norms and perfected them over a period of several centuries.

One of the main translations of the Turnovo school was the *Chronicle* of Constantin Manasius of the twelfth century, written in highly imaginative and eloquent verse. The translation was made for Tsar Ivan Alexander in 1335/36. Although not composed in verse form, the style of the translation is highly poetic.

Old Bulgarian translations prior to the eighteenth century: overview

In 1396, Bulgaria fell under Ottoman Turkish rule, which was to last for five centuries. There were no major translations during the second half of the fourteenth century and the fifteenth century, though at some centres, such as the Rila Monastery, copyists and translators tried to preserve translated literature. It was not until the sixteenth, and especially the following two centuries, that translation was pursued actively once again.

That last stage of the history of Old Bulgarian translated literature is known for the popular translations of a collection of religious sermons by Damascene Studit, a sixteenth-century Greek writer; these were written in the vernacular Greek and published in his book *Treasury*. Known as the *Damascenes*, the translations began a new trend of adapting texts to the new Bulgarian language through extensive use of the vernacular. Ten translations of these texts were produced in different Bulgarian dialects.

The Damascenes were modified in the eighteenth century by introducing non-canonical literary readings into the collection. Translators selected and added secular texts, which gradually attracted more interest than moral and religious sermons. Originals were adapted to suit the Bulgarian context, so that translations now set out to establish new relationships between writers and recipients.

It is perhaps worth summarizing the main features of translation activity prior to the eighteenth century at this point, before proceeding to discuss translation during the Bulgarian renaissance.

First, translation was a rather broad concept. Translations were integral parts of the national literature. Since there was little respect for authorship in the Middle Ages, even original texts incorporated translated elements and borrowed ideas, imagery and plots. Old Bulgarian translators were also writers and translation was considered an act of co-authorship and co-editing. It is therefore impossible to make a rigid distinction between original and translated literature during this period. There was no strict boundary and this allowed intermingling of the two types of creative work. Nevertheless, literary translation existed as an independent structural element in the system of Old Bulgarian literature.

Second, translated literature not only served Bulgarian readers but also spread among the other southern and eastern Slavs, especially Russians, Ukrainians, Serbs and, later on, Romanians. Having emerged a century earlier, Old Bulgarian literature provided the foundation for the literature which all southern and eastern Slavs were to share in due course. It was the mediating literature, in a mediating language, between the Byzantine culture and the Slavs, an exponent of the medieval civilization whose missionary basis was supported by translation; hence its all-Slavonic and international importance.

Finally, prior to the Renaissance, no other European people came as close to the ancient Greek philosophers as the Bulgarian translators. Neighbouring Byzantium gave Old Bulgarian literature its overall artistic identity, type of creative perception, genres and poetic vision and provided contact with Oriental literatures. Links with the Catholic West, on the other hand, were very weak during the Middle Ages.

It is difficult to compare Old Bulgarian and western European literatures in their medieval forms. The two literatures developed under different historical conditions and on the basis of different philosophies and aesthetic values. There are therefore fundamental differences between the two streams of Byzantine Orthodox and western European culture which were to come together on an all-European scale in the eighteenth century.

The Bulgarian Renaissance: eighteenth and nineteenth centuries

The Bulgarian Renaissance is generally thought to have started with the publication in 1762 of *Slavonic Bulgarian History* by Paisyi of Chilendar (1722–73), monk and enlightener. Translation followed the general development of Bulgarian literature during the eighteenth century but was characterized by a number of distinctive features.

Translation during the Bulgarian Renaissance assumed a new function as mediator between medieval and modern literature. Therefore many 'new translations' appeared, for example *Alexandria* (a heroic fictional epic about Alexander of Macedonia, 1796) and a collection of excerpts from the *Arabian Nights*, which had first been translated a few centuries earlier, the new translations were updated to reflect the modern idiom. These two translations provided continuity with the old literature and are therefore considered as marking the beginning of literary translation during the Bulgarian Renaissance.

Stories and Thoughts (1802), by Sophronius of Vratsa (1739–1813), marked a whole new stage in the development of translations during the early Renaissance. This is a collection of 144 fables of Aesop plus various narratives. Here, the new mediating function of translation was clearly understood to include interpreting the original; also, the old literary language was beginning to undergo a fundamental process of 'democratization'. This collection represents the first attempt to differentiate stylistic levels of the language and to adjust translation to the specific genre of the original.

Between the end of the eighteenth and the middle of the nineteenth century, translation was marked by a general tendency for

'Bulgarianization' (free interpretation and literary revision of the original to suit Bulgarian national, historical and psychological specificities). This was a natural result of the cultural and ideological overburdening of translation: due to the slow development of the Bulgarian intellectual elite, original works did not begin to appear until the late stages of the Bulgarian Renaissance. It was translators who laid the foundations of modern Bulgarian literature in terms of recurrent themes, images, plots, genres, vocabulary and stylistic diversity. Bulgarian culture needed to learn from new models and transform them into national ones. As part of the tendency to adapt the original to the reader's taste, translators also became semi-authors, developing the content of the original and adding their own text.

French, German and Russian sentimental literature was frequently 'Bulgarianized', especially since it provided a suitable context for using the clichés which Bulgarian readers had learned from sermons, hagiography and Damascenes.

Translations into Bulgarian were often based on intermediate versions in other languages. This can be explained in terms of a lack of appreciation of 'copyright' as we know it today and the urgent need to make contact with several European literatures at the same time.

The selection of translations depended on what was considered useful to the target reader rather than on the importance of the original text in its own national context. Translations essentially provided the Bulgarian Renaissance culture with its basic literary models, more specifically with works meant to teach human virtues or to present historical events.

Around the middle of the nineteenth century, translators were people who had acquired a high level of education and knowledge of the cultures of various European countries. They were therefore in a position to develop an individual approach to the originals they worked from and to strive towards achieving a balance between the need to preserve the artistic features of the original and, at the same time, produce readable translations. In the context of the Enlightenment, the practice of 'Bulgarianization' inevitably continued, but it slowly gave way to other methods of translation. The gradual development of the national language also played a

part in this process. Of particular importance were the translations by the greatest writers of the Bulgarian Renaissance, whose talents enabled them to use the full potential of the language (P. R. Slaveikov, L. Karavelov, C. Botev, N. Bonchev and others).

Diverse tendencies developed in the choice of certain foreign literatures. On the one hand, a much wider range of foreign literary texts became known in Bulgaria: French, Russian, German, Italian, English, American, Serbian, Greek, etc. On the other hand, translators had more opportunities to choose original texts, depending on the needs of the national liberation process. Writers of the French Enlightenment, for instance, were translated on a massive scale (but this did not stop the flow of translations of French sentimentalists); the same applied to Russian literature, which gradually assumed the function of mediator between the Bulgarian and European cultures. The most important translator from Russian, P. R. Slakeikov (1827–95), was one of the leading figures of the Bulgarian Renaissance. His translations of Russian, western European and Balkan authors contributed to the metric and prosodic development of Bulgarian verse. He used all forms of translation: Bulgarianization, adaptation (where he used other authors' ideas and plots for his own creative purposes), and literal translation.

Translated and original poetry began to appear simultaneously during this period. The Bulgarian poetic tradition developed out of the tension between folkloric forms and those of iambic poetry. A great deal of diversity existed, and stylistic and metric interpretations varied according to the translator's outlook and objectives. The 'revised translations' which were undertaken at the time were indicative of the literary aesthetics of the period.

Scientific and political translation influenced the development of national awareness and revolutionary ideology. It developed in response to a growing interest in the issues of governance, law, economics and in medical and natural sciences. The first Bulgarian schoolbook, *The Fish Primer*, which was written by Peter Beron (1800–71) and published in 1824, contained translations of eighteen fables of Aesop and works by ancient Greek authors. Unlike literary translations, scientific and political translations were always based on the original text. The usual practice was to translate excerpts rather than complete books. A tendency towards greater accuracy was evident, but different translations also frequently betrayed the ideological preferences of the intellectuals who undertook them.

Political articles were translated anonymously, as part of the struggle for independence. Some translations set out to give an accurate rendering of information (following the original without any substantial deviations); others took the form of free interpretation, adding comments, explanations and even appeals when the purpose was to achieve a particular patriotic goal.

Given the cultural and political vacuum which resulted from five centuries of Ottoman rule, the Bulgarian Renaissance was fundamentally different from developments in the rest of Europe. In Bulgaria, the various stages of European civilization had to be collapsed and absorbed in a very short time. Of utmost importance during this period was the need to defend the Bulgarian identity and to search for and identify the roots of national culture. This situation resulted in a functional overburdening of translation, which had to serve the urgent need to acquire basic literary and artistic models on a large scale; hence the co-existence of the three forms of translation during this period, namely Bulgarianization, adaptation and translation with commentary.

Translations gradually expanded the horizons of Bulgarian readers; the medieval genre system was now supplemented with sentimentalist imagery, popular educational material, pedagogical, historical and scientific texts, travel notes and political writings, not to mention the classics of European and neighbouring Balkan cultures. Bulgarians developed a lasting interest in Russian literature, which was perceived as both the mediating link to European civilization as well as the mainstay and guarantor of Bulgaria's Slavonic roots. In addition to importing new genres and imagery, translations during this period also became a testing ground for the national literary language, imagery, genre experiments, poetic culture and other major elements of art and culture in modern times.

Translation in the post-liberation period (1878 to the present)

The new perception of the functions and place of translations in the national culture, which was radically different from earlier perceptions, was most convincingly presented in the article 'Classical European writers in the Bulgarian language and the benefit of studying their works' (1873) by the literary critic Nesho Bonchev (1939–78). Bonchev rejected the idea of translating in response to national needs and called for re-orienting translation towards learning about and assimilating the finest examples of modern world literature. This marked a turning point from utilitarianism to the pursuit of artistic values. Bulgarianization naturally became obsolete as a translation method in this context.

At the beginning of the twentieth century, a group of writers associated with the journal *Misul* (1892–1907) suggested a new aesthetic programme for national literature, one in which the theory and criticism of translations occupied an important place. A new stage in the development of post-liberation translation activity began. This stage was characterized by continued orientation towards western Europe, mainly German literary and philosophical classics; at the same time, Russian influence remained strong and there was a growing interest in modern thinkers such as Nietzsche and Schopenhauer. In addition to western European literature, interest also grew in other geographical regions, themes and genres, for example Slavonic, Scandinavian and American poetry, prose and drama. With its ability to follow and draw inspiration from many European cultures, translated literature was able to keep up with world literature. The balance that was maintained among different influences was unprecedented and is the most distinctive feature of this period.

The quest for Europeanization provided the initiative for a number of outstanding translations of Francophone, German and English poetry by the poet Geo Milev (1895–1925). Building on the poetic language developed under the influence of the Symbolists, translators reached new standards of creativity and a new school of Bulgarian poetic translation was born, with well-developed artistic principles, high aesthetic criteria and modern literary orientation. At the same time, interest in the ancient classics remained strong and was particularly evident in the translations of Alexander Balabanov (1879–1955), classical philologist and Professor of ancient Greek literature at Sofia University, who translated works by Aeschylus, Sophocles, Euripides and Aristophanes, as well as Aesop's fables.

In the years between the two world wars, translators played an important role in introducing to the left-wing press the ideas of humanist and anti-fascist world writers, journalists and scientists.

After Geo Milev, the intense pace of translation slowed down. The change could be observed in such things as the choice of genres and themes and in the increasing specialization of publishers in areas such as classical literature on the one hand and mass entertainment literature on the other. The implementation of socialist cultural policy shortly after World War II was followed by the nationalization of private publishing houses in 1947/48. There followed a decade of national insularity, which clearly influenced the selection of books to be translated. However, the 1960s saw the beginning of quantitative and qualitative changes in terms of the orientation and quality of translations. These changes are still in evidence today. Translation began to win public recognition as a creative activity, and a national policy was implemented to fill existing gaps in the translation of foreign classics. New versions of older translations started to appear, and continue to appear to this day. Translated literature widened its scope to include authors of literary, scientific, journalistic and other texts from all corners of the globe, as well as a variety of publications, from complete works to anthologies, series, bilingual editions, etc.

Among the most important achievements during this period were the translation of the complete works of Shakespeare between 1970 and 1981 by the prominent Bulgarian poet Valeri Petrov and the translation of the scientific works of Kant between 1957 and 1987 by Tseko Torbov, who won the Vienna University Herder award in 1970 for his translation of *Critique of Pure Reason* and for his research activities in general. This period also saw the translation of political literature in series and other forms, as well as the works of outstanding scientists and scholars in various disciplines.

A new generation of translators has since joined the profession, having acquired substantial linguistic skills at various language schools. A special course for translators and interpreters was also established at Sofia University in 1974.

Further reading

Leskien 1903; Vaillant 1948; Georgiev 1955; Dinekov 1960; Picchio 1972; Trost 1978; *Prevodut i Bulgarskata Kultura* 1981; *Stara Bulgarska Literatura* 1980–89.

ANNA LILOVA

Translated from Bulgarian by Vera Georgieva

C

Canadian tradition

The 34 million inhabitants of Canada are mainly of French and British descent, but there are also a number of large minorities which include the original inhabitants (Indians who speak a variety of Huron-Iroquois and Algonquian, and the Inuit who speak Inuktitut), Germans, Italians, Chinese, Ukrainians and Dutch.

The exploration of Canada began in 1497 when John Cabot reached the coasts of Newfoundland and Nova Scotia. The first permanent settlements were established by the French in 1608 when the French explorer and colonizer Samuel de Champlain (c.1570–1635) established the settlement at Québec, known as 'New France', the name given to it by Jacques Cartier in 1534. In 1763, Canada was ceded to Britain by the Treaty of Paris. A member of the British Commonwealth, Canada also plays an active part in 'La Francophonie', the organization which represents French-speaking communities. The official languages are English and French.

Translation under French rule

The history of translation in Canada began with a kidnapping. While exploring the Gulf of St Lawrence in 1534, the French navigator Jacques Cartier (1494–1554) came into contact with several Indian tribes. In order to communicate with them, he had to resort to sign language. Before setting sail once again, Cartier unceremoniously 'recruited' the two sons of the Iroquois chief of Stadacona (present-day Québec City) and took them to France, where he taught them the rudiments of the French language. These two natives became the country's first interpreters.

On his second voyage, Cartier's new interpreters, Dom Agaya and Taignoagny, began to teach him about New France: its geographical features, natural resources and inhabitants. They even saved Cartier's expedition from catastrophe by teaching the 'pale faces' how to treat and cure scurvy, a terrible disease that had decimated Cartier's crew. When his exploratory expedition was completed, Cartier took his two interpreters back to France, for by now they had started to plot against him and his men. They settled in Brittany and collaborated on the compilation of two bilingual Iroquois–French lexicons, the first lexicographical works to which Canadian translators had contributed.

At the beginning of the seventeenth century, Champlain created an institution of resident interpreters in the new colony. He placed young French adventurers with the allied tribes and gave them the task of defending the interests of merchants, particularly those involved in the fur trade, and officials responsible for colonizing the shores of the St Lawrence River. These young men were resident interpreters in the sense that they lived among the natives, dressed like Indians, slept in tents, hunted, fished and took part in the feasts, dances and rites that made up the everyday life of their hosts. Through daily contact with the natives, the interpreters became familiar with their way of life and world view, and hence eminently qualified for dealing with the tribes. Among the first such interpreters were Étienne Brûlé, Nicolas Marsolet, Jean Nicolet, Olivier Letardif, Jean Richer, Jacques Hertel and François Marguerie.

The linguistic map of New France at that time was fragmented, with numerous dialects deriving from two language families: Algonquian and Huron-Iroquois. Although all the Indian languages belonged to one of these two families, a different interpreter was required for specific languages such as Micmac, Abenakis, Montagnais, Algonquian, Huron, Nipissing, Iroquois, Ottawa, and so on. Each language created a new linguistic barrier. In addition, the absence of written grammars, and of a written tradition, made the dialects difficult to master. Pronunciation (particularly of guttural sounds), intonation, breathing and rhythm, not to mention the difficulty inherent in translating abstract French vocabulary, created linguistic traps that could lead anywhere from a humorous mistranslation to a diplomatic incident. The missionaries, unlike the interpreters, did attempt to compile grammars and dictionaries, but they continued to run up against cultural taboos which complicated the translation of prayers. For example, it was no easy task to teach *Our Father, who art in heaven* ... to natives who had lost their fathers, for to speak of loved ones who had died was to insult them.

After Champlain's death, young people continued to go and live with the Indians to learn the challenging craft of interpreting. Pierre Boucher, Charles Le Moyne, Guillaume Couture and Nicolas Perrot were four eminent interpreters of this period. In the words of Bacqueville de La Potherie, 'The merchants could have offered 100,000 écus worth of merchandise, but they would not have sold even a pound of tobacco without the assistance of their interpreters' (Margry 1883: 186; translated).

In Montréal, the courts often required interpreters for Indian languages, as well as interpreters for English and Dutch, the languages used by merchants in the colonies to the south (New England and New Holland). Jean Quenet, Pierre Couc, René Cuillerier, Françoise Goupil (one of only two women to have served as interpreters at the time), Robert Poitiers du Buisson and Louis-Hector Piot de Langloiserie were among those who interpreted for the courts. They were essentially settlers, milliners, traders and manufacturers, and only occasionally worked as interpreters. Today, they would be considered freelancers.

Military interpreters formed another category. These men were members of the regular forces and often held command posts. Among the better known were Paul Le Moyne de Maricourt, Joseph Godefroy de Vieux Pont and François Hertel. In 1757, the army of the Marquis de Montcalm (1712–59), which had tried in vain to defend Québec against the troops of the British General James Wolfe (1727–59),

included over 1,700 Indians from various tribes, and ten interpreters.

In 1682, the governor of New France and successor to Frontenac, Joseph-Antoine de La Barre, wrote: 'One type of person who is indispensable to the service of the King in this country is the interpreter' (Biron 1969: 253; translated). But the interpreter's role was not limited to that of a language intermediary. In fact, these multilingual mediators, representatives of merchants and civil authorities to the tribes, also acted as guides, explorers, brokers, diplomats, ambassadors and advisers on Indian affairs. They formed a sort of buffer which helped to ease the culture shock that resulted from the encounter with the Indians. They had a deep understanding of the native way of thinking and demonstrated that true communication is achieved not at the superficial level of words, but rather through genuine interaction with the cultural, religious, economic and social institutions of a community. The understanding of others hinges more on what they are than on what they say. The interpreter who had the most influence over the Indians was the one who intimately understood the Indian soul. The Indians gave one of the interpreters from this period the nickname 'double man', while another was called 'two times a man', which indicates the extent to which the interpreters of early Canada were in tune with the Indian mentality.

Translation under English rule (1760–1867)

After the surrender of Montréal in 1760, and following the Treaty of Paris which gave control of the colonies to Britain in 1763, it was the turn of the English conquerors to organize the administration of Canada whose population had now grown to approximately 65,000. Brunet points out that 'although the Conquest minimized the professional options for [French] Canadians, there is no doubt that it presented them with a new career opportunity, namely translation' (1969: 24–5; translated). During the military rule (1760–64), English governors posted to Québec City, Trois-Rivières and Montréal appointed secretary-translators to translate into French (the language of the majority) the edicts and proclamations issued in English. Thanks to four

British officers who were descendants of French Huguenots (Cramahé in Québec City, Bruyères and Gugy in Trois-Rivières, and Maturin in Montréal), the French language enjoyed a semi-official status during these four transitional years. In 1764, the first year of civil government, *The Québec Gazette* made its début. It was the first bilingual newspaper in North America. Written in English and translated into French, this publication was used extensively for official government communications.

In 1767, Guy Carleton (1724–1808) replaced James Murray as governor and took up residence in Québec City. Sensitive to the needs of the French, he decided that it was essential to have the French laws and ordinances of the 'old régime' translated into English, a task the English magistrates declared to be beyond their abilities. Moreover, Carleton needed a French secretary to translate the new English proclamations and other official documents into French. The only Canadian who seemed capable of filling this dual role was the bilingual jurist François-Joseph Cugnet (1720–89). On 24 February 1768, Carleton appointed him 'French Translator and Secretary to the Governor and Council'; the day before, the Council had decided that such a good and sufficient translator shall have an appointment of 5 shillings sterling per day. For twenty-one years, Cugnet was responsible for official translation in the Province of Québec. When he died, his son Jacques-François (1758–97) succeeded him. Subsequently, the post was filled in turn by Xavier de Lanaudière, Philippe Aubert de Gaspé and Edward Bowen.

Following the establishment of the parliamentary system in 1791 and the division of the Province of Québec into two colonies (Upper Canada and Lower Canada), the Legislative Assembly also acquired a translator in 1793. In accordance with the wishes of the mother country, laws were enacted in English, but French was allowed as a language of translation. As of 1809, the work was carried out by two translators, one for French and the other for English.

Interpreters, so many and so visible under French rule, did not disappear after the Conquest. The large trading companies still employed many interpreters for their negotiations with native suppliers. The North West Company alone had 68 interpreters in 1804;

56 were francophone and 12 anglophone. The following interpreters and missionaries played a central role in the exploration and colonization of the Western plains and the Northern territories: Peter Ballenden, the Reverend John McKay, Felix Monroe, Father Albert Lacombe (1827–1916), Jean L'Heureux, Louis Léveillé, the Reverend James Evans (1801–46), Jerry Potts (*c*.1837–96) and Peter Erasmus (1833–1931). If there were few bloody battles between white men and natives in West Canada, it was due, in large part, to the efforts of interpreters such as Peter Erasmus and Jerry Potts, who acted with diplomacy on behalf of missionaries, explorers, surveyors and law-enforcement officers.

In 1840, Upper and Lower Canada were united. Section 41 of the Act of Union made English the sole official language of the united Canada. This was a consequence of Lord Durham's report of the previous year, which had advocated a policy of assimilating francophones in Lower Canada. Francophones were quick to react. On 18 September 1841, the Legislative Assembly of Canada passed a bill tabled by Étienne Parent (1802–74) which consisted of three sections. It provided for the translation into French, the printing and circulation of all legislation by the new Parliament and of all imperial laws relevant to Canadian affairs. Parent's bill was entitled: *An Act to provide for the translation into the French language of the Laws of this Province, and for other purposes connected therewith*. It was the first bill to deal specifically with translation and to be adopted by a legislative body in Canada. In 1854, one of the translators of the Legislative Assembly, Antoine Gérin-Lajoie (1824–82), submitted to the speaker a plan for reorganizing the assembly's translation bureaus. The plan provided for three subdivisions: laws, documents, and votes and proceedings. This organization of parliamentary translation services was to last for almost 100 years. Eugène-Philippe Dorion (1830–72) was another important figure in official translation immediately before and after Confederation in 1867. Appointed translator in the Assembly of the Province of Canada in 1855, Dorion was called upon to head its French translators' bureau in 1859, a post that he held subsequently with the House of Commons in Ottawa until 1870. His contemporaries spoke highly of his knowledge of classical languages, as well as of

English, French and some Indian languages. He is believed to have improved the stylistic quality of legislation translated into French.

During British rule, official translators served as mediators between the English and the French: they provided a link between two peoples who were destined to co-exist in the same territory. At the crossroads of two legal traditions, civil law and common law, these translators were among the first to tackle the difficult task of expressing British law and institutions in French terms.

The years following Confederation (1867–)

Literary translation has not enjoyed a long tradition in Canada (see below). On the other hand, the translation of non-literary texts (administrative, commercial, technical and legal) has continued to flourish, primarily as a result of the language laws and policies adopted by various government institutions. For example, Section 133 of the British North America Act (1867) places French and English on an equal footing in the House of Commons and in federal and Québec courts. During the first half of the twentieth century, the most prominent figures in non-literary translation were Achille Fréchette (1847–1929), Léon Gérin (1863–1951) and Pierre Daviault (1899–1964).

In 1934, the Secretary of State, Charles H. Cahan (1861–1944), tabled a bill providing for the centralization of federal government translation services and the creation of a Translation Bureau that would bring together some 100 translators working in various government departments. Over the years, especially those following the Royal Commission on Bilingualism and Biculturalism (1963) and the adoption of the *Official Languages Act* (1969), the Bureau has grown enormously. In its fiftieth year of service, it comprised over 900 translators, 100 interpreters, 100 terminologists and 550 support staff. It served 150 client-bodies from Ottawa and a number of regional offices and had an annual budget of over $85 million. The Bureau as a whole translated approximately 300 million words per year. Its multilingual department translated approximately 20 million words per year from and into some 60 languages,

and it contracted work out to a pool of 500 freelancers.

The competence of Canadian terminologists has been recognized throughout the world. They have devised a sound methodology for conducting terminological research, and have provided translators and language specialists with two increasingly effective computerized terminology banks. TERMIUM was developed by the Secretary of State and contains over one and a half million terms. The other bank, the BTQ, was created by the Gouvernement du Québec. Robert Dubuc, Marcel Paré, Pierre Auger, Nada Kerpan and Guy Rondeau have all played a vital role in the establishment of these terminology banks, and in the growth of the new profession of terminologist. Likewise, Québec's *Office de la langue française* (OLF), founded in 1961, has been responsible for countless initiatives in the field of language management in Québec and the francization of business and industry in particular. The *Office* has also gained recognition for the numerous glossaries it has published.

While developing TERMIUM in the 1970s, the Translation Bureau became interested in machine translation. In 1976, the machine translation research group at the Université de Montréal (TAUM) presented the Bureau with the prototype of METEO. Since then, over 85 per cent of all Canadian weather reports have been translated by computer.

Canada's Translation Bureau is not only the largest employer of translators and interpreters in the country, it also plays a vital role in implementing the policy of official bilingualism and multiculturalism (see Mossop 2006). The activities of the Bureau reflect broader national objectives related to the promotion of official languages. It should be noted, however, that over 85 per cent of all translation undertaken in Canada is from English into French, which raises the sensitive issue of the relative status of Canada's two official languages.

The organization of the profession

Canada is a virtual paradise for translators; it is probably the place where the profession is most structured. In a country of barely 34 million people, there are at least 25 different associations of translators, interpreters or terminologists. If we were to include the organizations that have disappeared since the first translators' association was founded in 1919 (the Cercle des Traducteurs des Livres Bleus), the total would be at least thirty-five. Between 1919 and 1984, a new association of translators, interpreters or terminologists was formed, on average, every two years.

In 1989, the Ontario Provincial Legislature recognized translators, terminologists, conference interpreters and court interpreters certified by the Association of Translators and Interpreters of Ontario (ATIO) and allowed them to use the reserved titles *certified translator, certified interpreter* and *certified terminologist* after their names. This was a real breakthrough which was initiated by André Séguinot, Julien Marquis and Richard Fidler (members of the ATIO Executive at the time), and Jean Poirier (MPP and former translator). A year later, the Corporation of Translators and Interpreters of New Brunswick (CTINB) received official recognition. And finally, after more than twenty-five years of hard work, the former Société des Traducteurs du Québec (STQ) was also recognized and, in March 1992, became the CPTIAQ, a professional corporation with a reserved title for its members. It was renamed Ordre des traducteurs, terminologues et interprètes agréés du Québec (QTTIAQ) in 2000.

There are two reasons for the proliferation of translators' associations. First, because professional associations fall under provincial jurisdiction, Canadian translators must organize themselves by province. Together, the associations make up the Canadian Translators, Terminologists and Interpreters Council (CTTIC), a national federation which represents Canada on international bodies such as the International Federation of Translators. The function of CTTIC is to coordinate the activities of the member societies and to set standards for governing the practice of translation. For example, CTTIC is responsible for organizing the national certification examination for translators, conference interpreters, court interpreters and terminologists.

The second reason for the proliferation of translators' associations has to do with the increased level of specialization in the profession. Since the mid-1970s, there has been a marked tendency for translators to group themselves into associations which reflect their fields of interest. Apart from the provincial associations, there are associations for visual language interpreters, literary translators, and a Canadian Association of Schools of Translation (CAST), to name but a few. Other groups bring together translators who specialize in education, in health or who work in the pharmaceutical industry. Moreover, at the initiative of Judith Woodsworth, a learned society of translation scholars was also founded in 1987: the Canadian Association for Translation Studies (CATS), the first of its kind in the world. Its primary objective is to promote and disseminate research in translation and related fields.

Publications

Canada is not only the promised land in terms of professional associations, it is also a country where publications on translation abound. Since 1940, a new translation, interpreting or terminology periodical has been launched on average every two years. Well-known scholarly periodicals include *Meta* (1955–), which is published by the Presses de l'Université de Montréal, and *TTR* (1988–), the official journal of the Canadian Association for Translation Studies.

Just as translators' associations have become increasingly specialized, so too have translation publications. This is true not only of periodicals but also of books. Until the 1960s, translators such as Sylva Clapin, Léon Gérin, Léon Lorrain, Pierre Daviault and Hector Carbonneau produced glossaries, vocabularies, bilingual dictionaries and works on usage. From 1970 onwards, a different type of book appeared on the market: the terminology and translation textbook. Authors include Irène de Buisseret (*Guide du traducteur*, 1972, revised and reprinted in 1975 as *Deux langues, six idiomes*); Geoffrey Vitale, Michel Sparer and Robert Larose (*Guide de la traduction appliquée*, I: 1978; II: 1980); Robert Dubuc (*Manuel pratique de terminologie*, 1978); Jean Delisle (*L'Analyse du discours comme méthode de traduction*, 1980, *La Traduction raisonnée*, 1993); Guy Rondeau (*Introduction à la terminologie*, 1981); Claude Bédard (*La Traduction technique*, 1986); Robert Larose (*Théories contemporaines de la traduction*, 1989). The history of translation is another field that seems to attract Canadian translation scholars, as evidenced by the following titles: Louis G. Kelly (*The True Interpreter*, 1979); Paul A. Horguelin (*Anthologie de la manière de traduire*, 1981); Jean Delisle (*Bridging the Language Solitudes*, 1984; *Translation in Canada, 1534–1984*, 1987; *The Language Alchemists*, 1990); Annie Brisset (*Sociocritique de la traduction. Théâtre et altérité au Québec, 1968–1988*, 1990). The predominance of books on translation pedagogy in the above list indicates the importance that translator training has assumed in Canada since the late 1960s.

Training

Professional translation has been taught at the University of Ottawa since 1936, at McGill University in Montréal since 1943, and at the Université de Montréal since 1951.

With the publication of their renowned *Stylistique comparée du français et de l'anglais* in 1958, Jean Darbelnet (1904–90) and Jean-Paul Vinay (1910–99) made a substantial contribution to translation pedagogy and have long since achieved international recognition for their work. They laid the groundwork for what Vinay himself called the 'Canadian school of translation' (Vinay 1958: 148). Translators and terminologists belonging to this school have shared a common tendency to focus on the concrete reality of language, rather than on abstract principles, and believe that 'the primary goal of an adequate translation theory is to facilitate the act of translating' (Vinay 1975: 17; translated).

In 1968, the translation section of the linguistics department at the Université de Montréal, chaired at the time by André Clas, offered the first full-time three-year programme leading to a degree in translation. Soon after, the degree became known as a BA Specialization (similar to an honours degree). Translation pedagogy flourished in the 1970s. Right across the country, but especially in Québec and Ontario, universities began to offer translator training programmes. Between 1968 and 1984, a new translation programme of one kind or another was launched every year, a new Bachelor's programme every two years, and a new Master's programme every four years.

The rapid growth of translator training since the late 1960s is reflected in numerous publications on teaching methods as well as a significant number of conferences devoted wholly, or in part, to this topic. On 5 November 1955, Canadian translators held their first general meeting in Montréal. Since that historic meeting, they have organized an average of three to five conferences, seminars or meetings annually.

The proliferation of professional associations, specialized publications, training programmes and conferences reflects the importance of translation in Canada. In addition, a true spirit of cooperation exists between professional associations, professional translators and university teachers of translation. This tripartite cooperation has led to the development of a variety of translation tools, machine translation systems and terminology banks. It has also resulted in translator training programmes that are better adapted to the needs of the market. Cooperation lies at the heart of the Canadian tradition and accounts for the current achievements of Canadian translators.

Literary translation

Although Canada is officially bilingual, the volume of literary translation is small compared to the mass of non-literary texts that are translated on a regular basis. According to the *Index Translationum* (1986), Holland publishes eleven times more literary translations than Canada, Sweden six times more, and Finland and Portugal twice as much. In Canada, there is a tendency to use the term 'literary translation' to refer not only to novels, poetry, essays and drama but also to works in the humanities and social sciences.

Literary translation as a genre made its debut around 1960: 'Before 1960 no significant novel was translated' (Stratford 1977: v). Prior to that time, Canada had produced no more than 60-odd titles (mainly accounts of French explorers and voyagers), half of which were translated and published elsewhere: in England, France or the United States. The relative success of literary translation since the 1960s can be attributed to the introduction of the Canada Council's Translation Grants Programme in 1972, the increase in the number of Québec and English-Canadian publishing houses, and the foundation in 1975 of the Association of Literary

Translators, which gave literary translators what Philip Stratford called a 'collective sense of identity' (1977: viii). Few translators are able to make a living out of literary translation alone, even today. Most are academics, civil servants, journalists, salaried translators within corporations, or freelancers. One exception worthy of mention is Sheila Fischman (1937–), who has translated over thirty books into English. These included works by some of the best-known Québec authors, such as Anne Hébert, Marie-Claire Blais, Michel Tremblay, Jacques Poulin, Victor-Lévy Beaulieu, Yves Beauchemin and Roch Carrier. Fischman was awarded the C.M. (Member of the Order of Canada) on 27 April 2000 for her services to Canadian–French Literature

Economic factors have contributed to the low volume of literary translation in Canada. The going rate for translators working in the commercial or administrative sector is twice the maximum rate paid by the Canada Council. Initially a mere 5 cents per word, this rate was still only 10 cents per word in 1993. Nevertheless, the Council's Translation Grants Programme has encouraged many publishers to launch translation collections. The Montréal-based publishing house Le Cercle du Livre de France (known today as les Éditions Pierre Tisseyre) was the first to launch such a series, in 1973, under the title *Collection des Deux Solitudes* (after Hugh MacLennan's novel *Two Solitudes*, 1945). The two solitudes refer to Canada's two main language groups, Francophones and Anglophones, who live side by side without really understanding one another. One of the specific objectives of the federal grants programme is to enable Canadians to become better acquainted with the other solitude through literature. In 1989, the publishing house Québec-Amérique launched a new series of translations called *Littérature d'Amérique*. Les éditions Boréal also publishes translated works. English literary translations have been published primarily by the following smaller presses: Harvest House, House of Anansi, New Press, Porcépic, Exile, Coach House, Talonbooks, Tundra, Guernica and NC Library.

Only two English–Canadian plays were translated prior to 1970, and very few have been translated since then. This can be explained by the activity of Québec playwrights, whose works

are promptly translated into English, and also by the preference within Québec theatre circles for American, British, Russian or Italian plays. Influenced by the new style of drama introduced by Michel Tremblay in 1968, growing nationalist sentiment, and the enhanced status of a typically Québecois language, translators who adapt works for the theatre began to naturalize foreign plays. The characters of Shakespeare, Chekhov, O'Neill, Lorca, Brecht or Goldoni were made to speak Québecois. Instead of self-effacing translations which aim to provide access to the foreign work, these adaptations provided a means of expressing the specificity of Québec (Brisset 1990).

And finally, where types of literary translation are concerned, it is impossible to ignore the intense, original, even avant-garde approach of feminist translators. These translators meet frequently at conferences and seminars. They work closely with the authors they translate and publish bilingual editions or special issues of magazines such as *Tessera*. The works they translate are all firmly rooted in feminist ideology, and the translations are carried out primarily from French into English. Québec novelists, poets or feminist thinkers such as Nicole Brossard, Loupy Bersianik, Lise Gauvin, France Théoret, Madeleine Gagnon and Jovette Marchessault are translated by their English-Canadian counterparts. Susanne de Lotbinière-Harwood (1991), Barbara Godard, Kathy Mezei, Marlene Wildeman, Fiona Strachan, Yvonne Klein and Gail Scott are leading representatives of the feminist approach to translation in Canada.

On the whole, the number of translated literary books doubled every five years during the 1970s. Until the 1980s, almost twice as many literary translations (in the strict sense of the term) were made from French into English than vice versa. In 1977, for example, the statistics were as follows: F→E: 380 titles; E→F: 190. Five years later, the gap had narrowed: F→E: 550 titles; E→F: 400. Three-quarters of all Canadian literary translations have appeared since 1972, and more than 80 per cent of these translations were subsidized.

In 1974, the Canada Council established a prize of $2,500 to be awarded each year to two outstanding translations: one French and one English. This prize, whose value doubled to

$5,000 in 1976, has become one of the Governor General's established Literary Awards. The recipients include Jean Paré, Sheila Fischman, Yvan Steenhout (all three of whom have won the award twice), Patricia Claxton, Ray Ellenwood, Colette Tonge, Frank Scott, Gilles Hénault, Philip Stratford, Charlotte Melançon and Jane Brierly. The 2007 prize was won by Nigel Spencer. In 1981, the Association of Literary Translators created the John Glassco Translation Prize in memory of the eminent writer and translator. The prize is awarded annually to the best book-length translation by a new translator.

By contrast with interpreting, the first profession practised in Canada following the arrival of the Europeans in 1534, literary translation has a short history. Were it not for generous government support, it might never have become a prominent activity. Nevertheless, the relatively small group of literary translators is as important and active as the whole profession of translation in Canada, a country which unquestionably ranks among the world's foremost translating nations.

Further reading

McLean 1890; Shipley 1966; Erasmus 1976; *Ellipse* 1977; *Meta* 1977; Stratford 1977; *Inuktitut* 1983; La Bossière 1983; Toye 1983; Delisle 1984, 1987; Fardy 1984; Simon 1989; Brisset 1990; Delisle 1990; Lotbinière-Harwood 1991; Brisset 1996.

JEAN DELISLE

Translated from French by Sara C. Lott.

Chinese tradition

Chinese, a Sino-Tibetan language, is an official language of the United Nations and is spoken by more people than any other language in the world. It is the official language of the People's Republic of China and Taiwan, one of the official languages in Hong Kong and Singapore, and is spoken by a large section of the population in Thailand, Malaysia and Vietnam.

The Chinese language of high antiquity, which goes back to the first millennium BC, has remained accessible to educated speakers of Chinese by virtue of having been recorded in the form of characters, i.e. ideographs. Unlike a phonetic script, ideographs are not affected by phonological evolution and are therefore largely immune to change. Inevitably, however, the spoken language developed along its own lines, and the gap between the written and spoken word grew wider and wider. By the time a literature in the vernacular emerged, the spoken form was already quite distinct from classical Chinese. The vernacular did not replace classical Chinese as the medium of formal written discourse until the first half of the twentieth century.

Classical Chinese is characterized by

(a) its high density, often compared to the style of telegrams,
(b) its grammatical versatility, whereby the same character can function as a noun, verb, adjective or adverb,
(c) its sparing use of tense and number, and
(d) its tonality, a feature which is particularly relevant in literary composition and hence in literary translation.

These characteristics have traditionally led to wide differences in interpretation, particularly evident in the case of translation. The vernacular language, now known as Mandarin or *putonghua*, is heavily polysyllabic, has more definite word classes, and makes much more use of grammatical markers, though by no means as extensively or obligatorily as, say, French or German. Translation from European languages, predominantly English, has progressively brought modern Chinese closer to those languages, at least in terms of writing styles.

A vast country with scores of regional languages, China has probably witnessed translation and interpreting activities since the first tribal battle or produce-exchange. Early historical works such as the first-century BC *Records of the Grand Historian* contain many references to translation in the context of diplomacy and commerce. As early as the Zhou Dynasty, in the ninth century BC, there were special government officials in charge of interpreting and translation work; their titles varied according to the group of languages they covered. An integral part of protocol, they were always present at meetings with foreign emissaries. The term for a government interpreter of this period was *sheren*, literally 'tongues-man'. The current Chinese word for 'translation', *yi*, forms the basis for the official title adopted since the Han Dynasty (195 BC–7 AD): *yiguan* or *yishi*, literally 'translation official'. Historical records also show that during the Han Dynasty, translators/interpreters (*yizhang*) were routinely employed by merchants on their long trips to Southeast Asia and India; they were also present in the merchant caravans bound for states such as Bactria to the north-west of China. During the Tang Dynasty (618–906), a period in which cultural exchanges between China and her neighbouring states reached new heights, a considerable number of foreigners who lived in China were employed as government interpreters and were allowed to accompany Chinese officials on diplomatic missions.

In the three thousand years from the Zhou Dynasty to the present, the bread-and-butter of the Chinese translator's work has always been in government and commerce. There are extant poetry translations dating back to at least the fourth century BC, but these early literary translations were mostly recorded as part of the experience of various diplomatic missions. There have been periods, however, when translation played a crucial role in China's cultural and social development, going far beyond the confines of government and commerce. The most significant of these periods relate to the translation of Buddhist scriptures, the work of Christian missionaries, the political and cultural events leading to the May Fourth Movement, and the emergence of the People's Republic of China and subsequent contact with European countries. But translation and interpreting have also had a role to play in China outside of such peak periods and, apart from the major languages involved in those periods, a significant number of Chinese books have been translated from the eleventh century onwards into such languages as Mongolian, Western Xia, Manchurian and Japanese.

Translation of Buddhist scriptures

The first wave of translation activities in China came in the wake of the spread of Buddhism. By the mid second century AD, the first Chinese translations of Buddhist sutras had been under-taken (though some sources put the year as early as AD 70). This marked the beginning of a massive translation movement, often sponsored by the government, which lasted for nine centuries. Given the time span and the number of translators involved, translation methods and approaches did not remain static; even the cultural and linguistic background of the translators changed considerably over the centuries.

The translation of Buddhist sutras from Sanskrit into Chinese can be divided roughly into three phases: Eastern Han Dynasty and the Three Kingdoms Period (*c.*148–265); Jin Dynasty and the Northern and Southern Dynasties (*c.*265–589); and Sui Dynasty, Tang Dynasty and Northern Song Dynasty (*c.*589–1100).

During the first phase, the translators were monks from Central Asia and Xinjiang; the majority were respected for their religious knowledge, but their command of the Chinese language was very poor. Monks like Parthamasiris from Parthia (the first translator of Buddhist sutras into Chinese), said to have achieved a fair command of Chinese not long after his arrival in the country, were few and far between. This linguistic disadvantage is reflected in the translations produced during this period: although the foreign monks had the assistance of their Chinese pupils or counterparts, many of the translations still read awkwardly. Moreover, a large number of the early Chinese Buddhist translations were not based on Indian texts, but were indirect translations via sources in the monk-translator's mother tongue.

The early translation method reflected the strength and weakness of these translators, as well as the emphasis placed on theological accuracy. Translation Forums, or *yichang*, were set up, with a highly revered Buddhist monk as Chief Translator (*yizhu*). The foreign monk's task was that of explaining in detail the precise meaning of the texts. Under the foreign monk were one or more interpreters (*duyu* or *chuanyu*) conversant with the monk's language; their task was to interpret the monk's explication into Chinese. In the audience were scores, sometimes hundreds, of Chinese monks and lay scholars who recorded in note form the foreign monk's explication. The Chinese translation was then compiled by the Recorder (*bishou*) – the person responsible for writing down the interpreter's words in Chinese.

The process involved consulting not just the Recorder's own notes, but also notes taken by others in the audience. The three steps of interpreting, recording and checking were the basis for all Translation Forum work. It is obvious that the forums were not only meant to produce Buddhist texts in Chinese, but were also a kind of intensive seminar on Buddhist sutras, and it was not unusual for the Chinese text and a detailed annotation to be produced simultaneously. Because of the strong theological emphasis, the foreign monk – despite his lack of knowledge of the target language – was always billed as the Translator, while the person who did the actual writing in Chinese was credited as the Recorder.

The second phase of sutra translation was marked by the officiation of prominent foreign monks (some directly from the Indian subcontinent) who had learned Chinese, and who were thus able to deliver a verbal Chinese translation of the texts in the Translation Forum without the assistance of an interpreter. Their verbal translations were put into writing by the Recorder, who then checked the written texts directly with the monk-translator. One of the most respected and productive monk-translators was Kumarajiva (344–413). Kumarajiva became a monk at the age of seven, when his mother, an Indian princess, decided to take the monastic vow. At twenty, he was a renowned teacher of the Larger Vehicle school of Buddhism. As a result of his fame, Kumarajiva was captured by the Chinese army which invaded his country, and he learned Chinese as a captive. He was assigned the task of translating Buddhist sutras, assisted by some 800 monks, and produced over 300 volumes. It was after the arrival of Kumarajiva in China (AD 401) that detailed records were kept of the number of participants in the Translation Forums. The scale of forums presided over by Kumarajiva was particularly grand, frequently numbering over 3,000 participants; the norm for attendance at forums held by other monks seems to have been in the hundreds rather than thousands. Not every foreign monk active in this period, however, had mastered the Chinese language; some still relied completely on interpreters during forum sessions. Moreover, one cannot presume the existence of a written text as a basis for translation. Buddhist sutras were often learned verbally and memorized by the monks, who first recited the sutra in Sanskrit in the Translation Forum, and then proceeded to translate and interpret it in Chinese. In such cases, a Sanskrit version was recorded during the same forum as the Chinese version.

The third phase of sutra translation showed a marked departure from previous practices in that the processes of theological explication and translation became separated. The size of Translation Forums was reduced dramatically – normally no more than three dozen monks were involved. This is true of all forums held from the late sixth century onwards, including those presided over by the most prolific monk-translator in Chinese history, Xuan Zang (602–64; original name Chen Wei), who rendered over 1,300 volumes of sutras into Chinese. Zang became a monk at the age of thirteen. At that time the sutras were open to extremely diverse interpretations, and Xuan Zang vowed that he would travel to where Buddhism originated to learn the truth. He left the Chinese capital Chang'an in 621 and did not return until 645. The twenty-five years of his itinerary were spent visiting major temples on his way to India and in the various subcontinental states, where he learnt Sanskrit and studied the most important Buddhist sutras under the guidance of renowned monks. Xuan Zang devoted the remaining twenty years of his life to translating Buddhist sutras into Chinese; he also established basic translation rules which were followed by many monk-translators who came after him. Many of his translations, such as the 'Heart Sutra', are still used by Chinese Buddhists today.

One major reason for the new translation practice was the increased linguistic and theological expertise of Chinese monks. Whereas almost anyone could join the old-style Translation Forums, the third-phase forums were highly selective: only monks or lay officials with special abilities were allowed to take part; all except those directly involved in the translation work were forbidden to enter the forum premises. Each participant was assigned a special duty, and the number of specialized posts increased to nine. Of these, the Polisher (runwen) was usually a government official noted for his literary ability; other posts were normally filled by monks. In the Song Dynasty (c.984), the government at one point established a Sanskrit school, recruiting some dozen pupils from various monasteries with the intention of fostering a new generation of Buddhist translators. However, the decline of Buddhism in India as well as a change in government policy led to a rapid decline in Buddhist translation activities towards the 1050s. The days of the Translation Forums were over, and the Buddhist translations done after this period were the works of individuals rather than the collective efforts of a unique translation establishment.

Sutra translation provided a fertile ground for the practice and discussion of different translation approaches. Generally speaking, translations produced in the first phase were word-for-word renderings adhering closely to source language syntax. This was probably due not only to the lack of bilingual ability amongst the forum participants, but also to a belief that the sacred words of the enlightened should not be tampered with. In addition to contorted target language syntax, transliteration was used very liberally, with the result that the translations were fairly incomprehensible to anyone without a theological grounding. The second phase saw an obvious swing towards what many contemporary Chinese scholars call *yiyi* (free translation, for lack of a better term). Syntactic inversions were smoothed out according to target language usage, and the drafts were polished to give them a high literary quality. Kumarajiva was credited as a pioneer of this approach. In extreme cases, the polishing might have gone too far, and there are extant discussions of how this affected the original message. During the third phase, the approach to translation was to a great extent dominated by Xuan Zang, who had an excellent command of both Sanskrit and Chinese, and who advocated that attention should be paid to the style of the original text: literary polishing was not to be applied to simple and plain source texts. He also set down rules governing the use of transliteration, and these were adopted by many of his successors.

Missionaries and translation in China

The second wave of translation activities was also related to religious activities, in particular those of Jesuit missionaries who arrived in China in the late sixteenth century. The Jesuits, notably

Matteo Ricci (1552–1610), who set up the first mission station in mainland China, decided that the best way to spread the gospels was to cultivate China's educated class. To this end, a large number of scientific works were translated into Chinese for circulation among scholars and government officials. Such works gained for the Jesuits a high respect from the government and the emperors, and as a result facilitated their missionary work. Missionary translation activities started shortly after Ricci arrived in China in 1583 and continued into the late seventeenth century. The missionaries active in China during that period numbered at least seventy, all of whom produced translations: some were direct translations, others were compilations based on existing Western works. Of the 300-plus titles produced by the missionaries, over a third dealt with various branches of science.

Missionary translation activities had several characteristics. First, a number of missionaries were actually appointed to the Chinese court, or were granted special favours by the emperors for their services in the field of science. Second, many of the books were commissioned with specific purposes in mind. A typical example was the large number of books on astronomy translated from 1628 to 1635 by Johann Adam Schall von Bell (1519–1666) and Jacobus Rho (1593–1638) for the Ming government, which was in the process of revamping the Chinese calendar. Third, collaboration between missionaries and Chinese government officials was common; many works were co-translations. Some Jesuits enjoyed a particularly close relationship with a number of converted Ming Dynasty Chinese officials such as Xu Guangqi (1562-1633), Yang Tingjun (1557–1627) and Li Zhizao (1565–1630). The books on astronomy translated by Schall and Rho, for instance, were all polished by Xu.

The scientific works translated jointly by the missionaries and Chinese scholars/officials fall into the following major categories:

(a) *Mathematics*: the pioneering work being Euclid's *Elements*, with the first six chapters translated by Ricci and Xu. Other notable works include those of Archimedes and Pardies, and the Qing emperor Kangxi is said to have taken part in the translation of works by Pardies;

(b) *Astronomy*: Schall, who was commissioned by both the Ming and the Qing governments to assist in the preparation of the new calendar, was the most prolific translator in this category;

(c) *Geography*: mostly in the form of annotated maps. Individual works on mineral resources and mining were also translated, notably Agricola's *De re metallica*;

(d) *Physics*: including such topics as hydraulic, mechanical and civil engineering. The best known title is *Qiqi tushou* (Illustrated Book of Miraculous Equipments), an amalgamation of materials gleaned from various European publications;

(e) *Religion*: the first extant translation of sections of the Bible was by Jean Bassett (1662–1702). The first translation of the Old and New Testaments into vernacular Mandarin was done by the Jesuit P. L. De Poirot (1735–1814). There were also several translations of the *Imitatio Christi* as well as translations of Catholic catechisms.

After the Papal suppression of the Society of Jesus, many Jesuits stayed on in China. Even when the government turned against them, they were protected by officials and Chinese converts and were generally able to continue with their translation and missionary work; a number of them continued to serve the Qing government. Jean François Gerbillon (1656–1730) and Thomas Pereira (1645–1708), for example, were appointed special Latin interpreters to a diplomatic mission to Nerchinsk, Russia in 1689.

The Jesuits, and later other missionaries, did not engage in one-way translation but were also instrumental in bringing the Chinese classics, and therefore Chinese philosophy, to Europe. Ricci translated the 'Four Books' (*Great Learning, Doctrine of the Mean, Confucian Analects* and *Mencius*) into Latin, while Nicolas Trigault (1577–1628) translated the 'Five Classics' (*Book of Songs, Book of Documents, Book of Changes, Book of Rites*, and *The Spring and Autumn Annals*), also into Latin. Some of the titles in the 'Books' and 'Classics' were later retranslated by missionaries active in the Qing Dynasty. This led to heightened interest in Europe in all things Chinese, particularly in the seventeenth century.

The end of empire

In the early nineteenth century the trading incursions of the European powers, backed by military might, grew too insistent to be ignored by the Peking government, and Lin Zexu (1785–1850) was despatched to Canton in 1838 to put the foreigners in their place. It was his insight that 'in order to control the foreigners we have to master their arts' that prompted the first official team of translators (four men schooled abroad) to tackle the English language. They translated excerpts from the local foreign press, such as the *Canton Register* (started 1827) and *Canton Press* (started 1835), and various English pamphlets on Chinese matters and international law. Their main achievement was *Haiguo tuzhi* (Geography of the Maritime Nations), published in 1844 and based on Murray's *Encyclopaedia of Geography* (1834).

Lin's mission eventually proved a failure, and after a series of military defeats the Manchu rulers agreed to found a College of Languages (*Tongwen guan*) in Peking in 1862. Students, first admitted in 1867, followed an eight-year course in languages – initially English, then French, Russian and German – and natural and social sciences. Their primary role was in the field of diplomacy, but the College also translated and published books on law, politics and natural sciences. Their efforts in the field of law were the most substantial: law books translated included Wheaton's *International Law*, the *Code Napoléon*, and Bluntschli's *International Law*.

In the south, the Jiangnan Arsenal set up its own translation bureau in Shanghai in 1865. It both complemented and rivalled the Peking *Tongwen guan*, concentrating on technical manuals but also extending its scope to embrace a broad spectrum of Western sciences. The bureau was responsible for Chinese translations of standard Western works like Herschel's *Outline of Astonomy*, J. D. Dana's *System of Mineralogy* (1872) and Charles Lyell's *Principles of Geology* (1873). Both the Peking and Shanghai bureaus employed foreign experts who had learned some Chinese, and several of them became known in their own countries as 'China hands'. The normal translation procedure was for the foreign experts to translate and explain verbally to Chinese collaborators, who took their words down and made a draft version.

Their manuscripts were then polished and improved stylistically by often monolingual Chinese scholars without further reference to the original. A number of Chinese translators employed by the bureaus, such as Li Shanlan (1810–82), were scientists in their own right and were therefore able to collaborate with the foreign experts as equals. The works by Herschel, Dana and Lyell were produced by such partnerships and had a long life as college textbooks.

Technical and scientific terms posed a particular problem. John Fryer, who served at the Jiangnan Arsenal for over twenty years, from 1867, explained their modus operandi (Xiong Yuezhi 1994: 497): first a check was made to see if a term was in the existing literature or in use in trade circles; if not, a translation was invented, either by concocting a new character, borrowing a disused one, or by coining a descriptive term (for example 'nourishing gas' for *oxygen* or 'light gas' for *hydrogen*), or by using polysyllabic phonetic representation. The invented term was then entered into a dictionary for later standardization. Despite this attempt at system, variation was rife.

The above institutions, and several more besides, were set up and run by Chinese officials. Alongside them, the missionary bodies were also active. Apart from religious texts, they also translated and published works of general educational interest. The first to be set up was the London Mission Press in Shanghai in 1843. The most productive was the Society for the Diffusion of Christian and General Knowledge among the Chinese, established in Shanghai in 1887. By 1903 they were said to have published around 250 books. Their translation procedures were similar to those employed by the official bureaus, but their technical books in particular suffered from the explicator's lack of expertise and his Chinese collaborator's lack of understanding, and the majority of them were dismissed by Ma Jianzhong (1845–1900), the eminent Chinese linguist, as unreadable or unintelligible.

The third force in the translation of Western works was neither official nor foreign. It emerged in the 1890s and was composed of native intellectuals and spearheaded by political reformers, the best known of them being Kang Youwei (1858–1927) and Liang Qichao (1873–1929). To impress upon their compa-

triots the need to struggle if they did not wish to perish, they introduced the ominous lessons of other empires in world history (all previously unknown to the ethnocentric Chinese); they also undertook translations in the fields of politics and sociology as a way of ensuring national survival. By now, the leading intellectuals had realized that Western thought and skills had to be made their own. Not only the focus but the channel of translation shifted; Japanese became the chief source language, both for original works in that language and also for Japanese translations of Western works. The reasons were simple: Japan was a generation ahead of China in its absorption of Western knowledge and culture, and written Japanese used Chinese characters. Liang Qichao estimated that it took five to six years for a Chinese to gain a reading knowledge of European languages, but only months to acquire an elementary understanding of Japanese. The drawbacks of translating from Japanese were that it was often based on only this elementary grounding in the language, and that it added another filter for the original message to pass through, assuming, as was frequently the case, that the Japanese translation was based on an English translation of an original in another language.

The reformists were very much involved in the rapid growth of independent publishing houses in the period 1895–1900. Their newspapers and magazines carried translations of items from the foreign press, and published in instalments translations of longer works. The most prestigious of the newspapers were the *Shiwu bao* (The Times) in Shanghai, edited by Liang Qichao, and the *Guowen bao* (National Register) in Tientsin, edited by Yan Fu (1853–1921). Yan Fu's translation of Thomas Huxley's long essay 'Evolution and Ethics' was first published in the *Guowen bao* in 1897 before being issued in book form under the title *Tianyan lun* (On Evolution).

This book was a milestone in Chinese translation history, both because its content (it popularized Social Darwinism) and style took the educated world by storm, and because Yan Fu laid down in his preface the three desiderata for translation that have been quoted ever since, namely Faithfulness, Communicability and Elegance. Elegance derived from the language of classical antiquity as the medium of translation. Undoubtedly the right choice for its time, because Yan Fu had to win over the educated class who revered antiquity, the term has since been interpreted as 'readability'. Yan's desiderata have been useful as general guidelines, but his preface is not the theoretical treatise it was later made out to be. He made no attempt to define any of his terms or follow a logical progression. In his preface as well as his translations he cultivated elegance.

Yan Fu set new standards by the depth of his understanding of the English language (he had spent three years in England as a naval cadet) and the breadth of his knowledge (he appended extensive commentaries to his translations), but his 'On Evolution' was not, and did not claim to be, a strict translation. Apart from being a loose rendering of the original, it incorporated some observations by Yan Fu himself. Yan went on to translate J. S. Mill, Herbert Spencer and Montesquieu in the same vein. After 1903, however, he swung towards literal translation, frequently revising his translations to ensure closer correspondence to the original. This had the negative effect of reducing intelligibility. In his last translations, from 1908 onwards, he reversed direction again, freely substituting material of his own for the original expositions. Thus Yan embodied in a single career the main translation trends of his age.

If Yan Fu can be considered the main translation figure in the field of philosophy and social science, the prize for fiction has to go to Lin Shu (1852–1924), his almost exact contemporary, and also from the coastal city of Fuzhou. Culturally an orthodox scholar, Lin Shu's first venture into translation was fortuitous: it is said that it was the recent death of his wife, in 1897, that made him sympathetic to the sad story of Marguerite in Dumas' *La Dame aux camélias* and led him to cooperate with his friend Wang Shouchang in translating the novel. Lin Shu knew no foreign languages; he composed into classical Chinese what Wang translated to him orally. Considerable care, however, was given to revising the draft by Wang and Wei Han. The publication of 'The life and death of the Parisian lady of the camellias' in 1899 was an instant success. Those who bought, read and praised it had no way of judging whether or not it was a good translation; they simply responded to the beauty of the writing. The story of a

beautiful young woman dying a tragic death contributed to its popularity, as this line had always gone down well in China; the more abandoned she was the better. In 1901, Lin's translation of Harriet Beecher Stowe's *Uncle Tom's Cabin* was published under the title 'The Black Slave Appeals to Heaven'; he had Wei Yi as collaborator and they were to form a lasting partnership. By 1911 (the year of the Republican revolution) Lin had translated over fifty books, and more than a hundred more were to come before he died; he worked with many collaborators, over twenty in all, translating from English and French. Interestingly, the actual translators were completely overshadowed by the 'rewrite man'. Nevertheless, Lin Shu's translations undoubtedly owed their popularity to his skill with words, and also to his discrimination: the leading contemporary scholar Qian Zhongshu has testified that despite their omissions and mistakes, the Lin Shu translations (he was referring particularly to Dickens and Montesquieu) have more wit and feeling than more 'faithful' renditions which were published later. Lin was inclined to expand on emotive passages and cut description. He also contributed enthusiastic prefaces and analyses of the chief virtues of the original works, which no doubt increased their impact. The younger generation which later overthrew the tradition that Lin Shu held dear and discarded the use of the classical Chinese in which he excelled admitted that they were engrossed in and indeed enraptured by his translations. His vast output included several works that have enjoyed lasting esteem, among them works by Dumas, Dickens, Balzac, Defoe, Scott, Cervantes, Conan Doyle, as well as many contemporary best-sellers and potboilers: he rendered into Chinese whatever came to hand. He also did not maintain a consistent quality: most critics agree that the quality of his writing deteriorated seriously after the revolution of 1911.

Though Lin Shu used classical Chinese to translate/rewrite long novels, the customary medium for that genre in China was the vernacular (Mandarin). For creative fiction the vernacular remained the dominant medium, indeed the trend was reinforced by the desire of reformist authors to put their message across to the masses. Some translators also adopted the vernacular, particularly in the early 1900s;

however, either because they found the style too verbose, were inexperienced in using it, or assumed that the readership for translations did not consist of the masses, the standard medium until the May Fourth Movement (1919) remained a relatively simple form of literary Chinese.

All the while, however, a cultural revolution was brewing, the most obvious manifestation of which was the use of Mandarin in all kinds of writing, rather than just writing designed for entertainment. Thus it was no coincidence that the Mandarin version of the complete Union Bible was also published in 1919 (see Wickeri 1995). If anything, the Bible translators were under greater democratic pressure than the new generation of cultural reformers to use a written language that reflected ordinary speech. The *Wenli* (i.e. classical language) Union Bible published in the same year soon receded from view, whereas the Mandarin version survived to become the standard text for Chinese Christians.

The twentieth century onwards

The May Fourth Movement, with its agenda of 'installing' a new culture in China, naturally accelerated the importation of Western writings in both original and translated forms. Previous translations, though produced in considerable numbers, had proceeded randomly in terms of choice of material. The new generation of intellectuals, almost all of whom seem to have engaged in translation, some on a massive scale, were much better educated in foreign cultures by virtue of having studied abroad or attended missionary schools in China; they were able to concentrate on works which enjoyed recognition in their own countries. The various vernacular language magazines that sprang up all had their own bias, but between them they more or less covered the map of the civilized world. It has been estimated that literary works from over thirty countries were translated in the 1920s, with the English-speaking countries significantly dropping down the league table to a position below Russia and France, on account of their conservatism (Chen Yugang 1989:95).

Political motivations also lay behind the increase in the translation of Soviet and other revolutionary literature in the 1930s, when the Chinese Communist Party transferred its emphasis from armed uprising to propaganda. The liberal left continued with its own programme of work, however, with perhaps the best expression of its aspirations being the launching in 1935 of the grand plan for a World Library, intended to encompass the ancient, medieval and modern literature of all major countries. The nation's top translators were recruited, and under the general editorship of Zheng Zhenduo (1898–1958) in Shanghai the Library published in 1935–6 over 100 classics from a dozen different countries. It is important to stress that most of the best creative writers of the age lent their skills to translation, which provided a guarantee of very readable products.

In the 1930s, the debate over translation principles that had begun in the 1920s rumbled on, the poles of contention as ever being 'fidelity' vs. 'licence'. In addition to the standard argument in support of fidelity, namely that the native features of the source text ought to be retained, there now emerged the additional, target-oriented objective of appropriating from European languages through translation wording and grammatical devices that the Chinese language was said to be in need of. This view was favoured by leftists who had the jargon of Soviet ideologues to contend with: with intelligent rephrasing being formidably difficult, they were – not surprisingly – inclined to mirror the original wording. The majority however gave more weight to the aesthetics of the Chinese language. Among those who argued the case for aesthetic licence was Lin Yutang (1895–1976), who translated more from Chinese into English than the other way round. There had been a few pioneers of Chinese–English translation around the turn of the century, like Su Manshu (1884–1918) and Gu Hongming (1857–1928), but it was not until the 1930s that the traffic in this direction was of any consequence.

The war with Japan, which broke out in 1937, disrupted large projects such as the World Library, but individual efforts were still very fruitful. Many nineteenth-century European novels were ably translated or re-translated, but perhaps the noblest effort of the war period was that of Zhu Shenghao (1912–44), who literally gave his life to translating the complete plays of Shakespeare. Born and educated in China's

Zhejiang province and accepted into Zhijiang University at the age of seventeen, where he read Chinese literature and English, Zhu graduated in 1921 and joined the Book Company in Shanghai as an English editor. At the age of twenty-three he started translating *The Tempest* into Chinese, with the understanding that the World Book Company would publish his complete translations of Shakespearean plays. The outbreak of the Sino-Japanese War shattered Zhu's translation schedule; his manuscripts were destroyed when he escaped from Japanese-occupied Shanghai. Zhu later returned to the Shanghai foreign concessions to resume his translation work, only to find himself on the run from the Japanese again with the outbreak of World War II, and his manuscripts were again destroyed. In failing health and stricken circumstances, Zhu worked on his translations of Shakespeare until his death in December 1944. He translated a total of thirty-one plays, all of which were published posthumously. Zhu's translations were in prose; his goal was intelligibility without simplification and, above all, speakability. His *Complete Plays* was published as a set in 1947, and reissued, with supplements, as *The Complete Works of Shakespeare* in 1978.

Following in his footsteps, Liang Shiqiu (1902–87) also translated the complete works of Shakespeare single-handed in Taiwan, in a more scholarly vein. Born and educated in Beijing before leaving for the United States to study at the universities of Colorado, Harvard and Columbia, Liang returned to China in 1926 with an MA in English literature and started lecturing at a number of Chinese universities, including Peking University. It was at this time that he started work on rendering the complete works of Shakespeare into Chinese, a task which took him half a century to complete. At the time of the Communist takeover in 1949, Liang left mainland China for Taiwan, where he continued his academic and translation work. Besides translating the complete plays and sonnets of Shakespeare (37 volumes) and other literary works, Liang was also the compiler of an English–Chinese dictionary. Another dedicated translator was Fu Lei (1908–66), best known for his translations of Balzac into rich and vibrant Chinese.

Under the People's Republic, the Soviet Union was the chief source of works for trans-

lation to begin with, but the literature of the Third World (Asia, Africa and Latin America) came to enjoy unprecedented attention. At the same time, the translation of Chinese works into other languages was stepped up through the agency of the Foreign Languages Press (set up in 1950), where native translators worked together with foreign experts. Perhaps the highest level of attention was lavished on *The Selected Works of Mao Tse-tung* (Mao Zedong), but a great many ancient and modern classics were also translated into several European languages. The doyens of translation into English were Yang Hsien-yi (Yang Xianyi) and Gladys Yang. After the cultural famine of the Great Proletarian Cultural Revolution (1966–76), there was an explosion during the 1980s (particularly 1982–6) in the translation of foreign works, right across the board from academic treatises to best-sellers, mainly from English. The quality of these translations has been uneven. The tide of published translations subsided noticeably in the late 1980s because of the financial as well as political constraints faced by publishers.

The state-supported Translators Association of China was set up in 1982 and publishes the bi-monthly 'Chinese Translators Journal' (in Chinese).

Training

The first extant record of a national school of foreign languages in Chinese history is of the National Academy of Persian (*Huihui guozi xue*), set up during the Yuan (Mongol) dynasty in China. Students were recruited from the upper classes of society and trained to be government translators and interpreters of Persian, which was the most important foreign language for the Mongols outside China in terms of their trade and military activities. There are no extant records of the academy's syllabus. The College of Languages, set up by the Manchu government in 1862, was the first multilingual Chinese academy devoted to the training of European language experts and translators. It offered English, French and Russian streams in an eight-year course covering Chinese and foreign languages, translation and such subjects as world history and geography, mathematics, international law, astronomy and economics. German was introduced in 1888 and Japanese in 1898. There were similar regional academies in Canton and Shanghai where the best students were sent to the College of Languages to continue their studies. After functioning independently for forty years, the College was incorporated into the National Capital University, the forerunner of Peking University. The responsibility of translator/interpreter training was taken over by the College of Interpreters (*Yixue guan*) which offered five-year courses in English, French, Russian, German and Japanese. The 'general studies' subjects were similar to those offered at the College of Languages.

After the establishment of the Chinese Republic in 1911, there was no fixed policy regarding translator/interpreter training, and most practitioners were self-trained. Under the People's Republic of China, in-service training was provided to those chosen to work in foreign affairs-related government departments. In Hong Kong, the training of simultaneous interpreters began in the mid-1970s to cater for the government's bilingual conference needs. Training is again in-service and provided by the government. However, some basic training in conference interpreting has been made available to university students in Hong Kong since the mid-1980s.

The first university degree course in translation offered by a Chinese community was the BA in Translation started in 1974 by the University of Hong Kong. An MA course in Translation/Interpreting has been running at GITIS, Fujen University in Taiwan since 1988. Other courses have since been introduced in numerous universities across the region.

Further reading

Ma Zuyi 1984; Cao Shibang 1986; Jiang Wehan 1987; Cheng Yugang 1989; Chan and Pollard 1994; Xiong Yuezhi 1994; Hung 1996.

EVA HUNG AND DAVID POLLARD

Czech tradition

Czech is a West Slavonic language. Typologically, it is an inflecting language whose word-endings perform a variety of functions and in which word order usually plays a grammatical role.

These characteristics are shared by the closest West Slavonic neighbour of Czech, namely Slovak.

Czech written records go back to the tenth century. Between the tenth and the twelfth centuries, the language underwent a rapid development. Literary Czech crystallized on the basis of fourteenth-century Central Bohemian dialects. It was significantly influenced by the work of the Czech thinker and religious reformer Jan Hus (born *c.*1372, burnt at the stake 1415), who was Rector of Prague University. Lexical codification of the language took place in the sixteenth century. The modern language shows an internal stratification into literary Czech (universally used in writing and, in a spoken form, in public communication) and conversational Czech, with original local dialects having coalesced into interdialects. The most widespread of these is known as *obecná čeština* or 'common Czech'. The spoken form of literary Czech has now adopted some of the features of *obecná čeština* and is consequently showing greater flexibility than standard literary Czech.

The Middle Ages

The earliest written evidence of interlingual contact on the territory of the present Czech Republic consists of Old Slavonic translations from Greek, dating from the second half of the ninth century. These are preserved largely in fragments and suggest that the Byzantine culture had some influence in the area, though this influence does not seem to have lasted long.

Latin became the principal cultural medium around the eleventh century and, consequently, the main source language in translation. The kinds of text translated during this period were primarily ecclesiastical and liturgical, but some texts on Church law were also translated.

Typical of the turn of the thirteenth and fourteenth centuries are free adaptations of Latin legendary and apocryphal material, such as the apocryphal legend of Judas. Czech hagiography of the period was also greatly influenced by a collection of the lives of the saints known as *Legenda aurea*. Also dating back to this period is a Czech version of the *Alexandreis*, a poem consisting of ten books in hexameter written around 1180 and attributed to Gaultier de Lille. The Czech version is based on a Latin translation of a French text and perhaps also on a German version produced in Bohemia.

From the thirteenth century onward, as interest in German culture spread among the Czech nobility, German epics of chivalry began to be translated. These were serious epics which portrayed chivalry as a noble pursuit. In the second half of the fourteenth century, translation turned to German texts of entertaining rather than serious tales of chivalry, mainly medieval Celtic and German themes with amorous motifs. From the 1360s onward, prose translations also began to be made of various genres of spiritual epic texts, with German as the main source language still. These were biblical and apocryphal stories, eschatological subjects, so-called 'hell novels' about the struggle between the Devil and God. *Trojánská kronika* ('The Trojan Chronicle'), a Czech translation and adaptation of the Latin *Historia Troiana* by Quido de Columna, was the first printed book in Czech (*c*.1470). The most important Czech translator of the second half of the fourteenth century was Tomáš Štítný ze Štítného (*c*.1333–1409), who translated religious and philosophical literature from Latin.

The age of humanism and Counter-Reformation (fourteenth to seventeenth centuries)

The fourteenth and fifteenth centuries witnessed a turning point in the development of the Czech language. Archaic structural elements were abandoned and Czech orthography was modernized. As a result of reformist endeavours, Latin also ceased to be the exclusive liturgical language around the beginning of the fifteenth century and liturgical texts in Czech translation began to be introduced into the Order of Service. During the first decade of the fifteenth century, further Czech translations were made of biblical texts. The first complete Czech translation of the Bible was printed in 1488.

Humanist translations from Latin represent two basic types of the artistic literature of the day. On the one hand, there is the detached style characteristic of some legendary accounts, for example the legend of St Procopius, and on the other a clear echo of courtly poetry, a passionate lyricism, and a blend of worldly eroticism and mystical ecstasy as can be seen in accounts of the legend of St Catherine of Alexandria. Apart from legends and biblical texts, the Czech humanists also translated the works of Erasmus of Rotterdam, the Latin classics, Greek authors, and the writings of the Fathers of the Church. One important translator of the period, Viktorin Kornel ze Všehrd (1460–1520), advocated the classical principle of *sensum de sensu*, giving priority to producing a functional translation in the spirit of the target language. Zikmund Hrubý z Jelení (also known as Gelenius: 1497–1554), a book publisher, brought out in 1537 and 1544 a comparative Latin–Greek–German–Czech dictionary by the title *Lexicon symphonum*.

The second half of the sixteenth century witnessed a flourishing of Czech literature among the urban mercantile class. Translations of classical and contemporary literature were undertaken, as well as translations of more specialized material from the natural sciences and the humanities. The source languages were predominantly Latin and German. Valuable aids to translation were also produced, including such lexicographical works as the Latin–Czech–German *Nomenclator tribus linguis* (1597) and the Czech–Latin–Greek–German *Silva Quadrilinguis* (1598), both compiled by the Czech humanist Daniel Adam z Veleslavína (1546–99). A major new version of the Bible, known as the *Kralice Bible*, was published between 1579 and 1594.

During the Counter-Reformation (from the second quarter of the seventeenth century), the majority of translations were of hagiographical literature, written by the Jesuits to consolidate the influence of the Catholic Church. They included translations of various writings on the cult of the Virgin Mary. One of the most popular translations of that period, reprinted many times during the seventeenth and eighteenth centuries, was a book of hymns rendered metrically by Jiří Třanovský (1592–1637) from German spiritual songs by Martin Luther.

The eighteenth and nineteenth centuries: the age of Czech National Revival

Literary translation into Czech flourished again in the eighteenth century, and translations were made of German classical works, of rococo and Anacreontic poetry. English and French literature were translated via the medium of German. Ballads and stories were translated from German, sometimes via intermediate versions in Polish. This period also witnessed an increased interest in historical prose and in drama. The works of the German dramatists Gotthold Ephraim Lessing and Friedrich von Schiller were translated from their originals, those of Shakespeare and Molière via German.

The National Revival programme was essentially one of enlightenment, and translation therefore tended to focus on topics which were accessible to the masses. The translations were intended to inspire a nation whose self-confidence had suffered during the Counter-Reformation, when the push for re-Catholicization supported by the Habsburg Empire had gone hand in hand with a vigorous programme of Germanization. The great works of world literature, especially poetry, were translated in order to make them part of the cultural repertoire available to the masses. The most significant translator of the early nineteenth century was Josef Jungmann (1773–1847), one of the leading representatives of the Czech movement of National Revival. He translated from English, French, German and Russian. From German, he translated mainly Goethe and Schiller, and from Russian the anonymous medieval epic *The Lay of Prince Igor*. Jungmann's five-volume Czech–German Dictionary (1834–9) was also a valuable contribution to translation practice. He is, however, best remembered for producing the first Czech version of Milton's *Paradise Lost* (1804, published 1811). In his translations, Jungmann enriched the Czech language by his use of neologisms, archaisms and borrowings from other Slav languages. His translation of Chateaubriand's *Atala* (1805) demonstrated the potential of modern poetic Czech in a way that had not been demonstrated before.

At the beginning of the nineteenth century, translation lay at the centre of a number of disputes, especially those concerning the legitimacy of old-fashioned lexical elements introduced by Humanists and the scale of lexical borrowings from Polish and from the southern and eastern Slavonic languages. Another topic of dispute was prosody. The leading Czech linguist of the day, Josef Dobrovský (1753–1829), demonstrated the unsuitability of quantitative metre for poetical writing in Czech; nevertheless this survived in translations from Latin and Greek poetry to the end of the last century.

The second half of the nineteenth century witnessed a rapid development of Czech literary and cultural life, including literary translation. A new attitude to foreign literatures was championed by the 'May' group (named after the almanac *May*), whose members believed in a democratic, sometimes radical-democratic, approach to progress. Translations began to account for a growing proportion of the literary output. In addition to ancient literature, translations now covered contemporary writing in all major languages: works by Gogol, Pushkin, Victor Hugo, Cervantes, Robert Burns, Byron, Shelley, Mickiewicz, Heine, Petöfi, and many more were translated into Czech. The May group focused on literature which was attractive in form and subject; they therefore tended to disregard many important poets and prose writers, such as Lamartine, Alfred de Vigny and Alfred de Musset. They also deliberately avoided translating from German sources in an attempt to free Czech literature from its entrapment in the German cultural sphere. At any rate, educated Czechs were able to read German literature in the original.

In the last quarter of the nineteenth century, known as the 'Lumír period' after the periodical *Lumír*, literary translation flourished as never before. The writers grouped around the periodical were cosmopolitans and were particularly active in translating poetry. Most prominent among them were the poets Jaroslav Vrchlický (1853–1912) and Josef V. Sládek (1845–1912). In Vrchlický's colossal œuvre as a translator, the Romance literatures predominated, especially French and Italian literature. He also translated from English and German, but his translations of English poetry were limited compared to those done by Sládek, whose favourite poet was Robert Burns. In addition to English poetry, Sládek's greatest achievement was that he translated thirty-three plays by Shakespeare and thereby enriched the Czech stage enormously. Between them, the various translators of the Lumír group provided Czech readers with a rich picture of contemporary literature in the major languages of Europe. Czech translations of Balzac, Dickens, Dostoyevsky, Flaubert, Goncharov, Maupassant, de Musset, Walter Scott, Thackeray, de Vigny, Zola and many others appeared very shortly after the publication of the originals. At the same time, works from less widespread European languages (such as those by Ibsen and Prešeren) and from oriental languages were also translated into Czech.

Towards the end of the nineteenth century, several scholars began to express their misgivings about Vrchlický's method of literal translation: it was felt that poetry translation needed to free itself from a slavish dependence on the form of the original. A greater freedom in this respect can be found in the work of Julius Zeyer (1841–1901) who translated from a variety of languages. The debate on literary translation, initiated by the Modernist movement in the 1890s, continued with minor interruptions even after World War I, perhaps until the late 1930s, with many outstanding writers, translators and literary scholars taking part in it.

The present

Developing the theoretical framework: the Prague School

The impulse for developing a modern theory of translation in general and of the translation of poetry in particular came from the Prague School, a group of scholars who were interested in poetic language as an autonomous mode of speech whose aesthetic function is directed at the linguistic sign itself. Their theory of poetic language strove from the outset for exactitude and formalization, but it did not operate with mathematical or statistical methods in the strict sense. It is therefore sometimes referred to as a 'pre-statistical' theory of poetic language. Demands by members of the Prague School around 1929 for elaborating the principles of a synchronic description of poetic language, an area they claimed was still neglected by linguistics, were already being addressed in a number of important publications by Roman Jakobson (1896–1982), including *O cheshskom stikhe* ('On

Czech Verse', 1923) and *Základy českého verše* ('Foundations of Czech Verse', 1926), as well as some studies by Jan Mukařovský (1883–1975). In the 1930s, Mukařovský published a number of studies on the structural characteristics of specific features of poetic language. He also developed a theory of poetic naming which does not confine itself to metaphor but attempts to account for a continuous transition between the two categories of descriptive and metaphorical naming. Generally speaking, Mukařovský's theory of poetry marked the beginning of a departure from the emphasis on formalism and on a static understanding of the separate components of the poetic text. This is particularly evident in *Kapitoly z české poetiky* ('Chapters from Czech Poetics', Mukařovský 1941).

In parallel with the development of a structural theory of poetic language, attempts were also made to develop a theory of the translation of poetry. The stimulus for a functional understanding of translation came from the founder of the Prague Structuralist School, Vilém Mathesius (1882–1945) in his article 'O problémech českého překladatelstv' ('On the problems of Czech translation', 1913). Among other significant studies in this area, mention should be made of Jakobson's essay 'O překladu veršů' ('On verse translation', 1930). Jakobson (1930) discusses differences in the semantic import of iambics in Czech and Russian and advocates the need for a functional reshaping of the metre of the translated text. This emphasis on the functional role of linguistic elements in the translated text proved highly influential and was adopted in the 1920s and 1930s by the leading practitioners of translation, resulting in many fine renderings of major works. Otokar Fischer (1883–1938) translated from German, English and French and expressed his belief in the functionalist approach in his study 'O překládání básnických děl' ('On translating works of poetry', 1929). Fischer's first major translation was of some of the writings of Friedrich Nietzsche (1914). Among his numerous translations, a special place is held by his epoch-making translation of Goethe's *Faust* (1928) and his selections from the work of the French poet François Villon (1927). Another milestone in the translation of poetry was the translation of Apollinaire's *Zone* by Karel Čapek (1890–1938), better known as a dramatist and prose writer. Since the 1920s, many outstanding Czech poets have continued to devote themselves to the translation of French poetry in particular. Modern translations of the poets of antiquity have also continued to be undertaken, for example by classical scholars such as Otmar Vaňorný (1860–1947), Otakar Jiráni (1879–1934) and Ferdinand Stiebitz (1894–1961).

The structuralist theory of poetic language proved valuable not only in providing a framework for developing a theory of poetry translation, but also in guiding the practice of translation in general and the translation of poetry in particular. Applied to bilingual communication, the functional view of language led to an emphasis on 'functional equivalence', stressing the relationship of the translated text to its receptors. In the translation of poetry, it marked the end of the mechanical copying of the formal features of the original. In addition, the development of exact methods for the analysis of poetic language meant that translation, in turn, began to be understood in terms of interpreting complex verbal signs in specific communicative contexts, and this led to a move away from irrational and subjective approaches.

The 1950s saw a revival of interest in translation theory, especially in the work of Jiří Levý (1926–67), published in book form as Umění překladu ('The Art of Translation') in 1963 and translated into German in 1969 as Die literarische Übersetzung. Theorie einer Kunstgattung and into Russian in 1974 as Izkusstvo perevoda. Although his method of analysis is usually described as literary, Levý succeeded in including in it and utilizing the findings of quantitative analysis and – in the context of contemporary Western theory – fully linking up with the Prague School. Jiří Levý's major contribution to the modern theory of poetry translation was his application of the methods of the exact sciences. With remarkable acuity, he pinpointed the main problems of poetry translation and in many respects marked out the lines along which future research would proceed. It was also largely due to him that, even during the period of pro-Soviet political orientation, Czech theoreticians and practitioners of translation rejected the Soviet tenets, which approached translation, especially that of poetry, from the point of view of formal correspondence. This is evidenced by the large number of outstanding translations of poetry and prose during that period; among these special mention should be made of the translations of American and Russian poetry by Jan Zábrana (1931–84). Modern Czech translation theory proceeds from the work of Jiří Levý, but endeavours to give greater weight to linguistic issues, increasingly turning its attention to exact methods of analysis of poetry translation.

Translation activity during the twentieth century

Despite the theoretical emphasis on the translation of poetry, the bulk of translation and publishing shifted towards prose by the beginning of the twentieth century. Major English, French and German works of realism were translated, along with Nordic, Slavonic, other Romance, and even Asian and African works of literature. This broad spectrum of translation was supported by the establishment of programmes in linguistics at Charles University in Prague and at the University in Brno, founded in 1918. Direct translations from oriental languages, for example the work of Tagore from Bengali, began to appear in the 1930s.

Typical of Czech translation work between the wars was an increased interest in American literature. With a few exceptions such as Mark Twain and Jack London, nineteenth-century American literature had until then been reaching Czech readers with a delay of at least one generation. Interest in contemporary American literature was so lively in the Czech Lands in the 1920s and 1930s that many novels appeared in translation very shortly after the publication of the English originals. The most successful American author in Czech translation was Upton Sinclair, many of whose novels were published from 1906 onward. Also successful in Czech translation were Willa Cather, Theodore Dreiser, Scott Fitzgerald, Sinclair Lewis, John Dos Passos, John Steinbeck, Thornton Wilder and, among dramatists, Eugene O'Neill. In the 1930s, anglophone literature was translated by the disciples of the Prague School linguist Vilém Mathesius (Aloys Skoumal, 1904–63, and Zdeněk Vančura, 1903–74) and those of Otokar Fischer (including Erik A. Saudek, 1904–62, whose translations of Shakespeare are considered outstanding). Russian literature of the Soviet period was represented between the wars by the poets Demyan Bednyy, Vladimir Mayakovskiy, and later Aleksandr Blok. Interest was shown also in novels and short stories with a civil war theme, such as those by Konstantin Fedin, Vsevolod Ivanov, Isaak Babel, Boris Pilnyak and Leonid Leonov.

Despite ideological constraints imposed by the ruling regime, the period from 1948 to 1989 witnessed a considerable increase in translations. Publishing policy, with financial support from the state, made it possible to bring out not only tendentious literature, but also translations of valuable (though not necessarily commercially viable) titles of world literature. During the past thirty years, translations into Czech were published from fifty-five languages, not counting the major international languages. Direct translations were also made from many smaller European languages, such as Flemish, Welsh, Icelandic, Lusatian Sorbian, Yiddish, Macedonian and Catalan. There exist now many direct translations of classical and contemporary works from Arabic, Chinese, Indonesian, Japanese, Korean, Farsi, Vietnamese, several languages of India (such as Bengali, Hindi, Hindustani, Malayalam, Marathi, Punjabi and Tamil) and from such 'exotic' languages as Swahili, Cakchiquel, Quiché, Yucatec and Eskimo. Nor has the literary heritage of the dead languages, such as Accadian, Assyrian, Aztec, classical Greek and Latin, Hebrew, Sanskrit and Sumerian, been forgotten.

One of the negative phenomena, especially in the 1970s and 1980s, was the marked spread of the translation of poetry with the aid of 'interlinear' or word-for-word translations; this was justified theoretically by the argument that poetry could only be translated by a poet. The real reason, however, was political rather than cultural, in that this practice followed what had become the norm in the former Soviet Union. On occasions, the collaboration between a linguist and a poet has undoubtedly resulted in fine translations, but in most instances this practice has not enriched the storehouse of Czech translation of foreign poetry.

After 1989, the great turning point in the political orientation of the Czech Republic and the switch to a market economy resulted in fundamental changes in the patterns of publishing translated literature. On the one hand, there was the definitive removal of ideological barriers, but on the other there was the loss of state subsidies. In the field of translation this meant a marked commercialization of the book market and a temporary decline in publishers' interest in more demanding genres, especially poetry. The boom in publishing commercially viable material, translated primarily from English and German, has inevitably attracted professionally less competent translators, though the high standard of translation into Czech has more or less been maintained.

Czech culture has at all times maintained a lively interest in what is happening abroad. In literary translation, this has meant that virtually every generation has made its own, sometimes more than one, translation of outstanding works of world literature. A small illustration of this is the fact that there exist thirteen published Czech translations of Edgar Allan Poe's poem 'The Raven'.

Non-literary translation

Unlike literary translation, commercial, medical, scientific and technical translation did not become the subject of academic study in the Czech Republic though it was, of course, practised (if on a limited scale) by specialists in their fields between the two wars. With the professionalization of translation after World War II, it became more common to employ non-literary translators in the translation departments of industrial and commercial enterprises, although of course many continued to work freelance in much the same way as literary translators. In 1989, when the country adopted a market economy, non-literary translation naturally gained in importance as it was recognized as a saleable commodity. At the same time, translation agencies were set up and individual translators of commercial texts began to work through them.

Interpreting

In the First Republic (1918–39), members of ethnic minorities had the right to plead in lower courts in their own language. Official (or authorized) interpreters were therefore needed in these and similar institutions, though they were not at the time strictly 'professional' nor, as a rule, full-time interpreters.

Interpreters were also used at the diplomatic and governmental levels. After World War II, in the 1940s and 1950s, simultaneous interpreting was provided primarily by the following categories: wartime émigrés (English), Jewish survivors of the concentration camps (German), second-generation Russian émigrés (Russian), educated Czechs from the pre-war francophile environment (French). Few of these had any linguistic training. A large number of ad-hoc interpreters were, and still are, also used as 'guide-interpreters' for foreign visitors: the Prague Information Service had some 2,500 guide-interpreters on its list in 1994. A very small number of the more highly qualified conference interpreters were/are members of AIIC.

Further reading
Levý 1957; *Acta Universitatis Carolinae, Translatologica Pragensia* (1984–); Galan 1988; Mánek 1990/91; Kufnerová *et al.* 1994.

ZLATA KUFNEROVÁ AND EWALD OSERS

Danish and Norwegian traditions

Danish and Norwegian are both Indo-European languages, historically and structurally related to Dutch, English and German. With the exception of Finnish, the Scandinavian languages constitute the sub-group termed 'Nordic', but Danish and Norwegian belong to different subtypes: Danish (with Swedish) belongs to the East Nordic group, Norwegian (with Icelandic and Faroese) to the West Nordic. However, the language situation in Norway is complicated by the fact that for over 400 years (1397–1814) Denmark and Norway formed one state, to which also belonged Schleswig-Holstein, Iceland, the Faroe Islands and, after its rediscovery in the eighteenth century, Greenland.

Copenhagen, in Denmark, was the capital and administrative centre of the realm, and Danish was consequently the language of administration and of the administrators. As a result, a literary language barely distinguishable from standard Danish developed in the towns of southern Norway, so that in the late nineteenth century, long after the severance of the union, the plays of Henrik Ibsen could be performed in their original versions at the Royal Theatre in Copenhagen.

But, long before that, a movement had been launched to create a new standard Norwegian language, *Nynorsk* (New Norwegian), on the basis of the dialects of rural areas uncontaminated by Danish influence. This resulted in a situation with two official languages and a movement away from Danish, even for the traditional literary medium, the near-Danish *Riksmål* or *Bokmål* (book language) of the south.

This entry treats Denmark and Norway as one area in the period up to 1800 and as separate areas for the modern period.

As the Scandinavian language communities are small, their need for translation is even greater than is the case for the languages of larger countries. There has, of course, been a considerable amount of mutual translation between Scandinavian languages, though the urge to communicate has sometimes been quelled by mutual animosity, as after the Danish–Swedish wars in the seventeenth century and Norway's struggle for independence during the nineteenth century. More important, therefore, has been the influence from and attraction to other European civilizations. From the earliest days and up to 1900 the attraction to Germany was by far the greatest. In the Middle Ages, the Hanse had settlements and trading posts all over Scandinavia, and German influence continued until the Schleswig wars of the mid-nineteenth century. English influence was by and large of minor importance throughout most of this period and was severely checked during the Napoleonic Wars, when Denmark/Norway was forced into an alliance with France, and Copenhagen was bombarded by the British navy in 1807. British influence was re-established in the latter half of the nineteenth century, to be strengthened in the twentieth by American influence, so that today by far the majority of translations are from and into English.

We do not know much about the translation situation in Scandinavia in early times; translation history begins with the introduction of Christianity around the year 1000, but the early Middle Ages have left few records. Latin, of course, was the literary language, but contrary to the practice of England and Iceland, few texts were translated into the vernacular. Therefore, the evidence we have of translation activity is mainly based on the emergence of Latin loanwords in the Danish documents that begin to appear after 1200. Saxo in his *Gesta Danorum*, written shortly after 1200, renders Scandinavian tradition, and in some cases undoubtedly translates Scandinavian sources, written and oral, into his ornate silver Latin; but no originals have been preserved.

In Norway, some legends were translated from Latin about 1150, and the Old Testament from the Vulgate in the thirteenth century. The first work of literature to be translated was *Tristram og Isond*, translated in 1226 by Brother Robert, at the request of King Haakon Haakonsen.

The Renaissance and after

Danish vernacular literature developed slowly, and Denmark therefore retained a tradition of original writing in Latin rather longer than the larger European countries. Consequently, many translations from the Renaissance to the beginning of the nineteenth century were into and from Latin. Many came fairly late: Ludvig Holberg's *Nicolai Climii Iter Subterraneum* (1741), an international best-seller inspired by Thomas More's *Utopia*, was translated into Danish for the first time by the poet Jens Baggesen in 1789. The main translation event for Denmark and Norway prior to the Enlightenment was undoubtedly Christiern Pedersen's translation of the Bible, influenced by Luther's Bible, and known as *Chr. III's Bible* (1550).

From the Middle Ages there was a considerable amount of translation from High and Low German into Danish, a tendency which was in no way diminished during the Reformation, when Danish theologians began to look to Wittenberg rather than to Rome for guidance and inspiration.

For other modern languages, Latin was often the relay language (Jakobsen 1988: 367). Thus a number of sixteenth- and seventeenth-century Danish works, mainly religious ones, were translated into Latin, and from Latin into English; and much of the traffic in the opposite direction followed the same route. Direct literary translation from English only began in the late seventeenth century with Daniel Collins's translation of Francis Quarles's *Enchiridion* (1640, Danish translation 1657), and that was still

exceptional: until well into the nineteenth century, most translation of English literature was via German.

In other respects, Collins's case is characteristic of the first translations from English: he was a merchant, he was English, working from his own language into Danish, and he spent much of his time in Norway. Until about the middle of the nineteenth century, English was regarded as a language of commerce rather than of culture, and, probably because of trade relations, English influence was stronger in Norway than in Denmark.

Large-scale translation from Romance languages, including French, only developed towards the end of the eighteenth century. Early examples of French influence typically took the form of loose imitation, as in Ludvig Holberg's *Peder Paars* (1719–20), which echoes passages from Boileau's *Le Lutrin*, but which is not a translation. Holberg's comedies were influenced by Molière, some of whose plays were actually translated for the 'Danish Stage' from its opening in 1722. One of the first large-scale translators from French, Spanish and other languages was Dorothea Biehl (1731–88), the first woman in Denmark to make a living as a writer. As her father did not believe in education for women, Biehl was largely self-taught, but she managed to acquire a number of European languages. She translated and adapted French, German and Italian plays for the stage, but she is best remembered for her celebrated translation of Cervantes' *Don Quixote* (1776–7).

The nineteenth century: Romantic translations

In the nineteenth century, translations became more frequent than before. The dominant source language was still German, but direct translations from English and the Romance languages were also found, especially after 1850. Works by all major European poets, dramatists and prose writers were translated at some point or other, and in addition, whole new genres were introduced, mainly as a result of translation. This is true of children's literature, which came into existence in Denmark rather later than in the larger European countries, and in the beginning was heavily dependent on translation

(Hjørnager Pedersen and Shine 1979). It would also be fair to say that the development of the Danish novel was much influenced by translations, notably of Walter Scott. Charles Dickens was translated by L. Moltke, who brought out an almost complete Dickens edition, the later volumes of which appeared almost simultaneously with the English book versions of the previously serialized novels. This translation was only supplanted in the course of the 1980s by Eva Hemmer Hansen's Dickens.

Towards the end of the eighteenth century, dramatic inspiration came mainly from Germany, and German influence continued into the nineteenth century, with translations and imitations of German romantic drama. Later, French influence was re-established, Eugène Scribe (c.1825–80) being one of the most popular dramatists. However, from the beginning of the century there was also interest in Shakespeare, Sille Beyer (1803–61) and the actor Peter Foersom being two of the most important translators and adaptors prior to Edvard Lembcke. Whereas, with *Hamlet Prinds af Danmark* (1813), Foersom was particularly interested from the beginning in the tragedies, which he translated with respect for Shakespeare's text, wishing to create roles in which he himself could shine, Sille Beyer from her first Shakespeare translation *Viola* (*Twelfth Night*) in 1847 tried to adapt his comedies to contemporary taste, with Mrs Heiberg, the leading lady of the Royal Theatre, taking an active part in shaping the speeches of the heroines. This meant extensive rewriting. Thus Malvolio and the plot centred around him were removed from the adaptation of *Twelfth Night* (Gad 1974).

In the course of the nineteenth century, the main writers and genres in all major European languages were covered. It is characteristic that many translations were by poets and dramatists. Thus the poet Oehlenschläger translated German fairy tales (1816), and the poet and philosopher N. F. S. Grundtvig translated *Beowulf* (1820). Hans Christian Andersen translated numerous plays for the Royal Theatre, and the poet Holger Drachmann produced a spirited version of Byron's *Don Juan* (Part I in 1880 and Part II in 1902).

Denmark in the present day

There has been considerable translation activity both from and into Danish throughout the twentieth century, and the volume of translations has increased steadily since 1950. In 1991, 2,336 books were translated, as against 1,976 five years previously; but here, as in other countries, the volume of literary translation has decreased in relation to that of non-literary translation: in 1986, two out of every three books translated were fiction, drama or poetry; in 1991 the figure had dropped to about 60 per cent.

At any rate, published books are only the tip of the iceberg. The majority of commercial and administrative translations are never registered as such, and this category would undoubtedly be even bulkier if many Danish companies had not adopted English (or, in some cases, German) as company language. Even so, the volume of translation is staggering.

English is more in demand than all other languages put together, both as source and target language; in 1991, it accounted for 1,528 of the 2,336 titles published, and this tendency undoubtedly also applies to non-published translations. However, there is also a fair amount of translation from and into German, which is followed in importance by French, Spanish, Italian and Russian. This fact is reflected in the training programmes available for commercial translators, which provide degrees in the languages mentioned. But translation takes place from and into practically all European languages and those of a great many other countries. This tendency is strengthened because, since the 1960s, there has been some immigration of ethnic groups who used to be very rare in Scandinavia. Apart from Turkey and former Yugoslavia, Vietnam, the Indian subcontinent, and Sri Lanka have also yielded a number of immigrants with varying language backgrounds. But small communities from all corners of the world can be found in modern Denmark: this entails a need for interpreters to and from a great number of languages. The training of such interpreters is unsystematic and haphazard.

It is impossible to mention more than a few of the many literary translators who have been active in the twentieth century. Kai Friis Møller (1888–1960) was a good translator of poetry, as was the poet and critic Tom Kristensen (1893–1974). One of the most productive translators of all time was Mogens Boisen (1910–87), who translated more than 800 books, mainly from English, German and French. Boisen was an army officer; he wrote books on military matters and was made lieutenant-colonel in 1951. By then, however, he had already started translating. Among his best known translations are Melville's *Moby Dick* (1955), Thomas Mann's *Dr. Faustus* (1957), and especially Joyce's *Ulysses*, which he first brought out in 1949 but kept revising till he published a third edition in 1980.

Research and publications

Interest in translation theory did not exist as such before 1900, although isolated remarks can be gathered from the introductions to various translations, ranging from A. Sørensen Vedel, who in the preface to his translation of Saxo's *Gesta Danorum* (1575) complains about Saxo's 'dark and difficult Latin', to the more considered and lengthier contributions of famous nineteenth-century translators such as Edvard Lembcke (Shakespeare) and Christian Wilster (Homer).

Lembcke is typical of his age in that he has little to say about the problems of translation but demonstrates his awareness of the difficulties through his analysis of the peculiarities of Shakespeare's subject matter and diction. Wilster, who is more outspoken, adopts a position very similar to that of Rossetti: that the translator should combine fidelity with a reasonable amount of freedom; he is also very much aware of the difficulties inherent in rendering a classical metre in a modern language.

Translation studies in the twentieth century began with the work of Paul Rubow, Professor of Comparative Literature at the University of Copenhagen, who wrote a little book on 'originals and translations' (1929) and a number of other studies of individual translators or translations. Eric Jacobsen's *Translation a Traditional Craft* (1958) was a major contribution to international translation scholarship, although it expressly dissociated itself from the budding discipline of translation theory. It is a study of Marlowe's translations of Ovid's elegies, viewed

against the background of Marlowe's education and language training. A combination of literary interest and classical scholarship is also characteristic of Knud Sørensen's *Thomas Lodge's Translation of Seneca's De beneficiis Compared with Arthur Golding's Version* (1960).

Translation theory proper, drawing on the tradition of Levý, was introduced into Denmark in L. L. Albertsen's *Litterær oversættelse* (Literary Translation, 1972), which maintains the importance of the translation over that of the original. From the early 1970s, a number of theses have been written on various aspects of translation, but most of these remain unpublished. One exception is Viggo Hjørnager Pedersen's *Oversættelsesteori* (Translation Theory, 1973), the third revised edition of which (1987) is the standard Danish introduction to translation studies. Gad (1974) is completely atheoretical but anticipates the work of the manipulators in concentrating on the historical and cultural background for Sille Beyer's adaptations of Shakespeare. Møller Nielsen (1974) is a scholarly study of Danish translations of Homer but is weak in general translation theory. Munch-Petersen (1976) is a mainly bibliographical account of nineteenth-century prose fiction translated into Danish. Lorentsen *et al.* (1985) discuss translation and new technology, whereas Baaring (1992) gives an introduction to interpreting. A number of other contributions have since appeared, but most of these are articles, and the majority are written in English or other major European languages. Mention should be made of Draskau (1987), Hjørnager Pedersen (1988), Jakobsen (1994) and Gottlieb (1994c).

Denmark is too small a country to have been at the forefront of a capital intensive area like machine translation. However, important work within the field has been done within the framework of the EU-financed EUROTRA programme, and IBM Denmark have developed a machine-assisted translation programme. The most original contribution in the field has probably been made by the small WINGER company, who have consistently developed translation programmes for PCs (Dunbar and Hjørnager Pedersen 1990; Dunbar and Andersen 1991).

Universities and other institutions of further education, together with associations of translators and private bodies, issue a number of series and journals devoted to translation. *DAO* is a monograph series in Danish on translation studies. Subjects range from general translation theory to subtitling and machine translation on PCs. The series is issued by the Centre for Translation Studies at Copenhagen University, which also edits a monograph series in English, *Copenhagen Studies in Translation*, and an international journal, *Perspectives in Translatology*. *ARK*, issued by the Copenhagen Business School, is a monograph series, several volumes of which have dealt with translation. *CEBAL*, likewise from the Copenhagen Business School, was the forerunner of the same institution's *Copenhagen Studies in Language*. Under both names this publication has printed many articles on translation. *Hermes* is a periodical on linguistics from the Åarhus Business School, often with articles on translation and lexicography.

The situation in Norway

Even before 1814, independent Norwegian translations had begun to appear. Thus translations of Shakespeare began in 1782, Nils Rosenfeldt's translation in 1790 comprising seven central works, and Johan Storm Munch translated Schiller's *Don Carlos* in 1812. Translations from Racine, Jean Paul, Goethe, Madame de Staël, Victor Hugo and others followed rapidly. However, many works of German, French or English origin were still read in Danish translation, whereas independent translations of the Old Icelandic sagas began with Jacob Aall's *Laxdøla saga* (1816–20).

The first translation into 'rural Norwegian' was Hans Hansen's translation of Horace (1797–1800). However, it was the pioneer of Norwegian as an independent language, Ivar Aasen, who really drew attention to the possibilities of this medium with his 1853 translation of poems and prose extracts from Shakespeare, Cervantes, Luther, Schiller and Byron into *landsmål*, the forerunner of Nynorsk. Aasen also planned a Bible in Nynorsk, and the New Testament, translated by Elias Blix, appeared in 1889. The complete Bible, however, only appeared in 1921, whereas the Samians of Northern Norway had had their own New Testament, translated by Niels Stockfleth, since 1834 (and the Greenland Inuits their Bible, translated by Paul Egede, since 1766).

The adherents of Nynorsk deliberately tried to enrich the new language and to give it prestige through translations from the classics. This is the background for translations of Shakespeare such as Arne Garborg and Olav Madshus's (*Macbeth* in 1901 and *Kaupmannen i Venetia* in 1905).

The first decades of the twentieth century were characterized by many translations from English, French and German, so that most major writers were represented in Norwegian before World War II. Mention must be made of Niels Kjær and Magnus Grønvold's translation of *Don Qixote* (1918) and translations of the classics: a free version of the *Odyssey* by Arne Garborg in 1918, followed by P. Østbye's *Iliad* (1920) and *Odyssey* (1922). Østbye also translated Greek tragedies by Sophocles (1924), Aeschylus (1926) and Euripides (1928).

The series *Klassiske bokværk*, 24 titles in all and containing translations of the classics, appeared in the 1920s, followed in the 1930s by *Bokverk frå millomalderen* with medieval classics like the *Rolandskvadet* (*Chanson de Roland*), translated by A. Dahle. The 1930s also saw a new translation of twenty-three Shakespearean plays by Henrik Rytter (1932–3), and two more plays followed in 1934. Shakespeare was also translated into the Riksmål, with twenty-one works by various translators during 1923–42, and a new collection of plays translated by A. Bjerke (1958–80). Most renowned in this category, however, are Hartvig Kiran's *Macbeth* (1962) and *Hamlet* (1967).

Many translations from Russian appeared throughout the twentieth century. Thus *Crime and Punishment* has appeared in no less than six different translations, and a complete new edition of Dostoyevsky was published in 1994.

English is the dominant language for translations into Norwegian, followed by German, Swedish, French, Danish, Russian and Spanish. The all-time best-selling translation is an Astrid Lindgren children's book (66,000 copies), followed by five detective stories by Ian MacLean (40–45,000 copies). Although English is the dominant language, this is less so than in Denmark and Sweden.

Well-known translators include Anna-Lisa Amadou, famous for her translation of Proust (1963–94), Ole Michael Selberg, who translated Musil (1990–94), Olav Angell, who translated Joyce's *Ulysses* (1993), and Kari and Kjell Risvik, famous for their 300 translations from fourteen languages.

As for translations from Norwegian, it is worth mentioning that Thor Heyerdahl's books have been translated into no less than 67 languages, Ibsen's plays into 50, and children's books by Aimée Sommerfeldt and Jostein Gaarder into 30 languages.

Research and publications

The first scholarly introduction to the area was Sylfest Lomheim's *Omsetjingsteori* (Translation Theory, 1989), and the anthology *Det umuliges kunst* (The Art of the Impossible), edited by Per Qvale, appeared in 1991. *Godt ord igjen* (edited by Morten Krogstad) was a festschrift on the occasion of the fortieth anniversary of the *Norsk Oversetterforening* (1988). The earliest introduction to the problems of translation is to be found in *Gyldendals Aktuelle Magasin* (volume 2, 1978). Among the most recent publications is Per Qvale's *From St. Jerome to Hypertext* (2003; originally published in Norwegian in 1988).

Mention should also be made of the exceptionally good English–Norwegian dictionary *Cappelens Store Engelsk-Norsk Ordbok*, compiled by the grand old man among Norwegian translators, Herbert Svenkerud: this could arguably serve as a model for bilingual dictionaries all over the world.

Further reading
Munch-Petersen 1976; Hjørnager Pedersen and Shine 1979; Hjørnager Pedersen 1988; Jakobsen 1988; Lomheim 1989; Qvale 1991.

VIGGO HJØRNAGER PEDERSEN
AND PER QVALE

Dutch tradition

The Dutch-language area comprises the Netherlands and Flanders, roughly the northern half of the federal state of Belgium. There are around 24 million speakers of Dutch, mostly in the Netherlands, with a substantial percentage in Flanders.

In the medieval period the area was politically divided, with some parts owing allegiance to France and others to the (German) Holy Roman Empire. In the fifteenth and sixteenth centuries the various duchies and counties of the Low Countries were gradually united under the Burgundian and then the Habsburg dynasties. The Eighty Years' War (1568–1648), which began as a rebellion against the Spanish Habsburg king Philip II, resulted in a north–south division, as the northern, Calvinist-dominated Dutch Republic gained independence and the Southern Netherlands remained Catholic under Spanish and subsequently Austrian rule. After the French Revolution of 1789 both countries came under French control. Following Napoleon's defeat in 1815 they formed the short-lived United Kingdom of the Netherlands, from which Belgium broke away in 1830. Originally dominated by a French-speaking bourgeoisie, Belgium is now a linguistically divided and politically decentralized state in which Dutch-speakers and French-speakers have exclusive rights in their own regions (Flanders and Wallonia, respectively); the capital Brussels is officially bilingual (Dutch–French) and the small German-speaking minority in the east enjoys constitutional protection. In the Netherlands, the northern province of Friesland is bilingual (Dutch–Frisian) as well, Frisian being spoken alongside Dutch by approximately 350,000 people, even though only a small proportion of these also use Frisian as a written language.

The history of translation into Dutch has yet to be written. Individual aspects have been investigated and documented in one way or another, but no general surveys or synthetic expositions are currently available.

The medieval period

Next to nothing is known about vernacular culture in the Low Countries during the early medieval period, since the written language was Latin. The very fragmentary evidence that has been preserved, however, leaves little doubt that the Dutch written tradition begins with translations. Among the very first words recorded in Old Dutch are isolated terms occurring as interlinear glosses in Latin manuscripts from the eighth and ninth centuries. The oldest discursive texts in an eastern form of Old Dutch known as Old Low Franconian are the tenth-century Carolingian (or Wachtendonck) psalms, interlinear versions of the Latin Vulgate; they probably came into being in the border region between the modern Netherlands and Germany but have been preserved only in fragmentary form in sixteenth-century copies and glosses.

A continuous tradition of written Dutch can be dated back to the late eleventh century, when the so-called *probatio pennae*, a single short sentence in Old Dutch together with its literal translation into Latin (or, less likely, vice versa), was written down by a West Flemish monk trying out a new quill in a monastery in England. The manuscript was discovered in Oxford in 1931, and our monk may well have crossed the Channel in or shortly after 1066 as part of the Flemish contingent accompanying William the Conqueror, who was married to the daughter of the Count of Flanders. The most substantial text in Old Dutch is the Egmond (or Leiden) *Willeram*. It dates from around 1100 and is a Dutch version of an Old High German commentary on the Song of Songs by the Benedictine monk Williram of Ebersberg in Bavaria. Although the two languages were still close to each other at this stage, the Dutch scribe writing in the monastery of Egmond in Holland systematically adapted his source text to fit his own pronunciation and vocabulary.

It is customary to refer to the language from the twelfth century onwards as Middle Dutch. Among the earliest literary products in Middle Dutch are the works of Henric van Veldeke, who wrote in the latter half of the twelfth century in an eastern dialect close to German. His rhyming *Life of Saint Servatius* of c.1160–70 was based on a Latin *vita* from a hundred years earlier. His *Eneid*, also in rhyming couplets, was altogether more innovative, as it went back to French secular sources: based on the Anglo-Norman *Roman d'Eneas* from around 1150, it introduced the courtly epic into both Dutch and German literature, for although Van Veldeke probably began his *Eneid* in Dutch he eventually finished it in Thuringia in a language that could readily be understood both by Dutch and by High German-speaking audiences. Van Veldeke's love lyrics, finally, harked back to the French troubadour tradition and helped introduce the courtly *Minnesang* into German literature.

On the whole, medieval Dutch literature and learning, and thus the written tradition generally, relied heavily on foreign-language sources, particularly Latin and French. In the twelfth and thirteenth centuries the economic and cultural centre of gravity in the Low Countries lay in Flanders, with flourishing towns like Bruges and Ghent. By the fourteenth century, the Duchy of Brabant, with towns like Brussels, Leuven and Antwerp, had begun to replace Flanders as the main cultural focus. Although the Counts of Flanders enjoyed a large degree of autonomy, they owed political loyalty to the French kings. The southern parts of the county (now in northern France) were French-speaking, and French was used frequently at court. The twelfth-century French poet Chrétien de Troyes wrote his *Conte du Graal* for the Flemish Count Philip of Alsace.

It is not surprising, then, that much secular and fictional writing in Middle Dutch is based on French models. Among the pre-courtly *chansons de geste*, i.e. the Carolingian or Frankish romances centred around the figure of Charlemagne, the Middle Dutch version (early thirteenth century) of the French *Renaut de Montauban* gives a good idea of the way the 'matter of France' was adapted. Although in a few places the French is followed almost word for word, the Dutch text cannot be traced back to one identifiable French manuscript but echoes different French versions. Many episodes have been very substantially altered, and they do not always occur in the same order. The most probable explanation for such divergencies is that they reflect an oral tradition, and that the written version was composed on the basis of memorized episodes – as is also suggested by the large store of formulaic phrases and the way in which some episodes are apparently shaped as self-contained entities.

The courtly Arthurian romances also reached the Low Countries via France. The techniques of radical *remaniement* (reshaping) and *entrelacement* (interweaving), and the complex textual relations between originals and adaptations which result from this, can be illustrated with reference to the massive *Lancelot* compilation – some 90,000 verses in all – put together around 1320 in Brabant. It contains ten Arthurian romances, the central three of which are translations from a French cycle. The others, inserted in different places (two romances between parts 1 and 2, the remaining five between parts 2 and 3), are rewritings of existing Middle Dutch versions of French sources, but here too the compiler freely added and omitted episodes, and provided linking passages in an attempt to hold the entire cycle together.

The impact of these works reached far. It is thought, for example, that the main Arthurian romance in Middle Dutch which is not a translation or adaptation, the *Walewein* begun by Penninc and completed by Pieter Vostaert, possibly around 1260, may have been written as an answer to the slightly earlier *Lantsloot vander Haghedochte*, a verse rendering of the French *Lancelot en prose*. The most important Middle Dutch animal epic, *Reynard the Fox*, can certainly be read as a satire on the courtly values of the Carolingian and Arthurian cycles.

But there are other reactions, which directly involve other cultural traditions and relations. The extremely prolific Jacob van Maerlant, the author of some 230,000 lines of verse who lived in the latter half of the thirteenth century, began his career with a number of courtly romances mostly based on French sources. Gradually, however, he turned away from fiction towards historical, didactic and encyclopaedic works, covering virtually every field of knowledge from geography to medicine, and including both biblical and secular history. In so doing, he replaced French source texts with Latin ones, the world of entertainment with the world of erudition. The switch from French to Latin as a source language is symptomatic. Latin, the high-status language of education, learning and the Church, marked a cultural divide. The translations of didactic and spiritual works from Latin into the vernacular clearly show the unequal relation between the two worlds. Scholastic theology, for example, remained the preserve of Latin, and only the more popularizing works on the subject, intended for a lay audience, were translated into Dutch. Texts containing practical meditation exercises and devotional treatises, on the other hand, were translated much more frequently. In some instances works of this kind were rendered both into prose and into verse: the verse translations tended to adopt modes of presentation reminiscent of the secular romances and of oral traditions, while the prose versions appear to have been intended for private reading or for reading aloud in the

small semi-religious communities typical of the medieval Low Countries.

As urbanization and literacy increased towards the end of the Middle Ages, the divide between Latin and vernacular culture narrowed. In some circles, such as the culturally influential semi-religious communities of the *Devotio Moderna* (also known as the 'Brethren of the Common Life') in the Northern Netherlands in the late fourteenth and fifteenth centuries, moralizing and didactic works were written in both Latin and Dutch, or translated very soon after their first appearance. In his *De libris teutonicalibus* ('On books in Dutch') Gerard Zerbold of Zutphen (died 1398) argued that it was immaterial whether books were read in Latin or the vernacular, as long as they were edifying and within the reader's intellectual grasp. At the same time, the emergence of an increasingly powerful merchant class in the towns created a demand for bilingual and even multilingual phrasebooks, of which the fourteenth-century Dutch–French *Livre des mestiers* ('Book of trades') is the first attested specimen.

The Renaissance

In the course of the fifteenth century several parts of the Low Countries came under the control of the Burgundian dukes. They set out to create a more centralized administration which used French as its dominant language. Although the Burgundians showed little interest in literary patronage, the so-called Chambers of Rhetoric, a kind of literary guild for well-to-do burghers which were introduced in the Low Countries in the fifteenth century, were modelled on French examples both in their organization and in the type of work they produced. Their output contained a significant number of translations from the French, and the high proportion of French loanwords in their vocabulary is indicative of the weight of French at this time.

The invention of printing around the middle of the fifteenth century was to have a profound impact on cultural life, but it did not immediately lead to translations. The very first printing presses in the Low Countries were set up in small northern towns; they published mostly Latin books but it soon became clear that the local markets were too limited, both financially and intellectually, to support such expensive enterprises. In the sixteenth century, Antwerp – by now the main economic and population centre and a cultural metropolis – became the most important publishing centre in the Low Countries. Here books could be printed for international markets in a range of languages and often in multilingual form. It was here also that from around the middle of the sixteenth century the European Renaissance would be translated into Dutch. The modern Dutch verb *vertalen* is first attested in its current meaning (to translate) in this period.

The role of translation around the beginning of the century may be gauged from the activity of a publisher like Thomas van der Noot, who was based mainly in Brussels rather than in Antwerp, and who was the first Low Countries printer to request and obtain, in 1512, copyright permission to protect his products. Between 1505 and 1523 Van der Noot brought out some 35 texts in approximately 40 printings. His early production ranged from saints' lives in Dutch to literature in French and a Latin work on logic. The later printings make it clear that Van der Noot, having identified his audience, carefully selected, translated and adapted his source texts to suit the wealthy, cultured, Dutch-speaking patrician circles of Brabant. Around half the books he printed were translations done by himself from Latin, French and German. In those cases where practical knowledge or moral instruction were the main reason for publication, he often removed, as irrelevant, any trace of the foreign-language origin of the texts. High-prestige works, on the other hand, whether of a professional or of a literary nature, would be brought out in luxurious, expensive editions and fully acknowledge their status as translations by parading their famous authors' names.

Later in the sixteenth century much of the translation activity associated with the break-through of the Renaissance in vernacular culture was intended for the same type of audience. Whereas the Humanist intellectual elite used Latin as its medium and various popularizing and chapbook versions in Dutch appealed to a more traditional public, the translations from the classics which began to appear in Antwerp around 1550 were aimed at a prosperous and culturally progressive urban elite. The first major translator of the Classics into Dutch was the Antwerp Rhetorician Cornelis van Ghistele (*c.*1510–73), who in the 1550s and 1560s produced commercially successful renderings of works by Ovid, Virgil, Terence and Horace, as well as of Erasmus and – via a Latin version – Sophocles. In his prefaces Van Ghistele chided the Humanists for writing only in Latin and, at the other end of the scale, voiced his contempt for 'worthless' medieval romances and other entertainment literature. He justified his own work by pointing not only to the intrinsic merit of his originals but also to translations being published in other modern languages. Typical of the early Renaissance translator was his acute awareness of the imperfection of the mother tongue compared with the purity, flexibility and abundance of the classical languages.

Whereas Van Ghistele stuck mostly to authors who were on the Latin school curriculum, the other major translator of the period, Dirk Volkertszoon Coornhert (1522–90), who worked in the northern Netherlands, was more interested in works containing practical or moral instruction. Apart from Homer, whom he translated through a Latin version, and Boccaccio, done via the French, Coornhert translated Boethius, Cicero and Seneca. In contrast to Van Ghistele, Coornhert showed a strong purist streak in his use of Dutch. In this, he went beyond translation: he actively encouraged those circles which in the 1580s produced the first Dutch grammar and the first Dutch treatment of dialectic and classical rhetoric; and he himself was the first to write a book on ethics in Dutch, devising the necessary terminology as he went along.

Coornhert's activity in this respect was symptomatic of the growing emancipation of Dutch as a vehicle for both arts and sciences. The latter half of the sixteenth century witnessed not only a huge increase in translations of all manner of practical and scientific works, but also the first works directly written in Dutch on subjects ranging from mathematics and logic to botany and music. Not surprisingly, the period also saw the first large-scale bilingual and multi-lingual dictionaries.

Another phenomenon of increasing importance was the translation of the Bible, mostly by Protestants, since the Protestant ethic expected believers to have direct access to the word of God. In the early phases of the Reformation a Dutch version derived from Luther's German Bible was commonly used. From the 1560s onwards the so-called 'Two Aces' Bible was widely read. This was a hybrid product, in which the Old Testament was based on Luther and the New Testament had been translated on very different principles from the original Greek. A standard version did not come about until the seventeenth century, when the Dutch States General commissioned an entirely new translation which was to be carried out along lines similar to the English Authorized Version, i.e. prepared by a collective, and as close to the source texts as the recipient language would permit. The Dutch 'States Bible' appeared in 1637. It was hugely influential as a linguistic and cultural point of reference, and remained the standard Dutch Bible until the twentieth century.

By the time the 'States Bible' appeared, the Eighty Years' War had run most of its course, the Dutch Republic had gained independence, and the political, economic and cultural centre of the Low Countries had shifted decisively from the southern to the northern Netherlands, and to Holland in particular. Amsterdam had replaced Antwerp as the new publishing capital. A supraregional Dutch standard language was gradually taking shape, a process to which the 'States Bible' contributed significantly. The prosperity of the new state, and the power of a self-conscious and highly literate merchant class in it, meant that the demand for translations could only increase. In the first decades of the seventeenth century Dutch culture continued the deliberate learning process associated with the vernacular Renaissance of the sixteenth century, but soon imitation turned into emulation. The mercantile base of the Dutch economy and the creation of a seaborne commercial empire fostered an active interest in practical knowledge and in things foreign. Moreover, in the politically and ideologically tolerant climate of the Dutch Republic, the sciences and modern philosophy flourished, and since by no means all the burghers of Holland read Latin or French, translations were called for.

The production of the seventeenth-century 'arch-translator' Jan Hendriksz Glazemaker (1619/20–82) can illustrate this wide-ranging

intellectual hunger. Glazemaker, who frequented the intellectual elite despite his modest social background, worked mostly from Latin and French, occasionally also from German and Italian. In all his translations, which ran to over sixty titles, he wrote a consciously purist Dutch. His professionalism is everywhere apparent, and he frequently criticized older translations for inaccuracies, priding himself on consulting existing versions in other languages as well. At the start of his career, in 1643, he translated a Latin text (John Barclay's *Argenis*) via the French; he returned to it in 1680, now rendering it directly from Latin. Originals in Greek, Portuguese or English, however, he translated via Latin or French intermediate versions. Glazemaker's early work ranged widely, and encompassed mostly history, didactic works and travel books. In 1658 he brought out the Qur'ān in Dutch, working from the French version by the orientalist André du Ryer (1647). While translations like these probably satisfied the general intellectual curiosity of his outwardlooking audience, the intense philosophical debates of the latter half of the seventeenth century were relayed to Dutch readers without sufficient knowledge of foreign languages in a long series of translations of virtually the complete works of Montaigne, Descartes and Spinoza. Many of Descartes' Latin works had been translated into French, and his French works into Latin; Glazemaker used both versions whenever possible, consulting mathematicians, musicologists and other specialists as the need arose. He was undoubtedly the first professional translator in Dutch.

The main literary translator of the period was arguably Joost van den Vondel (1587–1679), generally regarded also as the greatest poet and playwright of his age. His work as a translator illustrates some of the literary preoccupations of the time and the close interaction between translation and original writing. With his modest background and limited schooling, Vondel went to great lengths to learn first Latin and then Greek, as his ideas about literature matured. Early on, in the 1620s, when he was writing Dutch tragedies in the Senecan vein, he translated two of Seneca's plays. Following the translation in 1635 of the Neo-Latin play *Sophompaneas* by his compatriot Hugo Grotius, Vondel wrote two further plays concerning the Biblical Joseph, and the three were often performed together in the Amsterdam theatre. When his Humanist friends helped him discover Greek tragedy, he translated Sophocles' *Electra* and began consciously to develop an Aristotelian type of tragedy in Dutch. Apart from a number of translations, including Horace's poems and Ovid's *Heroides*, done purely as private exercises, he also rendered all of Virgil into Dutch, first in prose (1646) and then in verse (1660), before going on to write his own Christian epic *John the Baptist* (1662). His play *Jeptha* (1659), an emulation of George Buchanan's sixteenth-century Neo-Latin play *Jephthes*, was conceived as an Aristotelian model tragedy, and Vondel was still translating Sophocles and Euripides in the 1670s, when he had reached eighty.

By then, however, time had passed him by. The popular cash-box successes on the Amsterdam stage were non-classical plays, among which translations of Spanish comedies and tragi-comedies scored highly. Around 1670 however they too had to make way for the new cultural fashion. As France became the dominant power in Europe, French Classicism was introduced into the Netherlands via a large number of translations. Many of them were deliberately made to replace existing versions which did not follow the rules of French-Classicist poetics. Translation can rarely have played a more openly polemical and formative role than at this time. The triumph of French Classicism in the Amsterdam theatre was complete: in subsequent decades the number of translations consistently exceeded that of original works.

The modern period

The cultural dominance of France continued for the better part of the eighteenth century. At the same time, this very dominance brought about a certain patriotic reflex, while other forms of expression counteracted the French monopoly in particular domains. As a result, a more differentiated picture emerges. Dutch culture henceforth translated from a different range of source languages, and genre distinctions became more important in the selection.

With the further expansion of education and literacy the local market for Dutch books continued to grow, at a time when the Republic became more than ever an international, multi-lingual publishing centre. The Amsterdam publisher Isaac Tirion (1705–65) would be the first to publish exclusively books in Dutch. The phenomenon is related to the gradual decline of Latin as the obvious cultured medium, and its replacement with both French and Dutch. Whereas in the first half of the seventeenth century the proportion of Dutch as against Latin books printed in Holland was approximately 7 to 1, in the latter half of the century it had already changed to a proportion of 2 to 1. The trend continued in the first half of the eighteenth century, when the ratio of Dutch versus Latin books became 2 to 1. In the next fifty years Dutch books outnumbered works in Latin by 6 to 1. French, on the other hand, clearly strengthened its position. Following the revocation of the Edict of Nantes in 1685 French Huguenots fled to the Dutch Republic in such numbers that in Amsterdam alone an estimated twenty bookshops out of a total of some 250 sold almost exclusively French books.

Nevertheless the demand for Dutch translations continued to increase, particularly among the bourgeoisie with their interest in digestible versions of the new ideas in the sciences and philosophy, and in the new forms of literary prose. Until around the middle of the eighteenth century French was the main language from which Dutch translations were made, even though this was probably more true in a domain like the arts than in, say, religion. But, for the first time, English and German came into the picture. In the field of popular prose, for example, translated works consistently accounted for up to two thirds of the total production throughout the seventeenth and eighteenth centuries, with French, English and German as the main source languages. In the last quarter of the eighteenth century, however, the proportion of French translations decreased very noticeably, from around 50 per cent in 1600–1770 to around 20 per cent in the early nineteenth century. Translations from English remained insignificant until around 1700, established a constant presence for most of the century and declined only towards the end of the period – when French revolutionary armies had overrun the Netherlands. Translations from the German hardly played a part at all until around 1770, but by the end of the century

German had become far and away the most important source language. The pattern would remain the same for a good while: of all the novels printed in Holland in the 1820s and 1830s over 60 per cent were translations, and of these around 60 per cent were based on German originals. In the early nineteenth-century Dutch theatre too, well over half the plays were translations. Among the most popular authors for the stage were prolific writers like A.W. Iffland and August von Kotzebue. Between 1790 and 1830 around thirty of Iffland's and no fewer than 120 of Kotzebue's plays were translated into Dutch.

In the early eighteenth century English models and translations from English proved influential in launching spectatorial writings in the Netherlands. Addison and Steele's English *Spectator* was rendered into Dutch in its entirety in 1720–27. Justus van Effen (1684–1735), who had already tried his hand at a French-language 'Spectator' and translated Defoe's *Robinson Crusoe* and Swift's *A Tale of a Tub* into French, started a very successful *Dutch Spectator* in 1731. It would run to 360 issues until 1735, and was followed by a host of similar periodicals in which every subject under the sun was discussed. In all, the eighteenth century saw some seventy spectatorial series, both translated and original, in Holland alone. The other new prose genre, and one with a longer future, was the novel. Here English and German models, Laurence Sterne's *Sentimental Journey* and Goethe's *Werther* among them, combined to give rise to a Dutch wave of sentimental novels at the end of the eighteenth century. The epistolary genre, in which English examples predominated, lent itself particularly well to a portrayal of bourgeois values and virtues. The book now generally regarded as the first modern novel in Dutch, *Sara Burgerhart* (1782) by Betje Wolff and Aagje Deken, can hardly be imagined without Richardson's epistolary works as predecessors. Betje Wolff herself, who produced some 180 titles, published twenty-three translations from English, French and German.

The title page of *Sara Burgerhart* bore the proud inscription: 'Not Translated'. Considering the large numbers of translations coming onto the market at the time, the note of defiance in the inscription was unmistakable. There were other reactions as well. One critic complained towards the end of the century about the 'all-engulfing

ocean of translations', and in 1835 another writer remarked that Dutch translators were 'as numerous as locusts in Egypt, as indefatigable and probably as harmful'. Clearly, the cultural status of the translators had suffered, and they had come to be regarded generally as mere hacks. As early as 1787 J. Lublink de Jonge had published the first independent treatise in Dutch in defence of translation, and the debate for and against would continue in subsequent decades.

In broad outline, the pattern of translation established in the early nineteenth century continued into the twentieth. Translations from the classical languages retained high prestige but were numerically slight. English, French and German remained the most important source languages, even though their relative importance changed considerably. In the absence of reliable bibliographical surveys and of studies of sufficient scope and depth covering the vast area of Dutch-language book publishing and translation in the nineteenth and twentieth centuries, only one or two random aspects can be indicated here. As German came to be seen as a major language for the sciences in the nineteenth century, it consolidated its international position in other respects as well. Most of the Dutch translations of Scandinavian writers in the latter half of the nineteenth century, for example, were based on German versions. But in the literary field the historical novel was largely borne by translations from English, and the realist and naturalist novel by French works. Since the latter part of the twentieth century the ascendancy of English has been particularly noticeable in virtually every domain, from the sciences and the arts to the audiovisual media. While over the years the Netherlands has been among the top ten nations in the world in terms of book publishing, some 40 per cent of the total number of Dutch books brought out are translations, and around 20 per cent of these are translated from English. In the field of literary prose, well over half the total number of titles are translations, and of these around two thirds are from English.

In Flanders, where in the eighteenth and nineteenth centuries the upper echelons of the bourgeoisie had adopted French as their language of culture, much popular reading matter in Dutch was translated from the French.

When Belgium gained independence in 1830, the language of the administration was that of its leading classes, i.e. French. Over the next hundred years or so, the gradual emancipation of the Dutch-speaking population of Flanders meant that translation acquired an altogether new dimension. Following the Equality Law of 1898, which recognized Dutch alongside French as the country's official language, a massive effort of legal and administrative translation was set in motion, and continues to this day. All national laws are immediately translated into the other language, and the national Parliament has its simultaneous interpretation service. Whereas Dutch-speaking Flanders and French-speaking Wallonia are now monolingual territories, in the bilingual area of the capital Brussels all official documents appear in both languages.

The sheer volume of professional translating in the Netherlands and Flanders also led to translators' organizations being established. In Holland an association was first set up as early as 1931. The Dutch Society of Translators was founded in 1956; Dutch literary translators have their own section in the Society of Authors. The 'Belgian Chamber for Translators, Interpreters and Philologists', with Flemish and francophone subdivisions, came into being in 1955. The Dutch and the Belgian associations each have their own publications, and both are affiliated to the Fédération Internationale des Traducteurs (FIT).

In the Netherlands the prestigious Martinus Nijhoff Prize for literary translation was established in 1953, and several Dutch companies have developed and marketed machine translation systems. Since the 1950s and 1960s a number of higher education institutes for the training of translators have been set up in both countries. The last two decades also witnessed a remarkable flourishing of the new discipline of translation studies in the Low Countries.

Further reading

Hermans 1991b, 1991c; van Hoof 1991; De Rynck and Welkenhuysen 1992; Korpel 1993a.

THEO HERMANS

F

Finnish tradition

Finland has shaped its own identity in the space between major cultures. Successive phases of cultural and linguistic influence have created a society in which multi- or bilingualism and translation have played a significant role.

From the thirteenth century onwards, the dominant cultural influence in Finland came from Sweden; for five centuries Finland was part of the Swedish realm and shared in Sweden's cultural and military history. This period ended in the early nineteenth century, when Sweden lost military dominance in the north to Russia. Finland was ceded to Russia in 1809, to become an autonomous Grand Duchy within the Tsarist Empire. The Finnish nationalist movement gathered strength towards the end of the century, and independence was declared in 1917. The early decades after independence saw an increase in German influence, and this continued up to the end of World War II. The dominant cultural influence since then has been Anglo-American.

Today, Finland is primarily Scandinavian in terms of its cultural outlook. Its Swedish heritage is manifested in the presence of a Swedish-speaking minority and in the fact that Swedish is one of the two official national languages, alongside Finnish. Official documents, notices, product descriptions and the like all appear in both languages, and translation between them is thus widespread. The long-standing cultural links between Finland and Sweden have meant that this translation activity has been relatively unproblematic: the languages are now semantically close, despite the genetic difference. Attitudes to Swedish have remained ambivalent: the Swedish-speaking elite served in the nineteenth century as a channel for European influences, which fed into the rise of Finnish nationalism; on the other hand, the long centuries of Swedish rule had previously obstructed the emergence of Finnish as a national language.

Finland's historically precarious position between east and west is matched by the relative isolation of the Finnish language. Finnish is a Finno-Ugrian language, not part of the Indo-European family; it is thus unrelated to the Germanic languages to the west and the Slavonic ones to the east. A strongly agglutinating language, it is closely related to Estonian, and distantly to Hungarian. Finnish is the native language of about 93 per cent of the country's current population of five million. There are about 300,000 Swedish-speaking Finns.

The Swedish period (to 1809)

Finnish and Swedish speakers have lived alongside one another in Finland since the early Middle Ages. During the Swedish period, Finnish–Swedish bilingualism was normal among the upper classes and administrative corps. Official documents were issued in Latin, later in Swedish: this meant that the Finnish-speaking rural population had to rely on clerks or other educated people to translate or interpret for them when necessary. After the Reformation, the status of Finnish was raised, particularly following the first translations of the Bible.

Christianity had come to Finland around the end of the first millennium, but it was not until the fifteenth century that the Bible began to be translated into the vernacular. The first translator of any note was a fifteenth-century monk named Jöns Budde, who translated parts of the Bible into Swedish.

Translation into Finnish began to acquire historical importance with the work of Mikael

Agricola (*c.*1510–57), a Lutheran reformer and founder of literary Finnish. His translation of the New Testament appeared in 1548, followed by about a quarter of the Old Testament in 1551–2. A former student of Luther, Agricola translated with a clear sense of religious mission, in the belief that the Divine Word should be made accessible to all people. In his preface to the New Testament, he writes that the Word should be 'public, comprehensible to all men, and concealed from no-one' (translated). In addition, he states that his aim is to follow the original as closely as possible. Alongside the original source texts, Agricola also made use of existing translations into Greek, Latin, German and Swedish: this is evident in his Finnish, which introduced new loanwords and manifested some grammatical features which were borrowed from various languages, including the prenominal, article-like use of certain function words; Finnish had, and still has, no articles.

At the time Agricola was writing there was no written standard Finnish. There was a long tradition of homiletic Finnish which he could draw on, but he was in fact creating the written standard language as he translated. He based this standard on the dialect of south-west Finland, spoken around the city of Turku (Åbo in Swedish), which was the cultural centre of Sweden's Finnish province. The Swedish authorities encouraged the idea that the south-west dialect, rather than the eastern dialects spoken closer to Russia, represented the most authentic Finnish. Agricola was also conscious of the need to establish a general standard language.

A Finnish translation of the whole Bible did not appear until 1642. The translators were instructed to stay close to the original texts and to adhere to the Lutheran interpretation, to write a Finnish that was as good and natural as possible and could be understood in all parts of the country, and to maintain a stylistic unity between the various parts of the translation. The translators' committee, under Eskil Petraeus, built on the earlier work of Agricola and others but worked directly from the original languages. All the costs of translating and printing were covered by the state – an indication of the importance attached to the work. This translation of the Bible remained the standard version in Finland until the 1930s. It played an

enormous role in standardizing Finnish spelling and syntax, and the influence of its style can be seen in the work of many writers and poets, and even occasionally in the press (see Jääskeläinen 1989).

Translation into Finnish thus started with biblical translation. Legal translation, which developed later, proved much more problematic: the laws of the Finnish provinces were in Old Swedish, which was itself an unfamiliar language to many of the translators; there was no tradition of oral or written legal Finnish to build on, and many of the legal concepts had no Finnish equivalents. It took two more centuries for standard legal Finnish to take shape (Aaltonen 1986; Sandbacka 1986; Majamaa 1991).

The oldest Finnish translation of a legal text dates back to 1580; the manuscript is in the handwriting of Martti Olavinpoika, chaplain at the Swedish court, but the actual translation may have been done by Jaakko Pietarinpoika (Jacobus Petri Finno). The translation is heavily marked by Swedish interference. The first printed version of the Finnish law appeared in 1759, translated by Samuel Forsén (Forseen), an official translator in the Stockholm administration, but the Finnish he used was already archaic. Throughout Finnish history, legal texts have been significantly influenced by translations and by concepts borrowed from other languages, first Swedish and later Russian.

Translations of other types of administrative text during this period – statutes, royal decrees, etc. – were at first produced rather sporadically. Translations of edicts were read aloud from the pulpit (illiteracy was high and printed material scarce). In order to cope with the increasing load of administrative and legal translation and to maintain some degree of unified style, the first official post of Finnish translator (from Swedish) was established by the government in Stockholm in 1735. The translator was instructed to translate closely and accurately; the translations contained many loanwords and structures copied from Swedish, and some from Latin or French. In general, the official translators in the eighteenth century tended to adhere slavishly to source text forms and were less interested in achieving naturalness in the target language. The official Finnish translator's post was re-established after the official break with Sweden in 1809, and the number of official translators soon grew. One influential translator was the historian and linguist Reinhold von Becker, who sought to liberate legal Finnish from Swedish influence.

Literary translation was virtually non-existent during the Swedish period. Finnish literature itself did not begin to flourish until the nineteenth century. Literature was long considered to have a corrupting influence, and there was little demand yet for literary translations: the literate educated classes had access to literary works in Swedish and German, and to a lesser extent in French and English.

Education for literacy was undertaken by the Lutheran Church from the seventeenth century onwards. The campaign naturally produced a need for things to read, from an ABC primer to a translation of Luther's *Small Catechism*. In order to motivate the peasants to learn, in 1686 the authorities stipulated that permission to marry would not be granted until the young people could demonstrate a basic level of literacy. The combined influence of the Church and the administration thus ensured that early translation work had a definite pragmatic and didactic purpose, which tended to overrule considerations of target language naturalness or aesthetic value.

At the same time, part of the very motive for translation was to boost the status of the Finnish language. Towards the end of the Swedish period, the position of Finland – and therefore also Finnish – declined within the Swedish state, and in Finland itself bilingualism became less common, with the upper and middle classes retreating mainly to Swedish. Translation was thus a way of counteracting this trend.

During the Swedish period as a whole, translators often had a rather apologetic and defensive attitude to their target texts. The translator's work was not highly regarded, criticism was severe, and the translator's name was often not mentioned in the published work. At the beginning of the period, translation had nevertheless been seen in positive terms, as a way of enriching the Finnish language and educating the people; by the end of it, translation had become merely a means of defending the language and slowing down its decline.

The Russian period (1809–1917)

Finns had long been involved in Sweden's wars with Russia. The final defeat of Sweden in 1809 meant that Finland became part of the Russian Empire, but throughout the following century Finland acquired a large degree of legislative and cultural autonomy.

In the mid-19th century, Elias Lönnrot (1802–84, leading figure of the Finnish nationalist movement and compiler of the Finnish national epic *Kalevala*) set about revising and updating the Finnish legal language and retranslating some of the main legal texts. He also translated parts of Homer, poetry, hymns, history, scientific and medical texts. Through his translations and lists of technical terms he helped to create a basic Finnish vocabulary in botany, medicine and law. He was a prolific writer and published many articles on translation, dealing with matters as varied as the effects of shortening words in translations of hymns, the problems of translating poetry and ways of creating new Finnish terms in different fields. Finnish became an official language of Finland, alongside Swedish, in 1863, but Swedish remained the primary language of the law until well into the twentieth century. During this period, Russian was also used, for instance on street signs and in some official documents, but it never attained the status of an official national language.

The most important feature of this period is the emergence of literary translation, supported by a flourishing national literature, first in Swedish (many of the leading figures of the nationalist movement were Swedish-speaking) and then in Finnish (see Kovala 1985). One of the towering figures in the early days of the Finnish nationalist movement was the philosopher and cultural activist Johan Vilhelm Snellman (1806–81). In the late 1840s he proposed that a new journal be founded to publish Finnish translations of literary classics from other cultures, for artistic, patriotic and educational reasons. The idea was supported by Elias Lönnrot and also by the Finnish Literature Society (founded in 1831), which was aware of the need to introduce literary models into Finnish in order to stimulate the country's own literary culture. After some delay (partly for political reasons and partly because of the prevailing anti-literature attitudes among the religious revivalist movements) the plan came to fruition in 1869; the last decades of the century saw a significant boom in literary translation.

In 1871, an annual competition was set up by Snellman, who was now chairman of the Literature Society. The Society even drew up a list of writers and works to be translated, containing not only literary (e.g. Shakespeare, Dickens, Molière, Chateaubriand) but also historical and philosophical writings (Macaulay, Fox, Rousseau). A further list was compiled in 1887. The Literature Society thus played an important role as a commissioner of translations, either directly or indirectly, by suggesting cultural/literary gaps that needed to be filled and in many cases publishing the resulting translations. Some literary translations into Finnish were also published in the United States, where there was a lively community of Finnish emigrants.

In 1908, on the initiative of the Literature Society and other cultural circles, the Finnish Senate set up a fund to support Finnish translation (and original works) in literature and science. The stated aim was again to stimulate Finnish culture by incorporating the classic works of other cultures, which would then serve as catalysts for Finnish literature, science and scholarship. Adaptation to suit the tastes and needs of the Finnish readership was encouraged, except with literary texts (Lehto 1986).

During the first part of the Russian period translators were often civil servants or military personnel, whose work put them in touch with other languages. In the latter half, translators were more likely to be writers themselves: poets, university teachers and professors (for example Juhani Aho, Ilmari Kianto, J.W. Calamnius, Kaarlo Forsman). They translated partly for the general reader but partly also for the influential cultural circles in Finland, for students who would be the next elite and for artists who would be inspired by the translations to produce their own works of art – in Finnish. The motivation was thus both educational and aesthetic. Literary translation meant the creation of a culture, and the translators were well aware of this. Translating had a high status; there were many translators, and the Finnish readership valued their work.

Between about 1860 and 1917, a fairly representative selection of European literature became available in Finnish (some had already been available in Swedish). The peak of this translating activity came in the last three decades of the century. From Germany came Heine, Goethe, Schiller and other classics; especially popular were translations of stories of village life, which had quite an influence on the development of this popular genre in Finland. A Finnish version of Bunyan's edifying *Pilgrim's Progress* appeared in 1809 and Shakespeare's *Macbeth* in 1834. Scott and Dickens came later. Inspired by the opening of the Finnish National Theatre in Helsinki in the 1870s, Paavo Cajander (1846–1913) spent his life translating all Shakespeare's plays (except *Pericles*) into Finnish. His translations have had great influence on Finnish theatre and literature; they are still the only ones available for many of Shakespeare's plays.

Translations from French started with the works of Dumas père. The first Finnish translations from Russian date from the 1860s; Turgenev and Tolstoy were particularly popular. Scandinavian classics were translated during the same period; particularly influential were the translations of C. M. Bellman's Swedish songs, which (together with those of Schiller's lyrics) contributed to the weakening of the traditional strophe structure in Finnish lyric poetry and the rise of freer metres and rhythms towards the end of the century. Translations of the Greek and Latin classics got underway in the 1880s; translators were often schoolteachers translating specifically for school use, and there was some criticism of translations that were regarded as 'too sensual'. Italian literature arrived later, starting with the 1910s; the writer Joel Lehtonen was among those who translated from Italian.

The translation of literature for children and young people also started in the mid-19th century (Ollikainen 1985). Before this, most of the few books available for children had been religious and didactic; about half of these were translations, mostly from German, either directly or via Swedish. In 1847, three influential translations appeared: a collection of Estonian folk tales and two novels. Of the latter, one was the poet Antti Räty's translation of the uplifting story of the sufferings of Genoveva, by the German theologian Christoph von Schmid; this became extremely popular in Finland and went into several reprints. The other was postmaster Otto Tandefelt's abridged adaptation, based on Geyger's German adaptation, of Defoe's *Robinson Crusoe*. There followed translations from Andersen, the Grimm brothers, and the Finland Swede Zachris Topelius, the father figure of Finnish children's literature.

During the latter half of the nineteenth century, about half of all translations of children's literature were of German originals (directly or indirectly), and a quarter of English source texts. The exciting but overtly moralizing works of Franz Hoffmann were popular, as were Johanna Spyri's Heidi books. The 1860s and 1870s saw an English invasion of children's literature, perhaps partly influenced by the need felt by Baptist and Methodist missionaries for appropriate Sunday School material.

After Independence (1917–)

Finland gained its independence in 1917, following the Russian Revolution. Independence sparked off a new wave of literary translation; a foundation was set up to provide grants for both writing and translating works of literature. Literary translation now extended to more distant cultures. Cervantes' *Don Quixote* was translated in 1927–8 by Juho August Hollo (1885–1967). Hollo translated an enormous amount (over 200 titles), both literary and non-fiction, alongside his main academic occupation as a professor of education at the University of Helsinki and after retiring. He translated from many languages, European and non-European, including Arabic and Serbo-Croatian. He started with William James's speeches, then went on to educational classics (Pestalozzi, Montessori), philosophy (Bergson, Snellman, Russell, Descartes, Plato, Nietzsche) and literature; he also popularized works for the general public. Hollo had considerable cultural influence as a translator; he had such a reputation with publishers that he could himself suggest works that needed to be translated (for example Dostoevsky, Goethe, Tagore, France).

Latin-American literature did not arrive on the scene until the 1960s; the poet Pentti Saaritsa has been one of the main translators of this literature, especially of the works of Neruda. Chinese literature and philosophy were first translated in the 1920s, with a second peak of interest in the 1950s; most translations were done via German or English, but Pertti Nieminen, for example, works from Chinese originals directly. Translations of Japanese poetry (by Tuomas Anhava, and later Kai Nieminen) and Japanese drama started to flourish in the 1960s. Translations from African cultures are even more recent.

Throughout the history of literary translation in Finland, two traditions have held sway. In one, applying to translations from classical antiquity and to legal and biblical translation, the tendency has been to translate rather literally in the first instance, with an eye to the educational purpose of the texts in question; later versions of the same texts would then be produced, giving priority to a more natural Finnish. Imaginative fiction, on the other hand, was often rendered first in the form of adaptations (Macbeth first appears as a Finn, in a Finnish setting); later translations tended to show more respect for the source text. For instance, Modernist techniques such as stream of consciousness proved difficult to translate at first. In the 1940s, translators were still unhappy with an indirect free style and tended to prefer a more 'natural' direct or indirect speech. Later translations, such as those by Pentti Saarikoski (1937–83), were able to exploit and stretch Finnish more freely to accommodate the patterns of the source text. Saarikoski was a writer, poet and translator who became a legend in his time as a cultural radical and a leading figure of Finnish Modernism. He produced many translations of Greek classics (notably Homer's *Odyssey*) and modern prose (for example Salinger, Joyce, Bellow, Miller). His translation of Salinger's *Catcher in the Rye* into Helsinki slang was a sensational success. Some of his translations reflect the norm-breaking ideas of Ezra Pound, who was a major influence on Saarikoski's work.

The translations by poet Otto Manninen (1872–1950) have also become Finnish classics in their own right. A lecturer in Finnish, at the University of Helsinki, he translated a wide range of poetry and drama (over 100,000 lines) including Runeberg and Topelius from Swedish, Heine and Goethe from German, Molière from French, Petöfi from Hungarian and Homer, Sophocles and Euripides from Greek. He was also language reviser for the Bible translation committee (1921–37). His translations of Heine helped to introduce freer metres into Finnish poetry. In his translations from Molière he created his own equivalent of the alexandrine, known as 'Manninen's alexandrine', which resembled blank verse but retained rhyme and varied the caesura and syllable number.

Other influential literary translators of the twentieth century include the poets Eino Leino, and Yrjö Jylhä; literary scholar and poet V. A. Koskenniemi; writers Tyyni Tuulio, Eila Pennanen and Aale Tynni; also Esa Adrian, Anslem Hollo, Arto Häilä, Marja Itkonen-Kaila, Juhani Jaskari, Eino and Jalo Kalima, Kristiina Kivivuori, Juhani Konkka, Markku Mannila, Aarno Peromies, Annikki Suni, Oili Suominen, Inkeri Tuomikoski, Thomas Warburton (into Swedish) and Emil Zilliacus (Greek into Swedish).

Since independence, most official translation has been between Finnish and Swedish. Especially since the 1960s, the number of translators' posts has grown dramatically, as has the range of target languages translated into. The main European languages currently head the list.

By the end of the twentieth century translations accounted for just over 20 per cent of all titles published in Finland. A good 50 per cent of literary titles were translations; about half of these from English, followed by Swedish and German. Translations of children's literature accounted for as much as 75 per cent of all titles published (Kuivasmäki 1985).

Profession, training and research

Translator training, as a kind of master–apprentice arrangement, began with the 1908 Finnish Literature Fund already mentioned (Lehto 1986). The Fund's committee, which consisted of professors and other experts, took pains to select and train competent translators. Sample versions had to be submitted, and these were then checked and criticized in detail. Versions might be sent back for further revision several times, and the feedback process might continue for years. Even established poets and translators, such as Otto Manninen and Eino Leino, continued to submit samples of their work to other experts for comments and advice. A similar apprenticeship system has operated in some university language departments in recent decades: Eila Pennanen, for instance, trained many literary translators in her Helsinki seminars during the 1970s.

Institutional training of translators and interpreters started in the late 1960s, when four language institutes were set up (in Turku, Tampere, Savonlinna and Kouvola). They were independent, non-academic institutes running three-year diploma courses. In 1981, these institutes were upgraded and incorporated into the university system as departments or schools of Translation Studies (at the universities of Turku, Tampere, Joensuu and Helsinki, respectively). This change brought academic status and a longer period of study (five to seven years) leading to the MA degree and further to licentiate and doctoral degrees. It also provided a strong impetus for professional academic research in translation studies. A shorter BA degree was introduced in 1994. The languages most commonly offered are English, German and Russian. Student intake reflects the popularity of English.

The profession of translating and interpreting has grown enormously in Finland since World War II. This has led to improvements in standards and in the legal rights of translators and interpreters. Nordic cooperation has led to a joint agreement (in force since 1987) on citizens' rights to have access to an interpreter in certain contexts, at public expense. All Nordic countries seek to ensure that Nordic citizens can use their own native language in their dealings with the authorities. With the growth in immigration levels, community interpreting is now a feature of everyday life, but much of it is still done on an amateur basis.

The Finnish Association of Translators and Interpreters (SKTL) was founded in 1955 and has been a member of FIT since 1957. It is also a member of the Conseil Européen des Associations de Traducteurs Littéraires. The SKTL has five divisions: literary translation, non-fiction (document) translation, audiovisual media translation, interpreting, and research and teaching. By far the largest division is for the non-fiction, which includes scientific, business and technical translators. Membership is based on application and recommendation. The SKTL also keeps a membership register (indicating languages and fields of specialization) and a directory of Finnish interpreters.

The SKTL publishes the journal *Kääntäjä-Översättaren* ten times a year (the bilingual title consists of the Finnish and Swedish words for 'translator/the translator'). This is mostly in Finnish, but occasionally carries articles in other languages. It was awarded the FIT Journal Prize for 1988–90.

The SKTL also awards prizes: the Agricola Prize for an outstanding translation of prose or drama, the J. A. Hollo Prize for one of a non-fiction work, and the Uljas Attila Award for promoting interpreting or the status of interpreters in society. Translators are also eligible for grants by various state, library and private foundations.

The legal rights of translators are exceptionally well regulated in Finland. Translators (and their descendants) have been protected by Finnish copyright law since 1829. Copyright legislation has been developed in cooperation with other Nordic countries. Many translators work freelance, and many part-time only. In spite of an ample supply of professionals, translations also continue to be commissioned from non-professionals on an ad hoc basis. Because there are not enough native speakers of specific target languages – other than Swedish – working from Finnish, Finns often need to translate into a foreign language.

Before the schools of translation studies were founded, research on translation was sporadic, mostly undertaken as an offshoot activity of departments of literature or philology, and dealing almost exclusively with literary translation. More recently, however, more diverse areas of research have started to flourish. Areas of specialization include interpreting and cognitive processing (Turku), general theory, terminology and children's literature (Tampere), think-aloud protocol studies and assessment (Savonlinna), continuing training and assessment (Kouvola). The schools of translation studies also run several publication series.

Finnish research in computational linguistics and machine translation has made dramatic progress in recent years. Research has focused on term identification and retrieval, disambiguation, parsing of extensive corpora, Finnish–English machine translation, machine translation aids and hand-held electronic dictionaries (Brace 1994).

Further reading

Kovala 1985; Sorvali 1985; Aaltonen 1986; Lehto 1986; Ollikainen and Pulakka 1987; Sandbacka 1987; Majamaa 1991.

ANDREW CHESTERMAN

French tradition

Prior to the late Middle Ages, translation in France cannot be seen in isolation from the LATIN TRADITION of Western Europe. Though translation into vernacular languages began in the eleventh century in Europe, the first translations into Old French did not appear until the thirteenth century. Before then, translation was carried out into Latin and was usually undertaken in monasteries. During the eleventh and twelfth centuries, translation – both into Latin and into the vernacular – of Arabic philosophical and scientific writings and of Ancient Greek works and their related commentaries was undertaken by the Toledo School (see SPANISH TRADITION). This school is generally seen as providing a turning point in the history of translation in the West, which had begun with translation into classical Latin. Vulgar Latin, the language from which the romance languages and subsequently French evolved, was to become the target language of translation. The first documents written in Old French are literal translations of Latin liturgical texts which date back to the ninth century (van Hoof 1991).

The foundation of the first universities in France in the thirteenth century gave translation into French a real impetus. A century later, the use of Old French (as opposed to Latin) began to prevail in administrative documents, but Latin maintained its supremacy as the language of scholarship until the Renaissance signalled the decline of the great Latin tradition. However, this was a slow process and the use of Latin in scientific translations lasted well into the eighteenth century (Kelly 1979).

Guillaume de Loris's *Roman de la Rose* (*c*.1235) includes translations of Latin texts, and Virgil's *Aeneid* was also translated into Old French in the thirteenth century. Latin translations of Arabic medical treatises were themselves put into Old French, as were a number of chronicles of French history which had been written in Latin, for example *Historica Francorum* by Grégoire de Tours which dates from the sixth century, and the thirteenth-century work *Historia Regum Francorum*.

Under the reign of King Charles V (1337–80), translation of classical works was actively encouraged. Latin versions of Aristotle's works were retranslated into French by Nicolas Oresme (1330–82), one of the main translators at the royal court. Oresme is said to have introduced hundreds of new terms into French and produced several scientific translations; he also made interesting comments in the prefaces to his translations on such issues as the task of the translator, the need for accuracy and the introduction of new terms into the target language (Larwill 1934). However, this period of linguistic and intellectual activity was to be followed by decades of unrest which were not conducive to translation. The few translations which were produced during this period include those of Boccaccio's *Decameron* (1485), Titus Livius's *Decades* (1486) and Cicero's *De Oficie's* (1493), together with a small number of scientific works in Latin and Italian. To these can be added some translations from other European vernacular languages.

The sixteenth century: the development of French and translation of the classics

The sixteenth century witnessed a considerable increase in the number of translations due to the stimulating influence of the Renaissance and the introduction of printing technology. Renewed interest in the classics led the humanists to return to original sources and bypass medieval scholasticism, whilst the secularization of knowledge which was triggered by the Renaissance promoted translation into the vernacular for an expanding readership who did not have direct access to classical sources.

Specific terms were coined during this period to describe the process of translation: *traduire* (to translate) was introduced by Robert Esperre (1503–59) on the basis of the Italian *traducere*, and the humanist Etienne Dolet (1509–46) was responsible for introducing *traduction* (translation) and *traducteur* (translator). Dolet is a highly symbolic figure in Western translation history, having been accused of 'mistranslating'

one of Plato's works and burnt at the stake. He is credited with the first formulation of translation theory in *La manière de bien traduire d'une langue en l'autre* (How to translate well from one language into another), which was published in 1540. Dolet cites five rules for translation: understanding the meaning of the original text, mastering both source and target languages, avoiding word-for-word renderings, using the speech of ordinary people, and employing an appropriate tone. The fourth principle, using the speech of ordinary people, can be seen as a response to the tendency of sixteenth-century scholars and Latinists to introduce neologisms and Latin structures into the vernacular.

Initially, only a few translators were able to work directly into French from Greek texts. They included Thomas Sébillet, Jean Lalemant, Antoine Héroet and De la Boétie. Translation into Latin often constituted an intermediary stage before a French version could be produced, as in the case of Jean Laxary (or Lascaris) (1445–1534) and Claude de Seyssel (d. 1520), who worked as a team. Among their various joint efforts, Laxary translated Xenophon's Greek text *Anabassis* (fourth century BC) into Latin, and De Seyssel then translated Laxary's Latin version into French.

During this period, the use of Latin, the language of the Church, was firmly established in science and theology, and Latin was consequently the target language for many translations, especially those from other Romance languages, as well as Greek, Syriac and Hebrew. However, Plutarch's writings and Homer's *Iliad* were among the few sixteenth-century translations which were made into vernacular French. Several translations of Cicero's works were also undertaken into French: by Antoine Macault (in 1534 and again in 1549), Pierre Saliot (1537), Jehan Colin (1537) and Etienne Dolet (*c*.1542).

There were also numerous translations from Italian during this period. Both Marot (in 1544) and Peletier (in 1547) translated Petrarch's *Sonnets*. Translations from languages other than classical and Romance languages were restricted to English and Germanic works, perhaps the most important being François Baudoin's translation of Francis Bacon's *Essays*.

Translation was partly perceived as a means of disseminating knowledge to a wider audience, and in this respect translators assumed two associated tasks. They had to make classical writings more accessible to a wider readership and, in order to facilitate this task, they had to take part in developing the nascent French language.

One of the best-known French translators of the period, Jacques Amyot (1513–93), introduced several Greek works to French readers, including Plutarch's *Lives* and Longus's *Daphnis and Chloë*, the latter from the third century BC. Although his translations were to be criticized by subsequent translators for being too literal, the texts were written with the French reader in mind: Amyot provided glosses and definitions which did not exist in the source text. His translation of Longus's work, which was revised in the nineteenth century by Paul-Louis Courier, is said to be better known than Longus's original work. In parallel with attempts at achieving clarity of expression, the use of amplification as a rhetorical device is also evident in translations dating from this time, as can be seen in Michel de Tours' verse translation of Virgil's *Pastoral Poems* (1516), which is longer than its source text.

The historical and cultural context in which translation was practised and viewed in the sixteenth century is crucial to an understanding of its development. In 1539, a royal ordinance had decreed French to be the official language of the state, and the literary circle known as the *Pléiade* advocated the imposition of French and, through cultivating its use, its establishment as a language of equal status to Latin. In 1549, the poet and Latinist Joachim du Bellay (1522–60) wrote *Défense et illustration de la langue française*, a pamphlet which has been described as 'an anthology of all arguments against translation' (Mounin 1994: 13; translated). Translation, in other words, was seen as an obstacle to creativity in the vernacular. By contrast, the study and imitation in French of classical texts was regarded as a literary genre, and as poetry was the dominant literary form many verse translations were produced in that vein. Du Bellay, himself a translator of Virgil, distinguished between poetical and non-literary texts and considered the former untranslatable. The translated text was seen as unable to provide 'the grace and elegance of the original', the introduction into French of an alien language form being an unsurmountable obstacle. Du Bellay's

criticism of translation was not without consequences, as writers during this period tended to distance themselves from translation. The translations performed by the *Pléiade* can be described as a combination of literalism and innovation, with considerable coinage of neologisms derived from Latin and Greek.

A synthesis of sixteenth-century thought on translation can be found in Michel de Montaigne's *Essays* (1580–88). Montaigne talks about a hierarchical relationship between languages, with the vernacular being seen as the weaker idiom. He also draws a distinction between aesthetic and informative texts and sees the latter as being less problematic for the translator. The concept of a hierarchy of languages, with classical languages at the top and vernacular languages at the bottom, dominated sixteenth-century thought, and 'vulgar' vernacular languages were consequently regarded as unsuitable mediums for the dissemination of culture.

Translation activity prior to 1600 centred on classical literary texts. However, the translation of scientific texts increased considerably during this period, this aspect of translation being unaffected by the literary debates epitomized by the *Pléiade*. It is also worth noting that many classical works were translated in the fields of architecture, agriculture, natural history and medicine, to name but a few. As well as works by Pliny, Galen and Hippocrates, translations were made of Latin versions of Arabic works and of contemporary scientific texts. Overall, translation functioned as a means of spreading knowledge among the masses and of enriching the French language.

The seventeenth and eighteenth centuries: *Les Belles Infidèles*

The early part of the seventeenth century was the great age of French classicism, but translations were increasingly expected to conform to the literary canons of the day. The free dynamic translations known as *Les Belles Infidèles* aimed to provide target texts which are pleasant to read, and this continued to be a dominant feature of translation into French well into the eighteenth century. Classical authors were reproduced in a form which was dictated by current French literary fashion and morality. One of the main figures to adopt this approach was Nicolas Perrot D'Ablancourt (1606–64), who adapted classical texts to current canons and genres to such an extent that some of his translations are considered travesties of their originals. He not only 'censored' these works in the course of translating them but also 'corrected' any factual errors he encountered and generally aimed to 'improve' on the source text whenever he deemed it necessary. D'Ablancourt translated many Greek and Latin authors, including Cicero, Tacitus and Thucydides. Other translators who adopted this approach of 'improving' the source text by doctoring it to suit current sensibilities include Louis Giry (1596–1668), Benserade (1613–91), Pierre Perrin (1620–75), Paul Pellison (1624–93) and Jean Segrain (1624–1701). In 1681, Monsieur de la Valterie published a prose translation of Homeric verse; in a commentary accompanying the translation, he justified his adaptation of ancient customs in terms of propriety and, paradoxically, faithfulness to the author 'who did not intend to offend the reader' (quoted in Mounin 1955/1994: 62).

Several essays on the principles of translation were written in justification of this approach, including *Discours sur la traduction* by Gaspard Bachet de Méziriac (1581–1638). De Méziriac criticized the unfaithfulness of Amyot, who added or deleted material in his translations. In *De la traduction, ou règles pour bien apprendre à traduire*, Gaspard de Tende (1618–97) formulated the first genuine treatise on translation from Latin into French (Ballard 1992: 186). Reservations regarding the images used in the Homeric texts are expressed by subsequent translators such as Anne Marie Dacier (who was nevertheless a champion of faithful translation) in the introduction to her translation of the *Iliad* (1711), and also by Antoine de la Motte Houdar (1672–1731). Despite the fact that translators of the late seventeenth century paid more attention to the question of faithfulness to the source, their main priority continued to be providing texts which may appeal to the French reader.

However, as pointed out by Ballard (1992: 150), the *Belles Infidèles* approach was not universally accepted. In parallel with the literary trend of the *Belles Infidèles*, more literal approaches were put forward by Lemaistre de Sacy (1613–84), who translated a Latin version of the Bible into French, and Pierre-Daniel Huet (1630–1721), who, in *De Interpretatione* (1661), urged the translator to show humility towards the source text. Members of the Abbey of Port-Royal, near Paris, strived for fidelity in their many translations and retranslations of religious texts, including André Du Ryer's translation of the Qur'ān in 1647.

As well as ancient texts on architecture in Latin, contemporary works on medicine and pharmacology and texts in Flemish and Portuguese were translated. A growing number of Spanish, Italian and English works in both the literary and non-literary domains were also translated during the seventeenth century. They included Cervantes' *Don Quixote*, Marino's *Adonis* and Robert Green's *Pandisto*. Translations of Machiavelli's *Discourse*, Francis Bacon's *Moral Essays*, and John Locke's treatises, *Civil Government* and *Essay on Human Understanding*, contributed to a rich philosophical and political debate during this period.

The elegant eighteenth-century translations of the classics were the distorted looking-glass through which many viewed the classics in the age of Enlightenment. Translation lost popularity, both as a literary genre in itself and as an instructional tool, and to an increasing extent it was supplanted by an interest in contemporary foreign works in the fields of science and literature.

The eighteenth century saw a gradual loss of interest in classical languages and a growing interest in German and English cultures. The philosopher and encyclopedist Diderot (1713–84) was especially keen on English literature and produced an imitation of Samuel Richardson's *Pamela*. Voltaire (1694–1778) was instrumental in developing a passionate interest in English thought and literature in France. The dramatist Jean-François Ducis (1733–1816) adapted Shakespearean tragedies for the French stage, providing an alternative ending to *Othello*. This interest culminated in the widespread translation of English Gothic novels during the Gothic revival at the end of the century.

Translations of texts that were almost contemporary (from the seventeenth century) included Daniel Defoe's *Robinson Crusoe*, Jonathan Swift's *Gulliver's Travels*, Henry Fielding's *Tom Jones*, John Milton's *Paradise Lost* and some of Alexander Pope's *Essays*. Pierre le Tourneur (1737–88) translated the complete works of William Shakespeare. At the same time, French versions of works by Walpole, Reeve and Godwin were also hugely popular. Going beyond Europe for his sources, Antoine Galland (1646–1715) translated the *Arabian Nights*, combining fidelity to the dynamics of the source text with the observance of current literary conventions.

Throughout the eighteenth century translations from English outnumbered those from any other language. However, there were some translations of German and Italian works, for example Antoine de Rivarol translated Dante's *Divine Comedy* in 1783.

Theoretical discussions of translation continued during the eighteenth century. Jean le Rond d'Alembert (1717–83), who collaborated with Diderot on the compilation of *L' encyclopédie*, commented extensively on translation difficulties, seeing imitation rather than transcription as a suitable basis for the act of translation. Adaptation was not seen as betrayal but rather as a means of adjusting the foreign work to suit contemporary tastes. Charles Batteux (1713–80) stressed the need for grammatical restructuring in translation. Translation was also closely associated with the didactic function of literature during this period. On the whole, however, this was a period of transition during which translation theory was getting ready to leave the age of classicism behind and prepare the ground for the Romantic insistence on literalism.

The Romantic era

The Romantics brought literalism back into fashion in the nineteenth century, under the influence of German philosophy. They sought to 'transfer the creative power of great writers of other languages into their own' (Kelly 1979: 3), and empiricism gave way to a more philosophical approach. Among nineteenth-century translators, Jacques Dellile (1738–1813), Paul-Louis Courier (1772–1825), Leconte de Lisle (1818-1894), Charles Nodier (1780–1844), Alfred de Vigny (1797–1863), Alexandre Dumas (1802–70) and François Victor Hugo (1828–73) were particularly well known.

In the first half of the nineteenth century, the choice of translation strategy depended on whether the source text was a classical or a recent work. For example, Littré translated the first part of the *Iliad* in medieval verse in 1847: he deliberately used a form of language which pre-dated the codification of French in the seventeenth century.

In *De l'Esprit des traductions* (published in 1820), the writer, critic and translator Germaine de Staël (1766–1817) stressed the literary function of translation and its usefulness in the renewal of the target culture.

The preface to Leconte de Lisle's translation of the *Iliad* announced that the era of the *Belles Infidèles* was over, while Chateaubriand described his translation of Milton's *Paradise Lost* as 'traced' (*calqué*), using resources of the target language that were closest to those of the source language. The 'pleasing' form of the French text was now regarded as secondary to the close reproduction of the style of the source text; the Romantic age was looking for foreignness. Translation was once more regarded as an acceptable literary activity, and many classical works were retranslated in a spirit of historical restitution, which represented a clear split with the tradition of the *Belles Infidèles*. Among the many works which were retranslated were Virgil's *Eclogues*, his *Pastoral Poems* and the *Aeneid*, Homer's *Epics*, and Aristotle's *Metaphysics*, *Politics* and *Logic*.

A considerable number of English poets and writers were translated during this period, with numerous translations of Shakespearean texts being made. Milton's *Paradise Lost* was translated by Dellile and Chateaubriand (1768–1848). Translations of Byron, Coleridge, Scott and Dickens found an eager market, as did those of American literature. Charles Baudelaire (1821–67) was a fervent translator of the works of Edgar Allan Poe.

There was also a growing interest in science, with the philosopher Paul-Emile Littré (1801–1881) retranslating Hippocrates between 1839 and 1861, and many translations of contemporary works taking place in the fields of medicine, natural science and geography, among others. The internationalization of science and the constantly expanding potential readership fuelled an ever-growing demand for the translation of contemporary works.

The nineteenth century was also characterized by a practice of producing parallel translations in verse and prose. Given the difficulty and additional constraints under which verse translation has to be produced, prose translation became widespread and soon developed into a literary genre.

The contemporary period

The Romantic search for innovation through the use of translation was pursued well into the twentieth century, and intense translation activity by numerous author-translators characterized the first decades.

The number of author-translators who produced French versions of foreign works or retranslated the classics during this period is considerable. Among them, André Gide (1869–1951) translated Shakespeare, Valéry Larbaud (1881–1957) translated Samuel Butler and, more recently, Marguerite Yourcenar (1903–86), whose first translation in 1947 was of Virginia Woolf's *The Waves*, devoted much of her time to translation.

Translation was further promoted through the establishment of literary journals such as the *Nouvelle Revue Française*, *La Revue européenne* and *Europe*. In the aftermath of World War II, the increase in the level of international communication was to give a major impetus to the interpreting profession, hitherto very much in the background. Huge scientific and technological developments have also led to an enormous increase in the volume of specialized translation. The language planning policies of francophone countries in general (see CANADIAN TRADITION) have meant that stronger emphasis came to be placed on translation into French and on translation-related terminological work. A great deal of work has been done on coining neologisms in order to cope with new processes and techniques. And in an attempt to curb the influx of English/American foreign terms, much attention has also been paid to the question of standardization.

Translations of contemporary works now appear almost simultaneously with the originals, with translation from English leading the way. Most English and American best-sellers are translated into French; UNESCO statistics for the years 1981–3 indicate that approximately 3,500 translations were published in France during that period. More recent estimates suggest that translations represent just over 6 per cent of the 36,000 titles published in France every year, and for some publishing houses as much as 30 per cent of their output consists of translations. Problems of literary translation are frequently raised in the media and several awards have been created to acknowledge outstanding translations into French, perhaps the best known of these being the Prix Pierre-François Caillé, which was created in 1980.

Research and training

Theoretical issues have been addressed by linguists, philosophers and translators. In 1946, Valéry Larbaud (1881–1957) published his *Sous l'invocation de Saint Jérôme*, a compelling tribute to historical figures in the field of translation and a collection of heartfelt essays on its practice. In 1955, Georges Mounin (1910–93) published *Les Belles Infidèles*, a discussion of historical arguments against translation. He followed this in 1963 with *Les Problèmes théoriques de la traduction*, which represented a turning point in the theoretical study of translation. Other well-known contemporary French theorists include Jean-René Ladmiral, Henri Meschonnic and Antoine Berman. Both Meschonnic and Berman follow the Romantic tradition in arguing against the naturalization and appropriation of the source text by the target culture. Renewed interest in the history of translation theory and practice is illustrated in works by Michel Ballard (1992) and Lieven D'hulst (1990). Numerous publications on specialized translation have explored the didactics and practice of both translation and interpreting. The interrelation of translation and sociology is discussed in a special issue of *Actes de la Recherche en Sciences sociales* (2002). As far as interpreting is concerned, the best known researchers include Danica Seleskovitch and Marianne Lederer of ESIT (*Ecole Supérieure d'Interprètes et de Traducteurs*) and Daniel Gile.

France continues to be an important centre for research and training in translation and interpreting. ESIT, which is a part of the University of the Sorbonne Nouvelle in Paris, enjoys a worldwide reputation, being one of the few institutions which offer doctoral programmes in translation and interpreting. ISIT (*Institut Supérieur d'Interprétation et de Traduction*) is another well-known training centre, also based in Paris. In addition, several universities offer courses which include a component of translation and interpreting.

Collections of books on translation studies have been published by PUL (Presses Universitaires de Lille) and by Didier Erudition. Journals dedicated to translation include *Traduire* and *Palimpsestes*.

Organization of the profession

The *SFT* or *Société française des Traducteurs* (Association of French Translators) was founded in 1947 and publishes its own journal, *Traduire*. Until the early 1970s, when the *ATL* (*Association des traducteurs littéraires de France* – French Association of Literary Translators) was founded, the SFT represented all categories of translators, including literary translators. The aims of the SFT include protecting the rights of translators and setting appropriate rates of remuneration.

Since 1957, translators' rights have been covered by legislation, which puts them on an equal par with writers as regards copyright and social insurance. The Ministry of Culture has attempted since the 1980s to improve the situation and status of translators by means of legislation, whilst the *CNL* (*Centre national des Lettres*) provides grants to help with the translation of certain foreign works. A small number of bursaries are also awarded to translators to acknowledge outstanding translation work or to facilitate the translation of works which are unlikely to attract a wide readership.

Further reading
Larbaud 1946; Cary 1963; Kelly 1979; Horguelin 1981; Bassnett and Lefevere 1990; D'Hulst 1990; Van Hoof 1991; Ballard 1992; Mounin 1994; Casanova 1999; *Actes de la Recherche en Sciences Sociales* 2002.

MYRIAM SALAMA-CARR

G

German tradition

In the European context the term *deutsch* (German) is unusual in so far as it is not derived from an older name for a country or a tribe. Initially, it indicated a common vernacular; and even today linguistic and cultural connotations of the term *deutsch* are wider than present-day political and geographic realities suggest. In the eighth century, *theudisk* and the Latinate *theodiscus* referred to the dialects spoken by the Germanic tribes within Charlemagne's realm: Alemannic, Franconian, Saxon, Thuringian and Bavarian. The regional variants of the vernacular provided the linguistic matrix for the gradual development of German as a literary language, and eventually of modern High German (*Hochdeutsch*). The political borders – external as well as internal – of the German-speaking states hardly ever coincided with the linguistic borders: even today the same dialect is spoken on both sides of the German–Dutch border, in Luxembourg as in the Eifel, in French Lorraine as in the Southern Rhineland, in French Alsace as across the Rhine, in Northern Switzerland as in Southern Baden, in Austrian Tyrol, Salzburg and Upper Austria as in Bavaria. While modern High German is the literary language used by Austrians, Germans and (German-) Swiss alike, German literature paradoxically reflects both their common cultural heritage as well as their cultural plurality.

The Old High German period (eighth to tenth centuries)

The process of transforming German dialects rooted in oral pre-Christian traditions into a written, literal language began in the eighth century. Although there were numerous autoch-thonous texts, the bulk of writings in Old High German were translations from Latin. From a descriptive point of view, we may distinguish four basic types of texts:

(a) interlinear versions which are virtually incomprehensible without the Latin source texts;
(b) texts which resemble interlinear versions, such as the translation of the *Evangelical Harmony* by Tatian;
(c) 'free' or relatively 'free' translations such as the Old High German *Isidor* and Notker's works;
(d) adaptations and paraphrases such as *Christus und die Samariterin* and Psalm 138 (translated at Freising).

When attempting to assess the achievements of medieval translators one has to bear in mind the historical contingencies and the typological and functional constraints under which they were working. Bridging the linguistic and cultural gap which separated medieval translators from antiquity required enormous creative efforts. It would, therefore, be a misguided anachronism if one were to judge these Old High German translations by present-day norms and standards.

Initially, the German vernacular – which had no literary tradition – mainly served didactic purposes: glossaries, word-for-word translations and interlinear versions such as the Old High German Benedictine Rule, were used in monasteries in the teaching of Latin. However, there were some notable exceptions from this source text oriented didacticism. Located at different points of the typological spectrum and fulfilling quite distinct functions, texts such as the *Isidor* translation (*c.*800), Otfrid von Weissenburg's translation of the *Liber Evangeliarum* (*c.*863–71) and, later, Williram von Ebersberg's paraphrase of the Song of Songs (*c.*1060) brilliantly met the communicative challenge posed by Latin, by Christian doctrine and by classical culture. Notker von St Gallen (*c*.950–1022) was unique among translators in the Old High German period with regard to both the variety of texts he translated and his mode of translation. Apart from Christian theological literature, he turned his attention to philosophical and poetic texts, such as Boethius's *Philosophiae Consolatio* and Virgil's *Bucolica*, respectively. Drawing on the efforts, linguistic and philosophical, of previous generations of translators and German authors, he effectively transferred the most complex ideas and subtle notions from Latin into innovative, yet intelligible German. At the same time, he worked within the didactic tradition of the period, translating for his students' sake.

The Middle High German period (eleventh to fourteenth centuries)

It is hard to imagine the evolution of medieval German into a literary language without the assistance afforded by Latin. Existing side by side with Latin during the Middle High German period, the German language gradually opened up new and increasingly specialized areas of usage. The growing number and typological variety of translations produced during this period reflect an increasing need for communication on many levels, practical, speculative and entertaining: theological, philosophical, legal, educational and aesthetic. This need, in turn, led to further expansion and differentiation of German on the normative level, particularly of lexical inventories, but also of syntax. After 400 years of linguistic development, intensely influenced by Latin, the German language finally reached the stage when it could readily cope with the formal and intellectual challenge posed by Latin texts. For example, around 1210, Albrecht von Halberstadt not only translated Ovid's *Metamorphoses* into German, he also transposed them into the contemporary idealized world of courtly gallantry. Middle High German translations of Thomas Aquinas's and Meister Eckhart's writings effectively demonstrate that the German vernacular was now capable of expressing the subtleties of theological and philosophical discourses. By the fourteenth and fifteenth centuries, literary German had

evolved into a comprehensive communicative system covering all areas of human activity and interest. In this process, translations and related forms of interlingual and intercultural transfer of mainly Latin and French source texts, models and materials played an important part. As far as text production and reception are concerned, Latin–German bilinguality was the rule. Clerics as well as educated laymen wrote in Latin, or in German, or in both. Meister Eckhart and Heinrich Seuse, for instance, used Latin and German alternately, depending on their audiences; and Johann Geiler von Kaysersberg, the most popular fifteenth-century preacher, drafted most of his German sermons in Latin. As German gradually emancipated itself from Latin literary tradition, translations, parallel texts, compilations, adaptations and paraphrases, especially of literature for special purposes, warranted the continuing contacts between the two cultures. Eventually, in the fifteenth century, autochthonous German texts, covering specific areas of knowledge, were translated into other European languages, including Latin.

French influence on Middle High German began to be felt in the eleventh century; it increased during the twelfth and thirteenth centuries, continued through the fourteenth and weakened in the fifteenth century. This influence manifested itself in numerous loanwords, the formation of words and phraseology, but scarcely in Middle High German syntax. While in the twelfth and thirteenth centuries, Middle High German courtly epics and lyrical poetry were inspired by French models, this literary current did not interrupt the Latin tradition. Rather, it ran alongside the mainstream of religious and profane literature in medieval Latin and Middle High German. Despite the apparent effects of French literature on Middle High German literature, direct borrowings appear to have been relatively rare. Frequently, the exact status of German texts *vis-à-vis* presumed French sources is difficult to ascertain. For instance, scholars are uncertain whether the deviations of Hartmann von Aue's *Erec* from Chrétien de Troyes' *Erec et Enide* are due to Hartmann exercising considerable poetic licence, or whether he drew on an unknown French source text, or even on an intermediate Dutch version. In their handling of French material, German poets tended to exercise   considerable   freedom,   adapting, abridging or expanding and embellishing their material, sometimes adding commentaries. For historical and systematic reasons, it would be misleading and inappropriate to judge the relationships between Middle High German texts and their known or presumed French sources by reductive, source text-oriented standards.

The early modern High German period

In the fifteenth and sixteenth centuries the process of German developing into a literary language gathered momentum. Distinguished by their confident handling of style, the fifteenth-century translations of French novels by Elisabeth von Nassau-Saarbrücken, Eleonore von Österreich and Thüring von Ringoltingen bear witness to this development. Besides several written variants of German, a common literary language gradually established itself in the German language area. This phenomenon is closely associated with Martin Luther: his Bible translation and other writings helped to establish a literary form of German which was oriented towards, and modelled on, the vernacular rather than on Latin. Nevertheless, especially in the Humanist era, Latin continued as the dominant language in printing and writing, as well as in teaching. While poetry written in Latin was targeted at a social and intellectual elite, German was the language of the people and of popular poetry. Eventually, in the seventeenth century, this tension between Latin and German, between 'high' and 'low', was resolved in the poetry of Martin Opitz. As far as the history of translation into German and the history of German as a literary language are concerned, Opitz's poetry marks the transition to the modern High German period.

In the early modern High German period, translation concepts and principles of translation were a central topic of discussion even before these explicit discourses reached their climax in Luther's *Sendbrief vom Dolmetschen* (1530). For instance, the translations of the so-called 'Viennese School' of the fourteenth and early fifteenth century essentially fall into two classes, thus continuing the medieval tradition: on the one hand, what was called *aigne dewtsch*, a

scholarly source text-oriented German which submitted to Latin norms, and on the other hand translations into German in its current written forms, free from the constraints of Latin (this was called *gemaine Teutsch*). The characteristic forms and reader-oriented functions of these translations, based on Latin or French sources, were explained and justified in the prefaces.

A similar dichotomy may be observed in translations by early German Humanists. For instance, Niklas von Wyle (*c*.1410–78), who was convinced of the inherent primacy as well as the linguistic and stylistic superiority of his Latin sources, strove to translate them into German as literally as possible. Whether his texts would be intelligible to the common reader was of no concern to him. Not surprisingly, the more pragmatic, target-oriented translation method practised and propagated by the Humanists Albrecht von Eyb (1420–75) and Heinrich Steinhoewel (1412–82) proved to be more popular. As Albrecht was particularly concerned with the intelligibility of his translations, he adapted the language and subject matter of Plautus's comedies to fifteenth-century German popular culture and milieus, as well as to theatrical conventions. Steinhoewel followed similar translatorial principles. In his expansive translation of Aesop he introduced numerous proverbs, rhymed verses and allusions to topical events. This interpretive method of adaptive and re-creative translation Steinhoewel justified with reference to Horace's topos, as formulated in *De arte poetica*, and to Jerome's principles. Murner's German version of Virgil's *Aeneid* (1515) is another example of this 'naturalizing' translation method: he makes no attempt at imitating Latin participle constructions; antiquity is transposed to sixteenth-century Germany, reflecting her customs, traditions and ideas. While Murner is quite aware of the qualitative difference between Latin verse and German doggerel, he is nevertheless proud to have been instrumental in the resurrection of Virgil's epic from Latin death to German life.

Any account of the history and the theory of translation into German would be incomplete without Martin Opitz (1597–1639) and Justus Georg Schottel (1612–76). Both occupy particularly important positions in the transitional period from early modern to modern High

German. In *Deutsche Poeterey* (1624) Opitz argues that translation serves a dual purpose: translating from Greek and Latin poets is good exercise for the translator, and it is of benefit for German as a literary language by enhancing its latent potential. Both Opitz and Schottel went well beyond common fifteenth- and sixteenth-century practices in their use of German and in their translation methods because they were convinced that German was a fully-fledged literary language or, with practice, might become one, and that it was capable of poetic and oratorical style second to none.

Luther and Bible translation

The history of the German language since the Middle Ages is closely associated with translations of the Bible. Over a period of twelve hundred years these translations have formed a comprehensive corpus of texts which is representative, to a considerable degree, of German translation culture and its development through the ages. Bible translations have not only influenced the formation of Christian-ecclesiastic terminology and the language of ethics; Luther's translation, in particular, has had a formative and normative effect on modern High German. The enormous success of Luther's Bible translation may be attributed to his creative use of the German vernacular and to his principles of translation, but also to the mass circulation of his writings made possible by modern printing techniques, and to the historical dynamics – religious, social, political and economic – of the Reformation period. Luther chose to meet a daunting challenge: how to express the Word of God, as codified in the Bible, in the language of the common people who were unable to read Latin, Greek or Hebrew. As a rule, for Luther, expressing the biblical message in German meant translating 'freely', giving the 'letters their freedom', as it were. However, when essential theological 'truths' were concerned, Luther would sacrifice this principle of intelligibility and revert, for doctrinal reasons, to word-for-word translation.

As far as Bible translation into German is concerned, the period stretching from the late eleventh to the sixteenth century was an era of experimentation and consolidation: it produced special copies for the laity and for the poor, illustrated as well as extravagantly illuminated copies in the vernacular, collections of biblical texts for liturgical purposes, etc. The Reformation marked a turning point in the history of German Bible translation, with Luther and other Protestant reformers reverting to source texts in Hebrew and Greek for their translations of the Old Testament and the New Testament, respectively. Even the Bible translations of the Catholic Counter-Reformation, by Hieronymus Emser (NT, 1527) and others, were modelled on Luther's text. Indeed, since the second quarter of the sixteenth century, Luther's influence has pervaded the entire German tradition of Bible translation, irrespective of regional or denominational affiliations.

The modern High German period

Originating in the German Enlightenment period, the different strands of translation theory current in the past two centuries may be traced back to Johann Christoph Gottsched (1700–66) and his Leipzig circle, staunch defenders of Enlightenment values, and to their Swiss antagonists, Johann Jakob Bodmer (1698–1783) and Johann Jakob Breitinger (1701–76), respectively. Gottsched's and Breitinger's opposed views on translation, which clashed over Bodmer's translation of Milton's *Paradise Lost* (1732), reflect their distinct stance on poetics, aesthetics and literary language. Both subscribed to the rationalist view according to which there is an essential resemblance between languages and they are, therefore, translatable – at least in principle. Both agreed that different languages are not mirror images of each other. There was a difference of opinion as to whether a translation should be permitted to emulate linguistic, stylistic, and formal features of the source text and thereby violate target side norms. Gottsched maintained that a good translation had to be in agreement with the principles of enlightened, normative poetics. If the original or source text did not conform with these rules, the translator was duty-bound to improve, expand or abridge. The translation had to be a German text, through and through. Breitinger, in contrast, maintained that there were no superfluous words in literary works of art. In his *Kritische Dichtkunst* (1740) he rejected many of the more presumptuous claims of the Enlightenment, thus preparing the way for English in preference to French literature and its ideals. Anticipating Herder and Humboldt, he argued that the mentalities of different nations are reflected in the peculiarities of their respective languages. Therefore, a translation must not violate the 'thoughts' (*Gedancken*) of the original or deviate from its source in any other way. On the theoretical level, Breitinger's ideas were developed by Friedrich Gottlieb Klopstock (1724–1803) and Johann Gottfried Herder (1744–1803) who invested the 'spirit' of the original with the ultimate authority. This concept was put to the practical test by Johann Heinrich Voβ (1751–1826) in his translations of Homer (1793). The translations of Dante and Shakespeare by August Wilhelm Schlegel (1767–1845), of Rabelais by Gottlieb Regis, of Ariosto by Johann Gries, and of Cervantes by Ludwig Tieck (1773–1853) not only belong to the same tradition; they realize part of the Romantic project which aimed at accumulating world literature in the German language.

In seventeenth- and eighteenth-century continental Europe, France played a leading role in politics, the sciences and the arts. French intellectuals, including translators, shared a belief in the inherent superiority of their language and culture. Because of this conviction French translators felt justified in adapting translated texts in such ways as to make them conform not only to the grammatical, lexical and semantic norms and conventions of the French language, but also to typological, generic and aesthetic models prevalent in French literature. Strict classicist norms ruled drama and (epic) poetry, whereas the more flexible conventions of the *Belles Infidèles* were applied to translated prose fiction. French cultural predominance was reflected, in turn, by the large number of German imitations of French literary models, and of translations from French into German. And although many different types of texts were also translated from Latin, Greek and other modern European languages, German translators frequently used intermediate French translations as source texts, even if a copy in the original language was available. French mediation was particularly effective in introducing German readers to British philosophy, fiction and drama. French

translations of Locke, Pope, Addison, Defoe, Swift, Richardson and Fielding initially served as source texts for translations into German. Discussions by French translators and critics of British philosophy, of the idiosyncrasies of English novels, and especially of the apparent 'anomalies' of Shakespeare's plays met with considerable interest in Germany. Thus, ironically, the French themselves were instrumental in undermining their seemingly unassailable position as legislators in matters of good sense, taste and style. German writers grew familiar with British thought and literature, they began to resent what many of them came to perceive as distorting effects caused by French mediation. The gradual transition, in the course of the eighteenth century, from broad acceptability to virtual rejection of French models, including intermediate French texts, by German writers, both in theory and in practice, is a literary phenomenon with far-reaching cultural implications. Reflecting a significant change in the translational concepts and, more generally, in the underlying aesthetic, this transition is ultimately symptomatic of a paradigmatic change in the German history of thought: the emancipation from French intellectual and cultural hegemony, accompanied by the demise of rationalism, and the eventual propagation of an autonomous German national literature.

French meditation of English literature began early in the eighteenth century. It reached its peak, in the Protestant parts of Germany and in Switzerland, in the 1720s. At a time when in Zürich, Hamburg and somewhat later in Leipzig (in the 1740s) indirect translation was rejected in favour of direct translations of English novels and plays, French mediation continued elsewhere in Germany. As far as novels are concerned, it virtually ended with the 'birth' of the modern German novel, Wieland's *Don Sylvio von Rosalva* (1764), and with Blankenburg's essay on the novel (*Versuch über den Roman*, 1774).

As far as drama was concerned, France provided much of the material as well as the theatrical models; several German translations of English plays were based on intermediate French versions. Shakespeare, however, being the dramatic antidote to the rules and conventions of classicist French drama, was either read in French translation (e.g. by Voltaire), in its original English (e.g. Pope's edition), or he was translated directly from English into German. When, in 1741, Caspar Wilhelm von Borck published his translation of *Julius Caesar*, Johann Christoph Gottsched immediately condemned both the translation as well as the barbaric English original. Both ran counter to his strategy of reforming the German theatre. Gottsched favoured plays, mainly of French origin, which came closest to realizing his ideal of order by observing the Aristotelian rules, and by exercising moderation both with regard to action and to the use of language. When Edward Young's *Conjectures on Original Composition* (1759) was translated directly from English into German soon after its publication, the concepts of 'original genius' and of 'original composition' – which were to revolutionize aesthetic theory and poetic practice in Germany during the second half of the eighteenth century – were enthusiastically applied to Shakespeare and his works. Accordingly, Wieland's well-timed prose translation of twenty-two plays (1761–66) met with considerable public interest. Despite Gerstenberg's severe criticism, this translation considerably influenced the dramatists of the revolutionary literary movement known as *Sturm and Drang*, notably Johann Wolfgang von Goethe, Jakob Michael Reinhold Lenz and Friedrich Schiller. Johann Joachim Eschenburg's first translation of Shakespeare's complete works (1775–7/1782) marks a further important stage in German Shakespeare reception, a process at the end of which Shakespeare had acquired the status of a national German poet, and some of his works – notably *Hamlet* – occupied a place in the very centre of German literature.

Having started, in 1795, with the revision of a translation of *A Midsummer Night's Dream*, by 1810 August Wilhelm Schlegel had published another thirteen of Shakespeare's plays. Years later, Ludwig Tieck and others completed the project.

As a literary editor, critic, lecturer and translator, Schlegel prepared the way for Romanticism in Germany and elsewhere. In 1804 he became secretary to Mme de Staël, whom he accompanied on most of her travels through Europe until her death in 1817. Schlegel's principles of translation were based on the interpretation of works of art as organisms. Sharing Herder's

view, he considered every literary work of art as an entity comprising form and content. Unlike Herder and the *Sturm and Drang* poets, who argued that this entity was commensurate with 'nature', unconsciously created by a genius, Schlegel considered this entity as an 'organic created form' (*organische Kunstform*), which resulted from a conscious, intentional creative effort. Accordingly, each Shakespearean drama was a skilfully constructed organism, in which every detail (each scene, character etc.) was related to the whole by inherent necessity, and from which, in turn, it derived its meaning. Only by taking note of and translating every detail could justice be done to the original in its entirety; whereas any change distorted and destroyed the perfect organism. The language had to be light and pleasing; and the reader was to get the impression that s/he was reading an original German text, not a translation. In other words, Schlegel tried to combine the 'objective' and the 'subjective' aspects of translation: fidelity to the source text, on the one hand, and creative transformation and naturalization in accordance with target-side requirements, on the other.

The Romantic concept of translation, manifest in Schlegel's theory and practice of Shakespeare translation, was systematically analysed by Friedrich Schleiermacher. In his treatise *Über die verschiedenen Methoden des Übersetzens* (1813), Schleiermacher contrasted, with unprecedented sharpness of focus, the translatorial methods of 'alienation' and 'naturalization'. His reflections on the theories of language and of translation have occupied linguists and students of translation to the present day. Schleiermacher distinguished two major types of texts. In the first type, language serves as a vehicle mediating interlingual and intersubjective 'facts'. On principle, business-related texts are translatable because the vocabulary used is characterized by terminological constraints. In the second type, comprising poetic and philosophical texts, monolingual forms and the contents transported by them coalesce on a higher plane. This causes grave problems for translators because, in the course of time, the language of such texts has come to be associated with specific culture-bound concepts, conventions, attitudes and feelings. Because the associative complexes differ from language to language, and from culture to culture, transfer can only be accomplished by employing the 'alienating' method of translation: the translator takes his bearings from the unity of form and content of the source text, and from the source language. Schleiermacher advocated the use of a *proper* language for translation, which inevitably entailed language change. After all, only by deviating from established norms could the alien or foreign increment be visualized in the target language. Most important, though, Schleiermacher was convinced of the innovative, but also of the regenerative powers of translation.

Practically every modern translation theory – at least in the German-language area – responds, in one way or another, to Schleiermacher's hypotheses. There appear to have been no fundamentally new approaches. Translators and theorists, such as Ulrich von Wilamowitz-Moellendorff in the nineteenth and Emil Staiger in the twentieth century, advocated, with different emphases and for different reasons, the naturalizing method of translation. Walter Benjamin favoured the principle of alienation. Nevertheless, attempts have been made to transcend the antimony of naturalizing and alienating translation, to find a synthesis or a compromise (e.g. Schadewaldt 1927).

In the course of the nineteenth century translation activities in the German-speaking countries intensified and expanded. This applied not only to *belles lettres* but also to the natural sciences, medicine, engineering, the law, economics and general matters. While the bulk of translations continued to be based on the Romance languages, especially on French, and increasingly on English sources, other languages and cultures – including non-European ones – began to make their presence felt. Some of the significant developments, changes and characteristic shifts are reflected in anthologies of literature in translation, especially in so-called anthologies of world literature, which have been published in large numbers since the middle of the nineteenth century. For instance, until the end of the eighteenth century, German reception of French literature had focused on political, scientific and generally learned or informative matter, on the drama and the novel. It was not until well into the nineteenth century that French poetry, Romantic and contemporary, was being made available to German-speaking readers, mainly through anthologies. Growing economic and cultural contacts between Germany and the British Isles raised the awareness among German readers of British affairs. Yet, authors such as William Wordsworth and Lord Byron were mainly received as individual personalities rather than as representatives of their country or of British literature. In contrast, for a long time the translational mediation of Scandinavian and Hungarian literatures was primarily governed by imagological stereotypes and preconceptions relating to those countries, rather than by nineteenth-century historical realities. At times, texts were selected, and sometimes specifically translated, in accordance with the anthologists' personal tastes, or with their views and intentions concerning German literature and/or political affairs in a wider international context. In due course, Russian novels and Scandinavian drama took their place beside translations of French and English fictional prose and drama, respectively. While Scott, Dickens and Zola were translated promptly, Henry James was ignored for many decades. The British and American Modernist poets, too, had to bide their time.

During World Wars I and II translation activities were influenced by numerous factors, unavailability of source texts and politically motivated censorship being the most obvious ones. In varying degrees this also applies to the occupied zones of Germany in the immediate postwar period, and it continued in the German Democratic Republic until 1988. Nevertheless, the *Index translationum* for 1986 shows that nearly as many books were translated and published in East Germany (794) as in Great Britain (904). By comparison, 1,687 translated books appeared in France, and 8,017 in the Federal Republic of Germany. In divided Germany, the opposed ideologies, political and economic systems, and military alliances of the two German states had an effect on what texts were chosen for translation and, at times, even on the manner of translation. Systematic comparisons between translation activities in East and West Germany remain to be made.

From 1956 to 1986 the number of translated books published in the Federal Republic of Germany increased by 400 per cent. Bookshops in Germany were well stocked with translations in practically all areas, aiming at children as well as adults. However, in those areas of scientific research where time is of the essence, scholars were expected to rely on their own linguistic competence rather than on translations, especially from English. Conversely, in recent decades German scholars, especially those working in the natural sciences, in medicine and in related fields, have become accustomed to publishing their research results in English rather than waiting for them to be translated. In German cinemas and in television, where the proportion of foreign films, family series, children's programmes and documentaries is very high, dubbing is generally preferred to subtitling.

Profession, training and research

The *Bundesverband der Dolmetscher und Übersetzer e.V. (BDÜ)* and *Verband deutschsprachiger Übersetzer literarischer und wissenschaftlicher Werke e.V. (VDÜ)* are both member societies of FIT.

Courses for translators and/or interpreters are offered by many German universities, polytechnics and vocational academies: in Berlin (Humboldt), Bonn, Düsseldorf, Flensburg, Heidelberg, Hildesheim, Köln, Leipzig, Mainz, München and Saarbrücken, among other places. In addition, numerous other institutes, both public and private, offer training for translators and interpreters. Examinations administered outside the academic establishments are supervised by the regional Chambers of Commerce and/or by regional governments. As the curricula are not standardized, the quality of training and the proficiency of graduates vary considerably. In the absence of legal requirements, anyone may use the designation 'interpreter' or 'translator'.

The *Europäisches Übersetzer-Kollegium* at Strälen is a refuge for translators of literature and non-fiction. Founded in 1978 by Elmar Tophoven, *inter alia* translator of Beckett into German, this centre offers translators, established or budding, ideal facilities for their work: a specialized library, up-to-date electronic equipment, contact with colleagues, and a peaceful working environment. The *Deutsche Akademie für Sprache und Dichtung* and the *Deutsche Literaturfonds* award prizes to distinguished literary translators.

While for many years research on practical, functional, linguistic and pedagogical aspects of translation dominated, there has been increased interest in historical subjects in recent years, especially in the theory and practice of translation in the Middle Ages and in the Renaissance, and in eighteenth- and nineteenth-century theoretical discourses on translation. Gradually, more attention is being paid to the actual translations produced during the past three centuries, to the translators and the cultural contexts. Also, new research methods are being applied. As far as literature in translation is concerned, most research has traditionally tended to be source-text-oriented and, to some extent, prescriptive. With the growing involvement of literary scholars, historical–descriptive approaches have recently come into their own.

German scholars have been among the most active in the field of translation studies and have produced a very large and influential body of literature on the subject. Some of the best known names include Katharina Reiß, Hans Vermeer, Wolfram Wilss, Albrecht Neubert, Juliane House and Christiane Nord, among many others. Apart from individual publications by such scholars, there are a number of journals and book series devoted to the field of translation studies.

Further reading
Breitinger 1740/1966; Benjamin 1923/1963; Schadewaldt 1927; Schwarz 1945; Springer 1947; Schroebler 1953; Nordmeyer 1958; Schoendorf 1967; Huber 1968; Gebhardt 1970; Senger 1971; Haentzschel 1977; Sonderegger 1979; Apel 1982; Kittel 1988; Kittel and Frank 1991; Essmann 1992; Kittel 1992, 1995; Poltermann 1995; Essmann and Schoening 1996.

HARALD KITTEL AND
ANDREAS POLTERMANN

Greek tradition

Historically and culturally, the area in which Greek is spoken includes mainland Greece, the Aegean islands (including Crete and Cyprus) and, until 1922, the Ionian coast of Asia Minor. The colonizations of the sixth and seventh centuries BC extended this area to include regions around the Black Sea and areas in Southern France and Southern Italy (Magna Graeca), where Greek-speaking communities exist even today. Throughout the Hellenistic world, Greek was the lingua franca of the period and the language of culture and education. The Hellenized Eastern part of the Roman Empire adopted Greek as its official language and it remained so throughout the Byzantine period (AD 330–1453). During the following 400 years of Turkish rule, it was the language (together with religion) that was the main factor in keeping the national character alive and distinct. Following the War of Independence in 1821, the territory belonging to Greece expanded to include the Ionian Islands (1864), Thessaly (1881), Macedonia, Crete and the islands (1913), Thrace (1923) and the Dodecanese (1947). Historical, social and political factors led to widespread emigration and a large Greek diaspora, with particularly large Greek-speaking communities in North America and Australia.

The decipherment in 1952 by Chadwick and Ventris of the Linear B script as Greek gives the Greek language a 3,500-year-old history. This constitutes an unbroken, living tradition in the sense that aspects of all the major stages in that tradition survive and co-exist in the modern language. Thus the language of the Homeric epics (seventh and eighth century BC), the classical Greek of the fourth and fifth centuries BC, the Koine Greek of the New Testament, the Byzantine Greek of the fourth to fifteenth centuries AD and the popular language of folk literature throughout the 400 years of Turkish rule (1453–1821) are, to varying degrees, still accessible to Greeks today in a way that Anglo-Saxon or even Middle English is not accessible to speakers of modern English. With the birth of the modern nation and the growth of a national consciousness, the question of language became a national issue. What became known as the 'Language Question' in modern Greece was primarily a debate about the correct or desirable form of the written language. This debate developed into a contest between the popular spoken language (*demotic*) and its adherents (*demoticists*) on the one hand, and those who advocated a 'purified' form of the language (*katharevousa*) on the other. The latter is a language cleansed of foreign (mainly Turkish)

words and constituted a compromise between demotic and ancient Attic Greek. This strange 'diglossia' (the co-existence of two levels of language) became a national and political issue and cut across education, literature and, not least, the question of translation, often leading to violent confrontations between the proponents of each group. It was not until 1976 that demotic was finally established as the official language of education and, consequently, of the state.

Overview of translation activity

Despite their many and extensive contacts with other peoples and cultures, the ancient Greeks apparently attached little importance to translation: there is no discussion of either the practice or the process of translation throughout ancient Greek literature. And yet, they undoubtedly used both interpreters and translators. For example, one of the earliest forms of interpreting in the Greek world must surely have been interpreting the word of Apollo for those who travelled from foreign countries to consult the Oracle at Delphi. Similarly, there is evidence that early Greek philosophers had access to Egyptian texts, presumably in Greek translation. According to Kakridis (1971: 12–16), the ancient Greeks were rather like the English of some years ago: they did not learn foreign languages but expected others to learn theirs, nor did they want to allow foreign linguistic elements to influence the organic development of the Greek language and culture. This situation continued in the Hellenistic period, when the need for translation was again minimized by the fact that Greek was the lingua franca of the then civilized world. Similarly, in the first centuries AD, the two main incentives to early thinking on translation in other countries – namely, the translation of ancient Greek texts and of the New Testament – were not present in Greece, since the original texts were still accessible to Greek readers at that stage.

The first references to translation in the Greek context come from the early Byzantine period and concern the translation of legal texts (Troianos and Velissaropoulou-Karakosta 1993: 220–34). The division of the Roman Empire by Diocletian (284–305) into East and West had a direct influence on Roman Law in the East. The Eastern Empire consisted mainly of Greek-speaking peoples, or people who, at least, understood Greek. This meant that the laws and imperial decrees, which were written in Latin, were inaccessible to the greater part of the population. From the beginning of the fifth century, there was a systematic attempt in the law schools of Beirut and Constantinople to render Latin legal terminology into Greek. Here, the professors of law, known as *antikinsores* (vice-censors), made a significant contribution. They acted as both translators and translation teachers. They would make the Latin text accessible to their Greek-speaking students in class by first providing detailed introductions (*indeces*) in Greek to the particular Latin section. This was not, however, a word-for-word translation but took the form of an analysis or explanation of the text considered necessary for complete comprehension of the topic by the students. Then, with the help of these *indeces*, the students would attempt the translation of the Latin text. If the text in question was particularly difficult, the *antikinsores* would provide the students with the Greek translation of individual terms. This was known as interpreting *kata poda* (lit. 'on foot') and was followed by other activities designed to ensure full comprehension of the text. The work of the *antikinsores* is known to us only from their students' notes: they themselves left no written texts on their methods. It was from these annotations by students in the margins or between the lines of texts that the first legal dictionaries came into being. The impact of the new legal terminology which was formulated in Greek could be felt beyond the Byzantine area, and the translation of these texts into Slavic languages had considerable influence throughout the region. Thus the texts interpreted by the *antikinsores* and annotated by their students enabled the spread of various concepts, both legal and political, far beyond the confines of the New Rome.

Evidence of sustained, serious interest in translation and/or interpreting, however, does not emerge until the beginning of the Greek Enlightenment period and the growth of a national consciousness in the years leading up to the War of Independence against the Turks in 1821. And even then, this interest remained strictly within the confines of larger national issues concerning the language and education of the Greek people in the context of the new Greek state.

Intralingual translation

Bible translation naturally became an issue in Greece much later than it did in the rest of Europe. It was not until the nineteenth century that the need was recognized for a translation of the Koine Greek of the New Testament into the modern Greek vernacular. In addition to the usual theological and translation-related problems, the question of translating the Bible took on wider linguistic and national dimensions in the context of the establishment of the new Greek state following the War of Independence in 1821. Two diametrically opposed approaches to the subject are represented by Neophytos Vamvas (1776–1866), one of the translators of the Old and New Testaments, and Constantinos Economos (1780–1857). Economos believed that it was both impossible and pointless to translate the Bible into modern Greek. He insisted that the Greeks could understand the language of their forefathers and that their own language was common, vulgar and debased the lofty sense of the original; moreover, if the Scriptures could be read by everyone, this would lead to heresy and false interpretation. Vamvas, on his part, maintained that if a translation is intended to teach, then its diction and style must be simple; and, given Economos's criticisms of modern Greek, he distinguished between simple language and vulgar language. These were matters in which questions of translatability, the modern Greek language and national identity all became embroiled. The dispute continued to escalate, culminating in the *Evangelika* (Gospel Riots) in 1901, following the translation of the Gospels into modern Greek by Alexandros Pallis. Similar riots, known as the *Orestiaka*, were provoked by the performance of Aeschylus's tragedy in a modern demotic translation in 1903.

In Greece, translation practice and theory have focused to a large extent on intralingual translation – translation, that is, of ancient texts into the modern idiom. The great emphasis given to intralingual translation was in part meant to show the continuity of the Greek language rather than to produce a new Greek text and also to show the capacity of the modern idiom to act as a vehicle for the lofty ideas of the past. Talking at the literary remembrance service for Alexandros Pallis in 1939, Manolis Triandafyllidis (1883–1959), a leading member of the so-called 'Education Society' and author of a state-commissioned grammar of demotic Greek to be published in 1941, noted how in all nations the translation of the ancient classics of the particular literary tradition is seen as a unique source for rejuvenating the nation's culture. He lamented that for a long time in Greece there had been a lack of writers able to translate and that there was a tendency towards archaism and an insistence on a pure form of the language, which stifled every attempt to make the ancient texts available to people in their own modern tongue. This explains why so many major Greek writers and scholars have engaged in the translation of ancient texts into the modern idiom.

Since 1526, when the first paraphrase of the *Iliad* was published, 450 translators have translated the poetic works of 425 poets (Economou and Angelinaras 1979). The number of translators has actually increased in the 1980s and 1990s to include some of the best scholars, writers, theatre directors and critics: Phanis Kakridis, Yorgos Yatromanolakis, Pavlos Matessis, Costas Tachtsis, Dimitris Maronitis and Yorgos Heimonas, among others. Pallis (1851–1935) translated Euripides, Shakespeare, Thucydides and even Kant to demonstrate the possibility of using demotic Greek for so difficult a text. However, he is mainly remembered for his translations of the Gospels and the *Iliad*. The latter was both praised and condemned. He proceeded from the assumption that the Homeric poems were a popular creation, and boldly turned the epic into a contemporary demotic (folk) song, using the language and other features of the Greek traditional song. According to one historian of Greek literature (Politis 1973: 173), 'this translation of the *Iliad* is perhaps the most significant achievement of the generation of the first demoticists'. Nikos Kazantzakis and Ioannis Kakridis also produced a translation of the Homeric epics. Their effort to employ versification and rhythms easily recognizable by the layman from the rich tradition of Greek folk songs was an attempt to make

the works available but also attractive. It is also noteworthy that after fourteen years of work, they did not hesitate to state on its publication in 1962 that 'it was only a temporary form of translation'.

Publishing trends

Translation was not, however, limited to the intralingual variety, as a brief look at some recent statistics will show. The variety of texts translated by Greek scholars, clergymen, teachers, doctors and others between the sixteenth and nineteenth centuries is quite impressive, especially in view of the unconducive circumstances during the years of Turkish oppression. Zaviras (1972) records translations of an amazing number of foreign works written in Latin, Arabic, French, English, German, Russian, Italian, Slavonic and other languages. The list includes a great variety of religious texts and philosophical works, mainly by Aristotle and Plato, and also works by Cicero, Virgil, Plutarch, Cornelius Nepos, Shakespeare, Descartes and many others. The reiterated aim of the translators is to educate the subjugated Greeks, and later, following independence, to shape the identity of the liberated nation. In addition to making some of the wealth of their heritage available to their compatriots, Greek scholars translated works on astronomy, geography, history, mathematics, law, physics, arithmetic, geometry, biography, metaphysics, medicine, theology, philology, psychology, archaeology and other topics. They were eager to transmit the knowledge they had acquired for themselves in the European countries where they studied or worked or had made their homes.

Kassinis (1995) provides statistics for published literary translations in book form over the last five centuries, and this is indicative of the history of translation in Greece. Only one publication is recorded in the sixteenth century, five in the seventeenth, fifty-seven in the eighteenth, 3,000 in the nineteenth, 2,500 between 1901 and 1950 and 13,000 between 1950 and 1990. In terms of literary genre, the emphasis shifted from theatrical works to novels to poetry. In the eighteenth century, there were 16 translations of theatrical works, 13 narratives (five in verse form), and 29 works of popular literature. The names that predominate in this period of

Greek Enlightenment are Goldoni and, later, Molière. These are followed in the nineteenth century by Voltaire, Alfieri and Racine. From 1845 onwards, it is the novel that predominates, gradually coming to account for 57 per cent of all literature translated, with translations into Greek of Dumas, Sand and Mérimée. Of the 15 novelists translated in this period, 14 are French and only one (Walter Scott) English. Sixty-seven per cent of the total number of translations are from French, and this high proportion reflects the fact that many original works in English, German and Spanish were translated into Greek via French; it also reflects the French-orientation of culture and education in the new Greek state.

In the period between 1901 and 1950, literary translations were again undertaken mostly from French (36 per cent), though it is notable that the percentage of translations from English triples (25.4 per cent). This period saw the translation of works by Hugo, Verne, Zola, Balzac, Flaubert, Maupassant, Stendhal, Shakespeare, Wilde, Shaw, Maugham, Joyce, O'Neil and Eliot, but it also saw many translations of Russian, Scandinavian, German and Italian writers, including Tolstoy, Dostoyevsky, Chekhov, Gogol, Turgenev, Hamsun, Ibsen, Strindberg, Hauptmann, Nietzsche, D'Annunzio and Pirandello. English begins to play a predominant role on the translation scene after 1944, when Greece comes under Anglo-American influence and English is introduced into Greek schools after 200 years of French dominance. Between 1951 and 1990, English and American literature continues to predominate, though with a notable upsurge in translations of Latin American literature. Many of the most accomplished twentieth-century literary translators were major writers in their own right, for example Theotokis, Kazantzakis, Kosmas Politis, Seferis, Prevelakis and Elytis.

In 1994 approximately 4,200 books were published in Greece. Of these, one third were translations from other languages. This percentage is similar for the immediately preceding years. Literature accounts for 50 per cent of the total books translated, followed by the natural sciences (15 per cent) and social sciences (10 per cent). The predominant source language is English (62 per cent), followed by French (17 per cent), other European languages (17 per cent) and Asian and Latin American languages (2.8 per cent).

Translation theory and translation methods

Kakridis (1936) asserts that the history of translation theory in Greece begins with Nikolaos Sofianos, who lived and died in Venice in the first half of the sixteenth century. Sofianos was the first scholar to translate and write about translation into modern Greek and the first to write a Grammar of the common language of the Greeks, though this was not published until 1870. In his prologue-dedication to Dionysios, Bishop of Mylopotamos and Hersonesos, which prefaces his translation of Pseudo-Plutarch's *On the Education of Children* (printed in Venice in 1544), Sofianos raised for the first time in the Greek context what Koutsivitis (1994: 98) refers to as the 'how and why' of translation. His prime concern was with translation as a means of education and, consequently, with the use of a language where the emphasis would be on the naturalness of the target idiom and on facilitating the reader's understanding. However, it is Evgenios Vulgaris, in his *On the Discord in the Polish Churches. Historical and Critical Essay; Translated from French into the Popular Greek Language, with Historical and Critical Notes*, published in Leipzig in 1768, who actually dealt with some of the fundamental questions about translation and who attempted to answer them. This work is the translation of an essay by Voltaire which had been published in the preceding year in Basle. It is a bilingual edition with a comprehensive introduction and notes relating to the translation problems Vulgaris encountered. Vulgaris emphasized that translation should be into the current idiom of the target readership and should be checked by a native speaker (an early recognition of the need for editing), and be stressed the importance of using notes for clarification.

These and similar questions were examined more systematically by Dimitrios Katartzis (c.1730–1807) in the prologue to his translation in 1784 of *La Science du Gouvernement* by Real de Curban. This is the first time in the Greek context that we can talk of a theory of translation. The first question Katartzis raised regarding translation method was whether he should confine himself to scholastic translation, taking refuge behind ostensible fidelity and scholarliness, thus forcing the unfortunate reader into mental contortions rather than providing him with intellectual enjoyment. One distinctive feature of Katartzis's writing on translation is that he took his examples from the successful translations of others, rather than from his own translations. He opted for preserving the sense of the original text and ensuring the naturalness of the target language as his two prime concerns. Only in this way, he suggested, does the translation fulfil its mission in that it can thus be compared to the original and also stand as an independent text. The second question he discussed was the form of Greek to be used as the target language (a question that every Greek writer and translator felt obliged to consider). Katartzis's answer was to respect the living language of his age, enriching it with elements where necessary from older Greek and foreign languages.

Katartzis played a central role in the debate on the Greek language question. He wrote in the popular language (as spoken in Constantinopolitan circles) and without any compromise with the learned tradition. He was one of the most remarkable personalities of the years preceding the Greek Revolution of 1821 and a representative of the spirit of the Enlightenment. For Katartzis, language was not an end in itself but a means for the propagation of knowledge, and this conviction was reflected in the language of his translations and writings. He made what was for that time a revolutionary proposal, namely that ancient Greek should be taught through the medium of modern Greek: by means of translation both from ancient Greek and from modern European languages. In this way, he suggested, learning would be made available to all people, including those for whom ancient Greek remained a barrier, just as Latin was inaccessible to ordinary people in Europe for many years.

He then moved on to the problem of the lack of translation tools, dictionaries and reference books (a situation that has not changed very much today: the translator from and into modern Greek is still faced with a lack of good general and specialized bilingual dictionaries). He concluded with six rules concerning the rendering of literal and metaphorical expressions, changes in sentence structure, translation using corresponding TL phrases and expressions, the degree of freedom in the TL, the

transformation of unconnected sentences into cohesive discourse and the periphrastic or conceptual transliteration of terms. This fundamental text on translation theory and practice ends with a statement on the linguistic and educational usefulness of translation. According to Koutsivitis (1994: 113), '1784 can rightly be seen as the year in which translatology was born in modern Greece' (translated).

The language and literature of the new Greek state (after 1821) were very much influenced by translations from other languages. Korais, Rigas, Solomos and Kalvos, four founding figures of modern Greek culture, gave much time and thought to the problems of translation and were influenced in their original works by their activities as translators.

Adamandios Korais (1748–1833) was concerned with both inter- and intralingual translation. He made some interesting points concerning fidelity to ideas rather than words and justified in this way the addition of words in his translations that are not in the original but necessary in his view to render what the author 'means', which raised for the first time in the Greek context questions relating to intentionality and the sub-text. Korais also stressed the value of translation in terms of enriching the target langauge. His contribution to the Language Question was to elaborate three principles: first, that the language of the ancients is the key to a storehouse of learning to which their descendants must gain access in order to claim the right of national self-determination; second, that the modern (written) language must be consistent with the grammar and intuitions of today's (spoken) language; and third, that the way to break this vicious circle is to take the modern (spoken) language as the basis, and so far as is practicable to 'correct' it in order to minimize those elements which most distinguish it from its ancient predecessor (Beaton 1994: 301). Korais believed in education as the best means of equipping his fellow-countrymen for their future independence from Turkish rule, and was also one of the first Greek intellectuals to envisage the emancipation of the Greeks in the form of a nation state, defined in terms of its language and traditions.

Like Korais, Rigas Pherraios's interest in translation reflected his concern with language, education and politics. He played an important role in the development of a national Greek literature and was the first to draw up a 'political constitution' for a new order that might succeed the violent overthrow of the Ottoman empire. His 'call to arms' in verse, *Battle Hymn*, was appended to his 'political constitution' of 1797. His first work, *The School for Delicate Lovers*, published in Vienna in 1790, has in fact been shown to be a translation of three stories by Restif de la Bretonne, and although not the earliest translation of European fiction into Greek, it began a short-lived phase of interest in fiction dealing with contemporary urban life, which was taken up two years later with the anonymous original stories, *Results of Love*. This collection, in its turn, played its part in establishing modern Greek fiction. Pherraios introduced the idea of translation as a creative work, particularly beneficial to both translator and reader provided that it conveys faithfully the sense of the original and respects the peculiarities of the target language.

Solomos (1798–1857), the Greek national poet, and Kalvos (1792–1869), his contemporary, had very similar approaches. Both saw the translation process as an exercise and preparation for original work through assimilating and re-fashioning in their own way various elements from their sources. Following the death of Solomos, Iakovos Polylas (1826–96) undertook the task of editing the poet's work from his incomplete manuscripts. In addition to this, he translated Shakespeare's *Tempest* (1855) and *Hamlet* (1889). He was also one of the first to translate Homer's *Odyssey* (1875) and *Iliad* (1890) into modern Greek. His translations are a creative expression of his critical spirit – a result of his wish to make these classic works available to others. His original output is small, though he was one of very few writers of his generation in the Ionian Islands to write any prose fiction. In his well-known translations of Greek and foreign classical works, as well as in his own critical works, he discussed various methods of translation, touching on wider translation issues but also on issues specific to the Greek language. In the introduction to his translation of the third Elegy of Albius Tibullus, under the title 'Poetry Translation', he stressed the high demands made on the translator and also the important educational role of translation. He then proceeded to analyse the linguistic, stylistic and metrical problems arising from the translation of Latin poetry into Greek.

During the second half of the nineteenth century, various statements on translation methods specifically – rather than the role of translation in the wider context – began to appear frequently in prologues to translations and in articles in periodicals and newspapers. Influential in this general debate were the views of Emmanuel Roidis (1836–1904) who, in the prologue to his translation of Chateaubriand's *Itinéraire*, noted the difficulties he encountered and explained his preferences for sense-for-sense as against word-for-word translation, though at the same time paying particular attention to the linguistic idiom of the target language and trying to steer a middle course between the popular and purist forms of Greek. Roidis followed closely the translation approaches which were popular during his time and stressed the tremendously positive but also negative effects of good and bad translations. One translation which profoundly influenced Greek literary writing at the time was that of Zola's *Nana* by Ioannis Kambouroglou (1851–1902), published in 1880. Particularly important and innovative for the time were the views he expressed in the prologue, where he attempted to transcend both the linguistic and translation dilemma by arguing that his prime concern was to achieve an equivalent effect on the Greek reader and that his choice of linguistic idiom was dictated by this consideration alone. In a similar vein, Lorenzos Mavilis (1860–1912) believed that a translation should not be evaluated on the basis of a comparison with the original but in terms of its own conceptual coherence and formal appropriateness. Like most other writers on translation, he noted the influence of translated works on the nation's literature and on the development of the national language. Costis Palamas (1859–1941) for his part distinguished between the translator as interpreter and the translator as creator and examined the varying fates of the original and its author in their encounter with the two different types of translator. He did not seem to believe that a compromise could be achieved between the two positions, i.e. of the translator as interpreter and the translator as (re)creator.

The methods and theoretical issues associated with the translation of poetry in particular have been at the centre of the discourse on translation in Greece and were taken up by some of the best-known nineteenth- and twentieth-century Greek poets. One of the few studies in this period devoted entirely to translation theory was that by S. D. Valvis, *On the Translation of Poets*, published in 1878. Valvis raised the question of the translatability of poetry, beginning with an examination of the views of those who consider it impossible. In order to answer them, he examined what is meant by 'translation' and concluded with a realistic affirmation of its difficulty. In his view, any poetry translation should retain to some extent its foreign character and the 'parfum étranger' of its origin. The second main question that Valvis attempted to address was whether poetry should be translated into metrical verse or prose and, for aesthetic reasons, he expressed his preference for the former. Vivas also discussed various types of translation: free, word-for-word and sense-for-sense, and suggested that the model of 'les belles infidèles' should be avoided since it serves the purposes of the translator rather than the original writer. He considered literal translation the best, albeit the most demanding, form of translation, and concluded by recommending sense-for-sense, which represents the middle ground between free and literal translation.

The Nobel poet, George Seferis (1900–71), stressed that the main aim in his translations was that 'the [Greek] language be cleansed and enriched so as to become functional and able to "bear" a text coming either from the literature of the West or from the older literature of our land' (1980: 241; translated). He consequently divided his own translation work into interlingual, which he called *antigraphi* (copy), and intralingual, which he called *metagraphi* (transcription). An *antigraphi* of the original, he maintained, is successful and functions only when it follows the best literary models available in the target language. With intralingual translation, things are not so simple. Although the Greek translator of ancient Greek texts is obviously at an advantage over the foreign translator since the source text is accessible with less mediation, its transcription into the modern language is nevertheless not always easy or satisfactory. Similarly, Seferis maintained that ancient texts were often translated into the modern (demotic) language to prove the resourcefulness of the

latter, but without due attention being paid to enriching the modern idiom with elements from the ancient language.

Odysseus Elytis (1911–96), Greece's second Nobel poet, was also an accomplished translator, having translated mainly French, but also Russian, Spanish and Italian poets, and, of course, ancient Greek poets. He was one of the leading figures of the so-called 'Thirties' Generation', which also included Seferis. Like him, he translated the Apocalypse of St John. Elytis favoured free translation, with emphasis on the functionality of the target language. He made an important distinction between translating poems that one likes (and, of these, only those that lend themselves to translation), and poems that one feels obliged to translate because they are representative of a particular poet or belong to a whole that it would be wrong to split up. In the first instance, the translator is free to give up when faced with insurmountable problems. In the second instance, however, the translator's aim must simply be to achieve the best possible result. Like Seferis, Elytis introduced new terms to describe his translation practice: he referred to interlingual translation as a *defteri graphi* (second writing) and intralingual translation as a modern Greek *morphi* (form).

The contemporary period

Profession, training and research

The 1980s and 1990s in Greece saw the emergence of translation studies as an independent discipline. The questions that have concerned Greek translators and translation scholars (usually the same people) are, on the whole, similar to those that concern their colleagues in other countries. However, the issue of intralingual translation remains a distinctive and much debated topic (and practice) in the Greek context. Contributions to the theory and practice of both literary and non-literary translation have been informed in recent years mainly by linguistics, comparative linguistics and literary theory. A fair amount of work has been done in the areas of terminology and machine translation.

In 1978, a conference entitled *Prototypo ke Metaphrasi* (Original and Translation) was organized by the Department of Classical Philology at the University of Athens. This event is generally considered a landmark in the establishment of the academic discipline of translation studies in Greece, and the Proceedings (Soile 1980) remain a standard reference work on the theory of translation. This volume, together with the book by Kakridis (1936), were for years the only publications available on the theory of translation. Others keep being added to this still rather small list.

The Hellenic Society of Translators of Literature publishes an annual volume, *Greek Letters*, which contains translations of Greek literature. Special issues of Greek literary periodicals (*Diavazo* and *I Lexi*) have occasionally been devoted to literary translation. In September 1995, the first issue of *Metafrassi* appeared; this is a journal on literary translation (mainly French/Italian/Spanish-Greek) published by former students of the Centre de Traduction Littéraire at the French Institute in Athens. The online journal *Translatum* has been published since 2001.

The growing interest in translation as a discipline and as a profession is reflected in the number of translation conferences which have taken place in Greece since the 1990s. Several conferences have been organized by the Greek Office of the Commission of the European Communities on Translation and the Greek Language in Europe, the Ionian University in Corfu, the University of Athens, the University of Thessaloniki, and the Hellenic Association of Translators and Interpreters in the Public Sector. Annual symposia have also been organized in Delphi by the Ministry of Culture to address issues relating to the translation of Greek literature into various European languages.

Professional training in translation and interpreting exists in Greece on the tertiary level in both the public and private sectors. The first attempt to develop a comprehensive training programme for translators and interpreters was the founding in 1977 of KEMEDI (Centre for Translation and Interpreting) which began operation in Corfu in the mid-1990s. The need for such a centre had long been recognized, but its establishment was precipitated by Greece's imminent accession to the European Community and with Greek becoming one of the Community's official languages. Several foreign cultural institutes and various other private institutes in Greece offer training programmes for translators and interpreters (often in association with translation departments at foreign universities).

The existence of a number of professional interpreting agencies and the appearance in recent years of several professional translation agencies both in Athens and in Thessaloniki reflects a growing awareness in Greece of the need for professional translators and is helping to raise the profile of the profession, which nevertheless remains lacking in prestige and remuneration. Those engaged in the profession are beginning to realize the need for collaboration and cooperation and for a professional body that would be responsible for setting standards and promoting the profession. Moves are already being made in this direction.

Further reading

Kakridis 1936; Politis 1973; Vayenas 1989; Batsalia and Sella-Mazi 1994; Koutsivitis 1994.

DAVID CONNOLLY AND
ALIKI BACOPOULOU-HALLS

Hebrew tradition

Hebrew is a member of the north-western branch of the Semitic family of languages. It started as one of many Canaanite dialects, but its beginnings as a language in its own right can be identified with the adoption of that dialect by the Israelites who settled in the Land of Israel in *c.* 1000 BC and who continued to use it during their periods of national independence (*c.* 1000 BC–587 BC and 517 BC–AD 70). Outside these periods of national independence, spoken Hebrew was replaced, first by Aramaic and Greek, then – when the Jews were forced to leave their land – by the various languages amongst whose speakers they settled. At the same time, wherever Jewish identity was not lost, Hebrew continued to be used as the language of religious rites and retained the prestige that goes with its status as the 'Holy Tongue', this being a mixture of Hebrew and Aramaic. It also continued to be used in a limited range of written functions. All later uses of the language were thus closely related to Jewish life and culture. Contact with other languages resulted in constant changes to its original form, including some of its most fundamental traits, especially as more and more of the languages in question were non-Semitic.

Like the use of the language itself, translation into Hebrew is characterized by inherent discontinuity: its history is marked by a series of new beginnings, each one charting a set of new routes, to be followed for a limited period of time before being abandoned for yet another set. And since the centres of Jewish culture shifted continually, a new beginning normally coincided with a territorial shift. It is fair to say, however, that this description applies first and foremost to Western traditions; our knowledge of translational behaviour in other parts of the Jewish Diaspora is still too scanty to support a reliable account of non-western traditions.

Translation during antiquity

The Hebrew Bible includes clear references to translation, including liaison interpreting (for example Genesis 42: 23). In addition, several passages reveal traces of actual translation (for example Ezra 1: 7–8 in Hebrew vs. Ezra 5: 14 or 6: 5 in Aramaic). On the evidence of, among other things, the interference of other, often easily identifiable languages and textual traditions, it seems reasonable to suggest that quite a number of passages in the Old Testament may have been translated from other sources. There is very little one can say about these passages as the translations they presumably are.

There can be no doubt that some translation into Hebrew took place during the early phases of the post-biblical period. However, the actual texts that have come down to us are mainly confined to biblical verses quoted in Mishnaic texts and translated, as part of their interpretive treatment, into the new brand of Hebrew which was in use at the time (Bendavid 1967 and 1971). Later on, in the Land of Israel as well as in neighbouring countries where the Jews had settled (most notably Egypt), translation started to be carried out *from* Hebrew, mainly into Aramaic and Greek – first orally, then in writing. The main objective of this translational effort was to render the Scriptures accessible to the less learned so as to enable them to follow the services. Mishnaic literature also contains many important observations on the nature of translation and the proper ways in which it should be performed, as well as on the (in principle inferior) status of translating, translators and translated texts in the Jewish culture of the time.

In the post-Mishnaic history of Jewish culture, where Hebrew was retained as a privileged language but other languages were used for most communicative purposes, there were two periods/territories where translation into the Holy Tongue enjoyed a special status, both quantitatively and qualitatively; these were south-western Europe of the Middle Ages and certain parts of Central and Eastern Europe during the Enlightenment and Revival periods. In both cases, not only did translations account for a large percentage of all texts produced, but certain cultural and textual 'slots' were filled mainly, sometimes exclusively, by translations. In some instances, as in the case of the medieval *maqāmāt* and modern fables, translating served as a means of experimenting with, and later introducing in original composition, text types which were hitherto unknown in Hebrew.

The Middle Ages

Following a long interval, translation into Hebrew resumed in medieval Europe and was in full swing by the end of the twelfth century. Most of the texts translated were now 'works of wisdom', i.e. scientific texts.

Many of the scholarly works first selected for translation were treatises in Arabic on Jewish law (*Halakha*) and ethics (*Musar*) written by Jews in Muslim Spain or North Africa. No need for translation had arisen when the Jewish reader lived in areas where Arabic was a shared literary language, but, by the twelfth century, Jewish families had already moved to Christian territories, most notably in southern France and northern Italy, and their descendants were unable to read Arabic. Interest in the achievements of Jewish scholarship remained strong, and a pressing need to have the texts translated therefore emerged. Hebrew, which was in use as a privileged literary language, became the target language partly because Jews living in different places no longer shared any other means of communication. A recurrent pattern, even though not an exclusive one, was thus to have a treatise translated at the request of an interested patron, who merely required the prospective translator to be reasonably fluent in Arabic.

There is no explicit mention of remuneration, but it stands to reason that at least some translators received some payment, either from the individual 'commissioners' or from the local congregation, in which the commissioners often occupied key positions. Among the most influential translations of Jewish 'works of wisdom' completed during this period are Bahya ibn Paquda's *Hovot ha-Levavot* (Duties of the Heart), Maimonides' *Moreh Nevukhim* (Guide of the Perplexed), and Judah Halevi's *Sefer ha-Kuzari*.

Interest in scholarship soon spread to non-Jewish books and themes, leading to numerous translations into Hebrew of works of philosophy, logic, grammar, astronomy, medicine, physics, and various other medieval sciences. Here, Arabic was often a mediating language only, especially in the case of Greek and Latin, including many of Aristotle's works. Other source languages were later added to the list. The most comprehensive presentation of Hebrew translations in the Middle Ages and the Renaissance Period, as well as the role of Jews as cultural mediators between East and West, is still Steinschneider (1893); most of the texts mentioned throughout this 1,077-page volume are still buried in manuscripts.

Although the translation of medieval 'works of beauty' has had much less impact on the Jewish tradition, it was no doubt a lot more common than we have come to think, due to a tradition of devoting scholarly attention to 'serious' texts only. True, 'literary' translation was considered inherently inferior, at best on the threshold of legitimacy, and Jews indulged in it with some reluctance – whether for personal diversion or in an attempt to fill empty slots in the literary sector of their culture. However, it seems reasonable to assume that many of the texts that did exist at the time simply failed to reach us. Not having been submitted to copying and recopying, like many of the scientific texts, very few of them existed in more than one copy to begin with, and even these copies were soon lost. The number of literary translations which were subsequently considered fit to be printed was even smaller. Finally, when Hebrew medieval texts became an object of scholarly interest within modern Judaic Studies, it was again first and foremost 'scientific' writings which were taken into consideration and (re)printed.

A significant exception to this rule was *Mahbarot Iti'el*, the Hebrew translation by Judah Al-Harizi of Al-Hariri's *Maqāmāt* in Arabic. Al-Harizi undertook the translation as a preparatory exercise for writing his own collection of *maqāmāt*, entitled *Tahkemoni*. Probably as a result of the canonization of the *maqāmāt* in Arabic literature, as well as Al-Harizi's own prestige, *Tahkemoni* came to be held in high esteem in Jewish culture. Other literary translations which enjoyed considerable prestige and distribution include Abraham ibn Hasdai's *Ben ha-Melekh ve-ha-Nazir* (= *Barlaam and Josaphat*), *Kalila and Dimna*, *Mishle Sendebar* (a version of *The Seven Sages*) and the *Alexander Romance*. The marginalization of medieval literary translations in scholarly work, especially those which did not originate in the East, has lately begun to show signs of weakening, as witness the recent printing of a 1279 Hebrew translation of *King Artus* (Leviant 1969) and the reprinting of a 1541 translation of *Amadis de Gaula* (Malachi 1981).

Many medieval translations were preceded by lengthy introductions, which were overwhelmingly apologetic in tone. This may be explained in terms of the problematic image of translation in traditional Jewish culture, where there was long-standing resistance to translating the Hebrew Scriptures. Medieval Hebrew translators often felt obliged to ask the reader's forgiveness for indulging in the act of translating, especially if the translation was initiated by the translator himself. Many felt obliged to apologize for tackling the particular text they undertook to translate: in the case of 'works of wisdom', mainly because of their limited familiarity with the subject-matter; in the case of 'works of beauty', the apology reflected widespread apprehension regarding 'idle talk'. Finally, apologies were sometimes offered for the kind of language used in the translation, whether out of choice or out of necessity. These translators may or may not have had genuine reasons for apologizing to their readership, but their over-indulgence in apologetics should be seen first and foremost as a convention of medieval Hebrew translation.

The introductions also offer important insights into prevailing views of the nature of translation and the proper ways of handling it under the conditions of the time. Huge gaps existed between theoretical observations and normative pronouncements on the one hand and actual translational behaviour on the other, and the translators themselves were not totally blind to such discrepancies. In practice, many of the problems stemmed from the recurring need to translate from a rich language, which was well suited to the purpose it served, into a language with a rather small repertoire, an inevitable outcome of its having been so long confined to a limited range of uses, and ones that hardly concurred with the nature of the source texts. When the original at hand was written in Arabic, additional problems arose from the family resemblance between the source and target languages, which often led the translators astray.

Generally speaking, medieval translators had two different strategies to choose from, depending to a large extent on the prestige of the text submitted to translation. Translators of 'important' works – mostly scientific texts – usually chose to stay as close as possible to the Arabic wording, replacing small, relatively low-rank segments one at a time, and the resulting text consequently reflected the structure of the original. In an attempt to reduce the gap between the two lexical repertoires, new words were also coined, either through direct borrowing (with a measure of adjustment to the target language) or by way of loan-translation. The Hebrew texts thus abounded in interference at all levels, both deliberate, or at least controlled, and accidental. By contrast, when it came to literary and other less-privileged texts, the translators – sometimes the very same persons – stuck much closer to domestic models, especially those offered by the quasi-biblical language used in Hebrew medieval poetry. The two strategies can be seen most clearly in texts which are both scholarly and literary in nature, for example *Sefer ha-Kuzari*. These were sometimes translated as if they were pure science and sometimes as if they were basically literature.

While the way literary texts were translated had very little impact on Hebrew culture and next to none on the language, the strategy adopted by translators of scientific texts proved truly innovative. Originally a clear case of translationese, the resulting structures and vocabulary were gradually assimilated into the language at large. What came to be known as 'Tibbonid

Hebrew', after the most influential family of medieval translators, crystallized as a variety in its own right: not just a legitimate variety, but one which was considered most appropriate for particular uses. The Tibbonids were a family which produced several generations of highly influential medieval translators into Hebrew. From the first generation, Judah ibn Tibbon (c.1120–90) has come to be regarded in Jewish historiography as the 'father of all translators'. Among his major translations are Bahya ibn Paquda's *Duties of the Heart*, Judah Halevi's *Sefer ha-Kuzari* and Saʿadia's *Beliefs and Opinions*. His will to his son Shmuel ibn Tibbon (c.1160–1230) constitutes an important theoretical document on translation. The most important translation by Shmuel himself is Maimonides' *Guide of the Perplexed*. The introduction to this translation is not only unusually comprehensive, it is also one of the most important treatises on translation in the Middle Ages. Other well-known members of the family include Moses ibn Tibbon (1240–83) and Jacob ben Machir ibn Tibbon (c.1236–c.1312).

Translation into Hebrew continued in Renaissance Europe too, now mainly in Italy, which became a new centre of multilingual Jewish culture. Interesting as each instance of translation made between the sixteenth and the eighteenth century may be, whether in terms of choice of genre, author, text, or even translation strategy (including variation in the language of translation and the varying modes and extent of 'Judaizing' the texts), translation was hardly noticed as a distinct cultural activity during that period. For instance, the inventory of private Jewish libraries in Italy at the close of the Renaissance (Baruchson 1993) shows that owners were keen to collect Hebrew texts but that very few of these were translations. Moreover, unlike the Middle Ages, Hebrew translation during this interim period seems to have lacked any distinct profile. It certainly lagged behind almost anything Jews did in Hebrew, which in itself was no longer up to European standards anyway. Much of this was bound to change with the next beginning, which was intimately connected with the *Haskala*, the Hebrew Enlightenment movement aimed at bringing Jewish culture closer to the achievements of Central European cultures. The new beginning coincided with yet another territorial shift: the cultural centre moved first to Germany then further to the East. Finally, it also marked the end of interruptions in the evolution of the Hebrew tradition: from now on there would be an almost direct line of development in translation activity leading right up to the present.

The Enlightenment period

Even the uninitiated forerunners of the *Haskala* in the middle of the eighteenth century could see that there was virtually no chance of catching up with the civilized world without a major investment in translation. Translating was not only an obvious way of producing texts quickly and in quantity, which is one way of demonstrating the existence of the new culture, but it was also a convenient means of experimenting with anything that was thought worthy of treatment by virtue of its association with an existing culture of high prestige. However, right from the start a distressing tension revealed itself between these recognized needs and the inability of Hebrew to express everything that had been, let alone could have been, formulated in other cultures. It was ideology which was mobilized to alleviate the tension. The solution came from an ingenious reversal of medieval practices, which were still very much in force. Apologetics, which were based on exaggerating the deficiencies of translation, were replaced by a conscious effort to highlight the power and versatility of the language, even if this involved using false arguments. As early as 1755–6, a claim was made in the first pre-periodical of the *Haskala* to the effect that whereas 'words of wisdom' were indeed untranslatable, Hebrew could hardly be rivalled when it came to the translation of 'words of beauty', which were soon to become the centre of attention. By constantly asserting the ability of Hebrew to do precisely that which held so many difficulties in store, a favourable climate was created right from the start, and this made it possible to pursue a highly ambitious programme and to achieve many of its goals. This ideological solution was supplemented by another congruent move with far-reaching consequences: linguistic acceptability was posited as a major requirement, to an extreme marginalization of any real wish to reconstruct the features of the source text.

The priority thus assigned to complying with the norms of 'pure' Hebrew was to protect the emerging new culture from being submerged under the weight of a huge volume of imported texts.

The model within which a translator, like any writer, was obliged to manoeuvre was in fact much narrower than the sum total of Hebrew resources, because only the language documented in the Old Testament was made available for actual use. The decision to restrict the language used to the most classical form of Hebrew was ideologically motivated again: it was part of the overall struggle against anything that smacked of the Jewish Orthodoxy of the time. Paradoxically enough, this extreme archaization, which was to govern acceptability during the early *Haskala* period, had an important innovative effect on Hebrew, as the kind of language now made compulsory had for a long time been out of use. The Bible was now regarded both as a source of matrices, to be filled with new linguistic material, and as a reservoir of actualized forms, to be used as fixed expressions. Long and complex linguistic items came to be regarded as most appropriate *per se*. They were, in a sense, target-language segments in search of source-language items to replace. Long word-chains were often formed by concatenating a series of phrases taken out of their original contexts, and this preferred mode of usage obviously narrowed down the translators' options even further, which might explain the high level of uniformity in the texts produced throughout this period. Very often, texts were not identified as translations; at any rate, it was common practice to assign a translated text first and foremost to its translator. The range of activities, strategies and texts associated with translation was thus both broad and highly diffuse, especially as many compositions which did not draw directly on individual foreign texts were still based on imported models.

Given that Hebrew Enlightenment made its debut in Germany, it was naturally the local culture which was called upon to act as a supplier of texts and models, especially since mastery of German was another ideal of the *Haskala* itself. However, rather than turning to the model-culture in its contemporary state, the new cultural paradigm usually played it safe by using earlier forms of German as a reference point, selecting items and models which had once attained some canonization. Many of the texts and authors selected for translation had indeed occupied a position near the epicentre of the living German system, but most of them had since been relegated to a more peripheral position or were considered significant from a historical perspective only. For a while, inclusion in a German anthology, the kind of source which rarely reflects current tastes, seems to have been an important criterion for selecting a text for translation, especially since many *Haskala* writers initially came into contact with the German texts through such collections. This time lag explains why no poems of Schiller and Goethe, for example, were translated until the first quarter of the nineteenth century. Both poets later became extremely popular in Hebrew circles and remained so for at least a century, often obstructing the translation of contemporary writers and texts and hence perpetuating time lag and stagnation.

During the first decades of the *Haskala*, translation was largely restricted to short texts or fragments of longer ones, not only because short texts are inherently easier to handle, but also because they are particularly suitable for periodicals and readers, which is where all first translations and many of the subsequent ones were in fact published. This is partly why it took a long time for novels and dramatic texts, and even novellas and short(er) stories, to be selected for translation.

Quite a number of the texts which were translated from German were themselves translations from other languages. Thus, the emerging new Hebrew culture did come into contact with other cultures as well, if only through the mediation of German. The mediating culture naturally adapted the foreign texts and models to its own needs. A culture which gives priority to linguistic acceptability in terms of its own norms and pays little attention to the features of the source text is unlikely to question the adequacy of a mediating text and, indeed, for a very long time proponents of the Hebrew *Haskala* hardly stopped to ponder this point. The overall tolerance for indirect translation – again, quite a while after the German model-culture had come to regard it as no longer appropriate – was reflected in a proliferation of second-hand translations, starting with the very first modern translation into Hebrew, a fragment of Edward Young's *The Complaint, or Night Thoughts on Life, Death and Immortality*, undertaken in all likelihood by Moses Mendelssohn (Gilon 1979). Thus, even someone like Mendelssohn, who could just as easily have translated from the English original, adopted the approach favoured by the proponents of the emerging new literature when operating on its behalf, which was quite different from his own behaviour when he operated as a representative of the German culture (Toury 1988).

During the first decades of the *Haskala*, most indirect translations were of English and French origin, so that many ideas of the French Revolution, for instance, only reached the Hebrew reader in a mediated and mitigated form. Those few translations of non-German texts which were not mediated via German were seldom accepted as an integral part of the new paradigm, partly, at least, because they looked like relics of an earlier historical phase rather than forerunners of a new era.

An interesting example of many of the points made so far is offered by Shakespeare's fate in Hebrew (Almagor 1975): by the beginning of the nineteenth century, the Hebrew cultural milieu had come to regard the Bard, with whom it was acquainted mainly via German, as a major figure of world literature. In reality, this appreciation amounted to nothing more than paying lip-service to Shakespeare's importance in an attempt to emulate 'modern' cultures, and for a long time Shakespeare's position *vis-à-vis* Hebrew literature itself remained marginal. It was not until 1816 that the first known excerpt of a Shakespearean text was published. Before 1874, when the first play (*Othello*) was translated in its entirety, and from the original, only monologues and other short passages from his tragedies were translated, and every single one is likely to have been mediated. These fragments were normally presented and accepted as instances of poetry. At the same time, no sonnet – the Shakespearean short poem *par excellence* – was translated until 1916, most probably because Hebrew had had an uninterrupted sonnet tradition of its own and did not need to experiment in this area (Toury 1995, Chapter 6). Most nineteenth-century translations of Shakespeare were made by minor, if not totally obscure figures, and none of them won

any fame through these translations. In fact, the translations were mostly published in marginal periodicals, so that the great majority of the few fragments that did appear in print went virtually unnoticed.

No single translation undertaken during the Enlightenment period stands out as instrumental in the evolution of Hebrew culture. However, translation as a mode of generating texts, as well as the cumulative weight of translated products – texts and models alike – had an enormous impact on its course. The most outstanding domain in this respect is no doubt children's literature, the like of which Hebrew had never had and which was modelled almost exclusively on the German example (Shavit 1986, 1992). In spite of the relative brevity of close contact between the two cultures, traces of German influence can still be seen in some areas of Hebrew culture and language to this day.

The Revival period

During the nineteenth century, the cultural centre gradually moved further East, first within the German cultural domain itself and then out of it and into the Slavic region. Subsequent generations witnessed frequent changes of attitude and behaviour, but no need was now felt for a brand new beginning. Evolution was now proceeding more evenly and translational norms came closer and closer to those which operated in other Western cultures.

The gradual shift eastwards inevitably brought Hebrew writers into contact with ever new cultures. These contacts had two complementary effects: with the new systems in the background, new gaps were being identified and, at the same time, various options for filling them also presented themselves. Nor were the gaps now confined to the realm of text-type, theme and composition as they had been before. Rather, they manifested themselves on the language plane as well. In view of the new tasks it had to perform, the current form of Hebrew could no longer be regarded as adequate, not even by way of ideologically motivated wishful thinking. It soon became clear that many institutionalized modes of behaviour, including those imported from German a few decades back, could not fulfil the new purposes and had to be replaced. Starting in the 1820s, Russian had gradually become the closest available system, and it was this culture which would now present Hebrew with most of its new challenges and provide most of the options for meeting them. Russian also became the main source of texts for translation, both original and mediated. Indirect translation was still common, and at least one important literary complex, Scandinavian writing of the end of the century, was imported into Hebrew almost exclusively in a mediated form (Rokem 1982).

A key figure during this period was Avraham Shlonsky (1900–73). Born in the Ukraine, he emigrated to Palestine in 1921. A poet in his own right, Shlonsky was also one of the most prolific translators ever into Hebrew. He translated mainly from Russian (including many indirect translations), Yiddish and French. He also introduced significant changes in translational norms which were picked up by a growing number of translators. His translations include Gogol's *Revizor* (*The Inspector General*; 1935) and *Marriage* (1945), Sholokhov's *Virgin Soil Upturned* (1935–6) and *And Quietly Flows the Don* (1953–9), Pushkin's *Yevgeny Onegin* (1937ff.), Shakespeare's *Hamlet* (1946) and *King Lear* (1955), and De Coster's *Tyl Ulenspiegl* (1949).

The behaviour of Hebrew in relation to Russian during this period, which has come to be known in Hebrew historiography as the Revival Period, involved much more than a simple recognition of the latter's availability. One could say that Hebrew behaved as if the Russian system were part of it, and a dominant part at that. Especially since the 1860s, when the dependency patterns had already been established (Even-Zohar 1990), the new paradigm which took shape gradually replaced the previous one based on German and was to dominate Hebrew culture for many generations, even after the centre had moved out of Russia again. On the face of it, Hebrew purism was still strongly advocated, though no longer on the basis of the Bible alone. However, the underlying model which was applied to both original writing and translation, regardless of source language, was in fact highly Russified. This contributed much to the process of enriching and diversifying the available repertoire. Among other things, it made it possible for the first time to create a kind of simulated spoken language in prose fiction; this became necessary in view of the new kinds of literature which were now being translated, and despite the fact that Hebrew itself had hardly started to be used as a spoken language again. Extending the range of options available to the writer and translator, often one and the same person, made it possible to narrow down the concept of translation and increase the relative weight of dependence on the source text. The borderline between originals and non-originals thus became much clearer, and translations no longer pretended to be original writings, as they did during the German period; if anything, it was now original texts which were largely based on translational models. Interference in the translation of individual texts as well as in the composition of non-translated ones thus played an important role in the very revival of the language.

All these trends were further reinforced by the close contact which now developed between Hebrew and Yiddish, another language used by Jews but regarded throughout the Enlightenment as corrupt German, to be abandoned in favour of Hebrew and pure German. Yiddish, especially in its Eastern variety, was now rapidly becoming a literary language in its own right and was also increasingly being modelled on the Russian example. For a long period, Hebrew and Yiddish behaved as if they were two complementary components of the same culture, a canonized and a non-canonized system, respectively. Later on, Yiddish texts began to be translated into Hebrew, often by the authors themselves, not in order to increase their readership (the potential reader of Hebrew in Eastern Europe could normally read Yiddish anyway), but in a deliberate attempt to enhance their cultural prestige. This process also helped to fill many lacunae which were still felt in the Hebrew system and further reinforced its overall Russification, first and foremost in the literary domain.

Israel

Towards the end of the nineteenth century, with the rise of Zionism and the first waves of Jewish immigration to Palestine, the centre of Hebrew culture started to move back to the ancient homeland. The immigrants had been brought up in the Russified tradition, and the writers and translators among them carried on their activities in the new environment. Consequently, many of the old habits were perpetuated, especially as most of the readership was still in Europe. In the difficult years of World War I, literary translation in particular became an important means of supporting the Jewish intelligentsia, and many elaborate projects were put forward by various institutions for that purpose. Most of these projects were never realized in full, but their activities nevertheless led to a boom in translation production (Shavit and Shavit 1977).

At the beginning of the twentieth century, a secondary cultural centre was established in the United States by a similar group of immigrants from Eastern Europe. The main importance of this short-lived centre is that it subsequently provided a small number of writers and translators who were well versed in English and its literature. Many of them later moved to Palestine, by which time the local scene was ready to absorb them as the language of the British mandate over Palestine (1917–48) had become current in the country. English soon became the main source language in translation, but English texts were still translated in the old fashion, as if they were written in Russian. In the 1930s and 1940s, a struggle for domination ensued between the old Russified models and some new options associated with Anglo-American practices; it was finally settled in favour of the latter.

To be sure, the supremacy of the Palestinian centre was not established until the destruction of Jewish culture (in both Hebrew and Yiddish) had taken place in the Soviet Union and some six million Jews had been murdered by the Nazis. These events resulted in Hebrew culture becoming practically mono-territorial again. By this stage, Hebrew had developed a number of spoken varieties on its way to self-sufficiency. But written Hebrew continued to resist these varieties for quite a while. Translation took even longer to accept the new varieties of Hebrew, and it is only recently that the rich gamut of linguistic options which exist in practice began to be used in Hebrew translations (Ben-Shahar 1994). The emergence of translational norms which involve drawing on all varieties of Hebrew has increasingly made it possible to approximate

to the verbal formulation of the source text, and there is even a substantial subculture now which prefers foreignizing to domesticating translations. By the end of the century, translation was undergoing a process of cultural marginalization: while most Hebrew texts were still products of translation, there were clear signs that original compositions were beginning to be preferred by the reading public.

Profession, training and research

It is still the norm for an Israeli translator not to have had any specific training for the job, and many still practise translation as a sideline. This is particularly true of literary translators, most of whom are not even writers any more. A plea for more professionalism has often been made, but without much effect.

The first university to offer a fully-fledged programme in translation and interpreting was Bar-Ilan University in Ramat-Gan. For decades, other institutes of higher learning went on offering at most a handful of courses in translation theory and/or workshops in practical translation within a variety of departments, although new programmes have since been launched.

The Institute for the Translation of Hebrew Literature (ITHL), which promotes the translation of Hebrew literature into other languages, was founded in 1962. Until 1980, Israeli translators had no professional organization to represent them. In fact, translators were largely against the idea of being 'organized', and quite a number of attempts to establish an independent association therefore failed. For a long time, the interests of translators were partly taken care of by the Hebrew Writers Association, even though translators would not normally have been accepted as members. In 1980 the Israeli Translators Association was established, and in 1987 it became affiliated to FIT. Nowadays, several awards are offered to encourage translation into and out of Hebrew.

Concerning research, until the 1950s very little work was done in translation studies in Israel, except for some research on old translations of the Scriptures and on medieval translation practices. Unlike their counterparts in most Western cultures, translators and critics did not produce much writing on translation either, and very few of the articles that did get published had any real impact. Not a single book on modern translation was published until 1977, except for a concise monograph on the intriguing figure of Salkinsohn (Cohen 1942). Yitshak (Eduard) Salkinsohn (1820–83) was born in Russia and, after spending some time in Germany, moved to London, where he converted to Christianity. He translated Milton's *Paradise Lost* (1871) and Shakespeare's *Othello* (1874) and *Romeo and Juliet* (1878). His continental background, combined with his mastery of English, made him an ideal mediator between English literature and the Hebrew literary centre of the time. However, his missionary activities prevented his translations from being fully accepted. His unfinished translation of the New Testament was published posthumously.

Pioneering theoretical research was undertaken in the 1950s by the linguist Chaim Rabin, but since translation failed to acquire any academic status, very few scholars followed suit. The turning point occurred in the 1970s, when a series of high-quality doctoral dissertations were completed: Itamar Even-Zohar (1971), Menachem Dagut (1971, 1978), and Gideon Toury (1976, 1977). Toury's approach has inspired a number of doctoral dissertations and MA theses, mostly descriptive studies on aspects of literary translation into Hebrew. Interesting work in translation theory was also done by Yishai Tobin, Shoshana Blum-Kulka and Elda Weizman, mostly in English. Unlike the situation in many other countries, very little scholarly work has come out of the programmes for training translators and interpreters.

In 1973, Tel Aviv University established a Chair of Translation Theory with the mission of coordinating research and publications. The publication of the international journal *Target* (since 1989) can be counted among its successful outcomes.

Further reading
Halkin 1971; Shavit and Shavit 1977; Toury 1977, 1995.

GIDEON TOURY

Hungarian tradition

The migration of the Hungarian tribes began in the Volga-Kama region around the sixth century AD and continued until they conquered the basin of the Carpathian Mountains, where they settled in AD 896. The origin of some of the words which became assimilated into the language gives an indication of the peoples they met and partly absorbed during their travels. For example, *sajt* (cheese) is Volga-Turkish in origin, *asszony* (woman) was borrowed from the Iranians in the North-Caucasus, and *barát* (monk) is originally Russian.

The Hungarians call their language *Magyar*. It is the most important language of the Ugric branch of the Finno-Ugric family of languages and is spoken by the peoples of Hungary as well as by some minorities in neighbouring countries, mainly Rumania, the Czech Republic, Slovakia and the former Yugoslavia.

The Middle Ages

St Stephen I, or Szt István I as he is known in Hungary, was the first king of the Magyars (997–1038). In order to save his country from having to depend on the Western powers (German and Roman) or Eastern powers (the Byzantine Empire), he took the church as his ally and was crowned on Christmas Day, in the year 1000, with a crown sent by Pope Sylvester II. Stephen's promotion of the Catholic faith in his country led to his canonization in 1083. Latin, the lingua franca of the Christian Community, or *Respublica Christiana*, became the official language of the Hungarian Kingdom. Decrees and orders, documents, inscriptions, chronicles and notices were all written in Latin and no translation was undertaken into Hungarian or other minority languages.

The oldest texts known in Hungarian are nevertheless literary translations. The *Funeral Oration* (*c.*1195), which was found with its Latin original, is a free translation in rhythmic prose by an unknown clergyman. A translation of the Latin poem by Geoffroi de Breteuil (*c.*1280), found around 1300, was allegedly undertaken in Italy by an unknown Hungarian Dominican monk. In fact, the majority of Hungarian literary texts from the eleventh to the sixteenth century consist of translations from Latin, for example the *Legend of St Francis of Assisi* (*c*.1370).

Various fragments were also found of documents of endowments, gift-deeds, and certificates; these were translated from Latin and Greek by unknown hands. The biography of Alexander the Great, written in the third century by an author known as Pseudo-Callisthenes (because he was influenced by Callisthenes, *c*.370–27 BC), was translated from Greek. Some folk ballads show French influence. The translation of the *Golden Legend* by Jacobus de Voragine (*c*.1298) was widely read in Hungary in the late Middle Ages.

Bible translation

The Bible was read in Hungarian during church service as early as the beginning of the twelfth century. Fragments of the Hussite Bible (so called after Jan Hus, the Bohemian religious reformer and martyr) were translated after 1430 by two priests who had studied in Prague, where Jan Hus worked as a university teacher and popular preacher. Two complete translations of the Latin Vulgate, the fourth-century version of the Old and New Testament produced by St Jerome, also appeared: the first was translated in 1590 by Gáspár Károli (*c*.1530–91), a Protestant, and the second in 1626 by György Káldi (*c*.1530–1634), a Catholic. Both have been revised and re-published many times. Today, translations based on the Hebrew and Greek originals are available. A translation of the Hebrew version of the Pentateuch and the Haftaroth was issued in 1939 and reprinted in 1984.

Some religious texts translated from Latin into Hungarian for the benefit of nuns were found in the fifteenth and sixteenth centuries. Among these, the *Érdy Codex* (1527) stands out as the richest collection of contemporaneous Hungarian legends.

The sixteenth and seventeenth centuries

The Kingdom of Hungary remained a great power, with its own rich and receptive culture, until the end of the fifteenth century. Having conquered Constantinople in 1453, the Ottomans invaded the Balkan peninsula and finally, in 1526, they defeated the Hungarians and Bohemians at the Battle of Mohács. Hungary was split into three areas: the major, central part came under Turkish rule, the western and northern parts were ruled by the Habsburgs, and the eastern part by the princes of Transylvania. The Magyar language became the only remaining bond connecting the Magyars in the three areas. Literature, original and translated, flourished and was further stimulated by the Catholic–Protestant dispute. Non-literary translations, mostly of religious texts, also began to appear, but we have no records of any particularly outstanding non-literary translators. This flurry of translation was not the result of national planning but of individual ambitions and interests in literary, religious and philosophical issues.

Some of the major works translated during this period include Aesop's *Fables*, translated by Gábor Pesti in 1536 and by Gáspár Heltai in 1566; Sophocles' *Electra*, adapted by Péter Bornemisza in 1558; Castelleti's *Amarilli*, adapted by Bálint Balassi from Italian in 1588; and George Buchanan's *Jephte*, also adapted by Balassi from a Latin version in 1589. An outstanding version of Martin Luther's famous *Hymn*, translated into Hungarian by an unknown Protestant poet, also appeared in the sixteenth century. The *Psalms* were rendered into verse translations by István Székely (1548) and Albert Szenci Molnár (1607), the latter from the French texts by Clément Marot and the Swiss Théodore Béza. On the Catholic side, Cardinal Péter Pázmány (1570–1637) was one of the leading reformers of Hungarian style. Preacher, author, translator and an outstanding figure of the Counter-Reformation, he translated Thomas à Kempis' *Imitatio Christi* (Imitation of Christ) in 1624. In attempting to reform the Hungarian prose style, Pázmány's guiding principle was that, in a translation, the word should flow so smoothly as though it were written by a Hungarian in the Hungarian language.

The Enlightenment

Maria Theresa (1717–80) reigned as Empress of Hungary (or rather 'King of Hungary', as she was crowned according to the constitution) and Archduchess of Austria (1740–80) and established a regiment of Royal Guards which consisted of young Hungarian noblemen. This was an important period of Euro-American history: the age of the North American Declaration of Independence, the age which anticipated the Declaration of Human and Civil Rights in France and which witnessed the replacement of authoritarian beliefs by rational scientific inquiry in various fields of knowledge.

Several members of Maria Theresa's Royal Guard were poets, with a good command of foreign languages and a keen enthusiasm for the ideals of the Enlightenment. They tried to promote these ideals in Hungary by translating Western literature. Translation therefore acquired a new vocation for the Hungarians, and the different ideas and styles of the translated works helped to enrich their own native literature.

In the history of Hungarian literature, the year 1772 is considered the beginning of the New Age. This is the year which saw the publication of György Bessenyei's *Tragedy of Agis*, adapted from an unknown French drama according to the principles of Alexander Pope's *Essay on Man*, which Bessenyei had read in French. This work, plus the version of Jean-François Marmontel's *Stories* which appeared in Sándor Báróczi (1775), and various other works (some of which were also written or translated by members of the Royal Guard) formed the core of what became known as the French School. József Péczeli (1750–92), a Calvinist priest, also translated a variety of authors and works from French, including Voltaire (for example *Zaïre* in 1784 and *Henriade* in 1786) and Edward Young's *Night Thoughts* (1787).

Another school, founded by the Jesuit Dávid Baróti Szabó, concerned itself with translating Latin classics into Hungarian. Szabó translated Virgil's *Aeneid* (1810–13) and fragments of John Milton's *Paradise Lost* from a Latin version. With Szabó's and with Benedek Virág's translations began the glorious era of Horace's poetry in Hungary, and it was these translations which inspired the famous ode-writer Dániel Berzsenyi (1776–1836). An uninterrupted flow of translations of Horace followed and continued into the twentieth century. These translations are documented in the anthology *Horatius Noster*

(Our Horace) which appeared in 1935, edited by Imre Trencsényi-Waldapfel. They are also documented in *Opera Omnia* (The Complete Works of Horace) edited by Gábor Devecseri in 1961. Other well-known translators of the Latin School include Miklós Révai and József Rájnis.

As far as German is concerned, well-known works of that era, such as Aloys Blumauer's *Aeineid-travesty* and August von Kotzebue's plays, were adapted rather than translated into Hungarian. Ferenc Kazinczy (1759–1831) was one of the most important translators of German literature during that period. Reformer of the Hungarian language, Kazinczy was also a central figure on the national literary scene for half a century. He began his career in 1788 by translating the idylls of the Swiss poet Salomon Gesner. By the time he was arrested in 1794 as a member of a Jacobin society, he had already translated thirteen plays and various works by Lessing and Goethe.

The translation of Shakespeare

The golden era of Shakespeare in Hungary began with the work of Ferenc Kazinczy, who translated *Hamlet* from German in 1790. After Kasinczy, a few translators made some feeble attempts at rendering other major titles, but it was Sándor Petöfi (1823–49), Mihály Vörösmarty (1800–55), and János Arany (1817–82) who together planned to enrich Hungarian literature by translating all the plays of Shakespeare. This plan fell through when Petöfi, having only translated *Coriolanus* in 1848, died on the battlefield in 1849 during the war of independence. Vörösmarty, an outstanding figure of Hungarian national romanticism, went on to translate *Julius Caesar* and parts of *Romeo and Juliet* and *King Lear*. Arany translated *Hamlet*, *A Midsummer Night's Dream* and *The Life and Death of King John*.

The effort to provide more and better translations of Shakespeare in Hungarian continued after the great triad: Petöfi, Vörösmarty and Arany. During the first half of the twentieth century, a new group of renowned poet-translators, who published in the review *Nyugat* (West), undertook to provide the modern public with translations of the complete works of Shakespeare, including his *Sonnets*. Since World War II, several series have been published of the complete works of Shakespeare in Hungarian.

Translation in the eighteenth and nineteenth centuries

Following the expulsion of the Turks, which started in the late seventeenth century, the Habsburg kings tried to incorporate Hungary into their Empire. Consequently, German gradually replaced Latin as the source language in interpreting and non-literary translation, mostly of official documents. After centuries of almost total preoccupation with literary texts, the translation of official documents began in earnest in the eighteenth century, and the translation of technical texts followed in the nineteenth century.

Non-literary translation

Until the end of the eighteenth century, official and technical texts in the Kingdom of Hungary were written in Latin, as indeed they were in several other countries of Europe. While promoting and facilitating contact with other countries, this state of affairs delayed the development of national culture. One consequence of this was that no formal instruction of translators and interpreters was undertaken. The only exception was a few workshops for translation and interpreting from and into Hungarian and other minority languages of the country, which were offered at the offices of the central government.

After a brief interval in the 1780s, when King Joseph II tried to introduce German as the only official language, the struggle for Hungarian began. This ended in 1867 with Hungary gaining internal self-government as part of the dual Austro-Hungarian Monarchy. At this point, Hungary became a plurilingual country. To guarantee equal rights in legislation, administration and economy for citizens whose mother tongue was not Hungarian, the government established the Prime Ministerial Central Translating Office in 1869. This organization still functions as a bureau of translation and authentication today. However, translators and interpreters did not begin to organize themselves into professional bodies until after World War II.

As far as technical translation is concerned, the monthly periodical *Tudományos Gyüjtemény* (Scientific Collection; 1817–41) published articles on literary criticism and historical studies; the Hungarian Academy of Science, active since 1830, issued the review *Tudománytár* (Scientific Store), which covered a variety of technical fields: natural and physical sciences, medicine, geography, history, sociology, and so on. Most of the articles in this journal were translations, mainly from English, French and German. Gradually, other technical journals began to appear in Hungarian. These include a history journal, *Századok* (Centuries; 1867–), and the quarterly *Ethnographia* (1890–). These journals tend to contain many translated articles.

Finno-Ugric relations and the translation of folkloric texts

The Hungarian language differs substantially from other languages in the region and was generally considered to be of obscure origin. A number of scholars tried to trace it back to a variety of oriental languages, including biblical Hebrew. In 1769, János Sajnovics, a Hungarian member of an Austro-Hungarian group of astronomers working in Northern Norway, began to study the language of the local population. In 1770, he published a book in Latin in which he demonstrated that Hungarian is closely related to Lappish. Like Finnish and Estonian, Lappish belongs to the Finnic branch of the Finno-Ugric family of languages. This discovery inspired some authors to write poems and novels about Finnish-Estonian-Hungarian kinship. This was followed by a flurry of translation activity in this field.

From the middle of the nineteenth century until recent times, Hungarian linguists have been collecting folkloric texts of the small Finno-Ugric nations in Russia and making verbatim translations for linguistic and ethnographic analysis. Fragments of *Kalevala*, the national epic of the Finns, were first translated by István Fábián in 1826; the first complete translation of the text, by Ferdinánd Barna, appeared in 1871. The most popular version of *Kalevala*, by Béla Vikár, appeared in 1901 and has since been re-published several times. The Estonian epic, *Kalevipoeg*, was translated by Aladár Bán in 1911.

This special interest in the literature of the Baltic nations survived into the twentieth century. Translations of a series of works by Estonian novelists were published in the 1930s. The most popular Finn authors in Hungary include Mika Waltari and Väinö Linna, and the best known Estonian author is Jaan Kross. During the four decades of Communist rule in Hungary, readers also became acquainted with many older and modern authors of the various nations of the former USSR, and most of these authors were translated into Hungarian via Russian.

The beginnings of translation theory

Theoretical statements about translation began to appear in Hungary as early as the seventeenth century, when Cardinal Péter Pázmány advocated idiomatic, target language-oriented translation. Over a century later, and at the same time that Ferenc Verseghy's translation of *La Marseillaise* appeared (1794), another admirer of the French revolution, János Batsányi, attempted to offer a general theory of translation in which he concentrated on the old paradox of 'les belles infidèles' (see FRENCH TRADITION).

Other scholars advocated a variety of principles. The sentimentalist József Kármán (1769–95) objected that too much was translated. József Péczeli (1750–92) rejected the concept of freedom in translation, and Gábor Döbrentei (1758–1851) was more concerned with how Shakespeare would have written had he written in Hungarian.

Towards the mid-nineteenth century, Ferenc Toldy (1805–75), who is considered the father of Hungarian literary history, distinguished between fidelity to content and fidelity to form and denied the possible co-existence of the two types. Károly Szász (1829–1905), on the other hand, opposed this view and succeeded in translating great epic poems from several languages and introducing them to the Hungarian reader.

A summary of these views can be found in Radó (1883). Antal Radó (1862–1944) was a translator of Italian poetry, who also wrote a theoretical work on the art of translation (Radó 1909).

Beyond the nineteenth century

Translators of the late nineteenth and twentieth century introduced Hungarian readers to a wide range of foreign literatures. Nearly all the works of Goethe, Schiller, Dickens, Balzac, Verne, Dumas, Hugo, Zola, Ibsen and Poe appeared in Hungarian. *The Arabian Nights* was translated from French. Almost every decade from 1860 onwards witnessed the translation of another famous Russian novelist: Turgenev in the 1860s, Tolstoy in the 1870s, Dostoyevski in the 1880s, Chekhov in the 1890s and Gorky in the first decade of the twentieth century.

Three outstanding achievements of this period deserve special mention. Károly Bérczy began to translate Pushkin's *Yevgeny Onegin* from Bodenstedt's German version in 1863, but then, inspired by the atmosphere of the work, he learned the Russian language and finished translating it from the original in 1866. Vilmos Györy not only translated Cervantes' *Don Quixote* (1873–6) but also wrote a simplified version of it for young people (1875). With its highly effective rhythm and distinctive rhyme, Emil Ábrányi's *Cyrano*, based on a verse drama by Rostand (1896), has been as successful in its own right as its French original.

Prompted by the classical scholar Károly Kerényi (1897–1973), the publisher Officina launched a series of literary translations in the mid-1930s under the title *Bilingual Classics*, edited by Kerényi.

The best-known poet-translators of the twentieth century included Mihály Babits (1883–1941), Dezsö Kosztolányi (1885–1936) and Árpád Tóth (1886–1928), who belonged to the group which published in the review *Nyugat* and undertook to provide the complete works of Shakespeare in Hungarian (see above).

Among those who produced poetic translations of works by vanguard authors such as James Joyce and Marcel Proust, the most outstanding include Albert Gyergyai and Marcell Benedek for French, Aladár Schöpflin and Tivadar Szinnai for English, József Turóczi-Trostler for German, József Révay and Mihály András Rónai for Italian, Endre Gáspár for Spanish, Hugó Gallért and Zoltán Trócsányi for Russian, János Tomcsányi for Polish, Henrik Hajdu and Sándor Kreutzer for Scandinavian, and Gyula Germanus, Ervin Baktay and Rezsö Honti for

Oriental languages. Some of these translators worked closely with the authors they translated, for example Henrik Hajdu corresponded regularly with Selma Lagerlöf and Hugó Gellért with Gorky.

Some of the most outstanding poet-translators of this period became victims of the political and social turmoil of the time. György Faludy (1910–2006), who adapted – rather than translated – the work of the medieval French poet François Villon, survived jail and various painful experiences before emigrating (first to France, then North Africa, England and finally Canada) to escape from Nazi and Stalinist terror. Attila József (1905–37), who published anthologies of Rumanian, Czech and Slovak poetry at a time when friendship between neighbours was persecuted, broke down under the pressure of psychoanalytic experimentations and Communist party intrigues and eventually committed suicide. Miklós Radnóti (1909–44), translator of French poets and of the anthology *Orpheus nyomában* (In the Footsteps of Orpheus, 1942), fell victim to Nazi killers. Antal Szerb (1909–45), historian of literature, author, critic and translator, suffered the same fate. Szerb edited the bilingual anthology *Száz vers* (A Hundred Poems, 1944), a collection of the best Hungarian translations of modern poetry.

Like most other facets of life in Hungary, the course of translation was shaped during the period 1945 to 1989 by the Allied powers' decision to assign Hungary to the Soviet zone. Previously prohibited, works by Russians and other writers of the same region began to appear in Hungarian. The method of translation was influenced by the sudden demand to promote the literature of the Communist world, including the literature of languages unknown to anyone in Hungary except for a handful of linguists. The poet, unjustly called translator, received a prose or 'raw' translation made by a linguist. He or she then had to put into verse this raw translation of an original text whose cultural context he or she was often unfamiliar with. This is how the anthology of Albanian poets *Albán költők* (1952) and *A mongpé irodalom kistükre* (The Small Mirror of Mongolian Literature, 1965) were produced. This practice became widespread and was even followed sometimes in the case of languages known to the translators.

Political pressure and the general tolerance for poor-quality translations notwithstanding, the effort to promote high-quality literary translation continued unabated. Géza Komoróczy, Sándor Rákos and Sándor Weöres were among those who translated older works of literature, such as Sumerian lyrics and the *Gilgamesh Epic*. István Mészáros and Grácia Kerényia translated a range of classical and modern Polish works, of prose and poetry respectively. A number of South American and Caribbean authors were also translated during this period. In 1977, Zoltán Csuka was awarded the international FIT-Nathhorst Prize for his translations from Serbian, Croatian, Slovenian, Macedonian and Bulgarian.

In 1956, the monthly periodical *Nagyvilág* (Wide World) appeared; it continues to publish translations, articles and reviews of foreign literature in print. György Somlyó, translator of French and Spanish poetry, edited a regular almanac, *Arion*, which contained translations into and from Hungarian. The long-standing series *Lyra Mundi* (Lyric of the World) is published by Európa, and the series *A világirodalom gyöngyszemei* (The Pearls of World Literature) is published by Móra; both series consist of translations of world poetry.

The Translators' Section of the Hungarian Writers' Union became a member of FIT (Fedération Internationale des Traducteurs) in 1961. The FIT journal, *Babel*, was published from 1977 to 1988 in Budapest and edited from 1975 to 1988 by the Hungarian translator György Radó (1912–94), who was awarded the FIT-Nathhorst Prize in 1987.

After 1945, and particularly during 1956 and 1957, a number of authors and translators left Hungary. This was not the first wave of emigration by writers. Some Communist authors and translators had fled after 1919 into Austria, Germany, France and particularly the USSR. They carried on translating in their new environments but returned to Hungary after the Communist takeover and published their translations there. Those who emigrated to Israel and various Western countries after 1945 tried to promote Hungarian literature there by publishing translations into Hungarian. These included *The Unknown Tree* (1975), a collection of Polish poetry which was published in Hungarian translation by György Gömöri in

Washington in 1978. Román Rezek published his translations of works by the French Catholic philosopher Teilhard de Chardin in Brazil during the 1960s.

When the Communist political system in Hungary collapsed in 1989–90, its demands in terms of book publishing began to disappear. The obligatory translation of Communist literature ceased and some authors and translators who had emigrated to the West returned.

In 1966, Lóránd Tarnóczi published *The Translator's Handbook: Theory and Practice of Special Literature*. This is a compendium of general knowledge and information for non-literary translators. A collection of essays by twenty-nine leading translators, *A műfordítás ma* (Translation Today), was published in 1981.

Translator training

In 1973, the Training Centre for Translators and Interpreters (TCTI) was established at the University of Budapest. A year later, a number of other Hungarian universities began to introduce training programmes for translators, and today these programmes are offered by a wide range of academic institutions in – among other places – Budapest, Debrecen and Pécs.

Translation theory is now taught in various institutions, both from a linguistic and a literary perspective. The first international conference on translation studies to be held in Hungary took place in November 1992 and the second in September 1996.

In 1990, a professional translator of English literature, the playwright Árpád Göncz, was elected President of the Republic. He remained in office until 2000.

Further reading

Radó, A. 1883, 1909; Bayer 1909; Lenkei 1911; Tezla 1964; Rónay 1968; Szabó 1968; Rába 1969; Tezla 1970; Radó, Gy. 1971; Rákos 1975; Bart-Rákos 1981; Kurucz-Szörényi 1985; Radó, Gy. 1986; Kohn and Klaudy 1993.

GYÖRGY RADÓ

Icelandic tradition

It is not without reason that Iceland is sometimes described as a land of contrasts, both natural and social. Though situated in the North Atlantic, on the edge of the Arctic Circle, the island is warmed by the Gulf Stream, thus enjoying a much milder climate than one would expect at such a northerly latitude. The Mid-Atlantic ridge runs from north to south through the middle of Iceland and marks the juncture of two tectonic plates of the earth's crust. This ridge is geologically unstable and has been the site of frequent volcanic outbursts, causing the highest density of thermal activity to be found in any country of the world. But despite these fiery forces beneath its surface, the island remains capped by Europe's largest glaciers.

Like the natural environment in which they live, the Icelandic people are full of contrasts. Iceland first became inhabited in the late ninth century, when Norwegian and Celtic immigrants began to expand their settlements westward across the North Atlantic islands. The Icelanders formed one of Europe's last tribal societies, ruled by several dozen *goðar*, or local chieftains, with an annual assembly called the *Althing*. This commonwealth-type structure lasted for almost four centuries before submitting to the Norwegian Crown in 1262. Together with Norway, Iceland later passed to the Danish Crown in 1381. In 1944, with no more than 120,000 inhabitants, Iceland once more became an independent republic.

Living in this 'microstate', Icelanders today are both fiercely independent and highly dependent upon the rest of the world. Fish and marine products comprise almost 80 per cent of goods exports, and the limited domestic resources mean that almost all manufactured consumer goods, as well as many staple food products, have to be imported. Although very proud of their national language, Icelandic, and determined to support it against the onslaught of international mass media, almost all Icelanders are fluent in at least one foreign language (usually English) and many speak other European languages as well.

The language itself is living proof of the tenet that languages on the fringe of a linguistic area undergo little change through time. Icelandic maintains the complex and highly inflected Germanic grammar once common throughout northern Europe. The designation 'Saga Island' is well deserved too: not only has much of what we know about the literary tradition of northern Europe during the early Middle Ages been preserved in Icelandic manuscripts, but there are also few countries where learning and writing are held in higher esteem. This is a country where every twentieth person has written poetry, almost everyone nearing retirement age has written his or her autobiography and absolutely everyone has an opinion on how to say things in proper Icelandic! This can often make life rather difficult for the translator.

Translation in the Middle Ages

Strange as it may seem, the medieval northerners who inhabited Iceland do not appear to have had much need for translators or interpreters. In spite of the fact that they roamed from the Arctic to the Vatican, and even farther, only one medieval saga mentions ordinary people (that is, people other than the high church officials that populate the Bishops' Sagas) who spoke other, 'incomprehensible' languages. In *Ingvars saga víðförla*, the 'Saga of Ingvar the Far-travelled' which recounts the Norse voyages of discovery to Eastern Europe, the storyteller refers more than once to the variety of languages spoken. One of the main characters goes so far as to prepare for an expedition by embarking on a course of studies in vernacular languages. As a rule, however, everyone seems to have understood everyone else without difficulty in the medieval Northern world. Even those who travelled to Constantinople to join the Varangian guard do not seem to have had problems communicating with others; at least, if they did, they left us no record of such problems.

The oldest existing manuscripts indicate that, by the twelfth century at the latest, this linguistic paradise had become a thing of the past. The Christianization of Iceland around the year 1000 brought about a great need to translate all sorts of religious texts into a language that the new converts could understand. According to the *First Grammatical Treatise*, an Icelandic work on grammar dating back to the middle of the twelfth century, 'translations of holy works' existed in Iceland at the time. To judge from existing fragments and the earliest extant works, these would have primarily been expositions and other interpretive writings, rather than actual translations in the modern sense. It is also possible that accounts of the lives of some saints existed in Icelandic by 1150.

It is worth pointing out that the verb *að þýða*, now used to mean 'to translate', was not used in this sense in medieval times. It meant, as a rule, 'to oblige' or 'to obey', while the verb most commonly used for the process of translation was, it seems, *að snúa*, which literally means 'to turn'. In the large corpus of written Icelandic collected and excerpted over several decades by the University of Iceland Dictionary Project, examples of the use of the verb *að þýða* to mean 'translate' do not appear before the middle third of the sixteenth century, when the first translations of the New Testament were undertaken.

The oldest Icelandic book of homilies (now preserved in the Royal Library in Stockholm) dates from around 1200 and contains a collection of sermons, half of which at least are based on foreign models. These works have seldom been 'translated' directly; they are mostly retellings or even combinations of several works in one. Interestingly, one of the texts in this book of homilies addresses the listeners directly and bids them make allowances for the priests who had difficulty in expressing themselves in Icelandic.

In order to make Christian teachings as accessible as possible to the commoners, these early medieval translators, all of them clerically trained, adopted a simple, idiomatic style of prose, occasionally adorned with native proverbs and similitudes from everyday life. Latin-flavoured diction and syntax, which later came to characterize much of the Old Icelandic translation of religious prose, are not generally found in the early homilies. A number of classical rhetorical devices such as antithesis, chiasmus, anaphora, alliteration and word pairing were sometimes added to elevate the style of certain homilies.

Another form of popular medieval literature, the lives of saints, was also quick to take root in Iceland. Over 100 accounts of the lives of different saints exist in translation in manuscripts dating from the late twelfth century onwards. They are drawn primarily, but not exclusively, from Latin sources such as the apocryphal books of the New Testament and legends such as Jacobus de Voragine's *Legenda aurea* and Gregory's *Dialogues*.

In his authoritative work, *The Origins of Icelandic Literature*, Turville-Petre (1975) maintains that early religious writings taught Icelanders lessons that they later put to use in writing secular sagas. Like the homilies, the earliest translated accounts of the lives of saints show very little influence of Latin syntax and contain no more than a few loanwords from that language. Even the Greek and Roman gods are replaced by Norse ones: *Óðinn* for Mercury, *Þórr* for Jupiter and *Frigg* for Venus. Their lively, chatty style hardly differs from the style of Icelandic works such as the sagas of kings or of Icelanders. This situation did not endure, however, and from the mid-thirteenth to the fifteenth century many accounts of the lives of saints were written in a more ornate, florid style which consciously imitated Latin and often translated Latin constructions literally.

In addition to providing the common people with proper examples to follow in the form of the lives of saints, the churchmen, who in practical terms were the only educated class in the country, seem to have thought it important to introduce them to Christian religious and philosophical thought. One of the best-selling works of the Middle Ages (to judge by the number of translations and copies preserved) was the *Elucidarius* of Honorius

Augustodunensis, which dates back to the early twelfth century. Translated into Old Icelandic in the same century, the work takes the form of a debate on theology between master and pupil. The debate offers simple and reassuring answers to a large number of common questions, and the anonymous Icelandic translator of the twelfth century renders this in a language which preserves the simple, unassuming flavour of the original.

Several secular works were also translated during this period. The *History of the Kings of Britain*, compiled by Geoffrey of Monmouth around 1137, was translated around the end of the twelfth century. It is thought to have had considerable influence on the sagas which describe the missionary activities of the Norwegian kings; these sagas are among the most important Icelandic literary and historical achievements. Included in the principal manuscript of the Icelandic translation of Geoffrey's work is the poem *Merlínusspá*, a rare example of a verse rendering of a prose text, the original being Geoffrey's *Merlin's Prophecy*. Even more striking is the fact that, in the Icelandic version, the two sections of the poem are in reverse order, bringing the poem into closer correspondence with the ancient Icelandic eschatological poem *Völuspá* or *The Sybil's Prophecy*, to which the translation has been compared and which it does resemble. It could be argued that this is an early Germanic example of the reworking of a source text to fit a known pattern in the literary polysystem of the target culture.

All secular translations into Icelandic during the medieval period show a tendency towards extensive reworking of the source text. The so-called *riddarasögur* or 'courtly romances' were prose translations of vernacular metrical romances (from Old French, Low German or even English). At least one anonymous medieval translator of works on classical Rome, for instance, was fond of using direct speech, and often transformed indirect speech to suit his or her preference. This raises the question of whether the translations were intended to be read aloud and were therefore patterned, consciously or otherwise, to fit an oral format. Many of the stylistic devices characteristic of original Icelandic works of this period, such as repetition, references to time or to the audience, and alliteration, link the translations to an oral

tradition and suggest that they might have been delivered orally.

The prose translation by abbot Brandr Jónsson (d. 1264) of the poem *Alexandreis* by Galterus de Castellione (*c*.1180) is probably the most polished example of medieval translation from the Graeco-Roman classics into Icelandic. The dactylic hexameters of the original are expanded in the prose translation to give a slightly more diffuse narrative. Medieval translators obviously knew that they had to play to their own audiences. The original author, Galterus, expected his readers to be familiar with Middle Eastern geography, classical mythology and the story of Alexander the Great. Abbot Brandr, however, found it necessary to add explanations to his translations, or even shorten chapters which required such specialized knowledge. He used the Greek names of the gods, rather than translating them, and explained their roles. Where rhetorical exclamations occurred in the original, or where Galterus's opinion was clearly stated, the translator frequently added a comment to the effect that those words were not his own but those of Galterus.

Another popular entertainment during the late Middle Ages in Iceland was the *sagnadansar*, meaning 'folksongs' or 'ballads'. These are generally considered to have originated in France in the twelfth and thirteenth centuries and to have then spread fairly rapidly throughout Europe. There is reliable evidence confirming that they existed in translation in the Nordic countries early in the fifteenth century, but most scholars feel that they must have been known much earlier. The style of the ballads differs markedly from native Icelandic poetry: the word order is natural and the vocabulary rather limited. It is worth noting that many such Icelandic ballads were only partly translated from Norwegian versions and were not even completely adapted to the Icelandic conjugation system. This often presented a difficult problem when rhyme and rhythm were to be maintained without major alteration to the ballads. Typical features of original Old Icelandic epics, rhymed and unrhymed, hardly ever occur in these ballads. Such features include the convoluted word order of skaldic poetry, its kennings (i.e. expressions which work like riddles, for example 'the horse of the waves' = 'ship'), and the use of archaic poetic names for common nouns.

In Iceland, as elsewhere in Europe, the influence of the preaching friars in the late Middle Ages led to the increased popularity of the *exemplum*. This was a short tale which was often inserted in a sermon or text for explanatory purposes or as an example of a situation or moral, good or bad. *Exempla* were used by oriental and classical writers as well as the early fathers of the Christian Church. Examples of this genre include the *Dialogues* of Pope Gregory the Great, which are preserved in an Icelandic manuscript dating shortly after 1200. Another collection of *exempla* was translated from English in the late fifteenth century. The basic tale could be drawn from history, legend, the Bible, the lives of saints, classical literature, folk tales, and even from fables, animal tales and proverbs. Over 150 different stories have been found and edited in Icelandic translation. They appear to have been thought quite different from the native genre of *þáttr*, a short tale which focused on local heroes and which was firmly rooted in the Germanic warrior tradition. The characters in the *exempla* were foreigners – with obvious weaknesses that provided plenty of opportunity for religious moralizing.

The popularity of *exempla* waned in the wake of the Reformation, but manuscripts continued to be copied right up to the nineteenth century.

Official and legal translation in the Middle Ages

Even as they submitted to the Norwegian Crown in 1262, the Icelanders had no intention of bowing down meekly. With no fleet of ships in their possession, they managed to negotiate a settlement with the Norwegians which was intended to secure a minimum level of vital foreign trade. The agreement also stipulated that they were to be allowed to retain Icelandic laws, and this naturally meant continuing to use the language in which the laws were expressed. At that time, there were few differences to worry about among the languages concerned, and the differences which did exist were generally fudged or overlooked. In later centuries, any laws passed by the ruling monarchy, first in Norway and subsequently in Denmark, had to be translated if they applied to Iceland. It is also due to this persistence in using Icelandic for legal and official purposes that the Icelanders never

lost their written language as did their neighbours the Faroese, and indeed the Norwegians themselves after they came under Danish rule.

The vernacular was apparently used for official ecclesiastical correspondence very early on in Iceland, in the first century after the adoption of Christianity. It is generally assumed that two official written languages, Latin and Icelandic, were recognized practically from the beginning of the Christian era, and that according to an unwritten but widely followed rule, documents were composed and sent in the language which the intended receiver used and understood (*Kulturhistorisk leksikon for nordisk middelader fra vikingetid til reformationstid* 1982: articles on Norway and Iceland by Finn Hødnebø). Yet, even allowing for considerable lacunae in the records which have come down to us, it appears that the use of Latin for official written communication was very limited. Only an exceptionally small number of letters written in Latin have been preserved in Icelandic manuscripts; by contrast, extensive church correspondence in Icelandic can be found among the historical collections. Assuming Latin was the language used for church communication, these letters are likely to have been translated into Icelandic, perhaps to make them known to a wider audience.

The influence of Latin did not endure. It was replaced in later centuries by German and Danish, the preferred medium of the Lutheran Church and official administration respectively. This shift influenced the development of written Icelandic, especially in official use. What is known as the 'Chancellery' style, with Danicized Latinisms and extensive use of hypotaxis, was widely adopted; as a result, original written works from the seventeenth and eighteenth centuries remain among the most difficult Icelandic texts for modern readers to understand.

The Reformation and post-Reformation: the translation of religious texts

The period following the Reformation was almost exclusively devoted to the translation of religious works in Iceland. The national Lutheran Church, which controlled the printing press in the country, needed material for its services in the vernacular, including sermons, scriptural texts, and hymns. The first church ordinances from the Danish king Kristian III (1503–59), an ardent Lutheran, provided for the entire church service to be held in the vernacular, with the exception of a very small number of Latin hymns which were decreed to be acceptable. Furthermore, the publishing efforts of the Church were aimed at preaching and encouraging the spread of 'proper' doctrine. Among other things, this meant that native Icelandic religious works had to be purged of any non-conformist material before publication, and numerous edifying foreign works which followed the doctrinal lines approved by the Church were translated to complement this effort. Both the translation and writing of hymns flourished to fill the urgent need for religious melodies.

Most of the evidence indicates that it is unlikely that the entire Bible was translated into Icelandic before the sixteenth century. There is no mention of vernacular bibles among the lists of books owned by medieval libraries in Iceland. In those countries of Western Europe which exercised direct influence on Iceland during the late medieval period, complete versions of the Bible in the vernacular do not appear until quite late: in France and Germany the first ones date from the end of the thirteenth century; the first complete English Bible appeared a century later.

On the other hand, it has long been known that certain parts of the Bible were translated into Old Norse, the language spoken in Iceland and much of Scandinavia between the eighth and mid-fourteenth century. The work known as *Stjórn* (*c.*1310), attributed to a priest of the court of King Hákon Magnússon of Norway, includes substantial portions of the historical books of the Old Testament. Some of the glosses provided in this work confirm that the Psalter was translated during the medieval period, and the remarkable similarity between certain quotations from the Gospels in older and later texts indicates that an Old Norse translation of the Gospels must have existed in the thirteenth century.

Bible translation is important for language development for numerous reasons. First, texts which are used by a large number of the population naturally play an important role in standardizing the language. Second, the translation process itself generates new constructions, new meanings and new words (neologisms) to express the thoughts of both the Old and New Testament in different cultures. Studies of Icelandic have shown this to be very much the case here: an extraordinary number of words either make their first appearance in written Icelandic, or take on new meanings, in translations of the Bible dating back to the sixteenth century.

The Church maintained tight control of printing activities during this period, which meant that secular works were seldom if at all printed. However, handwritten copies of books intended for the amusement of the common people abounded during the sixteenth to eighteenth centuries. Books of this type, particularly the oldest among them, are known by their German name, *Volksbücher*; they were mainly retellings of older historical poems, courtly romances and fables. The German name is misleading as it obscures the fact that these works were originally intended for the upper classes; they did, however, spread rapidly in Germany from the end of the fifteenth century, with the advent of the printing press, and gradually became more and more common. Icelanders first became acquainted with these books in German editions and Danish translations: many of them had been translated into Danish early in the sixteenth century. A large number still exist in manuscript form, and many of the plots were adopted in the popular *rímur*, or rhymed epics, which flourished from the seventeenth to the nineteenth century.

Literary translation in Iceland

The late eighteenth and early nineteenth century in Iceland saw a renewed interest in the translation of Greek and Roman classics. Sveinbjörn Egilsson (1791–1852) was the headmaster of the only real school in Iceland at the time, which was transferred from the former Governor's residence at Bessastaðir to Reykjavík. He translated a number of such works into Icelandic, including Homer, often consciously imitating the style of classical, i.e. medieval Icelandic. His prose translations were (and still are) considered a milestone in Icelandic literature and pointed the way for others to follow; his translations of the *Iliad* and the *Odyssey* were reprinted as late as 1948–9. Egilsson also translated or assisted in translating medieval Icelandic works into Latin, including *Konungasögur* (Sagas of Kings) and *Snorra-Edda* (the Prose Edda).

Other translators of this era turned to modern European languages for their source texts. Benedikt Gröndal the Elder (1762–1825) translated Pope into the Icelandic metre *fornyrðislag*; this is the metre in which many of the ancient Eddic poems were written. Jón Þorláksson (1744–1819) followed his lead in translating Pope, Milton and Klopstock, among others. These were the first Icelandic translators who were not primarily clerics; although Jón Þorláksson admittedly started out as a minister, he was defrocked for a period and was obviously more interested in literature than in priesthood. From this time onwards, most translators were educated abroad (almost always at the University in Copenhagen) and were highly influenced by contemporary trends in European literature. This clearly played a role in shaping their views on translation as well. They aimed to bring the best and most edifying of foreign literature to Icelanders in their own language.

The first poets of the Romantic period, Bjarni Thorarensen (1786–1841) and Jónas Hallgr'msson (1807–45), translated a number of poems by Schiller, Oehlenschläger and Heine in the free style typical of that period. The following generation of poets discovered Goethe and the English Romantic poets: Byron, Shelley and Burns. Among the most productive translators of the nineteenth century were Steingr'mur Thorsteinsson (1831–1913) and Matthías Jochumsson (1835–1920). Thorsteinsson was referred to by the critics of the time as a *Kulturbringer*. He studied philosophy as well as classical and modern languages in Copenhagen and worked there for another ten years as a freelance poet and translator. His translations, which include *The Arabian Nights*, *King Lear*, *Robinson Crusoe* and Hans Christian Andersen's *Fairy Tales*, are characterized by a fine classical Icelandic style, often more his own than that of the original author. Surprisingly little difference is found between, for instance, the fantastic tales of *The Arabian Nights* and the carefully worded fables of Andersen. Thorsteinsson encouraged the young Jochumsson, a few years his junior, who had originally sailed for Copenhagen to learn commerce. Jochumsson eventually returned to Iceland where he became a minister, then newspaper editor, and eventually went back to the ministry. A great traveller, he was also an eager correspondent and one of the most productive of all Icelandic poets. In addition to composing poetry for every occasion and in great quantity, he wrote a number of popular dramas and translated the best-known works of Shakespeare. Jochumsson's translations of poems by Poe, Byron, Ibsen and numerous other Scandinavian writers are written in a sweeping and enthusiastic style that exalts the spirit, though it may at times lose the letter, of the original.

The numbers of both translators and translations have increased in Iceland with the upsurge in publishing activity during the twentieth century. Restrictions on imports, which applied to most consumer goods up until the 1970s and 1980s, had the effect of directing consumption to those areas of internal production where both high quality and a wide range of choice could be offered; only a few such areas were available, and they included publishing. The result was a high demand for books, and large numbers of published works were consequently translated, especially during the Depression,

Table 1: Translated works published in Iceland

Decade	1900–9	1910–19	1920–9	1930–9	1940–9	1950–9
original poetry	101	83	118	160	249	298
original fiction	46	72	102	142	244	278
translated fiction	136	120	135	277	760	548

(Source: Pálsson 1978: 166)

post-Depression and post-war years. Table 1 shows the increase in the number of works published in Iceland over six decades in three different literary genres: poetry, fiction and translated fiction.

Since the late twentieth century, almost half of the titles of the annual Icelandic book fair, which takes place mostly during the six-week period of the Christmas book-buying season, have consisted of translated works.

A language community of only 300,000 people is naturally limited in the amount of original literature it can produce. With the rise of professional theatre, the advent of serials in newspapers and radio and television dramatic productions, the demand for popular fiction and dramatic works in particular has far outgrown domestic production, and translation has subsequently flourished in these areas.

Translation from Icelandic

The existence of an extensive and varied corpus of medieval literature preserved in Icelandic manuscripts stimulated the translation of these works, which began in the seventeenth century. A small booklet entitled *Brevis commentarius de Islandia* was written by the cleric Arngrímur Jónsson, known as 'the learned', in 1593. It was intended to refute widespread lies and misconceptions about Iceland. With the passage of time, the polemics of Jónsson's work became irrelevant but the brief passages which he translated or retold from Icelandic medieval manuscripts in this work and his subsequent collection, *Crymogaea*, succeeded in arousing the interest of scholars in exploring these previously unknown treasures.

The following centuries witnessed an increased level of activity in collecting, editing and translating these manuscripts. The largest collection was put together in Copenhagen, under the auspices of Icelander Árni Magnússon (1663–1730). Magnússon served as Royal Archivist in Copenhagen and undertook numerous assignments for the Danish government in Iceland. He travelled extensively in Iceland in search of manuscripts and managed to find and hire Icelandic students or grammarians to record, copy, index and process the material in various ways. An estimated two-thirds of the manuscripts in Magnússon's

collection were destroyed by fire in 1728, but the Arnamagnean Collection and Institute has been the centre of Icelandic medieval scholarship for centuries.

A considerable part of the activity involving these manuscripts included making the material available in translations: first in Latin, then Danish. Sveinbjörn Egilsson translated most of the Sagas of Kings and the entire corpus of skaldic poetry into Latin; he also compiled a lexicon of the language of the skalds. With the rise of Romanticism in Europe, both scholars and poets found inspiration in the Icelandic material, especially in Germany and England. William Morris, for example, composed numerous poems based on Icelandic sagas and heroic poetry; he also translated many Icelandic works into English.

Apart from medieval Icelandic works, the *Hymns of the Passion* by the poet and cleric Hallgrímur Pétursson (1614–74) is probably the only older work in Icelandic to have been extensively translated into other languages. Written in 1659–60, the hymns describe in exceptionally figurative and lyrical, and yet easily understood language, how the poet identifies with the sufferings of Jesus and of mankind. During the next century and a half, no fewer than three different Latin translations were printed of the poems, in full or in part, in Copenhagen. One Chinese, one Hungarian, and several English translations have since been published. In addition to the *Hymns of the Passion*, other individual poems by Pétursson have also been translated into Danish.

In 1955, the novelist Halldór Kiljan Laxness was awarded the Nobel Prize for literature and a number of his works have since been translated into over a dozen languages, especially those of neighbouring cultures: Scandinavian languages, English, German and French. Other contemporary writers have been mainly translated into the Scandinavian languages and English.

The Icelandic view of quality and style in literary translation

Translation as it was undertaken during the medieval period set the tone for what was to follow in a very definitive manner. Icelandic translators have always been expected to deliver a text which reads well in Icelandic. Language-conscious Icelanders are quick to spot and criticize borrowings and unnatural phrasing or word order. A translation which sounds good in Icelandic is thus often considered a translation of quality. Newspaper reviews of new translations into Icelandic (on the few occasions when reviewers decide to devote any space to discussing aspects of translation as such) almost unfailingly point out that the works sound natural and are written in good style, or lack these qualities.

However, while the medieval translators knew their Latin, and very seldom made major errors or omissions, the same cannot be said of Icelandic translators today. One could speculate that the difference may lie partly in the fact that medieval translators were simply not paid by the page and that financial considerations did not therefore interfere with their quest for quality. Whatever the reasons, the fact remains that, even in works of recognized literary quality, sentences or even paragraphs are often missing, misunderstood or misconstrued. By and large, such changes appear to be unmotivated and the situation applies to translations both into and from Icelandic. Several articles have been published by literary scholars in Iceland in recent years pointing out these deficiencies. One can only imagine the quality of translations of less revered works, such as popular or pulp fiction, in comparison.

The present time

In today's world of mass media, small nations are obviously highly dependent on translation for their leisure as well as their work. Between 60 per cent and 70 per cent of television broadcasting in Iceland consists of subtitled foreign material; programmes for children are limited in number but are largely dubbed. Foreign news items on radio and television and in newspapers are almost all translated from foreign sources, as is a large part of the rest of the printed or broadcast material and advertisements. A great deal of translation is also carried out by or for small user-groups such as politicians and specialists in various fields; this includes official and legal documents, contracts, instructional materials, and so on. Given the size of the population and the level of translation

activity, it is no exaggeration to say that a much larger proportion of the population is occupied with translation in Iceland than in most other countries of the world.

It is surprising, given these facts, that there is not today and never has been in the past any programme of education for translators in Iceland, neither in the form of classroom-based instruction nor apprenticeship of any kind. A law passed in 1914, apparently as a result of the then current conflict and vague concern at impending hostilities in the North Atlantic, provided for 'legally approved document translators and court interpreters', but little provision was subsequently made for training or testing either group. Indeed, until relatively recently, anyone applying for permission to use this title was authorized to do so, provided he or she could demonstrate having either studied foreign languages or resided abroad for a considerable length of time. The Ministry of Justice now holds regular examinations for those applying to use the qualification. The exams are widely respected and considered a serious test of professional ability. There is no preparatory course offered, and no attempt is made to train or approve translators who specialize in areas other than legal translation.

Further reading

Einarsson 1961; *Kulturhistorisk leksikon for nordisk middelalder fra vikingetid til reformationstid* 1982; Seelow 1989; Zuck 1990; Pulsiano and Wolf 1993.

KENEVA KUNZ

Indian tradition

This entry sketches the history of translation in the Indian subcontinent rather than in the post-1947 nation state of India. The subcontinent is a roughly diamond-shaped area about 1,500 miles from north to south and the same east to west, bounded by the Himalayan mountains in the north and by the sea to the south. The languages currently spoken in this area fall into two main groups. About 70 per cent of the population, mainly in the northern half, speak Indo-European languages derived directly from Sanskrit, such as Hindi, Punjabi, Gujarati, Marathi, Bengali, and Nepali. Sinhalese, spoken in Sri Lanka, also belongs to this group. Another 20 per cent, mainly in the south, speak Dravidian languages, namely Tamil, Telugu, Kannada, and Malayalam. The rest speak Austric languages (mainly scattered tribal peoples), Tibeto-Burman languages (in the north-east), and Dardic languages (in the north-west). Urdu, the main language of Pakistan, is closely related to Hindi, but has adopted many Persian and Arabic words and uses the Arabic script. The main non-indigenous language, English, is used alongside their mother tongue by most educated people.

Several problems arise when attempting to deal with the earlier history of translation in the subcontinent. The evidence is extremely patchy, partly because of a predominantly oral tradition, partly because of the destruction of innumerable texts by climatic conditions, pests such as white ants, or hostile human agency. Extant copies of texts are often several centuries later than the date of their composition. The longevity and continuity of linguistic development in the area means that individual texts often exhibit features of more than one historical period. The chronology of texts is rarely exact and is often based largely on internal evidence such as references to previous authors and works. Similarly, the great geographical extent of the subcontinent often makes distinctions between language and dialect rather problematic. The evolving cultural homogeneity causes problems in distinguishing between retellings and variant renderings of common source material, adaptations of previous texts, and actual translations. Finally, little previous work has been done in the field of translation history for this region.

The ancient period (c.2500–800 BC)

The first need for inter-language communication in the subcontinent probably arose through trade. The oldest linguistic evidence is to be found in the characters inscribed on steatite seals found in the Indus valley in the north-west. These are said to date from 2500 to 1500 BC, but unfortunately the script has not yet been deciphered. The remains of a harbour have been unearthed in the area, and Indus-style artefacts have been found as far away as Mesopotamia. For some 2,000 years after this, until the inscriptions of the emperor Asoka in the third century BC, there is no material linguistic evidence at all. This is primarily due to the Aryans, bands of nomadic cattle-herders from central Asia who settled in the Indus area in the latter part of the 2nd millennium BC. They spoke Sanskrit, an Indo-European language, and brought with them a wealth of poetry which they subsequently collected together under the name *Rigveda* or 'hymns of wisdom'; another group of Aryans moved into Persia at around the same time and their sacred book, the *Avesta*, reflects a very similar culture to that of the *Rigveda*.

The Aryans regarded themselves as superior to the indigenous people and tried to preserve their cultural and linguistic purity. Once they had settled in the subcontinent, the *Rigveda* was endowed with extreme sanctity and mystic power by the priests. Only Aryans were allowed to learn and use the Rigvedic hymns. No reference to writing is found for several hundred years, so the linguistic and religious tradition was entirely oral, despite the continual elaboration of the original Rigvedic material. Even after the advent of writing, and the development of vernacular languages, so sacred were the Vedic texts considered that only commentaries written in Sanskrit are found until late medieval times, and certainly no translations until Western scholars gained access to them in the nineteenth century. However, ironically, even the *Rigveda* displays evidence of Dravidian influence in its use of retroflex sounds, and the *Atharvaveda*, the youngest of the four *Vedas*, contains magic spells and customs that are clearly non-Aryan. Some form of interaction, then, must have taken place between the Aryans and the indigenous linguistic communities, but its exact nature remains a matter of speculation.

The pre-classical period (c.800 BC–AD 100)

From about 800 BC onwards the Aryans began to spread out from the Indus region, eastwards into the Ganges valley and south towards the Deccan, and the Persian Achaemenid Empire took control of the Indus. Aryans also began to go beyond their tribal territories: students and traders travelled to Taxila in the kingdom of Gandhara in the north-west, soldiers mounted on elephants apparently fought in the Achaemenid army against the Greeks.

As the Aryans began to disperse, several major developments took place. A more scientific attitude became evident in their culture, and Sanskrit texts were composed on law, astronomy, astrology, and especially linguistic subjects such as etymology, metrics, prosody, and grammar. At the same time, the Aryan language started to fragment into dialectal or regional forms known as *Prakrits*. Panini's well-known grammar is regarded by some as a response to the Aryan diaspora, an attempt to fix the form of Sanskrit before it disintegrated into mutually unintelligible dialects. The disintegration process was reinforced by the great religious reformers of the sixth century BC, especially the Buddha and Mahavira (founder of Jainism), who propagated vernacular languages in order to make their teachings accessible to the masses. Panini's grammar may therefore also represent part of the orthodox religious backlash against these anti-Vedic movements.

Kautilya, the minister of the fourth-century BC Indian emperor Candragupta Maurya, wrote a treatise on statecraft (often compared to the work of the sixteenth-century Italian, Machiavelli) which gives us some indication of the status that a translator might have had during this period. Although the term 'translator' is not used, Kautilya mentions 'scribes' towards the end of a long list of occupations and salaries: the king's chief priest, other high priests, the prime minister, military commander, and members of the royal family (48,000 panas); chiefs of police, harem, armoury, prison, revenue, and treasury (24,000 panas); lesser royals, the chief of industry, counsellors (12,000 panas); guild masters, regimental heads, chariot-commanders, physicians, fortune-tellers, bards, professors and spies (500–8,000 panas); infantrymen, scribes, and accountants (500 panas). In the very last rank are craftsmen, servants, medical assistants and cowherds (with notional figures for slaves, elephants, horses, and oxen).

In the fourth century BC, contacts with the subcontinent are externally attested: we know that Alexander the Great of Macedon reached the Indus in 326 BC and that the Greek chronicler Megasthenes was the ambassador of Seleucus, Alexander's successor, at the Mauryan court. Among the earliest recorded translations are probably the names of places and rulers. The capital of Gandhara was known as *Takshashila* to the Indians and *Taxila* to the Greeks. The Greek historian Plutarch uses the Greek version, *Sandracottos*, for the name of the Indian emperor *Candragupta*.

With the arrival in India of Greeks from Bactria, we see coins issued with Greek legends on one face and the Indian Brahmi script on the other. Greek ideas on astrology, medicine, and drama are also perceived in Indian literature of the period. The Indo-Greek kings and the Bactrian kings of the Kushana tribe who ruled over parts of India often took imperial titles that seem to be borrowed from the Persians, such as *maharajatiraja* or 'king-of-kings' (cf. *shah-in-shah*), or from the Chinese, for example *daivaputra* or 'son of heaven'. The Kushana king Kanishka (*c*.AD 78–101) was a great patron of Buddhism, and Buddhist art flourished, especially in Gandhara. Kanishka also accelerated the spread of Buddhism into Central Asia and China.

Early Buddhism

Unlike the Vedic religion, Buddhism was an overtly proselytizing religion from the outset. Buddha himself urged his disciples to propagate his teachings. In the middle of the third century BC, the Indian emperor Asoka, after some particularly bloody campaigns, followed the general trend away from Vedic sacrifices and towards an ideology of non-injury and universal compassion (particularly stressed by Buddhism) and erected numerous pillars with inscriptions that record his edicts in local languages, probably in imitation of the Persian emperor Darius I. This must have required some translation-type activities on the part of the scribes. Various scripts are used on Asoka's pillars, and they name Syrian, Egyptian and Macedonian kings.

From about 250 BC onwards, Buddhist missions were sent south and west, and with notable success to Sri Lanka. The Buddhist canon (in Pali, one of the Prakrits) was probably written in Sri Lanka in the first century BC, about 500 years after Buddha's death. However, as well as being written in vernacular languages, Buddhist texts also began to be written in Sanskrit. Translation therefore became an important part of the transmission of the Buddha's teachings. In some cases, essentially the same texts, such as the *Jatakas* (stories of the Buddha's past lives, probably composed between the first century BC and the first century AD), are available in Sanskrit and Pali, though they may not strictly speaking be translations, but parallel texts with a common source. Indian Buddhist scholars travelled to China in the first century AD and were no doubt responsible for some of the earliest translations of Buddhist texts into Chinese (see CHINESE TRADITION).

Ashvaghosha's poem *Buddhacarita*, the 'life of Buddha', represents the earliest surviving Classical Sanskrit poetry (*c.* first century AD), but the manuscripts of it found at Turfan in Gobi are a Chinese translation by an Indian scholar.

The classical period (*c.*100–1000)

The Hindu Epics, two of the most important source texts for subsequent translation history, were consolidated during this period. *The Mahabharata* (*c.*300 BC to AD 300) tells the story of a major war, probably representing the Aryans' eastward expansion along the Ganges valley. *The Ramayana* (*c.*200 BC to AD 200) is about the abduction of Prince Rama's wife by the king of Lanka (Sri Lanka) and her subsequent rescue, probably echoing the Aryans' southward movement. These texts can also be said to represent the beginning of Hindu theism, as the heroes are gradually elevated to divine status as incarnations of the god Vishnu.

It is often difficult to tell which language a text was originally in, as opposed to the language of the extant version. However, small points of grammar and metre in these Epics suggest that the extant Sanskrit versions may have been translated from original Prakrit versions, or that at least the extant versions may represent attempts to 'Sanskritize' the Prakrit versions. Similar processes are certainly evident in the rewriting of the vernacular *Puranas* or 'Ancient Stories' (collections of legends, religious material, and pseudo-historical king-lists) in classical Sanskrit, with the idea of enhancing their status thereby.

In the case of Jainism and Buddhism, later texts were often written in Sanskrit, because by then the vernacular languages had either diverged too far to be mutually intelligible or were too regionally restricted. So, in the interests of the transmission of the teachings, scholars reverted to Sanskrit. However, later still, the trend is reversed once again, and translation mainly proceeded from Sanskrit into other languages. For example, the Bhakti religious movement not only composed original material in vernacular languages, but also translated many devotional poems, as well as the Epics and *Puranas*, from Sanskrit into local languages. There were also adaptations of the Epics and *Puranas* into Dravidian languages.

One area of literature which shows significant development in this period is drama. Some scholars attribute this to Greek influence, but this has not been proven. The importance of the rise of drama for translation is that Sanskrit plays started to allow characters who were not kings or brahmins (Hindu priests) to speak in Prakrits, which represent an intermediate stage between Classical Sanskrit and the modern Indian languages derived from Sanskrit. However, a *chaya* or 'gloss' was still provided in Sanskrit for the Prakrit speeches in the plays.

Another literary genre particularly important to translation history is the fable. This becomes popular with the *Pali Jatakas* and often involves talking animals. Some scholars again see Greek influence behind this development, but it is more likely that story-telling traditions from the Middle East through to China exchanged plots and characters. One collection of animal fables in particular, the *Pancatantra* or 'Five Treatises', has an astonishing translation history. It was first translated from Sanskrit into Pahlavi in the sixth century at the order of Khusrau Anushirwan, the Persian emperor. A Syriac translation followed in *c.*570, and an Arabic translation in the eighth century. The eleventh century saw new translations in Syrian, Arabic (as the story of *Kalila wa Dimna*), and Persian (as *Kalia Daman*), as well as a Greek translation from the Syrian which was used for a Hebrew version. A Latin version from this period is also known, and the stories gradually spread throughout Europe in all its major languages during the fifteenth and sixteenth centuries. The first English version, by Sir Thomas North, appeared in 1570 and was called *The Morall Philosophie of Doni*, after the name of the Italian translator. The fables of La Fontaine are explicitly acknowledged as based on the stories of Pilpay, the name by which their reputed Indian narrator Vidyapati was known in Europe. The *Pancatantra* was probably responsible for the stories of Reynard the Fox, common to many European folk traditions, which were given their finished European form by Goethe. Other stories of Indian origin, including some of the Sinbad stories, are to be found in *The Arabian Nights*.

Medical texts were the target of much translation activity during this period. Sanskrit treatises were translated first into Pali, and later into Bengali and Nepali. Outside India, translations are known in Korean, Khotanese, Tibetan, Mongolian, Chinese, and Arabic. The Muslim Caliphs at Baghdad, the seat of the Islamic Empire, also showed great interest in Indian science. The translation bureau set up by Caliph Al-Mansour (*c*.710–75) produced translations of Sanskrit texts on astronomy, medicine and mathematics (notably Aryabhata's fifth-century Sanskrit treatise), introducing the numeral system of Indian origin into Europe as well as various other Indian algebraic, geometrical, and astronomical concepts. Harun-al-Rashid (766–809) and al-Mamun (786–833) continued the translation work into the ninth century, but it ceased thereafter as Baghdad began to lose its political power.

Southern India and the Dravidian languages

The earliest literature of the south, unlike the *Rigveda*, is not particularly religious in content. Tradition tells us of three *sangams*, competitive poetic 'assemblies' at Madurai. No texts survive from the first, the Tamil grammar *Tolkappiyam* is supposedly a product of the second, and the eight anthologies of Sangam poetry (over 2,000 poems) are from the third. Tradition also attributes the introduction of Aryan culture into the south to the Vedic sage Agastya, claims that southern kings took part in the Mahabharata war and refers to them performing Vedic sacrifices. If nothing else, this reflects the extent of Aryan influence in the south at an early period. At the same time, archaeological evidence at Arikamedu near the south-eastern city of Pondicherry has revealed sea-trade with the Romans in the first century AD.

Early inscriptions found in this area are in Prakrit and Sanskrit, but Tamil soon replaces Prakrit. Education was initially dominated by Jains and Buddhists, but gradually the Hindu tradition overtook them. Jain texts, originally in Sanskrit and Prakrit, began to be written in Tamil, and Buddhism and Hinduism competed for royal patronage. Tamil literature naturally shows Jain influences, and Tamil epic poems such as *Silappadikaram* and *Manimekalai* have features of Sanskrit style. However, Tamil religious poetry of the highest quality was also being composed. There are references to an extensive early literature in Kannada as well, but very little has survived.

A religious movement known as Bhakti propagated the personal, devotional worship of the Hindu gods Vishnu and Siva. This gave rise to much poetic activity in the sixth and seventh centuries and won over many of the ordinary people. Education was mainly at orthodox Hindu temples and in Sanskrit, and many people were therefore excluded. They gained oral instruction from the Bhakti schools in Tamil instead. As the classical period of Sanskrit began to wane, works in Sanskrit became increasingly derivative, artificial, and lifeless. At the same time, local languages began to flourish: Kamban's version of the *Ramayana* is written in highly vigorous Tamil.

Tamil, Telugu, and Kannada had acquired much vocabulary from Sanskrit, but the connections were becoming looser. Sanskrit works, such as those of Kalidasa, and the Epics, were adapted to Telugu and made available to popular audiences. Kannada had been favoured by Jain patronage in Mysore, but again the first written Kannada texts are adaptations of Sanskrit originals. Marathi (although Indo-European) developed similarly: through patronage from Yadava kings, then used to render Sanskrit texts such as the *Bhagavad Gita* (a late interpolation in the *Mahabharata*), but also used for religious poems inspired by Bhakti texts introduced from the south.

Later Buddhism

As Buddhism developed, some sects began to follow similar paths to the Hindus, incorporating *Yoga* (physical exercises, meditation, and the philosophy of self-realization) and *Tantra* (visualization techniques involving a pantheon of iconic deities, symbolic rituals including sexual intercourse, and so on) into their practices. These sects, collectively termed *Mahayana* or 'the Northern school', as opposed to the more conservative *Hinayana* or 'Southern school', wrote mainly in Sanskrit rather than Pali.

The University of Nalanda in the north-east of India was particularly renowned for training translators from the fourth century onwards. Kumarajiva (344–413) went to China in 401 and translated the *Life of Nagarjuna* (a major Buddhist philosopher) into Chinese, and one of his pupils, Fa-hsien, came to India soon afterwards (405–11) to collect more texts. Jinagupta translated thirty-seven Sanskrit works into Chinese. Another translator, Paramartha, went to China in the fifth century and translated the *Life of Vasubandhu* (an earlier authority on Yoga at Nalanda). The Chinese Buddhist pilgrims Hsuan Tsang and I Tsing came to India in the seventh century and studied at Nalanda. Hsuan Tsang is said to have translated over thirty major Buddhist volumes, and I Tsing took several hundred texts back to China. Dharma Deva (960–1000) is credited with translating 118 Buddhist texts into Chinese. Some 8,000 Indian texts, many in translation, are preserved in the Sung-pao collection; they relate to Buddhism, Hinduism, astronomy, mathematics, and medicine. Among the earliest printed books in China are books in Sanskrit printed from wooden blocks, a technique probably taken from Tibet.

Tibetan culture was totally oral until the arrival of Buddhism. The alphabet was initially created solely for the purpose of receiving Buddhist texts in Sanskrit. The Nalanda scholars Arya Deva, Silabhadra, and Dharmapala went to Tibet, and their works were translated into Tibetan. Santarakshita and Padmasambhava were especially active in the transmission of Buddhism in the eighth century. After a period of persecution in the tenth century, the Bengali Atisa Dipankara Srijnana restored Buddhism in Tibet. The cooperation between Indian, Tibetan and Chinese scholars is evident in the *Mahavyutpatti*, a Sanskrit–Tibetan–Chinese dictionary of Buddhist technical terms which dates from the ninth or tenth century.

Long after Buddhism went to China, it passed to Japan in the form of Zen. In the turbulent times from the eleventh century onwards, Buddhist monks took Sanskrit manuscripts to Nepal, Tibet, or China, and many of those texts now survive only in their translated versions.

The medieval period (*c.*1000–1750)

Baghdad's decline from the tenth century onwards allowed the Turkic rulers of Afghanistan to grow in self-confidence, and they began to mount raids into northern India. Mahmud of Ghazni made seventeen such raids in the north-west between 1001 and 1027, destroying palaces, temples, and libraries. In the twelfth century, Mohammed of Ghor annexed Ghazni and its possessions in India, and his generals emulated Mahmud by destroying buildings, images, and texts as far as Bengal. However, Mohammed's successors subsequently became Indianized, settled in Delhi, resisted the Mongol invaders in the north-west, extended their sway into the Deccan and South India, and established an Islamic Sultanate which lasted in part until the arrival of the Moghuls.

Sanskrit competed to a certain extent with Persian at court during this period, but became increasingly redundant elsewhere as the vernacular languages flourished. Some Muslim poets began to write in Hindi. The increasing dominance of Persian in business and literature ironically gave regional tongues a great boost. In due course, however, even the Delhi Sultanate began to show interest in the indigenous culture. In 1357, after a visit to a library in Kangra, Sultan Firuz Shah ordered the translation of Sanskrit manuscripts on Hinduism into Persian and Arabic.

In 1398, Tamerlane destroyed the waning Sultanate and left its territories in the hands of local Muslim rulers. The Lodi Afghans briefly rebuilt the core in the fifteenth century, but Bengal remained outside their control, the Rajputs disputed the western areas with the kingdom of Gujarat, and the breakaway Muslim Bahmani kings ruled in the Deccan, with the Hindu Vijayanagar kingdom to the East.

Meanwhile in the south, as Islam and other religions such as Bhakti and Tantra started to erode orthodox Hinduism, scholars such as Sankara, Ramanuja and Madhva tried to incorporate some of the new ideas into the traditional Hindu framework. One particularly strong cult was the Virashaivas or Lingayats. The main exponent, Basava, was originally a Jain but was probably influenced by Buddhism and Islam as well as the Bhakti cults. His teachings, usually called simply the *Basava*, exist in one form in Palkurika Soma's Telugu *Basava* (1195). In the fourteenth century, this work was adapted into Kannada by Sumatibhima or Bhimacandra Kavi.

Puranas ('ancient stories') were composed in Kannada by Vishnu worshippers as well as by followers of Basava, and the Sanskrit *Bhagavata Purana* was translated into Kannada in the sixteenth century. Since then, most of the other major Puranas have been translated into Kannada. Hastimalla's *Adi Purana* is a Jain text in Kannada prose, but each of its sections begins with a Sanskrit verse identical with the opening verses of Jinasena's Sanskrit version. The Tamil Puranas are often far more complex and sophisticated than their Sanskrit counterparts. The *Bagavadam*, a Tamil version of the *Bhagavata Purana*, was translated into French at an early date. Telugu versions of the Puranas date back to the thirteenth century. However, Sanskrit retained its place at royal courts and among orthodox Hindu scholars. Major commentaries were written: on the *Dharmasastras* (Hindu Law) by Hemadri in the thirteenth century (keeping very close to the northern versions), and on the *Vedas* by Sayana in the fourteenth century. Although regional languages were diverging and flourishing, the population of the subcontinent was beginning to share a considerable degree of cultural homogeneity.

In 1337, the major southern kingdom of Vijayanagara was founded, and rapidly dominated the south. It shook off both the Delhi Sultans and the Muslim Bahmani kings of the Deccan, and restored Hinduism. Gradually, the centre of religious activity moved from the Tamil lands to Mysore and Maharashtra. The *Bhagavad Gita* was rendered in Marathi by Jnanadeva (1291), and he was followed in the fourteenth century by Namadeva, whose works denounce idol worship. The Vijayanagara kings had adopted a popular Marathi deity. Sanskrit works, especially the Epics and Puranas, continued to be adapted into Tamil, Telugu, Kannada, and Marathi, but Bhakti texts were steadily produced as well. Persian and Arabic had been introduced by the Muslim Bahmani kings in the northern Deccan. Malayalam, originally a western dialect of Tamil, started to enjoy an independent status as Malabar became less a part of the Tamil kingdoms, and more influenced by its foreign settlers, especially the Arabs.

Meanwhile, Hindu Bhakti still flourished, now propagated by the popular devotional poet Chaitanya in Bengal, and by the Marathi saints. Guru Nanak (1469–1539) incorporated Bhakti into a new religion, Sikhism. Orthodox Islam withdrew into an intellectual elite, but the Sufis shared the popular stage with Bhakti. Persian still dominated the courts.

The Moghul Empire

In 1504, Babur, a descendant of Tamerlane whose claims to kinship with the Mongol Genghiz Khan are the basis for the term *Moghul*, established himself in Afghanistan and, after a few initial raids, conquered Delhi in 1526. His memoirs were later translated from Turki into Persian and then into English. Babur's son Humayun conquered Gujarat. His son Akbar extended the empire, employing mainly non-Indian staff in his administration. He developed an eccentric religious system, engaging Hindus, Jains, Portuguese Christians, and Zoroastrians as advisers, and crushed a revolt by orthodox Muslims. Persia had by now freed itself from the Mongols. Pre-Islamic Persian culture was more acceptable to Hindus than Islam, the non-orthodox Persian Sufis being closer to Bhakti than Muslims, and Arabic therefore took second place to Persian.

Religion was a major spur to translation. Dara Shukoh, son of Shah Jahan, heard of the *Upanishads* (late Vedic and early Hindu philosophical texts) in Kashmir in 1640, and had about fifty of them translated from Sanskrit into Persian by 1657. These were later translated into Latin by Anquetil Duperron and published in Paris in 1802. The theologian Shah Wali Allah Dihlawi (1703–62) took the revolutionary step of translating the Qur'an into Persian. His annotated version was begun before 1730 and was not completed until 1738. He later compiled a set of instructions in Persian for scholars attempting to translate the Qur'àn. He also translated an Arabic grammar into Persian verse (c.1751–2) for the benefit of one of his sons and a Persian text ('Refutation of the Shi'ites') into Arabic. Until recently, his contribution to Islamic thought had been underestimated by both Western and Islamic scholars, who tended to pay far more attention to his political views.

Science also gave rise to translation activities: Sawai Jai Singh of Jaipur, mathematician, astronomer, and builder of several observatories, had some classical Greek texts on mathematics (including Euclid) translated into Sanskrit, as well as more recent European works on trigonometry and logarithms, and Arabic texts on astronomy.

During the Delhi Sultanate and the Moghul period, Hindu nobles and ministers used Persian at court, and many Hindus wrote books in Persian. Muslim scholars translated Sanskrit texts into Persian. Sanskrit Puranas have been discovered in Persian translations, one version of the *Bhagavata Purana* reputedly translated at Akbar's express command. Persian also gave rise to Urdu, which influenced both Hindustani, the vernacular language of the north, and Hindi.

The European period (c.1750–1947)

The Europeans had gradually begun to vie with the Arabs for trade dominance by the thirteenth century. Marco Polo visited the southern Pandyan kingdoms, Nicolo Conti, Athanasius Nikitin, and Duarte Barbosa travelled overland to Asia, and Vasco da Gama opened the sea route in 1498. In addition to these traders, Catholic missionaries arrived, especially the Portuguese, who soon translated the New Testament into Persian.

In 1600, the British East India Company was incorporated – essentially to trade in East Indian spices – but it soon came to exercise considerable political power in India as a whole. The need for translations of Indian texts was recognized early on by Company administrators. Muslim law had already been summarized in a digest at the order of the Moghul emperor Aurangzeb (1659–1707) and was universally acknowledged

by Indian courts. Hindu law, although much older, had never been systematically codified. Warren Hastings, the East India Company's Governor-General of Bengal, gathered together ten eminent Hindu pundits and commissioned them to prepare a digest of Hindu law for the courts. This had first to be translated from Sanskrit into Persian and then from Persian into English, because no English person as yet knew Sanskrit.

Indian scholars were initially reluctant to teach Sanskrit to the Europeans. Sir William Jones (1746–94), a judge of the Supreme Court in Calcutta, eventually managed to find a non-Brahmin medical practitioner who agreed to teach him, but only under the most stringent conditions. Sir William learned twenty-eight languages, including Chinese. In 1782, he translated seven pre-Islamic odes, *Mu'allaqaat*, from Arabic. In 1786, his presidential speech to the Asiatic Society contained his speculations on the common ancestry of Sanskrit and Greek, one of the earliest and most influential texts on comparative linguistics. Jones's translation in 1789 of the classical Sanskrit play *Sakuntala* by Kalidasa was almost immediately translated into German, French, Danish and Italian. Goethe was extremely impressed by the play, and the prologue of his *Faust* is widely considered to be modelled on that of *Sakuntala*. German scholars continued to show much interest in Sanskrit and played a prominent part in Sanskrit studies.

After the initial enthusiasm of Hastings, Jones and others, Indian culture in general and Sanskrit works in particular were increasingly subjected to negative judgements by English-speakers, who compared them with Victorian English models – rather than classical Greek or Latin models, which would have been a more appropriate basis for comparison – and ignored Sanskrit poetical rules and the opinions of native critics. The flow of translation began to move in the opposite direction (from European into Indian languages). Isolated attempts had been made to render Christian teachings into Indian languages during the eighteenth century. William Carey (1761–1834), a missionary, went to Calcutta in 1793, where he began his first Bible translation. Forced to leave British jurisdiction, he moved to the nearby Danish colony of Frederiksnagar in 1800. In 1801, he was appointed to teach Bengali, Sanskrit, and

Marathi at Fort William College. He translated the Bible into Bengali, Oriya, Marathi, Hindi, Assamese and Sanskrit. He also translated parts of it into twenty-nine other languages and dialects. In addition, he co-compiled dictionaries of Bengali, Sanskrit, and Marathi, and co-translated three volumes of the Hindu epic *Ramayana*. Carey is also credited with establishing a printing press at Serampore, urging the government to end infanticide and *sati*, and encouraging the use of Indians as missionaries. In 1813, the British opened India to missionaries, and their numbers rapidly increased.

Initially, the East India Company had followed the Moghul pattern of patronage to Indian learning, though on a much more modest level. Hastings set up a College of Arabic and Persian studies at Calcutta, and Jonathan Duncan a Sanskrit College at Benares. In 1813, the Charter Act granted £10,000 annually to 'the revival and improvement of literature and the encouragement of the learned Natives of India and for the introduction and promotion of a knowledge of the sciences among the inhabitants of the British Territories in India' (Spear 1970: 126). At first, under the influence of British orientalists, this led to the printing of classics and the translation of modern works into Sanskrit. However, in 1835 the Governor-General William Bentinck issued a resolution declaring that the funds should thereafter be used to impart 'knowledge of English literature and science through the medium of the English language' (ibid.: 127). English became the official state language instead of Persian; in the lower courts, Persian was replaced by the local languages, whose development was broadened by the needs of administrative and legal prose, rather than devotional poetry. Meanwhile, Indians began to realize the advantages of English for career advancement. The Hindu College, where English language and literature were taught, was founded in Bengal in 1816. The British founded three English-style universities between 1848 and 1856 and developed a grant system to enable Indians to open private colleges which were affiliated to them. The Aligarh College was founded by Sayyid Ahmad Khan in 1875 to cater for the needs of Muslims in Delhi.

The advent of the printing press had initially enabled prose translations of the Bible to be made available in the vernaculars. Various missionary societies also published translations of catechisms and other texts. But the presses also served to encourage other prose writing in the local languages: social reformers published tracts on women's education, child marriage, widow remarriage, and caste. Ram Mohan Roy (1772–1833) printed the first Indian newspaper and a bilingual English–Bengali magazine. Bengali and Hindi were his first languages, but he also spoke Sanskrit, Persian, Arabic, Hebrew, Greek and English. He criticized Hindu sectarianism and superstition, urging a return to a monotheism based on the Vedas and Upanisads, which he translated from Sanskrit into Hindi, Bengali, and English. The translations angered the orthodox tradition, but led to him being elected to honorary membership of the Société Asiatique in 1824. He also published some works on the teachings of Christ. As founder and editor of two of India's earliest newspapers, he urged the government to ban *sati*, which it did in 1829.

Indian religions also regained confidence, and Ramakrishna (a successor to the Bhakti tradition) inspired his disciple Vivekananda to found the Ramakrishna Mission, which began to play an important part in publishing Hindu texts in Sanskrit, with English glosses, and distributing them in India and abroad, especially in the United States. Puranas and Upanishads were also translated, for example by Durgaprasad into Hindi. Versions of Sanskrit and Persian tales began to appear in local languages, for example those of Raja Bhoj, Raja Birbal, Akbar, and Hakim Tai in Hindi.

European academics meanwhile sponsored the establishment of learned societies, such as the Royal Asiatic Society, the Pali Text Society, and so on, and continued the production of translations of Sanskrit and Pali texts. Dictionaries and grammars were compiled, serving the needs of both orientalist scholars and Christian missionaries. The Independence movement also encouraged considerable linguistic activity in local languages and in English, as well as in translation between them.

Rabindranath Tagore (1861–1941) translated his own work from Bengali into English, and was awarded the Nobel Prize for Literature in 1913 for the English version of what is probably his most enduring work, *Gitanjali*, 'Song

Offering'. He was knighted in 1915 but surrendered his knighthood in 1919 in protest at the Amritsar Massacre (where hundreds of Indian nationalists were killed by troops under British control). Many of his works have been translated into English, by himself and others (for discussions of his own translations of his work, see Mukherjee 1981 and Sengupta 1990).

The modern period (1947 to the present)

Gonda's ten-volume *History of Indian Literature* (1975–) contains innumerable references to translations between Indian languages and between them and English. Works translated include Vedic texts, the Hindu Epics, Puranas and Upanishads, and classical Sanskrit drama; English poetry by Keats and Tennyson; Shakespeare's plays and poems; Bengali plays, poetry, and novels; Hindi and Urdu fiction; the Gospels and other Christian texts; American literature, especially short stories and drama; European literature: Cervantes, Tolstoy, Ibsen – mostly via English translations.

Hindi, Urdu and, more recently, Punjabi are becoming important intermediaries in the translation process, both from English and other European languages and from the less widespread local languages. The dearth of children's literature in Indian languages is slowly beginning to receive attention.

Political and administrative needs have exerted their own pressures. For example a specialized prose had to be created for translating the Indian Constitution into Kashmiri, and the official Review Committee sadly noted the poverty of its vocabulary and the lack of a standard orthography (Kachru 1981: 97). However, the regional language academies do little to encourage translation work, and funding and publication are left to individual initiative and choice. Western publishers are playing their part in the translation of modern Indian writing into English; for example Heinemann followed their pioneering translations in the African Writers Series with the Asian Writers Series. The academic tradition is receiving a wider audience with publishers like Penguin and their translated editions of Sanskrit texts, the *Upanishads* and the *Bhagavad Gita*, Sanskrit drama and

poetry, the *Rgveda* and Hindu myths. Several Tibetan spiritual leaders in exile have translated key Buddhist works.

The output of Indian publishing houses varies from the Epics and other popular works translated by the Bharatiya Vidya Bhavan (Indian Institute of Culture) for the general Indian English-reading public, to the new editions of old translations published by Jaico Books (for example Sir Edwin Arnold's translation of the *Bhagavad Gita*), and the Indian University series of Sanskrit Classics with detailed pedagogic commentaries, published by Banarsidass. Religious publishers like the Ramakrishna Mission and the Advaita Ashrama have published highly literal glosses of the Upanishads and standard Sanskrit compendia of the Indian philosophical systems.

The study of translation and the organization of the profession

One might imagine that, with its multiplicity of languages and long tradition of translation, India would be a thriving centre for the theory and practice of translation in the modern era. However, as Mohanty (1994: 9) explains, 'the situation is just the reverse. Translation and Translation Studies hitherto have remained a marginalised affair.' Although the general situation is as Mohanty describes it, there are some reasons for cheer. The Centre for Applied Linguistics and Translation Studies (CALTS), created as a research centre in 1988 at the University of Hyderabad, now has a training programme for translators. A Centre for Literary Translation was set up in New Delhi, with an academic campus in Goa, in 1993.

The Indian Scientific Translators Association, based in New Delhi, is a member of FIT. The Sahitya Akademi, also in Delhi, has published a directory of translators and offers awards for translations.

Further reading
Humphreys 1951; Jesudasan and Jesudasan 1961; Dudley and Lang 1969; Dimock 1974; Gonda 1975; Mukherjee 1981; Dasgupta 1983; Niranjana 1992.

RAMESH KRISHNAMURTHY

Italian tradition

As a language directly developed from Latin, Italian has had to strive for many centuries in order to acquire an autonomous status. The process of identification, carried out in parallel with other European languages, took several centuries. The geographical features and the political vicissitudes of the country fostered a fragmentation of regional dialects with distinctive phonetic and lexical traits growing out from a common root, so-called Vulgar Latin. It was not until the sixteenth century that an identifiable Italian language finally emerged and was sanctioned as an official accepted standard.

Translation into the vernacular (tenth to fifteenth centuries)

The earliest written document in an Italian vernacular is in fact a translation from the Latin model of sworn deposition required by the Longobard bureaucracy for estate ownership records: a judge of Capua, in AD 960, wrote down the formula in words other than those of standard Latin for the benefit of witnesses who evidently could no longer understand it. This type of translation continued for a long time and stopped only when administrative practices had been completely taken over by the rising middle class. Day-to-day legal activities presumably required a massive use of interpreting in order to convey to the people the complex content of laws written in Latin and often already translated into that language from statutes originally written in the multitude of languages used by conquering armies and foreign rulers. The first systematic recourse to written translations in the vernacular appeared towards the middle of the thirteenth century in the Law Schools in Bologna and Florence, where it was felt that the application of classical rhetoric to a vernacular context required a close patterning of the style on Latin models (Maggini 1952). Thus Cicero's works were among the earliest examples of classical Latin texts translated into regional dialects with the obvious intent of raising the quality of the vernacular through a kind of mirror effect. This habit became very popular and generated numerous translations of rhetorics and philosophy texts.

At the same time, an analogous process took place on a more popular level with translations from French into Northern Italian dialects of entertainment literature such as the Arthurian legends and other narrative sources. Whereas in the first instance the names of the translators were often recorded because the translators concerned were major teachers of Law and Rhetorics (Brunetto Latini, Bartolomeo da San Concordio, Bono Giamboni, Lotario Diacono), the translators of the more popular kind of literature remain unknown. Here, attention focused on the work while the translator remained in the shadows, a situation that lasted well into the sixteenth century.

We notice also that among the learned translators working in the universities there was considerable awareness of the theoretical problems connected with translation. For instance, Bartolomeo da San Concordio (1262–1347) lists in his *Ammaestramenti degli Antichi* (Teachings of the Ancients) twelve important examples from classical religious authors in order to reinforce his tenet that 'in listening and in reading we shall attend more to the meaning than to the words' (Lapucci 1983: 14–15; translated). This tradition thrived throughout the fourteenth and fifteenth centuries and contributed to widening the spectrum of classical texts translated (besides the philosophical, historical, juridical and rhetorical works, there was in this period a definite emphasis on religious translations). The quality of the work produced, however, deteriorated steadily because later translators often plagiarized or tampered with earlier renditions, thus breaking the stylistic unity of the works. A notable exception is a series of translations of the Bible in central Italian vernacular made by anonymous monks among whom was Fra Domenico Cavalca (1270–1342). Such is the quality of their fourteenth-century texts that when Niccolò Malermi was editing the first printed Bible in Italian in 1471, he collected and referred to these texts, even though they were already more than a century old.

Around 1190, Raimbaut de Vaqueiras, a Provençal troubador, wrote a poem in which a Genoese lady answers in her own vernacular to the pleas of her Provençal suitor. This may be considered the first occurrence of an Italian dialect in poetry. Translation played a crucial role in establishing a poetical tradition in several parts of Italy. Jacopo da Lentini (first half of the thirteenth century) is among the earliest recorded Italian (more precisely Sicilian) poets, and one of his first compositions ('Madonna dir vi voglio') is a translation from Folquet de Marseilla, founding a well-established tradition that lasted over a century.

Dante Alighieri (1265–1321), following the accepted medieval notion, strongly asserted the impossibility of poetical translation. His *Convivio* (1304–8) contains the first Italian reference to the theory of translation: 'Anything harmonized through the bond of the Muses cannot be transmuted from its idiom into another without losing all its sweetness and harmony' (translated). Despite the categorical tone of this statement, Dante himself often tried his hand at the allegedly impossible task of translating Latin or Provençal poets into the Florentine dialect for inclusion in his works. The same practice was followed by Boccaccio and Petrarca.

Humanism and the Renaissance (1400–1550)

The huge number of translations produced in the vernacular paved the way for that rediscovery of the classics known as Humanism. During the second half of the fourteenth century and the whole of the fifteenth, numerous Greek and Latin authors were unearthed from the archives where they had lain buried, in many cases for centuries, under layers of dust.

During this period, which also witnessed a huge interest in the study of Greek, attitudes towards classical works were also changing. During the Middle Ages, the sole concern had been to pass on texts, copying acritically, occasionally adding to or removing from the original without hesitation. Now, however, the emphasis was on restoring the original to its ancient purity, removing the centuries of dust. An increase in translation output, with new principles and goals, emerged naturally alongside this new philological concern, the appearance of printing (*c.*1470), which increased the consumer market both in size and range, being crucial to such developments.

Almost all the translations carried out during this period were from Greek and Latin and, since Latin was still considered *the* language, the bulk of the work produced was from Greek into Latin, to be read mainly by scholars with limited proficiency in Greek. It was only later that translation was readily carried out from Greek into the Italian vernacular, often with reference to the Latin versions. All sorts of texts were translated: books on history, philosophy and religion, together with poetry, were the most frequent, although there were also works on medicine, agriculture, astrology, martial arts and mathematics (Paitoni 1766–7; Federici 1828).

Although it was Venice, with its traditional cultural openness and convenient geographical location, that practically dominated the printing industry (and therefore translation), the language into which almost all works were translated was the Tuscan vernacular, or to be more precise, the vernacular of Florence, the cradle of Humanism. There, a large group of lay intellectuals with humanist ideals who were able to understand Latin and (often) Greek had gathered around important figures such as Coluccio Salutati, Leonardo Bruni, Poggio Bracciolini, Marsilio Ficino and Giovanni Pico della Mirandola. Therefore it is hardly surprising that most translators were Florentine.

Looking through the surviving names, one realizes that the translators of the time were not always famous or eminent figures. Indeed, there is frequently no information about them whatsoever. Nonetheless, it was their anonymous work, together with the strong literary tradition which Florence had acquired during the two previous centuries, that led to the development of the Florentine vernacular as the basis of the Italian national language: from this point on, people started to talk of a common language of Italy, and of Italian, where they had previously spoken of Tuscan and Florentine vernaculars.

The translators of religious texts were generally monks and priests, whereas works on science and philosophy (excluding theology, of course) were translated by lay people. The basic purpose in all non-literary translation from the classical languages into the vernacular was to propagate the religious message or disseminate ideas of public usefulness among increasingly larger groups of people. This is exemplified in the title page of the first work on mathematics translated in Italy by the well-known mathematician Niccolò Tartaglia (alias Niccolò Fontana, 1499–1557): '... translated for common convenience and usefulness. It is so clear that every average, uninformed and inexpert mind will be able to understand it' (Tartaglia 1565; translated). This attitude was very widespread, and we find similar statements in Maestro Pietro Marino da Foligno's preface to his translation (1528) of the work by 'Palladius, worthy and ancient writer on agriculture, translated into the vernacular, so that those who don't know Latin may benefit, enjoy and gain useful information from his work' (translated).

It was a somewhat different matter where literary translations were concerned. The men of letters at court (e.g. Matteo Maria Bojardo) were often commissioned to translate literary works by patrons unfamiliar with the classical languages. In the case of works for the theatre, translation meant performance (above all, if not exclusively, at court). In addition, there was a huge amount of translation of ballads and French epic poetry, mainly for popular use, though this was marginal as a result of the large amount of home-produced works of a similar nature.

This was a dynamic period also for translation theory. In his brief treatise (*De interpretatione recta*, c.1420), the well-known Humanist Leonardo Bruni set out the rules a good translator should follow. Although Bruni's discussion dealt with translations from Greek into Latin, it was relevant also to the vernacular and greatly influenced subsequent generations of translators. The main thrust of his thesis was that the original work must be properly understood. The translator had to have perfect knowledge of both the source language and the target language, not only as regards their syntax and lexis, but also their rhetorical patterns. Indeed, the author's actual style was to be reproduced, together with the rhythm of the sentence (Folena 1973/1991). This interest in translation and the theoretical issues it raised became an increasingly important topic in Renaissance writings, which led to greater sophistication also in translation criticism.

Late Renaissance and Baroque (1550–1650)

Early Humanism, distinctly Latinophile in nature, gave way eventually to what could be called vulgar Humanism. The dignity of the vulgar tongue was almost universally recognized by the Italian intellectuals and scientists of the time, thanks also to the influence of Bembo's work (*Prose della volgar lingua*, 1525). Latin, however, was not discarded by the Roman Church, which indicated a conservative attitude in a changing world. The outcome of the Council of Trent (1545–63), whose influence was felt for many decades in Italy, was a fierce determination to defend Church ideology, the Holy Inquisition providing the means by which the Church was able to control the spread of ideas.

During this time, printing flourished: by 1550, no major town in Italy was without its printers. Prior to publication, however, every book was subject to approval by the religious authorities. If considered unsuitable for publication, it was placed on a list known as the 'Index of banned books'. Of course, this restricted quite considerably the translation work of the time, particularly in those regions of Italy where the political influence of the Church was stronger.

The lives of people such as Bruno, Galilei and Tasso testify to a significant extent to the dissent, difficulties and frustrations experienced by intellectuals who wished to assert their own views and thinking in a world ruled by the clergy. The translators, whose work did not require such independent thought, tended to be either men of letters at court, protected by benevolent patrons, or religious scholars. It is noteworthy, however, that many intellectuals of the period became clergymen themselves in order to further their literary careers.

Most of the translations done during this period were literary, especially concerning poetry, and religious. Indeed, because of the flourishing local production in Italian and Latin and the strict control exercised by the Court of Inquisition, translation of scientific texts was minimal. There was, however, a new genre in translation, namely, travel literature, which started with the publication (between 1550 and 1590) of *Navigazioni e viaggi*, a large collection of papers by Spanish and Portuguese travellers, translated by Giovanni Battista Ramusio of Treviso (1485–1557). Many classical authors were also translated; one of the most prolific translators of works for the theatre during the period was Lodovico Dolce, from Venice (1508–68).

A new feature of translation was the considerable artistic effort involved. In order to refine their literary skills, translators frequently competed against the original, which naturally meant moving away from the model of translation followed by the humanist philologists of the earlier period. There were experimental artistic translations in unrhymed hendecasyllables, in terza rima, in octave, etc., first following Petrarchan stylistic models and later baroque and mannerist ones.

Between 1563 and 1566, Virgil's *Aeneid* was translated by the famous man of letters Annibal Caro (1507–66), becoming what may be considered the first great work of translation produced in Italy. It is still studied at school today and is in many ways an unrivalled classic. Caro's *Eneide*, while excellent from a poetic standpoint, is, like all the works of its time, far removed from the original. The views of translator-poets such as Caro, for whom translation meant the creation of a text with the same value as the original, though distant from it, became the norm for poetic translation until Romanticism; these views are still held today by some practitioners.

One work which stands out as a classic of non-literary translation is Tacitus's *Annales*, translated by the Florentine scholar Bernardo Davanzati (1529-1606).

From Baroque to the Age of Enlightenment (1650–1800)

There were relatively few major innovations during the second half of the seventeenth century. Latin remained for a long time the only official language of scientific, economic and political communication. Since all foreign scientists and scholars could write Latin, sometimes translating into or from their first language, and since Italian scholars also knew Latin well, translation into Italian was rather pointless.

In the latter half of the eighteenth century, however, interest in French began to take over

from Latin. Between 1650 and 1800, French culture, not altogether ignored in Italy during the previous centuries, spread throughout the northern and central regions of Italy, as it did all over the rest of Europe. Prior to 1700, translations from French had been rare, done mainly by isolated amateurs operating in small cultural centres. After this point, however, there was a veritable outburst of translations from French.

The translations of the great seventeenth-century comedies and tragedies initiated what was to become an overwhelming influence of French culture in Italy. Molière, Racine and Corneille (two of whose works had already been translated in 1647 and 1651) were merely the best-known names among the huge army of playwrights whose work invaded eighteenth-century Italy. These translations (often done only a few years after their original staging in France) were sometimes inaccurate, concerned as they were with content and performability. Sometimes they entailed adaptation, with a variety of additions and cuts. After 1757, Italian tastes underwent a profound change, and interest in French comic theatre faded.

At the same time, the French novel had taken root in fertile ground. The best-loved author was Fénelon: after 1702 there were dozens of reprints of *Le avventure di Telemaco figliolo d'Ulisse*. Other favourites included Arnaud, Prévost, Riccoboni, Lesage, Marmontel, Rousseau, La Place, Florian and Voltaire. These French authors, often themselves translators from English, provided an important link between Italian and anglophone culture. La Place, for example, was responsible for bringing Fielding's *Tom Jones* and *Joseph Andrews* to Italy, and Riccoboni his *Amelia*, while Prévost brought Richardson's famous epistolary novels, *Pamela*, *Clarissa* and *Sir Thomas Grandison*.

During the latter half of the eighteenth century, French culture was spread further by the translation of works on philosophy, science, economics and politics, four areas which were of course inseparable in the writings of the French *philosophes*. The many translations undertaken, first from Voltaire's works and later from those of Diderot and D'Alembert, had a profound effect on late eighteenth-century Italy, significantly broadening the country's cultural horizons.

The translator in Italy now had little in common with the scholar–clergyman figure of the previous era, at least as far as translation from French was concerned. As Ferrari points out, with reference to translation of French tragic theatre,

> Everyone translated: renowned authors and unknown dilettantes; writers of tragedy, of comedy and of opera libretto; lyric poets, didactic poets and dialect poets; printers and journalists; university professors, seminary teachers and schoolteachers; women; nobles and diplomats; theologians; librarians; civil servants; adventurers; even doctors and soldiers. And this list includes only the translators whose work was printed. If manuscripts and bibliographical references were also taken into account, other names would be added, such as that of the infamous Casanova.
>
> (Ferrari 1925: xvi–xviii; translated)

Throughout this period, translations of Greek and Latin works continued uninterrupted, increasing after 1690, the year in which *Arcadia*, the Roman Academy of Letters, was founded. The Academy, where the major Italian literary figures of the time gathered, exercised considerable influence over literary production throughout the eighteenth century. The most important translations of classical poetry were the early Italian versions of Lucretius (1718), Catullus (1740), Propertius (1742) and Tibullus (1760). Important prose translations included Statius (1731), Phaedrus (1735) and Tertullianus (1756), while translations for the theatre included a number of works by Sophocles, Euripides and Plautus. It is worth noting that the translators of classical works – generally famous men of letters and academy members, unlike those working from French – tended to have similar backgrounds. Indeed, their tastes and ambitions reflected the ideal of the sixteenth-century religious intellectual. Nonetheless, their attitude towards the source text differed somewhat from that of earlier translators. According to Ferrari,

> The unlimited freedom of the seventeenth-century translators was criticized, particularly Annibal Caro for his famous translation of *The Aeneid*. Respect for the source text began to become the norm,

verse translation being preferred over prose translation. From 1725 on especially, literary translation moved closer to the original.

> (Ferrari 1925: xii; translated)

The transition towards a more modern approach to translation and translation theory is well represented by Melchiorre Cesarotti (1730–1808), who produced two versions of Homer's *Iliad*, one in verse and one in prose, 'one to let people enjoy Homer, one to let them get to know him' (Cesarotti 1786: 197; translated). He wrote a long essay to justify his choice and another one to go with his translations of Demosthenes' works, in which he emphasized the tension implied in translation work and the critical and artistic sophistication and agility required of a translator in order to 'respect the Genius of his language and let it walk, as it were, nimbly and fruitfully on a geometric line bridging two cliffs' (Cesarotti 1807: 162; translated).

From Romanticism to Neopositivism (1800–1900)

The trends of the eighteenth century were reinforced during the following period. First, Latin was replaced by modern languages, in so far as scientists, philosophers and economists began writing in their own language, leaving to Latin the role of official language of the Roman Church. Second, Italian culture was expanding in breadth and scope, though to different degrees in different parts of Italy. Third, culture was no longer the privilege of the few, but accessible to many, a social rather than individual phenomenon.

These changes also had a profound influence on translation, which was now being undertaken from a number of modern languages which had previously been almost completely ignored or else mediated through French. What is more important, a huge number of translations dealing with history, geography, science, philosophy and economics arrived on the scene, which until then had been dominated exclusively by literary translations.

Much has been written about the article by Madame de Staël published in *Biblioteca Italiana* in January 1816 under the title 'Sulla maniera e l'utilità delle traduzioni' ('On the manner and usefulness of translations'). In this article, which praised Vincenzo Monti's translation of the *Iliad* and the expressiveness of the Italian language, she urged Italians to undertake the translation of works of modern European literature. Everyday language, she claimed, was far superior to that learned from books; opening up to new languages meant enriching the existing vocabulary. In Madame de Staël's view, imitation of the classics should not be substituted with imitations of contemporary works: contact between literatures and cultures was useful above all for broadening minds and developing knowledge. The article also criticized the Italian culture of the time as being totally devoid of modernity, dominated as it was by obstinate nostalgics or by men of letters who cared only for the sounds of words and not the ideas they contained.

The reaction to this article, particularly to its criticism of Italy's men of letters, merely served to fire the age-old debate on the superiority of the classics over modern writing, imitation over originality, *labor limae* over artistic genius, a debate which held Italian intellectuals' attention, fruitlessly, for decades to come. Madame de Staël's article did not significantly affect the quantity of translation output (compare, for example, the poetry collection *Parnaso Straniero* of 1797 and that of 1848: nine-tenths of the total number of pages translated are still dedicated to Greek, Latin and Hebrew). The subsequent increase was due to the profound changes that had taken place during the previous period, namely, the growth in readership and the increasing importance of European national languages in all areas of life.

Some original ideas about translation in this period (running against the grain of Madame de Staël's argument) were expressed by Giacomo Leopardi (1798–1837), the great lyrical poet from Recanati. In his notebooks (*Zibaldone*, written between 1817 and 1832, but published only in 1898) there are many interesting observations derived from his experience as a meticulous and elegant translator, especially from Greek. Leopardi did not believe anything good could come from the translation of modern writers, convinced as he was that lessons in style could only come from a passionate study of classic literature. His thoughts on the necessarily artificial quality of translated language

and the difficult balance the translator must strike between the needs of the original text and those of the target language, together with his concept of imitation, continue to arouse interest even today. He stressed the importance of the aesthetic quality of translations, insisting that the work of a poet can be translated only by another poet. The main task of any good translation was to 'add beauty' and improve the expressive powers of the target language. There was an unprecedented increase in translation from English in nineteenth-century Italy. Although during the previous century Italy had shown some interest in anglophone works, the study and translation of those works had been undertaken by isolated practitioners or famous men of letters, some of whom worked at the English court. The most important names included Magalotti, Rolli, Baretti and Papi. The first translation of Shakespeare, dating from 1756, was carried out by Domenico Valentini, professor of Ecclesiastical History at the University of Siena. It was not until the following century, however, that these occasional attempts by a handful of men of letters were replaced by widespread interest in the anglophone world.

The poems of Ossian were hugely successful in Italy, as were those of Byron. Giulio Carcano (1812–84), poet and patriot, was the first and perhaps the greatest translator of Shakespeare in his century (Duranti 1979).

The early and successful translations by Domenico Cetti (1780–1812) of some of Nikolai Karamzin's poetry and prose, together with the *Saggio di poesie russe con due odi tedesca e inglese* (1816) by the Genoese nobleman Girolamo Orti (1769–1845) signalled the start of direct translation from Russian, without French as a mediating language. For more than half a century, however, these pioneers were the only ones working in this area. While translations from French continued throughout the nineteenth century very much as before, there was considerably less translation from either German or Spanish. Nonetheless, a 507-page volume of the *Parnaso Straniero* of 1848 deals with translation from Spanish.

Three great translations of the time deserve a special mention: Ippolito Pindemonte's translation of *The Odyssey* (1805–12), Vincenzo Monti's translation of *The Iliad* (completed in 1811), and Ugo Foscolo's translation of Laurence

Sterne's *A Sentimental Journey* (1804–06, but reworked and published in 1813). All three are still read and studied in Italy today.

An interesting quarrel arose between Monti and Foscolo upon the publication of Monti's translation of *The Iliad*. In a venomous epigram, Foscolo accused Monti (who had referred to other Italian and Latin translations for his own version) of being a 'great translator of the translators of Homer'. Foscolo's accusation was directed at a large group of translators-versifiers who, following the widespread stance of the earlier period, were less concerned with the original than with the translated product, this being conditioned by the rigorous norms of traditional metre. Foscolo himself, who knew Greek perfectly, attempted a translation of *The Iliad*, but, after translating books one and three, was unable to complete his task.

As far as non-literary translation is concerned, the century began with a sudden increase in the translation of scientific texts, now from English as well as from French. As the decades passed, the work of German positivist scientists began to be translated more regularly, reflecting the hegemony in research and applications they were acquiring. By the end of the century, the works of German scholars, even in the humanistic field (especially in Philology and Linguistics, the so-called Neogrammarians) had occupied the centre of the international cultural scene and begun to stimulate a great volume of translation. A similar pattern emerges for other branches of knowledge (politics, history, philosophy, psychology), with English and especially German acquiring an ever-growing importance.

The contemporary period

The transition between the nineteenth and twentieth centuries is marked by the gradual growth of publishing houses from mere printers or bookstores to family enterprises and then to larger and more complex industrial groups. This has influenced the quantity and the quality of translation output. As the reading public and the publishing market were rapidly growing along parallel lines, the figure of the translator also underwent deep changes: from the isolated intellectual who proposed a translation project

out of a deep personal interest in the foreign text, we gradually see the emergence of the professional figure of a translator commissioned by a publishing house and often performing his or her task under very unfavourable conditions. One remarkable exception is the role played by writers like Cesare Pavese, Elio Vittorini, and Eugenio Montale in the late 1930s and early 1940s; such writers actively rekindled interest in English, especially American, literature through an intense activity of translation. Especially in the case of Pavese and Vittorini, translating was a way of proposing a cultural and political alternative to the stifling and autarchic cultural policies of the Fascist regime.

The delay in the development of translation studies in Italy is probably due to the negative attitude of influential thinkers such as Benedetto Croce (1866–1952) who, following Dante, dismissed translation as a logically impossible task (see Croce 1902). An analogous attitude, although with a few differences of emphasis, was adopted by Giovanni Gentile (1920) and the neo-idealistic school of thought he represented. By contrast, Antonio Gramsci (1891–1937) invested translation with a more positive and necessary role, emphasizing its ability to bridge the gaps between different languages, connecting concepts on a superstructural, historically and culturally determined level (see Gramsci 1947/1975). Even though his theoretical considerations on the subject (along with the translations he did while in jail) were confined to his notebooks and were not available to the public until much later, Gramsci's position shows an active interest in translation on the part of Marxist intellectuals.

The most interesting Italian contributions to translation studies come from philologists and linguists such as Benvenuto Terracini (1886–1968) and Gianfranco Folena (1920–94). Their balanced and well-informed account of translation is grounded in a dynamic vision of the phenomenon, rather than in a static contraposition of principles as in the case of neo-idealist thinkers: exploring the ideal space between the formal and cultural contexts of the different languages, they emphasize the tension that sustains the work of the translator and the added value derived from the difficulties encountered. Since the 1990s there has been a renewed interest in translation studies and translation theory, and there are now several serious scholars in Italian universities analysing various aspects of translation, but no particularly original figure has yet emerged.

It is interesting to look at the quantitative trends in the output of published translations in Italy in relatively recent years. In 1982, out of a total 20,560 books published in Italy 22.5 per cent were translations. In 1991, the percentage increased to 26.1 per cent of a volume of books that is twice as large (40,142). In 1972, 45.9 per cent of translated pages were from English, 23.4 per cent from French and 13.7 per cent from German. Seventeen years later, in 1989, the percentage of pages translated from English had reached 54.4 per cent, whereas French dropped to 17.6 per cent and German remained stable at 13.4 per cent. In the same year, pages translated from Spanish amounted to 2.7 per cent, from Slavonic languages 2.3 per cent, from Classical languages (Latin and ancient Greek) 3.7 per cent, and from all other languages 4.3 per cent.

By and large, most published translations are of literature (43.9 per cent of translated pages in 1972; 44.8 per cent in 1989), followed by History (12.2 per cent in 1972, but only 8.5 per cent in 1989); Philosophy and Psychology (9.5 per cent in 1972 and 8.4 per cent in 1989); Religion (stable at 5.9 per cent); Political Science and Economics peaked to 5.6 per cent in 1972 but by 1989 were reduced to 2.5 per cent; the share of Medicine, by contrast, rose from a mere 2.1 per cent to 6.3 per cent.

The dubbing industry

In Italy, almost all foreign films are dubbed. Historically this has two concomitant causes: before World War II, it was felt that the use of subtitling would cut off a rather large section of popular audience as illiteracy rates were still fairly high. Moreover, the fascist regime was afraid of 'contaminating' the purity of the national idiom by exposing audiences to massive doses of foreign languages. At the end of the war, the second motivation all but disappeared, but the first was retained essentially because Hollywood executives did not want obstacles to the new market that was opening after Mussolini's isolationism. Their powerful

lobby even managed to have a clause added to the peace treaty signed with the Allies in 1943–5 making dubbing explicitly mandatory.

This situation has led to the development of a strong and well-organized dubbing industry, with specialized translators, adapters and actors. The massive use of American telefilms in the burgeoning television industry has resulted in lower standards, especially at the translation end of the process; adapters and actors barely manage to survive the loss of nuances and the sense of unease given sometimes by an asynchronous or faulty dubbing, but excessive simplifications and real howlers often noticeably mar the quality of the translated dialogue. There is a growing section of dedicated filmgoers that would prefer enjoying foreign films in the original form, with the help of subtitles, but the market situation seems to indicate that a radical change in this field is rather unlikely, at least in the near future.

The professional status of the translator

Whenever Italian translators meet, the complaint about their professional life is virtually unanimous. And they do not refer to exceptional vocational hazards like the one suffered by Ettore Capriolo, the translator of Salman Rushdie's *Satanic Verses*, who luckily survived stabbing. They refer to the low esteem in which their work is held, to the low earnings it yields, to the short time they are allowed to complete projects, to the insecurity of a steady flow of jobs, to the lack of control they have over the finished product. Even though working conditions have generally improved since the late twentieth century, the basic problem of a very unbalanced relationship between translators and publishers still exists.

The major factor sapping the translators' bargaining power is of course the existence of an immense reserve pool of would-be translators from which the publishers can draw the next candidate for a job – should one refuse their conditions, regardless of experience and technical or literary specialization. There is no need to emphasize that the main victim of this system, besides the professional translator, is the overall quality of most work, assigned as it is on the sheer basis of saving cost.

For decades now, the main translators'

unions (including AITI, Associazione Italiana Traduttori e Interpreti) have been trying to improve the status of the profession, but with very modest results, given the extreme fragmentation and isolation of translators as a group (out of some 10,000 people described as translators and interpreters in the 1981 census, only a fluctuating minority actually earn their living as full-time professionals, and most of them work freelance). The issues raised by the debate stimulated by the unions are slowly being understood by the general public and (still more slowly) by the institutional and legislative bodies. Some of the best and most sensitive publishing houses seem now to be interested in reaching a more advanced and (hopefully) balanced agreement in order to break the low cost/low quality cycle on a more consistent basis. There are many hypotheses under discussion (among which the institution of a National Registry of translators and interpreters seems to be the one more often mentioned) but the only real prospect of a short-term improvement of the situation probably lies in the 'harmonization' of rules regulating translation rights among members of the European Union.

Further reading
Maffei 1720; Carini 1894; Ferrari 1925; Zambon 1962; Folena 1973/1991; Duranti 1979; Santangelo and Vinti 1981; Lapucci 1983; Terracini 1983; *Atti del convegno 'In difesa dei traslocatori di parole, Editori e traduttori a confronto'* 1993; Bernascone 1994.

RICCARDO DURANTI

J

Japanese tradition

The Japanese language, which is spoken by over 125 million people in the Japanese archipelago to the east of China and Korea, has an affinity with Altaic languages, but its origins are much debated. Although syntactically somewhat similar to Korean, it is quite unrelated to Chinese.

Japan has been an empire since about AD 200, and Japanese emperors were regarded as divine until 1946. However, from 1186 until 1867 real power was in the hands of the military shoguns, the heads of three families (Minamoto, Ashikaga and Tokugawa) who were successively in actual control of the country, although the emperors retained formal sovereignty.

Japan's proximity to Asia and distance from Western countries has combined with historical factors to shape both the practice of and attitudes towards translating and interpreting in the area. Throughout much of Japan's history the motivation behind translation and interpreting has been the need for information, with interest in foreign civilization for its own sake being of secondary importance. Yet the outcome has been to introduce new ideas, literary forms, expressions and grammatical structures, thereby having an enormous impact on both the culture and language of the area.

Chinese–Japanese 'translation' in pre-modern times

Contact between Japan and China dates back at least as far as the first recorded official contacts in AD 57. In the third and fourth centuries, Korean scribes introduced the Chinese script to Japan, which lacked a script of its own, and by the sixth or seventh centuries this was widely used amongst the elite. Sometimes the sounds of the Chinese characters were used phonetically to write Japanese words, and sometimes the meanings were borrowed instead. Although two indigenous phonetic scripts were developed by the eighth century, enabling Japanese to be written without recourse to Chinese characters, the latter have remained in use to the present day because of their conciseness, formality and greater prestige (Twine 1991: 35).

China had a great impact on Japan's intellectual, religious and cultural life in the 1,300 years between the adoption of the writing system and the opening up of Japan to the West in 1854. Unofficial cultural and commercial contacts, as well as diplomatic missions that included monks, scholars and students, produced an exchange of ideas that resulted in many changes to Japanese institutions and society. Such contacts naturally required considerable language mediation. Rather than translating in the conventional manner, however, by the ninth century the Japanese had devised an ingenious annotation system called *kambun kundoku* (interpretive reading of Chinese), which enabled Chinese texts to be read without translation. Special marks were placed alongside the characters of Chinese texts to indicate how they could be read in accordance with Japanese word order, and a system of grammatical indicators was used to show inflections. This directly converted the Chinese texts into understandable, albeit rather unnatural, Japanese that retained a strong Chinese flavour.

Thus right up to the nineteenth century there existed two media of reading and writing in Japan: Chinese, used mainly for scholarly works, and Japanese, used chiefly for literature. Inevitably, however, there was a certain amount of interplay between the two traditions, resulting in a form of 'Japanized' Chinese as well as the sinicization of Japanese.

In 1611, the shogun Tokugawa Ieyasu encouraged Chinese merchants to trade in Nagasaki in south-western Japan, leading to a demand for interpreters of Tang Chinese and an influx of Chinese books. It was also about this time that the first true translations from classical and colloquial Chinese were produced, particularly colloquial fiction from the Ming dynasty (1368–c.1644). Whereas such writers as Asai Ryōi (?–1691) often followed the original text line by line (Keene 1987: 56), Ogyu Sorai (1666–1728), whose approach to translation is outlined in his introduction to *Yakubun sentei* (A Guide to Translation, 1711), produced free translations in colloquial Japanese (Kato 1983a: 63). The 1758 translation by Okajima Kanzan (1674–1728) of the Chinese romance *Shuihu zhuan* (All Men are Brothers) also had a great effect on the popular fiction of the late Edo period (1600–1868).

Pre-modern contacts with the West

The second wave of foreign languages reached the shores of Japan with the arrival of the Portuguese in the sixteenth and the Dutch in the early seventeenth century. The practice of *kambun kundoku* meant that there was already a precedent for adapting Japanese to the foreign language, rather than requiring the newcomer to conform to natural Japanese usage.

Portuguese

The desire to preach Christianity – combined with the need for trade – led the Portuguese to travel the world, and in 1543 a Portuguese shipwreck brought Japan into contact with the West for the first time. Another Portuguese ship visited Japan in 1546 and carried Anjirō, a fugitive samurai, back to Malacca, where he was introduced to Francis Xavier of the newly founded Society of Jesus. Xavier was inspired by Anjirō's accounts of Japan to commence missionary activities there. Anjirō, who could already speak broken Portuguese and who had become the first Japanese Christian, was sent to the College of St Paul in Goa, India, to study Christianity and Portuguese. There, he translated Christian materials such as the catechism into Japanese (Schurhammer 1982: 271).

Xavier arrived in Kagoshima in 1549, accompanied by Anjirō as his interpreter and translator. Gradually, the priests mastered Japanese and, with the help of converts, translated various Christian works into Japanese. This presented a major problem in terms of finding words to express new concepts such as 'God', 'angel', 'heaven' and 'cross', and led to inevitable discrepancies in meaning. One interpreter worthy of particular note was the Portuguese missionary João Rodrigues (c.1561–1633), who arrived in Japan in 1577. After studying Japanese, Rodrigues acted as the mission's chief interpreter, and interpreted at talks with the shogun Hideyoshi in 1591. He also compiled the *Arte da Lingoa de Iapam*, a grammar of Japanese in which he discussed Chinese poetry translated into Japanese and the difficulty of translating Portuguese into Japanese, and recommended translating the sense rather than giving a literal rendition (Cooper 1974).

A partial translation of Aesop's *Fables* was produced in romanized script in 1593 and was probably the first translation of a Western work apart from proselytizing materials. This was quite free and colloquial, and substituted the nearest Japanese equivalents for unfamiliar European objects. Partial translations of *Imitatio Christi* (1596) and Luis de Granada's *Guia do Pecador* (1599) also appeared, but there was little attempt to translate Portuguese works other than Christian literature.

By 1639 the Tokugawa shogunate had issued a series of seclusion orders closing the country off from 'destabilizing' outside influences. Traders and missionaries were banned, as was Christianity itself. Only the Dutch, who had arrived in 1609 and been ordered to reside in the town of Hirado in Kyushu, were allowed to stay because they made no attempt at proselytizing. The Chinese were restricted to Nagasaki, and the Koreans permitted to trade only in Tsushima. This move brought the already minimal translation of Western literature to a virtual halt.

Dutch

Some merchants, officials and samurai could speak foreign languages, but when the Dutch were ordered in 1641 to move to Dejima, an artificial island in Nagasaki, translating and interpreting became the sole province of government officials known as *Oranda tsūji* (Dutch interpreters), who also acted as customs officials. The position of *tsūji* was a hereditary one, although often it was inherited by adopted sons. Though paid well, the *tsūji* did not always have a good reputation, sometimes stealing foreign goods, sometimes being criticized for their poor linguistic abilities, and sometimes even being arrested for mistranslations. By the late eighteenth century, however, there was a fairly good system of training *tsūji*. They commenced studying Dutch at about the age of ten and had to pass an examination to qualify as trainee *tsūji*, from where they moved up the tsuji hierarchy (Sugimoto 1990).

There were usually about fifty *tsūji* at any one time, and every year two senior *tsūji* accompanied the head of the Dutch settlement to the capital Edo to meet the shogun and present a report on overseas affairs translated by the *tsūji*. They would interpret at talks with the shogun and with intellectuals thirsty for knowledge about the outside world, and this practice spread 'Dutch learning' to the capital.

The texts translated by the *tsūji* were overwhelmingly of a non-literary nature. Apart from trade-related documents, the first works translated were medical texts. The Dutch version of a Latin anatomical work was translated by Motoki Ryōi (1628–97) in 1682, although this is less well known than the later translation of another anatomical work, *Kaitai Shinsho*, published in 1774. Many *tsūji* became so well versed in the field that they switched to full-time medical careers. Medical texts were followed by works in the natural sciences and military science, with translation in the field of humanities coming last. The translations were undertaken into classical Chinese. The *tsūji* frequently had to coin equivalents to express new concepts, and a common method of doing this was to use existing Chinese words where possible.

The more scholarly of the *tsūji* played an important role in teaching Dutch and introducing Western knowledge and culture. Motoki Yoshinaga (1735–94) translated astronomical works and introduced Copernican theory into Japan. To a translation he undertook in 1792 he added a second volume, *Wage reigon*, explaining his method of translation, and this was probably

the first coherent essay on translation methods in Japan (Sugimoto 1990: 132). It compares Dutch and Japanese structures and discusses translation problems, the transcription of foreign words and different approaches to translation. But perhaps the most outstanding *tsūji*, both linguistically and scholastically, was Shizuki Tadao (1674–1728), who wrote nine books on the Dutch language, parts of which touch on translation issues, and who is widely regarded as the father of physics in Japan.

In 1808 the gifted young trainee *tsūji* Baba Sajūrō settled in Edo at the shogunate's orders, since there were no scholars there who could adequately read or translate Dutch. There Baba translated many Dutch grammars and taught Dutch to Japanese scholars. He was also in charge of translating the Dutch version of a French encyclopaedia, under the title *Kōsei Shimpen* (New Volumes for the Public Welfare). This translation, which commenced in 1811, consisted of seventy fascicles and is probably the largest national translation project ever undertaken in Japan, although it was never completed. It adopted an accessible style and Baba sometimes added explanatory comments, as did many *tsūji* of the time out of a belief that Japanese readers lacked sufficient familiarity with the West. This project was undertaken at a national bureau set up by the government in that year for the translation of 'barbarian books'. This translation bureau, which underwent several name changes, was a forerunner of the present University of Tokyo.

The *tsūji* also compiled dictionaries, often on the basis of existing dictionaries in other languages, and they helped in the compilation of a Dutch–Japanese dictionary by Hendrik Doeff, head of the Dejima settlement. The *Doeff Haruma*, the largest dictionary produced during the Edo period, was completed in 1833, a quarter of a century after it was started. Based on a Dutch–French dictionary, its colloquial style represented the birth of a new style of translation.

Other languages

The shogunate had gradually become aware of the need to learn languages other than Dutch. In 1808 an incident involving the British ship *Phaeton* prompted the shogunate to order the *tsūji* to study English, which they initially learnt from the Dutch. Increasing contacts with Russia highlighted the need to learn Russian, and several *tsūji* were based in Matsumae in northern Hokkaido. Baba also studied Russian and in 1820, when smallpox was a severe problem in Japan, he translated a Russian book on Jennerian vaccination. Baba earned a reputation as the first Russian linguist in Japan and was the first translator to introduce Russian literature to the area. Since many Russian documents of the time were written in French, in 1808 the authorities ordered the *tsūji* to learn French from Doeff. Probably at no other time in Japanese history have language and national affairs been as intertwined as they were in the early nineteenth century (Sugimoto 1990: 52). The emphasis in translation was overwhelmingly on works that would help Japan learn from the West, and there was still little literary translation being undertaken.

In 1853 Commodore Matthew Perry arrived to persuade Japan to start diplomatic and commercial relations with the United States. This led to the Kanagawa Treaty on 31 March 1854; there was a discrepancy between the Japanese translation of the treaty and the English, Dutch and Chinese versions, so the Japanese text was later changed to bring it into line (Roland 1982: 98). Perry's interpreters were Dr S.W. Williams, a Protestant missionary who had tried to translate the Bible into Japanese in China, Dr Bettelheim, another missionary, and the Dutch-speaking American diplomat Anton Portman. On the Japanese side, Nakahama Manjirō (1827–98), a shipwrecked fisherman who had been picked up by the Americans and spent several years in the United States, was used as a behind-the-scenes translator, while the interpreting was done by the *tsūji* Hori Tatsunosuke and Hatshisuko Tokushumo. In the second round of talks in 1854 Hori and Hatshisuko were joined by the *tsūji* Moriyama Einosuke.

When the first American consul in Japan met with the Japanese officials, his English was interpreted into Dutch by a Dutch-speaking American and then relayed into Japanese. Another prominent interpreter at the time was the Englishman Sir Ernest Satow, who had studied Japanese, thereby eliminating the need to use Dutch as the common medium. Thus the end of Japan's isolation also spelled the

end of the *tsūji*'s monopoly on interpreting and translating.

Meiji Period (1868–1912)

Another major change took place with the Meiji Restoration of 1868, which saw the end of the shogunate and the restoration of the emperor to power, and ushered Japan into the modern age. The opening up of Japan meant that more Japanese were able to study foreign languages in Japan or travel abroad, so that there was a growing supply of people capable of acting as interpreters to meet Japan's diplomatic, commercial and cultural needs during this period. The opening of the country also led to a flood of imported English, French, Russian and German works in an attempt to learn from the West, and the aim of many translations in the first decade of the Meiji Period was educational rather than aesthetic. The translations by the renowned educator Fukuzawa Yukichi (1835–1901), who acted as an interpreter on the first government missions to the United States and Europe, were particularly important because they introduced the thought and institutions of the West, coined many words to express foreign concepts and laid the groundwork for the transition from the difficult Chinese style to a more accessible vernacular style (Yoshitake 1959).

Also of particular influence in enlightening readers on modern values and social relations was the 1870–71 translation by Nakamura Keiu (1832–91) of *Self-Help* by Samuel Smiles. Nakamura made great efforts to make these stories of success through hard work readable, adding notes to explain unfamiliar objects and customs. He omitted or simplified parts that he thought were of no interest to Japanese readers or would hinder their understanding, and removed certain references to Christianity, which continued to be banned until 1872. The very title, *Saikoku Risshi Hen* (Success Stories of the West), was aimed at attracting readers, and this tendency to substitute emotive, eye-catching titles is evident in many translations of the time. Nakamura tried to reproduce the word order, punctuation, pronouns and relative pronouns of the original, and this helped create a new style of translation. Other important non-fiction translations included Nakamura's translation of John

Stuart Mill's *On Liberty* in 1871 and an 1882 translation by Nakae Chōmin (1847–1901) of Rousseau's *Social Contract*. Such works contained many unfamiliar concepts, and Meiji translators followed their Edo predecessors in using their knowledge of Chinese to coin new terms or to use existing terms in a new sense. Inevitably, however, this resulted in some distortions and a certain degree of incomprehensibility.

Reflecting this time of social and political upheaval, the 1877–86 period saw numerous translations of political novels; many of these translations took great liberties with the original work and focused on its content rather than on conveying its literary flavour. Bulwer Lytton's *Ernest Maltravers*, which appeared in 1879 under the title *Karyū Shunwa* (A Springtime Tale of Blossoms and Willows), was translated by Oda (Niwa) Jun'ichirō (1851–1919), who added explanatory notes and omitted passages which he considered of little interest to his readers. Also notable were a severely abridged version of Disraeli's *Coningsby* (*Shun'ōten*; The Chirping of Spring Warblers; 1884) and the 1885 translation of Bulwer Lytton's *Rienzi, the Last of the Roman Tribunes* by Tsubouchi Shōyō (1859–1935). These works inspired Japanese writers to produce their first political novels.

The Meiji Period also witnessed the advent of a golden age of literary translation, although in the first decade the choice of works translated was somewhat indiscriminate. The first translation of a Western literary work had been made back in the Edo Period (1850) from a Dutch rendition of Robinson Crusoe's *Record of Wanderings*, although another version appeared in 1857 before this was published. Yet neither had much impact, unlike later best-selling translations such as the 1878 translation by Kawashima Chūnosuke (1853–1938) of Jules Verne's *Around the World in Eighty Days*. The early translated novels often consisted of abridged or partial translations which followed the plot of the original but were very rough. Nevertheless, they opened up new vistas for Japanese literature, which at the time of the Meiji Restoration lacked vitality. Early Meiji translations were rendered into Chinese, because classical Japanese would have evoked associations regarded as inappropriate for foreign works, and a written style capable of reflecting the vernacular language had not yet been established (Twine 1991: 47).

Yet the early translations were very free and informal in their language, helping to break down the traditional Chinese-based style. Thus the Meiji Period witnessed a fusing of Japanese, Chinese and Western styles to form a new style.

Poetry was also greatly affected by translation. Traditional poetry consisted of *waka* and *haiku*, which had strict conventions concerning the number of syllables used, and longer free verse did not exist. Translations of European poetry adopted new forms and techniques – for instance, two of the fourteen translated poems in *Shintaishishō* (Selection of Poetry in the New Style, 1882) made an attempt at rhyming, which did not exist in traditional poetry. After about two decades of experimentation it was concluded that rhyming does not have any particular effect in Japanese (Oikawa 1994: 203). Although the *Shintaishishō* was criticized for its lack of poeticity, it marked the starting point of modern Japanese poetry by helping to create a new form.

After 1885 translations became more literal than in the early years of excessively free translation. In what was a radical pronouncement at the time, the preface to the translation of Bulwer Lytton's *Kenelm Chillingly* (*Keishidan*, 1885) stated that merely conveying the plot without paying attention to the style runs counter to the art of literary translation. The translation (there is some debate over who actually translated this work) attempted to convey the flavour of the original by reproducing as literally as possible its idiomatic expressions and personal pronouns, which traditionally were not used in Japanese. Precisely because no attempt was made to achieve naturalness of expression or to avoid unfamiliar figures of speech, this translation shaped not only later translations but also Japanese style in general. A literal approach was also adopted by Futabatei Shimei (1864–1909), an outstanding translator of Russian literature. His superb translation of Turgenev's 'The Rendezvous' (from *A Sportsman's Sketches*) was published as *Aibiki* in 1888. He tried to reproduce the original as exactly as possible, even down to the number of words and the punctuation, but his use of colloquial language opened new avenues of literary expression and he raised the task of translation to the level of an art.

Gradually, there emerged an interest in foreign literature for its own sake and as a reflection of the feelings of Europeans. Western plays, particularly Shakespeare's works, brought home the literary potential of drama. Literary periodicals introduced European literature in translation, and translated literature was regarded as being on an equal footing with original works. Many translators were writers themselves. Writers/translators such as Futabatei Shimei, Tsubouchi Shōyō, Mori Ōgai (1862–1922) and Ueda Bin (1874–1916) turned translation into an artistic form aimed at reproducing the flavour of Western literary works. Their struggle with the problem of skewing between the source and target texts shook traditional Japanese literature and led to new forms of literary expression. This meant, however, moving further away from the Japanese language and literary traditions. In an 1887 essay entitled 'Honyaku no kokoroe' (Hints on Translating) Morita Shiken (1861–97), the renowned translator of many of Victor Hugo's novels, discussed how far translators should go in assimilating the original work into readable Japanese. He advocated literal translation and letting the Japanese language be actively influenced by foreign style. His retranslation from the English version of Jules Verne's *Deux Ans de Vacances* (Jûgo Shōnen 1896) was highly influential.

The year 1889 saw the publication of *Omokage* (Vestiges), an anthology of German poetry translated by the writer Mori Ōgai and some colleagues. Although this used many traditional elegant words and ideas, it moved beyond traditional literature by using a wide range of translation methods, from merely conveying the sense to trying to convey the sense and the number of syllables per line, or the rhyming, or the wording (Kamei 1994: 42). It was successful as poetry, both in form and in concept, and was a source of inspiration for the Japanese Romantic movement, just as the 1894 translation of Zola's *Nana* by Nagai Kafû (1879–1959) spurred the Naturalist movement in Japan.

Bible translation has been one of the key translation enterprises in Japan ever since Xavier's arrival, with different versions of parts of the Bible being translated by both Protestants and Catholics. The translators were generally American missionaries, usually working as a committee aided by Japanese translators. By 1888 the first translation of the Bible was complete, but the New Testament was replaced in 1917 by a version which became standard until a colloquial Bible was published in 1955, followed by a new joint Protestant–Catholic translation in 1987. Yet it is the Meiji version of 1888 which has won the most praise for its literary merit.

Another Meiji masterpiece was *Sokkyō shijin*, Mori Ōgai's retranslation from the German of Hans Christian Andersen's *Improvisatoren*. Published serially between 1892 and 1901, it is considered a classic of modern Japanese literature and better than the original. Ōgai did not translate directly, focusing instead on conveying the meaning accurately and in good Japanese. Also noteworthy is *Kaichôon* (Sound of the Tide), which was translated by Ueda Bin and appeared in 1905. Although he also translated English and German poetry, it was his translations of French Symbolist poetry that had the most impact on Japanese poets and translators of poetry. Ueda's translations have been acclaimed as masterpieces, inspiring a generation of poets. His translations are far from being literal, but his refined classical Japanese successfully evoked the mood of the original poems.

In 1913 the translator of Arthur Symons's *The Symbolist Movement in Literature*, Iwano Hōmei (1873–1920), tried to translate each line separately and retain the order of the lines. He used non-Japanese structures and even tried to reproduce the original punctuation. His preface states that a new kind of word order is necessary to express new ways of thinking. The results worked reasonably well as poetry, and the Japanese is not particularly unnatural (Kawamura 1981: 18). The most outstanding translated anthology of the Taishō Period (1912–26), however, was Horiguchi Daigaku's *Gekka no ichigun* (A Moonlight Gathering, 1925). Horiguchi used colloquial language to express the images in the original poems, rather than forcing them to fit the traditional Japanese mould.

The impact of the war years

By the 1920s, nearly all of the major literary works of the world had been translated into

Japanese, and important works were being translated in the same year the original work appeared. Three strands of translation began to take shape from about the 1920s. The first consisted of socialist and communist literary works. Japanese Marxists translated treatises by Marx, Engels and Lenin, and these works influenced the proletarian literature movement. The second strand covered surrealist and stream-of-consciousness works, while the third consisted of American literary works (Takeda 1983: 247). However, the rise of militarism led to censorship of socialist and Communist translations – and the publication of best-selling translations of a biography of Mussolini in 1928 and an expurgated version of Hitler's *Mein Kampf* in 1940 – and the events leading up to World War II meant that American literature declined in popularity.

Chinese poetry continued to be translated, with Satō Haruo (1892–1964) being the pioneer in this field. Satō, who in 1927 translated *Shajinshū*, an anthology of forty-eight poems by female Chinese poets, was dissatisfied with the traditional approach of reading Chinese poetry in Japanese. Instead he translated creatively, capturing the flavour of the original poems, a method which subsequently became popular amongst translators. Even so, Satō continued to use the fixed form of verse, whereas Hinatsu Kōnosuke's (1890–1971) colloquial versions rendered Chinese poetry into modern poetry, focusing on the content without being constrained by the form and fixed rhythm (Kajima 1994).

Japan's defeat in World War II brought the Allied Occupation forces to its shores, with a concomitant need for interpreters and translators. General Douglas MacArthur's chief interpreter was Colonel Sidney Mashbir, and Matsui Akira served as interpreter at some of the meetings between the Emperor and MacArthur and at the Emperor's meetings with special U.S. envoy John Foster Dulles and MacArthur's successor, General Matthew Ridgway. At the Tokyo Trial of war criminals, over 50,000 pages of translation work was involved, with a Language Arbitration Board responsible for ruling on thorny translation problems. In the minor trials some Japanese interpreters were found guilty of war crimes (Roland 1982).

The end of the war ushered in a new age of translation unprecedented since the Meiji Restoration, with Japanese readers keen to read works that could not be published during the war. The quantity of translations, however, was not always matched by their quality, and the choice of works was controlled by the Occupation authorities. Books that criticized the United States or praised the military were suppressed, while translations of approved works were often given financial support (Satō 1987). During the war, the Japanese authorities had banned 2,120 foreign books and periodicals, many of which reported on Chinese resistance to the Japanese. Best-selling translations included *Ten Years in Japan* by a former US ambassador to Japan, George Orwell's *Animal Farm*, and *The Diary of Anne Frank*.

In the 1950s there were four recognizable trends in translation. American literature took over from European literature as mainstream Western literature in translation; translations of the works of existentialist writers such as Sartre, Camus, Kafka, Kierkegaard and Dostoevsky were undertaken and had a major impact; translations of literary works by Catholics began to appear; and literary works with explicit sexual scenes were translated (Takeda 1983: 248). Translations of books made into movies, such as *Gone with the Wind*, were also common.

Of particular note is *Yūkarashū* (1959–70), a nine-volume translation by Kindaichi Kyōsuke (1882–1971) of epics and other oral literature of the Ainu people, who live in the northern island of Hokkaido and are racially and linguistically distinct from the Japanese. The Ainu have no written language, and it was only after an Ainu woman began transcribing their epics in 1928 that translation of their literature became possible.

In 1960 the translator Itô Sei and the publisher of D. H. Lawrence's *Lady Chatterley's Lover* were charged for translating, publishing and distributing this work, which was alleged to contain obscene passages. A similar situation occurred with Marquis de Sade's *Juliette*. The 1960s also saw the translation of urban American Jewish literature and Black literature, although interest in translated literature waned somewhat, to be replaced to a large extent in the 1970s by translations of 'how-to' books and non-fiction works about US management methods or about Japan and its rise as a leading economy (Wilkinson 1990). Several 'complete works' translations, as well as translations in the field of popular entertainment such as the Hayakawa mystery and science fiction series, also began to appear.

By the end of the twentieth century translated books (mostly from English, French or German) accounted for more than 10 per cent of all books published each year. Best-seller lists in Japan almost always include some translations. Other genres in which translation has played a major role include film dubbing and subtitling, the translation of lyrics and children's books, and there is great demand for technical translations.

Profession, training and research

There is a large body of Japanese writing on translation, but Japanese writers are largely unacquainted with Western writing on translation and interpreting theory. This may, however, have allowed their ideas to develop along independent channels. Although Japanese writers have not developed a fully-fledged theory of translation, preferring discussions of specific works and problems to abstract theorizing, there are several distinct translation traditions in Japan, largely differentiated by their position on the issue of whether or not translations should actively transform Japanese language and style.

Nogami Toyoichirō (1883–1950) advocated a 'monochromatic' approach whereby no particular attempt is made to reproduce the tone and style of the original. He suggested that translations should sound foreign so as to introduce fresh expressions and forms into the language. Nogami also emphasized the importance of choosing what to translate based on whether or not it would contribute to Japanese culture – a recurring theme with many Japanese writers on translation. Other advocates of 'foreignizing' translations include Ikuta Chōkō (1882–1936) in his youth, Komiya Toyotaka (1884–1966) and Kawamori Yoshizô (1902–). These arguments are based on the idea that language is continually evolving and that the initially awkward style of such translations creates a new type of language – such expressions and style may initially shock, but if they have literary merit they will eventually be adopted.

Inevitably, however, translations that were 'faithful' to the original in an attempt to create a new style met with resistance from people who regarded this approach as detrimental to the Japanese language. Such writer/translators as Uchida Roan (1868–1929), Tsubouchi Shōyō, Hasegawa Futabatei and Mori Ōgai advocated rewriting foreign works into natural Japanese. The writer Tanizaki Jun'ichirō (1886–1965) was concerned that the intrusion of Western writing would lead to the demise of truly Japanese writing. He criticized 'translation-style' Japanese in his *Bunshō Tokuhon* (1960) – although his own writing was heavily influenced by English, claiming that translations in Japan are difficult to understand unless one is already familiar with foreign languages. The Nobel prize-winning author Kawabata Yasunari (1899–1972) regarded translations as the enemy of 'pure literature' and believed that they constitute a threat to Japan's cultural identity. Yet, already by around 1935 'pure' Japanese had largely disappeared, and there had emerged a new written language which absorbed the influence of Western languages rather well.

Taking a slightly different approach, Yanabu Akira (1928–), one of the few contemporary writers who have reflected on translation from a theoretical and historical rather than a literary viewpoint, claims that because anything foreign was accepted uncritically, expressions introduced through translation prevented a genuine understanding of Western thought, and that once the superficial attraction of these expressions faded, readers reverted to their old 'pre-modern' ways of thinking (Yanabu 1983).

Today the literal approach seems to be the more popular form in Japan, and free translation is generally considered in a rather negative light. However, unlike the 'neo-literalism' of such translators as Nogami, which aimed at enriching the Japanese language, the approach adopted by many contemporary translators who are willing to sacrifice natural Japanese for 'fidelity' to the original is based simply on the belief that literal translation equates with faithful translation. There is also considerable tolerance of literal translation on the part of readers, who have long been accustomed to a form of Japanese which is heavily influenced by Chinese and who expect translations to be unidiomatic. A further factor is the practice in Japanese schools of using literal translation as a means of learning English grammar, a habit which is carried through into the professional life of translators.

Books on translation in Japan fall into two broad categories: academic works that adopt an approach based on comparative literature, and more popular works such as 'how-to' books and examinations of mistranslations. Many works have strong sociolinguistic overtones, focusing on cultural differences between Japan and the West as manifest in language. Linguistic scholars in Japan have paid scant attention to translation, and translation theory is not regarded as a discipline in its own right.

On the interpreting side, the 1990s witnessed the first tentative but promising research into interpreting in Japan, particularly the cognitive aspects – a focus which is in sharp contrast to the product-oriented approach of Japanese writing on translation.

The fact that Japanese is a non-European language used in a non-Western culture means that there is potential for a significant contribution to translation and interpreting studies by Japanese practitioners and scholars from a somewhat different perspective, perhaps providing new insights into some perennial issues of translation studies.

Translation in Japan has become increasingly professionalized in recent years, with several translators' organizations, training institutions and journals aimed at aspiring translators and interpreters. The Japan Society of Translators was founded in 1934, the Japan Translation Association in 1986 and the Japan Translation Federation in 1981. The National Translation Institute of Science and Technology, which was founded in 1966, had about 13,000 members in 1995, admitted on the basis of success in the Licensed Technical Translators' Qualification test. The Japanese are amongst the world's leaders in developing machine translation.

Two events that symbolized the 'coming of age' of interpreting in Japan were interpreting during the 1964 Tokyo Olympics and the simultaneous interpreting on television during the landing on the moon by American astronauts. Interpreting in Japan today is a highly specialized profession, with specialist interpreters in the whole spectrum of interpreting tasks, from tour guide interpreting to liaison interpreting, broadcast interpreting and conference interpreting.

Further reading

Yoshitake 1959; Goodman 1967; Katō 1979; Kawamura 1981; Roland 1982; Katō 1983a, 1983b; Takeda 1983; Yanabu 1983; Keene 1987; Sugimoto 1990; Bekku 1994; Kamei 1994;

MASAOMO KONDO AND
JUDY WAKABAYASHI

Latin tradition

Latin is the language of Ancient Rome and the ancestor of modern Romance languages such as Spanish and French. Throughout the Middle Ages, it served as the language of science, philosophy, theology and other areas of knowledge. Until fairly recent times, knowledge of Latin was considered a prerequisite to any liberal education, and despite the almost exclusive use of vernacular languages in its reformed liturgies, Latin is still the official language of the Roman Catholic Church. As Latin remained the dominant cultural language of Western Europe until the end of the eighteenth century, translation into Latin has played a significant role in shaping European culture.

Rome (3rd century BC to 5th century AD)

Classical Rome

During the third century BC, Roman soldiers who were repatriated after garrison duty in the Greek East were coming back to Rome with a taste for Greek amusements, particularly theatre. Enterprising writers addressed this need by using free translation and adaptation from Greek sources. The first of these translators was Livius Andronicus (285–204 BC) with a Latin version of the *Odyssey* (250 BC) and a number of plays commissioned for the Roman Games of 240 BC. Gnaeus Naevius (c.270–c.199 BC) translated several Greek plays about the Trojan War, publicizing the legend that the Romans were descended from the Trojans who fled with Aeneas. The father of Latin literature, Quintus Ennius (239–169 BC), though most famous for his *Annales*, also translated for the theatre. Where Livius had worked on commission, Ennius worked under the patronage of Scipio Africanus the Elder, who had conquered Carthage, and Marcus Cato, known as 'the Censor'. The tradition of translation from Greek theatre was continued by Ennius's nephew, Pacuvius (c.220–130 BC), who played a leading role in turning Latin into a literary language, and by Caecilius Statius (d. 168 BC), regarded as the greatest comic writer of his time (Williams 1968: 363-6).

Although the majority of early work has been lost, we do have a considerable body of plays from the two most famous of these early dramatists, Plautus (d. 184 BC) and Publius Terentius Afer, known as Terence (190?–159? BC). Plautus and Terence are probably the world's first commercial literary translators. Terence's productions were based on the Greek plays of Menander and Apollodorus of Carystus. He was a somewhat more radical forerunner of the seventeenth-century *belles infidèles* (see FRENCH TRADITION), and in composing a text he often combined translated passages from several Greek originals. All of these Romans adapted freely for a Roman audience of coarser tastes than the original Greek audiences.

In the century following Terence, the Greeks introduced rhetoric to Rome, and translation was now taken to be a branch of rhetoric. There is no record of translation from other languages. The greatest age of Roman literary translation began with a translation of Homer by the otherwise obscure writer Matius (about 100 BC) and lasted until the middle of the first century AD. This age set the tradition which lasted well into the twentieth century of treating translation as a literary apprenticeship. Among the great names associated with developing a truly Roman literature are the poets Catullus (87–57 BC) and Horace (65–8 BC), and the statesman and jurist Cicero (106–43 BC). Cicero is one of the few Roman authors whose work is almost entirely preserved. Although only few of his translations from Greek remain, his discussion of translation in *De finibus honorum et Malorum* and in the *De optimo genere oratorum* had a formative influence on translation practice for the next 2000 years.

In terms of ordinary Romans who sought to improve themselves by translation, the crux of the matter was the rhetorical concept of rivalry through creative imitation, which Cicero defined as the imitation of outstanding virtues (*Tusculan Disputations* IV.17). In *De optimo genere oratum* ('The Best Kind of Orator') v. 14, Cicero makes two major points: that word-for-word translation is not suitable; and that translators should seek in their own language expressions that reproduce as much as possible the cogency of the original. His sensitivity to words made him an excellent terminologist, and his work prepared the ground for most modern philosophical terminology. Cicero is important for a verse translation of Aratus, *Phaenomena*, for much rhetorical translation which has not survived, and for his translations of Greek philosophy into Latin. There are discussions of the problems created by Greek terms in Cicero's philosophical writings, the most important being the discussions of Epicureanism in the *De finibus bonorum et malorum* ('The Ends of Good and Evil') II.iv.13–v.15. Of equal importance to the development of translation is Horace, whose discussion of literary imitation in the *Ars Poetica* ('The Art of Poetry') has had an influence on translation out of all proportion to his intent. The traditional theme of translator as rival to the author is discussed at length in Epistle VII. ix of Pliny the Younger (AD 61–112) and *Institutes of Oratory* X.v. by Quintilian (AD c.35–100). The essential point made in both is that one must imitate the author's virtues but still retain one's own individuality in translation.

Drawing on the talent at his disposal, the Emperor Augustus (63 BC–AD 14) set up a translation office as part of the imperial household to assist in administering the Empire. As long as the Roman Empire existed, translation remained important, although after the third century knowledge of Greek became less common in the West. There is no record of translation from languages other than Greek. As the teaching of medicine developed at Rome, an increasing amount of medical and pharmacological trans-lation began to appear, particularly after the fourth century. The Emperor Augustus's translation office in the imperial household seems to have had offshoots in the Eastern provinces. Most of this translation was done by Greeks who had come to Rome as slaves.

The Roman tradition of translation had a lasting effect on the translation theories of the next 1,500 years.

The Christians

Almost from its beginnings, Christianity spread from the Greek and Hebrew world into the rest of the Roman Empire. Formal translation begins with the Bible. The first Latin versions, collectively known as the *Vetus Latina*, date from the second century. There is considerable controversy over whether the earliest Christian liturgies in languages other than Greek were translations of Greek originals. It would seem from the evidence that these early liturgists worked in much the same way as the pre-classical Latin dramatists, by free adaptation of such canonical texts as existed in Greek.

Christians of different cultural traditions soon developed different slants, not necessarily heterodox, on the dogma handed down. This demanded translation, both written and oral. Among the very first of these translations was the important mystical tract, *Shepherd of Hermas*, translated during the second century from Greek into Latin. It is followed by a stream of biographies of saints and other doctrinal work, including Latin versions of the early Creeds, important not only as prayers but also as statements of belief. There seems to be very little from languages other than Greek. The extreme literality of these early Latin documents carries over from the Jewish ideas on the creative power of the Word (Kelly 1979: 69). But it would be a mistake to put this down completely to intellectual tradition: many of these early translators were uneducated. When they found translation necessary, they worked according to the still dominant assumption that word equals thing.

The emancipation of Christianity under Constantine in 312 allowed Christian culture to mature. Consequently, it acquired a scholarly tradition based on Classical education systems, with the result that the Christian Latin West continued the pagan tradition of learning from the Greeks. The number of juridical documents and Greek doctrinal texts translated into Latin increased, and these were often anonymous. The late fourth century and the early fifth are in many ways Rome's second classical period, centred on Rome and North Africa. It seems fairly certain that the Imperial Translation Office founded by the Emperor Augustus was still in operation, and something similar was taking shape in the Papal administration. From the early fourth century, a very skilled band of translators was centred on Rome and its schools. They were philosophers and theologians who took translation from what was going on in Greek as necessary to their enterprise. Among the most important of these are the philosopher Marius Victorinus (c.275–362), Rufinus (340?–416) – an enthusiast for Origen, who had a famous quarrel with Jerome, the philosopher Marius Mercator (c.400–50), and a large number of anonymous churchmen.

The Christian tradition culminates in the work of St Jerome (Eusebius Sophronius Hieronymus c.342–419/420), whose *Vulgate*, undertaken at the direct order of Pope Damasus, dominated biblical scholarship until the Reformation and is only now being displaced as the official version of the Catholic Church. Jerome was born of Christian parents at Strido, Dalmatia, and went to school in Rome. There, his teacher was the great grammarian Aelius Donatus. In 365 he was baptized and began studying theology at Trier, then second capital of the Western Empire. After going to a hermitage in the Syrian desert in 374, he was ordained priest at Antioch, and then, following the ancient Roman tradition, he studied at Constantinople under the Christian teachers Gregory of Nazianzen and Gregory of Nyssa, two of the greatest of the Greek Fathers. On his return to Rome, he attracted the notice of Pope Damasus and in 382 became his private secretary. Between 380 and 420 he produced a huge number of miscellaneous translations covering Church administration, monastic rules, theology and letters. Jerome is known as a first-class if somewhat rigorist and quarrelsome theologian, probably the most brilliant scholar of his time. He translated widely from contemporary Greek writers in a fairly classical style. His own thought on translation as expressed in letters and prefaces follows classical rhetorical precedent very closely. But his biblical style harked back to the early Christian literal style. He seems to have been the first to use truth (*veritas*) as a critical concept. His first concern being accuracy of the source text, he set about producing a critically accurate Greek text for the New Testament and, once this was established, he revised the traditional Latin lightly. For the Old Testament he went to the Hebrew, actually asking a friendly rabbi to guide him through the Hebrew text (*hebraica veritas*). Jerome cast doubt on the Old Testament books extant in Greek only, an attitude later to be taken up by Luther. But even Jerome soon ran into trouble. The correspondence between him and Augustine is peppered with St Augustine's warnings about religious innovation and pastoral difficulties caused by 'changing' familiar texts. To this, Jerome replies that God is on the side of the scholar (Kelly 1975).

Roman translation comes to an end and medieval translation begins with Manlius Anicius Severinus Boethius (AD 480–524), who came from a senatorial family that had become Christian quite early. Following a distinguished public career under the Ostrogothic emperor Theodoric, Boethius was imprisoned on trumped-up charges and died under torture in 524. He is most famous for his *De consolatione philosophiae*, which had a profound influence on the Middle Ages. The intellectual climate of the Middle Ages can be said to have been born of his Latin translation of Aristotle, begun early in his career. His well-known translations include most of Aristotle's *Organon*, Porphyry's *Isagoge*, and the *Geometria*, a rather free translation of Euclid's *Elements*. Boethius is at once last of the classical Romans and first of the Medievals. He lived during a period very much like our own, in which the social shape of the world was changing fast and political, intellectual and religious norms were being transformed. He intended to leave Latin versions of most of the great philosophers, so that when the world came to its senses, civilization could be rebuilt. Boethius is notable for his uncompromising espousal of literality. Though his stand owes much to Jerome's ideals of truth in translation, he harks back to the medical translators of the time of Cicero. Their literality had been condemned by Cicero and his kind, but their rhetorical training had made them aware that different topics demanded different styles, and that this spilled over into translation (Chadwick 1981: 123–41).

The Middle Ages (fifth to fifteenth centuries)

Principles of Latin translation

In practice, Jerome's method of translating the Bible proved more influential than the methods he used, and advocated, in other types of translation. Together with Boethius, he set the tone for translation into Latin. Literary translation with its rhetorical, poetic imperatives had disappeared, and translation was now in the hands of philosophers and theologians. And as scientific language lends itself naturally to Platonist ideals, the goal soon became truth in Seneca's sense: conformity between language, concept and thing. Literal translation was generally seen as the way to truth, though there were a few protests from those trained in ancient rhetoric, for example Pope Gregory the Great.

As the Western Roman Empire crumbled, the sense of urgency in the work of Boethius continued to grow. Cassiodorus (480?–550?), a Roman senator, founded the Vivarium, a monastery specializing in philosophical and theological translation from Greek. He intended to carry on Boethius's work, as far as it was possible. The main peculiarity of the work done in the Vivarium was its anonymity. The best known of the named translators of the period is Dionysius Exiguus (d. 556), who was on the fringes of the Vivarium and who specialized in contemporary theology (Berschin 1988: 74ff.). The most pressing task of Latin translators remained that of keeping in touch with the Greek East, which, as yet, had not suffered the social collapse of the West. The language of the Church Councils was still Greek: the various collections of Council minutes provide a record of the translation work that kept the Western Church in contact with the East.

A Greek monastery whose task was to liaise with Constantinople is attested in Rome in AD 649. Notable translators include Pope Zacharias (741–52), who translated Gregory the Great into Greek, and Joannes Scotus Erigena (c.810–c.877) whose *Periphysion* was at the centre of the Pseudo-Dionysian tradition in the West. Until the ninth century, Ravenna and Naples were centres of Greek studies with well-known schools of translation. Ravenna was particularly active in liturgical work. And until the thirteenth century, the Greek community of Sicily were active in administrative and religious translation; Sicily was still largely a Greek community ruled by speakers of Latin (Weiss 1950). Because there was a Greek presence in every part of the north coast of the Mediterranean, we find translation in Spain, for example the *Vitae Patrum graecorum* translated by Paschasius in 570 and *De ortu et obitu Patrum* translated by Isidore of Seville, both from Greek originals. Merovingian and Carolingian Gaul had a fund of expertise in Greek too, necessary for maintaining close diplomatic relations between France and the East, including marriage alliances.

One of the most important figures in the ninth century was the papal librarian, Anastasius Bibliothecarius (800?–879?). His major translations revolve around the Councils of the ninth century and the increasing tensions between East and West. He also did some translation of theology. He was known as a skilled translator, but his work does tend towards literality, without however doing violence to Latin style. He is also noted for a number of letters on translation practice (Kelly 1975). Translation of Greek conciliar documents ends about the fifteenth century with the final hardening of position, when the West withdrew its monasteries from Constantinople. The last of this stream of translators was Cardinal Bessarion (1403–72), a delegate of the Greek Church who changed sides and finally settled in Venice in the early fifteenth century. There was also some attempt at translation from vernacular languages into Latin during that period. The *Salic Law*, for instance, began as a German text in the ninth century, and was then translated into Latin. It underwent a number of retranslations back and forth after that.

By the eighth century, the Muslims had created a brilliant civilization with a number of schools and research centres at Baghdad, Basra, Toledo, Seville and Sicily. Through contact with the Greek world, they instituted an important programme of translation from Greek philosophy and physical science into Arabic (see ARABIC TRADITION). These translations were then commented on by a large number of scholars, including Averroës, Avicenna, al-Gazali and Alfarabi. Beginning in the eleventh century, philosophers and scientists from the West worked and studied in the Muslim East and came back with Latin translations of the Arabic versions of Greek philosophers, and of Arabic commentaries on them. The Arabs, at this point, were known primarily for advanced medicine. The substantial translation movement from Arabic into Latin was initiated by Constantine the African, who, late in the eleventh century, settled in the monastery at Monte Cassino after studying in North Africa. He specialized in the medical works of Galen. Constantine was followed by Bishop Alfanus of Salerno, who extended the field to Pythagoras, Plato, Aristotle and Hippocrates. During the twelfth century, most scientific and philosophical translation from Arabic into Latin was done in Spain and southern France. There arose a general pattern of cooperation or even collaboration between Christian and Arab. This was at the root of the formation of the School of Toledo, supposedly founded by Archbishop Raymond (1125–52). The best-known translators of this group worked under Raymond's successor, Archbishop John, for example Dominicus Gundisalvi, John of Seville, Gerard of Cremona (1114–87) and Peter of Toledo, all of whom translated Aristotle and the Arab commentators, Averroës and Avicenna. There were many translators working outside Toledo, for example Hermann of Carinthia, Plato of Tivoli, Adelard of Bath, and Michael Scot; the latter was working as late as 1217. A couple of Latin versions of the Qur'ān were also prepared during this period.

Aristotle and other Greek philosophers were introduced into the universities of the twelfth and thirteenth centuries through Latin versions of the Arabic translations. Jourdain (1843) gives a full list. Inevitably, the incursion of Aristotle in Arab dress caused intense disquiet in orthodox circles, and Aristotle was banned in several major places as a pagan influence. Aristotelians replied by translating directly from the Greek texts. The greatest of the twelfth-century translators from the Greek was James of Venice (fl. 1125–50). He was responsible for completing the Latin version of Aristotle's *Organon*, the *Physics*, *Metaphysics*, *De Anima*, and *Parva Naturalia*. The only Latin versions of Plato came

from Henricus Aristippus, whose *Meno* and *Phaedo* appeared in the late 1150s.

Two northerners stand out as important translators of this period. Robert Grosseteste, bishop of Lincoln and probably first chancellor of Oxford, translated the *Nicomachean Ethics* (1246?) and the *De Caelo*. He also translated a number of Greek commentaries on Aristotle, particularly those of Simplicius. Even more important was the Flemish Dominican, William of Moerbeke (1215?–86), who revised a number of the known translations of Aristotle and added to the Latin canon the *Politics* and the *Poetics*. Among the Greek commentaries of Aristotle, he translated Alexander on the *Meteorology* and the *De sensu*, Ammonius on the *De interpretatione*, Simplicius on the *Categories* and the *De Caelo*, and Themistius on the *De Anima*. In the Dominican schools of philosophy and theology, the Moerbeke versions replaced most others (D'Alverny 1982).

The Renaissance (fourteenth to sixteenth centuries)

In translation as in other matters relating to Classical traditions, the Renaissance was a time of rethinking, not a time of discovery of the past. Because literature was 'philosophy joined to eloquence' as Cicero had taught, Renaissance translation theory followed Ciceronian norms, and Horace's *Ars Poetica* (134–5) suffered a radical rereading, cf. Ben Jonson's translation:

> For being a poet, thou maist feigne, create,
> Not care, as thou wouldst faithfully translate,
> To render word for word.

In principle, literality here precludes fidelity: in Horace's original the distinction is not as clear cut.

Humanist translation begins in the great mercantile states of fourteenth-century Italy, in particular Florence and Venice. From the beginning of the fourteenth century, these cities welcomed Greek scholars fleeing the Turkish advance into the Byzantine Empire. They encouraged them to set up schools and built a classical culture around them. For the translator, patronage was essential, because it made possible the building of great libraries and the financing of scholarly searches of medieval libraries for classical manuscripts, both Latin and Greek.

One of the most important schools was that founded by Manuel Chrysoloras (1350–1415) in Florence. Because such schools were essentially philosophy schools with high respect for rhetoric, the translators coming from them were basically philosophers. The first humanist version of Aristotle was by Leonardo Bruni Aretino (1369–1444), whose 1423 version was prefaced by a pugnacious updating of Cicero's translation principles (Kelly 1979: 83). It was first printed in 1498. He also translated some Plato, the history of Xenophon, and the sermons of Basil the Great. In the 1460s, Marsilio Ficino (1433–99) made what was to remain the basic humanist Latin version of Plato. It was first printed in 1482. Other translators of Plato and Aristotle included Georgio Valla (1430–99), Theodore Gaza (1400–78) and Angelo Poliziano (1454–94). Translators of philosophy also translated medicine and science, often printing Latin and Greek on facing pages. Both Galen and Hippocrates were translated by Nicolo da Reggio (1280–1350). As the Humanist movement spread outside Italy, so did translation from Greek. One of the best-known translators of this early period was the Englishman Thomas Linacre (1460–1524), who specialized in Galen and prepared the ground for medical training in England.

Technical and literary translators were often the same people, as stylistic training did not privilege one genre over another. As well as the philosophical and religious texts mentioned above, Leonardo Bruni Aretino, for example, also translated Homer into Latin. Among this first wave of humanists were Lorenzo Valla (1405–51), Georgius Trapezuntius (1395–1472), and Poliziano, all of whom translated history, literature and the Greek Fathers.

Grammar and literary theory were of intense interest. Longinus, *On the Sublime*, was frequently translated (Weinberg 1950; Costa 1985). It is essential to remember that, at first, Latin translation was embedded in the Middle Ages. By the 1520s the standard of Latin had become less reminiscent of the late medieval style found in people like Linacre or Thomas More (1478–1534). Most of the great vernacular

translators, like Etienne Dolet (1509–36) and Melanchthon (1497–1560), produced Ciceronian Latin versions of Greek works. Publishers, like Froben of Antwerp and the Estienne family of Paris, flourished as editors, and even did some translation of their own.

This second wave of translators did not ignore science. Nor were they any more specialized than their predecessors. Typical of these Humanist scientists was Johann Hagenbut (Joannes Cornarius; 1500–58), Dean of Medicine at Jena. He was a prolific translator from the Greek. Cornarius is most famous as a medical writer, his translation of Hippocrates (1546) being his best known. Among his versions are the complete works of Basil the Great (1540), some Plato, some Galen and some Synesius. In mathematics, the Boethius translation of Euclid's *Elements* had several modern versions to compete with. The most important of these was that by Federico Commandino (1509–75), retranslated many times into modern languages. Commandino's works cover the whole range of Greek mathematics, including the *Conics* of Apollonius of Perge (1566), some Archimedes and some Ptolemy. Another influential translator of mathematics was the German Jesuit, Christophe Clavius (1537–1612). His Euclid appeared in 1574 and was followed by various books on calendar reform. By 1600, practically the whole of Greek science and medicine had been translated into Latin.

At a time when most poets were *poetae utriusque linguae* ('poets of both languages'), translation between the vernaculars and Latin became very common. It began in the time of Francisco Petrarch (1304–74), himself both translator and translated. As Italy was the centre of European culture, this sort of translation came about pretty casually as a compliment paid by one writer to another. Leonardo Bruni Aretino, for instance, translated Boccaccio's *Decameron* into Latin in about 1400. Probably the most influential translations were those of Machiavelli, done in the 1560s by Sylvestro Tegli (fl. 1590).

In England, Bartholomew Clerke (1537?–1609) translated Castiglione's *Il Cortegiano* into Latin, with a series of prefaces illustrating how England had come of age. At that time, hardly any English literature had been translated into Latin, apart from religious literature: there was some Chaucer translated by Sir Francis Kynaston. There is a full discussion of this issue in Binns (1990). France, however, translated its poets freely, in particular the poets of the Pléiade. Most of the translators remain anonymous. There was little activity of this type elsewhere in Europe (Briesemeister 1985).

The Bible

Of more immediate interest, because of its polemical value, was Bible translation. The humanists did have considerable qualms about the quality of the Latin in the *Vulgate* and there were well-founded doubts about the Greek text. Erasmus (*c.* 1466–1536) published a Greek text of the New Testament with his own Latin version in 1519. There followed a Latin version by Santi Pagnini (1528) which remained studiously neutral and literal. His Old Testament was done from the Hebrew, not the Greek. The next Latin version of the Bible, by Sebastian Münster of Basle (1535), was in better Latin: he took the Old Testament from the Hebrew and reprinted the Erasmus New Testament. These literal Bibles lost ground before the Zurich Bible of 1543, a squarely Protestant version edited by Leo Jud. In 1551 another Reformer, Sebastian Castellio, produced a Bible in almost Classical Latin. The most important of the Latin Bibles was by Theodore de Bèze, successor to Calvin. Though a Bible of immense scholarship, it soon acquired a reputation for twisting the biblical text to the dictates of Calvinism. The last of the Reformation Latin Bibles was that of Tremellius and Junius (1571). Among Latin versions of minor interest is the New Testament in verse by John Bridges, Bishop of Oxford (1620).

The Age of Reason (1600–1750)

In general, Humanist norms of translation remained in vogue, and translation into Latin was spared the excesses of the free translations current in France and England. This period is also notable for the appearance of bilingual Latin dictionaries. In England, one of the most extensive was by Adam Littleton, which included an English–Latin section. Similar dictionaries came out in other European countries. There were also a series of verse dictionaries, following

in the tradition of the humanist stylistic handbooks or *Elegantiae*. They culminated in François Noël's *Gradus ad Parnassum* (1755).

Technical translation

To a large extent, the Ancient Greek writers were still relevant. Euclid's *Geometry* was translated several times: in England in 1650 by Isaac Barrow, Professor of Greek and then Mathematics at Cambridge, and in 1703 by David Gregory, a member of Newton's circle. John Wallis, a member of the Royal Society, translated Archimedes in 1676. There were many versions of Hippocrates, most of them anonymous. The best known was made in 1717 by John Freind, a Royal physician, plainly for the instruction of medical students.

As an important centre of publication, free of censorship, Amsterdam had its own group of jobbing translators. These were not bound by any law of copyright, and translated all the latest work in all disciplines. Geneva seems to have had a similar group of scientific translators, and there was always the unemployed university graduate willing to free-lance anonymously. But the most important translations came from practitioners who saw translation as part of their job of publicizing the latest theories and research. Frans van Schooten, who translated Descartes' *Géométrie*, is a good example.

As vernacular languages began to compete with Latin, translation into Latin took on a rather desperate importance. There is a whole range of innovative works in alchemy, for example the works of the mythical 'Basil Valentine', that began life in a vernacular and gained an international reputation in Latin. Partington (1961) gives lists of significant translations. Scientists began writing in their own languages in the seventeenth century, with consequent difficulties for international distribution. Henry Oldenbourg, the Secretary of the Royal Society, established a custom of translating all foreign correspondence into Latin for publication in the *Philosophical Transactions*, and kept a watching brief over the standard of Latin in Continental translations of work from the Royal Society.

Pirating was a problem. To overcome it, Descartes had one of his friends, the Duc de Luynes, translate his French works for international distribution. His English contemporary,

Robert Boyle, after being translated without his permission by translators working for de Tournes of Geneva, arranged to be published simultaneously in English and Latin through Oxford presses. His example was followed by the philosopher Thomas Hobbes and later by Isaac Newton, on the rare occasions when Newton published in English. All of these authors kept very strict control over their translators. Newton's translator was a pupil, Samuel Clarke, who is also notable for an important Latin version of Rohault's *La physique* (1697), which became the prescribed text for Physics at Cambridge.

After 1700, scientific translation into Latin became sporadic. At times it was necessary, and Leeuwenhoek's Dutch books on the microscope were translated for the international market as were books on diet by the Scottish physician George Cheyne. Translation of scientific material into Latin ceased about 1750.

Religious translation

What religious translation there was during that period tended to remain technical. True, there were versions of the Anglican *Book of Common Prayer* and of the Lutheran Service, and Latin versions of vernacular spiritual writing found their way into the Catholic breviaries. But more typical of the period was the immense Old Testament with a Latin translation facing the Hebrew text by Charles Houbigant (1686–1783), France's finest Hebraist (1753). This is a study aid for the Old Testament containing commentary, translation and a justification of Houbigant's methods.

Literary translation

The bulk of translation into Latin was in verse following strictly Classical norms, and some very fine work was done. There were few Latinists of any note who specialized in translation, and most recognized poets tried their hand at Latin verse.

France is relatively typical of the Continental pattern. Training in Latin composition and translation was in the hands of the Oratorians, the Jesuits and the universities. A favourite author was La Fontaine, whose *Fables* were translated in full by the Oratorians, Modeste

Vinot (1672–1731), Pierre Tissard (1666–1790) and Jean-Baptiste Giraud (1702–76). Tissard and Vinot also translated Malherbe's Ode on Louis XIII's siege of La Rochelle (Lallemand 1888). Between 1669 and 1700 there was a steady stream of Latin versions of Nicholas Boileau-Despreaux's satires and letters. Notable among the otherwise obscure bunch of translators are Charles Rollin (1661–1741) and Michel Godeau (1656–1736), who had both been rectors of the Sorbonne. Fénelon's *Télémaque* was translated several times into Latin late in the seventeenth century, the most famous version being that of Etienne Viel (1737–87). Another version worth mentioning is that by Joseph-Claude Destouches (1764; see Vissac 1862). The rise of philology as a discipline in Germany was reflected by a spate of original composition, with a few lyrics by such as Goethe being translated into Latin.

The task of assessing the extent of translation into Latin in England is complicated by the immense Latin production of recognized poets such as Abraham Cowley. There are many passages translated from English or other languages in these Latin poems. Andrew Marvell also translated much of his own English work into Latin. As translation was accorded more respect then than it is now, translated pieces appear in the collected works of recognized Latin poets such as the Scot John Leech, who lived in the first half of the seventeenth century.

The major poet translated during that period was John Milton. A certain William Hogg translated a large proportion of Milton's major poetry into Latin in the 1670s and 1680s. This included *Paradise Lost*, *Comus* and *Lycidas*. Other translators of Milton included Thomas Power – Mathematics don at Trinity College in Cambridge – a translator known only as J. C., and a Mr Bold. John Dryden's *Alexander's Feast* was translated by George Bally in 1753 and his *Absalom and Achitophel* was translated by George Atterbury, later Bishop of Rochester, and Francis Hickman in 1682, and by William Coward, a somewhat notorious physician, in 1723. During the eighteenth century, Alexander Pope was widely translated, his *Essay on Man* and *Essay on Criticism* appearing in several versions. Among the translators of that period are the poet Christopher Smart, who translated *Ode on St Caecilia's Day* in 1743, and Usher

Gahagan, a classicist who went into coining (i.e. casting counterfeit coins of uncertain weight) after translating the *Essay on Criticism* in 1747, and – between his conviction and execution – translated Pope's *Temple of Fame* and *Messiah* in Newgate Prison. Among continental translators is the Dutch classicist Gotlieb Am-Ende, who translated the *Essay on Man*. Milton remained popular well into the eighteenth century and was translated in 1741 by Joseph Trapp, who had made his name in translations from classical languages, and by William Dobson, whose *Paradise Lost* came out in 1750.

1750 to the present

Paradoxically, as Latin ceased to be an international language and became a learned recreation, classicists came to know more about Roman composition techniques. Thus, as in Classical times, translation into Latin was governed more by ancient rhetorical practice than by contemporary translation theory.

Because Latin remains a working language for the Roman Catholic Church, translation is a fact of administration, particularly in the day-to-day running of diplomacy, and the Church at large. There is also some translation done for liturgical purposes, particularly in the compilation and revision of the Roman Breviary, as well as some translation of the Bible into Latin, most of it unofficial. A short-lived version of the Psalter (1945) was even used in the Breviary for about 25 years.

Literature

Bradner (1940) gives a fairly complete list of anthologies of Latin poetry from English sources, without systematically noting which anthologies published by the English public schools (particularly Eton and Westminster), Oxford and Cambridge admit translations. Translations gradually displace original work in the *Musae Etonienses* (1755, 1795) and the *Lusus Westmonasterienses* (1863–7). From the universities, the *Anthologia oxoniensis* (1846) contained a very large proportion of translations; the last nineteenth-century edition (1899) was almost entirely translations. Its Cambridge counterpart, *Arundines Cami* (1841), consisting entirely of

translations, went through six editions in twenty-five years. The prefaces of these anthologies are important statements of principle. Most classicists of any importance can be found among the translators published. Perhaps the greatest of nineteenth-century English translators into Latin was George Lyttelton, Fourth Baron of Frankley (1817–76), known for translations covering most English poets of the seventeenth and eighteenth centuries. The French Latinists' fascination with Boileau lasted until well into the nineteenth century, with versions of the *Art poétique* being published in 1820 by J. A. Chambonnet and in 1822 by J. J. Laval, and versions of *Le Lutrin* in 1846 by Dalidou and in 1824 by Laval.

In contemporary times, translation into Latin has become more and more of a learned game, typified by the *Liber quintus Odarum Q. Horati Flacci* (Horace, Odes V), translated by A. E. Godley, Ronald Knox, Rudyard Kipling and others in 1920. This is a collection of Latin versions of poems by Kipling, with a preface satirizing the classical profession. Other noteworthy translations of this type are Alexander Lenard's *Winnie ille Pu* (from the English original by A. A. Milne, tr. 1961), *Carruthers' Alicia in Terra Mirabili* (tr. 1967) and *Domus in Angulo Pui* (from the English original by Lewis Carroll), and L. G. Kelly's *Prorsus Taliter* (from the English original by Kipling, tr. 1985). On the continent, Auguste Haury's excellent Latin version of St Exupéry's *Le Petit Prince* appeared in 1961. But in Germany, as in Britain, the preference is for verse translation, usually short lyrics. These follow the great philological tradition of German universities, filtered through the Romantic movement of the late eighteenth and early nineteenth century. One important development in the early twentieth century is the rise of composition clubs, where a passage is proposed for a meeting, and the members gather to discuss their versions.

The retrenchment of Classical Studies after the Second World War occasioned various measures. The most important was the founding of periodicals such as *Latinitas* in Rome, *Vita Latina* in Avignon, and *Hermes Americanus* in Danbury, USA, all of which contain translations. Antonio Bacci, one of the best Latinists in the Vatican, worked on coining Latin words for twentieth-century innovations; his dictionary came out in 1963. For the moment, translation into Latin remains the property of the enthusiastic Latinist, but anthologies which contain Latin translations continue to be published.

Further reading
Jourdain 1843; Vissac 1862; Bradner 1940; Weiss 1950; *Cambridge History of the Bible* 1961; Williams 1968; *Oxford Classical Dictionary* 1970; Kelly, J. N. D. 1975; Wardman 1976; Kelly, L. G. 1979; Chadwick 1981; D'Alverny 1982; Berschin 1988; Binns 1990.

LOUIS G. KELLY

Latin American tradition

Like Latin America itself, the history of translation in the subcontinent is both uniform and diverse. This is a reflection of the basic cultural unity which grew out of that paradoxical merging of the Hispanic with the indigenous. Indeed, the most representative figure in Latin American translation, Malinalli Tenépal, is a veritable symbol of this cultural mix. Better known as Malinche, this controversial Aztec woman was among the first interpreters on the American continent to contribute to the process through which the peoples of the so-called New World enriched the knowledge and ideas of the Old (see Mirandé and Enríquez 1979).

Conquest (1492–1533)

When Columbus first arrived, about 1,000 languages from around 133 language families were spoken in America. The main ones were Aztec (with over twenty dialects) in Mexico and North and Central America; Maya-Quiche and Nahuatl in Mexico and Central America; Chibcha on the Colombian plateau; Carib in the Antilles and Venezuela; Tupí-Guaraní in Paraguay, Uruguay and northern Argentina; Aymara and Quechua in Ecuador, Peru and Bolivia; and Araucan in Chile. Despite the lack of historical evidence, there can be no doubt that substantial contact between the various

tribes took place, which in turn implies the existence of interpreters.

Interpreters were widely used from the very beginning of the Conquest, since the Spanish authorities and the Native Americans had no understanding of each other's languages. Indirect evidence can be found in the large number of terms by which interpreters were known, such as *lenguas, lenguaraces, farautes, trujumanes* and (in the case of Nahuatl) *naguatlatos*.

The Spanish monarchs took great pains to encourage their new subjects to learn the European language, issuing a stream of edicts to the effect that the Native Americans should be taught to read and write in Spanish. A 1550 law, for example, ordered sextons to teach the language to native children. However, such commands fell on deaf ears, both during this and later periods, because the evangelization process was carried out in the indigenous languages. The situation remained unchanged even when a 1770 royal edict, issued against the wishes of the missionaries, outlawed the Native American languages.

Thus, in practice the indigenous languages continued to be the vehicle for evangelization and oral contact, while Spanish (or Latin) was invariably used for written documents. The oldest translations printed on the American continent are – not surprisingly – religious works: in Mexico, *Breve y más enjundiosa doctrina cristiana en lengua mexicana y castellana*; and in Lima, a similar doctrinal text in Spanish, Quechua and Aymara.

The interpreters

It was appreciation of the important role interpreting would play in the Conquest that led Columbus to take two interpreters on his first voyage: Rodrigo de Jerez had spent some time in Guinea, while Luis de Torres supposedly spoke Hebrew, Chaldean and Arabic. They were obviously unable to use their foreign languages on the American continent. This initial experience made the colonizers aware of the need to train interpreters, and Columbus took ten natives back to Europe precisely so that they could acquire knowledge of the Spanish language and culture, a policy he maintained throughout future voyages. On his return to America, Columbus was accompanied by two interpreters, Alonso de Cáceres and a young boy from Guanahani (the Bahamas) who was given the name Diego Colón.

Subsequent expeditions followed the same pattern. In 1499 Alonso de Ojeda, Juan de la Cosa and Amerigo Vespucci took captives to serve as *lenguas* (literally, 'tongues'). Ojeda actually married his native interpreter and guide, Isabel. In 1518 Juan Grijalba took two natives to Yucatán as interpreters, Julianillo and Melchorejo, who had been captured the previous year by Captain Francisco Hernández de Córdoba. Melchorejo also accompanied Cortés on his first visit to Yucatán, along with another native called Francisco. Natives were captured along the Venezuelan coast by Admiral Vicente Yáñez Pinzón and taken to Santo Domingo for service as interpreters on future expeditions. Thus the first generation of Latin American interpreters were mainly natives who were captured and then taught Spanish. However, mention should also be made of those Spaniards who arrived on the early voyages and for various reasons ended up living among the indigenous tribes. Several of these eventually acted as interpreters, some after being recaptured and pressed into service, others reuniting voluntarily with the conquest group. Whether Native American or Spanish, these pioneering interpreters played an important part in the initial encounter between the two cultures.

Central America and the Antilles

It is reasonable to assume that interpreters were as important to Cortés as the warriors from Tlaxcala and the other allies who eventually enabled him to conquer Mexico. Bernal Díaz de Castillo (in Rosenblat 1990: 78–9) mentions that Cortés employed as many as three interpreters at one time: he would speak in Spanish to Aguilar, who would then translate into Maya for the Yucatec natives; Malinche would interpret from Maya into Nahuatl for the Mexican tribes; and Orteguita, a Mexican boy, would check whether Malinche's words corresponded to what Cortés originally said.

Aguilar (whose full name was Jerónimo de Aguilar) was a Spanish clergyman who survived Juan de Valdivia's shipwrecked expedition in 1511 and was taken captive on the island of Cozumel, where he lived with the Mayas for

eight years before being freed by Cortés; from thereon he accompanied Cortés as his *lengua* throughout the Mexican conquest campaign.

Malinche (also known as Malintzin and Doña Marina) was born in a village near Coatzacoalcos. As a girl she was sold to slave traders and ended up in Tabasco, where she formed part of a group of twenty women given away to Cortés in 1519. One day, when Aguilar was unable to understand the language of some Mexican natives, Malinche started to converse with them, and between the two they managed to establish communication with the natives, Malinche translating from Nahuatl to Maya and Aguilar from Maya to Spanish. This prompted Cortés to promise Malinche her freedom in return for her acting as his interpreter and secretary. She became much more than this – his companion, advisor, secret agent, and the mother of his child. It is widely thought, whether correctly or not, that without her aid, Cortés might not have been able to accomplish his mission of conquering Mexico. To this day, the term *malinchista* is used in Mexico to denote someone who sells out or otherwise betrays a cause.

Mexico, Santo Domingo and Cuba were the centres of gravity for the Conquest. From these positions numerous expeditions set off to the south and the north. Esteban Martín, the interpreter for Ambrosio Alfinger, who was the Santo Domingo agent for the Welser bankers from Germany, was sent to Coro (in Venezuela) with twenty men in 1529. Juan Ortiz, a Sevillian who was captured by the cacique Hirrihigua (or Ucita) at the age of eighteen and spent more than ten years with the natives, became Hernán de Soto's interpreter in the Florida and Texas campaigns up to 1542. Estevancio, the first known black interpreter in the Spanish-speaking world, sailed from Cuba for Florida in 1527 with Pánfilo de Narváez.

Peru and the rest of South America

In comparison with the Mexican campaigns, interpreters did not make such a deep impression on the Peruvian conquest. They did, however, play a vital role in the negotiations between the Inca Atahualpa and his counsellors on the one hand, and the Spaniards Francisco Pizarro, Hernando de Soto, Diego de Almagro and company on the other, negotiations which led to the Cajamarca ambush in 1532 and the execution of the Inca chief a year later. Among the interpreters about whom concrete information exists, pride of place goes to Felipillo (or Felipe) and Martinello, two young natives who accompanied Pizarro and Almagro on their various expeditions to Peru. Born on the island of Puná, Felipillo learnt Quechua in Túmbez from natives who spoke it as a second language, picked up Spanish from listening to soldiers, and was then taken – along with Martinello – to Panama by Pizarro. All historians agree that the interpreting provided by Felipillo of the conditions demanded of Atahualpa (recognition of the Church, the Pope and the Spanish monarchs) was far from faithful: indeed, the message was deliberately rendered in a manner offensive to the Inca king because Felipillo belonged to a rival tribe and was having an affair with one of Atahualpa's concubines.

Another colourful character was a Spanish soldier called Barrientos, a rogue and a thief who was condemned by Pizarro to be whipped and have his ears cut off. Disfigured, he fled southwards to northern Chile, which was then part of the Cuzco empire, where he lived with the natives. Diego de Almagro's expedition found him, transformed into a bearded native, and used him as an interpreter and intermediary.

Equally interesting was Francisco del Puerto, known as Paquillo, the first white interpreter in the River Plate area, where he arrived in 1515 with the explorer Juan Díaz de Solís. He spent ten years as a prisoner of the natives before being commissioned as a guide and interpreter for Sebastián Caboto. In 1526 he fell out with Gonzalo Núñez de Balboa and, by way of revenge, together with the natives prepared an ambush in which several Spaniards were killed.

Among Portuguese interpreters the most famous figure is the adventurer Gonzalo de Acosta, born in Portugal in 1490. He participated from the beginning in the discovery and conquest of the River Plate area and acted as interpreter for Alvar Núñez Cabeza de Vaca and Pedro de Mendoza.

Not a great deal is known about other interpreters in the southern part of the subcontinent during this period, but Arnaud (1950) mentions Antonio Tomás, Enrique Montes, Melchor Ramírez and Jerónimo Romero as interpreters who were active in the regions around what are now Buenos Aires, Montevideo and Asunción.

The colonial period (sixteenth to eighteenth centuries)

Once the various Native American kingdoms had been conquered, one of the main obstacles to evangelization was the diversity of languages in Latin America. Catholic clergymen became aware of the need for a lingua franca which could function as an intermediary between Spanish and the multitude of native languages. By way of solution, missionaries began to propagate the use of 'general languages': by 1584 Nahuatl was spoken from Zacatecas to Nicaragua; by the end of the sixteenth century Quechua spread from Peru down to northwest Argentina and from southern Colombia across to Ecuador and the Upper Amazon; Chibcha (or Muysca) was employed throughout the Colombian plateau; and Guaraní could be heard in Paraguay, the River Plate estuary and a large part of Brazil. Paradoxically, under the Spaniards Nahuatl and Quechua covered a greater expanse of territory than they had at the peak of their own respective empires.

However, leaving aside the necessities of daily communication, it must be pointed out that right up to the end of the colonial period the native languages were neglected by the Spanish authorities, an attitude which resulted in the loss of texts and translations of immense value, not to mention linguistic studies carried out by (among others) Jesuit, Franciscan and Hieronymite missionaries. In fact, since it was inconceivable that the sacraments of the Catholic Church be administered without a minimum of understanding of the basic articles of faith on the part of the convert, and since it was equally unacceptable that confession (for example) be undertaken through interpreters, priests dedicated themselves to a deep study of the local languages and even wrote grammars and dictionaries as well as translating several religious texts, such as breviaries, missals, devotional material, chants and hymns. These documents later fell into disuse, adding to the long list of scholarly works on the Native American languages that were produced during this period and then lost to posterity.

Interpreters and translators

In the course of colonization interpreters acquired an increasingly specific role and status within the emerging Latin American society. According to the *Recopilación de Leyes de los Reynos de las Indias* (Book II, Section XXIX; discussed in Gargatagli 1992), between 1529 and 1630 there were fifteen decrees relating to interpreters, signed by Carlos V, Philip II and Philip III. The first of these, in 1529, classified interpreters as assistants of governors and judges, and prohibited them from requesting or receiving jewellery, clothes or food from the natives. A 1537 law authorized natives to be accompanied by 'a Christian acquaintance' for the purpose of verifying the accuracy of interpretations. Professional status was achieved through the 1563 laws which fixed a salary according to the number of questions interpreted, determined working days and hours, and established how many interpreters should be allocated to each court. In addition, interpreters' obligations were specified in the form of an oath they had to take: 'to interpret clearly and openly, without omission or addition, without bias' (*Recopilación de Leyes de los Reynos de las Indias*; in Gargatagli 1992). Failure to fulfil such obligations meant that an interpreter could be accused of perjury and fined.

Similarly, Cobarruvias's *Primer Diccionario de la Lengua* (1611) offers a fairly detailed – if somewhat idealistic – definition of the interpreter, expecting not only accuracy but also 'Christianity and goodness'.

Translations

According to Leal (1979: 19), in the colonial period 'people read everything they could lay their hands on'. Given this appetite for reading, it was not likely that the circulation of books would be greatly affected by censorship or the activities of the Inquisition. A royal decree in 1531 forbade the exportation to the American continent of fictional works and of any text that impinged on the monarch's prerogatives or that was on the Inquisition's blacklist. The Crown was particularly keen to ban books that dealt with the New World, and most especially those written by foreigners. Among the most persecuted were the six volumes of the *Histoire*

Philosophique et Politique des établissements et du commerce des Européens dans les deux Indes by Guillaume Raynal, published in Amsterdam in 1770. But despite censorship this book appeared in thirty-eight editions before 1830 and circulated from Mexico to the River Plate, both in the French original and in the 1784 Spanish adaptation by Almodóvar del Río.

Such translations, together with the relatively free circulation of all types of books, contributed to the establishment of Spanish as the lingua franca in Latin America. However, books tended to lead rather ephemeral lives in colonial America. There were several factors that worked against the production and publication (and therefore the translation) of literary works, such as the wars of independence, the exodus of entire families (both Spanish and native) and the destruction of libraries, convents and public buildings. Indeed, it should come as no surprise that books were difficult to preserve in the colonial period in the New World since relatively few documents survived this epoch in Spain itself.

The disappearance of so many valuable texts appears at first sight to be a paradox, given that printing presses were installed early on in Mexico (1535) and Lima (1583), and that universities were soon founded in Santo Domingo (1538), Mexico (1553), Lima (1555), Bogotá (1580) and Quito (1586). But the determination of the authorities to control the written word at times reached fever pitch, as when the First Council of Mexico ordered the confiscation of all books of sermons in native languages on the grounds that they contained translation errors, or when grammars and dictionaries were included in the lists of prohibited texts.

At the southern tip of the continent the Jesuits carried out intense intellectual activity in which translation always played a pre-eminent role. Two works, P. Nieremberg's *Diferencia entre lo temporal y lo eterno* and P. Rivadeneira's *Flos Sanctorum*, were translated into Guarani and printed in Paraguay. But when the Jesuits were expelled, nothing remained of the printing presses nor of the works themselves.

Many other valuable translations were made of European works, but perhaps even more important were the translations of texts from the disappearing Native American cultures. For example, Juan Badiano from Xochimilco translated into Latin a book of native herbal medicines, *Libellus de medicinalibus indorum herbis*, which had been written in Nahuatl by a native called Martín de la Cruz in 1552. Around 1530 Fra Bernardino de Sahagún produced, in Nahuatl and Spanish, the *Libros de los Coloquios* or *Pláticas*, which dealt with a series of religious discussions between Franciscan monks and Aztec sages. The same author led a team that wrote, in Nahuatl, the *Historia de las Cosas de Nueva España*, which was based on the accounts of the old people in Tlatelolco and which Sahagún himself then translated into Spanish – a work that took a total of forty years to complete and ran into twelve volumes. A similar translation by Fra Diego de Durán, *Historia de las Indias de Nueva España y Islas de Tierra Firme*, was literally carried out from the Ramírez Codex. Such translations provide Americanists with material as valuable as the Rosetta stone because they facilitate the reconstruction of an almost completely obliterated past.

There are no records of any translations carried out between Native American languages during this period.

Independence and after (1800–1950)

The nineteenth and first half of the twentieth centuries were a prodigious period for intellectual activity throughout Latin America. At first, having shaken off the shackles of the Spanish colonists, nineteenth-century writers and artists were searching for a new identity and tended to look to (non-Hispanic) Europe and North America for models to imitate. The political and intellectual leaders of the emerging nations on the subcontinent generally had the opportunity to travel abroad in their formative years and were accustomed to sharing their ideas with their counterparts from other cultures and languages. Given this context of cultural interchange, it is not surprising that translation was virtually a necessity in post-independence Latin American society, a fact borne out by the volume of translations and the status acquired by some translators.

With some notable exceptions, translations during this period reflect more the genius of the original writer than the creativity of the

translator; in other words they tended to adhere closely to the source text. The predominant themes of the translated texts are related to politics, education, the theatre and literary matters, though religious and military topics also feature to some extent. Translation activity was greatly stimulated by the establishment of newspapers, literary journals, publishing houses and universities. French was the most commonly translated language at the beginning of the nineteenth century, with English gaining in importance later on. Italian and German also received attention, but fewer translations were carried out from Latin and Greek texts.

While the above-mentioned characteristics are to some extent shared by all the countries in the region, the true flavour of the period can only be fully appreciated by looking at some specific cases in more detail.

(a) *In Argentina*, various literary and drama societies, such as the *Sociedad del Buen Gusto del Teatro* (founded in 1817), translated and performed European works. Two of the republic's presidents took measures which had a direct impact on translation activity: in the early part of the nineteenth century Moreno ordered schools to teach an expurgated version of Rousseau's *Social Contract* (with the religious point of view eliminated); and later on Sarmiento imported North American teacher trainers, along with a package of didactic materials. As in other countries on the subcontinent, the rejection of everything Spanish led to increased interest in other cultures, which in turn stimulated translation. In addition, the waves of immigrants arriving on Argentine shores tended to promote cultural interchange and, consequently, translation activities. The major figures in translation in Argentina during this period include Bartolomé Mitre, Leopoldo Lugones, Manuel Galves, Ricardo Rojas and Jorge Luis Borges. Mitre and Borges are also important for their theoretical reflections on translation.

(b) *In Chile*, the history of translation goes hand in hand with that of publishing. The first newspaper to be founded in the country, *La Aurora de Chile* (1812), disseminated the ideas of Rousseau and other foreign philosophers. Government action, such as the creation of the University of Chile in 1842, was also crucial in the promotion of translation. It was quite common that texts destined for pedagogical use would be adapted to the Chilean context rather than translated literally. In the first half of this period French was the source language of the vast majority of texts translated, partly because of the enormous influence of authors like Voltaire, Rousseau, Diderot and Abbot Raynal on the processes of emancipation and formation of the new nation. The principal figures in the field of translation in Chile include Valentín Letelier and Jorge Lagarrigue, as well as Andrés Bello who, though Venezuelan, carried out most of his intellectual activity in Chile. Bello is regarded as one of the most prominent figures of Latin American jurisprudence, education and literature. He is best remembered as the author of the *Gramática de la lengua castellana* (1847) and of poems such as *Silvas americanas* and poetical imitations such as Victor Hugo's *La prière pour tous*. His translations in general (of Berni, Byron, Locke, Voltaire, Boyardo and Dumas, among others) are outstanding. Bello did not believe in translating in a servile manner; he wanted poetry to live in Spanish and in a Latin American tropical environment. He therefore imitated numerous poems of Victor Hugo, among others, taking great liberties in the process. Special mention should also be made of Pablo Neruda for his translation of literary works, including his excellent version of *Romeo and Juliet*.

(c) *In Cuba*, this epoch really starts at the end of the eighteenth century with the creation of the *Papel Periódico de La Habana*, in which a translation of Pope appeared. This was followed by a string of translations of the leading works of the contemporary philosophical and literary schools, translations which soon began to acquire a special Cuban flavour. The list of distinguished Cuban translators is headed by José María Heredia y Heredia, who was born in Mexico in 1803 and who translated Sir Walter Scott, Thomas Moore, Marie André Chenier, Vittorio Alfieri, Jean François Ducis, Voltaire, Roch

and Tytler, always enhancing the original text with his own creativity. In a similar vein, Gertrudis Gomez De Avellaneda (1814–73) translated the works of Victor Hugo, Lord Byron, Lamartine and Augusto de Lima into Spanish. Other notable female translators in nineteenth-century Cuba include Aurelia Castillo De Gonzalez and Mercedes Matamoros, whose translations included Byron, Chenier, Moore, Goethe and Schiller. In the fields of education and science, the major figures were the brothers Antonio and Eusebio Guiteras Font, Esteban Borrero Echevarria and José Del Perojo (who was the first to translate Kant and Fischer directly from German to Spanish). Finally, that major figure in universal letters, José Marti (1853–95), was also a noteworthy translator.

(d) *In Venezuela*, the same patterns can be detected: the predominance of literary translation, the importance of philosophical texts related to the emancipation process, the connection between translation and the pedagogical task of the emerging universities, and the creative freedom of the translator. The best representative of all these traits was undoubtedly the writer, educator and diplomat, Andrés Bello, mentioned above. The poet Juan Antonio Perez Bonalde (1846–92) was responsible for popularizing Heine and Poe in Latin America; his Spanish translation of Heine's *Das Buch der Lieder* has yet to be surpassed. Finally, Lisandro Alvarado (1858–1929) translated the chronicles of Nicholas Federman and – most importantly – Alexander von Humboldt's *Viaje a las regiones equinocciales del Nuevo Continente*.

The present day

Latin America constitutes a large, expanding market for the translator. Apart from the growing number of publishing houses for literary and other kinds of works, future demand for translations is guaranteed by the volume of commercial, industrial and technological exchange required by a community of fifteen countries and almost 400 million people.

In various countries there exists the figure of the public translator, appointed or authorized by the state for legal acts. Beyond this, however, the profession lacks official status throughout the subcontinent, a situation which has given rise to an intense struggle for recognition by Latin American translators and interpreters. This struggle has borne fruit in the creation of associations in practically all the countries of the region. Unfortunately these associations wield little power; indeed, there is a tendency towards proliferation rather than unity. For example, in Venezuela there are four different associations.

Training and research

Although it has been suggested that a translation school existed in Mexico as early as the sixteenth century, the first university programme aimed at forming translators was created in Argentina in 1945. This was followed by similar programmes in Uruguay (1954), Mexico (1966) and Cuba (1968). Then in the 1970s the first translation centres within university faculties in Latin America were founded: the Department of Translation at the Pontificia Universidad Católica de Chile in 1971, and the School of Modern Languages at the Universidad Central de Venezuela in 1974. Since then, several universities on the subcontinent have set up translation schools or departments, most of them offering degrees in translation (but rarely interpreting) after four or five years of study. On these degree courses English is the language with the greatest demand, followed by French and German, with Italian and Russian some distance behind. Portuguese is also now coming into its own in the Spanish-speaking parts of the subcontinent.

Although not specifically dedicated to training, the *Servicio Iberoamericano de Información en Traducción* (SIIT), created by UNESCO in 1986, deserves special mention for its efforts in the collection and dissemination of information related to translation throughout the subcontinent. Another significant development has been the increase, since the 1980s, in the number of national and international events (congresses, symposia and courses) dealing with translation and terminology.

Compared with other parts of the world, Latin America's contribution to the field of trans-lation studies has been rather modest. However, the region is not without its theorists: it is quite common, for example, to find a theoretical justification for the approach adopted to a particular work in the prologue to its translation. More often than not, such contributions have gone unnoticed, but Santoyo (1987) does acknowledge some of these efforts. The most widely recognized Latin American theorists are Miguel Teurbe Tolon from Cuba (1820–70), who was probably the first to write a didactic work on translation – *The Elementary Spanish Reader and Translator* (New York, 1852); Andrés Bello from Venezuela; Octavio Paz, Alfonso Reyes and Francisco Ayala from Mexico; Miguel Antonio Caro from Colombia; and Bartolomé Mitre and Jorge Luis Borges from Argentina. Borges was not only a prolific translator; he also wrote several articles on the translation process (see Gargatagli and Guix 1992). At the risk of over-generalizing, all these writers seem to emphasize mainly the creative freedom of the translator, particularly with reference to literary translations.

There are now quite a few journals dedicated wholly or partly to translation matters in Latin America. These publications are usually produced by the universities, as is the case of *Taller de Letras* (Pontificia Universidad Católica de Chile), *Núcleo* (Universidad Central de Venezuela), *Puente* (Universidad Femenina del Sagrado Corazón in Lima), *Cuadernos* (Universidad de Puerto Rico) and ISIT's *Boletín informativo* in Mexico. The SIIT distributes *Informaciones SIIT* three times a year. In addition, Latin American specialists are now contributing more regularly to international publications, for example to the journal *Meta* (see especially Volume 35(3), 1990: *Translation in the Spanish and Portuguese world*). Most translators' associations also issue regular bulletins.

Further reading
Arnaud 1950; Solano 1975; Santoyo 1987; Rosenblat 1990; de la Cuesta 1992; Fossa 1992; Gargatagli 1992; Gargatagli and Guix 1992; Arencibia 1993; Cabrera 1993; SIIT 1993; Bowen 1994; Vega 1994; Delisle and Woodsworth 1995.

GEORGES L. BASTIN

Translated from Spanish by Mark Gregson

P

Persian tradition

The Persian language spoken today in Iran, Afghanistan and parts of Central Asia is a member of the Indo-Aryan branch of the Indo-European family of languages, and a direct descendant of Old and Middle Persian. For over a millennium this language has been the primary means of daily discourse as well as the language of science, art and literature on the Iranian plateau. Before colonial rule, it was also the language of statecraft, jurisprudence and culture in the Indian subcontinent. At different times in the past it has been the language of literature in parts of the Caucasus and at the Ottoman courts. Today, all Iranians and Tajiks, and a majority of Afghans, use it. In the wake of the Iranian revolution of 1979, the civil war in Afghanistan, the collapse of the Soviet empire, and more recently the war in Afghanistan led by the USA and Britain following the September 2001 attacks on the Twin Towers, Persian is also emerging as the language of a large – and growing – diaspora community.

Translation into Persian has a long and eventful history; it has played an important part in the evolution of Iranian and Iranate civilizations throughout Western Asia and beyond. Information on translation activity before the advent of Islam in the seventh century is scant. In medieval Persia, the interaction between Arabic and Persian was the principal and determining feature of the activity. Following the Mongol and Tartar invasions of the thirteenth through fifteenth centuries, new patterns of interaction emerged between Persian on the one hand and a number of Indian and Turkic languages on the other, making this history even more complex and multifarious. Since the middle of the nineteenth century, translation from European languages has been an integral part of various modernization projects, both in Iran and in the Persian-speaking areas outside it.

Ancient Persian Empire

To the best of our knowledge, Old Persian was brought into the Iranian plateau in the second millennium BC by wave after wave of invading tribes from the Eurasian steppes. In time, it became the language of the Achamenians (559–330 BC), a dynasty of kings who established the largest, most powerful empire in the ancient world. However, Old Persian remained essentially the language of Persis, the south central region of present-day Iran, now known as Fars. Its literature is thought to have been transmitted orally, as we have no written records. We do have the *Avesta*, a religious book in what the scholars have termed Avestan, a language closely related to Old Persian. Even though it was committed to writing in the fourth century AD, *Avesta* contains some Zoroastrian hymns thought to be in older Iranian languages.

In time, Old Persian gave way to other languages, including Parthian and Median. However, Avestan remained the main language of Zoroastrian religion and culture throughout the centuries that separate the Achamenians from the Sasanians. The Achamenian empire was multilingual, and many of its documents were written not only in the various languages of the empire, but in Babylonian and Elamite as well. Still, our information about specific translation activities among these languages is too sketchy to allow any in-depth discussion of trends and patterns.

With the establishment of the Sasanian dynasty in Persia (AD 224–652) and the rise of Middle Persian, also known as Pahlavi, we begin to gain sufficient information about intercultural exchange to afford substantive discussions. We have Middle Persian translations of parts of *Avesta*, albeit in literal renditions which at times make the meaning unclear. Towards the end of the Sasanian period, the number of such translations increased considerably, perhaps as a way of combatting the rise of heretic tendencies within Zoroastrianism. Many surviving translations from Avestan into Middle Persian are religious in nature and contain a heavy dose of Semitic heterograms. Some contain translations from *Avesta* and other books, either in an Avestan alphabet known to us as Pazand, or in the Arabic script adopted in later centuries.

We also know that the Sasanian kings encouraged translations from Greek and Latin. Much historical knowledge, lost to the Persians as a result of the chaos that followed Alexander's conquest in 330 BC, was regained in this way. The Sasanian monarch Shapur I commissioned many translations from Greek and Indian works to be incorporated into collections of religious texts, and Shapur II laid claim to parts of the Roman empire on the basis of descriptions provided by Greek historians.

More importantly, the wide currency of Greek philosophy and sciences in Iran just before the advent of Islam may be attributed principally to translations which have now been largely lost. Early in the sixth century AD, King Khosrow the First, known as Anushirvan (the immortal soul), decreed the establishment of a clinic and medical school in the town of Gondishapur. There, Greek and Syrian philosophers and physicians worked side by side with their Iranian colleagues. The king also commissioned a translation into Pahlavi of *The Panchatantra*, an Indian collection of stories which provided the basis for numerous works in the Persian literature of the Islamic era.

Subsequently, this work formed the basis of many narratives in medieval Europe as well, possibly through later translations or abridged versions in Syriac. Arabic encyclopaedias and chronicles list the names of several significant sources of historical information on the Sasanians and incorporate the information they contained. According to these, early in the seventh century AD many famous Indian literary works had also been translated into Middle Persian. In addition to the above-mentioned *Panchatantra*, which was later modified and expanded into *Kalileh*

va Demneh, these included two of the Sinbad books, among many other tales.

Medieval Persia

In the second half of the seventh century, Islam began to spread over the Iranian plateau gradually but steadily. This marks a unique turning point in the life of the Iranians, not only religiously, but culturally and linguistically as well. The Persian language constitutes the most concrete link between Islamic and pre-Islamic Iranian cultures. It is true that the abandoning of the Pahlavi script – in favour of the Arabic script – resulted in significant linguistic changes. Still, the new script was far simpler and more advanced. In addition, where the Arabic script lacked essentially Persian consonants these were added to it. In short, the adoption of the Arabic script for Persian did not give rise to ruptures as significant as certain modernist reformers have assumed it did.

In the two centuries that followed, a succession of cultured Persians spearheaded a translation effort aimed at preserving pre-Islamic Iranian texts. They translated the most significant Middle Persian documents – literary, religious or otherwise – into Arabic, hoping to preserve the old content in the only garb likely to survive. Rozveh or Ruzbeh, better known by his Muslim name 'Abdollāh Ebn-Al-Moqaffa' (executed about 759), translated the *Panchatantra* and *Khotay-namak* (a collection of mythical legends of Persian kings and heroes) into Arabic. In all likelihood, he is also responsible for the translation into Arabic of accounts of the sixth-century reformist prophet Mazdak, and that of his followers.

Such texts, later translated from Arabic back into New Persian, formed the basis for much of our information about pre-Islamic Iranian culture, particularly its textual tradition. Among the extant Persian texts, the eleventh-century *Siāsat-Nāmeh* (Book on Statecraft), and the twelfth-century *Fars-Nāmeh* (Book about Fars), give a clear impression of being renditions of earlier works in Persian or Arabic. Those earliest texts, now largely lost, were themselves probably translations from Middle Persian. Thus throughout the eighth and ninth centuries, which was the period of Arab domination over cultural and political life on the Iranian plateau, translation activities were motivated by the desire to preserve an ancient civilization; these activities may be credited for what insights we have gained into pre-Islamic Iranian culture.

Persian, spoken throughout the Iranian plateau for over a millennium, has undergone few changes, remaining essentially at the same stage of morphological evolution. The proximity of neighbouring languages which belong to different linguistic families (the stronger influence of Arabic on Western Iran, and Uzbek and other Turkic languages on Eastern Iran), the push and pull of nationalism, and the fifty-year experiment with the Cyrillic alphabet in Soviet Tajikistan (1940–90), have had little effect on the structural ties among its varieties. Semantically, of course, its different varieties reflect complicated processes of linguistic absorption and appropriation. However, none has been substantial enough to create a new language.

Any discussion of the translation tradition in this language must begin with the very complex and multifaceted relationship between Arabic and Persian in the eighth and ninth centuries. It must take note of two parallel trends. The first, already mentioned, consisted of a series of translations made from extant texts into Arabic, later translated back into Persian. The second activity, undertaken by Persian converts to Islam, took the shape primarily of commentaries on the holy Qur'ān. As the word of God, the Qur'ān was considered untranslatable. Persian-speaking Muslims therefore produced important texts to propagate God's message to believers who did not understand Arabic. While technically conceived as commentaries, such texts nonetheless contained much word-for-word translation. Muslim commentators by and large kept the sentence structure and syntax of Qur'ānic verses intact, supplementing them with extensive commentaries. More often than not, such translations produced an effect of estrangement in Persian readers, signalling the alien character of the language in which God had revealed his message.

In addition to the first examples of a budding poetic tradition, the earliest extant documents in Persian include a number of translations. Among these we can count, interestingly, two important documents in scripts other than the

modified Arabic script used for writing Persian: a commentary on Ezechiel in the Hebrew script and a translation of the Psalms in the Syrian script. Besides these, the most significant early examples of non-religious translation into Persian were translations of Arabic works. For instance, the influential *Hodud al-ʿĀlam* (Frontiers of the World), an extremely important early Persian book of unknown authorship, is a translation of parts of Tabari's *History*. As philological documents, such works set the standard of admissibility of Arabic lexicon into Persian. As translations, they provided a model of prose writing in Persian which remained operative for many centuries.

In the tenth through twelfth centuries, translation into Persian gathered tremendous momentum, making available to Persian readers an impressive array of knowledge in fields as diverse as medicine, astronomy, geography, history and philosophy. The climate of religious tolerance and intellectual debate established in Baghdad by some Abbasid caliphs provided a model for local rulers in different parts of Iran, particularly in the northeastern regions of Khorāsān and Transoxiana. Under courtly patronage, works originating in Greek and Latin, Syriac and Aramaic, even Chinese and Sanskrit, began to appear in Persian, often through previous translations in Arabic.

In all these activities, the approach to translation was essentially utilitarian and pragmatic in nature. Translators thought it necessary, important or useful to translate certain works, and they did so efficiently and without much pretension. Typically, texts were subjected to a variety of changes; they were simplified, annotated, abridged, illustrated with pictures and diagrams, amended through sequels, or otherwise altered to suit the specific needs of the patron and the new readership. Translators of secular texts gave more priority to the grammatical features of Persian than had the translators of the Qur'ān and other Islamic texts. As a result, two rather dichotomous approaches to translation gained currency, one considered appropriate to religious and philosophic discourse, the other, freer approach, thought suitable for scientific translation.

Examples of the latter approach are too many to enumerate, but two are worth mentioning here. In the 1080s Mohammad b. Mansur of

Gorgān, known as Zarrindast, composed a Persian manual of ophthalmology entitled *Nur al-'Oyun* (Light of Eyes), on the basis of the Arabic work *Tazkerat al-Kahhālīn* (Advice to Oculists) by a scientist known to us as 'Ali b. 'Isā. In order to make it more useful to his local readers, the Persian translator recast the Arabic work in the form of question and answer. He also added much information that came from his own practice in the field of ophthalmic operations. Similarly, when the twelfth-century scholar Abu-Nasr Ahmad al-Qobavi was turning al-Narshakhi's tenth-century *History of Bukhara* into Persian, he updated the work with a sequel. Both works have subsequently been lost; only an extract from the latter, incorporated into another work some years after the author's death, survives.

This approach to translation made a great deal of scientific knowledge available to medieval Persia. Perhaps the best example is *Dāneshnāmeh-ye 'Alā'i*, an encyclopaedic work begun by the famous physician Avicenna and completed by his student Juzjani. It is a compendium of disciplines, more heavily tilted towards the sciences than towards literature and the arts. In a more or less systematic way, it addresses every imaginable sphere of human activity, from astronomy and its various offshoots to philosophy, theology, ethics and mysticism, as well as information about the properties of human and animal bodies, plants and minerals, poisons and antidotes, and numerous divinations and curiosities. Historically, *Dāneshnāmeh-ye 'Alā'i* is the first of many encyclopaedic Persian works which attempt to synthesize existing knowledge, both speculative and utilitarian. Without a translation tradition free from the constraints of attribution and propriety, such works might not have been possible.

As elsewhere in the Muslim world, in medieval Persia Arabic was the lingua franca. Almost all Persian writers and scholars were bilingual; and an extraordinary number of scientists and philosophers continued to write entirely or primarily in Arabic. In addition to the historian Tabari and physician and philosopher Avicenna, three of the greatest Islamic theologians – the Shi'ite Mohammad Tusi (d. 1076), the Sunni reformist Mohammad al-Ghazāli (d. 1111), and the Mo'tazelite Zamakhshari (d. 1144) – who was also a great grammarian and lexicographer

– can be counted among these, as can the jurist and philosopher Fakhr al-Din Rāzi (d. 1209). These men sometimes prepared Persian versions of the works they had written originally in Arabic, or supervised their students in such tasks. This is one reason why the border between translation and original work, as envisaged in that culture, appears blurred to us.

This fluidity enabled medieval Persian scientists and philosophers to be original authors and translators at the same time. The absence of proprietary concerns in medieval times further undermines modern-day efforts to distinguish writing from translation. Acts of borrowing, adaptation and appropriation were undertaken in ways that transcend modern classifications. The corpus of philosophical and scientific works in Persian is replete with bilingual texts or hybrids, as well as those in which text and commentary are in two different languages. There are also numerous texts of an indeterminate character; these may or may not be considered original works with later commentaries or annotated translations. Within the terms of medieval Persia, such works must be assumed to have originated in Arabic unless proven otherwise. They would subsequently be translated from Persian into Turkish, Urdu or Hindi.

Perhaps a trend could be mentioned here: before the Mongol invasions of the thirteenth century, Persian was primarily the language of literature and Arabic mainly the language of scientific inquiry in Western Asia. Medieval Persians, generally writing in Arabic, may be regarded as the custodians and successors of three pre-Islamic traditions in scientific writing: ancient Iranian, Hellenistic Greek and Indian. They frequently translated scientific works from Arabic, adding their own observations to them. Thus Nasir al-Din Tusi (d. 1274) translated the Greek basic manuals of mathematics and geometry, including Euclid's *Elements* and Theodosius's *Spherica* into Arabic, and the astrological judgements of Ptolemy from Arabic into Persian. In each case, he added his own comments to his translations. He also wrote Persian treatises on arithmetic based on Indian works unknown to us.

This makes a second trend visible: in medieval times, Persian was the second most important language of the Muslim world, a position which it has preserved ever since. It is the main language through which Islamic sciences have made their way to Eastern Muslim lands, particularly in the period that followed the Mongol invasion. At that time, many scientific works began to be written originally in Persian and were later translated into Arabic. We can list in this category the astronomical works based on direct observation and recorded on orders from Hulāgu in thirteenth-century Azerbaijan, or under the tutelage of Ologh-bayg, the scholarly ruler of Samarkand in the fifteenth century. The importance of this trend in the evolution of translation activity on the Indian subcontinent cannot be overemphasized.

The post-Mongol era

By the thirteenth century, Persian was becoming well established in India as the language of religious, literary and legal learning and communication. A number of important translations began to be made from Sanskrit and other Indian languages into Persian (see INDIAN TRADITION). Centuries of British colonial rule in India and the ascendancy of Modernism and nationalist ideologies in Iran and elsewhere in the Persian-speaking world have obscured the importance of these works. Still, some of the more important translations of this kind are known to us. They include 'Abdol-'Aziz Nuri-Dehlavi's fourteenth-century translation of an astronomical work by Varahra Mehera (d. 587), a 1587 translation of *Lilavati* (a treatise on arithmetic and geometry by the twelfth-century Indian scientist Bhaskara), and a treatise on algebra, entitled *Vija-Ganita*, which was translated in 1634. Scores of less important translations may also be mentioned, the best known being Najm al-Din Kakuravi's *Resaleh dar Jabr va Moqābeleh* (Treatise on Algebra and Reciprocity, 1814).

An Indian hub of translation activity can be found at the court of Emperor Akbar the Great in the latter part of the sixteenth century. In 1582, Akbar's minister Todar Mal issued a decree making Persian the official government language of the Moghul empire. As a result, Persian came to dominate the Indian subcontinent all the way to Bengal, and a great variety of works of Sanskrit literature were translated

into it. Chief among these were Abdol Qāder Badā'uni's translations of the *Mahabharata* and the *Ramayana* in the 1590s. In time, several significant translations were also made from English, making Persian the gateway to European sciences as well.

For a number of reasons, Persian cultural centres outside Iran became even more important between the sixteenth and nineteenth centuries. The officiating of Shi'ism in Iran in the sixteenth century shifted the emphasis in translation back to religious texts, particularly those of the prophetic tradition and the sayings of the Imams, collectively known as *Hadith*. In particular, *Nahj al-Balāgheh*, a compilation of aphorisms and wise sayings attributed to Imam 'Ali Ebn Abu-Taleb, cousin and son-in-law to the prophet and the first Imam of the Shi'is, emerged as an embodiment of the ideal of eloquence. The sayings contain a variety of rhetorical devices very difficult to maintain in translation. In the expanding network of Shi'i seminaries at Qom, Isfahan and other urban centres of Iran, translating this and similar Shi'i texts into Persian came to be regarded not only as the summit of literary achievement but as a great service to the community.

In India, the approach to translation was markedly different from that which prevailed in Persia. India was a far more multilingual environment than was Persia, and this fact was reflected in approaches to translation as well. Words trafficked more freely between Persian and other languages, and a degree of tolerance emerged towards mixed usages. This in turn gave rise to a divergence between the Persian of Iran proper and that of India and Central Asia. Furthermore, translations were now made into Persian not so much from Arabic but from Indian and Turkic languages, as well as English and Russian. Eventually, various historical developments contributed to divisions among the speakers of Persian. One principal reason, the rise of Shi'ism in Iran, has already been mentioned. British colonialism in India and Russian incursions into Central Asia were no less important. In 1832, the British initiated the process that resulted in the virtual obliteration of Persian from the Indian subcontinent. Similarly, with the fall of Central Asia to Russia in the latter part of the nineteenth century, almost all translation activity in Persian-speaking Central

Asia was realigned with Chaghatay (later Uzbek) and Russian languages.

All this affected translation activities in Persian, seriously undermining the international character of the language. The problem was compounded in modern times by several factors, among them the realignment of Central Asian Persian, renamed Tajiki by the Soviet Union, with Uzbek and Russian languages, as well as the emergence of a language reform movement in Iran which paid no attention to the consequences of its pronouncements and actions for the language as a whole. The result has been a crisis of mutual intelligibility which makes the impressive volume of translations into the modern Persian of Iran of little use outside Iran's borders. Coupled with the fact that in the last century or so no important translation movement has taken shape in Afghanistan or in Persian-speaking Central Asia, the fate of Persian as an international language can be said to stand at a critical juncture at the beginning of the twenty-first century.

The modern period in Iran

A number of developments resulted in a renaissance of translation activity in Iran in the latter part of the nineteenth century. After a century and a half of political instability, the Qajar dynasty (ruled 1795–1925) had returned a semblance of stability to Iranian society early in the century. More or less regular cultural contact with Europe had begun with the dispatch of Iranian students to Europe, adding to the pressing need for inter-governmental contact. Lithograph print had found its way to Persia, bringing in its wake the beginning of the Persian press and a fledgling book industry. All this led to greater familiarity with European languages and a resurgence of translation activity.

The new translation movement was propelled primarily by the perceived need to gain access to European sciences and technology. Anxious to modernize the Iranian army and bureaucracy, the Qajar state followed the dispatching of groups of students to Europe by the establishment of a polytechnic College, modelled after European institutions of higher education. Established in Tehran in 1852 and known as Dār al-Fonūn (House of Techniques), this insti-

tution played a crucial part in modernizing Iran. European teachers were hired to teach a variety of subjects, often with Iranians as their assistants and interpreters. They also prepared a number of textbooks in various sciences which were based largely on European scientific works. Thus, translation and interpreting began to play a crucial part in the evolution of pedagogical processes in modern Iran.

Many early Iranian translators of European works were graduates of Dār al-Fonūn. Chief among them was Mohammad-Hasan Khān, better known as E'temād al-Saltaneh, the last title the court bestowed on him. From 1871 to 1896 E'temad al-Saltaneh headed a new government office called Dār al-Tarjomeh (House of Translation), designed to coordinate government-sponsored translation and interpreting activities. The office was charged with supervising all state-sponsored translation activities. Under E'temād al-Saltaneh's tutelage, many significant European works were made available to Iranians, often from French and frequently in more or less free versions which approached adaptation.

Soon, translation activity was directed towards disciplines such as history, politics and literature and became an integral part of various modernization projects. It was almost always undertaken to make Iranians conscious of their own backwardness, in spite of a glorious past. European orientalists had been studying Persian literature and Iranian history with interest and enthusiasm for over a century, and the Romantics had glorified Persian culture and civilization, particularly of pre-Islamic times. Iranians had to be made aware of these works if they were to strive to regain the glory of their ancient culture.

The new translation movement was at least as significant in terms of its cultural impact as it was of the knowledge it transmitted or generated. Among the mix of works translated into Persian in the last decades of the nineteenth century, one can name Voltaire's historical narratives on Alexander the Great, Peter the Great, and Charles XII, Molière's Le Misanthrope and Le Médecin malgré lui, John Malcolm's History of Persia, as well as works by some of the best-known European authors of the time, including Dumas the Elder, Fénelon, Le Sage, Bernardin de Saint Pierre, Jules Verne and Daniel Defoe.

The availability of such works began to affect all aspects of the Iranian culture, from writing style to the position of women in society.

From the perspective of over a century, late nineteenth-century translations into Persian appear like a curious mix of ideology and fantasy, of fiction and history. However, if we begin to think of the phenomenon in terms of Iran's need for restructuring and reform, we may be in a better position to gauge the part such works have played historically. They made Iranians sorely aware of their backwardness, submitted the culture's assumptions and categories to unprecedented scrutiny, and intensified national desire for alignment with the West. Thus Persian translations of the nineteenth century may be said to have played a unique and significant part in Iran's drive towards modernization.

In terms of aesthetic quality, one work stands out from among all the nineteenth-century translations: Mirzā Habib Esfahānī's translation of James Morier's *The Adventures of Haji Baba of Esfahan*. Written in 1824, Morier's book was bitterly critical of Iranian society and has never been quite accepted by Iranians as the realistic work it is. Esfahānī's 1872 translation from French is unique in many respects. It attempts to indigenize the work through a variety of techniques: colloquialism, the use of a fairly heavy dose of Persian proverbs, and interspersing the work with Persian verse and humour. The strategy was so successful that it soon gave rise to a theory that Morier's work may have been based on a Persian original which was now being offered as a translation. As long as it provided the Iranians with some solace in thinking that the criticism may have been registered by an Iranian, the theory held some sway. More recently, it has been discredited fairly roundly.

By the end of the century, translation had made a considerable portion of European sciences and arts available to Iranians, and literary translation of European works had led to new movements aimed at modernizing Persian literature. Thus, Iran entered the twentieth century with an insatiable appetite for translation brought about by a deep thirst for restructuring its state, society and culture along European lines. Translated accounts of the French revolution played a significant part in driving forth the constitutional movement

(1905–11), and the Persian translation of the Belgian constitution of 1831 served as a draft document for the Iranian Constitution ratified in 1906. Throughout the twentieth century and until the present time, various translated texts of European and American origin – from the laws of nature and rules of etiquette to legal codes, political documents and bureaucratic regulations – have performed similar functions in Iran.

In broader terms, translation has been at the base of a great many philosophical and scientific enquiries, cultural speculations, social activities and political agendas in Iran throughout the modern period. It has been the chief means of introducing Iranians to new ideas, schools of thought and literary trends. It has been considered a necessary component of the drive towards modernity, no less so in the Islamic republic than in the monarchial state which preceded it. As a result, it has been pursued with an enthusiasm and determination unparalleled in the history of the Persian language. Today, almost all important works of Western civilization, from Aristotle and Plato to examples of the latest trends in American or French fiction, are available in Persian translation.

At the same time, translation has at times been viewed as an easy road to fame, if not to fortune, particularly in the social sciences and literature. While it has attracted much talent, it has at times had a negative impact on the evolution of the culture. It has certainly thwarted efforts to explore possibilities of political, social or cultural development which do not fit into Western patterns. Be that as it may, the importance of translation as a cultural activity has encouraged almost all notable intellectuals of contemporary Iran to try their hand at it. Rarely have these intellectuals specialized in fields such as literature or the social sciences. Instead, the impulse to translate seems to follow the search for relevance or the perceived need to buttress or justify one's own position, politically, philosophically or aesthetically.

Still, a distinction can be made between earlier translation activities and those prevailing since World War II. In the earlier period, translation was considered the best way to inform Iranians about the West. Typically, translators conceived of translation as a vehicle to speed up Iran's drive towards modernization. Whether literary, philosophical or historical, they envisioned translation as a vehicle for social or cultural change. In their hands, translation was used primarily as a means of education, and a tool for nation-building and cultural integration. Almost all the major translators of the time – Yusof E'tesām Al-Molk, Mohammad-'Ali Foruqi, 'Abbās Eqbāl Ashtiāni, Sa'id Nafisi, among many others – were concerned essentially with serving the Iranian culture through introducing European cultural achievements to Iranian readers. Almost all forums for disseminating ideas – the book industry, literary and political periodicals, as well as the institutions of higher education at a later stage – included translation-related activities as part of their agenda for acculturating and enlightening literate Iranians. To give only one example, Iranian journals – *Bahār*, *Dāneshkadeh*, *Ermaghān*, *Vafā*, and *Āyandeh*, among numerous others – relied on translation to inform Iranians about the history, politics and current affairs of European nations, with the express desire to propagate them as models for Iranians to follow. In doing so, they helped to bring about a new writing style, new means and methods of communication, and eventually a new literary tradition.

Following World War II, English gradually replaced French as the main European language taught at Iran's secondary schools and universities, as well as the principal medium for translation. At the same time, through a translation effort spearheaded by the pro-Soviet Tudeh Party of Iran, Marxist ideas, particularly in their Stalinist interpretations, began to gain currency in Iran. Soon, the Americans, having wrenched control of Iran from the British, entered the scene as well. By the 1960s translation activity had entered a new phase as competing political forces advanced their separate agendas, in part through translation.

In 1953, The Institute for Translation and Publication of Books (*Bongāh-e Tarjomeh va Nashr-e Ketāb*) was founded in Tehran on the initiative of a young Western-educated Iranian scholar named Ehsan Yarshater. Under the auspices of the royal court, the institute spearheaded a translation effort which resulted in several series of books, including the foreign literature series, the children and young adult series, the Iranology series, and the Persian texts series. Although the institute expanded the scope of translation-based publication substantially, its historic significance lies primarily in the standards it established to ensure authenticity, accuracy and editorial supervision. It also provided a model for other similar ventures, most notably the Franklin Institute of Iran, an American publishing enterprise founded in 1954. Such orgnaizations also tried to persuade the Iranian government to become a signatory to the Geneva Copyright Convention, to set copyright requirements for translations, and to set standards for editing translated texts. These efforts were only partially successful, as Iran saw no benefit in joining the international copyright convention.

Meanwhile, translation had remained a central component of the language learning process, particularly at university level. However, the activity was pursued in fairly traditional ways which were not always conducive to training competent, professional translators and interpreters. The main activity consisted of actual translations, with little discussion of the theoretical underpinnings or the principles governing the actual process of text production. Typically, students would offer their own translations, discussions would ensue, and a text would be suggested as the best possible rendition of a given original.

Through the 1970s, efforts were undertaken at Tehran University, the College of Translation and elsewhere, to introduce a new approach to teaching literary translation from English into Persian and vice versa. Teaching was based essentially on examining existing translations and discussing their relative merits and shortcomings. It also aimed to instil a sense of the comparative grammars of the languages and texts involved. Extensive discussions of the style, diction and context of each text replaced the requirement of text production. Important as it is, translation pedagogy has never been studied in Iran as a crucial component of translation activity.

Early in the 1980s, as part of the Islamic Republican State's efforts to redirect Iran's educational system towards its ideology, a Committee for Translation, Composition and Editing was established at the Headquarters for the Cultural Revolution. This committee seized the occasion provided by the temporary closure of the country's system of higher education to prepare textbooks that would better reflect the state ideology. Areas of knowledge were divided into some thirty different fields and university textbooks, often translated from English or French, were prepared for each field. In this way a series of textbooks, essentially translations and collations of Western works, were produced.

At present, translation pedagogy as well as the practical activity of translation and interpreting are diffuse, with no specific institution setting the agenda or guiding translation-based activities. In 1990, a professional journal called *Motarjem* (*The Translator*) began to be published at Ferdowsi University in Mashhad. This constituted the first attempt at stimulating the academic discourse on translation. The journal offers theoretical observations and practical guidelines for would-be translators. It also features occasional interviews with professional translators and edited texts designed to guide beginners. Its essays range from discussions of computerized and machine translation to the editing of translated texts, etc. Another journal, entitled *Mutala'āt Tarjama* (*Iranian Journal of Translation Studies*), was launched in 2003.

Translation activity continues to form an integral part of all academic studies and professional work involving foreign languages in Iran. It also features prominently as a means of social, cultural and literary communication between Iran and the rest of the world, more so in the light of continued restrictions on trade and travel. It may appear wanting in governing principles and institutional support but it is still a lively cultural activity and likely to remain so for the foreseeable future.

Further reading

Browne 1909–24; Rypka 1968; Storey 1970–72; Husain 1981; Balay and Cuypers 1983; Fouchecour 1986; Yarshater 1988; Karimi-Hakkak 1995.

AHMAD KARIMI-HAKKAK

Polish tradition

Polish is a West Slavonic language, closely related to Czech and Slovak, and ultimately traceable to an ancient language known as Protoslav. The dialects that gave rise to modern Polish cannot be accurately described, as no written records exist prior to the twelfth century. The earliest extant work written in Polish is the religious hymn *Bogurodzica* ('the-one-that-gave birth-to-God'), which dates back to the eleventh century. But while most medieval hymns are translations from Latin, no source text has been found for *Bogurodzica*. Interestingly, however, the title of the hymn is itself a translation of the Old Church Slavonic *bogorodica*, which in turn is a translation of the Greek *Theotokos*, meaning 'God-bearing'. Thus, in a sense *Bogurodzica* may be considered the first recorded translation into Polish.

Christianity made its way to Poland via Bohemia. In the ninth century AD, the Greek missionary St Cyril (BULGARIAN TRADITION) invented the Cyrillic alphabet and, with his brother St Methodius, introduced some Slavonic religious vocabulary into the language. St Methodius later translated the Bible into Slavonic. Many Czech and Slavic religious terms were consequently adopted in church services, but Latin remained the official language of the Catholic Church in Poland. During the Middle Ages, it was the only language used in schools, and the only official language of literature. Many authors continued to write in Latin well into the eighteenth century, but a few began to write in Polish during the Renaissance.

In the sixteenth century, Latin was used by both Church and state as an effective means of communication with what had by then become a highly heterogeneous population. Lithuanian and Ruthenian were spoken in rural areas in the eastern and southern parts of the country; German settlements in the west encouraged the predominance of German in this area; and there were large Jewish communities in most cities. Poland had become a multilingual and multicultural state.

A variety of languages were also spoken at the royal court. The court of the Italian-born Queen Bona Sforza (1494–1557) used Italian, a language which was familiar to the Polish social elite who had studied in Padua. King Zygmunt III (1566–1632) belonged to the Swedish House of Vasa, and his court consequently spoke German. In the seventeenth century, French established itself as the language of diplomacy and soon became the official language of the francophile court of King John Sobieski (1629–96). The subsequent rise of the Saxon House of Wettin towards the end of the seventeenth century brought to Poland a large number of Saxons, while the election of the last Polish king, Stanisław-August Poniatowski (1732–95), resulted in a massive influx of Russians: the king was a favourite of Empress Catherine the Great and adopted a policy of complete submission to the Russians. Every group introduced yet another language and culture into Poland.

Foreign intervention culminated in the partitioning of Poland by Russia, Austria and Prussia in 1795. Poland ceased to exist as a national state and Latin was no longer the official language of this area. The partitioning powers tried to impose their own languages, German and Russian, on the people of Poland. Polish consequently became the language of freedom, a symbol of national identity and integrity. It was to be cherished again as the symbol of resistance almost two centuries later, during the German occupation of 1939–45.

The instability of frontiers and the large-scale forced relocation of the population after World War II resulted in the establishment of an ethnic state, with a few small minorities (German in the west, Lithuanian in the east, and Ukrainian in the south). Today, Polish is practically the only language spoken in the country. In interacting with other members of the international community, the need to rely on translation in the new Polish state is as great now as it ever was in the past.

Languages and texts in translation

The Middle Ages

Little evidence remains of translational and other activities in the early Middle Ages, but the domination of Latin culture is well documented. Although they are not translations as such, the earliest works (historical chronicles written in Latin) show the strong influence of the Old French epic poetry known as 'chansons de geste'. The first known translations are *Psałterz floriański* (St Florian's Psalter), a fourteenth-century collection of psalms translated from Latin, and a number of extracts from the Bible. In the fifteenth century, it was mainly religious hymns that were translated, mostly from Latin, but some translations were also done from Czech and German. By contemporary standards, these translations are extremely free and might therefore be considered adaptations.

There is not much to say about interpreting during this period, but two historical facts are worth mentioning. In 1285, a synod of Polish bishops decreed that all masters appointed to teach in church schools had to know Polish well enough to be able to 'explicate Latin authors to the boys in the Polish language' (Stępień and Wilkoń 1983 (I): 8; translated). Less than a century later, in 1363, a meeting was held in Kraków and attended by several monarchs of medieval Europe. The guest of honour was the King of Cyprus, Pierre de Lusignan, who was visiting the courts of Europe in the hope of finding support for a crusade; he clearly needed interpreters to communicate with the kings and dukes who gathered at the Polish royal court.

The Renaissance: fifteenth to sixteenth centuries

The development of the Polish Humanist tradition began in the late fifteenth century, but its real source was the cosmopolitan court of King Zygmunt I (1467–1548) and his Italian Queen, Bona Sforza (1494–1557). The court attracted artists and scientists, many of them Italian, whose interest in the ancient world and contemporary Italy set the stage for the arrival of the Renaissance. Although some young Polish noblemen chose to study at the Protestant universities of Wittenberg, Zurich or Basel, the majority went to Padua and Bologna; they brought back manuscripts by Italian writers which ushered in a new intellectual climate.

Growing interest in antiquity encouraged Polish authors to look to the literature of the ancient world for inspiration. Similarly, the development of Humanist thought led to the revival of works by the great political writers of the classical era. The adaptation of foreign texts for a wider reading public became an established feature of that period. In addition to Latin and Italian, Greek became an important source language for translation.

Among the earlier attempts at non-literary translation was a rendering of some letters by Theophilactus Simokata, undertaken as an exercise by Nicolaus Copernicus in 1509. But it was not until the beginning of the following century that genuinely professional translations first appeared. Some, like Plutarch's *Treatises*, were anonymous. Others were done by famous philologists who combined a profound interest in the relevant languages with scholarly expertise in the source material. One of the most prominent translators of the time was Sebastian Petrycy (1554–1626), a physician, poet and philosopher, best known as a translator and commentator of Aristotle. In 1583, he was appointed lecturer in literary poetics at the University of Kraków. Petrycy was known as an author of both medical treatises and lyrics inspired by Horace. His annotated translations of Aristotle's *Politics* and *Economics*, dedicated to King Zygmunt III, were published in Kraków in 1605 and 1618 respectively. In the introduction to both works, he explained to the Polish reader his translation strategy of 'turning the foreign into our own' by 'softening the hard, silencing the shameful, filling in the gaps' (translated). Petrycy is considered one of the earliest theorists of translation in Poland. His contemporary Szymon Birkowski (1574–1626), professor of physics and medicine at the famous Academy of Zamość and a prominent philologist, translated *De collocatione verborum* by Dionysius of Halicarnassus and published what was probably the earliest bilingual edition of any text.

While in the Middle Ages texts were available mainly in the form of manuscripts, the Renaissance saw the revolutionary development of printing techniques. Several printing houses were set up in the 1570s to cater for this new market. The medieval tradition persisted in the printing of chronicles of the lives of saints and martyrs, prayer books and similar texts. But the development of printing techniques also aided the circulation of texts which marked the arrival of a new epoch. In 1535, Marcin Bielski (*c.* 1495–1575) published *Żywoty filozofów* (The Lives of Philosophers). This was a translation of a Czech version of Walter Burleus's *De*

vita et moribus philosophorum et poetarum, a compendium of knowledge about the ancient world. It was reprinted several times (the last reprint appeared around the middle of the sixteenth century) and translated into a number of the vernacular languages of Poland.

Eager to cater for a growing readership, Renaissance editors saw an opportunity to expand the book market by encouraging and supporting translators, whom they recruited mainly from the academic community at Kraków. Several scores of romances were published, as well as many collections of novellas. The quality of the translations was often very high, with many translators demonstrating great skill and inventiveness. Some books appeared in several editions; a few were still being reprinted as late as the eighteenth century. Some titles could even be bought at country fairs at the beginning of the twentieth century. Chivalric romances were quite popular; among the best-known was *Historia o Fortunacie* (A History of Fortunat, 1570), translated anonymously from German. However, it was the folk-tale type of romance that survived particularly well. The earliest recorded representative of this genre was *Żywot Aesopa Fryga* (The Life of Aesop of Frigia), published in 1522 by Biernat of Lublin (*c.*1465–*c.*1529). This was an adaptation of a Latin translation of a Greek story about a clever slave who outwitted his master, now set in the Polish context. The same protagonist appears in two more adaptations which count among the finest translation achievements of the time: the poem *Rozmowy, które miał król Salomon mądry z Marchołtem grubym a sprośnym* (Conversations between King Solomon the Wise and the fat and lewd Marcholt, 1521) translated by Jan of Koszyczki (date unknown), and the anonymous *Sowiźrzał krotochwilny i śmieszny* (The Witty and Funny Sowiźrzał, *c.*1530). The latter was the first Polish translation of the adventures of Till Eulenspiegel, a character from folk-tale type German romances of the Middle Ages.

These three translations illustrate what was to become the general practice of the time: that of appropriating original works. The idea of copyright was entirely alien to Renaissance authors, who treated the works of foreign colleagues as common property. This approach was advocated explicitly by the first Polish theorist of translation, Łukasz Górnicki (1527–

1603), who translated Baldassarre Castiglione's *Il Cortegiano*. In his version, *Dworzanin polski* (The Polish Courtier, 1566), Górnicki replaced the court of an Italian prince, which is the setting of the original story, with the court of a Polish bishop, and instead of Italian noblemen and noblewomen he introduced local characters. In the introduction to his version, Górnicki asks: 'Why is it that I differ from grof Balcer Kastilion?' In answer to this question, he details his reasons for changing such elements of the original cultural setting as he judged alien, offensive or difficult to understand for a Polish reader. This explanation earned him the position of the founding father of what came to be known as the 'method of Polonized adaptation', and his plea for the use of free paraphrase was to become the guiding principle for Polish translators over the next two centuries (Ziomek 1973). Indeed, it was fully acknowledged in the Golden Age of the Polish Renaissance. Several works by Mikolaj Rej (1505–69), known as the 'father of Polish literature', draw heavily on foreign sources, among them Paligenius, a Lutheran author by the name of Thomas Naogeorg, and the Dutch Humanist and writer Cornelius Crocus. The same principle is adopted in the work of the greatest poet of the Polish Renaissance, Jan Kochanowski (1530–84). Educated at the University of Padua, well travelled, and fully conversant with Latin and Greek, Kochanowski borrowed freely from various foreign sources. His famous *Pieśni* (Songs, published in 1586) consists mostly of adaptations of Horace. His greatest achievement in the field of translation is *Psałterz Dawidów* (David's Psalter, 1579). This is a poetic adaptation of the *Psalms of David*, but based on various source texts: apart from the Vulgate, Kochanowski used the Hebrew original and, as a source of inspiration, Latin poems by the Scottish humanist George Buchanan.

The first translations of drama appeared around the end of the sixteenth century. Górnicki produced an adaptation of Seneca's *Troas* in 1589, in 1592 an adaptation of Plautus's *Trinumus* was shown at the court of a Polish nobleman, and in 1616 Jan Andrzej Morsztyn (1621–92) published his translation of Corneille's *Le Cid*. As far as poetry is concerned, free verse was first introduced into Polish in 1699 by Krzysztof

Niemirycz, a minor poet, in a translation of La Fontaine's *Fables*.

The works of Polish authors who wrote in Latin were frequently translated into vernacular languages during this period, though some were not translated into Polish until the twentieth century. Many texts by Polish authors were printed outside Poland, either in the original Latin or in translation. A well-known example is *De optimo senatore*, a political treatise by Wawrzyniec Goślicki which was published in Venice in 1568; it was later translated *in extenso* into English and dedicated to Sir Robert Walpole in 1773 as one of the best books of its kind.

The Bible

Renaissance translations of the Bible deserve a separate chapter in the history of translation in Poland. More translations of the Scriptures were produced in this period than in any other, and this flurry of activity coincided with the developing role of translation as a powerful tool for promoting the Polish language.

The earliest Bible translation, printed in Prague and Vilnius (1517–25), was an old-Belorussian version produced by Franciszek Skoryna, a medical doctor at the University of Kraków. Fiercely attacked by both Orthodox and Protestant churches on account of his translation, Skoryna had to appeal to the king for protection. His translation marks the beginning of a long debate on how the Bible should be translated. At that time, the debate revolved around two main issues. The first was directly connected with the development, brief as it was, of the Polish Reformation. Making the Bible available in the vernacular was seen as a direct contribution to disseminating the ideas of the Reformation, and was therefore vehemently opposed by defendants of the Catholic Church. The second issue concerned an argument which is of central importance in most translation theories, namely the opposition between word and sense, the supremacy of the literal over the literary, or vice versa. As in other Christian countries, early translators of the Bible adhered to the former strategy, often at the cost of readability.

At least six complete translations of the Bible were made at the time: the Catholic version by Jan Leopolita (1561), the Calvinist Bible (1563), the Antitrinitarian Bible translated by Szymon Budny (1572), the Orthodox Bible which was translated into Old Church Slavonic (1589), the new Catholic Bible by the Jesuit Jakub Wujek (1593), and the Protestant Bible known as *The Bible of Gdańsk*, translated by Daniel Mikołajewski (1632). Though based essentially on the Vulgate, most later translations made some reference to the Greek and Hebrew originals (Frankowski 1975).

Controversies over the translation of the Bible gave rise to the earliest Polish form of translation studies as criticism directed at the representatives of rival denominations gradually developed into theoretical treatises.

The Enlightenment: seventeenth to eighteenth centuries

In the seventeenth century, the work of Piotr Kochanowski (1566–1620) deserves special mention. Kochanowski adapted for the Polish reader two masterpieces of Italian post-Renaissance literature: Tasso's *Jerusalem Delivered* and Ariosto's *Orlando Furioso*. The former became extremely popular; it was first printed in Kraków in 1618, and the last reprint appeared in 1968.

In diplomacy, contact with the West was easy to maintain, at least for the social elite versed in Latin, French, Italian or German. By contrast, interpreting services were required to maintain communication with the East. In transactions involving Russians and Tartars, for instance, each party used their own native tongue, and formal documents were issued in the two languages. The languages adopted in dealing with the Turks depended on the expertise of those interpreters who happened to be available at the time (often Polish ex-captives). The first qualified interpreter on record was probably the secretary of King Zygmunt-August II (1520–72); he was given a royal grant to study in Istanbul.

Whereas in the seventeenth century translating was considered almost the duty of a writer (cf. Balcerzan 1977: 444), with the dynamic development of Polish literature during the Enlightenment translations into Polish came to be seen mostly as sources of inspiration for original works. Apart from the authors of the ancient world, who remained very popular, it was representatives of French classicism who occupied a prominent position on translation

lists. The main principles established during the Renaissance underlay the poetics of translation in the eighteenth century: free adaptations existed as texts in their own right, totally independent of the originals. The 'beautification' of original works was considered a merit, drastic changes to the basic genre of the original (as in translating poetry into prose) were made as a matter of course, and indirect translation, that is translation based on other translations, was the norm. The eminent Polish translator of the time, Franciszek Ksawery Dmochowski (1762–1808), translated the poems of Edward Young from French versions, and the first Polish staging of *Hamlet* was based on a translation of a German version. James Macpherson's works of Ossian were first translated from French in 1792 by the greatest Polish poet of the time, Ignacy Krasicki (1735–1801). In the case of the classics, however, no mediation was needed: Dmochowski used the originals for his translations of Homer and Horace, as did Krasicki for his renderings of Plutarch and Hesiod. Dmochowski's chief achievement was an adaptation of Nicolas Boileau's *L'Art poétique* (1788), one of the most important theoretical works of the time.

The general disregard for the integrity of an original work is best seen in drama. Early Polish playwrights borrowed original plots and used them as a kind of basic canvas on which local pictures could be painted. The first attempt at imposing some restraint on this common practice came from a scientist and publicist, Stanisław Staszic (1755–1826), who suggested organizing translation contests for quality assessment. Staszic himself was mainly interested in the translation of scholarly treatises, but his activities influenced translation in general and signalled the end of the epoch of 'les belles infidèles'.

The novel, a genre which established itself in Poland in the early nineteenth century, was greatly influenced by earlier developments in European literature. One of the most influential works in this field was Rousseau's *La Nouvelle Héloïse*, some extracts of which appeared in a very good, annotated but anonymous translation in 1823. Tomasz Kajetan Węgierski (1756–84) translated Voltaire's *Zadig* (published in 1811) and Montesquieu's *Lettres persanes*. Unlike the sentimental novel, the gothic novel did not find many followers in Poland. The best of the few representatives of the genre is at the same time an example of an unusual translation activity: Jan Potocki (1761–1815), a Polish soldier, writer and traveller, wrote his *Manuscrit trouvé à Saragosse* in French; it was published in St Petersburg in 1804 and then translated into Polish by a Polish émigré in 1847. The twentieth century provides a similar example: the literary output of the great Joseph Conrad (1857–1924), a Pole who wrote in English, had to be translated into Polish. Another unusual case is the translation of Jan Kochanowski's Polish poems into Latin, published by one of the Polish bilingual poets of the Enlightenment, Franciszek Dionizy Kniaźnin, in a collection of poems by the title *Carmina* (1781).

The earliest translations from English were made during this period by Jan Ursyn Niemcewicz (1757–1841), a prominent poet who spent part of his life in the United States and translated Gray and Byron. At roughly the same time, the first English translations of Polish poetry began to appear: Maciej Kazimierz Sarbiewski (1595–1640), known in Europe as Casimire, was discovered by the English metaphysical poets; his poems appear in numerous anthologies.

The nineteenth and early twentieth centuries

During the first half of the nineteenth century the work of the translator did not in general merit much respect; this was a consequence of both the unorthodox principles which seemed to guide translation activities at the time and the sloppiness of mass production. The influx of badly translated, second-rate French novels which characterized that period is only comparable to the present-day influx of cheap British and American love stories. In this context, some of the best Polish poets and writers who also worked as translators found it extremely difficult to explain to their contemporaries that translation was as much of an art as original literature.

The Romantic opposition against classicism meant a change of genres and languages chosen for translation. One of the most original poets and at the same time best translators of the time, Cyprian Kamil Norwid (1821–83), translated Horace, Homer, Dante, Buonarotti, Béranger and Shakespeare into Polish. Shakespeare,

whose plays naturally attracted artists of the Romantic era, reached Polish audiences mainly via French adaptations or German translations. Poems by Goethe and Schiller were translated from German, and some novels by Walter Scott were translated via German. The feeling of nostalgia for the Golden Age, encouraged by the general situation in Poland (partitioned by Russia, Austria and Prussia in 1795), provided the impetus for translating Polish Renaissance poetry written in Latin. Increased contact with Russia resulted in the emergence of Russian as an important source and target language in translation. The works of the greatest Polish Romantic poet, Adam Mickiewicz (1798–1855), were translated into Russian, and Mickiewicz himself translated into Polish several poems by his Russian friend, Aleksandr Pushkin.

Following the failure of the January Uprising against the Russians in 1863, literature began to reflect an overall shift from romantic fantasy to positivist rationalism. The uprising and the ensuing events had changed both the social and economic situation of Poland as a significant number of intellectuals and some members of the wealthy elite were either sent into exile or left the country of their own accord. The central theme of most literary works (with the novel as the main genre) now became the plea of a stateless nation for its right to exist. The mission of translators, who no longer had to be creative authors in their own right, was clear: to enrich the literary canon available to the Polish reader. As always, the choices reflected the tastes and needs of the time: Zola, Balzac, Diderot, Gide, Stendhal, Voltaire (for fiction); Byron, Dante, Verlaine, Swinburne and Rimbaud (poetry); Maeterlinck and Ibsen (drama); Bergson and Kierkegaard (philosophy); Georges Brandes (criticism); and Russian theorists in general in the field of literary studies. The first translations of American poetry, including Whitman and Poe, were done by Zenon Przesmycki (1861–1944), a representative of Polish Modernism known as 'Miriam'.

The most prominent translator of the time was undoubtedly Tadeusz Żeleński, known as 'Boy' (1874–1941). A physician by profession and a great admirer and connoisseur of French literature, he published 112 translated volumes. Apart from the great French novelists of his time, he translated Molière, Pascal, Rabelais,

Rousseau, Villon, and Voltaire. Żeleński was killed by the Nazis in 1941 and did not complete his translation of Proust. It is largely due to his efforts that foreign literature occupies its present prestigious position in the literary canon of Poland. Equally important are the translations of the Russian Romantic poets (such as Pushkin and Lermontov) and Symbolists (such as Balmont, Blok, and Briusov) by one of the greatest Polish poets of the period, Julian Tuwim (1894–1953). Tuwim's well-known essay 'Traduttore – traditore', published in 1950, castigated incompetent translators and put forward a proposal for organizing regular diploma courses for translators. Tuwim suggested that candidates should pass a series of examinations on language, stylistics and culture; only those who successfully completed the course would then be allowed to publish their work.

In the first decades of the twentieth century Polish became a source language for translation. Polish novelists of the time contributed significantly to the world literary canon. *Quo vadis*, which earned Henryk Sienkiewicz (1846–1916) the Nobel Prize in 1905, was translated into many languages; it remained on the list of French best-sellers until quite recently. A modern American translation of Sienkiewicz's 3-volume historical saga about seventeenth-century Poland (*Ogniem i mieczem, Potop, Pan Wołodyjowski*, translated by S. Kuniczak as *With Fire and Sword, The Deluge, Fire in the Steppe*) appeared in the USA in 1991–2, and immediately gained considerable popularity. By 1916, the number of translations of novels by Sienkiewicz's contemporary, Eliza Orzeszkowa (1841–1910), had exceeded 200 in Russia alone. Various novels by another Polish Nobel prize winner, Władysław Reymont (1867–1925), were translated into several languages.

The present time

As in earlier periods, the choice of texts and languages for translation in contemporary Poland has been conditioned by the political situation. The revival of cultural life after World War II under Russian dominance resulted in prioritizing the translation and re-printing of works which were seen to be 'politically correct'. In 1956, labour riots in the city of Poznań were ruthlessly suppressed, resulting in the death of some fifty-three people. In the wake of these events, a period of political 'thaw' began, which stimulated an influx of works by such writers as Sartre, Saint-Exupéry and Camus. Polish translations of Faulkner, Steinbeck and Hemingway had a great impact on Polish readers, who also showed a growing interest in both classical and modern drama, including Shakespeare, Molière, Lope de Vega, Calderon, Goldoni, Goethe, Schiller, George Bernard Shaw, Brecht, Ionesco, Beckett, Dürrenmatt, and Genet. In 1969, Maciej Słomczynski (b. 1920) published his translation of James Joyce's *Ulysses*, which soon became a major cultural event. Several publishing houses launched thematic series of translations, for example on modern novels, Scandinavian authors, writers of Latin America, and contemporary Catholic writers.

Another significant shift came after the political upheaval of 1989. The abolishment of state censorship and the appearance of private publishing houses soon brought about an avalanche of translated books. The boom proved to be a mixed blessing. In addition to international best-sellers, a large number of substandard books began to appear in equally substandard Polish translations, and they were often promoted as highly representative of the long forbidden culture of the West.

In the humanities, translation has often proved to be the most effective means available for filling the gaps left by forty years of communist rule. Examples include two translations into Polish; one of a comprehensive history of Poland written by a British historian (*God's Playground* by Norman Davies, 1981; Polish edition 1990, 1991), and the other of *The History of Polish Literature* by Czesław Miłosz (1969; Polish edition 1993). Miłosz, a writer, poet and Nobel Prize-holder, is a Polish émigré who originally wrote the book for his American students.

Today, (American) English is by far the most important source language in literary as well as non-literary translation. The number of professional translators and interpreters, who often specialize in terms of translating a single author or translating within a single field of knowledge, continues to grow to meet the demands of an expanding book market and a free market economy.

The list of Polish writers whose works have been translated into other languages has also grown considerably. Readers in Europe now have access to works by contemporary Polish poets such as Herbert and Szymborska, dramatists such as Mrożek and Różewicz, and novelists such as Andrzejewski and Konwicki. In the academic field, works by Polish scholars have also begun to appear in translation. Growing interest in Poland as part of the new united Europe has stimulated the production of other types of publications, such as multilingual manuals, tourist guidebooks, and historical surveys in a variety of languages.

Theories and models

The earliest recorded attempt by a Polish scholar to formulate a theory of translation dates back to the 1440s. In an introduction to a treatise on spelling, an anonymous writer suggests that 'we may translate the same expression as meaning one thing or another, depending on the context' (translated from a quote in Balcerzan 1977: 29). The Polish verb *tłumaczyć* is ambiguous: it can mean 'explicate' or 'translate'. This dual interpretation partly explains the two conflicting principles of translation in the Polish tradition, namely the principle of 'appropriating foreign ideas and images, so that a foreign work is tailored after our own patterns' (Balcerzan 1977: 22; translated) versus the postulate that a foreign text must not be stripped of 'the features through which it can be recognized as being foreign' (Balcerzan 1977: 22; translated). The principle of adaptation, or 'Polonization', dominated translation practice mainly during the Renaissance and the Enlightenment, but it continued to feature in Modernist disputes between those who wanted to preserve the original local colour in their translations of foreign poetry and those who insisted that the foreign text should be domesticated. However, the more scientifically oriented philological and/or critical approach to translation which developed over the past few decades has resulted in a higher level of respect for the integrity of the original work. Fidelity in translation is now understood to mean preserving the original text rather than reconstructing it.

In contemporary thought, the old opposition is reworded in terms of a distinction between *samoistne* or 'self-sufficient' and *związane* or 'integrated' translations: while the former come to exist as independent texts, interpretations of the latter are achieved through confrontation with original works and their earlier translations. The distinction was first formally proposed by Stanisław Barańczak (b. 1946), a poet and one of the best contemporary translators of poetry, who combines the talent of a poet with the extensive knowledge of a literary critic. As a theorist, Barańczak represents the literary branch of Polish translation studies (Barańczak 1974, 1992). In general, literary translation theory in Poland has traditionally taken the shape of individual case studies in which practising translators discuss their own work or the work done by their colleagues. Although often interesting, such essays rarely offer anything more than passing observations and fragmented comments.

More theory-oriented contributions came from such scholars as Wacław Borowy and Edward Balcerzan (b. 1937), the latter a specialist in literary translation theory, who, as a university professor, supervised many scholarly dissertations on translation studies. Borowy's essays on translation are collected in *Studia i rozprawy* (Studies and Dissertations, 1952), a 2-volume anthology published posthumously by his colleagues and students. Theoretical aspects of translation have been discussed at length by Polish philosophers of language (for example in essays on the nature of literary work by Roman Ingarden, 1893–1970) and by linguists (most notably Zenon Klemensiewicz, 1891–1969). The linguistic branch of Polish translation studies is, however, a relatively young field. One of the most comprehensive early attempts at constructing a formal linguistic model of translation was offered by Olgierd Wojtasiewicz (1957/1993), who saw translation as a process consisting of two stages: at the initial stage, the surface structure of the text should be analysed and matched with a deep structure; at the second stage, such adaptations as might follow from an analysis of the context should be introduced. During the 1970s, the flourishing of contrastive linguistic studies (mainly Polish–English) gave rise to works which defined translation equivalence within the framework of transformational-generative grammar (Marton 1968; Krzeszowski 1974). In keeping with developments elsewhere, the approach to translation changed in the latter part of the twentieth century to reflect developments in the field of pragmatics and the popularity of the cognitive school in linguistics. Equivalence in translation has been redefined in terms of functional rather than formal criteria, and it is now widely recognized that equivalence is conditioned by cognitive and pragmatic factors (Krzeszowski 1981). As far as literary translation is concerned, the new model has the advantage of bridging the traditional gap between literary and linguistic studies (Tabakowska 1993), though theoretical works on non-literary translation remain heavily weighted towards linguistically-based models (Kopczyński 1980; Pisarska 1990).

The identity and status of translators

During earlier periods of history, translators were recognized as creators of literature and were accordingly granted rights equal to those of original authors. The gradual professionalization of the job, however, brought about a radical change in the status of translators. As early as 1772, Ignacy Krasicki felt obliged to make a plea in *Uwagi o tłumaczeniu ksiąg* (On Translating Books) for the importance and prestige of the profession to be recognized. Today, the translator is no longer seen as a mediator nor translation a guide to original literature; the translator is simply a professional engaged in a specific form of communication. A few translators continue to follow the old tradition, making their names mainly as writers, poets or literary critics.

Translation as a professional activity in Poland was first institutionalized with the founding of the Translators' Commission of the Union of Polish Writers in 1976. In 1981 a new organization was established: the Association of Polish Translators and Interpreters. Both organizations are affiliated to FIT (the International Federation of Translators). Soon after the latter was formed, Warsaw hosted the ninth World Congress of FIT (1981). In 1985, Zygmunt Stoberski, then member of the Editorial Committee of the journal *Babel*, became President of the International Organization for the Unification of Terminological Neologisms. It was at Stoberski's initiative that the list of International Scientific Terms – which appeared as a regular column in *Babel* from 1977 to 1985 – was upgraded into an independent publication: *NEOTERM*, a bulletin published in Warsaw from 1985 to 1997.

Further reading

Rusinek 1955; Ziętarska 1969; Ziomek 1973; Frankowski 1975; Pollak 1975; Balcerzan 1977; Kopczyński 1980; Krzeszowski 1981; Miłosz 1983; Balcerzan 1984, 1985; Pisarska 1990; Tabakowska 1993.

ELŻBIETA TABAKOWSKA

Romanian tradition

The Romanian language is a descendant of the Latin once spoken in the Eastern part of the Roman empire (Rosetti 1986: 76). After the Roman conquest in AD 106, the province of Dacia (roughly corresponding to modern Romania) was colonized and Latin became the vehicle of communication among its inhabitants. The variety of Latin which served as a basis for the Romanian language was not different from the Latin used in other Roman provinces, but it has since passed through continuous transformations, partly due to its normal evolution, partly owing to the influence of the languages with which it came into contact. Present-day Romanian has been influenced by non-Romance languages such as Hungarian, Albanian and various Slavic languages, which are spoken in neighbouring countries.

Romania switched from the Cyrillic to the Roman script in 1860. However, Romanian is also spoken in some parts of the former Soviet Union, where it is known as Moldavian, and there it is still written in the Cyrillic alphabet.

Early translations

In common with many other languages, the first translations into Romanian were of a religious nature and motivation. The basic Christian terminology is of Latin origin, for example *Dumnezeu* (from *Domine Deo*, 'Lord'), *boteza* (from *baptisare*, 'baptise'), and *cruce* (from *crux*, 'cross'). Sometime between the tenth and thirteenth centuries, the language and the organizational structures of the Slavonic church were officially adopted in Romania, signalling the incorporation of Romanian territory into the Byzantine sphere of influence. This development played a major role in shaping Romanian culture in subsequent centuries and is comparable to the adoption of Catholicism and Latin by the Poles and the Croatians of Slav origin in the tenth century (Ivaşcu 1969: 30). The cultural background which gave rise to the earliest Romanian translations was dominated by the merging of two traditions: the Byzantine tradition in the south and the occidental tradition in the east. The first recorded Romanian manuscript is a translation, probably from the first half of the sixteenth century, of a Slavonic *Acts of the Apostles* from the fifteenth century; it was discovered at the monastery of Voroneţ in Bucovina. There is no indication of when or where it was completed. There are, however, cultural and linguistic arguments which support placing it in the north of Transylvania, for instance the fact that it contains a large number of Hungarian elements such as *fuglu* (from Hungarian *fogoly* meaning 'captive') and *felelui* (from Hungarian *felelni* meaning 'to answer').

Given that Romanian was not a written language at the time, the official language being Slavonic in all contexts, the first Romanian translations of religious texts cannot be explained in terms of internal needs. These translations appear to have been driven by Lutheran and Calvinistic propaganda. The Lutheran Reformation was welcomed by the Magyars and Saxons of Transylvania, who then sought to attract the Romanians to their new faith; the distribution of printed translations of relevant texts provided an efficient means of achieving this aim. The first Romanian printed document was a Lutheran catechism published by the Saxons in Sibiu in 1544 (no longer extant). The Saxons in Braşov soon realized the benefits of being able to distribute books in Romanian on a large scale and began to use the existing paper mill and printing shop more extensively. They hired Deacon Coresi, who proved to be extremely active. In 1559, he published *Întrebare creştinească* (The Christian Inquiry), the first printed Romanian translation on record; in 1561 he published a Romanian Gospel, and in 1570 a Romanian Psalter and a Romanian missal. These translations enjoyed the support of the authorities. Prince Zápolya of Transylvania, for instance, personally commissioned the replacement of Slavonic books by Romanian ones.

Like the Lutherans, the Calvinists also used translations into Romanian to promote their faith. A book of psalms was translated from Hungarian in 1570 and printed with Latin characters in Oradea or Cluj. Bishop M. Tordási translated the books of Genesis and Exodus from the Hungarian Bible of Gáspár Heltai, which appeared in Cluj in 1551, and published them in Orăştie in 1582. Such large-scale distribution of printed translations throughout the region played a decisive role in developing and shaping the Romanian literary language.

In 1648, the whole of the New Testament was translated in Alba Iulia under the supervision of Metropolitan Simion Ştefan. Around the same time, and in the same region, the Apocrypha (the fourteen books appended to the Old Testament in the Septuagint and the Vulgate) were translated from Slavonic.

The seventeenth century

The seventeenth century was a time of political instability in the principalities and Transylvania, and this state of affairs naturally did nothing to stimulate an active cultural life. For almost fifty years no books of any kind were published. Nevertheless, even in these gloomy feudal times some translation and adaptation of folk tales continued to bear testimony to existing links with the Orient. At the same time, literary and printing activities gradually freed themselves from church authority, and contact with European humanism was established through Moldavian and Wallachian scholars who studied at Italian and Polish universities. This had the effect of diminishing the importance of Slavonic, and translations from other source languages began to appear. Nicolae Costin (1660–1712), statesman and historian, translated Antonio de

Guevara's famous book on Marcus Antonius, *Relox de Principes* (1529), from Latin. Spatharus Milescu (1636–1708), diplomat and great scholar, was the first to translate directly from a Greek original; he published his translation of the *Book with Many Questions* by Athanasius of Alexandria in 1661. Milescu also published the first translation of a philosophical text: *On Prevailing Reason* (1688), attributed to Flavius Josephus. But Milescu's most important contribution was translating the Old Testament in full from a version of the Septuagint which was published in Frankfurt in 1551. The translation appeared in 1688 under the title *Biblia de la Bucuresti* (The Bible from Bucharest), and all Romanian versions of the Septuagint have since been based on it.

The first poet translator in the Romanian tradition was Dosoftei (1649–93), the Metropolitan of Moldavia. His verse version of the *Psalter* (1673) remains one of the most highly valued translations of the *Psalms of David*, comparable in terms of its influence to famous versions such as those by Jan Kochanowski and Clement Marot. This was the first time high quality poetry had appeared in the Romanian language. The aesthetic quality of Dosoftei's verse is also evident in the fragment which he translated from the Cretan drama *Erofile*, a Greek adaptation of the Italian Baroque play *Orbecche* by Giraldi. Dosoftei also translated a prayer book (1681) and a missal (1679) from Greek versions. These translations, which were prepared for Moldavian churches, soon spread throughout the principalities and became far more popular than those done by Coresi approximately one hundred years earlier, thus making it possible to start conducting church services in Romanian.

The first law books and dictionaries were also translated and published during this period. They included *Pravila de la Govora*, 'The Law Books from Govora', translated by the monk Moxa from Slavonic and published in Wallachia in 1640, and *Pravilele Împărăteşti*, 'The Imperial Body of Law', translated by Eustratie from Greek and Latin sources and published in Moldavia in 1646. Both are among the earliest statements of legal codes written down in any national language in Europe. The first bilingual dictionary with Romanian as the source language was *Dictionarum valachico-latinum*. It contained

5,000 headwords and was compiled by Mihai Halici from the town of Caransebeş in 1643.

Lexicographic activity, combined with increased involvement in the practical problems of translation, stimulated thinking in this area. The lack of perfect correspondence between the words of two languages began to be noted and discussed. While translating the *Carte de pravile* (Book of Laws), for instance, I. B. Deleanu observed that there was no exact Romanian term for the German *Verbrechen* and noted that the lack of appropriate terminology posed a serious difficulty for the anonymous author of *Retorica*. This close link between practice and theory has remained the driving force behind translation studies in Romania down to the present day.

The Enlightenment

During the eighteenth century, when the Enlightenment was beginning to gain ground in Europe, the 'hospodars' or governors appointed by the Ottoman sultan began to rule in the Romanian principalities. Hungary had fallen under Turkish rule in 1526, after a long period of struggle between dynasties and threats from foreign powers, and eventually became part of the Habsburg Empire in the seventeenth century. Although this period is still viewed negatively by Romanians as well as Hungarians, the ensuing decades witnessed a thriving cultural life. The hospodars were functionaries and dragomen (interpreters) of the Porte, well educated and with a good command of French and Italian. They imposed the use of Greek in all contexts, including the church. More than three hundred books were printed between 1720 and 1820.

The principalities (Wallachia and Moldavia) and Transylvania went through a rapid process of secularization during this period, with translations and adaptations of popular literature gradually replacing those of religious works. French became the dominant source language in translation, with writers who expressed the spirit of the Enlightenment, such as Voltaire, Montesquieu and Rousseau, being among the most translated. The translators themselves were either educated members of the Romanian royal family, like Iancu Văcărescu and Iordache Golescu, or Greek scholars brought in by the

new rulers to teach at the royal academies in Iaşi and Bucharest.

It is to Transylvania's credit to have created the modern Romanian education system during this period. Numerous Greek handbooks on a variety of subjects such as logic, ethics and metaphysics were translated to cater for the demands of the new system. Eugen Vulgaris's translations of the French writer Fontenelle led Romanians to believe that the sun was the centre of the universe. Folk tales were also retranslated on the basis of Greek models such as *Halima*, the *Odyssey* and *Aesop's Fables*. Samuil Micu, one of the representatives of a movement known as Şcoala Ardeleana, 'The Transylvanian School', translated Baumeister's *Elementa Philosophiae* under the title *Logica* (Buda 1799); this was the first and most important contribution to the creation of a Romanian philosophical language.

During the last quarter of the eighteenth century and the first quarter of the nineteenth century, Romanians became particularly receptive to European science and philosophy in the principalities and Transylvania, actively assimilating Western literature and integrating it into the indigenous culture (Duţu 1970: 155). Free adaptation was the order of the day, with 'faithful' translations being the exception rather than the norm. The adaptations are both entertaining and instructive. Sappho, Anacreon, Petrarch, Ronsard, Metastasio and other representatives of the great European tradition in lyrical poetry were translated, often from intermediary versions (Greek in the principalities, Hungarian in Transylvania). Adaptations of Fénelon's *Adventures of Télémaque* by P. Maior in 1819 and Gr. Pleşoianu in 1831 enjoyed great popularity. Ion Barac published the first Romanian *Odyssey* in verse form in 1801, as well as the first *Hamlet* (c.1820). V. Aaron translated Ovid's *Metamorphoses* in 1803/4 and I. B. Deleanu translated *Themistocles*, by the Italian poet Metastasio, in 1801. Translations, or rather adaptations of works by Rousseau, Montesquieu, d'Arnaud, Marmontel, Pope and Florian portrayed man as a complex being; the pre-Romantic hero gradually found his way into Romanian literature. Theatrical performances given in the principalities by numerous French, Italian, German and Russian touring troupes provided further contact with European literature. The performances were hosted by the cultured members of the royal family, the boyars, who translated the plays into Greek as well as Romanian. The organizer of the first performance in the city of Iași was Gheorghe Asachi, who adapted *Mirthil and Chloe* by Florian in 1816 and later *Alzire* by Voltaire in 1818. Iancu Văcărescu translated Goethe (a fragment from *Faust*), Racine (*Britannicus*) and the German playwright Kotzebue (*The Evening Hour*).

Beyond the Enlightenment: the nineteenth century

During the 1840s and 1850s, translation activity continued to reflect the Romanian need for integration with European culture and literature. French continued to be the dominant source language, with the three genres of drama, epic poetry, and the lyric being well represented. Works translated during this period include *Phèdre* and *Athalie* by Racine, *Horace* by Corneille, *Le Misanthrope* and *Les Précieuses ridicules* by Molière, *Alzire* and *Mérope* by Voltaire, and *Marie Tudor* by Victor Hugo. Apart from drama, Romantic poets such as Hugo and Lamartine received special attention, but there were also several translations of prose writers such as Lesage, Prévost, George Sand, Dumas, Eugène Sue, and Balzac. The popularity of French culture also encouraged the translation of a great number of grammars and other types of handbooks.

In addition to French literature, works by Italian writers such as Dante, Ariosto, Tasso and Alfieri were also translated. English writers such as Young, Byron and Shelley were generally translated from French intermediaries. *Gulliver's Travels* became very popular shortly after it was first published in 1848 and was translated several times. German literature did not fare very well during this period, with a small number of writers such as Goethe and Schiller being translated. Interest in Russian literature was particularly strong in Moldavia, with Pushkin being the most popular writer: *The Gypsies* was translated by Al. Donici in 1837 and *The Black Shawl* by C. Negruzzi in 1834. European works of criticism, such as those by La Harpe, Marmontel, Saint-Marc Girardin, and Jules Janin also became available in translation.

Three outstanding scholars, Heliade Rădulescu (Wallachia), Gheorghe Asachi (Moldavia) and G. Barițiu (Transylvania), encouraged the Romanian public to read the masterpieces of various cultures and to adopt the moral values espoused in them. Heliade Rădulescu (1802–72) initiated a collection of classical authors in 1836; these included Homer, Xenophon, Demosthenes, Virgil, Tasso, Byron and Hugo, among others. In 1846, he published the *Biblioteca Universală* (Universal Library). This was a collection of 232 famous authors from various historical periods and representing various fields of knowledge, including philosophy, law, theology, natural science and aesthetics. Unfortunately, the Romanian public was not yet ready to receive and appreciate literary masterpieces or alternative moral and cultural values and could not assimilate European culture. The aristocracy continued to enjoy the masterpieces, while the less educated middle class preferred the melodrama, comedy or mawkish novelette. Heliade himself anticipated this reaction and tried to strike a balance between the needs of the common reader and the desirability of translating high literature. His translations of the latter type included Cervantes (an extract from *Don Quixote* appeared in 1840), Lamartine, Byron, Voltaire, Rousseau, Boileau, Goethe and Schiller; his translations of the kind of literature in which the common reader took an interest included Guinot, Marie Ayard Marville and Miss Norton. The popularity of ephemeral inferior literature in translation encouraged some intellectuals to accuse translation of being a 'dangerous mania' and to suggest that Romanian reception of foreign literature in the nineteenth century was motivated merely by 'supply and demand' (Cornea 1970: 109).

G. Barițiu (1812–93) played a leading role in the cultural life of Transylvania, especially in the field of translation. He was a great admirer of England as a 'model of political freedom' (Barițiu 1837) and one of the first translators of Shakespeare. In 1840, he published extracts from *Julius Caesar* and *The Merchant of Venice*; these were translated from German versions (as were his later extracts from works by Dickens). He published the full text of *Julius Caesar* in 1844; this was the first complete translation of a Shakespeare play to appear in Romania.

His translations of Schiller's *Don Carlos, Maria Stuart* and *Fiesko* appeared in 1843.

In the period heralding the rise of the revolutionary movement which swept much of Europe, including Romania, around the middle of the nineteenth century, Byron's personality and his fiery poems became very popular, and English literature, which by and large had been ignored until then, began to attract more attention. The first direct translation from English was probably Byron's *Manfred*, translated in 1843 by the Romanian revolutionary and writer C. A. Rosetti. The Byronic hero with his romantic and rebellious attitude became a distinctive feature, even a model, of Romanian cultural life. The first English novel to be translated was also to become one of the most popular; this was Defoe's *Robinson Crusoe*, translated and published by V. Drăghici in the city of Iaşi in 1835. Bulwer-Lytton's *The Last Days of Pompeii*, published in London in 1834, was serialized in Romanian magazines in 1838. Walter Scott's historical novels were well known to the Romanian public from the mid-1950s onwards.

Romanian magazines also carried the first news about the New World during this period, and translations of American literature soon began to appear. Washington Irving was the first author to be translated into Romanian, in 1836, followed by Benjamin Franklin, James Fenimore Cooper, Edgar Allan Poe and Mark Twain. Harriet Beecher Stowe's *Uncle Tom's Cabin*, published in 1852, was translated in Iaşi in 1853 and in Bucharest in 1854. This novel was particularly popular because of the topicality of its social message, which was consistent with the ideology of the democratic intellectuals striving to emancipate the gypsies.

The flourishing of translation activity during the nineteenth century had an enduring influence on Romanian cultural life and helped to bring Romania closer to the rest of Europe. The influence of French culture could be seen in the overall process of modernization which began to take place. The Schiller centenary in 1859 was followed by a boom in the translation of his work, as well as the work of other German authors such as Goethe, Heine and Lenau. German literature and philosophy helped shape the thinking of a number of influential Romanian personalities who studied in Berlin, Vienna and other German-speaking

universities. Titu Maiorescu, founder of the magazine *Convorbiri literare*, 'Literary Talk', was highly influenced by the ideas of Schopenhauer. The poet Mihai Eminescu (1850–89) was similarly influenced by German Romanticism. His excellent translations of the Austrian poet Lenau, *Bitte* (Request) and *Das dürre Blatt* (The Withered Leaf), were published in *Convorbiri literare* in 1879. Eminescu created a highly expressive poetic language, and in so doing made it possible for translations into Romanian to stand in their own right as equals of their European and American originals.

The last quarter of the nineteenth century witnessed an emphasis on translating works which focus on social issues. These included Gogol's *The Inspector-General*, published in 1874, Turgenev's *The Nest of Gentlefolk* (1880), Dostoyevsky's *Crime and Punishment* (1898), and Chekhov's *Motley Stories* (1899). Fragments of Dickens's *The Old Curiosity Shop* were published in the magazine *Contemporanul*, 'The Contemporary', in 1883, and the text appeared in full in 1894. Edgar Allan Poe's *The Murders in the Rue Morgue* appeared in translation in 1892 and Emile Zola's *The Dreyfus Affair* in 1898.

The contemporary period

Translation before World War II

During the first half of the twentieth century, a number of excellent translations were published by scholars who were established poets in their own right. The Transylvanian poet George Coşbuc translated from German as well as a number of other languages, including Greek (Homer's *Odyssey*), Latin (Virgil's *Aeneid* and *Georgics*), Sanskrit (*Rig-Veda*; Kalidasa's *Sákuntala, Ramayana* and *Mahabharata*), and Italian. His translation of Dante's *The Divine Comedy* was considered one of the best existing versions by C. Tagliavini, a well-known Italian scholar who had a special interest in Romanian. Another Transylvanian, Şt O. Iosif (1875–1913), was considered one of the best translators of German poetry during his time. He translated Heine, Goethe, Schiller, Bürger, and Lenau. He also translated work by the Hungarian poet Petôfi (*The Apostle*), as well as Shakespeare's *Romeo and Juliet* and *A Midsummer Night's Dream*. The *Iliad* and *Odyssey* were translated in perfect hexameters by G. Murnu. Other writers translated or retranslated during this period include Jules Verne, Oscar Wilde, Mikhail Lermontov, Ivan Goncharov, Rainer Rilke, Eugene O'Neill, François Villon, Mark Twain, Marcel Proust, and Balzac. These translations were the result of personal affinity and individual choice on the part of the translators rather than of official planning. Publishers were mainly interested in producing lucrative, popular literature. However, high-quality literature could also be successful. One of the most popular authors during this period was W. S. Maugham: almost thirty of his titles were translated by the Romanian writer J. Giurea and published between 1930 and 1945.

Translations from Hungarian were particularly well received during this period. This could be explained by the existence of a large core of shared elements and values in the history and the daily life of Romanians and Hungarians. The social theme was topical in both countries. For Romanians, the revolutionary verses of the Hungarian writer Sandor Petôfi carried much the same message as that derived by Hungarians from the poetry of the Romanian writer George Coşbuc. This stimulated translation activity between the two languages, at times even against official political trends. Liberally-minded intellectuals were conscious of the contribution made by translations in terms of achieving better understanding and harmony between the two peoples, especially against growing fascism in both countries. In 1935, for instance, G. Moşoiu, Lord Mayor of Oradea, offered a translation prize as a way of promoting mutual understanding between Romanians and Hungarians. One of the most successful translators from Hungarian during this period was the Transylvanian poet Octavian Goga (1881–1938). His versions of Petôfi, Ady and Madách were outstanding. He was awarded the National Prize for Literature in 1924 and his translation of Madách's *Tragedy of Man* is still considered one of the best in existence.

Translation after World War II

World War II and the years which followed it brought about a new isolation. Both original and translated literature were censored. The 1950s witnessed a growing demand for foreign literatures, with a definite need for translations since the majority of the Romanian public did not speak foreign languages. Many writers refused to publish their own works on literary or moral grounds, preferring instead to sign translation contracts with publishing houses. The result was that several masterpieces appeared in excellent translations during this period. For example, in 1955 two important works by Goethe were published: *Faust*, translated by the great poet and philosopher Lucian Blaga, and the autobiographical novel *From My Life. Poetry and Truth*, translated by Tudor Vianu, an outstanding scholar of the time. Translations of this type were the result of personal choice. Only the Russian classics were translated systematically in a series of complete works, including Gogol (1954–8), Chekhov (1954–63), and Turgenev (1953–62). The only non-Russian author whose works were translated and published in a complete edition was Shakespeare (1955–63, eleven excellent volumes by L. Leviţchi and D. Duţescu).

The early 1960s brought a gradual reappraisal of Romanian and foreign literature. High-quality translations appeared of outstanding works of literature from all over the world. The magazine *Secolul XX* ('The Twentieth Century') and the Editura pentru Literatură Universală ('Publishing House for World Literature', later known as Univers) played an important role in this process. Between 1961 and 1980, Univers published 2,700 titles by 2,100 different authors. In the following years, numerous other publishing houses were set up, for example Minerva, Albatros, and The Romanian Book. These, together with specialized journals such as *Familia*, *The Literary Romania*, *Horizon* and many others, ensured that all the classics from every country and epoch were translated. There is hardly an international writer who has not been translated into Romanian at least once, a fact often highlighted in UNESCO reports and statistics. As in previous decades, the most successful translators were writers, especially poets, in their own right.

One of the most valuable contributions of Univers was publishing seminal works in the fields of aesthetics, literary theory and criticism soon after they had appeared abroad. The *Essays* series included the main works of Croce, Curtius, Genette, Wellek, Eco, Greimas, Kaiser, Lotman, Alonso, Frye, Tomasevski, Vossler, Zumthor, Friedrich, Walzel and many others. A similar series was published by the Political Publishing House under the title *Idei contemporane* (Contemporary Ideas); this included works by Marshall McLuhan, Marcuse, Habermas, and Jaspers, among others.

Under the dictatorship of Ceauşescu, who was elected President of the State Council in 1967 and eventually President of Romania in 1974, translating was regarded as an ethically sound activity, whereas original literary works were subject to censorship and could only be published if they glorified the totalitarian regime. This further stimulated translation activity, and important works from all languages continued to be translated and retranslated into Romanian. In addition to individual works, a large number of anthologies were also published in the 1960s and 1970s. These included *Antologie Shakespeare bilingvă* ('A Bilingual Anthology of Shakespeare', 1964), *Antologia literaturii maghiare I-III* ('Anthology of Hungarian Literature I-III', 1965-8), *Antologia poeziei romantice germane* ('Anthology of German Romantic Poetry', 1969), *Sonetul italian* ('The Italian Sonnet', 1970), *Antologie bilingvă de poeziei franceză* ('Bilingual Anthology of French Poetry', 1970), and *Poeţi ai expresionismului* ('The Poetry of Expressionism', 1971). A comprehensive overview of the literature of the first half of the century is given by A. E. Baconsky in his *Panorama poezie universale* (1972), which covers ninety-nine poets from Ady to Yeats. The *Antologia poeziei americane*, compiled in 1979 by I. Caraion, covers all representative areas of American poetry: 130 poets from Anne Bradstreet (1612-72) to the present day. *Simbolismul european*, compiled in 1983 by Z. Molcuţ, is an imposing anthology (1,800 pages) of 160 authors, one of the most complete accounts of European symbolism in existence.

In recent decades, there has been a growing interest in non-Western literature. S. Al. George published a complete translation of *Bhagavad-Gita* from Hindi in 1971; this is one of the most famous philosophical poems of the oriental world. The *Antologia literaturii precolumbiene* (covering the literature of three cultures: Mayan, Mexican and Inca) appeared in 1973, and *Antologie Haiku* (Japanese lyric poetry from the sixteenth to the twentieth centuries) followed in 1974.

The relationship between national and translated literature is often one of close interdependence. Works by Gide and Proust, who greatly influenced the evolution of the Romanian novel in the first half of last century, remained largely untranslated during that period. By the 1960s and 1970s, the ground had been prepared by indigenous writings and their complete works became available in translation. Under the influence of Balzac, the novelist Cezar Petrescu created the 'Comédie humaine' of Romanian society between the two World Wars. It was only during the second part of last century, when the Romanian public had come to appreciate his own work, that he was able to publish successfully his excellent translations of Balzac's *Le Père Goriot* and *Eugénie Grandet*. The popularity of certain works in a foreign culture is also often aided by the relevance of their political and social themes, particularly when these themes cannot be addressed openly in the indigenous literature. The character of the dictator, developed in the context of a turbulent political situation, is a recurring feature of more recent South American literature, as in *The President* by Miguel Angel Asturias, *The Autumn of the Patriarch* by Gabriel García Márquez, as well as the novels of Alejo Carpenter; translations of all these works were very popular under the Ceauşescu dictatorship.

Translation today

Translation theory remains closely connected with practice in Romania. Most of the literature on translation is published by professional translators or teachers of translation. Titles such as 'How I Translated Faust' (Blaga 1955), 'Notes of a Translator' (Doinaş 1972b) and 'On the Faithful Translation of Poetry' (Doinaş 1988b) are good examples of theoretical studies which are grounded in genuine translation tasks. In 1965, the magazine *Secolul XX*, which has published works by theorists such as George Steiner, Jiří Levý and Ortega y Gasset on a regular basis, organized a debate on Georges Mounin's *Les problèmes théoriques de la traduction* to which many well-known translators contributed. A variety of linguistic, aesthetic and cultural issues were discussed. In the title of his contribution to this debate, Şt Aug. Doinaş (1965) expressed the view held by a generation of Romanian translators: 'Difficult, Risky but not Impossible'.

Interest in translation theory is also stimulated by the need to train translators and interpreters. Various manuals and handbooks have been published, as well as a number of translation-oriented linguistic studies. Doctoral dissertations on the subject have been presented at the universities of Bucharest, Timişoara and Cluj. Overall, however, the number of published books on translation remains relatively small.

The Translations and World Literature Section of the Writers' Union is a member of FIT. The Professional Union of Interpreters and Translators (UPIT) was established in 1990 and is responsible for protecting the rights of authors and promoting the professional status of translators and interpreters.

Further reading
Bariţiu 1838; Ivaşcu 1969; Cornea 1970; Duţu 1970; Kohn 1980; Rosetti 1986.

JÁNOS KOHN

Russian tradition

Russian is part of the East Slavonic family of languages and one of the six official languages of the United Nations. The history of modern Russia dates back to the ninth century AD, when a number of East Slavonic tribes united to form a new state known as Kiev Rus, after the name of its capital. Later the country's political centre moved to Moscow, which became the capital of a united Russia under Ivan the Great in the fifteenth century. Contact with Western Europe was initiated in the seventeenth century by Peter the Great, who established the educational system and built a new capital, St Petersburg (later to become known as Leningrad). Political unrest under the tsars culminated in a period of civil war (1918–22), after which the Communists established control of the country. The end of World War II saw the rise of the Soviet Union as one of the two major world powers. The mid-1980s saw the beginning of a period of social and political reform, known in the West as *perestroika*, and the progressive disengagement of Russia from Eastern Europe.

The recorded history of translation in Russia is as long and rich in events. The following is a brief overview of the main trends evident during different historical periods.

Translation in Kiev Rus

Writing, literature and translations were introduced in Kiev Rus in a relatively mature form. In the year 864, a Greek priest named Cyril and his brother Methodius, who were sent by the Byzantine emperor to do missionary work among Slavonic people, began with the creation of a new alphabet (now known as Cyrillic) which they used to translate a number of religious texts from Greek into Old Church Slavonic (see BULGARIAN TRADITION). Among their first translations were the New Testament, the Psalter and the Prayer Book. After Rus embraced Christianity in 988, numerous translations were made to give the converts access to the philosophical and ethical doctrines of the new religion and to the Church's rituals and customs. These included a variety of genres, such as Lives of Saints, Homilies, Chronicles and the like. Apocrypha also enjoyed great popularity with their stories of miracles, fantasies and exoticism, sometimes bordering on what was later called fiction. Most of these translations were made in Bulgaria but were used in Rus. The translators of religious books usually opted for word-for-word rendering of the source text.

A score of translations which were not exclusively religious and relatively less literal were also made in Rus at the time. Among them were such books as the *Zhitie Andreya Yurodivogo* (The Life of Andrei, the Man of God), *Pchela* (The Bee), *Kosmografiya* (Cosmography), and *Fiziolog* (The Physiologist), to mention just a few. One considerable achievement was the translation of Josephus Flavius's *The Judaic War*, in which the translator successfully avoided many pitfalls of literalness.

In this early period the translator's name was not mentioned as a rule, and it was often impossible to say whether a translation was made within the country or beyond its borders.

During the tragic years of the Mongol invasion (1228–1480) translations continued to play a major role in shaping the cultural character of the country. More parts of the Bible were translated and some of the previous translations were revised or replaced with new translations. Alongside religious translations, translations of non-religious material gradually began to appear, including *Istoriya Indiyskogo Korolevstva* (A Tale of the Indian Kingdom) and *Troyanskaya Voina* (The Trojan War). Most translations were made from Greek, some presumably used Latin and Old Hebrew sources.

This period also witnessed the gradual formation of the Russian language as a result of mutual influence between Old Church Slavonic and the people's vernacular. However, religious texts continued to be translated into Old Church Slavonic, which nobody spoke outside church services. At the same time, contact with other countries required the translation of political and business documentation, and here the new Russian language began to gain ground. Apart from translations, original texts during this period were themselves also written in a mixture of Slavonic and Russian.

Translation in the sixteenth and seventeenth centuries

From the sixteenth century onwards, Moscow began to emerge as the political as well as translation centre of the country. Important translations were no longer anonymous, and their contribution to the country's language and culture gained more recognition. Thus in 1515 Basil III, the Grand Prince of Moscow, asked for a learned translator to be sent to Moscow from a Greek monastery. The man, Mikhail Trevoles (b. 1475), came to Moscow in 1518 with a Greek embassy and became known as Maxime the Greek. During the rest of his life (he died in 1555 or 1556) he worked as a translator of religious books as well as some non-religious texts. In addition, he revised a number of existing translations and added commentaries to them. At first, he knew neither Russian nor Old Slavonic and his translations were made in two stages: he translated from Greek into Latin and then his assistants translated the Latin text into Old Slavonic. In his revisions of old translations, he often ignored long-established traditions and suffered accusations of heresy and blasphemy. Maxime the Greek was also a prolific writer, educator and philosopher. In his writings we can find numerous statements on

the art of translation, and these represent the first recorded exposition on the subject in Russia. He insisted on the need for a careful analysis of the source text in order to grasp all its nuances and allegories. To carry out such an analysis, the translator had to possess not only good linguistic but also extensive philological knowledge and had to undertake a great deal of preparatory work. Maxime backed up his prescriptions with ample observations about Greek vocabulary, rhythmical organization and phonetic features, which were to be accounted for in translation. Among his contributions to Russian philology was a dictionary which covered mostly Greek proper names but also included some Latin and Hebrew names. Maxime's active participation in Russia's political and ideological struggles brought him condemnation from the Church and he spent many years in exile.

Although the Russian scholars of the time seem to have already formed some ideas about the need for the translator to have a perfect command of the two languages and extensive background knowledge, in practice most translators lacked proper education. Their knowledge of languages and the resulting translations often left much to be desired.

In the seventeenth century, a greater number of translations of predominantly non-religious material began to appear. Scholarly translations included topics in astronomy and astrology, arithmetic and geometry, anatomy and medicine, as well as descriptions of various animals. Some translations could be described as works of literature in their own right. Also during this century, bilingual dictionaries were compiled for the first time to help translators in their work: Latin–Greek–Slavonic, Polish–Slavonic, Russian–Latin–Swedish and other combinations.

Translators of this period fell into four groups. First, there were staff translators in various administrative departments. These were mostly foreigners (Poles, Germans, Dutchmen) or natives from the southern or western parts of the country. As often as not, they had a good command of classical languages or of Polish but their knowledge of Russian and Old Slavonic was very scant. They were probably assisted by scribes, who wrote down and corrected their translations. The second group was small and consisted of a few monks who had a scholarly background and translated only religious and didactic books from Latin and Greek. The best known among them were Epiphanius, Slavinezky, Arsenius the Greek and Dionisius the Greek. The third group was the largest and its members could be described as part-time translators who occasionally made one or two translations in their spare time. Finally, there were translators who worked on their own initiative and chose the source texts they wanted to translate. Among them were some attendants of the tsar, for example Andrei Matveev, Bogdanov and Prince Kropotkin.

Translation in the eighteenth century

The eighteenth century proved decisive in the development of translation in Russia. Peter the Great's political reforms greatly expanded Russia's economic and cultural contacts with European countries, and this created a demand for numerous translations of scientific and technical texts, as well as works of fiction. Translators were now expected to produce work to higher standards. Tsar Peter issued a special decree on translation demanding a faithful rendering of the original sense. This was a period during which the Russian language began to develop its own literary models and many enlightened Russians saw translation as a means of enriching their language and of asserting its originality and its expressive potential.

Mikhail Lomonosov (1711–65), the great Russian scientist and poet, played an outstanding role in this process. Lomonosov and other prominent writers during this period, such as A. P. Sumarokov and V. K. Trediakovsky, produced many translations, predominantly of poetry. They often supplemented their translations with theoretical discussions, explaining why they rendered the source text the way they did and emphasizing the great value of the translator's work and its creative nature.

A new stage in translation activity began to develop in three directions. First, translation began to be institutionalized, with new structures emerging to organize and supervise the work. A group of translators were assembled in Tsar Peter's Foreign Collegium, and in 1735 the

St Petersburg Academy of Science established the Russian Assembly, which was the first professional organization of translators. Lomonosov, Trediakovsky and a few other members of the Academy were active in the Assembly, which had a body of staff translators. The Assembly selected books for translation, laid down some rules and principles and produced critical reviews of the work performed. It was also involved in training future translators. The Academy set up a language school whose graduates often became official translators. The general requirement at the time was that a translator had to be able to translate from at least three languages: Latin, German and French. Some students were sent by the Academy to study 'languages and sciences' abroad. Examinations were held to assess the professional performance of translators. The Academy also tried to stimulate public interest in translation. In 1748 its President announced an order from Tsarine Elisabeth to step up the translation of non-religious (secular) books. Later, the Academy Chancery published an appeal to the 'gentlefolk and people of other ranks' to produce translations. It was during this period that translators began to receive regular remuneration for their work.

In 1768, the Society for the Translation of Foreign Books was established with 114 members; among them were such eminent personalities as Trediakovsky, Sumarokov and Radishchev. The Society existed for fourteen years and produced many literary translations; it also stimulated discussions on the theoretical problems of translation.

The second dimension of this new stage of translation activity involved a change in terms of the selection of books to be translated. At the turn of the century, translations of classical authors began to be supplemented by a great number of books of a pragmatic nature; these were needed to support the Age of Reform. The process was accompanied by a change in the source languages: Polish texts now lost their popularity and the emphasis gradually shifted to modern European languages – mainly French, German and English.

Technical translations later lost their predominant position and literary translations came to occupy their place. Social reforms stimulated cultural life, and local literature was not yet at a stage when it could fulfil the cultural needs of Russian society. Literary translations were expected to fill the gap and to meet important social and cultural needs. Translators regarded their work as a service to their country, and they expressed this belief in forewords and prefaces to their translations. They believed that their mission was to enlighten and instruct their compatriots, to set moral standards and to create a new Russian literature. From that time on literary translations always enjoyed a high status in Russian culture.

This new awareness of the social importance of translation and translators constituted the third characteristic feature of the period. Translation was now considered a kind of creative writing, no less worthy of respect than original literature. The translator was regarded as a rival of the source text author, with the translated text being expected to aspire to higher standards and even to surpass the source text in terms of artistic quality.

The eighteenth century also witnessed the emergence of poetry translation in Russia, which later developed into a highly esteemed activity. Trediakovsky, for instance, made his reputation from his translation of P. Talman's *Voyage à l'île d'amour*, which included many verses that were successfully rendered in Russian rhyme. Less known but no less remarkable was A. Kantemir's translation of Horace's *Epistles* and other pieces of poetry from Latin and French. Especially numerous and varied were Lomonosov's translations from Latin, German, French and Greek, in which he showed remarkable skill both in rhymed and free verse. He paid much attention to reproducing the rhyming scheme of the source text, using various forms of choree and iambus to render the alexandrine of French epics and the hexameter of Greek tragedies. As Russian poetry of the time was not highly developed and was still based on the distribution of syllables, Lomonosov's innovations helped to enrich it and to establish new forms and traditions in the genres and metres of Russian verse.

The nineteenth and early twentieth centuries

The nineteenth century can be described as the golden age of Russian translation. If the previous age had made translation a professional activity,

the nineteenth century raised this activity to the level of high art.

The new Russian school of translation began to take shape thanks to the outstanding contributions of such prominent personalities as the historian Nikolai Karamzin and the poet Vasily Zhukovsky (1783–1852). At the end of the eighteenth and the beginning of the nineteenth century Karamzin published many translations in several periodicals. He regarded translation as an effective tool for improving a writer's style as well as an invaluable source of information, undertaken for the sake of curiosity, for establishing historical facts, for entertaining women, to provide material for new magazines, or to acquaint Russian readers with books that had not yet become well known. Karamzin's translation activity covered an impressive range of genres and languages: he translated the works of classical and contemporary authors from Greek, French, Latin, German, English, Italian and some oriental languages.

Pushkin referred to Zhukovsky as 'the genius of translation'. Zhukovsky was a talented Russian poet but translations accounted for a considerable part of his output. He translated from English, French, Old Russian, Latin and German. Thanks to him, Russian readers gained access to many works of Schiller, Goethe, Byron, Walter Scott and other giants of world literature. The range of his creative translation activity was staggering, covering, among other things, translations of fairy tales by Charles Perrault and the Grimm brothers, Firdausi's *Shah Nama*, a complete translation of Homer's *Odyssey* and a translation of the famous Old Russian epic *Tolkovanie imenam po alf avitu* (The Tale of Igor's Host). Zhukovsky is one of the leading names in the history of translation in Russia.

Like Karamzin, Zhukovsky advocated free translation, which sometimes resulted in a paraphrase or even a new story on the subject of the source text. He would occasionally transfer the setting to Russia, give the source text characters Russian names, and so on. His outstanding talent, however, enabled him to reproduce the style, rhythm and tone of the original poetry, and his best translations were remarkably faithful to their sources. The Russian school of translation owes much to Zhukovsky's legacy.

The practice of taking liberties with the source

text was also characteristic of prose translations of the period. Irinarkh Vvedensky, a talented and very popular translator of many novels by Charles Dickens and William Thackeray, would typically add several pages which had nothing to do with the source text. In his translation of Dickens's *David Copperfield*, for example, he introduced his own texts at the end of the second chapter, at the beginning of the sixth chapter and in some other parts of the novel. And he justified such contributions by the desire to please the reader, claiming that the translator had the right to freely re-create the spirit of the source text, to give a new life to the ideas of the author in a new situation – 'under another sky', as he put it.

Alexander Pushkin and Mikhail Lermontov, the two great Russian poets, also played a major role in the history of translation in Russia. Although translations occupied a relatively modest place in their poetry, they made a significant contribution to the improvement of literary translation in Russia. In their poetic paraphrases and imitations they managed to reproduce the most important features of foreign poetry and, above all, their renderings were remarkable works of art in their own right, in no way inferior to their original masterpieces. These free translations served as a model for other translators and established an important principle, namely that a good literary translation should be part and parcel of the national literature in the target language. The role played by Pushkin in the development of the Russian school of translation deserves special emphasis. He always showed great interest in the problems of translation, and his critical analyses of translations were exemplary and thought-provoking. He emphasized the importance of the initial selection of the literary works to be translated. His insistence on loyalty to the source text, coupled with the high quality and expressiveness of the translator's literary style, was a positive influence on the best Russian translators of the nineteenth and twentieth centuries.

Although the majority of translators during this period advocated and practised free translation, a few insisted on complete faithfulness to the source text, on literalism even to the detriment of sense and clarity. Among them were such prominent men of letters as P. A. Viasemsky, N. I. Gnedich and A. A. Fet, all of whom translated from a number of different languages. However, they did not always do as they preached. Sometimes the translator's artistic intuition and talent broke through the barrier of literalism. Viasemsky's translations of works by B. Constant and A. Mickiewicz, for instance, were not devoid of literary value, and Gnedich's translations, especially his translation of Homer's *Iliad*, were highly appreciated by Pushkin. Fet's extreme literalism adversely affected the quality of most of his translations, but he did come up with successful solutions sometimes.

Free translation was sometimes practised as a means of promoting democratic ideas, which would not have escaped official censorship in original works. Translators such as V. Kurochkin, D. Minaev and M. Mikhailov, among others, achieved this by choosing suitable source texts and/or by introducing in their translations subtle changes which triggered associations with the Russian context. It was during this period then that using translation as a vehicle of dissent became part of the Russian tradition.

The Soviet period

The years following the 1917 revolution saw a new upsurge in translation activity. On Maxim Gorky's initiative, a new publishing house was set up with an ambitious goal of publishing new or revised translations of all major literary achievements both in the West and in the East. In spite of enormous practical and administrative difficulties, this organization managed to publish in the following two decades or so translations of the works of such great authors as Balzac, Anatole France, Stendhal, Heine, Schiller, Byron, Dickens, Bernard Shaw, Mark Twain and many others.

A great number of translations were also published by other national and local presses in the 1930s and the following decades. The country's best scholars and writers participated in this work, elevating the art of translation to a new level of perfection. Many talented translators became known and respected in the Soviet Union and abroad during this period; they included M. Losinskij, T. Shchepkina-Kupernik, S. Marshak, N. Lubimov, E. Kalashnikova, N. Daruzes and many others.

The fact that the USSR was a multinational state contributed to the growing demand for translation. The scale of translation among national literatures was particularly impressive. Russian readers became familiar with the great epics of the Georgian, Armenian, Uzbek, Kazakh, Azerbaijani and other peoples. Much was done in this field by such prominent Russian poets and writers as Lev Ginsburg, Boris Pasternak and Nickolai Tikhonov.

The information explosion of the second half of the twentieth century gave a tremendous impetus to non-literary translation. The majority of translations were now of social, political, scientific and technical material. There was a growing demand for professional translators, but non-literary texts were still frequently being translated by non-professionals as part of their work in other spheres.

This unparalleled boom in translation activity brought many new people into the profession and resulted in structural and organizational changes. A network of translation services, agencies and departments was established in government offices and industrial and commercial enterprises. Many translators and interpreters became staff personnel; others worked part time or freelance. Given the scale and the overall high quality of translations, both literary and technical, the country was justly regarded as a great translation power during this period.

The increased demand for professional translators was met by numerous training establishments. A number of foreign language institutes set up translation departments, and translators were also trained in universities and technical colleges. Many educational establishments offered their students courses in translation alongside their main professional specialization.

Literary translators received their training at the Gorky Literary Institute, which was sponsored by the Soviet Writers Union. The emphasis here was on translating from the languages of the various ethnic groups of the USSR.

This rich and varied translation activity attracted much attention and recognition. Many periodicals regularly published translations from various languages as well as critical assessments of the strengths and weaknesses of specific translations.

Translation in the post-Soviet period

The years of *perestroika* radically changed the nature of translation practice in general and the market for translations in particular. The abolition of censorship has made it possible to translate many books which had been regarded as inadmissible on ideological or moral grounds. Publishing houses are no longer financed by the state, and many have since gone bankrupt or have had to reduce their output drastically. The market has been swamped by private commercial enterprises, with the result that book prices have risen sharply and standards have generally dropped. Emphasis has now shifted to translating popular fiction and pornographic material.

The new situation has had both positive and negative effects on the business side of translation. Most translations are now from English and translators receive better remuneration. Higher fees encouraged many non-professionals to try their hand at translation, and this has naturally produced a great number of poorly translated books. The new publishers set very tight deadlines in order to market the translations ahead of their competitors; they are no longer interested in supporting the kind of long and arduous effort that can result in a masterpiece.

There has also been a greater demand for English and German interpreters, and many of them earn good money working for national or foreign firms, or joint ventures. By contrast, translators from other languages often find it difficult to make a living. Especially hard hit have been the languages of limited diffusion and staff translators who had previously enjoyed a regular income in the state publishing houses.

The new market conditions highlight the absence of appropriate legislation to regulate translation activities in Russia. The Union of Translators has been trying hard to raise the social and financial status of its members and to restore the prestige of translation in Russia.

Translation theory in Russia

As an important aspect of the nation's culture, translation has been the object of scholarly discussion in Russia throughout its long history. It was not, however, until the second half of the twentieth century that the thought-provoking but often subjective ideas of critics, authors and members of the profession were supplemented by attempts to develop a coherent theory of translation. Since then, the level of growth in translation activity has been matched by numerous publications on theoretical aspects of translation.

Translation research in Russia stems from different schools of thought, reflects different areas of interest and expresses opposing views. Nevertheless, some common features can be singled out to identify what can be described as the Russian school of translation theory.

Russian translation theories are largely based on the assumption that translation is a phenomenon that can be studied and described in an objective and consistent way, using various methods of observation and analysis. The translator's decision-making process may seem subjective and intuitive, but it is ultimately governed by correlated linguistic and cognitive patterns in the source and target languages. Translation theory is expected to be descriptive in the first place, and its main task is to study observable facts, to discover the regular features of the translating process common to most individual acts of translation. It is only after discovering what translation actually is that conclusions can be drawn concerning what it should be. Theoretical generalization must therefore be based on facts rather than on subjective speculation. The main method of research used by Russian translation theorists is the comparative analysis of the source and target texts, as well as various experimental studies of the actual act of translation.

Theoretical investigations of translation in Russia are largely carried out within a linguistic framework. Most researchers regard the linguistic theory of translation as an important branch of the linguistic sciences, alongside general linguistics, comparative linguistics, psycholinguistics, sociolinguistics, text linguistics and other areas of linguistic research. This broad concept of macrolinguistics makes it possible to make extensive use of linguistic methods to describe the formal, semantic and cognitive aspects of translation. Most translation theorists in Russia are professional linguists as well as

practising translators. This helps to maintain a close link between theory and practice.

Scholars of translation in Russia carry out a wide range of investigations which embrace all aspects of the translating process and all the factors which are thought to influence it. They attempt to deal with general aspects of interlingual communication – its linguistic, cognitive and psychological dimensions – as well as problems associated with translation from one particular language into another. Much attention is paid to the concept of equivalence in translation, to the pragmatic and stylistic aspects of translation, to various models of the translating process and the meaningful text components which are replaced by equivalent elements in the target text. Translation problems are investigated through the analysis of translations from and between English, German, French, Spanish, Italian, Russian and other languages. The idea is that such complex studies of translation activity will eventually enable scholars to generalize from their findings and to develop a viable framework that can accommodate a general theory of translation.

Of no small importance is the fact that translation studies in Russia embraces all types of translation. Much attention is paid to the description of various aspects of non-literary translation, both written and oral, with an emphasis on political, technical, commercial and similar types of translation. Research in the field of literary translation considers both its linguistic and artistic features. In terms of oral translation, the object of interest is mainly conference interpreting, especially simultaneous interpreting. The investigation of such a wide range of translational activities has made it possible to describe both common features of all translations and the peculiarities of each particular type of translation.

Translation studies in Russia has always maintained close links with the practical training of future translators and interpreters. Specific types of research have often been prompted by the need to develop effective training syllabuses and curricula. Training establishments use the results of theoretical research to select appropriate teaching techniques and include courses in translation theory and practice.

Further reading

Fyodorov 1953; Chukovsky 1964; Revzin and Rozentsveyg 1964; Fyodorov 1968; Gachechiladze 1970; Kopanev 1972; Komissarov 1973; Shveitser 1973; Retsker 1974; Barkhudarov 1975; Chernyakhovskaya 1976; Komissarov 1980; Min'yar-Beloruchev 1980; Latyshev 1988; Shveitser 1988; Semenets and Panas'ev 1989; Komissarov 1990.

VILEN N. KOMISSAROV

S

Slovak tradition

Slovak is a West Slavonic language, typologically close to Czech. It has a literary form, used in official communications, in literature and in the media, and various dialects. The literary form is based on the Central Slovak dialects and has been taking shape since the middle of the nineteenth century. Until then, Czech (with an occasional admixture of Slovak lexical elements) was used as the literary language on the territory of what is now Slovakia. Towards the end of the eighteenth century, Anton Bernolák (1762–1813) attempted to create a literary Slovak language on the basis of western Slovak (now known as *Bernolákötina*, i.e. Bernolák language), but it was Ludovít Štúr (1815–56) who laid the solid foundations of literary Slovak. Full stylistic development did not begin until after 1918, with the establishment of the First Czechoslovak Republic (the first Slovak orthographical standards were laid down in 1931), and more especially after 1945, with the establishment of the Second Czechoslovak Republic.

Beginnings of Slovak translation

Until the turn of the eighteenth and nineteenth centuries, translation in the Slovak-speaking territories was mainly into Czech, though there were sporadic attempts at translation into spoken Slovak. Some ancient Greek texts were translated into Latin, exclusively for educated readers. Towards the end of the eighteenth century, a few translations were made from German into 'Bernolák Slovak'. The translators were generally Catholic priests. The most important figure of that period was Ján Hollý (1785–1849), a priest and poet, whose work marked a new epoch of translation: he translated the Greek

and Latin poets into 'Bernolák Slovak', including Virgil's complete *Aeneid* (1828). Bohuslav Tablic (1769–1823), a Protestant clergyman, poet, enlightener and organizer of cultural life in the Slovak region, translated German and English poetry (for example *Anglické múzy v česko-slovenském oděvu*: The English Muses in Czech-Slovak Garb). Shakespeare, Racine, Molière, Voltaire, Rousseau, Goethe, Pushkin, Mickiewicz and others were also translated into the newly created Slovak literary language during this period.

An outstanding figure in translation at the end of the nineteenth century was the poet and dramatist Pavol Országh Hviezdoslav (1849–1921), who translated from English, Hungarian, German, Polish and Russian. Hviezdoslav, together with the followers of Ludovít Štúr, transmitted the great literary works of the Renaissance, neoclassical and Romantic age to the Slovak reading public.

Translation in the contemporary period

After World War I and the establishment of Czechoslovakia there was an increase in translation activity in Slovakia, but complete emancipation from Czech was not yet achieved. For one thing, Czech translations of the world classics had to compensate for the shortage of native Slovak translations, and for another, these translations, all of them earlier than Slovak translations, frequently proved to be the Slovak translators' most important working aid in the absence of a native tradition of literary translation.

Not until after World War II did Slovak translation emancipate itself from Czech models, as a new generation of educated translators came to the fore. From the 1970s onward, the growing independence of Slovak literary translation was reflected in the fact that not only foreign, but also Czech literature was translated into Slovak.

In parallel with translation practice, though more slowly, a Slovak theory of translation came into being. This was based not only on the experience of the leading practitioners of modern literary translation, but also on the work of some theoreticians, principally those of what has come to be known as the Nitra School. Proceeding from the work of Jiří Levý, Slovak scholars elaborated a scientific definition of translation as a metatext within the system of literary communication. The founder of this school of thought was Anton Popovič (1933–84). He arrived in Nitra in 1967 and co-founded with František Miko the Centre for Literary Communication and Experimental Methodology with the objective of developing a theory of literary communication, and with it also a communicative theory of literary translation. Popovič outlined his theory in a number of publications, namely *Poetika umeleckého prekladu* (Poetics of literary translation, 1971) and *Umelecký preklad v ČSSR* (Literary translation in Czechoslovakia, 1974), and eventually formulated it more fully in his monograph *Teória umeleckého prekladu* (Theory of literary translation, 1975; translated into Hungarian, Russian and Serbo-Croatian). He also edited the volume *Originál/Preklad, Interpretačná terminológia* (Original/Translation, Interpretational terminology) in 1984. Another important publication by Popovič is *Dictionary for the Analysis of Literary Translation* (1976). Popovič's contribution to translation studies is analysed in Gentzler (1993).

An undesirable aspect, in the 1970s and 1980s, was – just as in the Czech Lands and elsewhere in the Soviet sphere of influence – the widespread practice of the translation of poetry with the aid of 'interlinear translations'. This was theoretically justified by the argument that poetry could only be translated by a poet. The real reason, however, was political rather than literary, in that the Slovak poets were simply copying the practice prevalent in the Soviet Union (see RUSSIAN TRADITION). Although on occasion the cooperation between a linguist and a poet undoubtedly resulted in fine translations, in most instances it failed to enrich the store-house of Slovak literary translation.

Because of the lack of qualified experts, non-literary translation prior to the 1940s – much as literary translation – largely relied on Czech translations. Emancipation from Czech as an intermediary language began only after World War II. The 1970s witnessed the beginning of a major translation drive from many languages, a process which has continued to gather momentum under the independent Slovak Republic.

While there must have been some interpreting at diplomatic and governmental level during Slovakia's brief wartime 'independence' as a German client state, professional interpreting did not begin in earnest until after World War II.

Professional organizations and translator training

As in the Czech Lands, literary translators in Slovakia after World War II were organized as a section of the Slovak Writers' Union; this became a member of FIT in 1970. Owing to a less drastic process of political 'normalization' in Slovakia, the Slovak Writers' Union was not dissolved and the Slovak translators' membership in FIT therefore continued uninterrupted. For internal purposes, however, there existed from the 1970s an organization under the Slovak Literary Fund, called the Slovak Translators' Centre; unlike its Czech parallel organization this included both literary and non-literary translators.

University-level teaching of translation in Slovakia began in 1968 in Bratislava, followed in 1973 by the establishment in Nitra of a postgraduate course for translators leading to a degree thesis and its defence. Thanks to the pioneering work of Anton Popovič, the department in Nitra gained international renown for its research and publications.

Further reading
Kochol 1968; Ferenčík 1982; Miko 1982; Vilikovský 1984; Hochel 1990.

ZLATA KUFNEROVÁ AND EWALD OSERS

Southeast Asian traditions

'Southeast Asia' is a relatively new term, having been devised during World War II to describe the geographical area south of China and east of India. This region can be divided into two parts. There are the 'mainland states' of Myanmar (Burma), Thailand, Cambodia, Laos and Vietnam. The cultures of these states remain strongly influenced by Hinduism and Buddhism. Below a latitude seven degrees north of the equator lie the 'island states' of Malaysia, Singapore, Indonesia, Brunei and the Philippines. Although historically these states were also influenced by Hinduism and Buddhism, they accepted Islam from the thirteenth century onwards. The northern part of the Philippines was converted to Catholicism under Spanish influence after 1565. Vietnam has been strongly influenced by its political relationships with China; other Southeast Asian states have also maintained strong commercial ties with China for over two thousand years.

Contact with the major world civilizations of India, the Middle East, China and Europe has involved exposure to a variety of languages, including Chinese, Sanskrit, Pali, Tamil, Arabic, Persian, Dutch, English and French. Southeast Asian translation practices reflect this complex intermingling of influences: on the one hand, extensive contact among local literary traditions; and on the other, the long-standing contact with major international religious and, later, secular literatures.

Contact, in general, has been expressed in a number of forms: through the direct translation of clearly identifiable source texts, but also through borrowing, adaptation, imitation and the creation of new works based on various degrees of knowledge of the source texts. This contact has been further complicated by the fact that written manuscripts have largely served as the basis for oral recitation in specific social contexts, and that these recitations must be further understood as intertextually related to other forms of performance, in particular the *wayang* shadow-puppet theatre and dance, as well as to the plastic arts of bas reliefs, murals, sculpture and temple architecture.

Classical South Asian sacred texts in Southeast Asia

There is evidence, from almost the beginning of the Common Era (CE), of the presence of powerful kingdoms in Southeast Asia whose major political, social and cultural practices were strongly influenced by South Asian models. Later there would be further influence from the expansion of Theravada Buddhism to the Pyu kingdom in the sixth century and then extensively throughout the mainland from the twelfth century.

Sacred languages and literatures

Sanskrit inscriptions, attesting to a knowledge of Indic literature, and in particular of Indian metres, are widespread from the fourth century, while inscriptions in indigenous languages appear two centuries later. The earliest surviving written record is a Khmer inscription (611 CE) in a Southern Indic script, which includes a number of Sanskrit terms. As the Khmer language developed in later centuries, Pali terms were also introduced. These same influences can also be seen in Burmese. The Mahayana Buddhist kingdom of Srivijaya in South Sumatra has left a small number of metrical inscriptions in Old Malay dating from 684 CE; they too are written in a Southern Indian script and contain many Sanskrit words. The first inscriptions in Old Javanese date from 732 CE, and again the presence of Indian words is pervasive. The earliest evidence of written Burmese dates from the eleventh century; this includes records incised on stone slabs and some fragments of palm leaf manucripts plastered on walls in the old capital of Pagan. Particularly significant is the Mya-zei-di Inscription of Prince Rajakumar (1113), which presents translations into Pyu, Mon and Pali of the same text.

Religious professionals maintained ritual texts in their original languages at the centre of the various literary polysystems. Commentaries in both the original language and in translation were, however, also important. A Chinese work of the sixth century, the *Gaoseng zhuan*, tells of a Kashmiri prince who was converted to Buddhism at the beginning of the fifth century and travelled to 'Java' to preach his new-found faith there. He translated a text of the Mulasarvastivada school into a local language. In a surviving, perhaps eighth-century, version of the Buddhist text, the *Sang Hyang Kamahayanikan*, each Sanskrit verse is followed by an Old Javanese paraphrase. The practice of the reading and immediate paraphrase of religious texts persists in Hindu Bali to the present day.

The epics

Among the nobility, less ascetic interests prevailed. The major translations and adaptions of the Classical period are based primarily on heroic texts: the two Sanskrit epics, the *Ramayana* by Valmiki and the *Mahabharata* by Vyasa. Other heroic texts include the tales of the Buddha's past lives (*jatakas*) from the *Khuddaka-nikaya* of the Pali Buddhist Canon and the extra-canonical *Pannyasa Jatakani*. A number of other Hindu and Buddhist texts were also translated, including the legendary *Harimvansa*, and the Buddhist fables of the *Panchatantra*.

Of the two epics, the *Ramayana* was the more prominent, and numerous versions are found throughout Southeast Asia. Santosh Desai believes that this epic travelled along two routes to Southeast Asia: along the southern sea route from Gujarat and south India into Java, Sumatra, and Malaya; and along the eastern land route from Bengal into Burma, Thailand and Laos. Cambodia and Vietnam may have received it partly from Java and partly from India (Ramanujan 1991: 33). One of the most ancient Sanskrit inscriptions from the eastern coast at Vo-canh can be dated to the third century CE and contains some words taken from that epic. Another inscription containing the name 'Valmiki' has been found at Tra-Kieu, an area ruled by the Campa king Prakasadharma from the second half of the seventh century CE. The earliest evidence for knowledge of the Valmiki *Ramayana* in Burma is once again found in early inscriptions.

Because of the variety of languages involved in transmission, not all of the written texts are based on Valmiki's original version. An exemplary Old Javanese *Ramayana,* displaying a large variety of Indian metres, was probably written before 930 CE. It seems to be based on a later Southern Indian Sanskrit text of the sixth to

seventh centuries, the *Ravana Vadha* (the Death of Rahwana, Rama's enemy). P. J. Zoetmulder suggests that the writer, known as Yogiswara in later Balinese tradition, gave himself a certain amount of liberty to depart from his model, by adding clarifications in certain places and abbreviating others (1974: 229). A focus on Rawana is also characteristic of the Malay *Hikayat Seri Rama*, which has survived only in the Arabic script, uses carefully modified terms to refer to God, and includes the Prophet Adam as a major character. This text may have been derived from Javanese versions used for shadow puppet performances.

In Cambodia, the earliest reference to the *Ramayana* is the Val Kantel inscription (seventh century), which mentions the recitation of both this epic and of texts from the scriptural tradition known as the *Purana* (myths). Bas reliefs illustrating stories from the *Mahabharata* indicate knowledge of this work as well. There are two later Khmer versions of the *Ramayana* – *Ramakerti I, II* (16th–18th centuries) – in which Sakyamuni Buddha is described as a bodhisattva, a potential Buddha who nevertheless refuses to enter into Nirvana until he is able to take all of created existence along with him. The best-known epic poem in Laos is *Prah lak Prah lam*, the Lao version of the *Ramayana* which is set in the Mekong Valley. The Tai-Loe version of the *Ramayana* is somewhat similar to the Khmer version: Rama is assimilated to the bodhisattva Sakyamuni, and his struggle with Ravana is linked to the Buddha's victory over Mara, the evil one who tried to tempt him with material pleasures. In Burma, U Aung Phyo composed a version of the *Ramayana* in verse, the *Rama Thagyin* (1775). Subsequently, U Tui (1751–96) composed a verse rendition of the Valmiki *Ramayana*. The Siamese version, *Ramakirti* (Rama's glory) or *Ramakian* (Rama's story), completed by King Rama I and his translator-poets in 1797, incorporates many Thai legends and customs in its 50,000 verses. The text shows possible influence from the Tamil *Ramayana* of Kamban since the names of many characters are clearly not Sanskrit.

In Island Southeast Asia, the *Mahabharata* overshadowed the *Ramayana* in importance. Translations of the major parts of the 'Northern' recension into Old Javanese were done before 1000 CE. A prose redaction of the fourth book, the 'Wirataparwa', bears a date equivalent to 996 CE; and some other books, although undated, are also dedicated to the same king. The translations were almost certainly done by a number of writers, judging by differences in language and style. The introductory verses to the 'Wirataparwa' describe the translator's aim as being to 'Javanize the work conceived in Vyasa's mind' (Zoetmulder 1974: 87). The story is to be told 'in accordance with the truth and exactly as it happened, without ambiguities and without verbosity'. These comments were clearly directed against other workers who were inclined towards 'embellishments' of their own making, and 'playful liberties' (ibid.: 88). The broad outlines of the original stories were followed, with some shortenings and omissions. Quotations in verse from the original Sanskrit remain scattered throughout the translations, both for their own intrinsic interest and as a way of anchoring the translations within the original source texts (ibid.).

An important poetic tradition developed in Old Javanese over the next two centuries, drawing on various stories from the *Mahabharata*. Increasingly, these literary works gained a local flavour. As Zoetmulder notes, '[t]hese men and women with Indian names are essentially Javanese, acting like Javanese, thinking like Javanese, and living in a Javanese environment' (ibid.: 188). These poetic narratives were preserved, and rewritten in Bali, and also spread to the Malay peninsula and Southern Thailand, together with the more indigenous Javanese love stories of Raden Panji. In Malaya, these imported tales had such prestige that texts were occasionally created which purported to be 'shifted from the Javanese', even though no original texts have as yet been found (Robson 1967: 7).

Buddhist texts

Popular hagiography of the Buddha, including both the canonical and apocryphal tales of his past lives, has also exerted an enormous influence on the form and content of Southeast Asian art and literature, most particularly on the Mainland; but their influence is also evident in the bas reliefs of temples and sculptures from the eighth to the twelfth centuries in Java and Sumatra. Frescoes in the twelfth-century Burmese Lokahteikpan Temple in Pagan depict the canonical *jataka* and are identified by lines written in Burmese. Many versions of the *Vessantara Jataka* exist throughout the different regions of Thailand and are still recited at the beginning of Buddhist Lent.

In the mid-eighteenth century two monks, Sayadaw Shin Kaweinda and U Awbatha, produced the first literary translations of the canonical jatakas into Burmese. U Awbatha (fl. 1752–87), whose prose style influenced the rest of Burmese literature, completed the first formal translation of the *Mahanipata*. Burmese scholar Htin Aung describes this translation as following the Pali originals closely 'as far as the incidents of the stories were concerned, but he [U Awbatha] portrayed character in detail, and made the characters more lifelike and therefore more interesting' (Htin Aung 1957: 47). This reflects the tendency in Burmese 'translation' towards redaction and adaptation rather than literal translation, a common trait throughout the region. The minor *jataka* of the *Khuddaka-nikaya* were subsequently translated by the Nyaung-gan Hsaya-daw (head of the Nyaung-gan Monastery). Later a Burmese translation was done of the apocryphal *Pannyasa Jatakani*, a text which became much more popular in Laos, Thailand and Cambodia.

Finally the Pali canon, or sections from it, was rendered into most major mainland Southeast Asian languages. During the Middle Period (16–19th centuries) in Cambodia, unknown translators developed Khmer versions of the Pali Tipitaka, with the most commonly preserved sections being the monastic rules (*vinaya*) and teachings (*sutta*). They also developed *samray*, the generic name for a Pali Buddhist religious treatise, containing both a Khmer translation and an explanatory commentary. This follows a popular oral tradition of reciting a religious text, translating it into Khmer, then commenting on it. Thailand's King Rama I (1782–1809) obtained the tipitaka from Sri Lanka and sponsored a grand council to standardize the Thai version in Pali.

Recent editions of sacred texts

Because of their continuing religious and cultural importance, major Buddhist texts have continued to be edited and translated to the present day. In 1856 the Burmese King Mindon, founder of the royal city of Mandalay and convenor of the Fifth Buddhist Council, ordered the engraving of the Burmese-Pali Tipitaka onto 729 stone stelae. One hundred years later, the Sixth Buddhist Council was convened in Burma (1954–6) to revise the engraved text and publish a print edition in Burmese.

In 1969 the Buddhist Institute of Cambodia published the complete Pali text of the Tipitaka based on a critical edition done in Thailand, together with a Khmer translation in 110 volumes. This edition was completed under French influence, with its more academic approach to editing and translation. Several Cambodian verse adaptations of the Mahanipata were made from this Tipitaka collection.

The *Ramayana* continues to be popular throughout Mainland Southeast Asia. Thailand's Rama IV (1920–25) commissioned a new translation of it based upon an English translation of the Sanskrit original; the first critical edition of the Lao *Phra Lok Phra Lam* was published in 1973. Most recently, the Cambodian Buddhist Institute published Thun Hin's Khmer translation of the *Ramayana* in 2005.

Islam in Island Southeast Asia

The coming of Islam to Island Southeast Asia after the beginning of the thirteenth century CE gradually put an end to the formal creation and consumption of Hindu and Buddhist texts in this region. Some texts survived in suitably adapted versions; others were not recopied, allowed to rot, or sometimes either burned or consigned to be used as waste paper for cleansing purposes (Sheikh Nuruddin ar-Raniri 1992: 29).

Again, religious texts (the QUR'ĀN and the stories of the life of the Prophet Muhammad, *hadith*), together with 'explanations' in indigenous languages, were at the centre of the system, while adventure stories continued to appeal strongly to the men of the court (and love stories to their women). The earliest legends derived from the Shia traditions, which were later considered to be unorthodox throughout the region. A. Samad Ahmad notes that 'the greater part' of Muslim chronicles in Malay from *c.*1300 to *c.* 1600s were 'translations or adaptations of Persian stories and most follow Persian writing styles' (A. Samad Ahmad 1987: xix).

A major example is the *Hikayat Muhammad Hanafiyyah*, which is based on a Persian text written in about 1350 and translated into an archaic form of classical Malay shortly thereafter. The text consists of two parts. The first tells of the martyrdom of Hasan and Husein, grandsons of the Prophet but destined never to succeed him as the leaders of Islam. The second part is a quite unhistorical account of the attempt of their half-brother, Muhammad Hannifiyah, to revenge their betrayal. The majority of the Malay text is fluent and idiomatic, although sections lapse into an unidiomatic 'translationese', which is distinguished by its 'clumsiness and weird constructions' (Brakel 1975: 44). These, however, later have a structural purpose: they are reserved for direct quotations from Arabic and Persian, for paraphrases of Arabic phrases and quotations, and for the finer points of religious law. The two styles, as editor L. Brakel states, are 'complementary', and their use is structurally determined in that the different forms serve opposing purposes (ibid.). Other translations of Middle Eastern warrior stories made prior to the sixteenth century include the *Hikayat Amir Hamzah*, describing the battles of the uncle of the Prophet in defence of the new faith, and the *Hikayat Iskandar Dzul-Karnain*, the life of Alexander the Great.

The *Taj as-Salatin* (Crown of Kings) by Bukhari al-Jauhari was completed in the Achehnese court of Alauddin Riayat Shah in 1603. The first three chapters deal in a pantheistic manner with the nature of mankind, of God, and of the world. The remaining twenty-three chapters deal, as the colonial scholar Sir Richard Winstedt writes, 'with such topics as death, the Caliphs and their honourable poverty, just and unjust rulers, Muslim and infidel, viziers, writers, envoys, officials, children, right conduct, intelligence, the science of physiognomy, the qualifications of rulers and their duties to subjects Muslim and infidel, their need to keep faith and be liberal' (Winstedt 1977: 140). Winstedt finds the Malay 'atrocious' (ibid.: 138). A more recent scholar, V. Braginsky, simply notes that the text includes Persian calques, a variety of Persian poetic forms and rhymed prose, and refers to over fifty Arabic and Persian sources (Braginsky 2004: 431).

Other works translated from Persian and Arabic to the end of the nineteenth century include extensive theological, legal and other scientific materials (Harun Mat Piah 2002). These translations were most commonly done in a fairly literal manner.

The colonial era, c.1800–1942

During the colonial era, the Malay Peninsula, Singapore and North Borneo were governed by the British; Indonesia by the Dutch. In more recent historical times, Myanmar was colonized by the British, Thailand remained independent, and the other states – Laos, Cambodia and Vietnam – became French colonies ('Indochina'). Increased translation activity between European and Chinese literatures is a hallmark of this period.

The first impact of European translation activity in the seventeenth century was associated with the Christian missions. In order to promote Christianity in Vietnam, Portuguese Jesuit missionaries created a Latin script for Vietnamese (*ngoc ngu*) in the seventeenth century, and used it to translate the Catechism, the Lives of the Saints, and other Christian works. French Catholic priests in the late seventeenth century and American Baptist missionaries in the early nineteenth century were also interested in producing Christian texts in Thai. Some Gospels in Thai were printed in the 1820s–1830s; others soon followed. Along with the spread of British colonial influence, Christian missionaries began their activities in Burma during the eighteenth century. The first Burmese translations of the Gospels appeared in 1815. The American Baptist Mission Press printed Christian tracts and catechisms in Burmese. Adoniram Judson's translation of the Gospel of St Matthew was printed in 1817. The Karen Mission Press, established in 1837, merged with the Moulmein Mission Press in 1855, and together they pioneered the translation and printing of the Bible in Sgaw, Pwo Karen and Mon languages.

Increasing poverty and political oppression in China led to the widespread dispersal of an overseas Chinese population throughout Southeast Asia during the late eighteenth and nineteenth centuries. This community was eager for reading material but, as a result of regular local intermarriage patterns, frequently preferred to read translations in indigenous languages. Some of these translations drew on Chinese heroic tales. The *Romance of the Three Kingdoms* (*Sanguo yanyi*) was popular in many Southeast Asian countries. It was translated into *quoc ngu* in Vietnam, rendered into a prose version by Thailand's Phra Khlang in 1802, and translated by Nou Kan into Cambodian, then serialized in the Buddhist Institute's literary magazine *Kambujasuriya* from 1948 and reprinted in 2005. Chinese literature in translation remained popular throughout the twentieth century. In Indonesia, it has been estimated that some 759 works of Chinese origin were translated into 'Low Malay' between about 1870 and 1950 (Sumardjo 2004: 27).

The impetus for the translation of European literature increased from the mid-nineteenth century, with French literature more popular in Laos, Vietnam and Cambodia and British literature elsewhere. The translation of fables and tales was intially quite popular. In Burma *Aesop's Fables* was translated from English in 1880, as were *One Thousand and One Nights* in 1886 and *Arab Tales* in 1889. Tales of adventure were also popular in this early modern period. During the latter part of the century, the novels of Sir Walter Scott, with their extensive dialogue, were published in Burmese translation; these significantly influenced the development of the modern Burmese novel.

In Indonesia, it has been estimated that over 230 works of European literature were produced during this period. A few were by major authors, such as Tolstoy, Shakespeare, Ibsen, Dickens, Victor Hugo and Guy de Maupassant. The overwhelming majority were more sensational works by popular authors such as Sir Arthur Conan Doyle, Edgar Rice Burroughs (Tarzan), Sax Rohmer (Fu Manchu), and the authors of adventure stories such as Alexandre Dumas, Rider Haggard and Jules Verne (Sumardjo 2004: 57).

Allowing for local tastes and the impact of the various colonial centres, these patterns were common throughout the rest of Southeast Asia. In Cambodia translations from Lao, French, Greek, Sanskrit, Vietnamese, Chinese, Japanese and English were made during the twentieth century. In 1901, the French institutionalized the academic study of Cambodia with the establishment of the École Française d'Extrême-

Orient, which subsequently took over the duty of caring for Angkor Wat in 1907. This influence encouraged Khmer translations of works by a number of French philosophers and writers, among them Molière, Corneille, Alexandre Dumas and Hector Malot.

In Vietnam, Nguyen Van Vinh's translations of Molière's plays became available in 1915, followed by Pham Quynh's translations of Corneille's plays in 1920. By 1920 Nguyen Van Vinh's translation of *Le Malade imaginaire* had been staged in Hanoi. The staffs of the two periodicals *Dong-duong tap-chi* (1913–16) and *Nam Phong tap-chi* (July 1917–December 1934) produced and published translations from Chinese and French, including Descartes' *Discours de la méthode*, Epictetus' *Enchiridion* (Manual), as well as Corneille's poems and Pham Quynh's translations of his tragedies *Le Cid* and *Horace*. The staff of *Nam Phong* also translated early Vietnamese texts in Chinese and *nom* into *quoc ngu*, for example *Hong Duc quoc-am thi-tap* (Collected Poems of the Hong Duc Period) and Phan Huy Chu's *Lich trieu hien chuong loai chi* (Regulations Made by the Various Dynasties, Arranged in Categories). *Dong-duong tap-chi* ran a section entitled 'Selections from French literature translated into Vietnamese'. Nguyen Trong-Thuat, the editor of *Dong-duong tap-chi,* translated a number of French novels including Antoine François Prévost's *Manon Lescaut* (1932), Alexandre Dumas' *Les trois mousquetaires* (1921), and Alain René Lesage's *Gil Blas*. By the late 1930s, the works of Western writers such as Balzac, Flaubert, Dickens, Tolstoy, Romain Rolland, Henri Barbusse, André Gide, Pascal, Dostoyevsky and Goethe were available to Vietnamese readers in translation.

Similarly, in Burma a large number of adapted Western novels had appeared by 1920, with favourites adopting themes of love and adventure. Shwei U-daung (1888–1974) was a master adaptor and translator of Victorian fiction, including works by Rider Haggard, Conan Doyle, G. W. M. Reynolds, Mrs. Henry Wood and Charles Dickens. Fiction writer P. Monin (1883–1940) also adapted Western books on sociology and psychology. In 1937 a group of Rangoon University students established the Red Dragon Book Club to publish translations of Marxist classics. One of their members, the young nationalist Ma Amar, translated Maurice

Collis' *Trials in Burma*, published in 1938, which influenced the development of nationalist literature in Burma.

World War II and after

The Japanese Occupation of much of Southeast Asia and the subsequent gradual dismantling of colonial empires led to the discovery and translation of new literary sources. These now included Russian, American and other European texts not previously available in particular colonies.

In Vietnam, while the war was still raging, a group of progressive French-educated intellectuals started a new weekly, *Thanh-nghi,* in 1943. They published translations of novels by French, English, American, Italian and Chinese writers, among them Somerset Maugham, Pearl Buck and Ts'ao Yu. From 1945 onwards there were many translations of Russian and Chinese works on political theory and Marxist economics under the influence of the Vietnamese Republic. In the South, between 1955 and 1963 existenialism was popularized through translations appearing in various books and newspapers.

The Burmese government established the Burma Translation Society in 1947, which provided the impetus for new translations. Shwei U-daung continued his tremendous translation activity, including his translation of Mikhail Sholokhov's *And Quiet Flows the Don*. Since the military coup in 1962, the government has exercised strict censorship on literature and the production of translations. This has not stopped the popularization of spy novels and romance, represented by the popular fiction of Mickey Spillane and James Hadley Chase.

The new translations gave Southeast Asian writers the chance to explore new literary styles as they worked to create new 'modern' literatures in their own languages. In Indonesia, for example, the innovative prose writer Idrus developed a sparse, cynical approach to the short story, which was influenced by his exposure to the Dutch writers of the 1930s. The anarchist poet Chairil Anwar studied (and plagiarized) T. S. Eliot, Rilke and the Dutch poets Slauerhoff and Marsmann. Pramoedya Ananta Toer, who was to become Indonesia's greatest prose writer of the twentieth century, learned eagerly from his translations of Steinbeck, Tolstoy, Sholokov, Gorky, Kuprin and Pasternak.

As the late twentieth century unfolded, the scope of works available in translation has continued to expand. In Indonesia, again, the range of writers translated has expanded to include Brecht, Neruda, Brodsky and Seamus Heaney. The list of a contemporary major publisher, Gramedia, includes works by Paulo Coelho, Amy Tan, Danielle Steel, John Grisham, Tolkien and Sydney Sheldon. Translation, in Indonesia and in other Southeast Asian nations, has entered the global marketplace. Harry Potter is everywhere. Occasionally, however, the opposite has also taken place. Different translation projects prioritizing different source languages/cultures have sometimes deliberately *deselected* specific source cultures. As reported in Stecconi and Torres Reyes (1997), not a single Anglo-American author featured in three anthologies of translations published in the Philippines in 1971 and 1975. This was done because the national resistance movement decried, among other things, an 'educational system set up by the American colonizers' to ensure that Filipinos remain 'estranged from themselves and their values' (1997: 71). Instead, prioritizing translations of literary texts from Asia, Africa and Latin America, as well as indigenous texts written in the different languages of the Philippines, these anthologies challenged Anglo-American literary hegemony and simultaneously participated in elaborating a narrative in which local Filipino resistance could be framed as part of a wider international movement of self-determination. Similarly, there have been few translations from Dutch into Indonesian after 1950, or from Russian into Vietnamese after the early 1980s.

Overall, the details of the contemporary situation described here confirm Richard Jacquemond's four hypotheses on 'the problems of translating across power differentials' (Jacquemond 1992; discussed in Robinson 1997: 31–2). Southeast Asian publishers translate extensively but still somewhat selectively from works controlled by major Western publishers, and are unable to sell much back in return. Except for a few major writers who confirm stereotypes of repressive Asian military regimes and the suffering of beautiful Asian women as victims of traditional patriarchal

authorities, there is little outside interest in a region best known for a foreign war lost as long ago as 1975. Some writers translate their own work into English, or have friends do it in the desire to reach a wider audience. Some also translate, or are translated into, other major regional languages, as happens particularly in the Philippines. Examples include Lina Sagaral-Reyes' 'Storya', originally in English, then translated into Cebuano and Tagalog (1990); and poet Jose F. Lacaba, who produces English translations of his own poems (1980, 1989). On the whole, however, barriers of nationalism and language differentials continue to limit the flow of literatures within the region itself.

Further reading
Iltin Aung 1957; Robson 1969; Zoetmulder 1974; Winstedt 1977; A. Samad Ahmad 1987; Ramanujan 1991; Sheikh Nuruddin Ar-raniri 1992; Stecconi and Torres Reyes 1997; Braginsky 2004.

HARRY AVELING AND
TERI SHAFFER YAMADA

Spanish tradition

The cultural diversity of Spanish history is not always visible in the modern Spain of 39 million inhabitants. The language known as Spanish, more correctly called Castilian, is now spoken throughout Spain but is only one of several Romance languages that developed from Latin after the Roman conquest of Hispania in the third century AD. The most active minority languages are Catalan in the northeast with its centre in Barcelona, Galician in the northwest, and Basque, a non-Romance language that has survived around the western French/Spanish border. The historical languages of Aragon, Leon and Asturias have also contributed to the linguistic mosaic. Collectively known as Romance, the Latin-derived languages were moreover spoken alongside the Arabic, Hebrew and Latin of medieval Spain. This considerable internal diversity has been both enhanced and repressed by translation. Translation took place into several languages throughout much of the medieval Reconquista, when Christians slowly 'reconquered' the peninsula from Islamic rule. The systematic privileging of Castilian as a target language can then be dated rather arbitrarily from 1492, initiating a long period of repression of internal diversity that lasted at least through to the death of Franco in 1975. A certain cultural plurality is nevertheless being rediscovered in present-day Spain.

The Reconquista (718–1492)

Major parts of Spain were under Islamic rule from 711 through to the thirteenth century, although Granada remained Islamic until 1492. The centuries of the Reconquista included long periods of co-existence and influence, made possible by the efforts of intercultural groups able to mediate between Arabic and Romance. Medieval translators in Spain were often Jews, Conversos (Jews publicly converted to Christianity) or Mozarabs (Christians who had lived under Islamic rule). There was also a rich variety of international scholars who translated into Latin. Like Sicily and Constantinople, Spain was a multicultural region between the Christian and Islamic worlds.

Islamic Spain had the most advanced scientific knowledge of the time, largely thanks to the Greek texts translated into Arabic in the ninth century. Regular translation efforts from Arabic into Latin date from the early twelfth century, when Adelard of Bath and the Converso Petrus Alphonsus brought knowledge of Arabic astronomy to England, and Bishop Michael of Tarazona, in the north of Spain, sponsored the translation of proto-scientific texts from Arabic into Latin, quite probably to meet a French demand. This northward flow was strengthened by Peter the Venerable (c.1092–1156), the French abbot of Cluny who visited Spain and organized the first Latin translation of the Qur'ān and explanatory documents in 1142–3. The translation was carried out by a team comprising Robert of Kent, Herman of Dalmatia, the Mozarab Peter of Toledo, the abbot's own French notary Peter, and a native informant called, with suitable anonymity, 'Mahumeth'. Robert and Herman were also part of a small network of foreign translators who were in Spain in search of Arabic science. The translations carried out by this group were mainly in the fields of astronomy, astrology and mathematics.

While in Spain, Peter the Venerable met Archbishop Raymond of Toledo, who was also French and also became interested in sponsoring translations from Arabic. There is little evidence that Raymond founded any 'college' of translators, but successive archbishops at Toledo did continue to favour the translative, and possibly educative activity that has been called the School of Toledo. According to González Palencia (1942), Raymond's prime interest was the accumulation of wealth and the gaining of power over the recently conquered lands. He met Peter the Venerable in Salamanca in 1142 and was presumably aware of the latter's project to have the Qur'ān translated into Latin. This might have inspired him to sponsor John of Spain's translation of Costa ben Luca's De differentia spiritus et animae, the only translation in which he is clearly named as a patron (d'Alverny 1964).

The main figure justifying talk of a 'School of Toledo' (Rose 1874) was Gerard of Cremona (c.1114–87), Italian translator of Arabic science into Latin. According to the Vita written by his associates or socii, Gerard went to Toledo in Spain for love of Ptolemy's Almagest, which he could not find among the Latins. He learned Arabic at Toledo and, according to the Vita, translated some seventy-one texts from Arabic into Latin, mostly in the fields of mathematics, astronomy, philosophy and medicine. Although he probably coordinated some kind of teamwork, Gerard's translations have a recognizable style. In the words of the Vita, 'To the end of his life he continued to transmit to the Latin world, as if to his own beloved heir, whatever books he thought finest, in many subjects, as accurately and as plainly as he could' (quoted in translation in McVaugh 1974). Translations undertaken in Toledo during the following century included those by the philosopher Michael Scot, who translated Aristotle and al-Butriji before moving to Bologna in 1220, and Herman of Germany, who translated Aristotle and Averroës from Arabic into Latin in the 1240s.

Most translations into Latin during this period were extremely literal, sometimes word-for-word. Traditionally applied to sacred texts, these strategies had been transferred to philosophical and scientific translating at least since

Boethius and John Scotus Eriugena. The resulting opacity was nevertheless offset by secondary discourses such as marginal notes, glosses and extended commentaries. Omissions and transformations were also used to Christianize certain texts.

As the translations from Arabic moved northwards, Christian epics in Latin or French were coming southwards, requiring translation or adaptation. Although troubadours visited the Spanish courts from the late twelfth century, major romances would not be translated before the second half of the thirteenth century, with anti-chivalrous elements omitted and adultery minimized in deference to the Spanish church.

From 1250 the Castilian vernacular was also receiving scientific texts from Arabic, significantly sponsored by Alfonso X (1221–84) possibly as part of a nation-building policy for Castile and to enhance his candidature to become Holy Roman Emperor. King of Castile (Spain) from 1252, Alfonso X is known as *el Sabio* ('the Wise') more for his sponsorship of learning than for his disastrous political and economic management of Castile. He was an 'active general editor' (Proctor 1951: 3) for numerous translations from Arabic, mostly into Castilian and mostly in the field of astronomy. These Alphonsine translations, mostly carried out at Toledo and mostly in the field of astronomy, should not be confused with the earlier church-sponsored work there. In some prominent twelfth-century cases, a Jew or Mozarab had rendered the Arabic text into an oral Romance version, which a Christian clerk had then translated into a written Latin version. The Alphonsine translators took over this method but now wrote down the Romance version. Collaboration was sometimes extended to include a *glosador* to supply explanatory comments, a *capitulador* to arrange the work into chapters, and an *emendador* to correct the Castilian. The main Alphonsine translators were Jewish, often working in collaboration with Christian clerks. A team of Italians associated with Alfonso's imperial candidature also rendered several of the Castilian translations into Latin and French.

Repeatedly opposed by the aristocracy, Alfonso X left Castile in political turmoil. The following century would see translations

into the rival Hispanic languages, especially into Catalan. Through numerous translations of classical and Renaissance Latin texts, to be followed in the fifteenth century by work from the Italian of Dante and Boccaccio, Catalan often functioned as a bridge to other Hispanic traditions. A small body of texts was translated into Galician, and a team in Avignon worked from Greek into Aragonese under Juan Fernández de Heredia (*c*.1310–96). Castilian was nevertheless the target language used by Pero Lopez de Ayala (1332–1407), whose calques from French and Latin texts helped move Castilian prose away from the Semitic structures introduced by the Alphonsine translators. A great survivor in very troubled times, Pero Lopez de Ayala had a long public career during which he was, among many other things, advisor to the king of France, negotiator with the house of Lancaster, and Royal Chancellor of Castile. He was twice taken prisoner, once by Edward the Black Prince for six months, later by the Portuguese. Late in life he retired to his estates where he wrote chronicles based on his observations and translated selections from Gregory the Great, Livy, Isidorus Hispanensis, Guido de Colonna and Boccaccio. These translations played an important role in the introduction of Italian humanism to Spain.

Serious contacts between Spanish scholars and Italian humanists might be dated from about 1392, when Coluccio Saluttati wrote to Juan Fernández de Heredia asking for a copy of his Aragonese version of Plutarch. These contacts resulted in translations and retranslations of the great texts of antiquity. Whereas the Italians translated into Latin, the Spanish worked into Romance. The transfer flow was thus generally from Italy into Spain, with many Greek texts being rendered into Hispanic Romance from intermediary Latin versions done in Italy. This would indeed be a distinctive feature of Spanish proto-humanism. But there was also significant mediation by French, particularly in the case of work into Catalan.

The contact between Spanish scholars and Italian Humanism was marked by theoretical differences. In the 1430s, Alonso de Cartagena (1384–1456), Bishop of Burgos and translator of Seneca and Cicero, criticized Leonardo Bruni's Latin version of Aristotle's *Ethics*. This attracted attention in Italy in 1436–7 and led to a debate. In *De interpretatione recta* Bruni had privileged target-language eloquence; Cartagena insisted on unadorned source-text fidelity, arguing that eloquence resided in substance and not style. Since Cartagena did not know Greek, he was in fact defending scholastic translations of Aristotle. Although opposing Humanist eloquence, Cartagena was not calling for word-for-word literalism. He instead recognized that 'each language has its own way of speaking', and that texts should be adapted to these differences except in the case of 'doctrines whose value derives from the authority of the person who pronounced them' (Santoyo 1987: 33). This restriction of course harks back to Jerome and would be picked up in about 1440 by Alfonso de Madrigal (c.1400–55). De Madrigal translated *Libro de las Cronicas o tienpos de Eusebio Cesariense* from Latin into Castilian and insisted on word-for-word methods *(interpretacion)* for such cases but then justified the use of 'exposition, commentary or glosses' for other text types (Norton 1984: 31–2). He thus distinguished two kinds of translation for two kinds of situation. The freer of the methods was supported by the belief that 'there is nothing that is signified by the words of one language that cannot be signified by the words of another' (Russell 1985: 31). This theory outlined a correction of Jerome, since special conditions were to apply to translations into the vernacular.

In practice, however, fifteenth-century Spanish translators were already remarkably free with their expositions, commentaries and glosses. One of the reasons for the increasing freedom in translation methods could have been the need to instruct a new class of readers. The main patronage of translations had shifted from the twelfth-century church to the thirteenth-century crown and, by the fifteenth century, to the Spanish nobility. The latter, which had limited knowledge of Latin, frequently contested the power of the king. Translations thus entered local power struggles. The Marquis of Santillana (1398–1458), who led the nobles against the king, was a particularly active sponsor, receiving Latin versions directly from Italy and having Virgil, Ovid and Seneca rendered into Castilian. A French military book could thus be translated into Castilian twice in the same year, once for Santillana and again for his arch political rival (Alvar and Gómez Moreno 1987). Similarly,

cognate languages had their own versions of certain texts. Paulo Orosio translated Aristotle's *Ethics* from Aragonese into Castilian, and the text also existed in Catalan; Enrique de Villena translated his own Catalan into Castilian. Other works from this period include Pero Diaz de Toledo's Castilian version of Plato's *Phaedo*, translated from Leonardo Bruni's Latin version in 1455. Many of these translators, including the Bishop of Burgos, were from Converso families, which formed a trading and intellectual class in the service of the various political powers.

In 1474–9 the Spanish nobility provoked civil war in Castile. Less than two decades later, in 1492, history looked very different. Under the Catholic Sovereigns, Castile was united with Aragon, the Inquisition had been set up, the Islamic kingdom of Granada had been defeated, the remaining Jews had been expelled, Columbus had seen the Americas, and Spain was gaining power and empire. These major changes affected translation in two ways. First, the Castilian language lost its supposed inferiority. Second, for some five centuries, the ideal of Castilian purity would periodically expel dissident cultural groups, notably Jews, Protestants, Jesuits, supporters of Napoleon, Romantic liberals, Carlists, Democrats and Republicans. All these exiled groups produced translators. Medieval translation had owed much to foreigners in Spain; translation after 1492 would often be indebted to Spaniards abroad.

The triumph of Castilian (1492–1975)

The year 1492 marks, among many other things, the first written grammar of a vernacular language, Castilian, written by Nebrija because, as he reportedly explained to Queen Isabel, 'language accompanies empire'. Spain became the dominant political force in Europe in the sixteenth and early seventeenth centuries, thanks not only to its colonial empire but also to Charles V's status as Holy Roman Emperor (1519–56), king of Burgundy and the Netherlands (1506–56) and, as Carlos I, king of Spain (1516–56). At the same time as it was imposed on the American colonies, Castilian thus gained political ascendance over French,

English and the languages of northern Europe, increasingly becoming an exporter of texts. This strengthening of Castilian culture moreover combined with the continued influence of Italian to squeeze out translations into other Hispanic languages, especially Catalan. The age of empire had little room for internal diversity.

One of the products of empire was a series of laws proclaimed from 1529 to 1630 in order to regulate interpreters in the American colonies. These laws stipulated the fees, workloads and ethical obligations of interpreters working between Castilian and the American tongues, as well as the extreme punishments awaiting those who did not comply. Quite probably without much effect in the colonies, one of the texts dating back to 1583 describes interpreters as 'the instrument by which justice is done, the natives are governed, and the injuries done to the natives are corrected' (Gargatagli 1992, unpublished). Whatever the actual practices, the legislative rationale was not without nobility.

Spanish translation theory adjusted to the new status of Castilian. For as long as the Latin-derived languages had collectively been called *Romance*, to translate into them had been to *romancear*, on a par with *vulgarizar*. However, the verb *traducir* and its cognates, gradually adopted from the Italian Humanists in the course of the fifteenth century, could now became part of an imperialist ideology, progressively doing away with the collectively inferior *Romance*. The most praised expression of this change was Juan Boscán's 1534 translation of Castiglione's *Il Cortegiano*, where the translator notes that 'to translate (*traducir*) this book is not really to put it into Romance (*romanzalle*), but to move it from one vernacular into another that is perhaps just as good' (Santoyo 1987: 59).

The new confidence was not restricted to work from Italian. In 1528 Fernán Pérez de Oliva (*c*.1494–*c*.1531) adapted Sophocles, probably from a Latin version, 'to show that classical ideas could be expressed in Castilian'. During the same period, Juan Luis Vives (1492–1540) developed a translation theory which distinguished between three kinds of translation: following *sensus*, following *verba*, or combining both such that 'words bring power and elegance to the senses'. This last option might be seen as an advance on classical binary oppositions, and an alternative would have been unthinkable without confi-

dence in the vernacular. Vives recommended that the translator select a method in accordance with text type, and he generally allowed that the figures and patterns of one language should not be expressed literally in another. Apart from *De ratione dicendi*, published in Leuven in 1533, where he presented his theory of translation, he published other works elaborating a critical empiricist philosophy. In *De disciplinis libri xx* he advocated the use of the vernacular in schools and the education of women. While at Oxford in 1523 he translated Isocrates from Greek into Latin.

In 1516 Pero Fernández de Villegas claimed to have improved not only the style but also the content of the *Divina Commedia*. In 1526 Alonso Fernández de Madrid amplified Erasmus's *Enchiridion* to about twice its original length, omitting some passages and adopting a preaching tone not to be found in the original. Although not typical of the period, such translations extended the notions of 'exposition, commentary or glosses' defended by Madrigal. Yet the use of amplification now also owed something to the translation methods of Erasmus, and to the growing influence of Protestantism.

Protestant and protesting translators

One of the main factors allowing the consecration of Castilian was the development of serious philology in Spain. Although certainly an offshoot of Italian Humanism, Spanish philology underwent a strong Erasmian influence, mediated by the scholars at the University of Alcalá de Henares who, under Cardinal Cisneros, prepared the first polyglot Bible to be printed (1502–17). Erasmus was translated into Castilian from 1511; Spain was one of the few countries where his works circulated freely. Cisneros even invited Erasmus to the University of Alcalá, without success. However, Erasmus's Bible was violently attacked when it arrived in Spain in 1520. The combination of philology and foreign Protestant ideas proved dangerous. It invited translators to assess religious source texts critically, increasingly challenging the orthodox Castilian–Catholic interpretations. One result was the evangelistic expansion of Fernández de Madrid's version of Erasmus. Another, more serious, was persecution by the Holy Office, the Inquisition.

The Counter-Reformation that put an end to Etienne Dolet in 1546 would make life difficult for many Spanish translators as well. Juan Luis Vives is said to have left Spain in order to avoid the Inquisition. The Erasmians who then went into exile in the mid-sixteenth century included the Bible translators Juan de Valdés, Francisco de Enzinas, Juan Pérez de Pineda (arrested by the Inquisition in 1557), Casiodoro de Reina and Cipriano de Valera (who revised Casiodoro's Bible and went unpunished). A further Protestant challenge to orthodoxy was Johannes Leizarraga's translation of the New Testament into Basque, carried out at the request of the Calvinist synod of Pau, France, in 1571.

Influenced by Protestant thought while in Leuven, Francisco de Enzinas (1520–52) moved to Wittenberg in 1541 where he began a Castilian version of the New Testament, published in Antwerp in 1543. Aware that Emperor Charles V had ordered all copies to be seized, Enzinas promptly dedicated the translation to him and went to Brussels to give him the first copy. When the emperor asked if he was the author Enzinas replied 'No, the Holy Spirit is the author ... I am only its faithful servant and weak instrument' (Menéndez y Pelayo 1952–3: 2.17). The title of the translation does indeed specify *Habla Dios* ('God Speaks'). The translation was nevertheless proscribed and Enzinas was imprisoned in Brussels, possibly to protect him from being sent to the Inquisition in Spain. He had no trouble escaping and ended up in England, where he became Professor of Greek at Cambridge. Enzinas also translated Plutarch, Lucian and Livy into Castilian, although his use of protective pseudonyms and anonymity makes the attributions uncertain.

One of a group of Protestants who fled from Seville, Casiodoro de Reina's (*c*.1520–94) translation of both testaments of the Bible (the *Biblia del Oso*) was the first in Castilian from the original languages. It reportedly took him ten years and was printed in Basle in 1569. Later revised by Cipriano de Valera, an exile who had also fled from Seville, the text was circulated in Spain by the Bible Society from the middle of the nineteenth century and remained the standard Bible of Spanish Protestants until the mid-twentieth century. In 1562 the Inquisition burned Casiodoro de Reina in effigy.

In these same years, Fray Luis de León (*c*.1527–91) was imprisoned partly because of eroticism in his translation of the Song of Songs. Fray Luis and the Protestant translators shared an insistence on work from the original tongues. This principle now applied beyond the religious sphere and was espoused by the likes of Diego Gracián, official secretary and 'interpreter of languages' to King Charles V and Felipe II. Gracián ostensibly rendered classical texts from Greek (to which he claimed Castilian was closer than any other language!), but his Plutarch was calqued on a French version and some of his other translations from Greek were mediated by Erasmus's Latin versions. The Protestants and philologists tended not to be so trustful of intermediary translations.

A major move towards Castilian purity came in 1558–9 when Felipe II, known to English history as the man who sent the Armada, set up an index of prohibited books and severely restricted study abroad. This move was associated with campaigns against Protestants and long-standing suspicion of Conversos. Spain virtually closed itself off from the movement of European ideas, becoming isolated from the secularization of philosophical and scientific thought. The translations of the late sixteenth and seventeenth centuries were thus mostly of classical texts, once again often from Latin or Italian intermediary versions, now with major degrees of ideological appropriation, as when Pero Sánchez de Viana translated Ovid in accordance with Christian beliefs. In order to perform such ideological acrobatics, explanatory glosses became full commentaries. Francisco de Quevedo thought nothing of publishing paragraphs of his own with passages translated more or less faithfully from Plutarch. But this Castilian confidence was no longer the expression of a triumphant empire.

The decline of Spain as a superpower

The seventeenth century, continuing the Golden Age of Spanish literature, translated mostly from Latin, Italian and French, alongside oddities like Garcilaso de la Vega Inca's translation of two lyrical texts from Quechuan in 1609, and the world's most famous pseudo-translation, Cervantes' *Don Quijote*, the first part of which was published in 1613. As France became the dominant political and cultural power, French was increasingly the intermediary language for texts from English, German and the Low Countries. This pattern would prevail for some two centuries. By the beginning of the eighteenth century, French was widely read in Spain. In 1759 Benito Jerónimo Feijóo complained that although many Spaniards could read and understand French, few of them could translate well (Santoyo 1987: 105). Fittingly, a manual for translation from French into Castilian was written by Antonio de Capmany in 1776.

All this time, however, there was a minor but direct flow from Italian and Latin, a directionality that was briefly enhanced by the 4,000 or so Jesuits exiled in Italy from 1767. The translators among this group included José Francisco Isla, Carlos Andrés, who translated the history of world literature that his brother Juan had written in Italian, and Pedro Montengón, who translated Ossian from an Italian version.

Yet the main threat to Castilian purity was not from Jesuits in Italy. The real danger lay in the French language, which now bore revolutionary ideals. In the 1770s, Tomás de Iriarte, sometime official translator at the Ministry of State in Madrid, was regarded with suspicion when he translated Destouches, Voltaire, and Molière for the Spanish stage. In 1792, Mariano Luis de Urquijo translated Voltaire with a preface that attacked the Inquisition, upon which the translator entered the diplomatic corps and was sent to London for his own good. Despite the ideological tensions, Spain nevertheless translated predominantly from French, particularly for the stage. At the beginning of the nineteenth century, 22 of the 28 plays published in the *Teatro Nuevo Español*, ostensibly the 'New Spanish Theatre', were translations or adaptations. A prominent example of this tendency was Tomás García Suelto's translation of *Le Cid*, performed successfully in Madrid in 1803. But ten years later, the same García Suelto had to leave Spain, together with the 10,000 or so *afrancesados* ('Frenchified Spaniards') who had supported the Napoleonic invasion of their country. This group of exiles included Francisco Javier de Burgos (1778–1848), who made Horace more 'noble' through omissions and substitutions; Juan María Maury (1772-1845), who published in Paris an influential bilingual historical anthology of Castilian poetry, and

Francisco Martínez de la Rosa (1787–1862), whose historical drama *Aben Humeya* was written in French and translated into Castilian.

A return to absolutism in 1823 led to a further expulsion, this time of the liberal Romantics, who emigrated to England, France and the Americas. Between 1824 and 1828 London was a centre of Spanish intellectual life, largely thanks to the German publisher Rudolph Ackermann's distribution of original texts and translations throughout Spanish America. Among the translators exiled in London was José Joaquín de Mora, who translated Walter Scott in 1825. In Spain, the intellectual closure was such that when Félix Torres Amat published his Catholic translation of the Bible in 1826 some said it had been financed by English Protestants (in fact it had been precensored by the church and was subsidized by the Spanish crown). After the July Revolution of 1830 many exiled liberals went from London to France, eventually returning to Spain in the course of the decade.

Translation into Castilian increased in the 1830s as a result of favourable publication laws. Texts that had many years previously been written were now translated for the first time: Diderot in 1831, Rousseau in 1836. Most of the translations came from or through French. Ideas about translation were also remarkably French, particularly with respect to adaptation to target-culture norms. In 1836 Mariano José Larra declared that the correct translation of comedies from French should be 'to seek equivalences not of the words but of the situations', adopting 'the customs of the country into which one is translating' (Santoyo 1987: 165). French influence was also visible in the common preference for rendering verse as prose. Byron thus entered Castilian from French not as a poet but as a writer of short stories. Translations in this period were generally free, hurried, and made with an eye to audience acceptability.

From as early as 1834 translation also played a role in the revival of Catalan as a literary language, often through indirect work and adaptations for the theatre. However, it was not until the 1880s that translators really enhanced the status of Catalan, setting up a strong translation culture that was later to be interrupted by the Franco dictatorship.

As the nineteenth century progressed, Spain lost its external colonies and suffered the internal strife of the Carlist wars. Reactions to the apparent decline modified the cultural dependence on France in two ways. First, the *Krausismo* movement, developed by Julián Sanz del Río from 1857 onwards, transformed the Heidelberg philosopher K. C. F. Krause into a peculiarly Spanish liberal-rationalism that combined populist elements with intellectual elitism. Through their struggles against various authorities and their insistence on the role of education, the Krausists introduced a more European intellectual vision that would survive well into the twentieth century. Opposed to them was the nationalism of Marcelino Menéndez y Pelayo (1856–1912), a scholar who sought to base Castilian purity on Roman-Christian foundations. His work had a far more direct influence on translations. In order to define Castilian purity, in 1880–81 Menéndez y Pelayo published his history of Spanish *heterodoxos* or 'dissidents', many of whom were great translators. Associated with this project were notes on some 283 Spanish translators, constituting a major source of information and misinformation on translation in Spain. Menéndez y Pelayo generally saw translation from classical sources as uplifting for both nation and language, but regarded many other sources as morally suspect. In his 1886 preface to a translation of Byron which broke with the previous dominance of prose, he claimed that prose translations of verse were simply the result of Spaniards copying the weaknesses of the French language (Santoyo 1987: 177–8). Although this position was modified in 1909 when he praised Luis Segalá y Estalella's prose version of the *Iliad*, Menéndez y Pelayo's preferences had a profound influence on Spanish philology.

Cultural nationalism was briefly opposed by various cosmopolitans who held allegiance neither to Spain nor to Castilian verse. In 1908, the Guatemalan Enrique Gómez Carrillo, prefacing Manuel Machado's prose versions of Verlaine, claimed that verse should be translated in simple prose, as Mallarmé had done with Poe. Almost all subsequent versions of French poetry were nevertheless in verse, largely because Symbolist poetry was read in French in Spain, turning the translations into mere stylistic exercises. European Naturalism, on the other hand, was massively translated from French after 1880, with Zola generally being translated in the same year as the French originals. English and German authors also entered Castilian after their acceptance in France, although the translations were increasingly from the original languages. Schopenhauer was translated into French in 1888, into Castilian in 1889. Ruskin reached French in 1900, notably through Proust, then Castilian the same year.

The contemporary period

Serious translations from non-French sources developed as the twentieth century progressed. Luis Astrana Marín (1889–1960) translated Shakespeare's complete works, published in 1929. On the level of theory, José Ortega y Gasset (1883–1955) published his famous essay 'Misery and Splendour of Translation' as a series of articles in the Buenos Aires newspaper *La Nación* in 1937. Initially neo-Kantian, he called for a revitalization of Spain based on individualism and elitism. One of the very few non-Germans to have resurrected Schleiermacher's arguments in favour of literalism, Ortega saw the translator as an idealist who should enable the reader to experience the strangeness of foreign works. His dualist reflections on the two classically opposed methods of translation can be related not just to his philosophical critiques of mass culture but also to the context of the Spanish civil war (1936–9).

The exile of Republicans in 1939 went beyond the well-worn pattern, dispersing major Spanish intellectuals throughout Europe and the Americas. Many of the exiled writers translated, often to earn a living but rarely as a full-time profession. These translators were mostly teachers or journalists, as distinct from previous generations that had often combined part-time translation with medium or high positions within the state structure. Dictatorship now separated the external translators from easy government jobs. And this time the rupture of exile was no momentary affair.

Franco's Spain lasted through to 1975, imposing varying degrees of censorship. Famous examples include the moralistic dubbing of films, where mistresses would be changed into aunts or sisters. More important, this relative closure repressed Spain's long-standing diversity. Internally, translation into languages other than

Castilian was for many years illegal. Externally, translation had to be into Castilian if it was going to find a market, either among exiles or in Spanish America. Castilian was thus privileged on both fronts. Spain's relative closure during decades of technological change also weakened direct contact with its former colonies. Iberian and Spanish-American terminologies increasingly diverged. Spanish Americans today tend to translate directly from American English (their computer is a *computadora*), whereas Iberian Spanish remains in close contact with European sources: an Iberian computer is an *ordenador*, corresponding to the French *ordinateur*.

Post-1975 Spain quickly developed a new internationalism that assisted the transition to strong democracy. Many previously banned works were now translated. Institutional programmes were also gradually set up to develop Spain's other languages, encouraging translation into them. There seemed to be a flood of translations on all fronts, many in great haste. And yet the statistics for book publication indicate a fairly constant growth in translations from the 1960s onwards.

The *Index Translationum* for 1947–86 showed Spain as among the three or four countries that translate the most, with its fairly constant rise in translations keeping slightly above the international average. More recent figures (Ganne and Minon 1992) showed that translated titles were 25 per cent of the Spanish total in 1986 and 26 per cent in 1991, well above the percentage for all larger European countries except Italy (25 per cent and 25 per cent respectively). Most book translations tend to be in the fields of general literature (42 per cent of all titles) and children's literature (51 per cent), predominantly from French and English.

In addition to book publication, translators and interpreters are employed in numerous aspects of social life, in the courts, at conferences, in the military, and in tourism, which is one of Spain's major industries. Spanish television has a generally high content of foreign programming, with a marked preference for dubbing. Regional television channels transmit in Catalan, Basque, and Galician, mostly in dubbed versions of foreign programmes. Some programmes on Basque television are dubbed in Basque and subtitled in Castilian.

Within the profession, recent trends suggest a move away from practices like Hispanizing foreign proper names (as in 'Carlos Marx') or the once common use of quite rigid literalism in legal translations. Certain unusual names like 'Pouchkine' have in most cases been Hispanized, effacing the fact that these authors originally reached Castilian through French.

Profession, training and research

The main professional association for the whole of Spain is APETI (Professional Association of Translators and Interpreters), founded in 1954. The official association of writers (Asociación Colegial de Escritores) has a section for translators. There are also regional associations. Further associations have been set up for sworn translators and interpreters (called *intérpretes jurados*), who have to pass a public exam. There is a regional society of the British Institute of Linguists. Despite these organizations, many translators still suffer from a lack of social prestige and remuneration.

Several Spanish ministries (those of Foreign Affairs, Education and Science, and Culture) as well as Spain's seventeen regional governments have undertaken initiatives to enhance the prestige of translators. Such initiatives take the form of national prizes, grants, subsidies for publication, and financial assistance to foreign publishers printing translations of literary and scientific works by Spanish authors.

In 1974, the Instituto Universitario de Lenguas Modernas y Traductores was set up at the Complutense University in Madrid primarily to train literary translators. A wider professional market was aimed for by the Escola Universitària de Traductors i Intèrprets at the Autonomous University of Barcelona. Although founded in 1972, its programme was not formally recognized by the Spanish Ministry of Education until 1980, perhaps indicating some resistance to its use of Catalan as well as Castilian as a home language. Similar profession-oriented programmes were established in Granada in 1979 and in Las Palmas in the Canary Islands in 1988. These university schools had three-year programmes until 1992–3, when a new four-year degree structure was phased in and the schools became faculties. Not achieved without conflict, the new structure reflected enhanced official recognition of translation as an academic discipline. In line with this trend, the Madrid institute changed its programme to offer a more general professional training for translators in 1990. There was then rapid expansion in the field, with further programmes set up in Málaga, Vigo, Salamanca, Barcelona, Vic, Madrid, Castellón, among others. Postgraduate courses in translation studies and specialized master's programmes are also offered by an increasing number of universities. The various university centres and departments of translation formed an association (*Conferencia*) in 1995.

Santoyo's 1996 bibliography lists some 6,000 Spanish and Spanish-American books and articles on translation. The current research is mostly on linguistic and pedagogical aspects, slightly less on historical subjects, and occasionally on problems of basic theory. This trend is generally borne out by the specialized journals: *Quaderns de Traducció i Interpretació* (Autonomous University of Barcelona, from 1982), *Sendebar* (University of Granada, from 1990), *Livius* (University of León, from 1992), *Gaceta de la traducción* (APETI, from 1993), *Boletín de Estudios de Traducción* (Vitoria and Leon, from 1994–5), *Hieronimus Complutensis* (Complutense in Madrid, from 1995) and *Viceversa* (University of Vigo, also from 1995), among others.

The prime mover behind recent historical research has been Julio-César Santoyo, whose many works on translation include bibliographies of English translations of Spanish literary classics as well as an extremely useful historical anthology of Spanish translation theory and criticism (1987). Work on the more practical aspects of translation has been strongly influenced by Valentín García Yebra, whose *Teoría y práctica de la traducción* (1982) adopts a basically linguistic approach found in most of the current manuals. A more formalized linguistic approach is proposed in Rosa Rabadán's *Equivalencia y traducción* (1991). Not surprisingly, the only official research category naming translation is 'Linguistics Applied to Translation and Interpretation'.

Further reading

Millás-Vallicrosa 1949; Proctor 1951; Menéndez y Pelayo 1952–3; Lemay 1963; d'Alverny 1964;

Kritzeck 1964; Gumbrecht 1976; García Yebra 1983; Russell 1985; Santoyo 1987; Santoyo *et al.* 1989; Round 1993; *Livius* 1994; Pym 1994; Navarro 1996; Santoyo 1996.

ANTHONY PYM

Swedish tradition

Swedish is spoken by more than 9 million people, predominantly in Sweden and parts of Finland, where the Swedish-speaking minority form some 6 per cent of the population. It is one of the two official languages of Finland.

In Sweden itself, Swedish has been the predominant language since the dawn of history and the sole official national language since the establishment of the modern state at the end of the Middle Ages. It is currently spoken as a native tongue by at least 90 per cent of the population of Sweden (including native descendants of immigrants). More than a million inhabitants of the country are immigrants or descendants of immigrants who arrived in the latter part of the twentieth century; they need – and the vast majority of them do have – a reasonable command of Swedish.

Swedish is the largest of the six Nordic languages in terms of number of speakers; the other languages spoken in Nordic countries are Finnish, Danish, Norwegian, Icelandic and Faroese. Of these, the three Scandinavian languages – namely Swedish, Danish and Norwegian – are spoken by over 19 million people; they are in principle mutually intelligible, and their present form and historical status are similar. While these languages can be analyzed and described within the same linguistic framework, they have distinct cultural and sociolinguistic backgrounds. In fact, the history of Swedish has been quite distinct from that of its close neighbours since the early Middle Ages.

Only with the final integration of Scandinavia into medieval European civilization does the impact of foreign influences begin to affect the vernacular language fundamentally. Thousands of runic inscriptions from the Viking Age, preserved on stone monuments in central parts of Sweden and Denmark, confirm this picture:

their linguistic form is entirely domestic. The decisive step in the integration process is the emergence of written vernaculars, using a script based on the Latin alphabet. This state of linguistic culture was attained in Sweden only as a result of the Christian mission and the subsequent introduction of Latin in the eleventh century (about one century later than in Denmark and Norway). The first 'books', which were written with Latin types in the vernacular language (i.e. in East Norse or classical Old Swedish), did not appear until the early thirteenth century; the oldest complete copies extant today date from c.1280.

These pioneering documents of Swedish literature are records of provincial law. Their linguistic form is characterized by an almost entirely domestic vocabulary and simple syntax and, above all, by a formulaic, repetitive style. These documents also mark, at least implicitly, the potential starting-point of Swedish trans-lation. Traditionally, the medieval legal style has been traced back to a domestic, pre-literary origin of the laws. Today, however, scholars question the immediate dependence of legal style upon a native oral tradition. Instead, attention has been drawn to striking similar-ities with continental legal writings, such as Roman jurisprudence and canon law. Given the present state of research, this means that we are not certain whether the history of trans-lation into Swedish actually begins with the first codification in script of internationally current legislation in the High Middle Ages.

The period of chivalry: early thirteenth to late fourteenth centuries

In Sweden, adaptation, rather than translation, may have played the main role in initiating the development of vernacular literature. Leaving aside the runic inscriptions, the domestic written tradition seems to have originated with paraphrases in the vernacular language of contemporary writing in West Norse, Middle Low German, Old French and Latin. This is part of a general pattern in Swedish literary creation in the High Middle Ages, an epoch often referred to as the golden age of East Norse literature. The translated literature of West Norse, Middle Low

German and Old French is closely related to 'chivalry', the cultural and ideological tradition prevailing in Western Europe at that time.

The ideology of chivalry was transmitted to the upper classes via 'chivalric' epic verse, expressed in rhymed chronicles, ballads and verse romances which were based on French and German originals, sometimes through the mediation of West Norse. An even more central task of writing for a large readership in this period consisted of the propagation of the Christian message in prayers and hymns, in preaching and in works of edification. Like chivalric poetry, these genres, usually written in Latin, were imported from abroad. Their rhetorical patterns were more or less fixed, like those of the various forms of chivalric poetry, but they were quite different from them in origin and structure; they also addressed a different public. Swedish religious texts from the High Middle Ages have been preserved primarily in the form of legends and biblical paraphrase.

The notion of paraphrase is crucial in this context. The 'swedification' of Low German, French and Latin originals generally meant very free reshaping, seldom restricted to remoulding the linguistic and stylistic form. The translators of that period took the liberty of adapting the original text by changing its content: adding, pruning and transposing material as they saw fit and, in many cases, substantially altering the message in the process. In fact, we have no evidence at this early period of anything like 'translation' in today's strict sense of the word.

The monastic period: late fourteenth to early sixteenth centuries

The Monastery of Vadstena is arguably the cradle of Swedish translation. This famous institution of late medieval Scandinavia was created by St Bridget and posthumously founded in accordance with her own, very exact instructions.

One of the first great enterprises of the new Bridgetine congregation consisted of retrans-lating the foundress's entire collection of *Revelationes* back from the Latin – into which they had been rendered by her confessors – into her own Swedish mother tongue. This major task seems to have been performed in connection with the inauguration of the Monastery in 1384. The printed edition available today occupies over 1,200 pages and is written in good, stylistically adequate Old Swedish.

This translation is substantially different from the free paraphrases of older medieval periods, so that the Bridgetine text may be regarded as the first translation – in the strict sense of the word – ever undertaken from a foreign language into Swedish. In fact, it is possible to follow the translator almost word for word as he proceeds through the eight books of Revelations. This monk translator clearly aimed at linguistic equivalence throughout – at the level of word, phrase and clause – and managed to fulfil this aim to a large degree.

While it may be argued that the Vadstena monks were, strictly speaking, the first Swedish translators, translation in general cannot be seen in isolation from the context in which it functions. During this early period, the vernacular (target) language was seen as inferior to the source language, and this naturally encouraged translators to copy the linguistic form of the original. This applied even to grammatical form: monastic translators tried to copy specific patterns of Latin syntax rather than just its rhetorical style. This does not detract from the value of their work as vernacular stylists; they successfully and skilfully manipulated the resources of late medieval Swedish, a rather basic idiom which lacked the kind of refinement that can only come from a long and rich literary tradition.

This great, pioneering enterprise provided the basis and inspiration for numerous subsequent translations which were undertaken at the Monastery throughout the Middle Ages. The printed editions of translated literature from Vadstena currently occupy the space of a whole shelf which is one metre in length. The Vadstena translators are mostly anonymous; we know only a few of them by name, the best known being Jöns Budde (also known as *Jöns Raek* or *Raeck*, from *c.*1436 to after 1491). Budde was the most industrious translator of the Vadstena monastic tradition and hence of medieval Scandinavia. He translated some twenty major works of different religious genres into Old Swedish. Significant items on his record include a number of books from the Old Testament, some from the Apocrypha (the books of Judith, Esther,

Ruth and the Maccabees); books of prominent mystics such as Mechtild of Hackeborn (*Liber specialis graciae*) and Suso (*Horologium divinae Sapientiae*), as well as the anonymous *Claustrum animæ*. He further translated a number of works of edification. Close study of his texts reveals that Budde was a skilful translator as well as an inspired preacher. His work was significant in terms of the development and refinement of literary Swedish in the late Middle Ages.

The Monastery of Vadstena dominated the production of literary texts in Scandinavia during the fifteenth century. With the introduction of paper, which was considerably cheaper and easier to handle than old parchment, the volume of text produced at the Monastery increased considerably. The majority of this monastic writing was in Latin, and versions produced in the vernacular were normally based on Latin originals. The Latin translators of the Monastery developed a system of their own. They learnt to write Swedish in an unprecedentedly routine fashion and produced a large volume of quality work at speed within a variety of domains, some of which were very abstract. They wrote with a certain degree of formal and linguistic consistency, which was quite an achievement for medieval Scandinavia. The translators at Vadstena in fact designed the moulds into which, some centuries later, a Swedish standard language was to be cast gradually and laboriously.

The Reformation and the great power period: early sixteenth to seventeenth centuries

One and a half centuries after the first Bridgetine translation, the leading men of the Swedish Reformation were entrusted by King Gustav Vasa with the important task of providing for the Swedish people a Holy Bible in their own language. The Vadstena tradition provided useful models for translation into effective Swedish, particularly but not exclusively of religious texts.

The Swedish New Testament appeared in 1526. The source text was probably the Latin version of the Renaissance edition of Erasmus. The oldest complete Swedish Bible, known as the Gustav Vasa Bible, was printed at Uppsala in 1541 and is thought to be based principally on Martin Luther's contemporary High German translation. Both Swedish translations are collective undertakings, and we do not know for certain which individual translators were responsible for particular sections of the two texts. However, there is convincing evidence that the leaders of the Swedish Reformation – the chancellor Laurentius Andrae, the royal secretary Olaus Petri and archbishop Laurentius Petri – were involved at different stages of the work. A printed copy of this text was distributed to each parish throughout the country. It was expected to be understood adequately everywhere, irrespective of dialect and individual local context. To fulfil this purpose, a certain uniformity in linguistic expression was seen as a prerequisite.

This sixteenth-century version was to become the official Bible of the Swedish State church until 1917, when it was replaced by a new official translation. The Vasa Bible holds a unique position in Sweden's literary and linguistic culture. For almost four centuries this text was recited aloud from the pulpit, read by the literate, quoted and referred to in literature and in everyday life. It naturally also played a major role in standardizing the written language. As far as the general history of Swedish is concerned, this translation is by far the most important text ever written in Swedish.

The historical and linguistic importance of the Swedish translation of the Bible, like that of contemporary translations in other Lutheran countries, has to be seen ultimately from the point of view of linguistic ideology rather than ecclesiastical authority. For Martin Luther, the Bible had to be translated in such a way as to allow common, unlearned people to understand the word of God. In Sweden, as in other countries influenced by the Reformation, this Lutheran translation doctrine had an extensive and lasting effect on attitudes to national language, as well as the national language itself. The translation achievements of Swedish reformers probably mark a definite departure from the Vadstena view of the vernacular as a vulgar language for everyday use, only imperfectly mirroring the magnificence of Latin. Translators of this period deliberately endeavoured to use an adequate national language effectively, and instead of copying the linguistic form of the original, translation now meant writing afresh.

This change in attitude was supported by other historical developments. The modern Swedish state was established by King Gustav Vasa, who implemented rigid measures of centralization. Printing, which was introduced during the Reformation, also played a role in fixing the form of written language. However, in spite of the fact that printing made the texts produced by Reformation writers and translators available on a large scale, and nothwithstanding the very real achievements of Bible translators, the literary culture of Sweden during the Reformation period was weak.

Sweden emerged from the Thirty Years' War as a major European power in the seventeenth century. King Gustav Adolf and Queen Christina had ambitions of cultural prestige. Their period of rule was characterized by a fairly open-handed cultural policy, Lutheran orthodoxy and an element of patriotic/historic fantasizing. During the concluding Caroline epoch, there was also a pronounced interest in orthography, grammar, and the preservation and regulation of the national language. All these factors supported the production of printed text in Sweden and influenced the development of translating activities in the seventeenth century.

Vernacular writing during this period was mainly original (Hansson 1982). In sharp contrast to conditions in medieval as well as modern periods, only one book out of five written in Swedish was a translation. Latin remained a major language in terms of the total production of printed text, almost as well represented as Swedish itself. As a source language for translation, though, Latin was now reduced to second position. Of the total 335 printed book translations into Swedish which appeared during the seventeenth century, the majority (203 titles or 61 per cent) are translations of German works of religious edification intended for the general public. A quarter (82 titles or 24 per cent) are based on Latin originals. Other source languages account for 15 per cent of titles translated: Gothic (i.e. Old Icelandic, 10 titles), French (14 titles), English (11), Danish, Spanish, Dutch and Polish (one each).

Devotional literature and collections of sermons translated from German were systematically used by the State church in anti-papist popular education, which was characterized by severe Lutheran orthodoxy. The translators of these works were mostly clergymen. Translation from Latin originals was generally carried out by lay people though some, for example Schroderus (*c.* 1570–1647), were influential professionals. They consisted of didactic literature of a more worldly character and a variety of historical and political works.

In line with the cultural ambitions of a new great power, many of the translations undertaken during this period were of medieval Icelandic sagas. Classical literature written in West Norse was presented as Gothic in origin (implying that it was Swedish); this act of patriotic forgery was undertaken with royal support. Icelanders could earn money by selling saga manuscripts and teaching the language to Swedish and Danish clients. The manuscripts, which were part of the literary heritage of Iceland, were eagerly exploited as relics of an alleged glorious past.

The academic period: early eighteenth century to *c.*1830

In the centuries immediately following the Reformation, written Swedish had slowly but steadily strengthened its position as a civilized European language. The position of Sweden as a major European power was undermined by the Great Northern War (1700–21), and the death of King Charles XII in 1718 marked an important transition to a new era. Sweden was now forced to give up its ambitions as a great power and began adjusting to its new role as a small, peaceful, fringe state in northern Europe. The national language could now quietly and steadily develop and be refined to accommodate all types of text and serve the needs of most literary genres. The educated classes began to develop a more international outlook, and the influence of French on Swedish culture reached its peak under the reign of King Gustavus III (1772–92).

Serious discrepancies in the historical records of the period unfortunately mean that we know very little about translating activities in general, and even less about individual translating achievements in eighteenth- and early nineteenth-century Sweden. As yet, no statistical information is available. What we do know can be summarized in a few general statements.

The creation of two learned academies in

Sweden, the Academy of Sciences in 1739 and the Swedish Academy in 1786, reflects a sober-minded and utilitarian view of language and literature, typical of the Age of Enlightenment. Along with the development of the natural sciences, inspired partly by the illustrious example of Carolus Linnæus (the universally acclaimed Swedish botanist who established the principles for naming and classifying plants and animals), a Swedish scientific prose was established in the middle of the century. It was based mainly on original production.

Rationalist ideas and severe French Classical demands on style and linguistic form governed literary writing. Quantitatively speaking, translation was probably rather insignificant as an activity – as it was during the seventeenth century – and this was to remain the case until the last decades of the eighteenth century, when two new genres of literary translation emerged. The first was sponsored by King Gustavus III himself. Under his protection, the theatre expanded rapidly, and this led to a strong demand for the translation of plays. The second, conditioned by political and economic factors, was that of prose fiction intended for cultivated entertainment of the bourgeois middle class that had grown in the eighteenth century. Most, if not all, of this *à-la-mode* literature consisted of commercial translations by self-employed professionals. French seems to have been the dominant source language at the beginning, but was later challenged by German and, at the very end of the period, English. The dissemination of books was dependent to a large extent on mobile libraries; there was a handful of them in Stockholm at the turn of the century (Björkman 1992).

The surrender of Finland to Russia in 1809, following a catastrophic war, deeply affected the Swedish nation and had significant implications for literary culture in Sweden, including translation. However, some of the developments that took place during the Gustavian era, particularly the translation of prose fiction, survived through to modern times.

The industrial period: *c.*1830 to the present

Swedish society has undergone some major changes since the beginning of the nineteenth century, including industrialization, various popular movements, emigration, the arrival of democracy and – since the latter part of the twentieth century – absorption of a considerable number of immigrants. And yet, translation activity during this last and most extended period is characterized by a remarkable degree of continuity, while at the same time being distinctly different on a number of counts from translation during earlier periods.

During this modern period, we see new genres of fiction being translated for mass production in order to provide simple entertainment for the general public. Commercialization requires high-speed production and the use of linguistic forms which can be understood by the ordinary reader. A logical consequence, or perhaps a necessary prerequisite of this, has been the appearance of the professional translator, a development which started in the previous period.

Within the literary establishment, on the other hand, priority was given to creativity and originality, and literary output was governed by the prevalent aesthetic values of German Romanticism. This naturally led to a lack of appreciation of imitative activities such as translation, and consequently also to an attitude of indifference towards translators and their achievements. In nineteenth-century Sweden, the professional translator was a humble craftsman who lacked the aura of romantic genius, a 'white collar proletarian' working under difficult conditions. A substantial number of translators during this period were women (Hjelm-Milczyn 1983).

As with the seventeenth century, a considerable amount of interesting statistical evidence is available today for literary book production (both original and translation) in nineteenth- and twentieth-century Sweden. We know, for instance, that 213 titles of prose fiction translated into Swedish from various languages were published between 1866 and 1870 (Torgerson 1982). Sixty years later, between 1926 and 1930, the corresponding figure was 1,490 titles. After another sixty years, in 1986-90, this figure rose to approximately 5,500 titles (Wollin 2002). The figures for original Swedish prose fiction published during the same three periods are 187, 1,120 and approximately 1,500 titles respectively. It seems evident from these figures that

there was a six- or seven-fold increase in the overall production of prose fiction, translated as well as original, during the first 60-year period; there also seem to have been more translations than original writing, notwithstanding minor temporary fluctuations within the period and changes in dominant source languages. In the second 60-year period, translated book production continues to increase, though in slightly lower proportions, whereas original writing remains relatively stagnant. The average translation ratio for the first two periods is 55 per cent, for the third it is roughly 80 per cent.

Today, non-literary genres are considerably less significant than literary genres in terms of total book production in Sweden. Fiction accounts for the majority of book translations and, in turn, translation dominates fiction writing. One reasonable hypothesis (as yet untested) is that this relative but constantly growing overlap between translation and fiction dates back to the emergence of commercial literary fiction some 200 years ago. If this is true, then the translation of fiction may be said to have historically marginalized non-literary book translation in Sweden.

The source languages of translations have changed over time. The dominance of French and German in the early nineteenth century was disrupted by the arrival of English in the mid-nineteenth century: the relevant figures for the period 1866–70 are 50 titles from German, 55 from French and 68 from English. For the period 1926–30, the figures are 178, 196 and 814 respectively; for 1986–90, the (approximate) figures are 140, 260 and no less than 4,400. American English has gradually gained ground at the expense of British, proceeding from almost no share of the English figures in the 1860s to roughly a quarter in the 1920s and considerably more than a half in the 1980s.

This growing Anglo-American dominance is partly counterbalanced by a parallel increase in the range of other source languages. For example, in the period 1926–30, source languages included Norwegian (99 titles), Danish (51), Russian (50) and Italian (30 titles), plus fewer titles from Spanish, Hungarian, Dutch, Polish and a dozen other source languages, practically all European. For 1986–90, the list is similar, though now slightly enriched by a few titles from major non-occidental languages such as Arabic,

Chinese and Japanese. Spanish, particularly the Latin American variety, now ranks fourth, with 92 titles; this may be partly due to the special preferences of the Swedish Academy's Nobel Prize committee.

Anglo-American dominance in modern literary translation has given rise to much criticism and serious concern in different circles of Swedish society, and it is a recurrent issue in public discussions of translation. What is often overlooked is the manifold nature of translated literature. Even today, more selective analyses of published titles, for instance in terms of restricting the analyses to authors of some literary distinction, suggests that the proportion of English source texts is dramatically lower than is often claimed, perhaps by some 40 per cent. The assessment of 'quality' is never a straightforward exercise, but we still cannot afford to ignore the issue.

Non-literary translation remains less productive than literary translation in modern Sweden. About one third (or fewer than 700) of all titles published in the quite typical year 1985 belong to a wide range of non-literary genres. As a total, this is of course not insignificant. English is less dominant as a source language than in literary translation.

Screen translation plays an important role in Sweden today. Dubbing was introduced in the 1920s but was soon abandoned, due to heavy costs, and replaced by subtitling. Today, dubbing is used only in children's movies, whereas subtitling has become extremely common (as it is in several minor language communities in Europe). Ivarsson (1992: 9) states that the amount of Swedish subtitling done in any one year during the 1980s or 1990s is equal to the total annual production of translated books of all genres (10,000 hours, which at the ratio of 30 pages per hour would correspond to about 1,500 average-sized books). The potential influence of this massive amount of subtitling on the national culture and language remains unknown at this stage.

Interpreting

Interpreting has been practised on and off in Sweden for several centuries. Training has been provided by the Swedish Army, particularly for Russian. Outside the military arena, interpreting has historically been more or less limited to diplomatic commissions and was of little significance in this principally monolingual country until the 1960s. This decade saw the beginning of extensive immigration from numerous countries, some of which are linguistically and culturally remote. The integration of immigrants (including second and third generations), has necessitated the implementation of many public policies, some of which relate to the provision of interpreting services. An immigrant in Sweden is legally entitled to the assistance of an interpreter in his or her contacts with the authorities, without charge. Training for interpreters working in these contexts is supported by the state, which also provides certification for professional interpreters.

Another important and steadily growing category of interpreters is engaged in signed language interpreting for the deaf and those with impaired hearing. There are at present several hundreds of sign language interpreters working in Sweden (which is far more than some decades ago, but still far less than needed).

Business and conference interpreting are not particularly active in Sweden. Swedish is not widely used outside Scandinavia and is hardly used even at international conferences held within Sweden itself. Nor is it taught for interpreting purposes at universities abroad. Sweden's membership of the European Community may however ultimately change this picture.

Professional organizations

The number of people who translate written documents from one language to another in Sweden was estimated in 1994 at 2,000; the majority, however, do not work full-time. More than 300 are authorized professional translators. Most translators work in large cities, mainly Stockholm, Göteborg and Malmö/Lund.

Literary translators (the majority), and translators of books in general, have been organized since 1970; the Translators' section of the Swedish Writers' Union had about 500 members in 1996. The majority of these are not full-time translators. Some one hundred theatre and opera translators are represented by the svenska dramatikerförbundet, while approximately seventy screen translators belong to the svenska teaterförbundet. The Swedish

Association of Professional Translators, with some 270 members in 1994, represents translators of professional and scientific texts, the majority of whom work full-time for clients in trade and industry. Many are also members of The Federation of Authorized Translators; members of this organization (240 in 1993) are authorized by the Kammarkollegiet (National Judicial Board for Public Lands and Funds). Authorized community interpreters are represented by a major organization, Sveriges tolkförbund (STOF).

The Institute for Interpretation and Translation Studies (IITS) at Stockholm University was founded in 1986, with responsibility for the coordination of research, training and information activities, as well as for Scandinavian cooperation within the fields of interpretation and translation in Sweden.

The most important Swedish periodical in the field is the quarterly *Tolkningsperspektiv*, which has been closely associated with the IITs since 1995.

Further reading

Hansson 1982; Torgerson 1982; Hjelm-Milczyn 1983; Andersson 1987; Wollin 1991a; Wollin 1991b; Björkman 1992; Wollin 2002.

LARS WOLLIN

T

Turkish tradition

The Turkish language was introduced into Asia Minor/Anatolia by the Seljuk Turks in the eleventh century and later became the official language of the Ottoman Empire (mid-thirteenth to twentieth centuries) and of the republic of Turkey (founded in 1923).

The Seljuk sultanate of Anatolia was an offshoot of the Ilkhanid empire and extended from Iran to Mesopotamia, Syria and Palestine in the eleventh century. The principality had a mixed population of Muslims, Christians, Armenians, Greeks, Syrians and Iranians; the Turkish element was dominant but tolerant of racial and religious differences. In administration and culture, the sultanate adopted mainly Iranian models and used Persian as the official language.

The Ottoman Empire that eventually grew out of various Anatolian principalities was also multi-ethnic, allowing for a plurality of languages within its boundaries which, at the peak of its power in the sixteenth century, had extended into central Europe in the west, Crimea in the north, and included the Middle East and North Africa. The dismemberment of the Empire after World War I led to the formation of the republic in 1923, in Asia Minor and part of Thrace. The republic retained, on a smaller scale, some of the ethnic/linguistic plurality of the empire. Today, Kurdish is the most widely spoken among the various minority languages, followed by Arabic, Armenian, Ladino and Greek.

Overview of pre-Ottoman and Ottoman period (thirteenth to nineteenth centuries)

In the Seljuk state, with Konya as its capital, the official interpreter-translator was known as *tercüman* (from Arabic *tarjaman*, of Aramaic origin). The *tercüman*, or 'dragoman' in English, was appointed by royal decree and held in high esteem. Dragomans were in charge of correspondence with foreign states and acted as intermediaries for foreigners and natives in court cases, interpreting for plaintiffs and defendants and referring them to their special clerks. At the time of Alaeddin Keykubad (d. 1237) there were two such appointed dragomans and two special translators' clerks.

The first imperial dragoman mentioned in Ottoman records is Lutfi Bey, who was sent as emissary to Venice in 1479 to deliver a treaty. The position of the official dragoman in the Ottoman state is therefore thought to have been established by Mehmed II (1432–81) after the conquest of Constantinople. Georgios Amirukis (Amirutzes in Turkish), who fell captive to Mehmet II following the conquest of the Greek Pontic Empire, is known to have translated for the Sultan in scholarly matters but not in political communications.

Professional translation/interpreting came to be institutionalized in the sixteenth century as the growing diplomatic and commercial activities of the Empire created more demand for professional dragomans. By the eighteenth century, the official function of dragomans was established in four separate areas:

(a) the foreign affairs department of the Imperial Chancery of State, known as the Sublime Porte;
(b) the administration of provinces, where

interpreters for law courts were appointed or dismissed on the recommendation of local judges but dragomans served, with a special warrant, as intermediaries in all official matters between the non-Turkish-speaking subjects of the Empire (who constituted the majority) and the local government;

(c) educational institutions such as the School of Military Engineering, the School of Naval Engineering and the Levent garrison for the training of the Nizam-i Cedid troops, all founded on European models in the late eighteenth century as part of military reforms. Here, dragomans interpreted for foreign instructors who did not speak Turkish. Of an institutional but altogether different nature was the position of the Naval Dragoman, established much earlier and the first important post to be made available to Christian subjects in the Ottoman Empire. The post was held exclusively by the Greek Phanariots of Istanbul, and the holder of the post was eventually promoted Chief Dragoman to the Sublime Porte. As the duty of the Naval Dragoman was to supervise the regular collection of taxes from non-Muslim subjects in the Mediterranean and Aegean islands under the jurisdiction of the Admiral of the Fleet, his authority far exceeded that of an interpreter. In 1839, however, a series of reforms known as *Tanzimat* and designed to Westernize the empire resulted in limiting the responsibilities of the Naval Dragoman to interpreting;

(d) in foreign embassies and consulates, dragomans were initially provided by the Ottoman government. In the seventeenth century, however, they were appointed by the foreign missions from among Christian subjects, who were exempted from the land and capitation tax levied on non-Muslims. The duty of the dragoman in the diplomatic corps was to interpret and facilitate communication between Ottoman statesmen and the embassies and to handle all correspondence. Some achieved considerable distinction: Mouradgea d'Ohsson, the Armenian dragoman of the Swedish Embassy in Istanbul, was one of the two Christians in the committee of twenty-two

dignitaries asked by Selim III (1761–1808) in 1791 to give their opinion on the reasons for the decline of Ottoman power. In the eighteenth century, the French Embassy started a school to train interpreters for its own use. At the time of Mahmut II (1785–1839) there were 218 consular dragomans, twenty-four with special warrants, most of whom were Greeks and some wealthy enough to purchase the position. In the final years of the empire foreign missions appointed their own subjects as dragomans.

Within the above hierarchy, the most important post was naturally that of the dragoman to the Imperial Chancery. Dragomans were initially chosen from Greek, Italian, German, Hungarian and Polish converts to Islam. At the time of Süleyman the Magnificent (1494–1566), Yunus Bey, of Greek origin, is known to have been influential in foreign policy and was entrusted twice with taking treaties to Venice. That he was held in high esteem is shown by the fact that a Translators' Mosque (*Durugman Mescidi*) was built in Istanbul, with the permission and no doubt the support of the Sultan, in recognition of his services. In the seventeenth century, four dragomans were employed at the Sublime Porte, the seat of government. In 1669, following the naval expedition to Crete and as a reward for his special services in the peace negotiations, the Grand Vezir Fazil Ahmed Pasha appointed Panagiotis Nicoussios Mamounas, a Greek from Chios educated in Padua, as Chief Dragoman. Until the Greek Insurrection in 1821, the office of the Chief Dragoman was henceforth held by the Greek Phanariots of Istanbul, frequently passing from father to son and becoming the cause of much rivalry between the families. Dragomans were allowed to grow a beard, wear fur, keep four servants and ride a horse, privileges denied to other Christian subjects. It was also officially established that Chief Dragomans should have a retinue of twelve servants and eight language apprentices, all of whom were held exempt from the capitation tax which non-Muslims had to pay.

In 1709, the Chief Dragoman Nikolaos Skarlatos was appointed governor of Moldavia and Walachia; promotion to this post at the end of the chief translator's term of office became regular practice after that. As the principal duties of the Chief Dragoman were to interpret for the Grand Vezir when he received foreign missions and to translate all documents other than those in Arabic, he was privy to state secrets and all details regarding foreign policy. In the second half of the eighteenth century it was felt that this position of responsibility was beginning to be abused by dragomans in their relations with the French, British and Russians, each rivalling the other in their attempts to gain more influence in the affairs of the empire.

In 1821, the Phanariot Chief Dragoman was executed on suspicion of being involved with Greek revolutionaries. Yahya Efendi, a convert to Islam who taught at the Military School of Engineering, was appointed to the post with the responsibility of organizing a training programme in Greek and French and supervising the work of an 'impartial' Greek appointed provisionally as dragoman. The breakdown of established practice and an increasing volume of work eventually led to the foundation of the Translation Chamber at the Porte in 1822; in 1833, the Chamber actively started training Turks and other Muslims as state translators and interpreters. Translation chambers of a similar nature were also set up in other government departments.

The translation chambers had a very significant function in the context of *Tanzimat*, the series of political, social and institutional reforms that initiated in 1839 the gradual but conscious shift towards a Western outlook. They served as the most important institutional centre for the penetration of European ideas (mainly through French) and for the education of the most distinguished statesmen, thinkers, scholars and literary innovators of the time. Despite conquests that reached into central Europe and active diplomatic and commercial relations, the Ottomans had generally remained indifferent to the ideas of the Enlightenment. It was only in the nineteenth century that the weakening Empire, forced by economic and political circumstances to turn to Europe, began to discover the stimuli for intellectual revival; the foundations of the Westernist modern Turkish Republic were laid in the nineteenth century. Two major phases of acculturation in the Turkish realm must therefore be recognized: Arab–Persian in the fourteenth–fifteenth centuries and European in the nineteenth to twentieth centuries.

The Arab–Persian phase: predominance of Islamic sources

Literary works began to appear in the thirteenth century and increased in number in the fourteenth century, when texts translated from Persian and Arabic played a vital role in the development of the Turkish language. At that stage, the selection of texts seems to have been made on a utilitarian basis, in terms of what was thought to be instructive and useful. Sacred texts and religious writing, therefore, held a very prominent place in the growing corpus of translations during this period. However, the Qur'ān (written in Arabic) was held sacrosanct; so much so in fact that when the Jews, who settled in the Ottoman Empire after their expulsion from Spain, first introduced the printing press in the sixteenth century, the mere possibility of printing in Arabic letters was ruled out by the chief religious dignitary.

The Qur'ān was eventually considered translatable but only on a word-for-word basis. The earliest known interlinear manuscript translations of the Qur'ān into Anatolian Turkish date back to the fourteenth century. Earlier translations into Eastern Turkic, following the mass conversion of Central Asian Turks to Islam in the tenth century, are mainly of two kinds: (a) interlinear, where 'each Turkic word or phrase is written in smaller characters at an angle of 45 degrees beneath each Arabic word', a practice which reflects the oral stage in the translation of the holy text, and (b) annotated, where 'each logical group of Arabic words (generally overlined in manuscripts in red ink) is translated en bloc by a group of Turkic words, forming sentences which use the grammatical, syntactical and literary norms of written Turkic' (Birnbaum 1990: 113–14). The same tradition was followed in Anatolian Turkish versions, while a third type of translation combined the two modes. Though very rare, there were also some fourteenth-to-fifteenth-century trilingual versions in Arabic, Persian and Anatolian Turkish, where the latter was written below the Persian, the first language into which the Qur'ān was translated in the tenth century.

The selection of texts for literary translation from Islamic sources is worth examining in some detail, because many have long been appropriated by the Ottoman-Turkish literary tradition as original works. Gülşehri's fourteenth-century translation of the Persian poet Feridüddin-i Attar's masterpiece *Mantiku't-Tayr* (The Language of Birds; an allegorical tale within a tale of birds in search of mystic union) is a case in point: this version is said to owe its excellence and 'originality' to what the translator contributed to the original in the form of tales from other sources and material of his own composition; and this he did without damaging the unity of Attar's work, which itself was a poetic 'elaboration' of the Arabic *Risalat al-Tayr* (Stories of Birds) by Ghazzali.

The work of Ahmed-i Dai, translator, poet, scholar and court tutor, provides further examples. Dai is described in the literary histories not as a translator but as a poet and scholar, on the basis of his two collections of poetry in Arabic and Persian. But of his nine prose works in Turkish, all were translations except *Teressül* (Copy-book for Writing), a guide to formal and informal correspondence, known as the first book on Turkish composition. Among his prose translations, the most important was the first Turkish version of the highly revered commentary on the Qur'ān by Ebu'l Leys-i Semerkandi, followed by an annotated translation of *Ayet-ul kursi* (the 256th verse of the second Sura of the Qur'ān), which included a glossary, hagiographies, and morality tales of Dai's choice and composition. Others were translations of *One Hundred Hadithî* (holy sayings) of the Prophet Muhammed and *Tibb-i nebeví* (The Prophet's Medical Advice), a collection of his sayings on hygiene and disease. The last was a part-translation of Ebu Naim Hafiz-i Isfahani's *Kitabu' ş-şifa fi-ahadisi'l Mustafa* (The Book of Remedies), which itself was based on the Persian summary-version by Imam Ahmed b.Yusuf et-Tifasi.

Ahmed-i Dai's discussions of the strategies he used are highly informative and revealing. In his preface to *Miftahu'l-cennet* (Key to Heaven, a guide to virtuous Islamic living) Dai claimed to have 'composed [the text] in eight sections' (Tekin 1992: 40–41; translated), i.e. gave it a different form from that of the Arabic original. Elsewhere, in the preface to his translation of Feridüddin-i Attar's *Tezkiretu'l-evliya* (Biographies of the Evliya – Muslim saints), he stated that he had 'liked [the work] so much that [he] could not help translating it' (ibid.:

45) although it had already been rendered from Persian into Turkish. Dai was thus engaged in some form of 'rewriting', an established practice which had long been popular in Eastern cultures. But Dai refers to all these works as 'translations', including another two 'translations' he undertook, one from Persian (*Nasir-i Tusi's Risale-i si-fasl*, 'Book of Thirty Chapters', a treatise on astrology and the calendar), and Ebu Bekr bin Abdullah el-Vasiti's *Kitabu't-ta'birname*, 'Book of Interpretations' (of dreams), originally in Arabic. In his prefaces, some of which were written in verse, he indicated the source texts and any other texts he used, explained why he had translated them, gave his name or pseudonym, and generally named his patrons, the princes who commissioned them or to whom they were dedicated.

Of the translations that Dai produced entirely in verse, the most interesting is his rhyming Arabic–Persian dictionary in 650 couplets. This is a shorter version of Reşidüddin-i Vatvat's *'ukudu'l-cevahir* (Strings of Jewels), which in some manuscripts had the Turkish equivalents written in interlinear form. The dictionary was designed to help teach Dai's young pupil, Prince Murat, and served not only as a lexicon but also as a guide to the Turkish forms of the (classical Arabic–Persian) *aruz* metre. Dai's most important verse translation is *Çengname* (The Book of Çeng-Lyre, an allegorical story of the Oriental lyre) which, as he explained, was partly a translation of the Persian poet Sadi's *mesnevi* (now lost) by the same title, expanded with verses by Dai himself. His translation of *Camasb-name* (The Book of Jamasb) by Nasir-i Tusi, also a Persian poet, was in the genre of 'Mirror for Princes', morality tales written as counsel for rulers. From the fourteenth century onward, the increasing popularity of 'Mirror for Princes' and of the narrative *mesnevi* form in rhyming couplets led to more translations in the same genre.

Other well-known examples from the fourteenth and fifteenth centuries include Kul Mesud's mainly prose translation of *Kelile ve Dimne* (Kelile and Dimne, animal fables translated from the Arabic version, itself a translation from Persian, originally written in Sanskrit), Şeyhoğlu's *Marzuban-name* (The Book of Marzuban – Governor, a collection of Persian animal fables combined with tales of kings and philosophers) and Mercimek Ahmed's *Kabus-name* (The Book of Kabus, a highly popular 'Mirror for Princes', by the Persian king Keykavus) commissioned for Sultan Murad II (1421–51) in the fifteenth century. Dai and his contemporaries played an important part in enriching the Turkish language, which was still in its early stages of development. They enjoyed the patronage of the rulers of Anatolian principalities, who resisted the dominance of Persian and were keen to be informed and instructed in Turkish.

However, by the end of the sixteenth century the canon of Ottoman poetry had become heavily Persianized. Translation activity, which had initially worked to elevate Anatolian Turkish to the level of a literary language and had provided excellent models in the fourteenth and fifteenth centuries, must have also played a part in this linguistic takeover at a later stage. The cultural policies of the Istanbul-based centralized government, which had replaced those of the more consciously Turkish former principalities, must also be recognized as a factor contributing to this change in literary and linguistic direction.

Translation of medical and scientific texts

In the fourteenth and fifteenth centuries, scientific texts were written almost entirely in Arabic, the medium of scholarship in *Medreses* (schools of higher learning). Among the earliest in Turkish were books on medicine, shorter versions of well-known Arabic texts, or compilations from Arabic sources: *Müfredat-i ibn Baytar* (Ibn Baytar's Book of Particulars), *Havass-ul-edviye* (Best Known Remedies), *Kamil-üs-sinaa* (Perfect Arts). An eminent doctor of that age, Celaleddin Hizir (known as Haci Pasha), wrote principally in Arabic but also produced two Turkish versions of his own work, a full translation (*Müntahab-üş-şifa*: Selected Remedies) and a shorter version omitting theoretical chapters (*Teshil-uş-şifa*: Facilitating Healing), in the preface of which he apologized for writing in Turkish for everyone to understand. Most translations of this kind were commissioned by Umur Bey and Isa Bey, princes of Aydin. Mukbil-zade Mümin's *Zahire-i Muradiye* (Diseases of the Body), which was dedicated to Murat II (1404–51), consisted

of translations – compiled from Arabic and Persian sources – in which Turkish terms were used along with their equivalents in the source languages, obviously in an attempt to develop medical terminology in the target language. It has also been discovered that among books on surgery, one by Sabuncu-oglu, rich in Turkish terms and claimed to be an original work by the author, was in fact a translation from the Arabic, known in Europe but not in Anatolia.

From the time of Mehmed I (1389–1421), a growing interest in encyclopaedic works prompted the writing and translation of many books on the 'wonders of the world', such as Zekeriya el-Kazvini's famous *Acaib-ül-mahlukât* (Strange Creatures) in Arabic (translated eight times over the centuries), which featured in particular natural and supernatural plants and animals, a favourite topic with some of the Ottoman sultans.

Contact with non-Islamic cultures

The interests of Mehmed II (1432–81), and his patronage of translations, were of a different nature. He was competent in Arabic and Persian and particularly interested in reading and discussing the works of the Greek Peripatetics and Stoics already translated into these languages. The Sultan is also said to have commissioned an Arabic translation of the New Testament.

Following his conquest of Constantinople and other territories, Mehmed II no doubt became aware of his role as patron of cross-cultural and scientific scholarship in the Islamic world, where Arabic was the principal language of learning. When he discovered Ptolemy's *Geography* among some Byzantine manuscripts in 1465, he had it translated into Arabic (rather than Turkish) by Georgios Amirukis, a renowned Pontic Greek scholar who lived in Mehmed II's court from 1461 till his death in 1475. He also had two treatises by Ali Kuscu on mathematics and astronomy translated from Persian into Arabic.

Three translations into Turkish from this period are worth mentioning. The first is Plutarch's *Lives* which, Gibbon (in Adivar 1970: 25–50) claimed, was translated from Greek on the Sultan's orders. The second is the life and deeds of Uzun Hasan, the King of Persia, from the Italian original by Giovanni Maria Angiolello, who took part in the expedition with the Sultan's son. The third text is of particular interest since it was a translation of a detailed exposition of the Christian creed by the Greek Orthodox Patriarch Gennadios Scholarios, who, soon after the conquest of Constantinople, was called into a debate with the Sultan; the debate took place through an interpreter, who was asked to record it in writing. The importance of this document is such that various translators over the centuries were asked to improve on it. The text was part-published in the *Mecmua-i Ebuzziya* (Journal of Ebuzziya) in Istanbul in 1911.

The scientific renaissance initiated under the patronage of Mehmed II did not continue under his successors. Ottoman science and medicine remained generally confined to the works of and commentaries on Aristotle, Ptolemy, Galen and Avicenna in Arabic, and interest in other cultures was not rekindled until the eighteenth century.

Translations from European sources in the eighteenth century

The liberal and aesthetic outlook characteristic of the reign of Ahmed III in the eighteenth century brought about a reawakening of interest in Western Europe. But this interest was mainly in non-literary works. The only European literary work to be translated (with additions) before the *Tanzimat* (the reforms initiated in the mid-nineteenth century) was Ali Aziz Efendi's *Muhayyelat* (Fantasies; 1797–8), a version of Petis de la Croix's *Les Mille et un jours*.

In 1717, a committee of twenty-five was appointed by Grand Vezir Ibrahim Pasha to translate from European as well as Oriental languages. Of this group, Esad Efendi translated Aristotle's *Physics* from Greek into Arabic, making note, for the first time in the East, of the telescope and microscope in his annotations. Furthermore, the need for military modernization to prevent further defeats led to the establishment of various schools such as the School of Military Engineering in 1734 and the Military Medical School in 1827; it also encouraged the learning of European languages

and the translation of scientific texts. For instance, following the founding of the first school of military engineering in 1734, there appeared two treatises: one on trigonometry, the first modern work on mathematics, part-translated from European sources, and an anonymous translation of *Memorie della guerra* by Count Raimondo Montecucculi (the Austrian general who fought against the Turkish invasion in 1661–4). Other works translated for the first time include Bernhardus Varenius's *Geographia Generalis* (1750), Herman Boerhaave's *Aphorismi* (1771) which introduced Harvey's anatomical treatise on blood circulation to Ottoman medicine, and Ibrahim Müteferrika's versions (1731) of two scientific works in Latin, discussing Galileo's and Descartes' theories, magnetism and the compass.

A major non-military innovation in the first half of the eighteenth century which also had a bearing on translations was the setting up of the printing press in 1727 by Ibrahim Müteferrika, a convert of Hungarian origin. Jewish (1493–94), Armenian (1567) and Greek (1627) printing presses had been established in Istanbul long before special permission could be obtained for a Turkish press to print books on non-religious subjects, i.e. excluding the Qur'ān and commentaries, holy traditions, theology and holy law (Lewis 1962: 51). Among the first books to be published by the Müteferrika press, starting in 1729, were the *Vankulu Lugati* (The Vankuli Dictionary, reprinted in 1755–6), which was 'translated' (i.e. rendered bilingual) from the Arabic in the sixteenth century, *Grammaire Turque*, a Turkish grammar in French, Muteferrika's treatises (1731), and his expanded version of *Cihannüma* (Showing the World), a geographical work, based on European sources, by Kâtip Çelebi (also known as Haci Halife). Çelebi was the translator of Mercator's *Atlas Minor* (1653–5) and a scientific thinker famous for his attempts to break down the barriers between Eastern and Western science in the seventeenth century.

The second printing press, set up at the School of Military Engineering in 1796, also chose a dictionary as its first book (printed in 1799); this was *Burhan-i Kaati* (Convincing Proof), 'translated' into a bilingual version from the Persian and compiled by Asim Efendi, known as Mütercim (Translator) Asim.

The Tanzimat period: 'Enlightenment' through translation in the nineteenth century

The principal revival in scientific and literary translations from European sources followed the setting up of the government Translation Chambers in 1833. However, translation from Persian and Arabic had also reached its peak during the nineteenth century. This state of affairs created tension between Eastern sources of canonical status and sources from the West, the latter as yet peripheral but gaining ground and becoming increasingly powerful. What provided an additional impetus not only to the modernizing reforms of Mahmut II but to acculturation with Europe was the earlier and more extensive Westernization programme of Mehmed Ali Pasha, the Khedive of Egypt, who was in open competition with the Sultan (see ARABIC TRADITION).

Among the new cultural institutions of the mid-nineteenth century was the Academy of Sciences (*Encümen-i Daniş*), established in 1851 and subsidized by the government, and the Ottoman Scientific Society (*Cemiyet-i Ilmiye-yi Osmaniye*), founded in 1860 by Münif Pasha, an eminent member of the Translation Chamber who was educated in Egypt. At these centres, which included non-Muslim members, translation activity from European sources was organized to provide teaching materials for a prospective university and to introduce and promote scientific and scholarly work. A translation of J. B. Say's *Catéchisme d'Économie Politique* (1852) and a biographical dictionary of eminent European statesmen, both by Abro Sahak Efendi, were among the first works to be published by the Academy. Several histories were also written or translated by the members of the Academy but remained in draft form and were never published; they included Ahmed Ağribozi's history of Ancient Greece, Todoraki Efendi's translation of a history of Europe, and Aleko Efendi's book on the last Napoleonic campaigns. The first history of Greek philosophy in Turkish, *Abrégé de la Vie des Plus Illustres Philosophes de l'Antiquité*, was translated by Cricor Chumarian and published independently in Izmir in 1854 in the form of parallel texts, with the original in French.

In 1865, three years after the Academy was closed, a Translation Committee was formed on similar lines, headed once again by Münif Pasha, the founder of the Scientific Society. The works known to have been published by this committee were translations of two books on history and geography, from English and French respectively. Münif Pasha also introduced a more influential medium for the dissemination of Western scientific thought with his *Mecmua-i Funun* (Journal of Sciences), the first Turkish journal of sciences, which also carried translations; it was published intermittently between 1862 and 1882 by the Scientific Society.

Münif Pasha was instrumental in introducing a new literary genre with his selection of translations of philosophical dialogues by Voltaire, Fénelon and Fontenelle, under the title *Muhaverat-i Hikemiye* (Philosophical Dialogues; 1859). This work is highly significant, given that it was the first to introduce the basic tenets of European Enlightenment in Turkish, and in an environment where 'philosophical speculation divorced from theology was considered heretical' (Mardin 1962: 234).

Two other translations appeared in the same year and marked the awakening of interest in European classics; they too were to have a lasting influence on forms and ideas that shaped modern Turkish literature. *Terceme-i Telemak* was a version of Abbé Fénelon's *Les aventures de Télémaque*, a political–philosophical novel, but also a 'mirror for princes', which was more readily acceptable in the Ottoman tradition that favoured Eastern examples of this genre. *Telemak* was first circulated in manuscript and was not published until 1862. The translator was the Grand Vezir Yusuf Kamil Pasha, who had served in Egypt, where the work had already been translated into Arabic and was well received. *Tercume-i Manzume* was a collection of verse by La Fontaine, Lamartine, Gilbert and Racine, translated by Ibrahim Şinasi to introduce European poetry in traditional *aruz* verse (adapted from classical Arabic and Persian) to facilitate its reception.

The first literary translators had thus served to introduce three new literary genres: Western poetry, philosophical dialogue and the novel. A year later, in 1860, Ibrahim Şinasi wrote the first Turkish domestic comedy and serialized it in the newspaper *Tercüman-i Ahval* (Interpreter of Conditions). Şinasi, who had trained at one of the departmental translation chambers and had visited France, was also the founder and chief editor of *Tasvir-i Efkâr* (Illustration of Ideas, established 1862), one of the first private Turkish newspapers to appear in Istanbul. A true innovator, the translations he serialized on literature, social and economic topics, as well as political thought, made his newspaper the most stimulating and popular of the time. He used journalism as a medium to put into practice his policy for simple Turkish prose, which had a lasting influence on the future of modern Turkish language and literature. Both literary and non-literary translations in newspapers and periodicals served as one of the most important means of implementing this policy, which was adopted by writers and journalists to communicate more easily with their readers.

Victor Hugo's *Les Misérables* was serialized in 1862, followed in subsequent years by Chateaubriand's *Atala* (1869), de Saint-Pierre's *Paul et Virginie* (1870), Voltaire's *Micromégas* (1871) and Dumas père's *Le Comte de Monte Cristo* (1871). The strategies followed in such translations of fiction, most of which were later published in book form, created a general awareness of the translators' norms and of the problems they faced. In his preface to *Atala* (published in book form in 1874), Recaizade Ekrem drew attention to the inadequacy of contemporary Turkish prose for the purposes of translation. To improve on the first serialized versions, *Micromégas* (1871) and the first eight chapters of *Les Misérables* (1879) were retranslated by Ahmed Vefik Pasha and Şemseddin Sami respectively. Ahmed Vefik Pasha, a renowned lexicographer like Şemseddin Sami, also retranslated *Les Aventures de Télémaque* (1881). In contrast to Yusuf Kamil Pasha's earlier translation in the traditional grand style, his version used simpler vocabulary and syntax, intended to be literal and accurate, as well as pleasing for the reader. Şemseddin Sami, criticized for being too literal in his version of *Les Misérables*, defended his strategy in his preface to his translation of *Robinson Crusoe* (1885), arguing that new ideas could not be conveyed in the conventional Ottoman style and that close adherence to the source text and the use of simple prose were conscious moves to use the full potential of the Turkish language. Their contemporary Ahmed Midhat Efendi, on the other hand, pursued not one but a variety of rewriting strategies in his numerous versions of classics and popular books rendered from French. In his prefaces, he frequently expressed his aversion for 'literal' translation because the result did not read like an original; he contributed to the elaboration of a critical/theoretical discourse which explored distinctions between concepts such as 'translation', 'interpretation' and 'appropriation'.

The years 1873–83 were the most productive for the writers/translators of the *Tanzimat*. Subsequently, censorship in Abdülhamid II's reign led mainly to the translation of popular French fiction. The Constitutional Revolution of 1908 and the deposition of Abdülhamid II were followed by a significant revival of translations of canonized works in history, philosophy and the social sciences, as well as English, German and Russian literature. Abdullah Cevdet, who translated Shakespeare, and journalists Hüseyin Cahit and Haydar Rifat were the most active and committed translators of the period.

Translation in the Republic (1923 to the present)

As in the nineteenth century, translation in the early twentieth century was instrumental in initiating the cultural revolution which supported the Westernizing programme of the secular republic of Turkey, founded by Mustafa Kemal (Atatürk) in 1923. In 1924, Remzi Kitabevi, a private publishing company, started its series *Translations from World Authors*. In the same year, a Commission for Original and Translated Works was formed by the Ministry of Education to produce publications for educational purposes. In 1928, the Roman script was officially adopted to replace Arabic letters. The first Turkish translation of the Qur'ān in the Roman alphabet appeared in 1932. The movement for simple Turkish that had begun in the nineteenth century ultimately resulted in the state-sponsored radical language reform of the Republic in the 1930s, whereby Turkish was also to be 'purified' of Arabic and Persian influence.

The revolutionary move made by Hasan Âli Yücel, Minister of Education, in setting up a Translation Committee in 1939 and a Translation Office in 1940 was intended to reinforce the new language policies and to organize a programme for cultural revival. The Office, composed largely of academics and prominent men of letters, was to select and translate 'world classics', beginning with Ancient Greek philosophy and literature. Such key texts were also essential for instruction in the new Humanities departments of the universities in Istanbul and Ankara. The general aim was to 'generate' the spirit of humanism by cultivating and assimilating foreign literatures through translation; this, it was felt, would bring about a renaissance and contribute to the development of the Turkish language and culture.

By the end of 1944, the most intensive translation period, 109 works were translated, headed by the Greek and French classics. By 1967 more than 1,000 translations were published, among which Eastern and Islamic texts constituted a very small proportion. A change in government policies and the dismissal of its leading members led to the Office losing its initial impetus after 1950. Throughout the 1960s, however, following the constitutional changes of 1961 that allowed for greater freedom of thought, private publishing companies became actively involved in the translation of Marxist/socialist literature, though such activity had its risks even for well-established translators and men of letters.

The Translation Office produced the periodical *Tercüme* (Translation; 1940–66), which was highly influential not only in terms of drawing attention to the activities of the Office but also in terms of creating a critical forum for the discussion of literary translation. Two prestigious translation journals, *Yazko Çeviri Dergisi* (Yazko Translation Journal; 1981–4) and *Metis Çeviri Dergisi* (Metis Translation Journal; 1988–92), continued in the same tradition. The launch in 1994 of a new quarterly periodical, *TÖMER Çeviri Dergisi* (Literary Translation Journal), under the auspices of Ankara University, suggests that interest in literary translation remains strong.

As shown in the *Index Translationum*, the total number of translated titles from 1982 to 1986 was 4,459. According to the Turkish Publishers' Association annual catalogue, the total number of translations (including intralingual translations from Ottoman into contemporary Turkish) on the market by October 1994 amounted to 6,028. Statistics supplied by a private bookshop (Pandora) show that in 1993, before the economic recession fully hit the market, 668 titles (more than two thirds) of a total of 1,518 new publications (excluding textbooks and publications by government ministries/official institutions) were translations.

Since the mid-1980s, Turkish publishers have kept up with the world market by publishing translations of international literature, from prize-winning fiction to popular best-sellers. Figures for the 1990s also indicate a growing interest in publishing translations in the fields of history, philosophy, psychology, social sciences, gender studies, children's literature, and the arts. Turkish versions of international encyclopaedias have enjoyed an unprecedented boom since the early 1980s.

A project launched by the Publications Department of the Yapi Kredi Bank in 1991, the Kâzim Taşkent Publication Series, pays generous fees for the translation of classics as yet unpublished in Turkish. Literary translation prizes were awarded by the Turkish Language Academy from 1959 to 1984.

Training, research and publications

The Economic and Social Studies Conference Board set up in 1961 by the Ford Foundation, Turkish industrialists and academicians was the first to initiate a training programme for conference interpreters in Switzerland, which subsequently continued to operate in Turkey. Some of the first professional interpreters to be trained by this programme are now also actively involved in training at the various universities.

In response to a growing demand for competent professional translators and conference interpreters in English, departments of translation and interpreting were set up in 1983–4 in two universities, Boğaziçi (Istanbul) and Hacettepe (Ankara). Apart from four-year degree courses, these departments also offer MA and PhD degrees in translation studies. The PhD programme at Boğaziçi University was the first to offer a course on the history of translation in Ottoman/Turkish society, with the aim of foregrounding the links between translation and literary/cultural history. Other institutions which offer training in translation include Yildiz Technical University (Istanbul) and Bilkent University (Ankara).

Further reading

Mardin 1962; Adivar 1970; Orhonlu 1974; Kut 1986; Paker 1991; Paker *et al.* 1991; Tekin 1992; Strauss 1994, 1995; Paker and Toska 1997; Paker 2002.

SALIHA PAKER

Bibliography

A. Samad Ahmad (1987) *Hikayat Amir Hamzah*, Kuala Lumpur: Dewan Bahasa dan Pustaka.

Aaltonen, H. (1986) 'Suomentamisen varhais-vaiheita' [Early Stages of Translation into Finnish], in J. Peteri *et al.* (eds) *10-vuotisjuh-lajilkaisu* [10th Anniversary Festschrift for the Turku Branch of the Finnish Association of Translators and Interpreters], Turku: Suomen kääntäjien ja tulkkien liitto, Turun paikallisosasto.

Aaltonen, Sirkku (1996) 'Rewriting Representations of the Foreign: The Ireland of Finnish Realist Drama', *TTR* IX(2): 103–22.

——(2000) *Time Sharing on Stage: Drama Translation in Theatre and Society*, Clevedon: Multilingual Matters.

——(2003) 'Retranslation in the Finnish Theatre', *Caderno de Tradução* 11: 141–59.

Abdel Haleem, M. A. S. (2004) *The Qur'ān, A New Translation*, Oxford: Oxford University Press.

Abdul-Raof, Hussein (2001) *Qur'ān Translation: Discourse, Texture and Exegesis*, Surrey: Curzon.

Abel, Jonathan E. (2005) 'Translation as Community: the Opacity of Modernizations of *Genji monogatari*', in Sandra Berman and Michael Wood (eds) *Nation, Language, and the Ethics of Translation*, Princteon, NJ: Princeton University Press, 146–58.

Abend-David, Dror (2003) *'Scorned My Nation'. A Comparison of Translations of* The Merchant of Venice *into German, Hebrew, and Yiddish*, New York: Peter Lang.

Abley, Mark (2003) *Spoken Here: Travels among Threatened Languages*, London: Arrow Books.

Aboulela, Leila (1999) *The Translator*, Edinburgh: Polygon.

Abril Martí, María Isabel (2006) *La interpretación en los servicios públicos: caracterización como género, contextualización y modelos de formación. Hacia unas bases para el diseño curricular.* Unpublished doctoral dissertation. University of Granada, Spain.

Abu Libdeh, A. (1991) *Metaphoric Expression in Literary Discourse with Special Reference to English–Arabic Translation*, Unpublished PhD Thesis, Edinburgh: Heriot-Watt University.

Abu-Lughod, Lila (1991) 'Writing Against Culture', in Richard G. Fox (ed.) *Recapturing Anthropology: Working in the Present*, Santa Fe: School of American Research Press, 137–62.

Access to Interpreters in The Australian Legal System (1991) Report by the Commonwealth Attorney-General's Department, Canberra: AGPS (AUSTRALIAN GOVERNMENT PUBLICATION SERVICE).

Ackerman, Seth (2006) 'Mixed Signals: When Hamas Hinted at Peace, US Media Wouldn't Take the Message', *Fair* (Fairness and Accuracy in Reporting), http://www.fair.org/index.php?page=2974 (accessed 8 March 2007).

Acta Universitatis Carolinae, Translatologica Pragensia (1984–), Prague: Charles University.

Actes de la Recherche en Sciences Sociales (2002) *Traduction: Les Échanges littéraires interna-tionaux*, Special Issue 144 (September).

Adab, Beverly (2000) 'Towards a More Systematic Approach to the Translation of Advertising Texts', in Allison Beeby, Doris Ensinger and Marisa Presas (eds) *Investigating Translation*, Amsterdam & Philadelphia: John Benjamins, 223–34.

——(2001) 'The Translation of Advertising: A Framework for Evaluation', *Babel* 47(2): 133–57.

——and Cristina Valdés (eds) (2004) *The Translator* 10(2) (special issue: *Key Debates in the Translation of Advertising Material*), Manchester: St Jerome.

Adams, Christine, Ann Corsellis and Anita Harmer (eds) (1995) *Basic Handbook for Trainers of Public Service Interpreters*, London: Institute of Linguists Educational Trust.

Adivar, A. Adnan (1970) *Osmanli Turklerinde Ilim* [Science in Ottoman Turkey], Istanbul: Remzi Kitabevi.

Agar, M. (1994) *Language Shock: Understanding the Culture of Conversation*, New York: William Morrow & Company.

Agorni, Mirella (2002) *Translating Italy for the Eighteenth Century: British Women, Translation and Travel Writing (1739–1797)*, Manchester: St Jerome.

Agost, Rosa María (1999) *Traducción y doblaje: palabras, voces e imágenes*, Barcelona: Ariel.

Ahamed, Syed Vickar (2003) *The Glorious Qur'ān, A Simplified Translation of the Meaning of The Qur'ān for Young People* (2nd edition), Elmhurst, New York: Tahrike Tarsile Qur'ān, Inc.

Ahrens, Barbara (2005) 'Prosodic Phenomena in Simultaneous Interpreting', *Interpreting* 7(1): 51–76.

AIIC (1979) *L'Enseignment de l'Interprétation. Dix ans de colloques (1969–79)*, Geneva: AIIC.

Aixelá, Javier Franco (2004) 'The Study of Technical and Scientific Translation: An Examination of its Historical Development', *Journal of Specialised Translation* 1: 29–49. Online http://www.jostrans.org/issue01/articles/Aixelá.htm (accessed 16 July 2007).

Akach, Philemon A.O. (2006) 'Colonisation of Sign Languages and the Effect on Sign Language Interpreters', in Rachel Locker McKee (ed.) *Proceedings of the Inaugural Conference of the World Association of Sign Language Interpreters, Worchester, South Africa, 31 October–2 November 2005*, Coleford, Gloucestershire: Douglas McLean, 32–43.

Aktaş Salman, Umay (2006) 'Hayırlı Sabahlar Hans!' (Good Morning Hans!), *Radikal*, 19 August. http://www.radikal.com.tr/haber.php?haberno=196195 (accessed 17 November 2007).

al-Ansari, Ahmad Makki (1405Hegira = 1984/1986 AD) *Nathariyyat al-Nahw al-Qur'āni* [The Theory of Qur'ānic Grammar], No place of publication: Dar al-Qiblah lil-thaqafah al-Islamiyyah, Abu-l-Futuh Printing Press.

Alawni, Khalil (2006) 'Sign Language Interpreting in Palestine', in Rachel Locker McKee (ed.) *Proceedings of the Inaugural Conference of the World Association of Sign Language Interpreters, Worchester, South Africa, 31 October–2 November 2005*, Coleford, Gloucestershire: Douglas McLean, 68–78.

al-Bawaba (2007) 'New Translation Initiative Set to Widen Access to Global Works for Arab Readers', 4 November.

Albertson, L. L. (1972) *Litteraer oversættelse* [Literary Translation], Copenhagen.

al-Bundaq, Muhammad Salih (1983) *Al-Mustashriqun wa tarjamat al-Qur'ān al-Karim* (The Orientalists and the Translation of the Holy Qur'ān), Beirut: Dar al-Afaq al-Jadida.

Alexander, Michael (1966) *The Earliest English Poems*, Harmondsworth: Penguin.

'Ali, Jawād (1986) *Al-Mufassal fi Tārikh al-'Arab Qabla al-Islām* [A Detailed History of the Arabs Prior to the Rise of Islam], vol. 1, Beirut: Dār al-'Ilm l-il-Mālayīn and Baghdad: Maktabat al-Nahda.

Ali, Saleh Salim (1992) 'Misrepresentation of Some Ellipted Structures in the Translation of the Qur'ān', *Meta* 37(3): 487–90.

Alifano, Roberto (1984) *Twenty-Four Conversations with Borges. Including a Selection of Poems (Interviews by Roberto Alifano 1981–1983)*, Housatonic, MA: Lascaux Publishers.

Allen, Beverley (1999) 'Paralysis, Crutches, Wings: Italian Feminisms and Transculturation', http://www.pum.umontreal.ca/revues/surfaces/vol3/allen.html (accessed January 2008).

Allen, Jeffrey (2003) 'Post-editing', in Harold Somers (ed.) *Computers and Translation: A Translator's Guide*, Amsterdam: John Benjamins, 297–317.

Allén, Sture (ed.) (1999) *Translation of Poetry and Poetic Prose: Proceedings of Nobel Symposium 110*, Singapore: World Scientific.

Allwood, Jens (1995) 'Action Theory', in Jef Verschueren, Jan-Ola Östman, Jan Blommaert and Chris Bulcaen (eds) *Handbook of Pragmatics. Manual*, Amsterdam: John Benjamins, 26–8.

Almagor, Dan (1975) 'Shakespeare ba-sifrut ha-ivrit bi-tkufat ha-haskala u-bi-tkufat ha-txiya: Skira bibliyografit u-bibliyografya' [Shakespeare in Hebrew Literature of the Enlightenment and Revival Periods: A Bibliographical Survey and a Bibliography], in Boaz Shahevitch and Menahem Perry (eds) *Sefer ha-yovel le-Shim'on Halkin* [Simon Halkin Jubilee Volume], Jerusalem: Rubin Mass, 721–84.

al-Shayyal, Gamal al-Deen (1951/2000) *Tarikh al-Tarjama wa al-Haraka al-Thaqafiyya fi Asr Muhammad Ali* (History of Translation and the Cultural Movement during the Reign of Muhammad Ali), Cairo: Maktabat al-Thaqafa al-Diniyya.

Altano, W. B. (1990) 'The Intricate Witness–Interpreter Relationship', in D. and M. Bowen (eds).

Altenberg, Bengt and Sylviane Granger (2002) 'Recent Trends in Cross-linguistic Lexical Studies', in Bengt Altenberg and Sylviane Granger (eds) *Lexis in Contrast: Corpus Based Approaches*, Amsterdam and Philadelphia: John Benjamins, 3-48.

Alvar, Carlos and Angel Gómez (1987) 'Traducciones francesas en el siglo XV', in Julius César Santoyo *et al.* (eds) 1989, vol. 1, 31–7.

Alvarez, Al (ed.) (1992) *The Faber Book of Modern European Poetry*, London: Faber & Faber.

Álvarez, Carmen (2005) Post on 'Demand for J->English / J->German translations ?', PROZ discussion forum, 23 June. http://www.proz.com/topic/30111 (accessed 16 August 2006).

Álvarez, Román and M. Carmen-África Vidal (eds) (1996) *Translation, Power, Subversion*, Clevedon: Multilingual Matters.

Alves, Fábio (ed.) (2003) *Triangulating Translation. Perspectives in Process Oriented Research*, Amsterdam & Philadelphia: John Benjamins.

——(2005) 'Ritmo cognitivo, meta-reflexão e experiência: parâmetros de análise processual no desempenho de tradutores novatos e experientes' [Cognitive rhythm, meta-reflection and experience: parameters of procedural analysis in the performance of novice and experienced translators], in Adriana Pagano, Célia Magalhães and Fábio Alves (eds) *Competência em Tradução: Cognição e discurso*, Belo Horizonte: Editora UFMG, 109–69.

——and José Luiz V.R. Gonçalves (2003)

'A Relevance Theory Approach to Inferential Processes in Translation', in Fábio Alves (ed.) *Triangulating Translation. Perspectives in Process Oriented Research*, Amsterdam & Philadelphia: John Benjamins, 3–24.

——and Célia M. Magalhães (2006) 'Investigando o papel do monitoramento cognitivo-discursivo e da metareflexão na formação de tradutores' [Investigating the role of cognitive-discursive monitoring and meta-reflection in translation training], *Cadernos de Tradução* XVII: 71–127.

al-Zafzaf, Muhammad (1984) *Al-Ta'rif bi-il-Qur'ān wa-l-Hadith* (Introducing the Qur'ān and Hadith), Kuwait: Maktabat al-Falah.

Ammann, Margret (1990) 'Anmerkungen zu einer Theorie der Übersetzungskritik und ihrer praktischen Anwendung', *TEXTconTEXT* 5: 209–50.

Amorim, Lauro Maia (2005) *Tradução e adaptação – Encruzilhadas da textualidade em Alice no país das maravilhas, de Lewis Carroll, e Kim, de Rudyard Kipling*, São Paulo: Editora UNESP.

Anderman, Gunilla (1993) 'Translation and Speech Acts', in Yves Gambier and Jorma Tommola (eds) *Translation and Knowledge: Proceedings of the 1992 Scandinavian Symposium on Translation Theory*, Turku: Centre for Translation and Interpreting.

——(2005) *Europe on Stage: Translation and Theatre*, London: Oberon Books.

——and Margaret Rogers (eds) (2005) *In and Out of English: For Better, for Worse*, Clevedon: Multilingual Matters.

Anderson, Benedict (1982) *Imagined Communities. Reflections on the Origin and Spread of Nationalism*, London: Verso.

——(1991/2004) *Imagined Communities*. Extracts from Introduction; Web page, produced by Martin Irvine. Available at http://www.georgetown.edu/faculty/irvinem/CCT510/Sources/Anderson-extract.html (accessed 23 January 2007).

Anderson, Bruce W. (1976) 'Perspectives on the Role of the Interpreter', in Richard Brislin (ed.) *Translation: Applications and Research*, New York: Gardner Press, 208–28.

——(1978) 'Interpreter Roles and Interpretation Studies: Cross-Cutting Typologies', in David Gerver and H. Wallace Sinaiko (eds) *Language*

Interpretation and Communication. Proceedings of the NATO Symposium on Language Interpretation and Communication, Venice, 26 September – 1 October 1977, New York: Plenum Press, 217–31.

Anderson, George K. (1949) *The Literature of the Anglo Saxons*, Princeton, NJ: Princeton University Press.

Andrade, Oswald de (1970) *Do pau-brasil à antropofagia e às utopias: Manifestos, teses de concursos e ensaios*, Rio de Janeiro: Civilização Brasileira.

Andrews, Richard (1991) *The Problem with Poetry*, Buckingham: Open University Press.

Angelelli, Claudia (2004) *Re-visiting the Role of the Interpreter: A study of conference, court and medical interpreters in Canada, Mexico and the United States*, Amsterdam & Philadelphia: John Benjamins.

Apel, Friedmar (1982) *Sprachbewegung: Eine historisch-poetologische Untersuchung zum Problem des Übersetzens*, Heidelberg: Carl Winter.

Apfelbaum, Birgit (1995) 'Interaktive Verfahren der Disambiguierung in Situationen des Gesprächsdolmetschens', *Kognitionswissenschaft* 5(3): 141–50.

Apollinaire, Guillaume (1970) *Calligrammes*, trans. Anne Hyde Greet, Berkeley, CA: University of California Press.

Appadurai, Arjun (1996) *Modernity at Large: Cultural Dimensions of Globalization*, Minneapolis, MN: University of Minnesota Press.

Appiah, Kwame Anthony (1993) 'Thick Translation', *Callaloo* 16(4): 808–19.

Appleyard, Joseph A. (1990) *Becoming a Reader: The Experience of Fiction from Childhood to Adulthood*, Cambridge: Cambridge University Press.

Apter, Emily (2004) 'Global *Translatio*: The "Invention" of Comparative Literature, Istanbul, 1933', in Christopher Prendergast (ed.) *Debating World Literature*, London and New York: Verso, 76–109.

Aquiline, Carol-Lee (2006) 'Interpreting: A Global Responsibility', in Rachel Locker McKee (ed.) *Proceedings of the Inaugural Conference of the World Association of Sign Language Interpreters*, Gloucestershire, UK: Douglas McLean, 141–8.

Arac, Jonathan, Wlad Godzich and Wallace Martin (eds) (1983) *The Yale Critics: Deconstruction in America*, Minneapolis, MN: University of Minnesota Press.

Arai, E. (1997) 'Court Interpreters', *Pacific Friend* (April): 4–8.

Arberry, Arthur J. (1955) *The Koran Interpreted*, Oxford: Oxford University Press.

Arencibia, L. (1992) 'Apuntes para una historia de la traducción en Cuba', *Livius* 3: 1–30.

Armstrong, Nigel and Federico M. Federici (eds) (2006) *Translating Voices, Translating Regions*, Rome: Aracne.

Armstrong, Richard H. (2005) 'Translating Ancient Epic', in John. M. Foley (ed.) *A Companion to Ancient Epic*, Oxford: Blackwell, 174–95.

Armstrong, Stephen, Colm Caffrey, Marian Flanagan, Dorothy Kenny, Minako O'Hagan and Andy Way (2006) 'Leading by Example: Automatic Translation of Subtitles via EBMT', *Perspectives: Studies in Translatology* 14(3): 163–84.

Arnau i Segarra, Pilar & Pere Joan i Tous, Manfred Tietz (eds) (2002) *Escribir entre dos lenguas: escritores catalanes y la elección de la lengua literaria = Escriure entre dues llengües: escriptors catalans i l'elecció de la llengua literària*, Kassel: Reichenberger.

Arnaud, V. (1950) *Los intérpretes en el descubrimiento, la conquista y la colonización en el Río de la Plata*, Buenos Aires: no publisher.

Arndorfer, Martin (1997) *Samuel Beckett: Fragen zur Identität eines zweisprachigen Schriftstellers*, Vienna: Praesens.

Arnett, Peter (1998) 'State of the American Newspaper, Goodbye, World', *American Journalism Review* 20 (November/December). http://www.ajr.org/Article.asp?id=3288 (accessed 17 April 2005).

Arnold, Denise and Juan de Dios Yapita (2006) *The Metamorphosis of Heads. Textual Struggles, Education, and Land in the Andes*, Pittsburgh, PA: Pittsburgh University Press.

Arnold, Doug, Lorna Balkan, Siety Meijer, R. Lee Humphreys and Louisa Sadler (1995) *Machine Translation: An Introductory Guide*, London: Blackwells. http://www.essex.ac.uk/linguistics/clmt/MTbook/ (accessed 28 November 2007).

Arnold, Matthew (1954) *Poetry and Prose*, edited by John Bryson, London: Rupert Hart-Davis.

——and F. W. Newman (1914) *Essays by M. Arnold*, London: Oxford University Press.

Arntz, Reiner (1993) 'Terminological Equivalence and Translation', in H. B. Sonneveld and K. Loening (eds) *Terminology: Applications in Interdisciplinary Communication*, Amsterdam & Philadelphia: John Benjamins, 5–19.

Arrojo, Rosemary (1994) 'Fidelity and the Gendered Translation', *TTR* 7(2): 147–63.

——(1995) 'Feminist "Orgasmic" Theories of Translation and their Contradictions', *TradTerm* 2: 67–75.

——(1998) 'The Revision of the Traditional Gap between Theory & Practice & the Empowerment of Translation in Postmodern Times', *The Translator* 4(1): 25–48.

——(1999) 'Interpretation as Possessive Love. Hélène Cixous, Clarice Lispector and the Ambivalence of Fidelity', in Susan Bassnett and Harish Trivedi (eds) *Post-colonial Translation. Theory and Practice*, London & New York: Routledge, 141–61.

——(2005) 'The Ethics of Translation in Contemporary Approaches to Translators' Training', in Martha Tennent (ed.) *Training for the New Millennium – Pedagogies for Translation and Interpreting*, Amsterdam & Philadelphia: John Benjamins, 225–45.

Arrowsmith, William and Roger Shattuck (eds) (1961) *The Craft and Context of Translation*, Humanities Research Centre, Austin, TX: University of Texas Press. Reprinted 1964; New York: Anchor Books, Doubleday & Co.

Arteaga, Alfred (ed.) (1994) *An Other Tongue: Nation and Ethnicity in the Linguistic Borderlands*, Durham–London: Duke University Press.

Asad, Talal (1986) 'The Concept of Cultural Translation in British Social Anthropology', in James Clifford and George E. Marcus (eds) *Writing Culture: The Poetics and Politics of Ethnography*, Berkeley, CA: University of California Press, 141-64.

——(1995) 'A Comment on Translation, Critique, and Subversion', in Anuradha Dingwaney and Carol Maier (eds) *Between Languages and Cultures: Translation and Cross-Cultural Texts*, Pittsburgh and London: University of Pittsburgh Press, 325–32.

Ascher, Marcia and Robert Ascher (1981) *Code of the quipu. A Study in Media, Mathematics and Culture*, Ann Arbor, MI: University of Michigan Press.

Ashcroft, Bill, Gareth Griffiths and Helen Tiffin (1989) *The Empire Writes Back: Theory and Practice in Post-colonial Literatures*, London: Routledge.

Ashton, R. (1980) *The German Idea: Four English Writers and the Reception of German Thought 1800–1860*, Cambridge: Cambridge University Press.

Atkins, Sue, Jeremy Clear and Nicholas Ostler (1992) 'Corpus Design Criteria', *Literary and Linguistic Computing* 7(1): 1–16.

Atti del convegno 'In difesa dei traslocatori di parole, Editori e traduttori a confronto' Trieste, 9–10 maggio 1991 (1993) (Libri e Riviste d'Italia, Ministero per i beni culturali e ambientali), Rome: Istituto Poligrafico e Zecca dello Stato.

Austermühl, Frank (2001) *Electronic Tools for Translators*, Manchester: St Jerome Publishing.

Austin, J. L. (1962) *How to do Things with Words*, Cambridge, MA: Harvard University Press.

Axel, Erik (1997) 'One Developmental Line in European Activity Theories', in Michael Cole, Yrjö Engeström and Olga Vasquez (eds) *Mind, Culture and Activity*, Cambridge: Cambridge University Press, 128–46.

Ayyad, Shukri (1993) *Kitab Aristotalis fi al-Shi'r: Tahqiq wa Dirasa fi Tarjamat Matta bin Yunis* (Aristotle's Poetics: A Critical Edition and Study of Matta bin Yunis's Translation). Cairo: General Egyptian Book Organisation.

Azevedo, Milton (1996) 'Sobre les dues versions de *Els Argonautes/Los Argonautas*, de Baltasar Porcel', in Suzanne S. Hintz, Everette E. Larson and Mario A. Rojas (eds) *Essays in Honor of Josep M. Sola-Sole: Linguistic and Literary Relations of Catalan and Castilian*, New York: Peter Lang, 53-67.

Baaring, I. (1992) *Tolkning – hvorhen og hvordan* [Interpretation – Where and How], Copenhagen.

Baccouche, Taïeb (2000) 'La traduction dans la tradition arabe', *Meta* 45(3): 395–9.

Bachmann-Medick, Doris (2006) 'Meanings of Translation in Cultural Anthropology', in Theo Hermans (ed.) *Translating Others*, Vol. 1, Manchester: St Jerome, 33–42.

Badawi, Muhammad Mustafa (1993) *A Short History of Modern Arabic Literature*, Oxford: Clarendon Press.

Baer, Brian J. and Geoffrey S. Koby (eds) (2003) *Beyond the Ivory Tower. Rethinking Translation Pedagogy*, Amsterdam: John Benjamins.

Baetens Beardsmore, Hugo (1978) 'Polyglot Literature and Linguistic Fiction', *International Journal of the Sociology of Language* 15: 91–102.

Bai, Xiaojing, Baobao Chang, Weidong Zhan and Yonghua Wu 柏晓静, 常宝宝, 詹卫东, 吴拥华 (2002) *Goujian daguimo de hanying shuangyu pingxing yuliaoku* [构建大规模的汉英双语平行语料库] [The construction of a large-scale Chinese–English parallel corpus], in Huang Heyan 黄河燕 主编(ed.) *Jiqi Fanyi Yanjiu Jinzhan — 2002 Nian Quanguo Jiqi Fanyi Yantaohui Lunwenji* [《机器翻译研究进展——2002年全国机器翻译研讨会论文集》] [Progress in Research of Machine Translation. Proceedings of the National Machine Translation Symposium 2002], Beijing: The Publishing House of Electronics Industry, 124–31.

Baigorri-Jalón, Jesús (2000) *La interpretación de conferencias: el nacimiento de une profesión. De París a Nuremberg*, Granada: Editorial Comares.

——(2004) *Interpreters at the United Nations: A History*, trans. by Anne Barr, Salamanca: Ediciones Universidad Salamanca.

——(2005) 'Conference Interpreting in the First International Labor Conference (Washington, D.C. 1919)', *Meta* 50(3): 987–96.

Bailyn, B. (ed.) (1965) *Pamphlets of the American Revolution, 1750–1776*, Cambridge, MA: Harvard University Press.

Baker, Mona (1992) *In Other Words: A Coursebook on Translation*, London & New York: Routledge.

——(1993) 'Corpus Linguistics and Translation Studies. Implications and Applications', in Mona Baker, Gill Francis and Elena Tognini-Bonelli (eds) *Text and Technology: In Honor of John Sinclair*, Amsterdam: John Benjamins, 233–50.

——(1995) 'Corpora in Translation Studies: An Overview and Some Suggestions for Future Research', *Target* 7(2): 223–43.

——(1996a) 'Corpus-based Translation Studies: The Challenges that Lie Ahead', in Harold Somers (ed.) *Terminology, LSP and Translation: Studies in Language Engineering,*

in honour of Juan C. Sager, Amsterdam & Philadelphia: John Benjamins, 175–86.

——(1996b) 'Linguistics and Cultural Studies: Complementary or Competing Paradigms in Translation Studies?', in Angelika Lauer, Heidrun Gerzymisch-Arbogast, Johann Haller and Erich Steiner (eds) *Übersetzungswissenschaft im Umbruch: Festschrift für Wolfram Wilss*, *Tübingen*, Tübingen: Gunter Narr, 9–19.

——(ed.) (1998) *Routledge Encyclopedia of Translation Studies* (1st edition), London & New York: Routledge.

——(2000) 'Towards a Methodology for Investigating the Style of a Literary Translator', *Target* 12(2): 241–66.

——(2004) 'The Status of Equivalence in Translation Studies: An Appraisal', in José María Bravo (ed.) *A New Spectrum of Translation Studies*, Valladolid: Universidad de Valladolid, 63–71.

——(2005a) 'Narratives in and of Translation', *SKASE Journal of Translation and Interpretation* 1(1): 4–13.

——(2005b) 'Linguistic Models and Methods in the Study of Translation', in Harald Kittel, Armin Paul Frank, Norbert Greiner, Theo Hermans, Werner Koller, José Lambert and Fritz Paul (eds) *Übersetzung, Translation, Traduction*, Berlin & New York: Walter de Gruyter, 285–94.

——(2006a) *Translation and Conflict: A Narrative Account*, London: Routledge.

——(2006b) 'Translation and Activism: Emerging Patterns of Narrative Community', *The Massachusetts Review* 47(III): 462–84.

——(2006c) 'Contextualization in Translator- and Interpreter-mediated Events', *Journal of Pragmatics* 38: 321–37.

——(2007) 'Reframing Conflict in Translation', *Social Semiotics* 17(2): 151–69.

——(in press) 'Resisting State Terror: Theorising Communities of Activist Translators and Interpreters', in Esperança Bielsa Mialet and Chris Hughes (eds) *Globalisation, Political Violence and Translation*, Basingstoke: Palgrave Macmillan.

——and Braňo Hochel (1998) 'Dubbing', in Mona Baker (ed.) *Routledge Encyclopedia of Translation Studies* (1st edition), London and New York: Routledge, 74–6.

Bakhtin, Mikhail (1981) *The Dialogic*

Imagination: Four Essays, trans. Caryl Emerson and Michael Holoquist, Austin, TX: University of Texas Press.

Bakker, Matthijs and Ton Naaijkens (1991) 'A Postscript: Fans of Holmes', in Kitty van Leuven-Zwart and Ton Naaijkens (eds) *Translation Studies: State of the Art*, Amsterdam: Rodopi, 193–208.

Bal, Mieke (2007) 'Translating Translation', *Journal of Visual Culture* 6(1): 109–24.

Balay, Christopher and Michel Cuypers (1983) *Aux Sources de la Nouvelle Persane*, Paris: French Institute of Iranology.

Balcerzan, E. (1971) 'Poetyka przekładu artystycznego' [The Poetics of Literary Translation], in *Oprócz głosu. Szkice historycznoliterackie* [Apart from the Voice. Studies in Literary Criticism: Collected Works of E. Balcerzan], Warsaw: Państwowy Instytut Wydawniczy.

——(1977) *Pisarze polscy o sztuce przekładu 1440–1974. Antologia* [Polish Authors on the Art of Translation 1440–1974. An Anthology], Poznán: Wydawnictwo Poznańskie.

Baldry, Anthony (2000) 'English in a Visual Society: Comparative and Historical Dimensions in Multimodality and Multimediality', in Anthony Baldry (ed.) *Multimodality and Multimediality in the Distance Learning Age*, Campobasso: Palladino, 41–90.

——and Paul J. Thibault (2006) *Multimodal Transcription and Text Analysis*, London & Oakville: Equinox.

Ballard, Michel (1992) *De Cicéron à Benjamin: Traducteurs, traductions, réflexions*, Lille: Presses Universitaires de Lille.

——(1997) 'Créativité et traduction', *Target* 9(1): 85–110.

Ballester, Ana (1995) *La política del doblaje en España*, Valencia: Ediciones Episteme.

——(2001) *Traducción y nacionalismo*, Granada: Comares.

Balliu, Christian (2005a) 'Clefs pour une histoire de la traductiologie soviétique', *Meta* 50(3): 934–48.

——(ed.) (2005b) *Enseignement de la traduction dans le monde*, Special issue of *Meta* 50(1).

Bandia, Paul (1993) 'Translation as Cultural Transfer: Evidence from African Creative Writing', *TTR* 6(2): 55–78.

——(2005) 'Esquisse d'une histoire de la traduction en Afrique', *Meta* 50(3): 957–71.

——(2008) *Translation as Reparation: Writing and Translation in Postcolonial Africa*, Manchester: St Jerome.

Bann, Stephen (1977) *Ian Hamilton Finlay*, London: Arts Council.

Baraldi, Claudio (2006) 'Diversity and Adaptation in Intercultural Mediation', in D. Busch (ed.) *Interkulturelle Mediation in der Grenzregion. Sprach- und kulturwissenschaftliche Analysen triadischer Interaktionsformen im interkulturellen Kontakt*, Frankfurt am Main: Peter Lang, 225–50.

Barańczak, S. (1974) 'Przekład jako "samoistny" i "związany" obiekt interpretacji (na marginesie niektórych polskich tłumaczeń Gottfrieda Benna)' [The Translation as a 'Self-sufficient' and 'Integrated' Object of Interpretation: Some Polish Translations of Gottfried Benn], in J. Baluch (ed.) *Z teorii i historii przekładu artystycznego* [Studies in the Theory and History of Translation], Krakow: Wydawnictwo Uniwersytetu Jagiellońskiego.

——(1992) *Ocalone w tłumaczeniu* [Saved during the Translation], Poznań: Wydawnictwo.

Barbieri, Daniele (2004) 'Samurai allo specchio' (Samurai in the mirror), *Golem – L'indispensabile* 8 (November). http://www.golemindispensabile.ilsole24ore.com/index.php?_idnodo=7958&_idfrm=62 (accessed July 2007).

Barbosa, Heloisa G. and Aurora M. S. Neiva (2003) 'Using think-aloud protocols to investigate the translation process of foreign language learners and experienced translators', in Fábio Alves (ed.) *Triangulating Translation. Perspectives in Process Oriented Research*, Amsterdam & Philadelphia: John Benjamins, 137–55.

Barițiu, G. (1938) 'Clasicii' [The Classics], *Foaie pentru minte inimă si literatură* 1(16): 1–2.

Barkhudarov, Leonid Sergeyevich (1975) *Yazik i perevod*, Moscow: Mezhdunarodniye otnosheniya.

Barnaby, Paul (2002) 'Scotland Anthologised: Images of Contemporary Scottish Identity in Translation Anthologies of Scottish Poetry', *Scottish Studies Review* 3(1): 86–99.

Barnett, Ian (2004) 'The Translator as Hero'. http://www.biblit.it/translator_hero.pdf (accessed 28 November 2007).

Barnstone, Willis (1993) *The Poetics of Translation: History, Theory, Practice*, New Haven, CT: Yale University Press.

Barnwell, Katharine (1975/1986) *Manual for Bible Translation: Introductory Course on Bible Translation*, Dallas, TX: Summer Institute of Linguistics.

Barrière, Caroline (2006) 'Semi-automatic Corpus Construction from Informative Texts', in Lynne Bowker (ed.) *Lexicography, Terminology and Translation: Text-based Studies in Honour of Ingrid Meyer*, Ottawa: University of Ottawa Press, 81–92.

Barsky, Robert F. (1993) 'The Interpreter and the Canadian Convention Refugee Hearing', *TTR* 6(2): 131–56.

——(1994) *Constructing a Productive Other: Discourse Theory and the Convention Refugee Hearing*, Amsterdam and Philadelphia: John Benjamins.

——(1996) 'The Interpreter as Intercultural Agent in Convention Refugee Hearings', *The Translator* 2(1): 45–63.

——(2001) *Arguing and Justifying: Assessing the Convention Refugee Choice of Moment, Motive and Host Country*, Aldershot, UK and Burlington, VT: Ashgate.

——(2005) 'Activist Translation in an Era of Fictional Law', *TTR* 18(2): 17–48.

Bart, I. and S. Rákos (eds) (1981) *A müfordítás ma* [Literary Translation Today], Budapest: Gondolat.

Barthes, Roland (1964) *Essais critiques*, Paris: Éditions du Seuil.

Bartsch, R. (1987) *Norms of Language. Theoretical and Practical Aspects*, London: Longman.

Baruchson, Shifra (1993) *Sfarim vekor'im: tarbut ha-kri'a shel yehude italya be-shilhe he-renesans* [Books and Readers: The Reading Interests of Italian Jews at the Close of the Renaissance], Ramat-Gan: Bar-Ilan University Press.

Bary, L. (1991) 'Oswald de Andrade's "Cannibalist Manifesto"', *Latin American Literary Review*, 19(38): 35–47.

Basalamah, Salah (2005) 'La traduction citoyenne n'est pas une métaphore', *TTR* 18(2): 49–70.

Bassnett, Susan (1980/1991) *Translation Studies*, London & New York: Routledge.

——(1985) 'Bilingual Poetry: A Chicano Phenomenon', *Revista Chicano-Riqueña* 13(3–4): 137–47.

——(1993) *Comparative Literature: A Critical Introduction*, Oxford: Blackwell.

——(1998a) 'Trapped in the Labyrinth: Further Reflections on Translation and Theatre', in Susan Bassnett and André Lefevere (eds) *Constructing Cultures: Essays on Literary Translation*, Clevedon: Multilingual Matters, 90–108.

——(1998b) 'The Translation Turn in Cultural Studies', in Susan Bassnett and André Lefevere (eds) *Constructing Cultures: Essays on Literary Translation*, Clevedon: Multilingual Matters, 123–40.

——(2000) 'Theatre and Opera', in Peter France (ed.) *The Oxford Guide to Literature in English Translation*, Oxford: Oxford University Press, 96–103.

——(2002a) *Translation Studies*, 3rd edition, London: Routledge.

——(2002b) 'Travel Writing and Gender', in Peter Hulme and Tim Youngs (eds) *The Cambridge Companion of Travel Writing*, Cambridge: Cambridge University Press, 225–41.

——and André Lefevere (eds) (1990) *Translation, History and Culture*, London & New York: Pinter Publishers.

——and Harish Trivedi (eds) (1999) *Postcolonial Translation: Theory and Practice*, London and New York: Routledge.

Bastin, Georges L. (1998) *¿Traducir o Adaptar?* Caracas: Universidad Central de Venezuela, CDCH/FHE.

——(2004) 'Introduction', *Meta* 49(3): 459–61.

——(2005) 'Les interventions délibérées du traducteur'. Paper presented at the XVII Conference of the Canadian Association of Translation Studies, London, Ontario.

——and Álvaro Echeverri (2004) 'Traduction et révolution à l'époque de l'indépendance hispano-américaine', *Meta* 49(3): 562–75.

——and Paul Bandia (2006) *Discourses on Translation and the Future of History*, Ottawa: University of Ottawa Press.

Batnag, Aurora E. (2002) 'Translation in the Philippines', National Commission for Culture and the Arts [Philippines] website. http://www.ncca.gov.ph/about_cultarts/comarticles.php?artcl_Id=212 (accessed 16 August 2006).

Batsalia, F. and E. Sella-Mazi (1994) *Glossologiki Prosengisi sti Theoria ke ti Didaktiti tis Metphrasis* [Linguistic Approach to the

Theory and Teaching of Translation], Corfu: Ionian University.

Battarbee, Keith (1986) 'Subtitles and Soundtrack', in Yves Gambier (ed.) *TRANS*, Turku: University of Turku, School of Translation Studies, 144–65.

Bauer, Heike (2003) '"Not a translation but a mutilation": The Limits of Translation and the Discipline of Sexology', *Yale Journal of Criticism* 16(2): 381–405.

Bauman, Zygmunt (1987) *Legislators and Interpreters: On Modernity, Post-Modernity and Intellectuals*, London: Polity Press.

Baumgardner, Robert J. (2006) 'The Appeal of English in Mexican Commerce', *World Englishes* 25(2): 251–66.

Baumgarten, Nicole (2005) 'On the Women's Service? Gender-conscious Language in Dubbed James Bond Movies', in José Santaemilia (ed.) *Gender, Sex and Translation. The Manipulation of Identities*, Manchester: St Jerome, 53–69.

——, Juliane House and Julia Probst (2004) 'English as Lingua Franca in Covert Translation Processes', *The Translator* 10(1): 83–108.

Baumgarten, Stefan (2007) *Translation as an Ideological Interface: English Translations of Hitler's Mein Kampf*, Unpublished doctoral dissertation, Birmingham: Aston University.

Bayer, J. (1909) *Shakespeare drámáh hazankban, I–II* [The Dramas of Shakespeare in our Country], Budapest: Franklin.

Baynham, Mike and Anna De Fina (eds) (2005) *Dislocations/Relocations: Narratives of Displacement*. Manchester: St Jerome.

Beal, Joan, Karen Corrigan and Hermann Moisl (eds) (2007a) *Creating and Digitizing Language Corpora. Volume 1: Synchronic Databases*, Basingstoke: Palgrave Macmillan.

——(eds) (2007b) *Creating and Digitizing Language Corpora. Volume 2: Diachronic Databases*, Basingstoke: Palgrave Macmillan.

Beard, Charles A. (1925) *An Economic Interpretation of the Constitution of the United States*, New York: Macmillan.

Beaton, Morven (2007a) 'Interpreted Ideologies in Institutional Discourse: The Case of the European Parliament', *The Translator* 13(2): 271–96.

——(2007b) *Competing Ideologies in the European Parliament: An Investigation into the Ideological Force of Recurring Cohesive Elements in Simultaneously Interpreted Political Debate*, Doctoral Thesis, Edinburgh: Heriot-Watt University.

Beaujour, Elizabeth Klosty (1989) *Alien Tongues: Bilingual Russian Writers of the 'First' Emigration*, Ithaca, NY: Cornell University Press.

Beckett, Sandra (ed.) (1999) *Transcending Boundaries: Writing for a Dual Audience of Children and Adults*, New York, London: Garland.

Bédard, Claude (1986) *La traduction technique: Principes et pratique*, Montreal: Linguatech.

——(2000) 'Mémoire de traduction cherche traducteur de phrases', *Traduire* 186: 41–9.

Beeby, Allison (1996) *Teaching Translation from Spanish to English*, Ottawa: University of Ottawa Press.

——(2003) 'Genre Literacy and Contrastive Rhetoric in Teaching Inverse Translation', in Dorothy Kelly, Anne Martin, Marie-Louise Nobs, Dolores Sánchez and Catherine Way (eds) *La direccionalidad en traducción e interpretación: perspectivas teóricas, profesionales y didácticas*, Granada: Atrio, 155–66.

Beekman, John and John Callow (1974) *Translating the Word of God*, Grand Rapids, MI: Zondervan.

Bekku, S. (1994) *Nihon no mei zuihitsu bekkan 45 Honyaku* [Celebrated Japanese Essays vol. 45: Translation], Tokyo: Sakuhinsha.

Bell, Alan (1991) *The Language of News Media*, Oxford: Basil Blackwell.

Bell, Anthea (1985) 'Translator's Notebook: The Naming of Names', *Signal* 46: 3–11.

——(1986) 'Translator's Notebook: Delicate Matters', *Signal* 49: 17–26.

Bell, Richard (1937/1939) *The Qur'ān, translated, with a critical re-arrangement of the Surahs by Richard Bell*, Edinburgh: T. & T. Clark.

Bell, Roger (1991) *Translation and Translating*, London: Longman.

Bem, Jeanne and Albert Hudlett (eds) (2001) *Écrire aux confins des langues*, Mulhouse: Centre de Recherche sur l'Europe littéraire de l'Université de Haute-Alsace.

Ben-Shahar, Rina (1994) 'Translating Literary Dialogue: A Problem and Its Implications for Translation into Hebrew', *Target* 6(2): 195–221.

Benis, Michael (1999) 'Translation Memory from O to R', *TransRef – The Translation Reference Centre*, http://www.transref.org/default.asp?docsrc=/u-articles/Benis3.asp (accessed April 2007).

Benjamin, Andrew (1989) *Translation and the Nature of Philosophy*, London & New York: Routledge.

Benjamin, Walter (1968/1996) 'The Task of the Translator', in Hannah Arendt (ed.) *Illuminations*, New York: Harcourt, Brace; reprinted in Marcus Bullock and Michael W. Jennings (eds) *Selected Writings of Walter Benjamin, Vol.1, 1913–1926*, Cambridge, MA & London: Belknap Press, 253–63.

Bennett, Karen (2007) ' "Epistemicide!" The Tale of a Predatory Discourse', *The Translator* 13(2): 151–69.

Bennett, Paul (1994) 'The Translation Unit in Human and Machine', *Babel* 40(1): 12–20.

Benninato, Renato and Don A. DePalma (2006) *Ranking of Top 20 Translation Companies*, Lowell, MA: Common Sense Advisory, Inc., http://www.commonsenseadvisory.com/members/res_cgi.php/060301_QT_top_20.php (accessed: 26 August 2007).

Bensimon, Paul (1990) 'Présentation', *Palimpsestes* 4: ix–xiii.

Benson, Elizabeth P. (1973) *Mesoamerican Writing Systems*, Washington DC: Dumbarton Oaks Research Library.

Benveniste, Emile (1958) 'Catégories de pensée et catégories de langue', *Les études philosophiques* 4: 419–29.

Bereiter, Carl and Marlene Scardamalia (1987) *The Psychology of Written Composition*, Hillsdale, NJ: Lawrence Erlbaum Associates.

Bergman, Robert D. (1994) *Biblical Hebrew and Discourse Linguistics*, Dallas, TX: Summer Institute of Linguistics.

Bergon, F. (ed.) (1989) *The Journals of Lewis and Clark*, New York: Viking.

Berk-Seligson, Susan (1988) 'The Impact of Politeness in Witness Testimony: the Influence of the Court Interpreter', *Multilingua* 7(4): 411–39.

——(1990/2002) *The Bilingual Courtroom*, Chicago: The University of Chicago Press.

Berman, Antoine (1984/1992) *L'Épreuve de l'étranger*, Paris: Editions Gallimard; trans-lated by S. Heyvaert as *The Experience of the Foreign: Culture and Translation in Romantic Germany*, Albany, NY: State University of New York.

——(1985/2000/2004) 'La traduction comme épreuve de l'étranger', *Texte* 4: 67–81; trans-lated by Lawrence Venuti as 'Translation and Trials of the Foreign' and reprinted in Lawrence Venuti (ed.) *The Translation Studies Reader*, 2000, London: Routledge, 284–97; reprinted in Lawrence Venuti (ed.) *The Translation Studies Reader* (2nd edition), 2004, London: Routledge, 276–89.

——(1986) 'Critique, commentaire et traduction. Quelques réflexions à partir de Benjamin et de Blanchot', *Poésie* 37(2): 88–106.

——(1990) 'La retraduction comme espace de la traduction', *Palimpsestes* 4: 1–8.

——(1995) *Pour une critique des traductions: John Donne*, Paris: Gallimard (unpublished extracts translated by Luise von Flotow).

——(1999) *La traduction et la lettre, ou l'auberge du lointain*, Paris: Seuil.

Bermann, Sandra and Michael Wood (eds) (2005) *Nation, Language and the Ethics of Translation*, Princeton, NJ: Princeton University Press.

Bernardini, Silvia (2005) 'The Theory Behind the Practice: Translator Training or Trans-lator Education?', in Kirsten Malmkjaer (ed.) *Translation in Undergraduate Degrees*, Amsterdam: John Benjamins, 17–29.

——and Federico Zanettin (2004) 'When Is a Universal Not a Universal? Some Limits of Current Corpus-based Methodologies for the Investigation of Translation Universals', in Anna Mauranen and Pekka Kujamäki (eds) *Translation Universals. Do They Exist?*, Amsterdam & Philadelphia: John Benjamins, 51–62.

Bernascone, Rossella (1994) *ABC della traduzione letteraria*, Turin: Tirrenia Stampatori.

Bessong, Aroga and Michel Kenmogne (2007) 'Bible Translation in Africa: A Post-Missionary Approach', in Philip Noss (ed.) *A History of Bible Translation*, Rome: Edizioni di Storia e Letteratura, 351–85.

Bey, Youcef, Christian Boitet and Kyo Kageura (2006) 'The TRANSBey Prototype: An Online Collaborative Wiki-Based CAT Environment for Volunteer Translators', in Elia Yuste (ed.) *Proceedings of the Third*

International Workshop on Language Resources for Translation Work, Research & Training (LR4Trans-III), 49–54.

Beylard-Ozeroff, Ann, Jana Králová and Barbara Moser-Mercer (1998) 'Introduction', in Ann Beylard-Ozeroff, Jana Králová and Barbara Moser-Mercer (eds) Translators' Strategies and Creativity, Amsterdam: John Benjamins, xi–xiii.

Bgoya, W. (1987) 'Books and their Reading in Tanzania. UNESCO Studies on Books and Readings', Babel 33(4): 224–31.

Bhabha, Homi (1994a) The Location of Culture, London and New York: Routledge.

——(1994b) 'How Newness Enters the World: Postmodern Space, Postcolonial Times and the Trials of Cultural Translation', in The Location of Culture, London: Routledge, 212–35.

Biau Gil, José Ramón and Anthony Pym (2006) 'Technology and Translation (a pedagogical overview)', in Anthony Pym, Alexander Perekrestenko and Bram Starink (eds) Translation Technology and its Teaching, Tarragona: Intercultural Studies Group, 5–19.

Biber, Douglas, Stig Johansson, Geoffrey Leech, Susan Conrad and Edward Finegan (1999) Longman Grammar of Spoken and Written English, London: Longman.

Bielsa, Esperança (2005) 'Globalisation and Translation: A Theoretical Approach', Language and Intercultural Communication 2(2): 131–44.

Biguenet, John and Rainer Schulte (eds) (1989) The Craft of Translation, Chicago and London: University of Chicago Press.

Billiani, Francesca (ed.) (2007a) Modes of Censorship and Translation. National Contexts and Diverse Media, Manchester: St Jerome.

——(2007b) Culture nazionali e narrazioni straniere. Italia 1903–1943, Florence: Le Lettere.

Billington, Michael (1984) 'Villains of the Piece', Guardian, 9 November.

Binns, J. W. (1990) Intellectual Culture in Elizabethan and Jacobean England: the Latin Writers of the Age, Leeds: Francis Cairas.

BIPE Conseil (1993) Statistical Approach to Literary Translation in Europe. A study produced at the request of the Unit Cultural Action of DG X of the Commission of the European Communities, November 1993.

Biron, H. (1969) 'Godefroy de Vieuxpont, Joseph', Dictionary of Canadian Biography, vol. II, Toronto: University of Toronto Press.

Bischoff, Alexander and Louis Loutan (1998) À mots ouverts: Guide de l'entretien médical bilingue à l'usage des soignants et des interprètes, Genève: Hopitaux Universitaires de Genève.

Björkman, M. (1992) Läsarnas nöje. Kommersiella lånbibliotek i Stockholm 1783–1809 [The Joy of Reading. Circulating Libraries in Stockholm 1783–1809], Uppsala: Avdelningen för litterartursociologi vid Litteraturvetenskapliga institutionen.

Black, J. K. (1977) United States Penetration of Brazil, Manchester: Manchester University Press.

Blaga, L. (1957) 'Cum am tradus pe Faust' [How I Translated Faust], Steaia 5: 85–90.

Blommaert, Jan (2001) 'Investigating Narrative Inequality: African Asylum Seekers' Stories in Belgium', Discourse and Society 12(4): 413–49.

——(2005) 'Bourdieu the Ethnographer: The Ethnographic Grounding of Habitus and Voice', The Translator 11(2): 219–36.

——(2007) 'On Scope and Depth in Linguistic Ethnography', Journal of Sociolinguistics 11(5): 682–8.

——and Chris Bulcaen (2000) 'Critical Discourse Analysis', Annual Review of Anthropology 29: 447–66.

Blum-Kulka, Shoshana (1981) 'The Study of Translation in View of New Developments in Discourse Analysis: The Problem of Indirect Speech Acts', Poetics Today 2(4): 89–95.

——(1986) 'Shifts of Cohesion and Coherence in Translation', in Juliane House and Shoshana Blum-Kulka (eds) Inter-lingual and Inter-cultural Communication: Discourse and Cognition in Translation and Second Language Acquisition Studies, Tübingen: Gunter Narr, 17–35.

——and Eddie A. Levenston (1983) 'Universals of Lexical Simplification', in Claus Faerch and Gabriele Casper (eds) Strategies in Inter-language Communication, London & New York: Longman, 119–39.

Bly, Robert (1984) 'The Eight Stages of Translation', in William Frawley (ed.) Translation: Literary, Linguistic and

Philosophical Perspectives, Newark, DE: University of Delaware Press, 67–89.

Boase-Beier, Jean (2003a) 'Mind Style Translated', *Style* 37(3): 253–65.

——(2003b) 'Style and Choice: Recreating Patterns in Translation', *Studies in Cross-Cultural Communication* 1: 1–28.

——(2004) 'Knowing and Not Knowing: Style, Intention and the Translation of a Holocaust Poem', *Language and Literature* 13(1): 25–35.

——(2006a) *Stylistic Approaches to Translation*, Manchester: St Jerome.

——(2006b) 'Loosening the Grip of the Text: Theory as an Aid to Creativity', in Manuela Perteghella and Eugenia Loffredo (eds) *Translation and Creativity: Perspectives on Creative Writing and Translation Studies*, London & New York: Continuum, 47–56.

——and Michael Holman (eds) (1998) *The Practices of Literary Translation. Constraints and Creativity*, Manchester: St Jerome.

Bobzin, Hartmut (1993) 'Latin Translations of the Koran: A Short Overview', *Islam: Zeitschrift für Geschichte und Kultur des Islamischen Orients* 70(2): 193–206.

Boéri, Julie (2008) 'A Narrative Account of the Babels vs. Naumann Controversy: Competing Perspectives on Activism in Conference Interpreting', *The Translator* 14(1): 21–50.

——and Stuart Hodkinson (2005) 'Babels and the Politics of Language at the Hearth of Social Forum'. *Euromovements*, http://www.euromovements.info/newsletter/babel.htm (accessed 13 July 2008).

Bolaños Cuellar, Sergio (2007) *Towards an Integrative Translation Approach. A Dynamic Translation Model Applied to the Analysis of the Translations of Gabriel Garcia Marquez' 'Cien Años de Soledad' into English, German, French, Portuguese and Russian*, Unpublished PhD Thesis, Hamburg: University of Hamburg.

Bolaños Medina, Alicia (2002) *Diseño y aplicación de un modelo didáctico innovador para la traducción de géneros digitales*. Unpublished doctoral dissertation, Universidad de Las Palmas de Gran Canaria.

Bolden, Galina (2000) 'Toward Understanding Practices of Medical Interpreting: Interpreters' Involvement in History Taking', *Discourse Studies* 2(4): 387–419.

Bolt, Ranjit, Michael Frayn, Christopher Hampton, Steven Pimlott, Jeremy Sams and Timberlake Wertenbaker (1989) *Platform Papers, 1 Translation*, London: Royal National Theatre.

Bontempo, Karen and Jemina Napier (2007) 'Mind the Gap! A Skills Analysis of Sign Language Interpreters', *The Sign Language Translator and Interpreter* 1(2): 275–99.

Boone, Elizabeth and Walter Mignolo (1994) *Writing without Words. Alternative Literacies in Mesoamerica and the Andes*, Durham, NC: Duke University Press.

Bordenave, M. C. R. (1990) 'State of the Art in Translation Teaching and Research in Brazil', *Meta* 35(3): 543–5.

Borges, Jorge Luis (1944/1999) *Ficciones*, edited by Gordon Brotherston and Peter Hulme, London: Duckworth.

Börsch, Sabine (1986) 'Introspective Methods in Research on Interlingual and Intercultural Communication', in Juliane House and Shoshana Blum-Kulka (eds) *Interlingual and Intercultural Communication: Discourse and Cognition in Translation and Second Language Acquisition Studies*, Tübingen: Gunter Narr, 195–209.

Bosseaux, Charlotte (2007) *How Does it Feel? Point of View in Translation. The Case of Virginia Woolf into French*, Amsterdam & New York: Rodopi.

Bot, Hanneke (2005) *Dialogue Interpreting in Mental Health*, Amsterdam & New York: Rodopi.

Böttger, Claudia (2004) 'Genre-Mixing in Business Communication', in Juliane House and Jochen Rehbein (eds) *Multilingual Communication*, Amsterdam & Philadelphia: John Benjamins, 115–29.

——and Kristin Bührig (2003) 'Translating Obligation in Business Communication', in Luis Pérez González (ed.) *Speaking in Tongues: Language across Contexts and Users*, València: Servei de Publicacions de la Universitat de València, 161–83.

Boudreau, Sylvie and Sylvie Vandaele (forthcoming) 'Un multi-outil adapté au parcours cognitif de l'étudiant en traduction spécialisée: application à la biomédecine'.

Boudreault, Patrick (2005) 'Deaf Interpreters', in Terry Janzen (ed.) *Topics in Signed Language Interpreting*, Amsterdam & Philadelphia: John Benjamins, 323–56.

Boulanger, Jean-Claude (1995) 'Présentation: images et parcours de la socioterminologie', *Meta* 40(2): 194–205.

Bourdieu, Pierre (1977) *Outline of a Theory of Practice*, trans. Richard Nice, Cambridge: Cambridge University Press.

——(1979/1984) *Distinction. A Social Critique of the Judgement of Taste*, trans. Richard Nice, London, Melbourne & Henley: Routledge & Kegan Paul.

——(1982) 'Censure et mise en forme', in *Ce que parler veut dire*, Paris: Librairie Arthème Fayar, 167–205.

——(1990) *The Logic of Practice*, trans. Richard Nice, London: Polity Press.

——(1991) *Language and Symbolic Power*, trans. Gino Raymond and Matthew Adamson, Cambridge: Polity Press.

Bourigault, Didier, Christian Jacquemin and Marie-Claude L'Homme (eds) (2001) *Recent Advances in Computational Terminography*, Amsterdam & Philadelphia: John Benjamins.

Bowen, David and Margareta Bowen (eds) (1990) *Interpreting: Yesterday, Today, and Tomorrow*, Binghamton, NY: SUNY at Binghamton.

Bowen, Margareta (1994) 'Negotiations to End the Spanish-American War', in Snell-Hornby, Pöchhacker and Kaindl (eds), 73–81.

Bowker, Lynne (2001) 'Towards a Methodology for a Corpus-based Approach to Translation Evaluation', *Meta* 46(2): 245–364.

——(2002a) *Computer-aided Translation Technology: A Practical Introduction*, Ottawa: University of Ottawa Press.

——(2002b) 'Information Retrieval in Translation Memory Systems: Assessment of current limitations and possibilities for future development', *Knowledge Organization* 29(3/4): 198–203.

——(2003) 'Terminology Tools for Translators', in Harold L. Somers (ed.) *Computers and Translation: A Translator's Guide*, Amsterdam & Philadelphia: John Benjamins, 49–65.

——and Jennifer Pearson (2002) *Working with Specialized Language: A Practical Guide to Using Corpora*, London & New York: Routledge.

Boyd-Barrett, Oliver (1980) *The International News Agencies*, London: Constable.

——and Terhi Rantanen (1998) *The Globalization of News*, London: Sage.

Boztepe, Emre (2006) 'Victor Hugo'yu da hidayete erdirdiler' [Victor Hugo Converts to Islam], *Radikal*, 25 August. http://www.radikal.com.tr/haber.php?haberno=196801 (consulted on 17 November 2007).

Bradford, W. (1952) *Of Plymouth Plantation 1620–1647*, ed. Samuel Eliot Morrison, New York: Modern Library.

Bradner, Leicester (1940) *Musae Anglicanae, A History of Anglo-Latin Poetry, 1500–1925*, New York: Modern Language Association of America.

Braginsky, Vladimir (2004) *The Heritage of Traditional Malay Literature*, Leiden: KITLV.

Bragt, Katrin van (1989) 'Corpus bibliographie et analyse des traductions. Un Programme d'analyse par ordinateur', *Revue de Littérature comparée* 63(2): 171–8.

Braine, George (ed.) (1999) *Non-Native Educators in English Language Teaching*, London: Lawrence Erlbaum Associates.

Brake, Terence, Danielle Medina-Walker and Thomas Walker (1995) *Doing Business Internationally: The Guide to Cross-Cultural Success*, Burr Ridge, IL: Irwin.

Brakel, Lode (1975) *Hkayat Muhammad Hanifiyyah*, The Hague: Nijhoff.

Brancati, Daniela (2002) *La pubblicità è femmina ma il pubblicitario è maschio. Per una comunicazione oltre i luoghi comuni*, Milan: Sperling & Kupfer.

Branchadell, Albert and Lovell Margaret West (eds) (2005) *Less Translated Languages*, Amsterdam & Philadelphia: John Benjamins.

Brand, C. P. (1957) *Italy and the English Romantics: The Italianate Fashion in Early Nineteenth-century England*, Cambridge: Cambridge University Press.

Bratcher, R. G. (1995) 'Current Trends in Translation', *The Bible Translator* 46(4): 439–44.

Braun, Sabine (2004) *Kommunikation unter widrigen Umständen? Fallstudien zu einsprachigen und gedolmetschten Videokonferenzen*, Tübingen: Gunter Narr.

Breckenridge, Carol A., Sheldon Pollock, Homi K. Bhabha and Dipesh Chakrabarty (eds) (2002) *Cosmopolitanism*, Durham & London: Duke University Press.

Breisemeister, Dietrich (1985) 'Französische Literatur in neulateinischen Übersetzungen', in R. Schoeck (ed.) *Acta Conventus neolatini Bononiensis*, Binghamton, NY: Medieval and Renaissance Texts and Studies, 205–15.

Breitinger, J. J. (1740/1966) 'Von der Kunst der Übersetzung', in J. J. Breitinger, *Kritische Dichtkunst*, 2 vols, Stuttgart: Metzlersche Verlagsbuchhandlung, 136–99.

Brennan, Mary (1999) 'Signs of Injustice', *The Translator* 5(2): 221–46.

——and Richard Brown (1997) *Equality before the Law: Deaf People's Access to Justice*, Durham: Deaf Studies Research Unit, University of Durham.

Bricker, Victoria R. (1988) *Epigraphy*, University of Texas Press: Austin, TX. Supplement to the *Handbook of Middle American Indians*, Vol. 4.

Brightman, Robert (1995) 'Forget Culture: Replacement, Transcendence, Relexification', *Cultural Anthropology* 10(4): 509–46.

Brisset, Annie (1989) 'In Search of a Target Language', *Target* 1(1): 10–27.

——(1990) *Sociocritique de la traduction. Théâtre et altérité au Québec (1968-1988)*, Montréal: Le Préambule.

——(1996) *A Sociocritique of Translation. Theatre and Alterity in Quebec*, Toronto: University of Toronto Press.

——(2002) 'Clémence Royer, ou Darwin en colère', in Jean Delisle (ed.) *Portraits de traductrices*, Ottawa: Presses de l'Université d'Ottawa, 173–203.

——(2004) 'Retraduire ou le corps changeant de la connaissance. Sur l'historicité de la traduction', *Palimpsestes* 15: 39–67.

Brotherston, Gordon (1992) *Book of the Fourth World. Reading the Native Americas through their Literature*, Cambridge: Cambridge University Press

——(2005) *Feather Crown: The Eighteen Feasts of the Mexican Year*, London: British Museum Press.

Brower, R. A. (ed.) (1959/1966) *On Translation*, Cambridge, MA: Harvard University Press/ New York: Oxford University Press.

Brown, Richard (1992) 'Bog Poems and Book Poems: Doubleness, Self-translation, and Pun in Seamus Heaney and Paul Muldoon', in Neil Corcoran (ed.) *The Chosen Ground: Essays on the Contemporary Poetry of Northern Ireland*, Bridgend: Seren, 171–88.

Brown, S. (1993) 'Access to Justice: The Role of

the Interpreter', *Judicial Officers Bulletin* 5(3): 17–18.

Browne, E. G. (1909–24) *The Literary History of Persia* (4 vols), Cambridge and London: Cambridge University Press.

Brownlie, Siobhan (2003) 'Distinguishing Some Approaches to Translation Research: The Issue of Interpretative Constraints', *The Translator* 9(1): 39–64.

——(2006) 'Narrative Theory and Retranslation Theory', *Across Languages and Cultures* 7(2): 145–70.

——(2007a) 'Situating Discourse on Translation and Conflict', *Social Semiotics* 17(2): 135–50.

——(2007b) 'Examining Self-Censorship: Zola's *Nana* in English Translation', in Francesca Billiani (ed.) *Modes of Censorship and Translation. National Contexts and Diverse Media*, Manchester: St Jerome, 205–34.

Brunette, Louise, Georges Bastin, Isabelle Hemlin and Heather Clarke (eds) (2003) *The Critical Link 3: Interpreters in the Community*, Amsterdam & Philadelphia: John Benjamins.

Bruns, Gerald (1992) *Hermeneutics Ancient and Modern*, New Haven & London: Yale University Press.

Bryant, W. C. (trans.) (1876) *The Iliad of Homer*, Boston: J. R. Osgood.

BS Broadcast Interpreters Group (BS Housout-suuyakuguruupu) (1998) *Housoutsuuyaku no sekai (The world of broadcast interpreting)*, Tokyo: Alc.

Budelmann, Felix (2005) 'Greek Tragedies in West African Adaptations', in Barbara Goff (ed.) *Classics and Colonialism*, London: Duckworth, 118–46.

Budge, E.A.Wallis (1967/1985) *The Book of the Dead. The Papyrus of Ani*, New York: Dover.

Bueno García, Antonio (2000) *Publicidad y traducción*, Soria: Universidad de Valladolid.

——(2003) 'Le concept d'autotraduction', in Michel Ballard and Ahmed El Kaladi (eds) *Traductologie, linguistique et traduction*, Arras: Artois Presses Université, 265–77.

Bühler, Hildegund (ed.) (1985) *Translators and their Position in Society: Proceedings of the Xth World Congress of FIT*, Vienna: Wilhelm Braumuller.

Bühler, Karl (1934) *Sprachtheorie: Die Darstellungsfunktion der Sprache*, Jena: G. Fischer.

Burke, David G. (2002) 'The Bible Societies and

the Deuterocanon as Scripture', *UBS Bulletin* 182/183: 223–40.

Burnard, Lou (ed.) (2007) *Reference Guide for the British National Corpus (XML Edition)*, Oxford: Oxford University Computing Services, http://www.natcorp.ox.ac.uk/XMLedition/URG/ (accessed 29 November 2007).

Burnett, Charles (2005) 'Arabic into Latin: The Reception of Arabic Philosophy into Western Europe', in Peter Adamson and Richard Taylor (eds) *The Cambridge Companion to Arabic Philosophy*, Cambridge: Cambridge University Press, 370–404.

Burns, E. B. (ed.) (1966) *A Documentary History of Brazil*, New York: Knopf.

——(1980) *A History of Brazil*, 2nd edn, New York: Columbia University Press.

Bush, Peter (1998/2001) 'Literary Translation, Practices', in Mona Baker (ed.) *Routledge Encyclopedia of Translation Studies* (1st edition), London: Routledge, 127–30.

——(2004/2005) 'Reviewing Translations: Barcelona, London and Paris', *EnterText* 4.3 Supplement http://people.brunel.ac.uk/~acsrrrm/entertext/4_3/ET43SBushEd.doc (last accessed 29 July 2007).

Butler, Judith (1990) *Gender Trouble. Feminisms and the Subversion of Identity*, London & New York: Routledge.

Butzkamm, Wolfgang (2001) 'Learning the Language of Loved Ones: On the Generative Principle and the Technique of Mirroring', *English Language Teaching Journal* 55(2): 149–54.

Buzelin, Hélène (2004) 'La traductologie, l'ethnographie et la production de connaissances' [Translation Studies, Ethnography and Knowledge Production], *Meta* 49(4): 729–46. Available at http://www.erudit.org/revue/meta/2004/v49/n4/009778ar.pdf (accessed 16 January 2007).

——(2005) 'Unexpected Allies: How Latour's Network Theory Could Complement Bourdieusian Analyses in Translation Studies', *The Translator* 11(2): 193–218.

——(forthcoming) 'Independent Publisher in the Networks of Translation', *TTR* 19(1).

Byrne, Jody (2006) *Technical Translation: Usability Strategies for Translating Technical Documentation*, Dordrecht: Springer.

Cabré, M. Teresa (1999) *Terminology: Theory, Methods and Applications*, Amsterdam & Philadelphia: John Benjamins.

Cabré Castellví, M. Teresa (2003) 'Theories of Terminology: Their Description, Prescription and Explanation', *Terminology* 9(2): 163–99.

——, Rosa Estopà Bagot and Jordi Vivaldi Palatresi (2001) 'Automatic Term Detection: A Review of Current Systems', in Didier Bourigault, Christian Jacquemin and Marie-Claude L'Homme (eds) *Recent Advances in Computational Terminography*, Amsterdam & Philadelphia: John Benjamins, 53-87.

Cabrera, P. I. (1993) 'El aporte de la traducción al proceso de desarrollo de la cultura chilena en el siglo XIX', *Livius* 3: 51–63.

Callow, Katharine (1974) *Discourse Considerations in Translating the Word of God*, Grand Rapids, MI: Zonderan.

Calógeras, J. P. (1963) *A History of Brazil*, P. A. Martin (trans. and ed.), first pub. 1939, first reissue, New York: Russell & Russell.

Calzada-Pérez, María (2001) 'A Three-Level Methodology for Descriptive–Explanatory Translation Studies', *Target* 13(2): 203–39.

——(ed.) (2003) *Apropos of Ideology: Translation Studies on Ideology – Ideologies in Translation Studies*, Manchester: St Jerome.

——(2005) 'Proactive Translatology vis à vis Advertising Messages', *Meta* 50(4): On unpaginated CD.

——(2007a) 'Translators and Translation Studies Scholars as Inoculators of Resistance', *The Translator* 13(2): 243–69.

——(2007b) *Transitivity in Translating: The Interdependence of Texture and Context*, Bern: Peter Lang.

Cambridge, Jan (1999) 'Information Loss in Bilingual Medical Interviews through an Untrained Interpreter', *The Translator* 5(2): 201–19.

——and Kirsty Heimerl-Moggen (2006) *DPSI Health Option. A Course Book*. http://www.spanish-interpreter.com/NEW_BOOK.html (accessed 7 January 2008).

Cameron, Deborah (1985) *Feminism and Linguistic Theory*, Houndmills & Basingstoke: Macmillan Press.

Caminade, Monique and Anthony Pym (1998) 'Translator-training institutions', in Mona Baker (ed.) *Routledge Encyclopedia of*

Translation Studies (1st edition), London: Routledge, 280–85.

Caminha, P. V. (1966) 'The Letter of Pero Vaz de Caminha', trans. E. B. Burns, in Burns (ed.) 20–29.

Campbell, J. A. (1993) 'Culture and Ideology in the Translation of Poetry', in Yves Gambier and Jorma Tommola (eds) *Translation and Knowledge: Proceedings of the 1992 Scandinavian Symposium on Translation Theory*, Turku: University of Turku, Centre for Translation and Interpreting, 139–53.

Campbell, Mary B. (1988) *The Witness and the Other World: Exotic European Travel Writing, 400–1600*, Ithaca & London: Cornell University Press.

Campbell, Stuart (1998) *Translation into the Second Language*, London: Longman.

Campos, Augusto de (1979) *Verso, reverso, controverso*, São Paulo: Editora Perspectiva.

——(1986) *O anticrítico*, São Paulo: Companhia das Letras.

——and Haroldo de Campos (1970) *Panorama de Finnegans Wake*, São Paulo: Editora Perspectiva.

——(1976a) 'Da tradução como criação e como crítica', in H. de Campos (ed.) *Metalinguagem*, São Paulo: Editora Cultrix.

——(1976b) *A operaçao do texto*, São Paulo: Editora Perspectiva.

——(1981) *Deus e o diabo no Fausto de Goethe*, São Paulo: Editora Perspectiva.

——, Decio Pignatari, Haroldo de Campos, Jose Lino Grunewald and Ronaldo Azeredo (1962) *Do verso a poesia concreta*, São Paulo: Massao Onho (Noigandres nos. 5).

Campos, Haroldo de (1975) *A arte no horizonte do provável*, São Paulo: Perspectiva, third edition.

Candlin, Chris (1985) 'Preface' to Malcolm Coulthard, *Discourse Analysis*, London: Longman.

——and Maurizio Gotti (2004) *Intercultural Aspects of Specialized Communication*, Bern: Peter Lang.

Canfield, G. W. (1983) *Sarah Winnemucca of the Northern Paiutes*, Norman, OK: University of Oklahoma Press.

Cannon, Garland (1986) 'The Construction of the European Image of the Orient: A Bicentenary Reappraisal of Sir William Jones as Poet and Translator', *Comparative Criticism: A Yearbook* 8: 167–88.

Canonica, Elvezio and Ernst Rudin (eds) (1993) *Literatura y bilingüismo. Homenaje a Pere Ramírez*, Kassel: Reichenberger.

Cao Shibang (1986) *Zhongguo fujiao yijing shi lunji* [Collected Essays on Chinese Buddhist Sutra Translations], Taipei: Dongchu Pub. Co.

Caputo, John (1997) *Against Ethics: Contributions to a Poetics of Obligation with Constant Reference to Deconstruction*, Bloomington & Indianapolis: Indiana University Press.

Carabelli, Angela (2003) 'A Brief Overview of IRIS – The Interpreter's Research Information System', in Jesús de Manuel Jerez (coord.) *Nuevas Tecnologías y Formación de Intérpretes*, Granada: Atrio, 113–39.

Carbonell, Ovidio (1996) 'The Exotic Space of Cultural Translation', in Roman Álvarez and M. Carmen-África Vidal (eds) *Translation, Power, Subversion*, Clevedon: Multilingual Matters, 79–98.

Carbonell i Cortés, Ovidio (2003) 'Semiotic alteration in translation. Othering, stereotyping and hybridization in contemporary translations from Arabic into Spanish and Catalan', *Linguistica Antverpiensia NS2* (Special Issue on Translation as Creation: the Postcolonial Influence): 145–59.

Cardenal, Ernesto (1992) *Los ovnis de oro*, trans. Russell Salmon, Bloomington, IN: Indiana University Press.

Carini, Isidoro (1984) *Le versioni della Bibbia in volgare italiano*, San Pier d'Arena: Salesiana.

Carlin, John (2005) 'Masters of American Comics: An Art History of Twentieth-Century American Comic Strips and Books', in John Carlin, Paul Karasik and Brian Walker (eds) *Masters of American Comics*, New Haven & London: Yale University Press, 25–175.

Carlson, Marvin (ed.) (2005) *The Arab Oedipus: Four Plays*, New York: Martin E. Segal Theater Publications.

Carr, Silvana E., Roda Roberts, Aideen Dufour and Dini Steyn (eds) (1997) *The Critical Link: Interpreters in the Community*, Amsterdam & Philadelphia: John Benjamins.

Carroll, J. (1994) 'Lawyer's Response to Language and Disadvantage before the Law', in J. Gibbons (ed.) *Language and the Law*, Sydney: Longman, 306–16.

Carroll, J. B. (1966) 'An Experiment in Evaluating the Quality of Translation', *Mechanical Translation* 9: 55–66.

Cary, Edmond (1956) *La traduction dans le monde moderne*, Geneva: Georg & Cie.

——(1963) *Les grands traducteurs français*, Geneva: Georg.

——(1969) 'La traduction totale', *Babel* 6(3): 110–15.

——and W. Jumpelt (1963) *Quality in Translation*, Oxford: Pergamon.

Casagrande, Joseph B. (1954) 'The Ends of Translation', *International Journal of American Linguistics* 20(4): 335–40.

Casanova, Pascale (1999/2005) *La République mondiale des lettres*, Paris: Éditions du Seuil; translated by M. B. Debevoise as *The World Republic of Letters*, 2005, Cambridge, MA.: Harvard University Press.

——(2002/in press) 'Consécration et accumulation de capital littéraire: la traduction comme échange inégal', *Actes de la recherche en sciences sociales* 144: 7–20; translated by Siobhan Brownlie as 'Consecration and Accumulation of Literary Capital: Translation as Unequal Exchange', in Mona Baker (ed.) *Critical Concepts: Translation Studies*, London: Routledge.

Castro-Klarén, S. and H. Campos (1893) 'Traducciones, Tirajes, Ventas y Estrellas: El "Boom"', *Ideologies and Literature* 4 (September–October): 319–38.

Catford, J. C. (1965) *A Linguistic Theory of Translation: An Essay in Applied Linguistics*, London: Oxford University Press.

——(1994) 'Translation Overview', in R. E. Asher and J. M. Y. Simpson (eds) *The Encyclopedia of Language and Linguistics*, Oxford & New York: Pergamon Press, 4738–47.

Cattaruzza, Lorella and Gabriele Mack (1995) 'User Surveys in SI: A Means of Learning about Quality and/or Raising Some Reasonable Doubt', in Jorma Tommola (ed.) *Topics in Interpreting Research*, Turku: University of Turku, 37–49.

Cattrysse, Patrick (2004) 'Stories Travelling Across Nations and Cultures', *Meta* 49(1): 39–51.

Cazdyn, Eric (2004) 'A New Line in the Geometry', in Atom Egoyan and Ian Balfour (eds) *Subtitles. On the Foreignness of Film*, Cambridge, MA. & London: The MIT Press, 403–19.

Celotti, Nadine (2000) 'Méditer sur la traduction des bandes dessinées: une perspective de sémiologie parallèle' [Reflections on the Translation of Comics: A Parallel Semiology Perspective], *Rivista internazionale di tecnica della traduzione* 5: 41–61.

——(2008) 'The Translator of Comics as a Semiotic Investigator', in Federico Zanettin (ed.) *Comics in Translation*, Manchester: St Jerome, pp. 33–49.

Certeau, Michel de (1984) *The Practice of Everyday Life*, trans. Steven F. Rendall, Berkeley: University of California.

Cesarotti, Melchiorre (1786) *L'Iliade d'Omero recata poeticamente in verso sciolto italiano*, Pisa: Molini Landi.

——(1807) *Le opera di Demostene tradotte e illustrate*, Florence: Molini Landi.

Chadwick, Henry (1981) *Boethius*, Oxford: Oxford University Press.

Chai, Mingjong and Ailing Zhang (eds) (2006) *Professionalization in Interpreting: International Experience and Developments in China*, Shanghai: Shanghai Foreign Language Education Press.

Chamberlain, Lori (1988/2004) 'Gender and the Metaphorics of Translation', *Signs* 13: 45–72; reprinted in Lawrence Venuti (ed.) *The Translation Studies Reader*, London & New York: Routledge, 306–22.

——(1998/2001) 'Gender Metaphorics in Translation', in Mona Baker (ed.) *Routledge Encyclopedia of Translation Studies* (first edition), London & New York: Routledge, 93–6.

Chan, Leo Tak-hung (ed.) (2004) *Twentieth-Century Chinese Translation: Modes, Issues and Debates*, Amsterdam: John Benjamins.

Chan Sin-wai and David Pollard (eds) (1994) *An Encyclopedia of Translation. Chinese/English*, Hong Kong: Chinese University Press.

Chang, Num Fung (2000) 'Towards a Macro-polysystem Hypothesis', *Perspectives: Studies in Translatology* 8(2): 109–23.

Charteris-Black, Jonathan and Timothy Ennis (2001) 'A Comparative Study of Metaphor in Spanish and English Financial Reporting', *English for Specific Purposes* 20(3): 249–66.

Chaume, Frederic (2002) 'Models of Research in Audiovisual Translation', *Babel* 48(1): 1–13.

——(2004) *Cine y traducción*, Madrid: Cátedra.

Chaves, María José (2000) *La traducción cinematográfica y el doblaje*, Huelva: Servicio de Publicaciones de la Universidad de Huelva.

Chen, Peng-hsiang (1975) *Translation History, Translation Theory* (in Chinese), Taipei: Hongdao wenhua shiye youxian gongsi.

Chen Yugang (ed.) (1989) *Zhongguo fanyi wenxue shigao* [History of Chinese Literary Translation], Beijing: Zhongguo duiwai fanyi Pub. Co.

Cheng, Mei (2003) 'Xuan Zang's Translation Practice', *Perspectives: Studies in Translatology* 11(1): 53–62.

Chernov, Gelij (1992) 'Conference Interpretation in the USSR: History, Theory, New Frontiers', *Meta* 37(1): 149–62.

Chernov, Ghelly (1979/2002) 'Semantic Aspects of Psycholinguistic Research in Simultaneous Interpretation', reprinted in Franz Pöchhacker and Miriam Shlesinger (eds) *The Interpreting Studies Reader*, London & New York: Routledge, 98–109.

——(2004) *Inference and Anticipation in Simultaneous Interpreting. A Probability-prediction Model*, Amsterdam & Philadelphia: John Benjamins.

Chernyakhovskaya, L. A. (1976) *Perevod i smyslovaya struktura* [Translation and Semantic Structure], Moscow: Mezhdunarodnye otnosheniya.

Chesterman, Andrew (1993) 'From "Is" to "Ought": Translation Laws, Norms and Strategies', *Target* 5(1): 1–20.

——(1994) 'Quantitative Aspects of Translation Quality', *Lebende Sprachen* 39: 153–6.

——(1997) *Memes of Translation: The Spread of Ideas in Translation Theory*, Amsterdam & Philadelphia: Benjamins.

——(1998) 'Causes, Translations, Effects', *Target* 10(2): 201–30.

——(1999) 'The Empirical Status of Prescriptivism', *Folia Translatologica* 6: 9–19.

——(2000) 'A Causal Model for Translation Studies', in Maeve Olohan (ed.) *Intercultural Faultlines. Research Models in Translation Studies 1: Textual and Cognitive Aspects*, Manchester: St Jerome, 15–27.

——(2001) 'Proposal for a Hieronymic Oath', *The Translator* 7(2): 139–54.

——(2002a) 'Semiotic Modalities in Translation Causality', *Across Languages and Cultures* 3(2): 145–58.

——(2002b) 'On the Interdisciplinarity of Translation Studies', *Logos and Language* 3(1): 1–9.

——(2004a) 'Beyond the Particular', in Anna Mauranen and Pekka Kujamäki (eds) *Translation Universals. Do they Exist?*, Amsterdam & Philadelphia: John Benjamins, 33–50.

——(2004b) 'Paradigm Problems?', in Christina Schäffner (ed.) *Translation Research and Interpreting Research. Traditions, Gaps and Synergies*, Clevedon: Multilingual Matters, 52–6.

——(2005) 'Problems with Strategies', in Krisztina Károly and Ágota Fóris (eds) *New Trends in Translation Studies: In Honour of Kinga Klaudy*, Budapest: Akadémiai Kiadó, 17–28.

——and Rosemary Arrojo (2000) 'Shared Ground in Translation Studies', *Target* 12(1): 151–60.

——and Emma Wagner (2002) *Can Theory Help Translators?*, Manchester: St Jerome.

Cheung, Martha (2004/2007) 'On Thick Translation as a Mode of Cultural Representation', in Dorothy Kenny and Kyongjoo Ryou (eds) *Across Boundaries: International Perspectives on Translation Studies*, Seoul: Sookmyung Women's University, 22–36. First presented at the 'Translation and the Construction of Identity' Conference (12–14 August 2004), Sookmyung Women's University, Seoul, Korea.

——(ed.) (2006) *An Anthology of Chinese Discourse on Translation. Vol 1: From Earliest Times to the Buddhist Project*, Manchester: St Jerome.

Cheyfitz, Eric (1991) *The Poetics of Imperialism. Translation and Colonization from 'The Tempest' to 'Tarzan'*, New York & Oxford: Oxford University Press.

Chi, Michelene T. H., Robert Glaser and M. J. Farr (eds) (1988) *The Nature of Expertise*, Hillsdale, NJ: Lawrence Erlbaum Associates.

Chiaro, Delia (1992) *The Language of Jokes. Analysing Verbal Play*, London: Routledge.

——(2004) 'Translational and Marketing

Communication. A Comparison of Print and Web Advertising of Italian Agro-Food Products', *The Translator* 10(2): 313–28.

Chilton, Paul (1985) *Language and the Nuclear Arms Debate: Nukespeak Today*, London: Frances Pinter.

Chladenius, Johann Martin (1742/1969) *Einleitung zur richtigen Auslegung vernünftiger Reden und Schriften*, Facsimile edition, Düsseldorf: Stern.

Choi, Jungwha (2002) 'The Status of Translators and Interpreters in Korea', *Meta* 47(4): 627–35.

Christ, Ronald (1982) 'On Not Reviewing Translations: A Critical Exchange', *Translation Review* 9: 16–23.

Christoffels, Ingrid K. and Anette M. B. de Groot (2005) 'Simultaneous Interpreting: A Cognitive Perspective', in Judith Kroll and Anette M. B. de Groot (eds) *Handbook of Bilingualism. Psycholinguistic Approaches*, Oxford: Oxford University Press, 454–79.

Chuansheng, He and Xiao Yunnan (2003) 'Brand Name Translation in China: An Overview of Practice and Theory', *Babel* 49(2): 131–48.

Church, Ken and William Gale (1991) 'Concordances for Parallel Text', *Using Corpora: Proceedings of the Seventh Annual Conference of the UW Centre for the New OED and Text Research*, Oxford: St Catherine's College.

Clément, Bruno (1994) *L'oeuvre sans qualités. Rhétorique de Samuel Beckett*, Paris: Seuil.

Clifford, James (1983) 'On Ethnographic Authority', *Representations* 1(2): 118–46.

——(1997) *Routes: Travel and Translation in the Late Twentieth Century*, Cambridge, MA: Harvard University Press.

——and George E. Marcus (eds) (1986) *Writing Culture: The Poetics and Politics of Ethnography*, Berkeley: University of California Press.

Clyne, Michael (1991) 'Zu kulturellen Unterschieden in der Produktion und Wahrnehmung englischer und deutscher wissenschaftlicher Texte', *Info DaF* 18(4): 376–83.

Cockerill, Hiroko (2006) *Style and Narrative in Translations: The Contribution of Futabatei Shimei*, Manchester: St Jerome.

Codde, Philppe (2003) 'Polysystem Theory Revisited: A New Comparative Introduction', *Poetics Today* 24(1): 91–126.

Coe, Michael (1992) *Breaking the Maya Code*, London: Thames & Hudson.

Cohen, Israel (1942) *Yitshak Eduard Salkinsohn: xayav u-mif'alo ha-sifruti* [Yitshak Eduard Salkinsohn: His Life and Literary Career], Tel Aviv: Mesila.

Cohen, J. M. (1962) *English Translators and Translations*, London: Longmans, Green.

Cohen, Jonathan (1988) 'Oquendo's "Rain": A Choral Rendering', *The American Voice* 10: 82–112.

Cohen, Robin (1997) *Global Diasporas: An Introduction*, London: UCL Press.

Cohn, Deborah (2006) 'A Tale of Two Translation Programs: Politics, the Market, and Rockefeller Funding for Latin American Literature in the United States during the 1960s and 1970s', *Latin American Research Review* 41(2): 138–64.

Cohn, Ruby (1961) 'Samuel Beckett Self-translator', *PMLA* 76: 613–21.

Cokely, Dennis (ed.) (1992) *Sign Language Interpreters and Interpreting*, Burtonsville, MD: Linstok Press.

——(2005) 'Shifting Positionality: A Critical Examination of the Turning Point in the Relationship of Interpreters and the Deaf Community', in Marc Marschark, Rico Peterson and Elizabeth A. Winston (eds) *Sign Language Interpreting and Interpreter Education*, Oxford: Oxford University Press, 3–28.

Coleridge, Samuel Taylor (1990) *Table Talk*, edited by C. Woodring, Princeton NJ: Princeton University Press.

Colin, Joan and Ruth Morris (1996) *Interpreters and the Legal Process*, Winchester: Waterside Press.

Colina, Sonia (2003) *Translation Teaching: From Research to the Classroom. A Handbook for Teachers*, Boston: McGraw Hill.

——(2008) 'Translation Quality Evaluation: Some Empirical Evidence for a Functionalist Approach', *The Translator* 14(1): 97–134.

Collados Aís, Ángela, E. Macarena Pradas Macías, Elisabeth Stévaux and Olalla García Becerra (eds) (2007) *La evaluación de la calidad en interpretación simultánea: parámetros de incidencia*, Granada: Editorial Comares.

——, María Manuela Fernández Sánchez and Daniel Gile (eds) (2003) *La evaluación de la calidad en interpretación: investigación*, Granada: Editorial Comares.

Collinge, Linda (2000) *Beckett traduit Beckett. De Malone meurt à Malone Dies, l'imaginaire en traduction*, Geneva: Droz.

Collins, Judith M. and John Walker (2006) 'What is a Deaf Interpreter?', in Rachel Locker McKee (ed.) *Proceedings of the Inaugural Conference of the World Association of Sign Language Interpreters*, Worcester, South Africa, 31 October–2 November 2005, Coleford, Gloucestershire: Douglas McLean, 79–90.

Concise Encyclopaedia of Islam (1989), edited by Cyril Glasse, London: Stacey International.

Congrat-Butlar, Stefan (ed.) (1979) *Translation and Translators, an International Directory and Guide*, New York: R. Bowker.

Conley, Tom (1986) 'Institutionalizing Translation: On Florio's Montaigne', *Demarcating the Disciplines: Philosophy. Literature. Art*, Glyph Textual Studies 1, Minneapolis, MI: University of Minnesota Press, 45–60.

Connolly, David (1998) 'Poetry Translation', in Mona Baker (ed.) *Routledge Encyclopedia of Translation Studies* (1st edition), London & New York: Routledge, 170–6.

Cook, Guy (2000) *Language Play, Language Learning*, Oxford: Oxford University Press.

——(2001) 'The philosopher pulled the lower jaw of the hen: Ludicrous invented sentences in language teaching', *Applied Linguistics* 22(3): 366–87.

——(2007) 'A Thing of the Future: Translation in Language Learning', *International Journal of Applied Linguistics* 17(3): 396–401

——(forthcoming) *Translation in English Language Teaching*, Oxford: Oxford University Press.

Cook, Michael (2000) *The Koran*, Oxford: Oxford University Press.

Cook, Stanley Arthur and Christian David Ginsburg (1911) 'Kabbalah', *Encyclopaedia Britannica*, New York, Vol. 15.

Cooper, Arthur (1978) *The Creation of the Chinese Written Character*, London: The China Society.

Cooper, M. (1974) *Rodrigues the Interpreter: An Early Jesuit in Japan and China*, New York: Weatherhill.

Copeland, Rita (1991) *Rhetoric, Hermeneutics and Translation in the Middle Ages: Academic Traditions and Vernacular Texts*, Cambridge: Cambridge University Press.

Corbett, John (1998) *Written in the Language of the Scottish Nation: A History of Literary Translation into Scots*, Clevedon: Multilingual Matters.

Cormier, Monique (1985) 'Glossaire de la théorie interprétative de la traduction et de l'interprétation', *Meta* 30(4): 353–9.

Cornea, P. (1970) ' "Cerere" şi "oferta" în determinarea profilului traducerilor de la jumătatea veacului trecut' ['Command' and 'Supply' in Determination of the Profile of Translations at the Middle of the Last Century], in Al. Dima, I. C. Chitimia, M. Novicov, P. Cornea, S. Velea and E. Popeangă (eds) *Probleme de literatură comparată şi sociologie literară*, Bucharest: Publishing House of the Romanian Academy.

Corsellis, Ann (2000) 'Turning Good Intentions into Good Practice: Enabling the Public Services to Fulfil their Responsibilities', in Roda Roberts, Silvana Carr, Diana Abraham and Aideen Dufour (eds) *Critical Link 2: Interpreters in the Community*, Amsterdam & Philadelphia: John Benjamins, 89–99.

——, Jan Cambridge, Nicky Glegg and Sarah Robson (2007) 'Establishment, Maintenance and Development of a National Register', in Cecilia Wadensjö, Birgitta Englund Dimitrova and Anna-Lena Nilsson (eds) *Critical Link 4: The Professionalisation of Interpreting in the Community*, Amsterdam & Philadelphia: John Benjamins, 139–50.

Cortesão, J. (1967) *A carta de Pêro Vaz de Caminha*, Lisbon: Portugália Editora.

Cosculluela, Cécile (2003) 'Semiotics and Translation Studies: An Emerging Interdisciplinarity', *Semiotica* 145(1–4): 105–37.

Coseriu, Eugenio (1977) *El hombre y su lenguaje*, Madrid: Gredos.

Costa, G. (1985) 'The Latin Translations of Longinus's Περί Ὕψους in Renaissance Italy', in R. Schoeck (ed.) *Acta Conventus neolatini Bononiensis*, Binghamton, NY: Medieval and Renaissance Texts and Studies, 224–38.

Coulmas, Florian (1992) *Language and Economy*, Oxford: Blackwell.

Coulthard, Malcolm (1975) *An Introduction to Discourse Analysis*, London: Longman.

Craig, Ian (2001) *Children's Classics under Franco*, Berne & Oxford: Peter Lang.

Crapanzano, Vincent (1986) 'Hermes' Dilemma: The Masking of Subversion in Ethnographic Description', in James Clifford and George E. Marcus (eds) *Writing Culture: The Poetics and Politics of Ethnography*, Berkeley: University of California Press, 51–76.

Crick, J. (2002) 'Freud's Literary Culture', *The Modern Language Review* 97(4): 1056–8.

Crisafulli, Edoardo (2002) 'The Quest for an Eclectic Methodology of Translation Description', in Theo Hermans (ed.) *Cross-cultural Transgressions: Research Models in Translation Studies II: Historical and Ideological Models*, Manchester: St Jerome, 26–43.

Croce, Benedetto (1902) *Estetica come scienza dell'espressione e linguistica generale*, Bari: Laterza.

Croft, William (1990) *Typology and Universals*, Cambridge: Cambridge University Press.

Cronin, Liam (2005) *Microsoft in Emerging Markets*, Limerick: Localisation Research Centre, http://www.localisation.ie/resources/conferences/2005/Online/Liam%20Cronin%202005.ppt (accessed 28 August 2007).

Cronin, Michael (1995) 'Altered States: Translation and Minority Languages', *TTR* 8(1): 85–103.

——(1996) *Translating Ireland*, Cork: Cork University Press.

——(2000) *Across the Lines: Travel, Language, Translation*, Cork: Cork University Press.

——(2002) 'The Empire Talks Back: Orality, Heteronomy and the Cultural Turn in Interpreting Studies', in Maria Tymoczko and Edwin Gentzler (eds) *Translation and Power*, Amherst and Boston: University of Massachusetts Press, 45–62.

——(2003) *Translation and Globalization*, London & New York: Routledge.

——(2005) 'Burning the House Down. Translation in a Global Setting', *Language and Intercultural Communication* 2(2): 108–19.

——(2006) *Translation and Identity*, London & New York: Routledge.

Cronon, W. (1983) *Changes in the Land: Indians, Colonists, and the Ecology of New England*, New York: Hill & Wang.

Crucefix, Martyn (tr.) (2006) *Rilke: Duino Elegies*, London: Enitharmon.

Crystal, David (1997a) *The Cambridge Encyclopedia of Language* (2nd edition), Cambridge: Cambridge University Press.

——(1997b) *English as a Global Language*, Cambridge: Cambridge University Press.

Culler, Jonathan (1982) *On Deconstruction: Theory and Criticism after Structuralism*, Ithaca, NY: Cornell University Press.

Cunico, Sonia and Jeremy Munday (eds) (2007) *Translation and Ideology: Encounters and Clashes*, Special Issue of *The Translator* 13(2).

d'Alverney, Marie-Therese (1982) 'Translation and Translators', in Robert L. Benson and Giles Constable (eds) *Renaissance and Renewal in the Twelfth Century*, Cambridge, MA: Harvard University Press, 421–62.

D'Andrade, R. and C. Strauss (eds) (1992) *Human Motives and Cultural Models*, Cambridge: Cambridge University Press.

D'hulst, Lieven (1987) *L'évolution de la poésie en France (1780–1830). Introduction à une analyse des interférences systémiques*, Leuven: Leuven University Press.

——(1990) *Cent ans de théorie française de la traduction: de Batteux à Littré (1748–1847)*, Lille: Presses Universitaires de Lille.

——(1991) 'Pourquoi et comment écrire l'histoire des théories de la traduction?', in Mladen Jovanovic (ed.) *Translation, a Creative Profession*, Proceedings of XIth World Congress of FIT, Belgrade, 1990, Belgrade: Prevodilac, 57–62.

Dadazhanova, Munavvarkhon (1984) 'Both Are Primary: An "Author's Translation" Is a Creative Re-creation', *Soviet Studies in Literature* 20(4): 67–79.

Dagut, Menachem B. (1971) 'A Linguistic Analysis of Some Semantic Problems of Hebrew–English Translation'. Unpublished PhD, Jerusalem: The Hebrew University.

——(1978) *Hebrew–English Translation: A Linguistic Analysis of Some Semantic Problems*, Haifa: The University of Haifa.

Daller, Helmut, Roeland Van Hout and Jeanine Treffers-Daller (2003) 'Lexical Richness in the Spontaneous Speech of Bilinguals', *Applied Linguistics* 24(2): 197–222.

Dam, Helle (1998) 'Lexical Similarity vs Lexical Dissimilarity in Consecutive Interpreting. A Product-based Study of Form-based vs Meaning-based Interpreting', *The Translator* (4)1: 49–68.

Danan, Martine (1991) 'Dubbing as an

Expression of Nationalism', *Meta* 36(4): 606–14.

Danby, Nicola (2004) 'The Space Between: Self-Translator Nancy Huston's *Limbes/ Limbo*', *La Linguistique* 40(1): 83–96.

Daniell, David (1994) *William Tyndale: A Biography*, New Haven & London: Yale University Press.

Danks, Joseph, Gregory Shreve, Stephen Fountain and Michael McBeath (eds) (1997) *Cognitive Processes in Translation and Interpreting*, Thousand Oaks, CA: Sage.

Danquah, J. B. (1928) *Gold Coast: Akan Laws and Customs*, London: Oxford University Press.

Dasenbrock, Reed Way (1987) 'Intelligibility and Meaningfulness in Multicultural Literature in English', *PMLA* 102(1): 10–19.

Dasgupta, Alokeranjan (ed.) (1983) *Problems of Translation from S. Asian Languages*, Heidelberg: S. Asia Institute, Heidelberg University. Originally published in 1978 as vol. 7 of *S. Asian Digest of Regional Writing*.

Davidson, Brad (2000) 'The Interpreter as Institutional Gatekeeper: The Social-linguistic Role of Interpreters in Spanish–English Medical Discourse', *Journal of Sociolinguistics* 4(3): 379–405.

——(2002) 'A Model for the Construction of Conversational Common Ground in Interpreted Discourse', *Journal of Pragmatics* 34: 1273–1300.

Davidson, Donald (1973/1984) 'Radical Interpretation', *Dialectica* 27: 313–28; reprinted in Donald Davidson (1984) *Inquiries into Truth and Interpretation*, Oxford: Clarendon Press.

Davies, N. (1981) *God's Playground. A History of Poland*, Oxford: Oxford University Press.

Davies, W.V. (1987) *Egyptian Hieroglyphs*, Berkeley: University of California Press.

Davis, Kathleen (2001) *Deconstruction and Translation*, Manchester: St Jerome.

Dayras, S. (1993) 'The Knox Version of the Trials of a Translator: Translation or Transgression', in Jasper (ed.), 44–59.

de Beaugrande, Robert (1978) *Factors in a Theory of Poetic Translating*, Assen: Van Gorcum.

de Bessé, Bruno (1997) 'Terminological Definitions', in Sue Ellen Wright and Gerhard Budin (eds) *Handbook of Terminology Management Vol. 1*, Amsterdam & Philadelphia: John Benjamins, 63–74.

de Certeau, Michel (1984) *The Practice of Everyday Life*, trans. Steven F. Rendall, Berkeley: University of California Press.

de Groot, Anette M. B. (1992a) 'Bilingual Lexical Representation: A Closer Look at Conceptual Representations', in Ram Frost and Leonard Katz (eds) *Orthography, Phonology, Morphology, and Meaning*, Amsterdam: North Holland, 389–412.

——(1992b) 'Determinants of Word Translation', *Journal of Experimental Psychology: Learning, Memory, and Cognition* 18(5): 1001–18.

——(1997) 'The Cognitive Study of Translation and Interpretation: Three Approaches', in Joseph Danks, Gregory Shreve, Stephen Fountain and Michael McBeath (eds) *Cognitive Processes in Translation and Interpreting*, Thousand Oaks, CA: Sage, 25–56.

De Jongh, E. M. (1992) *An Introduction to Court Interpreting*, Lanham, MD: University Press of America.

de la Cuesta, L.-A. (1992) 'Intérpretes y traductores en el descubrimiento y conquista del nuevo mundo', *Livius* 1: 25–34.

de Linde, Zoé and Neil Kay (1999) *The Semiotics of Subtitling*, Manchester: St Jerome.

de Lotbinière-Harwood, Susanne (1991) *Re-belle et infidèle. La traduction comme pratique de réécriture au féminin/The Body Bilingual. Translation as a Re-writing in the Feminine*, Québec: Les éditions du remue-ménage/The Women's Press.

——(1995) 'Geo-graphies of Why', in Sherry Simon (ed.) *Culture in Transit: Translating the Literature of Quebec*, Montreal: Véhicule Press, 55–68.

de Man, Paul (1986) *Resistance to Theory*, Minneapolis, MN: University of Minnesota Press.

de Manuel Jerez, Jesús (ed.) (2003) *Nuevas tecnologías y formación de interpretes*, Granada: Atrio.

——(2006) *La incorporación de la realidad profesional a la formación de intérpretes de conferencias mediante las nuevas tecnologías y la investigación-acción*. Unpublished doctoral dissertation, Granada: University of Granada.

——, Juan López Cortés and María Brander de la Iglesia (2004) 'Traducción e Interpretación, Voluntariado y Compromiso Social', *Puentes* 4: 5–72. Online <http://piit.beplaced.com/ECOSarticle.htm>.

de Mooij, Marieke (1998/2005) *Global Marketing and Advertising. Understanding Cultural Paradoxes*, Thousand Oaks, CA: Sage.

——(2003) *Consumer Behavior and Culture. Consequences for Global Marketing and Advertising*, Thousand Oaks, CA: Sage.

——(2004) 'Translating Advertising: Painting the Tip of an Iceberg', *The Translator* 10(2): 179–98.

de Pedro, Raquel (1996) 'Beyond the Words: The Translation of Television Adverts', *Babel* 42(1): 27–45.

De Regt, Lénart J. (ed.) (2006) *Canon and Modern Bible Translation in Interconfessional Perspective*, Istanbul: United Bible Socities.

de Rynck, P. and A. Welkenhuysen (eds) (1992) *De Oudheid in het Nederlands. Repertorium en bibliografische gids voor vertalingen van Grieks en Latijnse auteurs en geschriften* [Classical Antiquity in Dutch. Repertory and Bibliographical Guide for Translations of Greek and Latin Authors and Writings], Baarn: Ambo.

De Waard, Jan and Eugene A. Nida (1986) *From One Language to Another, Functional Equivalence in Bible Translating*, Nashville, TN: Thomas Nelson, Inc.

DeJean, Jean (1989) *Fictions of Sappho*, Chicago & London: University of Chicago Press.

Delabastita, Dirk (1989) 'Translation and Mass-Communication: Film and TV Translation as Evidence of Cultural Dynamics', *Babel* 35(4): 193–218.

——(1990) 'Translation and the Mass Media', in Susan Bassnett and André Lefevere (eds) *Translation, History and Culture*, London & New York: Pinter, 97–109.

——(1993) *There's A Double Tongue. An Investigation into the Translation of Shakespeare's Wordplay, with Special Reference to Hamlet*, Amsterdam & Atlanta: Rodopi.

——(ed.) (1997) *Traductio: Essays on Punning and Translation*, Manchester & Namur: St Jerome Press & Presses Universitaires de Namur.

——(2002) 'A Great Feast of Languages: Shakespeare's Bilingual Comedy in *King Henry V* and the French Translators', *The Translator* 8(2): 303–40.

——(2003) 'More Alternative Shakespeares', in A. Luis Pujante and Ton Hoenselaars (eds) *Four Hundred Years of Shakespeare in Europe*, Newark, DE: University of Delaware Press, 113–33.

——(2004) 'If I Know the Letters and the Language: Translation as a Dramatic Device in Shakespeare's Plays', in Ton Hoenselaars (ed.) *Shakespeare and the Language of Translation* (The Arden Shakespeare), London: Thomson, 31–52.

——(2005) 'Cross-Language Comedy in Shakespeare', *Humor* 18(2): 161–84.

——and Lieven D'hulst (eds) (1993) *European Shakespeares. Translating Shakespeare in the Romantic Age*, Amsterdam & Philadelphia: John Benjamins.

——and Rainier Grutman (eds) (2005a) *Fictionalising Translation and Multilingualism*, special issue of *Linguistica Antverpiensia: NS 4*.

——and Rainier Grutman (2005b) 'Fictional Representations of Multilingualism and Translation', *Linguistica Antverpiensia: NS 4*: 11–35.

DeLater, James Albert (2002) *Translation Theory in the Age of Louis XIV. The 1683 De optimo genere interpretandi of Pierre-Daniel Huet (1630–1721)*, Manchester: St Jerome.

Deledalle-Rhodes, Janice (1996) 'The Transposition of the Linguistic Sign in Peirce's Contributions to *The Nation*', *Transactions of the Charles S. Peirce Society* 32(4): 668–82.

——(1988–1989) 'La traduction dans les systèmes sémiotiques', *Etudes Littéraires* 21(3): 211–21.

Delisle, Jean (1980) *L'analyse du discours comme méthode de traduction: Initiation à la traduction française de textes pragmatiques anglais, théorie et pratique*, Ottawa: Presses de l'Université d'Ottawa.

——(1984) *Au cœur du trialogue canadien/ Bridging the Language Solitudes. Historique de l'évolution du Bureau fédéral des traductions, 1934–1984*, Ottawa: Ministère des Approvisionnements et Services.

——(1986) 'Dans les coulisses de l'adaptation théâtrale', *Circuit* 12: 3–8.

——(1987) *La traduction au Canada/Translation*

in Canada, 1534–1984, Ottawa: Les Presses de l'Universite d'Ottawa.

——(1988) Translation, an Interpretive Approach, translation of Part I of L'analyse du discours comme méthode de Traduction, trans. Patricia Logan and Monica Creery, Ottawa: University of Ottawa Press.

——(1990) Les alchimistes des langues/The Language Alchemists. Société des traducteurs du Québec (1940–1990), Ottawa: University of Ottawa Press.

——(1993/2003) La traduction raisonnée. Manuel d'initiation à la traduction professionnelle de l'anglais vers le français, Ottawa: Presses de l'Université d'Ottawa.

——(1998) 'Définition, rédaction et utilité des objectifs d'apprentissage en enseignement de la traduction', in Isabel García Izquierdo and Joan Verdegal (eds) Los estudios de traducción: un reto didáctico, Castellón: Universitat Jaume I, 13–44.

——(ed.) (2002) Portraits de traductrices, Ottawa: University of Ottawa Press.

——(2005) 'Les nouvelles règles de traduction du Vatican', Meta 50(3): 831–50.

——and Judith Woodsworth (eds) (1995) Translators through History, Amsterdam & Philadelphia: John Benjamins.

Deller, Sheila and Mario Rinvolucri (2002) Using the Mother Tongue, London/ Addleston: English Teaching Professional/ Delta Publishers.

Demers, Ginette (2003) 'L'interprétation en Colombie-Britannique à l'époque des explorations par voie terrestre et de la traite des fourrures dans les comptoirs (1793–1846)', TTR 16(2): 15–44.

——(2004) 'Colombie-Britannique: les missionnaires catholiques et les activités langagières (1842–1952)', Meta 49(3): 656–68.

Demerson, Geneviève (1984) 'Joachim Du Bellay traducteur de lui-même', in Grahame Castor and Terence Cave (eds) Neo-Latin and the Vernacular in Renaissance France, Oxford: Clarendon Press, 113–28.

Denison, Norman (1978) 'On Plurilingualism and Translation', in Lillebill Grähs, Gustav Korlén and Bertil Malmberg (eds) Theory and Practice of Translation, Bern/Frankfurt/Las Vegas: Peter Lang, 313–19.

Denissenko, Juri (1989) 'Communicative and Interpretative Linguistics', in Laura Gran and John Dodds (eds) The Theoretical and Practical Aspects of Teaching Conference Interpretation, Udine: Campanotto Editore, 17–20.

Derrida, Jacques (1967/1976) Of Grammatology, trans. Gayatri Chakravorty Spivak, Baltimore, MD: Johns Hopkins University Press.

——(1972a/1981) Positions, trans. Alan Bass, Chicago: University of Chicago Press; reprinted 2002, London & New York: Continuum.

——(1972b/1982) Margins of Philosophy, trans. Alan Bass, Chicago: University of Chicago Press.

——(1979) 'Living On/Borderlines', trans. James Hulbert, in Deconstruction and Criticism, New York: Continuum, 75–176.

——(1982/1985) The Ear of the Other. Otobiography, Transference, Translation, trans. Peggy Kamuf, Lincoln & London: University of Nebraska Press.

——(1985) 'Des Tours de Babel', trans. Joseph Graham, in Joseph Graham (ed.) Difference in Translation, Ithaca & London: Cornell University Press, 165–248; French original in Appendix to same volume, 209–48.

——(1987/1988) 'Letter to a Japanese Friend', trans. David Wood and Andrew Benjamin, in David Wood and Robert Bernasconi (eds) Derrida and Différance, Evanston, IL: Northwestern University Press, 1–5.

——(1988) 'Afterword', trans. Samuel Weber, in Limited Inc, Evanston, IL: Northwestern University Press, 111–60.

——(1990) Force de loi: Le 'fondement mystique de l'autorité'; Force of Law: The 'Mystical Foundation of Authority', Bilingual edition, trans. Mary Quaintance, Cardozo Law Review 11: 919–1045.

——(1992) '"This Strange Institution Called Literature": An Interview with Jacques Derrida', trans. Geoff Bennington and Rachel Bowlby, in Derek Attridge (ed.) Jacques Derrida: Acts of Literature, New York & London: Routledge, 33–75.

——(1996/1998) Monolingualism of the Other: or, The Prosthesis of Origin, trans. Patrick Mensah, Stanford, CA: Stanford University Press.

——(1999/2001) 'What is a "Relevant" Translation?', trans. Lawrence Venuti, Critical Inquiry 27: 174–200; reprinted in Lawrence Venuti (ed.) The Translation Studies Reader,

2004, London & New York: Routledge, 423–46.

Désilets, Alain (2007) 'Translation Wikified: How will Massive Online Collaboration Impact the World of Translation?', *ASLIB Translating and the Computer 29 Conference Proceedings*, London: ASLIB.

Desmet, Mieke (2007) *Babysitting the Reader: Translating English Narrative Fiction for Girls into Dutch*, Bern: Peter Lang.

Devarrieux, Claire (1993) 'Gallant: Paris est un jouet', *Libération (hors série: les 80 livres de l'année)* March: 14-15.

Dewdney, Selwyn (1975) *The Sacred Scrolls of the Southern Ojibway*, Toronto: University of Toronto Press.

Dharwadker, Vinay (1999) 'A. K. Ramanujan's Theory and Practice of Translation', in Susan Bassnett and Harish Trivedi (eds) *Postcolonial Translation: Theory and Practice*, London & New York: Routledge, 114–40.

Di Biase, Carmine G. (ed.) (2006) *Travel and Translation in the Early Modern Period*, Amsterdam & New York: Rodopi.

di Stefano, B. Follkart (1982) 'Translation as Literary Criticism', *Meta* 27(3): 241–56.

Díaz Cintas, Jorge (2001) 'Striving for Quality in Subtitling: The Role of a Good Dialogue List', in Yves Gambier and Henrik Gottlieb (eds) *(Multi)Media Translation, Concepts, Practices and Research*, Amsterdam & Philadelphia: John Benjamins, 199–211.

——(2003) *Teoría y Práctica de la subtitulación. Inglés–Español*, Barcelona: Ariel.

——(2005) 'El subtitulado y los avances tecnológicos', in Raquel Merino, José Miguel Santamaría and Eterio Pajares (eds) *Trasvases culturales: Literatura, cine y traducción* 4, Vitoria: Servicio Editorial de la Universidad del País Vasco, 155–75.

——and Aline Remael (2007) *Audiovisual Translation: Subtitling*, Manchester: St Jerome.

Diaz-Diocaretz, Myriam (1985) *Translating Poetic Discourse: Questions on Feminist Strategies in Adrienne Rich*, Amsterdam & Philadelphia: Benjamins.

Dick, Bernard (1990) *Anatomy of Film*, New York: St Martin's Press.

Dimock, Edward C. (1974) *The Literatures of India*, Chicago: University of Chicago Press.

Dina (2006) Post on 'European standard in translation', Chartered Institute of Linguists discussion forum, 25 July. http://www.iol. org.uk/discussion/viewtopic.asp?id=1749 (accessed 16 August 2006).

Dinekov, P. (1960) 'Über die Aufeinge der bulgarischen Literatur', *International Journal of Slavic Linguistics and Poetics*, vol. III.

Diop, Cheikh Anta (1974) *The African Origin of Civilization: Myth or Reality?*, New York: L. Hill.

Diriker, Ebru (1999) 'Problematising the Discourse on Interpreting – A Quest for Norms in Simultaneous Interpreting', *TEXTconText* 13: 73–90.

——(2004) *De-/Re-Contextualizing Conference Interpreting: Interpreters in the Ivory Tower?*, Amsterdam & Philadelphia: John Benjamins.

Diringer, David (1968) *The Alphabet. A Key to the History of Mankind*, 2 vols, London: Hutchinson.

Dizdar, Mak (1973) *Kameni spavač* (Stone Sleeper), Mostar: Prva književna komuna.

Doce, Jordi (1997) 'Two Extremes of a Continuum: On Translating Ted Hughes and Charles Tomlinson into Spanish', *Forum for Modern Language Studies* XXXIII(1): 46–59.

Dodds, John M. (1992) 'Translation Criticism in Defence of the Profession', *Rivista Internazionale di Tecnica della Traduzione* 0: 1–4.

——and David Katan (1997) 'The Interaction between Research and Training: Round table report', in Yves Gambier, Daniel Gile and Christopher Taylor (eds) *Conference Interpreting: Current trends in research. Proceedings of the international conference on 'Interpreting: what do we know and how?' Turku, 25–27 August 1994*, Amsterdam: John Benjamins, 89–107.

Dodson, Michael S. (2005) 'Translating Science, Translating Empire: The Power of Language in Colonial North India', *Comparative Studies in Society and History* 47(4): 809–35.

Doherty, Monika (1987) 'Text Connectors – A Reading Aid', *Babel* 33: 212–17.

Doinaș, Șt Aug. (1965) 'Dificil, riscant dar nu imposibil' [Difficult, Risky but not Impossible], *Secolul xx* 2: 157–62.

——(1972) 'Însemnarile unui traducator' [Notes of a Translator], in Șt Aug. Doinaș (ed.) *Poezie și modă poetică*, Bucharest: Eminescu Publishing House, 278–91.

Dollerup, Cay (2000a) 'Language Work at the United Nations', *Language International* 12(6): 12–16.

——(2000b) '"Relay" and "Support" Translations', in Andrew Chesterman, Natividad Gallardo San Salvador and Yves Gambier (eds) *Translation in Context: Selected Contributions from the EST Congress, Granada 1998*, Amsterdam & Philadelphia: John Benjamins, 17–26.

——(2003) 'Translation for Reading Aloud', *Meta* 48(1–2): 81–103.

——and Anne Loddergaard (eds) (1992) *Teaching Translation and Interpreting – Training Talent and Experience*, Amsterdam & Philadelphia: John Benjamins.

——and Annette Lindegaard (eds) (1994) *Teaching Translation and Interpreting 2. Insights, Aims, Visions. Papers from the Second Language International Conference, Elsinore, Denmark 4–6 June 1993*, Amsterdam: John Benjamins.

——and Vibeke Appel (eds) (1996) *Teaching Translation and Interpreting 3. New Horizons*, Amsterdam: John Benjamins.

Donaire, María Luisa and Francisco Lafarga (eds) (1991) *Traducción y adaptación cultural: España-Francia*, Oviedo: Universidad de Oviedo, Servicios de Publicaciones.

Dorr, Bonnie, Eduard Hovy and Lori Levin (2006) 'Machine Translation: Interlingual Methods', in Keith Brown (ed.) *Encyclopedia of Language and Linguistics*, 2nd edition, Amsterdam: Elsevier ftp://ftp.cfar.umd.edu/pub/bonnie/Interlingual-MT-Dorr-Hovy-Levin.pdf (accessed 10 October 2007).

Doughty, Catherine and Jessica Williams (eds) (1998) *Focus on Form in Classroom Second Language Acquisition*, Cambridge: Cambridge University Press.

Douma, Félix (1972) 'Reviewing a Translation: A Practical Problem in Literary Criticism', *Meta* 17(2): 94–101.

Dragsted, Barbara (2004) *Segmentation in Translation and Translation Memory Systems. An Empirical Investigation of Cognitive Segmentation and Effects of Integrating a TN System into the Translation Process*, Copenhagen: Copenhagen Business School.

——(2006) 'Computer-aided Translation as a Distributed Cognitive Task', in Stevan Harnad

and Itiel E. Dror (eds) *Pragmatics & Cognition* 14(2): 443–64.

Draskau, J. (1987) *The Quest for Equivalence: On Translating Villon*, Copenhagen: Atheneum.

Dreyer-Sfard, Regina (1965) *Die Verflechtung von Sprache und Bild: Sprache im technischen Zeitalter* 13: 1034–9.

Dries, Josephine (1995) *Dubbing and Subtitling. Guidelines for Production and Distribution*, Düsseldorf: The European Institute for the Media.

Dryden, John (1680/1992) 'On Translation', in Rainer Schulte and John Biguenet (eds) *Theories of Translation*, Chicago & London: University of Chicago Press, 17–31.

Drysdale, Helena (2001) *Mother Tongues: Travels through Tribal Europe*, London: Picador.

Du-Nour, Miryam (1995) 'Retranslation of Children's Books as Evidence of Changes of Norms', *Target* 7(2): 327–46.

Du Pont, Olaf (2005) 'Robert Graves's Claudian Novels: A Case of Pseudotranslation', *Target* 17(2): 327–47.

Dubuc, Robert (2002) *Manuel pratique de terminologie* (fourth edition), Montréal, Québec: Linguatech.

Dudley, D. R. and D. M. Lang (eds) (1969) *Penguin Companion to Literature vol. 4: Classical and Byzantine, Oriental and African Literature*, Harmondsworth: Penguin.

Duff, Anthony (1989) *Translation*, Oxford: Oxford University Press.

Duflou, Veerle (in progress) *Approaching Norms in Conference Interpreting: A Case Study*. Doctoral dissertation. Leuven: Katholieke Universiteit.

Dulles, J. W. F. (1969) 'The Contribution of Getúlio Vargas to the Modernization of Brazil', in E. N. Blakanoff (ed.) *The Shaping of Modern Brazil*, Baton Rouge, LA: Louisiana State University Press, 36–57.

Dunne, Keiran J. (2006a) (ed.) *Perspectives on Localization*, Amsterdam & Philadelphia: John Benjamins.

——(2006b) 'Putting the Cart Behind the Horse – Rethinking Localization Quality Management', in Keiran J. Dunne (ed.) *Perspectives on Localization*, Amsterdam & Philadelphia: John Benjamins, 95–117.

Duranti, Alessandro (1997) *Cultural Linguistics*, Cambridge: Cambridge University Press.

Duranti, Riccardo (1979) 'La doppia mediazione

di Carcano', in Laura Caretti (ed.) *Il teatro dei personaggio. Shakespeare sulla scena italiana dell'800*, Rome: Bulzoni.

Durban, Chris (2003) *Translation, Getting it Right: A Guide to Buying Translations*, http://www.fit-ift.org/download/getright-en.pdf (accessed 30 January 2007).

——(2004) http://translationjournalblogspot.com/2004/08/native-language.html (accessed 30 January 2007).

Duțu, Al. (1970) 'Traducere și modelare în cultura română din perioada luminilor' [Translation and Modelling in the Romanian Culture in the Period of Enlightenment], in Al. Dima, I. C. Chițimia, M. Novicov, P. Cornea, S. Velea and E. Popeangă (eds) *Probleme de literatură comparată și sociologie literară*, Bucharest: Publishing House of the Romanian Academy, 155–9.

d'Ydewalle, Géry, Johan van Rensbergen and Joris Pollet (1987) 'Reading a Message When the Same Message Is Available Auditorily in Another Language: The Case of Subtitling', in J. K. O'Regan and A. Lévy-Schoen (eds) *Eye Movements: From Physiology to Cognition*, Amsterdam & New York: Elsevier, 313–21.

Eades, Diana, Helen Fraser, Jeff Siegel, Tim McNamara and Brett Baker (2003) 'Linguistic Identification in the Determination of Nationality: A Preliminary Report', *Language Policy* 2(2): 179–99.

Eagleston, Robert (2005) 'Levinas, Translation and Ethics', in Sandra Bermann and Michael Wood (eds) *Nation, Language and the Ethics of Translation*, Princeton, NJ: Princeton University Press, 127–38.

Eagleton, Terry (2007) *How to Read a Poem*, Oxford: Blackwell.

Eco, Umberto (2001) *Experiences in Translation*, Toronto, Buffalo & London: University of Toronto Press.

——(2003) *Mouse or Rat? Translation as Negotiation*, London: Weidenfeld & Nicolson.

——and Siri Nergaard (1998) 'Semiotic Approaches', in Mona Baker (ed.) *Routledge Encyclopedia of Translation Studies* (1st edition), London & New York: Routledge, 218–22.

——, Stefan Collini, Richard Rorty, Jonathan D. Culler and Christine Brooke-Rose (1992) *Interpretation and Overinterpretation*, Cambridge: Cambridge University Press.

Edwards, Alicia (1995) *The Practice of Court Interpreting*, Amsterdam & Philadelphia: John Benjamins.

Eguíluz, Federico, Raquel Merino, Vickie Olsen, Eterio Pajares and José Miguel (eds) (1994) *Trasvases culturales: literatura, cine, traducción*, Vitoria: Universidad del País Vasco.

Einarsson, S. (1961) *Íslensk bókmenntasaga* [History of Icelandic Literature], Reykjavik: Snæbjörn Jónssón & Co.

Eisner, Will (1985) *Comics as Sequential Art*, Tamarac, FL: Poorhouse Press.

Eliot, J. (1666) *The Indian Grammar Begun, or An Essay to Bring the Indian Language into Rules: For the Help of Such as Desire to Learn the Same, for the Furtherance of the Gospel Among Them*, Cambridge, MA: Marmaduke Johnson.

Ellipse (1997) (Special Issue 21) 'The Translation of Poetry'.

Ellis, Roger and R. Tixier (eds) (1996) *The Medieval Translator 5*, Turnhout: Brepols.

——, J. Wogan-Browne, S. Medcalf and P. Meredith (eds) (1989) *The Medieval Translator 1*, Cambridge: D. S. Brewer.

Ellison, Julie (1990) *Delicate Subjects. Romanticism, Gender, and the Ethics of Understanding*, Ithaca & London: Cornell University Press.

Engeström, Yrjö and Reijo Miettinen (1999) 'Introduction', in Yrjö Engeström and Reijo Miettinen (eds) *Perspectives on Activity Theory*, Cambridge: Cambridge University Press, 1–16.

Englund Dimitrova, Birgitta (1993) 'Semantic Change in Translation – A Cognitive Perspective', in Yves Gambier and Jorma Tommola (eds) *Translation and Knowledge*, Turku: University of Turku, 285–97.

——(2002) 'Training and educating the trainers', in Eva Hung (ed.) *Teaching Translation and Interpreting 4 – Building Bridges*, Amsterdam: John Benjamins, 73–82.

——(2005) *Expertise and Explicitation in the Translation Process*, Amsterdam & Philadelphia: John Benjamins.

——and Kenneth Hyltenstam (eds) (2000) *Language Processing and Simultaneous Interpreting*, Amsterdam & Philadelphia: John Benjamins.

Enkvist, N. E. (1973) *Linguistic Stylistics*, The Hague: Mouton.

Erasmus, Mabel, Lebohang Mathibela, Erik Hertog and Hugo Antonissen (eds) (2003) *Liaison Interpreting in the Community*, Pretoria: Van Schaik.

Erasmus, P. (1976) *Buffalo Days and Nights*. As told to Henry Thompson. Introduction by Irene Spry, Calgary: Glenbow-Alberta Institute.

Ericsson, K. Anders and Herbert A. Simon (1984/1993) *Protocol Analysis: Verbal Reports as Data*, Cambridge, MA: MIT Press.

——(1987) 'Verbal reports on thinking', in Claus Faerch and Gabriele Kasper (eds) *Introspection in Second Language Research*, Clevedon: Multilingual Matters, 24–53.

Erikson, Thomas Hylland and Finn Sivert Nielson (2001) *A History of Anthropology*, London & Sterling, VA: Pluto Press.

Eskola, Sari (2004) 'Untypical Frequencies in Translated Language: A Corpus-based Study on a Literary Corpus of Translated and Non-translated Finnish', in Anna Mauranen and Pekka Kujamäki (eds) *Translation Universals. Do They Exist?*, Amsterdam & Philadelphia: John Benjamins, 83–100.

Esselink, Bert (2000) *A Practical Guide to Localization*, Amsterdam: John Benjamins.

Essmann, H. (1992) *Übersetzungsanthologien: Eine Typologie und eine Untersuchung am Beispiel der amerikanischen Verdichtung in deutschsprachigen Anthologien, 1920–1960* (Neue Studien zur Anglistik under Amerikanistik 57), Frankfurt: Peter Lang.

——and U. Schoening (eds) (1996) *Weltliteratur in deutschen Versanthologien des 19 Jahrhunderts* (Göttinger Beiträger zur Internationalen Übersetzungs-forschung 11), Berlin: Erich Schmidt.

Etman, Ahmed (2004) 'The Greek Concept of Tragedy in Arab Culture', in Freddy Decreus and Mieke Kolk (eds) *Re-reading Classics in 'East' and 'West'*, Documenta XXll(4): 281–99.

——(2008) 'Translation at the Intersection of Traditions: The Arab Reception of the Classics', in Lorna Hardwick and Christopher A. Stray (eds) *A Companion to Classical Receptions*, Oxford: Blackwell, 141–52.

Eugeni, Carlo (2007) 'Il rispeakeraggio televisivo per sordi. Per una sottotitolazione mirata del TG', *Intralinea* 9 http://www.intralinea. it/volumes/eng_more.php?id=513_0_2_0_ M60% (accessed 15 July 2007).

——and Gabriele Mack (eds) (2006) *New Technologies in Intralingual Subitling*, Special Issue on Respeaking, *inTRAlinia*, http://www.intralinea.it/specials/respeaking/eng_open.php (accessed August 2007).

Eustis, Richmond (2003) '"Notario" Loses Bid to Discredit Interpreter', *Fulton County Daily Report*, 27 October http://www.law.com/jsp/article.jsp?id=1067014195161 (accessed 7 January 2007).

Even-Zohar, Itamar (1971) 'Mavo le-teorya shel hatirgum ha-sifruti' [Introduction to a Theory of Literary Translation]. Unpublished PhD, Tel Aviv: Tel Aviv University.

——(1978a) 'The Position of Translated Literature within the Literary Polysystem', in James S. Holmes, José Lambert and Raymond van den Broeck (eds) *Literature and Translation: New Perspectives in Literary Studies with a Basic Bibliography of Books on Translation Studies*, Leuven: Acco, 117–27.

——(1978b) *Papers in Historical Poetics*, Tel Aviv: Porter Institute for Poetics and Semiotics.

——(1979) 'Polysystem Theory', *Poetics Today* 1(1–2): 287–310.

——(1981) 'Translation Theory Today', *Poetics Today* 2(4): 1–7.

——(1986) 'The Quest for Laws and Its Implications for the Future of the Science of Literature', in Janos Riesz and George M. Vajda (eds) *The Future of Literary Scholarship*, Frankfurt: Peter Lang, 75–80.

——(1990) *Polysystem Studies*, Special Issue of *Poetics Today* 11(1).

——(2000) 'The Position of Translated Literature within the Literary Polysystem'; revised version of 1978 text; in Lawrence Venuti (ed.) *The Translation Studies Reader*, London: Routledge, 192–7.

Fabbri, Paolo (2000) *Elogio di Babele*, Rome: Meltemi.

Fabre, Giorgio (1998) *L'elenco. Censura fascista, editoria e autori ebrei*, Torino: Zamorani.

Færch, Claus and Gabriele Kaspar (1980) 'Processes and Strategies in Foreign Language Learning and Communication', *Interlanguage Studies Bulletin* 5: 47–118.

——(eds) (1987) *Intraspection in Second Language Research*, Clevedon: Multilingual Matters.

Faiq, Said (ed.) (2004) *Cultural Encounters in Translation from Arabic*, Clevedon: Multilingual Matters.

Fairclough, Norman (1989/2001) *Language and Power*, London: Longman.

——(1995) *Media Discourse*, London: Longman.

Fardy, B. D. (1984) *Jerry Potts, Paladin of the Plains*, Langley, VA: Mr Paperback.

Farghal, Mohammed (1993) 'Managing in Translation: A Theoretical Model', *Meta* 38(2): 257–67.

Faulkner, P. (ed.) (1973) *William Morris: The Critical Heritage*, London and Boston: Routledge & Kegan Paul.

Fawcett, Peter (1995) 'Translation and Power Play', *The Translator* 1(2): 177–92.

——(1996) 'Translating Film', in Geoffrey Harris (ed.) *On Translating French Literature and Film*, Amsterdam: Rodopi, 65–88.

——(1997) *Translation and Language: Linguistic Theories Explained*, Manchester: St Jerome.

——(2000) 'Translation in the Broadsheets', *The Translator* 6(2): 295–307.

——(2001) 'Biggles's Friend André: A Study of Malraux in English Translation', *Target* 13(1): 103–24.

——(2003) 'The Manipulation of Language and Culture in Film Translation', in María Calzada Pérez (ed.) *Apropos of Ideology. Translation Studies on Ideology – Ideologies in Translation Studies*, Manchester: St Jerome, 145–63.

Feather, John (1993) 'Book Publishing in Britain: An Overview', *Media, Culture and Society* 15: 167–81.

Federici, Fortunato (1828) *Degli scrittori greci e delle italiane versioni delle loro opere*, Padua: Soc. Tip della Minerva.

Federman, Raymond (1987) 'The Writer as Self-translator', in Alan Warren Friedman, Charles Rossman and Dina Sherzer (eds) *Beckett Translating/Translating Beckett*, University Park, PA–London: Pennsylvania State University Press, 7–16.

Feldman, G. (1986) 'Going Global', *Publishers Weekly*, 19 December, 20–24.

Feleppa, Robert (1988) *Convention, Translation, and Understanding: Philosophical Problems in the Comparative Study of Culture*, Albany: SUNY Press.

Felstiner, John (1989) 'Kafka and the Golem: Translating Paul Celan', in Daniel Weissbort (ed.) *Translating Poetry: The Double Labyrinth*, London: Macmillan, 35–50.

The Feminist Sexual Ethics Project (n.d.), Brandeis University, http://www.brandeis.edu/projects/fse/Pages/islam.html (accessed October 2007).

Fenton, Sabine (2001) ' "Possess Yourselves of the Soil". Interpreting in Early New Zealand', *The Translator* 7(1): 1–18.

——and Paul Moon (2003) 'The Translation of the Treaty of Waitangi: A Case of Disempowerment', in Edwin Gentzler and Maria Tymoczko (eds) *Translation and Power*, Amherst, MA: University of Massachusetts Press, 25–44.

Ferenčík, Ján (1982) *Kontexty prekladu*, Bratislava: Slovenský spisovateľ.

Fernández López, Marisa (2000) 'Translation Studies in Contemporary Children's Literature: A Comparison of Intercultural Ideological Factors', *Children's Literature Association Quarterly* 25(1): 29–37.

Ferrara, A. (1980) 'Appropriateness Conditions for Entire Sequences of Speech Acts', *Journal of Pragmatics* 4: 321–40.

Ferrari, Luigi (1925) *Le traduzioni italiane del teatro tragico francese nei secoli xvii e xviii*, Paris: Librairie Ancienne Edouard Champion.

Ferrer Simó, María Rosario (2005) 'Fansubs y scanlations: la influencia del aficionado en los criterios profesionales' [Fansubs and Scanlations: The Influence of the Amateur on Professional Criteria], *Puentes* 6: 27–43.

Figueira, Dorothy Matilda (1991) *Translating the Orient: The Reception of 'Sakuntla' in Nineteenth-Century Europe*, Albany: SUNY Press.

Filippakopoulou, Maria (2005) 'Self-Translation: Reviving the Author?', *In Other Words* 25: 23–7.

Finch, C.A. (1969) *An Approach to Technical Translation: An introductory guide for scientific readers*, Oxford: Pergamon Press.

Findlay, Bill (1998) 'Silesian into Scots: Gerhart Hauptmann's *The Weavers*', *Modern Drama* XLI(I): 90–104.

——(2004) *Frae Ither Tongues: Essays on Modern Translations into Scots*, Clevedon: Multilingual Matters.

Finnegan, R. (1970) *Oral Literature in Africa*, Oxford: Clarendon Press.

Fiola, Marco A. (ed.) (2004) *Translation, Ethics and Society*, Special Issue of *TTR* 17(2).

Firth, John Rupert (1956a) 'Linguistic Analysis and Translation', *For Roman Jakobson: Essays on the Occasion of his Sixtieth Birthday*, The Hague; reprinted in F. R. Palmer (ed.) (1968) *Selected Papers of J. R. Firth 1952–59*, London & Harlow: Longmans, Green & Co., 74–83.

——(1956b) 'Linguistics and Translation', paper read at Birkbeck College, University of London, June 1956; reprinted in F. R. Palmer (ed.) (1968) *Selected Papers of J. R. Firth 1952–59*, London & Harlow: Longmans, Green & Co., 84–95.

——(1957) *Papers in Linguistics. 1934–1951*, London: Oxford University Press.

Fischbach, Henry (ed.) (1998) *Translation and Medicine*, Amsterdam & Philadelphia: John Benjamins.

Fischer, Michael M. J. and Mehdi Abedi (1990) 'Translating Qur'ānic Dialogics: Islamic Poetics and Politics for Muslims and for Us', *Hermeneutics and the Poetic Motion* (Translation Perspectives V), Binghamton, NY: State University of New York at Binghamton, 111–29.

Fischer, Otokar (1929) 'O překládání básnických děl' [On the Translation of Poetic Works], *Duše a slovo*, 263–83.

Fitch, Brian T. (1983) 'L'intra-intertextualité interlinguistique de Beckett: la problématique de la traduction de soi', *Texte* 2: 85–100.

——(1985) 'The Status of Self-translation', *Texte* 4: 111–25.

——(1988) *Beckett and Babel. An Investigation into the Status of the Bilingual Work*, Toronto, Buffalo & London: University of Toronto Press.

Fitts, D. (ed. and trans.) (1956) *Poems from the Greek Anthology*, New York: Directions.

Fitzgerald, E. (1880) *The Downfall and Death of King Oedipus*, Guildford: Billing & Sons.

Fitzpatrick, Elizabeth (2000) 'Balai Pustaka in the Dutch East Indies: Colonizing a Literature', in Sherry Simon and Paul St-Pierre (eds) *Changing the Terms: Translating in the Postcolonial Era*, Ottawa: University of Ottawa Press, 113–26.

Florence, H. (1941) *Viagem fluvial do Tietê ao Amazonas de 1825 a 1829*, São Paulo: Melhoramentos.

Flores, Lauro (1987) 'Converging Languages in a World of Conflicts: Code-switching in Chicano Poetry', *Visible Language* 21(1): 130–52.

Flynn, Peter (2004) 'Skopos Theory: An Ethnographic Enquiry', *Perspectives: Studies in Translatogy* 12(4): 270–85.

Fodor, István (1976) *Film Dubbing: Phonetic, Semiotic, Esthetic and Psychological Aspects*, Hamburg: Helmut Buske.

Folaron, Debbie (2006) 'A Discipline Coming of Age in the Digital Age', in Keiran J. Dunne (ed.) *Perspectives on Localization*, Amsterdam & Philadelphia: John Benjamins, 195–219.

Folena, Gianfranco (1973) '"Volgarizzare" e "tradurre"', in *La Traduzione* (Saggi e Studi), Trieste: LINT, 59–120.

——(1991) *Volgarizzare e tradurre*, Turin: Einaudi.

Forbes, Jill and Sarah Street (2000) *European Cinema*, New York: Palgrave.

Forsdick, Charles (2005) *Travel in Twentieth-Century French and Francophone Cultures: The Persistence of Diversity*, Oxford: Oxford University Press.

Forster, Leonard (1970) *The Poet's Tongues: Multilingualism in Literature*, London, New York & Sydney: Cambridge University Press.

Fossa, L. (1992) 'Los "Lenguas": Interpretación consecutiva en el siglo xvɪ', *Boletin Asociación de Traductores egresados de la Universidad Ricardo Palma* 4: 11–12.

——(2005) 'Juan Betanzos, The Man Who Boasted Being a Translator', *Meta* 50(3): 906–33.

Foucault, Michel (1972) *The Archeology of Knowledge*, trans. A. M. Sheridan-Smith, London: Tavistock.

——(1975/1977) *Discipline and Punish. The Birth of the Prison*, trans. Alan Sheridan, London: Penguin.

——(1976/1981) *The Will to Knowledge*, Vol. 1, trans. Robert Hurley, London: Penguin.

Fouchecour, Charles-Henri de (1986) *Moralia: Les Notions morales dans la Littérature persane de 3ᵉ/9ᵉ au 7ᵉ /13ᵉ siècles*, Paris: Editions Recherche sur les Civilisations.

Fowler, E. (1992) 'Rendering Words, Traversing Cultures: On the Art and Politics of Translating Modern Japanese Fiction', *Journal of Japanese Studies* 18: 1–44.

Fowler, Roger (1981) *Literature as Social*

Discourse: The Practice of Linguistic Criticism, London: Batsford.

——(1991) *Language in the News: Discourse and Ideology in the Press*, London: Routledge.

——(1996) *Linguistic Criticism* (2nd edition), Oxford: Oxford University Press.

——, Robert Hodge, Gunther Kress and Tony Trew (1979) *Language and Control*, London: Routledge.

Foz, Clara (1988) 'La traduction-appropriation: le cas des traducteurs tolédans des 12ᵉ et 13ᵉ siècles', *TTR* 1(2): 59–64.

—— (1998) *Le traducteur, l'Église et le roi (Péninsule ibérique XIIe–XIIIe siècle)*, Ottawa: Les Presses de l'Université d'Ottawa & Arras: Artois Presses Université.

——and María Sierra Cordoba Serrano (2005) 'Dynamique historique des (re)traductions du *Quijote* en français: questions méthodologiques et premiers résultats', *Meta* 50(3): 1042–50.

France, Peter (ed.) (2000) *The Oxford Guide to Literature in English Translation*, Oxford: Oxford University Press.

Frank, Armin Paul (1992) 'Towards a Cultural History of Literary Translation. "Histories," "Systems," and Other Forms of Synthesizing Research', in Harald Kittel (ed.) *Geschichte, System, literarische Übersetzung / Histories, Systems, Literary Translations*, Berlin: Erich Schmidt, 369–87.

——and Birgit Bödeker (1991) 'Transculturality and Interculturality in French and German Translations of T. S. Eliot's *The Waste Land*', in Harald Kittel and Armin Paul Frank (eds) *Interculturality and the Historical Study of Literary Translations*, Berlin: Erich Schmidt, 41–63.

Frank, Helen T. (2007) *Cultural Encounters in Translated Children's Literature: Images of Australia in French Translation*, Manchester: St Jerome.

Frankowski, J. (1975) '"Biblia Tysiąclecia" – tło i problematyka przekładu' [The 'Millennium Bible': Background and Some Theoretical Issues], in Pollak (ed.).

Fraser, Janet (1993) 'Public Accounts: Using Verbal Protocols to Investigate Community Translation', *Applied Linguistics* 14(4): 325–43.

——(2007) 'Negotiating the Transition from Study to (Self-)employment: Automatic

Progression or Conscious Process?', paper presented at the Seventh Portsmouth Translation Conference: Translation and Negotiation.

Frawley, William (1984) 'Prolegomenon to a Theory of Translation', in William Frawley (ed.) *Translation: Literary, Linguistic, and Philosophical Perspectives*, London & Toronto: Associated University Presses, 159–75.

Freitas, Elsa Simões Lucas (2004) 'Similar Concepts, Different Channels: Intersemiotic Translation in Three Portuguese Advertising Campaigns', *The Translator* 10(2): 291–311.

Frishberg, Nancy (1990) *Interpreting: An Introduction* (revised edition), Silver Spring, MD: Registry of Interpreters for the Deaf.

Fry, Deborah (2003) *The Localization Primer*, Localisation Industry Standards Association (LISA), http://www.lisa.org/interact/LISA primer.pdf (accessed 28 August 2007).

Fry, Donald (1985) *Children Talk About Books: Seeing Themselves as Readers*, Milton Keynes: Open University Press.

Fuentes Luque, Adrián (2001) 'Estudio empírico sobre la recepción del humor audiovisual', in M. Lourdes Lorenzo and Ana M. Pereira (coord.) *El subtitulado: (inglés–español/ gallego)*, Vigo: Universidade de Vigo, Servicio de Publicacións, 69–84.

Fuentes Luque, Adrián and Dorothy Kelly (2000) 'The Translator as Mediator in Advertising Spanish Products in English-Speaking Markets', in Allison Beeby, Doris Ensinger and Marisa Presas (eds) *Investigating Translation*, Amsterdam & Philadelphia: John Benjamins, 235–42.

Furniss, Tom and Michael Bath (1996) *Reading Poetry: An Introduction*, London: Prentice Hall.

Fyodorov, A. V. (1953) *Vvedenie v teoriyu perevoda* [An Introduction to the Theory of Translation], Moscow: Izdatelstvo literatury na inostrannykh yazykakh.

——(1968) *Osnovy obshchey teorii perevoda* [Foundations of a General Theory of Translation], Moscow: Vysshaya shkola.

Gachechiladze, G. R. (1970) *Vvedenie v teoriyu khudozhestvennogo perevoda* [An Introduction to the Theory of Literary Translation], Tbilisi: Izdatelstvo TGU.

Gadamer, Hans-Georg (1960/1989) *Truth and*

Method, trans. J. Weinsheimer and D. G. Marshall, London & New York: Continuum.

——(1977) *Philosophical Hermeneutics*, translated by David Linge, Berkeley: University of California Press.

Gaddis Rose, Marilyn (1995) 'Review of *The Family Idiot*, by Jean-Paul Sartre, trans. Carol Cosman', *Comparative Literature* 47(1): 82–4.

Gailliard, Françoise (1988) 'Expolangues 1988. Traduction et adaptation publicitaires', *Traduire* 137: 11–17.

Galan, František (1988) *Historic Structures, The Prague School Project 1928–1946*, Austin, TX: University of Texas Press.

Gambier, Yves (1991) 'Travail et vocabulaire spécialisés : Prolégomènes à une socio-terminologie', *Meta* 36(1): 8–15.

——(1992) 'Adaptation: une ambiguïté à interroger', *Meta* 37(3): 421–5.

——(1994) 'La Retraduction, Retour et Détour', *Meta* 39(3): 413–17.

——(2003a) 'Screen Transadaptation: Perception and Reception', in Yves Gambier (ed.) *Screen Translation*, Special Issue of *The Translator* 9(2): 171–89.

——(ed.) (2003b) *Screen Translation*, Special Issue of *The Translator* 9(2).

——and Jorma Tommola (eds) (1993) *Translation and Knowledge: Proceedings of the 1992 Scandinavian Symposium on Translation Theory*, Turku: Centre for Translation and Interpreting.

——, Daniel Gile and Christopher Taylor (eds) (1997) *Conference Interpreting: Current Trends in Research*, Amsterdam & Philadelphia: John Benjamins.

——and Henrik Gottlieb (eds) (2001) *(Multi) Media Translation, Concepts, Practices and Research*, Amsterdam & Philadelphia: John Benjamins.

García, Ignacio (2006) 'Translators on Translation Memories: A Blessing or a Curse?', in Anthony Pym, Alexander Perekrestenko and Bram Starink (eds) *Translation Technology and its Teaching*, Tarragona: Intercultural Studies Group, 97–105.

Garcia Yebra, V. (1983) *En torno a la traducción. Teoría. Crítica. Historia*, Madrid: Gredos.

Gardiner, Alan (1973) *Egyptian Grammar, being an Introduction to the Study of Hieroglyphs*, Oxford: Oxford University Press.

Gardner, Donald (tr.) (2007) *Remco Campert: I Dreamed in the Cities at Night*, Todmorden: Arc Publications.

Gargatagli, Ana (1992) 'La traducción de América', Unpublished paper presented at 'Primer congrès internacional sobre traducció', Universitat Autónoma de Barcelona.

——and J. G. Lopez Guix (1992) 'Ficciones y teorías en la traducción: Jorge Luis Borges', *Livius* 1: 57–67.

Garzone, Giuliana (2002) 'Quality and Norms in Interpretation', in Giuliana Garzone and Maurizio Viezzi (eds) *Interpreting in the Twenty-first Century: Challenges and Opportunities*, Amsterdam & Philadelphia: John Benjamins, 107–21.

——and Maurizio Viezzi (2002) *Interpreting in the Twenty-first Century: Challenges and Opportunities*, Amsterdam & Philadelphia: John Benjamins.

Gasca, Luis and Roman Gubern (1988) *El discurso del comic*, Madrid: Catedra.

Gaudin, François (1993) 'Socioterminologie: du signe au sens, construction d'un champ', *Meta* 38(2): 293–301.

Gaussier, Eric (2001) 'General Considerations on Bilingual Terminology Extraction', in Didier Bourigault, Christian Jacquemin and Marie-Claude L'Homme (eds) *Recent Advances in Computational Terminography*, Amsterdam & Philadelphia: John Benjamins, 167–83.

Gauvin, Lise and Rainier Grutman (1996) 'Langues et littératures: éléments de bibliographie', *Littérature* 101: 88–125.

Geertz, Clifford (1973) *The Interpretation of Cultures*, New York: Basic Books.

Gelb, Ignace J. (1974) *A Study of Writing*, Chicago: University of Chicago Press.

Genette, Gérard (1982) *Palimpsestes. La littérature au second degré*, Paris: Editions du Seuil.

Gentile, Adolfo, Uldis Ozolins and Mary Vasilakakos, with Leong Ko and Ton-That Quynh-Du (1996) *Liaison Interpreting: A Handbook*, Victoria: Melbourne University Press.

Gentzler, Edwin (1993/2001) *Contemporary Translation Theories*, London & New York: Routledge; second edition published 2001, Clevedon: Multilingual Matters.

——(2002a) 'Translation, Poststructuralism and Power', in Maria Tymoczko and Edwin Gentzler (eds) *Translation and Power*, Amherst

& Boston, MA: University of Massachusetts Press, 195–218.

——(2002b) 'What's Different about Translation in the Americas?', in Keith Harvey (ed.) *CTIS Occasional Papers* 2, Manchester: Centre for Translation & Intercultural Studies, 7–17.

——(2006) 'Translation and Border Writing in the Americas: Fiction, Performance Art, and Film', in Nigel Armstrong and Federico M. Federici (eds) *Translating Voices, Translating Regions*, Rome: Aracne, 356–71.

——and Maria Tymoczko (eds) (2002) *Translation and Power*, Amherst, MA: University of Massachusetts Press.

——(2008) *Translation and Identity in the Americas: New Directions in Translation Theory*, London and New York: Routledge.

Geoffrey of Monmouth (1966) *The History of the Kings of Britain*, trans. Lewis Thorpe, Harmondsworth: Penguin Books.

Georgiev, Emil (1955) 'Sazdavaneto na Preslavskata i Ohridskata Knozhovni Shkoli v Srednovekovna Bulgaria' [The Establishment of the Preslav and Ohrida Literary Schools in Medieval Bulgaria], in the *Annual Book of Sofia University,* Sofia: Department of Philology, Nauka i Izkustvo Publishers.

Gérard, A. (1986a and b) *European-language Writing in Sub-Saharan Africa*, vols I and II, Budapest: Akademiai Kiado.

Gerloff, Pamela (1988) *From French to English: A Look at the Translation Process in Students, Bilinguals, and Professional Translators.* Unpublished doctoral dissertation, Ann Arbor: University Microfilms International.

Gerver, David (1976) 'Empirical Studies of Simultaneous Interpretation: A Review and a Model', in Richard W. Brislin (ed.) *Translation: Applications and Research*, New York: Gardner, 165–207.

——and H. Wallace Sinaiko (eds) (1978) *Language Interpretation and Communication*, New York & London: Plenum Press.

Gibbels, Elisabeth (2004) *Mary Wollstonecraft zwischen Feminismus und Opportunismus*, Tübingen: Gunter Narr.

Giddens, Anthony (1979) *Central Problems in Social Theory*, London: Macmillan.

——(1990) *The Consequences of Modernity*, Stanford, CA: Stanford University Press.

Gilbert, G. N. and M. Mulkay (1984) *Opening Pandora's Box: A Sociological Analysis of Scientists' Discourse*, Cambridge: Cambridge University Press.

Gile, Daniel (1992) 'Les fautes de traduction: une analyse pédagogique', *Meta* 37(2): 243–62.

——(1994) 'Opening up in Interpretation Studies', in Mary Snell-Hornby, Franz Pöchhacker and Klaus Kaindl (eds) *Translation Studies. An Interdiscipline*, Amsterdam & Philadelphia: John Benjamins, 149–58.

——(1995a) *Basic Concepts and Models for Translator and Interpreter Training*, Amsterdam & Philadelphia: John Benjamins.

——(1995b) *Regards sur la recherche en interprétation de conférence*, Lille: PUL.

——(1998) 'Norms in Research on Conference Interpreting: A Response to Theo Hermans and Gideon Toury', *Translation and Norms*, Special Issue of *Current Issues in Language and Society* 5(1&2): 99–107.

——(1999) 'Testing the Effort Models' Tightrope Hypothesis in Simultaneous Interpreting – A Contribution', *Hermes* 23: 153–72.

——(2000) 'The History of Research into Conference Interpreting: A Scientometric Approach', *Target* 12(2): 297–321.

——(2005) 'Teaching Conference Interpreting: A Contribution', in Martha Tennent (ed.) *Training for the New Millennium. Pedagogies for Translation and Interpreting*, Amsterdam: John Benjamins, 127–52.

Gilon, Meir (1979) *Kohelet Mussar le-Mendelssohn al reka tkufato* [Mendelssohn's *Kohelet Mussar* in Its Historical Context], Jerusalem: The Israel Academy of Sciences and Humanities.

Global Initiative For Local Computing (2007) *About GILC*, GILC, http://www.gilc.info/about.php (accessed 28 August 2007).

Godard, Barbara (1984) 'Translating and Sexual Difference', *Resources for Feminist Research* 13(3): 13–16.

——(1990) 'Theorizing Feminist Theory/Translation', in Susan Bassnett and André Lefevere (eds) *Translation: History and Culture*, London: Frances Pinter, 87–96.

Godden, M. and M. Lapidge (eds) (1991) *The Cambridge Companion to Old English Literature*, Cambridge: Cambridge University Press.

Godijns, Rita and Michaël Hinderdael (eds) (2005) *Directionality in Interpreting: the*

'Retour' or the Native?, Ghent: Communication and Cognition.

Goff, Barbara (2007) 'Antigone's Boat: The Colonial and the Postcolonial in Tegonni: An African Antigone by Femi Osofisan', in Lorner Hardwick and Caro Gillespie (eds) *Classics in Postcolonial Worlds*, Oxford: Oxford University Press, 40–53.

Goffman, Erving (1959/1971) *The Presentation of Self in Everyday Life*, Harmondsworth: Penguin.

——(1970) *Strategic Interaction*, Oxford: Blackwell.

——(1981) *Forms of Talk*, Oxford: Basil Blackwell.

Goldblatt, David (1995) 'The Paradox of Power: Globalisation and National Government in Missionary Government', *Demos Quarterly* 7: 22–30.

Golder, John (1992) *Shakespeare for the Age of Reason: The Earliest Stage Adaptations of Jean-François Ducis 1769–1792*, Oxford: the Voltaire Foundation.

Gonçalves Rodrigues, A. A. (1992) *A tradução em Portugal 1495–1834*, Lisbon: Imprensa Nacional/Casa da Moeda.

Gonda, Jan (ed.) (1975–) *History of Indian Literature*, 10 vols, Wiesbaden: Otto Harrassowitz.

González, Palencia A. (1942) *El arzobispo Don Raimundo de Toledo y la escuela de traductores* [The archbishop Don Raimundo de Toledo and the translators' school] Barcelona: Labor.

González, Roseann. (1994) 'The Federal Court Interpreter Certification Project: Defining World Class Standards for Court Interpretation', in *Proceedings of IJET 4*, Brisbane: University of Queensland.

González, Roseann, Victoria Vásquez and Holly Mikkelson (1991) *Fundamentals of Court Interpretation: Theory, Policy and Practice*, Durham, NC: Carolina Academic Press.

González Davies, María (2004) *Multiple Voices in the Translation Classroom*, Amsterdam: John Benjamins.

Goodenough, William H. (1957/1964) 'Cultural Anthropology and Linguistics', in Dell Hymes (ed.) *Language in Culture and Society*, New York: Harper & Row, 36–9.

Goodman, G. J. (1967) *The Dutch Impact on Japan (1640–1835)*, Leiden: Brill.

Goris, Olivier (1993) 'The Question of French Dubbing: Towards a Frame for Systematic Investigation', *Target* 5(2): 169–90.

Gorlée, Dinda L. (1989) 'Wittgenstein, Translation and Semiotics', *Target* 1(1): 69–94.

——(1994) *Semiotics and the Problem of Translation: With Special Reference to the Semiotics of Charles S. Peirce*, Amsterdam & Atlanta: Rodopi.

Gostand, Riba (1980) 'Verbal and Non-verbal Communication: Drama as Translation', in Ortrun Zuber (ed.) *The Languages of Theatre. Problems in the Translation and Transposition of Drama*, Oxford: Pergamon Press, 1–9.

Gotti, Fabrizio, Philippe Langlais, Elliott Macklovitch, Didier Bourigault, Benoit Robichaud and Claude Coulombe (2005) '3GTM: A Third-Generation Translation Memory', in *Proceedings of the third Computational Linguistics in the North-East (CLiNE) Workshop*, Gatineau, Québec, 26 August 2005, 8-16; http://www.iro.umontreal. ca/~felipe/Papers/paper-cline-3gtm-2005.pdf (last accessed September 2007).

Gotti, Maurizio and Susan Sarcevic (eds) (2006) *Insights into Specialised Translation*, Bern: Peter Lang.

Gottlieb, Henrik (1994) *Tekstning – Synkron billedmedie-oversættelse* [Subtitling – Synchronous Screen Translation] (DAO 5), Copenhagen: Centre for Translation Studies, University of Copenhagen.

——(1995) 'Establishing a Framework for a Typology of Subtitle Reading Strategies. Viewer Reactions to Deviations from Subtitling Standards', *Translatio* 14(3–4): 388–409.

——(1997) *Subtitles, Translation and Idioms*, Copenhagen: University of Copenhagen.

——(1998) 'Subtitling', in Mona Baker (ed.) *Routledge Encyclopedia of Translation Studies* (1st edition), London & New York: Routledge, 244–8.

——(2005) 'Multidimensional Translation: Semantics turned Semiotics', in Heidrun Gerzymisch-Arbogast and Sandra Nauert (eds) *Challenges of Multidimensional Translation. Proceedings of the Marie Curie Euroconferences. MuTra: Challenges of Multidimensional Translation. Saarbrücken,*

2–6 May 2005, MuTra: np. http://www.euro conferences.info/proceedings/2005_Proceed ings/2005_proceedings.html (accessed 10 October 2007).

Gouadec, Daniel (2002) *Profession traducteur. Alias ingénieur en communication multi-lingue (et) multimédia*, Paris: Maison du Dictionnaire.

——(2007) *Translation as a Profession*, Amsterdam & Philadelphia: John Benjamins.

Gouanvic, Jean-Marc (1997) 'Translation and the Shape of Things to Come : The Emergence of American Science Fiction in Post-War France', *The Translator* 3(2): 125–52.

——(1999) *Sociologie de la traduction: la science-fiction américaine dans l'espace culturel français des années 1950*, Arras (France): Artois Presses Université.

——(2001) 'Ethos, Ethics and Translation. Toward a Community of Destinies', in Anthony Pym (ed.) *The Return to Ethics*, Special issue of *The Translator* 7(2): 203–12.

——(2002) 'A Model of Structuralist Constructivism in Translation Studies', in Theo Hermans (ed.) *Crosscultural Transgressions*, Manchester: St Jerome, 93–102.

Gramsci, Antonio (1947/1975) *Quaderni del carcere*, Turin: Einaudi.

Gran, Laura and John Dodds (eds) (1989) *The Theoretical and Practical Aspects of Teaching Conference Interpretation*, Udine: Campanotto Editore.

——and Christopher Taylor (eds) (1990) *Aspects of Applied and Experimental Research on Conference Interpretation*, Udine: Campanotto Editore.

Green, Julien (1987) *Le langage et son double/ Language and its Shadow*, Paris: Seuil.

Greenberg, J. (1955) *Studies in African Linguistic Classification*, Bloomington, IN: Indiana University Press.

Greimas, Algirdas Julien (1966) *Sémantique structurale. Recherche de méthode*, Paris: Larousse.

Grice, H. P. (1975) 'Logic and Conversation', in P. Cole and J. L. Morgan (eds) *Syntax and Semantics, Vol. 3: Speech Acts*, New York: Academic Press, 41–58.

Griffiths, J. and D. Pearsall (eds) (1989) *Book Production and Publishing in Britain 1375–1475*, Cambridge: Cambridge University Press.

Grimes, Joseph E. (1972) *Papers on Discourse*, Dallas, TX: SIL.

Grindrod, Margaret (1986) 'Portrait of a Profession: The *Language Monthly* Survey of Translators', *Language Monthly* 29: 9–11.

Groensteen, Thierry (1999) *Système de la bande dessinée* [The System of Comics], Paris: PUF.

Grosman, Meta, Mira Kadric, Irene Kovacic and Mary Snell-Hornby (eds) (2000) *Translation into Non-Mother Tongues in Professional Practice and Training*, Tübingen: Stauffenberg.

Grutman, Rainier (1991) 'L'écrivain flamand et ses langues. Note sur la diglossie des périphéries', *Revue de l'Institut de sociologie* 60: 115–28.

——(1993) 'Mono versus Stereo: Bilingualism's Double Face', *Visible Language* 27(1-2): 206–27.

——(1994) 'Honoré Beaugrand traducteur de lui-même', *Ellipse* 51: 45–53.

——(1997) *Des langues qui résonnent. L'hétérolinguisme au XIXᵉ siècle québécois*, Montréal : Fides.

——(2002) 'Les motivations de l'hétérolinguisme: réalisme, composition, esthétique', in Furio Brugnolo and Vincenzo Orioles (eds) *Eteroglossia e plurilinguismo letterario*, Vol. 2: *Plurilinguismo e letteratura*, Roma: Il Calamo, 291–312.

——(2003) 'La question linguistique en littérature', in Jean-Pierre Bertrand, Michel Biron, Benoît Denis and Rainier Grutman (eds) *Histoire de la littérature belge (1830–2000)*, Paris: Fayard, 357–67.

——(2006) 'Refraction and Recognition: Literary Multilingualism in Translation', *Target* 18(1): 17–47.

——(2007) 'L'autotraduction: dilemme social, entre-deux textuel', *Atelier de traduction* 7: 193–202.

Guidère, Mathieu (2000a) *Publicité et traduction*, Paris: L'Harmattan.

——(2000b) 'Aspects de la traduction publici-taire', *Babel* 46(1): 20–40.

——(2001) 'Translation Practices in International Advertising', *Translation Journal* 5(1) http://www.proz.com/translation-articles/articles/276/1/Translation-Practices-in-International-Advertising (accessed 14 July 2008).

Gumbrecht, H. U. (1976) 'Literary Translation

and its Social Conditioning in the Middle Ages: Four Spanish Romance Texts of the 13th Century', trans. H. Bennett, *Yale French Studies* 51: 205–22.

Gumul, Ewa (2006) 'Explicitation in Simultaneous Interpreting: A Strategy or a By-Product of Language Mediation?', *Across Languages and Cultures* 7(2): 171–90.

Gunneson, Ann-Mari (2005) *Écrire à deux voix. Eric de Kuyper, auto-traducteur*, Bruxelles: P.I.E.-Peter Lang.

Gurnah, Abdulrazak (1996) *Admiring Silence*, New York: New Press.

——(2001) *By the Sea*, New York: New Press.

Gutas, Dimitri (1975) *Greek Wisdom Literature in Arabic Translation. A Study of the Graeco-Arabic Gnomologia*, New Haven, CT: American Oriental Society.

——(1998) *Greek Thought, Arabic Culture: The Graeco-Arabic Translation Movement in Baghdad and Early Abbasid Society (2nd–4th/8th–10th Centuries)*, London: Routledge.

Gutiérrez Lanza, Camino (2002) 'Spanish Film Translation and Cultural Patronage: The Filtering and Manipulation of Imported Material during Franco's Dictatorship', in Maria Tymoczko and Edwin Gentzler (eds) *Translation and Power*, Amherst & Boston: University of Massachusetts Press, 141–59.

Gutt, Ernst-August (1990) 'A Theoretical Account of Translation – Without a Translation Theory', *Target* 2(2): 135–64.

——(1991/2000) *Translation and Relevance. Cognition and Context* (2nd edition), Oxford: Blackwell; Manchester: St Jerome.

——(2005) 'On the Significance of the Cognitive Core of Translation', *The Translator* 11(1): 25–49.

Hadas, Moses (ed. and trans.) (1973) *Aristeas to Philocrates (Letter of Aristeas)*, New York: Ktav Publishing.

Haddour, Azzedine (in press) 'Tradition, Translation and Colonization: The Greco-Arabic Translation Movement and Deconstructing the Classics', in Aleka Lianeri and Vanda Zajko (eds) *Translation and the Classic*, Oxford: Oxford University Press.

Haight, Lyon Anne (1970) *Banned Books* (3rd edition), New York & London: R. R. Bower Company.

Hale, Sandra (1997) 'The Treatment of Register Variation in Court Interpreting', *The Translator* 3(1): 39–54.

——(2004) *The Discourse of Court Interpreting: Discourse Practices of the Law, the Witness and the Interpreter*, Amsterdam & Philadelphia: John Benjamins.

——(2005) 'The Interpreter's Identity Crisis', in Juliane House, M. Rosario Martín Ruano and Nicole Baumgarten (eds) *Translation and the Construction of Identity. IATIS Yearbook 2005*, Seoul: IATIS, 14–29.

——(2007) *Community Interpreting*, Basinstoke: Palgrave Macmillan.

Hale, Terry (2006) 'Readers and Publishers of Translations in Britain', in Peter France and Kenneth Haynes (eds) *The Oxford History of Literary Translation in English*, Oxford: Oxford University Press, 34–47.

Halkin, A. S. (1971) 'Translation and Translators, Medieval', *Encyclopedia Judaica* 15, 1318–29.

Hall, Edward T. (1959/1990) *The Silent Language*, New York: Doubleday.

Hall, Edith (2008) 'Navigating the Realms of Gold: Translation as Access Route to the Classics', in Aleka Lianeri and Vanda Zajko (eds) *Translation and the Classic*, Oxford: Oxford University Press, 315–40.

Hall, Nigel (2004) 'The Child in the Middle: Agency and Diplomacy in Language Brokering Events', in Gyde Hansen, Kirsten Malmkjær and Daniel Gile (eds) *Claims, Changes and Challenges in Translation Studies*, Amsterdam & Philadelphia: John Benjamins, 285–96.

Hallewell, L. (1982) *Books in Brazil: A History of the Publishing Trade*, Metuchen, NJ, and London: The Scarecrow Press.

Halliday, Michael A. K. (1973) *Explorations in the Functions of Language*, London: Edward Arnold.

——(1992) 'Language as System and Language as Instance: The Corpus as a Theoretical Construct', in Jan Svartvik (ed.) *Directions in Corpus Linguistics*, Berlin: Mouton, 61–77.

Halverson, Sandra (1998) *Concepts and Categories in Translation Studies*, Doctoral Dissertation, University of Bergen.

——(1999) 'Conceptual Work and the "Translation" Concept', *Target* 11(1): 1–31.

——(2003) 'The Cognitive Basis of Translation Universals', *Target* 15(2): 197–241.

——(2006) 'Cognitive Aspects of Translation

(and Bilingualism)', Plenary lecture given at the Ninth Nordic Conference on Bilingualism, Joensuu, Finland, 10–12 August.

Hamburger, Maik (2004) 'Translating and Copyright', in Ton Hoenselaars (ed.) *Shakespeare and the Language of Translation*, London: Thomson Learning, 148–66.

Hamburger, Michael (1989) 'Brief Afterthoughts on Versions of a Poem by Hölderlin', in Daniel Weissbort (ed.) *Translating Poetry: The Double Labyrinth*, London: Macmillan, 51–6.

Hamilton, J. M. and E. Jenner (2004) 'Redefining Foreign Correspondence', *Journalism* 5(3): 301–21.

Hamilton, R. (1975) *Voices from an Empire: A History of Afro-Portuguese Literature*, Minneapolis, MN: University of Minnesota Press.

Hann, Michael (1992a) *The Key to Technical Translation, Volume 1: Concept Specification*, Amsterdam & Philadelphia: John Benjamins.

——(1992b) *The Key to Technical Translation, Volume 2: Terminology/Lexicography*, Amsterdam & Philadelphia: John Benjamins.

——(2004) *A Basis for Scientific and Engineering Translation*, Amsterdam & Philadelphia: John Benjamins.

Hanna, Blake T. (1972) 'Samuel Beckett traducteur de lui-même', *Meta* 17(4): 220–24.

Hanna, Sameh (2006) *Towards a Sociology of Drama Translation: A Bourdieusian Perspective on Translations of Shakespeare's Great Tragedies in Egypt*, Unpublished PhD Thesis, Manchester: University of Manchester.

Hannay, Margaret (ed.) (1985) *Silent But for the Word: Tudor Women as Patrons, Translators and Writers of Religious Works*, Kent, OH: Kent State University Press.

Hansen, Gyde (ed.) (1999) *Probing the Process in Translation: Methods and Results*, Copenhagen Studies in Language 24, Copenhagen: Samfundslitteratur.

——(ed.) (2002) *Empirical Translation Studies. Process and Product*, Copenhagen Studies in Language 27, Copenhagen: Samfundslitteratur.

——(2005) *Störquellen in Übersetzungsprozessen. Eine empirische Untersuchung von Zusammenhängen zwischen Profilen, Prozessen und Produkten*, Copenhagen: Copenhagen Business School.

Hansson, S. (1982) *Afsatt på Swensko. 1600-talets tryckta översättningslitteratur* [Translated into Swedish. Printed Translation Literature in 17th-century Sweden], Göteborg: Litteraturvetenskapliga institutionen.

Haraszti, Z. (ed.) (1956) *The Bay Psalm Book: A Facsimile Reprint of the First Edition of 1640*, Chicago: University of Chicago Press.

Hardwick, Lorna (2000) *Translating Words, Translating Cultures*, London: Duckworth.

——(2007a) 'Singing Across the Faultlines: Cultural Shifts in Twentieth-Century Receptions of Homer', in Barbara Graziosi and Emily Greenwood (eds) *Homer in the Twentieth Century: Between World Literature and the Western Canon*, Oxford: Oxford University Press, 47–71.

——(2007b) 'Shades of Multi-Lingualism and Multi-Vocalism in Modern Performances of Greek Tragedy in Post-Colonial Contexts', in Lorna Hardwick and Carol Gillespie (eds) *Classics in Post-Colonial Worlds*, Oxford: Oxford University Press, 305–28.

——and Carol Gillespie (eds) (2007) *Classics in Post-Colonial Worlds*, Oxford: Oxford University Press.

——and Christopher A. Stray (eds) (2008) *A Companion to Classical Receptions*, Oxford: Blackwell.

Hargreaves, H. (1969) 'The Wycliffite Versions', in G. W. Lampe (ed.) *The Cambridge History of the Bible*, vol. 2, Cambridge: Cambridge University Press, 362–415.

Harrington, Frank J. and Graham H. Turner (2001) *Interpreting Interpreting: Studies and Reflections on Sign Language Interpreting*, Coleford, Gloucestershire: Douglas McLean.

Harris, Brian (1990) 'Norms in Interpretation', *Target* 2(1): 115–19.

Harris, Roy (2001) *Rethinking Writing*, London & New York: Continuum.

Harrison, Stephen J. (2008) 'Virgilian Contexts', in Lorna Hardwick and Christopher A. Stray (eds) *A Companion to Classical Receptions*, Oxford: Blackwell, 113–26.

Harun Mat Piah (ed.) (2002) *Traditional Malay Literature*, Kuala Lumpur: Dewan Bahasa dan Pustaka.

Harvey, Keith (1995) 'A Descriptive Framework for Compensation', *The Translator* 1(1): 65–86.

——(1998/2000) 'Translating Camp Talk – Gay Identities and Cultural Transfer', *The Translator* 4(2): 295–320; reprinted in Lawrence Venuti (ed.) *The Translation Studies Reader*, London & New York: Routledge, 446–67.

——(2000) 'Gay Community, Gay Identity and the Translated Text', *TTR* 13(1): 137–65.

——(2003) *Intercultural Movements: 'American Gay' in French Translation*, Manchester: St Jerome.

Harwood, Richard (1977) *Did Six Million Really Die?*, Toronto: Samisdat.

Hatim, Basil (1986) 'Discourse/Text Linguistics in the Training of Interpreters', in Wolfram Wilss and Gisela Thome (eds) *Translation Theory and Its Implementation in the Teaching of Translating & Interpreting*, Tübingen: Gunter Narr.

——(1997) *Communication Across Cultures*, Exeter: Exeter University Press.

——(1998) 'Text Politeness: A Semiotic Regime for a More Interactive Pragmatics', in Leo Hickey (ed.) *The Pragmatics of Translation*, Clevedon: Multilingual Matters, 72–102.

——(2001) *Teaching and Researching Translation*, Harlow: Longman.

——and Ian Mason (1990a) *Discourse and the Translator*, Harlow, Essex: Longman.

——(1990b) 'Genre, Discourse and Text in the Critique of Translation', in Peter Fawcett and Owen Heathcock (eds) *Translation as Performance*, Bradford Occasional Papers No. 10, Bradford: University of Bradford, 1–13.

——(1997) *The Translator as Communicator*, London & New York: Routledge.

——and Jeremy Munday (2004) *Translation: An Advanced Resource Book*, New York & London: Routledge.

Haugerud, Joann (1977) *The Word For Us. Gospels of John and Mark, Epistles to the Romans and the Galatians*, Seattle: Coalition of Women in Religion.

Hawkes, David (2003) *Ideology* (2nd edition), London & New York: Routledge.

Hayes, John R. and Linda S. Flower (1980) 'Identifying the Organization of Writing Processes', in Lee W. Gregg and Erwin R. Steinberg (eds) *Cognitive Processes in Writing*, Hillsdale, NJ: Lawrence Erlbaum Associates, 3–30.

Haynes, Kenneth (2003) *English Literature and Ancient Languages*, Oxford: Oxford University Press.

He, Chengzhou (2001) 'Chinese translations of Henrik Ibsen', *Perspectives: Studies in Translatology* 9(3): 197–214.

Healy, Michele (2002) *The Cachet of Invisibility: Women Translators of Scientific Texts in England, 1650–1850*, Unpublished PhD dissertation, Ottawa: University of Ottawa.

Hearne, Betsy (1991) 'Coming to the States: Reviewing Books from Abroad', *The Horn Book Magazine* (September/October): 562–9.

Heidegger, Martin (1942/1996) *Hölderlin's Hymn 'The Ister'*, translated by W. McNeill and J. Davis, Bloomington, IN: Indiana University Press.

——(1975) *Early Greek Thinking. The Dawn of Western Philosophy*, translated by D. F. Krell and F. A. Capuzzi, New York: Harper & Row.

Heilbron, Johan (1999) 'Towards a Sociology of Translation: Book Translation as a Cultural World-System', *European Journal of Social Theory* 2: 429–44.

——and Gisèle Sapiro (eds) (2002) 'Traduction: Les échanges littéraires internationaux', Special issue of *Actes de recherche en sciences sociales* 144; Éditions du Seuil.

Heinemann, Ute (1998) *Schriftsteller als sprachliche Grenzgänger. Literarische Verarbeitung von Mehrsprachigkeit, Sprachkontakt und Sprachkonflikt in Barcelona*, Vienna: Praesens.

Heldner, Christina (1992) 'Une Anarchiste en Camisole de Force: Fifi Brindacier ou la métamorphose française de Pippi Langstrump', *La revue des livres pour enfants* 145: 65–71.

Heller, Joseph (1961) *Catch 22*, New York: Simon & Schuster.

Heltai, Pál (2005) 'Explicitation, Redundancy, Ellipsis and Translation', in Krisztina Károly and Ágota Fóris (eds) *New Trends in Translation Studies. In Honour of Kinga Klaudy*, Budapest: Akadémiai Kiadó, 45–75.

Hema, Zane (2007) 'WASLI–Past Present Future', *The Sign Language Translator and Interpreter* 1(1): 143–56.

Henderson, Harold G. (1958) *An Introduction to Haiku*, New York: Doubleday.

Hensel, Martin (1987) 'The Nuts and Bolts', *EBU Review* XXXVIII(6): 14–15.

Herbert, Jean (1952) *Manuel de l'interprète*, Genève: Georg.

——(1978) 'How Conference Interpretation Grew', in David Gerver and H. Wallace Sinaiko (eds) *Language Interpretation and Communication*, New York & London: Plenum Press, 5–10.

Herbst, Thomas (1994) *Linguistische Aspekte der Synchronisation von Fernsehserien. Phonetik, Textlinguistik, Übersetzungstheorie*, Tübingen: Niemeyer.

——(1997) 'Dubbing and the Dubbed Text – Style and Cohesion: Textual Characteristics of a Special Form of Translation', in Anna Trosborg (ed.) *Text Typology and Translation*, Amsterdam & Philadelphia: John Benjamins, 291–308.

Herder, Johann Gottfried (2002) *Philosophical Writings*, trans. and ed. Michael N. Forster, Cambridge: Cambridge University Press.

Hermann, Alfred (1956/2002) 'Interpreting in Antiquity', translated by Ruth Morris, reprinted in Franz Pöchhacker and Miriam Shlesinger (eds) *The Interpreting Studies Reader*, London & New York: Routledge, 15–22.

Hermans, Theo (ed.) (1985a) *The Manipulation of Literature. Studies in Literary Translation*, London & Sydney: Croom Helm.

——(1985b) 'Images of Translation: Metaphor and Imagery in the Renaissance Discourse on Translation', in Theo Hermans (ed.) *The Manipulation of Literature: Studies in Literary Translation*, London & Sydney: Croom Helm, 105–35.

——(1991a) 'Translational Norms and Correct Translations', in Kitty van Leuven-Zwart and Ton Naaijkens (eds) *Translation Studies. The State of the Art*, Amsterdam & Atlanta: Rodopi, 155–70.

——(1991b) 'Translating "Rhetorijckelijck" or "ghetrouwelijck". Some Contexts of Dutch Renaissance Approaches to Translation', in J. Fenoulhet and T. Hermans (eds) *Standing Clear. Festschrift for R. P. Meijer*, London: Centre for Low Countries Studies.

——(1991c) *Studies over Nederlandse vertalingen. Een Bibliografische lijst* [Studies in Dutch Translations. A Bibliographical List], The Hague: Bibliographia Neerlandica.

——(1993) 'On Modelling Translation: Models, Norms and the Field of Translation', *Livius. Revista de estudios de traducción* 4: 69–88.

——(1995) 'Toury's Empiricism Version One: Review of Gideon Toury's *In Search of a Theory of Translation*', *The Translator* 1(2): 215–23.

——(1996) 'Norms and the Determination of Translation', in Román Alvarez and Africa Vidal (eds) *Translation, Power, Subversion*, Clevedon: Multilingual Matters, 25–51.

——(1999) *Translation in Systems: Descriptive and System-Oriented Approaches Explained*, Manchester: St Jerome.

——(2002) 'Paradoxes and Aporias in Translation and Translation Studies', in Alessandra Riccardi (ed.) *Translation Studies: Perspectives on an Emerging Discipline*, Cambridge: Cambridge University Press, 10–23.

——(2003) 'Cross-Cultural Translation Studies as Thick Translation', *Bulletin of the School of Oriental and African Studies* 66(3): 381–9.

——(ed.) (2006) *Translating Others* (Vols. 1 and 2), Manchester: St Jerome.

——(2007) *The Conference of the Tongues*, Manchester: St Jerome.

——and Ubaldo Stecconi (2002) 'Translators as Hostages of History' (17–18 April 2002) http://europa.eu.int/comm/translation/theory/seminars.htm (accessed 7 February 2004).

Hernández-Bartolomé, Ana Isabel and Gustavo Mendiluce-Cabrera (2004) 'Audesc: Translating Images into Words for Spanish Visually Impaired People', *Meta* 49(2): 264–77.

Herrick, E. M. (1975) 'A Taxonomy of Alphabets and Scripts', *Visible Language* 8: 5–32.

Hertog, Erik (ed.) (2001) *Aequitas. Access to Justice Across Language and Culture in the EU*, Antwerp: Lessius Hogeschool.

——(2002) 'Language as a Human Right: The Challenges for Legal Interpreting', in Giuliana Garzoni and Maurizio Viezzi (eds) *Interpreting in the 21st Century: Challenges and Opportunities*, Amsterdam & Philadelphia: John Benjamins, 145–57.

——(2003a) 'From Aequitas to Aequalitas: Equal Access to Justice across Language and Culture in the EU (Grotius projects 98/GR/131 and 2001/GRP/015)', in Eric Hertog (ed.) *Aequalitas: Equal Access to Justice across Language and Culture in the EU (Grotius project 2001/GRP/015)*, Amberes: Lessius Hogeschool, 6–19.

——(ed.) (2003b) *Aequalitas. Equal Access to Justice across Language and Culture in the EU. Grotius Project 2001/GRP/015*, Antwerp: Lessius Hogeschool.

——and Bart van der Veer (eds) (2006) *Taking Stock: Research and Methodology in Community Interpreting*, Special Issue of *Linguistica Antverpientia* NS 5.

Hervey, Sándor (1998) 'Speech Acts and Illocutionary Function in Translation Methodology', in Leo Hickey (ed.) *The Pragmatics of Translation*, Clevedon: Multilingual Matters, 1–24.

Hess, Stephen (1996) *International News and Foreign Corrrespondents*, Washington, DC: Brookings Institution.

Hewson, Lance and Jacky Martin (1991) *Redefining Translation. The Variational Approach*, London & New York: Routledge.

Heylen, Romy (1993) *Translation, Poetics, and the Stage: Six French Hamlets*, London & New York: Routledge.

Heyn, Matthias (1998) 'Translation Memories: Insights and Prospects', in Lynne Bowker, Michael Cronin, Dorothy Kenny and Jennifer Pearson (eds) *Unity in Diversity? Current Trends in Translation Studies*, Manchester: St Jerome, 123–36.

Hickey, Leo (1998) *The Pragmatics of Translation*, Clevedon: Multilingual Matters.

——(2001) 'Politeness in Translation between English and Spanish', *Target* 12(2): 229–40.

Hill, Harriett (2006) *The Bible at Cultural Crossroads: From Translation to Communication*, Manchester: St Jerome.

Hirano, Cathy (1999) 'Eight Ways to Say You: The Challenges of Translation', *The Horn Book Magazine* 75(1): 34–41.

Hitti, Philip (1937/1970) *History of the Arabs*, Basingstoke & London: Macmillan.

Hjelm-Milczyn, G. (1983) 'Översättarna – kulturförmedlarna' [The Translators – Intermediaries of Culture], in H. Järv (ed.) *Den svenska boken 500 år* [The Swedish Book in 500 years], Stockholm: Liber, 158–84.

Ho, George (2004) 'Translating Advertisements across Heterogeneous Cultures', *The Translator* 10(2): 221–43.

Hochel, Braňo (1990) *Preklad ako komunikácia*, Bratislava: Slovenský spisovatel.

Hodkinson, Stuart and Julie Boéri (2005) 'Social Forums after London: The Politics of

Language', *Red Pepper*. http://www.redpepper.org.uk/Jan2005/x–Jan2005-ESF.html.

Hoenselaars, Ton (ed.) (2004) *Shakespeare and the Language of Translation* (The Arden Shakespeare), London: Thomson.

——(2006) 'Between Heaven and Hell: Shakespearian Translation, Adaptation, and Criticism from a Historical Perspective', *The Yearbook of English Studies* 36(1): 50–64.

——and Marius Buning (eds) (1999) *English Literature and the Other Languages*, Amsterdam & Atlanta, GA: Rodopi.

Hoffman, Eva (1989) *Lost in Translation: Life in a New Language*, London: Heinemann.

Hofstede, Geert (1980/2001) *Culture's Consequences, Comparing Values, Behaviors, Institutions, and Organizations Across Nations*, Newbury Park, CA: Sage.

——(1991) *Cultures and Organizations, Software of the Mind. Intercultural Cooperation and its Importance for Survival*, New York: McGraw Hill.

——and Gert Ian Hofstede (2005) *Cultures and Organizations. Software of the Mind*, New York: McGraw Hill. Revised and expanded edition of Hofstede 1991.

Hokenson, Jan Walsh and Marcella Munson (2007) *The Bilingual Text: History and Theory of Literary Self Translation*, Manchester: St Jerome.

Holes, Clive (1999) 'The Koran', in Peter France (ed.) *The Oxford Guide to Literature in English Translation*, Oxford: Oxford University Press, 141–5.

Hollindale, Peter (1997) *Signs of Childness in Children's Books*, Stroud: Thimble Press.

Holmes, James S. (1972) 'The Name and Nature of Translation Studies', Unpublished Manuscript, Amsterdam: Translation Studies Section, Department of General Studies; reprinted in Gideon Toury (ed.) *Translation Across Cultures*, 1987, New Delhi: Bahri Publications; reprinted in Lawrence Venuti (ed.) *The Translation Studies Reader*, London & New York: Routledge, 172–85.

——(1978/1988) 'Describing Literary Translations: Models and Methods', in James S. Holmes, *Translated! Papers on Literary Translation and Translation Studies*, Amsterdam: Rodopi, 80–91.

——(1988) *Translated! Papers on Literary Translation and Translation Studies*, Amsterdam: Rodopi.

——(1989) 'Translating Martial and Vergil: Jacob Lowland among the Classics', in Daniel Weissbort (ed.) *Translating Poetry: The Double Labyrinth*, London: Macmillan, 57–72.

——, José Lambert and Raymond van den Broeck (eds) (1978) *Literature and Translation: New Perspectives in Literary Studies with a Basic Bibliography of Books on Translation Studies*, Leuven: Acco.

Holstein, James A. and Jaber Gubrium (2005) 'Interpretative Practice and Social Action', in Norman Denzin and Yvonna Lincoln (eds) *The SAGE Handbook of Qualitative Research* (3rd edition), Thousand Oaks: Sage, 483–505.

Holz-Mänttäri, Justa (1984) *Translatorisches Handeln. Theorie und Methode*, Helsinki: Suoma-lainen Tiedeakatemia (Annales Academicae Scientiarum Fennicae B226).

——(1986) 'Translatorisches Handeln – theoretisch fundierte Berufsprofile', in Mary Snell-Hornby (ed.) *Übersetzungswissenschaft. Eine Neuorientierung*, Tübingen: Franke, 348–74.

——(1993) 'Textdesign – verantwortlich und gehirngerecht', in Justa Holz-Mänttäri and Christiane Nord (eds) *Traducere Navem. Festschrift für Katharina Reiß zum 70. Geburtstag* (studia translatologica A 3), Tampere: Tampereen Yliopisto, 301–20.

Homem, Rui Carvalho and Ton Hoenselaars (eds) (2004) *Translating Shakespeare for the Twenty-First Century*, Amsterdam & New York: Rodopi.

Honig, Edward (1985) *The Poet's Other Voice*, Amherst, MA: University of Massachusetts Press.

Hönig, Hans G. (1995) *Konstruktives Übersetzen*, Tübingen: Stauffenburg.

——(1997) 'Positions, Power and Practice. Functionalist Approaches and Translation Quality Assessment', *Current Issues in Language and Society* 4: 6–34.

——and Paul Kußmaul (1982/1991) *Strategie der Übersetzung. Ein Lehr- und Arbeitsbuch* (4th edition), Tübingen: Gunter Narr.

Hopkins, David (2008) 'Colonization, Closure or Creative Dialogue?: The Case of Pope's *Iliad*', in Lorna Hardwick and Christopher A. Stray (eds) *A Companion to Classical Receptions*, Oxford: Blackwell, 129–40.

Horn, Maurice (ed.) (1976/1999) *The World Encyclopaedia of Comics*, New York: Chelsea.

Horner, W. B. (1975) *Text Act Theory: A Study of Non-fiction Texts*. Unpublished PhD thesis, University of Michigan.

Hornikx, Jos (2007) 'An Empirical Study of Readers' Associations with Multilingual Advertising: The Case of French, German and Spanish in Dutch Advertising', *Journal of Multilingual and Multicultural Development* 28(3): 204–19.

Horton, R. and R. Finnegan (eds) (1973) *Modes of Thought: Essays on Thinking in Western and Non-Western Societies*, London: Faber.

House, Juliane (1977/1981) *A Model for Translation Quality Assessment* (2nd edition), Tübingen: Gunter Narr.

——(1988) 'Talking to Oneself or Thinking with Others? On Using Different Thinking Aloud Methods in Translation', *Fremdsprachen lehren und lernen* 17: 84–98.

——(1997) *Translation Quality Assessment: A Model Revisited*, Tübingen: Gunter Narr.

——(1998) 'Politeness and Translation', in Leo Hickey (ed.) *The Pragmatics of Translation*, Clevedon: Multilingual Matters, 54–71.

——(2002) 'Universality versus Culture Specificity in Translation', in Alessandra Riccardi (ed.) *Translation Studies. Perspectives on an Emerging Discipline*, Cambridge: Cambridge University Press, 92–110.

——(2004a) 'Explicitness in Discourse Across Languages', in Juliane House, Werner Koller and Klaus Schubert (eds) *Neue Perspektiven in der Übersetzungs- und Dolmetschwissenschaft, Festschrift für Heidrun Gerzymisch-Arbogast zum 60*, Bochum: AKS-Verlag, 185–208.

——(2004b) 'Concepts and Methods of Translation Criticism. A Linguistic Perspective', in Harald Kittel, Armin Paul Frank, Norbert Greiner, Theo Hermans, Werner Koller, José Lambert and Fritz Paul (eds) *Übersetzung–Translation–Traduction. An International Encyclopedia of Translation Studies*, Berlin: de Gruyter, 698–718.

——(2006a) 'Text and Context in Translation', *Journal of Pragmatics* 38(3): 338–358.

——(2006b) 'Communicative Styles in English and German', *European Journal of English Studies* 10(3): 249–68.

——(2007) 'Translation Criticism: From Linguistic Description and Explanation to Social Evaluation', in Marcella Bertuccelli Papi, Gloria Cappelli and Silvia Masi (eds) *Lexical Complexity: Theoretical Assessment and Translational Perspectives*, Pisa: Pisa University Press, 37–52.

——and Shoshana Blum-Kulka (eds) (1986) *Interlingual and Intercultural Communication: Discourse and Cognition in Translation and Second Language Acquisition Studies*, Tübingen: Gunter Narr.

——and Nicole Baumgarten (eds) (2007) *Übersetzungskritik: Modelle und Methoden*, Bochum: AKS Verlag.

Howatt, A. P. R. with H. G. Widdowson (2004) *A History of English Language Teaching* (2nd edition), Oxford: Oxford University Press.

Howe, Jeff (2006) 'The Rise of Crowdsourcing', *Wired* 14(6). http://www.wired.com/wired/archive/14.06/crowds.html (accessed 3 December 2007).

Htin Aung (1957) *Burmese Drama*, Calcutta: Oxford University Press.

Huittinen, Hetta (2001) *Konferenssitulkkaus 1900-luvun euroopan poliittisissa konteksteissa* [Conference Interpreting in the Twentieth Century in the European Political Context], Unpublished MA thesis, Turku: University of Turku.

Hulme, Peter and Tim Youngs (2002) 'Introduction', in Peter Hulme and Tim Youngs (eds) *The Cambridge Companion of Travel Writing*, Cambridge: Cambridge University Press, 1–13.

Humphrey, Janice H. and Bob J. Alcorn (1996) *So You Want to Be An Interpreter? An Introduction to Sign Language Interpreting* (2nd edition), Amarillo, TX: H&H.

Humphrey, Lawrence (1559) *Interpretatio Linguarum seu de ratione convertendi et explicandi auctores tam sacros quam profanos*, Basle: H. Frobenius & N. Episcopius.

Humphreys, Christmas (1951) *Buddhism*, Harmondsworth: Penguin.

Hung, Eva (1996) 'Translation Curricula Development in Chinese Communities', in Dollerup and Appel (eds).

——(ed.) (2002) *Teaching Translation and Interpreting 4 – Building Bridges*, Amsterdam: John Benjamins.

——(2005) 'Translation in China – An Analytical Survey', in Eva Hung and Judy Wakabayashi (eds) *Asian Translation Traditions*, Manchester: St Jerome, 67–108.

——and Judy Wakabayashi (2005a) 'Introduction', in Eva Hung and Judy Wakabayashi (eds) *Asian Translation Traditions*, Manchester: St Jerome, 1–17.

——(eds) (2005b) *Asian Translation Traditions*, Manchester: St Jerome.

Hurtado Albir, Amparo (ed.) (1999) *Enseñar a traducir. Metodología en la formación de traductores e intérpretes*, Madrid: Edelsa.

Husain, S. Rashid (1981) 'Some Notable Translations Rendered into Persian during Akbar's Time', *Islamic Culture*, vol. LV(4): 219–39.

Hutchins, John (1995) 'Reflections on the History and Present State of Machine Translation', in *MT Summit V* Proceedings, Luxembourg, 10–13 July.

——(1999) 'The Development and Use of Machine Translation Systems and Computer-based Translation Tools'. Paper presented at the International Symposium on Machine Translation and Computer Language Information Processing, 26–28 June, Beijing, China http://www.foreignword.com/Technology/art/Hutchins/hutchins99.htm (accessed 23 January 2007).

——(2001a) 'Machine Translation and Human Translation: In Competition or in Complementation?', *International Journal of Translation* 13: 5–20.

——(2001b) 'Machine Translation over Fifty Years', *Histoire, Epistemologie, Langage*, Tome XXII, fasc. 1: 7–31 http://ourworld.compuserve.com/homepages/wjhutchins/hel.htm (accessed 13 December 2003).

——(2005a) 'Example-based Machine Translation: A Review and Commentary', *Machine Translation* 19(3–4): 197–211.

——(2005b) 'Computer-based Translation Systems and Tools', http://www.bcs-mt.org.uk/nala_018.htm (accessed 25 January 2007).

——(2006) 'Computer-based Translation in

Europe and North America, and Its Future Prospects', *JAPIO 2006 Yearbook*, Tokyo: Japan Patent Information Organization, 170–74. Also available from http://www.hutchinsweb.me.uk/JAPIO-2006.pdf (accessed 28 January 2007).

——and Harold L. Somers (1992) *An Introduction to Machine Translation*, London: Academic Press.

Hyun, Theresa (1992) 'Translation Policy and Literary/Cultural Changes in Early Modern Korea (1895–1921)', *Target* 4(2): 191–208.

——(2003) *Writing Women in Korea. Translation and Feminism in the Colonial Period*, Honolulu, HI: University of Hawai'i Press.

Idema, Wilt (2003) 'Dutch Translations of Classical Chinese Literature: Against a Tradition of Retranslations', in Leo Tak-hung Chan (ed.) *One into Many: Translation and the Dissemination of Classical Chinese Literature*, Amsterdam: Rodopi, 213–42.

Idh, Leena (2007) 'The Swedish System of Authorizing Interpreters', in Cecilia Wadensjö, Birgitta Englund Dimitrova and Anna-Lena Nilsson (eds) *The Critical Link 4: Professionalisation of Interpreting in the Community*, Amsterdam & Philadelphia: John Benjamins, 133–6.

IGNITE (2007) *Linguistic Infrastructure for Localisation: Language Data, Tools and Standards*, http://www.igniteweb.org (accessed 3 December 2007).

Ihenacho, A. (1985) 'Translators and Aspects of Non-Literary Translation', in H. Bühler (ed.).

——(1988) 'How can Translation Play its Role Effectively in West Africa?', in Nekeman (ed.).

Ilg, Gérard (1959) *L'enseignement de l'interprétation à l'école d'interprètes de Genève*, Genève: Ecole d'interprètes.

An Inclusive Language Lectionary (1983) Division of Education and Ministry, Westminster: National Council of the Churches of Christ in the USA & Louisville, KY: John Knox Press & Presbyterian Publishing Corporation.

Inghilleri, Moira (2003) 'Habitus, Field and Discourse: Interpreting as a Socially Situated Activity', *Target* 15(2): 243–68.

——(2005a) 'Mediating Zones of Uncertainty: Interpreter Agency, the Interpreting Habitus

and Political Asylum Adjudication', *The Translator* 11(1): 69–85.

——(ed.) (2005b) *Bourdieu and the Sociology of Translation and Interpreting*, Special Issue of *The Translator* 11(2).

——(2005c) 'The Sociology of Bourdieu and the Construction of the "Object" in Translation and Interpreting Studies', *The Translator* 11(2): 125–45.

——(2007a) 'National Sovereignty vs. Universal Rights: Interpreting Justice in a Global Context', in Myriam Salama-Carr (ed.) *Translation and Conflict*, Special Issue of *Social Semiotics* 17(2): 195–212.

——(2007b) 'Macro social theory, linguistic ethnography and interpreting research', *Linguistica Antverpiensia* NS 5: 57–68.

——(2008) 'The Ethical Task of the Translator in the Geo-political Arena', *Translation Studies* 1(2): 212–23.

Ingram, Robert M. (1992) 'Interpreter's Recognition of Structure and Meaning', in Dennis Cokely (ed.) *Sign Language Interpreters and Interpreting*, Burtonsville, MD: Linstok Press, 99–119.

International Development Research Centre (2007) *PAN Localization – A Regional Initiative to Develop Local Language Computing Capacity in Asia*, IDRC, http://www.panl10n.net/english/about-pan.htm (accessed 28 August 2007).

International Federation of Translators (n.d.) *Bylaws, Article 6*, http://www.fit-ift.org/en/bylaws.php (accessed 12 June 2007).

Inuktitut (1983) 'Writing Systems and Translations' (special issue 53), Ottawa: Minister of Indian Affairs and Northern Development.

IRNA (2005a) http://web.lexis-nexis.com/executive/?ut=1130518062484 (accessed 28 October 2005).

——(2005b) http://web.lexis-nexis.com/executive/?ut=1130518062484 (accessed 28 October 2005).

Irving, Thomas B. (Al-Hajj Ta'lim 'Ali) (1992) *The Nobel Qur'ān, Arabic Text and English Translation*, Amman, Jordan: Dar Majdalawi.

Iser, Wolfgang (1978) *The Act of Reading: A Theory of Aesthetic Response*, London: Routledge & Kegan Paul.

Isham, William P. (1994) 'Memory for Sentence

Form after Simultaneous Interpretation: Evidence both for and against deverbalisation', in S. Lambert and B. Moser-Mercer (eds) *Bridging the Gap: Empirical Research in Simultaneous Interpretation*, Amsterdam: John Benjamins, 191–211.

——(1998) 'Signed Language Interpreting', in Mona Baker (ed.) *Routledge Encyclopedia of Translation Studies* (1st edition), London & New York: Routledge, 231–5.

Ishikawa, Luli (1999) 'Cognitive Explicitation in Simultaneous Interpreting', in Alberto Álvarez Lugris and Anxo Fernandez Ocampo (eds) *Anovar/Anosar estudios de traducción e interpretación*, Vol. 1, Vigo: Universidade de Vigo, 231–57.

ISO 704 (2000) *Terminology Work: Principles and Methods*, Geneva: International Organization for Standardization.

Israël, Fortunato (ed.) (2002) *Identité, altérité, équivalence? La traduction comme relation, Actes du Colloque international tenu à l'ESIT les 24, 25 et 26 mai 2000, en hommage à Marianne Lederer*, Paris, Caen: Lettres Modernes, Minard.

——and Marianne Lederer (eds) (2005) *La théorie interprétative de la traduction*, Paris: Minard, 3 vols.

Ivarsson, Jan (2002) 'Subtitling Through the Ages. A Technical History of Subtitles in Europe', *Language International* (April): 6–10.

Ivaşcu, G. (1969) *Istoria literaturii romane* [History of Romanian Literature], Bucharest: Scientific Publishing House.

Iyer, Pico (2000) *The Global Soul: Jet Lag, Shopping Malls, and the Search for Home*, New York: Knopf.

Jääskeläinen, Riitta (1993) 'Investigating Translation Strategies', in Sonja Tirkkonen-Condit and John Laffling (eds) *Recent Trends in Empirical Translation Research*, Joensuu: University of Joensuu, Faculty of Arts, 99–119.

——(1999) *Tapping the Process: An Explorative Study on the Cognitive and Affective Factors Involved in Translating*, University of Joensuu Publications in the humanities 22, Joensuu: University of Joensuu.

——and Sonja Tirkkonen-Condit (1991) 'Automatised Processes in Professional vs. Non-professional Translation: A Think-aloud

Protocol Study', in Sonja Tirkkonen-Condit (ed.) *Empirical Research in Translation and Intercultural Studies. Selected Papers of the TRANSIF Seminar, Savonlinna 1988*, Tübingen: Gunter Narr, 89–109.

Jacobsen, Eric (1958) *Translation: A Traditional Craft*, Copenhagen: Glydendale.

Jacquemet, Marco (2005) 'The Registration Interview: Restricting Refugees' Narrative Performances', in Mike Baynham and Anna De Fina (eds) *Dislocations/Relocations: Narratives of Displacement*, Manchester: St Jerome, 197–220.

Jacquemond, Richard (1992) 'Translation and Cultural Hegemony: The Case of French–Arabic Translation', in Lawrence Venuti (ed.) *Rethinking Translation*, London & New York: Routledge, 139–58.

Jaekel, Gary (2000) 'Terminology Management at Ericsson', in Robert C. Sprung (ed.) *Translation into Success: Cutting-edge Strategies for Going Multilingual in a Global Age*, Amsterdam & Philadelphia: John Benjamins, 159–71.

Jakobsen, Arnt Lykke (1988) 'The Earliest Translations from English into Danish', in G. Caie and H. Nørgaard (eds) *A Literary Miscellany Presented to Eric Jacobsen* (PDE vol. 16), Copenhagen: Atheneum.

——(1994) *Translating LSP Texts: Some Theoretical Considerations* (Copenhagen Studies in Language 16), Copenhagen: Copenhagen Business School.

——(1999) 'Logging Target Text Production with *Translog*', in Gyde Hansen (ed.) *Probing the Process in Translation: Methods and Results*, Copenhagen Studies in Language 24, Copenhagen: Samfundslitteratur, 9–20.

——(2002) 'Orientation, Segmentation and Revision in Translation', in Gyde Hansen (ed.) *Empirical Translation Studies: Process and Product*, Copenhagen: Samfundslitteratur, 191–204.

——(2003) 'Effects of Think Aloud on Translation Speed, Revision and Segmentation', in Fábio Alves (ed.) *Triangulating Translation*, Amsterdam: John Benjamins, 69–95.

——(2005) 'Investigating Expert Translators' Processing Knowledge', in Helle V. Dam, Jan Engberg and Heidrun Gerzymisch-Arbogast (eds) *Knowledge Systems and Translation*,

Berlin & New York: Mouton de Gruyter, 173–89.

——(2006) 'Research Methods in Translation – Translog', in Kirk P. H. Sullivan and Eva Lindgren (eds) *Computer Keystroke Logging: Methods and Applications*, Oxford: Elsevier, 95–105.

Jakobson, Roman (1930) 'O překladu veršů' [On Verse Translation], *Plán* 2: 9–11.

——(1959/2000) 'On Linguistic Aspects of Translation', in R. Brower (ed.) *On Translation*, Cambridge, MA: Harvard University Press, 232–9; reprinted in Lawrence Venuti (ed.) *The Translation Studies Reader*, London & New York: Routledge, 113–18.

——(1960) 'Concluding Statement: Linguistics and Poetics', in Thomas A. Seabok (ed.) *Style in Language*, Cambridge, MA: MIT Press, 350–77.

Jansen, Hanne (2004) 'Construals in Literary Translation: Spatial Particles and Spatial Imagery'. Paper presented at the fourth EST conference, Lisbon, Portugal, September 2004.

Jansen, Peter (1995) 'The Role of the Interpreter in Dutch Courtroom Interaction: The Impact of the Situation on Translational Norms', in Peter Jansen (ed.) *Translation and the Manipulation of Discourse: Selected Papers of the CERA Research Seminars in Translation Studies 1992-1993*, Leuven: CETRA, 133–55.

Janzen, Terry (ed.) (2005) *Topics in Signed Language Interpreting*, Amsterdam & Philadelphia: John Benjamins.

Jarniewicz, Jerzy (2002) 'After Babel: Translation and Mistranslation in Contemporary British Poetry', *European Journal of English Studies* 6(1): 87–104.

Jasper, D. (ed.) (1993) *Translating Religious Texts: Translation, Transgression, and Interpretation*, London: Macmillan.

Jenks, Chris (1993) *Culture*, London & New York: Routledge.

Jenn, Ronald (2006) 'From American Frontier to European Borders', *Book History* 9: 235–60.

Jensen, M. (1995) 'Simply Reading the Geneva Bible: The Geneva Bible and its Readers', *Literature and Theology* 9(1): 30–45.

Jentsch, Nancy K. (2002) 'Harry Potter and the Tower of Babel: Translating the Magic', in Land Whited (ed.) *The Ivory Tower and Harry Potter*, Columbia, MS: University of Missouri Press, 285–301.

Jervolino, Domenico (2000) 'Herméneutique et traduction. L'autre, l'étranger, l'hôte', *Archives de philosophie* 63: 79–93.

Jettmarová, Zuzana (1997) 'The Initiator and the Initial Norm in Advertisement Translation', in Kinga Klaudy and János Kohn (eds) *Transferre necesse est*, Budapest: Scholastica, 161–6.

——(1998) 'Literalness as an Overall Strategy for Translating Advertisements in the Czech Republic', in Ann Beylard-Ozeroff, Jana Králova and Barbara Moser-Mercer (eds) *Translators' Strategies and Creativity*, Amsterdam and Philadelphia: John Benjamins, 97–105.

Jiang Wenhan (1987) *Ming Qing jian zai Hua de tianshujiao yesuhui* [Jesuits in China in the Ming and Qing Dynasties], Shanghai: Zhishi Publishing Co.

Jianzhong, Xu (2003) 'Retranslation: Necessary or Unnecesary', *Babel* 49(3): 193–202.

Johansson, Stig (1998) 'On the Role of Corpora in Cross-Linguistic Research', in Stig Johansson and Signe Oksefjell (eds) *Corpora and Cross-linguistic Research*, Amsterdam & Atlanta: Rodopi, 1–24.

Johnson, Keith (2001) *An Introduction to Foreign Language Learning and Teaching*, London: Longman.

Johnson, Kristen (1992) 'Miscommunication in Interpreted Classroom Interaction', in Dennis Cokely (ed.) *Sign Language Interpreters and Interpreting*. Burtonsville, MD: Linstok Press, 120–61.

Johnson, Samuel (1759/1963) *The Idler; the Adventurer*, edited by W. J. Bate, John M. Bullitt and L. F. Powell, Yale Edition of the works of Samuel Johnson, v. 2, London; New Haven: Yale University Press, 211–17.

Johnston, David (1996) (ed.) *Stages of Translation*, Bath: Absolute Press.

——(2007) 'Mapping the Geographies of Translation', in Stephen Kelly and David Johnston (eds) *Betwixt and Between: Place and Cultural Translation*, Newcastle: Cambridge Scholars Press, 254–68.

Jones, Derek (ed.) (2001) *Censorship. A World Encyclopedia*, London & Chicago: Fitzroy Dearborn.

——and Steve Platt (eds) (1991) *Banned*, London: Channel 4/New Statements.

Jones, Francis R. (1989) 'On Aboriginal

Sufferance: A Process Model of Poetic Translating', *Target* 1(2): 183–99.

——(2006) 'Unlocking the Black Box: Researching Poetry Translation Processes', in Manuela Perteghella and Eugenia Loffredo (eds) *Translation and Creativity: Perspectives on Creative Writing and Translation Studies*, London: Continuum, 59–74.

——and Allan Turner (2004) 'Archaisation, Modernisation and Reference in the Translation of Older Texts', *Across Languages and Cultures* 5(2): 159–84.

——and Damir Arsenijević (2005) '(Re)-constructing Bosnia: Ideologies and Agents in Poetry Translating', in Juliane House, M. Rosario Martín Ruano and Nicole Baumgarten (eds) *Translation and the Construction of Identity: IATIS Yearbook 2005*, Seoul: IATIS (International Association of Translation & Intercultural Studies), 68–95.

Jones, Michèle H. (1997) *The Beginning Translator's Workbook: or the ABC of French to English Translation*, Lanham, New York & Oxford: University Press of America.

Jones, R. F. (1966) *The Triumph of the English Language*, Stanford, CA: Stanford University Press.

Jongh, Nicholas de (2000) *Politics, Prudery and Perversion – The Censoring of the English Stage 1901–1968*, London: Methuen.

Jourdain, Amable (1843 repr. 1960) *Recherches critiques sur l'âge et l'origine des traductions latines d'Aristote et sur les commentaires grecs ou arabes employés par les docteurs scholastiques*, New York: Franklin.

Julien, Catherine (2000) *Reading Inca History*, Iowa City: University of Iowa Press.

Jumpelt, Rudolf W. (1961) *Die Übersetzung naturwissenschaftlicher und technischer Literatur: Sprachliche Maßstäbe und Methoden zur Bestimmung ihrer Wesenszüge und Probleme*, Berlin: Langenscheidt.

Jung, Verena (2002) *English–German Self-translation of Academic Texts and its Relevance for Translation Theory and Practice*, Frankfurt: Peter Lang.

——(2004) 'Writing Germany in Exile – the Bilingual Author as Cultural Mediator: Klaus Mann, Stefan Heym, Rudolf Arnheim and Hannah Arendt', *Journal of Multilingual and Multicultural Development* 25(5–6): 529–46.

Jüngst, Heike Elisabeth (2004) 'Japanese Comics in Germany', *Perspectives: Studies in Translatology* 12(2): 83–105.

Kachru, B. B. (1981) 'Kashmiri Literature', vol. viii(4) of Jan Gonda (ed.) *History of Indian Literature*, Wiesbaden: Otto Harrassowitz.

Kade, Otto (1968) *Zufall und Gesetzmäßigkeit in der Übersetzung*, Leipzig: VEB Verlag Enzyklopädie.

Kadish, Doris and Françoise Massardier-Kenney (eds) (1994) *Translating Slavery. Gender and Race in French Women's Writing, 1783–1823*, Kent, OH: Kent State University Press.

Kadric, Mira and Klaus Kaindl (1997) 'Asterix – Vom Gallier zum Tschetnikjäger: Zur Problematik von Massenkommunikation und übersetzerischer Ethik', in Mary Snell-Hornby, Zuzana Jettmarová and Klaus Kaindl (eds) *Translation as Intercultural Communication: Selected Papers from the EST Congress, Prague 1995*, Amsterdam: John Benjamins, 135–45.

Kaindl, Klaus (1999) 'Thump, Whizz, Poom: A Framework for the Study of Comics under Translation', *Target* 11(2): 263–88.

——(2004) *Übersetzungswissenschaft im interdisziplinären Dialog* [Translation Studies in Interdisciplinary Dialogue], Tübingen: Stauffenburg.

Kakridis, I. (1936) *To Metaphrastiko Provlima* [The Translation Problem], Athens: no publisher.

Kalb, Marvin (1990) 'Introduction', in Nicholas Serfaty (ed.) *Media and Foreign Policy*, New York: St Martin's Press.

Kalina, Sylvia (1998) *Strategische Prozesse beim Dolmetschen: Theoretische Grundlagen, empirische Fallstudien, didaktische Konsequenzen*, Tübingen: Günter Narr.

Kamei, S. (ed.) (1994) *Kindai Nihon no Honyaku Bunka* [Translation Culture in Modern Japan], Tokyo: Chuo Koron-Sha.

Kang, Ji-Hae (2007) 'Recontextualization of News Discourse: A Case Study of Translation of News Discourse on North Korea', *The Translator* 13(2): 219–42.

Karamitroglou, Fotios (1998) 'A Proposed Set of Subtitling Standards in Europe', *Translation Journal* 2(2). http://www.accurapid.com/journal/04stndrd.htm (last accessed on 15 July 2007).

——(2000) *Towards a Methodology for the*

Investigation of Norms in Audiovisual Translation, Amsterdam & Atlanta: Rodopi.

Karimi-Hakkak, Ahmad (1995) 'From Translation to Appropriation: Poetic Cross-breeding in Early Twentieth-century Iran', *Comparative Literature* 47(1): 53–78.

Karttunen, Frances (ed.) (1994) *Between Worlds: Interpreters, Guides, and Survivors.* New Brunswick: Rutgers University Press.

Katan, David (1999/2004) *Translating Cultures: An Introduction for Translators, Interpreters and Mediators* (2nd edition), Manchester: St Jerome.

——(2006) 'It's a Question of Life or Death: Cultural Differences in Advertising Private Pensions', in Nicoletta Vasta (ed.) *Forms of Promotion. Texts, Contexts and Cultures*, Bologna: Pàtron Editore, 55–80.

——and Francesco Straniero Sergio (2001) 'Look Who's Talking. The Ethics of Entertainment and Talkshow', *The Translator* 7(2): 213–37.

Katō, S. (1979) *A History of Japanese Literature*, vol. 1, London: Macmillan.

——(1983a) *A History of Japanese Literature*, vol. 2: *The Years of Isolation*, London: Macmillan.

——(1983b) *A History of Japanese Literature*, vol. 3: *The Modern Years*, Tokyo: Kodansha International Ltd

Kaufert, Joseph M. and W. W. Koolage (1984) 'Role Conflict among Culture Brokers: The Experience of Native Canadian Medical Interpreters', *Social Science Medicine* 18(3): 283–6.

Kaufmann, Francine (2005) 'Contribution à l'histoire de l'interprétation consécutive: le *metourguemane* dans les synagogues de l'Antiquité', *Meta* 50(3): 973–86.

Kawamura, J. (1981) *Nihongo no Sekai 15 Honyaku no Nihongo* [Translating Japanese, in The World of the Japanese Language, vol. 15], Tokyo: Chūō Kōronsha.

Kay, Martin (2000) 'Preface', in Jean Véronis (ed.) *Parallel Text Processing. Alignment and Use of Translation Corpora*, Dordrecht, Boston & London: Kluwer Academic Publishers, xv–xx.

Kearns, John (2006a) *Bibliography of Publications on Translator and Interpreter Training*, IATIS training committee. Internal document. http://www.iatis.org/content/training.php# DATABASE (accessed 7 January 2008).

——(2006b) *Curriculum Renewal in Translator Training: Vocational Challenges in Academic Environments with Reference to Needs and Situation Analysis and Skills Transferability from the Contemporary Experience of Polish Translator Training Culture*, Unpublished doctoral dissertation, Dublin: Dublin City University, Ireland.

Keenaghan, Eric (1998) 'Jack Spicer's Pricks and Cocksuckers: Translating Homosexuality into Visibility', *The Translator* 4(2): 273–94.

Keene, D. (1987) *Dawn to the West: Japanese Literature in the Modern Era*, New York: Henry Holt & Company.

Keesing, Roger (1972) 'Paradigms Lost: The New Anthropology and the New Linguistics', *Southwest Journal of Anthropology* 28: 299–332.

Keiser, Walter (2004) 'L'interprétation de conférence en tant que profession et les précurseurs de l'Association Internationale des Interprètes de Conférence (AIIC) 1918–1953', *Meta* 49(3): 576–608.

Keith, Hugh (1989) 'The Training of Translators', in Catriona Picken (ed.) *The Translator's Handbook*, London: Aslib, 163–74.

——and Ian Mason (eds) (1987) *A Text Linguistic Approach to Translation Assessment: Translation in the Modern Language Degree*, London: CILT.

Keller, Gary D. (1984) 'How Chicano Authors Use Bilingual Techniques for Literary Effect', in Eugene E. García, Francisco A. Lomelí and Isidro D. Ortiz (eds) *Chicano Studies: A Multidisciplinary Approach*, New York: Teachers College Press, 171–90.

Kelly, Dorothy (1997) 'La enseñanza de la traducción inversa de textos generales', in Miguel Ángel Vega and Rafael Martín-Gaitero (eds) *La palabra vertida. Investigaciones en torno a la traducción*, Madrid: Universidad Complutense de Madrid, 175–82.

——(2005) *A Handbook for Translator Trainers. A Guide to Reflective Practice*, Manchester: St Jerome.

——, Anne Martin, Marie-Louise Nobs, Dolores Sánchez and Catherine Way (eds) (2003) *La direccionalidad en traducción e interpretación: perspectivas teóricas, profesionales y didácticas*, Granada: Atrio.

——(2006) 'Reflections on Directionality in Translator Training', *Forum* 4(1): 57–81.

Kelly, J. N. D. (1975) *Jerome: His Life, Writings and Controversies*, London: Duckworth.

Kelly, Louis G. (1969) *25 Centuries of Language Teaching*, Rowley, MA: Newbury House.

——(1979) *The True Interpreter. A History of Translation Theory and Practice in the West*, Oxford: Basil Blackwell.

Kenner, Hugh (1970) *The Translations of Ezra Pound*, London: Faber.

Kenniston, Ken (2005) *The Unfinished Saga of the Indian Language Software*, Limerick, Localisation Research Centre, http://www.localisation.ie/resources/conferences/2005/Audio/kken.m3u (accessed 28 August 2007).

Kenny, Dorothy (2001) *Lexis and Creativity in Translation. A Corpus-based Study*, Manchester: St Jerome.

——(2006) 'Corpus-based Translation Studies: A Quantitative or Qualitative Development?', *Journal of Translation Studies* 9(1): 43–58.

——(2007) 'Translation Memories and Parallel Corpora: Challenges for the Translation Trainer', in Dorothy Kenny and Kyongjoo Ryou (eds) *Across Boundaries: International Perspectives on Translation Studies*, Newcastle-upon-Tyne: Cambridge Scholars Publishing, 192–208.

——(forthcoming) 'Translation Units and Corpora', in Alet Kruger and Kim Wallmach (eds) *Corpus-based Translation Studies: More Research and Applications*, Manchester: St Jerome.

——and Kyongjoo Ryou (eds) (2007) *Across Boundaries: International Perspectives on Translation Studies*, Newcastle-upon-Tyne: Cambridge Scholars Press.

Kenny, Mary Ann (2007) *Discussion, Cooperation and Collaboration: Group Learning in an Online Translation Classroom*, Unpublished doctoral dissertation, Dublin: Dublin City University, Ireland.

Kent, Stephanie Jo (2007) 'Interpreters: "Guardians of Social Justice?"', Paper presented at *The Critical Link 5 Conference: Quality in Interpreting: A Shared Responsibility*, Sydney, Australia, 11–15 April 2007.

Kershaw, John (1966) *The Present Stage: New Directions in Theatre Today*, London: Collins.

al-Khūry, Shihāda (1988) *Al-Tarjama Qadīman wa Hadīthan* [Translation Past and Present], Sousa, Tunisia: Dar al-Maʿārif.

Kidwai, A. R. (1987) 'Translating the Untranslatable: A Survey of English Translations of the Quran', *The Muslim World Book Review* 7(4). http://soundvision.com/Info/quran/english.asp (accessed 27 January 2008).

Kilgarriff, Adam and Gregory Grefenstette (2003) 'Web as Corpus', *Computational Linguistics* 29(3): 333–47.

——, Michael Rundell and Elaine Uí Dhonnchadha (2006) 'Efficient Corpus Development for Lexicography: Building the New Corpus for Ireland', *Language Resources and Evaluation* 40(2): 127-52.

King, Graham (1978) *Garden of Zola: Emile Zola and his Novels for English Readers*, London: Barrie & Jenkins.

King, K. (1982) *English Reformation Literature: The Tudor Origins of the Protestant Tradition*, Princeton, NJ: Princeton University Press.

King, Russell, John Connell and Paul White (1995) *Writing across Worlds: Literature and Migration*, London & New York: Routledge.

Kinloch, David (2007) 'Lilies or Skelfs: Translating Queer Melodrama', *The Translator* 13(1): 83–103.

Kiraly, Don (1990) *Toward a Systematic Approach to Translation Skills Instruction*, Unpublished PhD Dissertation, Ann Arbor, UMI.

——(1995) *Pathways to Translation: Pedagogy and Process*, Kent, Ohio & London, England: Kent State University Press.

——(2000) *A Social Constructivist Approach to Translator Education. Empowerment from Theory to Practice*, Manchester: St Jerome.

——(2005) 'Project-Based Learning: A Case for Situated Translation', *Meta* 50(4): 1098–111.

Kirchhoff, Hella (1976a) 'Das Simultandolmetschen: Interdependenz der Variablen im Dolmetschprozess, Dolmetschmodelle und Dolmetschstrategien', in Horst Drescher and Signe Scheffzek (eds) *Theorie und Praxis des Übersetzens und Dolmetschens*, Bern & Frankfurt: Peter Lang, 59–71.

——(1976b) 'Das dreigliedrige, zweisprachige Kommunikationssystem Dolmetschen', *La Langage et l'Homme* 31: 21–7.

——(1976c/2002) 'Simultaneous Interpreting. Interdependence of Variables in the Interpreting Process, Interpreting Models and Interpreting Strategies', reprinted in Franz Pöchhacker and Miriam Shlesinger (eds) *The*

Interpreting Studies Reader, London & New York: Routledge, 111–19.

Kirkov, Dimiter (1988) 'Criteria for the Appraisal of *Belles-lettres* in Translation', *Babel* 34(4): 227–31.

Kitigaki, M. (1981) *Principles and Problems of Translation in Seventeenth-century England*, Kyoto: Yamaguchi Shoten.

Kittel, Harald (ed.) (1988) *Die literarische Übersetzung: Stand und Perspektiven ihrer Erforschung* (Göttinger Beiträge zur Internationalen Übersetzungs-forschung), Berlin: Erich Schmidt.

——(ed.) (1992) *Geschichte, System, Literarische Übersetzuung / Histories, Systems, Literary Translations* (Göttinger Beiträge zur Internationalen Übersetzungs-forschung 5), Berlin: Erich Schmidt.

——and Armin Paul Frank (eds) *Interculturality and the Historical Study of Literary Translations* (Göttinger Beitrage zur Internationalen Übersetzungs-forschung 4), Berlin: Erich Schmidt.

Kittredge, Richard I. (2003) 'Sublanguages and Controlled Languages', in Ruslan Mitkov (ed.) *Oxford Handbook of Computational Linguistics*, Oxford: Oxford University Press, 430–47.

Klaudy, Kinga (1993) 'On Explicitation Hypothesis', in Kinga Klaudy and János Kohn (eds) *Transferre necesse est ... Current Issues of Translation Theory. In honour of György Radó on his 80th birthday*, Szombathely: Dániel Berzsenyi College, 69–79.

——(1996a) 'Back Translation as a Tool for Detecting Explicitation Strategies in Translation', in Kinga Klaudy, José Lambert and Anikó Sohár (eds) *Translation Studies in Hungary*, Budapest: Scholastica, 99–114.

——(1996b) 'Concretization and Generalization of Meaning in Translation', in Marcel Thelen and Barbara Lewandoska-Tomaszczyk (eds) *Translation and Meaning Part 3* (Proceedings of the Maastricht Session of the 2nd International Maastricht–Łódź Duo Colloquium on 'Translation and Meaning', held in Maastricht, The Netherlands, 19–22 April 1995), Maastricht: Hogeschool Maastricht, 141–63.

——(2001) 'The Asymmetry Hypothesis. Testing the Asymmetric Relationship between Explicitations and Implicitations', Paper presented to the Third International Congress of EST 'Claims, Changes and Challenges in Translation Studies', Copenhagen 30 August–1 September 2001.

——(2003) *Languages in Translation. Lectures on the Theory, Teaching and Practice of Translation, With Illustrations in English, French, German, Russian and Hungarian*, Budapest: Scholastica.

——and Krisztina Károly (2005) 'Implicitation in Translation: Empirical Evidence for Operational Asymmetry in Translation', *Across Languages and Cultures* 6(1): 13–29.

Klein, Menachem (2003) 'Egypt's Revolutionary Publishing Culture, 1952–62', *Middle Eastern Studies* 39(2): 149–78.

Klein-Lataud, Christine (1996) 'Les voix parallèles de Nancy Huston', *TTR* 9(1): 211–31.

Klingberg, Göte (1986) *Children's Fiction in the Hands of the Translators*, Lund: Gleerup.

Kluckhohn, Florence Rockwood and Fred L. Strodtbeck (1961) *Variations in Value Orientations*, Evanston, IL: Row Peterson.

Knapp-Potthoff, A. and K. Knapp (1987) 'The Man (or Woman) in the Middle: Discoursal Aspects of Non-professional Interpreting', in K. Knapp, W. Enninger and A. Knapp-Potthoff (eds) *Analyzing Intercultural Communication*, Berlin: Mouton de Gruyter, 181–211.

Knight, Will (2005) 'Software Learns to Translate by Reading Up', NewScientist.com, http://www.newscientist.com/article.ns?id=dn7054 (accessed 22 January 2007).

Koch, Ernst (1947) 'Functionalism in Foreign Language Teaching', *The Modern Language Journal* 31(5): 266–71.

Kochol, Viktor (1968) 'Preklad a verš', *Slovenská literatúra* 15(3): 276–88.

Kocourek, Rostislav, Michael Bishop and Lise Lapierre (eds) (1997/1998) *Le Shakespeare français: sa langue / The French Shakespeare: his language* (special issue of *Alfa*, vol. 10/11), Halifax: Dalhousie University.

Koehn, Philipp (2005) 'Europarl: A Parallel Corpus for Statistical Machine Translation', Proceedings of *MT Summit X*, Phuket, Thailand, 13–15 September 2005, 79–86.

Kohlmayer, Rainer (1988) 'Der Literaturübersetzer zwischen Original und Markt. Eine Kritik funktionalistischer Übersetzungstheorien', *Lebende Sprachen* 33: 145–56.

——(1992) 'Übersetzung als ideologische Anpassung: Oscar Wildes Gesellschaftskomödien mit nationalistischer Botschaft', in Mary Snell-Hornby (ed.) *Translation Studies: an Interdiscipline*, Amsterdam: John Benjamins, 91–101.

Kohn, János (1980) 'Momente semnificative în istoria relaţiilor culturale româno-maghiare' [Important Moments in the History of the Romanian–Hungarian Cultural Relationship], in V. Coman (ed.) *Testimonies and Evocations*, Oradea: Publishing House of the Orthodox Bishopric.

——and Kinga Klaudy (eds) (1993) *'Transferre necesse est ...' Current Issues of Translation Theory*, proceedings of a symposium in honour of György Radó, Szombathely: Dániel Berzsenyi College.

Kohn, Kurt and Sylvia Kalina (1996) 'The Strategic Dimension of Interpreting', *Meta* 41(1): 118–38.

Koller, Werner (1979/2004) *Einführung in die Übersetzungswissenschaft*, Heidelberg & Wiesbaden: Quelle und Meyer.

——(1989) 'Equivalence in Translation Theory', in Andrew Chesterman (ed.) *Readings in Translation Theory*, Helsinki: Oy Finn Lectura Ab., 99–104.

——(1993) 'Zum Begriff der "eigentlichen" Übersetzung', in Justa Holz-Mänttäri and Christiane Nord (eds) *Traducere Navem. Festschrift für Katharina Reißzum 70. Geburtstag Yliopisto* (studia translatologica A 3), Tampere: Tampereen, 49–63.

——(1995) 'The Concept of Equivalence and the Object of Translation Studies', *Target* 7(2): 191–222.

Komissarov, V. N. (1973) *Slovo o perevode* [A Word About Translation], Moscow: Mezhdunarodnye otnosheniya.

——(1980) *Lingvistika perevoda* [The Linguistics of Translation], Moscow: Mezhdunarodnye otnosheniya.

——(1990) *Teoriya perevoda* [Translation Theory], Moscow: Vysshaya shkola.

Kondo, Fumiko (2007) 'Translation Units in Japanese–English Corpora. The Case of Frequent Nouns', Paper presented at *Corpus Linguistics 2007*, University of Birmingham, 27–30 July 2007, http://corpus.bham.ac.uk/corplingproceedings07/paper/203_Paper.pdf (accessed 21 January 2008).

Kopanev, P. I. (1972) *Voprosy teorii i istorii khudozhestvennogo perevoda* [Issues of the Theory and History of Literary Translation], Minsk: Izdatelstvo BGU.

Kopczyński, A. (1980) *Conference Interpreting: Some Linguistic and Communicative Problems*, Poznań: Uniwersytet im. Adama Mickiewicza.

Köpke, Barbara and Jean-Luc Nespoulos (2006) 'Working Memory Performance in Expert and Novice Interpreters', *Interpreting* 8(1): 1–23.

Korpel, Luc (1993) 'Rhetoric and Dutch Translation Theory (1760–1820)', *Target* 5 (1): 55–70.

Korsak, Mary Phil (1992) *At the Start. Genesis Made New. A Translation of the Hebrew Text*, New York: Doubleday.

——(1994/1995/2005) 'Eve Malignant or Maligned?', *Cross Currents*, USA and http://www.maryphilkorsak.com/eve.html(accessed December 2006).

Korzybski, Albert (1933/1958) *Science and Sanity* (4th edition), Lakeville, CT: The International non-Aristotelian Library Publishing Company.

Koskinen, Kaisa (2000a) *Beyond Ambivalence: Postmodernity and the Ethics of Translation*, Tampere: University of Tampere.

——(2000b) 'Institutional Illusions: Translating in the EU Commission', *The Translator* 6(1): 49–65.

——(2004) 'Shared Culture?: Reflections on Recent Trends in Translation Studies', *Target* 16(1): 143–56.

——and Outi Paloposki (2003) 'Retranslations in the Age of Digital Reproduction', *Cadernos de Tradução* 11: 19–38.

Koster, Cees (2000) *From World to World. An Armamentarium for the Study of Poetic Discourse in Translation*, Amsterdam & Atlanta, GA: Rodopi.

——(2002) 'The Translator In Between Texts: On the Textual Presence of the Translator as an Issue in the Methodology of Comparative Translation Description', in Alessandra Riccardi (ed.) *Translation Studies: Perspectives on an Emerging Discipline*, Cambridge: Cambridge University Press, 24–37.

Kothari, Rita (2003) *Translating India: The Cultural Politics of English*, Manchester: St Jerome.

Koutsivitis, V. (1994) *Theoria tis Metaphrasis* [Theory of Translation], Athens: Greek University Publications.

Kovačič, Irena (1994) 'Relevance as a Factor in Subtitling Reductions', in Cay Dollerup and Anne Lindegaard (eds) *Teaching Translation and Interpreting 2*, Amsterdam & Philadelphia: John Benjamins, 244–51.

Kovala, U. (ed.) (1985) *Maailmankirjallisuuden ja sen klassikkojen suomentamisesta Osat 1-III* [The Finnish Translation of World Literary Classics: English summaries in vol. III], Jyväskyla: Jyväskylan yliopiston kirjallisuuden laitoksen monisteet, nos 30–32.

Kraif, Olivier (2002) 'Translation Alignment and Lexical Correspondences', in Bengt Altenberg and Sylviane Granger (eds) *Lexis in Contrast: Corpus Based Approaches*, Amsterdam & Philadelphia: John Benjamins, 271–89.

——(2003) 'From Translational Data to Contrastive Knowledge', *International Journal of Corpus Linguistics* 8(1): 1–29.

Krashen, Stephen D. (1982) *Principles and Practice in Second Language Acquisition*, Oxford: Pergamon.

Krause, Corinna (2005) 'Finding the Poem – Modern Gaelic Verse and the Contact Zone', *Forum* 1; http://forum.llc.ed.ac.uk/issue1/Krause_Gaelic.pdf (accessed on 28 December 2007).

Krebs, Katja (2007a) 'Anticipating Blue Lines: Translational Choices as Sites of (Self)-Censorship – Translating for the British Stage under the Lord Chamberlain', in Francesca Billiani (ed.) *Modes of Censorship and Translation. National Contexts and Diverse Media*, Manchester: St Jerome, 167–86.

——(2007b) *Cultural Dissemination and Translational Communities: German Drama in English Translation, 1900-1914*, Manchester: St Jerome.

Kress, Gunther (1985) *Linguistic Processes in Sociocultural Practice*, Victoria: Deakin University Press.

——and Roger Fowler (1979) 'Interviews', Chapter 4 of Roger Fowler, Bob Hodge, Gunther Kress and Tony Trew, *Language and Control*, London: Routledge & Kegan Paul.

——and Theo Van Leeuwen (1996) *Reading Images. The Grammar of Visual Design*, London & New York: Routledge.

Krings, Hans P. (1986) *Was in den Köpfen von Übersetzern vorgeht. Eine empirische Untersuchung der Struktur des Übersetzungsprozesses an fortgeschrittenen Französischlernern*, Tübingen: Gunter Narr.

——(1988) 'Blick in die "Black Box" – Eine Fallstudie zum Übersetzungsprozeß bei Berufsübersetzern', in Rainer Arntz (ed.) *Textlinguistik und Fachsprache. Akten des Internationalen übersetzungswissenschaftlichen AILA-Symposions, Hildesheim, 13-16 April 1987*, Hildesheim: Olms, 393–412.

——(2001) *Repairing Texts: Empirical Investigations of Machine Translation Post-editing*, London & Kent, OH: Kent State University Press.

Kritzeck, J. (1964) *Peter the Venerable and Islam*, Princeton, NJ: Princeton University Press.

Krogstad, Morten (ed.) *Godt ord igjen. Festskrift ved Norsk Oversetterforenings 40-årsjubileum*. Mysen, Norway: Ruuds Antikvariat Mysen.

Kroll, Judith and Anette M. B. de Groot (eds) (2005) *Handbook of Bilingualism. Psycholinguistic Approaches*, Oxford: Oxford University Press.

——and Erika Stewart (1994) 'Category Interference in Translation and Picture Naming: Evidence for asymmetric connections between bilingual memory representations', *Journal of Memory and Language* 33: 149–74.

——and Natasha Tokowicz (2005) 'Models of Bilingual Representation and Processing: Looking Back and to the Future', in Judith Kroll and Anette M. B. de Groot (eds) *Handbook of Bilingualism. Psycholinguistic Approaches*, Oxford: Oxford University Press, 531–53.

Krontiris, Tina (1992) *Oppositional Voices: Women as Writers and Translators of Literature in the English Renaissance*, London & New York: Routledge.

Krouglov, Alexander (1999) 'Police Interpreting: Politeness and Sociocultural Context', in Ian Mason (ed.) *Dialogue Interpreting*, special issue of *The Translator* 5(2): 285–302.

Kruger, Alet (ed.) (1994) *New Perspectives on Teaching Translators and Interpreters in South Africa*, Department of Linguistics, University of South Africa.

——(ed.) (2004) *Corpus-based Translation Studies: Research and Applications*, Special Issue of *Language Matters* 35(1).

Krzeszowski, T. P. (1974) 'Contrastive Generative Grammar', *Studia Anglica Posnaniensia* 5: 105–12.

Kubati, Ron (2000) *Va e non torna*, Nardò: Besa Editrice.

Kufnerová, Zlata, Milena Poláčková, Jaromír Povejšil, Zdena Skoumalová and Vlasta Straková (1994) *Překládání a čeština* [On Translating and Czech], Prague: H + H.

Kuhiwczak, Piotr and Karin Littau (eds) (2007) *A Companion to Translation Studies*, Clevedon: Multilingual Matters.

Kujamäki, Pekka (2001) 'Finnish Comet in German Skies. Translation, Retranslation and Norms', *Target* 13(1): 45–70.

——(2004) 'What Happens to "Unique Items" in Learners' Translations? "Theories" and "Concepts" as a Challenge for Novices' Views on "Good Translation"', in Anna Mauranen and Pekka Kujamäki (eds) *Translation Universals. Do they Exist?*, Amsterdam & Philadelphia: John Benjamins, 187–204.

Kulturhistorisk leksikon for nordisk middelalder fra vikingetid til reformationstid [Cultural-historical Encyclopedia of the Nordic Middle Ages from the Vikings to the Reformation], 2nd edn (1982), Copenhagen: Rosenkilde og Bagger.

Kunz, Marco (1998) 'La variedad lingüística y su traducción: sobre un pasaje de Juan Goytisolo', in Maria Antonietta Terzoli (ed.) *Colloquium zu Ehren von Germán Colón* (*Acta Romanica Basiliensia* 9), Basel: Romanisches Seminar, 35–46.

——(2005) ' "In un placete de La Mancha of which nombre no quiero remembrearme": Don Quijote en spanglish y los desafíos de la traducción bilingüe', *Linguistica Antverpiensia: NS* 4: 231–42.

Kuo, Sai-Hua and Mari Nakamura (2005) 'Translation or Transformation? A Case Study of Language and Ideology in the Taiwanese Press', *Discourse & Society* 16(3): 393–417.

Kupsch-Losereit, Sigrid (1986) 'Scheint eine schöne Sonne? Oder: Was ist ein Übersetzungsfehler?', *Lebende Sprachen* 31: 12–16.

——(2000) 'Kognitive Prozesse, Übersetzerische

Strategien und Entscheidungen', in Alberto Gil, Johann Haller, Erich Steiner and Heidrun Gerzymisch-Arbogast (eds) *Modelle der Translation: Grundlagen für Methodik, Bewertung, Computermodellierung*, Frankfurt am Main: Peter Lang, 157–76.

Kure-Jensen, Lise (1993) 'Isak Dinesen in English, Danish, and Translation: Are We Reading the Same Text?', in Olga-Anastasia Pelensky (ed.) *Isak Dinesen: Critical Views*, Athens, OH: Ohio University Press, 314–21.

Kurucz, Gy. and L. Szorenyi (eds) (1985) *Hungaria Letteraria, Europae filia* [Literary Hungary, Daughter of Europe], Budapest: The Hungarian Publishers' and Booksellers' Association (Magyar Könyvkiadók és Könyvterjesztök Egyesülete).

Kurz, Ingrid (1989) 'The Use of Video-Tapes in Consecutive and Simultaneous Training', in Laura Gran and John Dodds (eds) *The Theoretical and Practical Aspects of Teaching Conference Interpretation*, Udine: Campanotto Editore, 213–16.

——(1991) 'The Interpreter Felipillo and His Role in the Trial of the Inca Ruler Atahualpa', *Jerome* 6(4): 3–4, 11.

——(1992) 'Shadowing Exercises in Interpreter Training', in Cay Dollerup and Anne Loddegaard (eds) *Teaching Translation and Interpreting: Training, Talent and Experience*, Amsterdam: John Benjamins, 245–50.

——(1996) *Simultandolmeschen als Gegenstand der interdisziplinären Forschung*, Wien: WUV-Universitätsverlag.

——(2002a) 'Physiological Stress Responses during Media and Conference Interpreting', in Giuliana Garzone and MaurizioViezzi (eds) *Interpreting in the 21st Century*, Amsterdam & Philadelphia: John Benjamins, 195–202.

——(2002b) 'Interpreting Training Programmes. The Benefits of Coordination, Cooperation and Modern Technology', in Eva Hung (ed.) *Teaching Translation and Interpreting 4 – Building Bridges*, Amsterdam: John Benjamins, 65–72.

——(2004) 'Dolmetschen gestern, heute, morgen', in *50 Jahre Universitas – Perspektiven im 21. Jahrhundert, Sonderausgabe Universitas* 4: 22–6.

Kußmaul, Paul (1991) 'Creativity in the Translation Process: Empirical approaches', in Kitty M. van Leuven-Zwart and Ton Naaijkens (eds) *Translation Studies: The State of the Art: Proceedings from the First James S. Holmes Symposium on Translation Studies*, Amsterdam: Rodopi, 91–101.

——(1994) 'Semantic Models and Translating', *Target* 6(1): 1–13.

——(1995) *Training the Translator*, Amsterdam & Philadelphia: John Benjamins.

——(2000a) 'Types of Creative Translating', in Andrew Chesterman, Natividad Gallardo San Salvador and Yves Gambier (eds) *Translation in Context*, Amsterdam & Philadelphia: John Benjamins, 117–26.

——(2000b) *Kreatives Übersetzen*, Tübingen: Stauffenburg.

Kut, Gunay (1986) '16. ve 17. Yuzyil Turk Edebiyatina Toplu Bakis' and '18. Yuzyil Turk Edebiyatina Toplu Bakis' [Survey of 16th-, 17th- and 18th-century Turkish Literature] in *Osmanlilarda ve Avrupa'da Cagdas Kulturun Olusumu 16-18. Yuzyillar* [The Evolution of Modern Culture in Europe and the Ottoman Empire in the 16th–18th Centuries], Istanbul: Metis Yayinlari, 129–49, 263–76.

Kwan-Terry, John (1992) 'Issues in Reception Aesthetics and Literary Translation', in Barbara Lewandowska-Tomaszczyk and Marcel Thelen (eds) *Translation and Meaning*, Maastricht: Rijkshogeschool Maastricht, Faculty of Translating and Interpreting, 207–18.

Kwieciński, Piotr (2001) *Disturbing Strangeness: Foreignisation and Domestication in Translation Procedures in the Context of Cultural Asymmetry*, Toruń, Poland: Wydawnictwo EDYTOR.

Kyle, Jim G. (1986) *Cognitive processes in deaf people. Final report to the Medical Research Council.* Unpublished report. Bristol University: School of Education.

——(2007) *Sign on Television: Analysis of Data. Based on Projects Carried Out by the Deaf Studies Trust 1993-2005*, Bristol: Deaf Studies Trust.

La Bossière, Camille R. (ed.) (1983) *Translation in Canadian Literature*, Ottawa: University of Ottawa Press.

Ladd, Paddy (2003) *Understanding Deaf Culture: In Search of Deafhood*, Clevedon: Multilingual Matters.

Ladmiral, Jean-René (1979) *Traduire: théorèmes pour la traduction*, Paris: Payot.

Lagarde, Christian (2001) *Des écritures «bilingues». Sociolinguistique et littérature*, Paris, L'Harmattan.

——(ed.) (2004) *Écrire en situation bilingue*, Perpignan: Presses Universitaires de Perpignan.

Lagoudaki, Elina (2006) 'Translation Memories Survey 2006: Users' Perceptions around TM Use', in *Proceedings of the ASLIB International Conference Translating & the Computer 28*, 15–16 November 2006, London: ASLIB.

Lai, John T. P. (2007) 'Institutional Patronage: The Religious Tract Society and the Translation of Christian Tracts in Nineteenth-Century China', *The Translator* 13(1): 39–61.

Lallemand, Paul (1888) *De Parnasso Oratoriano*, Paris: Thorin.

Lamb, M. (1985) 'The Cooke Sisters: Attitudes Toward Learned Women in the Renaissance', in Hannay (ed.), 107–25.

Lambert, José (1988) 'Twenty Years of Research on Literary Translation at the Katholieke Universiteit Leuven', in Harald Kittel (ed.) *Die literarische Ubersetzung: Stand und Perspektiven ihrer Erforschung. Band 2*, Berlin: Erich Schmidt Verlag, 122–38.

——(1993) 'History, Historiography and the Discipline. A Programme', in Yves Gambier and Jorma Tommola (eds) *Translation and Knowledge: Proceedings of the 1992 Scandinavian Symposium on Translation Theory*, Turku: Centre for Translation and Interpreting, 3–25.

——and Dirk Delabastita (1996) 'La traduction de texts audiovisuals: modes et enjeux culturels', in Yves Gambier (ed.) *Les Transferts Linguistiques dans les Médias Audiovisuels*, Villeneuve d'Ascq: Presses Universitaires du Septentrion, 33–58.

——and Hendrik van Gorp (1985) 'On Describing Translations', in Theo Hermans (ed.) *The Manipulation of Literature: Studies in Literary Translation*, London & Sydney: Croom Helm.

——and Barbara Moser-Mercer (1994) *Bridging the Gap: Empirical Research in Simultaneous Interpretation*, Amsterdam: John Benjamins.

Lambourne, Andrew (2006) 'Subtitle Respeaking. A New Skill for a New Age', in Carlo Eugeni and Gabriele Mack (eds) *New Technologies in Real Time Intralingual*

Subtitling, Special Issue of *InTRAlinea* http://www.intralinea.it/specials/respeaking/eng_more.php?id=447_0_41_0_M (last accessed on 15 July 2007).

Lamping, Dieter (1992) 'Die literarische Übersetzung als de-zentrale Struktur: Das Paradigma der Selbstübersetzung', in Harald Kittel and Horst Turk (eds) *Geschichte, System, literarische Übersetzung*, Berlin: Schmidt, 212–27.

Lane, Harlan, Robert Hoffmeister and Ben Bahan (1996) *A Journey into the Deaf World*, San Diego, CA: Dawn Sign Press.

Lang, Ranier (1976) 'Interpreters in Local Courts in Papua New Guinea', in W. M. O'Barr and J. F. O'Barr (eds) *Language and Politics*, The Hague/Paris: Mouton, 327–65.

——(1978) 'Behavioral Aspects of Liaison Interpreters in Papua New Guinea: Some Preliminary Observations', in D. Gerver and H. W. Sinaiko (eds) *Language Interpretation and Communication*, New York and London: Plenum, 231–44.

Langacker, Ronald (1987) *Foundations of Cognitive Grammar. Volume I. Theoretical Prerequisites*, Stanford, CA: Stanford University Press.

Language Technologies Institute at Carnegie Mellon University (2004) 'The (2004) LTI Projects', http://www.lti.cs.cmu.edu/research/cmt-projects.html (accessed 2 March 2006).

Lapucci, Carlo (1983) *Dal volgarizzamento alla traduzione*, Florence: Valmartina.

Larbaud, V. (1946) *Sous l'invocation de Saint Jérôme*, Paris: Gallimard.

Larkosh, Chris (1996) *The Limits of the Translatable Foreign: Fictions of Translation, Migration and Sexuality in 20th Century Argentine Literature*, Unpublished PhD dissertation, University of California Berkeley.

——(2004) 'Levinas, Latin American Thought and the Futures of Translational Ethics', *TTR* 17(2): 27–44.

——(2006) '"Writing in the Foreign": Migrant Sexuality and Translation of the Self in Manuel Puig's Later Work', *The Translator* 12(2): 1–21.

Larose, Robert (1989) *Théories contemporaines de la traduction* (2nd edition), Quebec: Presses de l'Université du Québec.

Laster, K. and V. Taylor (1994) *Interpreters and the Legal System*, Sydney: Federation Press.

Lathey, Gillian (2006a) 'The Translator Revealed: Didacticism, Cultural Mediation and Visions of the Child Reader', in Jan Van Coillie and Walter P. Verschueren (eds) *Children's Literature in Translation: Challenges and Strategies*, Manchester: St Jerome, 1–18.

——(2006b) *Translation for Children: A Reader*, Clevedon: Multilingual Matters.

——(forthcoming) *Invisible Storytellers: The Role of Translators in the History of English-language Children's Literature*, New York & London: Routledge.

Latour, Bruno (1979/1986) *Laboratory Life: The Construction of Scientific Facts*, Princeton, NJ: Princeton University Press.

——(1987) *Science in Action: How to Follow Scientists and Engineers through Society*, Cambridge, MA: Harvard University Press

——(2005) *Reassembling the Social: An Introduction to Actor-Network Theory*, Oxford: Oxford University Press.

Latyshev, L. K. (1988) *Perevod: problemy teorii, praktiki i metodiki prepodavaniya* [Translation: Problems of Theory, Practice and Teaching Methodology], Moscow: Prosveshchenie.

Laukkanen, Johanna (1993) *Routine vs. Non-routine Processes in Translation: A Think-aloud Protocol Study*. Uunpublished pro graduation thesis, University of Joensuu, Savonlinna School of Translation Studies.

——(1997) *Affective Factors and Task Performance in Translation*. Unpublished licentiate thesis, University of Joensuu, Savonlinna School of Translation Studies.

Lavigne, Claire-Hélène (2004) 'La traduction en vers des *Institutes* de Justinien 1er: mythes, réalités et entreprise de versification', *Meta* 49(3): 511–25.

Laviosa, Sara (1997) 'How Comparable Can "Comparable Corpora" Be?', *Target* 9(2): 289–319.

——(1998a) 'The English Comparable Corpus: A Resource and a Methodology', in Lynne Bowker, Michael Cronin, Dorothy Kenny and Jennifer Pearson (eds) *Unity in Diversity? Current Trends in Translation Studies*, Manchester: St Jerome, 101–12.

——(1998b) 'Core Patterns of Lexical Use in a Comparable Corpus of English Narrative Prose', in Sara Laviosa (ed.) *L' Approche basée sur le corpus/The Corpus-Based Approach*, Special Issue of *Meta* 43(4): 557–70.

——(ed.) (1998c) *L' Approche basée sur le corpus/ The Corpus-Based Approach*, Special Issue of *Meta*, Vol. 43(4). Available at http://www.erudit.org/revue/meta/.

——(2002) *Corpus-based Translation Studies: Theory, Findings, Applications*, Amsterdam & New York: Rodopi.

——(2007) 'Learning Creative Writing by Translating Witty Ads', *The Interpreter and Translator Trainer (ITT)* 1(2): 197–222.

Lawrence, D. H. (1960) *Women in Love*, Harmondsworth: Penguin.

——(1974) *Love (Femmes amoureuses)*, trans. Maurice Rancès and Georges Limbour, Paris: Gallimard.

Laygues, Arnaud (2004) 'La traducteur semeur d'éthique. Pour une application de la pensée d'Emmanuel Levinas à la traduction', *TTR* 17(2): 45–56.

Lecercle, Jean-Jacques (1990) *The Violence of Language: Interpretation as Pragmatics*, London: Palgrave.

Lecuona, Lourdes (1994) 'Entre el doblaje y la subtitulación: la interpretación simul-tánea en el cine', in Federico Eguíluz, Raquel Merino, Vickie Olsen, Eterio Pajares and José Miguel (eds) *Trasvases culturales: literatura, cine, traducción*, Vitoria: Universidad del País Vasco, 279–86.

Lederer, Marianne (1981) *La traduction simul-tanée – expérience et théorie*, Paris: Lettres Modernes.

——(ed.) (1990) *Etudes traductologiques, en hommage à Danica Seleskovitch*, Paris: Lettres Modernes Minard.

——(1993) 'Fondements de la théorie inter-prétative de la Traduction', in Catriona Picken (ed.) *Translation, The Vital Link*, Proceedings of the XIIIth FIT World Congress, vol.1, London: Institute of Translation and Interpreting, 632–41.

——(1994) *La traduction aujourd'hui*, Paris: Hachette.

——(2003) *Translation, the Interpretive Model*, translation of *La traduction aujourd'hui*, trans. Ninon Larché, Manchester: St Jerome.

——(2007) 'Can Theory Help Interpreter and Translator Trainers and Trainees?', *The Interpreter and Translator Trainer* 1(1): 15–36.

——and Fortunato Israël (eds) (1991) *La liberté en traduction*, Proceedings of the International Conference held at ESIT, Paris, June 1990, collection Traductologie no. 7, Paris: Didier-Erudition.

Lee, D. (1992) *Competing Discourses: Perspective and Ideology in Language*, London: Longman.

Lee, Seung-Jae, Cho-Lim Sung, Gye-Yon Lee, Hyang Lee, Young-Jin Kim, Hyun-Joo Jang, Sang-Won Lee and Sang-Eun Cho (2000) 'Kwuknay Kongkongkikwanuy Benyek Hyenhwang' [The Present Situation of Translation in Korean Public Organizations], *Penyekhak Yenkwu/The Journal of Translation Studies* 2(2): 57–107.

Lee, Tae-Hyung (2000) 'Temporal Aspects of Live Simultaneous Interpretation on TV: A Case of Academy Award Ceremonies', *Conference Interpretation and Translation* 2: 85–110.

Lee, Tzu-Yi (in progress) *The Translation of Race and Gender in Alice Walker's 'The Color Purple'*, Unpublished PhD thesis, Newcastle: Newcastle University.

Lee-Jahnke, Hannelore (ed.) (2001) *Evaluation: Parameters, Methods, Pedagogical Aspects*, Special Issue of *Meta* 46(2): 205–447.

——(2006) 'Le traducteur, passeur entre les cultures', in Martin Forstner and Hannelore Lee-Jahnke (eds) *CIUTI Forum Paris 2005: Regards sur les aspects culturels de la commu-nication*, Bern: Peter Lang, 61–86.

Leech, G. (1983) *Principles of Pragmatics*, London: Longman.

——(1992) 'Pragmatic Principles in Shaw's *You Never Can Tell*', in Michael Toolan (ed.) *Language, Text and Context: Essays in Stylistics*, London: Routledge.

Leeson, Lorraine (2001) 'The Provision of Sign Language Interpreters at European Institution Meetings. Some Points for Consideration'. Unpublished paper, Brussels: European Union of the Deaf.

——(2005a) 'Making the Effort in Simultaneous Interpreting', in Terry Janzen (ed.) *Topics in Signed Language Interpreting*, Amsterdam & Philadelphia: John Benjamins, 51–68.

——(2005b) 'Vying with Variation: Interpreting Language Contact, Gender Variation and Generational Difference', in Terry Janzen (ed.) *Topics in Signed Language Interpreting*,

Amsterdam & Philadelphia: John Benjamins, 251–92.

——and Susan Foley-Cave (2008) 'Deep and Meaningful Conversation: Interpreter Impartiality in the Semantics and Pragmatics Classroom', in Melanie Metzger and Earl Fleetwood (eds) *Translation, Sociolinguistic & Consumer Issues in Interpreting*, Washington, DC: Gallaudet University Press, 45–68.

——, John Saeed, Alison Macduff, Deirdre Byrne-Dunne and Cormac Leonard (2006) 'Moving Heads and Moving Hands: Developing a Digital Corpus of Irish Sign Language', Paper presented at the *Information Technology and Telecommunications Conference 2006*, Carlow, Ireland, 25–26 October 2006.

Leezenberg, Michiel (2004) 'Katharsis, Greek and Arab Style. On Averroes's Misunderstanding of Aristotle's Misunderstanding of Tragedy', in Freddy Decreus and Mieke Kolk (eds) *Re-reading Classics in 'East' and 'West'*, *Documenta* XXll(4): 300–15.

Lefevere, André (1975) *Translating Poetry: Seven Strategies and a Blueprint*, Assen: van Gorcum.

——(ed.) (1977) *Translating Literature: The German Tradition*, Assen: van Gorcum.

——(1981) 'Beyond the Process: Literary Translation in Literature and Literary Theory', in Marilyn Gaddis Rose (ed.) *Translation Spectrum: Essays in Theory and Practice*, Albany, NY: SUNY Press, 52–9.

——(1982/2000) 'Mother Courage's Cucumbers: Text, System and Refraction in a Theory of Literature', in Lawrence Venuti (ed.) *Translation Studies Reader*, London: Routledge, 233–49.

——(1983a) 'Voltaire, Shakespeare, Julius César et la traduction', *Équivalences* 14(2/3): 19–28.

——(1983b) 'Poetics (Today) and Translation (Studies)', in Daniel Weissbort (ed.) *Modern Poetry in Translation*, London & Manchester: MPT/Carcanet, 190–5.

——(1984) 'On the Refraction of Texts', in Mihai Spariosu (ed.) *Mimesis in Contemporary Theory: An Interdisciplinary Approach. Volume I: The Literary and Philosophical Debate*, Philadelphia: John Benjamins, 217–37.

——(1985) 'Why Waste Our Time on Rewrites? The Trouble With Interpretation and the Role of Rewriting in an Alternative Paradigm', in Theo Hermans (ed.) *The Manipulation of Literature. Studies in Literary Translation*, London & Sydney: Croom Helm, 215–43.

——(1987) ' "Beyond Interpretation" or the Business of (Re)Writing', *Comparative Literature Studies* 24(1): 17–39.

——(1992a) *Translation, Rewriting and the Manipulation of Literary Fame*, London & New York: Routledge.

——(ed.) (1992b) *Translation/History/Culture: A Sourcebook*, London & New York: Routledge.

——(1995) 'The Word in Two Languages: On Translating Hybrid Texts', in Henri Bloemen, Erik Hertog and Winibert Segers (eds) *Letterlijkheid Woordelijkheid/Literality Verbality*, Antwerp & Harmelen: Fantom, 223–33.

——(1998a) 'Chinese and Western Thinking on Translation', in Susan Bassnett and André Lefevere (eds) *Constructing Cultures: Essays on Literary Translation*, Clevedon: Multilingual Matters, 12–24.

——(1998b) 'Translation Practice(s) and the Circulation of Cultural Capital. Some Aeneids in English', in Susan Bassnett and André Lefevere (eds) *Constructing Cultures: Essays on Literary Translation*, Clevedon: Multilingual Matters, 41–56.

——and Susan Bassnett (1990) 'Introduction: Proust's Grandmother and the Thousand and One Nights: The "Cultural Turn" in Translation Studies', in Susan Bassnett and André Lefevere (eds) *Translation, History and Culture*, London & New York: Pinter, 1–13.

Léger, Benoit (2004) 'Nouvelles aventures de Gulliver à blefuscu: traductions, retraductions et rééditions des *Voyages de Gulliver* sous la monarchie de Juillet', *Meta* 49(3): 526–43.

Legge, M. Dominica (1963) *Anglo-Norman Literature and Its Background*, Oxford: Oxford University Press (repr. 1978, Westport, CT: Greenwood Press).

Lehto, L. (1986) 'The Finnish Literature Fund (1908–)', Prague: *Acta Universitatis Carolinae – Philologica* 1–3: 285–313.

Leighton, Lauren (1991) *Two Worlds, One Art: Literary Translation in Russia and America*, Dekalb, IL: Northern Illinois Press.

Lemay, R. (1963) 'Dans l'Espagne du xiie siècle. Les traductions de l'arabe au latin', *Annales Économies, Sociétés, Civilisations* 18(4): 639–65.

Lenkei, H. (1911) *Petőfi a világirodalomban* [Petőfi in World Literature], Budapest: Kunossy.

León-Portilla, Miguel (2003) *Códices. Los antiguos libros del Nuevo Mundo*, Mexico: Aguilar.

Leppihalme, Ritva (2000) 'The Two Faces of Standardization: On the Translation of Regionalisms in Literary Dialogue', *The Translator* 6(2): 247–69.

Leskien, A. (1903) 'Der Überzelonyskunst des Exarchen Johannes', *Archiv für slavische Philologie*, vol. 25.

Lévi-Strauss, Claude (1949) *Les structures élémentaires de la parenté*, Paris: Presses Universitaires de France.

Leviant, Curt (1969) *King Artus: A Hebrew Arthurian Romance of 1279*, New York: Ktav.

Levinas, Emmanuel (1989) 'Ethics as First Philosophy', in *The Levinas Reader*, edited by S. Hand, Oxford: Blackwell, 75–87.

Levine, Suzanne Jill (1991) *The Subversive Scribe: Translating Latin American Fiction*, St Paul, MN: Graywolf Press.

Levinsohn, Stephen H. (1987) *Textual Connections in Acts*, Atlanta, GA: Scholars Press.

——(2000) *Discourse Features of New Testament Greek: A coursebook on the information structure of New Testament Greek* (2nd edition) Dallas, TX: SIL International.

Levy, C. J. (1991) 'The Growing Gelt in Others' Words', *The New York Times*, 20 October, F5.

Levý, Jiří (1957) *Česke teorie překladu* [Czech Theories of Translation], Prague: SNKL.

——(1963) *Umění překladu*, Prague: Československý spisovatel. Trans. by W. Schamschula as *Die literarische Übersetzung. Theorie einer Kunstgattung*, Frankfurt and Bonn: Athenäum Verlag, 1969; 2nd edn, *Uměni překladu*, Prague: Panorama, 1983.

——(1969) *Die literarische Übersetzung. Theorie einer Kunstgattung*, trans. W. Schamschula, Frankfurt am Main: Athenäum.

Levy, Lital (2003) 'Exchanging Words: Thematization of Translation in Arabic Writing from Israel', *Comparative Studies of South Asia, Africa and the Middle East* 23(1–2): 106–27.

Lewis, Bernard (1962) *The Emergence of Modern Turkey*, London and New York: Oxford University Press.

Lewis, Philip (1985) 'The Measure of Translation Effects', in Joseph Graham (ed.) *Difference in Translation*, Ithaca, NY: Cornell University Press, 31–62.

L'Homme, Marie-Claude (2004) *La terminologie: principes et techniques*, Montréal : Les Presses de l'Université de Montréal.

Li, Jessica Tsui Yan (2006) 'Politics of Self-Translation: Eileen Chang', *Perspectives: Studies in Translatology* 14(2): 99–106.

Li, Sher-shiueh (2000) 'Stories Reinterpreted: The Jesuit Appropriation of Aesopic Fables in Late-Ming China' (in Chinese), *Chung Wai Literary Monthly* 29(5): 238–77.

——(2001) '*Exemplum* and *Apadana*: Buddhist Influences on the Chinese Writings of Late-Ming Jesuits' (in Chinese), *Bulletin of the Institute of Chinese Literature and Philosophy, Academia Sinica* 19: 451–97.

Lianeri, Alexandra and Vanda Zajko (eds) (in press) *Translation and the Classic*, Oxford: Oxford University Press.

Liddell, Scott K. (2003) *Grammar, Gesture and Meaning in American Sign Language*, Cambridge: Cambridge University Press.

Limbeck, Sven (1999) 'Plautus in der Knabenschule', in Dirk Linck (ed.) *Erinnern und Wiederentdecken: Tabuisierung und Enttabuisierung der männlichen und weiblichen Homosexualität in Wissenschaft und Kritik*, Berlin: Verlag Rosa Winkel, 15–68.

Lindberg, David C. (1978) 'The Transmission of Greek and Arabic Learning to the West', in Lindberg (ed.) *Science in the Middle Ages*, Chicago and London: The University of Chicago Press, 52–90.

Lindsay, Jennifer (ed.) (2006) *Between Tongues: Translation and/of/in Performance in Asia*, Singapore: Singapore University Press.

Littau, Karin (2000) 'Pandora's Tongues', *TTR* 13(1): 21–35.

Liu, Lydia H. (1995) *Translingual Practice: Literature, National Culture, and Translated Modernity: China, 1900-1937*, Stanford, CA: Stanford University Press.

——(1999) 'Legislating the Universal: The circulation of international law in the nineteenth century', in Lydia Liu (ed) *Tokens of Exchange: The problem of translation in global circulations*, Durham, NC: Duke University Press, 127–64.

Liu, Minhua (2001) *Expertise in Simultaneous*

Interpreting: A Working Memory Analysis, Doctoral dissertation, University of Texas at Austin.

Liu, Zhuo 刘倬. (2002) 'Jiqi fanyi de fazhan he tupo' [机器翻译的发展和突破] [Machine translation: developments and breakthroughs], in Huang Heyan 黄河燕 主编 (ed.) *Jiqi Fanyi Yanjiu Jinzhan Nian Quanguo Jiqi Fanyi Yantaohui Lunwenji* [《机器翻译研究进展——2002年全国机器翻译研讨会论文集》] [Progress in the Research of Machine Translation. Proceedings of the National Machine Translation Symposium], Beijing: The Publishing House of Electronics Industry, 1–6.

Livbjerg, Inge and Inger M. Mees (2003) 'Patterns of Dictionary Use in Non-domain-specific Translation', in Fábio Alves (ed.) *Triangulating Translation. Perspectives in Process Oriented Research*, Amsterdam & Philadelphia: John Benjamins, 123–36.

Localisation Research Centre (2003–6) *Localisation Reader*, Localisation Research Centre, Limerick, http://www.localisation. ie/resources/reader/reader.htm (accessed 28 August 2007).

Locke, Nancy A. (2003) 'New Organizations Serve the Localization Industry', *Multilingual Computing & Technology* 14: 34–8.

Locker McKee, Rachel (ed.) (2006) *Proceedings of the Inaugural Conference of the World Association of Sign Language Interpreters*, Worcester, South Africa, 31 October–2 November 2005, Coleford, Gloucestershire: Douglas McLean.

Logie, Ilse (2003) 'Plurilinguismo y traducción en la obra de Julio Cortázar', *Ciberletras* 10. http://www.lehman.cuny.edu/ciberletras/ v10/logie.htm (accessed 28 December 2007).

Lomheim, Sylfest (1989) *Omsetjingsteori* [Translation Theory], Oslo: Universitets Forlag.

Longacre, Robert (1989) *Joseph: A Story of Divine Providence. A Text Theoretical and Textlinguistic Analysis of Genesis 37 and 39–48*, Dallas, TX: SIL.

——(1996) *The Grammar of Discourse* (2nd edition), New York: Plenum.

Lorentsen, A., L. Mogensen and A. Fausing (1985) *Oversættelse og ny teknologi* [Translation and New Technology], Ålborg: Ålborg Universitets forlag.

Lorenzo, María Pilar (1999) 'La seguridad del traductor profesional en la traducción a una lengua extranjera', in Gyde Hansen (ed.) *Probing the Process in Translation: Methods and Results*, Copenhagen: Copenhagen Studies in Language 27, 85–124.

——(2003) 'La traducción a una lengua extranjera: una de los muchos desafíos a la competencia traductora', in Dorothy Kelly, Anne Martin, Marie-Louise Nobs, Dolores Sánchez and Catherine Way (eds) *La direccionalidad en traducción e interpretación: perspectivas teóricas, profesionales y didácticas*, Granada: Atrio, 93–116.

Lörscher, Wolfgang (1991) *Translation Performance, Translation Process and Translation Strategies: A Psycholinguistic Investigation*, Tübingen: Gunter Narr.

——(1993) 'Translation Process Analysis', in Yves Gambier and Jorma Tommola (eds) *Translation and Knowledge, SSOTT IV. Scandinavian Symposium on Translation Theory, Turku, 4–6.6. 1992*, Turku: University of Turku, Centre for Translation and Interpreting.

——(2005) 'The Translation Process: Methods and Problems of its Investigation', *Meta* 50(2): 597–608.

Lotman, Juri (2005) 'On the Semiosphere', *Sign Systems Studies* 33(1): 205–29.

Lowell, Robert (1958/1990) *Imitations*, New York: Farrar, Straus & Giroux.

Luhmann, Niklas (1985) *A Sociological Theory of Law*, London: Routledge & Kegan Paul.

——(1995) *Social Systems*, trans. John Bednarz, Stanford, CA: Stanford University Press (German original 1984).

——(2006) 'System as Difference', *Organisation* 13(1): 37–57.

Lung, Rachel and Donghui Li (2005) 'Interpreters as Historians in China', *Meta* 50(3): 997–1009.

Luyken, Georg-Michael, Thomas Herbst, Jo Langham-Brown, Helen Reid and Hermann Spinhof (1991) *Overcoming Language Barriers in Television. Dubbing and Subtitling for the European Audience*, Manchester: European Institute for the Media.

Lyons, John (1968) *Introduction to Theoretical Linguistics*, Cambridge: Cambridge University Press.

Ma Zuyi (1984) *Zhongguo fanyi jianshi* [A Brief

History of Translation in China], Beijing: Zhongguo duiwai Pub. Co.

Mack, Gabriele (2002) 'New Perspectives and Challenges for Interpretation. The Example of Television', in Giuliana Garzone and Maurizio Viezzi (eds) *Interpreting in the 21st Century*, Amsterdam & Philadelphia: John Benjamins, 203–13.

Mackenzie, Rosemary (2004) 'The Competencies Required by the Translator's Roles as Professional', in Kirsten Malmkjær (ed.) *Translation in Undergraduate Degree Programmes*, Amsterdam & Philadelphia: John Benjamins, 31–8.

Macklovitch, Elliott and Graham Russell (2000) 'What's Been Forgotten in Translation Memory', in John S. White (ed.) *Envisioning Machine Translation in the Information Future*, Mexico: Springer, 137–46.

Maffei, Scipione (1720) *Traduttori italiani, o sia notizia de' volgarizzamenti d'antichi scrittori latini e greci*, Venice: Sebastian Coleti.

Mahn, Gabriela (1988) 'Dialogue and Understanding: A Hermeneutical Approach to Translation', in Marilyn Gaddis Rose (ed.) *Translation Perspectives IV*, Binghamton, NY: National Resource Centre for Translation and Interpretation, 18–26.

Maier, Carol (1990–91) 'Reviewing Latin American Literature in Translation: Time to "Proceed to the Larger Questions"', *Translation Review* 34/35: 18–24.

——(1998) 'Issues in the Practice of Translating Women's Fiction', *Bulletin of Hispanic Studies* LXXV: 95–108.

——(ed.) (2000) *Evaluation and Translation*, Special issue of *The Translator* 6(2).

——(2006) 'The Translator as *Theorôs*: Thoughts on Cogitation, Figuration and Current Creative Writing', in Theo Hermans (ed.) *Translating Others I*, Manchester: St Jerome, 163–80.

——(2007) 'The Translator's Visibility: The Rights and Responsibilities Thereof', in Myriam Salama-Carr (ed.) *Translating and Interpreting Conflict*, Amsterdam: Rodopi, 255–66.

Maillot, Jean (1981) *La traduction scientifique et technique* (2nd edition), Paris: Technique et documentation.

Maitiniyazi, Rezhake (1994) *A History of Translation in Central Asia* (in Chinese), Urumqi: Xinjiang University Publishers.

Majamaa, R. (1991) 'Reunamerkintöjen historiaa eli kääntämisen historia 1800-luvulta lähtien' [Notes on Finnish Translation History from the Nineteenth Century], in I. Sorvali (ed.) *Käännöstutkimuksen suunnittelu-ja neuvottelupäivät, Oulu 5–6.3.1991* [Translation Research Planning Seminar, Oulu, 5–6 March 1991], Oulu: Oulun Yliopisto, Pohjoismaisten kielten laitos.

Malachi, Zvi (ed.) (1981) *Amadis de Gaula: Hebrew Translation by the Physician Jacob do Algaba, First Published in Constantinople, c. 1541*, Tel Aviv: Tel Aviv University.

Malena, Anne (ed.) (2003) *Traduction et (Im)migration/Translation and (Im)migration*, Special Issue of *TTR* 16(2).

Malmkjær, Kirsten (1992) 'Review of Translation and Relevance by E. A. Gutt', *Mind & Language* 7(3): 298–309.

——(1998a) 'Unit of Translation', in Mona Baker (ed.) *Routledge Encyclopedia of Translation Studies* (1st edition), London & New York: Routledge, 286–8.

——(1998b) 'Cooperation and Literary Translation', in Leo Hickey (ed.) *The Pragmatics of Translation*, Clevedon: Multilingual Matters, 25–40.

——(2000) 'Multidisciplinarity in Process Research', in Sonja Tirkkonen-Condit and Riitta Jääskeläinen (eds) *Tapping and Mapping the Process of Translation and Interpreting*, Amsterdam & Philadelphia: John Benjamins, 163–70.

——(ed.) (2004) *Translation in Undergraduate Degree Programmes*, Amsterdam: John Benjamins.

——(2005a) *Linguistics and the Language of Translation*, Edinburgh: Edinburgh University Press.

——(2005b) 'Translation and Linguistics', *Perspectives: Studies in Translatology* 13(1): 5–20.

Malone, Joseph L. (1988) *The Science of Linguistics in the Art of Translation: Some Tools from Linguistics for the Analysis and Practice of Translation*, Albany, NY: SUNY Press.

Manca, Elena (2008) 'From Phraseology to Culture: The Case of Qualifying Adjectives in the Language of Tourism', *International Journal of Corpus Linguistics* 13(3): 368–85.

Mánek, Bohuslav (1990/1991) 'První české

překlady Byronovy poesy' [The First Czech Translations of Byron's Poetry], *AUC* (Acta Universitatis Carolinae), Philologica-Monographica 12, Prague: Charles University.

Marco, Josep (2004) '¿Tareas o proyectos? ¿Senderos que se bifurcan en el desarrollo de la competencia traductora?', *Trans* 8: 75–88.

Mardin, Serif (1962) *The Genesis of Young Ottoman Thought – A Study in the Modernization of Turkish Political Ideas*, Princeton, NJ: Princeton University Press.

Margry, P. (ed.) (1883) *Découvertes et établissements des Français dans l'ouest et dans le sud de l'Amérique septentrionale (1614–1754)*, vol. 5, Paris: D. Jouast.

Marschark, Marc, Patricia Sapere, Carol Convertino, Rosemarie Seewagen and Heather Maltzen (2004) 'Comprehension of Sign Language Interpreting: Deciphering a Complex Task Situation', in *Sign Language Studies* 4(4): 345–68.

——(2005a) 'Educational Interpreting: Access and Outcomes', in Marc Marschark, Rico Peterson and Elizabeth A. Winston (eds.) *Sign Language Interpreting and Interpreter Education*, Oxford: Oxford University Press, 57–83.

——, Rico Peterson and Elizabeth A. Winston (eds) (2005b) *Sign Language Interpreting and Interpreter Education*, Oxford: Oxford University Press.

Martin, Anne (2003) 'La direccionalidad y la interpretación: epílogo', in Dorothy Kelly, Anne Martin, Marie-Louise Nobs, Dolores Sánchez and Catherine Way (eds) *La direccionalidad en traducción e interpretación: perspectivas teóricas, profesionales y didácticas*, Granada: Atrio, 427–34.

Martin, Elizabeth (2006) *Marketing Identities through Language: English and Global Imagery in French Advertising*, Houndsmills: Palgrave Macmillan.

Martin, Simon and Nicolas Grube (2000) *Chronicle of the Maya Kings and Queens: Deciphering the Dynasties of the Ancient Maya*, London & New York: Thames & Hudson.

Martín Ruano, M. Rosario (2003) 'Bringing the Other Back Home: the Translation of (Un) familiar Hybridity', *Linguistica Antverpiensia* NS 2: 191–204.

Martínez, José Matoe (1998) 'Be Relevant (Relevance, Translation and Cross-Culture)', *Revista Alicantina de Estudios Ingleses* 11 (Special Issue Devoted to Relevance Theory): 171–82.

Marton, W. (1968) 'Equivalence and Congruence in Transformational Contrastive Studies', *Studia Anglica Posnaniensia* 1: 53–62.

Maryns, Katrijn (2006) *The Asylum Speaker: Language in the Belgian Asylum Procedure*, Manchester: St Jerome.

Marzocchi, Carlo (2005) 'On Norms and Ethics in the Discourse on Interpreting', *The Interpreter's Newsletter* 13: 87–109.

Mason, Ian (1989) 'Speaker Meaning and Reader Meaning: Preserving Coherence in Screen Translation', in Henry Prais, Rainer Kölmel and Jerry Payne (eds) *Babel. The Cultural and Linguistic Barriers between Nations*, Aberdeen: Aberdeen University Press, 13–24.

——(1994) 'Discourse, Ideology and Translation', in Robert de Beaugrande, Abdulla Shunnaq and Mohamed H. Heliel (eds) *Language, Discourse and Translation in the West and Middle East*, Amsterdam: John Benjamins, 23–34.

——(ed.) (1999) *Dialogue Interpreting*, Special Issue of *The Translator* 5(2).

——(ed.) (2001) *Triadic Exchanges: Studies in Dialogue Interpreting*, Manchester: St Jerome.

——(2004) 'Text Parameters in Translation: Transitivity and Institutional Cultures', in Lawrence Venuti (ed.) *The Translation Studies Reader* (2nd edition), London & New York: Routledge, 470–81.

——(2006a) 'Projected and Perceived Identities in Dialogue Interpreting', in Juliane House, M. Rosario Martín Ruano and Nicole Baumgarten (eds) *Translation and the Construction of Identity*, Seoul: IATIS, 30–52.

——(2006b) 'On Mutual Accessibility of Contextual Assumptions in Dialogue Interpreting', *Journal of Pragmatics* 38(3): 359–73.

——and Miranda Stewart (2001) 'Interactional Pragmatics, Face and the Dialogue Interpreter', in Ian Mason (ed.) *Triadic Exchanges: Studies in Dialogue Interpreting*, Manchester: St Jerome, 51–70.

Massardier-Kenney, Françoise (1997) 'Towards a Redefinition of Feminist Translation Practice', *The Translator* 3(1): 55–69.

Matejka, Ladislav and Krystyna Pomorska (1971) *Readings in Russian Poetics: Formalist and Structuralist Views*, Cambridge, MA: MIT Press.

Mathesius, Vilém (1912/13) 'O problémech českého překladatelství' [On Problems of Czech Translation], *Přehled* 11: 807–8.

Matrat, Corinne Marie (1995) *Investigating the Translation Process: Thinking Aloud versus Joint Activity*, Ann Arbor, MI: University Microfilms International.

Matterson, Stephen and Darryl Jones (2000) *Studying Poetry*, London: Arnold.

Mauranen, Anna (2000) 'Strange Strings in Translated Language. A Study on Corpora', in Maeve Olohan (ed.) *Intercultural Faultlines. Research Models in Translation Studies 1: Textual and Cognitive Aspects*, Manchester: St Jerome, 119–41.

——(2004) 'Corpora, Universals and Interference', in Anna Mauranen and Pekka Kujamäki (eds) *Translation Universals. Do They Exist?*, Amsterdam & Philadelphia: John Benjamins, 65–82.

——and Pekka Kujamäki (eds) (2004) *Translation Universals. Do They Exist?*, Amsterdam & Philadelphia: John Benjamins.

May, H. F. (1976) *The Enlightenment in America*, Oxford: Oxford University Press.

May, Rachel (1994) *The Translator in the Text: On Reading Russian Literature in English*, Evanston, IL: Northwestern University Press.

Mayoral Asensio, Roberto (2001) 'Por una renovación en la formación de traductores e intérpretes: revisión de algunos de los conceptos sobre los que se basa el actual sistema, su estructura y contenidos', *Sendebar* 12: 311–36.

——, Dorothy Kelly and Natividad Gallardo (1988) 'The Concept of Constrained Translation. Non-Linguistic Perspectives on Translation', *Meta* 33(3): 356–67.

McAlister, Gerard (1992) 'Teaching Translation into a Foreign Language – Status, Scopes and Aims', in Cay Dollerup and Anne Loddergaard (eds) *Teaching Translation and Interpreting – Training Talent and Experience*, Amsterdam & Philadelphia: John Benjamins, 291–8.

——(2000) 'The Evaluation of Translation into a Foreign Language', in Christina Schäffner and Beverly Adab (eds) *Developing Translation Competence*, Amsterdam & Philadelphia: John Benjamins, 229–41.

McCloud, Scott (1993) *Understanding Comics*, Northampton, MA: Tundra.

——(2000) *Reinventing Comics*, New York: Paradox Press.

——(2006) *Making Comics*, New York, London, Toronto & Sydney: Harper.

McDonnell, Joseph (1997) *The Lexicon and Vocabulary of Signed English or Manually Coded English (MCE)*, Teanga 17, Dublin: ITÉ.

McGerr, R. P. (1988) 'Editing the Self-conscious Medieval Translator: Some Issues and Examples', *Text* 4: 147–61.

McGuire, James (1990) 'Beckett, the Translator, and the Metapoem', *World Literature Today* 64(2): 258–63.

McLean, J. (1890) *James Evans, Inventor of the Syllabic System of the Cree Language*, Toronto: Methodist Mission Press.

McNeil, Dougal (2005) *The Many Lives of Galileo: Brecht, Theatre and Translation's Political Unconscious*, Frankfurt & Berlin: Peter Lang.

McRae, John and Bill Findlay (2000) 'Varieties of English', in Peter France (ed.) *The Oxford Guide to Literature in English Translation*, Oxford: Oxford University Press, 34–8.

McVaugh, M. (trans.) (1974) 'Gerard of Cremona. A List of Translations Made from Arabic into Latin in the Twelfth Century', in E. Grant (ed.) *A Source Book in Medieval Science*, Cambridge, MA: Harvard University Press, 35–8.

McWilliam, G. H. (trans.) (1972) *Boccaccio: The Decameron*, Harmondsworth: Penguin.

Mead, Peter (2002) 'Exploring Hesitation in Consecutive Interpreting: An Empirical Study', in Giuliana Garzone and Maurizio Viezzi (eds) *Interpreting in the 21st Century*, Amsterdam & Philadelphia: John Benjamins, 73–82.

Medgyes, Peter (1994) *The Non-Native Teacher*, London: Macmillan.

Mediz Bolio, Antonio (1930/1973) *El libro de Chilam Balam de Chumayel*, Mexico: Universidad Autónoma de Mexico.

Mehanna, Ahmad Ibrahim (1978) *Dirasa hawl tarjamat al-Qur'ān al-Karim* [On Translating the Noble Qur'ān], Cairo: Al-Sha'b Publications.

Mehrez, Samia (1992) 'Translation and the Postcolonial Experience: The Francophone North African Text', in Lawrence Venuti (ed.) *Rethinking Translation: Discourse, Subjectivity, Ideology*, London & New York: Routledge, 120–38.

Menéndez y Pelayo, M. (1952–3) *Biblioteca de traductores españoles*, vols 54–7 of *Obras completas*, Santander: Consejo Superior de Investigaciones Científicas.

Merino, Rachel (1992) 'Profesión: adaptador', *Livius* 1: 85–97.

Merino Álvarez, Raquel (1994) *Traducción, tradición y manipulación: teatro inglés en España 1950-1990*, León, Spain: Universidad de León & Universidad del País vasco.

Merkel, Magnus (1998) 'Consistency and Variation in Technical Translation: A Study of Translators' Attitudes', in Lynne Bowker, Michael Cronin, Dorothy Kenny and Jennifer Pearson (eds) *Unity in Diversity? Current Trends in Translation Studies*, Manchester: St Jerome, 137–49.

Merkle, Denise (ed.) (2002) *Censorship and Translation*, Special Issue of *TTR* 15(2).

Meschonnic, Henri (1986) 'Alors la traduction chantera', *Revue d'esthétique* 12: 75–90.

Messner, Sabine and Michaela Wolf (eds) (2001) *Übersetzung aus aller Frauen Länder. Beiträge zu Theorie und Praxis weblicher Realität in der Translation*, Graz: Verlag Leykam.

Meta (1977) Special issue 22(1) 'The History of Translation in Canada'.

——(1995) Special Issue on *Translation and Interpretation in Japan* 33(1).

Metzger, Melanie (1999) *Sign Language Interpreting: Deconstructing the Myth of Neutrality*, Washington, DC: Gallaudet University Press.

Meurer, Siegfried (ed.) (1991) *The Apocrypha in Ecumenical Perspective*, trans. Paul Ellingworth, UBS Monograph Series No. 6, New York: UBS.

Mey, Kari-Anne L. (1998) 'Comics', in Jacob Mey (ed.) *Concise Encyclopedia of Pragmatics*, Amsterdam: Elsevier, 136–40.

Meyer, Bernd (2004) *Dolmetschen im medizinischen Aufklärungsgespräch. Eine diskursanalytische Untersuchung zur Wissensvermittlung im mehrsprachigen Krankenhaus*, Münster: Waxmann.

Meyer, Charles (2002) *English Corpus Linguistics: An Introduction*, Cambridge: Cambridge University Press

Meyer, Mike (2005) 'The World's Biggest Book Market', *New York Times*, 13 March.

Meyerhof, Max (1926) 'New Light on Hunain Ibn Ishaq and His Period', *Isis* 8(4): 685–724.

——(1937) 'On the Transmission of Greek and Indian Science to the Arabs', *Islamic Culture* 5 (January): 17–29.

Meylaerts, Reine (ed.) (2006) *Literary Heteroglossia in/and Translation*, special issue of *Target* 18(1).

Mezei, Kathy (1988) 'Speaking White: Literary Translation as a Vehicle of Assimilation in Quebec', *Canadian Literature* 117: 11–23.

——(1998) 'Bilingualism and Translation in/of Michele Lalonde's *Speak White*', *The Translator* 4(2): 229–47.

Mhina, G. A. (1970) 'The Place of Kiswahili in the Field of Translation', *Babel* 16(4): 188–96.

Microsoft (2007) 'Microsoft Launches Windows Vista and Microsoft Office 2000 to Consumers Worldwide', *PressPass – Information for Journalists (29 January 2007)*. http://www.microsoft.com/Presspass/press/2007/jan07/01-29VistaLaunchPR.mspx (accessed 26 August 2007).

Miguélez-Carballeira, Helena (2007) 'Perpetuating Asymmetries: The Interdisciplinary Encounter between Translation Studies and Hispanic Studies', *Hispanic Research Journal* 8(4): 359–74.

Mikkelson, Holly (1999) 'Relay Interpreting: A Solution for Languages of Limited Diffusion?', *The Translator* 5(2): 361–80.

——(2005) *The Interpreter's Edge* (3rd edition), Spreckels, CA: Acebo.

Miko, František (1970) 'La Théorie de l'expression et la traduction', in James S. Holmes, Frans de Haan and Anton Popovič (eds) *The Nature of Translation*, The Hague: Mouton, 61–77.

——(1982) *Hodnoty a literarny process*, Bratislava: Tatran.

Millán-Varela, Carmen (2004) 'Exploring Advertising in a Global Context. Food for Thought', *The Translator* 10(2): 245–67.

Millás Vallicrosa, J. M. (1949) *Estudios sobre historia de la ciencia española*, Barcelona: Consejo Superior de Investigaciones Científicas.

Miłosz, Cz. (1969/1983) *The History of Polish Literature*, Berkeley: University of California Press.

Milroy, Lesley (1987) *Language and Social Networks* (2nd edition), Oxford: Blackwell.

Milton, John (2001) 'Translating Classic Fiction for Mass Markets', *The Translator* 7(1): 43–69.

——(2003) 'Monteiro Lobato and translation: "Um país se faz com homens e livros"' *DELTA* 2003(19): 117–32.

——and Marie-Hélène Catherine Torres (eds) (2003) *Tradução, retradução e adaptação*, Special Issue of *Cadernos de Tradução* 11.

——and Eliane Euzebio (2004) 'The Political Translations of Monteiro Lobato and Carlos Lacerda', *Meta* 49(3): 481–97.

Mindess, Anna (1999) *Reading Between the Signs. Intercultural Communication for Sign Language Interpreters*, Yarmouth, ME: Intercultural Press.

Minhinnick, Robert (ed. & tr.) (2003) *The Adulterer's Tongue: Six Welsh Poets; A Facing Text Anthology*, Manchester: Carcanet.

Min'yar-Beloruchev, R.K. (1980) *Posledovatelny perevod* [General Translation Theory and Interpreting], Moscow: Voenizdat.

Miram, Guennadii Eduardovitch (2000) *Professia: perevodchik* [Profession: Interpreter], Kiev: Nika-tzentr Elga.

Mirandé, Alfredo and Enríquez Evangelina (1979) *La Chicana, The Mexican American Woman*, Chicago: University of Chicago Press.

Misak, Cheryl (ed.) (2004) *The Cambridge Companion to Peirce*, Cambridge: Cambridge University Press.

Modenessi, Alfredo Michel (2004) ' "A Double Tongue within Your Mask": Translating Shakespeare in/to Spanish-speaking Latin America', in Ton Hoenselaars (ed.) *Shakespeare and the Language of Translation*, London: Thomson Learning, 240–54.

Moeketsi, Rosemary and Kim Wallmach (2005) 'From Sphaza to Makoya!: A BA Degree for Court Interpreters in South Africa', *The International Journal of Speech, Language and the Law* 12(1): 77–108.

Molina, Lucía and Amparo Hurtado Albir (2002) 'Translation Techniques Revisited: A Dynamic and Functionalist Approach', *Meta* 47(4): 498–512.

Møller Nielsen, K. (1977) *Homeroversættelser og heksameterdigte* [Homer Translations and Hexameter Poems], Copenhagen.

Monacelli, Claudia (2000) 'Mediating Castles in the Air: Epistemological Issues in Interpreting Studies', in Maeve Olohan (ed.) *Intercultural Faultlines: Research Models in Translation Studies I, Textual and Cognitive Aspects*, Manchester: St Jerome, 193–214.

——(2005) *Surviving the Role: A Corpus-Based Study of Self-Regulation in Simultaneous Interpreting as Perceived through Participation Framework and Interactional Politeness*, Doctoral dissertation, Edinburgh: Heriott-Watt University.

Monaco, Marion (1974) *Shakespeare on the French Stage in the Eighteenth Century*, Paris: Didier.

Moner, Michel (1990) 'Cervantes y la traducción', *Nueva Revista de Filología Hispánica* 38(2): 513–24.

Montalt, Vincent and Maria Gonzalez Davis (2007) *Medical Translation Step by Step*, Manchester: St Jerome.

Montes Fernández, Antonia (2003) 'Die interkulturelle Dimension von Werbeanzeigen – eine übersetzungsrelevante kontrastive Textanalyse', *Translation Journal* 7(2) http://translationjournal.net/journal/24werbung.htm (accessed 14 July 2008).

Montgomery, Martin, Alan Durant, Nigel Fabb, Tom Furniss and Sara Mills (2000) *Ways of Reading: Advanced Reading Skills for Students of English*, London & New York: Routledge.

Montgomery, Scott L. (2000) *Science in Translation: Movements of Knowledge through Cultures and Time*, Chicago: University of Chicago Press.

Monticelli, Rita (2005) 'In Praise of Art and Literature: Intertextuality, Translations and Migrations of Knowledge in Anna Jameson's Travel Writing', *Prose Studies* 27(3): 299–312.

Montini, Chiara (2007) *«La bataille du soliloque». Genèse de la poétique bilingue de Samuel Beckett (1929-1946)*, Amsterdam & New York: Rodopi.

Moody, Bill (2007) 'Literal vs. Liberal: What Is a Faithful Interpretation?', *The Sign Language Translator and Interpreter* 1(2): 179–220.

Moosa, Matti (1983) *The Origins of Modern*

Arabic Fiction, Washington, DC: Three Continents Press.

Moretti, Franco (1998) *Atlas of the European Novel 1800–1900*, London & New York: Verso.

——(2004) 'Conjectures on World Literature', in Christopher Prendergast (ed.) *Debating World Literature*, London & New York: Verso, 148–62.

Morgan, E. (ed.) (1964) *The Founding of Massachusetts*, Indianapolis, IN: Bobbs-Merrill.

Morón, Marián and Elisa Calvo (2006) 'What do Translation Students Expect of Their Training in Spain?', *Current Trends in Translation Teaching and Learning*, Helsinki University Translation Studies Department Publication III, 105–19.

Morris, Ruth (1995) 'The Moral Dilemmas of Court Interpreting', *The Translator* 1(1): 25–46.

Moser, Barbara (1976) *Simultaneous Translation: Linguistic, Psycholinguistic and Human Information Processing Aspects.* Doctoral Dissertation, Innsbruck: University of Innsbruck, Austria.

——(1978) 'Simultaneous Interpretation: A Hypothetical Model and Its Practical Applications', in David Gerver and H. Wallace Sinaiko (eds) *Language Interpretation and Communication*, New York: Plenum, 353–68.

Moser-Mercer, Barbara (1997) 'Beyond Curiosity: Can Interpreting Research Meet the Challenge?', in Joseph Danks, Gregory Shreve, Stephen Fountain and Michael McBeath (eds) *Cognitive Processes in Translation and Interpreting*, Thousand Oaks, CA: Sage, 176–95.

——(2000) 'The Rocky Road to Expertise in Interpreting: Eliciting Knowledge from Learners', in Mira Kadric, Klaus Kaindl and Franz Pöchhacker (eds) *Translationswissenschaft. Festschrift für Mary Snell-Hornby zum 60 Geburtstag*, Tübingen: Stauffenburg, 339–52.

——(2008) 'Skill Acquisition in Interpreting: A Human Performance Perspective', *The Interpreter and Translator Trainer* 2(1): 1–28.

——and Robin Setton (2005) 'The Teaching of Simultaneous Interpreting: the First 60 Years (1929–1989)', *Forum* 3(1): 205–25.

——, Uli H. Frauenfelder, Beatriz Casado and Alexander Künzli (2005) 'Remote Interpreting: Issues of Multi-Sensory Integration in a Multilingual Task', *Meta* 50(2): 727–38.

Mossop, Brian (1988) 'Translating Institutions: A Missing Factor in Translation Theory', *TTR* 1(2): 65–71.

——(1996) 'The Image of Translation in Science Fiction & Astronomy', *The Translator* 2(1): 1–26.

——(2006) 'From Culture to Business: Federal Government Translation in Canada', *The Translator* 12(1): 1–27.

Mounin, Georges (1955/1994) *Les Belles Infidèles*, 2nd edn, Lille: Presses Universitaires de Lille.

Mousa, Kamel and 'Ali Dahrug (1992) *Kayfa Nafham al-Qur'ān* [How We Understand the Qur'ān], Beirut: al-Mahrusa.

Mouzourakis, Panayotis (2005) 'Remote Interpreting: A Technical Perspective on Recent Experiments', *Interpreting* 8(1): 45–66.

Moyal, Gabriel Luis (2005) 'Traduire l'Angleterre sous la Restauration: Gibbon et Shakespeare de Guizot', *Meta* 50(3): 881–950.

Mudimbe, Valentine Y. (ed.) (1997) *Nations, Identities, Cultures*, Durham & London: Duke University Press.

Mukařovský, Jan (1914/1948) *Kapitoly z Česképoetiky* [Chapters from Czech Poetics], Rev. edn in 2 vols, Prague 1948.

Mukherjee, Sujit (1981) *Translation as Discovery: Indian Literature in Translation*, Delhi: Allied Publishers; 1994 edition: London: Sangam Books.

Müller-Vollmer, Kurt (ed.) (1985) *The Hermeneutics Reader. Texts of the German Tradition from the Enlightenment to the Present*, Oxford: Blackwell.

Multiculturalism and the Law (1991) Report of the Ethnic Affairs Commission of New South Wales, Sydney.

Munch-Petersen, E. (1976) *Prosafiktion. Oversættelser til dansk 1800–1900* [Prose Fiction. Translation into Danish], Copenhagen: Rosenkilde og Bagger.

Munday, Jeremy (1998a) 'A Computer-assisted Approach to the Analysis of Translation Shifts', *Meta* 43(4): 542–56.

——(1998b) 'The Caribbean Conquers the World? An Analysis of the Reception of

García Márquez in Translation', *Bulletin of Hispanic Studies* 55: 137–44.

——(2001) *Introducing Translation Studies: Theories and Applications*, London & New York: Routledge.

——(2002) 'Systems in Translation: A Systemic Model for Descriptive Translation Studies', in Theo Hermans (ed.) *Crosscultural Transgressions. Research Models in Translation Studies II: Historical and Ideological Issues*, Manchester: St Jerome, 76–92.

——(2004) 'Advertising: Some Challenges to Translation Theory', *The Translator* 10(2): 199–219.

——(2007) *Style and Ideology: Translation and Latin American Writing*, New York & London: Routledge.

Muñoz Martin, Ricardo (2000) 'Translation Strategies: Somewhere Over the Rainbow', in Allison Beeby, Doris Ensinger and Marisa Presas (eds) *Investigating Translation: Selected Papers from the 4th International Congress on Translation, Barcelona, 1998*, Amsterdam & Philadelphia: John Benjamins, 129–38.

Muntefering, Matthias (2002) 'Dubbing in Deutschland: Cultural and Industrial Considerations', *Language International* (April): 14–16.

Murzaku, Alexander (2007) *Machine Translation*, available at http://www.lissus.com/resources_machine-translation.htm (accessed 14 December 2007).

Mveng, E. (1980) *L'art et l'artisanat africains*, Yaoundé: Editions Clé.

Mweri, Jefwa G. (2006) 'Complexities and Challenges of Interpretation in the Third World: The Kenyan Case', in Rachel Locker McKee (ed.) *Proceedings of the Inaugural Conference of the World Association of Sign Language Interpreters*, Gloucestershire, UK: Douglas McLean, 134–40.

Myers, Lora (1973) 'The Art of Dubbing', *Filmmakers Newsletter* (April): 56–8.

Naficy, Hamid (2001) *An Accented Cinema. Exilic and Diasporic Filmmaking*, Princeton & Oxford: Princeton University Press.

Naito, Mitio (1993) 'Einige Bemerkungen zu grundsatzlichen Problemen beim Übersetzen lyrischer Texte', in Armin Paul Frank, Kurt-Jürgen Maass, Fritz Paul and Horst Turk (eds) *Übersetzen, Verstehen, Bruckenbauen*, Berlin: Erich Schmidt, 516–24.

Nama, Charles A. (1993) 'Historical, Theoretical and Terminological Perspectives of Translation in Africa', *Meta* 33(3): 414–25.

Napier, Jemina (2006) 'A Time to Reflect: An Overview of Signed Language Interpreting, Interpreter Education and Interpreting Research', in Rachel Locker McKee (ed.) *Proceedings of the Inaugural Conference of the World Association of Sign Language Interpreters*, Worcester, South Africa, 31 October–2 November 2005, Coleford, Gloucestershire: Douglas McLean, 12–24.

——, Rachel McKee and Della Goswell (2006) *Sign Language Interpreting. Theory and Practice in Australia and New Zealand*, Sydney: The Federation Press.

Naudé, Jacobus A. and Christo H. J. van der Merwe (eds) (2002) *Contemporary Translation Studies and Bible Translation, a South African Perspective*, Bloemfontein: Acta Theologica, Supplementum 2.

Naumann, Peter (2005) 'Babels and Nomad – Observations on the Barbarising of Communication at the 2005 World Social Forum', *Communicate!* http://aiic.net/ViewPage.cfm/page1800.htm (accessed 28 December 2007).

Navarro, Fernando (1996) *Manual de bibliografía española de traducción e interpretación 1985-1995*, Alicante: Publicaciones de la Universidad de Alicante.

Navarro Errasti, María Pilar, Rosa Lorés Sanz and Silvia Murillo Ornat (eds) (2004) *Pragmatics at Work: The Translation of Tourist Literature*, Bern: Peter Lang.

Needham, Joseph (1958) 'The Translation of Old Chinese Scientific and Technical Texts', in A. D. Booth (ed.) *Aspects of Translation*, London: Secker & Warburg, 65–87.

Needham, Rodney (1972) *Belief, Language, and Experience*, Oxford: Blackwell.

Negroponte, Nicholas (1991) 'Multimedia', *Hightech* (August): 68.

Nekeman, Paul (ed.) (1988) *Translation, Our Future: xith World Congress of FIT*, Maastricht: Euroterm.

Nergaard, Siri and Giovanna Franci (eds) (1999) *VS: Quaderni di studi semiotici 82* (special issue: *La traduzione*), Milan: Bompiani.

Neubert, Albrecht (1994) 'Competence in Translation: A Complex Skill, How to Study and How to Teach it', in Mary Snell-Hornby,

Franz Pöchhacker and Klaus Kaindl (eds) *Translation Studies: An Interdiscipline*, Amsterdam & Philadelphia: John Benjamins, 411–20.

——and Gregory M. Shreve (1992) *Translation as Text*, Kent, OH: Kent State University Press.

Neunzig, Wilhelm (2003) 'Tecnologías de la información y traducción especializada inversa', in Dorothy Kelly, Anne Martin, Marie-Louise Nobs, Dolores Sanchez and Catherine Way (eds) *La direccionalidad en traducción e interpretación: perspectivas teóricas, profesionales y didácticas*, Granada: Atrio, 189–206.

——and Helena Tanqueiro (2007) 'Risikominimierung beim Übersetzen in die Fremdsprache – ein Thesenpapier aus spanischer Sicht', in Gerd Wotjak (ed.) *Quo vadis Translatologie? Ein halbes Jahrhundert universitäre Ausbildung von Dolmetschern und Übersetzern in Leipzig*, Berlin: Frank & Timme, 327–42.

Neves, Josélia (2005) *Audiovisual Translation: Subtitling for the Deaf and Hard-of-Hearing*, Unpublished PhD Thesis, London: University of Surrey Roehampton http://rrp. roehampton.ac.uk/artstheses/1 (accessed 15 July 2007).

——(2007) 'Of Pride and Prejudice: The Divide between Subtitling and Sign Language Interpreting on Television', *The Sign Language Translator and Interpreter* 1(2): 251–74.

Newman, Aryeh (1994) 'Translation Equivalence: Nature', in R. E. Asher and J. M. Y. Simpson (eds) *The Encyclopedia of Language and Linguistics*, Oxford & New York: Pergamon Press, 4694–700.

Newmark, Peter (1981) *Approaches to Translation*, Oxford: Pergamon Press.

——(1988) *A Textbook of Translation*, New Jersey: Prentice Hall.

——(1991) 'The Curse of Dogma in Translation Studies', *Lebende Sprachen* 36: 105–08.

——(1995) 'Debate', in Christina Schäffner and Helen Kelly-Holmes (eds) *Cultural Functions of Translation*, Clevedon: Multilingual Matters, 72–86.

Next Page Foundation (2004) *Lost or Found in Translation: Translations' Support Policies in the Arab World* (on CD ROM). http://www. npage.org/en (accessed 16 July 2008).

Ngũgĩ wa Thiong'o (1986) *Decolonising the Mind: The Politics of Language in African Literature*, London: James Currey.

Nicholson, Nancy Schweda (1994) 'Training for Refugee Mental Health Interpreters', in Cay Dollerup and Annette Lindegaard (eds) *Teaching Translation and Interpreting 2*, Amsterdam: John Benjamins, 211–15.

Nida, Eugene A. (1964) *Towards a Science of Translating*, Leiden: E. J. Brill.

——(1982) 'Why So Many Bible Translations?', in Lloyd R. Bailey (ed.) *The Word of God: A Guide to English Versions of the Bible*, Atlanta, GA: John Knox Press, 13–27.

——and Charles Taber (1969) *The Theory and Practice of Translation*, Leiden: E. J. Brill.

Nienhauser, Wiliam (ed.) (1986) *The Indiana Companion to Traditional Chinese Literature*, Taipei: CMC Publishing Inc.

Niranjana, Tejaswini (1992) *Siting Translation: History, Post-Structuralism and the Postcolonial Context*, Berkeley: University of California Press.

Nisbett, Richard E. and Timothy D. Wilson (1977) 'Telling More Than We Can Know: Verbal Reports on Mental Processes', *Psychological Review* 84/3: 231–59.

Nomura, Masa (2000) 'Text, Image, and Translation. The Example of Advertising in German and in Brazilian Portuguese in a Globalized Context', in Andrew Chesterman, Natividad Gallardo San Salvador and Yves Gambier (eds) *Translation in Context*, Amsterdam & Philadelphia: John Benjamins, 261–70.

Noraini, Ibrahim (2005) *Professionalization of Conference Interpreting: A Case Study of the Parliamentary Interpreting in Malaysia*, Unpublished pre-doctoral thesis, University of Granada.

Nord, Christiane (1988) *Textanalyse und Übersetzen*, Heidelberg: Groos.

——(1991a/2006) *Text-Analysis in Translation: Theory, Methodology and Didactic Application of a Model for Translation-Oriented Text Analysis*, Amsterdam : Rodopi.

——(1991b) 'Scopos, Loyalty, and Translation Conventions', *Target* 3(1): 91–109.

——(1997) *Translating as a Purposeful Activity. Functionalist Approaches Explained*, Manchester, St Jerome.

Nordmeyer, G. (1958) 'On the OHG Isidor

and its Significance for Early German Prose Writing', *PMLA* 73: 23–35.

Norlie, Olaf (1934) *The Translated Bible, 1534–1934*, Philadelphia, PA: The United Lutheran Publication House.

Nornes, Abe M. (1999) 'For an Abusive Subtitling', *Film Quarterly* 52(3): 17–34.

Norouzi, Arash (2007) '"WIPED OFF THE MAP" – The Rumor of the Century', *Global Research*, 20 January. http://www.globalresearch.ca/index.php?context=viewArticle&code=NOR20070120&articleId=4527 (accessed 5 March 2007).

Norton, D. (1993) *A History of the Bible as Literature*, 2 vols, Cambridge: Cambridge University Press.

Norton, G. P. (1984) *The Ideology and Language of Translation in Renaissance France and their Humanist Antecedents*, Geneva: Droz.

Noss, Philip A. (ed.) (2005) *Current Trends in Scripture Translation: Definitions and Identity*, UBS Bulletin 198/199, Reading: UBS.

——(ed.) (2007) *A History of Bible Translation*, Rome: Edizioni di Storia e Letteratura.

Nowell-Smith, Geoffrey and Steven Ricci (eds) (1998) *Hollywood and Europe. Economics, Culture, National Identity 1945–1995*, London: British Film Institute Publishing.

Nowotny, Karl A. (1961) *Tlacuilolli: Die mexikanischen Bilderhandschriften, Stil und Inhalt*, Berlin: Gebr. Mann.

Ntimbal, Peter (2006) 'Treason Trial Comes to Standstill', *WBS Television News*. Available at http://www.wbs-tv.com/besigyetrial.php (accessed 28 December 2007).

Nyberg, Eric, Teruko Mitamura and Willem-Olaf Huijsen (2003) 'Controlled Language for Authoring and Translation', in Harold Somers (ed.) *Computers and Translation: A Translator's Guide*, Amsterdam & Philadelphia: John Benjamins, 245–81.

Oates, Joyce Carol (1990) 'The Writer as Reviewer', *American Book Review* (November–December): 3.

O'Brien, Sharon (2006) 'Eye-Tracking and Translation Memory Matching', *Perspectives: Studies in Translatology* 14(3): 185–205.

O'Connell, Eithne (1998) 'Choices and Constraints in Screen Translation', in Lynne Bowker, Michael Cronin, Dorothy Kenny and Jennifer Pearson (eds) *Unity in Diversity?*

Current Trends in Translation Studies, Manchester: St Jerome, 65–71.

——(2003) *Minority Language Dubbing for Children: Screen Translation from German into Irish*, Berlin: Peter Lang.

——(2007) 'Screen Translation', in Piotr Kuhiwczak and Karin Littau (eds) *A Companion to Translation Studies*, Clevedon: Multilingual Matters, 120–33.

Ó Cuilleanáin, Corman (1999) 'Not in Front of the Servants. Forms of Bowdlerism and Censorship in Translation', in Jean Boase-Beier and Michael Holman (eds) *The Practices of Literary Translation. Constraints and Creativity*, Manchester: St Jerome, 31–44.

O'Hagan, Minako (2005) 'Teletranslation', in M. Pagani (ed.) *The Encyclopedia of Multimedia Technology and Networking*, Vol. 2, Hershey, PA: Idea Group, 945–50.

——and David Ashworth (2002) *Translation-mediated Communication in a Digital World: Facing the Challenges of Globalization and Localization*, Clevedon: Multilingual Matters.

O'Shea, José Roberto (ed.) (1999) *Accents Now Known: Shakespeare's Drama in Translation*, special issue of *Ilha do Desterro* nr 36.

O'Sullivan, Carol (2004–5) 'Translation, Pseudotranslation and Paratext: The Presentation of Contemporary Crime Fiction in Italy', *Enter text* 4(3), *Supplement*, http://www.brunel.ac.uk/4042/entertext4.3sup/osullivan_s.pdf (accessed 16 July 2008).

O'Sullivan, Emer (2000) *Kinderliterarische Komparatistik*, Heidelberg: C. Winter; English translation of a shortened version by Anthea Bell in *Comparative Children's Literature*, London: Routledge, 2005.

O'Tool, M. (1994a) 'Lawyers' Response to Language Constructing Law', in J. Gibbons (ed.) *Language and the Law*, Sydney: Longman, 188–92.

——(1994b) '"Communication" in the Courtroom: The Impact of Lawyers' Theories of Interpreting/Translation (I/T) upon the Administration of Justice in Australia', in *Proceedings of IJET 4*, Brisbane: University of Queensland, 166–241.

Obst, H. and R. H. Cline (1990) 'Summary History of Language Services in the U.S.

Department of State', in D. and M. Bowen (eds).

Oettinger, Anthony G. (1963) 'Review of *Die Übersetzung naturwissenschaftlicher und technischer Literatur: Sprachliche Maßstäbe und Methoden zur Bestimmung ihrer Wesenszüge und Probleme*, von Rudolf Jumpelt', *Language* 39(2): 350–52.

Ogden, Graham (1997) 'Is it "And" or "But"? Ideology and Translation', in Basil Rebera (ed.) *Current Trends in Scripture Translation*, UBS Bulletin 182/183, Reading: UBS, 213–21. See also *The Bible Translator* 52(3) (2001).

Oghli, Akmal al-Deen Ihsan (2006) *Al-Atrak fi Misr wa Turathahum al-Thaqafi* [Turks in Egypt and their Cultural Heritage], trans. S. Sa'dawi, Istanbul: Markaz al-Abhath lil-Tarikh wa al-Funun wa al-Thaqafa al-Islamiyya.

Oikawa, S. (1994) 'Shintaishi no Kyakuin' [Rhyme in New Style Verse], in Kamei (ed.).

Oittinen, Riitta (2000) *Translating for Children*, New York & London: Garland.

——(ed.) (2003) *Traduction pour les enfants*, Special Issue of *Meta* 48: 1-2.

Ojala-Signell, Raili and Anna Komarova (2006) 'International Development Cooperation Work with Sign Language Interpreters', in Rachel Locker McKee (ed.) *Proceedings of the Inaugural Conference of the World Association of Sign Language Interpreters*, Worchester, South Africa, 31 October–2 November 2005, Coleford, Gloucestershire: Douglas McLean, 115–22.

Okpewho, I. (1992) *African Oral Literature: Backgrounds, Character and Continuity*, Bloomington, IN: Indiana University Press.

Olk, Harald (2002) 'Critical Discourse Awareness in Translation', *The Translator* 8(1): 101–16.

Ollikaenen, A. and M. Pulakka (eds) (1987) *Kääntäjät kulttuurivaikuttajina* [Cultural Influences of Translators into Finnish], Jyväskylä: Jyväskylän yliopiston kirjallisuuden laitoksen moniste no. 35.

Olohan, Maeve (2004) *Introducing Corpora in Translation Studies*, London & New York: Routledge.

——and Mona Baker (2000) 'Reporting *that* in Translated English: Evidence for Subconscious Processes of Explicitation?', *Across Languages and Cultures* 1(2): 141–58.

Olson, Charles (1953/1968) *Mayan Letters*, London: Cape.

Ooi, Vicky (1980) 'Translating Culture: A Cantonese Translation and Production of O'Neill's *Long Day's Journey into Night*', in Ortrun Zuber (ed.) *The Languages of Theatre. Problems in the Translation and Transposition of Drama*, Oxford: Pergamon Press, 51–68.

Orengo, Alberto (2005) 'Localising News: Translation and the "Global–Local" Dichotomy', *Language and Intercultural Communication* 2(2): 168–87.

Orhonlu, Cengiz (1974) 'Tercuman' [Translator], *Islam Ansiklopedisi* [Encyclopedia of Islam – Expanded Turkish Version], vol. 12/I, Istanbul: Milli Egitim Bakanligi Yayinlari, 175–81.

Orloff, Ulrika (2005) 'Who Wrote this Text and Who Cares? Translation, Intentional "Parenthood" and New Reproductive Technologies', in José Santaemilia (ed.) *Gender, Sex and Translation. The Manipulation of Identities*, Manchester: St Jerome, 149–60.

Ortega y Gassett, José (1937/2000) 'The Misery and the Splendour of Translation', translated by Elizabeth Gamble Miller, in Lawrence Venuti (ed.) *The Translation Studies Reader*, London & New York: Routledge, 49–63.

Ostian, Emmanuel (2004) personal interview with Jerry Palmer, 8 October 2004.

Oustinoff, Michaël (2001) *Bilinguisme d'écriture et auto-traduction. Julien Green, Samuel Beckett, Vladimir Nabokov*, Paris: l'Harmattan.

Outtherenews, (2006) http://www.outtherenews.com/index.php?module=ContentExpress&func=display&ceid=5&meid=-1 (accessed 11 December 2006).

Øverås, Linn (1998) 'In Search of the Third Code: An Investigation of Norms in Literary Translation', in Sara Laviosa (ed.) *L'Approche basée sur le corpus/The Corpus-Based Approach*, Special Issue of *Meta* 43(4): 571–88.

Oxford Classical Dictionary (1970), 2nd edn, N. G. L. Hammond and H. H. Scullard (eds), Oxford: Oxford University Press.

Ozick, Cynthia (2007) 'Literary Entrails: The Boys in the Alley, the Disappearing Readers, and the Novel's Ghostly Twin', *Harpers Magazine* (April): 67–75.

Ozolins, Uldis (2000) 'Communication Needs and Interpreting in Multilingual

Settings: the International Spectrum of Response', in Roda Roberts, Silvana E. Carr, Diana Abraham and Aideen Dufour (eds) *The Critical Link 2: Interpreters in the Community*, Amsterdam: John Benjamins, 21–33.

PACTE (2003) 'Building a Translation Competence Model', in Fábio Alves (ed.) *Triangulating Translation. Perspectives in Process Oriented Research*, Amsterdam & Philadelphia: John Benjamins, 43–66.

——(2005) 'Investigating Translation Competence: Conceptual and Methodological Issues', *Meta* 50(2): 609–19.

Padilla Benítez, Presentación (1995) *Procesos de memoria y atención en la interpretación de lenguas*, Unpublished doctoral dissertation, University of Granada.

Paepcke, Friz (1986) *Im Übersetzen leben. Übersetzen und Textvergleich*, edited by K. Berger and H.-M. Speier, Tübingen: Gunter Narr.

Paes, J. P. (1990) *Tradução, a ponte necessária: Aspectos e problemas da arte de traduzir*, São Paulo: Editora Ática.

Pagano, Adriana S. (2000) 'Sources for Translation Theory: Fiction in Latin America', *ATA Chronicle* 29(4): 38–44.

——(2002) 'Translation as Testimony: On Official Histories and Subversive Pedagogies in Cortázar', in Maria Tymoczko and Edwin Gentzler (eds) *Translation and Power*, Amherst & Boston, MA: University of Massachusetts Press, 80–98.

Paitoni, Maria J. (1766–7) *Biblioteca degli autori antichi greci e latini volgarizzati*, Venice: Simoni.

Pajares, E. (2001) 'Literature and Translation: The First Spanish Version of *Tom Jones*', *Babel* 46(3): 193–210.

Paker, Saliha (1991) 'The Age of Translation and Adaptation in Turkey', in Robin Ostle (ed.) *Modern Literature in the Near and Middle East*, London: Routledge, 17–32.

——(2002) 'Translation as *Terceme* and *Nazire*: Culture-bound Concepts and their Implications for a Conceptual Framework for Research on Ottoman Translation History', in Theo Hermans (ed.) *Crosscultural Transgressions, Research Models in Translation Studies II Historical and Ideological Issues*, Manchester: St Jerome, 120–43.

——and Zehra Toska (1997) 'A Call for Descriptive Translation Studies on the Turkish Tradition of Rewrites', in Mary Snell-Hornby, Zuzana Jettmarová and Klaus Kaindl (eds) *Translation as Intercultural Communication*, Amsterdam & Philadelphia: John Benjamins, 79–88.

——, Işin Bengi, Nedret Pinar-Kuran and Suat Karantay (1991) '19th Century Adaptations of Molière', 'The Eloquent Mediator: Ahmed Midhat Efendi', 'The First Goethe Translations in Turkish', 'The Translation Office of the 1940s: Norms and Functions', in Douwe Fokkema (ed.) *Proceedings of the xiiith Congress of the International Comparative Literature Association*, vol. 5: *Space and Boundaries*, Munich: Iudicium Verlag, 382–405.

Palacio, Jean de (1975) 'Shelley traducteur de soi-même', *Revue des sciences humaines* 158: 223–44.

Palmer, Jerry (2000) *Spinning into Control. News Values and Source Strategies*, London: Continuum.

——and Victoria Fontan (2007) ' "Our Ears and Our Eyes". Journalists and Fixers in Iraq', *Journalism* 8(1): 5–24.

Palmer, Richard (1969) *Hermeneutics. Interpretation Theory in Schleiermacher, Dilthey, Heidegger, and Gadamer*, Evanston, IL: Northwestern University Press.

Paloposki, Outi and Kaisa Koskinen (2004) 'A Thousand and One Translations. Revisiting Translation', in Gyde Hansen, Kirsten Malmkjaer and Daniel Gile (eds) *Claims, Changes and Challenges in Translation Studies*, Amsterdam & Philadelphia: John Benjamins, 27–38.

Pálsson, Gísli (ed.) (1993) *Beyond Boundaries: Understanding, Translation, and Anthropological Discourse*, Oxford: Berg.

Pálsson, H. (1978) *Straumar og stefnur í islenskum bókmenntum fra 1550* [Tendencies and Periods in Icelandic Literature from 1550], Reykjavik: Iounn.

Paneth, Eva (1957/2002) *An Investigation into Conference Interpreting (with Special Reference to the Training of Interpreters)*, Unpublished MA thesis, University of London. Extracted in Franz Pöchhacker and Miriam Shlesinger (eds) *The Interpreting Studies Reader*, 2002, London and New York: Routledge, 31–40.

Pápai, Vilma (2004) 'Explicitation: A Universal of Translated Texts?', in Anna Mauranen and Pekka Kujamäki (eds) *Translation Universals. Do They Exist?*, Amsterdam & Philadelphia: John Benjamins, 143–65.

Papastergiadis, Nikos (2000) *The Turbulence of Migration: Globalization, Deterritorialization and Hybridity*, Cambridge: Polity Press.

Paquin, Robert (2001) 'In the Footsteps of Giants: Translating Shakespeare for Dubbing', *Translation Journal* 5(3) http://www.accurapid.com/journal/17dubb.htm (accessed 15 July 2007).

Parati, Graziella (2005) *Migration Italy: The Art of Talking Back in a Destination Culture*, Toronto, Buffalo & London: University of Toronto Press.

Parks, Tim (1998/2007) *Translating Style: A Literary Approach to Translation, A Translation Approach to Literature* (2nd edition), Manchester: St Jerome.

Parnell, A. and F. Villa (1986) 'Liaison Interpreting as a Method of Language Instruction', *Rassegna Italiana di Linguistica Applicata* 18(1): 25–32.

Parrish, Donna (2003) 'Localizing Songs and Software', *The Getting Started Guide: Localization*, Supplement to *Multilingual Computing & Technology*, 9.

Partridge, Eric (1966) *Origins: A Short Etymological Dictionary of Modern English*, (4th rev. enl. edn), London: Routledge & Kegan Paul.

Pasanen, Outi (1992) 'Positions on Translation: An Interview with Outi Pasanen', in Nicholas Royle, *Afterwords*, Tampere: Outside Books.

Paterson, Don (tr.) (2006) *Orpheus: A Version of Rilke's 'Die Sonette an Orpheus'*, London: Faber & Faber.

Pattanaik, Diptiranjan (2000) 'The Power of Translation: A Survey of Translation in Orissa', in Sherry Simon and Paul St-Pierre (eds) *Changing the Terms: Translating in the Post-Colonial Era*, Ottawa: University of Ottawa Press, 71–86.

Patton, Paul (2000) 'The Translation of Indigenous Land into Property: The Mere Analogy of English Jurisprudence . . .', *Parallax* 6(1): 25–38.

Pavesi, Maria (2005) *La Traduzione Filmica. Aspetti del Parlato Doppiato dall'Inglese all'Italiano*, Roma: Carocci.

Pavlović, Nataša (2007) *Directionality in Collaborative Translation Process. A Study of Novice Translators*, unpublished doctoral dissertation, Tarragona: Universitat Rovira I Virgili.

Payàs, Gertrudis (2004) 'Translation in Historiography: The Garibay/León-Portilla Complex and the Making of a Pre-Hispanic Past', *Meta* 49(3): 544–61.

Payne, Johnny (1993) *Conquest of the New Word: Experimental Fiction and Translation in the Americas*, Austin, TX: University of Texas Press.

Paz, Octavio (1966) *Poesía en movimiento*, Mexico: Siglo XXI.

Pazukhin, R. (1987) 'A Contribution to a General Theory of Models', *Semiotica* 67: 61–82.

Pearsall, D. (1977) *Old English and Middle English Poetry*, London, Henley and Boston: Routledge & Kegan Paul.

——(1989) 'Introduction', in Griffiths and Pearsall (eds) 1–10.

Pearson, Jennifer (2003) 'Using Parallel Texts in the Translator Training Environment', in Federico Zanettin, Silvia Bernardini and Dominic Stewart (eds) *Corpora in Translator Education*, Manchester: St Jerome, 15–24.

Pedersen, Viggo Hjørnager (1987) *Oversættelsesteori* [Translation Theory], Copenhagen.

——(1988) *Essays on Translation*, Copenhagen: Erhvervsøkonomisk Forlag.

——and Norman Shine (1979) 'Børnelitteratur i England og Danmark fra midten af det 18. århunderede til ca. 1830' [Children's Literature in England and Denmark from the Middle of the 18th Century to about 1830], I–II, *Børn og Bøger* 5: 222–30, and 6: 270–83.

Peirce, Charles Sanders (1992–8) *The Essential Peirce: Selected Philosophical Writings*, edited by the Peirce Edition Project, II vols, Bloomington, IN: Indiana University Press.

——(1931–58) *The Collected Papers of Charles Sanders Peirce*, edited by C. Hartshorne, P. Weiss and A. W. Burks, VIII vols, Cambridge, MA: Harvard University Press.

Peled, M. (1979) 'Creative Translation: Towards the Study of Arabic Translations of Western Literature since the Nineteenth Century', *Journal of Arabic Literature* 10: 128–50.

PEN American Center (2004) 'Reviewers Guide for Translated Books', http://www.pen.org/page.php/prmID/269 (last accessed 29 July 2007).

Pennarola, Cristina (2003) *Nonsense in Advertising. Deviascion in English Print Ads*, Naples: Liguori.

Penrod, Lynn K. (1993) 'Translating Hélène Cixous: French Feminism(s) and Anglo-American Feminist Theory', *TTR* 6(2): 39–54.

Perego, Elisa (2003) 'Evidence of Explicitation in Subtitling: Towards a Categorisation', *Across Languages and Cultures* 4(1): 63–88.

Pérez González, Luis (2006a) 'Interpreting Strategic Recontextualization Cues in the Courtroom', *Journal of Pragmatics* 38(3): 390–417.

——(2006b) 'Fansubbing anime: Insights into the Butterfly Effect of Globalisation on Audiovisual Translation', *Perspectives: Studies in Translatology* 14(4): 260–77.

——(2007) 'Appraising Dubbed Conversation. Systemic Functional Insights into the Construal of Naturalness in Translated Film Dialogue', *The Translator* 13(1): 1–38.

——(2008) 'Intervention in New Amateur Subtitling Cultures: A Multimodal Account', *Linguistica Antverpiensia* NS 6: 153–66.

Pergnier, Maurice (1973) 'Traduction et théorie linguistique', *Études de linguistique appliquée* 12: 26–38.

Perrin, Noel (1969) *Dr Bowdler's Legacy: A History of Expurgated Books in England and America*, London: Macmillan.

Perry, Menakhem (1981) 'Thematic and Structural Shifts in Autotranslations by Bilingual Hebrew–Yiddish Writers: The Case of Mendele Mokher Sforim', *Poetics Today* 2(4): 181–92.

Petrilli, Susan (ed.) (2003) *Translation Translation*, Amsterdam & New York: Rodopi.

Pevear, R. and L. Volokhonsky (trans.) (1990) F. Dostoevsky, *The Brothers Karamazov*, Berkeley: North Point Press.

Pfister, Manfred (ed.) (1996) *The Fatal Gift of Beauty: The Italies of British Travellers: An Annotated Anthology*, Amsterdam & Atlanta (GA): Rodopi.

Phillipson, Robert (1992) *Linguistic Imperialism*, Oxford: Oxford University Press.

Philpotts, Matthew (2007) 'Surrendering the Author-function: Günter Eich and the National Socialist Radio System', in Francesca Billiani (ed.) *Modes of Censorship and Translation. National Contexts and Diverse Media*, Manchester: St Jerome, 257–8.

Picchio, R. (1972) 'Questione della lingua slavia e Cirillometodiana', in *Studi sulla questione della lingua presso gli Slavi*.

Picht, Heribert (ed.) (2006) *Modern Approaches to Terminological Theories and Applications*, Bern: Peter Lang.

Picken, Catriona (ed.) (1989) *The Translator's Handbook* (2nd edition), London: Aslib.

Pickthall, Marmaduke (1930/1992) *The Meaning of the Glorious Koran, An Explanatory Translation*, Campbell, London: Everyman's Library.

——(1931) 'Arabs and Non-Arabs and the Question of Translating the Qur'ān', *Islamic Culture* July: 422–33.

Pieterse, Jan Nederveen (1995) 'Globalization as Hybridization', in Mike Featherstone (ed.) *Global Modernities*, London: Sage, 45–67.

Pihkala, Tuula (1998) 'Die Kompetenz des Dolmetschers auf die Probe gestellt: Relaisdolmetschen ohne Dolmetschanlage im Rahmen eines internationalen Bauprojekts' [Interpreting Competence Put to the Test: Relay Interpreting without Interpreting Facilities as Part of an International Construction Project], *TEXTconTEXT* 12(2): 129–47.

Pilcher, Tim and Brad Brooks (2005) *The Essential Guide to World Comics*, London: Collins & Brown.

Pilkington, Adrian (2000) *Poetic Effects*, Amsterdam: John Benjamins.

Piller, Ingrid (2001) 'Identity Constructions in Multilingual Advertising', *Language in Society* 30(2): 153–86.

——(2003) 'Advertising As A Site Of Language Contact', *Annual Review of Applied Linguistics* 23: 170–83.

Pinchuk, Isadore (1977) *Scientific and Technical Translation*, London: Deutsch.

Pinter, Ingrid (1969) *Der Einfluss der Übung und Konzentration auf Simultanes Sprechen und Hören*, Unpublished doctoral dissertation, University of Vienna.

Pinto, María and Dora Sales (2008) 'Towards User-centred Information Literacy

Instruction in Translation: the View of Trainers', *The Interpreter and Translator Trainer* 2(1): 47–74.

Piotrowska, Maria (2002) *A Compensational Model for Strategy and Techniques in Teaching Translation*, Kraków: Wydawnictwo Naukowe Akademii Pedagogicznej.

Pisarska, A. (1990) *Creativity of Translators. The Translation of Metaphorical Expressions in Non-literary Texts*, Poznań: Uniwersytet im. Adama Mickiewicza.

Pöchhacker, Franz (1994) *Simultandolmetschen als komplexes Handeln*, Tübingen: Gunter Narr.

——(1995) 'Simultaneous Interpreting: A Functionalist Perspective', *Hermes* 14: 31–53.

——(2003) 'El enfoque funcional en la interpretación simultánea', in Ángela Collados and José Antonio Sabio Pinilla (eds) *Avances en la investigación sobre interpretación*, Granada: Comares, 105–22.

——(2004) *Introducing Interpreting Studies*, London: Routledge.

——(2005) 'Quality Research Revisited', *The Interpreter's Newsletter* 13: 143–66.

——(2006) 'Interpreters and Ideology: from "between" to "within"', *Across Languages and Cultures* 7(2): 191–207.

——and Mira Kadric (1999) 'The Hospital Cleaner as Healthcare Interpreter: A Case Study', *The Translator* 5(2): 161–78.

——and Miriam Shlesinger (eds) (2002) *The Interpreting Studies Reader*, London & New York: Routledge.

Po-Fei Huang, Parker (1989) 'On the Translation of Chinese Poetry', in Rosanna Warren (ed.) *The Art of Translation*, Boston, MA: Northeastern University Press.

Pokorn, Nike K. (2003) 'The (In)competence of a Native Speaker in Translation Theory and Practice', in Dorothy Kelly, Anne Martin, Marie-Louise Nobs, Dolores Sanchez and Catherine Way (eds) *La direccionalidad en traducción e interpretación: perspectivas teóricas, profesionales y didácticas*, Granada: Atrio, 117–38.

——(2005) *Challenging the Traditional Axioms: Translation into a Non-mother Tongue*, Amsterdam & Philadelphia: John Benjamins.

Polezzi, Loredana (2000) 'Reflections of Things Past: Building Italy through the Mirror of Translation', *New Comparison* 29: 27–47.

——(2001) *Translating Travel: Contemporary Italian Travel Writing in English Translation*, Aldershot: Ashgate.

——(ed.) (2006) *Translation, Travel, Migration*, special issue of *The Translator* 12(2).

Politis, L. (1973) *A History of Modern Greek Literature*, Oxford: Clarendon Press.

Pöllabauer, Sonja (2004) 'Interpreting in Asylum Hearings: Issues of Role, Responsibility and Power', *Interpreting* 6(2): 143–80.

——(2005) *'I don't understand your English, Miss', Dolmetschen bei asylanhörungen*, Tübingen: Gunter Narr.

——(2006) ' "Translation Culture" in Interpreted Asylum Hearings', in Anthony Pym, Miriam Shlesinger and Zuzana Jettmarová (eds) *Sociocultural Aspects of Translating and Interpreting*, Amsterdam: John Benjamins, 151–62.

——(2007) 'Interpreting in Asylum Hearings: Issues of Saving Face', in Cecilia Wadensjö, Birgitta Englund Dimitrova and Anna-Lena Nilsson (eds) *The Critical Link 4: Professionalisation of Interpreting in the Community*, Amsterdam: John Benjamins, 39–52.

Pollak, S. (ed.) (1975) *Przekład artystyczny. O sztuce tlumaczenia. Kşiega druga* [Literary Translation. On the Art of Translating. Book Two], Wroclaw: Ossolineum.

Poltermann, Andreas (ed.) (1995) *Literaturkanon – Medienereignis – Kultureller Text: Formen interkultureller Kommunikation und Übersetzung* (Gottinger Beitrage Internationalen Übersetzungsforschung 10), Berlin: Erich Schmidt.

Poole, Adrian and Jeremy Maule (eds) (1995) *The Oxford Book of Classical Verse in Translation*, Oxford: Oxford University Press.

Popovič, Anton (1970) 'The Concept of "Shift of Expression" in Translation Analysis', in James S. Holmes (ed.) *The Nature of Translation: Essays on the Theory and Practice of Literary Translation*, The Hague & Paris: Mouton, 78–87.

——(1975) *Teoria umeleckého prekladu*, Bratislava: Tatran.

——(1976) *Dictionary for the Analysis of Literary Translation*, Edmonton: University of Alberta.

Pormann, Peter (2006) 'The Arab Cultural Awakening (Nahda), 1870-1950, and the Classical Tradition', *International Journal of the Classical Tradition* 13(1): 3–20.

Porter, Dennis (1991) 'Psychoanalysis and the Task of the Translator', in Alexandre Leupin (ed.) *Lacan and the Human Sciences*, Lincoln, NE: University of Nebraska Press, 143–63.

Posner, Michael (1988) 'Introduction: What is it like to be an expert?', in Michelene T. H. Chi, Robert Glaser and M. J. Farr (eds) *The Nature of Expertise*, Hillsdale, NJ: Lawrence Erlbaum Associates, xxix–xxxvi.

Pound, Ezra (ed.) (1936/1969) *Fenellosa. The Chinese Written Character as a Medium for Poetry*, San Francisco: City Lights.

Poyatos, Fernando (ed.) (1997) *Nonverbal Communication and Translation*, Amsterdam & Philadelphia: John Benjamins.

Prabhu, N. S. (1987) *Second Language Pedagogy*, Oxford: Oxford University Press.

Pratt, Mary Louise (1992) *Imperial Eyes: Travel Writing and Transculturation*, London & New York: Routledge.

——(2002) 'The Traffic in Meaning: Translation, Contagion, Infiltration', *Profession* (MLA Journal) 12: 25–36.

Prevodut i Bulgarskata Kultura [Translation and Bulgarian Culture] (1981), Sofia: Narodna Kultura Publishers.

Prickett, Stephen (1993) 'The Changing of the Host: Translation and Linguistic History', in David Jasper (ed.) *Translating Religious Texts: Translation, Transgression and Interpretation*, New York: St Martin's, 4–20.

Prins, Yopie (1999) *Victorian Sappho*, Princeton, NJ: Princeton University Press.

Proctor, E. S. (1951) *Alfonso X of Castile. Patron of Literature and Learning*, Oxford: Clarendon Press.

Prunč, Erich (2003) 'Óptimo, subóptimo, fatal: reflexiones sobre la democracia etnolingüística en la cultura europea de traducción', in Dorothy Kelly, Anne Martin, Marie-Louise Nobs, Dolores Sánchez and Catherine Way (eds) *La direccionalidad en traducción e interpretación: perspectivas teóricas, profesionales y didácticas*, Granada: Atrio, 67–92.

Pulsiano, P. and K. Wolf (eds) (1993) *Medieval Scandinavian: An Encyclopedia*, New York: Garland.

Putnam, S. (1948) *Marvelous Journey: A Survey of Four Centuries of Brazilian Writing*, New York: Knopf.

Puurtinen, Tiina (1995) *Linguistic Acceptability in Translated Children's Literature*, Joensuu: University of Joensuu.

——(1997) 'Syntactic Norms in Finnish Children's Literature', *Target* 9(3): 321–34.

——(2004) 'Explicitation of Clausal Relations: A Corpus-based Analysis of Clause Connectives in Translated and Non-translated Finnish Children's Literature', in Anna Mauranen and Pekka Kujamäki (eds) *Translation Universals. Do They Exist?*, Amsterdam & Philadelphia: John Benjamins, 165–77.

Pym, Anthony (1992a) *Translation and Text Transfer*, Frankfurt: Peter Lang.

——(1992b) 'Shortcomings in the Historiography of Translation', *Babel* 38(4): 221–35.

——(1994) 'Twelfth-century Toledo and Strategies of the Literalist Trojan Horse', *Target* 6(1): 43–66.

——(1995a) 'European Translation Studies, une science qui dérange, and Why Equivalence Needn't be a Dirty Word', *TTR: Traduction, Terminologie, Rédaction* 8(1): 153–76.

——(1995b) 'Translation as a Transaction Cost', *Meta* 40(4): 594–605.

——(1996a) 'Venuti's Visibility', *Target* 8(1): 165–77.

——(1996b) 'Material Text Transfer as a Key to the Purposes of Translation', in Albrecht Neubert, Gregory Shreve and K. Gommlich (eds) *Basic Issues in Translation Studies*, Kent, OH: Kent State University Institute for Applied Linguistics, 337–46.

——(1998) *Method in Translation History*, Manchester: St Jerome.

——(1999) 'Venuti's Scandals', *The European Legacy* 6(3): 416–18.

——(2000a) *Negotiating the Frontier. Translators and Intercultures in Hispanic History*, Manchester: St Jerome.

——(2000b) 'The European Union and Its Future Languages: Questions for Language Policies and Translations Theories', *Across Languages and Cultures* 1(1): 1–18.

——(ed.) (2001a) *The Return to Ethics*, Special Issue of *The Translator* 7(2): 139–54.

——(2001b) 'The Use of Translation in International Organizations', http://www.fut.

es/~apym/on-line/transinst.html (accessed 17 November 2004).

——(2001c) 'On Cooperation', in Maeve Olohan (ed.) *Intercultural Faultlines: Research Models in Translation Studies I. Textual and Cognitive Aspects*, Manchester: St Jerome, 181–92.

——(2003) 'Alternatives to Borders in Translation Theory', in Susan Petrilli (ed.) *Translation Translation*, Amsterdam & New York: Rodopi, 451–63.

——(2004) *The Moving Text: Localization, Translation and Distribution*, Amsterdam & Philadelphia: John Benjamins.

——(2005a) 'Explaining Explicitation', in Kinga Klaudy, Krisztina Károly and Ágota Fóris (eds) *New Trends in Translation Studies. In Honour of Kinga Klaudy*, Budapest: Akadémiai Kiadó, 29–45.

——(2005b) 'The Translator as Author: Two Quixotes', *Translation and Literature* 14(1): 71–81.

——, Miriam Shlesinger and Zuzana Jettmarová (eds) (2006) *Sociocultural Aspects of Translating and Interpreting*, Amsterdam: John Benjamins.

Quah, Chiew Kin (2006) *Translation and Technology*, Houndmills; UK & New York: Palgrave Macmillan.

Quillard, Geneviève (1998) 'Translation Advertisements and Creativity', in Ann Beylard-Ozeroff, Jana Králová and Barbara Moser-Mercer (eds) *Translators' Strategies and Creativity*, Amsterdam & Philadelphia: John Benjamins, 23–31.

——(1999) 'Publicité, traduction et reproduction de la culture', *Babel* 45(1): 39–52.

Quine, Willard van Orman (1959) 'Meaning and Translation', in Reuben Brower (ed.) *On Translation*, New York: Oxford University Press, 148–72.

——(1960) *Word and Object*, Cambridge, MA: MIT Press.

Quirion, Jean (2005) 'L' automatisation de la terminométrie: premiers résultats', in *Actes du 5ᵉ Congrès International: Langue et terminologie helléniques*, held in Nicosia, Cyprus (13–15 October 2005), Athens: Techniko Epimelitirio Elladas, 61–70.

Quirke, Stephen (2006) 'Translation Choices Across Five Thousand Years: Egyptian, Greek and Arabic Libraries in a Land of Many Languages', in Theo Hermans (ed.) *Translating Others II*, Manchester: St Jerome, 265–82.

Qvale, Per (ed.) (1991) *Det umuliges Kunst* [The Art of the Impossible], Oslo.

——(2003) *From St Jerome to Hypertext: Translation in Theory and Practice*, trans. by Norman R. Spencer, Manchester: St Jerome.

Rába, Gy. (1969) *Szép hűtlenek* [Belles infidèles], Budapest: Akadémiai.

Rabadán, Rosa (1991) *Equivalencia y traducción* [Equivalence and Translation], León: Universidad de León.

——(ed.) (2000) *Traducción y censura: 1939–1985. Estudio preliminar* [Translation and Censorship: 1939–1985. A Preliminary Study], León: Universidad de León.

Rabin, Chaim (1958) 'The Linguistics of Translation', in A. H. Smith (ed.) *Aspects of Translation: Studies in Communication 2*, London: Secker & Warburg, 123–45.

Radin, Charles (2004) 'Rumors of Rape Fan Anti-American Flames', *Boston Globe*, 4 January www.boston.com/news/nation/articles/2004/01/04/rumors_of_rape_fan_anti-american_flames.html (accessed 9 March 2007).

Radó, A. (1883) *A Magyar műfordítás története: 1772–1831* [A History of Literary Translation in Hungarian: 1772–1831], Budapest: Révai.

Radó, Gy. (1971) 'Shakespeare, Teacher of the Hungarian Poets', *Meta* 4: 215–21.

——(1979) 'Outline of a Systematic Translatology', *Babel* 25(4): 14–17.

——(1986) 'The Bible in Hungarian', *The Bible Translator: Technical Papers* 1: 144–5.

Rafael, Vicente L. (1988/1993) *Contracting Colonialism: Translation and Christian Conversion in Tagalog Society Under Early Spanish Rule*, Durham, NC: Duke University Press; 1988 edition – Ithaca, NY: Cornell University Press.

Raffel, Burton (1988) *The Art of Translating Poetry*, University Park, PA: Pennsylvania State University Press.

——(1992) 'Translating Cervantes: *Una vez más*', *Cervantes* 13(1): 5–30.

Rákos, S. (ed.) (1975) *Tanulmányok a műfordításról* [Studies in Literary Translation], Budapest: Union of Hungarian Writers, Literary Translation Section.

Ramanujan, Attipat Krishnaswami (1991)

'Three Hundred Ramayanas and Three Thoughts on Translation', in Paula Richman (ed.) *Many Ramayanas*, Berkeley: University of California Press, 22–48.

Rambelli, Paolo (2004) 'The Function of Pseudotranslation in the Redefinition of the Intellectual in the Second Half of the XVIII Century. The Case of *La magia bianca*', in Kevin B. Reynolds, Dario Brancato (general editors), Paolo Chirumbolo, and Fabio Calabrese (eds) *Transitions. Prospettive di studio sulle trasformazioni letterarie e linguistiche nella cultura italiana*, Firenze: Cadmo, 143–52.

——(2006) 'Pseudotranslations, Authorship and Novelists in Eighteenth-century Italy', in Theo Hermans (ed.) *Translating Others*, Amsterdam: St Jerome, 181–210.

Rayor, Diane (1991) *Sappho's Lyre: Archaic Lyric and Women Poets of Ancient Greece*, Berkeley: University of California Press.

Rebera, Basil (ed.) (1997) *Current Trends in Scripture Translation*, UBS Bulletin 182/183, Reading: UBS.

Reddy, Michael (1979/1993) 'The Conduit Metaphor: A Case of Frame Conflict in our Language about Language', in Andrew Ortony (ed.) *Metaphor and Thought* (2nd edition), Cambridge: Cambridge University Press, 164–201.

Reid, Ian (1980) 'Hazards of Adaptation: Anouilh's *Antigone* in English', in Ortrun Zuber (ed.) *The Languages of Theatre. Problems in the Translation and Transposition of Drama*, Oxford: Pergamon Press, 82–91.

Reiß, Katharina (1971) *Möglichkeiten und Grenzen der Übersetzungskritik*, München: Hueber.

——(1976) *Texttyp und Übersetzungsmethode. Der operative Text*, Kronberg: Scriptor.

——(1988) 'Der Text und der Übersetzer', in R. Arntz (ed.) *Textlinguistik und Fachsprache*, Hildesheim: Olms, 67–75.

——(1990) 'Das Mißverständnis vom eigentlichen Übersetzen', in R. Arntz and G. Thome (eds) *Übersetzungswissenschaft. Ergebnisse und Perspektiven*, Tübingen: Gunter Narr, 40–53.

——(2000) *Translation Criticism – The Potentials and Limitations*, translated by Erroll F. Rhodes, Manchester: St Jerome; New York: American Bible Society.

——and Hans J. Vermeer (1984) *Grundlegung einer allgemeinen Translationstheorie*, Tübingen: Niemeyer.

——(1991) *Grundlegung einer allgemeinen Translationstheorie* (2nd edition), Linguistische Arbeiten 147, Tübingen: Niemeyer.

Remael, Aline (2000) *A Polysystem Approach to British New Wave Film Adaptation, Screenwriting and Dialogue*, Unpublished Doctoral Dissertation, Leuven: KUL (Katholieke Universiteit Leuven).

——(1979) 'Outline of a Systematic Translatology', *Babel* 25(4): 14–17.

——(2003) 'Mainstream Narrative Film Dialogue and Subtitling', *The Translator* 9(2): 225–47.

Restaino, Franco (2004) *Storia del fumetto. Da Yellow Kid ai Manga* [A History of Comics. From Yellow Kid to Manga], Milano: UTET.

Retsjer, Ya. I. (1974) *Teoriya perevoda i perevodicheskaya praktika* [Theory and Translational Practice], Moscow: Mezhdunarodnye otnosheniya.

Revzin, I. I. and V. Yu. Rozentsveyg (1964) *Osnovy obshchego i mashinnogo perevoda* [Fundamentals of General and Machine Translation], Moscow: Vysshaya shkola.

Reyes, Rogelio (1991) 'The Translation of Interlingual Texts: A Chicano Example', *Translation Perspectives* 6: 301–08.

Richards, Jack C. and Theodore S. Rodgers (2001) *Approaches and Methods in Language Teaching* (2nd edition), Cambridge: Cambridge University Press.

Ricoeur, Paul (1981) *Hermeneutics and the Human Sciences*, edited and translated by John B. Thompson, Cambridge & Paris: Cambridge University Press and Editions de la Maison des Sciences de l'Homme.

——(2004/2006) *On Translation*, trans. Eileen Brennan, London & New York: Routledge.

Ripley, G. (ed. and trans.) (1838) *Philosophical Miscellanies*, vol. I of *Specimens of Foreign Standard Literature*, Boston: Hilliard, Gray & Company.

Risku, Hanna (1998) *Translatorische Kompetenz. Kognitive Grundlagen des Übersetzens als Expertentätigkeit*, Tübingen: Stauffenburg.

——(2002) 'Situatedness in Translation Studies', *Cognitive Systems Research* 1: 523–33.

Risset, Jacqueline (1984) 'Joyce Translates Joyce',

trans. Daniel Pick, *Comparative Criticism* 6: 3–21.

Roberts, Roda P., Silvana E. Carr, Diana Abraham and Aideen Dufour (eds) (2000) *The Critical Link 2: Interpreters in the Community*, Amsterdam & Philadelphia: John Benjamins.

Roberts-Smith, L. W. (1989) 'Communication Breakdown', *Law Society Journal* 27(7): 70–4.

Robinson, Douglas (1991) *The Translator's Turn*, Baltimore & London: Johns Hopkins University Press.

——(1993) 'Decolonizing Translation', *Translation and Literature* 2: 113–24.

——(1995) 'Theorizing Translation in a Woman's Voice', *The Translator* 1(2): 153–75.

——(1997a) *Translation and Empire*, Manchester: St Jerome.

——(1997b) *Becoming a Translator. An Accelerated Course*, London: Routledge (2nd edition 2003: *Becoming a Translator. An Introduction to the Theory and Practice of Translation*).

——(ed.) (1997c) *Western Translation Theory from Herodotus to Nietzsche*, Manchester: St Jerome.

Robinson, L. (1994) *Handbook for Legal Interpreters*, Sydney: The Law Book Company Ltd.

Robson, Stuart Owen (1969) *Hikayat Andaken Penurat*, The Hague: Nijhoff.

Rodrigues, Louis J. (1989) *Anglo-Saxon Verse Runes*, Barcelona: University of Barcelona Doctoral Dissertation.

Rodriguez, Liliane (1990) 'Sous le signe de Mercure, la retraduction', *Palimpsestes* 4: 63–80.

Rodwell, J. M. (1861) *The Koran*, London: Dent & Dutton.

——(1909/1992) *The Koran*, London: Dent, Everyman's Library.

Rogan, Eugene (2004) 'Arab Books and Human Development', *Arab Studies Quarterly* 26(2) http://www.eurozine.com/articles/2004–04–27–rogan-en.html (accessed 16 July 2008).

Rohdenburg, Günter (1996) 'Cognitive Complexity and Increased Grammatical Explicitness in English', *Cognitive Linguistics* 7(2): 149–82.

Rokem, Freddie (1982) *Scandinavian Literatures in Hebrew Translation, 1894–1980*, Tel Aviv:

The M. Bernstein Chair of Translation Theory, Tel Aviv University.

Roland, R. A. (1982) *Translating World Affairs*, Jefferson, NC: McFarland.

——(ed.) (1999) *Interpreters as Diplomats: A Diplomatic History of the Role of Interpreters in World Politics*, Ottawa: University of Ottawa Press.

Rónay, Gy. (1968) *Fordítás közben* [While Translating], Budapest: Magvető.

Ronda, J. (1984) *Lewis and Clark among the Indians*, Lincoln, NB: University of Nebraska Press.

Rosenblat, A. (1990) 'Los conquistadors y su lengua', in *Biblioteca Angel Rosenblat*, vol. 3, *Estudios sobre el español de América*, Caracas: Monte Avila Editores, 1–22.

Rosenthal, Franz (1975/1992) *The Classical Heritage in Islam*, trans. by Emile and Jenny Marmorstein (English version of the German original *Das Fortleben der Antike in Islam*, first published 1965); London and New York: Routledge.

Rosetti, Al (1986) *Istoria limbii române I. De la origini pînă la începutul secolului al xvii-lea* [A History of the Romanian Languages from the Beginnings to the Seventeenth Century], Bucharest: Scientific and Encyclopedic Publishing House.

Rossetti, D. G. (1911) *The Works of Dante Gabriel Rossetti*, W. M. Rossetti (ed.), London: Ellis.

Rota, Valerio (2008) 'Aspects of Adaptation. The Translation of Comics Formats', in Federico Zanettin (ed.) *Comics in Translation*, Manchester: St Jerome.

Rothe-Neves, Rui (2003) 'The Influence of Working Memory Features on Some Formal Aspects of Translation Performance', in Fábio Alves (ed.) *Triangulating Translation. Perspectives in Process Oriented Research*, Amsterdam & Philadelphia: John Benjamins, 97–119.

Rothenberg, Jerome (1968/1985) *Technicians of the Sacred*, Berkeley: University of California Press.

——(1971/1986) *Shaking the Pumpkin*, New York: A. van der Marck.

Round, N. (1993) '*Libro llamado Fedrón*'. Plato's '*Phaedo*' translated by Pero Díaz de Toledo, London: Tamesis.

Roxburgh, Angus (2004) 'Translating is EU's New

Boom Industry', *BBC online*, 8 April, http:// news.bbc.co.uk/1/hi/world/europe/3604069. stm (accessed 3 October 2007).

Roy, Cynthia (2000) *Interpreting as a Discourse Process*, New York and Oxford: Oxford University Press.

Roys, Ralph L. (1933/1967) *The Book of Chilam Balam of Chumayel*, Norman, OK: University of Oklahoma Press.

Rozan, Jean-François (1956) *La prise de notes en interprétation consécutive*, Genève: Georg.

Rubel, Paula G. and Abraham Rosman (eds) (2003) *Translating Cultures: Perspectives on Translation and Anthropology*, Oxford: Berg.

Rubow, P. V. (1929) *Originaler og oversættelser* [Originals and Translation], Copenhagen.

Rudin, Ernst (1996) *Tender Accents of Sound. Spanish in the Chicano Novel in English*, Tempe, AZ: Bilingual Press/Editorial bilingüe.

Rudvin, Mette (2006) 'Negotiating Linguistic and Cultural Identities in Interpreter-Mediated Communication for Public Health Services', in Anthony Pym, Miriam Shlesinger and Zuzana Jettmarová (eds) *Sociocultural Aspects of Translating and Interpreting*, Amsterdam & Philadelphia: John Benjamins, 173–90.

Rundle, Christopher (2000) 'The Censorship of Translation in Fascist Italy', *The Translator* 6(1): 67–86.

Rushdie, Salman (1992) *Imaginary Homelands: Essays and Criticism 1981–1991*, London: Penguin (1st edn London: Granta, 1991).

Rusinek, M. (ed.) (1955) *Sztuka przekładu* [The Art of Translation], Wroclaw: Ossolineum.

Russell, Debra (2003a) *Interpreting in Legal Contexts: Consecutive and Simultaneous Interpretation*, Burtonsville, MD: Linstock Press.

——(2003b) 'Contrasting Consecutive and Simultaneous Interpretation in the Courtroom', *International Journal of Disability, Community & Rehabilitation* 2(1) http://www.ijdcr.ca/ VOL02_01_CAN/articles/russell.shtml (accessed 16 July 2008).

——(2007) *Inclusion or the Illusion of Inclusion: A Study of Interpreters Working with Deaf Students in Inclusive Education Settings*. Paper presented at Critical Link, Sydney, Australia, 2007.

Russell, P. (1985) *Traducciones y traductores en la península ibérica (1400–1550)*, Bellaterra:

Servicio de Publicaciones de la Universidad Autónoma de Barcelona.

Rypka, Jan (1968) *History of Iranian Literature*, Dordrecht: D. Reidel Publishing Co.

Sa'adeddin, M. A. (1989) 'Text Development and Arabic–English Negative Transfer', *Applied Linguistics* 10(1): 36–51.

Sadgrove, P. C. (1966) *The Egyptian Theatre in the Nineteenth Century (1799–1882)*, Reading: Garnet.

Sager, Juan C. (1990) *A Practical Course in Terminology Processing*, Amsterdam & Philadelphia: John Benjamins.

——(1994) *Language Engineering and Translation: Consequences of Automation*, Amsterdam & Philadelphia: John Benjamins.

——(1997) 'Term Formation', in Sue Ellen Wright and Gerhard Budin (eds) *Handbook of Terminology Management Vol. 1*, Amsterdam & Philadelphia: John Benjamins, 25–41.

——(1998) 'What Distinguishes Major Types of Translation?', *The Translator* 4(1): 69–89.

Said, Edward (1978/2003) *Orientalism*, New York: Vintage Books.

——(1983) *The World, the Text, and the Critic*, Cambridge, MA: Harvard University Press.

Salama-Carr, Myriam (1996) 'The History of Translation'. Unpublished manuscript, University of Salford.

——(ed.) (2007) *Translating and Interpreting Conflict*, Amsterdam: Rodopi.

Saldanha, Gabriela (2004) 'Accounting for the Exception to the Norm: a Study of Split Infinitives in Translated English', *Language Matters, Studies in the Languages of Africa* 35(1): 39–53.

——(2005) *Style of Translation: An exploration of stylistic patterns in the translations of Margaret Jull Costa and Peter Bush*. Unpublished PhD thesis, Dublin: School of Applied Language and Intercultural Studies, Dublin City University.

Sale, George (1734) *The Koran*, Ghent.

Salkie, Ralph (2002) 'Two Types of Translation Equivalence', in Bengt Altenberg and Sylviane Granger (eds) *Lexis in Contrast*, Amsterdam & Philadelphia: John Benjamins, 51–71.

Salomon, Frank (2004) *The Cord Keepers. Khipus and Cultural Life in a Peruvian Village*, Durham, NC: Duke University Press.

Sammells, Neil (1992) 'Writing and Censorship: An Introduction', in Paul Hyland and Neil

Sammells (eds) *Writing and Censorship in Britain*, London & New York: Routledge, 1–14.

Sampson, Fiona (2006) 'Heidegger and the Aporia: Translation and Cultural Authenticity', *Critical Review of International Social and Political Philosophy* 9(4): 527–39.

Sampson, George (ed.) (1941) *The Concise Cambridge History of English Literature*, Cambridge: Cambridge University Press.

Sánchez, Manuela Fernández and José A. Sabio Pinilla (2004) 'Pour une mise en valeur de la connaissance historique: une anthologie de texts portugais sur la traduction', *Meta* 49(3): 669–80.

Sánchez-Cetina, Edesio (2007) 'Word of God, Word of the People: Translating the Bible in Post-Missionary Times', in Philip Noss (ed.) *A History of Bible Translation*, Rome: Edizioni di Storia e Letteratura, 387–408.

Sánchez-Gijón, Pilar (2004) *L'Ús de Corpus en la Traducció Especialitzada*, Barcelona: Univesitat Autònoma de Barcelona & Institut Universitari de Lingüística Aplicada, Universitat Pompeu Fabra.

Sandbacka, E. (1987) *Selvitys valtion käännöstoiminnasta* [Report on the Translation Operations of the Finnish State Administration], Helsinki: Valtiovarain-ministeriön järjestelyosasto 1/1986.

Sandrelli, Annalisa (2003) 'Herramientas informáticas para la formación de intérpretes: Interpretations y The Black Box', in Jesús de Manuel Jerez (ed.) *Nuevas tecnologías y formación de intérpretes*, Granada: Atrio, 67–112.

——and Jesús de Manuel Jerez (2007) 'The Impact of Information and Communication Technology on Interpreter Training: State-of-the-art and Future Prospects', *The Interpreter and Translator Trainer* 1(2): 269–303.

Santaemilia, Jose (ed.) (2005) *Gender, Sex and Translation: The Manipulation of Identities*, Manchester: St Jerome.

Santoyo, Julio César (1984) 'La traducción como técnica narrativa', *Actas del IV Congreso de la Asociación Española de Estudios Anglo-Norteamericanos*, Salamanca: Ediciones Universidad de Salamanca, 37–53.

——(1985) *El delito de traducir*, León: Universidad de León.

——(1987) *Teoría y crítica de la traducción:*

antología, Bellaterra: Servei de Publicacións de la Universitat Autónoma de Barcelona.

——(1989) 'Traducciones y adaptaciones teatrales: ensayo de una tipología', *Cuardernos de Teatro Clasico* 4: 96–107.

——, R. Rabadán, T. Guzmán and J. L. Chamosa (eds) (1989) *Fidus interpres: actas de las Primeras Jornadas Nacionales de Historia de la Traducción*, León: Secretariado de Publicaciones de la Universidad de León.

——(1989) *El delito de traducir*, León: Universidad de León.

——(2005) 'Autotraducciones: una perspectiva histórica', *Meta* 50(3): 858–67.

Sardin-Damestoy, Pascale (2002) *Samuel Beckett auto-traducteur ou l'art de "l'empêchement"*, Arras: Artois Press Université.

Sarkonak, Ralph and Richard G. Hodgson (eds) (1993) *Writing in Stereo*, special issue of *Visible Language* 27(1–2).

Sartiliot, Claudette (1988) 'Reading with Another Ear: Derrida's *Glas* in English?', *New Orleans Review* 15(3): 18–29.

Satō, R. (1987) *Honyaku Sōdōki* [A Time of Upheaveals in Translation], Tokyo: Sekai Ōraisha.

Satz, R. (1974) *American Indian Policy in the Jacksonian Era*, Lincoln, NB: University of Nebraska Press.

Saunders, David (1992) 'Victorian Obscenity Law: Negative Censorship or Positive Administration?', in Paul Hyland and Neil Sammells (eds) *Writing and Censorship in Britain*, London & New York: Routledge, 154–70.

Saussure, Ferdinand de (1959) *Course in General Linguistics*, edited by Charles Bally and Albert Sechahaye, trans. Wade Baskin, New York: Philosophical Library.

Savory, T. H. (1957) *The Art of Translation*, London: Cape.

Sawyer, David (2001) *The Integration of Curriculum and Assessment in Interpreter Education. A Case Study*. Doctoral Dissertation, Mainz: University of Mainz http//:archimed. uni-mainz.de/pub/2001/0097/diss.pdf (accessed 12 January 2006).

——(2004) *Fundamental Aspects of Interpreter Education*, Amsterdam & Philadelphia: John Benjamins.

Sayers Peden, Margaret (1989) 'Building a Translation, the Reconstruction Business:

Poem 145 of Sor Juana Ines de la Cruz', in John Biguenet and Rainer Schulte (eds) *The Craft of Translation*, Chicago & London: University of Chicago Press, 13–27.

Scarpa, Federica (2006) 'Corpus-based Quality-Assessment of Specialist Translation: A Study Using Parallel and Comparable Corpora in English and Italian', in Maurizio Gotti and Susan Sarcevic (eds) *Insights into Specialized Translation*, Bern: Peter Lang, 155–72.

Scatasta, Gino (2002) 'La traduzione dei fumetti' [Comics translation], in Romana Zacchi and Massimiliano Morini (eds) *Manuale di traduzione dall'inglese*, Milano: Bruno Mondadori, 102–12.

Scattergood, Damian (2003) 'Localization Management: Practical Automation Solutions', *The Getting Started Guide: Localization*, Supplement to *Multilingual Computing & Technology*, 12–17.

Schackman, Jane (1984) *The Right to Be Understood. A Handbook on Working with, Employing and Training Community Interpreters*, Cambridge: Cambridge National Extension College.

Schadewaldt, W. (1927) 'Das Problem des Übersetzens', in Hans Störig (ed.) *Das Problem des Übersetzens*, Darmstadt: Wissenschaftliche Buchgesellschaft, 233–41.

Schäffner, Christina (ed.) (1999) *Translation and Norms*, Clevedon & Philadelphia: Multilingual Matters.

——(2003) 'Third Ways and New Centres – Ideological Unity or Difference?', in María Calzada Pérez (ed.) *Apropos of Ideology. Translation Studies on Ideology – Ideologies in Translation Studies*, Manchester: St Jerome, 23–41.

——(ed.) (2004) *Translation Research and Interpreting Research: Traditions, Gaps and Synergies*, Clevedon: Multilingual Matters.

——(2005) 'Bringing a German Voice to English-speaking Readers: *Spiegel International*', *Language and Intercultural Communication* 2(2): 154–67.

——and Beverly Adab (eds) (2000) *Developing Translation Competence*, Amsterdam: John Benjamins.

Schäler, Reinhard (2001) 'Beyond Translation Memories', in Michael Carl and Andy Way (eds) *Proceedings of the Workshop on Example-Based Machine Translation*, held at the Machine Translation Summit VIII in Santiago de Compostela, Spain, 18 September 2001. Published on CD-ROM.

——(2003) 'Making a Business Case for Localisation', *ASLIB Translation and the Computer 25 Conference Proceedings*, London: ASLIB.

——(2007) 'Translators and Localization', *The Interpreter and Translator Trainer* 1(1): 119–35.

——and Pat Hall (2005) 'Development Localization', *Multilingual Computing & Technology* 16: 28–34.

Schein, Seth L. (2007) 'An American Homer for the Twentieth Century', in Barbara Graziosi and Emily Greenwood (eds) *Homer in the Twentieth Century: Between World Literature and the Western Canon*, Oxford: Oxford University Press, 268–85.

Scheiner, Corinne (1999) 'Writing at the Cross-Roads: Samuel Beckett and the Case of the Bilingual, Self-translating Author', in Ton Hoenselaars and Marius Buning (eds) *English Literature and the Other Languages*, Amsterdam & Atlanta, GA: Rodopi, 175–84.

Scheurich, James Joseph and Kathryn Bell McKenzie (2005) 'Foucault's Methodologies: Archeology and Genealogy', in Norman Denzin and Yvonna Lincoln (eds) *The SAGE Handbook of Qualitative Research* (3rd edition), Thousand Oaks, CA: Sage, 841–68.

Schjoldager, Anna (1995a) 'An Exploratory Study of Translational Norms in Simultaneous Interpreting: Methodological Reflections', in Peter Jansen (ed.) *Selected Papers of the CERA Research Seminars in Translation Studies 1992–1993*, Leuven: Katholieke Universiteit, 227–45.

——(1995b) 'Interpreting and the "Manipulation School" of Translation Studies', *Target* 7(1): 29–45.

Schleiermacher, Friedrich (1813/1963) 'Über die verschiedenen Methoden des Übersetzungs', in Hans Joachim Störig (ed.) *Das Problem des Übersetzens*, Darrnstadt: Wissenschaftliche Buchgesellschaft, 38–70.

——(1977a) *Hermeneutics: The Handwritten Manuscripts*, edited by Heinz Kimmerle, translated by J. Duke and J. Forstman, Missoula, MA: Scholars Press.

——(1977b) 'On the Different Methods of

Translating', in André Lefevere (ed. and trans.) *Translating Literature: The German Tradition from Luther to Rosenzweig*, Assen: Van Gorcum, 67–89.

——(1998) *Hermeneutics and Criticism and Other Writings*, edited and translated by Andrew Bowie, Cambridge: Cambridge University Press.

Schlesinger, Philip (1987) *Putting Reality Together* (2nd edition), London: Methuen.

Schmitt, David A. (2000) *International Programming for Microsoft Windows*, Redmond, WA: Microsoft Press.

Schogt, Henry G. (1988) *Linguistics, Literary Analysis, and Literary Translation*, Toronto–Buffalo–London: University of Toronto Press.

Schopp, Jürgen F. (2002) 'Typography and Layout as a Translation Problem', *Proceedings of the XVI FIT World Congress*, Vancouver, Canada, 189–93.

——(2005) *»Gut zum Druck«? - Typographie und Layout im Übersetzungsprozeß* ['Good for Print'? - Typography and Layout in Translation Process]. Unpublished Doctoral Dissertation, Tampere, Finland: University of Tampere, School of Modern Languages and Translation Studies.

Schreitmüller, Andreas (1994) 'Interlinguale Relationen', *Lebende Sprachen* 39: 104–6.

Schulte, Rainer (1990) 'Translation and the Publishing World', *Translation Review* 34–5: 1–2.

Schurhammer, G. (1982) *Francis Xavier: His Life, his Times*, vol. IV, *Japan and China 1549–1552*, Rome: The Jesuit Historical Institute.

Schwartz, Werner (1944) 'The Meaning of *Fidus Interpres* in Medieval Translation', *Journal of Theological Studies* 45: 73–8.

——(1963) 'The History of the Principles of Bible Translations in the Western World', *Babel* 9: 5–22.

Science Foundation Ireland (2007) *Government Science Strategy on Target as Minister Martin Announces €87 Million SFI Research Funding Awards*, 13 November 2007, http://www.sfi.ie/content/content.asp?section_id=226&language_id=1&publication_id=1532 (accessed 3 December 2007).

Scollon, Ron and Suzie Wong Scollon (2003) *Discourses in Place. Language in the Material World*, London & New York: Routledge.

Scolnicov, Hanna and Peter Holland (eds) (1989) *Plays out of Context. Transferring Plays from Culture to Culture*, Cambridge: Cambridge University Press.

Scott, Clive (2000) *Translating Baudelaire*, Exeter: University of Exeter Press.

Scott, Walter (1985) *Waverley*, edited by Andrew Hook, Harmondsworth: Penguin.

Searle, J. (1969) *Speech Acts: An Essay in the Philosophy of Language*, London: Cambridge University Press.

Seelow, H. (1989) *Die isländischen Übersetzungen der deutschen Volksbucher*, Reykjavik: Stofnun Árna Magnússonar.

Seferlis, Yorgos (2006) *Changes of Footing and Attention to Face in English–Greek Interpreted Dialogues*. Unpublished PhD thesis, Edinburgh: Heriot-Watt University.

Séguinot, Candace (1985) 'Translating Implicitation', *Meta* 30: 295–8.

——(1988) 'Pragmatics and the Explicitation Hypothesis', *TTR* 1(2): 106–14.

——(1989) 'The Translation Process: An Experimental Study', in Candace Séguinot (ed.) *The Translation Process*, Toronto: H.G. Publications, 21–53.

——(1995) 'Translation and Advertising: Going Global', in Christina Schäffner and Helen Kelly-Holmes (eds) *Cultural Functions of Translation*, Clevedon: Multilingual Matters, 55–71.

Seidlhofer, Barbara (1999) 'Double Standards: Teacher Education in the Expanding Circle', *World Englishes* 18: 233–45.

Seifert, Martina (2005) 'The Image Trap: The Translation of English-Canadian Children's Literature into German', in Emer O'Sullivan, K. Reynolds and R. Romøren (eds) *Children's Literature Global and Local: Social and Aesthetic Perspectives*, Oslo: Novus Press, 227–39.

Seleskovitch, Danica (1968/1983) *L'Interprète dans les conférences internationales, problèmes de langage et de communication*, Paris: Lettres Modernes.

——(1975) *Langage langues et mémoire, étude de la prise de notes en interprétation consécutive*, Paris: Lettres Modernes.

——(1976) 'Interpretation, a Psychological Approach to Translation', in R. Brislin (ed.) *Translation: Applications and Research*, New York: Gardner Press, 92–116.

——(1977) 'Take Care of the Sense and the Sounds will Take Care of Themselves or Why Interpreting is not Tantamount to Translating Languages', *The Incorporated Linguist* 16: 27–33.

——(1978/1994) *Interpreting for International Conferences*, translation of *L'Interprète dans les Conférences internationales*, 1968, trans. Stephanie Dailey and Eric Norman, Washington, DC: Pen & Booth.

——(1987) 'La Traduction interprétative', *Palimpsestes* 1: 41–50.

——(1988) 'Technical and Literary Translation, a Unifying View', in Catriona Picken (ed.) *ITI Conference 2*, London: Aslib, 83–8.

——(1989) 'Teaching Conference Interpreting', in Peter W. Krawutschke (ed.) *Translator and Interpreter Training and Foreign Language Pedagogy*, New York: SUNY Press, 65–88.

——(1991) 'Fundamentals of the Interpretive Theory of Translation', in *Expanding Horizons. Proceedings of the 12th National RID Convention 1991*, RID Press.

——and Marianne Lederer (1984/2001) *Interpréter pour traduire*, Collection Traductologie no. 1, Paris: Didier.

——(1989/2002) *Pédagogie raisonnée de l'interprétation*, Paris: Didier Erudition.

Selver, Paul (1966) *The Art of Translating Poetry*, London: John Baker.

Semenets, O. Ye. and A. N. Panas'ev (1989) *Istoriya perevoda* [The History of Translation], Kiev: Izdatelstvo KGU.

Senger, A. (1971) *Deutsche Übersetzungstheorie im 18. Jahrhundert (1734–1746)*, Bonn: Bouvier Verlag Herbert Grundmann.

Sengupta, Mahasweta (1995) 'Translation as Manipulation: The Power of Images and Image of Power', in Anuradha Dingwaney and Carol Maier (eds) *Between Languages and Cultures: Translation and Cross-Cultural Texts*, Pittsburgh, PA: University of Pittsburgh Press, 159–74.

Sergo, Laura and Gisela Thome (2005) 'Translation-related Analysis of the Textualisation of a Knowledge System on the Basis of Fauconnier's Concept of Mental Spaces', in Helle Dam, Jan Engberg and Heidrun Gerzymisch-Arbogast (eds) *Knowledge Systems and Translation*, Berlin & New York: Mouton de Gruyter, 207–25.

Serrano, Richard (2000) 'Translation and the Interlingual Text in the Novels of Rachid Boudjedra', in Mildred Mortimer (ed.) *Maghrebian Mosaic: A Literature in Transition*, Boulder, CO: Lynne Rienner, 27–40.

Setton, Robin (1998) 'Meaning Assembly in Simultaneous Interpreting', *Interpreting* 3(2): 163–99.

——(1999) *Simultaneous Interpretation. A Cognitive-pragmatic Analysis*, Amsterdam & Philadelphia: John Benjamins.

Shackman, Jane (1984) *The Right to be Understood: A Handbook on Working with, Employing and Training Community Interpreters*, Cambridge: National Extension College.

Shadbolt, David (2003) 'An Overview of Localization Tools', *The Getting Started Guide: Localization*. Supplement to *Multilingual Computing & Technology*, 8–11.

Shakir, A. and M. Farghal (1997) 'When the Focus of the Text is Blurred: A Textlinguistic Approach for Analyzing Student Interpreters' Errors', *Meta* 42(4): 629–40.

Shamma, Tarek (2005) 'The Exotic Dimension of Foreignizing Strategies', *The Translator* 11(1): 51–67.

Shanker, Thom (2004) 'U.S. Team in Baghdad Fights a Persistent Enemy: Rumors', *New York Times*, 23 March http://ics.leeds.ac.uk/papers/vp01.cfm?outfit=pmt&folder=1259&paper=1453 (accessed 5 March 2007).

Shannon, Claude and Warren Weaver (1949) *The Mathematical Theory of Communication*, Urbana, IL: University of Illinois Press.

Shavit, Zohar (1986) *Poetics of Children's Literature*, Athens, GA: University of Georgia Press.

——(1997) 'The Status of Translated Literature in the Creation of Hebrew Literature in Pre-State Israel (The *Yishuv* Period)', *Meta* 43(1): 1–8.

——and Yaakov Shavit (1977) 'Le-male et ha-arets sfarim: sifrut mekorit le-umat sifrut meturgemet be-tahalix yetsirato shel ha-merkaz ha-sifruti be-Erets Yisrael' [Translated vs. Original Literature in the Creation of the Literary Center in Erez Israel], *Ha-sifrut/Literature* 25: 45–86.

al-Shayyāl, Jamāl al-Dīn (1950) *Tārīkh al-Tarjama fi Misr fi Ahd al-Hamla al-Firinsiyya* [The History of Translation in Egypt during the French Invasion], Cairo: Dar al-Fikr al-Arabi.

Sheikh Nuruddin ar-Raniri (1992) *Sirat L-Mustaqin*, edited by Abu Hanifah, Jakarta: DPK.

Shih, Claire Yi-Yi (2006) *Translators' Revision Processes: Global Revision Approaches and Strategic Revision Behaviours*. Unpublished PhD thesis, University of Newcastle-upon-Tyne, School of Modern Languages.

Shipley, N. (1966) *The James Evans Story*, Toronto: The Ryerson Press.

Shippey, T. A. (1972) *Old English Verse*, London: Hutchinson.

Shlesinger, Miriam (1989a) *Simultaneous Interpretation as a Factor in Affecting Shifts in the Position of Texts in the Oral-Literate Continuum*. Unpublished MA thesis, Tel Aviv: Tel Aviv University.

——(1989b) 'Extending the Theory of Translation to Interpretation: Norms as a Case in Point', *Target* 1(1): 111–16.

——(1991) 'Interpreter Latitude vs. Due Process: Simultaneous and Consecutive Interpretation in Multilingual Trials', in Sonja Tirkkonen-Condit (ed.) *Empirical Research in Translation and Intercultural Studies: Selected Papers of the TRANS-SIF Seminar, Savonlinna 1988*, Tübingen: Gunter Narr, 147–55.

——(1994) 'Intonation in the Production and Perception of Simultaneous Interpretation', in Sylvie Lambert and Barbara Moser-Mercer (eds) *Bridging the Gap*, Amsterdam & Philadelphia: John Benjamins, 225–36.

——(1995) 'Shifts in Cohesion in Simultaneous Interpreting', *The Translator* 1(2): 193–214.

——and Franz Pöchhacker (eds) (2005) *Healthcare Interpreting: Discourse and Interaction*, Special issue of *Interpreting* 7(2).

Shorter Encyclopaedia of Islam (1974) edited by H. A. R. Gibb and J. H. Kramers, Leiden: Brill.

Shreve, Gregory and Joseph Danks (1997) 'Preface', in Joseph Danks, Gregory Shreve, Stephen Fountain and Michael McBeath (eds) *Cognitive Processes in Translation and Interpreting*, Thousand Oaks, CA: Sage, vii–ix.

Shuttleworth, Mark and Moira Cowie (1997) *Dictionary of Translation Studies*, Manchester: St Jerome.

Shveitser, A. D. (1973) *Perevod i lingvistika* [Translation and Linguistics], Moscow: Voenizdat; trans. as *Ubersetzung und Linguistik*, 1987, Berlin: Akademie Verlag.

——(1988) *Teoriya perevoda* [Translation Theory], Moscow: Nauka.

SIIT – Servicio Iberoamericano de Información sobre la Traducción (1993) *Repertorio de instituciones relacionadas con la traducción y la interpretación en los países de habla hispana y portuguesa*, Beccar (Argentina): SIIT.

Simeoni, Daniel (1998) 'The Pivotal Status of the Translator's *Habitus*', *Target* 10(1): 1–39.

Simões Lucas Freitas, Elsa (2004) 'Similar Concepts, Different Channels. Intersemiotic Translation in Three Portuguese Advertising Campaigns', *The Translator* 10(2): 291–311.

Simon, Sherry (1989) *L'inscription sociale de la traduction au Québec*, Quebec: Office de la langue française.

——(1996) *Gender in Translation: Cultural Identity and the Politics of Transmission*, London & New York: Routledge.

——(2002) 'Introduction', in Sherry Simon and Paul St-Pierre (eds) *Changing the Terms: Translating in the Postcolonial Era*, New Delhi: Orient Longman, 9–29.

——(ed.) (2005) *Translation and Social Activism*, Special Issue of *TTR* 18(2).

——and Paul St-Pierre (eds) (2000) *Changing the Terms: Translating in the Postcolonial Era*, Ottawa: University of Ottawa Press.

Simons, Margaret (1983) 'The Silencing of Simone de Beauvoir: Guess What's Missing from *The Second Sex*', *Women's Studies International Forum* 6(5): 559–64.

Simpson, Ekundayo (1975) 'Methodology in Translation Criticism', *Meta* 20: 251–62.

——(1978) *Samuel Beckett traducteur de lui-même: aspects de bilinguisme littéraire*, Quebec: International Centre for Research on Bilingualism.

——(1985) 'Translation Problems of African Countries', in H. Bühler (ed.) *Tenth World Congress of FIT: Translators and Their Position in Society*, Vienna: Braumüller.

Simpson, Michael (2007) 'The Curse of the Canon: Ola Rotimi's *The Gods are Not to Blame*', in Lorna Hardwick and Carol Gillespie (eds) *Classics in Post-Colonial Worlds*, Oxford: Oxford University Press, 86–101.

Simpson, Paul (1993) *Language, Ideology*

and Point of View, London & New York: Routledge.

Sinclair, John (1991) *Corpus, Concordance, Collocation*, Oxford: Oxford University Press.

——and Malcolm Coulthard (1975) *Towards an Analysis of Discourse*, Oxford: Oxford University Press.

Sinn, Elizabeth (1995) 'Yan Fu', in Sin-Wai Chan and David Pollard (eds) *An Encyclopaedia of Translation: Chinese–English, English–Chinese*, Hong Kong: Chinese University Press, 429–47.

Sirén, Seija and Kai Hakkarainen (2002) 'Expertise in Translation', *Across Languages and Cultures* 3(1): 71–82.

Sirois, Andrée (1997) *Les femmes dans l'histoire de la traduction. De la Renaissance au XIXe siècle, domaine français*, Unpublished MA Thesis, University of Ottawa.

Skutnabb-Kangas, Tove (2000) *Linguistic Genocide in Education – or Worldwide Diversity and Human Rights?*, Mahwah, NJ: Lawrence Erlbaum.

Smecca, Paola Daniela (2003) 'Cultural Migrations in France and Italy: Travel Literature from Translation to Genre', in Anne Malena (ed.) *Traduction et (im)migration/ Translation and (Im)migration*, special issue of *TTR* 16(2): 45–72.

Smith, Barbara Herrnstein (1987/1990) 'Value/ Evaluation', in Frank Letricchia and Thomas McLaughlin (eds) (1990) *Critical Terms for Literary Study*, Chicago: University of Chicago Press, 177–85.

Smith, Karen (2006) 'Rhetorical Figures and the Translation of Advertising Headlines', *Language and Literature* 15(2): 159–82.

SMT Group at the University of Edinburgh (2006) 'SMT at the University of Edinburgh' http://www.statmt.org/ued/ (accessed 5 November 2006).

Sneddon, Clive R. (2002) 'Rewriting the Old French Bible: The New Testament and Evolving Reader Expectations in the Thirteenth and Early Fourteenth Centuries', in Rodney Sampson and Wendy Ayres-Bennett (eds) *Interpreting the History of French*, Amsterdam: Rodopi, 35–59.

Snell, Barbara and Patricia Crampton (1989) 'Types of Translation', in Catriona Picken (ed.) *The Translator's Handbook*, London: Aslib, 59–70.

Snell-Hornby, Mary (1988) *Translation Studies. An Integrated Approach*, Amsterdam: John Benjamins.

——(1990) 'Linguistic Transcoding or Cultural Transfer? A Critique of Translation Theory in Germany', in Susan Bassnett and André Lefevere (eds) *Translation, History and Culture*, London & New York: Pinter Publishers, 79–86.

——(1999) 'The "Ultimate Confort": Word, Text and the Translation of Tourist Brochures', in Gunilla Anderman and Margaret Rogers (eds) *Word, Text, Translation: Liber Amicorum for Peter Newmark*, Clevedon: Multilingual Matters, 95–103.

——(2005) 'Of Catfish and Blue Bananas: Scenes-and-frames Semantics as a Contrastive "Knowledge System" for Translation', in Helle Dam, Jan Engberg and Heidrun Gerzymisch-Arbogast (eds) *Knowledge Systems and Translation*, Berlin & New York: Mouton de Gruyter, 193–206.

——(2006) *The Turns of Translation Studies*, Amsterdam & Philadelphia: John Benjamins.

——, Franz Pöchhacker and Klausb Kaindl (eds) (1994) *Translation Studies: An Interdiscipline*, Amsterdam: John Benjamins.

Softic, S. (1993) 'Communication in the Courtroom', *Judicial Officers Bulletin* 5(3): 18, 23.

Sohár, Anikó (1998) ' "Genuine" and "Fictitious" Translations of Science Fiction & Fantasy in Hungary', in Lynne Bowker, Michael Cronin, Dorothy Kenny and Jennifer Pearson (eds) *Unity in Diversity? Current Trends in Translation Studies*, Manchester: St Jerome, 38–46.

Solano, F. de (1975) 'El intérprete: uno de los ejes de la aculturación', in *Estudios sobre política indigenista española en America*, Universidad de Valladolid.

Soler Caamaño, Emma (2006) *La calidad en formación especializada en interpretación: Análisis de los criterios de evaluación de un jurado en un postgrado de interpretación de conferencia médica*, Unpublished doctoral dissertation, Barcelona: Universitat Pompeu Fabra.

Somekh, Sasson (1995) 'Biblical Echoes in Modern Arabic Literature', *Journal of Arabic Literature* 26: 136–200.

Somers, Harold (1999) 'Review Article:

Example-based Machine Translation', *Machine Translation* 14: 113–57.

——(2003a) 'Translation Memory Systems', in Harold L. Somers (ed.) *Computers and Translation: A Translator's Guide*, Amsterdam & Philadelphia: John Benjamins, 31–47.

——(ed.) (2003b) *Computers and Translation: A Translator's Guide*, Amsterdam & Philadelphia: John Benjamins.

Sonderegger, S. (1979) 'Geschichte deutschsprachiger Bibelübersetzungen in Grundzügen', in W. Besch, O. Reichmann and S. Sonderegger (eds) *Sprach-geschichte. Ein Handbuch zur Geschichte der deutschen Sprache und ihrer Erforschung*, Berlin & New York: de Gruyter, 129–85.

Soriano, Inmaculada (2007) *Evaluación de un programa de movilidad en la formación de traductores: expectativas, experiencias y grado de satisfacción de los participantes, profesores y gestores del intercambio MGLU-UGR-ULPGC*. Doctoral dissertation, Granada: Universidad de Granada, Spain. Available at: http://hera.ugr.es/tesisugr/16713266.pdf.

Sorvali, I. (1985) *Översättandets 200 år i Finland* [Two Hundred Years of Translation in Finland], Uleåborg: Institutionen för nordisk filologi vid Uleåborgs universitet.

Soukup, Paul A. and Robert Hodgson (eds) (1999) *Fidelity and Translation, Communicating the Bible in New Media*, Franklin, WI: Sheed & Ward and New York: American Bible Society.

Souza, M. (1990) Interview by G. Price, in Price (ed.) *Latin America: The Writer's Journey*, London: Hamish Hamilton, 123–33.

Spear, Percival (1970) *A History of India*, vol. 2, London: Penguin.

Sperber, Dan and Deirdre Wilson (1986/1995) *Relevance: Communication and Cognition* (2nd edition), Oxford: Blackwell.

Spivak, Gayatri Chakravorty (1992a) 'Acting Bits/Identity Talk', *Critical Inquiry* 18(4): 770–803.

——(1992b) 'The Politics of Translation', in Michèle Barrett and Anne Phillips (eds) *Destabilizing Theory: Contemporary Feminist Debates*, Stanford, CA: Stanford University Press, 177–200.

——(1993) 'The Politics of Translation', in *Outside in the Teaching Machine*, New York & London: Routledge, 179-200.

——(1994) 'Bonding in Difference', in Alfred Arteage (ed.) *An Other Tongue: Nation and Ethnicity in the Linguistic Borderlands*, Durham, NC & London: Duke University Press, 273-85.

——(1999) *A Critique of Postcolonial Reason: Toward a History of the Vanishing Present*, Cambridge & London: Harvard University Press.

Springer, O. (1947) 'Otfrid von Weissenburg: Barbarismus et Solœcismus. Studies in the Medieval Theory and Practice of Translation', *Symposium* 1: 54–81.

Sprung, Robert C. (2000a) 'Introduction', in Robert C. Sprung (ed.) *Translation into Success: Cutting-edge Strategies for Going Multilingual in a Global Age*, Amsterdam & Philadelphia: John Benjamins, ix–xxii.

——(ed.) (2000b) *Translating into Success: Cutting-edge Strategies for Going Multilingual in a Global Age*, Amsterdam & Philadelphia: John Benjamins.

Stachowiak, H. (1965) 'Gedanken zu einer allgemeinen Theorie der Modelle', *Studium Generale* 18: 432–63.

Stahuljak, Zrinka (2004) 'An Epistemology of Tension: Translation and Multiculturalism', *The Translator* 10(1): 33–57.

Stalnaker, R. C. (1972) 'Pragmatics', in D. Davidson and G. Harman (eds) *Semantics of Natural Language*, Dordrecht: Reidel.

St André, James (2003a) 'Retranslation as Argument: Canon Formation, Professionalization, and International Rivalry in Nineteenth Century Sinological Translation', *Cadernos de Tradução* 11: 59–93.

——(2003b) 'Modern Translation Theory and Past Translation Practice: European Translations of the Haoqiu zhuan', in Leo Tak-hung Chan (ed.) *One into Many: Translation and the Dissemination of Classical Chinese Literature*, Amsterdam: Rodopi, 39–66.

——(2004) '"But Do They Have a Notion of Justice?" Staunton's 1810 Translation of the Penal Code', *The Translator* 10(1): 1–32.

——(2006) 'Travelling Toward True Translation: The First Generation of Sino-English Translators', in Loredana Polezzi (ed.) *Translation, Travel, Migration*, special issue of *The Translator* 12(2): 189–210.

Stanton, Elizabeth Cady (1898/1985) *The*

Woman's Bible, intro. by Dale Spender, reprinted, Edinburgh: Polygon Books.

Stara Bulgarska Literatura [Old Bulgarian Literature] (1980–89), 7 vols, Sofia: Bulgarski Pisatel Publishers.

Staten, Henry (2005) 'Tracking the "Native Informant": Cultural Translation as the Horizon of Literary Translation', in Sandra Bermann and Michael Wood (eds) *Nation, Language and the Ethics of Translation*, Princeton, NJ: Princeton University Press, 111–26.

Stavans, Ilan (2003) *Spanglish. The Making of a New American Language*, New York: HarperCollins.

Stecconi, Ubaldo (1994/1999) 'Peirce's Semiotics for Translation', *Koinè* 4: 161–80; reprinted in Paul Soukup and Robert Hodgson (eds) *Fidelity and Translation*, Franklin, WI & New York: Sheed & Ward and American Bible Society, 161–80.

——(2004a) 'A Map of Semiotics for Translations Studies', in Stefano Arduini and Robert Hodgson (eds) *Similarity and Difference in Translation*, Modena: Guaraldi, 153–68.

——(2004b) 'Interpretive Semiotics and Translation Theory: The Semiotic Conditions to Translation', *Semiotica* 150(1/4): 471–89.

——(2007) 'Five Reasons Why Semiotics Is Good for Translation Studies', in Yves Gambier, Miriam Shlesinger and Radegundis Stolze (eds) *Translation Studies: Doubts and Directions. Selected Contributions from the EST Congress, Lisbon 2004*, Amsterdam & Philadelphia: John Benjamins, 15–26.

——and Maria Luisa Torres Reyes (1997) 'Transgression and Circumvention through Translation in the Philippines', in Mary Snell-Hornby, Zuzana Jettmarová and Klaus Kaindl (eds) *Translation as Intercultural Communication*, Amsterdam: John Benjamins, 67–78.

Steele, Jonathan (2006) 'Lost in Translation', *The Guardian*. Available online at: http://commentisfree.guardian.co.uk/jonathan_steele/2006/06/post_155.html (accessed 15 June 2006).

Steiner, George (1975/1992) *After Babel. Aspects of Language and Translation* (2nd edition), London: Oxford University Press.

——(1995) *What Is Comparative Literature?*, Oxford: Clarendon.

Steiner, T. R. (ed.) (1975) *English Translation Theory: 1650–1800*, Assen and Amsterdam: van Gorcum.

Steinschneider, Moritz (1893) *Die hebraeischen Uebersetzungen des Mittelalters und die Juden als Dolmetscher: Ein Beitrag zur Literaturgeschichte des Mittelalters, meist nach handschriftlichen Quellen*, Berlin: Kommissionsverlag des Bibliographischen Bureaus.

Stenzl, Catherine (1983) *Simultaneous Interpretation: Groundwork Towards a Comprehensive Model*. Unpublished MA Thesis, London: Birkbeck College, University of London.

Stern, Hans H. (1992) *Issues and Options in Language Teaching*, edited by P. Allen and B. Harley, Oxford: Oxford University Press.

Sternberg, Meir (1981) 'Polylingualism as Reality and Translation as Mimesis', *Poetics Today* 2(4): 221–39.

Sternberg, Robert J. and Todd I. Lubart (1999) 'The Concept of Creativity: Prospects and Paradigms', in Robert J. Sternberg (ed.) *Handbook of Creativity*, Cambridge: Cambridge University Press, 3–15.

Stetting, Karen (1989) 'Transediting: A New Term for Coping with a Grey Area Between Editing and Translating', in Graham D. Caie, Kirsten Haastrup, Arnt Lykke Jakobsen, Jørgen Erik Nielsen, Jørgen Sevaldsen, Henrik Specht and Arne Zettersten (eds) *Proceedings from the Fourth Nordic Conference for English Studies*, Copenhagen: University of Copenhagen, 371–82.

Stewart, David A., Jerome D. Schein and Brenda E. Cartwright (1998) *Sign Language Interpreting: Exploring Its Art and Science*, Needham Heights, MA: Allyn & Bacon.

Stewart, Dominic (2000) 'Conventionality, Creativity, and Translated Text: The Implications of Electronic Corpora in Translation', in Maeve Olohan (ed.) *Intercultural Faultlines. Research Models in Translation Studies 1: Textual and Cognitive Aspects*, Manchester: St Jerome, 73–91.

Stine, Philip C. (ed.) (1988) *Issues in Bible Translation*, UBS Monograph Series No. 3, Hong Kong: UBS.

——(2004) 'Dynamic Equivalence Reconsidered', *The Translator* 10(1): 129–35.

Stock, Brian (1978) 'Science, Technology and

Economic Progress in the Early Middle Ages', in David C. Lindberg (ed.) *Science in the Middle Ages*, Chicago and London: University of Chicago Press, 1–51.

Stockwell, Peter (2002a) *Cognitive Poetics: An Introduction*, London: Routledge.

——(2002b) 'Miltonic Texture and the Feeling of Reading', in Elena Semino & Jonathan Culpeper (eds) *Cognitive Stylistics: Language and Cognition in Text Analysis*, Amsterdam: John Benjamins, 73–94.

Stokoe, William B. (1960) *Sign Language Structure: An Outline of the Visual Communication Systems of the American Deaf*, Studies in Linguistics. Occasional Paper 8, Buffalo, New York: University of Buffalo.

Stolze, Radegundis (1992) *Hermeneutisches Übersetzen*, Tübingen: Gunter Narr.

——(2003) *Hermeneutik und Translation*, Tübingen: Gunter Narr.

Stone, Christopher (2006) *Towards a Deaf Translation Norm*. Unpublished doctoral dissertation, Bristol: University of Bristol, UK.

——(2007) 'Deaf Translators/Interpreters' Rendering Processes: The Translation of Oral Languages', *The Sign Language Translator and Interpreter* 1(1): 53–72.

Stoppard, Tom (1981) 'Across Nestroy with Map and Compass', in Royal National Theatre Programme Note to *On the Razzle*, London: Royal National Theatre.

Storey, C. A. (1970–72) *Persian Literature: A Biobibliographical Survey*, 2 vols, London: The Royal Asiatic Society of Great Britain and London.

St-Pierre, Paul and Prafulla C. Kar (eds) (2007) *In Translation: Reflections, Refractions, Transformations*, Amsterdam & Philadelphia: John Benjamins.

Straniero Sergio, Francesco (1999) 'The Interpreter on the (Talk) Show: Analysing Interaction and Participation Framework', *The Translator* 5(2): 303–26.

Stratford, P. (1977) *Bibliography of Canadian Books in Translation: French to English and English to French*, Ottawa: HRCC.

Strauss, Johann (1994) 'Romanlar, Ah! O Romanlar! Les Débuts de la lecture moderne dans l'Empire Ottoman (1850–1900)', *Turcica, Revue d'Études Turques*, vol. 26, Éditions Peeters, 125–63.

——(1995) 'The *Millets* and the Ottoman Language: The Contribution of Ottoman Greeks to Ottoman Letters (19th–20th Centuries)', *Die Welt des Islams* 35(2): 189–249.

Strümper-Krobb, Sabine (2003) 'The Translator in Fiction', *Language and Intercultural Communication* 3(2): 115–21.

Stubbs, Michael (1996) *Text and Corpus Analysis*, Oxford: Blackwell.

——(1997) 'Whorf's Children: Critical Comments on Critical Discourse Analysis (CDA)', in Ann Ryan and Alison Wray (eds) *Evolving Models of Language*, Clevedon: BAAL in association with Multilingual Matters, 110–16.

Sturge, Kate (1997) 'Translation Strategies in Ethnography', *The Translator* 3(1): 21–38.

——(1999) '"A Danger and a Veiled Attack". Translating in Nazi Germany', in Jean Boise-Beier and Michael Holman (eds) *The Practices of Literary Translation. Constraints and Creativity*, Manchester: St Jerome, 135–46.

——(2004) 'The Alien Within': Translation into German During the Nazi Regime*, Munich: Iudicium.

——(2006) 'The Other on Display: Translation in the Ethnographic Museum', in Theo Hermans (ed.) *Translating Others II*, Manchester: St Jerome, 431–40.

——(2007) *Representing Others: Translation, Ethnography and the Museum*, Manchester: St Jerome.

Sugimoto, T. (1990) *Nagasaju Tsūji Monogatari* [An Account of the Nagasaki Interpreters], Tokyo: Sotakusha.

Sumardjo, Jakob (2004) *Kesusasteraan Melayu Rendah*, Yogyakarta: Galang Press.

Sumberg, Carolyn (2004) 'Brand Leadership at Stake. Selling France to British Tourists', *The Translator* 10(2): 329–53.

Sunderland, Jane (2006) *Language and Gender. An Advanced Resource Book*, London & New York: Routledge.

Sundersingh, Julian (2001) *Audio Based Translation: Communicating Biblical Scriptures to Non-Literate People*, Bangalore: SAIACS Press & UBS.

Susam-Sarajeva, Şebnem (2003) 'Multiple-entry Visa to Travelling Theory', *Target* 15(1): 1–36.

——(2006) *Theories on the Move*, Amsterdam & New York: Rodopi.

Sutton, Martin (1996) *The Sin Complex: A Critical Study of English Versions of the Grimms' 'Kinder- und Hausmärchen' in the Nineteenth Century,* Kassel: Brüder Grimm Gesellschaft.

Sutton-Spence, Rachel and Bencie Woll (1999) *The Linguistics of British Sign Language: An Introduction,* Cambridge: Cambridge University Press.

Swales, John (1990) *Genre Analysis,* Cambridge: Cambridge University Press.

Swann, Brian (1992) *On the Translation of Native American Literatures,* Washington, DC: Smithsonian.

Swanton, M. (trans.) (1993) *Ango-Saxon Prose,* London: J. M. Dent; Vermont: Charles E. Tuttle.

Sweet, Henry (1899/1964) *The Practical Study of Languages: A Guide for Teachers and Learners,* edited by R. Mackin, Oxford: Oxford University Press.

Sykes, Mary (1985) 'Discrimination in Discourse', in Teun van Dijk (ed.) *Handbook of Discourse Analysis,* Vol. 4, London: Academic Press, 83–102.

Szabó, E. (1968) *A müfordítás* [Literary Translation], Budapest: Gondolat.

Tabakowska, Elżbieta (1993) *Cognitive Linguistics and the Poetics of Translation,* Tübingen: Gunter Narr.

——(2000) 'Is (Cognitive) Linguistics of Any Use for (Literary) Translation?', in Sonja Tirkkonen-Condit and Riitta Jääskeläinen (eds) *Tapping and Mapping the Processes of Translation and Interpreting,* Amsterdam & Philadelphia: John Benjamins, 83–95.

Tabbert, Reinbert (2002) 'Approaches to the Translation of Children's Literature', *Target* 14(2): 303–51.

Taft, Ronald (1981) 'The Role and Personality of the Mediator', in Stephen Bochner (ed.) *The Mediating Person: Bridges between Cultures,* Cambridge: Schenkman, 53–88.

Tahir-Gürçağlar, Şehnaz (2003) 'The Translation Bureau Revisited – Translation as Symbol', in María Calzada-Pérez (ed.) *Apropos of Ideology,* Manchester: St Jerome, 113–29.

——(2008) *The Politics and Poetics of Translation in Turkey, 1923–1960,* Amsterdam: Rodopi.

Tajadod, Nahal (2002) 'Les Premiers traducteurs de sutras bouddhiques en Chine, les Parthes An Shigao et An Xuan', in Philip

Huyse (ed.) *Iran: Questions et connaissances, Vol. I: La Période ancienne,* Paris: Association pour l'Avancement des Etudes Iraniennes, 363–80.

Takeda, K. (1983) 'Western Literature in Japanese Translation', in *Kodansha Encyclopedia of Japan,* vol. 8, Tokyo: Kodansha Ltd.

Tambiah, Stanley Jeyaraja (1990) *Magic, Science, Religion, and the Scope of Rationality,* Cambridge: Cambridge University Press.

Tannen, Deborah (1984) *Coherence in Spoken and Written Discourse,* Norwood, NJ: Ablex.

Tanqueiro, Helena (1999) 'Un traductor privilegiado: el autotraductor', *Quaderns: Revista de traducció* 3: 19–27.

——(2000) 'Self-Translation as an Extreme Case of the Author–Translator-Dialectic', in Allison Beeby, Doris Ensinger and Marisa Presas (eds) *Investigating Translation,* Amsterdam & Philadelphia: John Benjamins, 55–63.

Tanzmeister, Robert (1996) 'Sprachliches Relativitätsprinzip und literarische Selbstübersetzung am Beispiel von Jorge Semprúns *Federico Sánchez vous salue bien* und *Federico Sánchez se despide de Ustedes*', *Quo vadis, Romania?* 7: 67–100.

Tatilon, Claude (1990) 'Le texte publicitaire: traduction ou adaptation', *Meta* 35(1): 243–6.

Taviano, Stefania (2006) *Staging Dario Fo and Franca Rame: Anglo-American Approaches to Political Theatre,* Aldershot, Hants: Ashgate.

Taylor, B. (trans.) (1871) Johann Wolfgang von Goethe, *Faust: A Tragedy,* Boston: James R. Osgood & Company.

Tebbel, John (1987) *Between Covers. The Rise and Transformation of American Publishing,* Oxford: Oxford University Press.

Tebble, Helen (1999) 'The Tenor of Consultant Physicians: Implications for Medical Interpreting', *The Translator* 5(2): 179–200.

Tedlock, Dennis (1989) 'The Translator; or, Why the Crocodile was not Disillusioned: A Play in One Act', in Rosanna Warren (ed.) *The Art of Translation,* Boston, MA: Northeastern University Press.

Teele, Roy Earle (1949) *Through a Glass Darkly. A Study of English Translations of Chinese Poetry,* Ann Arbor, MI: University of Michigan Press.

Tekin, Gönül A. (1992) *Çengname – Ahmed-i Dai: Critical Edition and Textual Analysis*

[The Book of Ceng – Ahmed-i Dai], Sources of Oriental Languages and Literatures 16, Turkish Sources XIV, Cambridge, MA: Harvard University Press.

Temmerman, Rita (2000) *Towards New Ways of Terminology Description: The Sociocognitive Approach*, Amsterdam & Philadelphia: John Benjamins.

Tennent, Martha (ed.) (2005) *Training for the New Millennium: Pedagogies for Translation and Interpreting*, Amsterdam & Philadelphia: John Benjamins.

Tervoort, Bernard (1953) *Structurele Analyse van Visueel Taalgebruik binnen een Groep Dove Kinderen* [Structural Analysis of Visual Language Use within a Group of Deaf Children], Amsterdam: North-Holland Publishing.

Teubert, Wolfgang (2002) 'The Role of Parallel Corpora in Translation and Multilingual Lexicography', in Bengt Altenberg and Sylviane Granger (eds) *Lexis in Contrast*, Amsterdam & Philadelphia: John Benjamins, 189–214.

——(2004) 'Units of Meaning, Parallel Corpora, and their Implications for Language Teaching', in Ulla Connor and Thomas A. Upton (eds) *Applied Corpus Linguistics. A Multidimensional Perspective*, Amsterdam & New York: Rodopi, 171–89.

Tezla, A. (1964) *An Introductory Bibliography in the Study of Hungarian Literature*, Cambridge, MA: Harvard University Press.

——(1970) *Hungarian Authors*, Cambridge, MA: Harvard University Press.

Tharu, Susie and K. Lalita (eds) (1991/1993) *Women Writing in India*, Vols. 1 and 2, New York: The Feminist Press, City University New York.

Thieme, Jon (1995) 'The Translator as Hero in Postmodern Fiction', *Translation and Literature* 4(2): 207–18.

Thomas, L. H. C. (1951) 'Walladmor: A Pseudotranslation of Sir Walter Scott', *Modern Language Review* 46: 218–31.

Thomas, S. (1994) 'Relevance and Translation', in *Text Linguistics and Translation*, Special issue of *Turjuman* (École Supérieure Roi Fahd de Traduction, Tanger) 3(2): 37–49.

Thomson, Gaby (2005) 'Eastside Story – Westside Story: What is Happening in the Market of Translated Children's Books?', in Karin Aijmer and Cecilia Alvstad (eds) *New Tendencies in Translation Studies*, Göteborg: Göteborg University, 83–92.

Thomson, Greg (1982) 'An Introduction to Implicature for Translators', *Notes on Translation*, Special Edition: 1–82.

Thomson-Wohlgemuth, Gaby (2003) 'Children's Literature and Translation under the East German Regime', *Meta* 48(1–2): 241–49.

——(2004) 'A Socialist Approach to Translation: A Way Forward?', *Meta* 49(3): 498–510.

——(2007) 'On the Other Side of the Wall: Book Production, Censorship and Translation in East Germany', in Francesca Billiani (ed.) *Modes of Censorship and Translation. National Contexts and Diverse Media*, Manchester: St Jerome, 93–116.

Thrapp, D. L. (1988) *Encyclopedia of Frontier Biography*, 3 vols, Glendale, CA: Arthur H. Clark Company.

Timarová, Šárka Harry Ungoed-Thomas (2008) 'Admission Testing for Interpreting Courses', *The Interpreter and Translator Trainer* 2(1): 29–46.

Tirkkonen-Condit, Sonja (1986) 'Text Type Markers and Translation Equivalence', in Juliane House and Shoshana Blum-Kulka (eds) *Interlingual and Intercultural Communication*, Tübingen: Gunter Narr, 95–114.

——(1990) 'Professional vs. Non-professional Translation: A Think-Aloud Protocol Study', in Michael A. K. Halliday, John Gibbons and Howard Nicholas (eds) *Learning, Keeping and Using Language. Selected Papers from the Eighth-World Congress of Applied Linguistics. Sydney, 16–21 August 1987*, Amsterdam: John Benjamins, 381–94.

——(1992) 'A Theoretical Account of Translation – Without Translation Theory', *Target* 4(2): 237–45.

——(2000) 'Challenges and Priorities in Process Research', in Sonja Tirkkonen-Condit and Riitta Jääskeläinen (eds) *Tapping and Mapping the Processes of Translation and Interpreting*, Amsterdam & Philadelphia: John Benjamins, vii–ix.

——(2004) 'Unique Items – Over- or Under-represented in Translated Language?', in Anna Mauranen and Pekka Kujamäki (eds) *Translation Universals. Do they Exist?*,

Amsterdam & Philadelphia: John Benjamins, 177–86.

——and Riitta Jääskeläinen (2000) *Tapping and Mapping the Processes of Translation and Interpreting*, Amsterdam & Philadelphia: John Benjamins.

Titford, Christopher (1982) 'Subtitling – Constrained Translation', *Lebende Sprachen* 27(3): 113–16.

Togerson, S. (1982) *Översättningar till svenska av skönlitterär prosa 1866–1870, 1896–1900, 1926–1930* [Translations of Prose Fiction into Swedish 1866–1870, 1896–1900, 1926–1930], Göteborgs universitet, Litteraturvetenskapliga institutionen.

Toledano Buendía, C. (2001) 'Robinson Crusoe Naufraga en Tierras Españolas', *Babel* 47(1): 35–48.

Tomlinson, Charles (1979) *Renga. A Chain of Poems*, Harmondsworth: Penguin.

Toolan, Michael (1997) 'What is Critical Discourse Analysis and Why Are People Saying Such Terrible Things About It?', *Language and Literature* 6(2): 83–103.

Topping, Suzanne (2000) 'Sharing Translation Database Information: Considerations for Developing an Ethical and Viable Exchange of Data', *Multilingual Computing and Technology* 11(5): 59–61.

Torop, Peeter (2000) 'Towards the Semiotics of Translation', *Semiotica* 128(3/4): 597–609.

Torrens, A. (1994) 'Machine Translation Evaluation and Quality Benchmarks', *Terminologie et Traduction* 1: 375–415.

Torresi, Ira (2004) 'Women, Water and Cleaning Agents. What Advertisements Reveal about the Cultural Stereotype of Cleanliness', *The Translator* 10(2): 269–89.

——(2007a) 'Translating Dreams across Cultures: Advertising and the Localization of Consumerist Values and Aspirations', in Stephen Kelly and David Johnston (eds) *Betwixt and Between: Place and Cultural Translation*, Newcastle upon Tyne: Cambridge Scholars Publishing, 135–45.

——(2007b) 'Translating the Visual. The Importance of Visual Elements in the Translation of Advertising across Cultures', in Kyongjoo Ryou and Dorothy Kenny (eds) *Across Boundaries: International Perspectives on Translation Studies*, Newcastle upon Tyne: Cambridge Scholars Publishing, 38–55.

Tourniaire, Claudine (1999) 'Bilingual Translation as a Re-creation of the Censored Text. Rhea Galanaki in English and French', in Jean Boase-Beier and Michael Holman (eds) *The Practices of Literary Translation. Constraints and Creativity*, Manchester: St Jerome, 71–80.

Toury, Gideon (1976) 'Normot shel tirgum sifruti le-ivrit, 1930–1945' [Norms of Literary Translation into Hebrew, 1930–1945]. Unpublished PhD thesis, Tel Aviv University.

——(1977) *Normot shel tirgum ve-ha-tirgum ha-sifruti le-ivrit ba-shanim 1930–1945* [Translational Norms and Literary Translation into Hebrew, 1930–1945], Tel Aviv: The Porter Institute for Poetics and Semiotics, Tel Aviv University.

——(1978) 'The Nature and Role of Norms in Literary Translation', in James Holmes, José Lambert and Raymond van den Broeck (eds) *Literature and Translation*, Levine, Belgium: Acco, 83–100.

——(1980a) *In Search of a Theory of Translation*, Tel Aviv: Porter Institute.

——(1980b) 'The Translator as a Nonconformist-to-be Or: How to Train Translators to Violate Translational Norms', in Sven-Olaf Poulson and Wolfram Wilss (eds) *Angewandte Ubersetzungswissenschaft*, Arhus, Denmark, 180–84.

——(1984) 'Translation, Literary Translation and Pseudotranslation', *Comparative Criticism* 6: 73–86.

——(1985) 'A Rationale for Descriptive Translation Studies', in Theo Hermans (ed.) *The Manipulation of Literature: Studies in Literary Translation*, London: Croom Helm, 16–41.

——(1986) 'Translation. A Cultural-Semiotic Perspective', in Thomas A. Sebeok (ed.) *Encyclopedic Dictionary of Semiotics*, Berlin & New York: Mouton de Gruyter, 1111–24.

——(1988) 'Translating English Literature via German – and Vice Versa: A Symptomatic Reversal in the History of Modern Hebrew Literature', in Kittel (ed.), 139–57.

——(1990) 'The Coupled Pair of "Solution + Problem" in Translation Studies', in P. N. Chaffey, A. F. Rydning and S. S. Ulriksen (eds) *Translation Theory in Scandinavia*, Oslo: Universitet i Oslo, Institutt for britiske ogamerikanske studier, 1–23.

——(1991) 'What are Descriptive Studies into Translation Likely to Yield apart from Isolated Descriptions?', in Kitty van Leuven-Zwart and Ton Naaijkens (eds) *Translation Studies: The State of the Art*, Amsterdam: Rodopi, 179–92.

——(1993) 'Still in Search of Laws of Translational Behaviour: Closing in on Discourse Interference', in Kinga Klaudy and János Kohn (eds) *Transferre Necesse Est … Current Issues of Translation Theory*, Szombathely: Berzsenyi Dániel, 21–38.

——(1995) *Descriptive Translation Studies and Beyond*, Amsterdam & Philadelphia: John Benjamins.

——(1999) 'Culture Planning and Translation', in Alberto Alvarez Lugrís and Anxo Fernández Ocampo (eds) *Anovar-anosar, estudios de traducción e interpretación* (Vol. 1), Vigo: Universidade de Vigo, 13–26.

——(2004) 'Probabilistic Explanations in Translation Studies: Welcome as they are, would they Qualify as Universals?', in Anna Mauranen and Pekka Kujamäki (eds) *Translation Universals. Do they Exist?*, Amsterdam & Philadelphia: John Benjamins, 15–32.

——and José Lambert (1989) 'On *Target*'s Targets', *Target* 1(1): 1–7.

Townsend, R. F. (2004) *Hero, Hawk, and Open Hand. American Indian Art of the Ancient Midwest and South*, Chicago: Art Institute of Chicago & Yale University Press.

Toye, W. (ed.) (1983) *The Oxford Companion to Canadian Literature*, Oxford: Oxford University Press.

Traugott, Elizabeth Closs (1981) 'The Voice of Varied Linguistic and Cultural Groups in Fiction: Some Criteria for the Use of Language Varieties in Writing', in Marcia Farr Whiteman (ed.) *Variation in Writing: Functional and Linguistic-Cultural Differences*, Hillsdale, NJ: Erlbaum, 111–36.

Tribe, Rachel (1999) 'Bridging the Gap or Damning the Flow? Some Observations on Using Interpreters/Bicultural Workers When Working with Refugee Clients, Many of Whom Have Been Tortured', *British Journal of Medical Psychology* 72(4): 567–76.

——and Hitesh Raval (2003) *Working with Interpreters in Mental Health*, New York: Brunner Routledge.

Trivedi, Harish (2005) 'Translating Culture vs. Cultural Translation', *91st Meridian*, May 2005, http://www.uiowa.edu/91st/vol4_n1/index.html (accessed 16 July 2008).

——(2006) 'In Our Own Time, On Our Own Terms', in Theo Hermans (ed.) *Translating Others I*, Manchester: St Jerome, 102–19.

——(2007) 'Translating Culture vs. Cultural Translation', in Paul St-Pierre and Parfulla C. Kar (eds) *In Translation – Reflections, Refractions, Transformations*, Amsterdam and Philadelphia: John Benjamins, 277–87.

Troianos, S. and I. Veilssaropoulou-Karakosta (1993) *Istoria Dikaiou* [History of Law], Athens, Komotini: Sakkoulas.

Trosborg, Anna (1997) 'Translating Hybrid Political Texts', in Anna Trosborg (ed.) *Text Typology and Translation*, Amsterdam & Philadelphia: John Benjamins, 145–58.

Trost, Klaus (1978) 'Untersuchungen für Überekonystheorie und Praxis des späteren Kirchenslavischen', *Forum Slavicum* 43.

Trujillo, Arturo (1999) *Translation Engines: Techniques for Machine Translation*, Springer.

Tsai, Claire (2005) 'Inside the Television Newsroom: An Insider's View of International Translation in Taiwan', *Language and Intercultural Communication* 2(2): 145–53.

Tsuda, M. (2002) 'Non-Japanese Speaking Suspects/Defendants and the Criminal Justice System in Japan', *Interpretation Studies* (Journal of the Japan Association for Interpretation Studies) 2: 1–14.

Tumber, Howard and Frank Webster (2006) *Journalists Under Fire. Information War and Journalistic Practice*, London: Sage.

Turner, Graham and Kyra Pollitt (2002) 'Community Interpreting Meets Literary Translation: English–British Sign Language Interpreting in the Theatre', *The Translator* 8(1): 25–48.

Twine, N. (1991) *Language and the Modern State: The Reform of Written Japanese*, London: Routledge.

Tymoczko, Maria (1998) 'Computerized Corpora and the Future of Translation Studies', in Sara Laviosa (ed.) *L'Approche basée sur le corpus/ The Corpus-Based Approach*, Special Issue of *Meta* 43(4): 652–60.

——(1999a) *Translation in a Postcolonial Context: Early Irish Literature in English Translation*, Manchester: St Jerome.

——(1999b) 'Post-Colonial Writing and Literary Translation', in Susan Bassnett and Harish Trivedi (eds) *Post-Colonial Translation: Theory and Practice*, London and New York: Routledge, 19–40.

——(2000a) 'Translation and Political Engagement: Activism, Social Change and the Role of Translation in Geopolitical Shifts', *The Translator* 6(1): 23–47.

——(2000b) 'Wintering Out with Irish Poetry: Affiliation and Autobiography in English Translation (Review of Seamus Heaney's *Sweeney Astray*)', *The Translator* 6(2): 309–17.

——(2002a) 'Translation of Themselves: The Contours of Postcolonial Fiction', in Sherry Simon and Paul St-Pierre (eds) *Changing the Terms: Translating in the Postcolonial Era*, New Delhi: Orient Longman, 147–63.

——(2002b) 'Connecting the Two Infinite Orders: Research Methods in Translation Studies', in Theo Hermans (ed.) *Crosscultural Transgressions: Research Models in Translation Studies II, Historical and Ideological Issues*, Manchester: St Jerome, 9–25.

——(2003) 'Ideology and the Position of the Translator: In What Sense Is a Translator "In-between"?', in María Calzada Pérez (ed.) *Apropos of Ideology. Translation Studies on Ideology – Ideologies in Translation Studies*, Manchester: St Jerome, 181–201.

——(2006) 'Reconceptualizing Western Translation Theory', in Theo Hermans (ed.) *Translating Others I*, Manchester: St Jerome, 13–32.

——(2007) *Enlarging Translation, Empowering Translators*, Manchester: St Jerome.

——and Edwin Gentzler (eds) (2002) *Translation and Power*, Amherst & Boston, MA: University of Massachusetts Press.

Tynyanov, Yury N. (1929) *Arkhaisty I novatory* [Archaists and Innovators], Moscow: Akademia; reprinted 1967, Munich: Wilhelm Fink.

——(1971) 'On Literary Evolution', trans. C. A. Luplow, in Ladislav Matejka and Krystyna Pomorska (eds) *Readings in Russian Poetics: Formalist and Structuralist Views*, Cambridge, MA: MIT Press, 66–78.

Tytler, Alexander Fraser, Lord Woodhouselee (1791) *Essays on the Principles of Translation* (3rd edition) (1813), Edinburgh: Archibald Constable & Company.

Tyulenev, Sergei (in press) 'Translating Sexualities in Russia: Historical Aspects'.

UK Book Publishing Industry Statistics Yearbook (2007) London: The Publishers Association.

Ulrych, Margherita (2000) 'Domestication and Foreignisation in Film Translation', in Christopher Taylor (ed.) *Tradurre il Cinema*, Trieste: Dipartimento di Scienze del Linguaggio dell'interpretazione e della traduzione, 127–44.

UNESCO (2006) *Index translationum: Répertoire international des traductions. International bibliography of translations*, Paris: Unesco. http://www.unesco.org/culture/xtrans/ (accessed 22 January 2008).

UNESCO *COURIER* (1983) 'The Indian Languages of Latin America', Volume 7: 12–14.

Upton, Carole Ann (2000) *Moving Target: Theatre Translation and Cultural Relocation*, Manchester: St Jerome.

Ustinova, Irina P. (2006) 'English and Emerging Advertising in Russia', *World Englishes* 25(2): 267–77.

Utka, Andrius (2004) 'Phases of Translation Corpus: Compilation and Analysis', *International Journal of Corpus Linguistics* 9(2): 195–224.

Vaillant, A. (1948) 'La préface de l'évangéliaire vieux-slave', *Revue des études slaves* 24: 5–20.

Valdeón, Roberto A. (2005) 'The "Translated" Spanish Service of the BBC', *Across Languages and Cultures* 6(2): 195–200.

——(2007) 'Ideological Independence or Negative Mediation: BBC Mundo and CNN en Español's (translated) Reporting of Madrid's Terrorist Attacks', in Myriam Salama-Carr (ed.) *Translating and Interpreting Conflict*, Amsterdam & New York: Rodopi, 99–118.

Valdés, Cristina (2000) 'Reception Factors in Translated Advertisements', in Andrew Chesterman, Natividad Gallardo San Salvador and Yves Gambier (eds) *Translation in Context*, Amsterdam and Philadelphia: John Benjamins, 271–80.

Valentini, Cristina (2006) 'A Multimedia Database for the Training of Audiovisual Translators', *The Journal of Specialised Translation* 6: 68–83.

Valero Garcés, Carmen (2000) 'La traducción del cómic: retos, estrategias y resultados' [The Translation of Comics: Challenges, Strategies and Results], *Trans: Revista de traductología* 4: 75–88.

——(2002) 'Interaction and Conversational Constructions in the Relationships between Suppliers of Services and Immigrant Users', *Pragmatics* 12(4): 469–96.

Van Coillie, Jan and Walter P. Verschueren (eds) (2006) *Children's Literature in Translation: Challenges and Strategies,* Manchester: St Jerome.

Vandaele, Jeroen (2002) ' "Funny Fictions": Francoist Translation Censorship of Two Billy Wilder Films', *The Translator* 8(2): 267–302.

Vandaele, S. (2003) 'WebCT: une panacée pour l'enseignement de la traduction médicale?', *Meta* 48(3): 370–78.

Van den Broeck, Raymond (1984–1985) 'Verschuivingen in de stilistiek van vertaalde literaire teksten: een semiotische benadering', *Linguistica Antverpiensia* 18–19: 111–45.

——(1985) 'Second Thoughts on Translation Criticism: A Model of Analytic Function', in Theo Hermans (ed.) *The Manipulation of Literature: Studies in Literary Translation,* New York: St Martin's Press, 54–62.

——(1986) 'Generic Shifts in Translated Texts', *New Comparison* 1: 104–16.

——(1988) 'Translation for the Theatre', in J. T. Ydstie (ed.) *In Honour of Patrick Nigel Chaffey on the Occasion of his 50th Birthday, 22 September 1998 with Contributions from Friends and Colleagues,* Oslo: Centre for Applied Linguistics, University of Oslo.

——and André Lefevere (1979) *Uitnodiging tot de vertaalwetenschap,* Muiderberg: Coutinho.

van Dijk, Teun (1991) *Racism and the Press,* London: Routledge.

——(1998) *Ideology: A Multidisciplinary Approach,* London, Thousand Oaks & New Delhi: Sage.

——and Walter Kintsch (1983) *Strategies of Discourse Comprehension,* Orlando & London: Academic Press.

Van Hoof-Haferkamp, Renée (1989) 'Preface', in Danica Seleskovitch and Marianne Lederer, *Pédagogie raisonnée de l'interprétation* (1st edition), Paris: Didier Erudition, 3–4.

van Hoof, Henri (1991) *Histoire de la traduction en occident: France, Grande-Bretagne, Allemagne, Russie, Pays-Bas,* Paris and Louvain-la-Neuve: Duculot.

van Hoof, René (1962) *Théorie et pratique de*

l'interprétation *(avec application particulière à l'anglais et au français),* München: Max Hueber.

Van Kampen, Kimberly (1997) 'The Bible in Print in England before Tyndale', *Reformation* 2: 111–26.

Van Leeuwen, Theo (2006) 'Translation, Adaptation, Globalization: the Vietnam News', *Journalism* 7(2): 217–37.

van Leuven-Zwart, Kitty M. (1984) *Vertaling en origineel: Een vergelijkende beschrijvingsmethode voor integrale vertalingen, ontwikkeld aan de hand van Nederlandse vertalingen van Spaanse narratieve teksten,* Dordrecht: Foris Publications.

——(1989) 'Translation and Original: Similarities and Dissimilarities, I', *Target* 1(2): 151–81.

——(1990a) 'Translation and Original: Similarities and Dissimilarities, II', *Target* 2(1): 69–95.

——(1990b) 'Shifts of Meaning in Translation: Do's or Don'ts?', in Marcel Thelen and Barbara Lewandowska-Tomaszyk (eds) *Translation and Meaning,* Maastricht: Euroterm, 226–34.

Van Steen, Gonda (2007) 'Translating – or Not – for Political Propaganda: Aeschylus' *Persians* 402–405', in Francesca Billiani (ed.) *Modes of Censorship and Translation. National Contexts and Diverse Media,* Manchester: St Jerome, 117–41.

Vanderauwera, Ria (1985) *Dutch Novels Translated into English: The Transformation of a 'Minority' Literature,* Amsterdam: Rodopi.

Vanderschelden, Isabelle (2000a) 'Quality Assessment and Literary Translation in France', *The Translator* 6(2): 271–93.

——(2000b) 'Why Retranslate the French Classics? The Impact of Retranslation on Quality', in Myriam Salama-Carr (ed.) *On Translating French Literature and Film II:* Amsterdam & Atlanta: Rodopi, 1–18.

Vandewedhe, Willy, Sonia Vandepitte and Marc Van de Velde (eds) (2007) *The Study of Language and Translation,* Special Issue of *Belgian Journal of Linguistics* 21, Amsterdam: John Benjamins.

Vaseva, Ivanka (1980) *Teoriya i praktika perevoda,* Sophia: Nauka i isskustvo.

Vatican (2001) *Liturgiam authenticam: On the Use of Vernacular Languages in the Publication of the Books of the Roman*

Liturgy, http://www.vatican.va/roman_curia/congregations/ccdds/documents/rc_con_ccdds_doc_20010507_liturgiam-authenticam_en.html (accessed October 2007).

Vega, M. A. (ed.) (1994) *Textos clásicos de teoría de la traducción*, Madrid: Cátedra.

Vehmas-Lehto, Inkeri (1989) *Quasi-Correctness. A Critical Study of Finnish Translations of Russian Journalistic Texts*, Helsinki: Neuvostoliitto Instituutti.

Venneberg, Ute (1980) 'Problems in Translating Sean O'Casey's Drama *Juno and the Paycock*', in Ortrun Zuber (ed.) *The Languages of Theatre. Problems in the Translation and Transposition of Drama*, Oxford: Pergamon Press, 121–31.

Ventola, Eija (ed.) (2000) *Discourse and Community; Doing Functional Linguistics*, Tübingen: Gunter Narr.

Venuti, Lawrence (1986) 'The Translator's Invisibility', *Criticism* 28: 179–212.

—— (1991) 'Genealogies of Translation Theory: Schleiermacher', *TTR* 4(2): 125–50.

—— (ed.) (1992) *Rethinking Translation: Discourse, Subjectivity, Ideology*, London & New York: Routledge.

—— (1995a) *The Translator's Invisibility*, London & New York: Routledge.

—— (1995b) 'Translation, Authorship, Copyright', *The Translator* 1(1): 1–24.

—— (1996) 'Translation, Heterogeneity, Linguistics', *TTR* 9(1): 91–115.

—— (ed.) (1998a) *Translation and Minority*, Special Issue of *The Translator* 4(2).

—— (1998b) *The Scandals of Translation*, London: Routledge.

—— (2000a) 'Translation, Community, Utopia', in Lawrence Venuti (ed.) *The Translation Studies Reader*, London: Routledge, 468–88.

—— (2000b) '1990s', in Lawrence Venuti (ed.) *The Translation Studies Reader*, New York & London: Routledge, 333–42.

—— (2003) 'Retranslations: The Creation of Value', *Bucknell Review* 47(1): 25–38.

—— (ed.) (2004) *The Translation Studies Reader*, London & New York: Routledge.

Verdonk, Peter (2002) *Stylistics*, Oxford: Oxford University Press.

Vermeer, Hans (1978) 'Ein Rahem für eine Allgemeine Translationstherie', *Lebende Sprachen* 3: 99–102.

—— (1983a) 'Translation Theory and Lingusitics', in P. Roinila, R. Orfanos and Sonja Tirkkonen-Condit (eds) *Näkökohtia käänämisen tutkimuksesta*, Joensuu: University of Joensuu, 1–10.

—— (1983b) *Aufsätze zur Translationstheorie*, Heidelberg.

—— (1986) 'Übersetzen als kultureller transfer', in Mary Snell-Hornby (ed.) *Übersetzungswissenschaft – eine Neuorientierung*, Tübingen: Francke, 30–53.

—— (1987) 'What Does it Mean to Translate?', *Indian Journal of Applied Linguistics* 13: 25–33.

—— (1989a) *Skopos und Translationsauftrag*, Heidelberg: Universität Heidelberg.

—— (1989b/2000) 'Skopos and Commission in Translational Action', in Andrew Chesterman (ed.) *Readings in Translation Theory*, Helsinki: Oy Finn Lectura Ab, 173–87; reprinted in Lawrence Venuti (ed.) *The Translation Studies Reader*, London & New York: Routledge, 221–32.

—— (1992) 'Is Translation a Linguistic or a Cultural Process?', in Malcolm Coulthard (ed.) *Studies in Translation / Estudos in Tradução, Ilha do Desterro* 28: 37–49.

—— (1994) 'Hermeneutik und Übersetzung(swissenschaft)', *TEXTConText* 9(3–4): 161–82.

—— (1996) *A Skopos Theory of Translation (Some arguments for and against)*, Heidelberg: TEXTconTEXT.

Vernet, Juan (1978) *La cultura hispanoárabe en oriente e occidente*, Barcelona: Ariel.

Véronis, Jean (2000a) 'From the Rosetta Stone to the Information Society: A Survey of Parallel Text Processing', in Jean Véronis (ed.) *Parallel Text Processing*, Dordrecht, Boston & London: Kluwer Academic Publishers, 1–24.

Versteegh, Kees (1991) 'Greek Translations of the Qur'ān in Christian Polemics (Ninth Century A.D.)', *Zeitschrift der Deutschen Morgenlandischen Gesellschaft* 141(1): 52–68.

Vertovec, Steven and Robin Cohen (eds) (2002) *Conceiving Cosmopolitanism: Theory, Context, and Practice*, Oxford: Oxford University Press.

Vidal, Bernard (1991) 'Plurilinguisme et traduction. Le vernaculaire noir américain:

enjeux, réalité, réception à propos de *The Sound and the Fury*', *TTR* 4(2): 151–88.

Vieira, Else R. P. (1999) 'Liberating Calibans: Readings of *Antropofagia* and Haroldo de Campos' Poetics of Transcreation', in Susan Bassnett and Harish Trivedi (eds) *Postcolonial Translation: Theory and Practice*, London & New York: Routledge, 95–113.

Vienne, Jean (1994) 'Towards a Pedagogy of "Translation in Situation"', *Perspectives: Studies in Translatology* 2(1): 51–9.

——(2000) 'Which Competences Should We Teach to Future Translators, and How?', in Christina Schäffner and Beverly Adab (eds) *Developing Translation Competence*, Amsterdam & Philadelphia: John Benjamins, 91–100.

Vilikovský, Ján (1984) *Preklad ako tvorba*, Bratislava: Slovenský spisovateľ.

——(1988) 'Translation and Translation Criticism – the Elusive Criteria', in Paul Nekeman (ed.) *Translation, Our Future/La Traduction, notre avenir. XIth World Congress of FIT/XIe Congrès Mondial de la FIT*, Maastricht: Euroterm, 72–8.

Vinay, J.-P. (1975) 'Regards sur l'évolution des théories de la traduction depuis vingt ans', *Meta* 20(1): 7–27.

——and Jean Darbelnet (1958) *Stylistique comparée du français et de l'anglais*, Paris: Didier.

——(1995) *Comparative Stylistics of French and English: A Methodology for Translation*, translated and edited by Juan C. Sager and Marie-José Hamel, Amsterdam: John Benjamins.

Vissac, J. A. ([1862] 1971) *De la poésie latine en France*, Geneva: Slatkine.

Voigts, L. E. (1989) 'Scientific and Medical Books', in Griffiths and Pearsall (eds), 345–402.

Voldeng, Evelyne (1984) 'Trans Lata Latus', trans. Frances Morgan, *Tessera* 8(4): 82–96.

von Flotow, Luise (1991) 'Feminist Translation: Contexts, Practices and Theories', *TTR* 4(2): 69–84.

——(1997) *Translation and Gender: Translating in the 'Era of Feminism'*, Manchester: St Jerome.

——(1998) 'Dis-Unity and Diversity: Feminist Approaches to Translation Studies', in Lynne Bowker, Michael Cronin, Dorothy Kenny and Jennifer Pearson (eds) *Unity in Diversity?*

Current Trends in Translation Studies, Manchester: St Jerome, 3–13.

——(2000a) 'Translation Effects: How Beauvoir Talks About Sex in English', in Melanie Hawthorne (ed.) *Contingent Loves. Simone de Beauvoir and Sexuality*, Richmond, VA: Virginia University Press, 13–33.

——(2000b) 'Women, Bibles, Ideologies', *TTR* 13(1): 9–20.

——(ed.) (2000c) *Idéologie et traduction / Translation and Ideology*, Special Issue of *TTR* 13(1).

——(2002) 'Julia Evelina Smith, traductrice de la Bible: Doing more than any man has ever done', in Jean Delisle (ed.) *Portraits de traductrices*, 291–320.

——(2004) 'Sacrificing Sense to Sound: Mimetic Translation and Feminist Writing', in Katharina Faull (ed.) *Translation and Culture*, Special issue of *Bucknell Review* 2: 91–106.

——and Agatha Schwartz (eds) (2006) *The Third Shore. Short Fiction by Contemporary Women Writers from East/Central Europe*, Northwestern University Press.

von Schwerin-High, Friederike (2004) *Shakespeare, Reception and Translation*, London & New York: Continuum.

von Wright, G. (1971) *Explanation and Understanding*, London: Routledge & Kegan Paul.

Vuorikoski, Anna-Riitta (2004) *A Voice of its Citizens or a Modern Tower of Babel: The Quality of Interpreting as a Function of Political Rhetoric in the European Parliament*, Doctoral dissertation, Tampere, Finland: University of Tampere.

Waddington, Christopher (1999) *Estudio comparativo de diferentes métodos de evaluación de traducción general (inglés-español)*, Madrid: Universidad Pontificia Comillas.

Wadensjö, Cecilia (1992) *Interpreting as Interaction: On Dialogue Interpreting in Immigration Hearings and Medical Encounters*, Linköping Studies in Arts and Science 83, Linköping: Department of Communication Studies.

——(1998) *Interpreting as Interaction*, London & New York: Longman.

——(2000) 'Co-constructing Yeltsin – Explorations of an Interpreter-Mediated Political Interview', in Maeve Olohan (ed.) *Intercultural Faultlines. Research Models in*

Translation Studies 1: Textual and Cognitive Aspects, Manchester: St Jerome, 233–52.

——(2001) 'Interpreting in Crisis. The Interpreter's Position in Therapeutic Encounters', in Ian Mason (ed.) *Triadic Exchanges. Studies in Dialogue Interpreting*, Manchester: St Jerome, 71–85.

——(2004) 'Dialogue Interpreting – A Monologising Practice in a Dialogically Organised World', *Target* 16(1): 105–24.

——, Birgitta Dimitrova Englund and Anna-Lena Nilsson (eds) (2007) *The Critical Link 4: Professionalisation of Interpreting in the Community*, Amsterdam & Philadelphia: John Benjamins.

Wagner, Emma, Svend Bech and Jesús Martínez (2002) *Translating for the European Union Institutions*, Manchester: St Jerome.

Wakabayashi, Judy (2005) 'Translation in the East Asian Cultural Sphere', in Eva Hung and Judy Wakabayashi (eds) *Asian Translation Traditions*, Manchester: St Jerome, 17–66.

——and Eva Hung (eds) (2005) *Asian Translation Traditions*, Manchester: St Jerome.

Wallis, Julian (2006) *Interactive Translation vs Pre-translation in the Context of Translation Memory Systems: Investigating the effects of translation method on productivity, quality and translator satisfaction*, Unpublished MA dissertation, Ottawa: School of Translation and Interpretation, University of Ottawa. http://www.localisation.ie/resources/Awards/Theses/Thesis%20-%20Julian%20Wallis.pdf (accessed May 2007).

Walton, J. Michael (2006) *Found in Translation: Greek Drama in English*, Cambridge: Cambridge University Press.

——(2007) 'Good Manners, Decorum and the Public Peace: Greek Drama and the Censor', in Francesca Billiani (ed.) *Modes of Censorship and Translation. National Contexts and Diverse Media*, Manchester: St Jerome, 143–66.

Wang, Hui (2007) *A Postcolonial Perspective on James Legge's Confucian Translation: Focusing on His Two Versions of the* Zhongyong, PhD dissertation, Hong Kong Baptist University.

Wardman, Alan (1984) *Rome's Debt to Greece*, London: P. Elek.

Warren, Rosanna (1989) *The Art of Translation*, Boston, MA: Northeastern University Press.

Watt, W. M. (1994) *Companion to the Qur'ān*, Oxford: Oneworld Publications.

——and R. Bell (1970) *Introduction to the Qur'ān*, Edinburgh: The University Press.

Way, Catherine (2004) 'Making Theory Reality: An Example of Interdisciplinary Cooperation', in George Androulakis (ed.) *Proceedings of 'Translating in the 21st Century: Trends and Prospects'*, *Aristotle University of Thessaloniki, Greece, 27–30 September 2002*, Faculty of Arts AUTH, Thessaloniki, 584–92.

——(2008) 'Systematic Assessment of Translator Competence: In Search of Achilles's Heel', in John Kearns (ed.) *Translator and Interpreter Training: Ideas, Methods and Debates*, London: Continuum, 88–103.

Weinberg, B. (1950) 'Translations and Commentaries of Longinus' *On the Sublime* to 1600. A Bibliography', *Modern Philology* 48: 145–51.

Weiss, Roberto (1950) 'Translators from the Greek of the Angevin Court of Naples', *Rinascimento* 1: 194–226.

Weissbort, Daniel (ed.) (1989) *Translating Poetry: The Double Labyrinth*, London: Macmillan.

Wendland, Ernst R. (ed.) (1994) *Discourse Perspectives on Hebrew Poetry in the Scriptures*, UBS Monograph, No. 7, New York: UBS.

——(2002) 'Towards a "Literary" Translation of the Scriptures: with Special Reference to a "Poetic" Rendition', in Jackie A. Naudé and Christo H.J. van der Merwe (eds) *Contemporary Translation and Bible Translation. A South African Perspective*, Acta Theologica Supplementum 2, Bloemfontein, South Africa: University of the Free State, 164–201.

——(2004) *Translating the Literature of Scripture*, Dallas, TX: Summer Institute of Linguistics.

——(2006) *LIFE-Style Translating: A Workbook for Bible Translators*, Dallas, TX: Summer Institute of Linguistics.

Wheeler, Anne-Marie (2003) 'Issues of Translation in the Works of Nicole Brossard', *The Yale Journal of Criticism* 16(2): 425–54.

Wheen, John (July/August 2006) *Communicate*, http://www.atc.org.uk (accessed 31 January 2007).

Whitaker, Richard (2003) 'Issues in Multi-Cultural Translation: Translating the *Iliad* into Southern African English', in Lorna Hardwick and Carol Gillespie (eds) *Classics in Post-Colonial Worlds*, Oxford: Oxford University Press, 65–9.

Whiteside, T. (1981) *The Blockbuster Complex: Conglomerates, Show Business and Book Publishing*, Middletown, CT: Wesleyan University Press.

Whitman-Linsen, Candace (1992) *Through the Dubbing Glass*, Frankfurt: Peter Lang.

Whyte, Christopher (2002) 'Against Self-Translation', *Translation and Literature* 11(1): 64–71.

Wickeri, Janice (1995) 'The Union Version of the Bible and the New Literature in China', *The Translator* 1(2): 129–52.

Widdowson, H. (2000) 'On the Limitations of Linguistics Applied', *Applied Linguistics* 21(1): 3–25.

——(2003) *Defining Issues in English Language Teaching*, Oxford: Oxford University Press, 149–65.

Widlund-Fantini, Anne-Marie (2007) *Danica Seleskovitch, interprète et témoin du XXe siècle*, Lausanne: L'Age d'homme.

Wierzbicka, Anna (1996) 'Japanese Cultural Scripts: Cultural Psychology and "Cultural Grammar"', *Ethos* 24(3): 527–55.

——(2003) *Cross-Cultural Pragmatics. The Semantics of Human Interaction*, Berlin & New York: Mouton de Gruyter.

——(2006) *English: Meaning and Culture*, Oxford: Oxford University Press.

Wildeman, Marlene (1989) 'Daring Deeds: Translation as a Lesbian Feminist Language Act', *Tessera: La traduction au féminin. Translating Women* 6: 31–41.

Wilhelm, Jane Elisabeth (2004a) 'Herméneutique et traduction: la question de "l'appropriation" ou le rapport du "propre" à "l'étranger"', *Meta* 49: 768–76.

——(2004b) 'La traduction, principe de perfectibilité, chez Mme de Staël', *Meta* 49(3): 692–705.

Williams, Carolyn D. (1993) *Pope, Homer, and Manliness: Some Aspects of Eighteenth-Century Classical Learning*, New York: Routledge.

Williams, Gordon (1968) *Tradition and Originality in Roman Poetry*, Oxford: Clarendon Press.

Williams, Malcom (2004) *Translation Quality Assessment. An Argumentation-Centred Approach*, Ottawa: University of Ottawa Press.

Williams, R. (1973) *A Key into the Language of America*, Detroit, MI: Wayne State University Press.

Williams, Raymond (1983) *Keywords: A Vocabulary of Culture and Society*, London: Fontana.

Williams, Rowan (2002) *The Poems of Rowan Williams*, Oxford: The Perpetua Press.

Williams, Sarah (1995) 'Observations on Anomalous Stress in Interpreting', *The Translator* 1(1): 47–64.

Wilson, D. (1976) *The People and the Book: The Revolutionary Impact of the English Bible 1380–1611*, London: Barrie & Jenkins.

Wilss, Wolfram (1977) *Übersetzungswissenschaft. Probleme und Methoden*, Stuttgart: Klett.

——(1982) *The Science of Translation. Problems and Methods*, Tübingen: Gunter Narr.

Wilt, Timothy (ed.) (2003a) *Bible Translation: Frames of Reference*, Manchester: St Jerome Publishing.

——(2003b) 'Translation and Communication', in Timothy Wilt (ed.) *Bible Translation: Frames of Reference*, Manchester: St Jerome, 27–80.

Winch, Peter (1964) 'Understanding a Primitive Society', *American Philosophical Quarterly* 1: 307–24.

Winstedt, Richard Olaf (1977) *A History of Classical Malay Literature* (2nd edition), Kuala Lumpur: Oxford University Press.

Winters, Marion (2005) *A Corpus-based Study of Translator Style: Oeser's and Orth-Guttmann's German Translations of F. Scott Fitzgerald's* The Beautiful and Damned. Unpublished PhD thesis. Dublin: Dublin City University.

Witte, Heidrun (2000) *Die Kulturkompetenz des Translators. Begriffliche Grundlegung und Didaktisierung* (Studien zur Translation. Band 9), Tübingen: Stauffenburg.

Wojtasiewicz, O. A. (1957/1993) *Wstęp do teorii tłumaczenia* [An Introduction to the Theory of Translation], Wrocław: Ossolineum.

Wolf, Michaela (2000) 'The Third Space in Postcolonial Representation', in Sherry Simon and Paul St-Pierre (eds) *Changing the Terms: Translating in the Postcolonial Era*, Ottawa: University of Ottawa Press, 127–46.

——(2002) 'Culture as Translation – and Beyond: Ethnographic Models of Representation in

Translation Studies', in Theo Hermans (ed.) *Crosscultural Transgressions: Research Models in Translation Studies*, Manchester: St Jerome, 180–92.

——(2003) 'Feminist Thick Translation: A Challenge to the Formation of Feminist Cultural Identity?', *Tradução e Comunicação* 12: 115–31.

——(2006) 'The Female State of the Art: Women in the Translation Field', in Anthony Pym, Miriam Shlesinger and Zuzana Jettmarová (eds) *Sociocultural Aspects of Translating and Interpreting*, Amsterdam: John Benjamins, 129–41.

——and Alexandra Fukari (eds) (2007) *Constructing a Sociology of Translation*, Amsterdam & New York: John Benjamins.

Wollin, Lars (1991a) 'Två språk och flera skikt: uppenbarelsernas texttradition' [Two Languages and Several Layers: The Text Tradition of the Revelations], in T. Nyberg (ed.) *Birgitta, hendes vaerk og hendes klostre i Norden* [Birgitta, Her Work and Convents in Scandinavia], Odense: Odense Universitetsforlag, 407–34.

——(1991b) 'Kring det svenska bibelspråkets historia' [On the History of Biblical Swedish], in Svenska bibelsällskapet (ed.) *Den svenska bibeln. Ett 450-års jubileum* [The Swedish Bible. A 450th Anniversary], Stockholm: Proprius, 225–41.

——(2002) 'The Languages of the Nineteenth and Twentieth Centuries Translations I: Swedish', in Oskar Bandle (ed.) *The Nordic Languages: An International Handbook of the History of the North*, Walter de Gruyter, 1506–12.

Woodsworth, Judith (1998) 'History of Translation', in Mona Baker (ed.) *Routledge Encyclopedia of Translation Studies* (1st edition), London: Routledge, 100–5.

Woolard, Kathryn A. (1998) 'Language Ideology as a Field of Inquiry', in Bambi B. Schieffelin, Kathryn A. Woolard and Paul V. Kroskrity (eds) *Language Ideologies: Practice and Theory*, New York & Oxford: Oxford University Press, 3–47.

Woolf, Leonard (1939) 'Note', in Virginia Woolf, *Reviewing*, London: The Hogarth Press, 27–31.

Woolf, Virginia (1939) *Reviewing*, London: The Hogarth Press.

World Association of Sign Language Interpreters, Worchester, South Africa, 31 October – 2 November 2005, Coleford, Gloucestershire: Douglas McLean.

Wraxall, L. (trans.) (1862) Victor Hugo's *Les Misérables*, London: Hurst & Blackett.

Wright, Sue Ellen (1997) 'Representation of Concept Systems', in Sue Ellen Wright and Gerhard Budin (eds) *Handbook of Terminology Management Vol. 1*, Amsterdam & Philadelphia: John Benjamins, 89–97.

——and Leland D. Wright Jr. (1993) *Scientific and Technical Translation*, Amsterdam & Philadelphia: John Benjamins.

Wrigley, Amanda (2005) 'Aeschylus' *Agamemnon* on BBC Radio, 1946–1976', *International Journal of the Classical Tradition* 12(2): 216–44.

Wu, Andi and Zixin Jiang (1998) *Word Segmentation in Sentence Analysis*, Technical Report MSR-TR-99-10, Redmond, WA: Microsoft Corporation, Microsoft Research.

Wurm, Svenja (2007) 'Intralingual and Interlingual Subtitling. A Discussion of the Model and Medium in Film Translation', *Sign Language Translator and Interpreter* 1(1): 115–41.

Wüster, Eugen (1968) *The Machine Tool. An Interlingual Dictionary of Basic Concepts*, London: Technical Press.

——(1974) 'La théorie générale de la termi-nologie – un domaine interdisciplinaire impliquant la linguistique, la logique, l'ontologie, l'informatique et les sciences des objets', *Essai de définition de la terminologie. Actes du colloque international de termi-nologie*, held at Maoir du Lac Delage, Quebec (5–8 October 1974), Quebec: L'Éditeur officiel du Québec, 49–57.

Wyler, Lia (1993) 'Public Perception of Translation in Brazil', in Catriona Picken (ed.) *Translation: The Vital Link, Proceedings of the 13th FIT World Congress*, London: Institute of Translation and Interpreting, 550–3.

——(2005) 'A Promising Research Ground: Translation Historiography in Brazil', *Meta* 50(3): 851–7.

Xiong Yuezhi (1994) *Xixue dongjian yu wan-Qing shehui* [The Introduction of Western Learning and Late-Qing Society], Shanghai: Renmin Publishing Co.

——(1996) 'An Overview of the Dissemination of Western Learning in Late-Qing China', *Perspectives: Studies in Translatology* 4(1): 13–27.

Yahalom, Shelly (1980) 'Du non-littéraire au littéraire. Sur l'élaboration d'un modèle romanesque au XVIIIe siècle', *Poétique* 11: 406–21.

——(1981) 'Le système littéraire en état de crise', *Poetics Today* 2(4): 143–60.

Yanabu, A. (1983) *Honyaku gakumon hihan* [A Critique of Translation Studies], Tokyo: Nihon Honyakuka Yosei Centre.

Yarshater, Ehsan (1988) *Persian Literature*, New York: Bibliotheca Persica.

Yip, Wai Lim (1969) *Ezra Pound's Cathay*, Princeton, NJ: Princeton University Press.

Yorke, Gosnell (2000) 'Bible Translation in Africa: An Afrocentric Perspective', *The Bible Translator* 51(1): 114–23.

Yoshitake, Y. (1959) *Meiji. Taishō no Honyaku-shi* [A History of Translation in the Meiji and Taisho Periods], Tokyo: Kenkyusha.

Young, Iris (1990) *Justice and the Politics of Difference*, Princeton, NJ: Princeton University Press.

Yu, Chu Chi (2000) 'Translation Theory in Chinese Translations of Buddhist Texts', in Allison Doris Ensinger Beeby and Marisa Presas (eds) *Investigating Translation*, Amsterdam: John Benjamins, 43–53.

Yu, Shiwen, Huiming Duan, Xuefeng Zhu and Huarui Zhang俞士汉 段慧明 朱学锋 张化瑞 (2004) 'Zonghexing yuyan zhishiku de Jianshe yu liyong' [综合型语言知识库的建设与利用] [The construction and utilization of a comprehensive language knowledge-base], ICL/PKU website: http://www.icl.pku.edu.cn/icl_intra/internal_rev/icl_review_detail_public.asp?id=64&state=TR (accessed 6 March 2007).

Yuksel, Edip (n.d.) *Unorthodox Articles*, http://www.yuksel.org/e/religion/unorthodox.htm (accessed October 2007).

Zabalbeascoa, Patrick (2000) 'From Techniques to Types of Solutions', in Alison Beeby, Doris Ensinger and Maria Presas (eds) *Investigating Translation: selected papers from the 4th International Congress on Translation, Barcelona, 1998*, Amsterdam & Philadelphia: John Benjamins, 117–27.

Zabus, Chantal (1990) 'Othering the Foreign Language in the West African Europhone Novel', *Canadian Review of Comparative Literature* 17(3–4): 348–66.

Zacchetti, Stefano (1996) 'Il Chu sanzang ji ji di Sengyou come fonte per lo studio delle traduzioni buddhiste cinesi: Lo sviluppo della tecnica di traduzione dal II al V secolo d.C', *Annali di Ca' Foscari: Rivista della Facoltà di Lingue e Letterature Straniere dell'Università di Venezia* 35(3): 347–74.

Zambon, M. Rosa (1962) *Bibliographie du roman français en Italie*, Florence: Edizioni Sansoni Antiquariato; Paris: Librairie Marcel Didier.

Zanettin, Federico (1998) 'Fumetti e traduzione multimediale' [Comics and Multimedia Translation], *Intralinea* 1, http://www.intralinea.it/volumes/eng_open.php?id=P156 (accessed 16 July 2008).

——(2008a) 'The Translation of Comics as Localization. On Three Italian Translations of *La piste des Navajos*', in Zanettin (ed.), 200–19.

——(ed.) (2008b) *Comics in Translation*, Manchester: St Jerome.

——, Silvia Bernardini and Dominic Stewart (eds) (2003) *Corpora in Translator Education*, Manchester: St Jerome.

Zaro, Juan, J. (1999) 'Moratín's Translation of *Hamlet* (1798)', in Jean Boase-Beier and Michael Holman (eds) *The Practices of Literary Translation. Constraints and Creativity*, Manchester: St Jerome, 125–34.

Zatlin, Phyllis (2005) *Theatrical Translation and Film Adaptation: A Practitioner's View*, Clevedon: Multilingual Matters.

Zequan, Liu (2003) 'Loss and Gain of Textual Meaning in Advertising Translation: A Case Study', *Translation Journal* 7(4) http://www.accurapid.com/journal/26advert.htm (accessed 16 July 2008).

Zetzsche, Jost (2007) 'Translation Memory: State of the Technology', *Multilingual Computing* 8(6): 34–8.

Zhao, Wenjing (2005) *Hu Shi's Rewritings and the Construction of a New Culture*, Doctoral Thesis, Manchester, Centre for Translation & Intercultural Studies: The University of Manchester.

——(2006) *Cultural Manipulation of Translation Activities: Hu Shi's Rewritings and the*

Construction of a New Culture, Shanghai: Fudan University Press.

Zhu, Chunshen (2004) 'Repetition and Signification. A Study of Textual Accountability and Perlocutionary Effect in Literary Translation', *Target* 16: 227–52.

Zidan, Ahmad and Dina Zidan (1991) *Translation of the Glorious Qur'ān*, London: Ta-Ha Publishers.

Ziętarska, J. (1969) *Sztuka przekładu w poglądach literackich polskiego Oświecenia* [The Art of Translation in the Literary Theory of the Polish Enlightenment], Wrocław: Ossolineum.

Zilberdik, Nan Jacques (2004) 'Relay Translation in Subtitling', *Perspectives: Studies in Translatology* 12(1): 31–53.

Ziomek, J. (1973) *Renesans* [Renaissance], Warsaw: Państwowe Wydawnictwo Naukowe.

Zitawi, Jehan (2008) 'Disney Comics in the Arab World: A Pragmatic Perspective', in Federico Zanettin (ed.) *Comics in Translation*, Manchester: St Jerome, 152–71.

Zoetmulder, Petrus Josephus (1974) *Kalangwan*, The Hague: Nijhoff.

Zogbo, Lynell (2002) 'Ideology and Translation: the Case of *ruach elohim* and *ruach YHWH* in the Old Testament', in Philip A. Noss (ed.) *Current Trends in Scripture Translation*, UBS Bulletin No. 194/195, Reading: UBS, 121–33.

——and Ernst Wendland (2000) *Hebrew Poetry in the Bible: A Guide for Understanding and for Translating*, New York: United Bible Societies.

Zuber, Ortrun (ed.) (1980) *The Languages of Theatre. Problems in the Translation and Transposition of Drama*, Oxford: Pergamon Press.

Zuck, V. (ed.) (1990) *A Dictionary of Scandinavian Literature*, New York: Greenwood Press.

Index